C

EXPERIENCING SERIES

EXPERIENCING
FAMILY LAW

■

John E.B. Myers

Professor of Law
University of the Pacific
McGeorge School of Law

MAT#41219281

610 Opperman Drive
St. Paul, MN 55123
1-800-313-9378

Printed in the United States of America

ISBN: 978-0-314-27893-7

Table of Contents

Table of Cases

The principal cases are in bold type. Cases cited or discussed in the text are in roman type. References are to pages. Cases cited in principal cases and within other quoted materials are not included.

Introduction

Why would anyone *want* to practice family law? Many lawyers look down on family law. For them, family law is low prestige, too emotional, and too simple.

Simple? Hardly. The competent family law attorney is knowledgeable about a broad range of subjects, including marriage, domestic partnership, divorce, legal separation, annulment, child custody, child support, spousal support, modification of child and spousal support, intimate partner violence, paternity, marital property, adoption, guardianship, law office management, tax, bankruptcy, mediation, discovery, enforcement proceedings, including contempt, the psychological aspects of divorce, and trial and appellate practice. Each of these topics is complicated and evolving. Done well, family law is anything but simple.

Too emotional? There is no doubt that emotions run high in family law. But what is the meaning of "too emotional"? Too emotional for whom? Family law is not for everyone. The good family law attorney takes pride in helping clients work through what for many is the most difficult and emotional time of the client's life. Just as the psychologist or psychiatrist finds satisfaction helping others, so the family law attorney finds reward in helping clients through adversity. Don't choose family law unless you like people, and don't choose family law to resolve your own "issues." Choose family law if, deep down inside, you want to help others. Family law *is* emotional, but so long as you can cope with others' emotions without becoming cynical or inpatient, family law is a field in which you can do immense good.

Low prestige? Guilty as charged. Many lawyers view family law with disdain. Some judges share this sentiment. So, don't go into family law to become famous. Don't choose it to get rich. Choose family law to help others. If you go to work every day realizing you make the world a better place one client at a time, you will enjoy your work, you will make a contribution to your community, you will make a good living, and you will fulfill the highest aspiration of our profession: helping those in difficulty.

What is a Family?

The word "family" has many meanings[1]. Forty or fifty years ago, most Americans lived in two-parent married families. Andrew Cherlin writes, "The nuclear family of husband, wife, and children, which was predominant in the first half of the century, reached its zenith in the 1950s . . . . Since the 1960s, ... the overall percentage of children not living with both parents rose sharply to more than 40%."[2] When you think of your family, you probably think of your parents, brothers and sisters, grandparents, and relatives. Some of us include a stepparent, guardian, adoptive parent, or foster parent. Increasingly, kids have "two mommies" or "two daddies." When we grow up, most of us create a new family by getting married, entering a domestic partnership, or creating our own style of intimate relationship—our own family.

Family life—whether with your parents growing up, or with your spouse or partner as an adult—is a source of great happiness. If you have children, your happiness increases leaps and bounds. Kids drive us crazy, of course, but they also provide love without parallel.

Writing in the *West Virginia Law Review,* Martha Minow provides insight into the meaning of family:

> Both the growing diversity in groups across this nation who claim to be families and diversity within the families themselves carry consequences for three basic issues in family law: 1) who is in "the family," 2) what benefits accompany family membership, and 3) what obligations accompany family roles. It may once have seemed that these questions had obvious and uncontroverted answers. It may once have seemed that "family" referred to a natural or obvious social entity created by the biological ties of parent and child and the divine or contractual ties of marriage.

---

1   See Andrew J. Cherlin, Demographic Trends in the United States: A Review of Research in the 2000s, 72 *Journal of Marriage and Family* 403-419, 404 (2010).

2   Andrew J. Cherlin, Demographic Trends in the United States: A Review of Research in the 2000s, 72 *Journal of Marriage and Family* 403-419, 410 (2010).

I am skeptical of all stories of a past golden or untroubled age, however, and I do mean to dispute any claim that "family" as defined by law is natural or obvious. Certainly it is a legal rule, not a natural fact, that creates the presumption that a child born to a woman who is married is the child of the woman's husband. Rules about marriage eligibility and practices have also undergone sufficient historical changes to reveal the political, religious, and social choices embedded in that institution.

Scholars have also shredded the myth of the homogenous family with historical and sociological studies revealing enormous variance in the structures and functions of families. . . .

Today there can be no doubt that the variety of social practices poses new and pressing questions for legal definitions of family, family benefits, and family obligations. No neutral answers, tethered to "nature" or consensus, are available.[3]

Your Casebook

There are several excellent family law casebooks. A number of these books focus considerable attention on public policy and the family as well as constitutional law and the family. Policy oriented casebooks do not ignore the day-to-day practice of family law, but actual practice is not their focus. Your casebook is different. In your book, the primary focus *is* practice. The book does not ignore issues of policy or the impact of constitutional law on families. Your book, however, is designed to introduce you to the "real world" of family law—family law "in the trenches." Your book's primary goal is to give you a solid foundation in family law so you can hit the ground running if you decide to practice family law.

---

3 Martha Minow, All in the Family & In All Families: Membership, Loving, and Owing, 95 *West Virginia Law Review* 275 (1992/1993).

EXPERIENCING FAMILY LAW

CHAPTER 1

Cohabitation

HALF A CENTURY AGO, living together in an intimate relationship outside marriage was "living in sin." You may recall Bon Jovi's song "Living in Sin" in which he croons, "I don't need no preacher to tell me you're mine." Today, it is common for lovers to live together. Indeed, the federal government reports, "Cohabitation is increasingly becoming the first co-residential union formed by young adults."[1] In 2002, approximately nine percent of women between the ages of 15-44 were cohabiting in an intimate relationship.[2]

When a nonmarital cohabiting relationship ends, former lovers do not owe each other support. The system of marital/community property does not apply to unmarried cohabitants. Thus, cohabitants do not acquire marital property. When cohabitants have children, the rules for child custody and child support are the same as for married parents.

---

1 U.S. Department of Health and Human Services, Centers for Disease Control and Prevention, *Marriage and Cohabitation in the Unites States: A Statistical Portrait Based on Cycle 6 (2002) of the National Survey of Family Growth* p. 4 (2010); Andrew J. Cherlin, Demographic Trends in the United States: A Review of Research in the 2000s, *72 Journal of Marriage and Family* 403-419, 408 (2010)("Cohabitation continued to become more widespread . . . ."); Zhenchao Qian & Daniel T. Lichter, Changing Patterns of Interracial Marriage in a Multiracial Society, 73 *Journal of Marriage and Family* 1065-1084, 1068 (2011)("over the past 30 years, cohabitation has increased rapidly while replacing marriage as the first union transition for most young adults.").

2 U.S. Department of Health and Human Services, Centers for Disease Control and Prevention, *Marriage and Cohabitation in the Unites States: A Statistical Portrait Based on Cycle 6 (2002) of the National Survey of Family Growth* p. 1 (2010).

Contracts Between Unmarried Cohabitants

Unmarried cohabitants can contract with each other regarding property and support. The leading case is *Marvin v. Marvin*, decided by the California Supreme Court in 1976. Lee Marvin was a famous movie star. If you are curious, check him out in *The Dirty Dozen,* a war movie, or *Cat Ballou,* a western in which Marvin played a gun fighter too drunk to shoot straight. A much-shortened version of *Marvin* follows.

Marvin v. Marvin

California Supreme Court
18 Cal. 3d 660, 557 P.2d 106 (1976)

Tobriner, J.

During the past 15 years, there has been a substantial increase in the number of couples living together without marrying. Such nonmarital relationships lead to legal controversy when one partner dies or the couple separates.

We conclude: (1) The provisions of the Family Law Act do not govern the distribution of property acquired during a nonmarital relationship; such a relationship remains subject solely to judicial decision. (2) The courts should enforce express contracts between nonmarital partners except to the extent that the contract is explicitly founded on the consideration of meretricious sexual services. (3) In the absence of an express contract, the courts should inquire into the conduct of the parties to determine whether that conduct demonstrates an implied contract, agreement of partnership or joint venture, or some other tacit understanding between the parties. The courts may also employ the doctrine of quantum meruit, or equitable remedies such as constructive or resulting trusts, when warranted by the facts of the case.

In the instant case plaintiff [Michelle Marvin] and defendant [Lee Marvin] lived together for seven years without marrying; all property acquired during this period was taken in defendant's name. When plaintiff sued to enforce a contract under which she was entitled to half the property and to support payments, the trial court granted judgment on the pleadings for defendant, thus leaving him with all property accumulated by the couple during their relationship. Since the trial court denied plaintiff a trial on the merits of her claim, its decision conflicts with the principles stated above, and must be reversed. . . .

Plaintiff avers that in October of 1964 she and defendant "entered into an oral agreement" that while "the parties lived together they would combine their efforts and earnings and would share equally any and all property accumulated as a result of their efforts whether individual or combined." Furthermore, they agreed to "hold themselves out to the general public as husband and wife" and that "plaintiff would further render her services as a companion, homemaker, housekeeper and cook to defendant."

Shortly thereafter plaintiff agreed to "give up her lucrative career as an entertainer (and) singer" in order to "devote her full time to defendant as a companion, homemaker, housekeeper and cook;" in return defendant agreed to "provide for all of plaintiff's financial support and needs for the rest of her life."

Plaintiff alleges that she lived with defendant from October of 1964 through May of 1970 and fulfilled her obligations under the agreement. During this period the parties as a result of their efforts and earnings acquired in defendant's name substantial real and personal property, including motion picture rights worth over $1 million. In May of 1970, however, defendant compelled plaintiff to leave his household. He continued to support plaintiff until November of 1971, but thereafter refused to provide further support.

On the basis of these allegations plaintiff asserts two causes of action. The first, for declaratory relief, asks the court to determine her contract and property rights; the second seeks to impose a constructive trust upon one half of the property acquired during the course of the relationship. . . .

Defendant first and principally relies on the contention that the alleged contract is so closely related to the supposed "immoral" character of the relationship between plaintiff and himself that the enforcement of the contract would violate public policy. [The court rejected this argument.]

. . . The fact that a man and woman live together without marriage, and engage in a sexual relationship, does not in itself invalidate agreements between them relating to their earnings, property, or expenses. Neither is such an agreement invalid merely because the parties may have contemplated the creation or continuation of a nonmarital relationship when they entered into it. Agreements between nonmarital partners fail only to the extent that they rest upon a consideration of meretricious sexual services.

. . . We base our opinion on the principle that adults who voluntarily live together and engage in sexual relations are nonetheless as competent as any other persons to contract respecting their earnings and property rights. Of course, they cannot lawfully contract to pay for the performance of sexual services, for such a contract is, in essence, an agreement for prostitution and unlawful for that reason. But they may agree to pool their earnings and to hold all property acquired during the relationship in accord with the law governing community property; conversely they may agree that each partner's earnings and the property acquired from earnings remains separate property of the earning partner. So long as the agreement does not rest upon illicit meretricious consideration, the parties may order their economic affairs as they choose, and no policy precludes the courts from enforcing such agreements.

———————

In *Marvin v. Marvin,* the California Supreme Court referred to resulting and constructive trusts as possible remedies. The Iowa Supreme Court's decision in *Slocum v. Hammond* provides a good introduction to resulting and constructive trusts in the context of unmarried cohabitants.

Slocum v. Hammond

Supreme Court of Iowa
346 N.W.2d 485 (Iowa 1984)

Reynoldson, Chief Justice.

Plaintiff Dee Slocum filed a five-count petition against defendant Tom Otis Hammond, seeking under various theories to obtain one-half the value of property allegedly acquired during the period these parties cohabited. . . .

The evidence disclosed that defendant, a maintenance worker for Waldinger Corporation, had built several houses. These included the Hartford, Iowa, home he lived in when his wife died in October 1970. Plaintiff attended a New Year's Eve party at this home on December 31, 1970. After that plaintiff and defendant often were together. When plaintiff's Chicago employment terminated, she invited defendant to accompany her on a Caribbean vacation that extended February through the first part of March 1971, with each paying his or her own expenses.

Plaintiff testified she rejected defendant's marriage proposal but took up residence in his Hartford home in May 1971. Defendant characterized the arrangement as one for mutual sexual services; he was to "buy the groceries"; she was to cook them, and she was free to lead her own life, which in fact she did. Plaintiff characterized the relationship as one in which she was "to fix him breakfast, and lunch and dinner, clean house and just a lot of wife duties, take care of him."

In the fall of 1971 defendant renewed his interest in a rural tract near Hartford that he had attempted to buy several times. Although plaintiff testified she participated in the new negotiations, this was denied by defendant.

The sellers testified they never saw her during any phase of the transaction. It is uncontested that defendant borrowed the $4000 down payment for the ten and one-half acre tract, and that he had contemplated building another home for several years. At this point, however, plaintiff testified defendant asked her if she "wanted to be in on building a house" on the tract, and she responded that she did. Construction of a large house commenced in September 1971.

The final purchase payment of $2500 was made December 18, 1971. Plaintiff testified that was the day she "walked out" of defendant's Hartford home, and, although requested to do so by defendant, she refused to sign the mortgage or permit her name to be on the deed. She testified she said "no" because "the seven months I would have donated to whatever I did out there was to his benefit. I was ready to walk away and forget it, and now it's a different story." Defendant signed the note and mortgage to complete the purchase, and the deed ran to him alone.

From Hartford plaintiff moved into a Des Moines apartment rented by her brother and sister-in-law, and later the three occupied a Des Moines house plaintiff owned. Plaintiff moved back into defendant's home in June 1972. She testified defendant prevailed upon her to return and work on the house. When asked what defendant had said or done to convince her half the house belonged to her, she replied:

> He told me he loved me. He always told me that it was as much mine as his. The labors that I put into it, the labors that he accepted from me ... for the work I did, he accepted that labor from me knowing that I was doing it half and half ....

Upon cross-examination plaintiff could name no one other than defendant to whom she had claimed any interest in the property. She testified "from '73 on it was definitely a claim that I—that I—What do I want to say? That I displayed." On deposition she had testified that what she did for defendant and what he did for her "was all part of the love and affection and friendship" that they "had at that time for each other."

Plaintiff again moved back to her Des Moines home in October 1972 and did not return until after Christmas the same year. At that time she moved into the new house although it was not then completed; nor was it completely finished when this trial took place in October 1981. . . .

Plaintiff testified she assisted substantially in the construction of the house, a claim denied by defendant and all of his friends and co-workers on the construction site. . . .

The evidence disclosed plaintiff did much of the housekeeping and cooking following her return to the rural home in December 1972, although there was considerable testimony that she remained as defendant described her: a "free agent" who could and did "come and go" at will. . . .

Plaintiff also asserted she contributed financially to the house payment by depositing monies in a co-owned checking account. . . .

Plaintiff was served a notice that terminated her occupancy of the house on November 23, 1979. . . .

After these parties separated, plaintiff brought an action against defendant to dissolve a common-law marriage. Trial court filed a decree in that proceeding on February 20, 1980, holding there was neither an in praesenti intent to be married nor a public declaration sufficient to establish that the parties were husband and wife.

April 30, 1980, defendant was served with notice of this proceeding. Plaintiff variously describes "division" I of her petition as based on misrepresentation or implied contract resulting in a joint venture; count II pled the breach of an alleged oral contract. In count III she sought recovery on the doctrine of unjust enrichment, in count IV on an alleged resulting trust, and in count V on a constructive trust theory. In addition, on April 29, 1980, the same date this action was commenced, plaintiff filed a partition action for the division or sale of the real estate and undescribed personality. Upon plaintiff's motion, these two cases were consolidated for trial by order entered September 19, 1980.

[The trial court ruled against plaintiff, and she appealed.]

Appealing, plaintiff asserts she is entitled to recover under the equitable theories of unjust enrichment, resulting trust and constructive trust. . . .

At the outset we refer to an issue we are not required to explore extensively in this appeal. Over eight pages of plaintiff's brief are devoted to the proposition that "judicial resolution of disputes arising out of division of property accumulated by unmarried cohabiting couples does not contravene public policy." Plaintiff cites the well-known "palimony" decision, Marvin v. Marvin, 18 Cal.3d 660, 557 P.2d 106, 134 Cal.Rptr. 815 (1976), and its progeny spawned in a number of jurisdictions, most of which, unlike Iowa, do not recognize common-law marriages.

Defendant relies on other decisions, including *Hewitt v. Hewitt*, 77 Ill.2d 49, 394 N.E.2d 1204, 31 Ill.Dec. 827 (1979), a case that raises sobering public policy questions relating to property claims and other issues arising from such relationships. Michigan and New York have refused to adopt the entire *Marvin* holding; both limit such actions to enforcement of express contracts and deny judicial approval to any contract that must be implied. *See Carnes v. Sheldon,* 109 Mich.App. 204, 211-17, 311 N.W.2d 747, 752-53 (1981); *Morone v. Morone,* 50 N.Y.2d 481, 486-89, 413 N.E.2d 1154, 1157-58, 429 N.Y.S.2d 592, 595-96 (1980).

We considered a related issue in *Laws v. Griep,* 332 N.W.2d 339, 341 (Iowa 1983), where, in denying an unmarried cohabitant's loss of consortium claim, we wrote:

> The policy of this state is that the de jure family is the basic unit of social order. This policy is reflected in statutes governing the right to marry. It is reflected in the rule recognizing common law marriages. It is demonstrated by statutes defining the rights and responsibilities of husbands and wives toward each other and toward their children. The policy favoring marriage is not rooted only in community mores. It is also rooted in the necessity of providing an institutional basis for defining the fundamental relational rights and responsibilities of persons in organized society. This policy would be subverted if persons could gain marital legal rights without accepting correlative marital legal responsibilities. We need go no further than this in rejecting plaintiffs' invitation in the present case.

. . . In this case there are two reasons why we do not believe we are required to confront the basic issue plaintiff raises. First, it apparently was not urged by defendant in district court, and may not have surfaced here had plaintiff not voluntarily raised it. Second, we believe that even if the validity of plaintiff's proposition were conceded, under this record she nonetheless is not entitled to the relief she seeks.

Trial court filed "Findings of Fact, Conclusions of Law and Decree" in adjudicating plaintiff's three equitable claims. Among other facts, the court found the relationship between the parties was limited to their agreement to cohabit together without marriage; there was no substantial evidence of an agreement to share in the costs and expenses of building the house; defendant purchased the real estate and plaintiff refused to sign any of the related documents; defendant proceeded to construct his residence with the help of his friends and co-workers. The court further found "[t]hat the assistance that the plaintiff may have given in the selection, delivery, or application of any materials, like that of the defendant's other friends, was gratuitous and a part of the friendly relationship which then existed between the parties."

Trial court further found defendant furnished all the funds for construction of the house, furnished funds for plaintiff's personal needs, supplied her with various automobiles for her personal use, and paid for her tuition at a cosmetology school and for real estate sales classes. The court found that although plaintiff deposited monies in defendant's checking account, plaintiff withdrew for her personal use funds "far in excess" of those deposited. Further, defendant encouraged plaintiff to open her own savings account for her own funds and the proceeds of the sale of her Des Moines house.

In our de novo review, we find ample support in the record for each of the above factual findings, and adopt them as our own.

A. Unjust Enrichment

"Restitution" and "unjust enrichment" are modern designations for the older doctrine of quasi contracts or contracts implied in law, sometimes called constructive contracts. The doctrine rests upon the equitable principle that one shall not be permitted to unjustly enrich himself at the expense of another or to receive property or benefits without making compensation therefor. . . .

We do not perceive this doctrine to invest this court with a roving mandate to sort through terminated personal relationships in an attempt to nicely judge and balance the respective contributions of the parties. Plaintiff argues she "contributed all of her time, money and labor for seven years to help Tom Hammond build a house for the two of them, thus was entitled to recover half the value of the Hartford property, under the theory of unjust enrichment."

There is nothing in this record to show that defendant's retention of the house would be unjust or that it would be inequitable for the defendant to retain the benefit. . . . Clearly, plaintiff furnished less labor on this project than many of defendant's friends, in whom we would recognize no interest in the real estate. She contributed no capital and took no risk. We agree with trial court that the record discloses "no evidence to show that the defendant profited or enriched himself inequitably or unconscionably at the plaintiff's expense."

B. Resulting Trust

There are three situations in which a resulting trust may arise. Restatement (Second) of Trusts, Ch. 12 at 323 (1959). Plaintiff classifies her claim as a purchase money resulting trust. Ordinarily such a situation arises when the purchase price of the property is paid by one person and at his or her direction the vendor transfers the property to another. The latter is deemed to hold the property in trust for the person furnishing the consideration. The critical time occurs when the legal title to the property is acquired. A resulting trust cannot arise from matters coming into existence afterwards, and the person claiming to be the cestui que trust must occupy such position then as will entitle him or her to be substituted for the grantee. The plaintiff has the burden to establish all necessary facts with proof that is clear, certain, satisfactory and convincing.

Plaintiff argues consideration furnished by the cestui que trust may be only partial, and may be in the form of services, citing Restatement (Second) of Trusts, sections 454 and 455. Those sections, however, indicate that the consideration must flow to the vendor, not to the person taking title. Taking plaintiff's assertions at face value, the situation is that described in section 457 comment b:

> Where the transferee pays the purchase price to the vendor, the mere fact that another person subsequently pays the amount of the purchase price to the transferee or agrees to do so is not sufficient to create a resulting trust in his favor, if at the time of the purchase he did not agree to pay the purchase price or any part of it.

In this case we find, as did trial court, there was no evidence plaintiff paid or agreed to pay the vendor, and no agreement that she would provide any part of the consideration to anyone. The undisputed evidence is that she refused to sign the note and mortgage for the money to pay for the property, and the purchase price was borrowed and paid by defendant. A resulting trust is an intent-enforcing trust. Plaintiff's refusal to permit her name to be placed on the deed negates the necessary intent that she was to have an interest in the property.

Trial court was right in rejecting plaintiff's claim that a resulting trust arose in the circumstances shown by this record.

C. Constructive Trust

Plaintiff contends she is entitled to a constructive trust equal to an undivided one-half interest in the rural Hartford property. . . .

A constructive trust is a remedy, applied for purposes of restitution, to prevent unjust enrichment. It is an equitable doctrine. . . . A constructive trust is a creature of equity, defined as a remedial device by which the holder of legal title is held to be a trustee for the benefit of another who in good conscience is entitled to the beneficial interest. So, the doctrine of constructive trust is an instrument of equity for the maintenance of justice, good faith, and good conscience, resting on a sound public policy requiring that the law should not become the instrument of designing persons to be used for the purpose of fraud.

Constructive trusts fall into three categories: (1) those arising from actual fraud; (2) those arising from constructive fraud (appropriation of property by fiduciaries or others in confidential relationships); and (3) those based on equitable principles other than fraud. One seeking the remedy must establish the right by clear, convincing, and satisfactory evidence.

The distinguishing feature of the constructive trust is that it arises by construction of the court and ordinarily the result is reached regardless of and contrary to any intention to create a trust.

We agree with trial court's conclusion that plaintiff has produced no clear and convincing evidence showing defendant has enriched himself inequitably or unconscionably at plaintiff's expense. Plaintiff absented herself for months while much of the construction took place. The record reflects she is a bright, aggressive person who followed her own interests and who was fully capable of legally protecting any right she might have asserted in the real estate. It was only after the house virtually was completed and paid for that she presented defendant with a quitclaim deed to sign, conveying to her a one-half interest. Upon his refusal, she continued to live in the house until her occupancy was terminated, whereupon she commenced this action. There is a clear inference in the evidence that the services and benefits these parties conferred upon each other during the course of their cohabitation were gratuitously rendered and extended. We find nothing in this situation that would invoke the conscience of an equity court.

Affirmed and Remanded.

———————

Slocum v. Hammond was decided in 1984. At that time, the Iowa Supreme Court was not disposed to approve *Marvin* style contracts between unmarried cohabitants. States remain divided on the enforceability of contracts between unmarried cohabitants, although the trend is in the direction of approval. *See* George L. Blum, Property Rights Arising From Relationship of Couple Cohabiting Without Marriage, 69 A.L.R. 5th 219 (1999). States recognizing contracts between unmarried cohabitants do not distinguish between heterosexual and same sex unmarried couples.

Note: Palimony

"Palimony" is a term occasionally used to describe agreed upon or court-ordered support between former unmarried cohabitants. *See Trimmer v. Van Bomel,* 107 Misc. 2d 201, 434 N.Y.S.2d 82 (1980), where Justice Greenfield wrote:

> The complex and varied relationships between men and women, when they come to an end, oft leave a bitter residue and a smoldering irritation for which the salve, often the only soothing balm, is cash. It is a poor substitute for love, affection or attention, but for many its satisfactions are longer lasting. Ordinarily, alimony is the end product of the fission of matrimony and acrimony. More recently, the termination of informal live-in relationships has given rise to claims for palimony. Now, in this case, a man who claims to have been the constant companion of an elderly wealthy widow, who changed his life style from genteel poverty to luxury at her behest, sues at the breakup of their relationship for what may be called, for want of a better term, "Companiomony."

If the facts of *Trimmer v. Van Bomel* pique your curiosity, here's a summary:

> Plaintiff is a 67 year old gentleman, who was earning a modest but respectable living as a travel tour operator, when a person on one of his tours, the defendant, Mrs. Catherine Bryer Van Bomel, a wealthy widow with assets stated to be in excess of $40,000,000, began making demands on his time, and allegedly agreed to support him in luxurious fashion, if he would devote all his time and attention to her. He gave up his business career, in which he admits he was earning no more than $8,900 a year and became the ever-present companion of Mrs. Van Bomel. He moved to larger quarters and modified his wardrobe to suit her tastes. He accompanied her to lunch and dinner, escorted her to the theatre and parties, and travelled with her on her trips to Europe. All this was at the lady's expense, of course. He also acted as her confidant and her friends became his friends.
>
> For five years his life was constantly dominated by the needs, whims and desires of Mrs. Van Bomel. She spent money lavishly on him. Apart from taking care of his rent and his travel expenses, she had his suits hand tailored in Italy and in London, presented him

with two Pontiacs and a Jaguar and gave him a monthly stipend. All in all, she expended well over $300,000 for his personal needs. Then, suddenly, it all came to an end. Accustomed to a life of luxury, and now without the means to attain it, plaintiff sues his former benefactress for $1,500,000.

Mrs. Van Bomel filed a motion for summary judgment, and Justice Greenfield tossed Plaintiff's case out of court.

Questions and Problems

1. Judy and Wesley were lovers and lived together 15 years. They never married. Before Judy and Wesley met, Wesley had been married and had three children, all of whom were adults by the time Judy and Wesley started living together. Judy worked full time at Wal-Mart. Wesley owned and worked a farm. The couple lived on the farm. In addition to income from the farm, Wesley ran a hay bailing and hauling business that netted about $30,000 a year. During the relationship, Wesley purchased several pieces of farm land, putting title in his name alone. Judy and Wesley had a joint bank account into which they deposited their incomes. All bills were paid from the joint account. Wesley withdrew funds from the account to pay the mortgages on his various properties. During his relationship with Judy, Wesley used money from the joint account to make monthly contributions to a 401(k) retirement account in his name alone. Wesley developed cancer and died. When he died, the joint bank account contained $40,000. The 401(k) contained $75,000. In probate, Wesley's daughter is appointed personal representative. Does Judy have a claim against the estate for an interest in any of the property in Wesley's name? Would the results be different if Judy and Wesley had married? *Johnson v. Estate of McFarlin,* 334 S.W.3d 469 (Mo. Ct. App. 2010).

2. Abe was married when he started a sexual relationship with Beth. Abe never divorced his wife. Beth remained Abe's mistress until Abe died. During their ten year relationship, Abe did not live with Beth. Abe would visit Beth at her home a couple of times a week, but he did not stay the night. Upon Abe's death,

Beth seeks to enforce an oral agreement she says Abe made to support Beth for the rest of her life. The executor of Abe's estate refuses to make any payments to Beth. Can Beth enforce the agreement? *Cochran v. Cochran,* 89 Cal. App. 4th 283, 106 Cal. Rptr. 2d 899 (2001); *Bergen v. Wood,* 14 Cal. App. 4th 854, 18 Cal. Rptr. 2d 75 (1993); *Taylor v. Fields,* 178 Cal. App. 3rd 653, 224 Cal. Rptr. 186 (1986).

3. A cohabiting couple asks you to draft for them a contract that provides: "The parties shall be treated in all respects as a married couple under the laws of this state." Is it ethical for you to represent both parties to the contract? Putting aside the dual representation issue, would the proposed language accomplish the goals sought by the clients? That is, would the law treat the couple in all respects the same as a married couple?

4. Should the law require *Marvin* agreements to be in writing? In 2010, the New Jersey Legislature amended the Statute of Frauds to require palimony agreements to be in writing and signed by the parties. The New Jersey Statute provides: "No action shall be brought upon any of the following agreements or promises, unless the agreement or promise, upon which such action shall be brought or some memorandum thereof, shall be in writing, and signed by the party to be charged therewith . . . : A promise by one party to a non-marital personal relationship to provide support or other consideration for the other party, either during the course of such relationship or after its termination. For the purposes of this subsection, no such written promise is binding unless it was made with the independent advice of counsel for both parties."[3] Do you favor requiring a writing? Won't such a requirement occasionally lead to injustice?

---

3 N.J. Stat. Ann. § 25:1-5(h).

C

EXPERIENTIAL ASSIGNMENT

Practice Exercise: Draft **Marvin** *Agreement*

Rachel is a 20-year-old actor. Rachel has retained you to advise her about her plan to live with her boyfriend, Tim. Tim is also an actor. Rachel recently had a good supporting role in a popular film, and her acting career is taking off. Directors and producers are contacting her agent about possible starring roles. Tim has yet to "get a break," and is waiting tables. Rachel and Tim have been dating for a year, and are deeply in love. They don't plan to get married or have kids, at least not yet. Rachel and Tim recently decided to live together. Rachel heard from a friend that it might be a good idea for her to have a contract with Tim to sort out money issues, especially since her career is blossoming and Tim's isn't.

Assignments

1. You want Rachel to be fully advised about the pros and cons of a *Marvin* agreement. To that end, draft a letter to Rachel in which you outline the pros and cons. Explain what can and cannot be accomplished by a *Marvin* agreement. Explain why having an agreement is a good idea if the relationship ends. Finally, explain why the agreement should be in writing rather than informal. Your letter should be 1 to 2 single spaced pages.

2. Prepare a 1 to 2 page outline of Rachel's *Marvin* agreement. The final agreement will be 15 to 30 single spaced pages. For this assignment, you are simply preparing an outline of the subjects to be covered in the final agreement. Use resources in your law library and/or online to find out what goes into a *Marvin* agreement. In California, for example, there is a book on point titled *California Marital Settlement and Other Family Law Agreements*.

Premarital Agreements

AMERICAN LAW ALLOWS INDIVIDUALS in intimate relationships to contract with each other regarding many aspects of their relationship.[1] Contracts between unmarried cohabitants who are *not* planning to marry are often called *Marvin* agreements (Chapter 1). Contracts in contemplation of marriage are premarital or ante-nuptial agreements (Chapter 2). Contracts during marriage go by several names, including post-nuptial, transmutation, and partition and exchange.[2] (Chapter 3). Contracts between married couples who are separating but *not* divorcing are separation agreements. Contracts between divorcing spouses that are intended to settle their affairs in the divorce are referred to in some states as marital settlement agreements (Chapter 4).

Chapter 2 focuses on premarital agreements. The American Law Institute defines a premarital agreement as "an agreement between parties contemplating marriage that alters or confirms the legal rights and obligations that would otherwise arise under" applicable law.[3]

---

1 *See* Brett R. Turner & Laura W. Morgan, *Attacking and Defending Marital Agreements* (2d ed. 2012).

2 *See* American Law Institute, *Principles of the Law of Family Dissolution: Analysis and Recommendations* § 7.01(b), p. 946 (2002)("A marital agreement is an agreement between spouses who plan to continue their marriage that alters or confirms the legal rights and obligations that would otherwise arise under" the law.).

3 American Law Institute, *Principles of the Law of Family Dissolution: Analysis and Recommendations* § 7.01(a), pp. 945-946 (2002).

Relatively few engaged couples have a prenuptial agreement. Prenups traditionally have been used primarily by two groups: (1) wealthy individuals seeking to protect wealth from claims by new partners, and (2) older individuals with children from a previous marriage who desire to pass their property to their children.[4]

As for the first category, wealthy individuals, consider the following from the lives of the very rich.

Katrin is German. Nick is French. Katrin is heir to a fortune. Nick's parents are well off but not wealthy. Katrin and Nick met and fell in love in Europe. When they married in New York City, Katrin was 29, and Nick was 27. Nick worked on Wall Street, and earned a large income. Katrin did not work. During their eight year marriage they had two daughters. Three months prior to marriage, they signed a prenuptial agreement. Katrin wanted the prenuptial agreement to put her mind at ease that Nick was marrying for love, not money. The agreement provided in part, "In the event of divorce, the statutory matrimonial regime regarding property shall not apply. Each party shall manage his or her assets entirely independently. No marital or community property shall be acquired during the marriage. Neither party shall have any claim or ownership interest in the property of the other. Both parties waive any and all claims for maintenance or support if the marriage terminates in divorce. Both parties waive any statutory right to a portion of the estate of the first one of them to die."

The marriage did not last. Katrin left with the children and lives in Monaco. Nick wants joint custody of the children. Nick grew disenchanted with Wall Street, quit his high paying job, and enrolled at Yale to earn a Ph.D. in biotechnology. In the divorce, Nick argues the prenuptial agreement should not be enforced. Nick argues he did not sign the prenup voluntarily, did not read it at the time, and was not advised by an attorney about the meaning of the agreement. Nick asks the court to order Katrin to pay him $7 million in cash. This amount will allow Nick to earn about $150,000 a year for life and buy a home in New York City where the children can live while with him. In addition to the $7 million in property settlement, Nick asks $5,000 monthly spousal support and $3,000 monthly child support for the children.

Should the court enforce the premarital agreement? This case is loosely based on *Radmacher v. Granatino*, 2010 United Kingdom Supreme Court 42.

---

4 *See, e.g.*, Estate of Martin, 938 A.2d 812, 814 (Me. 2008)("James told his attorney he wanted a premarital agreement in order to protect the children of his first marriage.").

When you marry, you believe your relationship will last "'til death do us part." In addition to the couple's desire for a marriage that lasts, the state has an interest in supporting marriage. In the past, the state interest in stable marriage led courts to rule that premarital contracts that contemplate divorce violate public policy.[5] By contrast, premarital agreements focused only on distribution of property at death were acceptable because they did not encourage divorce.[6]

Courts have changed their views regarding premarital agreements that contemplate divorce. Today, premarital agreements that deal overtly with the possibility of divorce are enforceable.[7] The New York Court of Appeals wrote in *Van Kipnis v. Van Kipnis,*[8] "It is well settled that duly executed prenuptial agreements are generally valid and enforceable given the strong public policy favoring individuals ordering and deciding their own interests through contractual arrangements." The West Virginia Supreme Court of Appeals noted in *Ware v. Ware,*[9] "This Court has held that prenuptial agreements are presumptively valid."

---

5 *See* Marriage of Bonds, 24 Cal. 4th 1, 13-14, 5 P.3d 815, 99 Cal. Rptr. 2d 252 (2000)("At one time, a premarital agreement that was not made in contemplation that the parties would remain married until death was considered to be against public policy in California and other jurisdictions."); Hill v. Hill, 23 Cal. 2d 82, 86, 142 P.2d 417 (1943)(dealing with a separation agreement between married couple living separate: "Because, preservation of the marriage relationship is considered essential to the maintenance of organized society, it has been stated generally that the law will not countenance any contract having for its object the dissolution of a marriage."); American Law Institute, *Principles of the Law of Family Dissolution: Analysis and Recommendations* § 7.01 Comment (2002)("At one time, the law did not enforce agreements between prospective spouses that 'contemplated divorce,' as contrasted with agreements that applied only if the parties' marriage ended by death.").

6 *See* Marriage of Bonds, 24 Cal. 4th 1, 13, 5 P.3d 815, 99 Cal. Rptr. 2d 252 (2000)("There is nothing novel about statutory provisions recognizing the ability of parties to enter into premarital agreements regarding property, because such agreements long were common and legally enforceable under English law, and have enjoyed a lengthy history in this country.").

7 *See* Marriage of Bonds, 24 Cal. 4th 1, 5 P.3d 815, 99 Cal. Rptr. 2d 252 (2000)("At one time, a premarital agreement that was not made in contemplation that the parties would remain married until death was considered to be against public policy in California and other jurisdictions, but this court concluded in 1976 that the validity of a premarital agreement does not turn on whether the parties contemplated a lifelong marriage."); Hoyt v. Hoyt, 213 Tenn. 117, 372 S.W.2d 300, 303 (1963)("Antenuptial property settlements are favored by public policy."); W. Va. Code Ann. § 48-1-203 ("'Antenuptial agreement' or 'premarital agreement' means an agreement between a man and a woman before marriage, but in contemplation and generally in consideration of marriage, by which the property rights and interests of the prospective husband and wife, or both of them, are determined, or where property is secured to either or both of them, to their separate estate, or to their children or other persons. An antenuptial agreement may include provisions that define the respective property rights of the parties during marriage, or upon the death of either or both of the parties. The agreement may provide for the disposition of marital property upon an annulment or a divorce or separation of the parties."); Tenn. Code Ann. § 36-3-501 ("Notwithstanding any other provision of law to the contrary, except as provided in § 36-3-502, any antenuptial or prenuptial agreement entered into by spouses concerning property owned by either spouse before the marriage that is the subject of such agreement shall be binding upon any court having jurisdiction over such spouses and/or such agreement if such agreement is determined, in the discretion of such court, to have been entered into by such spouses freely, knowledgeably and in good faith without the exertion of duress or undue influence upon either spouse.").

8 11 N.Y.3d 573, 900 N.E.2d 977, 980, 872 N.Y.S.2d 426 (2008).

9 224 W. Va. 599, 687 S.E.2d 382, 387 (2009).

The National Conference of Commissioners on Uniform State Laws promulgated the Uniform Premarital Agreement Act in 1983 (UPAA). The UPAA has been adopted by more than half the states. The UPAA follows:

Uniform Premarital Agreement Act

§ 1. Definitions.

As used in this Act:

(1) "Premarital agreement" means an agreement between prospective spouses made in contemplation of marriage and to be effective upon marriage.

(2) "Property" means an interest, present or future, legal or equitable, vested or contingent, in real or personal property, including income and earnings.

§ 2. Formalities.

A premarital agreement must be in writing and signed by both parties. It is enforceable without consideration.[10]

§ 3. Consent.

(a) Parties to a premarital agreement may contract with respect to:

(1) the rights and obligations of each of the parties in any of the property of either or both of them whenever and wherever acquired or located;

(2) the right to buy, sell, use, transfer, exchange, abandon, lease, consume, expend, assign, create a security interest in, mortgage, encumber, dispose of, or otherwise manage and control property;

---

10 *See* Prell v. Silverstein, 114 Hawai'i 286, 162 P.3d 2, 11 (Ct. App. 2007)("other courts have held, and we agree, that marriage is adequate consideration for premarital agreements.").

(3) the disposition of property upon separation, martial dissolution, death, or the occurrence or nonoccurrence of any other event;

(4) the modification or elimination of spousal support;

(5) the making of a will, trust, or other arrangement to carry out the provisions of the agreement;

(6) the ownership rights in and disposition of the death benefit from a life insurance policy;

(7) the choice of law governing the construction of the agreement; and

(8) any other matter, including their personal rights and obligations, not in violation of public policy or a statute imposing a criminal penalty.

(b) The right of a child to support may not be adversely affected by a premarital agreement.

§ 4. Effect of Marriage.

A premarital agreement becomes effective upon marriage.

§ 5. Amendment, Revocation.

After marriage, a premarital agreement may be amended or revoked only by a written agreement signed by the parties. The amended agreement or the revocation is enforceable without consideration.

§ 6. Enforcement.

(a) A premarital agreement is not enforceable if the party against whom enforcement is sought proves that:

(1) that party did not execute the agreement voluntarily; or

(2) the agreement was unconscionable when it was executed and, before execution of the agreement, that party:

(i) was not provided a fair and reasonable disclosure of the property or financial obligations of the other party;[11]

---

11 What is fair and reasonable disclosure? *See* Friezo v. Friezo, 281 Conn. 166, 914 A.2d 533 (2007)(discussing states where couples entering premarital agreements are considered to be in a confidential relationship, the court wrote, "The overwhelming majority of jurisdictions that apply this standard do not require financial disclosure to be exact or precise. . . . We agree with the majority of jurisdictions that a fair and reasonable financial disclosure requires each contracting party to provide the other with a general approximation of their income, assets and liabilities, and that a written schedule appended to the agreement, although not absolutely necessary, is the most

(ii) did not voluntarily and expressly waive, in writing, any right to disclosure of the property or financial obligations of the other party beyond the disclosure provided; and

(iii) did not have, or reasonably could not have had, an adequate knowledge of the property or financial obligations of the other party.

(b) If a provision of a premarital agreement modifies or eliminates spousal support and that modification or elimination causes one party to the agreement to be eligible for support under a program of public assistance at the time of separation or marital dissolution, a court, notwithstanding the terms of the agreement, may require the other party to provide support to the extent necessary to avoid that eligibility.

(c) An issue of unconscionability of a premarital agreement shall be decided by the court as a matter of law.

The UPAA allows couples broad latitude to contract regarding property. If they want, a couple can contract completely out of their state's marital property system.[12] The New York Court of Appeals observed in *Van Kipnis v. Van Kipnis*[13] that a premarital agreement "may specifically designate as separate property assets that would ordinarily be defined as marital property subject to equitable distribution . . . . Such property would then remain separate property upon dissolution of the marriage." Indeed, the desire to avoid creation of marital property is the most common reason for premarital agreements.

Section 3(a)(4) of the UPAA allows premarital contracts that modify or eliminate spousal support on divorce. Under the UPAA, a contract limiting or eliminating spousal support is invalid only if enforcement of the agreement "causes one party to the agreement to be eligible for support under a program of public assistance . . . ." States vary on the enforceability of premarital contracts

---

effective method of satisfying the statutory obligation in most circumstances." 914 A.2d at 549-550. The court also wrote, "It is well established that the amount of time available to review a prenuptial agreement is relevant in assessing whether the agreement was voluntary or signed under duress, but not in determining whether the parties made a 'fair and reasonable' disclosure of their financial circumstances." *Id.* at 551.).

12 *See* Marriage of Bonds, 24 Cal. 4th 1, 13, 5 P.3d 815, 99 Cal. Rptr. 2d 252 (2000)("From the inception of its statehood, California has retained the community property law that predated its admission to the Union . . . . At the same time, applicable statutes recognized the power of parties contemplating a marriage to reach an agreement containing terms at variance with community property law."); Van Kipnis v. Van Kipnis, 11 N.Y.3d 573, 900 N.E.2d 977, 981, 872 N.Y.S.2d 426 (2008)("parties may expressly waive or opt out of the statutory scheme governing equitable distribution.").

13 11 N.Y.3d 573, 900 N.E.2d 977, 980, 872 N.Y.S.2d 426 (2008).

that modify or waive spousal support. In North Carolina, for example, couples may contract regarding modification or waiver of spousal support.[14] California provides that a premarital agreement waiving spousal support is enforceable at divorce only if the party seeking support was represented by an attorney when the agreement was signed.[15] Even if the party seeking support was represented by counsel, a waiver of support is unenforceable if the waiver is "unconscionable at the time of enforcement," that is, at the time of divorce.[16]

A premarital agreement cannot reduce or eliminate a parent's duty to support children.[17]

A premarital agreement is a contract, and "the rules applicable to the interpretation of contracts have been applied generally to premarital agreements."[18]

The Prenup Must Be Voluntary – UPAA § 6(a)(1)

Under the UPAA, a prenup must be "voluntarily." Interestingly, the UPAA does not define the term.[19] Courts have interpreted "voluntarily."[20] In *Marriage of Bonds*,[21] for example, the California Supreme Court wrote, "Courts frequently consult dictionaries to determine the usual meaning of words. *Black's Law Dictionary* defines 'voluntarily' as 'Done by design . . . Intentionally and without coercion.'"[22] The *Bonds* court outlined factors shedding light on voluntariness: (1) Presence or absence of coercion, fraud, duress, or undue influence, (2) Did the party understand the agreement and, in particular, understand the rights

---

14 N.C. Stat. Ann. § 52B-7(b). *See* Muchmore v. Trask, 192 N.C. App. 635, 666 S.E.2d 667 (2008).

15 Cal. Family Code § 1612(c).

16 Cal. Family Code § 1612(c).

17 *See* Cal. Family Code § 1612(b). "The right of a child to support may not be adversely affected by a premarital agreement."

18 Marriage of Bonds, 24 Cal. 4th 1, 13, 5 P.3d 815, 99 Cal. Rptr. 2d 252 (2000).

19 *See* Marriage of Bonds, 24 Cal. 4th 1, 17, 5 P.3d 815, 99 Cal. Rptr. 2d 252 (2000)("The commissioners, however, did not supply a definition of the term 'voluntarily,' nor was there much discussion of the term.").

20 *See* Marriage of Shanks, 758 N.W.2d 506, 512 (Iowa 2008)("Neither the IUPAA nor the UPAA defines the term 'voluntarily.' Black's Law Dictionary defines 'voluntarily' as '[i]ntentionally; without coercion.' In *Spiegal*, we intimated that a voluntarily executed premarital agreement was one free from duress and undue influence. We believe this is the appropriate formulation of the voluntariness inquiry under IUPAA as well. We therefore hold proof of duress or undue influence is required under section 596.8(1) to establish a premarital agreement was involuntarily executed.").

21 24 Cal. 4th 1, 5 P.3d 815, 99 Cal. Rptr. 2d 252 (2000). For baseball fans, you may be interested to know that this case involved the famous player Barry Bonds.

22 24 Cal. 4th at 16.

being waived? (3) Was there full disclosure of property and debts?[23] (4) Did the party have time to study the agreement, or was it presented shortly before the wedding? (5) Was the party represented by independent counsel?[24] (6) Was the party sufficiently mature and intellectually capable of understanding the agreement? (7) Were the parties of equal or unequal bargaining power and sophistication? The *Bonds* court concluded, "The question of voluntariness must be examined in the unique context of the marital relationship."[25]

Questions: Is the Prenup Voluntary?

1. Tom and Wendy are getting married in less than a month. Wedding plans are well-advanced. Invitations have been mailed. The wedding site is reserved. The caterer is employed. The cake is ordered. The wedding dress is at the seamstress following final fitting. Dresses for the bridesmaids are hanging in closets. Relatives and friends from far and wide have made airline and hotel reservations. In the midst of these happy but hectic preparations, Tom tells Wendy, "I think it would be a good idea for us to have a prenup. I asked my lawyer to draft one for us. Here it is. What do you think?" Should the advanced state of wedding preparations be a factor in deciding whether Wendy's signature on the prenup is voluntary?[26]

2. Deborah and Victor's wedding was just weeks away. Victor's attorney drafted a prenup and advised Deborah to review the prenup with an independent attorney. Victor's attorney recommended independent counsel, and Deborah consulted the attorney. The attorney advised Deborah that the prenup was "unfair."

---

23 *See* James O. Pearson, Jr., Failure to Disclose Extent or Value of Property Owned as Ground for Avoiding Premarital Contract, 3 A.L.R. 5th 394 (1992).

24 *See* Marriage of Bonds, 24 Cal. 4th 1, 23, 5 P.3d 815, 99 Cal. Rptr. 2d 252 (2000)(the court discussed at length whether the fact that a person was not represented by independent counsel rendered a premarital agreement involuntary. The court concluded that legal advice is an important factor in the voluntariness inquiry, but that a premarital agreement can be voluntarily entered into without legal advice. "It seems evident that the commissioners who enacted the Uniform Act intended that the presence of independent counsel (or a reasonable opportunity to consult counsel) should be merely one factor among several that a court should consider in examining a challenge to the voluntariness of a premarital agreement."); Friezo v. Friezo, 281 Conn. 166, 914 A.2d 533, 557 (2007)(a reasonable opportunity to consult an attorney "means simply that the party against whom enforcement is sought must have had sufficient time before the marriage to consult with an attorney other than the attorney representing the party's future spouse.").

25 Marriage of Bonds, 24 Cal. 4th 1, 26, 5 P.3d 815, 99 Cal. Rptr. 2d 252 (2000).

26 *See* Edwards v. Edwards, 16 Neb. App. 297, 744 N.W.2d 243 (2008)(the fact that wife had made wedding plans did not mean she was coerced into signing prenuptial agreement); Barocas v. Barocas, 94 A.D.3d 551, 942 N.Y.S.2d 491 (2012)("Defendant's claims that she believed that there would be no wedding if she did not sign the agreement, that the wedding was only two weeks away and that wedding plans had been made, is insufficient to demonstrate duress.").

The attorney advised Deborah not to sign the prenup. Victor paid the fee charged by Deborah's attorney. Deborah understood the prenup and decided to sign it. A few years later, Deborah files for divorce and claims the prenup is invalid because Victor paid the fee of the attorney she consulted. Should the fact that Victor paid the attorney invalidate the prenup? *Barocas v. Barocas*, 94 A.D.3d 551, 942 N.Y.S. 2d 491 (2012).

> **Practice Note:** A key component of an informed and voluntary agreement is full knowledge of what is gained and lost in a prenuptial agreement. The attorney representing the party with greater assets should assure full disclosure of the client's wealth.

Should an Unconscionable Premarital Agreement be Enforceable? – UPAA § 6(a)(2)

Section 6(a)(2) of the UPA provides that an unconscionable prenup is not enforceable unless certain conditions are met. As is true with the word "voluntary," the UPA does not define unconscionable. The North Dakota Supreme Court grappled with the meaning of unconscionable in *Sailer v. Sailer*,[27] where the court wrote, "Although the issue of whether a premarital agreement is unconscionable presents a question of law, the analysis turns on factual findings related to the relative property values, the parties' financial circumstances, and their ongoing need." Courts ask, how one-sided is the agreement?

Careful reading of the UPAA reveals that some unconscionable agreements *are* enforceable![28] Section 6(a)(2) states that an unconscionable agreement *is* enforceable if the disadvantaged party was given fair and reasonable disclosure of the other party's property, or waived the right to disclosure.[29]

Is it good public policy to enforce an unconscionable premarital agreement so long as the disadvantaged party understood and agreed to the agreement? On one hand, absent coercion or fraud, parties have the right to make

---

27 788 N.W.2d 604, 606 (N.D. 2010).

28 *See* Marriage of Bonds, 24 Cal. 4th 1, 16, 5 P.3d 815, 99 Cal. Rptr. 2d 252 (2000).

29 For analysis of fair and reasonable financial disclosure, *see* Friezo v. Friezo, 281 Conn. 166, 914 A.2d 533 (2007).

bad deals. Contract law usually is not so paternalistic that it protects us from our folly. On the other hand, there are differences between signing a contract for a box of chocolates and signing a premarital contract, aren't there?[30] If you enter a one-sided contract with a merchant, you have no one to blame but yourself. But should the result be the same if you sign a one-sided premarital agreement? Is it fair to allow one party—typically the party with the most to lose—to be bound by an *unconscionable* premarital agreement?[31] The American Law Institute's

---

30 *See* American Law Institute, *Principles of the Law of Family Dissolution: Analysis and Recommendations* § 7.02, p. 956, Comment (2002).

31 The California Supreme Court discussed the differences between commercial contracts and premarital agreements in Marriage of Bonds, 24 Cal. 4ᵗʰ 1, 24-27, 5 P.3d 815, 99 Cal. Rptr. 2d 252 (2000): A commercial contract most frequently constitutes a private regulatory agreement intended to ensure the successful outcome of the business between the contracting parties—in essence, to guide their relationship so that the object of the contract may be achieved. Normally, the execution of the contract ushers in the applicability of the regulatory scheme contemplated by the contract, and the endeavor that is the object of the contract. As for a premarital agreement (or clause of such an agreement) providing solely for the division of property upon marital dissolution, the parties generally enter into the agreement anticipating that it never will be invoked, and the agreement, far from regulating the relationship of the contracting parties and providing the method for attaining their joint objectives, exists to provide for eventualities that will arise only if the relationship founders, possibly in the distant future under greatly changed and unforeseeable circumstances.

Furthermore, marriage itself is a highly regulated institution of undisputed social value, and there are many limitations on the ability of persons to contract with respect to it, or to vary its statutory terms, that have nothing to do with maximizing the satisfaction of the parties or carrying out their intent. Such limitations are inconsistent with the freedom-of-contract analysis. We refer to rules establishing a duty of mutual financial support during the marriage and prohibiting agreements in derogation of the duty to support a child of the marriage; the unenforceability of a promise to marry; the circumstance that a party may abandon the marriage unilaterally under this state's no-fault laws; and the pervasive state involvement in the dissolution of marital status, the marriage contract, and the arrangements to be made for the children of the marriage—even without consideration of the circumstance that marriage normally lacks a predominantly commercial object. We also observe that a premarital agreement to raise children in a particular religion is not enforceable. We note, too, that there is authority—as conceded by the commissioners who considered the Uniform Act to the effect that a contract to pay a spouse for personal services such as nursing cannot be enforced, despite the undoubted economic value of the services. These limitations demonstrate further that freedom of contract with respect to marital arrangements is tempered with statutory requirements and case law expressing social policy with respect to marriage.

There also are obvious differences between the remedies that realistically may be awarded with respect to commercial contracts and premarital agreements. Although a party seeking rescission of a commercial contract, for example, may be required to restore the status quo ante by restoring the consideration received, and a party in breach may be required to pay damages, the status quo ante for spouses cannot be restored to either party, nor are damages contemplated for breach of the marital contract. In any event, the suggestion that commercial contracts are strictly enforced without regard to the fairness or oppressiveness of the terms or the inequality of the bargaining power of the parties is anachronistic and inaccurate, in that claims such as duress, unconscionability, and undue influence turn upon the specific context in which the contract is formed.

We also have explained generally that we believe the reference to voluntariness in the Uniform Act was intended to convey an element of knowing waiver that is not a consistent feature of commercial contract enforcement. Further, although the Uniform Act contemplated that contract defenses should apply, in the sense that an agreement should be free from fraud (including constructive fraud), duress, or undue influence, it is clear from the debate of the commissioners who adopted the Uniform Act and the cases cited in support of the enforcement provision of the Uniform Act that subtle coercion that would not be considered in challenges to ordinary commercial contracts may be considered in the context of the premarital agreement. The obvious distinctions between premarital agreements and ordinary commercial contracts lead us to conclude that factual circumstances

Principles of the Law of Family Dissolution analyze the differences between a marrying couple and a couple of merchants:

> While there are good reasons to respect contracts relating to the consequences of family dissolution, the family context requires some departure from the rules that govern the commercial arena. The relationship between contracting parties who are married, or about to marry, is different than the usual commercial relationship in ways that matter in the law's treatment of their agreements. Persons planning to marry usually assume that they share with their intended spouse a mutual and deep concern for one another's welfare. Business people negotiating a commercial agreement do not usually have such expectations of one another. (When courts sometimes say that parties to a premarital agreement are in a relationship of trust with one another, they are making the same point in different language.) The distinctive expectations that persons planning to marry usually have about one another can disarm their capacity for self-protective judgment, or their inclination to exercise it, as compared to parties negotiating commercial agreements.[32]

Iowa's version of the Uniform Premarital Agreement Act (IUPAA) allows a judge to refuse to enforce an unconscionable premarital agreement. The Iowa Supreme Court wrote in *Marriage of Shanks*,[33] "In contrast to the UPAA approach, unconscionability alone is sufficient to render a premarital agreement unenforceable under the IUPAA, notwithstanding fair and reasonable financial disclosure. . . . Under the IUPAA, courts may address unconscionability claims whether or not appropriate financial disclosures are made."

---

relating to contract defenses that would not necessarily support the rescission of a commercial contract may suffice to render a premarital agreement unenforceable. The question of voluntariness must be examined in the unique context of the marital relationship.

Because the Uniform Act was intended to enhance the enforceability of premarital agreements, because it expressly places the burden of proof upon the person challenging the agreement, and finally because the California statute imposing fiduciary duties in the family law setting applies only to spouses, we do not believe that the commissioners or our Legislature contemplated that the voluntariness of a premarital agreement would be examined in light of the strict fiduciary duties imposed on persons such as lawyers, or imposed expressly by statute upon persons who are married.

32 American Law Institute, Principles of the Law of Family Dissolution: Analysis and Recommendations § 7.02, p. 956 (2002).

33 758 N.W.2d 506, 514 (Iowa 2008).

Which approach to you favor? Do you favor upholding unconscionable premarital agreements that were signed voluntarily? Or do you prefer the more paternalistic approach that allows judges to set aside unconscionable prenups?

Should a Premarital Agreement Be Enforceable Years After It Is Signed If Enforcement Would be Unfair *at the Later Date*?

The American Law Institute's *Principles of the Law of Family Dissolution* grapple with the enforceability of premarital agreements that turn out to be unfair when they are sought to be enforced years after they are signed. The *Principles* state that a premarital agreement should not be enforced if enforcement would "work a substantial injustice."[34] The *Principles* conclude, "When many years have passed since the agreement was executed, when the parties first have children in common after execution, or when the circumstances of the parties have unforeseeably changed, courts must examine the agreement before enforcing it to ensure . . . that such enforcement will not work a 'substantial injustice.'"[35]

What is a "substantial injustice"? Does the "substantial injustice" language create a potential escape hatch from virtually any prenup? Should parties be entitled to rely on their prenup in the event of divorce? Put differently, if you voluntarily sign a prenup, shouldn't you be stuck with it?

---

34 American Law Institute, *Principles of the Law of Family Dissolution: Analysis and Recommendations* § 7.05, p. 982 (2002).

35 American Law Institute, *Principles of the Law of Family Dissolution: Analysis and Recommendations* § 7.02, p. 955 (2002). Elsewhere, the Comment to Section 7.05 states, "In sum, nearly all premarital agreements involve special difficulties arising from unrealistic optimism about marital success, the human tendency to treat low probabilities as zero probabilities, the excessive discounting of future benefits, and the inclination to overweigh the importance of the immediate and certain consequences of agreement—the marriage—as against its contingent and future consequences." p. 987.

Questions on Premarital Agreements

1. Who should have the burden of proof regarding enforceability of a pre-marital agreement? The party seeking to enforce the agreement? Or the party seeking to invalidate the agreement? The UPAA places the burden of proof on the party challenging a premarital agreement. The American Law Institute takes the opposite approach, placing the burden of proof on the party seeking to enforce a premarital agreement.[36] Which position to you prefer?

2. How much time does a person need between their wedding day and the day they are given a premarital agreement to read and consider? Should a premarital agreement be enforced if the groom sees it for the first time a few minutes before he walks down the aisle? What about the night before the wedding? A week before? A month? The American Law Institute's *Principles of the Law of Family Dissolution* presume at least 30 days should be provided.[37] California law provides that a premarital agreement is not voluntary unless "the party against whom enforcement is sought has not less than seven calendar days between the time that the party was first presented with the agreement and advised to seek independent legal counsel and the time the agreement was signed."[38] Should the law specify a specific time limit, or should each case be decided on its own facts? Suppose a statute requires a week, but a party signed an agreement in a shorter time after going over the agreement with a lawyer. Should the seven day period apply when a lawyer advised the individual and the individual understood the prenup?[39]

3. Married couples are in a confidential relationship, and owe each other duties of honesty and candor (See Chapter 3). Is a couple planning to marry, and thinking about a premarital agreement, in a confidential relationship?[40] The Connecticut Supreme Court discussed this issue in *Friezo v. Friezo*.[41] The court wrote: "Our review of this case law indicates that when a party's independent knowledge is insufficient and the other party must disclose financial informa-

---

36 American Law Institute, *Principles of the Law of Family Dissolution: Analysis and Recommendations* § 7.04, p. 960 (2002)("(2) A party seeking to enforce an agreement must show that the other party's consent to it was informed and not obtained under duress.").

37 American Law Institute, *Principles of the Law of Family Dissolution: Analysis and Recommendations* § 7.04(3)(a), p. 960 (2002).

38 Cal. Family Code § 1615(c)(2).

39 *See* Marriage of Cadwell-Faso, 191 Cal. App. 4th 945, 119 Cal. Rptr. 3d 818 (2011).

40 *See* Marriage of Rudder, 230 Or. App. 437, 217 P.3d 183, 193 (2009)("the relationship between the parties to a premarital agreement is 'fiduciary in character' if entered into in contemplation of marriage.").

41 281 Conn. 166, 914 A.2d 533, 549 (2007).

tion in a prenuptial agreement, the extent of the required disclosure depends on how the court views the relationship. Courts in the majority of jurisdictions regard the parties as involved in a confidential relationship of mutual trust that demands the exercise of the highest degree of good faith, candor and sincerity in all matters bearing on the proposed agreement. . . . Jurisdictions that treat the parties as involved in an arm's-length relationship on the theory that parties who are not yet married are not presumed to share a confidential relationship, impose a duty on each spouse to inquire and investigate the financial condition of the other, and consequentially, the disclosure requirement is less demanding. Connecticut regards the parties to a premarital agreement as involved in a confidential relationship." Which is the better position?

In *Hood v. Hood,* the Alabama Court of Civil Appeals enforced a premarital agreement. Do you agree with the court's decision?

Hood v. Hood

Court of Civil Appeals of Alabama
72 So. 3d 666 (2011)

Bryan, Judge.

Kristi L. Hood ("the wife") appeals from a judgment entered by the Etowah Circuit Court ("the trial court") that divorced her from Frank L. Hood ("the husband").

[Husband sought divorce. Husband argued that a premarital agreement regarding property division and spousal support was enforceable. Wife argued the premarital agreement was not enforceable.]

. . . The trial court . . . conducted a hearing on the enforceability of the antenuptial agreement. The only testimony presented at this hearing was from the wife on the issue whether she signed the antenuptial agreement while under duress. The wife testified that she had met the husband in Natchez, Mississippi, when she was working as a registered nurse. There is an indication in the record that the husband is a doctor. At that time, the wife had custody of two children from a previous marriage, and the parties began living together in the wife's home in Natchez with her two children. The husband paid the mortgage on that residence while they lived together. After the parties became engaged, the husband moved to Gadsden, and, approximately one month before the wife and her children moved to Gadsden in the summer of 1998, the husband purchased the home on Hood Drive, i.e., the marital residence. After the wife moved with her children to live with the husband in the marital residence, she decided to make her home in Natchez available to rent.

The wife stated that the parties had never set a wedding date, but, she stated, at midnight on December 28, 1998, the husband asked her if she wanted to get married at the courthouse that day, and she agreed. The wife stated that she did not learn that the husband expected her to sign an antenuptial agreement until they were on the way to the courthouse to be married. According to the wife, the husband told her that they had to stop at his attorney's office to sign "the marriage papers" and it was not until she was at the husband's attorney's office that she realized that the husband wanted her to sign an antenuptial agreement. Apparently, the wife was shocked at the request and began crying.

The wife stated that the husband's attorney had discussed the antenuptual agreement with her, and she admitted that she had understood that in the event the parties divorced the husband "would reserve control over certain things that he had," including the marital residence. The wife also testified that she had understood that she would not have a claim to the husband's IRA, pension plans, and stocks that he owned before the marriage, but she also stated that she did not know what pension plans the husband owned. The wife admitted that while she was at the husband's attorney's office she understood that she would not have a claim to the property listed in the agreement if the parties divorced.

The wife further testified that the husband's attorney had sent the wife and the husband to another attorney, "his good friend," so the wife could review the agreement with a separate attorney. According to the wife, the husband was approximately 10 feet away outside an open door when she was discussing the agreement with her "independent" counsel. The wife stated that the attorney that she met with only browsed through the agreement because the parties were trying to make it to the courthouse before it closed. The wife stated that she was crying and was trying to whisper to the attorney because the husband looked mad and that she did not understand what the attorney told her. The wife testified that, initially, she refused to sign the agreement, so she and the husband left the attorney's office and returned to their home. According to the wife, the husband told her that he would not have the nerve to get married if she did not sign the antenuptial agreement. The parties subsequently returned to the second attorney's office, and she signed the antenuptial agreement.

The wife claimed that she did not know that the second attorney was supposed to be her attorney, and she stated that she did not understand that she had waived a right to alimony in the event the parties divorced. The wife stated that she was never able to read through the entire agreement, but she agreed that she knew that she was giving up rights by signing the agreement that she otherwise would have had if she had not signed the agreement.

According to the wife, her former husband had been threatening to take custody of their children because she was living with the husband in violation of their divorce judgment. The wife stated that the husband was aware of that fact, and the wife thought that, if she did not sign the agreement, she and the husband would not get married and there was a possibility that she would lose custody of her children. She stated that her children were ages one and three years old at the time she signed the antenuptual agreement and that she had no money and no place to live because her home in Natchez was occupied by renters.

The husband's attorney offered the parties' antenuptual agreement into evidence, but no other exhibits were offered or admitted during that hearing. That agreement states, in pertinent part:

"WHEREAS, the parties to this agreement contemplate entering into the marriage relation with each other, and;

"WHEREAS, [the husband], individually owns certain tangible and intangible property, a list of which is set out hereinafter in Exhibit 'A', the nature and extent of which has been disclosed to the [wife], and he desires that all property now owned or hereafter acquired by either [sic] shall be free, for purposes of testamentary disposition, divorce or otherwise, from any claim of the [wife], that may arise by reason of their contemplated marriage, other than as set out herein:

"NOW THEREFORE, in consideration of the premises and the mutual covenants herein contained, it is agreed as follows:

" 1. Both before and after the solemnization of the marriage between the parties, [the husband] shall separately retain all rights in his own property, including all interest, rents and profits which may accrue or result in any manner from increases in value, and he shall have the absolute and unrestricted right to dispose of his property, free from any claim that may be made by the [wife] by reason of their marriage, and with the same effect as if no marriage had been consummated between them, whether such disposition be made by gift, conveyance, sale, lease; by will or codicil or other testamentary means; by laws of intestacy; or otherwise. *Any property, real, personal or mixed, acquired after the date of said marriage shall be considered joint property unless agreed to in writing, signed by both parties.* [emphasis supplied by the court]

" . . . .

" 8. [The wife] has examined the financial statements attached hereto and made a part hereof as Exhibit 'A' and has had the opportunity to question and examine all items therein, and acknowledges that fair disclosure has been made by [the husband], as contemplated under the provisions of Section 43–8–72, Code of Alabama (1975). Each certifies that he or she has had an independent and separate counsel and has been independently advised and has been given, without limitation, all information requested. Each further certifies that counsel has advised and informed him or her of the legal effects of this document.

" 9. In the event of the death of [the husband] or the granting of a final divorce decree, [the wife] shall have no right to any claim against the estate of [the husband] based on spousal or marital rights including, but not limited to maintenance, support, or property settlements, by reason of or on account of dissolution of the marriage, or by reason of death." [emphasis added by the court]

Exhibit A, which was a document attached to the antenuptial agreement, was labeled "Property to be Retained by [the husband], Individually, Without Any Claims by [the wife]," and it included six paragraphs identifying real and personal property . . . .

On May 5, 2009, the trial court entered an order finding that the antenuptual agreement was "voluntarily entered into by the husband and the wife for good and valuable consideration and that the agreement was fair, just and reasonable from the [wife]'s point of view so as to be valid under general principles governing antenuptual agreements." . . .

On March 31, 2010, the trial court entered a judgment divorcing the parties on the grounds of incompatibility of temperament and an irretrievable breakdown of the marriage. The parties were awarded joint legal custody of their child, and the wife was awarded primary physical custody of the child, subject to the husband's visitation rights as specifically set forth in the judgment. The husband was ordered to pay the wife child support in the amount of $250.56 a month, and the wife was required to maintain health-insurance coverage for the child. . . .

On appeal, . . . the wife argues that the trial court erred by concluding that the antenuptual agreement is valid and enforceable because, she says, (1) her testimony indicated that she was under duress when she signed the agreement, (2) she did not have the opportunity to obtain the advice of independent counsel, and (3) the husband failed to provide full disclosure of the existence and/or value of his assets. . . .

Alabama law has long held that antenuptial agreements are generally enforceable in equity, but because of the confidential relationship of the two parties, such contracts are scrutinized by the courts to determine their justice and reasonableness. . . . The proponent of an antenuptual agreement has the burden of showing that the consideration was adequate and that the entire transaction was fair, just and equitable from the other party's point of view or that the agreement was freely and voluntarily entered into by the other party with competent independent advice and full knowledge of the other party's interest in the estate and its approximate value.

After a review of the evidence in the record and in light of our standard of review on appeal, we conclude that the trial court could have concluded that the wife voluntarily signed the antenuptual agreement. Although the wife presented evidence indicating that she believed that she would not have had a place to live with her children if she had not signed the agreement, there was no indication that the husband had told her that she and her children would be immediately required to vacate his home if she did not sign the agreement. Moreover, there was no indication that the wife's former husband had filed an action to modify custody based on the wife's living arrangement with the husband. In short, the wife did not present any evidence indicating that there was a need to sign the antenuptual agreement shortly after she became aware of the agreement in order to prevent losing custody of her children.

We also conclude that the trial court could have determined that the wife had signed the agreement after receiving competent independent advice. . . . The wife signed the agreement that stated that she had been advised by independent counsel and that she had been informed of the legal effects of the agreement. Relying on that certification from the wife, the trial court could have concluded that the wife had received competent independent advice.

Finally, the wife contends that the antenuptual agreement should be unenforceable because the agreement did not provide "full disclosure" of the husband's assets. However, this court has required only that the party against whom the agreement is being enforced have a general knowledge, not a full knowledge, of the other's estate. The record indicates that the husband and the wife had dated for approximately one and a half years before they were married, and the wife does not contend that she did not have a general knowledge of the husband's estate.

. . . Because we conclude that the trial court could have determined that the wife had voluntarily signed the agreement, with independent advice, and with a general knowledge of the husband's estate, we affirm that part of the trial court's judgment concluding that the antenuptual agreement is valid and enforceable.

The decision in *Hood v.* Hood reflects the deference appellate courts give factual findings and credibility assessments of triers of fact (whether trial judge or jury). The appellate court in *Hood* does *not* say it would have reached the same conclusion as the trial court. Rather, the appellate court says, "the trial court *could have* determined that the wife voluntarily signed the agreement . . . ."

In *In re Michael G.*,[42] the California Court of Appeal reminds us of the different functions of trial and appellate courts. *Michael G.* was a termination of parental rights case in juvenile court. The Court of Appeal wrote:

> At oral argument, we found it necessary to restate, more than once, the standard of review that applies when the issue on appeal challenges the juvenile court's resolution of disputed factual questions, and to remind the appellants that this court does not substitute its judgment for that of the juvenile court. Appellate practitioners would be well advised to remember it is the function of the trier of fact, not the appellate court, to determine the facts . . . .

In *Lang v. Levi*, the Maryland Court of Special Appeals analyzes a premarital agreement in the context of an arbitration agreement. Arbitration in family law is discussed in Chapter 4.

Lang v. Levi

Court of Special Appeals of Maryland
198 Md. App. 154, 16 A.3d 980 (2011)

Zarnoch, J.

This appeal challenges the correctness of the reduction of a claimed marital award by a Jewish arbitration panel, the Beth Din,[43] and the outright denial of an award on post-arbitration applications by a representative of the Av Beth Din.[44] Appellant Julie Lang and Appellee Zion Levi signed a prenuptial agree-

---

42 203 Cal. App. 4th 580, 137 Cal. Rptr. 3d 476 (2012).

43 The Beth Din of America is a rabbinical court. One of the purposes of the Beth Din is to "provide a forum where adherents of Jewish law can seek to have their disputes resolved in a manner consistent with the rules of Jewish law." Rules and Procedures of the Beth Din of America, Preamble (a).

44 The Av Beth Din is "the most senior jurist who may join in the adjudication of cases or advise the presiding *dayanim* [judges]. The Av Beth Din is a highly respected *rabbi* and *posek* [decider] ..." *New World Encyclopedia*,

ment, which stated in part that Levi had an obligation to pay Lang $100 a day from the time they no longer resided together until Levi granted Lang a get, a Jewish divorce. They also signed an arbitration agreement giving the Beth Din the authority to decide any disputes that arose regarding this prenuptial agreement.

When the marriage fell apart, Lang and Levi appeared before the Beth Din in 2008. The panel rejected Lang's claim that she was entitled to a cumulative amount of $108,000 in stipulated per diems, but granted her an award of $10,200. However, the award was later reduced to zero by a representative of the Av Beth Din who found, on the basis of Jewish law, that Levi was not obligated to pay any amount to Lang. In 2009, Lang petitioned the Circuit Court for Montgomery County to vacate the arbitration award, and Levi moved for summary judgment. The circuit court found no grounds to vacate the award, and granted Levi's motion. For the reasons set forth below, we affirm the decision of the circuit court.

Appellant Julie Lang and Appellee Zion Levi were married on June 22, 2003, and entered into both a secular marriage under Maryland law and a Jewish marriage. That same day, the parties signed a prenuptial agreement and an arbitration agreement. The prenuptial agreement provided that if the parties did not continue to reside together, Levi would pay Lang $100 a day from the day they no longer resided together until the end of their Jewish marriage. The arbitration agreement provided that if the parties no longer lived together as husband and wife, they authorized an arbitration panel, the Beth Din, to decide all issues involving the Jewish divorce and premarital agreements, including monetary disputes. This agreement stated: "The decision of the Beth Din shall be made in accordance with Jewish Law (Halakhah) and/or the general principles of arbitration and equity (Pesharah) customarily employed by rabbinical tribunals."

The parties had one child together, Victoria, who was born on September 21, 2004. By 2005, the marriage had deteriorated and on October 1, 2005, the parties separated. In 2006, Levi sued for a divorce and Lang counter-claimed, requesting sole custody, alimony, attorney's fees, determinations regarding property, and a monetary award. The trial court entered a consent order resolving custody and visitation disputes. Around the same time, the parties agreed that Levi would pay *pendente lite* child support.

The circuit court entered a decree of absolute divorce on March 28, 2008. The court denied Lang's request for alimony, ordered the parties to evenly divide

Beth Din, http://www.newworldencyclopedia.org/entry/Beth_Din (last visited February 16, 2011). *See also* Tal Tours (1996) Inc. v. Goldstein, 9 Misc.3d 1117(A), 808 N.Y.S.2d 920 (Sup.Ct.2005) (The Av Beth Din is "the supervisor of the Beth Din.").

their child's school expenses, required Levi to provide health insurance for the child, and denied both parties' requests for attorney's fees.

Levi also petitioned the Beth Din to arrange the get. The Beth Din notified Lang on July 3, 2008 and requested she contact the Beth Din if she wished to participate. When she agreed, the Beth Din scheduled an arbitration session for September 17, 2008 before a panel of three rabbis. At the session, the Beth Din heard arguments on both the prenuptial agreement and the get. At that time, Levi offered and Lang accepted the get. Six weeks later, the panel addressed the remaining issue and rejected as "unjust and improper" Lang's claim for a per diem obligation of $108,000, computed up to the moment she was summoned to the Beth Din. Finding that the purpose of the prenuptial agreement was to ensure the timely offering of a get by the husband, the panel concluded that Lang was entitled to $100 a day from October 1, 2005, when the parties no longer resided together, to January 10, 2006, when Levi first offered her a get, a cumulative amount of $10,200.

In November 2008, Lang and Levi both applied for modification of the decision under the Rules and Procedures of the Beth Din. Rabbi Mordechai Willig, the Segan [Assistant] Av Beth Din, was designated to hear the post-arbitration applications. Although he was not present when evidence was taken before the panel, and he did not entertain argument or hear additional evidence, he rendered a decision. In a March 30, 2009 ruling, he rejected the panel's determination and eliminated the monetary award to Lang. Rabbi Willig held that he had authority to modify the decision under Section 1(b) of the Beth Din Rules and Procedures. He reasoned that under Jewish law, even when language seems unambiguous, the intent of the parties is still relevant to the interpretation of a contract. The Segan Av Beth Din also noted that "a beth din is especially empowered to avert an unintended consequence that may result from a literal reading of a contractual provision when the beth din is authorized to decide a case based on the equities of the matter." For these reasons, he concluded that the intent of the parties in the present case was not "to provide the wife with a mechanism to demand additional money beyond any negotiated or court imposed settlement." Instead, the intent of the parties was to require Levi to pay economic costs if he failed to give a timely get. Because Levi was willing to give Lang a get soon after the parties stopped residing together and Lang refused, she was not entitled to any award. Further, because Lang consistently failed to demand a monetary award that was supposed to be paid in weekly installments, it was "likely" that she "implicitly waived" her right to it. Finally, Lang already participated in a secular court proceeding on her financial divorce claims and Rabbi Willig found that "generally, a party that appears before a secular court may not later bring a claim in beth din."

On April 29, 2009, Lang brought an action in the Circuit Court for Montgomery County petitioning the court to vacate the decisions of the Beth Din and Av Beth Din, and alleging breach of contract under the Jewish pre-nuptial agreement. On July 28, 2009, the court granted Levi's motion for summary judgment, finding that the parties submitted to the jurisdiction of the Beth Din for arbitration in an arbitration agreement enforceable in Maryland, that the Beth Din had the authority to interpret Jewish law and to delegate to Rabbi Willig the rendering of a decision under the Rules and Procedures of the Beth Din, and that the Av Beth Din's decision was not "an irrational decision on a question of law that is so extraordinary that it is tantamount to the arbitrator's exceeding his powers to warrant the court's intervention." Lang timely noted this appeal.

Appellant presents the following question for our review: Did the circuit court err by denying appellant's petition to vacate the arbitration award? For the reasons that follow, we shall affirm the decision of the circuit court. . . .

Because the Beth Din is an arbitration panel, we must . . . consider the standard for vacating an arbitration panel's decision. The Maryland Uniform Arbitration Act ("MUAA"), Md.Code, §§ 3–201 et seq. governs the enforceability of arbitration agreements. The MUAA severely restricts the role the courts play in the arbitration process in order to further the policy of favoring arbitration as an alternative method of dispute resolution, which conserves judicial resources. Under the MUAA, a court may only vacate an arbitration award where: (1) An award was procured by corruption, fraud, or other undue means; (2) There was evident partiality by an arbitrator appointed as a neutral, corruption in any arbitrator, or misconduct prejudicing the rights of any party; (3) The arbitrators exceeded their powers; (4) The arbitrators refused to postpone the hearing upon sufficient cause being shown for the postponement, refused to hear evidence material to the controversy, or otherwise so conducted the hearing as to prejudice substantially the rights of any party; (5) There was no arbitration agreement, the issue was not adversely determined in proceedings, and the party did not participate in the arbitration hearing without raising the objection.

It is important to emphasize that a court's power to vacate an arbitration award is narrowly confined to the above circumstances. Factual findings by an arbitrator are virtually immune from challenge and decisions on issues of law are reviewed using a deferential standard on the far side of the spectrum away from a usual expansive de novo standard. An arbitrator's mere error of law or failure to understand or apply the law is not a basis for a court to disturb an arbitral award. Only a completely irrational decision by an arbitrator on a question of law, so extraordinary that it is tantamount to the arbitrator's exceeding his powers, will warrant the court's intervention.

Here, Lang alleges only that the Beth Din exceeded its powers, and that its decision was irrational. She has the burden to prove these assertions.

To begin, Lang argues that we must vacate Rabbi Willig's decision reversing the Beth Din's award because it is "irrational" based on the plain language of the parties' contract. Lang argues that the prenuptial agreement plainly states that from the time the parties no longer reside together until the delivery of the get, Levi must pay her $100 per day under any circumstances. Because the Beth Din's award ignored this plain language, she asserts, it was thus irrational and must be reversed.

In our opinion, the Beth Din appropriately exercised its authority within the confines of its own rules and procedures, which both Lang and Levi agreed to be subject to under the arbitration agreement. Under that agreement, the parties conferred upon the Beth Din the authority to settle any marital disputes, including monetary disputes, between the parties "in accordance with Jewish law (Halakhah) and/or general principles of arbitration and equity (Pesharah) customarily employed by rabbinical tribunals." Under Jewish law, the provision in the contract that is the basis for Lang's claim for $108,000 was intended to facilitate the timely delivery of a get, preventing what is referred to as agunah or "chained wives." This is an issue in the Orthodox Jewish community that arises because under traditional Jewish law, a civil divorce does not dissolve the marriage. Only a religious divorce, provided by a signed writ of divorce called a "get," completely dissolves the marriage for a person who wishes to remarry within the Orthodox Jewish religion. By tradition, only the husband has the power to grant or withhold the get. The rabbinic authorities may not compel the husband to grant the get if he does not wish to do so. Until a woman receives a get she may not remarry within her religion. If she does remarry without the get, the new marriage is not considered valid. The woman is considered an adulterer, and any children from the new marriage are considered illegitimate.

Thus, the intent of the parties in signing the $100–a–day–penalty was to prevent Levi from withholding a get from Lang. The provision was not necessary here because Levi was willing to give Lang a get and Lang was reluctant to accept it. Requiring Levi to pay Lang any monetary award under the provision, Rabbi Willig found, would be an "unintended consequence" of a "literal reading of a contractual provision when the beth din is authorized to decide a case based on the equities of the matter." As Segan Av Beth Din, he determined that it would be inequitable under Jewish law to require any payment because Levi "was willing to give a Get early in the process." The parties agreed to arbitrate in the Beth Din and granted that body authority to interpret as well as determine matters of Jewish law, including a consideration of the equities. Since this Court cannot interpret Jewish law or gauge equities as determined by rabbinical tribunals, we decline to vacate the decision of the Beth Din as contrary to the parties' agreement.

We further point out, as Levi notes, that Rabbi Willig's interpretation of the $100–a–day penalty is consistent with the prenuptial agreement. The very first line in the instructions for the agreement states: "This Agreement is intended to facilitate the timely and proper delivery of a get." Thus, the agreement was not designed to confer a windfall on a wife, who refuses to receive the get, but rather it was intended only to prevent Lang from becoming a "chained wife."

Lang argues that Rabbi Willig's decision reversing the Beth Din's award was beyond his authority under the arbitration agreement. We disagree for two reasons. First, the parties agreed to submit any marital disputes to the Beth Din and abide by its rules and procedures, which include the authority of the Av Beth Din to reverse the panel's decision. Second, because of the religious nature of the Beth Din, the First Amendment prohibits us from determining whether reversal by the Av Beth Din is appropriate under Jewish law and the principles of equity as determined by a religious tribunal. Thus, we do not find that Rabbi Willig was without authority to reverse the panel's decision. . . .

Were we less convinced of the rationale of Rabbi Willig's determination, we would still find it exceedingly difficult to scrutinize the Beth Din decision in the manner Lang urges. As noted earlier, the standard for vacating an arbitrator's decision is a narrow standard to begin with. The addition of the religious context further narrows the standard to make our intervention nearly impossible. As has been clear since secular courts were first faced with intrachurch property disputes, courts have jurisdiction over these cases, but are prohibited from interpreting the underlying religious dogma. This is known as the religious question doctrine. While the parties do not raise the doctrine on appeal, we cannot ignore it when considering the extent of our reach into the Beth Din's final decision.

The Supreme Court has held that both the Free Exercise and Establishment Clauses of the First Amendment prohibit judicial review of religious questions. As the Court articulated in *Serbian Eastern Orthodox Diocese v. Milivojevich*, 426 U.S. 696, 708-709 (1976): "Civil courts do not inquire whether the relevant (hierarchical) church governing body has power under religious law (to decide such disputes). Such a determination frequently necessitates the interpretation of ambiguous religious law and usage. To permit civil courts to probe deeply enough into the allocation of power within a (hierarchical) church so as to decide religious law (governing church policy) would violate the First Amendment in much the same manner as civil determination of religious doctrine." . . .

Therefore, we cannot delve into whether under Jewish law there is legal support for Rabbi Willig's reversal of the panel's decision. As far as the rigor of our review is concerned, this is an area where treading lightly is not enough. Here, we cannot tread at all. . . .

Affirmed.

Can One Get a Get Through Specific Performance?

Jodi and Earl married in a Jewish ceremony. Years later, Earl obtained a civil divorce. Earl refused to grant Jodi a get. As a result, they remained married in the eyes of Orthodox Jewish law. When they were married, Jodi and Earl signed a Jewish marriage contract called a ketubah. The ketubah provided in part: "The said Bridegroom made the following declaration to his bride: 'Be thou my wife according to the law of Moses and Israel. I faithfully promise that I will be a true husband unto thee; I will honor and cherish thee; I will work for thee; I will protect and support thee and will provide all that is necessary for thy due sustenance as it beseemeth a Jewish husband to do. I also take upon myself all such further obligations for thy maintenance, as are prescribed by our religious statute.'" Jodi sued Earl, seeking specific performance of the ketubah, which Jodi argued should be interpreted to require Earl to give her a get. Does a secular court have authority to order Earl to execute a get for Jodi? *See Schneider v. Schneider*, 408 Ill. App. 3d 192, 945 N.E.2d 650 (2011); *Marriage of Goldman*, 196 Ill. App. 3d 785, 554 N.E.2d 1016 (1990).

In Islamic law, a mahr is a prenuptial agreement by which a wife is guaranteed a dowry. The mahr provides an amount of money to be paid at the time of marriage, and an amount to be paid in the event of divorce.[45] In the following case, the Washington Court of Appeals evaluates the enforceability of a mahr.

---

45 *See* Ahmed v. Ahmed, 261 S.W.3d 190 (Tex. Ct. App. 2008)(Mahr was not enforceable).

Marriage of Obaidi and Qayoum

Court of Appeals of Washington
154 Wash. App. 609, 226 P.3d 787 (2010)

Kulik, C.J.

A mahr is a prenuptial agreement based on Islamic law that provides an immediate and long-term dowry to the wife. Husna Obaidi and Khalid Qayoum, both children of Afghan immigrants, signed a mahr agreement written in Farsi during an engagement ceremony known as a Nikkah ceremony. Mr. Qayoum, who does not speak, read, or write Farsi, did not know about the mahr until 15 minutes before he signed it. An uncle explained the mahr to Mr. Qayoum after he had signed it. After a 13–month marriage, Ms. Obaidi filed a petition for dissolution of the marriage. Ms. Obaidi asserts that the mahr requires Mr. Qayoum to pay her $20,000 upon divorce.

The question presented here is whether the mahr is a valid agreement. We conclude that under neutral principles of contract law, the parties did not enter into an agreement for payment of $20,000 to the wife upon divorce. Therefore, we reverse the trial court's enforcement of the mahr. We affirm the trial court's award of attorney fees.

At the time of the marriage, Ms. Obaidi was 19 and Mr. Qayoum was 26. Mr. Qayoum is a United States citizen and has lived in the United States since he was three. Ms. Obaidi is from Canada.

The parties are both children of Afghan immigrants and the couple was married according to Afghan custom. As part of these customs, the parties signed a "mahr" agreement during an engagement or Nikkah ceremony held on December 30, 2005. The Nikkah ceremony is a religious ceremony that is similar to a wedding reception at a typical Christian wedding. At some point during the Nikkah ceremony, Ms. Obaidi and Mr. Qayoum, along with a small group of family and friends, went into a smaller room. Verses from the Koran were read and Ms. Obaidi and Mr. Qayoum each swore to take the other as his or her spouse. As part of the ceremony, the parties signed the mahr.

A mahr is an agreement based on Islamic law under which a husband agrees to pay a dowry to his wife. Generally, there is a short-term portion and a long-term portion. The short-term portion is due immediately. The long-term portion is the amount that the wife is entitled to take with her in the event of a divorce. In the mahr at issue here, the short-term portion was $100 and the long-term portion was $20,000.

The Nikkah ceremony was conducted in Farsi, except when Mr. Aji-sab, who performed the ceremony, asked Mr. Qayoum if he wanted to marry Ms. Obaidi. Mr. Qayoum does not speak, read, or write Farsi. Mr. Qayoum has lived in the United States for all but two or three years of his life. He considers himself "American first." He explained that he went through the Afghan marriage process because his mother was concerned that he would lose even the small amount of cultural knowledge he had about Afghanistan.

Mr. Qayoum testified that he had never heard the word "mahr" before the day of the Nikkah ceremony. He acknowledged that he had previously attended a couple of receptions, but he stated that he was unfamiliar with the Nikkah ceremony. According to Mr. Qayoum, he was not informed of the Nikkah ceremony until 10 or 15 minutes before the event took place. At some point, Mr. Qayoum selected an uncle to act as his representative during the discussions that took place as part of the Nikkah ceremony. The mahr, in total, states:

Marriage Certificate (Nekah Certificate)

Marriage Ceremony between Mr. Khalid Qayoum and Ms. Husna (the daughter of Mr. Habebullah Khan Obaidi) on December 29, 2005 took place in the presence of:

Witnesses:

1—Mr. Abdullah Khan {Signed}

2—Mr. Mohammad Aref Khan {Signed}

The proxy for groom (Khalid) was
    Mr. Abdul Sabour Khan {Signed}

The proxy for bride (Husna) was
    Mr. Hafezullah Khan {Signed}

Experts:

Haji Hayatullah Khan, Lateefullah Khan, Hemayetullah Khan, Abdul Khalil Qayoum, Javid, and Ehsan Khan {Signatures}

Short term marriage portion: One hundred Canadian Dollars

Long term marriage portion: 20,000.00 Dollars

The organizer: Mohammad–Ullah Faizi

Signatures of each witnesses [sic], proxies and experts {Signed and dated 12–29–2005}

In the Afghan culture, the couple is considered married upon the completion of the Nikkah ceremony and, after this ceremony, Ms. Obaidi and Mr. Qayoum began holding themselves out as husband and wife. They later had an Islamic marriage ceremony on July 21, 2006, and solemnized their marriage civilly in Whitman County on November 6, 2006.

The parties lived with Mr. Qayoum's mother, starting in August 2006. On May 8, 2007, Ms. Obaidi, at her husband's request, went to Afghanistan for three and one-half months. Shortly after her return, she was asked to leave her mother-in-law's house. On December 7, Ms. Obaidi filed a petition for dissolution of marriage in King County Superior Court. In February 2008, the case was moved to Whitman County.

After the dissolution trial, the court entered findings of fact and conclusions of law. The written findings of fact and conclusions of law incorporate the court's oral ruling. The trial court concluded that Ms. Obaidi was entitled to the $20,000 mahr. This appeal followed.

On appeal, Mr. Qayoum contends the mahr contravenes the Washington policy of no fault divorce [and] the mahr is not enforceable as a contract or as a prenuptial agreement . . . .

A New Jersey case, *Odatalla v. Odatalla*, 355 N.J.Super. 305, 309, 810 A.2d 93 (2002), provides a helpful framework for considering the application of state law to a mahr agreement. In *Odatalla*, the trial court ordered the specific performance of the mahr agreement. The husband appealed, arguing that review of the mahr by a state court was precluded under the doctrine of separation of church and state. The husband also argued that the agreement was not a valid contract under New Jersey law.

The *Odatalla* court looked for guidance to *Jones v. Wolf*, 443 U.S. 595, 602–03, 99 S.Ct. 3020 (1979), which explained the "neutral principles of law" approach that allows agreements to be enforced based on neutral principles of law, not religious doctrine. In *Jones*, a dispute over the ownership of church property was taken to a civil court in Georgia. The court set aside the separation of church and state issues by applying the neutral principles of law doctrine. Justice Blackmun explained, "We cannot agree, however, that the First Amendment requires the States to adopt a rule of compulsory deference to religious authority in resolving church property disputes, even when no issue of doctrinal controversy is involved." In other words, the court determined that the controversy over the ownership of the property could be decided on neutral principles of law, not upon religious beliefs or policies.

Based on *Jones*, the *Odatalla* court determined that the mahr did not violate the separation of church and state doctrine if the court could apply neutral principles of law to the enforce the mahr. The court concluded that the mahr could be enforced by applying neutral principles of contract law. Notably, the court found all the elements of a contract even though the husband argued that the mahr was too vague to apply because it did not state when the money would be due. Because the court determined that the mahr was simply a contract between two consenting adults, the court concluded that the mahr was not against public policy. . . .

Applying the neutral principles of contract law, we can resolve this case by using these neutral principles of law, not Islamic beliefs or policies. We apply Washington law to resolve the issues of the formation and validity of the agreement.

Mr. Qayoum raises arguments under the law applying to prenuptial agreements and the law of contract. Prenuptial agreements are subject to the principles of contract law. Mr. Qayoum asserts the mahr agreement was invalid under contract law. We agree. For a valid contract to exist, there must be mutual assent, offer, acceptance, and consideration. Here, there was no meeting of the minds on the essential terms of the agreement. A valid contract requires a meeting of the minds on the essential terms. Mr. Qayoum was not told that he would be required to participate in a ceremony that would include the signing of a mahr until 15 minutes before he signed the mahr. Here, Mr. Qayoum was unaware of the terms of the agreement until they were explained to him by an uncle after the mahr had been signed. The negotiations preceding the execution of the agreement were conducted in Farsi. Also, the document was written in Farsi which Mr. Qayoum does not read, write, or speak. Mr. Qayoum did not have the opportunity to consult with counsel although he was advised by his uncle, who is neither an attorney nor an expert in Islamic law, after the agreement was signed. Because Mr. Qayoum could not speak, write, or read Farsi, there was no meeting of the minds as to the terms of the mahr agreement. . . .

The trial court's finding that the mahr was a valid contract was not supported by substantial evidence. . . .

Problems on Premarital Agreements

1. Bill was a wealthy seventy-seven-year-old businessman when he married Rabha, who was much younger. Rabha was born and grew up in Morocco. Rabha met Bill when she travelled to the United States to visit her brother. Within two months, Bill and Rabha were engaged. Bill had his attorney draft a premarital agreement. The agreement provided that in the event of divorce, each party waived their interest in the other party's property and their rights to equitable distribution of property, spousal support, retirement, life insurance, and attorney's fees. The agreement provided that each party gave up the right to inherit from the other. The only asset Rabha was entitled to under the agreement was $100,000 if she and Bill were still married and living together when Bill died. The agreement did not disclose Bill's assets. Rabha's native language is Arabic, and when she signed the premarital agreement, she spoke little English. She relied on translators for oral and written communication in English. The parties were married 15 years. Now, they are divorcing. Rabha testifies that she thought she was signing a "paper for marriage, like a license or something. I signed it without reading it." Rabha was not given a copy of the agreement to review before signing. Rabha was not advised on the agreement by an attorney. Is the agreement enforceable? *Chaplain v. Chaplain,* 54 Va. App. 762, 682 S.E.2d 108 (2009).

2. Randall is an attorney in private practice. Teresa has a bachelor's degree in business. Teresa has worked in the marketing department of a casino, as a secretary, and as a bookkeeper and office manager. Randall and Teresa were married in Jamaica. At the time of the marriage, Randall owned valuable commercial properties. Teresa had no assets to speak of. Randall has a large income. It is the second marriage for both, and each has children from their first marriage. While contemplating marriage, Randall and Teresa discussed Randall's desire for a premarital agreement. Randall said he wanted to preserve his assets for his children in the event the marriage failed. Randall said he would not marry again without a premarital agreement protecting his property "for my kids." Teresa agreed, stating that she was not marrying Randall for his money. Randall drafted a premarital agreement and presented it to Teresa ten days before the wedding. The agreement stated that each party would maintain separate ownership of their assets acquired before and during marriage, and that they did not intend to hold jointly-owned property except the marital home and a joint bank account. The agreement contained a mutual waiver of alimony. The agreement disclosed Randall's assets. Randall encouraged Teresa to consult an attorney, which she did. The attorney explained the agreement to Teresa. Randall and Teresa signed the agreement the day before leaving for Jamaica. Prior

to and during the six year marriage, Teresa worked in Randall's office as a bookkeeper and secretary. In the divorce, Teresa argues that the premarital agreement was not signed voluntarily and that the agreement was unconscionable. Teresa seeks division of marital property and spousal support. Teresa acknowledges that she is employable, but points out that the jobs she is qualified for will require her to live at a standard much lower than she enjoyed while married to Randall. Is the premarital agreement enforceable? Does the fact that Randall said he would not marry again without a premarital agreement render the agreement unenforceable? Do the facts that Randall is an attorney and that Teresa worked for him render the agreement unenforceable? Does the fact that enforcement of the agreement means Teresa will have to lower her standard of living render the agreement unenforceable? *Marriage of Shanks,* 758 N.W.2d 506 (Iowa 2008).

3. Debra and Dave have been married 10 years. They have one child, who is nine. Four days before their wedding, the parties signed a premarital agreement. At the time, Dave was represented by counsel; Debra was not. The premarital agreement, which was drafted by Dave's attorney, stated that both parties had "fully disclosed his or her present approximate net worth," that "each party had full opportunity to review the agreement," and that "both parties acknowledge their understanding of the effect and content of the agreement." The agreement listed Dave's separate property as six parcels of real property. The agreement did not list the values of the properties. Debra had no assets at the time of marriage. The agreement provided that neither party would acquire any interest in the property of the other, whether that property was acquired prior to or during marriage. During the marriage, Dave's income was derived entirely from buying and selling real property, all of which was titled in his name alone. Over the course of the marriage, Dave bought and sold 75 parcels of real estate. Debra was a full time homemaker. Recently, Debra filed for divorce. In the divorce, Debra challenges the premarital agreement, arguing that she did not enter into the agreement voluntarily and that the agreement is unconscionable. Debra asks the judge to declare the premarital agreement invalid and to characterize all of the property owned by Dave before marriage, during marriage, and at divorce as marital property. Dave argues the premarital agreement is valid and should be enforced, meaning that all of the real property owned by Dave in his business, including the property he owns at the time of divorce, is his separate property. What should be the outcome? *Marsocci v. Marsocci,* 911 A.2d 690 (R.I. 2006).

4. When Joyce and Robert married, she was 44, he was 52. It was the second marriage for each. Joyce is a teacher. Robert owns and works a large farm. Robert owned the farm before marrying Joyce. During the marriage, Robert paid the monthly mortgage on the farm with income from farming. During the marriage, Robert purchased five additional pieces of farm land, paying for the land with income from his farming operation. Joyce helped with the farm, including doing the books for the operation.

Two days before their wedding, Joyce and Robert entered into a prenuptial agreement prepared by Joyce's attorney. The agreement follows:

> This antenuptial contract entered into this [two days prior to the wedding], between Robert Jones, hereinafter for convenience referred to as Husband, and Joyce King, hereinafter for convenience referred to as Wife, Witnesseth:
>
> I. Husband and Wife intend to marry each other soon, and it is agreed that after such marriage, all of the properties of any name or nature, real, personal or mixed, wherever they may be found, belonging to Husband before marriage shall be and remain forever his personal estate, and that this shall include all interest, rents, and profits which may in time accrue or result in any manner from increase in value, or be collected for the use of the same in any way.
>
> II. All properties of any name or nature, real, personal or mixed, wherever the same shall be found which belong to Wife before marriage shall be and remain forever her personal estate, and this shall include all interest, rents, and profits which may in time accrue or result in any manner from increase in value, or be collected for the use of the same in any way.
>
> III. Each party agrees to sign with the other, all title paper, deeds or other papers necessary to transfer property when sold to a purchaser, in any event, it is necessary that such title papers be executed by a man and wife, either in this state or any other state, and this courtesy shall be prompt at any time and in any place.
>
> IV. Husband agrees to, from his own personal estate, assume necessary expense of support and maintenance of Wife.
>
> V. Nothing herein shall be construed to be a bar to either party to this agreement, giving any property of which they may be possessed to the other party by will or otherwise. Each party to this agreement shall control their personal estate as described herein, and do with the

properties thereof whatsoever they wish and will, by his or her orders or directions or by will, the same as either could or would do if no marriage existed between them. That upon the demise of each party, their personal estates shall pass by their individual Wills, or by law to their individual heirs, and each party waives any claim participation they may otherwise be entitled to by law in the estate of the other.

The agreement did not list what property Joyce or Robert owned prior to the marriage. After 25 years of marriage, Joyce filed for divorce. In the divorce action, Joyce argues the premarital agreement is invalid for two reasons. First, the agreement did not specify what property Robert owned at the time of the marriage. Second, the agreement did not mention divorce or separation. It mentioned only property rights during marriage and at death. Because the agreement did not mention property rights at divorce, the agreement should not apply at divorce. Robert admits that the premarital agreement did not disclose the nature and extent of his property. He claims, however, that the agreement should be enforced because during their 14 month courtship, Joyce learned the extent of Robert's property. As for the argument that the agreement did not mention divorce, Robert argues that "common sense" indicates the agreement should be applied in the event of divorce. How should the judge rule on these two issues? How would you draft the agreement differently to avoid such issues? *Smetana v. Smetana,* 726 N.W.2d 887 (S.D. 2007).

Professional Responsibility and Issues Regarding Premarital Agreements

Can one attorney represent both parties to a premarital agreement? The West Virginia Supreme Court of Appeals addressed this question in *Ware v. Ware,*[46] where the court wrote:

> This Court has previously recognized that, in certain instances, dual representation is never appropriate, even if both parties are willing to consent. It is improper for a lawyer to represent both the husband and the wife at any stage of the separation and divorce proceeding, even with full disclosure and informed consent. The likelihood of prejudice is so great with dual representation so as to make

---

46   224 W. Va. 599, 687 S.E.2d 382, 390 (2009).

adequate representation of both spouses impossible, even where the separation is "friendly" and the divorce uncontested.

Like divorce actions, the nature of prenuptial agreements is such that the parties interests are fundamentally antagonistic to one another. Indeed, the purpose of a prenuptial agreement is to preserve the property of one spouse, thereby preventing the other from obtaining that to which he or she might otherwise be legally entitled. . . . Accordingly, the Court holds that one attorney may not represent, nor purport to counsel, both parties to a prenuptial agreement.

How to Broach the Subject of a Prenup

Broaching the subject of a premarital agreement can be tricky. Imagine two people madly in love and planning to marry. One evening, over a romantic dinner, Sue says to Sam, "I love you so much, and I can't wait to be married. But just in case our marriage ends in divorce, I think we should have a premarital agreement so I can keep all my property for myself, and I won't have to support you. What do you think, sweetie?" Do you think Sue's statement might put a damper on the evening? What is the most appropriate way to raise the topic of a prenup?

EXPERIENTIAL ASSIGNMENT

Practice Exercise: Draft Prenuptual Agreement

Maria is a 23-year-old hip hop artist. She is extremely successful. Maria has several platinum CDs. She regularly performs on television. She sells out concerts around the world. Maria is not only extremely successful, she is extremely wealthy. Maria's fortune from her entertainment career is valued at approximately $45 million.

Raul is a 25-year-old aspiring actor. A synonym for "aspiring actor" is "starving artist." Raul works as a waiter, takes acting classes, shows up for auditions, and waits for his "big break."

Maria's finances are handled by a management firm that has many entertainment and sports clients. Maria owns real estate in the United States, Mexico, and Japan. She owns a large investment portfolio. She owns the mansion in which she lives. Although Maria is wealthy and lives the lifestyle of an important entertainer, she is frugal. For example, she drives a four-year-old Honda Civic and does her own shopping and cooking. As Maria says, "I was poor when I was little. Mom and dad worked hard to put food on the table. When I'm not performing, I like being a regular person. It is more fun to buy your own food at the farmers market and cook at home than to go to some fancy restaurant. Besides, I'm a good cook." Maria is careful about her spending and lives well within her means. Maria understands that fame can be fleeting. Her money is conservatively invested, and she will be wealthy for the rest her life even if she retires today.

Maria and Raul met at a party. They were instantly attracted to each other and started dating. You can see their picture together on the covers of *People, US, Rolling Stone,* and similar magazines. After dating a year, Raul asked Maria to marry him. Maria said "yes," and the wedding is planned for six weeks from today.

Recently, Maria met with her investment advisor, Rachel. Rachel suggested that Maria consider a prenuptial agreement. Rachel said, "I know you two are madly in love, and that's wonderful. But you know the statistics, Maria. Lots of marriages don't work, and that seems especially true for entertainers." Maria received similar advice from a number of friends. One friend was blunt, "Listen, you are a wealthy woman. How do you know Raul isn't marrying you for your money? You should get a prenup to protect you if he's a gold digger, or if it doesn't work out."

Maria has retained you to prepare a prenuptial agreement for her. Maria hopes her marriage lasts "til death do us part," but if it doesn't, Maria believes each party should keep as their own all the property they bring into the marriage and all the property they earn during marriage. In other words, Maria would like a prenuptial agreement that maintains her property—including her earnings—as her separate property. Similarly, Raul will keep his property as his separate property. In the event of divorce, both spouses will waive any right to spousal support.

Assignment: Draft a premarital agreement for Maria.

CHAPTER 3

Marriage and Domestic Partnership

MARRIAGE IS A deeply personal relationship.[1] In 1891, Joel Bishop, the nineteenth century's most influential U.S. commentator on family law, opined, "Marriage being the source of population, of education, of domestic felicity—being the all in all without which the State would not exist—it is the very highest public interest."[2] A long line of United States Supreme Court decisions extol the virtues of marriage and family. In 1888, the Court wrote that marriage is "the most important relation in life."[3] In 1923, the Court stated that the right "to marry, establish a home and bring up children" is protected by the Due Process Clause.[4] In 1942, the Court added that marriage is "fundamental to the very existence and survival of the race."[5] In 1965, the Court waxed lyrical, "Marriage is a coming together for better or for worse, hopefully enduring, and intimate

---

1   *See* U.S. Department of Health and Human Services, Centers for Disease Control and Prevention, *Marriage and Cohabitation in the Unites States: A Statistical Portrait Based on Cycle 6 (2002) of the National Survey of Family Growth* p. 4 (2010)("Married persons have generally better mental and physical health outcomes compared with unmarried persons. Married persons also live longer . . . . Research also indicates that marriage is positively associated with the health and well-being of children.").

2   Joel P. Bishop, *New Commentaries on Marriage, Divorce, and Separation* vol 1., § 38, p. 16 (1891).

3   Maynard v. Hill, 125 U.S. 190, 8 S. Ct. 723 (1888).

4   Meyer v. Nebraska, 262 U.S. 390, 43 S. Ct. 625 (1923).

5   Skinner v. Oklahoma, 316 U.S. 535, 62 S. Ct. 1110 (1942).

to the degree of being sacred. It is an association that promotes a way of life, not causes; a harmony of living, not political faiths; a bilateral loyalty, not commercial or social projects."[6] In 1978, the Court affirmed that "the right to marry is of fundamental importance for all individuals."[7]

In earlier times, many Americans married young. Recently, age at marriage has risen. Andrew Cherlin writes, "The typical age at marriage continued its decades-long rise in the 2000s: The median age at first marriage rose to 27.4 for men and 25.6 for women in 2008."[8]

The Marriage Contract

Marriage is a contract.[9] Section 300(a) of the California Family Code is typical of statutes around the country, and provides, "Marriage is a personal relation arising out of a civil contract between a man and a woman, to which the consent of the parties is necessary." Of course, marriage is no ordinary contract.[10] In 1948, the California Supreme Court observed, "Marriage is thus something more than a civil contract subject to regulation by the state; it is a fundamental right of free men."[11]

How does marriage differ from a commercial contract? Many ways. The parties to a typical commercial contract can rescind the agreement by mutual agreement. Not so with marriage, which can only be terminated by a court or death.[12] Marriage is deeply personal and founded on love and trust. Commercial contracts are arms-length.

---

6   Griswold v. Connecticut, 381 U.S. 479, 85 S.Ct. 1678 (1965).

7   Zablocki v. Redhail, 434 U.S. 374, 98 S. Ct. 673 (1978).

8   Andrew J. Cherlin, Demographic Trends in the United States: A Review of Research in the 2000s, 72 *Journal of Marriage and Family* 403-419, 404 (2010).

9   *See* Okla. Stat. Ann. § 1 ("Marriage is a personal relation arising out of a civil contract to which the consent of the parties legally competent of contracting and of entering into it is necessary, and the marriage relation shall only be entered into, maintained or abrogated as provided by law."); Rev. Code. Wash. Ann. § 26.04.010(1) ("Marriage is a civil contract between a male and a female who have each attained the age of eighteen years, and who are otherwise capable.").

10   *See* Joel P. Bishop, *New Commentaries on Marriage, Divorce, and Separation* vol 1., § 11, p. 5 (1891)("it is also more than a contract, and differs from all other contracts.").

11   Perez v. Sharp, 32 Cal. 2d 711, 714, 198 P.2d 17 (1948).

12   *See* Okla. Stat. Ann. Tit. 43 § 1, which provides that marriage "shall only be . . . abrogated as provided by law."

Brief History of Marriage

In England prior to 1754, a couple could marry informally. No license or ceremony was required. In *The Family, Sex and Marriage in England: 1500-1800*, Lawrence Stone observes that most people viewed marriage as "a personal affair of no concern to external authorities . . . ."[13] A couple merely exchanged the words "I accept you as mine."[14] This simple exchange of vows created a marriage.[15] A vow to marry in the future—*per verba de futuro*—was an engagement and became marriage upon consummation.[16] A vow stated in the present tense—*per verba de praesenti*—created an immediate marriage.[17] Philip Reynolds remarks, "It became possible to marry suddenly and casually, without any preparations, negotiations, or permission."[18]

Informal marriage caused problems. Some unscrupulous individuals married multiple times. Incestuous marriages occurred. A man interested in a young woman's fortune might convince her to elope with him to London, where unethical clergymen married anyone for a fee. Many of these clandestine marriages occurred near Fleet prison, and were known as Fleet marriages.[19]

---

13 Lawrence Stone, *The Family, Sex and Marriage in England: 1500-1800* p. 30 (1977).

14 Or, "I do take thee to my wife" and "I do take thee to my husband."

15 Lawrence Stone, *The Family, Sex and Marriage in England: 1500-1800* p. 31 (1977)("Any sort of exchange of promises before witnesses which was followed by cohabitation was regarded in law as a valid marriage.").

16 *See* Joel P. Bishop, *New Commentaries on Marriage, Divorce, and Separation* vol. 1, § 313, p. 130 (1891) ("The agreement of future marriage is termed espousals *de future*, or a contract *per verba de future*; that superinducing the status, espousals *de praesenti*, or a contract *per verba de praesenti*." Vol. 1 § 313, p. 130. "The books speak of three forms of consent,—*per verba de presaenti, per verba de future cum copula*; and, in Scotland, consent by habit and repute. But these three forms signify only three different channels of proof; for the only consent which will create matrimony is the mutual one to present marriage,—not necessarily *per verba*, but always and indispensably *de praesenti*." Vol. 1, § 341, p. 142).

The canon law expert Gratian wrote in his *Decretum* (c. 1140) that marriage occurred in two stages, first consent, then consummation, that is sexual intercourse. Gratian's view may account for the belief among some that a marriage is not compete until it is "consummated." Experts following Gratian disputed the idea that marriage requires consummation. Today, of course, there is no requirement that a marriage be consummated to be valid.

17 Today's common law marriage, discussed in Chapter 3, is a descendent of the old informal marriage.

18 Philip L. Reynolds, Marrying and Its Documentation in Pre-Modern Europe: Consent, Celebration, and Property. In Philip L. Reynolds & John Witte (Eds.), *To Have and To Hold: Marrying and Its Documentation in Western Chrisendom, 400-1600* pp. 1-42, at 10 (2007).

19 Lawrence Stone, *The Family, Sex and Marriage in England: 1500-1800*, p. 33 (1977)("The most flourishing trade of all was done by decayed clergymen in the vicinity of the Fleet in London, particularly in the first half of the eighteenth century when official weddings were heavily taxed and those around the Fleet were both legally valid and very cheap.").

Church authorities argued against informal marriage. Churchmen believed marriage should be presided over by clergy, and should take place in church. Rebecca Probert writes that informal marriage was not on a par with marriage that complied with church requirements.[20]

The tug-of-war between church control and informality motivated Parliament to enact Lord Hardwicke's Marriage Act in 1754. The Act required church weddings. Marriage should not occur until the proposed marriage was announced in church on three Sundays—a ceremony known as banns. The banns allowed anyone to come forward who knew of an impediment to the marriage. We see the residue of banns in many modern weddings, when the person officiating says, "If anyone knows a reason why these two should not marry, let that person speak now or forever hold their peace."

At earlier times, marriage subjected women to legal disadvantages. For example, getting married meant that a woman lost control of her property.[21] In 1863, the California Supreme Court wrote, "At common law, the effect of a marriage was to deprive the wife of all separate legal existence, her husband and herself being deemed at law but one person," and the "one" was the husband.[22] In the nineteenth century, states adopted Married Women's Property Acts, which granted women some legal rights, especially regarding of property.

Among other disabilities accompanying marriage, "custom dictated that the wife give up her surname and assume the husband's. She could no longer contract or litigate in her own name; nor could she manage property or earn money."[23] A husband could insist that children bear his name.

In 1869, the Illinois Supreme Court ruled that Myra Bradwell—a married woman—could not obtain a license to practice law.[24] The primary reason was that married women could not enter into the legally binding contracts that a lawyer must consummate with clients. Mrs. Bradwell—who met all the requirements for admission to the bar—appealed to the United States Supreme Court,

---

20 Rebecca Probert, The Misunderstood Contract Per Verba De Praesenti, in R. Probert (ed.), *Marriage Law and Practice in the Eighteenth Century: A Reassessment* (2009).

21 *See* Joel P. Bishop, *New Commentaries on Marriage, Divorce, and Separation* vol. 2, § 829, pp. 336-337 (1891)("By the unwritten law, marriage invests the husband with all the wife's available means of support, with ownership of her future earnings, and with the right to appropriate to himself her acquisitions. In return for which, it casts on him the duty, not in any considerable degree taken away by the modern statutes, suitably to maintain her, according to his ability and condition in life.").

22 Miller v. Newton, 23 Cal. 554, 563 (1863).

23 Marriage of Schiffman, 28 Cal. 3d 640, 643 (1980).

24 In re Bradwell, 55 Ill. 535 (1869).

asserting that denial of a license to practice law denied her constitutional rights. The Supreme Court rejected her arguments.[25] In a concurring opinion, Justice Bradley expressed the views of many in authority:

> The civil law, as well as nature herself, has always recognized a wide difference in the respective spheres and destinies of man and woman. Man is, or should be, woman's protector and defender. The natural and proper timidity and delicacy which belongs to the female sex evidently unfits it for many of the occupations of civil life. The constitution of the family organization, which is founded in the divine ordinance, as well as in the nature of things, indicates the domestic sphere as that which properly belongs to the domain and functions of womanhood. The harmony, not to say identity, of interest and views which belong, or should belong, to the family institution is repugnant to the idea of a woman adopting a distinct and independent career from that of her husband. So firmly fixed was this sentiment in the founders of the common law that it became a maxim of that system of jurisprudence that a woman had no legal existence separate from her husband, who was regarded as her head and representative in the social state; and, notwithstanding some recent modification of this civil status, many of the special rules of law flowing from and dependent upon this cardinal principle still exist in full force in most States. One of these is, that a married woman is incapable, without her husband's consent, of making contracts which shall be binding on her or him. This very incapacity was one of the circumstances which the Supreme Court of Illinois deemed important in rendering a married woman incompetent fully to perform the duties and trusts that belong to the office of an attorney and counselor.

> It is true that many women are unmarried and not affected by any of the duties, complications, and incapacities arising out of the married state, but these are exceptions to the general rule. The paramount destiny and mission of woman are to fulfill the noble and benign offices of wife and mother. This is the law of the Creator.

---

25 Bradwell v. State, 83 U.S. 130 (1872).

Requirements for Valid Marriage

Legal requirements to marry vary in detail from state to state.[26] In all states, the consent of the parties is required.[27] Consent has been a bedrock of marriage for centuries.[28] Conor McCarthy writes, "When the Church canonists of the central Middle Ages considered the question of what created a marriage between two people, the conclusion that they came to was that it was the consent of the persons to be married which created the marital bond."[29]

A couple obtains a marriage license from a county official.[30] The Oklahoma statute, for example, provides that persons desiring to marry must submit a sworn application to the clerk of the district court setting forth basic information about the couple, including a statement that "the parties are not disqualified from or incapable of entering into the marriage relation." If the clerk is satisfied, the clerk issues a marriage license and a marriage certificate. Following the marriage ceremony, the marriage certificate is completed and returned to the court clerk.[31]

A marriage must be solemnized before witnesses.[32] Washington State law provides, "In the solemnization of marriage no particular form is required, except that the parties thereto shall assent or declare in the presence of the minister, priest, or judicial officer solemnizing the same, and in the presence of at least two attending witnesses, that they take each other to be husband and wife."[33]

---

26 *See* Pickens v. Pickens, 490 So.2d 872, 875 (Miss. 1986)("the legal relationship of husband and wife may be created only in conformity with the procedures authorized by the statute law of this state.").

27 Joel P. Bishop, *New Commentaries on Marriage, Divorce, and Separation* vol. 1., § 295, p. 123 (1891)("the status of marriage is cast upon the parties by the law, yet the course of the law is to impose it only on those who seek it, not upon the non-consenting.").

28 *See* Conor McCarthy, *Marriage in Medieval England: Law, Literature and Practice*, p. 19 (2004)("the Roman emphasis on consent as a fundamental aspect of the marriage bond.").

29 Conor McCarthy, *Marriage in Medieval England: Law, Literature and Practice*, p. 19 (2004).

30 *See, e.g.,* Rev. Code. Wash. Ann. § 26.04.140 ("Before any persons can be joined in marriage, they shall procure a license from a county auditor . . . .").

31 Okla. Stat. Ann. tit. 43, § 5.

32 *See, e.g.,* Okla Stat. Ann. tit. 43, § 7.

33 Rev. Code. Wash. Ann. § 26.04.070.

Practice Exercise: Go online and find the requirements for a marriage license in your state and your county or parish. Where would you go for a license? How much does a license cost? Does the law require or encourage marrying couples to take classes before they get married? What information is provided to couples about to marry? Is there a waiting period between when you get the license and when you can tie the knot? Should there be a waiting period?

Interracial Marriage

According to the Pew Research Center, one in seven U.S. marriages is interracial or interethnic.[34] The rate of "marrying out" more than doubled between 1980 and 2008.[35] Yet, interracial marriage was not always popular, socially acceptable, or legal.

Laws against interracial marriage—anti-miscegenation laws—were established in colonial times, and endured in many states into the twentieth century.[36] Three attempts—1871, 1912, and 1913—were made to amend the U.S. Constitution to forbid interracial marriage. The racism motivating the proposed amendments is clear in a speech in Congress on December 11, 1912 by Congressman Roddenberry of Georgia. Roddenberry was particularly outraged that the famous African American boxer Jack Johnson married not one but

---

34 Jeffrey S. Passel, Wendy Wang & Paul Taylor, Marrying Out: One-in-Seven New U.S. Marriages is Interracial or Interethnic (June 4, 2010. Pew Research Center).

35 *See* Zhenchao Qian & Daniel T. Lichter, Changing Patterns of Interracial Marriage in a Multiracial Society, 73 *Journal of Marriage and Family* 1065-1084 (2011)("To varying degrees, Blacks, Hispanics, Asians, and American Indians have all experienced increases in out-marriage with Whites since the 1970s." p. 1065. "We find that intermarriage rates overall have continued to increase and that this upward trend is due in part but not entirely to changing population composition. Ethnoracial boundaries are blurring or are being crossed. But, at the same time, intermarriage rates among new immigrant groups have slowed, especially among Hispanics and Asians." p. 1082).

36 *See* Joel P. Bishop, *New Commentaries on Marriage, Divorce, and Separation* vol. 1., § 683, p. 297 (1891)("It is the policy of many of our States, originally adopted when the distinctions of race were broader legally than now, yet still widely continued, to inhibit by statutes intermarriages between persons of the negro, including sometimes the Indian, and the white races."); Eva Saks, Representing Miscegenation Law. In Kevin R. Johnson (Ed.), *Mixed Race America and the Law* p. 11-12, 11 (2003)("Maryland passed this country's first miscegenation statute in 1661. The statute criminalized marriage between white women and black men").

three white women. Not only that! Johnson had the annoying habit of knocking out white boxers.[37] Roddenberry spewed forth his venom:

> The resolution to which I make reference is one already introduced by me, providing for an amendment to the Constitution of the United States, with the usual resolving clause, and the article is as follows: "The intermarriage between negroes or persons of color and Caucasians or any other character of persons within the United States or any territory under their jurisdiction, is forever prohibited; and the term 'negro' or person of color, as here employed, shall be held to mean any and all persons of African descent or having any trace of African or negro blood."

> The newspapers, glaring in their headlines, announce that Jack Johnson again marries a white woman. Thank God such an outrage is impossible anywhere in the Southland. No brutality, no infamy, no degradation in all the years of southern slavery possessed such villainous character and such atrocious qualities as the provision of the laws of Illinois, New York, Massachusetts, and other States, which allow the marriage of the negro Jack Johnson to a woman of the Caucasian strain. [Applause.] Gentlemen, I offer this resolution that the proper committee may consider it and that the State of the Union may have an opportunity to ratify it. This is no amendment peculiarly favorable to one portion of our great land. In that section far to the south of us such is the relation between the two races that no African within all of Dixie land carries in his heart the hope or cherishes in his mind the aspiration that he can ever lead there to the altar of matrimony a woman of Caucasian blood. With all the impositions we are alleged to have placed upon this inferior race, such is our harmony, such is the fellowship between the blacks and the whites of the South, such is the black's respect for the superiority of his former master, that they would commit self-destruction before they would entertain the thought of matrimony with a white girl beneath southern skies.

> You have some negro problems up North yourselves. The negro question stands out in the example of Johnson's marriage in Chicago as presenting to you as grave a negro question as ever confronted your brethren in the South; and I say to you, in no bitterness but in the

---

37 You may have heard the phrase "the great white hope." The origin of the phrase lay with white people who hoped for a white boxer who could defeat Jack Johnson.

depths of good fellowship, that we in that far-off land will be glad, in the spirit of love and fraternity, to aid you in its proper and its wise and its permanent solution. The case we cite is not an isolated one. The records of Boston, of Chicago, and of other cities show that negroes less prominent, of less notoriety, are from time to time binding themselves in matrimony with weak and unfortunate women of the white race. Gentlemen, that does not happen in the South. May God spare you, our brethren of the North, of its recurrence. It does transpire in the North; it does occur in the West; and I say to you that we are ready now, without the arbitrament of war, without an appeal to arms, without a terrific four years deluge of fratricidal blood, to join with you in peace, in harmony, and in amity in solving this great negro problem that now confronts you in the North and in the West. Every son of the south will offer his life to lift the pall of its infamy from your homes and perish if need be to free your white girls from the accursed thralldom.[38]

At mid twentieth century, twenty-nine states prohibited interracial marriage.[39] The beginning of the end of anti-miscegenation laws occurred in California.[40] In 1947, Andrea Perez, who was of Mexican descent, and Sylvester Davis, who was black, applied for a marriage license in Los Angeles County. The clerk denied the license because California law stated, "No license may be issued authorizing the marriage of a white person with a Negro, Mulatto, Mongolian or member of the Malay race." Perez and Davis sought a writ of mandamus to compel the clerk to issue a license. Before the California Supreme Court, the county justified the ban on interracial marriage with arguments that blacks are inferior. In a lengthy repudiation of the county's position, Justice Traynor ruled the law unconstitutional. Justice Carter concurred, writing, "It is my considered opinion that the statutes here involved are the product of ignorance, prejudice and intolerance, and I am happy to join in the decision of this court holding that they are invalid and unenforceable." With their legal victory in hand, Andrea and Sylvester slipped out of public view. Apparently, that's the way they wanted it.

---

38 Congressional Record—House, December 11, 1912, pp. 502-503.

39 *See* Kevin R. Johnson (Ed.), *Mixed Race America and the Law,* p. 5 (2003).

40 Perez v. Sharp, 32 Cal. 2d 711, 198 P.2d 17 (1948).

The death knell of anti-miscegenation laws sounded in 1967 with the U.S. Supreme Court's decision in *Loving v. Virginia*.[41] The case involved Richard Loving and Mildred Jeter. Richard and Mildred grew up in rural Virginia and knew each other since childhood. Their legal battle against Virginia's anti-miscegenation law went to the U.S. Supreme Court and was a cause célèbre. The case was covered in *Newsweek, Life*, and other magazines.

Mildred and Richard Loving; 13 June 1967. Time & Life Pictures/Getty Images

Robert Pratt knew the Loving family personally, and wrote a touching remembrance, part of which is reproduced here:

Crossing the Color Line: A Historical Assessment and Personal Narrative of *Loving v. Virginia*

Robert A. Pratt
41 *Howard Law Journal* 229 (1998)

On many evenings just before sunset, my grandmother and I would sit on our front porch. We lived in the rural black community of Battery, Virginia (approximately forty-five miles east of Richmond) which is located in Essex County. Suddenly, I would hear my grandmother remark: "Well, I see Richard's gone in for the night." I would then turn my head to follow the direction of her

---

gaze, where I would see a white man driving his car down the dirt road leading to a house owned by my great-uncle. It was a two-story wood-frame house, which was one of the biggest in the neighborhood. Most of the rooms were usually rented out to various family-friends, relatives, and occasionally to the families of those who worked at the sawmill—jointly operated by my great-uncle and his older brother, my grandfather.

Raymond and Garnet Hill, along with their two sons, lived there for a time in the early 1960s. Garnet's younger sister, Mildred, was a frequent visitor, especially on weekends. Mildred's three children usually accompanied her on these visits, but her husband never did—at least not during daylight hours. As my grandmother later explained, the white man who occasionally visited my great-uncle's house near nightfall was Richard Loving. The woman whom I knew as Mildred was his wife, and the three children with whom I occasionally played were their children. . . .

Richard Perry Loving and Mildred Delores Jeter had known each other practically all of their lives, as their families lived just up the road from each other in the rural community of Central Point, Virginia, located in Caroline County. . . .

Richard Loving spent most of his time in the company of [his black neighbors, who accepted him] in part, because . . . Richard's parents had lived among these people for most of their lives without asserting any of the prerogatives generally associated with white supremacy. For twenty-three years, Richard's father had defied the racial mores of southern white society by working for Boyd Byrd, one of the wealthiest black farmers in the community; and apparently, he never had any qualms about doing so. While the elder Lovings were not oblivious to racial differences, the close-knit nature of their community required a certain degree of interdependence which could sometimes lead to an acceptance of personal relationships in a particular setting that would have been anathema elsewhere. So when white Richard Loving, age seventeen, began courting "colored" Mildred Jeter, age eleven, their budding romance drew little attention from either the white or the black communities.

Mildred (part-black and part-Cherokee) had a pretty light-brown complexion accentuated by her slim figure, which was why practically everyone who knew her called her "Stringbean" or "Bean" for short. Richard (part-English and part-Irish) was a bricklayer by trade, but spent much of his spare time drag-racing a car that he co-owned with two black friends, Raymond Green (a mechanic) and Percy Fortune (a local merchant). Despite their natural shyness, both Richard and Mildred were well-liked in the community, and the fact that they attended different churches and different schools did not hinder their courtship. When he was twenty-four and she was eighteen, Richard and Mildred decided to legalize their relationship by getting married.

Mildred did not know that interracial marriage was illegal in Virginia, but Richard did. This explains why, on June 2, 1958, he drove them across the Virginia state line to Washington, DC, to be married. With their union legally validated by the District of Columbia, Mr. and Mrs. Loving returned to Central Point to live with Mildred's parents; however, their marital bliss was short-lived. Five weeks later, on July 11, their quiet life was shattered when they were awakened early in the morning as three law officers "acting on an anonymous tip" opened the unlocked door of their home, walked into their bedroom, and shined a flashlight in their faces. Caroline County Sheriff R. Garnett Brooks demanded to know what the two of them were doing in bed togeth-er. Mildred answered, "I'm his wife," while Richard pointed to the District of Columbia marriage certificate that hung on their bedroom wall. "That's no good here," Sheriff Brooks replied. He charged the couple with unlawful cohabitation, and then he and his two deputies hauled the Lovings off to a nearby jail in Bowling Green.

At its October term in 1958, a grand jury issued indictments against the couple for violating Virginia's ban on interracial marriages. Specifically, they were charged with violating Virginia's 1924 Racial Integrity Act. The Act stipu-lated that all marriages between a white person and a colored person shall be absolutely void without any decree of divorce or other legal process, and it pro-hibited interracial couples from circumventing the law by having their marriag-es validated elsewhere and later return to Virginia. The Lovings waived their rights to a trial by jury and pled guilty to the charges. On January 6, 1959, Judge Leon M. Bazile, sentenced each of them to one year in jail, but he suspended the sentences on the condition that they leave the state of Virginia and not return together or at the same time for a period of twenty-five years. The Lovings paid their court fees of $36.29 each and moved to Washington, DC, where they would spend their next five years in exile.

During their years in the nation's capital, the Lovings lived with Mildred's cousin, Alex Byrd, and his wife Laura at 1151 Neal Street, Northeast. Their first child, Sidney, was born in 1958; Donald was born in 1959; and Peggy, the only girl, was born in 1960. The years in Washington were not happy ones for the couple. Richard struggled to maintain permanent employment while Mildred busied herself tending to the needs of their three children. During this time, they remained oblivious to the civil rights movement that was unfolding in their midst. "I just missed being at home," she told me years later. "I missed being with my family and friends, especially Garnet [her sister]. I wanted my children to grow up in the country, where they could run and play, and where I wouldn't worry about them so much. I never liked much about the city."

Virginia law would not allow Richard and Mildred Loving to live together as husband and wife in the state, nor would they be allowed to raise their mixed-race children (considered illegitimate under state law) in Virginia. They could visit Virginia, but they could not do so together. They were not even allowed to be in the state at the same time; however, that did not stop them from trying or from succeeding on various occasions. Mildred and the children made frequent visits to Battery, Virginia, the rural black community where her sister and brother-in-law lived. When Mildred would arrive in Battery, some of the neighbors would begin to look at their watches to see how long it would be before Richard's car came cruising through the neighborhood. During those early years, Richard's visits to the "Big House" (the common nickname for my great-uncle's boarding house) occurred almost exclusively after dark; but after a time, he became less cautious. Perhaps, he was confident in the belief that our community would keep his secret, or he was convinced that the local authorities in Essex County (which was adjacent to Caroline County) were not that interested in monitoring his whereabouts. It was on those occasions that I played with the Loving children, especially Sidney who was exactly my age.

The Lovings had not really been that interested in the civil rights movement, nor had they ever given much thought to challenging Virginia's law. But with a major civil rights bill being debated in Congress in 1963, Mildred decided to write to Robert Kennedy, the Attorney General of the United States. The Department of Justice referred the letter to the American Civil Liberties Union. Bernard S. Cohen, a young lawyer doing pro bono work for the ACLU in Alexandria, Virginia, agreed to take the case. He would later be joined by another young attorney, Philip J. Hirschkop.

In October 1964, Cohen and Hirschkop filed a class action suit in the U.S. District Court for the Eastern District of Virginia. In January 1965, Judge Bazile presided over a hearing of the Lovings' petition to have his original decision set aside. In a written opinion, he rebutted each of the contentions made by Cohen and Hirschkop that might have resulted in a reconsideration of their clients' guilt. After citing several legal precedents he concluded: "Almighty God created the races white, black, yellow, Malay and red, and he placed them on separate continents. And but for the interference with his arrangement, there would be no cause for such marriages. The fact that he separated the races shows that he did not intend for the races to mix." The Lovings' attorneys appealed to the Virginia Supreme Court of Appeals, but their luck was no better there. On

March 7, 1966, a unanimous court upheld Judge Bazile's decision. The convictions remained intact. Having exhausted their appeals in Virginia's courts, the Lovings proceeded to the U.S. Supreme Court.

On December 12, 1966, the U.S. Supreme Court agreed to hear the case. The NAACP, the NAACP Legal Defense and Education Fund, the Japanese American Citizens League, and a coalition of Catholic bishops also submitted briefs on the couple's behalf. In preparing the brief for their clients, Cohen and Hirschkop reviewed the history of Virginia's miscegenation statutes dating back to the seventeenth century, referring to them as "relics of slavery" and "expressions of modern day racism." In concluding his oral argument on April 10, 1967, Cohen relayed a message to the Justices from Richard Loving: "Tell the Court I love my wife, and it is just unfair that I can't live with her in Virginia."

Two months later on June 12, 1967, Chief Justice Earl Warren delivered the opinion of a unanimous Supreme Court. The Court rejected each of the state's arguments, as well as the legal precedents upon which they rested. . . .

The Lovings had chosen not to witness the Court's proceedings. Their attorneys, Bernard Cohen and Philip Hirschkop, were in their offices when a newspaper reporter called and informed them of the Court's decision. They then relayed the good news to the Lovings, who later attended a press conference at the lawyers' office in Alexandria. "We're just really overjoyed," said Richard Loving. "My wife and I plan to go ahead and build a new house now." As for Mildred, she said simply, "I feel free now." Then, a photographer snapped a picture of the couple; it has appeared in every newspaper story and magazine article ever written about them--his arm around her neck, both of them smiling, and with law books in the background. They had waited more than nine years for vindication, and it had finally come. . . .

Richard and Mildred Loving, along with their children, took up legal residence in Virginia almost immediately after the Court's ruling. Richard was finally able to build the white cinderblock house he had always wanted for his family. Those of us who lived in Battery did not see quite as much of the famous family as we once did, now that they had officially moved back home to Caroline County, off of Route 72 (also referred to as Sparta Road). But we still saw them sometimes, especially in the town of Tappahannock. The Lovings had made history and, by our community standards, become famous, but they were treated no differently after the Supreme Court ruling than they had been before. To us, they were still just Richard and Mildred, and that was exactly how they wanted it. As far as Richard was concerned, there was really only one major change worth mentioning: "For the first time, I could put my arm around her and publicly call her my wife."

Richard Loving was killed in a car accident in 1975. Mildred and the children lived on in the modest cinderblock home Richard built for them.

————————

In *Loving v. Virginia*,[42] Chief Justice Warren wrote that Virginia's statute "to prevent marriages between persons solely on the basis of racial characteristics violates the Equal Protection and Due Process Clauses of the Fourteenth Amendment. . . . Marriage is one of the basic civil rights of man, fundamental to our very existence and survival. To deny this fundamental freedom on so unsupportable a basis as the racial classifications embodied in these statutes, classifications so directly subversive of the principle of equality at the heart of the Fourteenth Amendment, is surely to deprive all the State's citizens of liberty without due process of law. The Fourteenth Amendment requires that the freedom of choice to marry not be restricted by invidious racial discriminations. Under our Constitution, the freedom to marry or not marry, a person of another race resides with the individual and cannot be infringed by the State."[43]

Restrictions on Marriage

Loving v. Virginia teaches there are limits on the power of government to regulate marriage. The California Supreme Court observed, "There can be no prohibition of marriage except for an important social objective and by reasonable means."[44] That said, states have authority over many aspects of marriage.[45] States prohibit marriage below a specified age.[46] States require couples to obtain a marriage license and solemnize the marriage. Solemnization can be secular

———————————

42   388 U.S. 1, 87 S. Ct. 1817 (1967).

43   After *Loving v. Virginia* in 1967, interracial marriage "increased significantly from 310,000 in 1970 to 651,000 in 1980, and to 1,161,000 in 1992." Zhenchao Qian, Breaking the Racial Barriers: Variations in Interracial Marriage Between 1980 and 1990, 34 *Demography* 263-276, at 263 (1997). Marriages between Blacks and Whites increased from 51,000 in 1960 to 395,000 in 2002. Zhenchao Qian & Daniel T. Lichter, Changing Patterns of Interracial Marriage in a Multiracial Society, 73 *Journal of Marriage and Family* 1065-1084, 1066 (2011).

44   Perez v. Sharp, 32 Cal. 2d 711, 714, 198 P.2d 17 (1948).

45   The California Supreme Court spoke for other courts when it wrote, "The regulation of marriage is considered a proper function of the state." Perez v. Sharp, 32 Cal. 2d 711, 713, 198 P.2d 17 (1948).

46   California Family Code § 302 provides: "(a) An unmarried male or female under the age of 18 years is capable of consenting to and consummating marriage upon obtaining a court order granting permission to the underage person or persons to marry. (b) The court order and written consent of the parents of each underage person, or of one of the parents or the guardian of each underage person shall be filed with the clerk of the court, and a certified copy of the order shall be presented to the county clerk at the time the marriage license is issued."

or religious. Marriages are forbidden that are bigamous or incestuous.[47] Later in this chapter you will see that many states prohibit same-sex marriage, although the status of same-sex marriage may be decided in 2013 by the U.S. Supreme Court.

Common Law Marriage

A "common law" marriage occurs when a couple considers themselves married and acts as a married couple, but the couple does not meet the legal requirements of a license and marriage ceremony. In *People v. Lucero*,[48] the Colorado Supreme Court wrote, "A common law marriage is established by the mutual consent or agreement of the parties to be husband and wife, followed by a mutual and open assumption of a marital relationship."

The requirements for common marriage are: (1) Agreement between the parties to be married at that time; (2) The parties are competent to marry; (3) The parties cohabit as a married couple; (4) The parties hold themselves out to the world as married; and (5) The parties have a reputation as a married couple.[49]

Common law marriage is available in Alabama, Colorado, Iowa, Kansas, Montana, Rhode Island, South Carolina, Texas, and Washington, D.C.

States that do not allow common law marriage will recognize as valid a common law marriage from a state that allows common law marriage.

Question Regarding Common Law Marriage

Mary and John lived in Texas. Nine years ago, Mary and John began dating. John got a new job in Atlanta, GA. Eight years ago, Mary moved to Atlanta to live with John. Seven years ago they separated and Mary moved back to Texas. Two weeks after returning to Texas, Mary discovered she was pregnant. After learning Mary was pregnant, John moved back to Texas. The couple's daughter was born six years ago. Mary and John purchased a home together in Texas six

---

47 *See* Okla. Stat. Ann. Tit. 43, § 2, which states: "Marriages between ancestors and descendants of any degree, of a stepfather with a stepdaughter, stepmother with stepson, between uncles and nieces, aunts and nephews, except in cases where such relationship is only by marriage, between brothers and sisters of the half as well as the whole blood, and first cousins are declared to be incestuous, illegal and void, and are expressly prohibited."

48 747 P.2d 660, 663 (Colo. 1987).

49 *See* Zharkova v. Gaudreau, 45 A.3d 1282 (R.I. 2012) for a good description of the elements of common law marriage.

years ago. They got a Veterans Administration loan for the home and the loan papers listed them as husband a wife. Four years ago, John began working in Kuwait. When John returned to the U.S. on vacation, he stayed with Mary and their child. While working in Kuwait, John had medical insurance, and Mary and the child were insured on John's policy, with Mary listed as his spouse. During the relevant time, Mary and John had separate bank accounts and filed their taxes as single persons. After finishing his work in Kuwait, John returned to live with Mary. After learning that Mary had been unfaithful, John filed for divorce in Texas. Does a common law marriage exist between Mary and John?

Marriage and Immigration

Federal immigration law allows United States citizens to help family members immigrate to the United States.[50] Two steps are required. First, a family immigrant visa petition is filed with U.S. Citizenship and Immigration Services. Second, once the visa petition is approved, an application to immigrate is filed. Immediate relatives—spouses and children—can immigrate quickly. Other family members may have to wait months or years.

Federal immigration law defines "spouse" as an individual who is legally married, and whose marriage is not a sham entered in order to facilitate immigration. A marriage entered in order to circumvent immigration laws is a sham and does not allow an alien spouse to gain immigration benefits.[51] Once an alien is determined to have perpetrated marriage fraud, the alien is permanently barred from becoming a U.S. citizen.[52]

A U.S. citizen who is engaged to be married to a foreign national may petition for a special visa to allow the fiancé to enter the United States to get married. Following marriage, the non-citizen spouse may apply for permanent residency.

---

50 *See* Immigrant Legal Resource Center, *A Guide for Immigration Advocates* vol. 1, § 4.1, p. 4-2 (2010).

Lawful permanent residents of the United States may apply for spouses and children, as well as other relatives, to immigrate the United States. Unlike U.S. citizens, however, whose spouses and children can immigrate quickly, spouses and children of permanent residents may have to wait. In 2000, Congress created a new non-immigrant visa to allow spouses and children of lawful residents to move to the United States more quickly.

51 *See* 8 C.F.R. § 204.2(a)(1)(ii).

52 *See* Ettienne v. Holder, 659 F.3d 513 (6th Cir. 2011)("Under 8 U.S.C. § 1154(c), a person who has previously attempted to gain permanent residency through a fraudulent marriage is barred from procuring an immigrant visa, regardless of other eligibility.").

Immigration law is a highly complex specialty, beyond the scope of this text. It is worth mentioning that an attorney with expertise in both family law and immigration can be helpful to many families and individuals.

Marriage Equality—Same-Sex Marriage

Prior to the 1970s, there was little public discussion of marriage equality. Heterosexual marriage was a given. In 1891, Joel Bishop defined marriage as "the civil status of one man and one woman legally united for life . . . ."[53] Statutes in several states defined marriage without mentioning that it was between a woman and a man—Why mention the obvious?

In the 1970s, advocates for gay and lesbian rights began a political, scholarly, and legal campaign for marriage equality.[54] An early voice was the National Coalition for Gay Organizations which, in 1972, advocated repeal of laws restricting same-sex marriage.[55]

Timothy Biblarz and Evren Savci write, "In the 1990s, marriages between same-gender partners were not legally recognized anywhere in the world . . . . Beginning in September 2000, when the Netherlands extended to right to marry to include sex-sex couples, the ensuing decade brought significant expansion of legal rights and recognitions. Same-sex marriage became legal in Belgium, Norway, Sweden, Spain, South Africa, Canada, and Mexico City, and in the United States in Massachusetts, Connecticut, Iowa, Vermont, New Hampshire, and Washington, D.C. Dozens of other nations and states granted same-sex couples rights associated with marriage via domestic partnerships, civil unions, and the like."[56]

In the United States, early legal efforts to achieve marriage equality foundered. In *Anonymous v. Anonymous*,[57] decided in 1971, plaintiff and defendant met in Georgia in 1968. According to plaintiff, he believed, incorrectly, that defendant was a woman. Three months later they went through a marriage ceremony in Texas. Upon returning to plaintiff's apartment after the wedding, plain-

---

53 Joel P. Bishop, *New Commentaries on Marriage, Divorce, and Separation* vol 1, § 11, p. 5 (1891).

54 See William N. Eskridge, Jr., *The Case for Same-Sex Marriage: From Sexual Liberty to Civilized Commitment* (1996).

55 Quoted in William N. Eskridge, Jr., *The Case for Same-Sex Marriage: From Sexual Liberty to Civilized Commitment* (1996).

56 Timothy J. Biblarz & Evren Savci, Lesbian, Gay, Bisexual, and Transgender Families, 72 *Journal of Marriage and Family* 480-497, at 480 (2010).

57 67 Misc.2d 982, 325 N.Y.S.2d 499 (Supreme Court 1971).

tiff fell asleep. Plaintiff awoke in the middle of the night and touched defendant, only to find, to his surprise, that defendant was a man. Plaintiff and defendant never lived together or had sex. In his home state of New York, plaintiff brought an action to declare the "marriage" invalid. The trial court wrote, "The law makes no provision for a 'marriage' between persons of the same sex. Marriage is and always has been a contract between a man and a woman." The court ruled that the "so-called marriage ceremony" did not create a marriage.

Also in 1971, the Minnesota Supreme Court decided *Baker v. Nelson.*[58] John Baker and his partner James Michael McConnell were denied a marriage license by a county clerk. The Minnesota Supreme Court wrote that Minnesota law "does not authorize marriage between persons of the same sex . . . . The institution of marriage as a union of man and woman, uniquely involving the procreation and rearing of children within a family, is as old as the book of Genesis. . . . The equal protection clause of the Fourteenth Amendment, like the due process clause, is not offended by the state's classification of persons authorized to marry. There is no irrational or invidious discrimination."

In 1973, the Kentucky Court of Appeals upheld a trial judge's decision to deny a marriage license to a lesbian couple.[59] The Court of Appeals wrote, "The sections of Kentucky statutes relating to marriage do not include a definition of that term . . . [H]owever, marriage has always been considered as a union of a man and a woman . . . . It appears to us that appellants are prevented from marrying . . . by their own incapability of entering into a marriage as that term is defined."

In 1974, the Washington Court of Appeals joined the chorus. In *Singer v. Hara,*[60] two men were denied a marriage license. The Court of Appeals wrote, "The courts known by us to have considered the question have all concluded that same-sex relationships are outside of the proper definition of marriage." The court concluded that defining marriage to exclude same-sex relationships did not create a suspect classification subject to heightened scrutiny under the equal protection clause.

---

58 291 Minn. 310, 191 N.W.2d 185 (1971).

59 Jones v. Hallahan, 501 S.W.2d 588 (Ky. Ct. App. 1973).

60 11 Wash. App. 247, 522 P.2d 1187 (1974).

The legal dam burst in Hawai'i in 1993, when the Hawai'i Supreme Court's decided *Baehr v. Lewin*.[61] The court held that the equal protection clause of the state constitution may require recognition of marriage equality.

In response to *Baehr v. Lewin*, in 1996, Congress passed the Defense of Marriage Act (DOMA).[62] The House Judiciary Committee Report on DOMA states: "It is critical to understand the nature of the orchestrated legal assault being waged against traditional heterosexual marriage by gay rights groups and their lawyers. . . . The legal assault against traditional heterosexual marriage laws achieved its greatest breakthrough in the State of Hawaii in 1993."[63] The House committee continued: "The Defense of Marriage Act has two primary purposes. The first is to defend the institution of traditional heterosexual marriage. The second is to protect the right of the States to formulate their own public policy regarding the legal recognition of same-sex unions, free from any federal constitutional implications that might attend the recognition by one State of the right for homosexual couples to acquire marriage licenses."[64]

DOMA provides: "In determining the meaning of any Act of Congress, or of any ruling, regulation, or interpretation of the various administrative bureaus and agencies of the United States, the word 'marriage' means only a legal union between one man and one woman as husband and wife, and the word 'spouse' refers only to a person of the opposite sex who is a husband or wife. No State, territory, or possession of the United States, or Indian tribe, shall be required to give effect to any public act, record, or judicial proceeding of any other State, territory, possession, or tribe respecting a relationship between persons of the same sex that is treated as a marriage under the laws of such other State, territory, possession, or tribe, or a right or claim arising from such relationship."[65]

In *Massachusetts v. United States Department of Health and Human Services*,[66] the federal First Circuit Court of Appeals ruled DOMA unconstitutional insofar as it denied federal benefits to same-sex couples legally married in Massachusetts.

---

61   74 Haw. 530, 852 P.2d 44 (1993). Interesting personal information on Ninia Baehr and Genora Dancel can be found in William N. Eskridge, Jr., *The Case for Same-Sex Marriage* (1996).

62   1 U.S.C.A. § 7 and 28 U.S.C.A. § 1738C.

63   House Report (Judiciary Committee). P.L. 104-199, 110 Stat. 2419. Report No. 104-664. pp. 2-3. July 9, 1996

64   House Report (Judiciary Committee). P.L. 104-199, 110 Stat. 2419. Report No. 104-664. July 9, 1996.

65   1 U.S.C.A. § 7; 28 U.S.C.A. § 1738C.

66   682 F.3d 1 (1st Cir. 2012).

Returning to the issue of marriage equality, in 1999, the Vermont Supreme Court ruled in *Baker v. State*[67] "that the State is constitutionally required to extend to same-sex couples the common benefits that flow from marriage under Vermont law. Whether this ultimately takes the form of inclusion within the marriage laws themselves or a parallel 'domestic partnership' system . . . rests with the Legislature." In response to *Baker*, the Vermont Legislature legalized same sex marriage.

In *Kerrigan v. Commissioner of Public Health*,[68] the Connecticut Supreme Court in 2008 grappled with "whether the state statutory prohibition against same sex marriage violates the constitution of Connecticut." The court wrote, "We conclude that, in light of the history of pernicious discrimination faced by gay men and lesbians, and because the institution of marriage carries with it a status and significance that the newly created classification of civil unions does not embody, the segregation of heterosexual and homosexual couples into separate institutions constitutes a cognizable harm. We also conclude that (1) our state scheme discriminates on the basis of sexual orientation, (2) for the same reasons that classifications predicated on gender are considered quasi-suspect for purposes of the equal protection provisions of the United States constitution, sexual orientation constitutes a quasi-suspect classification for purposes of the equal protection provisions of the state constitution, and, therefore, our statutes discriminating against gay persons are subject to heightened or intermediate judicial scrutiny, and (3) the state has failed to provide sufficient justification for excluding same sex couples from the institution of marriage."

In *Varnum v. Brien*[69] the Iowa Supreme Court in 2009 addressed same-sex marriage. The court ruled that the Iowa statute limiting marriage to a woman and a man violated the equal protection clause of the state constitution.

In 2000, California voters approved Proposition 22, which added Family Code § 308.5, providing, "Only marriage between and man and a woman is valid or recognized in California." In 2008, the California Supreme Court struck down Proposition 22. Following the Supreme Court's decision, approximately 18,000 California same-sex couples married. Opponents of same-sex marriage fought back with Proposition 8, which passed later in 2008, and which amended the state constitution to prohibit same-sex marriage. In 2009, the California Supreme Court upheld Proposition 8. Undaunted, proponents of same-sex marriage repaired to federal court where, in 2010, the U.S. District Court ruled

---

67 170 Vt. 194, 744 A.2d 864 (1999).

68 289 Conn. 135, 957 A.2d 407 (2008).

69 763 N.W.2d 862 (Iowa 2009).

California's constitutional ban on same-sex marriage violated the Fourteenth Amendment of the U.S. Constitution.[70] The District Court ruled, "California has no interest in differentiating between same-sex and opposite-sex unions." The court noted that the proponents of same-sex marriage "do not seek recognition of a new right. . . . Rather, [the proponents] ask California to recognize their relationships for what they are: marriages." On appeal to the Ninth Circuit, the Court of Appeals affirmed the District Court. The appellate court wrote:

> Prior to November 4, 2008, the California Constitution guaranteed the right to marry to opposite-sex couples and same-sex couples alike. On that day, the People of California adopted Proposition 8, which amended the state constitution to eliminate the right of same-sex couples to marry. We consider whether that amendment violates the Fourteenth Amendment to the United States Constitution. We conclude that it does.
>
> Although the Constitution permits communities to enact most laws they believe to be desirable, it requires that there be at least a legitimate reason for the passage of a law that treats different classes of people differently. There was no such reason that Proposition 8 could have been enacted.[71]

In 2011, the New York Legislature legalized same sex marriage. The statement of legislative intent provides: "Marriage is a fundamental human right. Same-sex couples should have the same access as others to the protections, responsibilities, rights, obligations, and benefits of civil marriage. Stable family relationships help build a stronger society. For the welfare of the community and in fairness to all New Yorkers, this act formally recognizes otherwise-valid marriages without regard to whether the parties are of the same or different sex." New York's Domestic Relations Law now reads: "A marriage that is otherwise valid shall be valid regardless of whether the parties to the marriage are of the same or different sex."[72] The law provides that religious organizations and clergy opposed to same sex marriage do not have to perform such marriages and cannot be sued for such refusal.

---

70   Perry v. Schwarzenegger, 704 F. Supp. 2d 921 (E.D. Cal. 2010).

71   Perry v. Brown, 671 F.3d 1052 (9th Cir. 2012).

72   N.Y. Dom Rel. L. § 10-a(1).

As of late 2012, same sex marriage was legal in Maine, Maryland, Massachusetts, Connecticut, Iowa, Vermont, New Hampshire, New York, and Washington. In early 2013, the U.S. Supreme Court agreed to hear cases dealing with marriage equality and DOMA.

Public attitudes toward marriage equality are evolving. Yet, opposition is robust. A number of religions oppose same-sex marriage. Some twenty-nine states amended their constitutions to declare same sex marriage illegal.

Regarding children, psychological research indicates that "children raised by lesbian partners (mostly co-mothers) have been found across a large number of tests to be generally similar to children raised by heterosexual parents on dimensions of psychological well-being, peer relations, and social and behavioral adjustment."[73]

Scholars are divided on same-sex marriage.[74] Writing in the *Texas Review of Law and Politics*, George Dent argued in 2011 that "Straight is Better."[75] Dent wrote, "Society has valid reasons to prefer heterosexuality and traditional marriage over other options, including homosexuality and 'same-sex marriage.' Heterosexuality is a normal part of human nature. It is conducive to the happiness of most people to treat it as such. Traditional marriage and the biological family are not inherently sexist and are beneficial to both sexes. They also benefit society by making adults better and more productive citizens and by providing the best upbringing for children. When a husband and wife bear and raise children they are not merely affecting their personal lifestyle preference; they are helping to ensure the future of our society. Homosexuals—and all people—should be treated with decency and civility, but not all behavior merits equal respect." Dent's views are in the minority among scholars writing today.

Civil Union; Domestic Partnership

Unmarried couples lack many legal rights enjoyed by married couples. For example, married couples inherit from each other. A married person can be on their spouse's employment-related health insurance. Spouses automatically come within the system of marital property. Spouses have the right to visit each

---

73 Timothy J. Biblarz & Evren Savci, Lesbian, Gay, Bisexual, and Transgender Families, 72 *Journal of Marriage and Family* 480-497, at 484 (2010).

74 See David Orgon Collidge, Playing the Loving Card: Same-Sex Marriage and the Politics of Analogy, *BYU Journal of Public Law* 201 (1998).

75 George W. Dent, Jr., Straight is Better: Why Law and Society may Justly Prefer Heterosexuality, 15 *Texas Review of Law and Politics* 359 (2011).

other in hospital. A married person can sue for wrongful death. Married couples can file joint tax returns. The list goes on.

Before barriers to marriage equality started falling, lesbian and gay couples who were unable to marry agitated for rights similar to the rights enjoyed by married couples.[76] States responded with laws authorizing civil unions or domestic partnerships. At the level of local government, many cities extended health insurance and other benefits to domestic partners of city employees.[77]

When the Washington State legislature enacted Washington's domestic partnership law, the legislature made the following findings:

> Many Washingtonians are in intimate, committed, and exclusive relationships with another person to whom they are not legally married. These relationships are important to the individuals involved and their families; they also benefit the public by providing a private source of mutual support for the financial, physical, and emotional health of those individuals and their families. The public has an interest in providing a legal framework for such mutually supportive relationships, whether the partners are of the same or different sexes, and irrespective of their sexual orientation.[78]

> It is the intent of the legislature that for all purposes under state law, state registered domestic partners shall be treated the same as married spouses.[79]

New Jersey's Domestic Partnership Act defines domestic partnership as: "Both persons have a common residence and are otherwise jointly responsible for each other's common welfare as evidenced by joint financial arrangements

---

76 *See* Marriage Cases, 43 Cal. 4th 757, 801, 183 P.3d 384 (2008)("In 1999, the Legislature enacted the initial legislation creating a statewide domestic partnership registry.").

77 Challenges to extending benefits to same-sex partners have largely failed. *See* National Pride at Work, Inc. v. Governor of Michigan, 481 Mich. 56, 748 N.W.2d 524, 529 (2008)("We granted leave to appeal to consider whether the marriage amendment, Const. 1963, art. 1, § 25, which states that 'the union of one man and one woman in marriage shall be the only agreement recognized as a marriage or similar union for any purpose,' prohibits public employers from providing health-insurance benefits to their employees' qualified same-sex domestic partners. Because we agree with the Court of Appeals that providing such benefits does not violate the marriage amendment, we affirm its judgment."); Council of the City of New York v. Bloomberg, 6 N.Y.3d 380, 846 N.E.2d 433 (2006); Heinsma v. City of Vancouver, 144 Wash. 2d 556, 29 P.3d 709 (2001)(city could define its employees' "dependents" to include domestic partners); Robin C. Miller, Validity of Governmental Domestic Partnership Enactments, 74 A.L.R.5th 439 (1999).

78 Wash. Rev. Code Ann. § 26.60.010.

79 Wash. Rev. Code Ann. § 26.60.015.

or joint ownership of real or personal property. . . . Both persons have chosen to share each other's lives in a committed relationship of mutual caring . . . ."[80] Nevada law is similar, describing domestic partners as persons who "have chosen to share one another's lives in an intimate and committed relationship of mutual caring . . . . Domestic partners have the same rights, protections and benefits, and are subject to the same responsibilities, obligations and duties under law . . . as are granted to and imposed upon spouses."[81]

Some domestic partnerships, like some marriages, end in dissolution. Marriage is terminated only by judicial divorce. Domestic partnership can be dissolved in similar fashion. In some states, domestic partners can agree to "simplified termination" of the relationship, accomplished by filing the necessary documents with the proper government office.[82]

Married Couples and Domestic Partners Can Do Whatever They Like With Their Property (Almost)

Married couples and domestic partners can do pretty much whatever they like with their property. Marital property is analyzed in Chapter 9.

During marriage and domestic partnership, agreements regarding property go by different names: transmutation in California; post-nuptial agreement in some states; partition and exchange in Texas. A Texas statute provides: "At any time, the spouses may partition or exchange between themselves all or part of their community property, then existing or to be acquired, as the spouses may desire."[83] Another Texas statute allows spouses to change property from separate to community.[84] A related provision states that a partition or exchange agreement is enforceable without consideration.[85]

Married couples and domestic partners can change separate property into marital/community property and visa-versa.[86] A recurring example is a single

---

80   N.J. Stat. Ann. § 26:8A-4(b). The statute provides that the partners must be at least 18, must agree to be financially responsible for each other, must not be married or in another domestic partnership, must not be too closely related, must be of the same sex or, "except that two persons who are each 62 years of age or older and not of the same sex may establish a domestic partnership."

81   Nev. Rev. Stat. § 122A.200(1).

82   *See* Nev. Rev. Ann. § 122A.300.

83   Tex. Family Code § 4.102.

84   Tex. Family Code § 4. 202.

85   Tex. Family Code § 4.104.

86   *See* Shaw v. Shaw, 87 So. 3d 235 (La. Ct. App. 2012)("Spouses may enter into a matrimonial agreement dur-

person who owns a home, gets married, and changes title of the property from their name alone to concurrent ownership with their spouse (joint tenancy, tenancy in common, tenancy by the entirety, or community property). States differ on the formalities required to change property ownership between spouses, although the norm is a writing.

States limit transfers by one spouse or domestic partner of marital/community property to third persons. Thus, in many states, one spouse cannot give away marital/community property without the consent of the other spouse. Similarly, in many states, both spouses must consent to the sale of marital/community real property.

Although married couples and domestic partners have great freedom to deal with their property as they see fit, there is one thing they can't do: Transfer property between themselves or to others in order to avoid paying debts. They can't transfer property to hide it from creditors. All states have laws against so-called transfers in fraud of creditors. The majority of states have adopted a version of the Uniform Fraudulent Transfer Act (FTA) promulgated by the National Conference of Commissioners on Uniform State Laws.[87] Section 4 of the FTA states:

> A transfer made . . . by a debtor is fraudulent as to a creditor, whether the creditor's claim arose before or after the transfer was made . . . , if the debtor made the transfer . . . (1) with actual intent to hinder, delay, or defraud any creditor of the debtor; or (2) without receiving a reasonably equivalent value in exchange for the transfer or obligation, and the debtor: (i) was engaged or was about to engage in a business or transaction for which the remaining assets of the debtor were unreasonably small in relation to the business or transaction; or (ii) intended to incur, or believed or reasonably should have believed that he or she would incur, debts beyond his or ability to pay as they became due.

The California Court of Appeal's decision in *State Board of Equalization v. Woo*[88] illustrates the FTA in action. Husband owed back taxes to the state tax

---

ing marriage to modify or terminate the matrimonial regime only upon a joint petition and a finding by the court that it serves the parties' best interests. A matrimonial agreement is a contract establishing a regime of separation of property or modifying or terminating the legal regime. Spouses are free to establish by matrimonial agreement a regime of separation of property or modify the legal regime as provided by law.").

87 National Conference of Commissioners on Uniform State Laws, Uniform Fraudulent Transfer Act, vol. 7A.

88 82 Cal. App. 4th 481 (2000).

authority—the Board of Equalization (Board). Husband and wife suspected the Board was planning to collect the taxes by garnishing community property. Husband and wife wanted to protect wife's salary (community property) from garnishment, so they agreed that wife's income from employment would be her separate property rather than community property. The Board could not garnish wife's separate property. The plan failed. Changing wife's income from community property to separate property was done with the intent to defraud husband's creditor, the Board.

EXPERIENTIAL ASSIGNMENT

Practice Exercise: *Uniform Fraudulant Convenances Act*

Susan Sanchez is a local restaurateur who owns and operates a popular eaterie. In addition to being a regular patron at Sue's restaurant, you have occasionally reviewed contracts for her. Recently, while enjoying a desert coffee at Sue's restaurant, Sue sat at your table and said, "May I ask you a legal question?" You replied, "Sure." Sue relays the following: Sue and her husband Phil own the real estate housing the restaurant. They own it as joint tenants. A year ago, a customer slipped and fell in the restaurant and broke her hip. Sue recently received a demand letter from an attorney representing the injured customer. The letter demands that Sue pay the customer $500,000 or the customer will sue. Unfortunately, at the time the accident happened, Sue did not have insurance to cover the accident. After relating these facts, Sue says, "Phil and I are thinking we should sell the restaurant to my mom for a nominal amount so we don't own it if this lady sues us and gets a judgment. If the lawsuit goes against us, the property won't be ours and we won't lose it. Can we do that?" You say, "I'll look into it and get you an answer."

Assignment: (1) Locate your state's Fraudulent Convenances Act. Read the Act and cases interpreting it. Draft a letter to Sue answering her question. (2) Is your conversation with Sue in the restaurant covered by the attorney-client privilege? (3) Will your letter to Sue be covered by the attorney-client privilege?

In the Shadow of Divorce—
Agreement In Hopes of Saving Marriage

Sometimes, a married couple or domestic partners are near divorce, but want to try to save their marriage. To that end, they may enter a "postnuptial agreement."[89] The Connecticut Supreme Court described postnuptial agreements in *Bedrick v. Bedrick*,[90] "A postnuptial agreement is distinguished from both a prenuptial agreement and a separation agreement. Like a prenuptial agreement, a postnuptial agreement may determine, *inter alia*, each spouse's legal rights and obligations upon dissolution of the marriage. As the name suggests, however, a postnuptial agreement is entered into during marriage—after a couple weds, but before they separate, when the spouses plan to continue their marriage." The *Bedrick* court wrote, "We conclude that postnuptial agreements are valid and enforceable and generally must comply with contract principles. We also conclude, however, that the terms of such agreements must be both fair and equitable at the time of execution and not unconscionable at the time of dissolution."

The *Bedrick* court's emphasis on fairness is echoed by the Minnesota statute on postnuptual contracts, which provides in part: "Spouses who are legally married under the laws of this state may enter into a postnuptial contract or settlement which is valid and enforceable if it [is] . . . procedurally and substantively fair and equitable both at the time of its execution and at the time of its enforcement . . . A postnuptial contract or settlement is valid and enforceable only if at the time of its execution each spouse is represented by separate legal counsel."[91]

In *Ansin v. Ansin*, the Massachusetts Supreme Judicial Court discusses postnuptual agreements.

---

89 *See Shaw v. Shaw*, 87 So. 3d 235 (La. Ct. App. 2012)("Spouses may enter into a matrimonial agreement during marriage to modify or terminate the matrimonial regime only upon a joint petition and a finding by the court that it serves the parties' best interests. A matrimonial agreement is a contract establishing a regime of separation of property or modifying or terminating the legal regime. Spouses are free to establish by matrimonial agreement a regime of separation of property or modify the legal regime as provided by law.").

90 300 Conn. 691, 17 A.3d 17, p. 21 n. 1 (2011).

91 Minn. Stat. Ann. § 519.11(1).

Ansin v. Ansin

Supreme Judicial Court of Massachusetts
457 Mass. 283, 929 N.E.2d 955 (2010)

Marshall, C.J.

We granted direct appellate review in this divorce proceeding to determine whether so-called "postnuptial" or "marital" agreements are contrary to public policy and, if not, whether the marital agreement at issue is enforceable. A "post-nuptial" or "marital" agreement is an "agreement between spouses who plan to continue their marriage that alters or confirms the legal rights and obligations that would otherwise arise under ... [the] law governing marital dissolution." American Law Institute, *Principles of the Law of Family Dissolution: Analysis and Recommendations* § 7.01(1)(b) (2002) (*ALI Principles of Family Dissolution*). Consistent with the ALI, we adopt the term "premarital" agreement for what is often termed a prenuptial or antenuptual agreement, and the term "marital" agreement for what is often termed a postnuptial agreement.

The dispute is between Kenneth S. Ansin (husband) and Cheryl A. Craven–Ansin (wife) concerning the validity of their 2004 written agreement "settling all rights and obligations arising from their marital relationship" in the event of a divorce. Two years after the agreement was executed, in November, 2006, the husband filed a complaint for divorce and sought to enforce the terms of the agreement. At the time of the complaint, the parties had been married for twenty-one years and had two sons.

A judge in the Probate and Family Court upheld the agreement, finding that it was negotiated by independent counsel for each party, was not the product of fraud or duress, and was based on full financial disclosures by the husband, and that the terms of the agreement were fair and reasonable at the time of execution and at the time of divorce. Judgment was entered enforcing the marital agreement. The wife appealed . . . . We now affirm.

. . . At the time of the execution of the marital agreement in 2004, the value of the combined assets of the husband and wife was approximately $19 million. One of the assets, now at issue, is the husband's interest in certain trusts and business entities established by his grandfather, currently managed by his uncle. The assets of these various entities are substantial real estate holdings in Florida. The husband's interest in the Florida real estate is passive; he was not involved in the management of the properties, and did not have or exercise control over the sale or other disposition of the properties. During the course of the marriage, the husband received, and the wife was aware of, distributions from his interest in the Florida real estate. The timing and amount of the distributions was unpredictable, and varied widely, as the wife knew.

During the course of their marriage the couple retained RINET Company LLC (RINET) to provide financial advice to them and to prepare their joint tax returns. The parties' primary financial planner from RINET met with the couple on a quarterly basis, and RINET prepared "periodic summary reports" to permit the couple to monitor their financial affairs. Because the husband's interest in the Florida real estate was "fractional" and "non-controlling," and because "speculation" is "inherent in any attempt to assign any values to such interests," there was no attempt by RINET to assign concrete values to these assets. Rather, on the reports prepared by RINET, the husband's interest in the Florida real estate was given a "placeholder" value of $4 million to $5 million (the amount varied from time to time), of which the wife was well aware. The wife understood that the husband's principal objective in executing a marital agreement was to protect his interest in the Florida real estate in the event of a divorce.

The parties were married in July, 1985. The execution of their marital agreement nineteen years later was precipitated by marital problems that began toward the end of 2003. At the time the couple sought the assistance of a marriage counselor. In early 2004, the husband informed his wife that he "needed" her to sign an agreement if their marriage was to continue. He testified that his "uncertainty" about the wife's commitment to their relationship was the reason for this request. It caused the wife a "great deal of stress"; she told her husband that she would not sign any such agreement, and that discussion of the issue made her "physically ill." The parties separated, as it turned out, for some six weeks. While the parties were separated, the husband promised his wife that he would recommit to the marriage if she would sign a marital agreement. She agreed to do so, she said, in an attempt to preserve the marriage and the family. The parties resumed living together, and went on a "second honeymoon."

In April, 2004, they began negotiating the terms of the agreement, which we describe below. Each retained counsel. The judge's detailed description of the negotiations depicts back-and-forth discussions between counsel for the wife and counsel for the husband, during which the wife negotiated terms more favorable to her. Several draft agreements were exchanged. The judge found that in the course of the negotiations the wife was "fully informed" of the marital assets, and that she was "satisfied" with the disclosures made by the husband with respect to the Florida real estate, which included the financial summaries prepared by RINET that used the "placeholder" values. Finally, with the assistance of their respective counsel, the parties reached an agreement; it was signed in July, 2004.

We briefly summarize key provisions of the marital agreement. The agreement sets forth the parties' intent that, in the event of a divorce, the terms of the agreement are to be "valid and enforceable" against them, and "limit the rights" that "otherwise arise by reason of their marriage." The agreement recites that the parties are aware of the rights to which they may be entitled under Massachusetts law, that each has retained independent legal counsel, and that each executed the agreement "freely and voluntarily." The agreement states that the parties are "aware of the other's income," warrants that each has been provided with "all information requested by the other," and affirms that each "waives his or her rights to further inquiry, discovery and investigation." The agreement further recites that each is "fully satisfied" that the agreement "will promote marital harmony" and "will ensure the treatment of Husband's property to which the parties agreed before their marriage and since their separation."

As for the distribution of property in the event of a divorce, the agreement states that the wife "disclaims any and all interest she now has or ever may have" in the husband's interest in the Florida real estate and other marital assets. The husband agreed to pay the wife $5 million, and thirty per cent of the appreciation of all marital property held by the couple from the time of the agreement to the time of the divorce. The agreement provides that the wife could remain in the marital home for one year after any divorce, with the husband paying all reasonable expenses of that household. The husband agreed to pay for the wife's medical insurance until her death or remarriage, and he agreed to maintain a life insurance policy to the exclusive benefit of the wife in the amount of $2.5 million while the parties remained married.

On execution of the marital agreement, the relationship between the husband and wife took on, in the judge's words, a "light and optimistic tone" and both were "looking forward to strengthening their marriage." The two engaged in numerous activities together, including training for a marathon and traveling. However, in August, 2004, the parties had a discussion that "led the wife to believe that their marriage was over." The husband had not decided to divorce his wife, and the judge credited his testimony that he was "unwilling" to abandon the marriage at that time.

In response to their marital difficulties, the parties again considered separating, but decided not to do so at least until their younger son graduated from high school. They remained living together from August, 2004, until June, 2005, engaged in an intimate relationship, and "attempted to preserve the appearance of their marriage." During this time, they purchased a new home for $790,000, and paid $500,000 for its renovations.

Meanwhile, the husband applied for and was accepted to Harvard University's Kennedy School of Government; his decision to enroll as a student there was not supported by his wife. The wife began to increase her consumption of alcohol, leading to more arguments with her husband. In June, 2005, at the wife's request, the husband moved out of the house. He did not file for divorce at that time, believing that while things looked "grim," filing for divorce would have been the "ultimate declaration" that his marriage was over. After separating from her husband, the wife maintained contact with their RINET financial advisor, inquiring on multiple occasions what the value of any payment to her would be under the terms of the marital agreement. In 2006 the wife became involved in a serious relationship with another man. In February of that year, the wife informed the husband that "one of us has to be strong enough to take the steps to bring closure to our relationship." She did not commence divorce proceedings. In November, 2006, the husband filed a petition for divorce.

Whether a marital agreement should be recognized in Massachusetts is a long-deferred question of first impression. Consistent with the majority of States to address the issue, *see Bratton v. Bratton,* 136 S.W.3d 595, 599–600 (Tenn.2004), we conclude that such agreements may be enforced. *See e.g., Matter of Estate of Harber,* 104 Ariz. 79, 86, 449 P.2d 7 (1969); *Casto v. Casto,* 508 So.2d 330, 333 (Fla.1987); *Lipic v. Lipic,* 103 S.W.3d 144, 149 (Mo.Ct.App.2003); *Matter of Estate of Gab,* 364 N.W.2d 924, 925 (S.D.1985).

Several States have enacted statutes that permit the enforcement of marital agreements. *See, e.g., Tibbs v. Anderson,* 580 So.2d 1337, 1339 (Ala.1991); *Boudreaux v. Boudreaux,* 745 So.2d 61, 63 (La.Ct.App.1999); *Button v. Button,* 131 Wis.2d 84, 87–88, 388 N.W.2d 546 (1986). *But see Ohio Rev.Code Ann.* § 3103.06 (West 2005) ("A husband and wife cannot, by any contract with each other, alter their legal relations, except that they may agree to an immediate separation and make provisions for the support of either of them and their children during the separation"). Many States have not addressed the issue. We are aware of no jurisdiction that has declined to enforce such agreements unless required to do so by statute.

Our decision is consistent with our established recognition that a marital relationship need not vitiate contractual rights between the parties. We have, for example, recognized the validity of premarital agreements, and separation agreements, reasoning that it was important to respect the parties' freedom to contract and that such agreements may serve a useful function in permitting the parties to arrange their financial affairs as they best see fit.

The wife argues that marital agreements are different in kind and should be declared void against public policy because they are "innately coercive," "usually" arise when the marriage is already failing, and may "encourage" divorce. The wife provides no support for, and we reject, any assumption that marital agreements are typically executed amid threats of divorce or induced by illusory promises of remaining in a failing marriage. Marital contracts are not the product of classic arm's-length bargaining, but that does not make them necessarily coercive. Such contracts may inhibit the dissolution of a marriage, or may protect the interests of third parties such as children from a prior relationship. In any event, a marital agreement will always be reviewed by a judge to ensure that coercion or fraud played no part in its execution.

A marital agreement stands on a different footing from both a premarital and a separation agreement. Before marriage, the parties have greater freedom to reject an unsatisfactory premarital contract. A separation agreement, in turn, is negotiated when a marriage has failed and the spouses intend a permanent separation or marital dissolution. The family unit will no longer be kept intact, and the parties may look to their own future economic interests. The circumstances surrounding marital agreements in contrast are pregnant with the opportunity for one party to use the threat of dissolution to bargain themselves into positions of advantage.

. . . We join many other States in concluding that marital agreements must be carefully scrutinized. Before a marital agreement is sanctioned by a court, careful scrutiny by the judge should determine at a minimum whether (1) each party has had an opportunity to obtain separate legal counsel of each party's own choosing. We do not require, as do some other States, that a marital agreement will be enforceable only if each spouse is represented by separate counsel. . . . Reliance on the advice of experienced, independent legal counsel, however, will go a long way toward ensuring the enforceability of an agreement; (2) there was fraud or coercion in obtaining the agreement; (3) all assets were fully disclosed by both parties before the agreement was executed; (4) each spouse knowingly and explicitly agreed in writing to waive the right to a judicial equitable division of assets and all marital rights in the event of a divorce; and (5) the terms of the agreement are fair and reasonable at the time of execution and at the time of divorce. Where one spouse challenges the enforceability of the agreement, the spouse seeking to enforce the agreement shall bear the burden of satisfying these criteria.

We now elaborate on those points as they apply to the marital agreement here.

As with contracts generally, marital agreements are not enforceable if tainted by fraud or coercion. . . .

Even though the judge in this case did not utilize a burden-shifting analysis, we see no reason to question her ultimate finding that the marital agreement was not the product of coercion or fraud. The agreement was the product of lengthy negotiations between the parties, each represented by separate, experienced counsel. The wife's attorney testified that, consistent with the instructions of her client, she intended to negotiate an enforceable marital agreement. A vigorous exchange ensued with the husband's counsel in which she was able to negotiate significant gains for the wife. The evidence is clear that the wife made an informed, voluntary choice to sign the agreement.

As to fraud, the wife argues that the husband misrepresented his intention to stay in the marriage in order to induce her to sign the agreement. The judge found to the contrary, and her findings are fully supported by the evidence. . . .

We have explained with respect to premarital agreements that full and fair disclosure of each party's financial circumstances is a significant aspect of the parties' obligation to deal with each other fairly because they stand in a confidential relationship with each other and must have such information in order to make an informed decision about the terms of the agreement. The obligation is greater with respect to marital agreements because each spouse owes a duty of absolute fidelity to the other. . . . The requirement of full disclosure may be satisfied if "prior to signing the agreement the party seeking to enforce it provided the other party with a written statement accurately listing (i) his or her significant assets, and their total approximate market value; (ii) his or her approximate annual income . . . and (iii) any significant future acquisitions, or changes in income, to which the party has a current legal entitlement, or which the party reasonably expects to realize" in the near future. ALI *Principles of Family Dissolution* § 7.04(5). The disclosure need not be exact, but must approximate the value of the assets.

We agree with the judge that the disclosures here were sufficient to meet this rigorous standard. The wife argues that the husband undervalued his interest in the Florida real estate, and that he committed a breach of the warranty in the agreement that such disclosures were "accurate and truthful." The facts as found by the judge belie this claim. . . .

The wife acknowledged when she executed the marital agreement that she had "been provided with all information requested," that she was "afforded sufficient opportunity to inquire and investigate further financial circumstances" of her husband, and that she waived her "rights to further inquiry." There is nothing in the record to suggest that those representations were inaccurate.

By the terms of their agreement, the husband and wife agreed that they intended the marital agreement to limit their rights in the event of divorce, and that the agreement should govern "in lieu of and in full discharge and satisfaction of the rights which otherwise arise by reason of their marriage." As we explained in the context of premarital agreements, waiver is important because it underscores that each party is exercising a meaningful choice when he or she agrees to give up certain rights. In determining whether there was a meaningful waiver of rights, a judge should consider whether each party was represented by independent counsel, the adequacy of the time to review the agreement, the parties' understanding of the terms of the agreement and their effect, and a party's understanding of his or her rights in the absence of an agreement. Here, the wife was represented by independent counsel, who represented her over the course of several weeks as the terms of the agreement were negotiated. The wife affirmed in writing that she understood the rights she was waiving, and she does not claim that she did not understand any terms of the agreement. The evidence supports the conclusion that the wife's waiver was meaningful. . . .

In evaluating whether a marital agreement is fair and reasonable at the time of execution, a judge should . . . consider the entire context in which the agreement was reached, allowing greater latitude for agreements reached where each party is represented by separate counsel of their own choosing. A judge may consider the magnitude of the disparity between the outcome under the agreement and the outcome under otherwise prevailing legal principles, whether the purpose of the agreement was to benefit or protect the interests of third parties (such as the children from a prior relationship), and the impact of the agreement's enforcement upon the children of the parties. Other factors may include the length of the marriage, the motives of the contracting spouses, their respective bargaining positions, the circumstances giving rise to the marital agreement, the degree of the pressure, if any, experienced by the contesting spouse, and other circumstances the judge finds relevant.

Viewed at the time of execution, we agree with the judge that the marital agreement at issue here was fair and reasonable. As noted earlier, the wife was represented by experienced, independent counsel throughout the negotiations. In the event of a divorce, the wife was to receive a substantial fixed sum payment from her husband. If the marital estate appreciated in value after execution of the agreement, she would receive, in addition, a percentage of the increase in value; she did not forgo the fixed payment if the marital assets, including the husband's interest in the Florida real estate, declined substantially. There is no basis to the wife's claim that the judge "ignored" the husband's legal obligation of disclosure of value of the Florida real estate. As we discussed in detail earlier, the basis of the valuation was known to and accepted by the wife and her lawyer. We see no reason to disturb the judge's ruling on this point. . . .

The gravamen of the wife's complaint is that she will be left with a disproportionately small percentage of the couple's marital assets. A marital agreement need not provide for an equal distribution of assets, as long as a judge has concluded that the agreement is fair and reasonable. . . . We again see no reason to conclude that the judge was erroneous in her conclusion.

Judgment affirmed.

Questions Based on *Ansin v. Ansin*

1. Did Wife *really* sign voluntarily? The court makes much of the fact that Wife was represented by counsel. But what of the fact that Husband said he "needed" Wife to sign an agreement "if their marriage was to continue"? As well, Husband said he would recommit to the marriage "*if*" Wife "would sign a marital agreement"? Does this sound like coercion to you? On the other hand, Husband *is* entitled to his reasons for wanting an agreement, isn't he?

2. The court cites Ohio law that provides: "A husband and wife cannot, by any contract with each other, alter their legal relations, except that they may agree to an immediate separation and make provisions for the support of either of them and their children during the separation." Do you prefer the Ohio approach, which would forbid a postnuptial agreement, or the approach taken by the Massachusetts Supreme Judicial Court? The Ohio approach is highly paternalistic, isn't it?

EXPERIENTIAL ASSIGNMENT

Practice Exercise: Is the Postnuptual Agreement Adequate?

Maria and Hugo Jones have been married nine years. They have four young children. Throughout the marriage, Hugo physically abused Maria. Maria estimates Hugo hit her more than 35 times over the years. The children are often aware of the violence. Six years ago, Hugo pleaded guilty to misdemeanor domestic battery against Maria and was placed on probation. Two months ago, Hugo threw Maria to the ground and kicked her. Hugo was arrested, but the prosecutor decided against prosecution. Following the violence two months ago, Hugo moved out of the family home. He stopped paying the mortgage and the utility bills. A week after he moved out, Hugo texted Maria, "Give our marriage another try. I love you. Do this for the kids." This is the cycle of their marriage. Hugo would get mad, usually after getting drunk, beat Maria, then say he was sorry, ask forgiveness, and promise, "It won't happen again." Over and over, Maria took Hugo back, believing his promises to "get help for his drinking and violence." Over and over, the violence returned. Maria responded to Hugo's text, "No. I'm not doing this no more. I'm getting a divorce." Hugo replied, "I will take the kids away from you. You have no job. You have no money. I have all the money, and money buys justice." Hugo hired a lawyer. Hugo told the lawyer that Maria had physically abused their oldest child. On the basis of this accusation, which Maria says is a lie, the attorney obtained an ex parte order of temporary custody. The sheriff went to the home and removed the children from Maria's custody, giving the children to Hugo. After the children were given to Hugo, Maria contacted you and you agreed to help Maria even though she has no money to pay you. You file for divorce, and you file a motion to get custody of the children returned to Maria. The judge grants your motion and orders the children returned to Maria pending a trial on custody. A few days ago, Maria called you and said, "I have decided to give the marriage one more try. Hugo has promised to get therapy for his violence and his alcohol problem. He called me crying and begged me not to divorce him. He says he knows he has a problem, and he wants to get help. The kids are asking me to stay married to their dad." You counsel Maria about the cycle of violence in abusive relationships. She says, "I know, I understand, but I need to do this." You offer to draft a postnuptual agreement for Maria and Hugo's signatures. By the agreement you hope to offer Maria some protection. Your first draft of the agreement follows:

BINDING LEGAL AGREEMENT/CONTRACT BETWEEN MARIA JONES AND HUGO JONES, A MARRIED COUPLE

1. This agreement is made between Maria Jones, hereafter referred to as Maria, and Hugo Jones, hereafter referred to as Hugo.

2. Maria and Hugo are married and are the proud parents of four wonderful children. It is primarily because of their love for their children that Maria and Hugo enter into this agreement. This agreement is enforceable without consideration.

3. This agreement is binding by and between Maria and Hugo. Maria and Hugo understand and agree that any violation of the terms of this agreement may result in liability for breach of contract.

4. Maria and Hugo hope to avoid dissolution of their marriage. The goal of this agreement is to try to save their marriage for the benefit of themselves and their children.

5. Maria and Hugo agree that it is never justifiable for a married person to inflict domestic violence on their spouse. Maria and Hugo agree the domestic violence includes any use of physical force, including hitting, slapping, grabbing, kicking, pushing, and any use of a weapon. Maria and Hugo agree that domestic violence also includes threats to use violence. Maria and Hugo agree that domestic violence includes preventing a spouse from calling 911 for help, threatening a spouse to prevent the spouse from calling 911 for help, or in any other way using force or fear to prevent a spouse from obtaining help from any source.

6. Maria and Hugo understand that married couples sometimes disagree and argue. Disagreements and arguments are normal. Maria and Hugo agree that a disagreement or argument is never a justification for the use of domestic violence. Maria and Hugo also agree that a disagreement or argument is never a justification to threaten a spouse with domestic violence.

7. Maria and Hugo agree that neither of them will use any type of domestic violence against the other.

8. Maria and Hugo agree that any use or threat of domestic violence by either of them is a violation of this agreement.

9. Hugo acknowledges that in the past he has committed domestic violence against Maria. Hugo agrees that he will get professional counseling to help him learn not to use or threaten domestic violence in the future. Hugo agrees that he will begin domestic violence counseling on or before _____. Hugo realizes that a promise to get help is not good enough. Therefore, Hugo agrees to provide written proof that he is enrolled in and participating in domestic violence treatment. Hugo will provide this written proof to Maria and to Maria's attorney, _____. Hugo agrees to remain in domestic violence counseling until his counselor certifies in writing that Hugo has satisfactorily completed counseling. Hugo agrees that if he drops out of counseling or fails to regularly attend counseling, then he has violated this agreement.

10. Maria and Hugo agree that domestic violence is harmful to children. This is true whether or not the children see the violence with their own eyes.

11. Maria and Hugo agree that any use of domestic violence is evidence that the person using domestic violence is not a fit person to have custody of children. Maria and Hugo agree that if one of them inflicts domestic violence on the other, evidence of that domestic violence can be used in any family law case regarding custody.

12. Maria and Hugo agree that either of them may video or audio record any communication between them that either of them views as inappropriate.

13. Maria and Hugo agree that neither of them will disparage the other in the presence of any of their children. Maria and Hugo agree that they will not do anything to alienate the children from the other parent. Maria and Hugo agree that the children need and want both parents. Maria and Hugo agree that any behavior that amounts to alienation or disparagement amounts to evidence that the adult engaged in such inappropriate behavior is not acting as a competent parent.

14. Maria and Hugo own a home at _____ . The parties agree that for the time being, and until they agree otherwise in writing, Maria will have sole occupancy of the home. If Hugo wants to enter the home, he agrees to knock and ask Maria's permission to enter. Hugo agrees to immediately resume making the mortgage payment on the home, and to pay the mortgage payment every month, without fail. The mortgage is currently in arrears. Hugo agrees to immediately pay the arrears on the mortgage. Hugo agrees to provide written proof to Maria and her attorney that he has paid the arrears, and he will provide this written proof by _____. Hugo also agrees to pay all utility bills on the home.

15. Regarding custody of the children, Maria and Hugo agree to abide by the terms and conditions of the custody order that is now in force in family court. A true and correct copy of the custody order is attached to this agreement.

16. Maria is not working at this time, but she agrees to look for work. Because Maria is not presently working, Hugo agrees to pay monthly child support of $1,000 to Maria on the first of every month, beginning _____, and continuing thereafter. Maria and Hugo agree

that when Maria finds work, they will recalculate child support according to the uniform child support guidelines.

17. Hugo has several cars, and Hugo agrees to provide a car for Maria's use. Hugo agrees to maintain insurance on the car. Hugo agrees to provide the car to Maria on or before_____.

18. Maria and Hugo understand that as a married couple, the law requires that they be completely honest with each other about their finances. Hugo owns his own business, and Hugo agrees that he will inform Maria in writing of his exact income from his business. Hugo agrees that by signing this agreement, he consents to allowing Maria or her attorney to learn about any and all accounts or moneys in which Hugo has any interest in any institution of any kind in any location.

19. Maria and Hugo agree that they have not separated as that term is defined in the Family Code. Because they have not separated, any and all income from Hugo's business is marital property, and has been marital property since their marriage.

20. Under this agreement, Hugo undertakes to refrain from any use of domestic violence. Hugo also undertakes substantial financial obligations. Hugo agrees that if he violates any of the terms of this agreement, that in addition to fulfilling the obligations, he will be liable for attorneys fees required to enforce this agreement. Hugo also agrees to liquidated damages in the amount of $100.00 per day for every day he is in violation of any of the term of this agreement.

21. Maria and Hugo agree that they are aware of and understand the contents of this agreement, and they have entered into this agreement voluntarily, without duress, undue influence, fraud, or coercion of any kind.

22. This agreement contains the entire agreement of the parties on these matters, superseding any previous agreement between them.

23. This agreement may be amended or revoked only by written agreement signed by the parties. Any amended agreement will be enforceable without consideration.

24. This agreement will be governed by, and interpreted in accordance with, the law of this state.

25. If any provision of this agreement is held in whole or in part to be unenforceable for any reason, the remainder of that provision and of the entire agreement will be severable and remain in effect.

26. The effective date of this agreement will be the date of its execution by the second of the parties to do so.

27. Each party has been represented in the negotiations and in preparation of this agreement by an independent attorney of his or own choosing. The foregoing is agreed to by:

Date: _____

Maria Jones

Date: _____

Hugo Jones

Approved as conforming to the agreement of the parties:

Date: _____

Attorney for Hugo Jones

Date: _____

Attorney for Maria Jones

Assignment: Lawyers are communicators, orally and in writing. One of the most valuable skills you can develop is to become a good critic of your own writing. After you complete a draft, put it aside for an hour or a day and come back to it with a fresh eye. Critique your writing for substance, style, punctuation, persuasion, thoroughness, and polish. Be a ruthless self-editor. As well, ask a trusted colleague, secretary, or paralegal to read your "stuff." It is amazing the errors someone else sees that you don't.

With these admonitions in mind, critique the agreement you drafted for Maria. What is good about it? What did you leave out that you should include? What could you say differently or better? If the parties sign it, do you think the agreement will help stop the violence?

_____

Duty of Honesty and Fair Dealing Between Spouses

In many states, spouses are considered fiduciaries to one another.[92] In California, for example, the Family Code provides, "Each spouse shall act with respect to the other spouse in the management and control of the community assets and liabilities in accordance with the general rules governing fiduciary relationships . . . ."[93] In some states, although spouses are not fiduciaries, they are in a "confidential relationship." When a person in a "confidential relationship" engages in a financial transaction that benefits the actor and disadvantages the other party, the actor has the burden of proving the transaction was fair.[94]

In a few states, spouses are not fiduciaries, nor are they automatically in a confidential relationship. In *Lasater v. Guttmann*,[95] the Maryland Court of Special Appeals stated that Maryland spouses are not fiduciaries, and are not always in a confidential relationship.[96] In Maryland, the existence of a confidential relationship between spouses is decided on a case-by-case basis.

Conclusion

Marriage and domestic partnership is one of the most deeply meaningful and gratifying relationships in life. Lawyers play a limited role in intact marriages and domestic partnerships; a fact that is *just fine* with couples. In the next chapter we turn from the happy subject of marriage and domestic partnership to the challenging and often sad topic of divorce. It is at that juncture—when relationships fall apart—that our profession makes its appearance.

---

92 Fiduciary relationships include attorney-client, trustee-beneficiary, and agent-principal. *See* Lasater v. Guttmann, 194 Md. App. 431, 456, 5 A.3d 79 note 16 (2010)(the court states that the in following states, spouses are fiduciaries toward each other: Arizona, California, Idaho, Louisiana, Nevada, New Mexico, Oregon, and Washington).

93 California Family Code §§ 721(b), 1100(e). California law establishes financial sanctions—penalties—when one spouse breaches the duty of honesty and fair dealing with the other. California Family Code § 1101.

94 *See* Lasater v. Guttmann, 194 Md. App. 431, 457, 5 A.3d 79 note 18 (2010)(the court states, "the spousal relationship is presumed to be a confidential one . . . " in Florida, North Carolina, South Dakota, and Virginia).

95 194 Md. App. 431, 457, 5 A.3d 79 note 18 (2010).

96 Interestingly, the Lasater court wrote, "Maryland law does not presume that spouses are in a confidential relationship. That is not the case with people who are engaged to marry, however. Maryland presumes that an engaged couple occupies a confidential relationship. Therefore, in the case of a prenuptial agreement, the party who is the proponent of the agreement bears the burden to show that there was not 'overreaching.'" Note 19).

CHAPTER 4

Divorce

MOST DAY-TO-DAY WORK of family law attorneys concerns divorce. The details of the job are endless, and include meeting with clients and prospective clients; helping clients understand the divorce process; counseling clients about whether they want to divorce or whether the marriage can be saved; gathering detailed financial information; drafting and filing pleadings; conducting discovery; filing motions; conducting research; negotiating settlements; consulting experts (*e.g.*, forensic accountants, psychologists); and preparing for and appearing in court.

Divorce rates fluctuate over time. Andrew Cherlin writes, "The aggregate risk of a marriage ending in divorce appears to have declined from the peak that occurred around 1980. Perhaps half of marriages that were begun around that time will end in divorce, but the lifetime level of divorce may not be as high for marriages begun recently. . . . Divorce rates are diverging by education. During the 1960s and 1970s, the probability that a marriage would end in divorce rose sharply for all groups. Since then, however, the probability of divorce has declined among married couples in which the spouses have college degrees, whereas divorce probabilities have stayed roughly the same or even increased for the less educated."[1]

When you enter practice, you will learn to deal with opposing counsel. Most of the attorneys you deal with will be honest and well intentioned. It is critical that the attorneys you oppose view *you* as honest and reliable. While you don't want to give the impression you are a push over, you will accomplish more for your clients if you are perceived as reasonable and willing to compromise.

---

1 Andrew J. Cherlin, Demographic Trends in the United States: A Review of Research in the 2000s, 72 *Journal of Marriage and Family* 403-419, 405 (2010).

Of course, there will be times when you have to be hard-nosed. Most of the time, however, mutual good will between counsel leads to proper results.

Your most important asset in practice is your integrity. If the lawyers and judges you interact with view you as a person of integrity, you will prosper. If lawyers and judges view you as dishonest, incompetent, or lazy, you will have great difficulty. It takes time and effort to build a reputation for integrity. It takes only one foolish act to lose your good reputation.

In addition to purely legal work, family law attorneys need to decide how much "hand holding" to do. Many clients are in crisis, especially early on. They are going through the worst experience of their life. Many clients are angry, scared, depressed, anxious, and uncertain about the future. When children are involved, emotions run even higher. Attorneys have an important counseling role, but lawyers are not mental health professionals. Sometimes it is appropriate to refer a client to a mental health professional who can help the client with the emotional side of divorce.

There is no escaping the emotional aspects of family law. If you are uncomfortable dealing with strong emotions, and with people who are hurting or angry, family law may not be for you. You can do a great deal of good as a family law attorney, but it is not for everyone.

Brief History of Divorce

Divorce existed in antiquity. In ancient Greece, an Athenian could petition a magistrate for divorce. Divorce was available in Rome. As the Catholic Church gained power, the law of domestic relations fell under ecclesiastical control. The church considered marriage a sacrament instituted by God. By the tenth century, the church put a stop to divorce.

Although complete divorce—divorce *a vinculo matrimonii*—was not available under church law, the church allowed "legal separation"—divorce *a mensa et thoro,* or divorce from bed and board. Divorce *a mensa et thoro* authorized a married couple to live apart. Importantly, however, the couple remained married. Today, legal separation is available, although it is seldom used because absolute divorce is readily available, and most couples who break up choose divorce.

Why would a couple today prefer legal separation to divorce? One reason is to maintain employment-related medical insurance. Suppose Husband has a serious medical condition that requires expensive treatment. Husband is covered by Wife's employment-related medical insurance. If Husband and Wife divorce, Husband's coverage under the insurance will eventually end. The couple decides that in order to maintain husband's eligibility for insurance, they will obtain a legal separation rather than a divorce. With a legal separation, they are still married, and husband remains eligible for wife's employment-related insurance. Not all insurance plans go along with this approach.

A second reason some couples choose legal separation is because they don't want to take that final step to end the marriage. They don't want to live together, but they share the hope that someday down the road they might reconcile.

Returning to our historical sojourn, in addition to permitting divorce *a mensa et thoro*, the church authorized annulment of marriage. Annulment is discussed in Chapter 10.

Divorce as we know it today—*a vinculo matrimonii*—did not become widely available in England until 1857. Prior to that time, a few wealthy individuals obtained divorces by act of Parliament—that is, a legislative divorce.[2] When the United States became a nation, legislative divorce was available and was used occasionally.[3] Legislative divorce died out during the nineteenth century as state legislatures authorized courts to grant divorce.

Fault-Based Divorce

When divorce became more readily available in the nineteenth century, it was based on marital fault.[4] Only a spouse who was innocent of fault could obtain a divorce. A spouse seeking a divorce commenced a divorce action and had to prove that their spouse was at fault. Grounds for fault-based divorce varied slightly from state to state. States generally included as grounds adultery,[5] physical or mental cruelty, desertion, fraud, impotence, conviction of felony, habitual drunkenness, failure to support, and incurable insanity.

---

2 *See* Lawrence Stone, *The Family, Sex and Marriage in England 1500-1800* (1977)("Between 1670 and 1799, there were only one hundred and thirty-one" divorces granted by Parliament.).

3 Maynard v. Hill, 125 U.S. 190, 205-206, 8 S. Ct. 723 (1888)("When the object of the relation has been thus defeated, and no jurisdiction is vested in the judicial tribunals to grant a divorce, it is not perceived that any principle should prevent the legislature itself from interfering, and putting an end to the relation in the interest of the parties as well as of society.").

4 Divorce was disfavored, and would only be tolerated if there was serious marital fault. In 1891 Joel Bishop wrote of divorce, "Evils numberless, extending to the demoralization of society itself, would follow the abandonment of marriage as a permanent status, and permitting it to be the subject of experimental and temporary arrangements and fleeting partnerships. Wisely, therefore, the law holds it to be a union for life." Joel P. Bishop, *New Commentaries on Marriage, Divorce, and Separation* vol. 1, § 40, p. 16 (1891).

5 Another name for adultery was "criminal conversation." See Joel P. Bishop, *New Commentaries on Marriage, Divorce, and Separation* vol. 1, § 1365, p. 570 (1891)("'Criminal conversation' . . . is adultery committed by a third person with the wife . . . .").

Defenses to Divorce During the Era of Fault

During the era of fault, which lasted into the 1980s, a spouse who was sued for divorce could raise one of three defenses: recrimination, connivance, or condonation. If a defense was established, the divorce case was dismissed and the parties remained married.

With recrimination, the spouse charged with marital fault—the defendant— filed a counter suit charging the plaintiff with fault.[6] For example, a defendant who was sued for divorce based on mental cruelty might counter sue based for mental cruelty. Or a spouse charged with adultery might counter sue for cruelty. If both spouses were "guilty" of marital fault, *neither could obtain a divorce!* In the 1894 case *Brenot v. Brenot,*[7] husband sued wife for divorce, accusing her of adultery. Wife counter sued claiming extreme cruelty. The trial court found the allegations of both parties true, denied all relief, and dismissed the case. The California Supreme Court approved, writing, "There is also no question but that a court of equity is authorized to enter a judgment dismissing an action of divorce, where both parties are seeking a decree, and the evidence discloses them to be equally guilty of the misconduct alleged." So, if you're both bad, you're stuck with each other!

To ameliorate the harsh result sometimes brought about by strict application of recrimination, some states adopted the doctrine of comparative rectitude. Under comparative rectitude, if both spouses were at fault, the spouse whose fault was less serious could get a divorce.

The defense of connivance applied when the spouse seeking divorce connived for the other spouse to commit fault.[8] In *Sargent v. Sargent,*[9] husband sued

---

6 *See* Joel P. Bishop, *New Commentaries on Marriage, Divorce, and Separation* vol. 2, (1891)(Section 340, p. 165: "Recrimination in divorce law is the defense that the applicant has himself done what is ground for divorce either from bed and board or from the bond of matrimony. It bars the suit founded on whatever cause, whether the defendant is guilty or not.").

7 102 Cal. 294, 296 (1894).

8 *See* Joel P. Bishop, *New Commentaries on Marriage, Divorce, and Separation* vol. 2, § 203, p. 110 (1891) ("Connivance in divorce law is a married party's corrupt consenting to evil conduct in the other whereof afterward he complains." Section 204 states: "It excludes the right of divorce on the double ground, that in a court of justice one will not be heard to complain of an act tainted by his own wrong; and that, in the words of Lord Stowell, by reason of the consent 'no injury has been done and therefore there is nothing to redress.'" pp. 110-111. Bishop wrote at Section 249, p. 128: "Collusion in divorce law is a corrupt combining of married parties to procure a sentence or judicial order by some false practice; as, for one of them to appear to or in fact do what otherwise would be ground for divorce, or in any way to deceive the court in a cause, thus seeking its interposition as for a real injury." At Section 250, p. 128, Bishop wrote, "it is perceived, therefore, that collusion is closely allied to the connivance treated of in the last chapter. Commonly but not necessarily, connivance comes from collusion, while ordinarily collusion is a species of connivance." At Section 251, p. 128, he wrote, "To the extent to which collusion is connivance, it bars divorce on the principles explained in the last chapter.").

9 114 A. 428 (N.J. Chancery 1920).

for divorce based on wife's adultery with the family chauffeur. Husband suspected the chauffeur's motives, but did not fire the chauffeur. Rather, husband kept the chauffeur in his employ, realizing his wife would often be alone with the chauffeur. Husband hired detectives to spy on them. When adultery occurred, husband sued for divorce. Wife raised the defense of connivance, and the court denied husband's suit for divorce.

Condonation as a defense applied when one spouse committed marital fault, and the innocent spouse forgave the trespass.[10] So long as the forgiveness—condonation—was voluntary, it foreclosed a later suit for divorce. In *Murphy v. Murphy*,[11] husband committed burglary and armed robbery. Shortly following the crimes, wife allowed husband to hide in their home. She also spent some of the ill-gotten gain. Husband was sent to prison. Wife filed for divorce, but the court denied divorce because wife condoned her husband's crimes. She was not an "innocent and injured spouse."

Circumventing Limits on Divorce

During the era of fault, many couples who wanted to end their marriage contrived grounds for divorce. (*See Pratt v. Pratt and Mug*, below). Another tactic when both spouses wanted to end the marriage was for one spouse to file a complaint for divorce, and for the other spouse to default. A third tactic was for one spouse to leave the state and move temporarily to a state that had liberal grounds for divorce. Such states—notably Nevada—became known as "divorce mills."

This postcard from Reno, Nevada—Washoe County—shows a happy divorcee. Note the well-paid lawyer and the judge.

---

10 *See* Matter of Dube, 163 N.H. 575, 44 A.3d 556 (2012)("The affirmative defense of condonation is the forgiveness of an antecedent marital offense on condition that it shall not be repeated. Under the doctrine, if either party to a marriage thinks proper to forgive the infidelity of the other, it cannot afterwards be set up as a ground of divorce without evidence of a further injury."); Joel P. Bishop, *New Commentaries on Marriage, Divorce, and Separation* vol. 2, (1891)(Section 269, pp. 134-135 "Condonation is the remission, by one of the married parties, of an offence which he knows the other has committed against the marriage, on the condition of being continually afterward treated by the other with conjugal kindness,—resulting in the rule that while the condition remains unbroken there can be no divorce, but a breach of it revives the original remedy.").

11 205 A.2d 647 (Pa. Super. Ct. 1964).

During the early twentieth century, thousands of married Americans got divorced in Nevada. Indeed, the practice was so common that "Going to Reno" was understood to mean going there for a divorce.

Young women kick up their heels outside a Reno, Nevada boarding house catering to married women seeking to divorce.

One of the women shows off a new dress.

The following case, *Pratt v. Pratt and Mug*, is not real. It springs from the fertile imagination of Sir Alan Patrick Herbert (1890-1971) and was published in his 1936 book *Uncommon Law*. A.P. Herbert studied jurisprudence at Oxford and was admitted to bar in 1919. He never practiced law, but was an influential advocate for law reform. He served as a Member of Parliament for Oxford University. Among other causes, Herbert advocated reform of English divorce law. In *Pratt v. Pratt and Mug*, Herbert pokes fun at the practice then common in England by which married couples wanting to divorce fabricated evidence of non-existent adultery.

Pratt v. Pratt and Mug

A Swan Song

(Before Mr. Justice Foot)

MUCH COMMENT WAS CAUSED in legal circles today by an unconventional speech of Sir Oliver Slick, K.C., M.P.,[12] opening a case in the Probate and Divorce Division. Sir Oliver is retiring from practice in a few days' time, and it is thought that he may be suffering from overstrain.

---

12 K.C. stands for Kings Counsel; M.P. stands for Member of Parliament.

Sir Oliver: May it please your Lordship, my dear old fellow, in this case I appear for the petitioner, Mrs. Gladys Eleanor Pratt, who is praying for a dissolution of marriage on account of—well, I mean, she wants to get rid of the man and that's all about it, milord. Milord, this is probably the last case in which I shall ever appear, so, to tell you the truth, I take a pretty detached view of the whole proceedings. Well, I mean, look at old Twopenny here *(Mr. Albert Twopenny, of the firm of Twopenny and Truelove, solicitors for the petitioner) – he'll* never give me a brief[13] again after this, *but I don't care!* And that's what makes the whole thing so terribly *funny*!

(Sir Oliver here laughed heartily.)

The Judge: Sir Oliver, if this is your swan song, I am sure that you would wish it to be in tune with the traditions of the Bar and with your own fine record.

Sir Oliver: Certainly, milord; you're a good sort, milord, and I don't want to offend you, though you've given me a packet of trouble from time to time. Well, milord, the facts are these. The parties were married only a year ago at Westminster, and lived happily together for about three weeks, milord. Temperamentally, perhaps, they were unsuited; the husband was fond of golf and the woman of lawn tennis. However, the wife remained and is to this day devoted to her husband; but last year, milord, on July 20th—no, 21st—Mrs. Pratt noticed that Mr. Pratt's affections were cooling, and on the 24th, milord, she found him telephoning to a strange woman, a Miss Elizabeth Mugg, milord, who has been cited in this case as a—what-d'you-call-it ?—

The Judge: Sir Oliver, I'm not sure that I follow you.

Sir Oliver: 'Woman Named', milord, that's the expression I wanted. *(Sir Oliver then lowered his voice and continued in tones suggestive of profound moral indignation.)* Milord, there seems to be no doubt that this woman, by a protracted course of duplicity and cunning, has deliberately stolen away this husband from his wife. It is difficult, milord, to frame language strong enough to describe a woman who, without any provocation, it appears, from her unfortunate partner in guilt, has wormed her way into the affections of an English husband, and invaded, corrupted, and finally broken up an English home. Picture, milord, the state of mind of my unfortunate client as, day by day and bit by bit, she sees that devotion which is her right transferred to the supplanter. On the 26th, milord, this poor woman had a nervous breakdown; on the 29th she had fits. Milord, do you think I've done enough of this?

The Judge: I beg your pardon, Sir Oliver?

---

13 For an English barrister, a "brief" is a case.

Sir Oliver: I mean, need I give the Court any more of this gup? Because, of course, you know the whole case is a put-up job –

The Judge: Sir Oliver, I think you are not very well. Perhaps it would be fairer to your client to adjourn.

Sir Oliver: Never was better, old boy. Fit as yourself, and fitter. Well, I wasn't playing bridge half the night, milord, as I happen to know you were!

(Sir Oliver here laughed again in a genial manner.)

The Judge: If you are in good health, Sir Oliver, we will continue the hearing, but you will please confine yourself to the facts of the case.

Sir Oliver: Well, milord, the facts are very simple. This is just one of the ordinary trumped-up upper-class divorce cases, you know, which nowadays, as a rule, we don't bother to open at all. The lady's just bored with him, that's all. Well, I mean, in these days, living with the same husband, week after week, for a whole year—Society girls can't stand it. There's nothing unpleasant in the case, nobody's done anything wrong, but my client wants to marry a chap in the Guards—Jack Filter—you know, milord, fellow with the eyeglass you met at the club the other day, so we've pitched this yarn about Pratt and Elizabeth Mugg— Don't interrupt, Twopenny!

(Mr. Twopenny spoke earnestly to Sir Oliver at this point, and subsequently on several occasions, but Sir Oliver did not appear to hear what was said.)

Sir Oliver (continuing): I'm sorry for Pratt in a way—that's the respondent, milord—he's a very good fellow and adores Mrs. Pratt. But it's his own fault, really. The trouble was, you see, milord, that he married the girl for her money and then fell in love with her. I can tell you, between ourselves, my dear Old Lordship, we had a job to get him to agree to this divorce at all. Didn't like it, not a bit. But in the end we got him over the money. You see, he's terribly in debt, milord, and she's going to pay him a decent maintenance. Of course, technically, I know, milord, we shall ask the man to pay Mrs. Pratt maintenance, and a fat maintenance, too; but that's all eyewash. Besides, we made things easy for him over Elizabeth Mugg, and that helped to turn the scale, because he thought he had to go to Brighton with her, and he hates Brighton. But when he found he needn't even see Elizabeth Mugg he didn't mind being divorced because of her so much. In point of fact he never has seen Elizabeth Mugg. I mention that because I don't want anyone here to take too seriously what I said about Elizabeth Mugg just now, because Elizabeth Mugg is really a very nice woman and knows her job thoroughly. Elizabeth has been in eighty-nine divorce cases, she tells me, under various names, and has never met one of the parties yet. In this case, of course, she went down to Brighton and stayed a night at the 'Cosmopole'. Pratt's valet stayed there the same night, and put a pair of Pratt's boots outside Elizabeth's room. During the night her boots met Pratt's, and the next day the valet met one of the chambermaids and identified the boots, and there you are. You'll have all the evidence, of course, Pratt's bill, and the cloak-room ticket and the menu and everything, but that's all there is to the case.

The Judge: Sir Oliver, I never like to interrupt counsel when opening a case, but are you materially assisting your client?

Sir Oliver: I should be sorry if you thought I wasn't, milord, because Mrs. Pratt is really quite a decent little woman. In fact, everybody in the case is thoroughly decent, including your Lordship, if I may say so, and it seems to me a great pity that all these decent people should be put to all this trouble and expense and publicity when the whole thing might easily be done in two minutes at a registry office or through one of the big stores. On the other hand, of course, I have to live, and you have to live, milord, and Elizabeth Mugg has to live, so we mustn't complain. Speaking for myself, I'm doing very well out of this case, because my client is not only decent but rich, and old Twopenny here knows how to make 'em cough up—well, I mean he's marked me a pretty fat fee on the brief—well, I mean for a potty little bogus divorce. I mention these points, milord, because it is so nice to get a touch of reality in a case like this. How you can sit up there, milord, day after day, swallowing all the stuff served up to you by members of the Bar like me, who ought to know better—

The Judge: Sir Oliver, this is an occasion without precedent in all my long experience, and I find a difficulty in dealing with it. But if you are unable to conduct yourself in accordance with the traditions of your profession and the interests of your client I shall be compelled to ask you to withdraw from this Court.

Sir Oliver (bowing): Milord, I bow to your ruling. Milord, I have little to add at this stage of the case. My client will now go into that box and tell the tragic story of her married life. She will tell you of affection blighted, of a homemade desolate, and a heart destroyed. She will tell you that even at this late hour she is ready to hold out the hand of forgiveness and clasp to her bosom the rightful partner of her life, if he will but tear himself from the embraces of the supplanter, Mugg, a woman, milord, who, as you will shortly hear, has from first to last— from first to last, milord—played a part in the lives of these two people which is without precedent, milord, in my experience for treachery, deceit, ingratitude, and cunning. Call Gladys Pratt.

The Judge: At two o'clock?

The Court adjourned.

Note on *Uncommon Law*

Late one night when I was in law school a hundred years ago, I stumbled upon Herbert's *Uncommon Law* sitting on a dusty shelf in the library. I opened the book and started reading cases. Before long I was laughing out loud. I don't know about you, but I seldom laugh aloud when reading cases. When you are bored with law school (not that that ever happens, of course) see if your school has *Uncommon Law* or another of Herbert's compilations of imaginary cases. Reading a few of his cases is a wonderful tonic for the tedium of law study.

The following case from the Missouri Court of Appeal was decided in 1926, at the height of fault based divorce. The decision discusses traditional defenses to divorce, and is an interesting study of divorce law at an earlier time.

Ratcliff v. Ratcliff

Missouri Court of Appeals
288 S.W. 794 (1926)

Arnold, J.

This is an action for divorce . . . .[14] The facts developed are that the parties were married in Holt County on March 26, 1910. No children were born of the marriage. It appears that Wife is about 14 years the senior of Husband. Prior to the said marriage, Wife had lived on a farm in Holt County with her widowed mother. Husband, a single man, then about 19 years of age, came to said county from the state of Virginia and entered the employ of Wife's mother as a farm hand. Both Wife and Husband had lived with Wife's mother on the farm for a period of about 18 years, when Wife's mother died. After the death of Wife's mother, the two continued to live on the farm for a year or two previous to their marriage and for a time thereafter. The evidence shows that at the time of the said marriage Wife was the owner of two tracts of land, one consisting of 80 acres and the other of 105 acres, both of which were encumbered. At this time Husband possessed a little property, probably a team or two and a few farm implements, but no real estate. After their marriage, the parties prospered, and within a few years had accumulated considerable personal property, and had paid off the encumbrances on Wife's lands. . . .

---

14   Throughout the opinion, the Court of Appeals refers to Wife as Plaintiff and Husband as Defendant. For ease of reading, I've substituted "Wife" for "Plaintiff" and "Husband" for "Defendant."

Sometime in the fall of 1923, one Fred Wallace, who had been employed to gather corn, moved, with Jennie his wife, into a small house on the farm near the dwelling occupied by Wife and Husband. Wallace and his wife continued to live there until sometime in December, when Fred Wallace left, and Jennie moved into the house occupied by Wife and Husband. . . . Wife's testimony shows that adulterous relations between Jennie Wallace and Husband began in February, 1924, and continued daily until the latter part of June following. . . .

Wife testified that, when she would arise in the morning to build the fires and prepare breakfast, Husband would get out of his bed and go into the room occupied by Jennie and would get into bed with her; that she saw him do this from the latter part of February until the latter part of June, when Wife left home. It is in evidence that, when Husband went into the bedroom of Jennie Wallace, the door between the two rooms was always left open; that Wife would continue the preparation of breakfast, and when the meal was ready she would go into Jennie's bedroom and call her and Husband to breakfast. Wife testified she remonstrated with Husband on his relations with Jennie and also had some mutual friends speak to him about it; that Husband became offended thereat and said she would only "make things worse." Considerable trouble developed between the parties over the woman, which resulted in Wife leaving her home and going with some relatives who had come to visit them, thus leaving Husband and Jennie Wallace together in the home. However, Jennie remained only a day or so, when she left. It appears Wife remained away from her home until the latter part of August, 1924, when she returned and continued to live and cohabit with Husband as his wife until January 15, 1925, when she again left and thereafter instituted this suit.

The petition alleges adultery by Husband after his marriage with Wife, and that he has offered Wife such indignities as to render her condition intolerable . . . .

The answer admits the marriage, as alleged in the petition, that Wife and Husband had lived together as husband and wife until January 15, 1925, and generally denies all other allegations. Upon the issues thus made, the cause was submitted to the court, resulting in a judgment and decree in favor of Wife, granting her an absolute divorce,[15] restoration of her maiden name, and alimony in the lump sum of $4,000. . . . Husband has appealed. . . .

It is urged that Wife was not entitled to a divorce, because the only offense proved sufficient to entitle her to a divorce was that of adultery. It is urged that, under the evidence, if Husband committed adultery, he did so with the knowledge and consent of Wife, and she is therefore guilty of connivance which would

---

15 The court means a complete divorce—divorce *a vinculo matrimonii*—rather than a legal separation—a divorce from bed a board, or a divorce *a mensa et thoro*.

bar her right to divorce. It is also argued that the testimony shows that Wife resumed cohabitation with Husband after knowledge of the alleged adultery, and she thereby condoned the offense; that the subsequent misconduct, as shown in the evidence, was wholly insufficient to revive the alleged adultery as grounds for divorce.

Condonation is defined as the conditional forgiveness or remission, by a husband or wife, of a matrimonial offense which the other has committed. The word also has been defined as "a blotting out of an imputed offense" against the marital relation "so as to restore the offending party to the same position he or she had before the offense was committed." It is Husband's position that condonation herein was implied from the fact that Wife and Husband lived together as husband and wife after the alleged adulterous offense.

It has been held, under conditions where a husband's infidelity was condoned, such infidelity was revived by his subsequent cruelty to her, or by subsequent adultery, or by subsequent desertion. And so, in the case at bar, the testimony of Wife is that repeated acts of cruelty were indulged by Husband against Wife after she returned to live with him, such as neglect when she was ill, leaving her at home alone to care for and feed the stock and provide herself with wood, and even assaulting her at one time. No testimony was offered by Husband, and therefore the testimony of Wife in this behalf is undisputed. Under the above rulings, such conduct on the part of Husband rendered the condonement inoperative. Every condonation is upon the implied condition that the party forgiven will thereafter abstain from the commission of a like offense, and will treat the forgiving spouse in all respects with conjugal kindness. It is not necessary, therefore, that the subsequent injury be of the same kind, or proved with the same clearness, or sufficient of itself, when proved, to warrant a divorce or separation. Accordingly, a course of unkind and cruel treatment will revive condoned adultery . . . . It is clear the court did not err in granting a decree of divorce on the showing made.

It is Husband's contention that Wife connived at the adultery charged and therefore is barred from urging such act as ground for divorce. We think this position is untenable. The general rule in this respect is stated in 19 C. J. 90, § 12, as follows: "Mere passive permission of misconduct, however, does not make the party guilty of connivance, if he does nothing to encourage the other to commit the offense and does not directly or indirectly throw opportunities therefor in the way; and connivance cannot be implied from mere negligence, folly, dullness of apprehension, or indifference."

A corrupt intent in the mind of one party that the other shall commit the offense is an essential element of connivance. Wife's testimony, and that is all we have here, is to the effect that she made repeated attempts, pathetically inef-fectual, to induce her husband to refrain from his adulterous indulgences with Jennie Wallace. There is no showing, even inferentially, that the trial court erred in the respect charged. . . .

We find no reversible error of record, and the judgment and decree are affirmed.

Question based on *Ratcliff v. Ratcliff*

It is pretty clear Husband did not like Wife, let alone love her. Why do you suppose Husband put up such a fight to stay married? Here's a clue: The answer is a five letter word.

No Fault Divorce

The 1960s brought calls to do away with fault-based divorce.[16] As a step in that direction, a number of states passed laws allowing divorce when the parties lived apart for a number of years. In 1969, California became the first state to adopt no-fault divorce. Indeed, in California today, it is improper even to mention fault in a petition for divorce.[17] By 1985, all states had some form of no-fault divorce.

With no-fault divorce, a married person files a petition asserting the mar-riage is "irretrievably broken" or that "irreconcilable differences" have caused the irremediable breakdown of the marriage.[18] Basically, "irreconcilable dif-ferences" is whatever one spouse thinks is a good reason to end the marriage. Judges seldom second guess claims of irreconcilable differences.

Although all states have some form of no fault divorce, a number of states also retain traditional fault-based grounds for divorce.[19]

In the era of no fault, the defenses of condonation, connivance, and recrim-

---

16   As early as 1952, the California Supreme Court recognized the emerging movement away from fault. In De Burgh v. De Burgh, 39 Cal. 2d 858, 868 (1952), the court wrote, "Marriage failure, rather than the fault of the par-ties, is the basis upon which such divorces are granted."

17   Cal. Family Code § 2335 provides: "Except as otherwise provided by statute, in a pleading or proceeding for dissolution of marriage or legal separation of the parties, including depositions and discovery proceedings, evidence of specific acts of misconduct is improper and inadmissible."

18   Cal. Family Code § 2310(a).

19   *See, e.g.,* Matter of Dube, 163 N.H. 575, 44 A.3d 556 (2012).

ination are largely irrelevant. A few states retain watered down versions of the traditional defenses.[20]

Divorce can be unilateral. That is, one spouse can get a divorce even if the other spouse wants to stay married. Another way of saying this is that today there is no defense that can defeat an action for divorce.

Covenant Marriage—Reintroducing Fault?

Concerned about the high divorce rate, Arizona, Arkansas, and Louisiana created so-called covenant marriage. The Arizona version of covenant marriage provides:

> § 25-901(A). Persons who have the legal capacity to marry pursuant to this title may enter into a covenant marriage . . . . (B). A declaration of intent to enter into a covenant marriage shall contain all of the following: (1). The following written statement: We solemnly declare that marriage is a covenant between a man and a woman who agree to live together as husband and wife for as long as they both live. We have chosen each other carefully and have received premarriage counseling on the nature, purposes and responsibilities of marriage. We understand that a covenant marriage is for life. If we experience marital difficulties, we commit ourselves to take all reasonable efforts to preserve our marriage, including marital counseling.

> § 25-902. [This section allows Arizonans to convert existing marriages to covenant marriages.]

> § 25-903. . . If a husband and wife have entered into a covenant marriage . . . the court shall not enter a decree of dissolution of marriage . . . unless it finds any of the following: (1) The respondent spouse has committed adultery. (2) The respondent spouse has committed a felony and has been sentenced to death or imprisonment . . . . (3) The respondent spouse has abandoned the matrimonial domicile for at least one year before the petitioner filed for dissolution of marriage and refuses to return. . . . (4) The respondent spouse has physically or sexually abused the spouse seeking the dissolution of marriage, a child, a relative of either spouse permanently living in the matrimonial domicile or has committed domestic violence . . . . (5) The spouses have been living separate and apart continuously without reconcili-

---

20 *See, e.g.*, Ware v. Ware, 7 So.3d 271 (Miss. Ct. App. 2008); Matter of Dube, 163 N.H. 575, 44 A.3d 556 (2012); Chastain v. Chastain, 672 S.E.2d 108 (S.C. Ct. App. 2009).

ation for at least two years . . . . (7) The respondent spouse habitually abused drugs or alcohol. (8) The husband and wife both agree to a dissolution of marriage.

Louisiana's grounds for dissolution of covenant marriage are similar to Arizona's except Louisiana does not provide for dissolution when "the husband and wife both agree to a dissolution of marriage."

Will covenant marriage lower the divorce rate? Would you prefer a covenant marriage for yourself?

Authority of the State Regarding Marriage and Divorce

The state has a substantial interest in supporting marriage and regulating divorce. The California Supreme Court described the state interest in *De Burgh v. De Burgh:*[21]

> The family is the basic unit of our society, the center of the personal affections that ennoble and enrich human life. It channels biological drives that might otherwise become socially destructive; it ensures the care and education of children in a stable environment; it establishes continuity from one generation to another; it nurtures and develops the individual initiative that distinguishes a free people. Since the family is the core of our society, the law seeks to foster and preserve marriage. But when a marriage has failed and the family has ceased to be a unit, the purposes of family life are no longer served and divorce will be permitted. Public policy does not discourage divorce where relations between husband and wife are such that the legitimate objects of matrimony have been utterly destroyed.

Judicial Recognition of Out of State Marriage and Divorce

States recognize and enforce out of state marriages and divorces. What happens, however, with same sex marriage? For example, Sue and Ellen marry in State X, where marriage equality applies. Later, Sue and Ellen move to State Y. State Y does not permit same sex marriage. Sue files for divorce in State Y. Should the courts of State Y entertain the divorce action? Or, suppose Sue and Ellen divorced in State X, then Sue moves to State Y where she seeks to enforce a

---

21   39 Cal. 2d 858, 863-864 (1952).

term of the State X divorce. Must courts in State Y accord full faith and credit to the State X divorce?

In the 2009 decision in *Lewis v. New York State Department of Civil Service*,[22] the state Department of Civil Service had announced it would recognize the validity of the marriage of a same sex couple whose marriage was valid in the state where the marriage occurred. At that time, marriage equality had not reached New York. Opponents sued, seeking a declaration that the Department's recognition of same sex marriage was illegal. The Appellate Division of the Supreme Court ruled that New York law recognizing valid marriages from other states applied to same sex marriages that are valid in the jurisdiction where the marriage is solemnized.

Similar issues arise with domestic partnerships. New Jersey's domestic partnership law states, "A domestic partnership, civil union or reciprocal beneficiary relationship entered into outside of this State, which is valid under the law of the jurisdiction under which the partnership was created, shall be valid in this State."[23]

Jurisdiction in Divorce Litigation

A divorce action is a lawsuit, and like all lawsuits, the court must have jurisdiction. In analyzing jurisdiction, it is helpful to break divorce into three parts: (1) the divorce itself, (2) child custody, and (3) the financial aspects of divorce— child support, spousal support, property division, and attorney fees.

As you recall from civil procedure, in the normal civil case, the court must have subject matter jurisdiction *and* personal jurisdiction. In divorce litigation, subject matter jurisdiction is always necessary. Personal jurisdiction, by contrast, is not always required.

Jurisdiction to Grant Divorce

A court has subject matter jurisdiction to grant divorce if at least one spouse is domiciled in the state. All states have a residency requirement for divorce.[24] California, for example, provides, "A judgment of dissolution of marriage may

---

22 60 A.D.3d 216, 872 N.Y.S.2d 578 (2009).

23 N.J. Stat. Ann. § 26:8A-6(c).

24 *See, e.g.,* Del. Code Ann. Tit. 13 § 1504(a); Kan. Stat. Ann. §60-1603(a) (resident of the state for 60 days); Minn. Stat. Ann. § 518.07 (resident of the state "not less than 180 days immediately preceding the commencement of the proceeding"); Tex. Family Code Ann. § 6.301 (domiciled in Texas for 6 months and in the county 90 days).

not be entered unless one of the parties to the marriage has been a resident of this state for six months and of the county in which the proceeding is filed for three months next preceding the filing of the petition."[25] Mississippi law grants jurisdiction "where one of the parties has been an actual bona fide resident of this state for six months next preceding the commencement of the suit."[26]

If a couple born and raised in Texas gets married in Texas, and later divorces in Texas, no jurisdictional issues are likely to arise. The court clearly has subject matter jurisdiction *and* personal jurisdiction over the parties. Similarly, if a couple married in Iowa, but moved to Texas years ago, jurisdictional issues are unlikely to arise. But what of the following situation? A married couple lives in Virginia. One of them moves to Texas and meets the Texas residency requirement. The other spouse has never set foot in Texas. Can the spouse living in Texas get divorced in Texas? Texas has no personal jurisdiction over the spouse in Old Dominion. The U.S. Supreme Court's decision *Williams v. North Carolina* provides the answer.

Williams v. North Carolina

United States Supreme Court
317 U.S. 287, 63 S. Ct. 207 (1942)

Mr. Justice Douglas delivered the opinion of the Court.

Petitioners were tried and convicted of bigamous cohabitation under § 4342 of the North Carolina Code, and each was sentenced for a term of years to a state prison. The judgment of conviction was affirmed by the Supreme Court of North Carolina. The case is here on certiorari.

Petitioner Williams was married to Carrie Wyke in 1916 in North Carolina and lived with her there until May, 1940. Petitioner Hendrix was married to Thomas Hendrix in 1920 in North Carolina and lived with him there until May, 1940. At that time petitioners went to Las Vegas, Nevada and on June 26, 1940, each filed a divorce action in the Nevada court. The defendants in those divorce actions entered no appearance nor were they served with process in Nevada. In the case of defendant Thomas Hendrix service by publication was had by publication of the summons in a Las Vegas newspaper and by mailing a copy of the summons and complaint to his last post office address. In the case of defendant Carrie

---

25　Cal. Family Code § 2320.

26　Miss. Code Ann. § 93-5-5(a).

Williams a North Carolina sheriff delivered to her in North Carolina a copy of the summons and complaint. A decree of divorce was granted petitioner Williams by the Nevada court on August 26, 1940, on the grounds of extreme cruelty, the court finding that "the plaintiff has been and now is a bona fide and continuous resident of the County of Clark, State of Nevada, and had been such resident for more than six weeks immediately preceding the commencement of this action in the manner prescribed by law." The Nevada court granted petitioner Hendrix a divorce on October 4, 1940, on the grounds of willful neglect and extreme cruelty and made the same finding as to this petitioner's bona fide residence in Nevada as it made in the case of Williams. Petitioners were married to each other in Nevada on October 4, 1940. Thereafter they returned to North Carolina where they lived together until the indictment was returned. Petitioners pleaded not guilty and offered in evidence exemplified copies of the Nevada proceedings, contending that the divorce decrees and the Nevada marriage were valid in North Carolina as well as in Nevada. The State contended that since neither of the defendants in the Nevada actions was served in Nevada nor entered an appearance there, the Nevada decrees would not be recognized as valid in North Carolina. . . . The State further contended that petitioners went to Nevada not to establish a bona fide residence but solely for the purpose of taking advantage of the laws of that State to obtain a divorce through fraud upon that court. [Petitioners were convicted.] The Supreme Court of North Carolina in affirming the judgment held that North Carolina was not required to recognize the Nevada decrees under the full faith and credit clause of the Constitution (Art. IV, § 1).

Article IV, § 1 of the Constitution not only directs that "Full Faith and Credit shall be given in each State to the public Acts, Records, and Judicial Proceedings of every other State" but also provides that "Congress may by general Laws prescribe the Manner in which such Acts, Records and Proceedings shall be proved, and the Effect thereof." Congress has exercised that power. Congress has provided that judgments "shall have such faith and credit given to them in every court within the United States as they have by law or usage in the courts of the State from which they are taken." . . .

[The U.S. Supreme Court ruled that domicile is required to grant a divorce.] Domicile creates a relationship to the state which is adequate for numerous exercises of state power. Each state as a sovereign has a rightful and legitimate concern in the marital status of persons domiciled within its borders. The marriage relation creates problems of large social importance. Protection of offspring, property interests, and the enforcement of marital responsibilities are but a few of the commanding problems in the field of domestic relations with which the state must deal. Thus it is plain that each state by virtue of its command over its domiciliaries and its large interest in the institution of marriage can alter within its own borders the marriage status of the spouse domiciled there, even though the other spouse is absent. There is no constitutional barrier if the form and nature of the substituted service meet the requirements of due process.

[I]f one is lawfully divorced and remarried in Nevada and still married to the first spouse in North Carolina, . . . we would then have . . . a most perplexing and distressing complication in the domestic relations of many citizens in the different states. Under the circumstances of this case, a man would have two wives, a wife two husbands. The reality of a sentence to prison proves that that is no mere play on words. Each would be a bigamist for living in one state with the only one with whom the other state would permit him lawfully to live. Children of the second marriage would be bastards in one state but legitimate in the other. . . .

So when a court of one state acting in accord with the requirements of procedural due process alters the marital status of one domiciled in that state by granting him a divorce from his absent spouse, we cannot say its decree should be excepted from the full faith and credit clause merely because its enforcement or recognition in another state would conflict with the policy of the latter. . . .

. . . The judgment is reversed and the cause is remanded to the Supreme Court of North Carolina for proceedings not inconsistent with this opinion.

Williams teaches that subject matter jurisdiction to grant a divorce requires that at least one spouse be domiciled in the divorcing state. To grant a divorce that is binding on both parties and that is entitled to full faith and credit, the divorcing state does *not* have to have personal jurisdiction over the absent spouse, although due process does require notice to the absent spouse.

The prosecutor in *Williams* was not about to let his defeat in the U.S. Supreme Court frustrate his desire to throw the Williamses in the slammer. The prosecutor indicted them again; this time arguing that the Nevada divorces were a sham because the Williamses never intended to change their domicile from North Carolina to Nevada. Since the Nevada divorces were void for want of subject matter jurisdiction, the prosecutor argued the Williamses were guilty of bigamy. Over the Williams' strenuous objection that the second prosecution violated double jeopardy, the couple was convicted *again*. And again the U.S. Supreme Court took the case, but this time the Court sided with the prosecutor. *Williams v. North Carolina.*[27] (*Williams* II).

---

27   325 U.S. 895 (1945).

In *Williams* II the Court reiterated, "Under our system of law, judicial power to grant a divorce, jurisdiction, strictly speaking—is founded on domicile." The Court went on to hold, however, that North Carolina was not bound by the Nevada court's determination that the Williamses were actually domiciled in Nevada. The Supreme Court wrote, "The State of domiciliary origin [North Carolina] should not be bound by an unfounded, even if not collusive, recital in the record of a court of another State. As to the truth or existence of a fact, like that of domicile, upon which depends the power to exert judicial authority, a State not a party to the exertion of such judicial authority in another State but seriously affected by it has a right, when asserting its own unquestioned authority, to ascertain the truth or existence or that crucial fact."

After *Williams* II, the following scenario arose: Wife left the marital home in Massachusetts and traveled to Florida where she filed for divorce. Husband filed an answer contesting the Florida court's jurisdiction. At trial in Florida, Husband appeared and was represented by counsel. Wife testified that she was domiciled in Florida. The Florida judge ruled against Husband on the question of jurisdiction and granted a divorce to Wife. Divorce in hand, Wife returned to Massachusetts. Husband commenced an action in Massachusetts. Citing *Williams* II, husband argued the Florida divorce was void because Wife was not really domiciled in Florida. Does *Williams* II control? Or does the fact that Husband appeared in the Florida case and contested jurisdiction foreclose the issue to collateral attack? In *Sherrer v. Sherrer*,[28] the U.S. Supreme Court ruled the Florida divorce was valid and entitled to full faith and credit. Husband availed himself of the court in Florida and lost. He could not re-litigate the issue of jurisdiction in Massachusetts.

In sum, jurisdiction to grant a divorce requires domicile of at least one of the parties. Personal jurisdiction over the absent party is not required.

Domicile of Members of the Armed Forces

Domicile is the basis for subject matter jurisdiction over divorce. Members of the armed forces move from place to place. What is a service member's domicile for purposes of divorce? In *The Military Divorce Handbook*, Mark Sullivan writes:

> Many courts hold that the domicile of SMs [service members] continues from that which exists at entry into the armed forces until such time as the requisite intent and relocation occur, even though

---

28 334 U.S. 343 (1948).

one may be stationed in a different state or country for years. The rule that a SM may retain his or her initial domicile, however, does not mean that the SM cannot change his or her domicile. To do so, however, the SM must show unequivocally by his or her actions an intent to abandon the initial domicile and take on a new domicile. A change of residence is not necessarily a change of domicile.[29]

Several states (e.g., Georgia,[30] North Carolina,[31] Texas,[32] Virginia[33]) have statutes allowing service members to divorce if they are stationed in the state for a period of time (*e.g.*, 6 months). Colonel Sullivan emphasizes that jurisdiction to grant divorce is based on domicile, and that residence at a particular location is not the same as domicile. He writes, "When confronted with such a statute, counsel should proceed cautiously. Residence alone is not domicile. Residence pursuant to military orders is not domicile. True domicile requires physical presence in addition to the intent to remain in that state indefinitely . . . ."[34]

Jurisdiction Over Financial Aspects of Divorce

If a divorce court has subject matter jurisdiction *and* personal jurisdiction over both parties, the court has authority to adjudicate the financial aspects of divorce, including property division, support, and attorneys fees. Suppose, however, that the court lacks personal jurisdiction over one of the spouses, typically because that spouse does not live in the divorce state and is not subject to the state's long arm statute. In *Kulko v. Superior Court*, the U.S. Supreme Court grappled with this question.

---

29 Mark E. Sullivan, *The Military Divorce Handbook: A Practical Guide to Representing Military Personnel and Their Families* p. 400 (2d ed. 2011).

30 Ga. Code Ann. § 19-5-2.

31 N.C. Stat. Ann. § 50-18.

32 Tex. Stat. Family Code § 6.304.

33 Va. Code Ann. § 20-97.

34 Mark E. Sullivan, *The Military Divorce Handbook: A Practical Guide to Representing Military Personnel and Their Families* p. 405 (2nd ed. 2011)..

Kulko v. Superior Court

U.S. Supreme Court
436 U.S. 84, 98 S. Ct. 1690 (1978)

Mr. Justice Marshall delivered the opinion of the Court.

The issue before us is whether, in this action for child support, the California state courts may exercise *in personam* jurisdiction over a nonresident, nondomiciliary parent of minor children domiciled within the State. For reasons set forth below, we hold that the exercise of such jurisdiction would violate the Due Process Clause of the Fourteenth Amendment.

Appellant Ezra Kulko married appellee Sharon Kulko Horn in 1959, during appellant's three-day stopover in California en route from a military base in Texas to a tour of duty in Korea. At the time of this marriage, both parties were domiciled in and residents of New York State. Immediately following the marriage, Sharon Kulko returned to New York, as did appellant after his tour of duty. Their first child, Darwin, was born to the Kulkos in New York in 1961, and a year later their second child, Ilsa, was born, also in New York. The Kulkos and their two children resided together as a family in New York City continuously until March 1972, when the Kulkos separated.

Following the separation, Sharon Kulko moved to San Francisco, Cal. A written separation agreement was drawn up in New York; in September 1972, Sharon Kulko flew to New York City in order to sign this agreement. The agreement provided, *inter alia*, that the children would remain with their father during the school year but would spend their Christmas, Easter, and summer vacations with their mother. While Sharon Kulko waived any claim for her own support or maintenance, Ezra Kulko agreed to pay his wife $3,000 per year in child support for the periods when the children were in her care, custody, and control. Immediately after execution of the separation agreement, Sharon Kulko flew to Haiti and procured a divorce there; the divorce decree incorporated the terms of the agreement. She then returned to California, where she remarried and took the name Horn.

The children resided with appellant during the school year and with their mother on vacations, as provided by the separation agreement, until December 1973. At this time, just before Ilsa was to leave New York to spend Christmas vacation with her mother, she told her father that she wanted to remain in California after her vacation. Appellant bought his daughter a one-way plane ticket, and Ilsa left, taking her clothing with her. Ilsa then commenced living in California with her mother during the school year and spending vacations with her father. In January 1976, appellant's other child, Darwin, called his mother from New York and advised her that he wanted to live with her in California. Unbeknownst to appellant, appellee Horn sent a plane ticket to her son, which he used to fly to California where he took up residence with his mother and sister.

Less than one month after Darwin's arrival in California, appellee Horn commenced this action against appellant in the California Superior Court. She sought to establish the Haitian divorce decree as a California judgment; to modify the judgment so as to award her full custody of the children; and to increase appellant's child-support obligations. Appellant appeared specially and moved to quash service of the summons on the ground that he was not a resident of California and lacked sufficient "minimum contacts" with the State under *International Shoe Co. v. Washington*, 326 U.S. 310 (1945), to warrant the State's assertion of personal jurisdiction over him.

The trial court summarily denied the motion to quash, and appellant sought review in the California Court of Appeal . . . . The appellate court affirmed the denial of appellant's motion to quash, reasoning that, by consenting to his children's living in California, appellant had "caused an effect in the state" warranting the exercise of jurisdiction over him.

The California Supreme Court granted appellant's petition for review, and in a 4-2 decision sustained the rulings of the lower state courts. It noted first that the California Code of Civil Procedure demonstrated an intent that the courts of California utilize all bases of *in personam* jurisdiction "not inconsistent with the Constitution." Agreeing with the court below, the Supreme Court stated that, where a nonresident defendant has caused an effect in the State by an act or omission outside the State, personal jurisdiction over the defendant in causes arising from that effect may be exercised whenever "reasonable." It went on to hold that such an exercise was "reasonable" in this case because appellant had "purposely availed himself of the benefits and protections of the laws of California" by sending Ilsa to live with her mother in California. While noting that appellant had not, "with respect to his other child, Darwin, caused an effect in California"—since it was appellee Horn who had arranged for Darwin to fly to California in January 1976—the court concluded that it was "fair and reasonable for defendant to be subject to personal jurisdiction for the support of both children, where he has committed acts with respect to one child which confers [*sic*] personal jurisdiction and has consented to the permanent residence of the other child in California."

. . . The existence of personal jurisdiction . . . depends upon the presence of reasonable notice to the defendant that an action has been brought, and a sufficient connection between the defendant and the forum State to make it fair to require defense of the action in the forum. In this case, appellant does not dispute the adequacy of the notice that he received, but contends that his connection with the State of California is too attenuated, under the standards implicit in the Due Process Clause of the Constitution, to justify imposing upon him the burden and inconvenience of defense in California.

The parties are in agreement that the constitutional standard for determining whether the State may enter a binding judgment against appellant here is that set forth in this Court's opinion in *International Shoe Co. v. Washington, supra:* that a defendant "have certain minimum contacts with the forum State such that the maintenance of the suit does not offend traditional notions of fair play and substantial justice." . . .

. . . We believe that the California Supreme Court's application of the minimum-contacts test in this case represents an unwarranted extension of *International Shoe* and would, if sustained, sanction a result that is neither fair, just, nor reasonable.

In reaching its result, the California Supreme Court did not rely on appellant's glancing presence in the State some 13 years before the events that led to this controversy, nor could it have. Appellant has been in California on only two occasions, once in 1959 for a three-day military stopover on his way to Korea, and again in 1960 for a 24-hour stopover on his return from Korean service. To hold such temporary visits to a State a basis for the assertion of *in personam* jurisdiction over unrelated actions arising in the future would make a mockery of the limitations on state jurisdiction imposed by the Fourteenth Amendment. Nor did the California court rely on the fact that appellant was actually married in California on one of his two brief visits. We agree that where two New York domiciliaries, for reasons of convenience, marry in the State of California and thereafter spend their entire married life in New York, the fact of their California marriage by itself cannot support a California court's exercise of jurisdiction over a spouse who remains a New York resident in an action relating to child support.

Finally, in holding that personal jurisdiction existed, the court below carefully disclaimed reliance on the fact that appellant had agreed at the time of separation to allow his children to live with their mother three months a year and that he had sent them to California each year pursuant to this agreement. . . . To find personal jurisdiction in a State on this basis, merely because the mother was residing there, would discourage parents from entering into reasonable visitation agreements. Moreover, it could arbitrarily subject one parent to suit in any State of the Union where the other parent chose to spend time while having custody of their offspring pursuant to a separation agreement. . . . The unilateral activity of those who claim some relationship with a nonresident defendant cannot satisfy the requirement of contact with the forum State. It is essential in each case that there be some act by which the defendant purposefully avails himself of the privilege of conducting activities within the forum State.

The "purposeful act" that the California Supreme Court believed did warrant the exercise of personal jurisdiction over appellant in California was his "actively and fully consenting to Ilsa living in California for the school year and sending her to California for that purpose." We cannot accept the proposition that appellant's acquiescence in Ilsa's desire to live with her mother conferred jurisdiction over appellant in the California courts in this action. A father who agrees, in the interests of family harmony and his children's preferences, to allow them to spend more time in California than was required under a separation agreement can hardly be said to have purposefully availed himself of the benefits and protections of California's laws. . . .

In light of our conclusion that appellant did not purposefully derive benefit from any activities relating to the State of California, it is apparent that the California Supreme Court's reliance on appellant's having caused an "effect" in California was misplaced. . . .

California's legitimate interest in ensuring the support of children resident in California without unduly disrupting the children's lives . . . is already being served by the State's participation in the Revised Uniform Reciprocal Enforcement of Support Act of 1968. This statute provides a mechanism for communication between court systems in different States, in order to facilitate the procurement and enforcement of child-support decrees where the dependent children reside in a State that cannot obtain personal jurisdiction over the defendant. California's version of the Act essentially permits a California resident claiming support from a nonresident to file a petition in California and have its merits adjudicated in the State of the alleged obligor's residence, without either party's having to leave his or her own State. New York State is a signatory to a similar Act. Thus, not only may plaintiff-appellee here vindicate her claimed right to additional child support from her former husband in a New York court, but also the Uniform Acts will facilitate both her prosecution of a claim for additional support and collection of any support payments found to be owed by appellant.

It cannot be disputed that California has substantial interests in protecting resident children and in facilitating child-support actions on behalf of those children. But these interests simply do not make California a fair forum in which to require appellant, who derives no personal or commercial benefit from his child's presence in California and who lacks any other relevant contact with the State, either to defend a child-support suit or to suffer liability by default.

. . . [W]e conclude that the appellant's motion to quash service, on the ground of lack of personal jurisdiction, was erroneously denied by the California courts. The judgment of the California Supreme Court is, therefore,

Reversed.

Kulko makes clear that personal jurisdiction over *both* parties is required to adjudicate the financial aspects of divorce.

In *Kulko*, the Supreme Court mentioned the Uniform Reciprocal Enforcement of Support Act, which was first promulgated in 1950 to assist with interstate enforcement of child support. All states have a version of this law, now called the Uniform Interstate Family Support Act. The Act is discussed in Chapter 7.

Problem on Jurisdiction

Rachel and Michael married in Texas where they were born, grew up, and went to college. Their son is three. The couple separated and Michael moved to Missouri with the child. Seven months after moving to Missouri, Michael filed in Missouri a petition for divorce and child custody. Rachel was personally served in Texas. Rachel did not file a response to Michael's petition. A Missouri judge entered a default judgment against Rachel. The court granted a divorce, awarded custody to Michael, and ordered Rachel to pay child support and to pay part of the marital debts. Shortly following entry of the default judgment, Rachel filed a special appearance in the Missouri court challenging subject matter and personal jurisdiction. Specifically, Rachael argues that Missouri lacked subject matter jurisdiction to grant a divorce, award custody, award child support, or divide property or debts. Rachel asserts that Missouri lacks personal jurisdiction over her. Missouri has a long-arm statute. Rachel has never lived in Missouri or conducted business there. She was personally served in Texas, not Missouri. Did the trial court err in any aspect of its default judgment? *Ketteman v. Ketteman*, 347 S.W.3d 647 (Mo. Ct. App. 2011).

Jurisdiction Over Child Custody

Personal jurisdiction over both parents is *not* required to adjudicate child custody. Jurisdiction over child custody is governed by two statutes, the Parental Kidnapping Prevention Act and the Uniform Child Custody Jurisdiction and Enforcement Act. Both acts are analyzed in Chapter 6.

Domestic Relations Exception to Federal Jurisdiction

Actions for divorce, support, and child custody cannot be litigated in federal court. In *Ankenbrandt v. Richards*,[35] the U.S. Supreme Court ruled that the so-called domestic relations exception to federal jurisdiction "divests the federal courts of power to issue divorce, alimony, and child custody decrees."

The United States is a party to the Hague Convention on the Civil Aspects of International Child Abduction, a treaty that facilitates return of children wrongfully removed from their home country. Civil actions under the Hague Convention *may* be brought in federal or state court. The Convention is discussed in Chapter 6.

Problem on the Domestic Relations Exception

Pam was a young single school teacher living in Ohio. Pam began a romantic relationship with Dan, a wealthy married man from Arizona. Dan urged Pam to quit her job and be his companion. According to Pam, Dan repeatedly promised he would divorce his wife and marry her. The relationship between Pam and Dan lasted ten years, but Dan never divorced his wife. During their relationship, Dan purchased a home in Ohio for Pam. Dan purchased cars for Pam, paid her living expenses, and gave her a generous "allowance." Pam and Dan often traveled the world together, living extravagantly. After ten years, Dan ended the relationship with Pam and asked her to vacate the Ohio home where she had been living. Pam began a civil action against Dan in Arizona state court for damages based on promissory estoppel, intentional infliction of emotional distress, outrage, fraud, and breach of promise to marry. Dan removed the case to federal court based on diversity of citizenship. Pam asks the federal court to remand the case to state court. Does this case fall within the domestic relations exception to federal jurisdiction? *Norton v. McOsker*, 407 F.3d 501 (1st Cir. 2005).

---

35 504 U.S. 689 (1992).

Jurisdiction in International Divorce

In our mobile world, many married couples live together or apart in different countries. Jurisdiction over international divorce is complex, and you may wish to consult two law review articles: J. Thomas Oldham, What if the Beckhams Move to L.A. and Divorce? Marital Property Rights of Mobile Spouses when They Divorce in the United States, 42 *Family Law Quarterly* 263 (2008), and Ann Laquer Estin, International Divorce: Litigating Marital Property and Support Rights, 45 *Family Law Quarterly* 293 (2011).

Alternatives to Litigation— Mediation; Arbitration; Collaborative Law

Litigating family law issues takes a toll on couples' pocketbooks and egos. The breakdown of marriage is often accompanied by hurt feelings, sadness, and anger. Pitting one spouse against the other in court blows this pain and anger through the roof. Much of the work of family law attorneys is helping clients *avoid* litigation. The vast majority of family law cases settle out of court.

Progress has been made integrating nonadversarial techniques into family law as alternatives to litigation.[36] Nancy Ver Steegh describes nonadversarial techniques in her article titled "Family Court Reform and ADR: Shifting Values and Expectations Transform the Divorce Process":[37]

> *Mediation:* Almost nonexistent in the family courts fifty years ago, mediation has since become the workhorse of family dispute resolution. Indeed, some states mandate participation. The Model Standards of Practice for Family and Divorce Mediation define mediation as: "A process in which a mediator, an impartial third party, facilitates the resolution of family disputes by promoting the participants' voluntary agreement. The family mediator assists communication, encourages understanding and focuses the participants on their individual and common interests. The family mediator works with the participants to explore options, make decisions and reach their own agreements." ...
>
> *Concerns About Alternative Processes and Services: Domestic Violence.* Although alternative processes and services clearly benefit

---

36 *See* Mason v. Mason, 256 S.W.3d 716 (Tex. Ct. App. 2008)("Texas strongly encourages alternative dispute resolution, particularly in family law matters.").

37 Nancy Ver Steegh, Family court Reform and ADR: Shifting Values and Expectations Transform the Divorce Process, 42 *Family Law Quarterly* 659 (2008).

most families, this may not be true in cases involving domestic violence. In such situations, participation in some processes and services
may place family members in danger. At the same time, excluding families from participation may deny them access to programs that could
be beneficial, if safe. Because researchers agree that families experiencing domestic violence differ significantly from each other, blanket
inclusion or exclusion from processes and services makes little sense.
Rather, each situation should be assessed, and families should receive
sufficient information to make informed choices about participation. . . .

Collaborative Law. Some lawyers have chosen to focus their
practices entirely on settlement of cases. Under the collaborative law
model both parties retain collaborative lawyers . . . . The parties and
lawyers agree at the outset that the matter will be resolved without
going to court and that the collaborative lawyers will be disqualified from continued representation if impasse is reached and court
action is required. In that event, the parties must retain new litigation counsel.

Collaborative law, as an alternative to litigation, has grown steadily since
it was conceived by Stu Webb in 1990.[38] In 2009, the National Conference of
Commissioners on Uniform State Laws promulgated the *Uniform Collaborative
Law Act*. Versions of the Act have been enacted in California, North Carolina,
Texas, and Utah.[39] The Prefatory Note to the Act states:

> Collaborative law is a voluntary, contractually based alternative
> dispute resolution process for parties who seek to negotiate a resolu-
> tion to their matter rather than having a ruling imposed upon them
> by a court or arbitrator. The distinctive feature of collaborative law,
> as compared to other forms of alternative dispute resolution such as
> mediation, is that parties are represented by lawyers ("collaborative
> lawyers") during negotiations. Collaborative lawyers do not repre-
> sent the party in court, but only for the purpose of negotiating agree-
> ments. The parties agree in advance that their lawyers are disqualified
> from further representing parties by appearing before a tribunal if
> the collaborative law process ends without complete agreement ("dis-
> qualification requirement"). Parties thus retain collaborative lawyers

---

[38] *See* Stu Webb, An Idea Whose Time Has Come, Collaborative Law: An Alternative for Attorneys Suffering
Family Law Burnout,18 *Matrim. Strategist* 7 (July 2000).

[39] Cal. Family Code § 2013; N.C. Gen Stat. §§ 50-70 to 50-79; Tex. Family Code Ann. § 6.603(b), § 153.0072
(a); Utah R. Jud. Admin. 4-510(1)(D).

for the limited purpose of acting as advocates and counselors during the negotiation process.

The basic ground rules for collaborative law are set forth in a written agreement ("collaborative law participation agreement") in which parties designate collaborative lawyers and agree not to seek tribunal (usually judicial) resolution of a dispute during the collaborative law process. The participation agreement also provides that if a party seeks judicial intervention, or otherwise terminates the collaborative law process, the disqualification requirement takes effect. Parties agree that they have a mutual right to terminate collaborative law at any time without giving a reason.

The goal of collaborative law is to encourage parties to engage in "problem-solving rather than "positional" negotiations. . . .

Lawyers can and do, of course, encourage clients to engage in problem-solving negotiations without formally labeling the process collaborative law. The distinctive feature of collaborative law is, however, the disqualification requirement—the enforcement mechanism that parties create by contract to ensure that problem-solving negotiations actually occur. The disqualification requirement enables each party to penalize the other party for unacceptable negotiation behavior if the party who wants to end the collaborative law process is willing to assume the costs of engaging new counsel. Each side knows at the start that the other has similarly tied its own hands by making litigation expensive. By hiring two Collaborative Law practitioners, the parties send a powerful signal to each other that they truly intend to work together to resolve their differences amicably through settlement. . . .

To encourage problem-solving negotiations, collaborative lawyers emphasize that no threats of litigation should be made during a collaborative law process and the need to maintain respectful dialogue. . . .

Both collaborative law and mediation offer parties the benefits of a process to promote agreement through private, confidential negotiations, the promise of cost reduction, and the potential for better relationships. . . .

Mediation and collaboration law do, however, have differences which might make collaborative law more or less attractive to some parties as a dispute resolution option. A neutral is not present during collaborative law process negotiation sessions unless agreed to by the parties, while mediation sessions are facilitated by a neutral third party. . . . Despite their limited purpose of representation in negotiating a resolution of a dispute, collaborative lawyers are not neutrals but are advocates for their clients.[40]

Harry Tindall and Jennie Smith describe their experience with collaborative law in an article in the *Family Law Reporter*:

> The superiority of collaborative law is multidimensional. One such dimension greatly valued by clients is the economy of the process with regard to time. While cases in traditional litigation may drag on for months with time consuming court appearances, the average length of time between the start of the process with signing of the participation agreement and court approval of resolution within the firm has been approximately six months. . . .
>
> Clients benefit from and greatly appreciate the predictability of the collaborative process . . . .
>
> In family law, the outcome of a case results in a shift in family life. For families in transition, one of the most advantageous qualities of collaborative law is that it provides more integrity and peace to the process. In contrast to litigation, collaborative law pushes parties to recognize and acknowledge the other party's goals and interests, even if not shared.
>
> Collaborative law is further unlike litigation as the process is intended to result in a mutually beneficial outcome rather than one party prevailing over the other.[41]

Is collaborative law appropriate when a relationship is infected with domestic violence? The Prefatory Note to the Uniform Collaborative Law Act states: "The rules/act systematically address the problem of domestic violence. The most significant provision of the rules/act's approach to domestic violence is the obligation it places on collaborative lawyers to make 'reasonable inquiry whether the [party or] prospective party has a history of a coercive or violent

---

40 National Conference of Commissioners on Uniform State Laws, Uniform Collaborative Law Rules and Uniform Collaborative Law Act, Prefatory Note (2010).

41 Harry L. Tindall & Jennie R. Smith, Collaborative Law: An Innovation Here to Stay, Bureau of National Affairs, 38 *Family Law Reporter* 1132-1138, at 1137 (January 17, 2012).

relationship with another [party or] prospective party.' If the lawyer 'reasonably believes' the party the lawyer represents has such a history, the lawyer may not begin or continue a collaborative law process unless the party so requests and the lawyer 'reasonably believes' the party's safety 'can be protected adequately during the collaborative law process.'"

Arbitration is a form of alternative dispute resolution in which parties agree, *i.e.*, contract, to resolve a dispute without litigation.[42] Arbitration is common in business, and is gaining popularity in family law.[43] The New Jersey Supreme Court ruled, "The constitutional guarantee of parental autonomy includes the right of parents to choose arbitration as the forum in which to resolve their disputes over child custody and parenting time."[44]

All states have statutes on arbitration, and several states have statutes focused on arbitration of family law matters.[45] Indiana's Family Law Arbitration Act, for example, "permits a broad range of family law matters to be submitted to arbitration, including dissolution actions in their entirety, actions to establish child support, custody, or parenting time, or petitions to modify any decree, judgment, or order . . . ."[46]

Arbitration is an *alternative* to litigation.[47] If a party who is dissatisfied with an arbitration award were able to seek judicial review of the award, the purpose of arbitration—avoiding litigation—would be undermined. In commercial arbitration, judicial review of an arbitration award is available only in narrow circumstances, usually where an award was obtained by fraud or corruption, or where the arbitrator exceeded her authority.[48] The same judicial reluctance to review arbitration decisions applies in family law. When child custody is arbitrated, however, the judiciary must ensure that children's interests are protected. The New Jersey Supreme Court ruled in *Fawzy v. Fawzy*[49] that arbitration awards regarding child custody are subject to judicial review.

---

42 *See* Lippman v. Lippman, 20 So.3d 457 (Fla. Ct. App. 2009)(there was no agreement to arbitrate).

43 Mason v. Mason, 256 S.W.3d 716 (Tex. Ct. App. 2008).

44 Johnson v. Johnson, 204 N.J. 529, 9 A.3d 1003, 1004-1005 (2010). *See* Fawzy v. Fawzy, 199 N.J. 456, 973 A.2d 347 (2009).

45 *See*, e.g., Ind. Code Ann. § 34-57-5; Tex. Fam. Ann. §§ 6.601, 153.0071; Wis. Stat. § (Rule) 802.12(3). *See also* Brockmann v. Brockmann, 938 N.E.2d 831 (Ind. Ct. App. 2010).

46 Brockmann v. Brockmann, 938 N.E.2d 831, 835 (Ind. Ct. App. 2010).

47 *See* Tuetken v. Tuetken, 320 S.W.3d 262 (Tenn. 2010).

48 *See* Franke v. Franke, 268 Wis. 2d 360, 674 N.W.2d 832, 838-839 (2004)("Our cases and secondary authority support the principle that judicial review of an arbitral award is narrow.").

49 199 N.J. 456, 973 A.2d 347 (2009).

Client Intake

The first in-person meeting with a prospective client is typically designed to find out the nature of the case, determine whether the attorney is willing to take the case, and decide whether the client wishes to retain the attorney. Among other things, the attorney discusses her fee structure. It is advisable to have a written retainer agreement. The agreement spells out the scope of the representation.

Many family law attorneys ask clients to fill out a "Client Intake Form" before coming to the office. The form asks detailed questions about the family, children, property, and finances. Completing the form in advance saves time and money.

> **Practice Note:** Family law attorneys must to be sensitive to the possibility of domestic violence. Victims of domestic violence are sometimes embarrassed to disclose their abuse. The skillful attorney builds rapport and trust with the client in order to create an atmosphere in which the client can be completely honest.

Discovery in Divorce Litigation

The family law attorney needs a large amount of information about both spouses. When divorcing couples are on good terms, and when they are honest, most or all of the information can be obtained informally, without the need for formal discovery. When litigation is required, however, the full panoply of discovery tools is available.[50] Thus, it is sometimes necessary to depose the parties and their experts. Interrogatories, requests for production of documents, and subpoenas are available.

A discovery issue that arises in some contested child custody cases involves the effort by one parent to gain access to the other parent's medical or mental health records.[51] The parent seeking access argues that the records are needed to determine the physical or mental health and parenting capacity of the parent in treatment. The parent in treatment argues medical and mental health records

---

50 *Family Law Financial Discovery* (2011)(Continuing Education of the Bar, California).

51 *See* Kinsella v. Kinsella, 150 N.J. 276, 696 A.2d 556 (1997).

are highly confidential and are covered by the psychotherapist-patient or phy-sician-patient privilege. The California Court of Appeals' decision in *Manela v. Superior Court* balances with the competing interests.

Manela v. Superior Court

California Court of Appeal
177 Cal.App.4th 1139, 99 Cal. Rptr. 3d 736 (2009)

Kitching, J.

This is a marital dissolution action brought by Real Party in Interest David Y. Manela (father) against Petitioner Mira R. Manela (mother). One of the prin-ciple issues in the case is whether father should be granted joint custody over the couple's 4-year-old son, Jacob. In connection with that issue, father and mother became embroiled in a discovery dispute that is the subject of our opinion.

Mother contends that father has a "seizure" disorder that affects his abil-ity to care for Jacob. Father denies mother's allegations and contends that he merely has a "tic" that is controlled by medication. Mother subpoenaed the med-ical records of two of father's physicians, Dr. Hart C. Cohen and Dr. Andrea H. Morrison, claiming that the records will support her allegations regarding father's seizures. The trial court, however, granted father's motion to quash the subpoenas on the ground that the documents were protected by the physician-patient privilege. Mother filed a petition for a writ of mandate requiring the trial court to vacate its order quashing the subpoenas.

We hold that the trial court abused its discretion by quashing the sub-poena to Dr. Cohen because father waived the physician-patient privilege with respect to certain records of Dr. Cohen. . . . We further hold, however, that the trial court did not abuse its discretion with respect to quashing the subpoena to Dr. Morrison because the documents mother sought from Dr. Morrison were privileged.

Mother claims that father suffers from regular "seizures" which last from 45 seconds to 2 ½ minutes. The seizures usually occur when father awakens from sleep. Although father does not lose consciousness when the seizures occur, mother claims the seizures cause father's head, neck, shoulders, and one arm to seize and that the seizures are "extremely loud and very frightening." Mother further claims that the seizures cause father to temporarily lose his ability to speak and often cause him to vomit. Father denies that he has a seizure disorder. Instead, father contends, he has a "tic" which is controlled by medication.

On June 17, 2008, father filed a petition for dissolution of marriage. In his petition, father requested that custody of Jacob be awarded "consistent with the best interest of the minor child." In her response to father's petition, mother requested that the court award custody of Jacob to her alone. . . .

[As the divorce was pending,] the court "temporarily" prohibited father from driving Jacob until it obtained more information regarding father's alleged seizure disorder.

Father filed a declaration from Dr. Benjamin Gross, a neurologist. Dr. Gross stated in his declaration that he had treated father for the past nine years for hypnagogic movements, also known as a tic disorder. Dr. Gross further stated that father's condition has been controlled by Tegretol and that there was no neurological reason to restrict father's ability to drive an automobile or to prevent father from caring for Jacob.

The court issued an order granting father and mother joint legal custody over Jacob. The court granted mother primary physical custody over Jacob and father secondary physical custody, specifying the days and nights on which Jacob would be with father. The court did not place any limitations on father's right to drive Jacob.

The court stated that the evidence was "quite clear that father does not suffer from seizures as the term is generally recognized to me." The court further stated that father's tics only occurred "when he's ready to go to bed. Presumably he's not about to go to sleep before he's put the child to bed. And even under anybody's characterization, the most the alleged seizure lasts is about two and a half minutes, generally quite less. I don't see that it in any way impairs this father's ability to be involved, to have the child overnight." . . .

Mother issued subpoenas to Dr. Cohen and Dr. Morrison. The subpoenas demanded that Dr. Cohen and Dr. Morrison produce "all medical records pertaining to David Manela."

Father filed a motion to quash the subpoenas and for a protective order and monetary sanctions. Father argued that the subpoenas should be quashed because the documents mother sought were protected by the physician-patient privilege.

In response to father's motion, mother alleged that the medical records she sought would support her allegations regarding father's alleged seizure disorder. Mother claimed that Dr. Morrison treated father for seizures when father was 11 years old and for several years thereafter. Mother also alleged that on August 29, 2007, Dr. Cohen examined father regarding his neurological condition and that she was present during the exam. Mother further alleged that at that exam, father stated to Dr. Cohen in her presence a detailed account of father's seizures. The trial court granted father's motion to quash the subpoenas....

Mother claims that father waived the physician-patient privilege by filing the declaration of Dr. Gross and by speaking about his medical condition to Dr. Cohen in the presence of mother. This waiver, mother argues, extends to father's privilege relating to Dr. Morrison. Mother also contends that the patient-litigant exception to the physician-patient privilege applies because father "tendered" the issue of his alleged seizure condition.

Father contends that the physician-patient privilege protects all of the documents mother seeks....

We begin with the premise that there can be no discovery of materials which are privileged. The physician-patient privilege is codified in Evidence Code section 994, which provides, in part, that "the patient ... has a privilege to refuse to disclose, and to prevent another from disclosing, a confidential communication between patient and physician if the privilege is claimed by: (a) The holder of the privilege. . . ." To the extent the physician-patient privilege applies, "it bars discovery of even relevant information."

Section 912(a) [of the Evidence Code] provides, in part: "The right of any person to claim a privilege provided by [the] physician-patient privilege is waived with respect to a communication protected by the privilege if any holder of the privilege, without coercion, has disclosed a significant part of the communication or has consented to disclosure made by anyone." ...

Here, father does not dispute that mother was present during his August 29, 2007, intake exam by Dr. Cohen, and that father consented to disclosure of at least a significant part of the communication between father and Dr. Cohen on that date. . . . Mother's presence at the examination caused father to waive the physician-patient privilege, *i.e.,* rendered father's communications with Dr. Cohen non-confidential and unprivileged, unless mother's presence was reasonably necessary for Dr. Cohen's diagnosis and treatment of father. Although father argues that mother's presence was necessary, he offers no evidence supporting that assertion. Accordingly, father waived the physician-patient privilege with respect to Dr. Cohen's exam on August 29, 2007. . . .

[The Court of Appeal ruled that father waived the physician-patient privilege between father and Dr. Gross because father asked Dr. Gross to file a declaration about father's medical condition.]

Mother argues that father's waiver of the physician-patient privilege with respect to Dr. Cohen's and Dr. Gross's medical records also caused a waiver of the privilege with respect to Dr. Morrison's medical records. However, we may not extend the waiver of privileges, including the physician-patient privilege, beyond the express limits of section 912. In light of the important public policies underlying privileges, moreover, the scope of the waiver of a privilege is generally construed narrowly. . . .

Further, the scope of a waiver should be determined with reference to the purpose of the privilege. The physician-patient privilege has two purposes: (1) to preclude humiliation of the patient that might follow disclosure of his ailments and (2) to encourage the patient's full disclosure to the physician of all information necessary for effective diagnosis and treatment of the patient.

In this case, father's interest in precluding his "humiliation" of disclosing his alleged medical condition to mother is belied by his voluntarily disclosure to mother of his communications with Dr. Cohen and his filing of Dr. Gross's declaration. But the disclosure of father's communications with Dr. Cohen and Dr. Gross did not relate back to father's communications with Dr. Morrison many years earlier when father was a teenager. When father spoke to Dr. Morrison, father reasonably believed he could fully and freely discuss his medical condition. If we allow father's litigation adversary access to Dr. Morrison's records, father's interest in disclosing all necessary information to his treating physician will be undermined. We therefore hold that father's waiver of the physician-patient privilege with respect to Dr. Cohen and Dr. Gross did not also constitute a waiver of that privilege with respect to Dr. Morrison.

One exception to the physician-patient privilege is the patient-litigant exception. Section 996 [of the Evidence Code] provides: "There is no privilege under this article as to a communication relevant to an issue concerning the condition of the patient if such issue has been tendered by the patient." Mother claims that father tendered the issue of his seizure/tic disorder, and therefore father's communications with his physicians regarding that medical condition are not privileged. We disagree.

There are two grounds for the patient-litigant exception. First, the courts have noted that the patient, in raising the issue of a specific ailment or condition in litigation, in effect dispenses with the confidentiality of that ailment and may no longer justifiably seek protection from the humiliation of its exposure. Second, the exception represents a judgment that, in all fairness, a patient should not be permitted to establish a claim while simultaneously foreclosing inquiry into relevant matters.

The patient-litigant exception usually arises in an action for personal injuries. A plaintiff seeking to recover damages arising out of a particular injury cannot claim the physician-patient privilege with respect to that injury because plaintiff's action tenders the issue.

A defendant, however, does not tender his or her medical condition by simply denying the plaintiff's allegations regarding the same. . . .

In *Koshman v. Superior Court* (1980) 111 Cal.App.3d 294, 168 Cal.Rptr. 558 (*Koshman*), the court addressed the issue of whether the patient-litigant exception applied in the context of a custody dispute between parents. After the mother was awarded custody of the parents' two children, the father moved to modify the custody order on the ground that the mother was hospitalized for treatment for an overdose of narcotics. The father sought medical records related to the mother's hospitalization. The court, however, held that the mother did not tender the issue of her alleged overdose, and thus the patient-litigant exception did not apply.

The present case is analogous to *Koshman*. Like the mother in *Koshman*, father did not raise the issue of his tic/seizure disorder in his pleadings or his application for custody of Jacob. It was mother who first raised the issue in her response to father's application. Mother was also the first party to file evidence in connection with the issue. Father, by contrast, merely denied mother's allegations and submitted evidence in support of that denial.

Allowing father to invoke the physician-patient privilege does not raise the same concern for fairness that is raised in a typical personal injury case. It is grossly unfair to allow the plaintiff to pursue a claim for personal injuries without allowing the defendant to obtain medical records related to the alleged injuries. Here, by contrast, father does not seek custody of Jacob on the ground that he has a tic/seizure disorder. Indeed, if father had his way, his alleged disorder would not be an issue in the case. Father thus did not tender the issue of his alleged disorder within the meaning of section 996.

> **Practice Note:** You observe in *Manela v. Superior Court* use of motions and orders to show cause. Family law litigation is in large measure a motions practice: motion for temporary custody; motion for support; motion for sanctions; motions for attorney fees, etc.

Practice Note: Many clients struggle financially during divorce, and one of the biggest expenses is paying YOU! To keep costs down, some clients are willing to do some of the non-legal leg work entailed in the process. In one of my cases, for example, my client tracked down her husband's DUI convictions in various counties. In another case, a client living in a foreign country obtained essential documents from her government that would have taken me weeks to get through the mail. She also obtained a certified copy of her divorce decree from a different American state. Your client is not a professional investigator, of course, and should not be asked to perform legal tasks or functions that entail risk. There are times though when a client is happy to help and happy to save some money. Obviously, you must be careful not to have a client do work you should do. You will find the right balance.

Attorney Fees in Family Law Matters

The matter of attorney fees arises in two settings. First, unless an attorney is representing a client *pro bono*, the client and the attorney enter a contract regarding attorney fees. Second, in some cases one spouse files a motion asking the court to order the other spouse to pay some or all of the moving spouse's attorney fees.

Agreement Regarding Attorney Fees

A written agreement should be executed regarding attorney fees. In many cases, the attorney requires a retainer, that is, an advance payment of fees. The advance is placed in the client trust account, and may not be commingled with the attorney's own funds. Contingent fee agreements are not typically used in family law proceedings. Reproduced below is a Professional Services and Fee Agreement drawn from a California practice guide.[52] You will craft your own agreement.

---

52 *California Family Law: Practice and Procedure.* Mathew Bender 2012.

Professional Services and Fee Agreement

[Date] _____

[Address] _____

Dear Mr./Ms. _____ *[name of client]*:

You have requested that this office represent you in a proceeding for _____ [dissolution of your marriage with or legal separation from or a judgment of nullity regarding your marriage with] _____ *[name of other spouse]*. This letter will confirm the terms on which we have agreed to represent you in that matter.

You understand, of course, that we cannot and do not guarantee or even speculate regarding the outcome of negotiations or court proceedings. Our experience has shown that there are too many uncertainties in these kinds of proceedings, as well as in the courts and the legal system generally, to allow anyone to predict or even speculate regarding the results in these matters.

Also, as we have told you, we cannot determine at this time what the ultimate total of your fees and costs will be. The total amount will depend on a number of factors, including the amount of time that we are required to spend on the matter, whether the time is spent in our offices or the courtroom, the complexities of the case, and the extent to which the proceedings are contested by you or your spouse.

Please read this agreement and be sure you understand its terms before signing it. If this letter conforms to your understanding of our agreement, please sign it in the space provided at the end of the letter. We invite you to consult with independent counsel of your choice before entering into the agreement and have provided you with a copy of this agreement for that purpose before you sign it.

Until we receive a signed copy of this letter from you, along with the amount of the fee deposit provided in Paragraph 2, no agreement will exist between us, and we will not be obligated to provide any services.

1. General Description of Services. [Except for the services described below,] I and/or other attorneys from this Office will provide all professional services that are reasonably necessary and appropriate to represent your interests in the proceeding described above, until such time as we are discharged from service or otherwise cease to represent you in this matter. [The services that will not be provided under this agreement are as follows: (specify)].

2. Deposit and Use of Fee Advance. You _____ [have paid or agree to pay by _____ *(date)*] to this office the sum of $_____ by _____ [check or cash or credit card] as an advance on fees for the services to be provided under this agreement [and for any costs incurred in representing you in this matter, such as costs for filing fees, court reporters, and expert witnesses]. This payment will assure the availability of my/our services in this matter and will act as a credit toward any actual fees or expenses incurred in this matter. We will deposit these funds in our office's client trust account. You authorize this office to transfer these funds from our trust account to our own accounts at the time that the fees are actually earned [or the costs are actually incurred]. If the fees [and costs] actually incurred in this proceeding do not exhaust the amount you have paid by the time that the proceeding has been finally resolved or by the time that our office otherwise ceases to represent you, you will be refunded the difference.

3. Hourly Rate and Determination of Fee. The fee in this matter will be based on time actually spent by me and/or other attorneys and paralegals in this office in representing you according to the standard hourly rates in effect for this office at the time that the services are actually rendered. Hourly rates may vary as different rates may be in effect for my personal time or for that of a colleague and may also depend on the type of work being done. The current hourly rates for the persons who may render services in this matter are as follows:

[Specify schedule of hourly rates, such as the following]

Myself: $_____ per hour.

My associate, _____ *[name]*: $_____ per hour.

Our paralegal(s): $_____ per hour.

You will be notified in writing of any change in the above hourly rates. Any change in the hourly rates will not be effective until _____ days after the notice of change.

This office may seek a court order requiring the other party to pay all or part of our attorney's fees and costs. If the court grants such an order, any amounts that this office receives from the other party will be credited against your balance due for attorney's fees and costs. However, you will be liable for fees and costs if the amount awarded by the court is less than your balance due under this agreement for fees and costs. If the total amount of your payments and payments received from the other party exceeds the balance due for fees and costs, the excess payments will be refunded to you.

4. Other Expenses and Costs. Expenses and costs may be advanced by this office on your behalf for filing fees, court reporters, investigators, expert witnesses, and other costs pertaining to the proceeding. You will be separately charged for reimbursement of these advances [and the amounts billed will be deducted from any balance remaining on your fee deposit]. [In lieu of advancing some types of costs, such as fees for outside experts (e.g., accountants), we may instead arrange for you to pay the third-party service provider directly. In that event, you understand and agree that you will be directly responsible for promptly paying for those services and that this office will not be responsible for your failure to do so.]

5. Billing. You will receive a billing statement from this office every _____ [*specify, e.g.,* two months]. Each statement will show the services rendered since the preceding statement, the fees charged for those services, and any costs (as described in Paragraph 4) incurred since the preceding statement. The statement will also list the fee advance credit or balance due from the previous statement and any credits for any payments made by you or on your behalf during the statement period. Any balance due is payable no later than _____ [*specify, e.g.,* the date on which this matter is finally concluded or the date on which this office otherwise ceases to represent you, whichever occurs first].

6. No Errors and Omissions Insurance. As required by Business and Professions Code Section 6148(a)(4), we hereby advise you that this office does not maintain errors and omissions insurance coverage applicable to the services to be rendered on your behalf, nor has this office filed a written agreement guaranteeing payment of errors and omissions claims pursuant to Rule IV(B)(1) of the Law Corporation Rules of the State Bar . . . .

7. Your Responsibilities. In order to effectively represent you in this matter, this office will need your full cooperation in providing needed financial and other information. You agree to provide this information when requested by this office. You also agree to inform this office immediately of any change in your address and telephone number.

We reserve the right to ask the court for permission to withdraw from representing you in the event that you fail or refuse to accept or follow our advice on any important aspect of this matter. We also reserve the right to request permission to withdraw from representation in the event of any fact or occurrence that we believe would make it unlawful for us to continue to represent you.

You agree to honor and comply with all court orders and rules. It is a material condition of our agreeing to represent you that you agree to honor all orders and rules issued by the court. We will not knowingly be a party to any intentional violation of a court order or rule.

You may be assured of the full commitment of my services and those of my office to your representation in this matter and of my best efforts to achieve the most satisfactory disposition of your case. You will be kept fully informed of our progress in this matter. We appreciate the privilege of being able to serve you in this matter.

Very truly yours,

[Firm name]

_____ [signature]

By:

_____ *[Name of attorney]*

I have read the above agreement [consisting of _____ pages] and understand its terms. I hereby accept and agree to the terms, conditions, and recitals set forth in this agreement. I also hereby acknowledge that I have received a copy of this agreement.

_____ [signature]   Date:_____

Court-Ordered Attorney Fees

The court has authority to order one party to pay some or all of the other party's attorney fees. Such orders place the spouses on an equal footing in court. As the Colorado Supreme Court put it in *Marriage of Ikeler*,[53] "Attorney's fees are intended to equalize the parties and ensure neither party suffers undue economic hardship because of the dissolution of marriage." An award of attorneys fees is based on the parties' income, needs, and ability to pay.

---

53   161 P.3d 663, 668-669 (Colo. 2007).

Problem on Attorney Fees

Should the judge order attorney fees in the following case? Linda and Charles are divorcing. Linda's attorney files a motion requesting a court order that Charles pay Linda's attorney fees and litigation costs. The motion requests that Charles be ordered to pay Linda $1 million for attorney fees already incurred, and an additional $2 million for future fees. Linda files a declaration stating that her monthly income is $350,000. Linda lists approximately $2 million in liquid assets, $70 million in additional assets, and monthly expenses of approximately $650,000. In her declaration, Linda states she is unable to pay the attorney fees incurred in the divorce without liquidating assets. In response, Charles does not dispute his ability to pay reasonable fees. Rather, he argues Linda has no need for a fee award and that any disparity in income or assets is an insufficient ground to justify a fee award. Charles' monthly income is approximately $10 to 16 million (that's right, $10 to 16 million each month). Charles has assets over $290 million, debt of $216,000, and monthly expenses of $2.1 million. Should Charles be ordered to pay some or all of Linda's attorney fees? *Marriage of Brandes,* 2008 WestLaw 4989173 (Cal. Ct. App. 2008)(nonpublished).

Servicemembers Civil Relief Act

In 1940, Congress enacted the Soldiers and Sailors Relief Act (SSRA). SSRA puts civil litigation against servicemembers on temporary hold while servicemembers are deployed. The purpose of SSRA is to allow servicemembers to devote their full attention to military duties, without worrying about lawsuits back home. Congress updated the law in 2003 and renamed it the Servicemembers Civil Relief Act (SCRA).[54]

A servicemember can apply to a court for a 90 day stay of proceedings in civil litigation, including divorce, custody, or paternity.[55] The service member must support the application for stay with a "letter or other communication from the servicemember's commanding officer stating that the servicemember's current military duty prevents appearance and that military leave is not authorized for the servicemember at the time of the letter."[56]

---

54 50 U.S.C. App. § 501 et seq.

55 Filing a request for a stay does not constitute a general appearance. Thus, the service member does not forfeit the argument that the court lacks personal jurisdiction.

56 50 U.S.C. App. § 522(b)(2)(B).

The non-servicemember party can argue a stay is unnecessary. Mark Sullivan, in his book *The Military Divorce Handbook*[57] writes, "Counsel for the nonmilitary party should request that the court examine whether the SM [servicemember] acted in good faith. Most courts hold that a SM must exercise due diligence and good faith in trying to arrange to appear in court. When a SM demonstrates bad faith in his or her dealings with the court, no stay will be granted. . . . A stay is not expected to last forever. . . . A stay is intended to last only as long as the [need for the stay] lasts." If a stay is granted, it can be extended. SCRA limits the ability to obtain a default judgment against a service member.

The Maine Supreme Judicial Court's decision in *Real v. Real* illustrates SCRA in action:

Real v. Real

Supreme Judicial Court of Maine
3 A.3d 1196 (2010)

Alexander, J.

In this appeal from the entry of a protection from abuse judgment, the appellant challenges only that part of the court's judgment ordering spousal support payments. Because the judgment was entered against a member of the Armed Services on active duty who did not appear at the hearing, federal law, specifically, the Servicemembers Civil Relief Act, 50 U.S.C.S. app. § 521 (2006), requires that we vacate the challenged support order.

This matter is before us on appeal by Adam M. Real from the judgment of the District Court entered in a protection from abuse action pursuant to 19-A M.R.S. § 4007 (2009). . . .

Crystal M. Real and Adam M. Real began living together sometime in the spring of 2009. Also living with them was Crystal's two-year-old daughter from a prior relationship. Adam also has a child, not living with him, from a prior relationship. The parties have no children together.

Adam was employed with the Maine National Guard and, at some point, transferred to active duty with the United States Army. In the summer of 2009, as part of Adam's Army duty, he was transferred to Fort Belvoir, Virginia. The

---

57 Mark E. Sullivan, *The Military Divorce Handbook: A Practical Guide to Representing Military Personnel and Their Families* (2d ed. 2011. American Bar Association).

couple then began living in the vicinity of Fort Belvoir. They were married in Virginia on August 19, 2009.

One month later, on September 19, 2009, Crystal filed an application for a protection from abuse order in the District Court for Fairfax County, Virginia. A temporary order was issued, on or about that date, barring Adam from having any contact with Crystal. The temporary order was to expire on September 25, 2009. Crystal's application for a temporary order did not seek any payments for support, and the resulting court order did not mandate any payment of funds by Adam to Crystal.

Filings by both parties in the record of this appeal indicate that an order, extending the original temporary order, was to expire on or before October 8, 2009, when a final hearing on the protection from abuse petition was scheduled to be held. No hearing was apparently held on that petition. At some point during this time period, Crystal moved back to Maine from Virginia. . . .

On December 10, 2009, Crystal filed a protection from abuse action in the District Court at South Paris. The application for the protection from abuse order indicated that the relief Crystal was requesting included a support payment of $681 a month, which she characterized as a share of Adam's military housing allowance.

The court granted a temporary order for protection from abuse and scheduled a hearing on the final order for December 29, 2009. . . . The hearing was held as scheduled on December 29, 2009. Adam did not appear, nor did counsel appear on his behalf. The court granted the final protection from abuse order as requested, including an award of $681 a month support to be paid to Crystal for the two-year duration of the order. . . .

The order included no findings addressing the propriety of entering what was, in essence, a default judgment requiring the payment of money by a person, not present at hearing, who was on active duty with the United States Army. *See* 50 U.S.C.S. app. § 521 . . . .

Adam filed a timely appeal from the court's order. He does not contest the no-contact provisions of the protection from abuse order, but he does specifically contest the requirement that he pay Crystal $681 each month for two years.

We take this opportunity to address the special needs and protections of law afforded to members of our Armed Forces on active duty, when those servicemen and women are parties to litigation. The "Servicemembers Civil Relief Act" of 2003, prohibits entry of a civil judgment against a member of the active duty military who, although served, does not appear for a hearing, unless further protective steps are taken. . . . Section 521 was not called to the trial court's attention and is not explicitly cited by Adam in his appeal. However, unless there has been an affirmative waiver of the protections of the Act by the servicemember, section 521 constitutes a statutory bar to the trial court's authority to enter a judgment in the absence of an appearance by the servicemember or his counsel. . . .

The parties to this matter were married. Thus, the court had the authority in the protection from abuse proceeding to enter a temporary support order for a brief period of time, because a legal obligation to support a spouse is found in Maine's divorce laws. In any proceeding against a servicemember, however, federal law requires that, before granting the requested relief in the absence of that party or his or her attorney, the court appoint an attorney to inquire into and represent the servicemember's interest in the action. Section 521 "applies to any civil action or proceeding . . . in which the defendant does not make an appearance." Section 521(b)(2) requires that "if in an action covered by this section it appears that the defendant is in military service, the court may not enter a judgment until after the court appoints an attorney to represent the defendant."

From the face of the pleadings, it was apparent that Adam was on active duty in the military. The court did not, however, appoint an attorney for Adam after noting his absence as required by 50 U.S.C.S. app. § 521(b)(2). Rather, the court proceeded to hear the case in the absence of an appearance by Adam or his attorney, and entered a judgment requiring Adam to pay Crystal $681 a month for two years, presumably to come from his military pay.

Setting aside the concern that the support awarded in this case does not appear to have been "temporary," the support payment requirement was imposed in a proceeding in which Adam had been served, but had not appeared. That judgment, entered in a proceeding against a member of the Armed Forces on active duty who has not appeared, was prohibited by 50 U.S.C.S. app. § 521, and must be vacated.

Question based on *Real v. Real*

In *Real v. Real,* it was apparent from the "face of the pleadings" that one party was in the military. But suppose it is not apparent from the pleadings or from other evidence available to the court that an absent party is a servicemember. If the judge enters a default judgment against the absent servicemember, does the judgment violate the Servicemember's Civil Relief Act?

EXPERIENTIAL ASSIGNMENT

Draft Divorce Complaint/Petition and Summons

A divorce is a lawsuit, and like other lawsuits a divorce is commenced by filing a pleading, typically a petition or a complaint. The party commencing the divorce is the petitioner or plaintiff. In addition to drafting and filing the petition/complaint, the commencing party drafts a summons. States differ in the wording of the petition/complaint and summons. In some states official government forms must be used for the petition/complaint and summons. In other states there are no required forms and the party commencing the divorce drafts the necessary documents.

1. Find out whether your state requires the use of government forms for the petition/complaint and summons. The easiest way to find out may be to go on line. Use a search term like "Idaho divorce complaint" or "New York divorce petition." If you are in California, type in "California family law forms." If your state requires use of official forms, download and print out blank forms or get them from the law library. If your state does not use official government forms, you can find sample petitions/complaints and a summons on line or in the library. Depending on your state, either fill in the required forms or draft a petition/complaint and summons. Make up the facts of the case.

2. Find out if your county has local requirements for filing a petition/complaint for divorce. Does your county have relevant local court rules? Are there local forms you must use? In law school you learn the importance of statutes and cases. Less emphasis is placed on state-wide rules of court and local (county or parish) court rules. In day-to-day practice, you must know the state-wide and local rules as thoroughly as you know the statutes and cases. Just to make life interesting, local rules vary from county/parish to county/parish. If you practice in more than one county/parish, you have to know the local rules for each jurisdiction. Finally, keep in mind that every judge is different. Judge X may like things done one way in her courtroom, while Judge Z prefers a slightly different approach. And of course the judge is king or queen of the courtroom. We are mere lawyers. We do things their way, not the other way around!

3. What is the filing fee to commence a divorce in your county/parish? If your client is poor and can't afford the filing fee, is there a procedure for a judge or court clerk to waive fees?

4. Once the petition/complaint is filed, what do you do with it? Serve it on the respondent/defendant, of course. Find out the law regarding service of process in your state. Who can serve the petition/complaint and summons? What does service of process cost? What if the client is poor and can't afford to pay for service of process? What do you do if the process server can't locate the respondent/defendant? What if the respondent/defendant lives outside your county/parish, your state, your country? How do to serve the absent respondent/defendant?

5. Are you convinced yet that this is complicated?!

CHAPTER 5

Parent-Child Relationship: Establishing Parentage

IN MOST CASES THERE is no doubt about parentage. Giving birth generally establishes the mother-child relationship although, as we will see, some children have two mommies. As for the father-child relationship, if a woman and man are married and living together at the time of birth, the law creates a strong presumption that husband is the father. Of course, not every child born during marriage is the biological offspring of the husband, and the law grapples with this reality.

Issues of paternity arise most often when mother is not married. To use the antiquated phrase, her child is born "out of wedlock." If the father steps forward and assumes his parental responsibilities, issues of paternity seldom arise. Sometimes, however, father is less than enthusiastic about assuming the mantle of parenthood, including child support. In some cases, more than one man could be the father. When an unwed mother receives public benefits to support her child, child support officials are keen to establish paternity and enforce father's duty to support his children.

This chapter introduces the complicated and evolving topic of parentage.

"Illegitimate" Children

At common law, a child born out of wedlock was "illegitimate"—a "bastard." Early law treated "illegitimate" children harshly.[1] William Blackstone

---

1 *See* Solangel Maldonado, Illegitimate Harm: Law, Stigma, and Discrimination Against Nonmarital Children, 63 *Florida Law Review* 345 (2011). Maldonado writes: "No one would dispute that for most of U.S. history, 'illegitimate' children suffered significant legal and societal discrimination. Under the common law, nonmarital

(1723-1780) wrote in his *Commentaries on the Laws of England* about "illegitimate" children:

> I proceed next to the rights and incapacities which appertain to a bastard. The rights are very few, being only such as he can *acquire;* for he can *inherit* nothing, being looked upon as the son of nobody, and sometimes called *filius nullius*, sometimes *filius populi*. Yet he may gain a surname by reputation, though he has none by inheritance. All other children have their primary settlement in their father's parish; but a bastard in the parish where born, for he hath no father. The incapacity of a bastard consists principally in this, that he cannot be heir to any one, neither can he have heirs but of his own body; for, being *nullius filius*, he is therefore of kin to nobody, and has no ancestor from whom any inheritable blood can be derived.

In Shakespeare's *King Lear*, Edmund is the "illegitimate" son of the Earl of Gloucester. Because Edmund is *fillius nullius*—the son of no one—Edmund cannot inherit from the Earl. Edmund devises a plan to become Earl himself by getting rid of his brother, who is the Earl's "legitimate" son and heir, as well as the Earl. To learn how Edmund's nefarious plan worked out, I'm afraid you'll have to read the play. You'll get the hint that things didn't turn out as planned from the following Note in the *Harvard Law Review*:

> The common law was content to leave the bastard Edmund with nothing but his remedy of self-help and its tragic consequences. He was *fillius nullius*, the son of no one and the heir of no one. He had no right to support from his parents and no heirs than those of his own body. In the eyes of the law his separation from his parents was complete and permanent, for by no subsequent act could they ever legitimate him.
>
> Had Edmund lived in the United States, even as late as the nineteenth century, he would have fared little better, for virtually

---

children had no right to parental support and no right to inherit from or through a parent. They faced legal and societal barriers when they sought public office, entry into professional associations, or to transfer their own property at death." Maldonado argues that "the law continues to discriminate against nonmarital children, imposing economic, social, and psychic harms. First, federal and state laws still treat nonmarital children differently in a number of areas, including support for post-secondary education and rules of intestacy and citizenship. These laws place heavier economic burdens on nonmarital children than on their marital counterparts. These laws also signal to society that there is a material distinction between marital and nonmarital children. Moreover, lawmakers and courts continue to express disapproval of nonmarital families, thereby reinforcing societal biases against nonmarital children."

every state adopted this common law doctrine. Some legislative ame-
lioration of its harshness has followed, but though Edmund's outlook would be less dismal today [1962], he would by no means have
attained equality . . . . Today he could almost everywhere be made
legitimate by the subsequent marriage of his parents. Even as an illegitimate he usually would be entitled to inherit from his mother, but
his right to inherit from her or her kindred would be much more limited. Only a minority of states would permit him to inherit from or
through his father . . . .[2]

In 1881, the California Supreme Court decided *Estate of Wardell*.[3] The issue
was whether an "illegitimate child" could inherit from her father. The California
court described early law: "It is well settled that at common law the word 'children' means those born in lawful wedlock . . . . Those only were considered as
legitimate whose blood was traceable to the legal marriage of a common pair.
A person not born in lawful wedlock was not regarded as a member of the group
known in law as the family; and consequently was not entitled to the privileges
of members of the family, or to any right of inheritance or succession." By 1881
and *Estate of Wardell*, the law had softened, and the court ruled an "illegitimate"
child could inherit from her parent.

A series of United States Supreme Court decisions beginning in the 1960s
struck down many restrictions on the rights of children born out of wedlock. Today,
the term "illegitimate child" is falling into disuse. Many states and the Uniform
Parentage Act (UPA) abolish the concept of illegitimacy.[4] The UPA does so with
the words: "A child born to parents who are not married to each other has the same
rights under the law as a child born to parents who are married to each other."[5]

Uniform Parentage Act of 2000

As mentioned above, with most children there is no doubt about the mother-child relationship. In many cases, the father-child relationship is equally

---

2 Note, The Rights of Illegitimates Under Federal Statutes, 76 *Harvard Law Review* 337, 337 (1962).

3 57 Cal. 484, 490 (1881).

4 *See, e.g.,* Rev. Code Wash. Ann. tit. 26 § 26.26.106 ("A child born to parents who are not married to each
other or in a domestic partnership with each other has the same rights under the law as a child born to parents
who are married to each other or who are in a domestic partnership with each other.").

5 *Uniform Laws Annotated,* Vol. 9B Uniform Parentage Act of 2000, § 202. *See, e.g.,* California Family Code
§ 7602 ("The parent and child relationship extends equally to every child and to every parent, regardless of the
marital status the parents.").

clear. Yet, cases arise daily in which the answer to the question, "Who's your daddy?" is, to put it mildly, complicated. Every state has complex statutes governing paternity. No two states have exactly the same law, although results are generally consistent.

Throughout the twentieth century, the National Conference of Commissioners on Uniform State Laws promulgated model laws on paternity. The Uniform Parentage Act (UPA) of 2000 is the latest effort. Selected sections of the 2000 UPA are reproduced below:

§ 102. Definitions.

In this Act:

(1) "Acknowledged father" means a man who has established a father-child relationship.

(2) "Adjudicated father" means a man who has been adjudicated by a court of competent jurisdiction to be the father of a child.

(3) "Alleged father" means a man who alleges himself to be, or is alleged to be, the genetic father or a possible genetic father of a child, but whose paternity has not been determined. The term does not include:

(A) a presumed father;

(B) a man whose parental rights have been terminated or declared not to exist; or

(C) a male donor.

(4) "Assisted reproduction" means a method of causing pregnancy other than sexual intercourse. The term includes:

(A) intrauterine insemination;

(B) donation of eggs;

(C) donation of embryos;

(D) in-vitro fertilization and transfer of embryos; and

(E) intracytoplasmic sperm injection.

* * *

(7) "Determination of parentage" means the establishment of the parent-child relationship by the signing of a valid acknowledgment of paternity under Article 3 or adjudication by the court.

(8) "Donor" means an individual who produces eggs or sperm used for assisted reproduction, whether or not for consideration. The term does not include:

(A) a husband who provides sperm, or a wife who provides eggs, to be used for assisted reproduction by the wife;

(B) a woman who gives birth to a child by means of assisted reproduction, except as otherwise provided in Article 8 [Article 8 deals with surrogacy]; or

(C) a parent under Article 7 or an intended parent under Article 8.

* * *

(11) "Gestational mother" means an adult woman who gives birth to a child under a gestational agreement.

(15) "Paternity index" means the likelihood of paternity calculated by computing the ratio between:

(A) the likelihood that the tested man is the father, based on the genetic markers of the tested man, mother, and child, conditioned on the hypothesis that the tested man is the father of the child; and

(B) the likelihood that the tested man is not the father, based on the genetic markers of the tested man, mother, and child, conditioned on the hypothesis that the tested man is not the father of the child and that the father is of the same ethnic or racial group as the tested man.

(16) "Presumed father" means a man who, by operation of law under Section 204, is recognized as the father of a child until that status is rebutted or confirmed in a judicial proceeding.

(17) "Probability of paternity" means the measure, for the ethnic or racial group to which the alleged father belongs, of the probability that the man in question is the father of the child, compared with a random, unrelated man of the same ethnic or racial group, expressed as a percentage incorporating the paternity index and a prior probability.

§ 106. Determination of Maternity.

Provisions of this Act relating to determination of paternity apply to determinations of maternity.

§ 201. Establishment of Parent—Child Relationship.

(a) The mother-child relationship is established between a woman and a child by:

(1) the woman's having given birth to the child, except as otherwise provided in Article 8 [surrogacy];

(2) an adjudication of the woman's maternity; or

(3) adoption of the child by the woman; or

(4) an adjudication confirming the woman as a parent of a child born to a gestational mother if the agreement was validated under Article 8 or is enforceable under other law.

(b) The father-child relationship is established between a man and a child by:

(1) an unrebutted presumption of the man's paternity of the child under Section 204;

(2) an effective acknowledgment of paternity by the man under Article 3, unless the acknowledgment has been rescinded or successfully challenged;

(3) an adjudication of the man's paternity;

(4) adoption of the child by the man; or

(5) the man's having consented to assisted reproduction by a woman under Article 7 which resulted in the birth of the child; or

(6) an adjudication confirming the man as a parent of a child born to a gestational mother if the agreement was validated under Article 8 or is enforceable under other law.

§ 202. No Discrimination Based on Marital Status.

A child born to parents who are not married to each other has the same rights under the law as a child born to parents who are married to each other.

§ 204. Presumption of Paternity in Context of Marriage.[6]

(a) A man is presumed to be the father of a child if:

---

6 The 1973 version of the UPA had a presumption of paternity that applied when "a man 'receives the child into his home and openly holds out the child as his natural child. . . .' This presumption was not carried forward [to the 2000 UPA] because genetic testing is a far better means of determining paternity." 2000 UPA, Comment to § 204. You will observe that this now omitted presumption *is* the law in the California and Colorado cases in the book.

(1) he and the mother of the child are married to each other and the child is born during the marriage;

(2) he and the mother of the child were married to each other and the child is born within 300 days after the marriage is terminated by death, annulment, declaration of invalidity, or divorce, or after a decree of separation;

(3) before the birth of the child, he and the mother of the child married each other in apparent compliance with law, even if the attempted marriage is or could be declared invalid, and the child is born during the invalid marriage or within 300 days after its termination by death, annulment, declaration of invalidity, or divorce, or after a decree of separation;

(4) after the birth of the child, he and the mother of the child married each other in apparent compliance with law, whether or not the marriage is or could be declared invalid, and he voluntarily asserted his paternity of the child, and:

   (A) the assertion is in a record filed with [state agency maintaining birth records];

   (B) he agreed to be and is named as the child's father on the child's birth certificate; or

   (C) he promised in a record to support the child as his own; or for the first two years of the child's life, he resided in the same household with the child and openly held out the child as his own.

(b) A presumption of paternity established under this section may be rebutted only by adjudication under Article 6.

§ 301. Acknowledgment of Paternity.[7]

The mother of a child and a man claiming to be the genetic father of the child may sign an acknowledgment of paternity with intent to establish the man's paternity.

§ 302. Execution of Acknowledgement of Paternity.

(a) An acknowledgment of paternity must:

---

7 A "voluntary declaration of paternity has long been an alternative to a contested paternity suit." 2000 UPA, Prefatory Comment to Article 3.

(1) be in a record;

(2) be signed, or otherwise authenticated, under penalty of perjury by the mother and by the man seeking to establish his paternity;

(3) state that the child whose paternity is being acknowledged:

(A) does not have a presumed father, or has a presumed father whose full name is stated; and

(B) does not have another acknowledged or adjudicated father;

(4) state whether there has been genetic testing and, if so, that the acknowledging man's claim of paternity is consistent with the results of the testing; and

(5) state that the signatories understand that the acknowledgment is the equivalent of a judicial adjudication of paternity of the child and that a challenge to the acknowledgment is permitted only under limited circumstances and is barred after two years.

(b) an acknowledgment of paternity is void if it:

(1) states that another man is a presumed father, unless a denial of paternity signed or otherwise authenticated by the presumed father is filed with the [agency maintaining birth records];

(2) states that another man is an acknowledged or adjudicated father; or

(3) falsely denies the existence of a presumed, acknowledged, or adjudicated father of the child.

(c) A presumed father may sign or otherwise authenticate an acknowledgment of paternity.

§ 303. Denial of Paternity.

A presumed father may sign a denial of paternity. The denial is valid only if:

(1) an acknowledgment of paternity signed, or otherwise authenticated, by another man is filed pursuant to Section 305;

(2) the denial is in a record, and is signed, or otherwise authenticated, under penalty of perjury; and

(3) the presumed father has not previously:

(A) acknowledged his paternity, unless the previous acknowledgment has been rescinded pursuant to Section 307 or successfully challenged pursuant to Section 308; or

(B) been adjudicated to be the father of the child.

§ 304. Rules for Acknowledgment and Denial of Paternity.

(a) An acknowledgment of paternity and a denial of paternity may be contained in a single document or may be signed in counterparts, and may be filed separately or simultaneously. If the acknowledgement and denial are both necessary, neither is valid until both are filed.

(b) An acknowledgment of paternity or a denial of paternity may be signed before the birth of the child.

(c) Subject to subsection (a), an acknowledgment of paternity or denial of paternity takes effect on the birth of the child or the filing of the document with the [agency maintaining birth records], whichever occurs later.

(d) An acknowledgment of paternity or denial of paternity signed by a minor is valid if it is otherwise in compliance with this Act.

§ 305. Effect of Acknowledgment or Denial of Paternity.

(a) Except as otherwise provided in Sections 307 and 308, a valid acknowledgment of paternity filed with the [agency maintaining birth records] is equivalent to an adjudication of paternity of a child and confers upon the acknowledged father all of the rights and duties of a parent.

(b) Except as otherwise provided in Sections 307 and 308, a valid denial of paternity by a presumed father filed with the [agency maintaining birth records] in conjunction with a valid acknowledgment of paternity is equivalent to an adjudication of the nonpaternity of the presumed father and discharges the presumed father from all rights and duties of a parent.

§ 307. Proceeding for Rescission.

A signatory may rescind an acknowledgment of paternity or denial of paternity by commencing a proceeding to rescind before the earlier of:

(1) 60 days after the effective date of the acknowledgment or denial, as provided in Section 304; or

(2) the date of the first hearing, in a proceeding to which the signatory is a party, before a court to adjudicate an issue relating to the child, including a proceeding that establishes support.

§ 308. Challenge After Expiration of Period for Rescission.

(a) After the period for rescission under Section 307 has expired, a signatory of an acknowledgment of paternity or denial of paternity may commence a proceeding to challenge the acknowledgment or denial only:

(1) on the basis of fraud, duress, or material mistake of fact; and

(2) within two years after the acknowledgment or denial is filed with the [agency maintaining birth records].

(b) A party challenging an acknowledgment of paternity or denial of paternity has the burden of proof.

§ 401. Establishment of Registry.

A registry of paternity is established in the [agency maintaining the registry].

§ 402. Registration for Notification.

(a) Except as otherwise provided in subsection (b) or Section 405, a man who desires to be notified of a proceeding for adoption of, or termination of parental rights regarding, a child that he may have fathered must register in the registry of paternity before the birth of the child or within 30 days after the birth.

(b) A man is not required to register if:

(1) a father-child relationship between the man and the child has been established under this Act or other law; or

(2) the man commences a proceeding to adjudicate his paternity before the court has terminated his parental rights.

(c) A registrant shall promptly notify the registry in a record of any change in the information registered. The [agency maintaining the registry] shall incorporate all new information received into its records but need not affirmatively seek to obtain current information for incorporation in the registry.

§ 403. Notice of Proceeding.

Notice of a proceeding for the adoption of, or termination of parental rights regarding, a child must be given to a registrant who has timely registered. Notice must be given in a manner prescribed for service of process in a civil action.

§ 404. Termination of Parental Rights: Child Under One Year of Age.

The parental rights of a man who may be the father of a child may be terminated without notice if:

(1) the child has not attained one year of age at the time of the termination of parental rights;

(2) the man did not register timely with the [agency maintaining the registry]; and

(3) the man is not exempt from registration under Section 402.

§ 405. Termination of Parental Rights: Child at Least One Year of Age.

(a) If a child has attained one year of age, notice of a proceeding for adoption of, or termination of parental rights regarding, the child must be given to every alleged father of the child, whether or not he has registered with the [agency maintaining the registry].

(b) Notice must be given in a manner prescribed for service of process in a civil action.

§ 501. Scope of Article.

This article governs genetic testing of an individual to determine parentage, whether the individual:

(1) voluntarily submits to testing; or

(2) is tested pursuant to an order . . . .

§ 502. Order for Testing.

(a) Except as otherwise provided in this article and Article 6, the court shall order the child and other designated individuals to submit to genetic testing if the request for testing is supported by the sworn statement of a party to the proceeding:

(1) alleging paternity and stating facts establishing a reasonable probability of the requisite sexual contact between the individuals; or

(2) denying paternity and stating facts establishing a possibility that sexual contact between the individuals, if any, did not result in the conception of the child.

(b) A support-enforcement agency may order genetic testing only if there is no presumed, acknowledged, or adjudicated father.

(c) If a request for genetic testing of a child is made before birth, the court or support-enforcement agency may not order in-utero testing.

(d) If two or more men are subject to court-ordered genetic testing, the testing may be ordered concurrently or sequentially.

§ 505. Genetic Testing Results; Rebuttal.

(a) Under this Act, a man is rebuttably identified as the father of a child if the genetic testing complies with this article and the results disclose that:

(1) the man has at least a 99 percent probability of paternity, using a prior probability of 0.50, as calculated by using the combined paternity index obtained in the testing; and

(2) a combined paternity index of at least 100 to 1.

(b) A man identified under subsection (a) as the father of the child may rebut the genetic testing results only by other genetic testing satisfying the requirements of this article which:

(1) excludes the man as a genetic father of the child; or

(2) identifies another man as the possible father of the child.

§ 601. Proceeding Authorized.

A civil proceeding may be maintained to adjudicate the parentage of a child. The proceeding is governed by the rules of civil procedure.

§ 602. Standing to Maintain Proceeding.[8]

Subject to Article 3 and Sections 607 and 609, a proceeding to adjudicate parentage may be maintained by:

(1) the child;

(2) the mother of the child;

(3) a man whose paternity of the child is to be adjudicated;

(4) the support-enforcement agency [or other governmental agency authorized by other law];

---

8 "This section grants standing to a broad range of individuals and agencies to bring a parentage proceeding." 2000 UPA, Comment to § 602.

(5) an authorized adoption agency or licensed child-placing agency; or

(6) a representative authorized by law to act for an individual who would otherwise be entitled to maintain a proceeding but who is deceased, incapacitated, or a minor [; or

(7) an intended parent under Article 8 [surrogacy].

607. Limitation: Child Having Presumed Father.

(a) Except as otherwise provided in subsection (b), a proceeding brought by a presumed father, the mother, or another individual to adjudicate the parentage of a child having a presumed father must be commenced not later than two years after the birth of the child.

(b) A proceeding seeking to disprove the father-child relationship between a child and the child's presumed father may be maintained at any time if the court determines that:

(1) the presumed father and the mother of the child neither cohabited nor engaged in sexual intercourse with each other during the probable time of conception; and

(2) the presumed father never openly held out the child as his own.

§ 609. Limitation: Child Having Acknowledged or Adjudicated Father.

(a) If a child has an acknowledged father, a signatory to the acknowledgment of paternity or denial of paternity may commence a proceeding seeking to rescind the acknowledgement or denial or challenge the paternity of the child only within the time allowed under Section 307 or 308.

(b) If a child has an acknowledged father or an adjudicated father, an individual, other than the child, who is neither a signatory to the acknowledgment of paternity nor a party to the adjudication and who seeks an adjudication of paternity of the child must commence a proceeding not later than two years after the effective date of the acknowledgment or adjudication.

(c) A proceeding under this section is subject to the application of the principles of estoppel established in [an omitted Section of the UPA].

§ 622. Consequences of Declining Genetic Testing.

(a) An order for genetic testing is enforceable by contempt.

(b) If an individual whose paternity is being determined declines to submit to genetic testing ordered by the court, the court for that reason may adjudicate parentage contrary to the position of that individual.

(c) Genetic testing of the mother of a child is not a condition precedent to testing the child and a man whose paternity is being determined. If the mother is unavailable or declines to submit to genetic testing, the court may order the testing of the child and every man whose paternity is being adjudicated.

Many states that adopt the UPA alter the Act. Thus, only about half the states have a putative father registry. Some states add to the list of presumed fathers. California and Colorado, for example, add as a presumed parent a man or woman who receives a child into her or his home and openly holds out the child as his or her natural child.[9]

Case Law on Parentage—UPA in Action

The cases in this section grapple with various aspects of parentage. We begin with the Colorado Supreme Court's decision in *N.A.H and A.H. v. S.L.S.*, which is a good introduction to the day-to-day workings of the UPA.

N.A.H. and A.H. v. S.L.S.

Supreme Court of Colorado
9 P.3d 354 (2000)

Kourlis, J.

This case concerns the interpretation of Colorado's Uniform Parentage Act (the UPA), and causes us to determine what considerations that Act directs the courts to include in making paternity decisions. Specifically, the case involves a young girl, S.R.H., who was born in 1994, when her mother was married to N.A.H. (Husband). N.A.H. was identified on the birth certificate as her father and accepted the child into his home. However, genetic tests demonstrate that, in fact, S.L.S. (Biological Father) is the biological father of S.R.H.. Pursuant to

---

9 Cal. Family Code § 7611(d).

Colorado statutes, both men can claim a presumption of being S.R.H.'s legal father. Because a child can have only one legal father, the court must resolve the competing presumptions afforded these two men and adjudicate paternity for the child. Colorado's UPA specifies that in the face of conflicting presumptions, courts should look to the weight of policy and logic in settling the conflict and adjudicating paternity. Accordingly, we determine that a question of paternity is not automatically resolved by biological testing, but rather calls upon the courts to consider the best interests of the child in analyzing policy and logic as directed by the statute.

We hold that the best interests of the child must be of paramount concern throughout a paternity proceeding, and therefore, must be explicitly considered as a part of the policy and logic analysis that is used to resolve competing presumptions of fatherhood.

In this case, the magistrate did not make express findings on the best interests of the child when he adjudicated Biological Father as the child's legal father. The court of appeals upheld the magistrate's adjudication, even absent such findings. Since we conclude that the court must address the best interests of the child, we reverse the court of appeals and remand the case for further proceedings.

On June 28, 1994, A.H. (Mother) gave birth to a baby girl, S.R.H. At the time of S.R.H.'s conception and birth, Mother was married to Husband and they lived together. Husband attended the child's birth, was listed on the birth certificate as the father, and accepted S.R.H. as his own child.

During their twenty-year marriage, the couple periodically experienced marital difficulties and had a history of domestic violence. On one occasion, Mother temporarily moved out of state, and on another occasion, she visited a safe house for counseling for victims of domestic violence.

At a time when she and Husband were having difficulties, Mother became involved in an extramarital affair with a coworker, Biological Father. Mother would visit Biological Father's home, telling him that she did not want to return to her home because she feared Husband. During this time, Mother and Biological Father conceived S.R.H. Mother told Biological Father that he was the real father and that he would be listed on the birth certificate. For approximately eighteen months after S.R.H. was born, Mother left the child in Biological Father's care for ten hours every Friday while Mother worked. Biological Father also took S.R.H. on a weeklong trip out of state to meet his relatives.

Mother and Husband separated in November 1995, and she filed for dissolution of marriage. She alleged that Husband had assaulted her, and that he had not bonded with S.R.H. Shortly thereafter, however, Mother and Husband reconciled and began attending marriage counseling. In January 1996, Mother abruptly terminated Biological Father's visits with S.R.H.

As a result, Biological Father petitioned for a determination of his parent-child relationship with S.R.H. on March 5, 1996. Husband was unaware that S.R.H. was not his biological daughter until Biological Father initiated this action.

After an initial hearing on April 22, 1996, the magistrate ordered genetic testing of the parties to determine whether Biological Father was, in fact, S.R.H.'s biological father. . . . The tests revealed that Biological Father could not be excluded as S.R.H.'s biological father, and that the probability of his parentage was 99.68% when compared to an untested, unrelated Caucasian male.

[T]he magistrate issued an order declaring Biological Father to be the legal father. The magistrate recognized that under state law, Husband and Biological Father each were entitled to a presumption of legal fatherhood. He also recognized that the paternity statute required him to resolve the competing presumptions by considering policy and logic. He then stated,

In this case the logically persuasive presumption is that the DNA testing is the most accurate way to determine who the father of the child may be. That individual is [Biological Father]. Therefore, unless this presumption is outweighed by considerations of public policy, it must control. The facts in this case do not rise to the level of showing that public policy would be served by declaring the respondent, [Husband], to be the father of the child. The Court acknowledges that [Husband] is and will continue to be an excellent and committed parent. However, this is not a case in which the Court is to select which male will do a better job of being the father of the child. [Biological Father] isn't just the sperm donor. He has shown that he wishes to be actively involved in the child's life. The record reflects that, throughout the life of the child, [Biological Father] has made reasonable attempts to see the child and be a part of the child's life. Although the Court recognizes that there continues to be a strong presumption of legitimacy, that presumption is overcome by the logic of the scientific evidence.

. . . The court then took additional testimony, which was directed at allocating parenting time, the reintroduction of Biological Father into S.R.H.'s life, and child support. . . . He also ordered S.R.H.'s name to be changed, and the parties to work with a psychologist to formulate a plan to integrate Biological Father into S.R.H.'s life. . . .

The court of appeals upheld the . . . ruling that Biological Father is S.R.H.'s legal father.

At the outset, we note the extraordinary importance of the outcome of a paternity proceeding. Such a proceeding determines who a child's legal father will be, and therefore, who will enjoy the rights and responsibilities of legal fatherhood. Parenthood in our complex society comprises much more than biological ties, and litigants increasingly are asking courts to address issues that involve delicate balances between traditional expectations and current realities. The determination of parenthood includes the right to parenting time; the right to direct the child's activities; the right to make decisions regarding the control, education, and health of the child; and the right to the child's services and earnings. Legal fatherhood imposes significant obligations as well, including the obligation of support and the obligation to teach moral standards, religious beliefs, and good citizenship.

The UPA recognizes this by providing a mechanism to choose among competing presumptions: If two or more presumptions arise which conflict with each other, the presumption which on the facts is founded on the weightier considerations of policy and logic controls. Competing presumptions must be resolved, because although a child certainly can have emotional attachments to more than one father figure, she can have only one legal father.

In this case, competing presumptions of legal fatherhood arise. Husband benefits from two presumptions: the presumption of legitimacy and the presumption occasioned by accepting the child into his home and holding her out as his own. The presumption of legitimacy declares that a man is presumed to be the natural father of a child if: he and the child's natural mother are or have been married to each other and the child is born during the marriage. A strong public policy supports this presumption. The presumption associated with accepting the child as his own is closely related to the presumption of legitimacy and arises when a man receives the child into his home and openly holds out the child as his natural child.

Biological Father benefits from a competing presumption that presumes a man to be a child's legal father if genetic testing reveals that he is the biological father. . . .

The presumption of legitimacy of a child born during wedlock is overcome if the court finds that the conclusion of the experts conducting the tests, as disclosed by the evidence based upon the tests, shows that the husband or wife is not the parent of the child. . . .

Our task in this case is to determine what the General Assembly has directed courts to do in the situation presented by the facts of this case. The first question must be whether there are genuine competing presumptions, or whether one of the men who claims fatherhood is entitled to a conclusive determination.

We note that the parties have not themselves argued that biology defeats all other presumptions and conclusively establishes fatherhood. However, we address the issue in the interest of completeness.

Nowhere in the statutes does the General Assembly identify any presumption as conclusive. Specifically, section 19–4–105 does not indicate that the presumption of legitimacy automatically outweighs the presumption of biology, or that the converse is true. In fact, no section of the UPA suggests that one presumption of fatherhood should be absolute or conclusive. Rather, the paternity statute indicates that any of the presumptions may be rebutted by clear and convincing evidence. . . .

Similarly, the evidentiary statute does not conclusively elevate a biological presumption over other presumptions. That statute indicates that the presumption of legitimacy is overcome "if the court finds that the conclusion of the experts conducting the tests, as disclosed by the evidence based upon the tests, shows that the husband or wife is not the parent of the child," it does not state that blood evidence is conclusive of fatherhood in all circumstances, or that it automatically eliminates other presumptions of fatherhood. Additionally, although the evidentiary statute states that evidence of biological fatherhood must be admitted and that a biological presumption must attach, the presumption based on biology is still rebuttable. . . .

. . . We conclude that the statute contemplates that neither the presumption of legitimacy nor the presumption based on biology is conclusive. Rather, the statutory scheme as a whole indicates that all presumptions are rebuttable, including the presumption based on biology. The statutes allow for the creation of various presumptions in favor of men who have claims to fatherhood of a child. When those presumptions conflict, then the statute directs the courts to resolve them on the basis of policy and logic. Accordingly, the next step is to analyze what the courts must consider in the policy and logic equation.

The petitioners, Husband and Mother, argue that we should reverse the magistrate's determination of paternity because the magistrate failed to consider explicitly the best interests of the child as part of the policy and logic used to resolve competing presumptions. We agree, and hold that the best interests of the child must be considered as part of the policy and logic analysis used to decide legal fatherhood. . . . All the facts considered by the trial judge should bear directly on the child's best interests. In some cases, the child's best interests may not match the best interests of any of the adults involved. Perhaps, as King Solomon observed many centuries ago in a battle over parentage, the true parent is the one who can elevate the best interests of the child over his or her own best interests. . . .

Given our conclusion that a court must apply the best interests of the child standard in weighing competing presumptions, we must now turn to the ultimate question of whether the magistrate in this case did so. We conclude that the findings are insufficient to convince us that he did apply the best interests standard, and thus, we remand the case.

Justice Coats, dissenting:

Today a majority of the court holds that in a paternity proceeding in Colorado, the question of paternity is not automatically resolved by establishing the genetic or biological father of the child. Rather, the majority holds that the best interests of the child are paramount and must be explicitly considered by a court in deciding which of two presumptive natural fathers should be declared the legal father of the child, even after court-ordered genetic testing has proven as a matter of scientific fact that one cannot possibly be, and the other almost certainly is, the child's biological father. Because I do not understand Colorado's statutes the same way, I respectfully dissent. . . .

In light of the legislature's evidentiary treatment of genetic tests that definitively exclude certain individuals from the class of possible parents, I do not believe this case calls for us to resolve conflicting presumptions of paternity. . . . While I wholeheartedly agree with the majority that the best interests of the child are paramount in affixing the incidents of the parent-child relationship, . . . it seems clear to me from the statutory scheme as a whole that the first requirement of a paternity proceeding is to determine, to the extent possible, the natural or biological father of the child. That being the case, the best interests of the child can be (and expressly are) taken into account in a host of other ways by the statutes, but they cannot change the fact of paternity. . . .

[O]nce the husband has been excluded by genetic testing, at least any presumption of his fatherhood arising from the timing of the marriage has been rebutted and ceases to exist.

In the proceeding below, the presumption of legitimacy favoring the husband of the child's mother was rebutted in precisely this manner. The husband enjoyed a presumption that he was the child's "natural" father . . . simply because he was married to the child's mother when the child was born. Belatedly, he submitted to DNA testing, the results of which were admitted into evidence without objection. The unchallenged conclusion from those tests was that he could not be the child's biological father. Therefore, without regard to the genetic testing of anyone else, and whether or not a presumption arose in any other man as the result of additional genetic testing, the presumption of legitimacy was overcome . . . .

[A]ny presumption of paternity is overcome by genetic testing that conclusively excludes the beneficiary of that presumption from the class of possible fathers. . . .

In this case, the petitioner, who was claiming to be the child's biological father even though he had not been married to the child's mother at the time of the birth, also submitted to genetic testing. The result of those tests, which were also admitted into evidence without objection, indicated a probability of 99.68% that he was the biological father . . . .

Colorado's Uniform Parentage Act contains a number of indications that the term "paternity" refers to actually fathering a child. . . .

The majority concludes that the General Assembly intended the whole paternity proceeding to be about the best interests of the child and therefore that the trial court must focus on best interests in resolving conflicting presumptions of paternity. . . .

Today's holding, in effect, permits biological fathers to be divested of all parental rights without any showing of waiver, estoppel, or forfeiture brought about by their conduct. . . .

Because I understand the existing statutory scheme to require a declaration of the existence of the father-child relationship between a child and an alleged father who has proven himself to be the child's biological father to the satisfaction of the court in an action pursuant to section 19–4–107, I would affirm the judgment below. I therefore respectfully dissent.

Questions based on *N.A.H. and A.H. v. S.L.S.*

1. The majority in *N.A.H. and A.H. v. S.L.S.* states, "although a child certainly can have emotional attachments to more than one father figure, she can have only one legal father." Apparently, the majority believes it is established beyond peradventure that there can be only one legal father. Is a "one and only one father" rule established beyond question in *your* mind? There can be no doubt that the tradition in our society is one mother and one father. Might it be time to rethink the "one and only one" rule? The majority of the Colorado Supreme Court emphasized the overriding importance of the child's best interests. Is it possible that, in some cases, a child's best interests are best served by recognizing two fathers?

Suppose a child's mother is dead, and two men are presumed fathers. Obviously, a child can have two parents. Could the two parents be men—two fathers?

2. Do you favor the majority or the dissent in *N.A.H. and A.H. v. S.L.S.*? Does it make sense to conclude that biology should always prevail? Isn't the majority correct when it concludes that the overriding factor should be the child's best interests? On the other hand, Justice Coats makes a credible argument in favor of biology. We will encounter the idea that blood is thicker than water again in this chapter and in chapters discussing adoption and visitation with children by adults who are not biological parents.

3. How would *N.A.H. and A.H. v. S.L.S.* be decided under the Uniform Parentage Act, *supra*?

The next case is also from Colorado. Again we see competing presumptions under the UPA.

Interest of C.L.S.

Colorado Court of Appeals
2011 WL 5865898 (2011)

Bernard, J.

When two men seek to be declared the father of a child, Colorado's paternity statutes establish a process to resolve their claims and to declare which man will be the child's father under the law. The statutes accomplish this end by creating presumptions of paternity. . . . If two men each establish a presumption that is not rebutted, the statutes prescribe a method for resolving the conflict between them: the trial court determines which presumption should control based on the weightier considerations of policy and logic. Our supreme court addressed this method in *N.A.H. v. S.L.S.*, 9 P.3d 354, 359–65 (Colo.2000), concluding that it must include consideration of the child's best interests.

In this case, two men each established presumptions of paternity that were not rebutted. To resolve these competing presumptions, the magistrate applied the statutory method and, as a result, named one of them the child's legal father. . . .

S.V. (mother) and T.V. (husband) had been married a short time when a son, C.L.S., was conceived in early 2006. Mother also had a short, intimate relationship with T.R.S. (boyfriend) at the same time.

Mother filed for dissolution of marriage later in 2006, before the son was born. Mother and husband executed a separation agreement a few days before the son's birth, which did not refer to any children or a pregnancy. The dissolution decree, issued in February 2007 after the son was born at the end of 2006, also does not refer to any children.

At the time of the son's birth, his birth certificate did not list a father.

Mother and boyfriend began dating again in the spring of 2007, about three months after the son was born. Genetic testing was performed a short time later. It excluded boyfriend as the son's biological father. However, although he was aware of these results, boyfriend acted as the son's father, signed an acknowledgement of paternity, and added his name to the son's birth certificate as the son's father.

Mother did not notify husband that boyfriend had been listed on the birth certificate as the son's father. Husband did not know that boyfriend had formally acknowledged being the son's father.

Boyfriend, mother, and the son then began to live together. Mother and boyfriend had another child. They ended their relationship in the summer of 2008. Boyfriend then asked a court to grant him parental responsibilities for the son. The court awarded him some parenting time. He paid mother child support, and maintained health insurance on both children.

In the course of applying for governmental benefits, mother worked with the local child support enforcement unit. Based on information that mother provided, the enforcement unit sought an order establishing husband as the son's legal father and requiring him to pay mother a regular amount to support the son. In October 2008, genetic testing established a 99.99% probability that husband was the son's biological father.

Once the enforcement unit learned that boyfriend had signed an acknowledgement that he was the son's father and that boyfriend's name had been placed on the son's birth certificate, the unit filed this case to determine the son's legal father, naming both husband and boyfriend. Husband then sought an allocation of parental responsibilities for the son.

After a hearing, the magistrate entered a series of findings. First, he found that there were competing statutory presumptions of paternity. On the one hand, husband was presumed to be the son's legal father because he was married to mother when the child was conceived and born, and genetic testing indicated that he was the son's biological father. On the other hand, boyfriend was presumed to be the son's legal father because he voluntarily acknowledged that he was the son's father, and he held the son out as his child.

Second, the magistrate made findings about husband's and boyfriend's conduct. Husband knew mother was pregnant when they separated and before their marriage was dissolved; however he did not take any action to claim the son as his child. Boyfriend knew that he was not the son's biological father, but he decided to have his name entered on the son's birth certificate as the son's father, and he cared for the son as his own child while he lived with mother.

Third, the magistrate resolved the competing presumptions of paternity by finding that it was in the child's best interests to declare boyfriend to be the son's legal father.

Husband asked the district court to review the magistrate's order. He asserted that the facts did not establish the statutory presumption that boyfriend voluntarily acknowledged that he was the son's father. . . .

The district court concluded that the magistrate's finding that boyfriend satisfied the statutory presumption that he voluntarily acknowledged paternity "appeared to be error." This statutory presumption requires that any other man presumed to be the father must consent in writing to the acknowledgement. That did not happen here. However, the district court concluded that this error was "ultimately harmless" because boyfriend had also established a second presumption of paternity.

. . . Reviewing the magistrate's order . . . , the district court upheld the magistrate's decision. . . .

Colorado's paternity statutes are based on the Uniform Parentage Act (UPA). . . . Our paternity statutes establish a mechanism for establishing a father-child relationship. The first step in this process is determining whether a man is presumed to be a child's father. There are six statutory presumptions. § 19–4–105(1)(a)–(f).

The magistrate found that four of these presumptions existed here. Two applied to husband:

- § 19–4–105(1)(a) (the man and the child's mother were married and the child was born during the marriage) (also known as the presumption of legitimacy); and

- § 19–4–105(1)(f) (genetic tests establish that the probability of a man's parentage of the child is 97% or higher) (also known as the presumption of biology).

Two applied to boyfriend:

- § 19–4–105(1)(d) (the man received the child into his home and openly held the child out as his natural child); and

- § 19–4–105(1)(e) (the man acknowledges his paternity in writing, but, if another man is also presumed to be the father, the other man has given written consent to the acknowledgement).

Once presumptions are established, they may be rebutted by clear and convincing evidence. That did not occur here. However, on review, the district court determined that the evidence did not support one of the presumptions applying to boyfriend because husband did not provide written consent for boyfriend to acknowledge the son as his child. Thus, the district court concluded, this presumption was rebutted, in effect, because one of the factors necessary to establish it was not met.

The second step in the process occurs after the presumptions are established and have not been rebutted. If two or more presumptions arise which conflict with each other, the presumption which on the facts is founded on the weightier considerations of policy and logic controls. . . .

None of the statutory presumptions of paternity is conclusive. That means, as relevant here, that neither the presumption of biology, nor the presumption of legitimacy, is conclusive, and neither presumption automatically eliminates other presumptions of fatherhood.

Assuming that competing presumptions have not been disproved by clear and convincing evidence, the trial court must then decide . . . which man should be declared the child's legal father based on the weightier considerations of policy and logic. This is a fact-intensive inquiry; all the facts considered should bear directly on the child's best interests; and the trial court resolves the competing presumptions by focusing on the best interests of the child and making determinations of paternity with that standard at the forefront. . . .

The result of a final determination of paternity is to render one presumptive father the child's parent. The other presumptive father becomes a nonparent who does not have rights to visit a child or to make any decisions about the child's education, health, or upbringing. This is because a child can have only one legal father.

The legislature [added] eight factors that the judge or magistrate shall consider when evaluating the weightier considerations of policy and logic. At least five of the eight factors focus on the child, such as the length of time during which the presumed father has assumed the role of father of the child, the nature of the father-child relationship, the age of the child, the relationship of the child to any presumed father or fathers, and any other factors that may affect the equities arising from the disruption of the father-child relationship between the child and the presumed father or fathers or the chance of other harm to the child. . . .

[The Court of Appeal agreed with the lower court's decision and affirmed].

Comment and Question

1. You are probably familiar the saying, "It takes a village to raise a child." Well, apparently the village is only big enough for only one dad. The man who loses a paternity fight has no rights. As the Colorado Court of Appeals put it, the losing "presumptive father becomes a nonparent who does not have rights to visit a child or to make any decisions about the child's education, health, or upbringing. This is because a child can have only one legal father." To repeat an earlier question, does the "one and only one father" rule make sense?

2. How would *Interest of C.L.S.* play out under the Uniform Parentage Act, *supra*.?

The 2000 version of the Uniform Parentage Act allows a man who is not a presumed father to bring a paternity action (UPA § 602). California parentage law is more restrictive. Under California law, only presumed fathers normally can sue to establish paternity. In *Adoption of Kelsey S.*, the California Supreme Court crafted a remedy for men who are *not* presumed fathers but who *are* biological fathers and who actively attempt to assume the responsibilities of parenthood.

Adoption of Kelsey S.

California Supreme Court
1 Cal. 4ᵗʰ 816, 823 P.2d 1216 (1992)

Baxter, J.

The primary question in this case is whether the father of a child born out of wedlock may properly be denied the right to withhold his consent to his child's adoption by third parties despite his diligent and legal attempts to obtain custody of his child and to rear it himself, and absent any showing of the father's unfitness as a parent. We conclude that, under these circumstances, the federal constitutional guarantees of equal protection and due process require that the father be allowed to withhold his consent to his child's adoption and therefore that his parental rights cannot be terminated absent a showing of his unfitness. . . .

Kari S. (mother) gave birth to Kelsey, a boy, on May 18, 1988. The child's undisputed natural father is petitioner Rickie M. He and Kari S. were not married to one another. . . . Father was aware that mother planned to place their child for adoption, and he objected to her decision because he wanted to rear the child.

Two days after the child's birth, father filed an action in superior court . . . to establish his parental relationship with the child and to obtain custody of the child. . . .

On May 24, 1988, Steven and Suzanne A., the prospective adoptive parents, filed an adoption petition . . . . Their petition alleged that only the mother's consent to the adoption was required because there was no presumed father under [California's version of the Uniform Parentage Act, Family Code section 7611].

On May 31, 1988, the prospective adoptive parents filed a petition to terminate father's parental rights. The superior court consolidated that proceeding with the adoption proceeding.

The parties subsequently stipulated that father was the child's natural father. The superior court, however, ruled that he was not a "presumed father" within the meaning of section 7611. The court held four days of hearings to determine whether it was in the child's best interest for father to retain his parental rights and whether the adoption should be allowed to proceed. On August 26, 1988, the court found "by a bare preponderance" of the evidence that the child's best interest required termination of father's parental rights. Father appealed.

[Since shortly after the child's birth, the child resided in the home of the prospective adoptive parents. The child never lived with Ricky, the biological father.]

Family Code Section 7611 states, "A man is presumed to be the natural father of a child" if the man meets any of several conditions set forth in the statute. Whether a biological father is a "presumed father" under section 7611 is critical to his parental rights. [If a man is a presumed father, his consent to adoption is required. If a presumed father refuses to consent, the adoption cannot proceed unless his parental rights are terminated. His parental rights can only be terminated upon a showing of parental unfitness. By contrast, if a man is an alleged father and not a presumed father, California's adoption statutes give the alleged father no right to withhold consent to adoption. The alleged father has a right to notice of the adoption and the right to be heard. However, if the man is "only" an alleged father, the adoption can proceed if adoption is in the child's best interest. With an alleged father, no showing of parental unfitness is required.]

This statutory scheme creates three classifications of parents: mothers, biological fathers who are presumed fathers, and biological fathers who are not presumed fathers (i.e., natural fathers). A natural father's consent to an adoption of his child by third parties is not required unless the father makes the required showing that retention of his parental rights is in the child's best interest. Consent, however, is required of a mother and a presumed father regardless of the child's best interest. The natural father is therefore treated differently from both mothers and presumed fathers. With this statutory framework in mind, we now examine father's contentions.

A man becomes a "presumed father" under section 7611(d) if he receives the child into his home and openly holds out the child as his natural child. It is undisputed in this case that father openly held out the child as being his own. Father, however, did not physically receive the child into his home. He was prevented from doing so by the mother, by court order, and allegedly also by the prospective adoptive parents.

Mother and the prospective adoptive parents (respondents) contend the statutory scheme allows a mother to preclude her child's father from acquiring presumed father status and thereby eliminate the need for his consent regardless of whether he is a demonstrably fit parent. Father responds that such result is impermissible under the federal constitutional guarantees of equal protection and due process. He claims he should be deemed to be the presumed father under section 7611(d) because he did all that he could do under the circumstances to receive the child into his home. He contends we should not construe the statute in such a way that the mother can unilaterally bar the father from receiving their child into his home and thereby deprive him of presumed father status and the concomitant right . . . to withhold consent to the child's adoption by third parties. . . .

The precise question before us has not been addressed by the United States Supreme Court. We are guided, however, by a series of high court decisions dealing with the rights of unwed fathers. From those decisions, we must attempt to distill the guiding constitutional principles.

In *Stanley v. Illinois*, 405 U.S. 645 (1972), the court held that under the due process clause of the Fourteenth Amendment to the federal Constitution an unmarried father was entitled to a hearing on his fitness as a parent before his children were taken from him. *Stanley* is factually distinguishable because the father in that case had lived intermittently with his children and their mother for 18 years. As the court put it, he had "sired and raised" the children. Unlike in the present case, the children were not infants, and the father had maintained a close relationship with them for many years. Despite these differences from our case, *Stanley* does illuminate our task. The court noted that it had "frequently emphasized the importance of the family. The rights to conceive and to raise one's children has been deemed essential . . . . Nor has the law refused to recognize those family relationships unlegitimized by a marriage ceremony." A father's "interest in retaining custody of his children is cognizable and substantial." More important, the court seemed to indicate that a father's parental rights could not be terminated absent a showing of his unfitness, and that a showing of the child's best interest would be an insufficient basis for termination of the father's rights. . . .

If father is not a presumed parent under section 7611(d) [accepting child into his home and holding the child out as his child], his parental rights may be terminated under [California law] merely by showing that termination would be in the child's best interest. No showing of father's unfitness is required under the statutes. The statutory scheme therefore appears to conflict with the emphasis in *Stanley* on the need for a particularized finding of unfitness. Father was never found to be unfit.

In its next case dealing with unwed fathers, *Quilloin v. Walcott*, 434 U.S. 246 (1978), the court was faced with a situation more similar to the present case. A child was born out of wedlock and was in the custody and control of his mother for his entire life. She and the natural father never married or established a home together. She married another man, and several years later he attempted to adopt the child with her consent. The child was then 11 years old. The natural father attempted to block the adoption and to secure visitation rights, but he did not seek custody or object to the child's continuing to live with the mother and her husband. Under the Illinois statutory scheme, the trial court denied the father's petition to legitimate the child and thereby precluded him from gaining veto power over the child's adoption, on the ground that legitimation was not in the child's best interests. The father claimed he was entitled to recognition and retention of his parental rights absent a showing of unfitness. . . .

A unanimous court in *Quilloin* reiterated that "The relationship between parent and child is constitutionally protected." The court, however, found no denial of either due process or equal protection. As to due process, the court explained, "We have little doubt that the Due Process Clause would be offended if a State were to attempt to force the breakup of a natural family, over the objections of the parents and their children, without some showing of unfitness and for the sole reason that to do so was thought to be in the children's best interest. But this is not a case in which the unwed father at any time had, or sought, actual or legal custody of his child. Nor is this a case in which the proposed adoption would place the child with a new set of parents with whom the child had never before lived. Rather, the result of the adoption in this case is to give full recognition to a family unit already in existence, a result desired by all concerned, except [the father]. Whatever might be required in other situations, we cannot say that the State was required in this situation to find anything more than that the adoption, and denial of legitimation, were in the best interests of the child."

The court also restricted its holding as to equal protection. The father contended he should have the benefit of the same standards applied to married fathers. In rejecting this claim, the court explained, "He has never exercised actual or legal custody over his child, and thus has never shouldered any significant responsibility with respect to the daily supervision, education, protection, or care of the child. Appellant does not complain of his exemption from these responsibilities and, indeed, he does not even now seek custody of his child."

The present case has several of the earmarks the court found lacking in *Quilloin*, and which the court suggested might render invalid a termination of a father's rights based only on a showing of the child's best interest. Those factors are as follows:

(i) Unlike the father in *Quilloin*, father asked the mother for custody of their child and, when rebuffed, immediately (as soon as the child was born) went to court seeking legal custody. He continues to seek legal recognition of his parental rights.

(ii) The mother does not seek to retain the child and have it adopted by a husband. As put by the *Quilloin* court, "The proposed adoption would place the child with a new set of parents with whom the child had never before lived." Of course, we recognize that as a result of the lower courts' decisions the child has now been living with the prospective adoptive parents for more than three years. This fact, however, is not relevant to the analysis of whether father's rights were violated *ab initio*.

(iii) The parties disagree as to the amount of care and support that father provided to the child and its mother. The record is unclear as to whether and to what extent, if any, this dispute affected the trial court's decision that the adoption was barely in the child's best interest. The record is clear, however, that father is not like the natural father in *Quilloin*, who avoided contact with his child until several years after its birth and came forward only when another man tried to adopt it. More important for this part of our analysis, father, also unlike the father in *Quilloin*, did attempt through legal channels to shoulder full responsibility for his child.

In short, the present case is the type of case the high court emphasized it was not deciding in *Quilloin*. By implication, however, the *Quilloin* decision strongly suggests that the parental rights of a [parent in father's] position may not properly be terminated absent a showing of his unfitness as a father. On the present facts, a showing of the child's best interest would appear to be insufficient under *Quilloin*. This conclusion is reinforced by the high court's next decision on the subject. . . .

The high court again considered the rights of biological fathers . . . in *Lehr v. Robertson*, 463 U.S. 248 (1983). The father and mother lived together before the child's birth, and he visited the child in the hospital when the child was born. He did not, however, live with either the mother or child after its birth, and he did not provide them with any financial support. Nor did he offer to marry the mother. Eight months after the child's birth, the mother married another man. When the child was two years old, the mother and her new husband began adoption proceedings. One month later, the biological father filed an action seeking a determination of his paternity, an order of support, and visitation with the child. Shortly thereafter, the biological father learned of the pending adoption proceeding, and almost immediately he sought to have it stayed pending the determination of his paternity petition. The state court informed him that it had already signed the adoption order earlier that day, and then dismissed his paternity action.

Relying on *Stanley* . . . , the biological father contended the New York statutory scheme was unconstitutional on due process and equal protection grounds. First, he argued that a putative father's actual or potential relationship with his child born out of wedlock is a liberty interest that could not be destroyed without due process of law. He therefore contended he had a right to prior notice and an opportunity to be heard before he was deprived of that interest. Second, he contended the equal protection clause of the Fourteenth Amendment was violated because the statutes denied him the right to consent to the adoption and accorded him fewer procedural rights than were given to the mother.

The *Lehr* court rejected the biological father's due process challenge, on the ground that under New York law he could have enrolled in that state's "putative father registry." If he had done so, he would have been statutorily entitled to receive notice of any proceeding to adopt his child. The high court held that the statutory scheme "adequately protected appellant's inchoate interest in establishing a relationship with [the child]." In the present case, father claims no violation of procedural due process based on lack of notice. (He has participated fully in these proceedings since their inception.) Thus, the discussion in *Lehr* of procedural due process does not resolve the substantive question before us.

The court's rejection in *Lehr* of the father's equal protection claim is more relevant to our decision. Under New York law, as in California, the mother of a child (born either in or out of wedlock) is guaranteed the right to veto an adoption of her child unless the mother is found to be unfit as set forth in the statutes. Only some fathers, however, are included within this favored class. In upholding this distinction, the court observed, "The existence or nonexistence of a substantial relationship between parent and child is a relevant criterion in evaluating both the rights of the parent and the best interests of the child." . . .

On its face, *Lehr* does not resolve the dilemma before us. The stated premise of the court's holding was that the equal protection clause does not prevent a state from according a child's biological father fewer rights than the mother if he has "never established a relationship" with the child. The court did not purport to decide the legal question in the present case, that is, whether the mother may constitutionally prevent the father from establishing the relationship that gives rise to his right to equal protection. The *Lehr* court, however, recognized the uniqueness of the biological connection between parent and child. "The significance of the biological connection is that it offers the natural father an opportunity that no other male possesses to develop a relationship with his offspring. If he grasps that opportunity and accepts some measure of responsibility for the child's future, he may enjoy the blessings of the parent-child relationship and make uniquely valuable contributions to the child's development." *Lehr* can fairly be read to mean that a father need only make a reasonable and meaningful attempt to establish a relationship, not that he must be successful against all obstacles. . . .

Although the foregoing high court decisions do not provide a comprehensive rule for all situations involving unwed fathers, one unifying and transcendent theme emerges. The biological connection between father and child is unique and worthy of constitutional protection if the father grasps the opportunity to develop that biological connection into a full and enduring relationship. . . .

Father asserts a violation of equal protection and due process under the federal Constitution; more specifically, that he should not be treated differently from his child's mother. In constitutional terms, the question is whether California's sex-based statutory distinction between biological mothers and fathers serves important governmental objectives and is substantially related to achievement of those objectives. Does the mother's ability to determine the father's rights substantially serve an important governmental interest? The question is the same whether the analysis is undertaken as a matter of due process or equal protection.

There is no dispute that the State's interest in providing for the well-being of illegitimate children is an important one. Although the legal concept of illegitimacy no longer exists in California, the problems and needs of children born out of wedlock are an undisputed reality. The state has an important and valid interest in their well-being.

The more difficult issue is whether the statutory treatment of natural fathers (*i.e.*, biological fathers without presumed status under section 7611) is substantially related to the achievement of that objective. On the facts of this case, the question must be framed as follows: Is the state's important interest in the well-being of a child born out of wedlock substantially furthered by allowing the mother to deny the child's biological father an opportunity to form a relationship with the child that would give the father the same statutory rights as the mother (or a presumed father) in deciding whether the child will be adopted by third parties?

Respondents do not adequately explain how an unwed mother's control over a biological father's rights furthers the state's interest in the well-being of the child. The linchpin of their position, however, is clear although largely implicit: Allowing the biological father to have the same rights as the mother would make adoptions more difficult because the consent of both parents is more difficult to obtain than the consent of the mother alone. This reasoning is flawed in several respects.

Respondents' view too narrowly assumes that the proper governmental objective is adoption. As we have explained, the constitutionally valid objective is the protection of the child's well-being. We cannot conclude in the abstract that adoption is itself a sufficient objective to allow the state to take whatever measures it deems appropriate. Nor can we merely assume, either as a policy or factual matter, that adoption is necessarily in a child's best interest. . . .

If the possible benefit of adoption were by itself sufficient to justify terminating a parent's rights, the state could terminate an unwed mother's parental rights based on nothing more than a showing that her child's best interest would be served by adoption. Of course, that is not the law; nor do the parties advocate such a system. We simply do not in our society take children away from their mothers—married or otherwise—because a "better" adoptive parent can be found. We see no valid reason why we should be less solicitous of a father's efforts to establish a parental relationship with his child. Respondents seem to suggest that a child is inherently better served by adoptive parents than by a single, biological father but that the child is also inherently better served by a single, biological mother than by adoptive parents. The logic of this view is not apparent, and there is no evidence in the record to support such a counterintuitive view.

Nor is there evidence before us that the statutory provisions allowing the mother to determine the father's rights are, in general, substantially related to protecting the child's best interest. As a matter of cold efficiency, we cannot disagree that eliminating a natural father's rights would make adoption easier in some cases. That, however, begs the question because it assumes an unwed mother's decision to permit an immediate adoption of her newborn is always preferable to custody by the natural father, even when he is a demonstrably fit parent. We have no evidence to support that assumption. . . .

The lack of any substantial relationship between the state's interest in protecting a child and allowing the mother sole control over its destiny is best demonstrated by the results that can arise when a mother prevents the father from obtaining presumed status under section 7611. We attribute no blame to a mother who seeks to place her child for adoption. Under the statute, the father has basically two ways in which to achieve that status: he can either marry the mother, or he can receive the child into his home and hold it out as his natural child. Of course, the first alternative is entirely within the mother's control. She cannot be forced to marry the father. The second alternative is, for the most part, also within her control. She can deny the father the right to come into her home. She can also deny him the right to take the child into his home. Faced with the mother's denial, the father has only one recourse aside from illegal self-help. He must seek a court order granting him custody so that he can take the child into his home and thereby gain presumed father status. As in this case, however, the trial court may deny him custody based on its view that the child is better served by remaining with the mother or third parties, *e.g.*, prospective adoptive parents. . . .

The anomalies under this statutory scheme become readily apparent. A father who is indisputably ready, willing, and able to exercise the full measure of his parental responsibilities can have his rights terminated merely on a showing that his child's best interest would be served by adoption. If the child's mother, however, were equally of the opposite character—unready, unwilling, and unable—her rights in the child could nevertheless be terminated only [on a showing of unfitness]. Such a distinction bears no substantial relationship to protecting the well-being of children. Indeed, it has little rationality.

The system also leads to irrational distinctions between fathers. Based solely on the mother's wishes, a model father can be denied presumed father status, whereas a father of dubious ability and intent can achieve such status by the fortuitous circumstance of the mother allowing him to come into her home, even if only briefly—perhaps a single day. . . .

Under the statutory scheme, two fathers who are by all accounts equal in their ability and commitment to fulfill their parental missions can be treated differently based solely on the mothers' decisions whether to allow the father to become a presumed father.

. . . . Clearly, the father is treated unfairly under [existing law], but equally important is the loss to the child. The child has a genetic bond with its natural parents that is unique among all relationships the child will have throughout its life. . . . It therefore would be curious to conclude that the child's best interest is served by allowing the one parent (the mother) who wants to sever her legal ties to decide unilaterally that the only other such tie (the father's) will be cut as well. Absent a showing of a father's unfitness, his child is ill-served by allowing its mother effectively to preclude the child from ever having a meaningful relationship with its only other biological parent.

In summary, we hold that [California law that allows adoption of an alleged father's child without proof of unfitness] violates the federal constitutional guarantees of equal protection and due process for unwed fathers to the extent that the statutes allow a mother unilaterally to preclude her child's biological father from becoming a presumed father and thereby allowing the state to terminate his parental rights on nothing more than a showing of the child's best interest. If an unwed father promptly comes forward and demonstrates a full commitment to his parental responsibilities—emotional, financial, and otherwise—his federal constitutional right to due process prohibits the termination of his parental relationship absent a showing of his unfitness as a parent. Absent such a showing, the child's well-being is presumptively best served by continuation of the father's parental relationship. Similarly, when the father has come forward to grasp his parental responsibilities, his parental rights are entitled to equal protection as those of the mother.

A court should consider all factors relevant to that determination. The father's conduct both before and after the child's birth must be considered. Once the father knows or reasonably should know of the pregnancy, he must promptly attempt to assume his parental responsibilities as fully as the mother will allow and his circumstances permit. In particular, the father must demonstrate a willingness himself to assume full custody of the child—not merely to block adoption by others. A court should also consider the father's public acknowledgement of paternity, payment of pregnancy and birth expenses commensurate with his ability to do so, and prompt legal action to seek custody of the child.

We reiterate and emphasize the narrowness of our decision. The statutory distinction between natural fathers and presumed fathers is constitutionally invalid only to the extent it is applied to an unwed father who has sufficiently and timely demonstrated a full commitment to his parental responsibilities. Our statutes are constitutionally sufficient when applied to a father who has failed to make such a showing. . . .

The trial court found that adoption was in the child's best interest. The court, however, did not have the benefit of our decision in this case and thus did not decide the threshold constitutional question of whether father demonstrated a sufficient commitment to his parental responsibilities. Father and the prospective adoptive parents sharply disagree on that question, and the evidence is conflicting in several respects as to father's attempts to fulfill his responsibilities, especially during the period before the child's birth. We therefore conclude the more prudent approach is to remand to the trial court to make the determination in the first instance. In doing so, the trial court must take into account father's conduct throughout the period since he learned he was the biological father, including his conduct during the pendency of this legal proceeding, both in the trial and appellate courts, up to the determination in the trial court on remand by this court. We recognize that during these proceedings father may have been restricted, both legally and as a practical matter, in his ability to act fully as a father. Nevertheless, the trial court must consider whether father has done all that he could reasonably do under the circumstances.

If the trial court finds on remand that father failed to demonstrate the required commitment to his parental responsibilities, that will be the end of the matter. He will not have suffered any deprivation of a constitutional right. If, however, the required commitment is found, the result under our constitutional analysis will necessarily be a decision that father's rights to equal protection and due process under the federal Constitution were violated to the extent that he was deprived of the same statutory protections granted the mother. Therefore, if (but only if) the trial court finds father demonstrated the necessary commitment to his parental responsibilities, there will arise the further question of whether he can be deprived of the right to withhold his consent to the adoption. . . .

Questions and Comments Based on *Kelsey S.*

1. In *Kelsey S.*, the California Supreme Court emphasized the importance of "the biological connection between father and child," describing the connection as "unique and worthy of constitutional protection." The court wrote, "The child has a genetic bond with its natural parents that is unique among all relationships the child will have throughout its life." In *N.A.H. and A.H. v. S.L.S., supra,* the Colorado Supreme Court majority seemed to downplay the importance of biology, and to play up the significance of a child's best interest. What do you think? Is there something unique about the biological parent-child relationship that deserves special protection? If so, why is biology so important? When a judge must select between a fit biological father and a fit presumed father with no genetic connection to a child, should biodad get a "head start" of some kind? Should the scales tip in his favor? If so, what rule do you propose? How much of a head start?

2. In *Kelsey S.*, the California Supreme Court describes several U.S. Supreme Court decisions grappling with the rights of unwed fathers. Can you distill from the U.S. Supreme Court a guiding principle to decide these cases? The California Supreme Court wrote, "One unifying and transcendent theme emerges. The biological connection between father and child is unique and worthy of constitutional protection if the father grasps the opportunity to develop that biological connection into a full and enduring relationship." Did the California Supreme Court capture the essence of the U.S. Supreme Court's thinking?

3. In *Kelsey S.*, the court stated, "We simply do not in our society take children away from their mothers—married or otherwise—because a 'better' adoptive parent can be found." The reality is, however, that there are some pretty terrible parents. Many children would unquestionably be better off with adoptive parents. Yet, unless an incompetent parent meets the legal standard of "unfitness"—a difficult standard to meet—the child remains with the incompetent parent. Would it really be wrong to allow adoption of children whose parents, although falling short of unfitness, *are* incompetent?

By the way, what does "unfit" mean? Can you define it? And when I say, "Can you define it?," I mean, can you define it with sufficient precision that your definition can be applied in court to permanently sever the parent-child relationship? If you succeed in defining "unfit," try your hand at defining "incompetent," which must fall somewhere between "great parenting" and "unfit parenting." Good luck.

4. Cases take years to work their way through the trial and appellate systems.[10] But a child's needs and a child's development are not tied to legal timelines! A child who is an infant-in-arms when her case begins may be in kindergarten when the legal system finally grinds to a conclusion. *Kelsey S.* illustrates the mismatch between child development and the plodding process of litigation. By the time the California Supreme Court decided *Kelsey S.,* the child had been living with her prospective adoptive parents more than three years—her whole life! And the Supreme Court remanded the case for additional time consuming proceedings. What if the trial court decides the biological father's rights were violated, and Kelsey is ordered removed from the only parents she has ever known—the people who loved and cared for her since birth—in order for the child to be turned over to her father, a stranger. Would that make *any* sense? Would such a move sacrifice Kelsey on the altar of her biological father's constitutional rights? Do the adoptive parents have any rights?

5. The core teaching of *Kelsey S.* is that if an unwed father who is not a presumed father wants parental rights, he must act and act quickly. As the California Supreme Court put it, "If an unwed father promptly comes forward and demonstrates a full commitment to his parental responsibilities—emotional, financial, and otherwise—his federal constitutional right to due process prohibits the termination of his parental rights absent a showing of his unfitness as a parent."

6. In *Kelsey S.,* the Supreme Court listed factors to consider in deciding whether biodad acted to preserve his rights: (1) Biodad's conduct before and after the child's birth; (2) Once biodad knows or reasonably should know of the pregnancy, he must promptly attempt to assume his parental responsibilities as fully as mother will allow and his circumstances will permit; (3) Biodad must be willing to assume parental responsibilities himself, not simply seek to block adoption; (4) Did biodad publicly acknowledge paternity?; (5) What financial contributions did biodad make?; (6) Did biodad promptly bring legal action to protect his rights?

Suppose Bobby Sue and Billy Bob date briefly and have sex once. After they have sex, they "break up" and don't socialize. Bobby Sue becomes pregnant, but she does not tell Billy Bob. Is Billy Bob on notice of the pregnancy? The California Supreme Court wrote that biodad must step forward when he knows or *should* know of the pregnancy. Should Billy Bob know of the pregnancy?

---

10 A noteworthy exception to the slow pace of litigation is found in proceedings under the Hague Convention on the Civil Aspects on International Child Abduction, discussed in Chapter 6. Hague Convention cases are often completed with astonishing speed.

7. For a thorough analysis of case law on the right of unwed fathers to block adoption of their children, *see* Ardis L. Campbell, *Rights of Unwed Father to Obstruct Adoption of His Child by Withholding Consent*, 61 A.L.R. 5th 151 (originally published in 1998).

The next case, like *Kelsey S.*, illustrates the potential for heartache when different adults seek custody of a child.

Adoption of O.M.

California Court of Appeal
169 Cal. App. 4th 672, 87 Cal. Rptr. 3d 135 (2008)

Ruvolo, P.J.

A biological father who does not qualify as a statutory presumed father, but who also has not been shown to be an unfit parent, is constitutionally entitled to prevent the termination of his parental rights if, as soon as he knew or should have known of the mother's pregnancy, he demonstrated a full commitment to his parental responsibilities. This entitlement may also exist when the father's attempt to demonstrate such a commitment is unilaterally frustrated by the child's mother. [*See Kelsey S., supra*].

In this case, a biological father's effort to assume his parental responsibilities was frustrated, in part, by the child's mother, who broke off their relationship and decided to relinquish the child for adoption. However, the father's ability to demonstrate his commitment was impeded to a far greater extent by the predictable consequences of his own criminal activity. Under these circumstances, we hold that the father did not make a showing of commitment to his parental responsibilities sufficient to entitle him to a hearing on his fitness before his parental rights could be terminated. Accordingly, we affirm the trial court's order granting the prospective adoptive parents' petition to terminate the biological father's parental rights.

The minor who is the subject of this appeal is O.M., who was born in San Bernardino County on September 11, 2006. O.M.'s biological father is appellant B.R., who was 28 years old at the time of the hearing in the trial court. O.M.'s biological mother is a woman named L.T., who is not a party to this appeal. B.R. and L.T. knew each other for several years before O.M. was born, but were never married, and never lived together.

In February 2006, B.R. learned that L.T. had received a positive result on a home pregnancy test, and he took her to a medical clinic to confirm the result. L.T. was expected to deliver on or about October 17, 2006. B.R. was happy about the pregnancy, and he and L.T. discussed raising the child together. They told B.R.'s parents about the pregnancy, and they were also happy about it.

B.R. has a history of drug use, and between 1998 and 2006, he was convicted of numerous crimes, including possession of marijuana for sale; attempted kidnapping; criminal threats; vandalism; and various Vehicle Code violations. He was on parole when he learned that L.T. was pregnant, but even after he took her to the clinic, he continued to use methamphetamine and marijuana, and avoided his parole officer because he knew he could not pass a drug test. About a week after L.T.'s pregnancy was confirmed, B.R. was arrested for a parole violation, which resulted in his being incarcerated for about four months.

While B.R. was incarcerated, he maintained contact with L.T. by telephone and email, but did not provide her with any material support. She remained on good terms with his parents B.R. Sr. and W.R., however, and they provided her with maternity clothes and some money. During this time, L.T. was arrested for shoplifting, and B.R.'s parents told her they would care for the child if she went to prison.

After B.R. was released from prison, around June 10, 2006, he saw L.T. at least once. At that time, B.R. stopped using drugs for a while. However, L.T. soon resumed her relationship with another man, who was the father of her older child, and began to avoid contact with B.R. He made some efforts to find her, both by physically searching for her and through mutual friends and her mother, A.T., but was unable to contact her. He did not give A.T. or any of L.T.'s friends any correspondence to transmit to L.T., however, and did not attempt to provide her with any money or material support through them, even though he was working and living with his parents at the time.

Meanwhile, respondents T.M. and J.R., who are O.M.'s current caretakers and his prospective adoptive parents, learned through an adoption facilitator that L.T. might be willing to surrender her baby to them, and contacted her in early July 2006. T.M. is a veterinarian, and J.R. is a registered nurse. They are residents of San Francisco, had been domestic partners for over seven years, and had decided to start a family by adopting a child. After making that decision, they contacted an adoption agency in 2005, and successfully completed its screening process for potential adoptive parents.

When T.M. and J.R. met with L.T. in July 2006, she told them that she was interested in placing her baby with a same-sex couple. She also told them, falsely, that she had gotten pregnant from a one-night stand at a party and was not in contact with the baby's father. During L.T.'s pregnancy, T.M. and J.R. helped her move into new housing, and gave her some financial assistance.

L.T. never talked to B.R. about giving up the baby for adoption, but in July or August 2006, he learned from A.T. that she was planning to do so. B.R. wanted to "have some say-so" over his child, and made an appointment with a lawyer to discuss the issue. By then, however, B.R. had begun using methamphetamine again. On August 6, 2006, the day before he was scheduled to meet with the lawyer, B.R. was arrested. He was charged with being a felon in possession of a handgun and ammunition, and possession of methamphetamine for sale. These crimes were alleged to have been committed on the day of his arrest.

On September 10, 2006, T.M. and J.R. learned that L.T. had gone into labor, and they immediately drove to the hospital, where they arrived before O.M. was born. After the birth, L.T. promptly relinquished O.M. to T.M. and J.R., who have had physical custody of him ever since. While L.T. was at the hospital, a friend of B.R.'s, who was dating L.T.'s sister, told B.R.'s parents that L.T. was about to give birth, and they rushed to the hospital. When L.T. saw them there, she confessed to T.M. and J.R. that she had deceived them about her relationship with the baby's father, and explained that he was in prison. She also told them that B.R. had not been very involved with her during the pregnancy.

Later that day, B.R. filed a petition asking the San Bernardino Superior Court to determine that he was the father of L.T.'s baby; to halt any adoption proceedings until his paternity was established; and to grant guardianship or visitation to B.R. Sr. and W.R. T.M. and J.R. did not learn about the filing of these proceedings until about a month later. In the meantime, on September 25, 2006, T.M. and J.R. filed an adoption request, and a notice to terminate B.R.'s parental rights, in the San Francisco Superior Court.

While the adoption request was pending, B.R. entered into a plea bargain in the criminal case arising out of his arrest in August 2006, under which he received a sentence of 12 years in state prison. He is not scheduled to be released until January 9, 2016, by which time O.M. will be 9 years old. Nonetheless, on November 1, 2006, B.R. filed an objection to the adoption in the San Francisco Superior Court proceedings, stating that he had not known of the adoption plan during L.T.'s pregnancy (a statement later contradicted by his own testimony), and that if his parental rights were not terminated, B.R. Sr. and W.R. would care for the child until B.R. was released from prison.

On January 15, 2008, the San Francisco Superior Court held a hearing regarding T.M. and J.R.'s request that B.R.'s paternal rights be terminated, and that they be permitted to adopt O.M. At the hearing, an expert clinical psychologist testified that O.M. was securely attached to T.M. and J.R., and identified them as his parents. [Note: Attachment is discussed in Chapter 6.] The psychologist opined that T.M. and J.R. were "very competent parents," and that O.M. would suffer serious trauma and detriment if he were removed from their custody and placed with B.R.. Similarly, a social worker from the adoption agency testified that her post-placement visits with T.M. and J.R. had demonstrated that they were "wonderful parents" and that O.M. was healthy, happy, and well-adjusted in their care, and very attached to them. She recommended that T.M. and J.R. be permitted to adopt O.M.

At the conclusion of the hearing, the trial court announced its decision, later memorialized in a written order, that B.R. did not qualify as a statutory presumed father, and was not entitled to the rights afforded to unmarried fathers by the *Kelsey S. . . . .* case. The court found by clear and convincing evidence that O.M.'s best interests would be served by terminating B.R.'s parental rights, and ordered that his adoption by T.M. and J.R. should proceed despite B.R.'s lack of consent. This timely appeal ensued.

Under the applicable statutory scheme in California, the consent of a child's biological father is not needed for an adoption unless he has qualified as a presumed father. B.R. acknowledges that he is not entitled to statutory status as a presumed father. In arguing that his parental rights nonetheless should not have been terminated without a finding of unfitness, B.R. relies on the non-statutory paternal rights (*Kelsey S.* rights) established by *Kelsey S.*

. . . *Kelsey S. . . . .* held . . . that an unwed father who has no *statutory* right to block a third party adoption by withholding consent may nevertheless have a *constitutional* right to do so under the due process and equal protection clauses of the Fourteenth Amendment and thereby to preserve his opportunity to develop a parental relationship with his child. . . .

Under the *Kelsey S.* standard, if an unwed father promptly comes forward and demonstrates a full commitment to his parental responsibilities—emotional, financial, and otherwise—his federal constitutional right to due process prohibits the termination of his paternal relationship absent a showing of his unfitness as a parent. Once the father knows or reasonably should know of the pregnancy, he must promptly attempt to assume his parental responsibilities as fully as the mother will allow and the circumstances permit. . . . [A]father cannot compensate for his failure to promptly come forward to offer support by attempting to assume his parental responsibilities many months after learning of the pregnancy.

The burden is on a biological father who asserts *Kelsey S.* rights to establish the factual predicate for those rights. B.R. does not contend that he actually met the criteria set forth in *Kelsey S.* Rather, he contends that he should be excused from doing so, because his efforts to maintain contact with L.T. and gain legal custody of O.M. after his birth were blocked by L.T.'s refusal to see him after the first four or five months of her pregnancy. In so arguing, he relies on the Supreme Court's holding in *Kelsey S.* that the statutory scheme governing unwed biological fathers' rights violates equal protection and due process to the extent that the statutes allow a mother unilaterally to preclude her child's biological father from becoming a presumed father.

In the present case, however, it was not L.T.'s unilateral action alone that prevented B.R. from meeting the requirements necessary to acquire *Kelsey S.* rights. One of those requirements is that once the father knows or reasonably should know of the pregnancy, he must promptly attempt to assume his parental responsibilities as fully as the mother will allow and his circumstances permit. Here, B.R. learned of the pregnancy in February 2006, and L.T. did not start refusing to see him at least until sometime in June 2006. B.R. has not established that during the intervening four months, he provided support to L.T. of any kind—financial, emotional, or practical. All he has shown is that his *parents* furnished her with some clothing and money, though apparently not enough to prevent her from needing the support of T.M. and J.R. once they came into the picture.

The record supports the conclusion that B.R. was prevented from supporting L.T. during the initial period of her pregnancy, before she began refusing to see him, not because of any unilateral action on her part, but by his own actions in committing the parole violations, including the use of illegal drugs, that led to his incarceration. We do not discern any violation of equal protection or due process in holding an unwed father's own criminal activity against him when assessing whether he has met the criteria for *Kelsey S.* rights.

Even after B.R.'s release from incarceration on June 10, 2006, the record does not reflect any significant effort on his part to assume the mantle of responsible fatherhood notwithstanding L.T.'s repudiation of him. He was working and living with his parents, yet he admittedly made no attempt to furnish L.T. with any money or material support, despite his ability to get messages to her through L.T.'s mother and their mutual friends. Once B.R. learned that L.T. planned to relinquish the baby for adoption, he did promptly attempt to consult an attorney so as to assert his legal rights. By then, however, he had begun using drugs again, and had illegally taken possession of a handgun and ammunition. As a result of this conduct, B.R. was arrested again, and pleaded guilty to charges that resulted in a 12-year prison sentence.

In short, L.T.'s refusal to communicate with B.R. played only a relatively small role in his failure to qualify for *Kelsey S.* rights. Far more of the responsibility lies with B.R.'s own actions in violating the law. Thus, on the facts, this is not a case in which a biological father has become entitled to *Kelsey S.* rights by making good faith attempts to fulfill his parental responsibilities, only to have those attempts frustrated by the unilateral actions of his child's mother. . . .

This conclusion is also in accord with the *Kelsey S.* court's statement that in order to be entitled to equal protection of his parental rights, an unwed father must, in particular, demonstrate a willingness *himself* to assume *full* custody of the child—not merely to block adoption by others. In the present case, B.R. does not seek to assume full custody of O.M. himself. Rather, he seeks to obtain only legal custody, while relegating physical custody to his parents until he is released from his present lengthy incarceration. Such a result would not serve the interest in stability and continuity in a child's family life, which has also been identified as an important public policy in the *Kelsey S.* context. . . .

The trial court's order is affirmed.

NOTE based on *Adoption of O.M.*

Can you imagine the stress experienced by the adoptive parents? They took the baby into their home on his birth day in 2006. They litigated with the father in the trial court, not knowing whether they would keep the child or be ordered to turn him over to father. After trial, it was not until 2008 that the Court of Appeal handed down its decision. Father sought review in the California Supreme Court. The Supreme Court ended the matter in 2009, when it refused to hear the case. Father did not seek review in the U.S. Supreme Court. Every day, from the first inkling that father would fight for custody, through time consuming and expensive litigation at the trial and appellate levels, the adoptive parents wondered, "Will we keep our child? Is he really ours?" Of course, father had similar longings, "Will I ever get my child." I confess my sympathy lies with the adoptive parents, not dad. Clearly, there is no easy solution. Litigation takes time. Yet, the stress and heartache are palpable.

Unmarried and married same-sex couples often decide to have children. Complex parentage issues can arise in such cases. Consider the Washington Supreme Court's decision in *Parentage of L.B.*

Parentage of L.B.

Supreme Court of Washington
155 Wash. 2d 679, 122 P.3d 161 (2005), *cert. denied*,
547 U.S. 1143 (2006)

Bridge, J.

In 1989, after dating for several months, Page Britain and Sue Ellen ("Mian") Carvin began living together as intimates. Five years later, they decided to add a child to their relationship and together artificially inseminated Britain with semen donated by a male friend. . . . The parties conducted the artificial insemination in their home, with Carvin personally inseminating Britain with the donor sperm. Carvin accompanied Britain to her prenatal appointments, and they participated together in prenatal birthing classes. On May 10, 1995, Carvin was present at and assisted in the birth of L.B. When she was born, the parties gave L.B. family names representing both Carvin's and Britain's family. In L.B.'s baby book, Britain listed herself under "mother" and altered "father" to also read "mother," listing Carvin.

For the first six years of L.B.'s life, Carvin, Britain, and L.B. lived together as a family unit and held themselves out to the public as a family. Carvin and Britain shared parenting responsibilities, with Carvin actively involved in L.B.'s parenting, including discipline decisions, day care and schooling decisions, and medical care decisions. Both parties were named as "parents" on L.B.'s kindergarten and first grade records. While the parties now dispute the nature of their relationship and the extent of Carvin's role as a "mother," the record reflects that Carvin provided much of the child's mothering during the first six years of her life. This conclusion is supported by the fact that L.B., in her interactions with the two women, referred to Carvin as "mama" and Britain as "mommy."

L.B. was nearly six years old when the parties ended their relationship. After initially sharing custody and parenting responsibilities, Britain eventually took measures to limit Carvin's contact with L.B. and in the spring of 2002, unilaterally terminated all of Carvin's contact with L.B. L.B. was then seven years old.

Seeking to continue her relationship with L.B., on November 15, 2002, Carvin filed a petition for the establishment of parentage in King County Superior Court. In it she sought, in relevant part, (1) that she be declared the legal parent of L.B. pursuant to the Uniform Parentage Act (UPA) [and], (2) that she be declared a parent by equitable estoppel or that she be recognized as a *de facto* parent.

On December 13, 2002, the family court commissioner dismissed Carvin's petition based on a determination that Carvin lacked standing under the UPA and that the UPA does not grant standing to "psychological" parents. Carvin moved for a revision of the commissioner's ruling. On revision, the trial judge found that "there is a substantial relationship between Petitioner Carvin and the child in this case" and that "both parties care deeply" for the child. He further found neither Britain nor Carvin to be "unfit." Finally, he found that "there is a substantial showing in the record that terminating visitation between [Carvin] and the child harmed the child." However, he "reluctantly" affirmed the commissioner's ruling, holding that Carvin lacked standing under the UPA and as a *de facto* parent.

In the face of advancing technologies and evolving notions of what comprises a family unit, this case causes us to confront the manner in which our state, through its statutory scheme and common law principles, defines the terms "parents" and "families." . . .

Inevitably, in the field of familial relations, factual scenarios arise, which even after a strict statutory analysis remain unresolved, leaving deserving parties without any appropriate remedy, often where demonstrated public policy is in favor of redress. And so we turn to the question before us: whether our state's common law recognizes *de facto* parents and, if so, what rights and obligations accompany such recognition. Specifically, we are asked to discern whether, in the absence of a statutory remedy, the equitable power of our courts in domestic matters permits a remedy *outside* of the statutory scheme, or conversely, whether our state's relevant statutes provide the exclusive means of obtaining parental rights and responsibilities.

Two Court of Appeals cases support Carvin's claim that Washington's common law recognizes the status of *de facto* parents. Implicitly recognizing *de facto* parentage status, these courts have awarded custody to nonbiological "parents" over the objection of otherwise fit biological parents. . . . The cases . . . support the proposition that Washington common law recognizes the significance of parent-child relationships that may otherwise lack statutory recognition. In addition, both cases make clear that individuals may comprise a legally cognizable family through means other than biological or adoptive.

Our legislature has been conspicuously silent when it comes to the rights of children like L.B., who are born into nontraditional families, including any interests they may have in maintaining their relationships with the members of the family unit in which they are raised. In assessing whether our common law may recognize such relationships as well as the extent of the rights accorded *de facto* parents, if any, we consider the relevant legislative enactments concerning parentage, child custody, and visitation, for two critical purposes: (1) to discern legislative pronouncements of our state's public policy and (2) to determine whether there exists a clear legislative intent to preempt the establishment of any common law rights in this context.

In 2000, Washington adopted the then-current version of the UPA to govern statutory determinations of parentage in our state. Several sections of the UPA shed light on our state's public policy concerning disputes which touch on the rights and interests of children. Specifically, the legislature established that questions of parentage are to be considered without differentiation on the basis of the marital status or gender of the child's parent. Additionally, the UPA establishes that at least in the case of artificial insemination, the intent of the parties is the principal inquiry in determining legal parentage. While not directly controlling here, these related policy pronouncements inform our decisionmaking regarding recognition of a common law right to *de facto* parentage. . . .

A study of Washington's common law confirms that, particularly in disputes touching on the rights and protection of minors, Washington courts have historically exercised broad equitable powers in considering cases regarding the welfare of children . . . .

Our state's current statutory scheme reflects the unsurprising fact that statutes often fail to contemplate all potential scenarios which may arise in the ever changing and evolving notion of familial relations. Yet, simply because a statute fails to speak to a specific situation should not, and does not in our common law system, operate to preclude the availability of potential redress. This is especially true when the rights and interests of those least able to speak for themselves are concerned. We cannot read the legislature's pronouncements on this subject to preclude any potential redress to Carvin or L.B. In fact, to do so would be antagonistic to the clear legislative intent that permeates this field of law—to effectuate the best interests of the child in the face of differing notions of family and to provide certain and needed economical and psychological support and nurturing to the children of our state. While the legislature may eventually choose to enact differing standards than those recognized here today, and to do so would be within its province, until that time, it is the duty of this court to endeavor to administer justice according to the promptings of reason and common sense.

Reason and common sense support recognizing the existence of *de facto* parents and according them the rights and responsibilities which attach to parents in this state. We adapt our common law today to fill the interstices that our current legislative enactment fails to cover in a manner consistent with our laws and stated legislative policy.

To establish standing as a *de facto* parent we adopt the following criteria: (1) the natural or legal parent consented to and fostered the parent-like relationship, (2) the petitioner and the child lived together in the same household, (3) the petitioner assumed obligations of parenthood without expectation of financial compensation, and (4) the petitioner has been in a parental role for a length of time sufficient to have established with the child a bonded, dependent relationship, parental in nature. In addition, recognition of a *de facto* parent is limited to those adults who have fully and completely undertaken a permanent, unequivocal, committed, and responsible parental role in the child's life.

We thus hold that henceforth in Washington, a *de facto* parent stands in legal parity with an otherwise legal parent, whether biological, adoptive, or otherwise. As such, recognition of a person as a child's *de facto* parent necessarily authorizes a court to consider an award of parental rights and responsibilities based on its determination of the best interest of the child. A *de facto* parent is not entitled to any parental privileges, as a matter of right, but only as is determined to be in the best interests of the child at the center of any such dispute.

Britain asserts the recognition of Carvin as a *de facto* parent, and granting her rights akin to a biological or adoptive parent violates Britain's constitutionality protected liberty interest to care for and control her child without unwarranted state intervention, in contravention of United States Supreme Court precedent. She notes that the law presumes that biological parents are not only fit, but will act in the best interest of their children, and there is no indication that she is in anyway unfit as a parent. Carvin counters that common law recognition of *de facto* parents does not implicate . . . constitutional infirmities . . . and that the first of the four *de facto* parent standards, that the "natural or legal parent consented to and fostered the parent-like relationship," incorporates the constitutionally requisite deference to the legal parent. We agree with Carvin.

Johnson, J. (dissenting).

I disagree with the majority's resolution of this case and am saddened by the impact caused by this judicial rewrite of our parentage laws on this child—poor little L.B. At the outset, I note that the sexual orientation history of the parties in this case should be irrelevant under the straightforward analysis the statute and constitution require. Regardless of the various sexual orientation claims, the outcome must be that a mother has a fundamental right to make decisions for her child. The Washington Uniform Parentage Act (UPA) requires the same analysis and conclusion as do the state and federal constitutions: L.B.'s mother, Page Britain, is fit (no contrary allegation has been made), and therefore the courts must presume that she acts in her child's best interests.

Under the majority's holding, the parties in this case will return to the trial court for a determination of whether Sue Ellen ("Mian") Carvin, the claimant, is a "*de facto*" parent—even though she is not a parent under any reading of our constitution or statute. If or when the court below decides she is a "*de facto*" parent, Carvin will magically obtain the fundamental rights of a parent—rights equal to those of L.B.'s biological and legal mother, Britain. Unfortunately, the court will then likely divide custody on some unspecified basis.

This outcome is unconstitutional and in derogation of rights of the mother because it interferes with an admittedly fit parent's fundamental right to make child rearing decisions.

It will be shown below that this "*de facto*" claimant meets *none* of the qualifications of a parent under the UPA. Further indicative of Carvin's motives here, her counsel admitted at argument that Carvin has not contributed to L.B.'s support since this litigation began. Instead of helping support L.B., she has chosen to engage in protracted litigation that is costly, financially and emotionally— undoubtedly causing agonizing stress on little L.B., who has become a battleground for this interpersonal and political debate.

The majority purports to dispose of the constitutional issue by waving a magic wand and creating "*de facto*" parents. However, it is this court's creation of this new class of parents that is the constitutional violation. In this case there is a real, fit, actual, biological parent whose fundamental interest in the care, custody, and raising of her child is infringed by the majority's elevating of a nonparent to "*de facto*" parental status.

This is a constitutional matter. The United States Supreme Court found in *Troxel v. Granville,* 530 U.S. 57, 120 S.Ct. 2054 (2000)] that the Washington trial court had erred when it failed to apply the constitutionally *required* presumption that a fit parent acts in the child's best interests (and thus failed to require proof that the parent was unfit before making a custody determination against the parent's wishes).

Here, the majority errs, as the Washington statute and trial court did in *Troxel,* by allowing a court to assume that it is in a child's interests to continue a relationship with a nonparent over objection of the legitimate parent. Second, the majority's ruling fails to provide any protection for Britain's fundamental constitutional right as a fit mother to make decisions concerning the upbringing of her own daughter.

Worse, in my view, the majority here looks beyond a detailed and complete statutory scheme adopted by the Washington legislature and creates by judicial decree a new method for determining parentage. The UPA, adopted by many states, is avowedly intended to provide the exclusive remedy for determining parentage . . . .

Here, the UPA unambiguously defines a "parent." A parent is "an individual who has established a parent-child relationship under RCW 26.26.101." A mother-child relationship is established in five situations: (1) when a woman gives birth to a child, (2) through an adjudication of maternity, (3) through adoption, (4) by a surrogate parentage contract, or (5) by an affidavit and physician's certificate stating a person's intent to be bound as a parent of a child born through alternative reproductive medical technology.

Britain qualifies under RCW 26.26.101(1)(a), . . . as she is the birth mother of L.B. Carvin does not qualify under any section. This should end the analysis.

The statute does contemplate various other ways in which a person may establish a true parent relationship. Absent from these definitions of parent, which the legislature intended as exclusive, is any mention of a "*de facto*" parent or any provision that Carvin fits.

The majority improperly concludes that the legislature's failure to speak is somehow an invitation for this court to add further definitions or provisions to a statute that is clear, unambiguous, and all encompassing. The majority's conclusion is wrong on the facts and violates our long-standing rules of statutory construction.

The majority wishes to act with the wisdom of Solomon in not only implementing but making the law in this sensitive family law area. Solomon's famous case with two women claiming the same baby had a different point, however, badly misapprehended by the majority. Solomon threatened to cut the baby in half in order to determine the *real* mother, to whom he restored full custody. 1 *Kings* 3:16–28. The court today holds an actual division more wise and sends the case and the child to lower courts for that division. Poor little L.B.

———————————

Questions based on *Parentage of L.B.*

1. Which opinion appeals to you, majority or dissent?

2. Justice Johnson, in dissent, is upset with Ms. Carvin. According to Justice Johnson, during the litigation, Ms. Carvin did not contribute to the support of the child, but chose "to engage in protracted litigation that is costly, financially and emotionally . . . ." But what was she supposed to do? Ms. Britain completely cut off contact between Ms. Carvin and the child. Is the justice suggesting Ms. Carvin should have sent money to the person who refused to allow a relationship with the child? Was it wrong to resort to the courts to seek a remedy for what Ms. Carvin—and the majority—saw as a wrong?

3. If the case arose in California, could Ms. Carvin qualify for parental rights under *Kelsey S.*?

4. We don't know why Ms. Britain decided to completely cut Ms. Carvin out of the child's life. Maybe she had good reason. But suppose she cut off Ms. Carvin not because Ms. Carvin was a bad "parent," but because Ms. Britain and Ms. Carvin could not get along with each other. Could it be credibly argued that cutting the child off from Ms. Carvin rendered Ms. Britain "unfit"?

5. In dissent, Justice Johnson criticizes the majority for wishing "to act with the wisdom of Solomon." In a previous decision, *N.A.H. and A.H. v. S.L.S.*, the Colorado Supreme Court also mentioned King Solomon's wise judgment. The Biblical story of Solomon speaks to the power of parental love. Two women claimed to be the mother of a child—an early parentage case! The woman lived in the same house, and each had a baby. One of the babies died, and both women claimed to be the mother of the living child. They took their dispute to the king. One of the women told the king that the other woman had accidentally smothered her baby while they slept.[11] When she discovered her baby dead, the mother quietly exchanged her dead baby for the living baby and claimed the living baby as her own. The other women said this was a lie. King Solomon said, "Bring a sword and split the baby in two. Each woman shall have half." Hearing this, the true mother said, "Don't kill the child! Give the baby to her." The lying woman said, "Divide it!" Solomon's trick worked. He realized that a true parent would rather give up her baby than see it sacrificed. The liar's lack of concern for the baby revealed her an imposter.

---

11 So-called "overlying" occurs when an adult sleeping with a baby rolls over and accidentally smothers the baby. Overlying has caused death throughout time.

In *N.A.H. and A.H. v. S.L.S., supra,* the court concluded that a child cannot have two fathers. In *In re M.C.,* the California Court of Appeal considers whether a child can have three parents.

In re M.C.

California Court of Appeal
195 Cal. App. 4th 197, 123 Cal. Rptr. 3d 856 (2011)

Johnson, J.

[In California, a juvenile court proceeding to protect a child from maltreatment is commenced by a child protective services agency.] This dependency action involves the question of whether a child, born during the marriage of two women but conceived as the result of a premarital relationship between one of the women and a man, may have three presumed parents, one of whom is the child's biological mother, one of whom is the child's presumed mother because she and the child's biological mother were married when the child was born, and one of whom is the child's presumed father because he promptly came forward and demonstrated his commitment to his parental responsibilities, to the extent the biological mother and circumstances allowed.

The juvenile court found the child has three presumed parents. The biological and presumptive mothers appeal, arguing the juvenile court erred when it found the father to be a presumed father. We conclude substantial evidence supports the parentage findings, but the juvenile court's work is incomplete. The matter must be remanded for the juvenile court to resolve the conflicting presumptions of parentage. . . .

Appellant Melissa V. (Melissa) and appellant Irene V. (Irene) met in June 2006, and began living together within two weeks. The relationship was stormy from the start, marked by physical and verbal abuse by both women, and allegedly peppered throughout with problems arising from Melissa's mental illness and drug and alcohol abuse.

Melissa and Irene became registered domestic partners in February 2008; they separated on May 25, 2008. During that separation, Melissa began an intimate relationship with appellant and respondent Jesus Perez (Jesus). In June 2008 Melissa became pregnant with minor M.C. (or "the child"), and informed Jesus he was the child's father. Jesus was supportive of Melissa's pregnancy, and invited Melissa to live with him. Melissa lived with Jesus and his family for the first few months of her pregnancy. During that time, Jesus provided financial support for Melissa, and ensured that she received prenatal medical care.

On July 24, 2008, Melissa filed a petition to dissolve the domestic partnership with Irene. . . . Melissa and Irene reconciled in September 2008. Melissa told Jesus "she did not feel comfortable with him and preferred to live with Irene and that Irene had agreed to care for her and the baby," and moved out. At first, the women lived in a car. In late September they moved into an apartment. When she left Jesus, Melissa did not tell him where she would be living. She did not provide him any contact information, and did not have a phone for more than a few weeks. Melissa and Irene were married on October 15, 2008, when same-sex marriage was legal in California.

M.C. was born M.C.V. in March 2009. Melissa is the only parent listed on the child's birth certificate. Irene was present at the child's birth. Melissa, Irene and M.C. lived together for about three to four weeks, until Melissa moved out taking the child with her. Jesus did not assert a right to visitation with or custody of M.C. after she was born, nor did he pay any child support. Jesus did not know where Melissa was living and made no effort to contact her through her family. . . .

In June 2009, Melissa resumed contact with Jesus, who had moved to Oklahoma in February 2009 to pursue an employment opportunity. Melissa told Jesus she had left Irene, and needed financial assistance for M.C. Jesus agreed to send her money for the child's support and, on three occasions between July and August 2009, sent $100 to Melissa through Western Union. Melissa and Jesus maintained internet contact with one another and, at Jesus's request, Melissa regularly took M.C. to visit Jesus's family.

M.C. was taken into protective custody in mid-September 2009, after Melissa's new boyfriend, Jose A., attacked Irene with a knife, stabbing her in the neck and back and causing severe injuries. Melissa was arrested and charged as an accessory to attempted murder in connection with that attack.

[The court's lengthy discussion of Melissa and Irene's dysfunctional relationship and neglect of M.C. is omitted. The juvenile court found the child was neglected and assumed jurisdiction over the child.]

The principle issue on appeal concerns the juvenile court's novel finding that M.C. has three presumed parents, a biological presumed mother, a statutorily presumed mother and a constitutionally presumed father under *Adoption of Kelsey S.* (1992) 1 Cal.4th 816 (*Kelsey S.*). Melissa and Irene insist the juvenile court erred when it found Jesus to be M.C.'s presumed father. Jesus, not surprisingly, contends that finding was correct, but maintains the court erred when it refused immediately to place M.C. in his custody . . . .

The Uniform Parentage Act of 1973 (UPA), Family Code section 7600 et seq., provides the statutory framework for judicial determinations of parentage, and governs private adoptions, paternity and custody disputes, and dependency proceedings.

Under the dependency law scheme, only mothers and presumed parents have legal status as "parents," entitled to the rights afforded such persons in dependency proceedings, including standing, the appointment of counsel and reunification services. In an appropriate case, a man or a woman who is not a child's biological parent may be deemed his or her "presumed parent."

Under the UPA, the parent-child relationship between a child and his or her natural mother is presumptively established, most often and easily, by proof of her having given birth to the child.

Establishing a father's status is often more difficult. Nevertheless, the need to establish a father's status in a dependency proceeding is pivotal; it determines the extent to which he may participate in the proceedings and the rights to which he is entitled.

The UPA distinguishes between "alleged," "biological," and "presumed" fathers. A man who may be the father of a child, but whose biological paternity has not been established, or, in the alternative, has not achieved presumed father status, is an alleged father. A biological or natural father is one whose biological paternity has been established, but who has not achieved presumed father status.

Presumed father status ranks highest. Presumed fathers are vested with greater parental rights than alleged or biological fathers. Only a presumed father is a parent entitled to receive reunification services [from the juvenile court] . . . and custody of the child . . . .

Section 7611 sets forth several rebuttable presumptions under which a man may qualify as a presumed father, two of which are pertinent here. They are: if the man is or has been married to the child's mother and the child is born during (or soon after) the marriage, or the man receives the child into his home and openly holds out the child as his natural child. The statutory purpose of Family Code section 7611 is to distinguish between those fathers who have entered into some familial relationship with the mother and child and those who have not. A man who has neither legally married nor attempted to legally marry the mother of his child cannot become a presumed father unless he *both* receives the child into his home *and* openly holds out the child as his natural child. Therefore, to become a presumed father, an unwed biological father must not only openly and publicly admit paternity, but must also *physically* bring the child into his home. . . .

An unwed father may also, under narrow circumstances, assert constitutional paternity rights, even though he does not qualify under a statutory presumption under section 7611. Such a quasi-presumed, or *Kelsey S.* father, as they are most commonly known, is an unwed biological father who comes forward at the first opportunity to assert his paternal rights after learning of his child's existence, but has been prevented from becoming a statutorily presumed father under 7611 by the unilateral conduct of the child's mother or a third party's interference.

The principles regarding the presumptions of paternity also have been applied with equal force to a woman seeking presumed mother status.

Increasingly, as aptly illustrated here, the complicated pattern of human relations and changing familial patterns gives rise to more than one legitimate claimant to the status of presumed parent, and the juvenile court must resolve the competing claims. Although more than one individual may fulfill the statutory criteria that give rise to a presumption of paternity, there can be only one presumed father. The procedure for reconciling competing presumptions . . . provides that . . . the presumption which on the facts is founded on the weightier considerations of policy and logic controls.

[The child's attorney and] amicus curiae invite us to employ this case as a vehicle to highlight the inadequacies of the antiquated UPA to accommodate rapidly changing familial structures, and the need to recognize and accommodate novel parenting relationships. We agree these issues are critical, and California's existing statutory framework is ill-equipped to resolve them. But even if the extremely unusual factual circumstances of this unfortunate case made it an appropriate action in which to take on such complex practical, political and social matters, we would not be free to do so. Such important policy determinations, which will profoundly impact families, children and society, are best left to the Legislature. . . .

Moreover, the reasons M.C. and amicus curiae urge judicial recognition of extended parental relations illustrate why such recognition could be unwise here . . . . In the abstract, it is not difficult to opine a child might be well served by judicial recognition and preservation of a relationship with three legal "parents," all of whom love and care for her, and each of whom has evinced a commitment to providing her a safe and stable family environment. This is not that case.

Here we have a child who was detained [by child protective services] as an infant and who has never found safety or stability with any individual claiming parental status. The biological mother has a lengthy history of drug and alcohol abuse and serious emotional disturbance or mental illness, has never been capable of providing her daughter a stable home and will, in all likelihood, never be able to do so . . . .

The presumed mother likely developed a superficial attachment, at best, to M.C. when the newborn lived with her for three weeks. If Melissa is to be believed, Irene rarely held the infant when they lived together, and became irritated when the baby cried. Thus, the child may never have begun to form an early attachment to Irene. While Irene has begun consistently to visit M.C., she has never occupied a parental role in the child's life. Her relationship with M.C. cannot, at least on this record, approach the level of a parent-child relationship the state seeks to protect in dependency actions. And, it is questionable whether Irene will be able to pull her own life together within the legally allotted time to allow such a relationship with M.C. to flourish. Irene has significant issues related to domestic violence to address before she can be deemed a suitable caretaker, she resides in inappropriate housing, and lacks parenting skills, employment and transportation. Nor is there any family relationship to preserve here, as the fleeting marriage during which the child was born no longer exists, and the marital partners agree there is no chance of reconciliation. The parental presumptions are driven by state interest in preserving the integrity of the family and legitimate concern for the welfare of the child.

Finally, although viewed against the backdrop of the two women, Jesus appears to be the most stable and capable "parent" available to M.C., we cannot ignore the fact that he made no attempt to forge a parent-child bond with M.C. before this dependency proceeding began. Even since, on this record, he appears to have remained a relative stranger to M.C., not by choice, but by virtue of physical distance and his inability to spend more time with his daughter during this pivotal bonding period of her life. . . . .

Under the UPA, the parent-child relationship between a child and his or her natural mother is established by proof of her having given birth to the child. No one disputes Melissa's presumptive status as M.C.'s biological or natural mother.

According to section 7611, a man is presumed to be the natural father of a child if, as pertinent here, "(a) He and the child's natural mother are or have been married to each other and the child is born during the marriage. . . . (d) He receives the child into his home and openly holds out the child as his natural child." The statute is written in masculine form but, where it is practicable to do so, the statutory presumptions regarding parentage apply equally to women. . . .

Melissa and Irene were married when M.C. was born. In addition, Melissa, M.C. and Irene lived in the same home for a few weeks after the child was born. Irene claims she and Melissa planned to raise the child together as a family, or to co-parent even if they were not together. She considers herself M.C.'s parent, and claims to have spent every day with the child after she was born until Melissa moved out, and always to have held out M.C. as her natural child although she has provided no support for M.C. since Melissa left. Evidence of the circumstances of the relationship between Irene and the child during the period between M.C.'s birth and Melissa's departure is sparse. It is however, undisputed the three people shared a home for a few weeks. It is also undisputed that Irene took steps, even before this action was initiated, to obtain custody of and visitation with M.C., and that, once she was permitted to see the child, her visits were consistent and appropriate. Applying the UPA in a gender neutral fashion, the juvenile court concluded Irene qualified as a "presumed mother" under both section 7611(a), due to the marital presumption, and subdivision (d), because she had received M.C. into her home and openly held her out as her natural child. No one seriously disputes either finding. . . . Irene satisfies the statutory requirements as a presumed mother . . . .

Jesus cannot qualify as a statutorily presumed father. He never married or attempted to marry Melissa, so section 7611(a) is clearly inapplicable. To qualify under subdivision (d), Jesus must have received the child into his home and openly held out the child as his natural child. There is no question that, since he learned Melissa was pregnant, Jesus consistently and openly held out M.C. as his natural child. He opened his home to Melissa, supported her financially during the first four months of her pregnancy, told his family she was pregnant with his child, and ensured that she received prenatal medical care.

When Melissa moved out, she cut off contact with Jesus until June 2009 when she sought financial help for M.C. from him. Jesus immediately responded to Melissa's request, and began providing minimal financial support. . . . Jesus arranged for M.C. to visit his parents on a regular basis, so she could establish a relationship with her paternal relatives. In addition, when DCFS contacted him about this action, Jesus immediately proclaimed his intention to parent M.C., and expressed his desire to have M.C. placed in his custody and care. He appeared at every court hearing thereafter, travelling from Oklahoma to do so, during a period during when he was not yet entitled to vacation leave at his new job.

Although Jesus argues he should be found a presumed father pursuant to section 7611(d), the trial court correctly concluded he does not qualify under that section. Jesus, who has lived in Oklahoma all of M.C.'s life, never "received" M.C. into his own home. M.C.'s visits and contact with paternal relatives are not sufficient to satisfy this requirement. Section 7611(d) does not apply unless a child has been physically present for some period of time in his or her father's home; "constructive receipt" is not sufficient.

Although he does not qualify as a statutorily presumed father, the juvenile court did find Jesus to be a presumed father under *Kelsey S.* based on the facts outlined above. That conclusion was correct. . . . To satisfy the *Kelsey S.* criteria, a child's biological father must show he promptly stepped forward to assume full parental responsibilities for his child's well-being, the child's mother or some third party thwarted his efforts to assume his parental responsibilities, and that he demonstrated a willingness to assume full custody of the child. . . . The father's conduct both *before and after* the child's birth must be considered. Once the father knows or reasonably should know of the pregnancy, he must promptly attempt to assume his parental responsibilities as fully as the mother will allow and his circumstances permit. In particular, the father must demonstrate a willingness himself to assume full custody of the child—not merely to block adoption by others. A court should also consider the father's public acknowledgement of paternity, payment of pregnancy and birth expenses commensurate with his ability to do so, and prompt legal action to seek custody of the child.

We agree Jesus satisfies the requirements of a *Kelsey S.* father. From the time he learned Melissa was pregnant, he held himself out as M.C.'s father. He believed the child was his biological child and told others Melissa was pregnant with his child. Melissa lived with him the first four months of her pregnancy. He acknowledged paternity to Melissa, his family and his fiancée, financially provided for Melissa for a time and ensured that she received prenatal care. He told [child protective services] he had always intended to be a father to M.C., regardless of the nature of his relationship with Melissa. It was beyond Jesus's control that Melissa left him to return to her volatile relationship with Irene. She did not tell Jesus where she was moving, nor leave him any contact information. But, once Melissa renewed contact in June 2009, Jesus responded promptly and began providing support for M.C. He maintained communications with Melissa until she was imprisoned, expressed his desire to be part of M.C.'s life and facilitated arrangements so his daughter could begin to know her paternal relatives. When the dependency action was initiated, Jesus came from Oklahoma to attend each hearing and continued to fight for custody of M.C.

Arguably, Jesus might have expended more effort to maintain ties with Melissa throughout her pregnancy, acted sooner to establish his paternity by seeking to have his name on M.C.'s birth certificate, or made an effort to visit M.C. after she was born. But the law does not require Jesus to do everything he possibly can. Rather, he is required to promptly attempt to assume his parental responsibilities as fully *as the mother will allow and his circumstances permit.* The juvenile court implicitly found Jesus was operating under the financial, time and distance constraints of a new job in another state and his commitment to his pregnant fiancée in Oklahoma, which prevented him from coming to California as often as he might otherwise have done, at least until he was entitled to vacation time. . . .

We are left with three individuals claiming legal status as parents: a biological mother, a statutorily presumed mother, and a *Kelsey S.* father. Only two of these individuals may retain that status. A juvenile court faced with conflicting claims of presumed parentage must apply section 7612 to determine which presumption controls. . . .

Here, no individual claiming parental status has been shown by clear and convincing evidence to be unfit to retain his or her status. The juvenile court declined to weigh the presumptions, content to leave M.C. with three presumed parents. While we empathize with the desire to leave all options open, particularly in a case such as this in which, at least at the time the parentage determination was made, no available choice was optimal, that conclusion was improper. The court's ruling was not wrong—as far as it went. M.C. does have three presumed parents . . . . But the juvenile court must take the next step to reconcile the competing presumptions to determine which of them are founded on the weightier considerations of policy and logic. . . .

The matter must be remanded to the juvenile court to resolve the conflicting fact-intensive presumptions as between the three parents . . . .

Questions based on *In re M.C.*

1. Suppose you are the juvenile court judge to whom the case is remanded. You have three "parents" vying for parentage. Only two can prevail. How will you cut the Gordian knot?

2. In *In re M.C.,* the biological mother, Melissa, had major mental health and criminal issues. Irene had only a superficial relationship with the child and had violence issues. Jesus lived far away. Suppose the facts were different. Consider the following scenario:

> For years, Melissa and Irene were in a stable same sex relationship. Melissa is a pediatrician. Irene is a first grade teacher. Three years ago, Melissa and Irene broke up. Melissa started dating James, a surgeon, and became pregnant by him. James and Melissa did not live together, and their dating relationship ended when Melissa was three months pregnant. Soon thereafter, Melissa and Irene got back together. Irene, Melissa, and James decided to co-parent. All three attended prenatal appointments. Irene and James were present at the

birth of Zoey. The three agreed that Irene would stop teaching and stay home with Zoey until she reached school age. All three adults parent Zoey. In addition to spending a great deal of time with Zoey, James faithfully provides financial support.

How many parents does this lucky little one have? Two or three? If the adults stay on good terms, the question will never need to be answered. Life will go on and Zoey will benefit from her two mommies and her daddy. Irene, Melissa, and James will have to finesse some legal issues along the way—Who consents to medical care? Who makes decisions about Zoey's education?—but these are not insurmountable. Their private family life will remain private.

Suppose, however, that relationships fray and a custody dispute erupts in court. Can Zoey have three parents? According to *In re M.C.*, Zoey is limited to two. One of these dedicated, loving, competent, deserving "parents" must lose. This hardly seems fair to the adults. And it sure doesn't seem fair to Zoey. Look at it from Zoey's point of view. Ask Zoey, "Who are your parents?" Is there any doubt in your mind what she will say?

Problems on Parentage

The following problems give you an opportunity to work with the UPA and the cases you studied. Your professor may prefer that you answer the questions under your state's version of the UPA. In any event, enjoy!

1. Ruth and John married 11 years ago. They live together. Ruth gives birth. Is John a presumed father?

2. Sally and Harry are married. From January to March, Sally had an affair with Fred. Sally and Harry are still married and living together. In December, Sally gives birth to a child. Is Harry a presumed parent? Is Fred a presumed parent? Can Fred seek to establish paternity?

3. Sandy and Sam married 9 years ago. They separated two years ago, but continued to have sex. Today, Sandy gave birth. Is Sam a presumed parent?

4. Kee got pregnant in January by Bill. Kee and Bill never married. In May, Kee and Harry get married. Kee gives birth in October. Is Harry a presumed father? Is Bill?

5. Virginia and Seth never married. They moved in together two years ago and have a sexual relationship. Recently, Virginia gave birth. Seth and Virginia take the baby home and tell everyone they are the parents. Is Seth a presumed parent?

6. Becky and Bob dated and had a sexual relationship from January to June. They never lived together. In November, Becky gave birth. Becky has custody. Bob has visited the child at Becky's home. He has never taken the child to his home. Is Bob a presumed parent?

7. Nancy had sexual relations with two men she dated from January to May. Nancy gave birth in November. Nancy does not know which man is the father. Nancy made no attempt to inform the men she was pregnant. In December, Nancy relinquished the baby for adoption. Can the baby be adopted without discovering who the father is?

8. Crystal and Ray married 3 years ago and tried unsuccessfully to have a child. They decided to try artificial insemination with sperm from an anonymous donor. Crystal became pregnant and recently gave birth. Who are the parents?

9. Melissa and Frank dated from January to March last year. Melissa became pregnant and gave birth in December last year. Melissa and Frank never lived together. The baby lived with Melissa. Frank visited with the baby regularly, and often had custody of the baby at his place on weekends. In November of this year, Melissa decided that she didn't want Frank to have any further contact with the baby, and stopped allowing visits. What, if anything, can Frank do?

10. Linda and Julie are lovers. They have lived together five years. They decided to have a child. A doctor removed eggs from Julie, and the eggs were fertilized with sperm from a sperm donor selected by Linda and Julie. The fertilized eggs were implanted in Linda. Linda gave birth a year ago, and both women parented the child. When the child was old enough to speak, she referred to both women and "mommy." Recently, Linda and Julie separated. Linda refuses to allow Julie to see the child. What, if anything, can Julie do?

11. Wife and Husband married eight years ago. Four years ago, Wife began an affair with Lover. Last year, Wife became pregnant, and gave birth. Who is daddy? Husband? Lover? Husband is listed on the birth certificate and has always held out the child as his own. Blood tests reveal, however, that Lover is probably the bio dad. Wife spent time with Husband, but much of the time they were separated. Wife broke up with Lover and moved back in with Husband. Lover wants to spend time with the child, but Wife says no. Lover files an action seeking to establish that he is daddy. Husband files a motion for summary judgment arguing that because he and Wife were married and cohabiting at the time of conception, he is presumed to be daddy. Lover argues that because he is the bio dad, his right to a relationship with the child is protected by the Constitution. What result?

12. Mom was dating Powers. Two years ago, Mom briefly dated Sinicropi and became pregnant by him. Without knowing she was pregnant, Mom went back to Powers. When the child was born, Mom and Powers executed a voluntary acknowledgement of paternity. Mom and Powers raised the child as their own. It was not until recently that anybody suspected Sinicropi might be the biological father. Mom suspected Sinicropi was the bio dad based on the child's appearance. DNA testing indicates Sinicropi is probably bio dad. Mom and Powers broke up and Powers and mom agreed on joint custody. Mom then moved away without the child, and Powers and Sinicropi are fighting for custody. The trial court rules that the child has two fathers: Powers, the man who raised him, and Sinicropi, the bio dad, who has had no previous relationship with the child. The trial court gives custody to Powers, but also gives parenting time to Sinicropi. Is this a correct ruling? *Sinicropi v. Mazurek*, 273 Mich. App. 149, 729 N.W.2d 256 (2006).

13. Wife and Husband married six years ago and were "swingers." A year ago, Wife had sex with Lover and became pregnant by him. Wife told Husband he might not be the dad. The baby was born this year. Husband was present at the birth, was named the father on the birth certificate, and the couple gave the baby Husband's name as a middle name. A month later, DNA testing excluded Husband as the father. According to Husband, he took no further role in caring for the baby. Wife and Husband split up soon thereafter. Wife attempted to contact Lover—the bio dad—to give him the good news that he was a daddy, and Lover made himself scarce. Wife eventually found Lover, who promised to start a college fund for the tike. DNA testing confirmed Lover as daddy, and he started making regular support payments. Husband filed a petition seeking to disestablish himself as the father and to adjudicate Lover as the father. Lover seeks dismissal. Should Husband be allowed to obtain a ruling that he is *not* the father?

14. Melissa and Bill date and Melissa becomes pregnant. Bill is involved in prenatal care, and when the baby is born, Bill establishes a relationship with the baby. However, Bill does not take the baby into his own home and hold the baby out as his own. He always visits the baby at Melissa's house. Bill does not execute a voluntary declaration of paternity. Nor is Bill listed on the birth certificate. Not long after the baby is born, Melissa marries Tim, and the two begin raising the baby as their own. Tim holds the baby out as his own. Bill seeks custody of the child. Does Bill have standing?

15. Husband and Wife are married. Husband has an affair with Lover, and Lover becomes pregnant and has Husband's child. The child is Lover's only child. Husband argues that Lover agreed to bear a child for Husband and Wife to adopt. Lover argues the baby resulted from a romantic relationship, and she always intended to be the mom. When the child is 1 month old, and in Lover's care, Husband presents Lover with a document called "Agreement for Custody and Adoption." The agreement provides that Lover consents to a stepparent adoption of the child by Wife. Lover and Husband sign the agreement, and Husband leaves with the 1-month-old baby, who has lived since then with Husband and Wife as their child. A month after the agreement is signed, Lover files an action seeking custody. She argues she was coerced to sign the agreement. Wife argues that she is the baby's mother even though she is not the bio mom. What result?

16. Elisa entered into a sexual relationship with Emily eight years ago. They began living together six months later. They exchanged rings, opened a joint account at the bank, and referred to themselves as "partners." They discussed having a child. Because Elisa earned more than twice as much as Emily, they decided Emily would give birth and be a stay-at-home mother. Elisa would be the primary breadwinner. At a sperm bank, they chose a donor, and Emily and Elisa were present when Emily was inseminated. During pregnancy, both attended childbirth classes, and both were present at birth. They agreed on the baby's name. Elisa claimed the child as a dependent on her tax returns. Elisa obtained a life insurance policy and named Emily as the beneficiary. Both women parented the child. After the child's birth, Emily stayed home and Elisa worked full time. Elisa and Emily separated two years ago. At first, Elisa paid the mortgage on their home and paid Emily $1,500 per month support. Recently, Elisa lost her job due to downsizing, and stopped paying support. After six months, Elisa found employment and now earns $200,000 per year. Elisa refuses to pay any support and argues that Emily should find work. For her part, Emily refuses to allow Elisa to see the child. What can each party do?

EXPERIENTIAL ASSIGNMENT

Practice Assignment: *Letter to Client*

In this assignment you will write a letter to a client, Tamara Vincellette. The facts of the case follow:

> Tamara Vincellette and Emily Sorenson were lovers ten years. They met in college. After college, Tamara was commissioned a officer of the line in the U.S. Navy.[12] Tamara has been a naval officer ten years. Tamara intends to remain in the Navy as a career. Her plan is to remain on active duty at least 20 years, possibly 30. Presently, Tamara has the rank of

---

12 An officer of the line or line officer is an officer trained to assume combat command. For example, the captain of a navy warship is an officer of the line.

Lieutenant Commander.[13] Emily is an accountant specializing in corporate tax. Because Tamara is in the military, she moves to new assignments every few years. With her accounting skills, Emily is able to switch jobs fairly easily, so when Tamara receives a new assignment, Emily moves too and gets a job at the new location.

Until 2011, the American military did not allow lesbian or gay individuals to serve openly. The military policy from 1993 to 2011 was "don't ask don't tell." If a gay or lesbian servicemember "came out" or was discovered, the member could be discharged from the service. To keep their relationship secret, Tamara and Emily always maintained separate addresses. They spent most nights together. When "don't ask don't tell" ended, Tamara and Emily dropped the charade and began living together.

For some years, Tamara and Emily discussed the idea of having a child. They discussed adoption. They also discussed assisted reproduction. They are in their early 30s, and Emily said, "The biological clock is running. We'd better do this baby thing if we're gonna." Now that they can finally live openly together without jeopardizing Tamara's military career, they decide it is time to have a baby. The question is: Where is this baby going to come from?

Tamara and Emily decide to try artificial insemination. They obtain sperm from a mutual friend, and Emily is inseminated by a physician. It works, and Emily becomes pregnant! Tamara and Emily attend birthing classes together. Tamara is at the bedside when Emily gives birth to a healthy baby girl, Emma. Tamara and Emily are listed on Emma's birth certificate as the parents. Tamara and Emily co-parent Emma.

When Emma is five, Tamara receives orders to serve aboard the U.S.S. *Ronald Reagan*, an aircraft carrier. The ship is deployed at sea many months at a time. While as sea, Tamara receives the following letter from Emily: "Dear Tamara, I believe our relationship is at an end. I'm very sorry to say this, but I've been thinking it over for a long time. Now that you have been away so many months, it has finally become clear to me that I need to be on my own with Emma. We are moving back home.

---

13 To give you an idea where Tamara is at this point in her naval career, the officer ranks are Ensign, Lieutenant Junior Grade, Lieutenant, Lieutenant Commander, Commander, Captain, Admiral. Tamara's rank of Lieutenant Commander is about where you would expect to be with ten years active service. Most career officers retire at Commander or Captain. Only a small percentage of officers reach the rank of Admiral.

I'll give you the address when I have one. I want you to continue to be part of Emma's life, and you can visit her when you are home. I do believe that she needs to be with me, that is, in my custody. Your military duties make it impossible for you to give her the day-to-day care she needs as a young child. Again, I'm so sorry it has come to this. We had many good and wonderful years together, but now it is time to move on. I'm sorry you have to read this in the middle of the ocean."

Tamara contacts you and asks, "What legal rights do I have regarding my daughter Emma? Can I get custody?"

Assignment: Write a letter to Tamara explaining her legal rights regarding Emma. Base your letter on the law in your state. Your letter should explain the governing legal principles in language comprehensible to an intelligent layperson.

CHAPTER 6

Child Custody

THIS CHAPTER ADDRESSES the most emotionally charged aspect of family law, child custody. Fortunately, most divorcing parents agree on the custodial arrangement they believe is best for their family, and custody litigation is avoided.[1] When parents agree on custody, the judge seldom second guesses the parents. This is not to say parental decisions regarding custody are binding on the court.[2] In the final analysis, judges—not parents—decide custody.

When parents cannot agree on custody, litigation is necessary, and full blown custody litigation breeds tremendous—almost indescribable—ill will and heartache. Custody fights are hard on clients and kids. Even lawyers, who ostensibly are detached professionals, lose sleep over these cases. Indeed, there are family law attorneys who won't litigate custody. They'll do everything else, but not custody. You will have to judge for yourself whether you have the temperament for this aspect of family law. On the bright side, in your role as counselor at law, you can help some estranged parents reach agreement about children. You may decide to train as a mediator, increasing your skill in helping parents reach agreement.

Impact of Divorce on Children

Psychologists have studied the impact of divorce on children.[3] Most studies suggest divorce is a risk factor for adjustment problems.[4] Paul Amato reviewed

---

1 *See* American Psychological Association, Guidelines for Child Custody Evaluations in Family Law Proceedings, 65 *American Psychologist* 863-867, at 863 (2010)("When parents agree to a child custody arrangement on their own—as they do in the overwhelming majority (90%) of cases—there may be no dispute for the court to decide.").

2 *See Harvey v. Harvey*, 470 Mich. 186, 680 N.W.2d 835 (2004).

3 *See* Gary B. Melton, John Petrila, Norman G. Poythress & Christopher Slobogin, *Psychological Evaluations for the Courts: A Handbook for Mental Health Professionals and Lawyers* pp. 549-550 (3d ed. 2007).

4 *See* Hyun Sik Kim, Consequences of Parental Divorce for Child Development, 76 *American Sociological*

the literature available in 2010 and wrote, "Research during the last decade continued to show that children with divorced parents, compared with children with continuously married parents, score lower on a variety of emotional, behavioral, social, health, and academic outcomes, on average."[5] Gary Melton and colleagues wrote:

> Divorce obviously has a negative effect. . . . During the first year after the divorce, conflict typically escalates as both parties deal with the depression and anger engendered by the divorce, as well as the practical problems resulting from separate households. The crisis for the children is exacerbated if there is very high conflict between the parents. In such cases, children are worse off when their parents remain in contact. . . .

> Long-term effects may be very different from those during the first months or even years following the divorce. For example, preschoolers were the age group most traumatized by separation and divorce, but ten years later they were minimally affected by the experience. . . .

> The available [psychological] literature on the effects of divorce gives little basis for either policy or individual dispositions . . . . [The] literature gives little help in decisionmaking about custody. Indeed, if anything, it suggests the pitfalls in making predictions from clinical assessments at the time of divorce.[6]

Hyun Kim writes, "Children with divorced parents are disadvantaged regarding various life outcomes, including likelihood of dropping out of high school, cognitive skills, psychosocial well-being, and social relations."[7] Yet, many

---

Review 487-511 (2011); Daniel Potter, Psychosocial Well-Being and the Relationship Between Divorce and Children's Academic Achievement, 72 *Journal of Marriage and Family* 933-946 (2010)("divorce generally has a negative association with children's outcomes." p. 933. "Divorced families tend to have lower annual incomes and fewer material resources than non-divorced families. In addition, parenting quality is often lower and less consistent in divorced families." p. 934. "Children from divorced families tend to do less well in school than children from nondivorced families." pp. 934-935. "divorce diminishes children's psychosocial well-being, and the decline in well-being helps explain the poorer performance of divorced children at school." p. 944).

5   Paul R. Amato, Research on Divorce: Continuing Trends and New Developments, 72 *Journal of Marriage and Family* 650-666, 653 (2010)("Similarly, adults with divorced parents tend to obtain less education, have lower levels of psychological well-being, report more problems in their own marriages, feel less close to their parents (especially fathers), and are at greater risk of seeing their own marriages end in divorce.").

6   Gary B. Melton, John Petrila, Norman G. Poythress & Christopher Slobogin, *Psychological Evaluations for the Courts: A Handbook for Mental Health Professionals and Lawyers* pp. 550-551 (3d ed. 2007).

7   Hyun Sik Kim, Consequences of Parental Divorce for Child Development, 76 *American Sociological Review*

children of divorce do well. Many of your law school classmates—if not you—are "children of divorce." Getting through college and into graduate school is no mean feat, yet your colleagues pulled it off despite divorce. Divorce is a risk factor for kids, not a fate accompli.[8] Indeed, a divorce that ends a bad, abusive marriage can be good for kids in the long run.[9] Gary Melton and colleagues write, "High conflict in *intact* families is even more deleterious for children than divorce."[10] Although divorce is a risk factor for problems, a more potent risk factor is continuing conflict and animosity between parents. Pamela Ludolph and Milfred Dale write:

> There is a substantial body of literature on the harmful effects of family conflict on children . . . . As early as 1971, Michael Rutter wrote that divorce-related conflict negatively influenced child behavior. He believed that it was conflict, not parental separation, that caused the harm to children of divorce . . . . Many subsequent studies have supported the idea that marital conflict is predictive of attachment difficulties and emotional insecurity in young children and that marital harmony contributes to security.[11]

Primer on Child Development

You are training to become a lawyer, not a psychologist. Yet, if you practice family law, it behooves you to know something about child development. This section introduces leading theories of child development.

Bronfenbrenner's Ecological Systems Theory

American psychologist Urie Bronfenbrenner (1917-2005) pioneered the "Ecological Systems Theory" of child development.[12] Bronfenbrenner described

---

487-511, at 487 (2011).

8 Hyun Sik Kim, Consequences of Parental Divorce for Child Development, 76 *American Sociological Review* 487-511, at 488 (2011)("it remains to be seen whether children of divorce successfully catch up with their counterparts or whether these children experience further developmental setbacks after divorce.").

9 Hyun Sik Kim, Consequences of Parental Divorce for Child Development, 76 *American Sociological Review* 487-511 (2011).

10 Gary B. Melton, John Petrila, Norman G. Poythress & Christopher Slobogin, *Psychological Evaluations for the Courts: A Handbook for Mental Health Professionals and Lawyers* p. 549 (3d ed. 2007).

11 Pamela S. Ludolph & Milfred D. Dale, Attachment in Child Custody: An Additive Factor, Not a Determinative One, 46 *Family Law Quarterly* 1, 21 (2012).

12 *See* Urie Bronfenbrenner, *The Ecology of Human Development* (1979).

Although Ecological Systems Theory provides a useful way to understand child development, the theory plays almost no role in court. A July 2010 Westlaw search for "Bronfenbrenner" revealed two cases.

five interconnected systems that surround and influence a child's development: (1) Microsystem—Environment closest to the child, including family, neighborhood, friends, and school. (2) Mesosystem—Interactions between Microsystems (*e.g.*, parents interacting with teachers). (3) Exosystem—External social systems that indirectly impact a child (*e.g.*, the working conditions of parents). (4) Macrosystem—Larger social context in which the child lives, including public policy and law. (5) Chronosystem—Events over the course of a lifetime. A child's development is affected by how well or poorly the systems function.[13]

Piaget's Stages of Development

Jean Piaget (1896-1980) was a Swiss psychologist. Piaget described four stages of development: sensorimotor, preoperational, concrete operations, and formal operations.

Sensorimotor. The sensorimotor stage lasts from birth through age two. During the sensorimotor stage the child develops a basic understanding of the self as separate from the world.

The pace of cognitive and physical development during the sensorimotor state is astonishing, reinforcing the importance of providing babies an environment rich in appropriate stimulation. Ponder the damage to a baby who is confined to a crib in a sterile institution (or home) devoid of love and stimulation. Similarly, consider the harm inflicted on a baby who is neglected because the parents are often strung out on drugs.

Preoperational. The preoperational stage lasts from age two to six or seven. The child gains in ability to use symbols, especially language. The child's vocabulary expands dramatically. The child is egocentric. Robert Siegler and Martha Alibali note that due to their immaturity and egocentricity, preschool children "often speak right past each other, without appearing to pay any attention to what others are saying."[14] Between ages four and seven, children expand the capacity to engage in meaningful two way discussions.[15]

---

13 James Garbarino is a psychologist and an important contributor to our understanding of the impact of social forces on child development. Garbarino was a graduate student under Bronbenbrenner. See James Garbarino, *Lost Boys: Why Our Sons Turn Violent and How We Can Save Them* (1999).

14 Robert S. Siegler & Martha Wagner Alibali, *Children's Thinking* 40 (4th ed. 2005). Of course, "talking past each other" is not unique to children. Attend a party and listen in on "conversations" between adults. You will often hear something very like the one sided "conversation" between four-year-olds.

15 Robert S. Siegler & Martha Wagner Alibali, *Children's Thinking* 32 (4th ed. 2005).

Concrete Operations. The stage of concrete operations extends from six or seven to eleven or twelve.[16] The child gains capacity to see the world from another person's perspective. The child can solve complex problems, but lacks understanding of many abstract principles.

Formal Operations. This stage arrives for most children at approximately eleven or twelve and continues developing into adulthood. The child reasons at progressively higher levels of abstraction and sophistication. Siegler and Alibali put it this way, "Perhaps the most striking development during the formal operations period is that adolescents begin to see the particular reality in which they live as only one of an infinite number of imaginable realities. This leads at least some of them to think about alternative organizations of the world and about deep questions concerning meaning, truth, justice, and morality."[17]

Piaget believed children progress from stage to stage via three processes: assimilation, accommodation, and equilibration. With assimilation, a child makes sense of new information by evaluating it in light of what the child already knows. For example, when my son Will was four, I tried to explain how corporations make money. (Why on earth I tried to explain this to a four-year-old is a mystery). I asked, "How does Southwest airlines make money? What does Southwest sell?" Will had taken several flights on Southwest, and I expected him to say they charge people to fly. Nope. His answer was, "They sell peanuts." If you have flown Southwest, you know they provide peanuts. Four-year-old Will remembered the peanuts, so he solved the problem by drawing on what he knew: Southwest Airlines makes money selling peanuts—assimilation.

Piaget used the word accommodation to describe the way children change their thinking to understand new information. A young child touches a hot object and experiences pain. The child incorporates the new information into understanding.

Equilibration is the process by which children "put the pieces together" to make sense of the world. Through the interactive processes of assimilation, accommodation, and equilibration the child develops a model of how the world works. Siegler and Alibali observe, "Piaget believed that children generalize the assimilations, accommodations, and equilibrations involved in these particular changes into a broad shift from emphasizing external appearances to emphasizing deeper, enduring qualities."[18]

---

16   Robert S. Siegler & Martha Wagner Alibali, *Children's Thinking* 43-44 (4th ed. 2005).

17   Robert S. Siegler & Martha Wagner Alibali, *Children's Thinking* 44 (4th ed. 2005).

18   Robert S. Siegler & Martha Wagner Alibali, *Children's Thinking* 32 (4th ed. 2005).

Bowlby's Attachment Theory

John Bowlby (1907-1990) was an English psychoanalyst. Bowlby is the "father" of attachment theory.[19] As a young psychiatrist, Bowlby was interested in helping troubled children.[20] Bowlby focused on the quality of the relationship between infant and parent, especially mother. Bowlby believed the quality of the mother-child relationship has a profound impact on the developing child—an impact that reverberates down the years.[21]

In the aftermath of World War II, Bowlby was commissioned by the World Health Organization to prepare a report on homeless children, a major concern in post-war Europe. Bowlby's report, *Maternal Care and Mental Health*, was published in 1951 and was a watershed.[22] Bowlby eloquently described the importance of "mother-love which a young child needs." Bowlby's report, written more than sixty years ago, rings true today and reminds us of the profound implications of disrupting relations between parents and children:

> The services which mothers and fathers habitually render their children are so taken for granted that their magnitude is forgotten. In no other relationship do human beings place themselves so unreservedly and so continuously at the disposal of others. This holds true even of bad parents—a fact far too easily forgotten by their critics, especially critics who have never had the care of children of their own. It must never be forgotten that even the bad parent who neglects her child is none the less providing much for him. Except in the worst cases, she is giving him food and shelter, comforting him in distress, teaching him simple skills, and above all is providing him with that continuity of human care on which his sense of security rests. He may be ill-fed and ill-sheltered, he may be very dirty and suffering from disease, he may be ill-treated, but, unless his parents have wholly rejected him, he is secure in the knowledge that there is *someone* to

---

19   Robert Karen, *Becoming Attached: First Relationships and How They Shape Our Capacity to Love* (1998) (Oxford University Press. New York)(this book provides interesting biographical information and insights regarding John Bowlby).

20 Although Bowlby was a psychoanalyst by training, he drew from all sources of knowledge, including evolutionary theory, ethology, genetics, biology, experimental psychology, etc.

21   Robert Karen, *Becoming Attached: First Relationships and How They Shape Our Capacity to Love* (1998) (Oxford University Press. New York)("Bowlby, founder of attachment theory, believed that it is in our first relationship, usually with our mother, that much of our future well-being is determined." p. 5).

22 John Bowlby, *Maternal Care and Mental Health* (1951)(World Health Organization. Geneva).

whom he is of value and who will strive, even though inadequately, to provide for him until such time as he can fend for himself.[23]

Scholars before and after Bowlby echo the concern that disrupting the connection between child and parent can be traumatic.[24] Roger Kobak and Stephanie Madsen write, "Unchallenged maintenance of an attachment bond contributes to a feeling of security. . . . When an individual perceives a threat to a caregiver's availability, he or she will feel anxious and angry. . . . A persistent disruption of an attachment bond will result in feelings of sadness and despair."[25]

Bowlby's most famous student was Mary Ainsworth (1913-1999), an American psychologist who conducted ground breaking research on attachment in Uganda and at Johns Hopkins University in Baltimore.[26] Ainsworth's research provided empirical support for Bowlby's theory of attachment. Ainsworth devised the famous Strange Situation procedure which provides a way to evaluate attachment.[27] With the Strange Situation, children age one year to twenty months are brought to the psychology laboratory.[28] The child and the parent enter a small room with interesting toys. The child is encouraged to play with the toys. A stranger enters the room and the child's reaction is observed. Eventually, the parent leaves the room, and again the child's reaction

---

23 John Bowlby, *Maternal Care and Mental Health* pp. 67-68 (1951)(World Health Organization. Geneva).

24 Mary Dozier & Michael Rutter, Challenges to the Development of Attachment Relationships Faced by Young Children in Foster and Adoptive Care. In Jude Cassidy & Philip R. Shaver (Eds.), *Handbook of Attachment: Theory, Research, and Clinical Applications* 698-717, at 699 (2nd ed. 2008)("During the second half of the first year of life, children typically develop attachment relationships to specific caregivers. . . . Thus experiences of separation, maltreatment, and privation, even early in the first year of life, may have long-term developmental consequences."); Roger Kobak & Stephanie Madsen, Disruptions in Attachment Bonds: Implications for Theory, Research, and Clinical Intervention. In Jude Cassidy & Philip R. Shaver (Eds.), *Handbook of Attachment: Theory, Research, and Clinical Applications* 23-47 (2nd ed. 2008).

25 Roger Kobak & Stephanie Madsen, Disruptions in Attachment Bonds: Implications for Theory, Research, and Clinical Intervention. In Jude Cassidy & Philip R. Shaver (Eds.), *Handbook of Attachment: Theory, Research, and Clinical Applications* 23-47, at 24 (2nd ed. 2008).

26 Jude Cassidy, The Nature of the Child's Ties. In Jude Cassidy & Philip R. Shaver (Eds.), *Handbook of Attachment: Theory, Research, and Clinical Applications* pp. 3-22 (2nd ed. 2008)("Ainsworth conducted two pioneering naturalistic observation studies of mothers and infants in which she applied the ethological principles of attachment theory as a framework. One of these investigations was conducted in the early 1950s in Uganda; the other was carried out in the early 1960s in Baltimore."); Robert Karen, *Becoming Attached: First Relationships and How They Shape Our Capacity to Love* (1998).

27 Robert Karen, *Becoming Attached: First Relationships and How They Shape Our Capacity to Love* (1998).

28 Catherine R. Lawrence, Elizabeth A. Carlson & Byron Egeland, The Impact of Foster Care on Development, 18 *Development and Psychopathology* 57-76, at 62-63 (2006)("the Strange Situation, a standardized laboratory procedure designed to assess infant patterns of attachment and exploration in relation to the primary caretaker.").

A version of the Strange Situation procedure can be used outside the laboratory.

is observed. The parent returns, and the researcher observes the child's reaction—does the child go to the parent? Ignore the parent? Finally, the stranger leaves.[29] Based on research with the Strange Situation procedure, Ainsworth described three types of attachment—secure, insecure-avoidant, and insecure-ambivalent/resistant.

Secure attachment is most likely to occur when parents are loving, warm, consistent, and sensitive to their baby's needs.[30] In the United States, approximately 70% of babies become securely attached.[31] The securely attached baby views the parent as a "secure base." The baby feels comfortable exploring the environment, confident that the secure base is there for them. The typical securely attached baby is relatively easy to sooth when upset. In the Strange Situation, the securely attached baby seeks the parent when distressed, calms down well, and is able to get back to play.

During the preschool years, the securely attached child is likely to develop good self-esteem, be popular, and be flexible and able to problem solve. These positive attributes continue as the child matures.[32] Lisa Berlin, Jude Cassidy, and

---

29 On the internet, search for "Strange Situation" and you will find videos of the Procedure.

30 Jay Belsky & R.M. Pasco Fearon, Precursors of Attachment Security. In Jude Cassidy & Philip R. Shaver (Eds.), *Handbook of Attachment: Theory, Research, and Clinical Applications* 295-316 at 299 (2nd ed. 2008) ("Furthermore, security is associated with prompt responsiveness to distress, moderate, appropriate stimulation, as well as with warmth, involvement, and responsiveness."); Robert Karen, *Becoming Attached: First Relationships and How They Shape Our Capacity to Love* 444 (1998); Martha Farrell Erickson & Byron Egeland, Child Neglect. In John E.B. Myers (Ed.), *The APSAC Handbook on Child Maltreatment* 103-124 (2011)(Sage. Thousand Oaks, CA). Erickson and Egeland write:

> Longitudinal observational research using carefully standardized measures of the quality of attachment shows that babies become securely attached when their parents are consistently sensitive and responsive to their needs, comforting them when they are distressed, playing and talking and singing to them when they seek interaction, and allowing quiet time when the baby gives cues that indicate they don't want to be hugged or fed or tickled right now. With sensitive, responsive care, babies learn to trust their caregivers and perceive the world as a safe place.

> Babies also learn that they have the power to solicit what they need. When their signals to caregivers bring results, babies have their first experience of competence and what developmental psychologists call "effectance"—discovering that they have an effect on those around them. This is what we want for all children. With that foundation of trust and security, children venture out with confidence and enthusiasm, using their attachment figures as a secure base from which to explore and learn about the world around them. Securely attached children also regulate their emotions more effectively and are more likely to enter into cooperative, caring relationships with other adults and children than children who do not have the firm foundation of a secure attachment. p.112.

31 Martha Farrell Erickson & Byron Egeland, Child Neglect. In John E.B. Myers (Ed.), *The APSAC Handbook on Child Maltreatment* 103-124 (2011)(Sage. Thousand Oaks, CA).

32 Michelle Deklyen & Mark T. Greenberg, Attachment and Psychopathology in Childhood. In Jude Cassidy & Philip R. Shaver (Eds.), *Handbook of Attachment: Theory, Research, and Clinical Applications* 637-665, at 637 (2nd ed. 2008)("Numerous empirical findings link secure attachments to caregivers in the first two years of life with sociability, compliance with parents, and effective emotion regulation.").

Karen Appleyard write, "Individuals with secure attachments to their mothers during infancy also have more harmonious and mutually supportive relationships with siblings, friends, peers, and romantic partners, even 20 years later."[33]

Parents who are in a loving relationship of their own are in the best position to nurture their child toward secure attachment.[34] Jay Belsky and R.M. Fearon write, "An abundance of evidence indicates that a supportive relationship with a spouse or partner during the infancy and toddler years is correlated with the very kinds of parenting theorized (and found) to predict attachment security."[35]

Insecure-Avoidant attachment may develop when the primary caretaker is often emotionally unavailable or rejecting of the child.[36] The baby cannot count on the parent for consistent nurturance. The baby may become unpredictably angry and unresponsive to the parent. In the Strange Situation, the avoidantly attached child does not turn to the parent when distressed.

Insecure-Ambivalent attachment is more likely to develop when the primary caretaker is inconsistent or disorganized. The parent does not seem "in tune" with the baby. The baby cannot predict the behavior of the most important person it the baby's life. This leads to insecurity and, often, anger. In the Strange Situation, the ambivalently attached child has difficulty calming down when upset, and may appear angry and needy at the same time.

Some children in the Strange Situation do not fit neatly into one of Ainsworth's three categories of attachment.[37] Main and Solomon described a

---

33 Lisa J. Berlin, Jude Cassidy, & Karen Appleyard, The Influence of Early Attachments on Other Relationships. In Jude Cassidy & Philip R. Shaver (Eds.), *Handbook of Attachment: Theory, Research, and Clinical Applications* 333-347, at 343 (2nd ed. 2008).

34 Jay Belsky & R.M. Pasco Fearon, Precursors of Attachment Security. In Jude Cassidy & Philip R. Shaver (Eds.), *Handbook of Attachment: Theory, Research, and Clinical Applications* 295-316 at 307 (2nd ed. 2008).

35 Jay Belsky & R.M. Pasco Fearon, Precursors of Attachment Security. In Jude Cassidy & Philip R. Shaver (Eds.), *Handbook of Attachment: Theory, Research, and Clinical Applications* 295-316 at 307 (2nd ed. 2008).

36 Jay Belsky & R.M. Pasco Fearon, Precursors of Attachment Security. In Jude Cassidy & Philip R. Shaver (Eds.), *Handbook of Attachment: Theory, Research, and Clinical Applications* 295-316 at 299 (2nd ed. 2008)("insecure-avoidant attachments are related to intrusive, excessively stimulating, controlling interactional styles" p. 299).

37 Judith Solomon & Carol George, The Measurement of Attachment Security and Related Constructs in Infancy and Early Childhood. In Jude Cassidy & Philip R. Shaver (Eds.), *Handbook of Attachment: Theory, Research, and Clinical Applications* 383-416 at 386-387 (2nd ed. 2008)("About 15% of attachments in normative samples, and much higher percentages in high-risk samples, are difficult to classify with the original [three categories]. Main and Solomon described the range of behaviors found in such unclassifiable infants, and developed guidelines for a fourth classification group termed 'disorganized/disoriented.' . . . [T]he child lacks a coherent attachment strategy with respect to the parent.").

fourth type of attachment observed in a small number of children: Disorganized/disoriented.[38] As explained by Kobak and Madsen:

> A traditional focus on the availability of an attachment figure assumes that the attachment relationship will serve as a source of safety; however, children exposed to abuse or extreme forms of punishment must manage a profound dilemma, as their attachment figures are potential sources of danger. Main and Hesse (1990) noted that infants who have been unpredictably frightened by their attachment figures are caught in a conflict when placed in a situation that normally elicits attachment behavior. Although these infants may display the typical secure and insecure attachment strategies, many show temporary lapses in their strategies; such lapses are marked by fear, freezing, and disorientation. Main and Solomon (1986) developed a new classification, "disorganized/disoriented" for infants showing these behaviors in the Strange Situation. . . . The infant and adult disorganized classifications have been consistently linked to a variety of adjustment difficulties and to psychopathology.[39]

Insecure attachment is a risk factor for problems down the road.[40] Michelle Deklyen and Mark Greenberg write, "Most of the research linking attachment with psychopathology has considered attachment as a potential risk or protective factor . . . . Attachment exerts its influence *in the context of other risk factors* within the child and the family ecology."[41] Not all insecurely attached

---

38   M. Main & J. Solomon, Discovery of a New, Insecure Disorganized/Disoriented Attachment Pattern. In T.B. Brazelton & M. Yogman (Eds.), *Affective Development in Infancy* pp. 95-124 (1986).

See Jay Belsky & R.M. Pasco Fearon, Precursors of Attachment Security. In Jude Cassidy & Philip R. Shaver (Eds.), *Handbook of Attachment: Theory, Research, and Clinical Applications* 295-316 at 301 (2nd ed. 2008)("at least six independent studies have found that disorganized attachment is associated with disturbances in parenting behavior that could be considered frightening to the infant (rather than insensitive").

39   Roger Kobak & Stephanie Madsen, Disruptions in Attachment Bonds: Implications for Theory, Research, and Clinical Intervention. In Jude Cassidy & Philip R. Shaver (Eds.), *Handbook of Attachment: Theory, Research, and Clinical Applications* 23-47, at 35-36 (2nd ed. 2008).

40   Michelle Deklyen & Mark T. Greenberg, Attachment and Psychopathology in Childhood. In Jude Cassidy & Philip R. Shaver (Eds.), *Handbook of Attachment: Theory, Research, and Clinical Applications* 637-665, at 637 (2nd ed. 2008).

41   Michelle Deklyen & Mark T. Greenberg, Attachment and Psychopathology in Childhood. In Jude Cassidy & Philip R. Shaver (Eds.), *Handbook of Attachment: Theory, Research, and Clinical Applications* 637-665, at 638 (2nd ed. 2008)(emphasis in original).

Deklyen and Greenberg discuss "risk factors":

> Research on risk factors for disorder leads to five general conclusions. First, it is unlikely that a single cause will be either a necessary or a sufficient cause for most pathology; even the expression of disorders

babies and toddlers have adjustment problems as they mature. Alan Sroufe writes, "Variations in infant-caregiver attachment do not relate well to every outcome, nor do they relate inexorably to any outcome whatsoever. They are related to outcomes only probabilistically and only in the context of complex developmental systems and processes."[42] Insecure attachment is a risk factor, not a death sentence.[43] Moreover, insecure attachment is *not* itself a disorder or mental illness.[44] Deklyen and Greenberg write, "It is clear that insecure attachment is not itself a form of psychopathology but may set a trajectory that, along with other risk factors, can increase the risk for either externalizing or internalizing psychopathology."[45] Thus, Deklyen and Greenberg observe, "Insecure attach-

---

with established biochemical or genetic mechanisms will be potentiated or buffered by other biological or environmental factors. Thus it is doubtful that attachment insecurity alone will lead to disorder, although it may increase its likelihood. . . .

A second tenet of developmental psychopathology states that multiple pathways exist to and from disorder. . . .

Third, risk factors occur at multiple levels, including the individual, the caregiver, and the broader ecological context. . . .

Fourth, the relations between risk and outcome may be nonlinear . . . .

A fifth guiding principle is that certain risk factors may have differential influence in different developmental periods.

42 L. Alan Sroufe, Attachment and Development: A Prospective, Longitudinal Study from Birth to Adulthood, 7 *Attachment & Human Development* 349, 365 (2005).

43 *See* Pamela S. Ludolph & Milfred D. Dale, Attachment in Child Custody: An Additive Factor, Not a Determinative One, 46 *Family Law Quarterly* 1 (2012). The authors write:

Other longitudinal research has not supported a long-term link between attachment status and social and emotional outcome variables, or even the maintenance of secure or insecure attachment status over time. Two twenty-year studies found some indicators of continuity, but did not find an association between results of the Strange Situation administered in toddlerhood and measures of attachment and relationship quality in young adults. . . .

While two other longitudinal studies reported that nearly two-thirds of their samples maintained the same attachment classification over time, these authors also emphasized the importance of negative life events as moderators of attachment status. In one study, divorce in early childhood was particularly likely to result in the maintenance or creation of an insecure attachment, especially when there were high levels of parental conflict. In the second study, several factors tended to increase the likelihood of a change in attachment status over time, including divorce, loss of a parent, life-threatening illness of a parent or child, parental psychiatric disorder, and physical or sexual abuse by a family member. . . .

Finally, recent longitudinal research on infant-mother attachment has found significant variability of outcome for children reared in similar circumstances and has pointed to the importance of cumulative stressors in predicting attachment status.

44 Michelle Deklyen & Mark T. Greenberg, Attachment and Psychopathology in Childhood. In Jude Cassidy & Philip R. Shaver (Eds.), *Handbook of Attachment: Theory, Research, and Clinical Applications* 637-665, at 657 (2nd ed. 2008).

45 Michelle Deklyen & Mark T. Greenberg, Attachment and Psychopathology in Childhood. In Jude Cassidy & Philip R. Shaver (Eds.), *Handbook of Attachment: Theory, Research, and Clinical Applications* 637-665, at 657 (2nd ed. 2008).

ment to a caregiver during infancy has been related to poor peer relations, anger, and poor behavioral self-control during the preschool years and beyond."[46]

During the preschool years, the avoidantly attached child may demonstrate excessive anger and aggression. The child may be unpopular, setting the stage for isolation. The ambivalently attached preschooler may be immature and easily overwhelmed. Difficulties with intimacy and friendship may persist.

Attachment—secure or insecure—typically occurs between ages six months to a year.[47] Babies become attached to abusive and neglectful parents.[48] The quality of attachment may suffer, but attachment occurs.[49] Babies can become attached to more than one person.[50] Jude Cassidy writes, "The majority of children become attached to more than one familiar person during their first year."[51]

It is not uncommon for expert witnesses in child custody litigation to use the terms "attachment" and "bonding."[52] One also finds these terms in legisla-

---

46　Michelle Deklyen & Mark T. Greenberg, Attachment and Psychopathology in Childhood. In Jude Cassidy & Philip R. Shaver (Eds.), *Handbook of Attachment: Theory, Research, and Clinical Applications* 637-665, at 637 (2nd ed. 2008).

47　Mary Dozier & Michael Rutter, Challenges to the Development of Attachment Relationships Faced by Young Children in Foster and Adoptive Care. In Jude Cassidy & Philip R. Shaver (Eds.), *Handbook of Attachment: Theory, Research, and Clinical Applications* 698-717, at 699 (2nd ed. 2008).

48　Jude Cassidy, The Nature of the Child's Ties. In Jude Cassidy & Philip R. Shaver (Eds.), *Handbook of Attachment: Theory, Research, and Clinical Applications* 3-22 (2nd ed. 2008)("findings that infants become attached even to abusive mothers suggest that the system is not driven by simple pleasurable associations." p. 5).

49　Mary Dozier & Michael Rutter, Challenges to the Development of Attachment Relationships Faced by Young Children in Foster and Adoptive Care. In Jude Cassidy & Philip R. Shaver (Eds.), *Handbook of Attachment: Theory, Research, and Clinical Applications* 698-717, at 706 (2nd ed. 2008)("Except under very atypical circumstances, all infants become attached to their primary caregivers. Even when children have maltreating parents, they appear to develop specific attachment relationships with those parents. It is quality of attachment that differentiates most children, rather than whether they have developed attachment relationships of a certain relative strength or intensity.").

50　Jay Belsky & R.M. Pasco Fearon, Precursors of Attachment Security. In Jude Cassidy & Philip R. Shaver (Eds.), *Handbook of Attachment: Theory, Research, and Clinical Applications* 295-316 at 303 (2nd ed. 2008)("If, as is now widely recognized, infants and young children can establish relationships with more than a single individual . . . ."); Jude Cassidy, The Nature of the Child's Ties. In Jude Cassidy & Philip R. Shaver (Eds.), *Handbook of Attachment: Theory, Research, and Clinical Applications* 3-22 (2nd ed. 2008).

51　Jude Cassidy, The Nature of the Child's Ties. In Jude Cassidy & Philip R. Shaver (Eds.), *Handbook of Attachment: Theory, Research, and Clinical Applications* 3-22, at 14 (2nd ed. 2008).

52　J.W. v. C.M., 627 N.W.2d 687 (Minn. Ct. App. 2001)(in custody case, child had been cared for since birth by "foster parents" to whom the child was attached; "The district court found a strong attachment existed between A.K.M. and the Brauns but none existed between A.K.M. and appellant because of his canceled and failed visitations." p. 693); In re K.C.F., 928 A.2d 1046 (Pa. Super. Ct. 2007)(expert in termination of parental rights case used attachment terminology loosely); In re C.L., 178 Vt. 558, 878 A.2d 207 (2005)(expert's report said child was attached to foster parents and it would be risky to remove child from foster parents and return child to father).

tion.[53] Often, the terms are used loosely and have little connection to the "attachment theory" developed by Bowlby, Ainsworth, and others. What the expert is typically referring to is the psychological connection between child and caretaker. Regarding "bonding," Pamela Ludolph and Milfred Dale observe that the word "is bandied about regularly but has no consensual definition within psychology. . . . There is currently no commonly used assessment tool for 'bonding' or even a common understanding of the meaning of the term. Nonetheless, attorneys and judges frequently order 'bonding assessments' of unknown quality to help them make important decisions in the best interests of children."[54]

An article by David Arredondo and Leonard Edwards offers guidance on the use and misuse in court of the terms "attachment" and "bonding."[55] Arredondo and Edwards conclude, "The term 'attachment' (as usually conceived) is too narrow to be of much use to the court . . . ."[56] They write:

> Modern attachment theory addresses the dyadic nature of relationships but excludes the wider system of relatedness in which most children participate. It draws on historical and experimental psychological theory as its basis. Forensic mental health professionals, however, have extended the concept of attachment beyond its scientific and theoretical basis. . . .
>
> Forensic testimony based on attachment theory may mislead courts in three ways. First, the concept of attachment draws distinctions in black and white, whereas courts often need to decide questions in the gray areas of human relations. For heuristic purposes, theoreticians and research scientists classify attachments into four or five rigidly defined categories (secure, insecure-avoidant, insecure-resistant, ambivalent, or disorganized). Though appropriate for research purposes, these categories are insufficiently subtle to describe in a forensic setting the rich and complex spectrum of dimensions of human interrelatedness. Forensic experts need to recognize and openly

---

53 California Welfare and Institutions Code § 361.5. This statute lies at the heart of California's system of family reunification services for children living in foster care. At one point the statute states, "the child is closely and positively attached to that parent" (361.5(c)). At another point in the same statute the section refers to "the degree of parent-child bonding . . . ." (361.5(e)(1)).

54 Pamela S. Ludolph & Milfred D. Dale, Attachment in Child Custody: an Additive Factor, Not a Determinative One, 46 *Family Law Quarterly* 1, 17 (2012).

55 David E. Arredondo & Leonard P. Edwards, Attachment, Bonding, and Reciprocal Connectedness, 2 *Journal of the Center for Families, Children and the Courts* 109-125 (2000).

56 David E. Arredondo & Leonard P. Edwards, Attachment, Bonding, and Reciprocal Connectedness, 2 *Journal of the Center for Families, Children and the Courts* 109-125, at 110 (2000).

acknowledge this limitation of their testimony. The full range and complexity of human relationships and the developmentally dynamic context in which they occur do not permit categorization in a manner sufficiently valid to make them useful to juvenile and family court. In a forensic setting, attachment theory is critically limited because it describes attachment in terms of categories instead of more accurately conceptualizing interrelatedness as a spectrum of continuously distributed variables. . . .

Second, attachment theory may mislead courts because it excludes from its scope the attitudes of adult caregivers . . . .

Third, the concept of attachment is vague. As applied in both research and forensic psychology, the terms "bonding" and "attachment" have multiple meanings that sometimes diverge from their ordinary meanings. When several experts and child protection workers testify in court about attachment, each may use the term to mean something different from the others.[57]

Instead of testimony about attachment or bonding, Arredondo and Edwards recommend the concept of "reciprocal connectedness," which they define as follows:

"Reciprocal connectedness" paints a more comprehensive and subtle picture of relationships than do "bonding" and "attachment." In the context of decisionmaking in the family court setting, we can define it as a mutual interrelatedness that is characterized by two-way interaction between a child and an adult caregiver and by the caregiver's sensitivity to the child's developmental needs.[58]

---

57 David E. Arredondo & Leonard P. Edwards, Attachment, Bonding, and Reciprocal Connectedness, 2 *Journal of the Center for Families, Children and the Courts* 109-125, at 110-111 (2000).

58 David E. Arredondo & Leonard P. Edwards, Attachment, Bonding, and Reciprocal Connectedness, 2 *Journal of the Center for Families, Children and the Courts* 109-125, at 112 (2000)(authors describe the "dimensions of reciprocal connectedness with younger children [to] include: Frequency and quality of eye contact; Frequency of affectionate touching or soothing; Spontaneous anticipation of the child's needs or desires; Empathic response to the needs of the child for attention; Spontaneous smiling in both directions; Bilateral initiation of affectionate interactions; Understanding of the child's unique temperament; Affectionate speech or 'cooing'; Singing, reading, and playing with the child. Dimensions with older children might include: Recognition of the child as a unique individual; Recognition of the particular needs of the developmental stage of the child; Valuing the child for who he or she is; Trying to understand the child's world from his or her perspective; Trying to teach the child; Trying to learn from the caregiver; Seeking guidance or comfort from the caregiver; Sharing positive experiences; Maintaining a relationship that allows the child some measure of control while setting limits and maintaining boundaries." pp. 113-114).

Erickson's Stages of Development

Erik Erikson (1902-1994) was born in Europe, where he studied psychology and psychoanalysis. Erikson described eight stages of development from infancy to old age. Each stage presents a conflict the successful resolution of which paves the way to healthy development. Erickson's stages are summarized below.

Trust vs. Mistrust. Birth to 18 months. The focus of this period is whether the young child's basic needs are fulfilled by parents. If the child receives consistent loving attention, the child learns to trust. By contrast, if the child is neglected, the child may develop a basic mistrust of the world—the world is not a safe, dependable place. The overlap with attachment theory is apparent.

Autonomy vs. Shame and Doubt. Age 18 months to 3 years. When parents are consistent and encouraging, the child develops autonomy and self-confidence. When parents are not supportive, or when parents expect too much, children may develop a sense of shame and self-doubt.

Initiative vs. Guilt. Age 3 to 5 years. The child is learning how the world works, and the child takes the initiative to solve problems. When parents and other adults encourage the child while, at the same time, making sure the child is safe, the child gains a sense of independence and initiative. On the other hand, if the child's efforts to explore the world are stymied or ridiculed, the child may develop self-doubt, shame, and guilt.

Industry vs. Inferiority. Age 6 to 12 years. At this stage, children are more responsible and able to share and work together. Children want to master new skills. Children are developing moral values. This is a critical time for the development of self-confidence. A child who is encouraged makes progress in these dimensions, whereas a child who is criticized and doubted acquires a sense of inferiority.

Identity vs. Role Confusion. Age 12 to 18 years. The critical period of transition from childhood to adulthood, with the angst that accompanies the teenage years.

Intimacy vs. Isolation. The young adult, age 18 to 35. The young adult asks basic questions like, Who am I? What do I want out of life? Can I find love and intimacy? Is the world for or against me?

Generativity vs. Self-Absorption or Stagnation. Middle adulthood from 35 up to 65. If things go well, the adult finds fulfillment in work and family. As the kids grow up and leave the nest, the adult finds new challenges or stagnates and begins to get "old."

Ego Integrity vs. Despair. Late adulthood, from the 50s or 60s until death. When we look back on life, do we feel we accomplished something? Made a contribution? If the answer is yes, Erikson calls this a sense of integrity. If the answer is no, we may despair that life was not worthwhile.

Brief History of Child Custody Law

For much of the nineteenth century, courts ruled that fathers normally had the right to custody.[59] Gradually, the presumption in favor of dad was replaced by the "tender years" presumption, which held that children of tender years should normally be with mom.[60] In the 1960s, critics argued the tender years presumption constituted gender-based discrimination. The tender years presumption gave way to a gender-neutral preference for the "primary caretaker," that is, the parent who provides most of the day-to-day parenting.[61] The overarching priority is a custody decision that serves the best interests of the child.

The following case was decided by the California Supreme Court in 1860, and provides insight into judicial thinking about custody at an earlier time. As you read the decision, note the growing awareness of the importance of the child's best interests.

Wand v. Wand

California Supreme Court
14 Cal. 512 (1860)

Baldwin, J.

No questions arise in Courts of Justice more interesting or important than those which affect the domestic relations of society. The happiness of the community is deeply concerned in the right establishment and just understanding

---

59 Joel P. Bishop, *New Commentaries on Marriage, Divorce, and Separation* vol. 2, § 1152, p. 449 (1891)("To an extent not necessary to be here defined, the father is at the common law the guardian of his minor children.").

60 *See* Joel P. Bishop, *New Commentaries on Marriage, Divorce, and Separation* vol. 2, § 829, pp. 336-337 (1891)("if the good of the child requires, she, other things being equal, will be preferred to him and to all other persons for custodian. This is often so emphatically where the infant is of a tender age, especially requiring a mother's care.").

61 Weinberger v. Weinmeister, 268 P.3d 305 (Alaska 2012)("we defined the tender years doctrine as the presumption that, other factors being equal, a mother will be given preference for custody. . . . We reaffirm our precedent holding that a presumption in favor of the mother is an improper basis on which to award custody.").

of the rules which govern these relations. The record in this case involves the question, whether the father or the mother is entitled to the custody of an infant child, under the circumstances hereinafter stated.

The plaintiff brought her bill for a divorce, *a vinculo*, from her then husband, the defendant, upon the ground of extreme cruelty. This cruelty consisted, as averred and proved on the trial, in an attempt to kill her, by snapping a loaded pistol at her breast. This effort failing, he shot himself, inflicting a dangerous wound. This conduct seems to have been the result of jealousy, but we look in vain into the record for anything to justify it. There is no allegation in the answer, impeaching the fidelity of the plaintiff, nor is there anything in the proofs which even throws suspicion upon the purity of her conduct, apart from these acts of the defendant, which seem to have been unaccompanied by explanation. The defendant appears to have been a man of peaceable general demeanor; and this act is charged as the sole deviation from a course of affectionate and becoming conduct in his marital relations.

The judge below made a decree dissolving the marriage, and giving the custody of the child to the father. The child is an interesting girl of some six or seven years of age. The plaintiff, since the decree, has married—the defendant is single.

This appeal is taken from so much of the decree as fixes the custody of the child. Possibly, the plaintiff might have some difficulty in maintaining the decree of divorce upon the ground of extreme cruelty, founded upon this single act, under all the circumstances; although, as no appeal has been taken from that portion of the record, it is not necessary to consider the point, or intimate any opinion upon it.

The question of law raised by this statement is this: Is a husband, divorced from his wife, at her instance, for extreme cruelty, entitled to the custody of a female child of tender years—the conduct of the wife being without blame? . . .

It is not denied that the husband, as the head of the family, has the direction and control of the family, and of family affairs, and that his will and judgment are paramount to those of the wife, as well in respect to the custody of the children of the marriage, as to other things. But after the marriage has been dissolved, the question is different.

It is difficult to see upon what principle he is to be regarded as the superior, or as having superior rights, on the cessation of the matrimonial connection, to the other partner, now released from all marital obligations of obedience to him. Bishop on Marriage and Divorce (Sec. 641), uses this language: . . . "That from parentage necessarily flow both the right and duty to educate and maintain the offspring; and from these flows, also, the right to their custody; that as between the parents, the law having placed the husband at the head of the family, and made his will paramount whenever he and the wife differ in judgment, and having likewise vested in him the property from which the children must be supported, it follows, of necessity, that he is entitled, in preference to her, to their custody also. . . . Upon principle, therefore, the rule would seem to be, that *prima facie*, after a separation, the father is entitled to the custody of the children, unless there be a divorce for his fault; in which case, the mother is entitled; yet, that this *prima facie* right must always be subject to the superior claims, that is, the good of the children."

. . . That a child of the tender age of this could be better cared for by the mother, with whom she could be almost constantly, than the father, whose necessary avocations would withdraw him, in a great measure, from personal superintendence and care of her, is plain enough. Indeed, if the dominion of the child should be given to the father, it is very evident that he must confide her person to some female to care for and keep her; and upon the person thus selected would depend, in a great degree, the happiness and welfare of the infant. We do not see why the mother should not, in the first instance, be intrusted with this office, for which she seems, upon every ground of humanity and natural right, to have the claim. For it does not at all follow that, in the present unhappy state of relations of these parties, the care or protection of the father is to be relinquished, or his parental duties or obligations destroyed. On the contrary, he has a right to be admitted to see the child at all convenient times when he may desire it. For the purpose of insuring him in the enjoyment of this right, he may have leave at any time to apply to the District Court for the necessary orders—for which the cause may be considered as open, so as to provide the necessary relief, if application be unhappily necessary. But it is to be hoped that this matter can be, as it should be, amicably settled by the parties so as to give the full benefit of parental protection and care to this child, and at the same time give to both parents the comfort of her society.

The Court reverses the decree below giving the custody of the child to the father, and orders that the child be restored to the mother . . . .

Observations bed on *Wand v. Wand*

1. Wife sought a divorce based on extreme cruelty because husband put a gun to her chest and pulled the trigger, intending to kill her. Yet, the Supreme Court wrote, "Possibly, the plaintiff might have some difficulty in maintaining the decree of divorce upon the ground of extreme cruelty, founded upon this sin-

gle act . . . ." What?! Trying to kill your spouse might not be grounds for divorce? Are you kidding?

2. *Wand* offers insight into gender roles in bygone days. A wife was obliged to obey her husband. The husband was the head of the family. His decisions were paramount. He had control of all property. (*See* Chapter 9.) The court assumed men work and women stay home to care for children.

3. The court wrote that the case "may be considered open" to allow father to return to court if mother frustrates his right to visit the child. This is the law today. The family court retains continuing jurisdiction to revisit custody and visitation until children reach age 18.

Custody Terminology

States vary slightly in the terms used to describe custody.[62] A distinction exists between legal and physical custody. Legal custody is the right to make decisions about a child's medical care, where the child goes to school, and innumerable day-to-day issues. Physical custody is the right to have the child live with the custodial parent all or part of the time. Sole physical custody means the child lives full time with the custodial parent. Joint physical custody means the child lives part of the time with each parent.[63] Parents can have joint legal and joint physical custody, or one parent can have sole physical custody while the parents share legal custody.

The law's preference in custody matters is to maximize involvement of both parents in the child's life. In Illinois, "unless the court finds the occurrence of ongoing abuse . . . , the court shall presume that the maximum involvement and cooperation of both parents regarding the physical, mental, moral, and emotional well-being of their child is in the best interest of the child."[64] In Michigan, "If the parents agree on joint custody, the court shall award joint custody unless the court determines on the record based upon clear and convincing evidence that joint custody is not in the best interests of the child."[65] California's Legislature

---

62 For example, Texas uses the term "managing conservator." In North Dakota, the parent with whom children live most of the time has "primary residential responsibility."

63 *See* Mich. Comp. Laws Ann. § 722.26a(7) ("As used in this section, 'joint custody' means an order of the court in which 1 or both of the following is specified: (a) That the child shall reside alternately for specified periods with each of the parents. (b) That the parents shall share decision-making authority as to the important decisions affecting the welfare of the child.").

64 750 ILCS 5/602(c).

65 Mich. Comp. Laws Ann. § 722.26a(2).

stated, "It is the public policy of this state to assure that children have frequent and continuing contact with both parents after the parents have separated or dissolved their marriage . . . ."[66]

Best Interests of the Child

As stated earlier in this chapter, most divorcing parents agree on custody, and the judge approves their agreement. When parents cannot agree on custody, the judge employs the best interests of the child standard. The Vermont Supreme Court discussed the best interest standard in *Miller-Jenkins v. Miller-Jenkins*:[67] "The family court's sole focus in a custody dispute must be the best interests of the child. Although the parents are the ones who appear before the court in a custody dispute, and it is therefore easy to become caught up in their rights and interests rather than the child's welfare, the family court must not take into consideration the competing, often antagonistic, desires of the parents without upsetting the delicate nature of custody proceedings and trivializing the welfare of the child."

The question is always: What custody arrangement is best for this child? In conducting a best interest analysis, the judge considers all evidence shedding light on a child's short- and long-term interests—the totality of the circumstances.[68] The judge has broad discretion.[69] Statutory definitions of "best interests" are similar around the country. The Illinois and Michigan statutes are illustrative:

750 ILCS 5/602

(a) The court shall determine custody in accordance with the best interest of the child. The court shall consider all relevant factors including:

(1) the wishes of the child's parent or parents as to his custody;

(2) the wishes of the child as to his custodian;

---

66 Cal. Family Code § 3020(b).

67 12 A.3d 768 (Vt. 2010).

68 *See* Parris v. Parris, 319 S.C. 308, 460 S.E.2d 571, 572 (1995)("the totality of the circumstances peculiar to each case constitutes the only scale upon which the ultimate decision can be weighed.").

69 *See* Marriage of Smithson, 407 Ill. App. 3d 597, 943 N.E.2d 1169 (2011)("The determination of child custody rests largely within the discretion of the trial court, and its decision will not be disturbed on appeal unless it is against the manifest weight of the evidence or the trial court abused its discretion.").

(3) the interaction and interrelationship of the child with his parent or parents, his siblings and any other person who may significantly affect the child's best interest;

(4) the child's adjustment to his home, school and community;

(5) the mental and physical health of all individuals involved;

(6) the physical violence or threat of physical violence by the child's potential custodian, whether directed against the child or directed against another person;

(7) the occurrence of ongoing or repeated [violence] whether directed against the child or directed against another person; and

(8) the willingness and ability of each parent to facilitate and encourage a close and continuing relationship between the other parent and the child;

(9) whether one of the parents is a sex offender . . . .

Mich. Comp. Laws Ann. § 722.23

As used in this act, "best interests of the child" means the sum total of the following factors to be considered, evaluated, and determined by the court:

(a) The love, affection, and other emotional ties existing between the parties involved and the child.

(b) The capacity and disposition of the parties involved to give the child love, affection, and guidance and to continue the education and raising of the child in his or her religion or creed, if any.

(c) The capacity and disposition of the parties involved to provide the child with food, clothing, medical care or other remedial care recognized and permitted under the laws of this state in place of medical care, and other material needs.

(d) The length of time the child has lived in a stable, satisfactory environment, and the desirability of maintaining continuity.

(e) The permanence, as a family unit, of the existing or proposed custodial home or homes.

(f) The moral fitness of the parties involved.

(g) The mental and physical health of the parties involved.

(h) The home, school, and community record of the child.

(i) The reasonable preference of the child, if the court considers the child to be of sufficient age to express preference.

(j) The willingness and ability of each of the parties to facilitate and encourage a close and continuing parent-child relationship between the child and the other parent or the child and the parents.

(k) Domestic violence, regardless of whether the violence was directed against or witnessed by the child.

(l) Any other factor considered by the court to be relevant to a particular child custody dispute.

Although the best interest standard is ubiquitous, it has always had critics.[70] The basic problem is that the best interest standard is standardless. Decision-making standards that lack relatively clear guidelines for making decisions result in unpredictable outcomes, especially in close cases. Every judge conducting a best interest analysis has a unique personal history. Most judges are parents, and judges almost certainly are influenced by their experience with their own kids. Not only is every judge different, every judge was once a lawyer. Not a psychologist or social worker trained in child development, but a lawyer trained in contracts, torts, and crimes. What makes us think judges have any particular skill in deciding what is best for children? On the other hand, judges have a solemn responsibility to do justice—a responsibility the vast majority of judges take very seriously. Judges understand that few decisions they make are more important than decisions about children. As well, judges are skilled at sorting through conflicting evidence to find kernels of truth. Thus, we can be fairly confident that the gravity of the office, combined with experience and an appreciation of the importance of "getting it right," equips judges to reach correct decisions most of the time. In the final analysis, although the best interests of the child standard has shortcomings, no one has offered a viable alternative. Can you think of a better way to decide custody cases? Before you answer that question, read the excerpt from Robert Mnookin's famous 1975 article.

---

70 *See* Steven N. Peskind, Determining the Undeterminable: The Best Interest of the Child Standard as an Imperfect But Necessary Guidepost to Determine Child Custody, 25 *Northern Illinois University Law Review* 449 (2005).

Child-Custody Adjudication:
Judicial Functions in the Face of Indeterminacy

Robert H. Mnookin
39 Law and Contemporary Problems 226-293 (1975)

Who should decide custody disputes and by what process? Are custody disputes, by their very nature, somehow inappropriate for resolution by adjudication? Adversary proceedings are said to distort the fact-finding process in custody disputes and unnecessarily injure the parties. Commentators have argued that judges are ill-equipped to make the necessary determinations and that social workers, psychologists, or psychiatrists should have a more important role in the ultimate decision, perhaps as part of a family court.

The determination of what is "best" or "least detrimental" for a particular child is usually indeterminate and speculative. For most custody cases, existing psychological theories simply do not yield confident predictions of the effects of alternative custody dispositions. Moreover, even if accurate predictions were possible in more cases, our society today lacks any clear-cut consensus about the values to be used in determining what is "best" or "least detrimental."

Because what is in the best interests of a particular child is indeterminate, there is good reason to be offended by the breadth of power exercised by a trial court judge in the resolution of custody disputes. But the underlying reasons for this indeterminacy—our inability to make predictions and our lack of consensus with regard to values—make the formulation of rules especially problematic. In all events, the debate over rules versus discretion is best understood when the indeterminacy of what is best is candidly admitted. Moreover, examination of the reasons for this indeterminacy suggests that procedural changes in custody disputes, greater use of experts, or a change in the nature of the forum may avoid some mistakes and make the process more fair but will not correct the underlying difficulty.

An inquiry about what is best for a child often yields indeterminate results because of the problems of having adequate information, making the necessary predictions, and finding an integrated set of values by which to choose. But some custody cases may still be comparatively easy to decide. While there is no consensus about what is best for a child, there is much consensus about what is very bad (*e.g.*, physical abuse); some short-term predictions about human behavior can be reliably made (*e.g.*, chronic alcoholism or psychosis is difficult quickly to modify). Asking which alternative is in the best interests of a child may have a rather clear-cut answer in situations where one claimant exposes the child to substantial risks of immediate harm and the other claimant already has a substantial personal relationship with the child and poses no such risk. In a private dispute between two parents, for example, if a judge could predict that one parent's conduct would seriously endanger the child's health, it would not be difficult to conclude that the child's expected utility would be higher if he went with the other parent, whose conduct did not, even without the necessity of defining utility carefully. More generally, where one alternative plainly risks irreversible effects on the child that are bad and the other does not, there is no need to make longer-term predictions or more complicated psychological evaluations of what is likely to happen to the child's personality.

But to be easy, a case must involve only one claimant who is well known to the child and whose conduct does not endanger the child. If there are two such claimants or none, difficult choices remain. Most custody disputes pose difficult choices.

Custody disputes are now decided on the basis of broad, person-oriented principles that ask for highly individualized determinations. The trial judge has broad discretion, but the question asked often has no meaningful answer. What are some of the implications of the use of indeterminate standards in custody disputes? Would more precise standards that ask an answerable question be better?

More rule-like standards would avoid or mitigate some obvious disadvantages of adjudication by an indeterminate principle. For one thing, the use of an indeterminate standard makes the outcome of litigation difficult to predict. This may encourage more litigation than would a standard that made the outcome of more cases predictable. Because each divorcing parent can often make plausible arguments why a child would be better off with him or her, a best-interests standard probably creates a greater incentive to litigate than would a rule that children should go to the parent of the same sex.

Indeterminate standards also pose an obviously greater risk of violating the fundamental precept that like cases should be decided alike. Because people differ and no two custody cases are exactly alike, the claim can be made that no process is more fair than one requiring resolution by a highly individualized, person-oriented standard. But with an indeterminate standard, the same case presented to different judges may easily result in different decisions. The use of an indeterminate standard means that state officials may decide on the basis of unarticulated (perhaps even unconscious) predictions and preferences that could be questioned if expressed. Because of the scope of discretion under such a standard, there is a substantial risk that decisions will be made on the basis of values not widely shared in our society, even among judges.

But the choice between indeterminate standards and more precise rules poses a profound dilemma. The absence of rules removes the special burdens of justification and formulation of standards characteristic of adjudication. Unfairness and adverse consequences can result. And yet, rules that relate past events or conduct to legal consequences may themselves create substantial difficulties in the custody area. Our inadequate knowledge about human behavior and our inability to generalize confidently about the relationship between past events or conduct and future behavior make the formulation of rules especially problematic. Moreover, the very lack of consensus about values that makes the best-interests standard indeterminate may also make the formulation of rules inappropriate: a legal rule must, after all, reflect some social value or values. An overly ambitious and indeterminate principle may result in fewer decisions that reflect what is known to be desirable. But rules may result in some conspicuously bad decisions that could be avoided by a more discretionary standard. What balance should be struck?

Three assumptions guide what follows. First, family autonomy is given a high value. Second, continuity and stability in relationships are assumed to be important and desirable for children, especially for young children. This proposition cannot be proven beyond any doubt by existing empirical studies, and accurate predictions for a particular child about the effects of the lack of stability are beyond existing techniques. But a substantial and impressive consensus exists among psychologists and psychiatrists that disruption of the parent-child relationship carries significant risks. Third, legal rules, especially in an area touching upon substantial intrafamilial relationships, should not contradict deeply held and widely shared social values.

The use of an indeterminate standard for private dispute resolution does raise a number of questions related to fairness. In addition, the best-interests test probably encourages the judicial delay and lack of finality that plague custody law. Given a hopelessly ambitious standard that asks the impossible, judges may seek to avoid making an initial determination in a private custody dispute and may be more willing later to reopen and reconsider an initial decision. Finally, the use of an indeterminate standard for adjudication may result in more cases being litigated than would be true if more rule-like standards governed custody disputes requiring the private dispute-settlement function. Because of these various disadvantages of an indeterminate standard, the analysis of more precise alternatives would seem very much in order.

[Professor Mnookin searches] for more rule-like standards for the adjudication of private custody disputes. Apart from three intermediate rules that will help dispose of only a small number of cases, this safari returns with no game worth keeping. The quest continues by examining alternative methods of dispute resolution: mediation, informal adjudication, and random selection. My conclusion is hardly comforting: while the indeterminate best-interests standard may not be good, there is no available alternative that is plainly less detrimental.

Three intermediate rules seem justifiable for private dispute settlement. First, custody should never be awarded to a claimant whose limitations or conduct would endanger the health of the child under the minimum standards for child protection [established by law]. The correct resolution of a private dispute is obvious where one claimant poses an immediate and substantial threat to the child's physical health and the other does not. Second, the court should prefer a psychological parent (*i.e.*, an adult who has a psychological relationship with the child from the child's perspective) over any claimant (including a natural parent) who, from the child's perspective, is not a psychological parent. [The term "psychological parent" was coined by Joseph Goldstein, Anna Freud, and Albert Solnit in their 1973 book *Beyond the Best Interests of the Child*.] Third, subject to the two rules noted above, natural parents should be preferred over others. In a dispute where the natural parent poses no danger to the child's physical health and is viewed by the child as his psychological parent, a preference for the natural parent over a third party gives expression to broadly shared social values about parental responsibilities for the welfare of their offspring and reflects the importance to the child of a sense of lineage.

These three standards could be even-handedly and fairly applied, are consistent with the best-interests-of-the-child principle, and would dispose of some cases. . . . These three standards would not, however, dispose of a very large class of private disputes: controversies between two natural parents, neither of whom would endanger a child's physical health, where both are psychological parents.

For these disputes between parents, should additional rules be adopted? Alternative standards include awarding custody (1) on the basis of the sex of the parent (*e.g.*, maternal preference); (2) to the parent of the same sex as the child; (3) to the richer parent; (4) to the parent who would spend more time with the child; (5) to the parent chosen by the child; or (6) to the parent whose psychological relationship with the child would be "less detrimental." None of these seems preferable to the best-interests standard.

Compared to the best-interests standard, the sex or wealth-based rules would be capable of even-handed application. By making the results of adjudication more predictable, such rules would also tend to discourage litigation. But the reduction of litigation would be achieved by substantially changing the spouses' relative bargaining power in private negotiations. A standard providing for maternal preference, for example, does more than affect the outcome of the small number of disputes that are actually litigated. It also gives mothers as a class more bargaining power than fathers in negotiations over custody. Therefore, in comparing some more determinate standard with the best-interests principle, it is not enough simply to suggest that fewer disputes will be litigated. One must also consider whether the effects of the alternative standards on private negotiations are desirable.

The best-interests-of-the-child standard provides a more "neutral" backdrop for both private negotiations and adjudication than a rule providing a preference on the basis of sex; and in my view, this is desirable. There appears to be no substantial empirical evidence to justify, from the child's perspective, a rule that systematically "tilts" the process in favor of the mother where the parents disagree . . . . Sex-based rules have been tried historically and are now being discarded (correctly in my view) because they reflect value judgments and sexual stereotypes that our society is in the process of rejecting. A wealth-based standard has similar weaknesses, for wealth and child rearing ability are not known to be coincident, and a test that preferred the richer parent for that reason alone would be seen as unfair. It might be thought that, other things being equal, a richer parent would be more likely to provide the child with certain material advantages. But child-support payments can be used to reallocate family wealth. Moreover, a wealth-based test would be offensive to many people, because they would see it as implicitly treating the child as a possession to be allocated by a market, even though the application of the standard itself would involve no exchange.

A standard that awards custody to the parent able to spend more time with the child would ignore qualitative differences in time spent with the child and thus might not be justifiable from the perspective of what is good for the child. In all events, because the test would require a prediction of the amount of time each parent would spend with the child, it would be very difficult to apply and would invite exaggeration and dishonesty in litigation.

Having the child choose has much to commend it. The child, after all, is the focus on social concern. Moreover, in the face of indeterminacy, why not have the child's values inform the choice? The child, better than the judge, may have an intuitive sense of the parent's love, devotion, and capacity. But particularly for infants, this standard is little more than a random process, and for the younger child, what would this standard mean? Would the child be able to express a preference? If so, would the child's choice be pressured or corrupted by the prelitigation behavior of one parent? Is it desirable or fair to ask the child to choose? This rule might make the child, in the parents' eyes, responsible for the choice. This might often be a very great burden for the child. Furthermore, if the child were made responsible, the child's relationship with the nonchosen parent might be substantially injured. Many states now require a judge to consider a child's expressed preference in applying the best-interests standard, and the choice of those young people twelve to fourteen years of age or older is by statute often made dispositive. Perhaps this age could be lowered, but in all events, the existing practice appears preferable to a rule that would require the child to choose and then make that choice determinative for all cases.

The final "standard"—choosing the parent whose psychological relationship with the child would be "less detrimental"—is suggested by Goldstein, Freud, and Solnit [in *Beyond the Best Interests of the Child*] and represents the most recent of a related series of proposals that the insights of psychology and psychiatry be used as a basis for the reformulation of custody standards. . . . I accept the conclusion that a "psychological parent" who is biologically unrelated to the child should prevail over a natural parent who is a stranger to the child. While the proposition has not been empirically proven, the risks of removing the child from a "psychological parent" for placement with a psychological "stranger" would seem to outweigh the psychological benefits the child might receive by maintaining a better sense of lineage by living with the natural parent. Moreover, I believe that psychologists and psychiatrists can rather consistently differentiate between a situation where an adult and a child have a substantial relationship of the sort we characterize as parent-child and that where there is no such relationship at all. But I do not think that existing psychological theories provide the basis to choose generally between two adults where the child has some relationship and psychological attachment to each.

Having custody disputes determined by embracing more and more of the niceties of psychological and psychiatric theories requires careful analysis of the limits of these theories, their empirical bases, and the capacity of our legal system to absorb this new doctrine. In cases where, from the child's perspective, each claimant has a psychological relationship with the child, I doubt whether there would often be widespread consensus among experts about which parent would prove psychologically better (or less detrimental) to the child. Often each parent will have a different sort of relationship with the child, with the child attached to each. One may be warm, easy-going, but incapable of discipline. The other may be fair, able to set limits, but unable to express affection. By what criteria is an expert to decide which is less detrimental? Moreover, even the proponents of psychological standards have acknowledged how problematic it is to evaluate relationships from a psychological perspective unless a highly trained person spends a considerable amount of time observing the parent and child interact or talking to the child. Superficial examinations by those without substantial training may be worse than nothing. And yet, that is surely a high risk.

Even with the best trained experts, the choice would be based on predictions that are beyond the demonstrated capacity of any existing theory.

The problems posed by the use of an indeterminate standard, coupled with the difficulties of formulating more precise rules that would dispose of many cases, invite explicit consideration of modes of dispute resolution other than traditional adjudication. Since a primary goal for cases of these sorts should be facilitating private resolutions, mediation is an obvious possibility. A negotiated settlement has considerable advantages over one imposed by a court. The adults seeking custody avoid the cost—both financial and emotional—of an adversary proceeding.

We would more frankly acknowledge both our ignorance and the presumed equality of the natural parents were we to flip a coin. Whether one had a separate flip for each child or one flip for all the children, the process would certainly be cheaper and quicker. It would avoid the pain associated with an adversary proceeding that requires an open exploration of the intimate aspects of family life and an ultimate judgment that one parent is preferable to the other. And it might have beneficial effects on private negotiations.

Resolving a custody dispute by state-administered coin-flip would probably be viewed as unacceptable by most in our society. Perhaps this reaction reflects an abiding faith, despite the absence of an empirical basis for it, that letting a judge choose produces better results for the child. Alternatively, flipping a coin might be unacceptable for some because it represents an abdication of the search for wisdom.

While forceful arguments can be made in favor of the abandonment of adjudication and the adoption of an openly random process, the repulsion many would probably feel towards this suggestion may reflect an intuitive appreciation of the importance of the educational, participatory, and symbolic values of adjudication as a mode of dispute settlement. Adjudication under the indeterminate best-interests principle may yield something close to a random pattern of outcomes, while at the same time serving these values, affirming parental equality, and expressing a social concern for the child. Insofar as judges as a group may have value preferences that systematically bias the process and make the pattern less than random, these value preferences may reflect widespread values that have not been acknowledged openly in the form of legal rules.

In child-custody disputes, the determination of what is "best" or "least detrimental" for a particular child is usually indeterminate. . . . On the one hand, the very inability to make predictions about the consequences of alternative custody dispositions and the lack of a social consensus about the values that should inform child rearing make the formulation of rules—by the court or the legis-lature—very problematic at the present time. On the other hand, the use of an indeterminate standard such as "best interests" raises fundamental questions of fairness. But neither offers assurance of being plainly superior to adjudication under the indeterminate best-interests principle.[71]

Now that you have digested Professor Mnookin's ideas, have you come up with something better than the best interests of the child standard?

> **Practice Note:** We live in the era of no fault divorce. In child cus-tody litigation, however, fault is alive and well. To determine a child's best interests, the judge considers the strengths and weaknesses of each parent. Each parent in a contested custody case looks for as much mud to sling at the other parent as possible. It can get ugly. It is critical that you have the trust of your client so your client feels free to reveal the skeletons in her or his own closet. Impress on your client the impor-tance of being completely honest with you. It is better for you to know in advance about that DUI a year ago or that "little drug problem" than to find out about it for the first time in court!
>
> While it is true that fault is relevant in custody litigation, it is a delicate matter to decide how and when to bring parental fault to the court's attention. In some cases, you can attain a settlement favorable to your client by letting the other side know about the evidence you will present if the case goes to trial. If the other parent has a lot of baggage, that parent may "give up without a fight." If the case goes to trial, be thoughtful about presenting evidence of fault. Simply because a parent has done some bad things does not mean the parent doesn't love their child. If you or your client come across a little too self-righteous or holier than thou, or if you or your client exaggerate the other parent's faults, the judge may hold it against your client. Mudslinging requires finesse, discretion, and a good aim.

---

71 *Id.* at 228-230, 233-236, 261-265, 282-288, 290-292.

Should the Judge Talk to the Kids?

In custody litigation, should children testify? Can you think of anything *less* appropriate than putting a child on the witness stand and asking the child to "pick a parent"? With older children, judges sometimes talk to the child in chambers, without the parents.[72] The Oklahoma Supreme Court's decision in *Ynclan v. Woodward* provides a thorough analysis of in-chambers interviews of children.

Ynclan v. Woodward

Supreme Court of Oklahoma
237 P.3d 145 (2010)

Kauger, J.:

This is a case of first impression. We have never determined under what circumstances and conditions a trial court may: (1) conduct *in camera* interviews of children who are the subject of child custody and/or visitation proceedings; and (2) provide the transcript of the proceedings to the parents after the private *in camera* interview occurs. An *in camera* interview is generally an "in chambers" interview which is essentially an approved ex-parte communication because it is a communication that involves fewer than all of the parties who would ordinarily be legally entitled to be present during the discussion. . . . We assume original jurisdiction to address these questions, and to delineate the guidelines for trial courts to follow when conducting an *in camera* interview of children in custody/visitation matters. We also hold that unless one party or both parties appeal the custody determination, due process does not require that either parent have access to the transcript of the *in camera* interview of the children merely to satisfy their own curiosity. . . .

Nancy Ynclan (the mother) and Nolan Shawn Ynclan (the petitioner/father) were married on Valentine's Day 1996. The couple had four children born in 1996, 1997, 1999, and 2004, and on February 27, 2008, the mother filed for divorce . . . .

The matter proceeded to trial on January 14 and January 30, 2009. On the second day of trial, the trial judge interviewed the three oldest children, in chambers, without counsel or the parents being present. However, a court reporter was present to take notes. The three interviews lasted less than fifteen minutes.

---

72 *See* Cal. Family Code § 3042.

The mother insists that counsel for both sides agreed not to be present in the interview, but that written questions were submitted. According to the father, after the interview, he promptly made an informal request for the transcript of the children's interviews and tendered his cost deposit. This request was denied and at the conclusion of the trial, the court granted the divorce and awarded the mother custody of the children.

On February 13, 2009, the father made a formal request to the court to review the transcript of the children's testimony. The court held a hearing on March 2, 2009, and denied the father's request for the transcript. . . . .

The procedure of a trial judge conducting a private, *in camera* interview with a child, depending upon age and maturity, has been widely used as a means of discovering the child's custodial preference. The purposes of conducting an interview in private, rather than in open court in the presence of the parents include:

(1) elimination of the harm a child might suffer from exposure to examination and cross-examination and the adversarial nature of the proceedings generally;

(2) reduction of added pressure to a child to an already stressful situation;

(3) enhancement of the child's ability to be forthcoming;

(4) reduction of the child's feeling of disloyalty toward a parent or to openly choose sides;

(5) minimization of the emotional trauma affecting the child, by lessening the ordeal for the child;

(6) protection of the child from the tug and pull of competing custodial interests; and

(7) awarding custody without placing the child in an adverse position between the parents.

Obviously, the purpose of such a hearing is not to lessen the ordeal for the parents, but, rather, to lessen the ordeal for the child. Nor is it intended to make a secret of the basis for the court's findings. The preference of the child is only one of many factors to be considered when determining the child's best interest concerning custody. It should never be the only basis for determining custody. Nor should a child be directly asked where the child would rather live because specifically asking preference provides an opportunity for parental manipulation or intimidation of the child as well as an opportunity for the child to manipulate the parents. It also gives the child the impression that their preference is "the" deciding factor for custody. Rather, the trial court should conduct such an interview so as to discern the child's preference, while at the same time, being sensitive to how the child is coping with the divorce, the pressures put on the child by the divorce and stating a preference, as well as to ascertain the motive of the child in stating a preference. When the trial court determines the child's best interest will be served by considering the child's preference, whether to hold such an interview is generally within the trial court's discretion.

Because the interview is not held in open court, in the presence of the parents, courts have also recognized that such a procedure is contrary to the basic concepts of an adversarial system. For instance, in *KES v. CAT,* 107 P.3d 779 (Wyo. 2005), a case in which one parent objected to the child being interviewed by the trial court in private, the Supreme Court of Wyoming noted that: "the fundamental principal of Anglo-Saxon law that the decision must be based on evidence in open court lest the guaranty of due process be infringed." The flip side of the coin is that "the conviction of those trained in the social and medical sciences that the informal procedure of obtaining the infant's preference, outlook, and interest in the calm of the judge's chambers, away from the pressure of the parents, provides best for the welfare of the child and of society as a whole." Undeniably, conducting such an interview raises due process and fundamental fairness issues, insofar as the parents are concerned. At conflict with the parents' basic due process rights is the child's right to be heard and to express a preference as to where he or she will live.

The Wyoming Court also noted several due process implications which arise in custody litigation such as the parent's right to associate with and rear his or her child, or to enjoy their children's companionship, and to direct upbringing. When an *in camera* interview is proposed, other implications also arise such as the right to be apprised of all the evidence upon which an issue is to be decided and the right to examine, explain or rebut such evidence including the right to hear or cross-examine witnesses. The Wyoming Court noted that when a judge interviews a child in private without the consent of a parent, the parent is deprived of due process inasmuch as he or she is unable to hear the evidence, and is not given an opportunity to explain or rebut statements made by the child. . . .

In spite of the due process implications, *in camera* interviews are widely used as a means of discovering a child's custodial preference. In most cases, if the parents consent or agree to the interview, a trial court may hold an *in camera* custody preference interview without the parents. If a parent does not object to the procedure at the time of the interview, then any objection is generally waived on appeal. Even when consent is given, the courts usually protect the parents' due process rights by either allowing or requiring the parents' lawyers to be present during the interview or at least allowing the lawyers to either submit or ask questions, or both. However, if the parent is acting pro se, the pro se parent is excluded from the interview altogether.

Other various procedures have been developed, in attempts to resolve the conflict between the parental due process rights with the child's right to be heard. For instance, a number of states require, either by statute or judicial holding, that *in camera* conversations with children must be recorded. In other states, the presence of a court reporter can be waived, or the record must be made only if requested by the parties.

Taken together, [Oklahoma statutes] do not fully resolve the conflicts between the parental due process rights of having an *in camera* interview transcribed with the child's right to be heard. For instance, 43 O.S. § 113, does not expressly address parental consent to holding an *in camera* interview. What it does do is:

(1) require the court to determine that the best interest of the child will be served by expressing preference;

(2) generally give the trial court discretion to consider a child's preference unless the child is of sufficient age, [presumably 12 or older], in which case the court is required to consider the expression of preference or other testimony;

(3) expressly allow counsel to be present, but provides that if the lawyers are not allowed in the interview, the reasons for their exclusion must be expressly stated by the trial court;

(4) in no case is the child's preference binding on the court or the only factor the court should consider;

(5) if the child is of sufficient age to form an intelligent preference, and the court does not follow the child's preference, the court shall make specific findings of fact supporting such action if requested by either party; and

(6) either party may also request that a transcript of the in chamber proceedings be made, but the statutes do not address whether or if the party is entitled to access of the transcript.

In order to provide a proper balance of parental due process rights with the child's right to be heard, we hereby adopt the following guidelines for trial courts to utilize when planning to conduct an *in camera* custodial or visitation child preference interview:

(1) If the trial court or the parties consider the possibility of an *in camera* interview of the children, then the trial court must make and state on the record its preliminary determinations concerning whether the child's best interest is served by conducting such an *in camera* interview and whether the child is of a sufficient age to form an intelligent preference;

(2) If the parents consent to the interview being in chambers, or otherwise waive their own presence, the judge may proceed with an *in camera* interview.

(3) If one or both parents object to being excluded, the trial court must consider whether the parents want counsel present. This consideration should include whether to allow counsel to be present, allow counsel to question the child, or allow counsel to submit questions to be asked. Whether the trial court allows the counsel to participate in the questioning or submit questions is within the trial court's discretion. If no objection is made regarding this issue, the parties waive objection to the issue on appeal. If the judge proceeds with an *in camera* interview without counsel present, the reason for counsel's exclusion must be stated on the record.

(4) The next issue to be considered on the record is whether either or both parents request that a court reporter be present. If a request for a court reporter is made, the court reporter must be present and the interview shall be recorded—otherwise the parties waive objection to the issue on appeal. . . .

Once a record is made, the question becomes whether it must be made available to the parties, and if so when? Again, the procedures vary from state to state. In some states, the record must be made available to the parties. In other states, the record may be sealed from the parties, but must be made available for appellate review in an effort to protect the children's confidentiality, while still providing a basis of appellate review to protect the parents' due process rights. . . .

We hold that unless a parent or the parents appeal the custody or visitation determination, due process does not require that either parent have access to the transcript of the *in camera* interview of the children merely to satisfy their curiosity. . . .

Watt, J., dissenting:

I dissent . . . . Although the majority gives lip service to a plethora of reasons why an *in camera* interview serves the child's best interests, today, its opinion . . . may well sound the death knell to the utilization of this invaluable tool in future contested child custody matters. . . .

The opinion most certainly destroys the foundational principle for courts to conduct "*in camera* hearings" with the children which principle is also the basis for any custody decision, that being "the best interests of the child/children." Today's order not only robs the trial court of its discretion but also destroys the court's most vital tool in making decisions with regard to custody and that is obtaining the trust of the child or children. No longer can a judge promise that degree of protection of CONFIDENTIALITY so that a child will be more likely to be forthright and honest in expressing his or her views during these *in camera* proceedings.

I would adopt the rationale expressed in *Myers v. Myers*, 170 Ohio App.3d 436, 867 N.E.2d 848 (2007), where the court stated, as follows: "The requirement that the *in camera* interviews be recorded is designed to protect the due-process rights of the parents. The due-process protection is achieved in this context by sealing the transcript of the *in camera* interview and making it available only to the court for review. This process allows appellate courts to review the *in camera* interview proceedings and ascertain their reasonableness, while still allowing the child to feel safe and comfortable in expressing his opinions openly and honestly, without subjecting the child to any additional psychological trauma or loyalty conflicts."

Accordingly, the sealing of the transcript and its inclusion in the record on appeal for review by the appellate courts in Oklahoma and using an abuse of discretion standard of review would protect the rights and best interests of the children while also affording the parents their right of due process.

By today's opinion, absent a complete waiver by all of the parties, "*in camera* hearings" as we have known them for decades will disappear.

With today's pronouncement and rule change, either parent need only file their petition in error, pay the filing fee, and obtain and pay for a copy of the transcript and then be free to "beat the child/children over the head with it" for comments made to the judge in chambers. . . . No responsible parent would want access to hearing results unless they intended to, at some future date, use it against the child or a former spouse.

Under today's order, thousands of children, at best, will leave the courthouses across this state with a bitter taste in their mouth for the judicial system or, at worst, result in mental or physical scarring that will remain for the rest of their lifetime.

Furthermore, instead of protecting the children and acting in their best interest, warring parents, consumed with bitterness for one another will now use their children as weapons in their domestic battle with the opposing spouse. . . .

Accordingly, I dissent.

Question based on *Ynclan v. Woodward*:

Do you side with the majority of the dissent?

American Bar Association Guidelines
for Judges on Talking to Children About Custody

The American Bar Association's Center on Children and the Law published guidelines for judges making custody decisions. The guidelines contain information to help judges talk to children in chambers.

Practice note: Before you read the guidelines from the ABA Center on Children and the Law, permit me to bend your ear about the benefits of active membership in the bar. The American Bar Association's Section of Family Law has useful publications, including *Family Advocate,* a quarterly magazine that publishes short, practice-oriented articles. The Section also publishes the *Family Law Quarterly,* a scholarly journal with in-depth articles. Your state bar association has a family law section. In California, where I teach and practice, the Family Law Section of the State Bar publishes *Family Law News,* which updates family law practitioners on recent cases, changes in legislation, developments in practice, news about conferences, and opportunities to fulfill continuing legal education requirements. Your county bar association may have a family law section. In my county, for example, the family law section of the Sacramento County Bar Association has monthly meetings. Involvement in the ABA, the state bar, and the county bar is a great way to meet other attorneys with similar interests. Bar associations have numerous committees, and you can volunteer for committees on family law. The ABA, state, and local bar associations have student memberships. You can join today and get involved!

A Judge's Guide: Making Child-Centered Decisions in Custody Cases

American Bar Association Center on Children and the Law (2d ed. 2008)

The Toddler-preschool aged child (18 months to 5 years)

At this age, the court sometimes seeks additional information directly from the child. It is important to keep in mind the following when conducting these interviews:

- Be flexible and have limited expectations or agendas when trying to interview a toddler or preschooler. In many cases, an interview may not be possible for this age group. In particular, a toddler has limited language skills and likely would not be comfortable speaking with a judge without a parent present or nearby. Have a qualified evaluator observe the parent-child interaction.

- If you choose to meet with a child of this age, try to fit into the child's schedule as much as possible. For example, a meeting should be scheduled only when the child is well rested and fed.

- Prior to the meeting, allow the child to safely explore the environment. It may be helpful to have a few small toys or crayons and paper. Respect and acknowledge any security objects, such as a blanket or stuffed animal that the child brings to the interview.

- Use simple words and brief explanations. At the same time, even toddlers may understand a lot despite the fact that they are not very verbal.

- Be aware of the child's difficulty understanding the concept of time and the sequence of events, especially if you discuss scheduled transitions between households. For example, even the idea of "the day after tomorrow" is a difficult concept. A four-year-old, however, might understand the concept of "weekend" if it is explained as the days when Mommy and Daddy don't go to work.

The Early Elementary School-Aged Child (5 to 7 Years)

You may wish to conduct an in-chambers interview with a child of this age. The following are age-appropriate tips for a successful interview:

- Reassure the child that he or she is not responsible for the separation and divorce.

- Allow the child to share excitement about new skills and/or let him or her draw or play with a puzzle during the session. There are books that attorneys can read with young children.

- Ask open-ended questions that are parent neutral; "Let's talk about what you do when you are with each parent." Ask the same questions about both parents.

- Acknowledge that a child of this age may be experiencing a loyalty conflict and reassure the child that it is not their responsibility to decide where they should live.

- Find out what activities are most important to the child. What activities give the child a sense of mastery and purpose? Their enthusiasm is usually apparent.

- Recognize the child's sense of time at this age. Be as concrete as possible and speak in present terms. Relate a future event to an occasion or situation known to the child, such as "When school ends during the summer, you will live with your Mom/Dad."

- Draw out a child's feelings by using the third person or generalizing, such as "Some children feel sad when . . ."

The Older Elementary School-Aged Child (8 to 10 Years)

You may wish to conduct an in-chambers interview with a child of this age. The following are age-appropriate tips for a successful interview:

- Remember that children of this age, because of their sense of loyalty and fairness, may ask you to allow them to see parents for equal amounts of time. This option may be unworkable for a number of reasons, including the parent's inability to communicate effectively. Children are often relieved to hear that it is not their responsibility to make such a decision.

- For rapport building: Ask the child about favorite school subjects, extracurricular activities, or hobbies. What kinds of activities does the child like to do with a parent? What are the names of the child's friends?

- Ask the child what has changed since the separation. How has it affected friendships, activities, and schoolwork?

- Assess whether the child has assumed a parental role. How is time spent with the parent? What does the child do after coming home from school?

Note if the child tends to take care of a parent or assumes too many responsibilities.

- Be aware that the child may surprise you with a fairly clear understanding of the divorce process form overhearing the parents' discussions.

The Middle School-Aged Child (11 to 13 Years)

An in-chambers interview may be appropriate with children of this age. You may want to consider the following points:

- Explain the role and the purpose of the interview clearly. Children of this age tend to exaggerate their sense of responsibility. They may assume that in talking to you they are being asked to make a definitive decision about what will happen to them following the separation or divorce.

- Assess whether the younger adolescent is assuming too many adult responsibilitites following the separation and may be at risk for becoming a "parental child." The child may even be encouraging this unhealthy dynamic because it gives them a sense of control.

- How does the younger adolescent report progress in school and homework completion? Is there a consistent place in each household in which the younger adolescent can work independently yet still have a parent available for help?

- How organized does the younger adolescent feel? Does he worry excessively about losing something or forgetting to transport something between households? Does he feel like he has enough privacy?

- How much time does the younger adolescent spend unsupervised in each home and how comfortable is he or she with these arrangements?

- What kind of peer activities does the younger adolescent participate in? How does he or she spend time with friends? Is the time spent with friends unsupervised or is an adult nearby?

The Adolescent or High School-Aged Child (14 to 18 Years)

When conducting an in-chambers interview, consider the following strategies:

- Find a way to show respect for the adolescent's independence, such as a choice of when to meet or where to sit during an interview.

- Ask the adolescent to take you through a typical day in his or her life. What kinds of responsibilities does he or she have in and outside the home? What kind of encouragement and support does he or she receive to be independent and responsible?

- How does the adolescent see the future: "Where do you hope to be next year at this time; two years down the road; five to ten years down the road?" How does each parent support these goals? Note the adolescent's body language during the interview. Does he or she seem weighted down or optimistic about the future?

- Adolescents are usually acutely aware of how future plans may be affected by school performance. Assess how the adolescent is doing in school without making them feel more pressured. Instead ask general questions about what courses the adolescent is taking and what interests them.

- How does the adolescent perceive his or her parent's relationship? How does this perception affect the adolescent's relationships outside the family? Who does the adolescent spend the most time with outside the family and how do they spend their time together?

An Attorney for the Child?

Family court judges have discretion to appoint an attorney for children in contested custody cases.[73] Appointment of counsel occurs most often in high conflict cases and where there are accusations of abuse.

Psychological Evaluation in Custody Cases

In contested custody cases, judges sometimes order custody evaluations performed by mental health professionals.[74] The Association of Family and Conciliation Courts approved *Model Standards of Practice for Child Custody Evaluation* (AFCC *Model Standards*).[75] The AFCC *Model Standards* define

---

73 *See e.g.*, Cal. Fam. Code § 3150; Conn. Gen. Stat. Ann. § 46b-54 (court may appoint counsel if in the best interest of the child); Fla. Stat. Ann. § 61.401 (if the court finds it is in the best interest of the child, the court may appoint a guardian ad litem to act as next friend of the child . . . ."); American Bar Association Section on Family Law, *Standards of Practice for Lawyers Representing Children in Custody Cases* (2003); Ann M. Haralambie, *The Child's Attorney: A Guide to Representing Children in Custody, Adoption, and Protection Cases* (1993).

74 Who is qualified to serve as a child custody evaluator? *See* Association of Family and Conciliation Courts, *Model Standards of Practice for Child Custody Evaluation* (2006).

75 Association of Family and Conciliation Courts, *Model Standards of Practice for Child Custody Evaluation* (2006).

custody evaluation: "The child custody evaluation process involves the compilation of information and the formulation of opinions pertaining to the custody or parenting of a child and the dissemination of that information and those opinions to the court, to the litigants, and to the litigants' attorneys."

In normal litigation, each side hires experts to support its position. Child custody litigation is different. A custody evaluator should be neutral. The AFCC *Model Standards* state, "Evaluators shall always function as impartial examiners."[76] Many custody evaluators will only take cases if they are appointed by the court. Court appointment enhances neutrality.

A custody evaluation cannot answer the ultimate question of a child's best interest. There is no psychological test or battery of tests that determines best interests.[77] Evaluators do not have a crystal ball that makes custody decisions easy.

A good custody evaluation gives the judge insight into parenting style and psychological functioning. The evaluator provides information about the child's psychological needs. The evaluator offers suggestions regarding the "fit" between parenting attributes and a child's psychological needs.[78] The American Psychological Association's *Guidelines for Child Custody Evaluations* (APA *Guidelines*) remark, "The most useful and influential evaluations focus upon skills, deficits, values, and tendencies relevant to parenting attributes and a child's psychological needs. Comparatively little weight is afforded to evaluations that offer a general personality assessment without attempting to place

---

76 Association of Family and Conciliation Courts, *Model Standards of Practice for Child Custody Evaluation* Preamble ¶ 2 (2006).

77 *See* Gary B. Melton, John Petrila, Norman G. Poythress & Christopher Slobogin, *Psychological Evaluations for the Courts: A Handbook for Mental Health Professionals and Lawyers*, pp. 559-560 (3d ed. 2007)("It is our contention that psychological tests assessing clinical constructs (*e.g.*, intelligence, depression, personality, academic achievement) are frequently unnecessary and often used inappropriately. Tests of intellectual capacity, achievement, personality style, and psychopathology assess constructs that are linked only indirectly, at best, to the key issues concerning custody and visitation. . . . [W]e recommend the use of traditional psychological tests only when specific problems or issues that these tests were designed to measure appear salient in the case."); American Psychological Association, Guidelines for Child Custody Evaluations in Family Law Proceedings, 65 *American Psychologist* 863-867, at 866 (2010)("Multiple methods of data gathering enhance the reliability and validity of psychologists' eventual conclusions, opinions, and recommendations. . . . Direct methods of data gathering typically include such components as psychological testing, clinical interview, and behavioral observation. Psychologists may also have access to documentation from a variety of sources (*e.g.*, schools, health care providers, child care providers, agencies, and other institutions) and frequently make contact with members of the extended family, friends and acquaintances, and other collateral sources when the resulting information is likely to be relevant.").

78 American Psychological Association, Guidelines for Child Custody Evaluations in Family Law Proceedings, 65 *American Psychologist* 863-867, at 864 (2010)("Issues that are central to the court's ultimate decision-making obligations include parenting attributes, the child's psychological needs, and the resulting fit.").

results in the appropriate context."[79] Thus, an evaluation that says, "Mother is depressed" does little to help the judge. Plenty of depressed parents are wonderful with their children. The judge needs concrete information about the impact of parental strengths and weaknesses on day-to-day parenting.

Custody evaluators prefer to interview both parents. A mental health professional who has not personally evaluated a parent should not opine on the parent's psychological functioning. The APA *Guidelines* provide: "Psychologists provide an opinion of an individual's psychological characteristics only after they have conducted an examination of the individual adequate to support their statements and conclusions. The only exception to this occurs in those particular instances of record review, consultation, or supervision (as opposed, in each case, to evaluations) in which an individual examination is not warranted or necessary for the psychologist's opinion. The court typically expects the psychologist to examine both parent as well as the child."[80]

Custody evaluators provide valuable information. But should custody evaluators take the final step and offer specific recommendations regarding custody? Many evaluators do. The APA *Guidelines* caution, "The profession has not reached consensus about whether psychologists should make recommendations to the court about the final child custody determination."[81] Gary Melton and his colleagues argue mental health professionals have little to offer regarding which parent should have custody.[82] Melton writes:

> Thus the state of the literature does not promote confidence about the validity of opinions concerning dispositions judges might consider in custody cases. Indeed, there is probably no forensic question on which overreaching by mental health professionals has been so common and so egregious. Besides lacking scientific validity, such

---

79 American Psychological Association, Guidelines for Child Custody Evaluations in Family Law Proceedings, 65 *American Psychologist* 863-867, at 864 (2010).

80 American Psychological Association, Guidelines for Child Custody Evaluations in Family Law Proceedings, 65 *American Psychologist* 863-867, at 866 (2010)("While the court eventually will have no choice but to make a decision regarding persons who are unable or unwilling to be examined, psychologists have no corresponding obligation. Psychologists do have an ethical requirement to base their opinions on information and techniques sufficient to substantiate their findings. . . . Nonexamining psychologists also may share with the court their expertise on issues relevant to child custody (*e.g.*, child development, family dynamics) as long as they refrain from relating their conclusions to specific parties in the case at hand.").

81 American Psychological Association, Guidelines for Child Custody Evaluations in Family Law Proceedings, 65 *American Psychologist* 863-867, at 866 (2010).

82 Gary B. Melton, John Petrila, Normal G. Poythress & Christopher Slobogin, *Psychological Evaluations for the Courts: A Handbook for Mental Health Professionals and Lawyers* (3d ed. 2007).

opinions have often been based on clinical data that are, on their face, irrelevant to the legal questions in dispute. . . .

Determining a child's best interest is difficult. Mental health professionals can assist courts, but custody evaluators do not appear to have skills superior to those possessed by experienced, patient, compassionate judges.

> **Practice Note:** A thorough custody evaluation from a respected mental health professional often carries great weight with the judge. Learn who the competent custody evaluators are in your community. Get to know them and the kinds of information they can provide in an evaluation.
>
> An impediment in many cases to a thorough custody evaluation is cost. In my community, Sacramento, California, a full custody evaluation can cost three to five thousand dollars. This is beyond the financial reach of many parents.

As you can imagine, it frequently happens that one parent is very unhappy with the result of a custody evaluation. Can the unhappy parent sue the evaluator? If the evaluator was appointed by the court, courts rule the evaluator has absolute immunity from suit. *See, e.g.,* Cooney v. Rossiter, 976 N.E. 2d 441 (Ill. Ct. App. 2012), aff'd in part and vacated in part, 2012 WL 6721091 (Il.. 2012).

Sexual Orientation and Child Custody

In the not so distant past, gay and lesbian parents faced a steep uphill battle for custody of their children. In *Bachman v. Bradley,*[83] decided in 1952, a father acknowledged bisexuality. The trial judge denied him custody, and the Pennsylvania appellate court affirmed, writing, "We think the cumulative weight of the evidence is to the effect that the children in the custody of [father] may be exposed to improper conditions and undesirable influences." In 1967, a California trial judge ruled, "The homosexuality of [mother] as a matter of law constitutes her not a fit or proper person to have the care custody and con-

---

83   171 Pa. Super. 587, 91 A.2d 379 (1952).

trol of the minor child of the parties." The judge refused even to consider the facts of the case, concluding, essentially, that no gay or lesbian parent is fit for custody.[84] In *Roe v. Roe*,[85] decided in 1985 by the Virginia Supreme Court, father lived with his same-sex partner. They slept in the same bed and were affectionate in front of father's child, but did not "flaunt" their homosexuality. The Virginia court wrote, "The father's continuous exposure of the child to his immoral and illicit relationship renders him an unfit and improper custodian as a matter of law."

Times have changed. Courts today hold that sexual orientation itself has no bearing on custody. In *Miller-Jenkins v. Miller-Jenkins*,[86] the Vermont Supreme Court wrote, "The State of Vermont has determined that same-sex couples have the same rights and responsibilities as opposite-sex couples—thus, the sexual orientation of the parents is irrelevant in a custody determination."

What *can* be relevant is sexual behavior, not sexual orientation. Exposing a child to inappropriate sexual behavior—gay or straight—between a parent and their partner or spouse can be relevant to custody.[87] The South Carolina Court of Appeals explained in *Reed v. Pieper*,[88] "A parent's morality, while a proper consideration in custody disputes, is limited in its force to what relevancy it has, either directly or indirectly, to the welfare of the child."

Race, Ethnicity, and Child Custody

Race or ethnicity is generally not relevant in custody decisionmaking. The United States Supreme Court's decision in *Palmore v. Sidoti* addresses the constitutional dimension of race and child custody.

---

84 Nadler v. Superior Court, 255 Cal. App. 2d 523, 63 Cal. Rptr. 352 (1967)(the Court of Appeal ruled "that the trial court erred in failing to exercise its discretion and ruling as a matter of law that petitioner was an unfit mother.").

85 228 Va. 722, 324 S.E.2d 691 (1985).

86 12 A.3d 768 (Vt. 2010).

87 *See* DiStefano v. DiStefano, 60 A.D.2d 976, 401 N.Y.S.2d 636 (1978)("While the sexual life style of a parent may properly be considered in determining what is best for the children, its consideration must be limited to its present or reasonably predictable effect upon the children's welfare.").

88 393 S.C. 424, 713 S.E.2d 309 (Ct. App. 2011).

Palmore v. Sidoti

United States Supreme Court
466 U.S. 429, 104 S.Ct. 1879 (1984)

Chief Justice Burger delivered the opinion of the Court.

We granted certiorari to review a judgment of a state court divesting a natural mother of the custody of her infant child because of her remarriage to a person of a different race.

When petitioner Linda Sidoti Palmore and respondent Anthony J. Sidoti, both Caucasians, were divorced in May 1980 in Florida, the mother was awarded custody of their 3-year-old daughter.

In September 1981 the father sought custody of the child by filing a petition to modify the prior judgment because of changed conditions. The change was that the child's mother was then cohabiting with a Negro, Clarence Palmore, Jr., whom she married two months later. . . .

After hearing testimony from both parties and considering a court counselor's investigative report, the court . . . made a finding that "there is no issue as to either party's devotion to the child, adequacy of housing facilities, or respectability of the new spouse of either parent."

The court then addressed the recommendations of the court counselor . . . for a change in custody because "the wife petitioner has chosen for herself and for her child, a life-style unacceptable to the father and to society. The child is, or at school age will be, subject to environmental pressures not of choice."

The court then concluded that the best interests of the child would be served by awarding custody to the father. The court's rationale is contained in the following: "The father's evident resentment of the mother's choice of a black partner is not sufficient to wrest custody from the mother. It is of some significance, however, that the mother did see fit to bring a man into her home and carry on a sexual relationship with him without being married to him. Such action tended to place gratification of her own desires ahead of her concern for the child's future welfare. This Court feels that despite the strides that have been made in bettering relations between the races in this country, it is inevitable that Melanie will, if allowed to remain in her present situation and attains school age and thus more vulnerable to peer pressures, suffer from the social stigmatization that is sure to come."

The Second District Court of Appeal affirmed. We granted certiorari, and we reverse.

The judgment of a state court determining or reviewing a child custody decision is not ordinarily a likely candidate for review by this Court. However, the court's opinion, after stating that the "father's evident resentment of the mother's choice of a black partner is not sufficient" to deprive her of custody, then turns to what it regarded as the damaging impact on the child from remaining in a racially mixed household. This raises important federal concerns arising from the Constitution's commitment to eradicating discrimination based on race. . . .

The court correctly stated that the child's welfare was the controlling factor. But that court was entirely candid and made no effort to place its holding on any ground other than race. Taking the court's findings and rationale at face value, it is clear that the outcome would have been different had petitioner married a Caucasian male of similar respectability.

A core purpose of the Fourteenth Amendment was to do away with all governmentally imposed discrimination based on race. Classifying persons according to their race is more likely to reflect racial prejudice than legitimate public concerns; the race, not the person, dictates the category. Such classifications are subject to the most exacting scrutiny; to pass constitutional muster, they must be justified by a compelling governmental interest and must be necessary to the accomplishment of their legitimate purpose. . . .

It would ignore reality to suggest that racial and ethnic prejudices do not exist or that all manifestations of those prejudices have been eliminated. There is a risk that a child living with a stepparent of a different race may be subject to a variety of pressures and stresses not present if the child were living with parents of the same racial or ethnic origin.

The question, however, is whether the reality of private biases and the possible injury they might inflict are permissible considerations for removal of an infant child from the custody of its natural mother. We have little difficulty concluding that they are not. The Constitution cannot control such prejudices but neither can it tolerate them. Private biases may be outside the reach of the law, but the law cannot, directly or indirectly, give them effect. Public officials sworn to uphold the Constitution may not avoid a constitutional duty by bowing to the hypothetical effects of private racial prejudice that they assume to be both widely and deeply held. . . . The effects of racial prejudice, however real, cannot justify a racial classification removing an infant child from the custody of its natural mother found to be an appropriate person to have such custody.

The judgment of the District Court of Appeal is reversed. It is so ordered.

In 2011, the American Academy of Child and Adolescent Psychiatry summarized the literature on multiracial children.[89] The Academy wrote:

> Multiracial children are one of the fastest growing segments of the U.S. population. The number of mixed-race families in America is steadily increasing, due to a rise in interracial marriages and relationships, as well as an increase in transracial and international adoptions. . . .

> About two million American children have parents of different races. . . .

> Recent research has shown that multiracial children do not differ from other children in self-esteem, comfort with themselves, or number of psychiatric problems. Also, they tend to be high achievers with a strong sense of self and tolerance for diversity. . . . Research has shown that children with a true multiracial or multicultural identity generally grow up to be happier than multiracial children who grow up with a "single-race" identity.

> Some interracial families face discrimination in their communities. Some children from multiracial families report, teasing, whispers, and stares when with their family.

> Parents can help their children cope with these pressures by establishing open communication in the family about race and cultures, and by allowing curiosity about differences in skin color, hair texture, and facial features among family members.

Indian Child Welfare Act

The Federal Indian Child Welfare Act (ICWA) governs "child custody proceedings" concerning Indian children.[90] ICWA defines "child custody proceeding" to include foster care, termination of parental rights, preadoptive placement, and adoption. ICWA does not apply to child custody litigation between parents.[91] ICWA is discussed in Chapter 14.

---

89   American Academy of Child and Adolescent Psychiatry, *Facts for Families: Multiracial Children* (March 2011).

90   25 U.S.C. § 1903.

91   25 U.S.C. § 1903(1) (the term "child custody proceeding" "shall not include . . . an award, in a divorce proceeding, of custody to one of the parents.").

Custody to Non-Parent?

Most custody litigation is between parents. Occasionally, litigation is waged between a parent and a non-parent. The Pennsylvania Supreme Court's decision in *Charles v. Stehlik* is instructive.

Charles v. Stehlik

Supreme Court of Pennsylvania
560 Pa. 334, 744 A.2d 1255 (2000)

Cappy, Justice.

This is a custody matter. The question at issue is whether the lower courts properly determined that Randall Charles ("Appellee"), who is the step-parent of the child in question, should have primary custody rather than Richard Stehlik ("Appellant"), who is the child's biological father. After careful review of this matter, we affirm.

Appellant and Linda Bauer ("Mother") were married on December 6, 1986. A son, who was named Matthew, was born to Appellant and Mother on March 3, 1989; this was the only child resulting from this marriage. In August of 1989, a few months after Matthew was born, Appellant and Mother separated. At that juncture, Mother moved from the marital residence in New Jersey to reside with her parents in Pittsburgh. Mother took with her Matthew and her two children from her first marriage, Kimberly and Kevin Bauer (referred to as "Kimberly" and "Kevin").

Mother subsequently met Appellee in Pittsburgh and married him on July 21, 1990. Mother and Appellee set up house with their new blended family consisting of the then one year old Matthew, Kimberly, Kevin, and Appellee's daughter, Jennifer. During Mother's marriage to Appellee, Mother had primary physical custody of Matthew. Appellee was very active in Matthew's life; so close was the relationship between the two that Matthew has always called Appellee "daddy."

In November of 1993, Mother was diagnosed with cancer. She ultimately succumbed to this disease, dying on September 4, 1995.

After Mother's death, Kimberly and Kevin moved to Virginia to live with their father without incident. Custody of Matthew, however, became a contested issue. On September 15, 1995, Appellee filed a complaint seeking primary custody of Matthew. This matter was assigned to the Honorable Ronald W. Folino.

Extensive evidence was presented by several witnesses, including Appellant, Appellee, Jennifer, a few character witnesses, the therapist who treated Matthew following the death of Mother, and from William F. Fischer, Ph.D. ("Dr. Fischer"), a court-appointed psychologist.

The trial court relied heavily on the testimony of Dr. Fischer, whom the trial court found both credible and persuasive. In formulating his opinion in this matter, Dr. Fischer conducted interviews and tests with the parties, Matthew, and Jennifer, Matthew's stepsister. Dr. Fischer also conducted telephone interviews with the therapist who helped Matthew cope with the death of Mother as well as a counselor who had been working with Appellant. After gathering all of this data, Dr. Fischer opined that it was "in Matthew's best interest to remain in the primary custody of [Appellee], at least for the present time."

The trial court summarized the many factors on which Dr. Fischer based this opinion. First, Dr. Fischer pointed to the fact that on two separate occasions, Matthew spontaneously indicated[92] that "he wanted to stay with his dad here in Pittsburgh (*i.e.*, [Appellee])." Dr. Fischer also testified that Matthew was more cheerful and relaxed when he accompanied Appellee to the sessions with Dr. Fischer than when Matthew accompanied Appellant. Also, the pictures that Matthew drew while in the company of Appellant showed chaotic and sad scenes, while the ones he drew in the company of Appellee were "much more cheerful. . . . " Finally, Dr. Fischer testified that Matthew's loss of his mother would make it "extremely difficult, if not traumatic, for Matthew to move to New Jersey at this time."

The trial court also relied on the testimony provided by Jennifer LaRosa ("Ms. LaRosa"), the therapist who treated Matthew after Mother's death. Ms. LaRosa testified that Matthew felt a strong sense of abandonment whenever he would visit Appellant in New Jersey, and that he worried that he would not be brought back to Pittsburgh.

Appellant and Appellee both testified. As to Appellant, the trial court found that he loves Matthew very much. Although the trial court was concerned about displays of "questionable judgment" and of anger on the part of Appellant, it noted that its "overall impression of [Appellant] was that he is a good man and truly wants to be a loving (and loved) father." The trial court, however, expressed concerns over Appellant's "capacity to withdraw and isolate himself from others," a trait which was clearly not in Matthew's best interests.

---

92   Dr. Fischer stressed that he never asked Matthew whether he would prefer to reside with Appellant or Appellee as to do so would be "to ask a child to betray one of the parents." N.T., 08/15/1996, at 21.

The trial court found that Matthew's life centers on his home in Pittsburgh. The trial court referred to Appellee, who has lived with Matthew since Matthew was a year old, as Matthew's "day-to-day father." The trial court found Appellee credible when he testified "that Matthew calls him dad or daddy, and that Appellee treats Matthew like his son." The trial court further noted that Pittsburgh is the only home that Matthew had ever known in his eight years of life. The court stated that "Matthew's school is here, his stepsister (Jennifer) is here, his maternal grandparents are here and his school friends are here."

The trial court, therefore, concluded that as "Matthew has had such serious and traumatic changes and losses in his life recently, it would not be healthy for him to suffer the additional loss of his day-to-day home and father and be required to move to a new home in New Jersey." The trial court noted that it made this determination by applying the standard which states that a biological parent has a prima facie right to custody as against a third party, and that the scales are thus tipped hard in favor of the biological parent at the outset of the analysis. The trial court found that this presumption in favor of the biological parent had been overcome in this matter as "the instant case offers compelling and convincing reasons why [Appellee] should retain primary custody of Matthew at the present time." The trial court, however, stressed that "Matthew's relationship with his biological father should continue and should be expanded." The trial court's order thus provided that Appellant would have partial custody of Matthew, and the length of the summertime visits Matthew would spend with Appellant in New Jersey would gradually increase over the next several years.

The Superior Court affirmed on appeal. . . . Appellant then filed a petition for allowance of appeal with this court and we granted allocatur. . . .

It is axiomatic that in custody disputes, the fundamental issue is the best interest of the child. In a custody contest between two biological parents, the burden of proof is shared equally by the contestants. Yet, where the custody dispute is between a biological parent and a third party, the burden of proof is not evenly balanced. In such instances, the parents have a prima facie right to custody, which will be forfeited only if convincing reasons appear that the child's best interest will be served by an award to the third party. Thus, even before the proceedings start, the evidentiary scale is tipped, and tipped hard, to the biological parents' side.

In the matter *sub judice*, the trial court properly noted that "the evidentiary scales were tipped hard in [Appellant's] favor." Yet, even with Appellant having this presumption in his favor, the trial court nonetheless found that there were convincing reasons which compelled it to award primary custody of Matthew to Appellee. . . . The trial court gave extensive reasons to support this conclusion. The most important factors to the trial court were that Matthew felt most at home in Pittsburgh with Appellee, the man he has known as "dad or daddy," since he was a baby. Furthermore, the trial court noted that considering the recent loss of his mother and his half-siblings, uprooting Matthew from his home, school, and the man he considers his "dad" could prove devastating to Matthew's present mental condition. In light of the circumstances of this case, we find that the trial court did not abuse its discretion when it ordered Matthew to remain in the custody of Appellee. . . .

. . . Appellant argues that Appellee should have been required not only to prove that there were convincing reasons as to why Matthew should remain with Appellee, but also that Appellant was an unfit parent. In support of his position, Appellant notes that several of our sister states have adopted the standard whereby a biological parent will always prevail over a third party in a custody dispute unless there has been an affirmative showing that the biological parent is unfit or has abandoned the child. He claims that if this court were to adopt such a standard, we would have to reverse the trial court for not only did Appellee fail to establish that Appellant was an unfit parent, but Appellant also presented extensive evidence showing his fitness to have custody of Matthew.

We agree with Appellant that some of our sister states do employ such a standard. This court, however, has explicitly declined to follow such a path. In *Albright v. Commonwealth. ex rel. Fetters*, 491 Pa. 320, 421 A.2d 157, 161 (1980), we stressed that the biological parent's *prima facie* right to custody is not to be construed as precluding a custody award to a non-parent, absent a demonstration of the parent's dereliction. We again emphasize that the standard seeks only to stress the importance of parenthood as a factor in determining the best interests of the child. However, other factors which have significant impact on the well-being of the child can justify a finding in favor of the non-parent, even though the parent has not been shown to have been unfit.

We see no reason to abandon our *Albright* holding. . . . The cardinal concern in all custody cases is the best interest and permanent welfare of the child. In staying true to that maxim, we have decreed that there will be instances where it is proper to award custody to the third party even where there has been no showing that the biological parent is unfit. While this Commonwealth places great importance on biological ties, it does not do so to the extent that the biological parent's right to custody will trump the best interests of the child. In all custody matters, our primary concern is, and must continue to be, the well-being of the most fragile human participant—that of the minor child. We therefore reject Appellant's argument.

For the foregoing reasons, the order of the Superior Court is affirmed.

Nigro, Justice, dissenting.

I respectfully dissent, as I believe that the standard set by the cases from our sister jurisdictions is the one we should follow. The supreme courts of North Carolina, Iowa, Arkansas, Alabama and Wisconsin have all upheld a presumption in favor of granting custody to a natural parent as against a third party which shall only be overcome by showing that the natural parent is unfit or unable to assume parental responsibilities.

When two natural parents each seek custody of their child pursuant to a separation or divorce, the courts are forced to choose and therefore "best interests of the child" is the proper standard. Thus, absent true joint custody, one parent will prevail over the other—even if by the slimmest of margins. In a highly mobile society, additionally fraught with the vagaries of modern relationships, those initial custody decisions may have a long-term effect of severing the child/non-custodial-parent ties equivalent to terminating that parent's parental rights. "The day to day contact between the child and one having custody can create a relationship that may leave the birth parent almost an intruder. All of the day to day interactions between a parent and child are bound to be diminished if not eliminated where the parent comes on the scene as a court permitted 'visitor'." *Barstad v. Frazier*, 118 Wis.2d 549, 348 N.W.2d 479, 483 (1984).

I believe, as does the Supreme Court of Alabama, that

> [t]he prima facie right of a natural parent to the custody of his or her child, as against the right of custody of a nonparent, is grounded in the common law concept that the primary parental right of custody is in the best interest and welfare of the child as a matter of law. So strong is this presumption, absent a showing of voluntary forfeiture of that right, that it can be overcome only by a finding, supported by competent evidence, that the parent seeking custody is guilty of such misconduct or neglect to a degree which renders that parent an unfit and improper person to be entrusted with the care and upbringing of the child in question.

Terry v. Sweat, 494 So.2d 628 (Ala.1986).

Furthermore, I believe that natural parents have a constitutionally protected paramount right to custody, care and control of their child whenever there is no evidence that the parents were unfit or neglected the child's welfare....

As the natural parent's rights in this regard are so fundamental, I would abrogate them only rarely and only in the most extraordinary circumstances, as where there is a judicial finding of persistent neglect of parental responsibilities.

Therefore, similar to this Court's majority opinion, I would find that as between a natural parent and a third party the presumption of custody is tipped hard in the natural parent's favor. I differ from the majority, however, in that I would find that the presumption can only be overcome by placing on the nonparent third party the considerable burden of establishing the extraordinary circumstance that the natural parent has violated his parental responsibilities or has been determined to be judicially unfit.

In the instant matter, as the third party nonparent failed to establish that the natural father violated his parental responsibilities or was unfit, I would award primary custody to the natural father.

Questions based on *Charles v. Stehlik*

1. The majority in *Charles v. Stehlik* ruled that a finding of parental unfitness is not required to award custody to a non-parent. In dissent, Justice Nigro argued that a finding of unfitness should be required. In 2000, the New Jersey Supreme Court agreed with Justice Nigro. In *Watkins v. Nelson*,[93] the New Jersey court grappled with "the appropriate standard for deciding a custody dispute between a biological parent and a third party following the death of the custodial parent. . . . We hold that . . . a presumption exists in favor of the surviving biological parent. That presumption can be rebutted by proof of gross misconduct, abandonment, unfitness, or the existence of exceptional circumstances, but never by a simple application of the best interests." Where do you come out on this issue?

2. When you studied the cases on parentage in Chapter 5, you saw judges struggling to balance two interests. First, respect for the biological connection between parent and child; a respect rooted not only in the U.S. Constitution, but in human nature. Second, a desire to enhance children's happiness and welfare by maintaining established parent-like attachments between children and caretakers who are not biological parents. In this chapter, judges again struggle to balance these interests. How do you strike the balance? Should biology nearly always prevail over non-parent caretakers? If not, should there be a presumption in favor of biology? If so, can you put the presumption into words *without* using the term "best interests of the child"? Or, is the only proper standard, What is best for *this* child?

---

93   163 N.J. 235, 748 A.2d 558 (2000).

In re Mullen from the Ohio Supreme Court grapples with another custody contest between a biological parent and a nonparent.

In re Mullen

Supreme Court of Ohio
129 Ohio St. 3d 417, 953 N.E.2d 302 (2011)

Cupp, J.

The issue raised in this case is whether a parent, by her conduct with a nonparent, entered into an agreement through which the parent permanently relinquished sole custody of the parent's child in favor of shared custody with the nonparent. For the reasons that follow, we hold that competent, credible evidence supports the juvenile court's conclusion that the parent did not enter into such an agreement. . . .

This matter is a dispute between a biological parent and a nonparent over the biological parent's minor child. Michele Hobbs, appellant, met Kelly Mullen, appellee, in May 2000. The two began a relationship and eventually commenced living together. In 2003, Mullen expressed a desire to have a child. Hobbs asked a friend, appellee Scott Liming, who lived in Atlanta, Georgia, to donate his sperm to Mullen for an in vitro fertilization procedure. Liming agreed. Mullen and Liming signed a purported "Donor–Recipient Agreement on Insemination," prepared by an attorney, in which Liming agreed to provide his semen to Mullen to use for purposes of her insemination. The agreement provided that Liming would be listed as the father on the birth certificate of any child conceived, but that he otherwise relinquished all parental rights and waived any action for future custody of, or visitation with, any children born to Mullen from the insemination procedure. Mullen agreed not to hold Liming legally or financially responsible for any child conceived. Hobbs was not a party to the agreement.

In 2004, the women began the in vitro fertilization process, in which Mullen was the female recipient of the implantation. The women shared the financial responsibility of the process. Mullen became pregnant and delivered a baby on July 27, 2005. Hobbs was present at the birth. The birth certificate identified Mullen as the child's mother and Liming as the father. The birth certificate is on file in the Office of Vital Statistics at the Ohio Department of Health. The women created a ceremonial birth certificate that listed the two of them as the baby's parents. Liming also formally acknowledged paternity.

Before the baby's birth, Mullen, through counsel, executed a will, in which she nominated Hobbs the guardian of her minor child. Mullen also executed a health-care power of attorney for her child and a general durable power of attorney for her child. In each of the latter two documents, Mullen gave Hobbs the authority to act as Mullen's agent and to make decisions regarding the child. In each document, Mullen acknowledged that she was the legal parent of the child, but that she considered Hobbs "to be [her] child's co-parent in every way."

Shortly after the child's birth, Liming moved back to Ohio and began visiting the child. For the two years after the child's birth, the women coparented. In 2007, the women's relationship deteriorated. In October 2007, Mullen and the child moved out of the house that they had shared with Hobbs.

In December 2007, Hobbs filed a verified complaint for shared custody in the Hamilton County Juvenile Court . . . and a motion for visitation during the proceedings. Hobbs alleged that Mullen had created a contract through her conduct with Hobbs to permanently share legal custody of the child. Hobbs asked the court to grant her immediate visitation rights with the child and to enter an order . . . granting her equal and shared custody of the child. In January 2008, Liming also petitioned for shared custody of the child.

A magistrate determined that Hobbs had actively participated in the decision and process to have a child, that Mullen and Hobbs had had an understanding that they would act as equal coparents, and that Mullen had made an agreement taking away Liming's parental rights and responsibilities while, in three other documents, listing Hobbs as an equal coparent. Thus, the magistrate concluded that Mullen's conduct had created an agreement with Hobbs in which Mullen relinquished partial custody of her child to Hobbs and that it was in the child's best interests to maintain ties with Hobbs.

Both Mullen and Liming filed objections to the magistrate's report. The juvenile court rejected the magistrate's decision. In its entry, the juvenile court focused on the legal relationship of each party to the child: Mullen was the biological and natural mother of the child and had acquired legal custody by operation of law; Liming was the legal, natural, biological father with potential to obtain full custodial rights; Hobbs was a nonparent under Ohio law despite her active role in raising and caring for the child.

Based on the testimony provided by Mullen, Liming, Hobbs, and others, as well as documentary evidence, the juvenile court concluded that a preponderance of the evidence did not conclusively demonstrate that Mullen's conduct created a contract that permanently gave partial custodial rights of the child to Hobbs. The juvenile court concluded that the magistrate had incorrectly required Mullen to share custody of her child, and the court dismissed Hobbs's complaint for shared legal custody.

Parents have a constitutionally protected due process right to make decisions concerning the care, custody, and control of their children, and the parents' right to custody of their children is paramount to any custodial interest in the children asserted by nonparents. *Troxel v. Granville* (2000), 530 U.S. 57. A parent's right to make decisions concerning the care, custody and control of his or her children, however, is not without limits. For example, Ohio does not recognize a parent's attempt to enter into a statutory "shared parenting" arrangement with a nonparent, same-sex partner because the nonparent does not fall within the definition of "parent" under the current statutes. Rather, a parent may voluntarily share with a nonparent the care, custody, and control of his or her child through a valid shared-custody agreement. The essence of such an agreement is the purposeful relinquishment of some portion of the parent's right to exclusive custody of the child. A shared-custody agreement recognizes the general principle that a parent can grant custody rights to a nonparent and will be bound by the agreement. A valid shared-custody agreement is reviewed by the juvenile court and is an enforceable contract subject only to the court's determinations that the custodian is a proper person to assume the care, training, and education of the child and that the shared-legal-custody arrangement is in the best interests of the child.

This appeal concerns whether a parent's conduct with a nonparent created an agreement for permanent shared legal custody of the parent's child. The determination of whether such a contract is present is essential. If there is no such contract, then the parent retains all parental rights. If there is such a contract, then the juvenile court must engage in a suitability and best interests analysis. . . .

Whether a parent has voluntarily relinquished the right to custody is a factual question to be proven by a preponderance of the evidence. Likewise, whether a parent, through words and conduct, has agreed to share legal custody with a nonparent is also a question of fact. . . .

In this case, the juvenile court engaged in an extensive analysis to determine whether Mullen's conduct created any agreement by which she had permanently ceded partial legal custody rights to Hobbs. The evidence the juvenile court cited to support Hobbs's allegations that Mullen agreed to permanently share custody with Hobbs included that (1) Hobbs and Mullen had planned for the pregnancy together, (2) Hobbs was present at the child's birth, (3) Hobbs's name appeared on the ceremonial birth certificate, (4) Hobbs and Mullen jointly cared for the child, (5) Hobbs and Mullen held themselves out as and acted like a family, (6) Mullen's will named Hobbs as the child's guardian, and (7) Mullen executed a general durable power of attorney and a health-care power of attorney giving Hobbs the ability to make school, health, and other decisions for the child.

Thereafter, the court detailed the counterevidence. The court noted that all the documents created by Mullen that gave Hobbs some custodial responsibilities not only were revocable, but were, in fact, revoked by Mullen. Testimony supported Mullen's statement that she did not intend to relinquish sole custody of the child in favor of shared custody with Hobbs. The juvenile court also stated that although the evidence was unclear whether a shared-custody agreement was actually drafted by the parties or presented to Mullen, the evidence did show that Mullen had consistently refused to enter into or sign any formal shared-custody agreement when presented with the opportunity to do so. In an apparent acknowledgment that the parties had presented conflicting evidence, the juvenile court commented that "under circumstances such as are present in this case a writing of the agreement between the petitioner and the mother would be instructive and preferred to determine whether a contractual relinquishment was made and how much custody was relinquished."

The juvenile court also analyzed the role of the child's father when considering whether Mullen permanently gave over partial legal custody rights. Mullen and Liming each testified that they consider the donor agreement, executed prior the child's birth, no longer in effect, and they are not abiding by it. Like Hobbs, Liming has also had regular contact with the child, and he is a consistent presence in the child's life. He is listed on the child's official birth certificate and has formally acknowledged paternity. The juvenile court indicated that before Hobbs could be determined to have any shared custody right, the father's pending parental rights must also be considered.

On this conflicting and disputed evidence, the juvenile court concluded that there was reliable, credible evidence that Mullen's conduct did not create an agreement to permanently relinquish sole custody of her child in favor of shared custody with Hobbs. . . . Like that of the juvenile court . . . , our review of the record shows that not only was there evidence indicating that Mullen had intended to share custody of the child, there was contrary evidence indicating that Mullen did not agree to permanently cede partial legal custody rights to Hobbs.

In this regard, . . . the best way to safeguard both a parent's and a nonparent's rights with respect to children is to agree in writing as to how custody is to be shared, the manner in which it is shared, and the degree to which it may be revocable or permanent, or to apply to a juvenile court for an order establishing the scope of the legal custody that the parent desires to share, or both.

Finally, we do not agree with appellant's argument that "coparent" equals "shared legal custody" and that because the parties' statements and various documents used the "coparent" terminology, the parties therefore clearly agreed to "shared legal custody." "Coparenting" is not synonymous with an agreement by the biological parent to permanently relinquish sole custody in favor of shared legal parenting. "Coparenting" can have many different meanings and can refer to many different arrangements and degrees of permanency. The parties' use of the term, together with other evidence, however, may indicate that the parties shared the same understanding of its meaning and may be considered by the trial court in weighing all the evidence.

Because the holding of the juvenile court . . . [is] supported by the evidence and [is] not clearly against the manifest weight of the evidence, we must affirm . . .

Pfeifer, J., dissenting.

Is filial love something to be dangled and then snatched away, promised and then reneged upon? Once a natural parent promises a coparenting relationship with another person and acts on that promise, she has created a relationship between the coparent and the child that has its own life. The natural parent cannot simply declare that relationship over. That is what Kelly Mullen attempts to do in this case and what the majority decision allows. Now, no court will ever determine whether it is in Lucy Mullen's best interests to have a continuing relationship with the woman she calls "Momma," Michele Hobbs. Because the juvenile court in this case at the very least should have gotten to the point of making that best-interests determination, I dissent.

Custody Problems

1. Pam and Dan are divorcing. They have one child, a preschooler. Upon separation, Dan moved from the marital home to a city 50 miles away. Pam and Dan could not agree on custody. The trial judge found that the marital relationship was filled with strife. The trial court ordered primary physical custody of the child to alternate between Pam and Dan every other year—one year with Pam, one with Dan, and so on. Neither parent agreed with the judge's decision, and both parents appeal. What result?

2. Kim and John are divorcing. They have three young children. Kim and John practice Wicca, which is a form of paganism. The court awarded joint legal and physical custody, and ordered Kim and John to "take such steps as are needed to shelter the children from involvement and observation of non-mainstream religious beliefs and rituals." Both parents appeal the trial judge's order. What result?

3. Mary and Bob are divorcing. They have three children, aged four, six, and ten. The parties agreed that while the divorce is pending, the children will live temporarily with Bob in the marital home. With the divorce still pending, Bob begins dating Wendy. After a few months, Wendy moves in with Bob and the kids. Mary believes it is wrong to cohabit outside marriage, and seeks a court order changing temporary custody from Bob to her. What result?

4. Marsha and Martin married. Martin is Jewish. One month before their marriage, Marsha, who was Baptist, converted to Judaism. At the time of her conversion, she executed a "Declaration of Faith," witnessed by three rabbis, "pledging to rear all their children in loyalty to the Jewish faith and its practices." The parties have a son, age eight. Recently, Martin filed for divorce. The parties could not agree on custody. Marsha returned to her Baptist faith and is attending a Baptist church. She enrolled the child in Sunday school at her church. In addition, the child attends a youth group at the church on Wednesday evenings and went to the church camp the previous summer. Martin acknowledges Marsha has the right to expose the child to her religion, but objects to the child's being indoctrinated in the Christian faith or being enrolled in any activity "that would be contrary to his Jewish faith." The trial court refrained from restraining either parent's religious activity with the minor. The trial court ruled: "The parties are awarded joint physical and legal custody of the minor. The minor is to spend every Monday and Tuesday with Marsha and every Wednesday and Thursday with Martin. Each party is awarded alternate weekends, from Friday after school until Monday morning." As for religious holidays, Martin was awarded the first and second day of Passover, Yom Kippur, and Rosh Hashanah. Marsha was allotted Purim and the third night of Passover, conditioned upon her taking the minor to a synagogue service on those holidays. In addition, she was awarded Christmas Eve, Christmas Day, and Easter Sunday. With respect to enrollment in religious studies, Martin was permitted to enroll the child "in a Hebrew Jewish Studies program, up to two times per week, regardless of his custody schedule. This religious training program shall have priority over any other schedule or activity. Except as provided herein above, nothing in this Order is deemed to prevent either party from enrolling the child in or having the child participate in other religious programs or activities during their respective custodial time." Marsha appeals. What result? *Marriage of Weiss,* 42 Cal. App. 4th 106, 49 Cal. Rptr. 2d 339 (1996).

5. Christi and Porter married 6 years ago. They have four children aged one, three, five, and seven. The couple separated, and Christi filed for dissolution. They cannot agree regarding custody. The crux of the case is Christi's lesbian relationship with a 19-year old woman, Shannon Maloney. Christi and Porter entered into a stipulation referred to as the "Shannon clause," which provided, "Christi shall not

allow Shannon Maloney to be associated with the minor children and shall not allow Shannon to live or visit in Christi's home." Porter filed a petition to modify the stipulation because Christi had allowed Shannon to associate with the children, including living in the house with the children. The judge appointed James Fullilove, a mental health counselor, to examine the parties and the children. Mr. Fullilove sharply criticized Christi for seeing nothing wrong with co-parenting with Shannon, and warned that the children would suffer greatly if brought up in a homosexual environment. This view was informed by his belief that a lesbian partner would distort the children's (especially the girls') perception of female role models. Christi secured her own expert, Dr. Sally Thigpen, a psychologist. Dr. Thigpen wrote a report detailing her assessments of Christi, Porter and the children, as well as her critique of Mr. Fullilove's report. Dr. Thigpen disagreed with Mr. Fullilove's assessment of "the Shannon situation." Dr. Thigpen testified that there was no reliable clinical evidence showing that children raised by lesbian couples were more likely to grow up lesbian or to have more psychological problems than the general population. She admitted, however, that the situation had been unfavorable in that Christi had instructed the children not to tell Porter that Shannon was living part time in the home. Dr. Thigpen reiterated that Christi was the more capable and involved parent. Porter's pastor, Gary Hahler, admitted that Christi took the children to Springhill Baptist Church more often than Porter did, but he fervently disapproved of homosexuality as a sin. Although the pastor never personally observed Christi and Shannon engaged in any immoral conduct, he recalled that three unnamed church members had voiced displeasure over Christi's lifestyle. Porter testified that homosexuality is a choice and a sin, that kids raised by lesbian parents are more likely to grow up lesbian, and he disagreed with Dr. Thigpen's professional opinion to the contrary. He requested primary custody, allowing Christi all the supervised visitation she wanted. The court found that exposing the children to an openly lesbian relationship "could very well be destructive emotionally" for the children since it would place them in conflict with "the ordinary morals of society." Purportedly on the strength of Mr. Fullilove's and Dr. Thigpen's testimony, the court found that Christi and Shannon simply could not be discreet in their relationship. The court accepted pastor Hahler's testimony that the lifestyle violated Baptist standards; he found the children needed "stable predictable living in a conflict free environment" which Porter was better able to provide. The court named Porter the primary domiciliary parent. Christi appeals. What result? *Cook v. Cook,* 970 So.2d 960 (La. 2007).

6. Sharon and Paul have been married 10 years. They have three children, ages 8, 6, and 3. Paul is a highly paid engineer with a high tech corporation. Sharon is a child psychologist in private practice. A year ago, Sharon was diagnosed with multiple sclerosis (MS), a neurological disorder. Sharon's prognosis is guarded. MS

affects each patient differently. A few months ago, Sharon began using an electric wheel chair because she is no longer able to walk. She drives with an adapted mini-van. Because of MS related fatigue, Sharon has reduced her psychology practice to part time, and it is likely that eventually she will be unable to work. Sharon has contacted you about the possibility of divorce. She tells you that Paul has been unfaithful to her. Sharon informs you that Paul is a good father, but he works all the time and has little time for the children. Sharon has always been the primary caretaker. If she goes through with a divorce, Sharon would like to divide the property equally, but she wants the family home because that's where the children have always lived. As well, the home has been adapted for her wheelchair. Sharon will need spousal support. As for the children, Sharon would like joint legal custody, but sole physical custody. If Sharon divorces, she will eventually lose her health insurance through Paul's employer. With her MS, she needs good medical insurance. Advise Sharon.

Courts agree the fact that a parent is disabled is not a sufficient basis to deny custody. The California Supreme Court expressed the uniform judicial sentiment in *Marriage of Carney:* [94]

> We do not mean, of course, that the health or physical condition of the parents may not be taken into account in determining whose custody would best serve the child's interests. In relation to the issues at stake, however, this factor is ordinarily of minor importance; and whenever it is raised—whether in awarding custody originally or changing it later—it is essential that the court weigh the matter with an informed and open mind. In particular, if a person has a physical handicap it is impermissible for the court simply to rely on that condition as prima facie evidence of the person's unfitness as a parent or of probable detriment to the child; rather, in all cases the court must view the handicapped person as an individual and the family as a whole. To achieve this, the court should inquire into the person's actual and potential physical capabilities, learn how he or she has adapted to the disability and manages its problems, consider how the other members of the household have adjusted thereto, and take into account the special contributions the person may make to the family despite—or even because of—the handicap. Weighing these and all other relevant factors together, the court should then carefully determine whether the parent's condition will in fact have a substantial and lasting adverse effect on the best interests of the child.

---

94   24 Cal. 3d 725, 598 P.2d 36 (1979).

7. In another case involving physical disability, consider Mary and Bill. They have been married nearly twenty years. Two years ago, Mary was involved in a car accident that left her quadriplegic. Mary and Bill have four children, who are now 15, 13, 9, and 5. Mary has always been a stay-at-home parent. Bill works as an electrician. Mary and Bill love their children and are good parents. Mary's injury is so severe that she can no longer breathe on her own. She is bedridden, and is attached to a respirator that "breathes for her." She can move her eyes and talk in a whisper. With the help of Bill's insurance, the state, and their church, Mary is able to live at home. Her room is like a hospital room. Mary is in a hospital bed, with the respirator humming at her side. The state pays for a nurse to be in attendance when Bill works. The nurse arrives at 7 in the morning and stays until Bill returns from work at 5 or 6 in the evening. The kids wander in and out of Mary's room, and although she cannot physically care for them, she is in constant communication with them. She mothers them despite her disability. Recently, Mary learned that Bill is having an affair with the nurse. Mary told her next door neighbor and long-time friend Sue about the affair. Mary is furious and deeply hurt. At Mary's request, Sue calls you and tells you Mary would like to consult you about a divorce. You visit the home while Bill is at work. What should/can Mary do?

8. Mother and father have a baby. Mom and dad are divorcing. Mom believes the baby should not receive vaccinations against common childhood diseases. Father believes the baby should receive vaccinations recommended by the baby's pediatrician. The pediatrician submits a letter to the judge recommending that the baby receive routine vaccinations. Should the judge order vaccinations over mom's objection? Based on *In re A.J.E.*, 372 S.W. 3d 696 (Tex. Ct. App. 2012).

Modification of Child Custody

A custody decision is *res judicata*. A parent dissatisfied with a custody decision can appeal. The disappointed parent cannot, however, return to the trial court to relitigate the *same* facts. The custody decision is final regarding the facts before the court.

Although a custody decision is *res judicata* regarding the facts before the court, the court retains continuing jurisdiction to modify custody if the facts change months or years down the road. A parent seeking modification of custody must prove that a substantial change in circumstances occurred since the initial custody decision—a change that warrants a fresh look at custody.[95] Continuing jurisdiction over custody lasts until the child turns 18.

The California Supreme Court described the changed circumstances rule in *Marriage of Brown and Yana*,[96] "Once the trial court has entered a final or permanent custody order reflecting that a particular custodial arrangement is in the best interest of the child, the paramount need for continuity and stability in custody arrangements—and the harm that may result from disruption of established patterns of care and emotional bonds with the primary caretaker—weigh heavily in favor of maintaining that custody arrangement. In recognition of this policy concern, we have articulated a variation on the best interest standard, known as the changed circumstance rule . . . . Under the changed circumstance rule, custody modification is appropriate only if the parent seeking modification demonstrates a significant change of circumstances indicating that a different custody arrangement would be in the child's best interest." In a similar vein, the Arkansas Supreme Court wrote in *Alphin v. Alphin*,[97] "A judicial award of custody should not be modified unless it is shown that there are changed conditions that demonstrate that a modification of the decree is in the best interest of the child . . . . [C]ourts impose more stringent standards for modifications of custody than they do for initial determinations of custody. The reasons for requiring these more stringent standards for modifications . . . are to promote stability and continuity in the life of the child, and to discourage the repeated litigation of the same issues."

What constitutes substantially changed circumstances? The facts of each case are considered. Remarriage of either parent is seldom a change of circumstance warranting changed custody. If the custodial parent dies, the non-custodial parent automatically has the right to custody, and does not have to get a court order.

---

95 *See* 750 Ill. Stat. 5/610(b) ("The court shall not modify a prior custody judgment unless it finds by clear and convincing evidence, upon the basis of facts that have arisen since the prior judgment or that were unknown to the court at the time of entry of the prior judgment, that a change has occurred in the circumstances of the child or his custodian . . . ."); Collier v. Harris, 261 P.3d 397, 403 (Alaska 2011)("A parent seeking a modification of legal custody must make a prima facie showing of substantially changed circumstances sufficient to justify a modification hearing. The change in circumstances requirement is intended to discourage continual relitigation of custody decisions, a policy motivated by the judicial assumption that finality and certainty in custody matters are critical to the child's emotional welfare. For this reason, the change must be demonstrated relative to the facts and circumstances that existed at the time of the prior custody order that the party seeks to modify."); Minter v. Minter, 29 So.3d 840 (Miss. Ct. App. 2010)("The law on custody modification is well established. A non-custodial party must prove that: (1) there has been a substantial change in circumstances affecting the child; (2) the change adversely affects the child's welfare; and (3) a change in custody is in the best interest of the child.").

96 37 Cal. 4th 947, 956 (2006).

97 364 Ark. 332, 219 S.W.3d 160, 165 (2005).

In a recurring scenario, a parent with custody frustrates the non-custodial parent's ability to visit the child. Does such obstructionist behavior amount to substantial changed circumstances? Judges seldom change custody on this basis, although a protracted course of deliberate interference with visitation might persuade a judge to revisit custody.[98]

At the outset of a divorce case, one parent may seek an order for temporary custody. A temporary order remains in place until the trial court decides custody on the merits. The court may alter temporary custody without evidence of changed circumstances. Nor does the changed circumstances rule apply when parents reach an informal custody agreement without involving a court. Of course, if an informal arrangement persists a long time, the court will take this into account in deciding custody.

The Alaska Supreme Court discusses custody modification in *Heather W. v. Rudy R.*

Heather W. v. Rudy R.

Supreme Court of Alaska
274 P.3d 478 (2012)

Fabe, Justice.

Rudy R. moved to modify the agreement through which he and Heather W. share 50–50 custody of their daughter. He argued that recent legal troubles and instability in Heather's life amount to changed circumstances that required modifying the custody agreement in the child's best interests. The superior court agreed. Heather now appeals, arguing that the evidence does not show that any of her changed circumstances affected her child. The superior court also found that it was in the child's best interests for Rudy to have primary physical custody. Heather argues this was an abuse of discretion because the trial court considered impermissible character evidence, gave disproportionate weight to some factors while ignoring others, and refused to consider evidence of past domestic violence between the parties.

We conclude that the superior court did not abuse its discretion by finding changed circumstances and did not assign disproportionate weight to certain statutory best interest factors. But because the issue of domestic violence has never been adjudicated, we remand for an evidentiary hearing to determine

---

98 *See* Miller-Jenkins v. Miller-Jenkins, 189 Vt. 518, 12 A.3d 768 (2010)(to deliberately sabotage visitation rights is evidence of unfitness).

whether Rudy has a history of domestic violence, and, if so, whether he has rebutted the statutory presumption against an award of custody.

Heather W. and Rudy R. have one daughter, born in May 2000. In September 2002 Heather and Rudy stipulated to a custody agreement whereby Heather had primary physical custody of their daughter. Shortly thereafter, when the child was two or three, the parties began an informal arrangement in which they shared physical custody week on-week off. In 2006 the parties formally stipulated to modifying their custody agreement to reflect the informal, alternate-week schedule they had been following.

In July 2010 Rudy filed a motion to modify the parties' custody arrangement. Rudy argued that there had been "a material change of circumstances" that justified modifying the custody agreement and that it was now in his daughter's best interests that Rudy have primary physical custody. Rudy argued that several factors in Heather's life constituted a material change of circumstances that warranted modifying the custody agreement, including: Heather's criminal charges for driving under the influence and driving with a suspended license in November 2009 and for driving with a suspended license in April 2010; the revocation of Heather's license; the bad behavior of people close to Heather; and the instability of Heather's living situation.

Heather opposed the requested modification. She argued that there had not been a material change in her circumstances and that even if Rudy's allegations were true, he had failed to show how those allegations affected the child.

The superior court held a custody modification hearing in February 2011. At the evidentiary hearing, the testimony concentrated largely on Heather's alleged shortcomings as a parent. Heather was questioned about the circumstances surrounding her DUI charge. Heather pleaded guilty to reckless driving. Throughout the hearing, Heather and others were questioned about her drinking, and Rudy suggested in closing that Heather had a drinking problem.

At the hearing, Rudy also emphasized two instances of concern between Heather and men with whom she was romantically involved. In one instance, immediately preceding her DUI charge, Heather and then-boyfriend Adam returned to Heather's house after several drinks when Adam began "destroying Heather's house." Heather testified that she was "absolutely terrified," and felt compelled to drive to a nearby gas station to call the police. In another incident in October 2008, police were called to the home Heather shared with then-boyfriend Charles. Charles was intoxicated and had a gun. Heather, who was also intoxicated, refused a police officer's commands to move away from Charles, and was eventually handcuffed, though not arrested.

Both Heather and the citing police officer testified about the charge for driving with a license suspended/revoked. This case was dismissed. Heather claimed that she needed to drive her daughter to the emergency room because of a high fever, but the superior court found her story less than credible.

Heather also testified about her various residences during the preceding five years. In her affidavit she stated that she had lived in four residences, but Rudy presented evidence that Heather may have lived at another address and been untruthful about the dates of her various residences.

Throughout the hearing, Heather argued that her daughter was not affected by Heather's alleged conduct, pointing out that her daughter was not present during the DUI or the incidents involving Adam and Charles. Heather maintained that her lack of a driver's license had not affected her daughter's attendance in school or extracurricular activities. Heather argued that she had lived in her current address for over a year and that the child had a stable home life and good home.

Finally, Heather's credibility was at issue during the hearing. Rudy called two witnesses to support his contention that Heather had provided the court with two forged letters and suggested that someone had subsequently removed one of the letters from the court file. The superior court found that some of Heather's explanations for her behavior were less than convincing.

Following the three-day hearing, the superior court issued an order, supported by findings of fact and conclusions of law, awarding primary physical custody to Rudy. Heather filed a motion for reconsideration, which was denied, and she now appeals. . . .

Alaska Statute 25.20.110(a) provides that "an award of custody of a child or visitation with the child may be modified if the court determines that a change in circumstances requires the modification of the award and the modification is in the best interests of the child." Heather makes two sets of arguments, the first of which claims that the trial court erred in finding a material change in circumstances, and the second of which claims that the trial court abused its discretion in applying the statutory best interests of the child factors. We address these arguments in turn.

As a threshold matter, a party seeking a modification of custody must make a prima facie showing that a substantial change in circumstances has occurred. The required change in circumstance must be significant or substantial, and must be demonstrated relative to the facts and circumstances that existed at the time of the prior custody order that the party seeks to modify. Further, to be material, a change in circumstances must affect the children's welfare. We require a movant to clear this threshold in order to maintain continuity of care and to avoid disturbing and upsetting the child with repeated custody changes. We have expressed concern that children not be shuttled back and forth between parents unless there are important circumstances justifying such change as in their best interests and welfare.

The superior court found a substantial change in circumstances, concluding: "The things that constitute a change of circumstances are Heather's DUI case which was pled out, the restrictions on her driver's license, there is the stability issue, including at least two incidents of potential domestic violence in Heather's relationships, and the deterioration in the parents' relationship."

Heather argues that the superior court erred in finding a material change in circumstances. Her argument presents a mixed question of fact and law: She argues that a change in circumstances can only be found material if the change affects the child and that the superior court erred because Rudy did not demonstrate a nexus between his allegations against Heather and any effect on the child. Rudy responds that "there is no Alaska case law that prohibits a trial court from finding that a series of events can constitute a substantial change of circumstance."

Rudy is correct. When reviewing whether a trial court was justified in finding a change in circumstances, we do not parse each alleged factual assertion of change, but instead look to see whether the circumstances in the aggregate establish a change of circumstances. The superior court certainly did not abuse its discretion in taking into account all of the circumstances raised in this case in concluding that there had been a substantial change of circumstances. Heather's DUI arrest, subsequent arrest for driving with a suspended license, and conduct with her boyfriends—one of which involved domestic violence and another of which involved a gun—demonstrate a pattern of conduct that presents a substantial change of circumstances.

Although Heather argues that none of these events were shown to affect her daughter because her daughter was not present to witness them, the superior court characterized this argument as "way too narrow." The superior court was well within its broad discretion to find that such bad behavior was a substantial change of circumstances affecting the child.

Once the trial court has found a substantial change in circumstances justifying custody modification, it must then determine whether modification of the arrangement is in the best interests of the child. In making a determination as to best interests, a court is required to consider the statutory factors enumerated in AS 25.24.150(c)[99] and, if there is a history of domestic violence by a parent, to apply the presumption under AS 25.24.150(g).[100]

Heather argues that the trial court abused its discretion in three separate ways in applying the statutory factors. First, Heather argues that the court impermissibly relied on evidence of her lifestyle that did not affect her daughter. Second, she argues that the trial court assigned disproportionate weight to certain factors while ignoring others. Finally, she argues that the court failed to take into consideration Rudy's history of domestic violence.

As Heather points out, a parent's lifestyle, habits or character is only relevant as it may be shown to negatively affect the child or the parent's parenting ability. Heather argues that the superior court impermissibly relied on evidence of her "lifestyle, habits, or character" by focusing on her DUI charge, license restrictions, frequent moving, and relationship troubles, particularly without any direct evidence that these adversely impacted her daughter.

Rudy responds that Heather's behavior is covered under numerous statutory factors. The DUI charge, he argues, and the fact that Heather was intoxicated when the police were called on the incidents involving Adam and Charles, goes to substance abuse, one of the statutory factors. He argues that the frequent moves can properly be considered under the stability factor. Finally, he argues

---

99 AS 25.24.150(c) provides:

In determining the best interests of the child the court shall consider

(1) the physical, emotional, mental, religious, and social needs of the child;

(2) the capability and desire of each parent to meet these needs;

(3) the child's preference if the child is of sufficient age and capacity to form a preference;

(4) the love and affection existing between the child and each parent;

(5) the length of time the child has lived in a stable, satisfactory environment and the desirability of maintaining continuity;

(6) the willingness and ability of each parent to facilitate and encourage a close and continuing relationship between the other parent and the child, except that the court may not consider this willingness and ability if one parent shows that the other parent has sexually assaulted or engaged in domestic violence against the parent or a child, and that a continuing relationship with the other parent will endanger the health or safety of either the parent or the child;

(7) any evidence of domestic violence, child abuse, or child neglect in the proposed custodial household or a history of violence between the parents;

(8) evidence that substance abuse by either parent or other members of the household directly affects the emotional or physical well-being of the child;

(9) other factors that the court considers pertinent.

100 AS 25.24.150(g) provides:

There is a rebuttable presumption that a parent who has a history of perpetrating domestic violence against the other parent, a child, or a domestic living partner may not be awarded sole legal custody, sole physical custody, joint legal custody, or joint physical custody of a child.

that Heather's "relationships with violence" involving Adam and Charles could properly be considered under the domestic violence factor.

In *Craig v. McBride*, we concluded that residential stability was a proper consideration in the best interest analysis.[101] It was therefore not an abuse of discretion for the superior court to consider this evidence.

Similarly, the superior court pointed to Heather's relationship history as evidence of instability. The court said it had "concerns regarding Heather's relationship with Charles. Her relationship with Adam is unclear. The court has concerns about both geographic and emotional stability." But because a parent's history of relationships marked by violence speaks to the statutory factor of the length of time the child has lived in a stable, satisfactory environment and the desirability of maintaining continuity, the superior court did not abuse its discretion in considering this evidence.

Further, the court's reference to Heather's relationship history was only mentioned in passing under the stability factor. The superior court addressed Heather's questionable decision-making with her boyfriends in more detail in addressing her capability of meeting the needs of her child. The court found that Heather's having continued living with Charles after he was arrested for drunkenly waiving a gun and her return to a house where Adam was having a violent outburst (and potentially her resumption of a relationship with Adam) were evidence of her poor judgment that suggested a potential inability to meet her daughter's needs, a statutory factor under the best interest analysis. Heather makes no argument that this reliance was impermissible or erroneous, and it appears the superior court properly considered Heather's relationship history as it related to her daughter.

Heather also argues that the superior court abused its discretion by giving insufficient weight to certain factors, while focusing too heavily on others.

First, she argues that the trial court failed to properly consider her capability and desire to meet her daughter's needs. To support her argument, she points to evidence that she was involved in her daughter's schooling, that she met her daughter's basic needs, and that she successfully co-parented with Rudy. But the superior court emphasized that due to Heather's lack of credible testimony as to what was going on in her life, it did not really have a good idea of Heather's capability in meeting her child's needs. Further, the trial court noted that Heather's choice to continue to live with Charles after the gun incident, as well as her actions on the night of her charge for driving with a suspended license, raised concerns

---

101　639 P.2d 303, 305 (Alaska 1982).

about her judgment as a parent. In short, the trial court did not, as Heather argues, give insufficient weight to this statutory factor; the court simply disagreed with Heather as to how well she met it. Trial courts are given broad deference to make these determinations, and here the trial court did not abuse that discretion.

Heather also argues that the trial court abused its discretion by failing to give sufficient weight to the bond between her and her daughter. The trial court only briefly addressed this factor, but it did say that there was "love and affection" between the child and both of her parents, suggesting that the factor did not cut toward one parent or another. This issue was not in dispute during the trial. A trial court acts within its discretion when it summarily deals with a factor that is not in dispute and that does not favor one parent over the other.

Heather also argues that the trial court abused its discretion by giving insufficient weight to the importance of maintaining continuity. A modification decision effectively takes this factor into consideration with its threshold question whether circumstances were changed sufficiently to warrant modification. Because the superior court did not abuse its discretion in finding a substantial change of circumstances, there is no basis for concluding that it abused its discretion in finding that instability in Heather's life weighed in favor of awarding custody to Rudy, despite the fact that it represented a change in the status quo.

Finally, Heather argues that the superior court gave undue weight to considerations of Heather's credibility. The court emphasized what it believed to be Heather's lack of credibility. In its written findings of fact, the superior court found that "the real issue in this case is that it is very difficult to gauge exactly what is going on in Heather's life. The court has concerns about Heather's credibility. The court can't believe what Heather is saying." Heather argues that this emphasis on her credibility was improper because a parent's character is only relevant as it may be shown to negatively affect the child or the mother's parenting ability. But the superior court did not frame the credibility issue as a character flaw that weighed against granting Heather custody. In fact, the superior court expressly declined Rudy's invitation to address Heather's credibility as a separate factor, saying, "I don't take away children because I think parents have lied on the stand. Never have done that. Never will." Instead, the superior court focused on how Heather's lack of credibility made it difficult for the court to evaluate what was actually going on in her life and raised concerns about her judgment as a parent. The court observed that Heather's lack of credibility left "a vacuum of information" for the court to determine Heather's capability in meeting her daughter's needs, while the evidence showed that Rudy "appeared to have a very stable life." The court also noted that Heather's lack of credibility "called into question her judgment as a parent." This is not the sort of irrelevant character evidence we have previously deemed improper for the trial court to consider.

Heather finally argues that the superior court erred by failing to consider Rudy's history of domestic violence. Heather argues both that the superior court failed to consider Rudy's history of domestic violence in the best interest analysis as required by AS 25.24.150(c)(7) and that the superior court failed to apply the presumption against awarding custody to a parent with a history of domestic violence as required by AS 25.24.150(g). Rudy responds that he has presented evidence sufficient to overcome this rebuttable presumption. Rudy also seems to suggest that Heather had no subjective or objective concerns about continued domestic violence when she entered the stipulated custody agreement and that thus Rudy's history is now irrelevant to the issue of custody.

Sometime in 2001, while they were still together, Rudy was convicted of assaulting Heather. Heather testified that this domestic violence was the reason she initially took physical custody of her daughter and that it was only after Rudy had completed "anger management" that the two began the informal arrangement that they formalized with the 2006 modification stipulation. Rudy testified that he completed a six-month domestic violence intervention at the Men's Center for Change in Cordova, but it appears that no court has made a finding as to (1) whether Rudy has a history of domestic violence as defined by AS 25.24.150(h), or (2) whether Rudy's completion of this program satisfied his burden of overcoming the presumption under AS 25.24.150(h). Both the original 2002 custody order and the 2006 custody modification were entered by stipulation.

At the most recent trial, the parties' first contested custody proceeding, the superior court refused to consider Rudy's domestic violence. When Heather's attorney questioned Rudy about the domestic violence incident, the trial court indicated that it would not consider evidence of an assault that occurred before the parties' 2006 custody modification and that collateral estoppel applied to Heather's claim of assault. In its written findings of fact, the court noted that Heather had asked the court to consider the episode of domestic violence perpetrated by Rudy, but that "there have been no further episodes or threats of violence between the parents since the 2001 episode." In its oral findings, the court elaborated a bit, saying "this event occurred well before the parents' agreement to share custody in 2006."

We addressed a very similar situation in *McAlpine v. Pacarro*.[102] In that case, the father had assaulted the mother, and the parties had entered into a stipulated custody agreement granting the mother primary legal custody. The

---

102   262 P.3d 622 (Alaska 2011).

parties subsequently modified that custody arrangement, though the mother retained physical custody. The father later moved for a modification of custody and was granted primary physical custody. In 2009, ten years after the initial assault, the mother petitioned for a modification of custody and asked the trial court to determine the legal effect of the father's previous assault. The trial court refused to hear evidence of domestic violence on the ground that anything that had happened prior to the most recent custody order was barred by collateral estoppel and res judicata. We concluded that collateral estoppel did not bar a consideration of evidence of previous domestic violence in a custody case where the issue was not adequately addressed at the initial custody determination or subsequent proceedings. In this case, it does not appear that evidence of Rudy's domestic violence has ever been heard in a custody proceeding, and thus the superior court erred in refusing to consider evidence of domestic violence.

Accordingly, we remand this case to the superior court for an evidentiary hearing solely on the issues whether Rudy has a history of domestic violence under AS 25.24.150(g), and, if so, whether Rudy has successfully rebutted the presumption of AS 25.24.150(h).

Practice Note based on *Heather W. v. Rudy R.*: The trial judge had serious doubts about Heather's credibility. The judge said, "The court can't believe what Heather is saying." In court, credibility is everything! If a judge gets the impression your client is lying, you are done— stick a fork in it. Yet, the temptation to stretch the truth is powerful, especially in child custody litigation where so much is at stake. A critical part of your job is helping clients understand the importance of telling the truth, and preparing them to testify truthfully and credibly.

Problems and Questions on Modification of Custody

1. Sue and Abe dated, and Sue became pregnant. Their daughter Rachel was born three years ago. Sue and Abe agreed to share custody. Eventually, however, they could not get along, and Sue sought sole legal and physical custody. Abe sought joint legal and physical custody. The court decided the parents would have joint legal custody, and that Sue would have primary physical custody, largely because Abe is a long-haul truck driver, and is away from home weeks at a time. Abe has liberal visitation. Sue met Paul, and they married a year ago. Paul is a smoker. When Abe found out Paul was smoking in the home with Rachel present, he asked Paul to not smoke near Rachel. Paul agreed to smoke outside. On several occasions when he picked Rachel up for visitation, Abe noted that her hair and clothes smelled of smoke. Once, at a city park, he saw Paul smoking right next to Rachel at a family picnic. Abe told Sue that if she could not keep their daughter away from second hand smoke, he would go back to court and seek full custody. Sue told Abe that Paul had a right to smoke outside, and that he (Abe) should calm down. Can Abe go to family court and change custody based on Rachel's exposure to second hand smoke? *Heagy v. Kean,* 864 N.E.2d 383 (Ind. Ct. App. 2007); *Johnita M.D. v. Davis D.D.,* 191 Misc.2d 301, 740 N.Y.S.2nd 811 (2002); *Michael Scott M. v. Victoria L.M.,* 192 W. Va. 678, 453 S.E.2d 661 (1994).

Would it make a difference if it was second hand marijuana smoke as opposed to second hand tobacco smoke? How about second hand smoke from methamphetamine or crack cocaine?

2. A parent persistently violates a custody order by failing to pick up and return a child on time. Can persistent failure to abide by the timing requirements of a custody order amount substantial changed circumstances warranting a fresh look at custody? *Collier v. Harris,* 261 P.3d 397 (Alaska 2011).

3. Three years ago, mom received full custody of two young children in a divorce. Dad has liberal visitation, which he always uses. Mom stayed home with the kids while she finished her undergraduate education. She graduated a month ago, and was recently hired by the fire department. Firefighters work 24 hour shifts. When dad learns mom will soon be working 24 hour shifts, he tries to convince mom to switch custody to him because his work schedule is more flexible. Mom says no. Does mom's new profession constitute a substantial change in circumstances warranting a new look at custody? *Collier v. Harris,* 261 P.3d 397 (Alaska 2011).

4. Steve and Celeste were married five years. They have one daughter, Michelle, who is four. In their divorce Celeste and Steve agreed to joint legal and physical custody. Conflict arose between the parties due to their different religions. Celeste joined the United Pentecostal Church, Steve is Roman Catholic. Michelle was baptized in the Catholic Church while her parents were still married. Celeste's church has several lifestyle restrictions that affect Michelle. Steve filed a motion to change custody, asking for sole physical custody. Celeste filed a similar motion, seeking sole physical custody. A court appointed custody evaluator wrote:

> The parties' conflict stemming from their differing beliefs and values is having a negative effect on Michelle. Some examples of Celeste's religious practices which have a direct effect on Michelle include: Celeste's insistence that Michelle can only swim if she wears a dress and there are no boys in the water. Michelle cannot wear pants or shorts. Michelle can only wear dresses that are below the knees and cover three-quarters of her arms. Celeste does not believe females should cut their hair, wear make-up, jewelry or nail polish. Celeste will not allow Michelle to watch television. Celeste does not support or approve of Michelle participating in sports or dance. Michelle attends St. Charles Catholic School where she wears a uniform. According to Celeste, this uniform does not conform to her religion's requirements. In my professional opinion, the two conflicting faiths have fostered fear, deceitfulness, guilt and confusion for Michelle. I recommend that Michelle not attend religious services with Celeste. Although Michelle is bonded to both parents, she is tormented by keeping secrets on both sides. The child is too young to deal with this form of conflict. Michelle told me that she fears that if she does the things permitted by her father, such as wearing jeans or playing sports, then she is going to go to Hell according to her mother.

If the court credits the custody evaluator's report, what should the court do? *Holder v. Holder,* 171 Ohio App. 3d 728, 872 N.E.2d 1239 (2007).

5. Brenda and Martin are divorced. They have a daughter, Sue. Sue was a baby when her parents divorced. Brenda and Martin have joint legal custody. Brenda has primary physical custody. Martin exercises regular visitation. Brenda and Martin are excellent parents. Sue is now old enough for first grade. Brenda wants to home school Sue. Martin wants Sue enrolled in public school. Brenda's desire to home school Sue is based partly on her religious beliefs. Martin believes public school would benefit Sue because it would expose her to children outside Brenda's religion. Brenda and Martin cannot agree on the school issue. What is in Sue's best interest?

Does a family court judge have any particular expertise in selecting between home schooling and public school? *In re Kurowski,* 161 N.H. 578, 20 A.3d 306 (2011).

6. Lisa and Wayne were married and had one child, a daughter Sally, who is now nine. Two years ago, they divorced and agreed on joint legal and physical custody. Sally lives most of the time with Lisa. Three months ago, Lisa started dating John, a convicted sex offender. John pled guilty to performing oral sex on his own daughters when they were six and eight years old. John was honest with Lisa about his past. Lisa was concerned, but John promised he would not do anything inappropriate. Lisa talked to John's therapist, who informed Lisa that John understood his conduct was wrong and that he had made good progress in therapy. John spends a quite a bit of time at Lisa's home, and sometimes spends the night. Wayne learned John was a convicted sex offender by looking at an online sex offender registry. Wayne thought Lisa probably didn't know, so Wayne immediately called Lisa to inform her. Lisa told Wayne she was aware of John's past, but that Sally was safe. Wayne didn't buy it. When Lisa refused Wayne's request to prohibit any contact between John and Sally, Wayne brought an action in family court to restrain Lisa from exposing Sally to John. Should the judge grant the restraining order? *Argabright v. Argabright,* 727 S.E.2d 748 (S.C. 2012).

Move Away Cases

Beth and John fell in love and married while in law school. They had a baby girl, Joy, during their third year. Upon graduation, John got a job with the state. Beth went to work for a large corporate law firm, and worked crazy hours. They bought a home and settled in. Unfortunately, the marriage deteriorated, and they divorced. They agreed on joint legal custody. They also agreed that John would have primary physical custody because John's work schedule for the state was more flexible than Beth's long hours at the firm. Beth has visitation three days a week, mostly on weekends. Several years pass, with Beth and John working cooperatively to co-parent. Then John got an offer to join the faculty at a law school across the country. John proposes to take Joy with him. Beth says, "No way. If you move and take her with you, how am I supposed to be a mother?" This scenario plays out daily in our mobile society, and I'm sure you see there are no easy answers.

A large body of case law addresses the move away scenario.[103] Quite a few states have move away statutes.[104] The Colorado statute, for example, applies when a parent with primary custody plans a move that will substantially change the non-custodial parent's ties to the child.[105] The statute instructs judges to consider all factors relevant to the child's best interests. Specifically, the judge considers the reasons for the proposed move, objections of the non-moving parent, quality of each parent's relationship with the child, educational opportunities for the child here and there, presence or absence of extended family here and there, advantages of the child remaining with the moving parent, and likely impact of the move on the child.

Like Colorado judges, New York judges consider all evidence shedding light on a proposed move. The New York Court of Appeals captured the complexity of the move away issue in *Tropea v. Kenward*:[106]

> Relocation cases . . . present some of the knottiest and most disturbing problems that our courts are called upon to resolve. In these cases, the interests of a custodial parent who wishes to move away are pitted against those of a noncustodial parent who has a powerful desire to maintain frequent and regular contact with the child. Moreover, the court must weigh the paramount interests of the child, which may or may not be in irreconcilable conflict with those of one or both of the parents. . . .

103 *See, e.g.*, Jennings v. Yillah-Chow, 84 A.D.3d 1376, 924 N.Y.S.2d 519 (2011)("The disposition of a petition for permission to relocate with minor children rests upon a determination of the best interests of the children. Relocation may be allowed if the custodial parent demonstrates, by a preponderance of the evidence, that the proposed move is in the child's best interests. When evaluating whether a proposed move will be in the child's best interests, the factors to be considered include, but are certainly not limited to, each parent's reasons for seeking or opposing the move, the quality of the relationships between the child and the custodial and noncustodial parents, the impact of the move on the quantity and quality of the child's future contact with the noncustodial parent, the degree to which the custodial parent's and child's life may be enhanced economically, emotionally and educationally by the move, and the feasibility of preserving the relationship between the noncustodial parent and the child through suitable visitation arrangements."); Pember v. Shapiro, 794 N.W.2d 435 (N.D. 2011)("We use a four-factor test in assessing a custodial parent's request to move to another state. . . . (1) The prospective advantages of the move in improving the custodial parent's and child's quality of life, (2) The integrity of the custodial parent's motive for relocation, considering whether it is to defeat or deter visitation by the noncustodial parent, (3) The integrity of the noncustodial parent's motives for opposing the move, (4) The potential negative impact on the relationship between the noncustodial parent and the child, including whether there is a realistic opportunity for visitation which can provide an adequate basis for preserving and fostering the noncustodial parent's relationship with the child if relocation if allowed, and the likelihood that each parent will comply with such alternate visitation.").

104 *See, e.g.*, Colo. Rev. Stat. Ann. § 14-10-129.

105 Colo. Rev. Stat. Ann. § 14-10-129.

106 87 N.Y.2d 727, 665 N.E.2d 145 (1996).

In reality, cases in which a custodial parent's desire to relocate conflicts with the desire of a noncustodial parent to maximize visitation opportunity are simply too complex to be satisfactorily handled within any mechanical . . . analysis that prevents or interferes with a simultaneous weighing and comparative analysis of all of the relevant facts and circumstances. Although we have recognized and continue to appreciate both the need of the child and the right of the noncustodial parent to have regular and meaningful contact, we also believe that no single factor should be treated as dispositive or given such disproportionate weight as to predetermine the outcome. There are undoubtedly circumstances in which the loss of midweek or every weekend visits necessitated by a distant move may be devastating to the relationship between the noncustodial parent and the child. However, there are undoubtedly also many cases where less frequent but more extended visits over summer and school vacations would be equally conducive, or perhaps even more conducive, to the maintenance of a close parent-child relationship, since such extended visits give the parties the opportunity to interact in a normalized domestic setting. In any event, given the variety of possible permutations, it is counterproductive to rely on presumptions whose only real value is to simplify what are necessarily extremely complicated inquires. . . .

We hold that each relocation request must be considered on its own merits with due consideration of all the relevant facts and circumstances and with predominant emphasis being placed on what outcome is most likely to serve the best interests of the child. While the respective rights of the custodial and noncustodial parents are unquestionably significant factors that must be considered, it is the rights and needs of the children that must be accorded the greatest weight, since they are innocent victims of their parents' decision to divorce and are the least equipped to handle the stresses of the changing family situation.

Of course, the impact of the move on the relationship between the child and the noncustodial parent will remain a central concern. Indeed, even where the move would leave the noncustodial parent with what may be considered meaningful access, there is still a need to weigh the effect of the quantitative and qualitative losses that naturally will result against such other relevant factors as the custodial parent's reasons for wanting to relocate and the benefits that the child may enjoy or the harm that may ensue if the move is or is not permitted. Similarly, although economic necessity or a specific health-related concern may present a particularly persuasive ground for permitting the proposed move, other justifications, including the demands of a second marriage and the custodial parent's opportunity to improve his or her economic situation, may also be valid motives that should not be summarily rejected, at least where the over-all impact on the child would be beneficial. While some have suggested that the custodial spouse's remarriage or wish for a "fresh start" can never suffice to justify a distance move, such a rule overlooks the value for the children that strengthening and stabilizing the new, post-divorce family unit can have in a particular case.

In addition to the custodial parent's stated reasons for wanting to move and the noncustodial parent's loss of access, another factor that may well become important in a particular case is the noncustodial parent's interest in securing custody, as well as the feasibility and desirability of a change in custody. Obviously, where a child's ties to the noncustodial parent and to the community are so strong as to make a long-distance move undesirable, the availability of a transfer of custody as a realistic alternative to forcing the custodial parent to remain may have a significant impact on the outcome. By the same token, where the custodial parent's reasons for moving are deemed valid and sound, the court in a proper case might consider the possibility and feasibility of a parallel move by an involved and committed noncustodial parent as an alternative to restricting a custodial parent's mobility.

Other considerations that may have a bearing in particular cases are the good faith of the parents in requesting or opposing the move, the child's respective attachments to the custodial and noncustodial parent, the possibility of devising a visitation schedule that will enable the noncustodial parent to maintain a meaningful parent-child relationship, the quality of the life-style that the child would have if the proposed move were permitted or denied, the negative impact, if any, from continued or exacerbated hostility between the custodial and noncustodial parents, and the effect that the move may have on any extended family relationships. Of course, any other facts or circumstances that have a bearing on the parties' situation should be weighed with a view toward minimizing the parents' discomfort and maximizing the child's prospects of a stable, comfortable and happy life. . . .[107]

---

107 665 N.E.2d at 150-151.

In *Rego v. Rego*,[108] the Alaska Supreme Court described Alaska move away law:

> A custodial parent's decision to move out-of-state amounts to a substantial change in circumstances as a matter of law. . . . The superior court must assess whether there are legitimate reasons for the move and the impact of the move on the child. A move is legitimate if it is not primarily motivated by a desire to make visitation more difficult. . . . Once the relocating parent has made the threshold showing that a legitimate move justifies custody modification, there is no presumption favoring either parent when the court considers the child's best interests. The relocating parent secures primary custody by showing that living with that parent in a new environment better serves the child's interests than living with the other parent in the current location. In undertaking this analysis, the superior court must assume that the legitimate move will take place and consider the consequences that the move will have on the child—both positive and negative.

West Virginia's move away statute provides:

(a) The relocation of a parent constitutes a substantial change in the circumstances . . . of the child only when it significantly impairs either parent's ability to exercise responsibilities that the parent has been exercising.

(b) A parent planning to move for more than 90 days must give a minimum of 60 day's notice to the other parent. The notice must include a proposal for how custodial responsibility shall be modified, in light of the intended move.

(c) When changed circumstances are shown under subjection (a) of this section, the court shall, if practical, revise the parenting plan so as to both accommodate the relocation and maintain the same proportion of custodial responsibility being exercised by each of the parents. In making such revision, the court may consider the additional costs that a relocation imposes upon the respective parties for transportation and communication, and may equitably allocate such costs between the parties.

---

108 259 P.3d 447 (Alaska 2011).

(d) When the relocation constituting changed circumstances under subsection (a) of this section renders it impractical to maintain the same proportion of custodial responsibility as that being exercised by each parent, the court shall modify the parenting plan in accordance with the child's best interests and in accordance with the following principles:

(1) A parent who has been exercising a significant majority of the custodial responsibility for the child should be allowed to relocate with the child so long as that parent shows that the relocation is in good faith for a legitimate purpose and to a location that is reasonable in light of the purpose. The percentage of custodial responsibility that constitutes a significant majority of custodial responsibility is seventy percent or more. A relocation is for a legitimate purpose if it is to be close to significant family or other support networks, for significant health reasons, to protect the safety of the child or another member of the child's household from significant risk of harm, to pursue a significant employment or educational opportunity or to be with one's spouse who is established, or who is pursuing a significant employment or educational opportunity, in another location. The relocating parent has the burden of proving the legitimacy of any other purpose. A move with a legitimate purpose is reasonable unless its purpose is shown to be substantially achievable without moving or by moving to a location that is substantially less disruptive of the other parent's relationship to the child.

(2) If a relocation of the parent is in good faith for legitimate purpose and to a location that is reasonable in light of the purpose and if neither has been exercising a significant majority of custodial responsibility for the child, the court shall reallocate custodial responsibility based on the best interest of the child, taking in to account all relevant factors including the effects of the relocation on the child.

(3) If a parent does not establish that the purpose for that parent's relocation is in good faith for a legitimate purpose to a location that is reasonable in light of the purpose, the court may modify the parenting plan in accordance with the child's best interests and the effects of the relocation on the child. Among the modifications the court may consider is a reallocation of primary custodial responsibility, effective if and when the relocation occurs, but such a reallocation shall not be ordered if the relocating parent demonstrates that the child's best interests would be served by the relocation.

(4) The court shall attempt to minimize impairment to a parent-child relationship caused by a parent's relocation through alternative arrangements for the exercise of custodial responsibility appropriate to the parents' resources and circumstances and the developmental level of the child.

In *Marriage of Brown and Yana,* the California Supreme Court grapples with the move away dilemma.

Marriage of Brown and Yana

California Supreme Court
37 Cal. 4ᵗʰ 947, 127 P.3d 28 (2006)

Baxter, J.

In this case, a parent who had been awarded sole legal and sole physical custody of a child after a contested custody dispute sought to relocate with her child to Nevada. The noncustodial parent opposed the relocation . . . . The trial court denied the noncustodial parent's applications to restrain the relocation and to modify custody . . . . We conclude the trial court did not err . . . .

The relevant facts are undisputed. In 1994, Nicole F. Brown and Anthony Yana obtained a dissolution of their marriage. In 1999, the court awarded Brown sole legal custody and sole physical custody of their son, Cameron, following a psychological evaluation of the parties and a contested evidentiary hearing on custody. After these events, Brown and Yana each continued to reside in San Luis Obispo County. Brown remarried and has two children with her second husband.

[In 2003], Brown informed Yana she was moving with Cameron to Las Vegas, Nevada, at the end of the summer. . . . Yana filed an order to show cause to restrain any change of residence for Cameron . . . .

Brown filed an order to show cause to adjust Yana's visitation schedule upon her move to Nevada. She stated in a supporting declaration that her husband had taken a job in Las Vegas and that the family would be residing in Green Valley, Nevada. She also stated Cameron was extremely close to his two half siblings, and that they miss one another when apart. Brown asserted there was no basis for Yana's requested relief because, as Yana admitted, Cameron was doing well in her sole custody. Moreover, she contended, she had a legitimate reason for the residential move, and the move would not constitute a change of circumstances. . . . With the planned relocation in mind, Brown offered an increase in Yana's summer visitations with Cameron . . . .

The trial court temporarily restrained Brown from moving away with Cameron, appointed an attorney for Cameron, and set the matters for a hearing. At the hearing, the trial court expressed its reluctance to grant Yana's requests for relief. Although Yana acknowledged that Brown was not seeking to relocate in bad faith, he argued that Cameron's removal could be restrained "if it would prejudice the rights or the welfare of the child." . . . Yana [stated] he was prepared to offer "a lot of evidence about Las Vegas, Nevada, such as the high student-to-teacher ratio; the fact that the state of Nevada has one of the highest dropout rates in junior high and high school of any state in the nation; the amount of crime over there; the volume of the people moving in and out of the community of Las Vegas, Nevada, and what the transient effect has upon people in that community."

Cameron's court-appointed attorney reported at the hearing what Cameron had told him during interviews at each parent's home. The attorney offered his opinion, based on everything Cameron had said and done, that Cameron was "a conflicted young man," who said "different things at different times, based upon who he happened to be with at the time."

At the hearing's conclusion, the trial court denied Yana's requests for relief. . . .

Brown argues, in effect, that [California law permits] a parent with sole legal and sole physical custody to unilaterally supervise and make all decisions regarding a minor child's residence and schooling, thereby conferring a right to relocate with the child without interference from the noncustodial parent. . . . We are not persuaded.

Brown concedes, as she must, that . . . Family Code section 7501 expressly addresses the right of a custodial parent to relocate with a child. By its terms, section 7501 unambiguously provides the right is not absolute and may be curtailed if the move would result in detriment to the child: "A parent entitled to the custody of a child has a right to change the residence of the child, subject to the power of the court to restrain a removal that would prejudice the rights or welfare of the child." (§ 7501(a)). Notably, the statute contains no qualifying language purporting to limit its application to parents with only certain custodial rights. . . . Section 7501, fairly read, contemplates that even a parent with sole legal and sole physical custody may be restrained from changing a child's residence, if a court determines the change would be detrimental to the child's rights or welfare.

Not only does section 7501 undermine any notion of a custodial parent's absolute right to relocate with a child, but so does the lack of any California decision supporting such a proposition. The seminal decision of *Marriage of Burgess*, 13 Cal.4th 25 (1996) referred to the right of a custodial parent to change the residence of a child as a *presumptive* right that might not prevail if the move would result in detriment to the child. Decisions subsequent to *Burgess* uniformly acknowledge that, even where a permanent custody order is in place, the custodial parent's right to relocate with a child remains subject to the changed circumstance rule....

A custodial parent seeking to relocate after dissolution of marriage need not establish the move is "necessary" in order to be awarded physical custody of a minor child, or to retain physical custody under an existing custody order. Moreover, while a decision to change a child's residence ordinarily does not reflect upon the parent's suitability to retain custody, an obvious exception is a custodial parent's decision to relocate simply to frustrate the noncustodial parent's contact with the minor child. In this regard, even if the custodial parent is otherwise fit, such bad faith conduct may be relevant to a determination of what permanent custody arrangement is in the minor child's best interest.

When a final judicial custody determination is in place, and a noncustodial parent seeks to modify custody in response to a proposed relocation, the trial court must apply the changed circumstance rule. Although the noncustodial parent is not required to show a custody modification is "essential" to prevent detriment to the child from the planned move, he or she bears the initial burden of showing that the proposed relocation of the child's residence will cause detriment to the child, requiring a reevaluation of the existing custody order. Imposing this burden on the noncustodial parent is consistent with the recognition that the paramount need for continuity and stability in custody arrangements—and the harm that may result from disruption of established patterns of care and emotional bonds with the primary caretaker—weigh heavily in favor of maintaining ongoing custody arrangements.

The changed circumstance rule requires a substantial showing to modify a final judicial custody determination. In a move-away case, a change of custody is not justified simply because the custodial parent has chosen, for any sound good faith reason, to reside in a different location, but only if, as a result of relocation with that parent, the child will suffer detriment rendering it essential or expedient for the welfare of the child that there be a change....

If the noncustodial parent makes the required initial showing of detriment, the court is then obligated to perform the delicate and difficult task of determining whether a change in custody is in the best interests of the child. Among the factors the court ordinarily should consider when deciding whether to modify custody in light of a proposed move are the following: the child's interest in stability and continuity in the custodial arrangement; the distance of the move; the child's age; the child's relationship with both parents; the relationship between the parents, including, but not limited to, their ability to communicate and cooperate effectively and their willingness to put the child's interests above their individual interests; the child's wishes if the child is mature enough for such an inquiry to be appropriate; the reasons for the proposed move; and the extent to which the parents currently share custody.

The trial court enjoys wide discretion to order a custody change based upon a showing of detriment, including detriment caused to the relationship between the noncustodial parent and the child, if such a change is in the best interests of the child in light of all the relevant factors. . . .

The record reflects that Yana's orders to show cause and his supporting papers did not identify any detriment to Cameron that might result from the proposed move. At the court hearing, Yana conceded that Brown was not seeking to relocate in bad faith. Consistent with this concession, and with Brown's proposal for a slight modification in visitation, Yana made no claim that Brown sought to use the relocation to limit his contact with Cameron.

The record additionally shows that when the court pressed Yana for a description of the detriment he claimed, Yana merely offered to produce "a lot of evidence about Las Vegas, Nevada, such as the high student-to-teacher ratio; the fact that the state of Nevada has one of the highest dropout rates in junior high and high school of any state in the nation; the amount of crime over there; the volume of people moving in and out of the community of Las Vegas, Nevada, and what the transient effect has upon people in that community." Like the trial court, we conclude this was insufficient . . . .

The . . . matter is remanded . . . for further proceedings consistent with the views expressed herein.

Move Away Questions

1. Distill from the preceding materials a list of factors to govern decision-making in move away cases.

2. In move away cases, which parent should shoulder the burden of proof? Should a custodial parent who is planning to move have the burden of proving that the move will benefit the child? Or should the noncustodial parent opposing the move have the burden of proving that the move will be detrimental? Another possibility is that neither parent has a burden of proof—they are on equal footing—and the judge considers all the circumstances to reach the best decision. In *Marriage of Brown and Yana,* the California Supreme Court concluded that a noncustodial parent opposing a move has the burden of proving detriment. In *Rego v. Rego,* the Alaska Supreme Court placed a burden on the relocating parent to make a threshold showing of a legitimate reason to move. Which approach do you prefer?

3. Should a proposed move by a custodial parent automatically constitute substantial changed circumstances, warranting a fresh look at custody? The Alaska Supreme Court in *Rego v. Rego* wrote, "A custodial parent's decision to move out-of-state amounts to a substantial change in circumstances as a matter of law." The West Virginia statute provides that a proposed move is a substantial change of circumstances "only when it significantly impairs either parent's ability to exercise responsibilities that the parent has been exercising." The Wyoming Supreme Court wrote in *Hanson v. Belveal,*[109]"A parent's relocation, by itself, is not a material change in circumstances warranting modification of a custody order."What do you think? Should any proposed move constitute substantial changed circumstances? Did the Alaska court rule as it did because nearly any move away from Alaska is a long distance move?

4. Several states give judges authority to order "electronic visitation" when parents live far apart. Utah law provides for "virtual parent-time," which is "parent-time facilitated by tools such as telephone, e-mail, instant messaging, video conferencing, and other wired or wireless technologies over the Internet or other communication media to supplement in-person visits . . . ." Utah Code Ann. § 30-2-32(f). Wisconsin law provides, "The court may grant to either or both

---

109   280 P.3d 1186 (Wyo. 2012).

parents a reasonable amount of electronic communication at reasonable hours during the other parent's period of physical placement . . . ." Wis. Stat. Ann. § 767.41(4)(e). *See also* Tex. Family Code § 153.015; Jason LaMarca (Note) Virtually Possible—Using the Internet to Facilitate Custody and Parenting Beyond Relocation, 38 *Rutgers Computer and Technology Law Journal* 146 (2012).

Virtual visitation is better than nothing, but is a virtual hug really a hug?

Move away cases are difficult when the moving parent has sole custody. What if parents have joint custody, and one parent decides to move? Consider the Massachusetts Supreme Judicial Court's decision in *Mason v. Coleman.*

Mason v. Coleman

Supreme Judicial Court of Massachusetts
447 Mass. 177, 850 N.E.2d 513 (2006)

Cowin, J.

The defendant, Betsy Shanley Coleman (mother), appeals from a judgment of the Probate and Family Court enjoining removal from the Commonwealth of children whose legal and physical custody she shares with the plaintiff, James R. Mason (father). General Laws c. 208, § 30, governs removal from the Commonwealth of children of divorced parents where one of the parents seeks to relocate without the consent of the other parent. Removal of the children may be authorized by the court only "upon cause shown," meaning a showing that removal is in the children's best interests. In *Yannas v. Frondistou-Yannas*, 395 Mass. 704, 711, 481 N.E.2d 1153 (1985), we addressed removal where one parent had sole physical custody of the children.[110] Today we consider the appropriate

---

110   Editor's footnote: In Yannas v. Frondistou-Yannas, 395 Mass. 704, 711-712, 481 N.E.2d 1153 (1985), the Massachusetts Supreme Judicial Court applied a "best interests" analysis. The court wrote: "The interest of the custodial parent in moving must also be assessed. The relative advantages to the custodial parent from the move, the soundness of the reason for moving, and the presence or absence of a motive to deprive the noncustodial parent of reasonable visitation are all likely to be relevant considerations. That the move is in the best interests of the custodial parent does not mean that it is automatically in the best interests of the child. Finally, the interests of the noncustodial parent must be considered. If that parent is unfit or has not exercised his or her rights of visitation, the judge's problem is less difficult than in the case of a diligent noncustodial parent. The reasonableness of alternative visitation arrangements should be assessed. The fact that visitation by the noncustodial parent will be changed to his or her disadvantage cannot be controlling. In this process, the first consideration is whether there is a good reason for the move, a 'real advantage.' If the custodial parent established a good, sincere reason for

standard where parents have joint physical and legal custody. We conclude that in such a situation "cause shown" pursuant to G.L. c. 208, § 30, means a showing that removal is in the "best interests" of the children taking into account all the circumstances and weighing the factors as described below.

On the facts in this case, the judge appropriately considered the "best interests" of the children, and did not abuse her discretion in concluding that removal of the children would not serve their best interests. Refusal to authorize removal did not violate the mother's constitutional right to interstate travel . . . . We affirm.

We summarize the facts found by the judge. The mother and father married in 1985. Two children were born of their marriage in 1992 and 1994, respectively, in New Hampshire. The parents divorced there in 1998. The judge found that during the marriage each parent took the part of a "primary caretaker" to the children. After the marriage, by stipulation the father and mother entered into a joint physical and legal custody agreement that was incorporated into their divorce decree. Under the agreement, the parents divided physical custody of the children approximately equally. The parties agreed to move within twenty-five miles of Chelmsford, and agreed that, in light of uncertainty as to where each would locate in Massachusetts, the children would attend school in the district of the mother's residence.

Some years passed, and each parent remarried. The mother and father obtained modification of the divorce decree by the Probate and Family Court as required by their changing needs. The father eventually relocated to Nashua, New Hampshire, approximately seventeen miles from Chelmsford. The mother objected privately but had little advance notice of the move and did not file suit to prevent it.

Weeks after the father gave notice of his plan to move to Nashua, the mother gave notice of her intent to relocate with the stepfather to Bristol, New Hampshire. The mother's parents live in Bristol; she planned to move into her parents' home with her family and eventually into her own home nearby. The stepfather's children from a previous marriage (of whom the stepfather had joint custody) and his former wife were also to move to Bristol, and the stepfather promised them that he would follow.

In 2002, testing revealed that the older child, then ten years old, had attention deficit disorder/attention hyperactivity disorder and related learning prob-

---

wanting to remove to another jurisdiction, none of the relevant factors becomes controlling in deciding the best interests of the child, but rather they must be considered collectively."

lems. Although kind and athletic, he lacked appropriate social skills and had trouble making friends. As a result of medication, the hard work of both parents, and a dedicated school staff, the child was able to succeed in fifth grade.

The Chelmsford school district has initiated a student accommodation plan for the child, and his middle school has established an "active and effective support system for him." The judge found that the child is making "great strides" both socially and educationally in his middle school. The judge further found that, based on the State's standardized achievement tests, the Chelmsford school system is one of the better school systems in the Commonwealth, and that the Bristol, New Hampshire, middle school ranks below the State average on New Hampshire's standardized achievement test. The judge concluded that, in light of the disruptions to his developmental process that would be occasioned by the challenges of a new home, school, and sibling, and reduction in the time spent with the father, the move to New Hampshire would be "detrimental" to the older child's socialization and education.

In addition to the developmental issues, the judge found that the mother's children claimed one of them was inappropriately touched by the son of the mother's new husband. The allegation caused considerable acrimony between the mother and father. This tension left the child, who subsequently recanted and then reasserted his claim of abuse, feeling "scared about his role in the family" and "emotionally harmed" by his parents' ongoing conflict.

When the mother informed the father of her intention to move to New Hampshire, the father refused to consent to removal of the children from the Commonwealth and filed a complaint for modification of the divorce decree in the Probate and Family Court seeking, among other things, sole physical custody and a temporary order enjoining the mother from removing the children from the Commonwealth. The mother counterclaimed for modification granting her sole physical custody and for a temporary order permitting the planned relocation to Bristol, New Hampshire.

A probate judge allowed the father's temporary order enjoining removal . . . . After some time, and a four-day trial, a different judge weighed the best interests of the children and determined that removal to New Hampshire in the manner requested by the mother was not in the best interests of the children and thus would not be authorized by the court. The judge found that Chelmsford schools were preferable to those of Bristol, particularly for the child with special needs; that uprooting the children would be detrimental to their interests; that the move would cause a reduction of the father's parenting time that would not be in the children's interests; that misconduct allegations against a stepsibling weighed against increased time in the mother's household; and that there was insufficient evidence of financial imperative to justify the mother's move to Bristol. The judge determined that the father's move to Nashua did not provide ground for the relief requested by the mother, and the judge did not award sole physical custody to either party, deciding instead to order continued shared legal and physical custody. The mother appealed . . . .

In this case, the mother wishes to remove the children from the Commonwealth, and the father, who shares legal and physical custody with her, has refused to consent. The mother has thus requested permission from the court to remove the children. General Laws c. 208, § 30, provides that "a minor child of divorced parents who is a native of or has resided five years within this Commonwealth and over whose custody and maintenance a probate court has jurisdiction shall not ... be removed out of this Commonwealth ... if under the age of consent, without the consent of both parents, unless the court upon cause shown otherwise orders." The words "upon cause shown" mean only that removal must be in the best interests of the child. The best interests of the child standard is one grounded in the particular needs and circumstances of the individual child in question. . . .

Where physical custody is shared, the "best interest" calculus pertaining to removal is appreciably different from those situations that involve sole physical custody. Where physical custody is shared, a judge's willingness to elevate one parent's interest in relocating freely with the children is often diminished. No longer is the fortune of simply one custodial parent so tightly interwoven with that of the child; both parents have equal rights and responsibilities with respect to the children. The importance to the children of one parent's advantage in relocating outside the Commonwealth is greatly reduced.

Where physical custody is shared and neither parent has a clear majority of custodial responsibility, the child's interests will typically favor protection of the child's relationships with both parents because both are, in a real sense, primary to the child's development. Distant relocation often impedes frequent and continued contact with the remaining joint custodian.

Joint physical custody need not necessarily be impeded by relocation outside the Commonwealth. In some cases, distance between the parents may not greatly increase as a result of removal. In addition, there are significant differences in the individual tolerances of the custodians and the children. It is a question for a judge, taking into account all of the facts, whether an increase in travel time between households and schools brought about by removal, and other burdens of distance, will significantly impair either parent's ability to exercise existing responsibilities, and ultimately whether removal is in a child's best interests.

We turn to the propriety of the judge's order denying permission for the mother to remove the children. The order is based on the judge's findings that the children's best interests would be negatively affected by this move. She made detailed written findings that their current schools were superior, that uprooting the children would be difficult for them, that the move would impair the father's parenting to the detriment of their interests, that potential misconduct by other siblings in the mother's household weighed against increased physical custody by the mother, and that any financial or other advantage of the move to the mother was unclear. From this the judge determined that it was not in the children's best interests to be removed to Bristol. . . .

The mother advances several arguments with regard to the judge's findings of fact, none of which is persuasive. The judge was not required to adopt the opinions of a guardian ad litem, therapist, psychologist, school official, and other evaluator, each of which were different from those of the judge in certain particulars. The judge's findings regarding financial matters are also not internally inconsistent or unsupported by evidence. Her findings regarding the situation are warranted by the evidence and, based on them, her conclusion that removal is not in the children's best interests is not an abuse of discretion.

The mother contends in passing, without citation to directly relevant judicial authority, that the judge's refusal to authorize removal of the children from the Commonwealth offended her right to freedom of movement pursuant to the Fifth and Fourteenth Amendments to the United States Constitution. To the contrary, G.L. c. 208, § 30, does not restrict the mother's right of travel, only her right to remove children within the law's scope. The judge here determined that removal would clearly not serve the best interests of the children. Thus, we are satisfied that the mother's travel was not unconstitutionally impeded by the application of G.L. c. 208, § 30.

For the foregoing reasons, the judgment of the Probate and Family Court is affirmed.

Move Away Problems

1. Marry and Todd married and had two kids. They divorced when the kids were quite young. By agreement, the divorce decree granted primary physical custody to Mary, with both parents sharing legal custody. The decree included a "relocation provision" that required automatic transfer of physical custody from Mary to Todd if Mary moved out of state. Four years following the divorce, Mary informed Todd she planned to move to a neighboring state for a new job. She intended to take the children with her. Todd objected and said, "I can't stop you from moving, but if you leave it will be very hard for me to be with the kids. If you move, our divorce decree says I get custody of the kids. So I'm asking you not to move. Or, if you move, leave the children with me." Mary moved with the kids. When Todd found out, he filed a motion in family court to enforce the "relocation provision" and transfer custody to him. Mary responds that the "relocation provision" is unenforceable. How should the court rule? *Taylor v. Elison,* 263 P.3d 448 (Utah Ct. App. 2011).

2. Aleena and Aadil married and had two children. When the parties divorced, the children were 4 and 6. In the divorce, Aleena and Aadil received joint legal custody. Aleena received primary physical custody. The children stayed with Aadil alternate weekends and Wednesday nights. The children have a strong bond with their dad and with his parents, the paternal grandparents. Aleena remarried. Aleena's new husband is in the U.S. Marines. Aleena's husband received orders to relocate to a Marine base in another state, approximately 400 miles away. Aleena notified Aadil of the transfer and of her plan to move with the children to the new location. Aleena proposed that the children live with her during the school year, and spend half the summer vacation, a week during the Muslim holy days, and half the Thanksgiving break with Aadil. Aadil disapproves of the move. The matter is before the family court for decision. Should the judge approve the move? *Storrie v. Simmons,* 225 W. Va. 317, 693 S.E.2d 70 (2010).

3. Maria and Phil have two children, 4 and 6. In their divorce, Maria and Phil agreed that Maria would have custody of the children, with liberal visitation for Phil. Maria and Phil are good parents. Both work full time. They live in Big City. Maria decided to move from Big City to Small Town, 200 miles away. Phil objected, and Maria filed a petition in family court seeking permission to move. Maria explains that she has a job lined up in Small Town. Maria's parents live on a farm near Small Town. Maria wants to move away from the violence and drug dealing in her Big City neighborhood. Maria has rented an apartment in Small Town, within walking distance of schools and parks. Phil argues that if Maria wants to move, she should move to a

safer location in Big City rather than 200 miles away. Phil points out that his parents and extended family live in Big City. Moreover, Phil explains that if the children move to Small Town, they will no longer have ready access to the cultural benefits offered by Big City. Finally, Phil complains that if Maria moves, his ability to have a day-to-day role in his children's lives will be severely impaired. He will not be able to coach his kids' sports teams, attend school functions, see them on a spontaneous basis, or fill in for Maria when she is sick or has to stay late at work. *Jennings v. Yillah-Chow,* 84 A.D.3d 1376, 924 N.Y.S.2d 519 (2011).

4. Ioannis and Stamatia were born in Greece, but have lived many years in the United States and are U.S. citizens. Both have Ph.D.s from prestigious universities, are university professors, and are famous in their respective fields. The parties have two minor children. Both parents love their children and play important roles in their lives. In their divorce, the judge awarded joint legal custody of the children, with Stamatia to have sole physical custody. Later, Stamatia asks the judge to allow her to move with the children to Greece, where she has been offered the position of president of a university. Ioannis objects to the children moving to Greece. The children are fluent in English and Greek. During their marriage, the family traveled to Greece nearly every summer. Both parents come from prominent Greek families. The children's grandparents live in Greece. Should the judge allow Stamatia to move to Greece with the children over Ioannis' objection? *Yannas v. Frondistou-Yannas,* 395 Mass. 704, 481 N.E.2d 1153 (1985).

5. Should a child who is old enough to have an opinion on the subject be able to veto a custodial parent's decision to move to another state? A Massachusetts statute provides: "A minor child of divorced parents who is a native of or has resided five years within this commonwealth and over whose custody and maintenance a probate court has jurisdiction shall not, if of suitable age to signify his consent, be removed out of this commonwealth without such consent . . . ." Mass. Gen. Laws Ann. Ch. 208 § 30. Do you favor such a law? How old is old enough to make such a decision? In intact families, kids don't have veto power over their parents' decision to move. Why should a child of divorced parents have such power?

Custody Issues When a Parent is in the Military

Members of our armed forces defend the nation at considerable sacrifice—sometimes the ultimate sacrifice. Servicemembers who are parents endure long separations from their children. In intact military marriages, the stay-at-home parent keeps the home fire burning and cares for the kids. Things are more challenging for single parent servicemembers. Often, the servicemember's relatives step in when the parent is deployed.

When a servicemember/parent is divorced and has custody, the noncustodial parent often assumes custody during deployment. Problems arise when the noncustodial parent who "takes over" during deployment decides to start court proceedings to change custody while the servicemember remains deployed. In this scenario, the Servicemembers Civil Relief Act (SCRA)—discussed in Chapter 4—applies, and the custody action can be stayed.[111]

In custody disputes involving servicemembers, should the judge consider the impact on children of lengthy military deployments? Jeri Hanes grapples with this question in an article in *Army Lawyer*, an excerpt of which appears below.

Fight for Your Country, Then Fight to Keep Your Children: Military Members May Pay the Price . . . Twice

Jeri Hanes
***Army Lawyer* 27-50 (2011)**

"After Iraq Tour, National Guard Soldier Loses Custody of Son;" "A Soldier's Service Leads to a Custody Battle Back Home;" "Deployed Troops Battle for Child Custody;" "Custody Battles Can Become a Rude 'Welcome Home' for Military Parents." These various media headlines reveal the entirely different battlefield servicemembers face upon return from combat. These headlines are followed by narratives of servicemembers who were the primary physical custodians of their children prior to their mobilization or deployment in support of the War on Terror. Upon their return, each of these military parents found themselves in a fight to regain custody of their children . . . .

---

111   *See* Ex parte K.N.L., 872 So.2d 868 (Ala. Civ. App. 2003); Marriage of Grantham, 698 N.W.2d 140 (Iowa 2005)(the Act does not require a stay in every case); Cole v. Cole, 971 So.2d 1185 (La. Ct. App. 2007); Henneke v. Young, 145 Ohio App.3d 111, 761 N.E.2d 1140 (2001).

Lieutenant Eva Slusher (previously Eva Crouch) had physical custody of her daughter for six years in accordance with her divorce order, when she was subsequently mobilized for eighteen months with her Kentucky National Guard unit. During her mobilization, Slusher's ex-husband received a temporary order to keep their child. A month after Slusher was released from active duty, a family court judge permanently modified the original custody order because it was "in the best interests of the child." Slusher stated, "[e]very time I went to court ... I kept thinking there was no way they could rule against a mother because she was serving her country."

Specialist Tonya Towne maintained physical custody of her son for eight years before being deployed to Iraq in 2004. When she returned home in 2005, a New York family court modified her original custody order and gave permanent physical custody to her ex-husband. Despite finding Towne to be an "excellent mother," the appellate court refused to overturn the family court's decision. Towne's opinion: "I don't care how they word it; it's a punishment to the Soldier. The whole reason I'm in this situation is because I did a job for the military." ...

The United States needs a uniform custody act for servicemembers which prohibits state courts from considering the military deployments of all servicemembers, Active and Reserve Components, during permanent child custody modification proceedings (the "deployment rule"). ...

The 2008 National Defense Authorization Act added the words "including any child custody proceeding" to the default judgment and ninety-day stay of proceedings provisions of the Servicemember's Civil Relief Act (SCRA). Despite this explicit clarification of the applicability of the SCRA to child custody proceedings, the change offers little relief to servicemembers. This is because deployments are typically longer than the minimum ninety-days courts are required to stay proceedings pursuant to the SCRA, and courts are authorized to refuse additional requests. Additionally, courts are not precluded from issuing temporary modification orders that may affect the best interests of the child analysis during permanent modification proceedings after the servicemember redeploys. ...

State Statutes Regarding Custody of Servicemembers

A number of states have statutes addressing custody issues of servicemember parents. The Arizona statute provides that if the parent with whom a child resides a majority of the time is deployed a substantial distance away, a court shall not enter a final order modifying custody until 90 days after the deployment ends.[112] Arizona law also states, "The court shall not consider a parent's absence caused by deployment or mobilization or the potential for future deployment or mobilization as the sole factor supporting a real, substantial and unanticipated change in circumstances . . . ."[113] Arkansas law states, "A court shall not permanently modify an order for child custody or visitation solely on the basis that one of the parents is a mobilized parent."[114] California law provides that a parent's failure to comply with custody or visitation orders is not sufficient, by itself, to modify custody or visitation if the reason for the failure is the parent's deployment.[115] California law goes on to state that when a parent with sole or joint physical custody is deployed, any modification of custody "shall be deemed a temporary custody order, which shall be subject to review and reconsideration upon the return of the party from military deployment . . . . There shall be a presumption that the custody order shall revert to the order that was in place before the modification, unless the court determines that it is not in the best interest of the child."[116] A Florida statute provides that if a motion to modify custody is filed because a parent is deployed, the court may not modify a previous custody judgment, except on a temporary basis. The statute specifies that deployment may not be the sole factor in a decision to change custody.[117] An Indiana statute provides, "A court may not consider a parent's absence or relocation due to active duty service as a factor in determining custody or permanently modifying a child custody order. If a court temporarily modifies a custody order due to a parent's active duty service, the order temporarily modifying the custody order terminates automatically not later than ten days after the parent notifies the temporary custodian in writing that the parent has returned from active duty service."[118] Oregon law provides that a parent's inability to comply with a joint custody order does not constitute a change of circumstances when the inability is due to military service.[119] South Carolina law provides, "If a military parent is required to be separated from a child due to military service, a court shall not enter a final order modifying the terms establishing custody or visitation contained in an existing order until ninety days after the military par-

---

112   Ariz. Rev. Stat. Ann. § 25-411(B).

113   Ariz. Rev. Stat. Ann. § 25-411(C).

114   Ark. Code Ann. § 9-13-110(b).

115   Cal. Family Code§ 3047(a).

116   Cal. Family Code § 3047(b)(1).

117   Fla. Stat. Ann. § 61.13002(1).

118   Indiana Code § 31-17-2-31.3

119   Ore. Rev. Stat. Ann. § 107.169(6)(a).

ent is released from military service. A military parent's absence or relocation because of military service must not be the sole factor supporting a change in circumstances or grounds sufficient to support a permanent modification of the custody or visitation terms established in an existing order."[120]

Question Regarding Custody by Servicemembers

A number of statutes provide that military deployment cannot be the "sole" factor in determining custody or visitation. Should military services be a factor *at all*? Would you favor a law requiring judges to ignore military service when considering best interests?

C

EXPERIENTIAL ASSIGNMENT

Practice Exercise: *A Memo for Your Boss*

Six months ago you passed the bar. Congratulations! Now you are an inexperienced but eager young attorney working for a lawyer with years of experience in family law. Your boss just sent you the following e-mail:

> I have been retained to represent Dr. Judith Wallenstein. Dr. Wallenstein is a prominent surgeon in our city. The doctor was divorced three years ago from her husband Dr. William Wallenstein, also a well known local physician. I was not involved in the divorce. Under the divorce, the Wallensteins have joint legal custody. Judith has primary physical custody. The three kids—aged 7, 5, and 3—live in Judith's home. The kids spend every other weekend with their dad at his house. Judith has a full time nanny to take care of the children while Judith works. Mother and father are good parents. There are no substance

---

120 S.C. Code Ann. § 63-5-920(A).

abuse issues or other problematic parenting behaviors. Both sets of grandparents live here and are involved with their grandkids. Recently, Judith received an offer to join the faculty at the medical school in our neighboring state. She wants to accept the offer and move there with the kids. The move will put the kids almost 200 miles from their dad. Dr. Wallenstein asked me whether she can move and take the children with her. She believes her ex-husband will object to the move. It has been a long time since I handled a move away case. I'd like you to research the law in our state on move aways and summarize the law for me in a brief memo. One or two pages should be fine. Just a summary; not a long treatise, please! With the law in mind, give me your opinion on whether you think a judge will approve the move if it is opposed by father. Thanks. Oh, and I need the memo tomorrow. Hope you didn't have plans for tonight. Sorry.

Assignment: Prepare the requested memo for your boss.

Jurisdiction Regarding Child Custody

Subject matter jurisdiction regarding child custody is governed by two statutes, the federal Parental Kidnapping Prevention Act (28 U.S.C. § 1738A), which is binding on the states, and the Uniform Child Custody Jurisdiction and Enforcement Act (UCCJEA), a version of which is in force in every state. Personal jurisdiction over both parents is *not* required to adjudicate child custody.

Some cases of international child abduction by parents are governed by The Hague Convention on the Civil Aspects of International Child Abduction (Hague Convention).

The first version of the UCCJEA was the Uniform Child Custody Jurisdiction Act (UCCJA), promulgated in 1968 by the National Conference of Commissioners on Uniform State Laws. The UCCJA was intended to remedy uncertainty about interstate child custody determinations. Prior to the UCCJA, courts ruled that jurisdiction over child custody could be based on a child's domicile, residence, or temporary presence in the state. The drafters of the UCCJA described the problems caused by pre-UCCJA law:

> There is a growing public concern over the fact that thou-
> sands of children are shifted from state to state and from one fam-
> ily to another every year while their parents or other persons battle

over their custody in the courts of several states. Children of sepa-rated parents may live with their mother, for example, but one day the father snatches them and brings them to another state where he petitions a court to award him custody while the mother starts cus-tody proceedings in her state; or in the case of illness of the mother the children may be cared for by grandparents in a third state, and all three parties may fight over the right to keep the children in sev-eral states. These and many similar situations constantly arise in our mobile society where family members often are scattered all over the United States and at times over other countries. A young child may have been moved to another state repeatedly before the case goes to court. When a decree has been rendered awarding custody to one of the parties, this is by no means the end of the child's migrations. It is well known that those who lose a court battle over custody are often unwilling to accept the judgment of the court. They will remove the child in an unguarded moment or fail to return him after a visit and will seek their luck in the court of a distant state where they hope to find—and often do find—a more sympathetic ear for their plea for custody. The party deprived of the child may then resort to similar tactics to recover the child and this "game" may continue for years, with the child thrown back and forth from state to state, never com-ing to rest in one single home and in one community. . . .

In this confused legal situation the person who has possession of the child has an enormous tactical advantage. Physical presence of the child opens the doors of many courts to the petitioner and often assures him of a decision in his favor. It is not surprising then that custody claimants tend to take the law into their own hands, that they resort to self-help in the form of child stealing, kidnapping, or vari-ous other schemes to gain possession of the child. The irony is that persons who are good, law-abiding citizens are often driven into these tactics against their inclinations; and that lawyers who are reluctant to advise the use of maneuvers of doubtful legality may place their clients at a decided disadvantage.[121]

---

121 Commissioner's Comment to UCCJA, 9 *Uniform Laws Annotated* 116-117 (1988).

Questions using pre-UCCJA law:

Before the UCCJA, jurisdiction to decide custody could be based on a child's physical presence in a state. Use pre-UCCJA law to answer the following questions:

1. Mom and Dad marry in Washington and have a child. The marriage breaks down and mom files for divorce. Dad is afraid the court will award child custody to mom, so one night, without telling mom, Dad packs the car, plops junior in the car seat, and leaves for Missouri, where he has family. Once in Missouri, he files an action for custody. Does Missouri have jurisdiction?

2. Mom and Dad divorce in Georgia. After a custody battle, Mom is awarded custody. Dad relocates to North Dakota. A year later, dad puts the kids on an airplane and takes them to North Dakota, where he files a custody modification action. Does North Dakota have jurisdiction?

3. Mom and Dad divorce in Nevada and dad gets custody. Mom moves to Utah, where she grew up and went to college. According to the divorce decree, Mom gets a month visitation in the summer with the kids in Utah. At the end of a summer visit, mom refuses to return the kids to Nevada, and mom commences custody modification proceedings in Utah. Does Utah have jurisdiction?

Pre-UCCJA law encouraged warring parents to scoop up the kids, head for the border, and litigate elsewhere. The UCCJA was designed to end this practice

.

UCCJA Gets a Facelift—UCCJEA

The UCCJA was designed to bring uniformity to interstate child custody determinations, and to reduce forum shopping. Although the UCCJA worked reasonably well, states had slightly different versions of the UCCJA, and the law had loopholes. The result was continued uncertainty. Congress stepped in in 1980 with the Parental Kidnapping Prevention Act (PKPA). The UCCJA was updated in 1997 to achieve consistency with the PKPA. The new version of the UCCJA is the Uniform Child Custody Jurisdiction and Enforcement Act (UCCJEA).

The PKPA and the UCCJEA are lengthy and do not make for interesting reading. Nevertheless, the statutes are so important to your understanding of child custody jurisdiction, and play such a prominent role in practice, that the statutes are set forth in their entirety, and deserve careful study.

Before you launch into the PKPA and the UCCJEA, keep in mind that child custody litigation occurs at two stages. First, an initial custody determination. Second, proceedings to modify an initial custody determination. Keep the two stages in mind as you study the PKPA and the UCCJEA.

Federal Parental Kidnapping Prevention Act

28 U.S.C. § 1738A.
Full faith and credit given to child custody determinations

(a) The appropriate authorities of every State shall enforce according to its terms, and shall not modify except as provided in subsections (f), (g), and (h) of this section, any custody determination or visitation determination made consistently with the provisions of this section by a court of another State.

(b) As used in this section, the term—

(1) "child" means a person under the age of eighteen;

(2) "contestant" means a person, including a parent or grandparent, who claims a right to custody or visitation of a child;

(3) "custody determination" means a judgment, decree, or other order of a court providing for the custody of a child, and includes permanent and temporary orders, and initial orders and modifications;

(4) "home State" means the State in which, immediately preceding the time involved, the child lived with his parents, a parent, or a person acting as a parent, for at least six consecutive months, and in the case of a child less than six months old, the State in which the child lived from birth with any of such persons. Periods of temporary absence of any of such persons are counted as part of the six-month or other period;

(5) "modification" and "modify" refer to a custody or visitation determination which modifies, replaces, supersedes, or otherwise is made subsequent to, a prior custody or visitation determination concerning the same child, whether made by the same court or not;

(6) "person acting as a parent" means a person, other than a parent, who has physical custody of a child and who has either been awarded custody by a court or claims a right to custody;

(7) "physical custody" means actual possession and control of a child;

(8) "State" means a State of the United States, the District of Columbia, the Commonwealth of Puerto Rico, or a territory or possession of the United States; and

(9) "visitation determination" means a judgment, decree, or other order of a court providing for the visitation of a child and includes permanent and temporary orders and initial orders and modifications.

(c) A child custody or visitation determination made by a court of a State is consistent with the provisions of this section only if—

(1) such court has jurisdiction under the law of such State and

(2) one of the following conditions is met:

(A) such State (i) is the home State of the child on the date of the commencement of the proceeding, or (ii) had been the child's home State within six months before the date of the commencement of the proceeding and the child is absent from such State because of his removal or retention by a contestant or for other reasons, and a contestant continues to live in such State;

(B) (i) it appears that no other State would have jurisdiction under subparagraph (A), and (ii) it is in the best interest of the child that a court of such State assume jurisdiction because (I) the child and his parents, or the child and at least one contestant, have a significant connection with such State other than mere physical presence in such State, and (II) there is available in such State substantial evidence concerning the child's present or future care, protection training, and personal relationships;

(C) the child is physically present in such State and (i) the child has been abandoned, or (ii) it is necessary in an emergency to protect the child because the child, a sibling or parent of the child has been subjected to or threatened with mistreatment or abuse;

(D) (i) it appears that no other State would have jurisdiction under subparagraph (A), (B), (C), or another State has declined to exercise jurisdiction on the ground that the such court assume jurisdiction; or

(E) the court has continuing jurisdiction pursuant to subsection (d) of this section.

(d) The jurisdiction of a court of a State which has made a child custody or visitation determination consistently with the provisions of this section continues as long as the requirement of subsection (c)(1) of this section continues to be met and such State remains the residence of the child or of any contestant.

(e) Before a child custody or visitation determination is made, reasonable notice and opportunity to be heard shall be given to the contestants, any parent whose parental rights have not been previously terminated and any person who has physical custody of a child.

(f) A court of a State may modify a determination if the custody of the same child made by a court of another State, if—

(1) it has jurisdiction to make such a child custody determination; and

(2) the court of the other State no longer has jurisdiction, or it has declined to exercise such jurisdiction to modify such determination.

(g) A court of a State shall not exercise jurisdiction in any proceeding for a custody or visitation determination commenced during the pendency of a proceeding in a court of another State where such court of that other State is exercising jurisdiction consistently with the provision of this section to make a custody or visitation determination.

(h) A court of a State may not modify a visitation determination made by a court of another State unless the court of the other State no longer has jurisdiction to modify such determination or has declined to exercise jurisdiction to modify such determination.

Uniform Child Custody Jurisdiction and Enforcement Act

Article 1
General Provisions

§101. Short Title.

This Act may be cited as the Uniform Child-Custody Jurisdiction and Enforcement Act.

§102. Definitions.

In this Act:

(1) "Abandoned" means left without provision for reasonable and necessary care or supervision.

(2) "Child" means an individual who has not attained 18 years of age.

(3) "Child-custody determination" means a judgment, decree, or other order of a court providing for the legal custody, physical custody, or visitation with respect to a child. The term includes a permanent, temporary, initial, and modification order. The term does not include an order relating to child support or other monetary obligation of an individual.

(4) "Child-custody proceeding" means a proceeding in which legal custody, physical custody, or visitation with respect to a child is an issue. The term includes a proceeding for divorce, separation, neglect, abuse, dependency, guardianship, paternity, termination of parental rights, and protection from domestic violence, in which the issue may appear. The term does not include a proceeding involving juvenile delinquency, contractual emancipation, or enforcement under Article 3.

(5) "Commencement" means the filing of the first pleading in a proceeding.

(6) "Court" means an entity authorized under the law of a State to establish, enforce, or modify a child-custody determination.

(7) "Home State" means the State in which a child lived with a parent or a person acting as a parent for at least six consecutive months immediately before the commencement of a child-custody proceeding. In the case of a child less than six months of age, the term means the State in which the child lived from birth with any of the persons mentioned. A period of temporary absence of any of the mentioned persons is part of the period.

(8) "Initial determination" means the first child-custody determination concerning a particular child.

(9) "Issuing court" means the court that makes a child-custody determination for which enforcement is sought under this Act.

(10) "Issuing State" means the State in which a child-custody determination is made.

(11) "Modification" means a child-custody determination that changes, replaces, supersedes, or is otherwise made after a previous determination concerning the same child, whether or not it is made by the court that made the previous determination.

(12) "Person" means an individual, corporation, business trust, estate, trust, partnership, limited liability company, association, joint venture, government; governmental subdivision, agency, or instrumentality; public corporation; or any other legal or commercial entity.

(13) "Person acting as a parent" means a person, other than a parent, who:

    a. has physical custody of the child or has had physical custody for a period of six consecutive months, including any temporary absence, within one year immediately before the commencement of a child-custody proceeding; and

    b. has been awarded legal custody by a court or claims a right to legal custody under the law of this State.

(14) "Physical custody" means the physical care and supervision of a child.

(15) "State" means a State of the United States, the District of Columbia, Puerto Rico, the United States Virgin Islands, or any territory or insular possession subject to the jurisdiction of the United States.

(16) "Tribe" means an Indian tribe or band, or Alaskan Native village, which is recognized by federal law or formally acknowledged by a State.

(17) "Warrant" means an order issued by a court authorizing law enforcement officers to take physical custody of a child.

103. Proceedings Governed By Other Law.

This Act does not govern an adoption proceeding or a proceeding pertaining to the authorization of emergency medical care for a child.

104. Application to Indian Tribes.

(a) A child-custody proceeding that pertains to an Indian child as defined in the Indian Child Welfare Act, 25 U.S.C. § 1901 et seq., is not subject to this Act to the extent that it is governed by the Indian Child Welfare Act.

(b) A court of this State shall treat a tribe as if it were a State of the United States for the purpose of applying Articles 1 and 2.

(c) A child-custody determination made by a tribe under factual circumstances in substantial conformity with the jurisdictional standards of this Act must be recognized and enforced under Article 3.

105. International Application of Act.

(a) A court of this State shall treat a foreign country as if it were a State of the United States for the purpose of applying Articles 1 and 2.

(b) Except as otherwise provided in subsection (c), a child-custody determination made in a foreign country under factual circumstances in substantial conformity with the jurisdictional standards of this Act must be recognized and enforced under Article 3.

(c) A court of this State need not apply this Act if the child custody law of a foreign country violates fundamental principles of human rights.

106. Effect of Child-Custody Determination.

A child-custody determination made by a court of this State that had jurisdiction under this Act binds all persons who have been served in accordance with the laws of this State or notified in accordance with Section 108 or who have submitted to the jurisdiction of the court, and who have been given an opportunity to be heard. As to those persons, the determination is conclusive as to all decided issues of law and fact except to the extent the determination is modified.

110. Communication Between Courts.

(a) A court of this State may communicate with a court in another State concerning a proceeding arising under this Act.

(b) The court may allow the parties to participate in the communication. If the parties are not able to participate in the communication, they must be given the opportunity to present facts and legal arguments before a decision on jurisdiction is made.

(c) Communication between courts on schedules, calendars, court records, and similar matters may occur without informing the parties. A record need not be made of the communication.

(d) Except as otherwise provided in subsection (c), a record must be made of a communication under this section. The parties must be informed promptly of the communication and granted access to the record.

Article 2
Jurisdiction

201. Initial Child-Custody Jurisdiction.

(a) Except as otherwise provided in Section 204, a court of this State has jurisdiction to make an initial child-custody determination only if:

(1) this State is the home State of the child on the date of the commencement of the proceeding, or was the home State of the child within six months before the commencement of the proceeding and the child is absent from this State but a parent or person acting as a parent continues to live in this State;

(2) a court of another State does not have jurisdiction under paragraph (1), or a court of the home State of the child has declined to exercise jurisdiction on the ground that this State is the more appropriate forum under Section 207 or 208, and:

(A) the child and the child's parents, or the child and at least one parent or a person acting as a parent, have a significant connection with this State other than mere physical presence; and

(B) substantial evidence is available in this State concerning the child's care, protection, training, and personal relationships;

(3) all courts having jurisdiction under paragraph (1) or (2) have declined to exercise jurisdiction on the ground that a court of this State is the more appropriate forum to determine the custody of the child under Section 207 or 208; or

(4) no court of any other State would have jurisdiction under the criteria specified in paragraph (1), (2), or (3).

(a) Subsection (a) is the exclusive jurisdictional basis for making a child-custody determination by a court of this State.

(b) Physical presence of, or personal jurisdiction over, a party or a child is not necessary or sufficient to make a child-custody determination.

202. Exclusive, Continuing Jurisdiction.

(a) Except as otherwise provided in Section 204, a court of this State which has made a child-custody determination consistent with Section 201 or 203 has exclusive, continuing jurisdiction over the determination until:

(1) a court of this State determines that neither the child, the child's parents, and any person acting as a parent do not have a significant connection with this State and that substantial evidence is no longer available in this State concerning the child's care, protection, training, and personal relationships; or

(2) a court of this State or a court of another State determines that the child, the child's parents, and any person acting as a parent do not presently reside in this State.

(b) A court of this State which has made a child-custody determination and does not have exclusive, continuing jurisdiction under this section may modify that determination only if it has jurisdiction to make an initial determination under Section 201.

203. Jurisdiction to Modify Determination.

Except as otherwise provided in Section 204, a court of this State may not modify a child-custody determination made by a court of another State unless a court of this State has jurisdiction to make an initial determination under Section 201(a)(1) or (2) and:

(1) the court of the other State determines it no longer has exclusive, continuing jurisdiction under Section 202 or that a court of this State would be a more convenient forum under Section 207; or

(2) a court of this State or a court of the other State determines that the child, the child's parents, and any person acting as a parent do not presently reside in the other State.

204. Temporary Emergency Jurisdiction.

(a) A court of this State has temporary emergency jurisdiction if the child is present in this State and the child has been abandoned or it is necessary in an emergency to protect the child because the child, or a sibling or parent of the child, is subjected to or threatened with mistreatment or abuse.

205. Notice; Opportunity to be Heard; Joinder.

(a) Before a child-custody determination is made under this Act, notice and an opportunity to be heard in accordance with the standards of Section 108 must be given to all persons entitled to notice under the law of this State as in child-custody proceedings between residents of this

State, any parent whose parental rights have not been previously terminated, and any person having physical custody of the child.

(b) This Act does not govern the enforceability of a child-custody determination made without notice or an opportunity to be heard.

206. Simultaneous Proceedings.

(a) Except as otherwise provided in Section 204, a court of this State may
not exercise its jurisdiction under this Article if, at the time of the commencement of the proceeding, a proceeding concerning the custody of
the child has been commenced in a court of another State having jurisdiction substantially in conformity with this Act, unless the proceeding
has been terminated or is stayed by the court of the other State because
a court of this State is a more convenient forum under Section 207.

207. Inconvenient Forum.

(a) A court of this State which has jurisdiction under this Act to make a
child-custody determination may decline to exercise its jurisdiction
at any time if it determines that it is an inconvenient forum under the
circumstances and that a court of another State is a more appropriate
forum. The issue of inconvenient forum may be raised upon motion of a
party, the court's own motion, or request of another court.

(b) Before determining whether it is an inconvenient forum, a court of
this State shall consider whether it is appropriate for a court of another
State to exercise jurisdiction. For this purpose, the court shall allow the
parties to submit information and shall consider all relevant factors,
including:

(1) whether domestic violence has occurred and is likely to continue
in the future and which State could best protect the parties and the
child;

(2) the length of time the child has resided outside this State;

(3) the distance between the court in this State and the court in the State
that would assume jurisdiction;

(4) the relative financial circumstances of the parties;

(5) any agreement of the parties as to which State should assume jurisdiction;

(6) the nature and location of the evidence required to resolve the pending litigation, including testimony of the child;

(7) the ability of the court of each State to decide the issue expeditiously and the procedures necessary to present the evidence; and

(8) the familiarity of the court of each State with the facts and issues in the pending litigation.

(c) If a court of this State determines that it is an inconvenient forum and that a court of another State is a more appropriate forum, it shall stay the proceedings upon condition that a child-custody proceeding be promptly commenced in another designated State and may impose any other condition the court considers just and proper.

(d) A court of this State may decline to exercise its jurisdiction under this Act if a child-custody determination is incidental to an action for divorce or another proceeding while still retaining jurisdiction over the divorce or other proceeding.

208. Jurisdiction Declined by Reason of Conduct.

(a) Except as otherwise provided in Section 204 or by other law of this State, if a court of this State has jurisdiction under this Act because a person seeking to invoke its jurisdiction has engaged in unjustifiable conduct, the court shall decline to exercise its jurisdiction unless:

(1) the parents and all persons acting as parents have acquiesced in the exercise of jurisdiction;

(2) a court of the State otherwise having jurisdiction under Sections 201 through 203 determines that this State is a more appropriate forum under Section 207; or

(3) no court of any other State would have jurisdiction under the criteria specified in Sections 201 through 203.

209. Information to be Submitted to Court.

(a) In a child-custody proceeding, each party, in its first pleading or in an attached affidavit, shall give information, if reasonably ascertainable, under oath as to the child's present address or whereabouts, the places where the child has lived during the last five years, and the names and present addresses of the persons with whom the child has lived during that period.

Article 3
Enforcement

302. Enforcement Under Hague Convention.

Under this Article a court of this State may enforce an order for the return of the child made under the Hague Convention on the Civil Aspects of International Child Abduction as if it were a child-custody determination.

303. Duty to Enforce.

A court of this State shall recognize and enforce a child-custody determination of a court of another State if the latter court exercised jurisdiction in substantial conformity with this Act or the determination was made under factual circumstances meeting the jurisdictional standards of this Act and the determination has not been modified in accordance with this Act.

305. Registration of Child-Custody Determination.

(a) A child-custody determination issued by a court of another State may be registered in this State.

306. Enforcement of Registered Determination.

(a) A court of this State may grant any relief normally available under the law of this State to enforce a registered child-custody determination made by a court of another State.

(b) A court of this State shall recognize and enforce, but may not modify, except in accordance with Article 2, a registered child-custody determination of a court of another State.

307. Simultaneous Proceedings.

If a proceeding for enforcement under this Article is commenced in a court of this State and the court determines that a proceeding to modify the determination is pending in a court of another State having jurisdiction to modify the determination under Article 2, the enforcing court shall immediately communicate with the modifying court. The proceeding for enforcement continues unless the enforcing court, after consultation with the modifying court, stays or dismisses the proceeding.

311. Warrant to Take Physical Custody of Child.

(a) Upon the filing of a petition seeking enforcement of a child-custody determination, the petitioner may file a verified application for the issuance of a warrant to take physical custody of the child if the child is immediately likely to suffer serious physical harm or be removed from this State.

PKPA and UCCJEA Work as a Team

The UCCJEA dovetails with the PKPA. The statutes are a team. The Colorado Supreme Court's decision in *Parental Responsibilities of L.S.* illustrates the collaboration between UCCJEA and PKPA.

Parental Responsibilities of L.S.

Supreme Court of Colorado
257 P.3d 201 (2011)

Chief Justice Bender delivered the Opinion of the Court.

This case concerns a child custody dispute between a divorced mother and father. The child currently lives in Colorado with her mother, Tatanjia Willyard Spotanski McNamara. The father, Stacy Joe Spotanski, lives in Nebraska. Seeking to gain custody of his daughter, the father filed a custody action in Nebraska. Although the mother objected to Nebraska's exercise of jurisdiction, a Nebraska district court entered an initial child custody determination awarding custody to the father. Subsequently, the mother filed her own custody action in Colorado. A Colorado district court awarded custody to the mother, refusing to enforce the prior Nebraska custody determination on the basis that Nebraska did not have jurisdiction. Reversing the district court, the Colorado Court of Appeals held that, although Nebraska did not have jurisdiction over the custody determination, Colorado must nevertheless accord that determination full faith and credit.

This interstate child custody dispute requires us to determine whether Colorado is obligated to recognize and enforce the prior child custody determination rendered by the Nebraska court. To reach this determination, we focus on the Parental Kidnaping Prevention Act of 1980, 28 U.S.C. § 1738A (PKPA), which extends the requirements of the Full Faith and Credit Clause to custody determinations and, thereby, furnishes a rule of decision for courts to use in adjudicating interstate custody disputes. We conclude that, because Nebraska failed to exercise jurisdiction in accordance with the requirements of the PKPA, the PKPA does not require Colorado to give full faith and credit to the Nebraska custody determination. Hence, we hold that Colorado does not have to enforce the Nebraska custody determination.

Consequently, we reverse the judgment of the court of appeals and remand the case to that court to return the case to the trial court for proceedings consistent with this opinion.

The child who is the subject of this case was born in 2001 and resided in Colorado with her mother and father beginning in August 2003. The parties separated in January 2004, and the father moved to Nebraska. In May 2004, the mother and father signed a written agreement, which stated that all custody matters would be under Colorado jurisdiction, that the child would continue to live in Colorado with her mother, and that the father would be allowed visitation rights.

In the summer of 2004, the father took the child to Nebraska for an agreed-upon visit. At the conclusion of the visit, the father refused to return the child to Colorado. In November 2004, the father filed in the district court for Howard County, Nebraska an action for dissolution of marriage and asked to be awarded custody of the child. In a pro se answer to the dissolution action, the mother alleged that the child had resided in Colorado for almost two years and that she was supposed to visit her father in Nebraska for no more than three months, "not to establish residency for a court action." The next month, the mother filed a pro se dissolution action in the district court for Adams County, Colorado. She then filed in the Nebraska district court a motion to dismiss the Nebraska dissolution action based on the pending dissolution action in Colorado. Meanwhile, in the Adams County district court action, after a January 2005 hearing in which the mother appeared pro se, the district court issued a minute order dismissing the dissolution action. By way of explanation, the district court's minute order stated only that "the State of Nebraska has jurisdiction over the matter." It made no reference to child custody.

On September 21, 2006, the Nebraska district court issued a final decree, dissolving the marriage and awarding custody of the child to the father. The decree stated that the court had jurisdiction, but it only made findings regarding jurisdiction over the dissolution action and failed to find whether the court had jurisdiction over the custody determination or whether Nebraska is the child's home state. . . .

[Father admitted the child had not been in Nebraska 6 months when he sought custody. Mother appealed to the Nebraska Court of Appeals, but the

Court of Appeals dismissed her case on procedural grounds. Eventually, mother prevailed in a Colorado trial court, but the Colorado Court of Appeals ruled against her. The Colorado Court of Appeals ruled that even though Nebraska lacked jurisdiction, Colorado was bound by the Nebraska custody order. The Colorado Supreme Court accepted Mother's appeal].

Currently, the child lives with the mother in Colorado, and the mother refuses to comply with the Nebraska district court order awarding custody to the father. Because the mother refuses to comply with its order, the Nebraska district court issued a warrant for the mother's arrest in May 2008. The warrant orders law enforcement to take physical custody of the child and return the child to the father.

This case involves competing custody determinations entered by Colorado and Nebraska. The mother argues that the Nebraska court failed to exercise jurisdiction in accordance with the PKPA, and, therefore, the court of appeals erred when it held that Colorado must enforce the Nebraska determination. The father argues that the court of appeals correctly held that the Nebraska district court's exercise of jurisdiction complied with the PKPA, and, consequently, the PKPA obligates Colorado to enforce the Nebraska custody determination.

Parallel federal and state statutes—the PKPA (28 U.S.C. § 1738A) and the UCCJEA, a uniform state law adopted by both Colorado and Nebraska—govern whether Nebraska had jurisdiction to enter an initial child custody determination and whether Colorado must enforce that determination. To untangle these applicable laws, we first discuss the PKPA, which, by imposing rules for a state's exercise of jurisdiction over child custody matters, dictates whether a state must enforce a child custody determination entered by the court of a sister state. . . .

We then consider whether Nebraska exercised jurisdiction in accordance with the PKPA. This inquiry requires us to determine whether Nebraska exercised jurisdiction in accordance with both its own law and the jurisdictional provisions of the PKPA. We conclude that Nebraska did not have jurisdiction, under either its own law or the PKPA, to enter an initial child custody determination in this case. Consequently, the PKPA and parallel Colorado law do not require Colorado to recognize or enforce the Nebraska determination.

. . . Congress signaled that its chief aim in enacting the PKPA was to extend the requirements of the Full Faith and Credit Clause to custody determinations. . . . The PKPA acts as a rule of determination in interstate custody disputes by imposing a duty on the States to enforce a child custody determination entered by a court of a sister State if the determination is consistent with the provisions of the Act. . . . Section 1738A(a) states: "The appropriate authorities of every State shall enforce according to its terms, and shall not modify except as provided in this Act, any custody determination made consistently with the provisions of this section by a court of another State."

In *Thompson v. Thompson*, 484 U.S. 174, 108 S.Ct. 513 (1988), the United States Supreme Court interpreted this provision to mandate that "once a State exercises jurisdiction consistently with the provisions of the PKPA, no other State may exercise concurrent jurisdiction over the custody dispute and all States must accord full faith and credit to the first State's ensuing custody decree."

Conversely, if a state court's custody determination fails to conform to the PKPA's requirements, then the custody determination is not entitled to full faith and credit enforcement in another state. Both the legislative scheme of the PKPA and *Thompson* confirm this conclusion. First, the PKPA specifically conditions interstate enforcement of a custody determination on the determination having been "*made consistently* with the provisions of the PKPA by a court of another State." . . . . Second, in *Thompson*, the Supreme Court stressed that "the sponsors and supporters of the PKPA continually indicated that the purpose of the PKPA was to provide for nationwide enforcement of custody orders *made in accordance with its terms*." . . .

Colorado statutes and case law incorporate the requirements of the PKPA. . . . The UCCJEA is a uniform state law which was promulgated after the PKPA and intended to harmonize state law with the provisions of the PKPA. Because Colorado enacted the UCCJEA, its statutes regarding jurisdiction over child custody disputes and enforcement of foreign custody decrees are substantively identical to the PKPA.

As relevant to whether Colorado has jurisdiction to enter an initial custody determination, section 14–13–201, C.R.S. provides the same bases to establish initial jurisdiction as does the PKPA, as relevant here: (1) home state and (2) significant connection. Likewise, both the PKPA and section 14–13–201, C.R.S. prioritize home state jurisdiction over significant connection jurisdiction.

Regarding whether Colorado must enforce a custody determination rendered by a another state, Colorado statutes mandate that a Colorado court is obligated to enforce the child custody determination of another state when it determines that the sister state made the determination in "substantial conformity" with or under factual circumstances satisfying the jurisdictional requirements of the UCCJEA, [which provide], "A court of this state shall recognize and enforce a child-custody determination of a court of another state if the latter court exercised jurisdiction in substantial conformity with this article or the determination was made under factual circumstances meeting the jurisdictional standards of this article." . . . When another state has already entered a child custody determination, we inquire whether the first-in time court's exercise of jurisdiction was in accordance with the PKPA.

Because Colorado statutes and case law incorporate the requirements of the PKPA, if a sister state exercised jurisdiction in accordance with the PKPA, then its exercise of jurisdiction would necessarily be in substantial conformity with Colorado law. Accordingly, we now consider whether the Nebraska court's exercise of jurisdiction was in accordance with the PKPA such that Colorado must recognize and enforce the Nebraska custody determination.

The PKPA dictates whether Colorado must accord full faith and credit to the Nebraska custody determination. If Nebraska exercised jurisdiction consistently with the provisions of the PKPA, then Colorado must accord it full faith and credit. However, if the Nebraska determination was not made consistently with the requirements of the PKPA, then the custody determination is not entitled to full faith and credit enforcement in Colorado.

The PKPA provides that a state's custody determination is made consistently with the PKPA when: (1) the court of the state has jurisdiction under its own law, and (2) the exercise of jurisdiction meets one of the conditions set out in 28 U.S.C. § 1738A(c)(2). Because we determine that the Nebraska district court did not have jurisdiction over this custody determination under its own law—as it was not the child's home state, and the home state did not decline jurisdiction—we therefore conclude that the PKPA does not obligate Colorado to accord the Nebraska determination full faith and credit.

Nebraska Revised Statutes section 43–1238(a), which sets out the requirements for Nebraska to exercise jurisdiction to make an initial child custody determination, provides four independent bases for jurisdiction to make an initial child custody determination. Only the first two are relevant here: (1) home state and (2) significant connection. . . .

As with the PKPA, Nebraska Revised Statutes section 43–1238(a) gives priority to home state jurisdiction. To have jurisdiction to enter an initial custody award, Nebraska Revised Statutes section 43–1238(a)(1) requires that, at the commencement of the custody proceeding, Nebraska must be the home state of the child or have been the home state of the child within the last six months. A court's jurisdiction must exist at the time an action is filed and cannot be attained after such date regardless of the amount of time spent by the children in the state subsequent to the filing of a custody action. . . .

If Nebraska is not the home state of the child, then it may exercise significant connection jurisdiction only if: (1) another state does not have jurisdiction as the child's home state; or (2) the home state has declined to exercise jurisdiction on the ground that Nebraska is the more appropriate forum under section. To confer significant connection jurisdiction to Nebraska based on the home state declining jurisdiction, Nebraska Revised Statutes section 43–1238(a)(2) requires that the child's home state declined jurisdiction on the ground that either the home state is an inconvenient forum or the party seeking jurisdiction in the home state engaged in unjustifiable conduct . . . .

In this case, the child lived in Colorado with at least one parent from August 2003 until the summer of 2004, more than six consecutive months. Then, after the child's scheduled visit with her father in Nebraska, the father refused to return the child to Colorado. After the father refused to return the child to Colorado, the child lived in Nebraska with her father for just over five months before her father commenced the Nebraska custody action in November 2004. In its September 2006 order giving custody of the child to the father, the Nebraska district court failed to state its grounds for exercising jurisdiction under the UCCJEA.

Because the child had lived in Colorado for six consecutive months immediately before the father commenced the custody proceeding and had not lived in Nebraska for six consecutive months, Colorado, and not Nebraska, was the child's home state. To allow the father to establish jurisdiction in Nebraska by refusing to return the child to the mother, as required by the parties' agreement that the child would reside in Colorado with her mother, would contravene the purposes of the UCCJEA and the PKPA, both of which seek to prevent parental kidnapping and equivalent misconduct. Because Nebraska was not the child's home state at the time the father commenced the custody proceeding, the Nebraska court could only have properly exercised jurisdiction if Colorado declined to exercise jurisdiction on the ground that Nebraska is the more appropriate forum . . . .

The Nebraska court based its determination that Colorado declined jurisdiction on the decision of the Adams County district court to dismiss the mother's action for dissolution of marriage. In its minute order dismissing the case, the Adams County district court stated only that "the State of Nebraska has jurisdiction over this matter." It failed to provide reasons for declining jurisdiction and to engage in even a cursory consideration of whether Nebraska is a more appropriate forum. The district court did not mention child custody, the UCCJEA, home state jurisdiction, inconvenient forum, or unjustifiable conduct.

The Adams County district court failed to engage in any consideration of the relevant statutory factors for inconvenient forum . . . . It also failed to consider whether the party seeking to invoke its jurisdiction engaged in unjustifiable conduct . . . . The district court did not consider that the parties agreed that the child would reside in Colorado with the mother and that the father likely engaged in unjustifiable conduct by retaining the child in Nebraska after the termination of her scheduled visit and, thus, did not decline jurisdiction on those grounds.

Accordingly, because Colorado, and not Nebraska, had jurisdiction as the child's home state and Colorado did not decline jurisdiction on the ground that Nebraska is the more appropriate forum . . . , Nebraska did not have jurisdiction over this matter under its own law. As Nebraska did not have jurisdiction under its own law, the PKPA does not require Colorado to accord the Nebraska custody determination full faith and credit.

For these reasons, we reverse the judgment of the court of appeals and remand the case to that court to return the case to the trial court for proceedings consistent with this opinion.

Justice Coats, dissenting.

I decline to join the majority opinion, not from any particular dispute over its interpretation of the jurisdictional standards and priorities of the PKPA or UCCJEA but because I believe our enactment of the UCCJEA requires us to accept Nebraska's own determination of its jurisdiction. . . . By construing the UCCJEA to sanction its collateral attack on Nebraska's jurisdictional determination, expressly made under the provisions of that act, the majority merely perpetuates the promulgation of conflicting state child-custody orders and, therefore, the very jurisdictional stalemate the UCCJEA was drafted to end. Because I believe our own jurisdictional statute forbids us from modifying a child-custody order of another state that was made under a provision of law in substantial conformity with our own, I respectfully dissent. . . .

Nowhere . . . does the UCCJEA state or (at least in my opinion) even imply that a modifying or enforcing state is to disregard established principles of finality and res judicata and re-determine for itself the correctness of jurisdictional determinations, made by applying the identical provisions of the UCCJEA, by other jurisdictions responsible for initial child-custody determinations. Once the question of initial jurisdiction has been fully and finally litigated in another state, according to provisions in substantial conformity with the UCCJEA, that determination is entitled to credit, whether or not a court of this state would have reached the same conclusion. . . .

Questions based on *Parental Responsibilities of L.S.*

1. A Nebraska judge made a custody order, but the Colorado Supreme Court refused to give the order full faith and credit. The Colorado court examined the basis for the Nebraska judge's order and concluded the Nebraska court lacked jurisdiction to make a custody order. In dissent, Justice Coats argues that a Colorado court may not "re-determine for itself the correctness of jurisdictional *determinations*" of other states. In defense of the majority, surely a court must have authority to determine the legitimacy of a sister state's assertion of jurisdiction, mustn't it? *See* the discussion of the U.S. Supreme Court's decision in *Williams v. North Carolina* on pages 111-112.

2. Note that the child was in Nebraska only five months when dad commenced custody proceedings in Nebraska. It takes six months for a state to become a child's home state. Should dad have waited a month longer before commencing his custody case so he could claim Nebraska as the child's home state?

Jurisdiction at Two Stages of Custody Litigation: Jurisdiction to Make an Initial Custody Determination; Jurisdiction to Modify Custody

The Colorado Supreme Court's decision in *Parental Responsibilities of L.S.* helps you understand the inner workings of the UCCJEA and the PKPA. Now that you are familiar with the statutes, analysis focuses on jurisdiction at two stages of child custody litigation. First, jurisdiction to make an *initial* custody determination. Second, jurisdiction to *modify* a custody determination of *another* state.

Jurisdiction to Make an Initial Child Custody Determination

UCCJEA § 102(8) defines "initial determination" as "the first child-custody determination concerning a particular child." Jurisdiction to make an initial custody determination is governed by § 201. The next two cases—*Prizza v. Prizza* and *Marriage of Sareen*—analyze jurisdiction to make an initial custody determination.

Prizza v. Prizza

Court of Appeals of Virginia
58 Va. App. 137, 707 S.E.2d 461 (2011)

Petty, Judge.

Gary Prizzia ("husband") and Judit Prizzia ("wife") were married in Hungary on August 28, 1999. While they were living there, their only child was born on February 3, 2000. In April 2000, the Prizzias moved to Virginia, where they resided until December 15, 2002. On that date, both parties took the child to Hungary for a visit over the Christmas holidays. Husband returned to Virginia on December 25, 2002, and wife and the child remained in Hungary. On February 4, 2003, wife filed for divorce in Hungary, requesting custody of the child. Upon learning of wife's actions, husband filed for divorce in the Circuit Court of Henrico County on May 6, 2003. Husband's complaint also requested the court to award him custody of the child and to make an equitable distribution of the marital estate.

On December 30, 2003, the trial court entered an order finding "that Hungary had proper jurisdiction over the parties as to divorce, custody, visitation and child support," and accordingly "declined to exercise jurisdiction over those matters at that time." . . .

On March 19, 2005, the Hungarian court granted the parties a divorce and awarded custody of the child to wife, with visitation rights to husband. The Hungarian court did not award child support, nor did it divide the parties' property. Husband then sought to revive the dormant proceeding in Henrico County . . . . Wife did not return to Virginia for the hearings, but was granted permission to present testimony by telephonic deposition.

On May 24, 2010, the trial court entered a final decree. The final decree addressed the issues of equitable distribution, child support, and spousal support. The trial court declined to enter any order dealing with the issues of divorce or child custody, choosing instead to defer to the Hungarian court's ruling on those issues.

Husband first argues that the trial court erred in finding that the Hungarian court had jurisdiction to decide the issues of child custody and visitation. Thus, he posits, the trial court erred in failing to exercise its jurisdiction over those issues. Where multiple states or foreign countries have potential initial jurisdiction over child custody, the Uniform Child Custody Jurisdiction and Enforcement Act (UCCJEA) dictates where actual jurisdiction shall be exercised. Here, we conclude that the trial court failed to follow the requirements of the UCCJEA.

To determine whether a court of this Commonwealth has jurisdiction to make an initial child custody determination, we look to Code § 20–146.12:

A. Except as otherwise provided in § 20-146.15 [the section providing for temporary emergency jurisdiction], a court of this Commonwealth has jurisdiction to make an initial child custody determination only if:

(1) This Commonwealth is the home state of the child on the date of the commencement of the proceeding, or was the home state of the child within six months before the commencement of the proceeding and the child is absent from this Commonwealth but a parent or person acting as a parent continues to live in this Commonwealth;

(2) A court of another state does not have jurisdiction under subdivision 1, or a court of the home state of the child has declined to exercise jurisdiction on the ground that this Commonwealth is the more appropriate forum . . . , and (i) the child and the child's parents, or the child and at least one parent or a person acting as a parent, have a significant connection with this Commonwealth other than mere physical presence and (ii) substantial evidence is available in this Commonwealth concerning the child's care, protection, training, and personal relationships;

(3) All courts having jurisdiction under subdivision 1 or 2 have declined to exercise jurisdiction on the ground that a court of this Commonwealth is the more appropriate forum to determine the custody of the child . . . ; or

(4) No court of any other state would have jurisdiction under the criteria specified in subdivision 1, 2, or 3.

Subsection A is the exclusive jurisdictional basis for making a child custody determination by a court of this Commonwealth. Thus, to determine whether a court of this Commonwealth had jurisdiction to make an initial child custody determination in this case, we must first decide what the "home state" of the child was on May 6, 2003, the date this proceeding was commenced.

The UCCJEA defines "home state" as "the state in which a child lived with a parent or a person acting as a parent for at least six consecutive months immediately before the commencement of a child custody proceeding. . . . A period of temporary absence of any of the mentioned persons is part of the period." Code § 20–146.1. Hence, a child's "home state" is where the child has lived with one or more of his parents for the consecutive six-month period immediately preceding the date on which a child custody proceeding is filed.

However, this is not the only six-month period we must consider in analyzing initial jurisdiction over child custody under Code § 20–146.12(A)(1). Where, as here, the child was not living in Virginia on the date the proceeding was filed, we must determine if Virginia was the child's home state at any time during the six months before the filing date. If so, Virginia would continue to have initial jurisdiction. This alternate basis for jurisdiction becomes relevant in instances where a child has acquired a new residence less than six months before the commencement of a custody proceeding, thus rendering the child technically without a home state as of the date of the commencement of the proceeding. In such a case, the court must examine whether the child had a home state at any point within the six-month period preceding the date of filing. In other words, the court must ask whether at any point throughout the six months preceding the date of filing, it could be said that on a particular date, the child had lived with a parent in a particular state for at least six consecutive months. The purpose behind this statutory scheme is to extend a state's home state status throughout the six-month period it would take for another state to become the child's new home state.

Thus, if a child lived with a parent in Virginia for six months and then moved to another state (or another country, for that matter), Virginia would continue to have jurisdiction to make an initial child custody determination under Code § 20–146.12(A)(1) until the child had lived long enough in the other state (*i.e.*, six months) for that state to become the child's new home state.

With this understanding of the UCCJEA's basic jurisdictional scheme in mind, we need not decide whether the child's presence in Hungary from December 15, 2002 to May 6, 2003 constituted a "period of temporary absence" within the meaning of Code § 20–146.1, thus rendering Virginia the home state as of the date of filing, or whether the child had actually changed residence from Virginia to Hungary during that time. Even if the child's residence had permanently changed on December 15, 2002 from Virginia to Hungary, Virginia continued to have initial child custody jurisdiction for six months after that date. Thus, as of May 6, 2003, the date on which husband commenced this custody proceeding, Virginia either was the child's home state or had been the child's home state within the previous six months. This means that under Code § 20–146.12(A)(1), Virginia had jurisdiction to make an initial child custody determination.

Having concluded that Virginia had jurisdiction to make an initial child custody determination, we must next analyze whether the trial court properly declined to exercise its jurisdiction under the UCCJEA. In analyzing this issue, we must decide as a subsidiary issue whether Hungary also had jurisdiction under the UCCJEA's jurisdictional framework. In considering this question, we treat the Hungarian court as we would a court of another state in the United States ....

Code § 20–146.4(B) directs that "a child custody determination made in a foreign country under factual circumstances in substantial conformity with the jurisdictional standards of this act must be recognized and enforced under Article 3 (§ 20–146.22 et seq.) of this chapter." In other words, a Virginia court must recognize and enforce a foreign custody determination if the facts of the case would have supported a finding of jurisdiction by the foreign court had it applied the jurisdictional standards of the UCCJEA.

Here, when we apply the jurisdictional standards of the UCCJEA to the facts before the Hungarian court as of February 4, 2003, when wife first filed her divorce and custody petition, we conclude that the Hungarian court did not exercise jurisdiction "under factual circumstances in substantial conformity with" the UCCJEA's jurisdictional standards. Essentially, we are faced with the question, "Under the standards of Code § 20–146.12, did the Hungarian court have jurisdiction to make an initial child custody determination as of February 4, 2003?" We hold that it did not.

First, Hungary was not the "home state" of the child in February 2003, when wife filed her divorce and custody petition in the Hungarian court. The child had not yet lived in Hungary for six months as of February 4, 2003. Furthermore, Hungary had not been the home state of the child at any time during the six-month period immediately preceding the date of wife's filing on February 4, 2003. Thus, Hungary did not have jurisdiction under Code § 20–146.12(A)(1) at the time of wife's filing. Rather, Virginia continued to have home state jurisdiction at that time.

Second, Hungary did not have jurisdiction pursuant to any of the other potential avenues for obtaining jurisdiction under Code § 20–146.12(A) .... This is for two reasons: (1) Virginia retained home state jurisdiction under Code § 20–146.12(A)(1); and (2) the Virginia trial court did not decline to exercise jurisdiction on the ground that the Hungarian court was the more appropriate forum .... We have already discussed the first reason. We will now explain the second.

Although the trial court said it was "declining to exercise jurisdiction" over child custody matters in this case, the trial court did not decline to exercise its jurisdiction in a manner that conformed either to Code § 20–146.18 or to Code § 20–146.19.

Code § 20–146.18(A) provides: "A court of this Commonwealth that has jurisdiction under this act to make a child custody determination may decline to exercise its jurisdiction at any time if it determines that it is an inconvenient forum under the circumstances and that a court of another state is a more appropriate forum." However, Code § 20–146.18 does not permit a court simply to declare that it has decided to decline to exercise jurisdiction. Rather, Code § 20–146.18(B) requires: "Before determining whether it is an inconvenient forum, a court of this Commonwealth *shall* consider whether it is appropriate for a court of another state to exercise jurisdiction. For this purpose, the court *shall allow the parties to present evidence and shall consider all relevant factors. . . . "* The statute then lists eight specific factors the court must consider in determining whether to decline to exercise jurisdiction under this section. . . .

Here, the trial court failed to do what the statute requires. The trial court made no specific determination that Virginia was an inconvenient forum under the circumstances or that the Hungarian court was a more appropriate forum. Moreover, the trial court did not allow the parties to present all relevant evidence, as husband requested, on the issue of whether it was more appropriate for the Hungarian court to exercise jurisdiction. Because it did not allow the parties to present evidence pertaining to the statutory factors, the trial court could not have based its decision on a proper review of those factors. Thus, we conclude that by failing to follow the requirements of Code § 20–146.18, the trial court did not properly decline to exercise its jurisdiction pursuant to that section.

The second way a trial court can decline to exercise its jurisdiction over child custody is set forth in Code § 20–146.19, which states that "if a court of this Commonwealth has jurisdiction under this act because a person seeking to invoke its jurisdiction has engaged in unjustifiable conduct, the court shall decline to exercise its jurisdiction unless one of certain enumerated exceptions is met." Code § 20–146.19(A). Here, there is no evidence that Virginia had home state jurisdiction because husband had engaged in unjustifiable conduct. The trial court did not make this finding, nor did it base its decision to decline to exercise jurisdiction on Code § 20–146.19. Therefore, this second avenue for declining to exercise jurisdiction does not apply to this case.

Because the trial court did not properly decline to exercise its jurisdiction . . . , its vague, unexplained, general decision to decline to exercise jurisdiction was improper . . . . Moreover, since Virginia had jurisdiction to make an initial child custody determination . . . , and since the Virginia trial court did not properly decline to exercise this jurisdiction . . . , Hungary did not have jurisdiction to make an initial child custody determination . . . . Therefore, under the jurisdictional standards of the UCCJEA, Virginia had jurisdiction to make an initial child custody determination, and Hungary did not. Accordingly, it was error for the trial court to defer to the Hungarian court on the issue of child custody in the manner that it did. We thus reverse this decision of the trial court and remand for the trial court to decide whether to exercise its jurisdiction and award custody pursuant to Virginia law. In making that determination, the trial court must allow the parties to present evidence and must consider all relevant factors . . . . If, based on that consideration, the trial court concludes that Virginia is an inconvenient forum under the current circumstances and that Hungary is currently a more appropriate forum for determination of child custody, the trial court may decline to exercise its jurisdiction . . . .

Questions based on *Prizza v. Prizza*

1. Assume husband prevails after the case is remanded to the trial court. The trial judge awards custody to husband. Problem is: The child is in Hungary! How is husband going to enforce his Virginia custody order? Go to Hungary and enforce his Virginia custody order there? Recall, Hungary already awarded custody to wife. What do you suppose husband's odds of success are before a Hungarian court?

2. Look at the extraordinary amount of time it took to litigate this case! Wife filed for divorce in 2003. It wasn't until 2010 that the trial court finally rendered its decision. The Court of Appeals handed down its decision in 2011, but that didn't end the matter. By the time the litigation finally grinds to a halt the child may be 18!

Marriage of Sareen

California Court of Appeals
153 Cal. App. 4th 371, 62 Cal. Rptr. 3d 687 (2007),
cert. denied, **552 U.S. 1259 (2008)**

Cantil-Sakauye, J.

Reema Sareen (wife) appeals the trial court's grant of (husband) Vikas Sareen's motion to quash jurisdiction in wife's child custody petition. Wife contends the trial court erred in concluding India was their child's home state under the Uniform Child Custody Jurisdiction and Enforcement Act (UCCJEA or Act) (Fam.Code, § 3400 et seq.) and that, absent an order from the court in India declining jurisdiction, California did not have jurisdiction. Wife contends

California has jurisdiction under the UCCJEA. We agree with wife and shall reverse the order granting husband's motion to quash.

On February 17, 2002, husband and wife were married in New Delhi, India. In July 2002 they moved from India to New York State. Husband is a United States citizen and wife is a legal resident of the United States. Their daughter, S., was born in New York on February 20, 2004. She is a United States citizen.

According to wife, on August 20, 2004, husband told her the family was going to Switzerland for a vacation. However, when they got to Frankfurt, Germany, they changed planes not for Switzerland, but for India. They arrived in India on August 21, 2004. Less than a week later, on August 27, 2004, husband filed for divorce in an Indian court. Three days later, on August 30, 2004, husband filed a petition for custody of S. in the Indian court and an application to restrain wife from leaving India with S. Husband then returned alone to New York.

According to wife, husband abandoned wife and six-month-old S. in New Delhi without financial support, taking with him wife's United States residency documents, her Indian passport, and S.'s United States passport. Wife tried to obtain replacement documents to allow her return to the United States with S. When wife tried to obtain a replacement passport for S., husband refused to sign the necessary consent "for purposes relating to certain pending court proceedings." Wife was able to temporarily return to the United States in February/March 2005 to work on her own immigration papers and request S.'s passport. She then rejoined her daughter in India in March 2005. S.'s new United States passport was eventually issued on September 21, 2005. Wife and S. were able to leave India on November 5, 2005. They flew to New York and then a few days later flew to California where they took up residence.

Husband denied he abandoned wife and S. in India. He declared it was understood they were going to vacation there, but that wife's continued tantrums, threats, and cruel behavior compelled him to file for divorce shortly after their arrival. He claimed he voluntarily left S. with wife while the divorce and custody proceedings were pending, after making provisions for their support. He denied taking wife's or S.'s passports or documents. He claimed wife had property and family in New Delhi. He contended wife was legally required to stay in India while the divorce and custody proceedings were pending there.

The divorce and custody proceedings in India, started by husband in August 2004, continued with husband and wife both flinging accusations of mistreatment, abuse, lies, threats, neglect, misrepresentations, and fraud against each other. Wife apparently filed a dowry action against husband. Husband sought to change his divorce petition to an annulment proceeding based on allegations that wife fraudulently induced their marriage on a false representation of her educational background. On application by wife, the India trial court entered an order in May 2005 requiring husband to pay child and spousal support. The record contains evidence of husband paying only two months of the ordered support. The Indian court did not enter any order restraining wife or S. from leaving the jurisdiction and the statute referenced by husband as barring wife's leaving applied only where a guardian was appointed, which had not occurred.

On January 31, 2006, wife filed, in the Sacramento County Superior Court, a petition for child custody and support, including a request for child abduction prevention orders.

Husband filed a motion to quash jurisdiction premised on the grounds that (1) India has jurisdiction of the custody proceedings for S. and wife illegally kidnapped S. to come to California, (2) S. did not have minimum contacts with California, (3) husband did not have minimum contacts with California, and (4) that husband did not cause an effect in California.

Wife opposed husband's motion to quash denying husband's factual contentions and claiming she did not violate Indian law or any Indian court order by moving back to the United States when she was able to do so, that she never intended to go to India or stay there, that her presence in India was not voluntary, and that she was now lawfully living in California with the permission of the Indian government. Wife argued personal jurisdiction over husband was not necessary for a custody determination under the UCCJEA, that the Indian proceedings did not preempt exercise of California jurisdiction, and that California could exercise jurisdiction premised either on California being S.'s home state or on there being no home state and S.'s significant connection with California. Wife stated in November 2005 she came to Sacramento where her brother lives and works and is able to give her and S. considerable moral support. She is working part-time here and is receiving Temporary Assistance to Needy Families (TANF)....

. . . The trial court filed a ruling . . . granting husband's motion to quash. In pertinent part, the ruling stated: "In this case, the divorce case commenced in India, one week after wife and S. arrived there. Thus, India was not the home state under the UCCJEA for purposes of the proceeding in Delhi. At the time S.'s home state was New York. This action was filed on January 31, 2006. At the time S. had resided in India for a year and thus under the statutory definition India was the home state for purposes of the UCCJEA. The Court in India has not declined to exercise its jurisdiction . . . . The UCCJEA is clear, at this time absent an order from the Delhi court declining jurisdiction in favor of California, this Court does not have jurisdiction under the UCCJEA."

It is well-settled in California that the UCCJEA is the exclusive method of determining subject matter jurisdiction in custody disputes involving other jurisdictions. The UCCJEA applies to international custody disputes as well as interstate disputes. Under the Act, foreign countries are to be treated as states for the purpose of determining jurisdiction, unless the child custody law of the country violates fundamental principles of human rights. Nothing in the record suggests the custody law of India in any way violates principles of human rights.

Although there is some conflict in the parties's version of events in this case, the relevant jurisdictional facts are largely undisputed. We are not bound by the trial court's findings regarding subject matter jurisdiction, but rather independently reweigh the jurisdictional facts. Subject matter jurisdiction either exists or does not exist at the time the action is commenced, and cannot be conferred by stipulation, consent, waiver, or estoppel. The action is commenced when the first pleading is filed; here, January 31, 2006.

The first issue we address is whether the trial court was precluded from exercising jurisdiction due to the pendency of the custody proceedings in India. Husband admits he filed for custody in India before the family had been in the country for six months, which would have been a requirement under the UCCJEA for home state jurisdiction, but claims his action came within the jurisdictional requirements of Indian law and that the proceeding in India precludes the exercise of jurisdiction by a California court under section 3426(a).

Section 3426(a), reads: "Except as otherwise provided in Section 3424 [temporary emergency jurisdiction], a court of this state may not exercise its jurisdiction under this chapter if, at the time of the commencement of the proceeding, a proceeding concerning the custody of the child has been commenced in a court of another state *having jurisdiction substantially in conformity with this part,* unless the proceeding has been terminated or is stayed by the court of the other state because a court of this state is a more convenient forum under Section 3427." (Italics added.)

On January 31, 2006, when wife filed her custody petition in this case, custody proceedings had been commenced and were pending in India. The pertinent question under section 3426(a), is not whether the Indian court had jurisdiction under its own laws for such proceeding, but whether such jurisdiction was in substantially in conformity with the UCCJEA. Here it is undisputed husband filed his custody petition on August 30, 2004, only nine days after the family arrived in India. Such a miniscule amount of time in India does not come close to establishing the connection to the state required by the UCCJEA for the exercise of custody jurisdiction. India's jurisdiction in the pending custody proceeding, while presumably adequately established under Indian law, was not in substantial conformity with the UCCJEA. Nor did the India court's order on application of wife requiring husband to pay child support confer jurisdiction on India under the UCCJEA. Under section 3402(c) a child custody determination does not include an order relating to child support. The trial court was not precluded from exercising its jurisdiction, if it had it, because of the pendency of the proceeding in India.

We turn to the question of whether the trial court had jurisdiction to exercise in this case under the Act. Section 3421(a), confers jurisdiction on a California court "only if any of the following are true: (1) This state is the home state of the child on the date of the commencement of the proceeding, or was the home state of the child within six months before the commencement of the proceeding and the child is absent from this state but a parent or person acting as a parent continues to live in this state. (2) A court of another state does not have jurisdiction under paragraph (1), or a court of the home state of the child has declined to exercise jurisdiction on the grounds that this state is the more appropriate forum under Section 3427 or 3428, and both of the following are true: (A) The child and the child's parents, or the child and at least one parent or a person acting as a parent, have a significant connection with this state other than mere physical presence. (B) Substantial evidence is available in this state concerning the child's care, protection, training, and personal relationships. (3) All courts having jurisdiction under paragraph (1) or (2) have declined to exercise jurisdiction on the ground that a court of this state is the more appropriate forum to determine the custody of the child under Section 3427 or 3428. (4) No court of any other state would have jurisdiction under the criteria specified in paragraph (1), (2), or (3)."

Section 3402(g), provides the definition for the term "home state" as used in section 3421. "Home state means the state in which a child lived with a parent or a person acting as a parent for at least six consecutive months immediately before the commencement of a child custody proceeding. A period of temporary absence of any of the mentioned persons is part of the period."

On January 31, 2006, wife and S. had lived in California for a period of under three months (they arrived a few days after November 5, 2005). Therefore, California was not the home state of S. on the date of the commencement of this proceeding. Nor is there any evidence that California "was the home state of S. within six months before the commencement of the proceeding and S. is absent from this state but a parent or person acting as a parent continues to live in this state" so as to give California jurisdiction under the second sentence of subdivision (a)(1) of section 3421 for recent home state jurisdiction. S. had never previously lived in California with either parent for any consecutive period of six months, much less a period ending within the previous six months to January 31, 2006. The trial court did not have jurisdiction under subdivision (a)(1) of section 3421.

For California to exercise jurisdiction under subdivision (a)(2) of section 3421, we must first determine if there was any other state with home state jurisdiction under subdivision (a)(1) at the time of the commencement of wife's proceeding. The trial court concluded that on January 31, 2006, S. "had resided in India for a year and thus under the statutory definition India was the home state" under the UCCJEA. It is undisputed S. lived in India from August 20, 2004 until November 5, 2005. However, we part company with the trial court in concluding such period of residence can be counted towards India being S.'s home state on January 31, 2006.

Although we have not found any California case holding on point, cases in other states have concluded time spent in a forum after the filing of a child custody petition may not be counted towards the time necessary for home state jurisdiction. For example, . . . in *Irving v. Irving* (1985) 682 S.W.2d 718, a Texas court of appeal concluded Texas did not have jurisdiction to award custody in an action filed in Texas by a father four days after he had brought his children to Texas, when the children had otherwise lived in Illinois and had been taken from their grandmother's home in Mississippi where they were temporarily staying. The court stated: "During the three-year duration of this legal battle, the children have undoubtedly developed roots in Texas. However, we cannot allow the appellee to bootstrap his way into a Texas court based on relationships developed after suit was commenced."

. . . We are persuaded a parent may not take a child to a jurisdiction, file a premature custody petition, and then use the time the child remains in that jurisdiction pending resolution of the petition to meet the six-month UCCJEA home state period, either in that custody proceeding or as a defense to the other parent's competing custody proceeding in another state. To do so would condone blatant forum-shopping, particularly here where it appears husband's actions were responsible for keeping S. in India after his filing of the divorce and custody actions.

We conclude India was not the home state of S. under the UCCJEA on January 31, 2006 when wife filed her petition in this case.

The only other state that could possibly have been S.'s home state on January 31, 2006, when wife filed her petition in this case, was New York. However, neither wife nor husband claim New York was then S.'s home state and indeed it is clear S. had not lived in New York since August 2004 and had only spent a few days in New York when wife and she came back to the United States in November

2005. Admittedly, periods of temporary absence of a child and parents from a state are counted in determining whether the period for home state jurisdiction has been met. It would, however, be a stretch of imagination on these facts to consider an absence, with the exception of a few days, of almost *seventeen months* to be a "temporary" absence from New York.

We conclude there was no state with home state jurisdiction on January 31, 2006, when wife filed her petition for child custody in the trial court.

In such a situation California may exercise jurisdiction under section 3421(a)(2) when "both of the following are true: (A) The child and the child's parents, or the child and at least one parent or a person acting as a parent, have a significant connection with this state other than mere physical presence. (B) Substantial evidence is available in this state concerning the child's care, protection, training, and personal relationships." The evidence established both were true in this case.

Here S. was not quite two years old at the time of wife's filing of the petition in California. Wife submitted a declaration in support of her opposition to husband's motion to quash in which she stated she and S. came to California approximately three months earlier and they were now "settled" in California, where she has the moral support of her brother who also lives here. Wife is working part-time and is receiving temporary public assistance. Husband did not submit any evidence contradicting wife's claims or establishing an alternate location of available important information regarding S.

Therefore, the undisputed evidence established wife's significant connection with this state beyond mere physical presence. She had family, work and financial connections to Sacramento. In addition, the undisputed evidence established that the relevant current information relating to S., her daycare, her family relationships, her friends and her activities, as well as the relevant information regarding her future care, protection, and schooling was available in California, where wife and she had settled. Although some past information regarding S. might be located in New York and India, such information would not be as significant as the information regarding S.'s current and future circumstances available in California, particularly where the information in New York would relate to only a few months of S.'s infancy and the information in India would most likely reflect the temporary living arrangements of wife and S. while wife sought to return to the United States.

The trial court erred in concluding it did not have jurisdiction under the UCCJEA. The evidence before it established jurisdiction under section 3421, subdivision (a)(2).

The judgment (order) of the trial court granting respondent's motion to quash is reversed. Appellant is awarded her costs on appeal.

Comments on Initial Jurisdiction

1. Studying *Marriage of Sareen* and *Prizza v. Prizza,* you gain an appreciation of the complexity of UCCJEA litigation. You may recall that the Introduction to this book states, "Many lawyers look down on family law. For them, family law is low prestige, too emotional, and too simple. Simple? Hardly." When you delve into the UCCJEA and the PKPA, you see why family law is anything but simple.

2. Do you sometimes wonder, how on earth do parents afford to litigate cases in different jurisdictions, up and down the appellate ladder? What must it cost in attorneys fees, court costs, and travel expenses to wage an interstate or international custody battle?[122] Not to mention the cost in stress and heartache.

Jurisdiction to Modify a Custody Determination of *Another* State

When a court makes an initial child custody determination, the court retains continuing jurisdiction until the child reaches adulthood. (*See* UCCJEA § 202). Complex issues arise when a child who has a custody determination in place moves to another state, and a court of the new state is asked to modify the custody determination of the original state. (UCCJEA § 102(11) defines "modification"). Section 203 governs jurisdiction to modify custody, and provides that a court of the "new" state may not modify a custody determination made by a court of the "original" state unless certain requirements are fulfilled. The UCCJEA and PKPA are designed so that only one state has jurisdiction to modify custody. In other words, there can be no concurrent modification jurisdiction.

The following three cases discuss jurisdiction to modify sister state custody determinations.

---

122 Few attorneys can afford to take complex interstate or international custody jurisdiction cases pro bono. These cases often take hundreds of attorney hours. The cases can be intellectually challenging and personally and professionally rewarding, but the cost in time is significant. As I type this footnote, I'm looking at a 100 page stack of documents that arrived today asking my pro bono assistance with an international child abduction case. I'll take a couple of hours to see if I want to and can afford to help.

Graham v. Superior Court

California Court of Appeal
132 Cal. App. 4ᵗʰ 1193, 34 Cal. Rptr. 3d 270 (2005)

Hastings, J.

Petitioner, father in a child custody matter, seeks a writ of mandate requiring the family court to vacate an order entered on March 29, 2005, in which it determined that it no longer had exclusive jurisdiction to modify its original child custody/visitation order. The original custody order was entered in October 2003, after the parties stipulated to a judgment of dissolution of their marriage. The family court awarded the parties joint custody of their twin girls, born in California on October 2001, but physical custody was awarded to [mother]. One month before entry of the judgment, mother had moved with the twins to New York, with the consent of father.

[Father] continued to seek relief on visitation issues in California, including make-up visitation time and a request to take the children on a cruise. [Father] subsequently filed a motion to modify visitation orders and one month later, a motion to modify custody, requesting sole legal custody and primary physical custody of his two daughters.

Father's consolidated motions were heard on March 1, 2005. The court declined to exercise jurisdiction, relying upon Family Code section 3422. . . .

Father contends that the family court erred in its interpretation of section 3422. In relevant part, section 3422 provides that a California court has "exclusive, continuing jurisdiction" over the child custody determination *until* both of the following conditions are met: "a court of this state determines that neither the child, nor the child and one parent . . . have a significant connection with this state *and* that substantial evidence is no longer available in this state concerning the child's care, protection, training, and personal relationships." Thus, only when there is both a lack of significant connection and lack of substantial evidence in this state, may California terminate exclusive jurisdiction. We conclude the trial court erred in its interpretation of the statute.

[In the trial court, the judge] stated to counsel for [father]: "Whatever I think of your request for changing custody, I think you need to address it to a New York court which could then make an appropriate decision based on the evidence there *because that's where I think the evidence is.* So, I'm going to decline to exercise my jurisdiction any further in this matter and defer to the court of New York for further modification to my order if a court in New York wants to do that." A few moments later, the court stated: "The court has jurisdiction. I have jurisdiction until something occurs. And what occurs is my making a determination that neither—and I just love the way this is phrased. Neither the child nor the child and one parent nor the child and a person acting as a parent have a significant connection with this state and that substantial evidence is no longer available in this state concerning the child's care, protection, training, and personal relationship. *I am making that determination today.*" In its written order, the family court stated: "[Mother] and the parties' two minor children ... have continuously resided in the State of New York since September 2003, and no longer have a significant connection with the State of California."

It is apparent from the order that the family court focused on [mother] and the twins when it concluded that no further "significant connection" remained within California.

Father argues the court erred when it concluded the out-of-state residency of the children and [mother] terminated a significant connection with California. He relies upon *Kumar v. Superior Court* (1982) 32 Cal.3d 689 (*Kumar*), which held that a "significant connection" to the original state continues to exist as a matter of law as long as a parent who is exercising visitation rights still lives in that state. . . .

[The goal regarding continuing jurisdiction] . . . was expressed by Professor Bodenheimer: "The continuing jurisdiction of the prior court is exclusive. Other states do not have jurisdiction to modify the decree. They must respect and defer to the prior state's continuing jurisdiction. Exclusive continuing jurisdiction is not affected by the child's residence in another state for six months or more. Although the new state becomes the child's home state, significant connection jurisdiction continues in the state of the prior decree where the court record and other evidence exists and where one parent or another contestant continues to reside."

Professor Robert G. Spector, the reporter for the committee which drafted the [UCCJEA], explained the intended application of section 3422: "So long as one parent, or person acting as a parent, remains in the state that made the original custody determination, only that state can determine *when the relationship between the child and the left-behind parent has deteriorated sufficiently so that jurisdiction is lost.*" The *Kumar* interpretation advances this objective. If the remaining parent continues to assert and exercise his visitation rights, then the parent-child relationship has not deteriorated sufficiently to terminate jurisdiction.

The negative phrasing of section 3422 reinforces California's intent to retain exclusive jurisdiction. California courts must retain continuing jurisdiction *unless both* conditions are met that cause that jurisdiction to be terminated: neither the child, nor the child and the parent have a significant connection with the state and substantial evidence is no longer available in this state.

. . . California has sufficient contacts for a significant connection. The twins were born in California and resided in California for half of their current life. Father was granted specific periods of custody in California during the summer and alternating holidays, as well as at least four visits each year in New York. Relatives of the twins in California were granted reasonable visitations. . . .

We . . . conclude that the original state retains continuing exclusive jurisdiction as long as the parent who is exercising visitation rights still lives in that state and the relationship between that parent and the child has not deteriorated to the point at which the exercise of jurisdiction would be unreasonable.

By focusing on the wrong parent, the family court failed to properly assess the first factor addressed in section 3422. The matter must be remanded for the family court to reassess the matter.

Question based on *Graham v. Superior Court*

The court that makes an initial custody award retains *exclusive* modification jurisdiction. Only one state has modification jurisdiction at any one time. The court of a state that did not make an initial custody award cannot modify the initial custody award unless (1) the state that made the initial award determines it no longer has continuing jurisdiction, or (2) the state that made the initial award determines it is an inconvenient forum, or (3) the child and parents have left the state that made the initial award. *See* UCCJEA § 203.

With these principles in mind, consider the following: Hillary and Bill marry in Iowa and have two kids in the Hawkeye state. They divorced 5 years ago, and Bill was awarded sole custody. Hillary was awarded visitation. Four years ago, Bill and the children moved to Oregon. Hillary remained in Iowa. Hillary is a teacher, and she visits the kids in Oregon every summer for a month or two. The children have not been back to Iowa since they moved to Oregon. Recently, Hillary decided to seek full custody of the children. She files a petition for custody modification in Iowa. Bill argues there is no evidence about the children in Iowa—all the recent relevant evidence is in Oregon. Bill argues Iowa no longer has modification jurisdiction. Who is right? Where should custody litigation occur?

Custody of A.C.

Supreme Court of Washington
165 Wash. 2d 568, 200 P.3d 689 (2009)

Chambers, J.

A child and his mother are from Montana but moved to Washington. The child's former foster parents [the Nagals], still living in Montana, asked Washington courts to grant them custody. Washington has adopted the Uniform Child Custody Jurisdiction and Enforcement Act (UCCJEA). Under that act, because the foster parents live in Montana and seek to modify a custody determination initially made by Montana, and because Montana has never declined jurisdiction, Washington courts do not have jurisdiction to determine custody. Washington's exercise of jurisdiction in this case both offends the goals and violates the provisions of the UCCJEA. We reverse both the trial court and the Court of Appeals and remand to the trial court with orders to dismiss.

A.C. was born to Holly Cork on August 28, 1997, in Montana when Cork was 14. Both A.C. and Cork were placed in foster care by a Montana court. On January 7, 1999, the district court in Montana awarded the State legal custody of both Cork and A.C. On January 27, 2000, the State of Montana petitioned for permanent custody of A.C. and for termination of Cork's parental rights. A.C. was placed with David Nagel and Anita Bangert (the Nagels) as foster parents. The trial court terminated Cork's parental rights but the Montana Supreme Court reversed the termination, concluding that due process required that Cork have an attorney during the formulation of her treatment plan. In 2002, Cork obtained her GED, completed a 75-hour nurse's aide certification, and participated in a transition program for reunification with A.C. Montana's temporary custody of A.C. was terminated, A.C. was returned to Cork's custody, and on May 15, 2002, Cork and A.C. moved to Spokane, Washington.

In early October 2002, Washington's Child Protective Services (CPS) received an anonymous phone call from someone who claimed that A.C. had been punched and thrown around by his mother. The caller claimed that Cork had extensive involvement with Montana's social services, that she "wasn't ever interested in parenting but was interested in winning in court," and that she had received A.C. "back on a technicality" and then "fled the state of Montana." Around the same time, the Nagels sent a letter to the Washington Department of Social and Health Services (DSHS) stating that A.C. had been returned to Cork "due to a legal technicality" and offering to provide "foster/adoptive care" to A.C. "should the need arise."

DSHS began an investigative assessment of Cork. A DSHS case worker contacted Cork's social worker in Montana. The social worker opined that the Nagels had called with the anonymous allegations of abuse, noting the similarities between the call and the Nagel's letter and stating, "it's too much information." She said that the Nagels were vindictive when A.C. was returned to his mother. She also mentioned that Cork "is and was interested in parenting," and that "Holly did not flee to Washington, she had the support of the Montana agency." DSHS ended its investigation, finding little or no risk. The case worker concluded that although A.C. was still defiant and did not believe that Cork was his real mother, he was in no danger of abuse and should be fine with counseling. Cork did not provide A.C. with the recommended counseling.

On October 29, 2002, although they continued to live in Montana, the Nagels filed a petition in Spokane County for nonparental custody of A.C. The Nagels' petition claimed Cork was not a suitable custodian and requested that she have only limited visitation with her son. The Washington trial court ordered Cork to allow the Nagels visitation with A.C. Later the court appointed a guardian ad litem for A.C. The Nagels then moved for a temporary order of visitation and for a bonding and attachment assessment. In August 2003, the trial court granted temporary custody of A.C. to the Nagels in Montana and set out a schedule of visitation for Cork. In October 2003, Cork obtained new counsel and in January 2004, she moved to dismiss the nonparental custody petition, arguing for the first time that Washington did not have subject matter jurisdiction under the UCCJEA. The court denied the motion and at trial awarded custody of A.C. to the Nagels in Montana, with Cork having visitation rights and paying child support. Cork appealed. The Court of Appeals affirmed.

The UCCJEA arose out of a conference of states in an attempt to deal with the problems of competing jurisdictions entering conflicting interstate child custody orders, forum shopping, and the drawn out and complex child custody legal proceedings often encountered by parties where multiple states are involved. It is, in a sense, a pact among states limiting the circumstances under which one court may modify the orders of another. Most states have adopted the UCCJEA in order to reduce conflicting orders regarding custody and placement of children.

Both Montana and Washington have adopted the UCCJEA, making the act the exclusive basis to determine jurisdiction of this interstate child custody dispute. The UCCJEA determines when one state may modify an "initial child custody determination" made by another state. Under the UCCJEA, a Washington court may modify Montana's initial child custody determination only if either Montana declines jurisdiction or all parties have left that state.

The UCCJEA provides, in pertinent part: "Except as otherwise provided in RCW 26.27.231, a court of this state may not modify a child custody determination made by a court of another state unless a court of this state has jurisdiction to make an initial determination under RCW 26.27.201(1)(a) or (b) and: (1) The court of the other state determines it no longer has exclusive, continuing jurisdiction or that a court of this state would be a more convenient forum; or (2) A court of this state or a court of the other state determines that the child, the child's parents, and any person acting as a parent do not presently reside in the other state."

In essence, the UCCJEA provides that unless all of the parties and the child no longer live in the state that made the initial determination sought to be modified, that state must first decide it does not have jurisdiction or decline jurisdiction. Montana has jurisdiction over this dispute because Montana made the initial child custody determination regarding A.C.; the Nagels are persons acting as parents under the act who still reside in Montana; and Montana has not declined jurisdiction.

The Nagels argue that there is no current Montana custody decree in effect so there is no initial determination to be modified. But the definitions of the UCCJEA are quite broad. The definition of "child custody determination" includes "a judgment, decree, parenting plan, or other order of the court providing for the legal custody, physical custody, or visitation with respect to a child," and includes even temporary orders. Most recently, the Montana district court dismissed the termination case and ended the State's temporary protective custody of A.C. This order returned custody to Cork and, therefore, meets the definition of an initial child custody determination. The statutory definition of modification is similarly broad and includes any child custody determination that "changes, replaces, supersedes, *or is otherwise made after* a previous determination concerning the same child." Since the trial court's action in this case occurred after Montana's prior determination concerning custody of A.C., it was a modification of Montana's initial determination.

The Nagels also argue that they are not persons acting as parents and thus all relevant parties have left Montana. But a "person acting as a parent" is defined as a person other than a parent who (1) had physical custody of the child for a period of six consecutive months within one year before the commencement of the proceeding and (2) claims a right to legal custody under Washington law. In the year before this action began, the Nagels had custody of A.C. from October 29, 2001 until May 15, 2002, over six months. In addition, by filing a petition for nonparental custody, they have claimed a legal right to custody under Washington law. The Nagels are persons acting as parents under the act.

. . . Our conclusion rests . . . on current controlling Washington law, which states that "a court of this state *may not* modify a child custody determination made by a court of another state *unless* . . . (1) *[t]he court of the other state* determines it no longer has exclusive, continuing jurisdiction . . . or that a court of this state would be a more convenient forum." As Montana has also adopted this provision of the UCCJEA, under both Washington and Montana law, the Nagels must petition Montana and obtain an order that Montana has declined jurisdiction before Washington courts have jurisdiction to modify Montana's custody order. . . .

Observation and question based on *Custody of A.C.*

1. The initial custody order in *Custody of A.C.* was entered by a juvenile court exercising jurisdiction over a maltreated child, rather than by a family law court. As the Washington Supreme Court points out, however, the UCCJEA definition of "child-custody proceedings" is broad, and covers family court proceedings for custody *as well as* juvenile court proceedings to protect children from maltreatment. *See* UCCJEA § 102(3) and (4).

2. If the Nagels return to Montana and try to convince a Montana judge to decline jurisdiction, do you think they will succeed?

The next case is long. I shortened it, but it is still long (sorry). Despite the length, the case is worth studying. When you finally reach the end, you will have a deep understanding of the UCCJEA.

Marriage of Nurie

California Court of Appeal
176 Cal. App. 4th 478, 98 Cal. Rptr. 3d 200 (2009)

Richman, J.

This case graphically confirms what we said long ago: "controversies over custody are oftentimes long drawn out and bitter. This one involves an acrimonious six-year international custody battle, in which lawyers on two continents seemingly have left no stone unturned, while the parties themselves have left no rock unhurled. The accusations and counter-accusations include kidnapping, fraud, and domestic violence, all set against a backdrop of Interpol warrants, armed gunmen, and flights from justice. In both California and Pakistan, mud has been slung, court orders flouted, and reputations challenged.

The issue on appeal, however, is the far less dramatic one of jurisdiction under the Uniform Child Custody Jurisdiction and Enforcement Act (UCCJEA). We conclude the well-reasoned decision of the trial court was correct: the California court that dissolved the marriage had initial home state jurisdiction, it never lost jurisdiction, and its order granting custody to Husband was valid when entered and remains valid. Wife, of course, remains free to request modification.

Fizza Rizvi (Wife) and Ghulam Nurie (Husband) were both born in Pakistan, but Husband had lived in the United States for his entire adult life and is a naturalized United States citizen. They were married in a religious ceremony in Karachi on October 30, 2001. Shortly after the wedding, Wife came to live with Husband in his home of 16 years in Fremont, California. The couple were again married in a civil ceremony in Reno, Nevada, on January 31, 2002, and resided together in Fremont for the duration of their brief marriage. On September 16, 2002, their son (Son) was born in San Ramon, California.

On or about February 19, 2003, Wife took five-month-old Son to Pakistan, ostensibly on a four-week visit with the extended families. Husband bought round-trip airfare for them on that understanding. At the end of that time, Wife said she wanted to extend her visit for a few more weeks, and Husband agreed. Husband later learned through a third party that Wife did not plan to return.

Husband traveled to Pakistan in late May 2003 to attempt to persuade Wife to return with their Son. His efforts failed, and he returned to California alone. Wife did not directly communicate to Husband that she did not intend to return to California until the "end of May" 2003.

On June 20, 2003, Husband filed for dissolution of the marriage in Alameda County Superior Court. He sought custody of Son under the UCCJEA. On July 29, 2003, he obtained an ex parte order to show cause granting him temporary custody. Wife was served in Pakistan on September 16, 2003.

On September 30, 2003, Margaret Gannon, an Oakland attorney, made a special appearance on Wife's behalf to contest subject matter jurisdiction under the UCCJEA and to quash service of summons. At that hearing, a briefing schedule was established and a hearing on the merits set for November 4, 2003.

Wife substituted in as her own attorney on October 16, 2003, before any briefs had been filed. Wife filed no briefs, did not appear at the November 4 hearing, and took no further action to challenge the court's jurisdiction. The court found that Wife had been served and had notice of the hearing. After hearing testimony from Husband about Son's birth and first months of life, as well as the circumstances under which Son was taken to Pakistan, the court found it had home state jurisdiction and awarded sole legal and physical custody to Husband. The court issued a written order on November 5, 2003 (2003 Custody Order), with a substantially identical amended order filed November 12, 2003.

Meanwhile, on October 1, 2003, Wife filed an action seeking custody of Son in the Court of the Civil Judge and Guardian Judge (Guardian Court) in Pakistan. She neglected to disclose the pendency of the California Dissolution Action. On October 3, the Pakistani court issued an order forbidding Husband to remove Son from Pakistan. In the custody application, Wife alleged she had been physically abused by Husband during their marriage.

Husband filed responsive papers, informing the Guardian Court of California's 2003 Custody Order. On December 1, 2003, the Pakistani court dismissed Wife's custody application, deferring to the California court's jurisdiction.

Wife appealed that decision to the district court in Karachi, which issued an order temporarily forbidding the removal of Son from Pakistan. The parties agreed to settle the appeal by entering into an agreement on December 16, 2003, under which they were to reconcile as a couple in the United States and share custody of Son (2003 Compromise). Husband agreed not to "maltreat" Wife or her family, and if he broke that agreement, Wife was entitled to recourse under California law. Husband also agreed to furnish the California court with a copy of the 2003 Compromise after both parties returned to California. Incorporating the terms of the parties' agreement, the Pakistani court issued an order disposing of the appeal (December 2003 Order).

Under their agreement, Wife was to return to California with Son on or about December 31, 2003. She failed to do so, however, claiming that Husband had verbally abused her after the agreement was signed. Husband returned to the United States alone in late December 2003 or early January 2004.

The Alameda County District Attorney's Office then got involved. Wife corresponded by e-mail with its investigator, detailing her allegations of abuse and neglect by Husband. Nevertheless, on March 1, 2004, the district attorney's office issued an arrest warrant for Wife, alleging two felonies for child abduction and unlawful deprivation of custody (Pen.Code, §§ 278, 278.5).

On March 1, 2004, Wife, represented by new California counsel, Hannah Sims, sought an ex parte order to show cause in California, requesting that the court modify the 2003 Custody Order or, in the alternative, "abdicate" jurisdiction to Pakistan. Wife's request included a declaration by her alleging physical and psychological abuse at Husband's hands during their marriage, and detailing events in Pakistan leading up to and following the December 2003 Order. Husband responded, in part, by requesting judicial notice of a number of documents that had been filed in the Pakistani courts.

On March 5, 2004, the court denied Wife's ex parte application and set a hearing for May 5, 2004. Wife's attorney subsequently took her motion off calendar, as Wife would not risk arrest and prosecution to appear at the hearing.

Sometime in 2004, Husband returned to Karachi, where Wife alleges he bought a house in October 2004. She claims he lived there almost continuously for three years thereafter, enjoying regular visitation with Son. Husband acknowledges that he visited Pakistan frequently from 2004 through October 2007 and that he did exercise some supervised visitation with Son, but claims their time together was "unconscionably limited" by Wife. Husband claims he was only in Pakistan temporarily to fight for custody of Son and always intended to return to his home in California.

Husband did initiate substantial litigation in Pakistan over the years, most of it aimed at either enforcing, or obtaining relief from, the December 2003 Order, which the Pakistani courts treated as binding on the issue of joint custody. Husband also sought orders for visitation with Son, the most recent being the July 12, 2006 order that Wife seeks to enforce in this proceeding (July 2006 Order).

Meanwhile, on October 29, 2004, while Husband was evidently in Pakistan, his attorney had Wife's default entered in the Dissolution Action in California, with notice to Wife's attorney of record. On January 21, 2005, judgment of dissolution was granted, with legal and physical custody awarded to Husband, again with notice to Wife's counsel. On February 1, 2005, Hannah Sims formally withdrew as Wife's counsel. Wife claims, however, that she had no knowledge of the default judgment until December 18, 2007.

Though the circumstances are disputed, it is fairly clear that Husband was not in Pakistan from October 2005 until April 2006, and we may infer that he returned to California.[FN7] He again returned to Pakistan in April 2006 and began to seek court-ordered visitation with Son. In mid-June, believing Wife was going to flee with Son, Husband sought an order prohibiting Son's removal from Pakistan. A hearing was scheduled for June 27, 2006, and "in the meantime" the court ordered that Son not be removed from its jurisdiction. Wife and Son were detained by Pakistani immigration officials at the airport, although she claimed she was simply taking him on a pre-planned family vacation to Turkey. Another order was issued June 27, 2006, continuing the matter until July 5, 2006, and retaining the non-removal order in effect "in the meanwhile."

FN7. Wife alleges that Husband, along with three or four armed accomplices, tried to kidnap Son in October 2005 and that shots were fired during the attempt. According to Wife, Husband then fled Pakistan to avoid being arrested for attempted murder and kidnapping. Husband denies this account, claiming that he was assaulted and stoned by Wife and her siblings when he came to Wife's family home to visit Son. In January 2007, the criminal charges against Husband were dropped by Wife and her family, resulting in his acquittal.

On July 12, 2006, the [Sindh High Court] SHC, in accordance with the parties' agreement, ordered supervised visits for two hours each week between Husband and Son, to be conducted at the office of Wife's attorney in Karachi. There was no explicit non-removal clause in the July 2006 Order. According to Wife, this arrangement continued for approximately 15 months.

Then, Wife alleges that on October 26, 2007, Husband and three armed accomplices kidnapped Son from outside her lawyer's office in Karachi, as she brought him for the scheduled visitation. An order prohibiting Son's removal from Pakistan was issued by the SHC on October 29, 2007, which was followed by a warrant for Husband's arrest and placement of Son's and Husband's names on an "Exit Control List" to prevent them from leaving Pakistan. Husband somehow escaped the country and returned to California with Son. On April 18, 2008, the SHC authorized issuance of an INTERPOL red warrant for Husband's arrest.

Husband, for his part, claims the seizure of Son was perfectly legal and was conducted by the Pakistani Federal Investigation Agency (FIA), which was enforcing an INTERPOL yellow warrant issued as a result of the abduction charges against Wife in California. Husband declares that he and Son left Pakistan with the cooperation of the United States government and arrived back in the United States on November 21, 2007.

Either way, Son was brought back to California and kept at an undisclosed location. He now lives with Husband in California and attends school here.

On January 8, 2008, Wife registered the July 2006 Order from Pakistan in Alameda County Superior Court, and shortly thereafter filed an order to show cause to modify the earlier California custody order and to enforce the foreign order under section 3405. The trial court consolidated the Registration Action with the Dissolution Action.

A hearing was held on the Registration Action on February 19, 2008. On February 21, 2008, the court denied registration and enforcement of the July 2006 Order, and refused to take judicial notice of unauthenticated documents from Pakistan filed by both parties. In that order the court found that: (1) its jurisdiction under the UCCJEA and the issue of service were litigated and resolved in Husband's favor in the Dissolution Action; (2) the November 5, 2003 custody order entered in that action, and subsequently incorporated into the January 21, 2005 default judgment, was valid and enforceable; (3) Wife's then counsel was served with notice of entry of judgment; and (4) the time limitations for seeking relief from entry of a default judgment had passed. . . .

The court issued a written order on May 12, 2008, reaffirming its findings in the February 21 order and concluding that California's jurisdiction under the UCCJEA was exclusive and continuing, that it did not lose jurisdiction by reason of Husband's prolonged presence in Pakistan or the loss of "significant connections" with Son, that the alleged kidnapping of Son by Husband did not require California to relinquish jurisdiction, and that California would not voluntarily decline jurisdiction as an inconvenient forum. The court's lengthy and well-reasoned order will be cited further in our opinion, as we affirm its conclusions.

Thankfully, it is not our task to decide all of the hotly contested factual issues between these warring parties. We are, however, asked to decide between two core concepts in child custody jurisdiction that appear to compete in this case, namely "home state" jurisdiction and "exclusive, continuing" jurisdiction. We conclude the method for resolving any conflict between these legal principles is dictated by the UCCJEA, and decide the case accordingly.

The exclusive method of determining subject matter jurisdiction in custody cases is the UCCJEA. Under the UCCJEA, a California court must treat a foreign country as if it were a state of the United States for the purpose of determining jurisdiction. Moreover, with limited exception, a child custody determination made in a foreign country under factual circumstances in substantial conformity with the jurisdictional standards of this part must be recognized and enforced in California.

Subject matter jurisdiction either exists or does not exist at the time an action is commenced. There is no provision in the UCCJEA for jurisdiction by reason of the presence of the parties or by stipulation, consent, waiver, or estoppel.

Under the UCCJEA, the state with absolute priority to render an initial child custody determination is the child's home state on the date of commencement of the first custody proceeding, or alternatively, the state which had been his home state within six months before commencement if the child is absent from the home state but a parent continues to live there. "Home state" means the state in which a child lived with a parent or a person acting as a parent for at least six consecutive months immediately before the commencement of a child custody proceeding. In the case of a child less than six months of age, the term means the state in which the child lived from birth with any of the persons mentioned. A period of temporary absence of any of the mentioned persons is part of the period.

A court that properly acquires initial jurisdiction has exclusive, continuing jurisdiction unless one of two subsequent events occurs: (1) a court of the issuing state itself determines that neither the child, nor the child and one parent, nor the child and a person acting as a parent have a significant connection with this state and that substantial evidence is no longer available in this state concerning the child's care, protection, training, and personal relationships, or (2) there is a judicial determination by either the issuing state or any other state that the child, the child's parents, and any person acting as a parent do not presently reside in the issuing state.

The UCCJEA takes a strict first in time approach to jurisdiction. Basically, subject to exceptions not applicable here, once the court of an appropriate state has made a child custody determination, that court obtains exclusive, continuing jurisdiction. The court of another state cannot modify the child custody determination; and must enforce the child custody determination.

Wife urges us to consider the overriding interest of the child in making our decision on jurisdiction. She asks us to take into account the trauma Son must have suffered in being torn away from his mother, his familiar culture, and his extended family in Pakistan, where he had spent most of his first five years.

While we are not unconcerned with the child's best interests, the UCCJEA in fact eliminates the term best interests from the statutory language to clearly distinguish between the jurisdictional standards and the substantive standards relating to child custody and visitation. As the trial court aptly noted, "The issue currently before the court is not what is in the best interest of the child. Rather the issue now before the court is which jurisdiction has the *authority* to engage in that inquiry and adjudicate the competing claims." . . .

The trial court found that California properly assumed initial UCCJEA jurisdiction over the child custody matter as Son's home state when the Dissolution Action was commenced. That initial assertion of jurisdiction gave California exclusive, continuing jurisdiction . . . .

Nevertheless, Wife argues that the California dissolution judgment is void or should be set aside on three grounds: (1) she was deprived of due process and notice by the procedures employed; (2) Husband failed to notify the California court of the proceedings in Pakistan, as required by section 3429(d); and (3) Husband made misrepresentations in the dissolution action that acted as a fraud upon the court.

The trial court found the due process and notice issues had been litigated in the Dissolution Action and that the time had expired for Wife to contest those matters. Nevertheless we discuss the merits to dispel Wife's claim of a void judgment.

The requirements of due process of law are met in a child custody proceeding when, in a court having subject matter jurisdiction over the dispute, the out-of-state parent is given notice and an opportunity to be heard. Personal jurisdiction over the parents is not required to make a binding custody determination, and a custody decision made in conformity with due process requirements is entitled to recognition by other states.

Wife acknowledges that she "received" the summons and order to show cause on September 16, 2003. And the proceedings below leave no doubt that she had actual notice of the hearing on the order to show cause.

Wife now claims, however, that she had no actual notice of the November 4 hearing and that "actual notice" was required under section 3408. In fact, the statute requires only notice *"reasonably calculated to give* actual notice." Notifying Wife's attorney of record in open court clearly satisfied the statute. The trial court properly found that Wife had an opportunity to be heard and simply failed to avail herself of it.

Wife also claims she had no knowledge of the dissolution judgment until December 18, 2007, despite the fact that she was represented by counsel throughout the default proceedings. The court itself served Wife's attorney with notice of entry of default and entry of judgment—notice necessarily imputed to wife. There was ample support for the trial court's finding that Wife's attorney was properly served and time has run out for any challenge on the various alternatives that might theoretically have been available to her. Although Wife appeals to the court's inherent power to set aside a void judgment at any time, the judgment was not void for lack of subject matter jurisdiction or failure to comply with due process.

Wife claims the custody order in the Dissolution Action should also be set aside because Husband did not comply with section 3429(d), which imposes upon each party a "continuing duty to inform the court of any proceeding in this or any other state that could affect the current proceeding."

Perhaps Husband could have provided the California court with more prompt notice of Wife's custody action in Pakistan and more details of the various Pakistani orders. However, when Wife sought to modify the 2003 Custody Order on March 1, 2004, or alternatively to transfer jurisdiction to Pakistan, Husband did file a request for judicial notice, attaching multiple documents from the Pakistani proceedings, including the December 2003 Order and Husband's subsequent contempt proceeding against Wife. Thus, the court was aware of those proceedings before the final judgment of dissolution was entered. Neither party further updated the court about the various Pakistani actions during the default proceedings.

However, the absence of this information was not material to the court's assertion of jurisdiction or entry of default judgment. It is primarily the existence of prior-in-time proceedings of which the court must be apprised for jurisdictional purposes. Since California's custody order was first-in-time and was based on home state jurisdiction, and since Wife had been in violation of its custody orders for more than a year, it is unlikely the California court would have taken any different action even if it had been provided with more up-to-date details regarding the proceedings in Pakistan.

Section 3429 does not specify a remedy for a party's failure to comply with his or her continuing disclosure obligations. It certainly does not require the first-in-time court to relinquish jurisdiction. Moreover, since the duty to inform the court of other proceedings rested equally with Wife, neither party should benefit from the mutual neglect of duty, if there was one.

Wife claims the judgment of dissolution should be declared void because of alleged misrepresentations in Husband's court filings which amounted to a fraud upon the court. Specifically, wife claims he accused her of taking Son from California "illegally" and "without [Husband's] permission," implying that she had kidnapped him. In context, though, Husband's statements were not misleading. He explained that Wife "told [him] she was only going on vacation and then refused to return home."

Husband's statements in his proposed judgment that Wife kept Son "hidden" in Pakistan and that he had not seen his son in "over one year" were not literally true. Nevertheless, Husband does contend that Wife kept Son cloistered away in her parents' home and deprived Husband of contact except on her own "unconscionably limited" terms, enforced by her family's private security guards. Even if Husband exaggerated the length of time since he had last seen Son, that was not material to the court's exercise of jurisdiction or its entry of default judgment. Given that Wife had filed no responsive pleading and had long been in knowing violation of a California court order, the exact date of last father-son contact was not material.

Wife argues vigorously that the motivating force behind the UCCJEA is to prevent parental kidnapping, and that our decision in this appeal must be guided by that principle. While that is certainly one of the UCCJEA's underlying objectives, it is not the only one. We have previously identified the primary purposes of its predecessor, the Uniform Child Custody Jurisdiction Act (UCCJA), as (1) preventing the harm done to children by shifting them from state to state to relitigate custody, and (2) preventing jurisdictional conflict between the states after a custody decree has been rendered. Thus, among the primary purposes of the uniform acts is to encourage states to respect and enforce the prior custody determinations of other states, as well as to avoid competing jurisdiction and conflicting decisions.

Wife argued in the trial court that on October 1, 2003, when she filed her action for custody in Pakistan, California and Pakistan had "concurrent jurisdiction." Such claim ignores the fact that a major aim of the UCCJEA is to *avoid* "concurrent jurisdiction." . . .

Other provisions of the UCCJEA reinforce the drafters' intent to avoid competing forums and conflicting orders. Thus, section 3423 "complements" section 3422 by restricting the conditions under which one state may modify the custody orders of another state. The UCCJEA requires deference to another state's earlier issued custody determination in the absence of specified findings, thereby requiring at least a conscious, reasoned, and statutorily limited basis for asserting modification jurisdiction. And section 3426 provides, in substance, that a court may not exercise its jurisdiction under this chapter if, at the time of the commencement of the proceeding, a proceeding concerning the custody of the child has been commenced in a court of another state having jurisdiction substantially in conformity with this part.

More than once the drafters cited this triad of provisions as the central mechanism for avoiding competing forums and conflicting orders, thereby minimizing parents' motivation to snatch children and remove them to a different jurisdiction. These provisions, taken together, provide a comprehensive, integrated system designed to provide that one—and only one—court may exercise jurisdiction over custody determinations at any given time.

Wife argues that even if the California court properly exercised jurisdiction in the first instance, it lost jurisdiction under section 3422(a)(2), which provides in significant part that "a court of this state that has made a child custody determination consistent with Section 3421 or 3423 has exclusive, continuing jurisdiction over the determination until ... a court of this state or a court of another state determines that the child, the child's parents, and any person acting as a parent do not presently reside in this state."

The parties disagree on the interpretation of section 3422. Wife argues that California lost jurisdiction as soon as Husband acquired a residence in Pakistan, essentially advocating the view that jurisdiction is self-terminating when the specified parties move out of the decree state. Accordingly, Wife goes to some length to prove that Husband "resided" for a substantial period in Pakistan from sometime in 2004 until October 2007, pointing out that he bought a house there and enjoyed regular visitation with Son. And, she argues, husband is estopped to deny residency in Karachi because he used a Karachi address on his pleadings in Pakistan.

Husband acknowledges that he visited Pakistan frequently, but insists he was there only to try to regain custody of Son and to keep in contact with him. Husband claims he stayed with his parents or friends while he was there. He claims the house in Karachi was purchased by his mother and is held in her name (Qamar Nurie). He never was employed in Pakistan, and never bought property or owned a car there. He always intended to return to California, not to move to Pakistan.

The trial court found that Wife's own assertions with respect to Husband's continuous residence in Karachi were without foundation. And we cannot conclude that Husband deceived the Pakistani courts into thinking he had abandoned his California residence. It was Wife who first listed Husband's address in Karachi when she sued him for custody of Son, even though she knew he lived in California. In his responsive pleading, Husband told the Guardian Court that he had not lived in Karachi since 1973 and that he worked in the Silicon Valley. Thus, at least as of December 2003, when Pakistan initially assumed jurisdiction, it was well aware that Husband lived in California. Using a Karachi address in his pleadings in Pakistan did not operate as an estoppel or mislead the Pakistani courts.

More importantly, the crucial question under the statute is not whether Husband "resided" in Pakistan, but whether he *stopped* residing in California. On that point, Husband claims he never stopped residing in California because he continuously owned a house here, which he kept for his own use and never rented out, even paying a gardener to maintain the grounds in his absence. He always maintained a car, telephones and a fax machine here, paid taxes and utilities here, and had built his career as an electrical engineer and marketing manager in the Silicon Valley. He has lived in California since 1983 and considers it his permanent home. We may infer from his declaration that he maintained furnishings and other personal possessions in his home in Fremont. We infer from the record that he physically resided in California at least from October 2005 to April 2006, and his residence here during other periods has not been precluded. These factors convince us that Husband continuously maintained a residence in California despite his physical presence in Pakistan for prolonged periods. By contrast, none of the cases cited by Wife held that a parent was "not presently residing" in the decree state when he or she continued to maintain a fully functional household there. . . . It is well established that a party may have more than one residence.

We also agree with the trial court that a judicial determination that all parties no longer reside in the decree state is required to divest that state of continuing, exclusive jurisdiction. Indeed, the language of the statute would seem to admit of no other construction. It is not the parties' departure itself that terminates the decree state's exclusive, continuing jurisdiction. Rather, it is when a "court determines" that all parties have ceased residing there that jurisdiction is lost. Without such a finding either in Pakistan or California, the statutory condition terminating jurisdiction simply has not occurred. . . .

The requirement of a judicial determination under the UCCJEA is more than a procedural technicality. It reflects a deliberate effort to provide a clear end-point to the decree state's jurisdiction, to prevent courts from treading on one another's jurisdiction, and to ensure that custody orders will remain fully enforceable until a court determines they are not. By requiring a modifying state to first determine whether all the parties have vacated the prior decree state, the UCCJEA forces the court to pay conscious deference to pre-existing custody orders. This arrangement furthers the statutory demand that only one state exercise jurisdiction at any given time, thereby reducing the temptation to litigants to decide for themselves that they are free to disregard an earlier order. . . .

Wife emphasizes the importance of "home state" jurisdiction, and insists that Pakistan became Son's home state, even as California lost connections entitling it to continuing jurisdiction. She claims that home state jurisdiction is "paramount" under the UCCJEA because it is ultimately in the child's best interests for that state to make the custody determination.

It is true that in initial custody determinations the child's home state is given absolute priority. That is, in fact, the basis upon which California asserted initial jurisdiction in this case. However, it is not true that a change in the child's home state will automatically allow the new home state to acquire modification jurisdiction.

Wife argues that the December 2003 Order in Pakistan was a valid modification of the earlier California order. She also contends that even if Pakistan was not Son's home state in 2003, as the trial court found, it had become his home state at least by July 12, 2006, when the SHC issued the order Wife seeks to enforce.

Under sections 3422 and 3423, however, it is not enough that a jurisdiction qualify factually as the child's home state to exercise modification jurisdiction. Rather, the UCCJEA makes clear that a change in the child's home state after a court has initially assumed jurisdiction does not result in the shifting of jurisdiction to the new home state. The principles of the UCCJEA require a state at least to deferentially assess the status of any pre-existing order before acting. For Pakistan to assume modification jurisdiction, either California would have had to voluntarily cede jurisdiction (which it did not), or else the Pakistani court would have had to find that "the child, the child's parents, and any person acting as a parent do not presently reside" in California.

Not only was that finding never made, but there was no substantial evidence to support such a finding on October 1, 2003, when Wife's custody action was commenced in Pakistan. Nor was there when the December 2003 Order was filed, as Husband was still living and working in California. Indeed, even by the time the July 2006 Order was issued, there would have been no basis for Pakistan to assume modification jurisdiction. Husband had evidently been in California from October 2005 until April 2006. That he was in Pakistan from April until mid-July 2006 does not provide a substantial basis for concluding that he was not "presently residing" in California. In short, Wife cannot point to any specific court order issued at a time when the Pakistani courts would have been justified in exercising modification jurisdiction in compliance with UCCJEA principles. . . .

As discussed above, the parties engaged in significant litigation in Pakistan involving custody and visitation issues. These actions all had their genesis in Wife's initial attempt to gain custody of Son *after* she had been served with the California summons and ex parte order awarding custody to Husband. This is precisely the kind of forum-shopping the UCCJEA deplores. Although we have already determined that California had exclusive, continuing jurisdiction, we alternatively hold that the July 2006 Order was not enforceable because Pakistan's jurisdiction was not exercised in substantial conformity with UCCJEA principles.

The Pakistani Guardian Court initially declined to exercise jurisdiction . . . . Wife asserts that Pakistan gained jurisdiction two weeks later because she and Husband entered into the 2003 Compromise. As the trial court noted, "it is unclear how a compromise regulating visitation pending the parents' return to California changed [the Guardian Court's] analysis."

As the trial court found, Pakistan appears to have asserted jurisdiction based on the parties' consent. This view is confirmed by subsequent observations in the Pakistani court filings, that Husband had "surrendered" or "submitted" to Pakistan's jurisdiction. However, as noted, subject matter jurisdiction cannot be created by consent. . . .

We conclude that the July 2006 Order did not substantially comply with UCCJEA principles and need not be enforced by a California court. In so holding, we conclude that the concepts of exclusive continuing jurisdiction, restraint in exercising modification jurisdiction, and deference to prior-in-time decrees (except in limited circumstances) are among the key jurisdictional standards that must be adhered to by a foreign jurisdiction before its custody orders are entitled to enforcement in California. In other words, a party seeking to enforce a foreign custody order must show not only factual circumstances in substantial conformity with the initial jurisdictional requirements of section 3421, but also that the foreign order substantially conforms to the policies of enforcing prior decrees and avoiding conflicting jurisdiction embodied in sections 3422, 3423 and 3426. . . .

Wife claims California has also lost jurisdiction based on subdivision (a)(1) of section 3422, which provides that a court may lose exclusive, continuing jurisdiction if "A court of this state determines that neither the child, nor the child and one parent, nor the child and a person acting as a parent have a significant connection with this state and that substantial evidence is no longer available in this state concerning the child's care, protection, training, and personal relationships."

The statute unambiguously gives the decree state sole power to decide whether jurisdiction has been lost on this basis. The assessment of a state's "significant connections" with a child is made at the time the jurisdictional determination is made, rather than at the time of commencement of the proceeding. We understand this rule to have required the court below to assess California's connections to Son as of May 2008, when it ruled on Wife's jurisdictional challenge, rather than in June 2003, when the Dissolution Action was commenced, or January 2008, when Wife filed the Registration Action.

"Significant connections" [continue] until the state loses all or almost all connection with the child. Jurisdiction continues as long as the parent who is exercising visitation rights still lives in the decree state and the relationship between that parent and the child has not deteriorated to the point at which the exercise of jurisdiction would be unreasonable.

Applying that standard, California did not lose significant connections with Son after the initial custody order was entered. Husband, who continued to reside in California, also made frequent visits to Pakistan to maintain contact with Son. In such a situation, Husband's continued residence in California gives this state a legitimate connection to the custody dispute, and Husband has not shown disinterest in maintaining contact with Son such that the state's connection to the child has been lost. California, after all, had an outstanding arrest warrant based on Wife's continuing unlawful retention of Son in Pakistan. The fact that the child was in the center of a continuing criminal investigation in this state shows that California retained a connection to him—and a legitimate concern for his welfare.

Moreover, regardless of how he got here, Son is now residing in California. He lives with his father in California, goes to school in this state, receives medical treatment, and sees a therapist here. Son has significant connections with the state and substantial evidence exists here with respect to his care and upbringing such that the courts of this state have a legitimate interest in deciding issues related to his custody.

Wife argues that "significant connections" cannot be created as a result of kidnap. But the trial court declined—and we decline—to determine the truth of Wife's kidnapping allegations on the basis of declarations alone. We also cannot ignore the fact that the deterioration of Son's connection to California was the direct result of Wife's willful disobedience of a California court order. A parent should not be allowed to unilaterally withhold a child from his home state in defiance of a valid court order, and then use the child's prolonged absence to argue that he has lost connection to the state.

We do not question that Pakistan also has a substantial connection to Son. Earlier in Son's life, Pakistan may, in fact, have been the site of more evidence concerning his wellbeing. The relevant inquiry, however, is not which jurisdiction has the most evidence or the most significant connection to the minor, but whether California has so thoroughly lost connection that an exercise of its jurisdiction would be unreasonable. Clearly, it has not. . . .

Finally, Wife argues that even if California technically could retain jurisdiction, it should nevertheless cede jurisdiction to Pakistan because it is a more convenient forum. Whether a trial court stays its proceedings on that basis is purely discretionary, and the ruling will not be disturbed on appeal unless there was a clear abuse of discretion.

The trial court examined each of eight factors pertinent to the inconvenient forum decision under section 3427. We find its reasoning cogent and concise, and quote it in full:

> "a. *Whether [domestic violence] has occurred and which state may be in the best position to protect the parties and the child:* There are allegations of domestic violence in this forum dating back to 2002-2003. Upon an appropriate application, this court is in a position to

protect the alleged victim pending hearing on both the domestic violence issues and the custody issues. The court has no information suggesting that Pakistan is better suited to afford such protection.

"b. *Length of time child has resided outside California:* The minor has been outside California for over four years, and this may weigh on the scale in favor of Pakistan. On the other hand, the minor's lengthy absence from this forum has been due to Wife's refusal to obey the prior orders of this court, and the court is reluctant to allow her to use this disobedience to her advantage. Moreover, the child is here now and available to this court.

"c. *The distance between the two forums:* The distance is as great as one could imagine, but it is unclear how this weighs in favor of one forum over the other.

"d. *The financial hardship to the parties in litigating in one forum vs. the other:* Each forum presents a hardship to one of the parties; however, there are tools available to this court to mitigate the financial hardship . . . .

"e. *Any agreement as to which state should assume jurisdiction:* Wife might argue that the 2003 compromise reflects such an agreement, but on its face it was an interim agreement in anticipation of the parties returning to California. Thus on balance it reflects an agreement to litigate in California rather than Pakistan.

"f. *The nature/location of evidence including testimony from the child:* Evidence is available in both jurisdictions, but the child is available here and the current therapist is here. This factor tips toward California.

"g. *The ability of each court to decide the matter expeditiously:* Whatever the issues regarding custody and visitation, a final trial on the merits is available here within a matter of months. The only information regarding Pakistan is the record of the parties and the child being there for the better part of four years without a resolution. This may be because Pakistan only asserted temporary jurisdiction, but in any event on this record, this court concludes it offers the 'fastest track.'

"h. *The familiarity of the court in each state with the facts:* The Pakistani courts know more about the procedural wrangling of the past four years and have more ready access to the facts regarding the alleged kidnapping and other events that preceded it, and this factor may tip towards Pakistan. However, there are procedures available that might enable this court to receive the benefit of evidence available in Pakistan or even judicial proceedings in Pakistan leading to factual findings on key issues."

In light of this thoughtful analysis, we cannot say that the trial court abused its discretion in refusing to declare Pakistan a more convenient forum. A court should decline jurisdiction as an inconvenient forum only when there is concurrent jurisdiction elsewhere. Here, as discussed, California had exclusive, continuing jurisdiction, and Pakistan had no modification jurisdiction under UCCJEA principles.

The judgment is affirmed.

Observation based on *Marriage of Nurie*

Whew! That was quite a marathon. Thanks for sticking with it. The Court of Appeal did a nice job of explaining many aspects of the UCCJEA.

Problems on Jurisdiction in Child Custody Litigation

1. Mom and dad live in California and have 2 kids, ages 6 and 8. Mom separates from dad and returns with the kids to New Mexico where she grew up. After living in New Mexico 9 months, mom commences a divorce action in New Mexico and seeks custody of the children. Does New Mexico have jurisdiction to adjudicate custody?

2. Mom and dad live in New York. They have two kids. They divorce in New York and mom gets custody. Two years later, dad moves to Kentucky to take a new job. When the children are in Kentucky for a visit, dad refuses to return them to New York. When the kids have been in Kentucky seven months, dad starts a custody modification proceeding in Kentucky. What result?

3. Mom and Dad divorce in Michigan. They agree on joint physical and legal custody of the children, who are two and three, and their agreement becomes part of the divorce decree. Dad moves to Oregon. The kids go back and forth every 3 months according to an agreed upon schedule that is part of the decree. When the

older child is ready for kindergarten, Mom believes the older child should remain in Michigan during the school year. Dad insists that the parties follow the original custody arrangement. Mom files a motion in Michigan to modify the custody. Does Michigan have jurisdiction?

Suppose that while mom's motion is pending, the children are in Oregon, and Dad files a motion in Oregon to change custody to him. Does Oregon have jurisdiction?

4. Mom and dad are from Kansas. They have two kids. They begin law school together in Texas. During their second year of law school in Texas, they divorce in Texas. By agreement, mom gets primary custody. Upon graduation, mom moves back to Kansas with the children. Dad takes a job in Dallas. The children visit dad in Texas four or five times a year. The kids live full time in Kansas with mom, where they go to school. Four years after the divorce, dad files a motion in a Texas court to modify custody. Does Texas have jurisdiction to modify?

5. Mom and dad marry in Tennessee and have a child there. They divorce in Tennessee, and mom gets custody of junior. Not long after the divorce, Dad moves to Arizona. Junior visits dad in Arizona two or three times a year. Dad files a petition in Arizona seeking a change of custody to him. Does Arizona have jurisdiction to modify the Tennessee decree?

Suppose the facts are different. Mom got custody in the Tennessee divorce. A year later, mom and dad agreed that junior would live in Arizona with dad. After junior has been living in Arizona 8 months, mom insists that junior return to Tennessee. Dad says no and files a petition in Arizona to modify the Tennessee custody decree. Does Arizona have jurisdiction?

6. Mom and dad have lived many years in California. They divorced in California, and mom was awarded sole physical and legal custody of their child. Following the divorce, dad moved to Washington State. A year after the divorce, dad becomes concerned about the care afforded the child by mom in California. While the child is visiting dad in Washington, dad brings an action in Washington seeking to modify custody to award custody to him. Mom asks the Washington court to dismiss the proceeding. What should the Washington court do?

7. Mom and dad live in Idaho, and have one child. They divorce in Idaho and mom receives custody. Dad receives visitation. Mom moves to Maryland and lives

there 5 years. Mom brings an action in Maryland to modify dad's visitation. Dad asks the Maryland court to dismiss the matter.

8. Mary and John are both physicians on active duty with the United States Navy. Mary and John married in 2010, just after they completed their residency training. Mary is a surgeon and John is a pediatrician. Their daughter Kim was born at the Balboa Naval Hospital in San Diego, California on January 2, 2011, while Mary and John were both stationed at the hospital. On May 1, 2011, Mary and John were deployed overseas. When her parents deployed overseas, Kim went to live with her maternal grandparents in Seattle, Washington. Kim stayed in Seattle with the maternal grandparents from May 1, 2011 until September 1, 2011, when she moved to Cleveland, Ohio to live with the paternal grandparents. The move from Seattle to Cleveland was necessitated by the sudden death of Kim's maternal grandfather. Kim lived with the paternal grandparents from September 1, 2011 until January 1, 2012, when Mary returned to the United States and was stationed at the Naval Academy in Annapolis, Maryland. Kim joined her mother in Maryland on January 1, 2012. On March 1, 2012, John returned from deployment and was assigned to the Naval Air Station in San Diego, California. Kim was sent to stay with John in San Diego on March 3, 2012, and Kim remained in California from March 3, 2012 until June 5, 2012, when she returned to Mary in Maryland. On September, 16, 2012, John filed a petition for dissolution of marriage in the California Superior Court for San Diego County. Mary was served with the summons and petition at her home in Maryland. In his dissolution action, John seeks legal and physical custody of Kim plus child support and division of marital property. Mary hires an attorney who files a motion in California seeking dismissal of John's petition. Mary's argues that the divorce should occur in Maryland.

Once it is determined where the divorce and custody case will occur, the issue of child custody will arise. Assuming Mary and John cannot agree on custody, how should the judge rule on custody? Consider the following facts: As physicians, Mary and John work long hours, although as a surgeon, Mary works longer hours than John. John plans to get out of the service in 2014 and to enter private medical practice in pediatrics in San Diego. John's parents—who recently retired—plan to move to San Diego in 2014 to be near their son and granddaughter. When Kim's paternal grandparents move to San Diego, they will care for Kim while John works, and Kim will not attend day care. Mary plans to stay in the Navy as a career. Every two to four years, Mary will be deployed overseas and to different duty stations around the United States. When Mary is at work, Kim will attend day care. Mary can afford good day care. When Mary is deployed overseas, Kim will be able to live abroad, with the advantages that living abroad brings. When Mary and Kim are living abroad, Kim will be able to attend schools operated by the military. Mary and John are both loving parents, and Kim is attached to both parents. Unfortunately, Mary and John cannot agree on joint custody and each is determined to gain sole legal and physical custody with reasonable visitation to the noncustodial parent. Once the divorce is final, Mary plans to marry Phil, a career Navy Chaplain who has two children of his own.

9. Sue was a senior at Harvard in Boston, Massachusetts when she met Juan, also a Harvard student. Sue and Juan dated for about two months during the late fall of 2011, and had sex once. They stopped dating soon after sleeping together. A month later, to her surprise, Sue discovered she was pregnant. Sue decided not to tell Juan. Sue was not sure whether Juan was the father because Sue had had sex with another man not long after breaking up with Juan. Sue graduated from Harvard in January, 2012, and moved to Ann Arbor, Michigan to live with her parents. The baby was born in August, 2012 in Ann Arbor. The birth certificate listed the father as "unknown." Sue posted pictures of the baby on her Facebook page, and Juan saw the pictures. Juan wrote to Sue, "Am I the father? Please contact me. If I am the dad, I want to be a dad." Sue did not write back. Juan travelled to Ann Arbor to try to find Sue, but he could not locate her. Sue and the baby stayed in Ann Arbor from August, 2012 until April, 2013, when Sue and the baby moved to Berkeley, California, where Sue began a Ph.D. program at the University of California at Berkeley. In August, 2013, Juan located Sue in Berkeley and commenced an action for child custody in the appropriate California court. Assume that Sue denies that Juan is the father. Can Juan seek to establish himself as the child's father? Does California have jurisdiction to determine paternity, child custody, and child support?

10. Amber and Bryant live in Tennessee. Amber and Bryant dated but never married. Amber gave birth to Marquise. When the child was 3, Amber brought a paternity action against Bryant, seeking child support. The Tennessee court entered an Order of Paternity establishing Bryant as the father. Bryant was ordered to pay child support and was given visitation. When Marquis was 6, Amber got in trouble with the law. Amber asked her mother Kimberli to take custody of Marquis while she worked through her legal problems. Kimberli lived in Indiana. Kimberli cared for Marquis at her Indiana home for 30 months, enrolling him in school and sports, and serving as a parent. After Marquis had been living with Kimberli for 30 months, Bryant filed a motion in Tennessee seeking to modify custody from Amber to him. Kimberli intervened and asked the Tennessee court to dismiss Bryant's motion to modify custody. Kimberli argues that Tennessee lacks jurisdiction, and any proceedings should be in Indiana. How should the Tennessee judge rule on the question of jurisdiction?

Hague Convention on Civil Aspects of International Child Abduction

Imagine you are married. You have two kids, 9 and 11. One day you arrive home to find the children gone and the following note from your spouse, "I can't handle this relationship. I'm going to Germany to stay with my parents, and I'm taking the children with me. We won't be back. I'll e-mail you when we arrive. I'm sorry, but I have to do this." Once you recover from the initial shock, you wonder to yourself, "What can I do about the kids? I want them here. This is their home. This is nuts."

The Hague Convention on Civil Aspects of International Child Abduction was promulgated to deal with international parental child abduction. Selected provisions of the Convention are reproduced below.

Chapter I – Scope of the Convention

Article 1

The objects of the present Convention are --

(a) to secure the prompt return of children wrongfully removed to or retained in any Contracting State; and

(b) to ensure that rights of custody and of access under the law of one Contracting State are effectively respected in other Contracting States.

Article 3

The removal or the retention of a child is to be considered wrongful where—

(a) it is in breach of rights of custody attributed to a person, an institution or any other body, either jointly or alone, under the law of the State in which the child was habitually resident immediately before the removal or retention; and

(b) at the time of removal or retention those rights were actually exercised, either jointly or alone, or would have been so exercised but for the removal or retention.

The rights of custody mentioned in sub-paragraph (a) above, may arise in particular by operation of law or by reason of a judicial or administrative decision, or by reason of an agreement having legal effect under the law of that State.

Article 4

The Convention shall apply to any child who was habitually resident in a Contracting State immediately before any breach of custody or access rights. The Convention shall cease to apply when the child attain's the age of 16 years.

Article 5

For the purposes of this Convention -

(a) "Rights of custody" shall include rights relating to the care of the person of the child and, in particular, the right to determine the child's place of residence;

(b) "Rights of access" shall include the right to take a child for a limited period of time to a place other than the child's habitual residence.

Chapter II – Central Authorities

Article 6

A Contracting State shall designate a Central Authority to discharge the duties which are imposed by the Convention upon such authorities.

Article 7

Central Authorities shall co-operate with each other and promote co-operation amongst the competent authorities in their respective States to secure the prompt return of children and to achieve the other objects of this Convention.

Chapter III – Return of Children

Article 8

Any person, institution or other body claiming that a child has been removed or retained in breach of custody rights may apply either to the Central Authority of the child's habitual residence or to the Central Authority of any other Contracting State for assistance in securing the return of the child.

The application shall contain [all information relevant to the case].

Article 10

The Central Authority of the State where the child is shall take or cause to be taken all appropriate measures in order to obtain the voluntary return of the child.

Article 11

The judicial or administrative authorities of Contracting States shall act expeditiously in proceedings for the return of children.

If the judicial or administrative authority concerned has not reached a decision within six weeks from the date of commencement of the proceedings, the applicant or the Central Authority of the requested State, on its own initiative or if asked by the Central Authority of the requesting State, shall have the right to request a statement of the reasons for the delay. If a reply is received by the Central Authority of the requested State, that Authority shall transmit the reply to the Central Authority of the requesting State, or to the applicant, as the case may be.

Article 12

Where a child has been wrongfully removed or retained in terms of Article 3 and, at the date of the commencement of the proceedings before the judicial or administrative authority of the Contracting State where the child is, a period of less than one year has elapsed from the date of the wrongful removal or retention, the authority concerned shall order the return of the child forthwith.

The judicial or administrative authority, even where the proceedings have been commenced after the expiration of the period of one year referred to in the preceding paragraph, shall also order the return of the child, unless it is demonstrated that the child is now settled in its new environment.

Where the judicial or administrative authority in the requested State has reason to believe that the child has been taken to another State, it may stay the proceedings or dismiss the application for the return of the child.

Article 13

Notwithstanding the provisions of the preceding Article, the judicial or administrative authority of the requested State is not bound to order the return of the child if the person, institution or other body which opposes its return establishes that -

> (a) the person, institution or other body having the care of the person of the child was not actually exercising the custody rights at the time of removal or retention, or had consented to or subsequently acquiesced in the removal of retention; or

> (b) there is a grave risk that his or her return would expose the child to physical or psychological harm or otherwise place the child in an intolerable situation.

The judicial or administrative authority may also refuse to order the return of the child if it finds that the child objects to being returned and has attained an age and degree of maturity at which it is appropriate to take account of its views.

In considering the circumstances referred to in this Article, the judicial and administrative authorities shall take into account the information relating to the social background of the child provided by the Central Authority or other competent authority of the child's habitual residence.

Article 16

After receiving notice of a wrongful removal or retention of a child in the sense of Article 3, the judicial or administrative authorities of the Contracting State to which the child has been removed or in which it has been retained shall not decide on the merits of rights of custody until it has been determined that the child is not to be returned under this Convention or unless an application under the Convention is not lodged within a reasonable time following receipt of the notice.

Article 19

A decision under this Convention concerning the return of the child shall not be taken to be determination on the merits of any custody issue.

Article 20

The return of the child under the provision of Article 12 may be refused if this would not be permitted by the fundamental principles of the requested State relating to the protection of human rights and fundamental freedoms.

Chapter VI – Rights of Access

Article 21

An application to make arrangements for organizing or securing the effective exercise of rights of access may be presented to the Central Authorities of the Contracting States in the same way as an application for the return of a child.

The Central Authorities are bound by the obligations of co-operation which are set forth in Article 7 to promote the peaceful enjoyment of access rights and the fulfillment of any conditions to which the exercise of such rights may be subject. The central Authorities shall take steps to remove, as far as possible, all obstacles to the exercise of such rights. The Central Authorities, either directly or through intermediaries, may initiate or assist in the institution of proceedings with a view to organizing or protecting these rights and securing respect for the conditions to which the exercise of these rights may be subject.

Article 26

Each Central Authority shall bear its own costs in applying this Convention.

Central Authorities and other public services of Contracting States shall not impose any charges in relation to applications submitted under this Convention. In particular, they may not require any payment from the applicant towards the costs and expenses of the proceedings or, where applicable, those arising from the participation of legal counselor advisers. However, they may require the payment of the expenses incurred or to be incurred in implementing the return of the child.

Upon ordering the return of a child or issuing an order concerning rights of access under this Convention, the judicial or administrative authorities may, where appropriate, direct the person who removed or retained the child, or who prevented the exercise of rights of access, to pay necessary expenses incurred by or on behalf of the applicant, including travel expenses, any costs incurred or payments made for locating the child, the costs of legal representation of the applicant, and those of returning the child.

Defenses to Return of Child Under Hague Convention

If the Convention applies because a child was wrongfully removed from the country of habitual residence, then the child must be returned to the habitual residence unless one of five defenses to return applies. The defenses are described by the court in *Trudrung v. Trudrung*[123]:

> Upon a showing of wrongful removal or retention, return of the child is required unless the Respondent establishes one of several affirmative defenses. Two of the defenses must be supported by clear and convincing evidence: (1) that return would expose the child to a "grave risk" of "physical or psychological harm or otherwise place

---

123   686 F. Supp. 2d 570 (M.D. N.C. 2010).

the child in an intolerable situation" and (2) that return of the child would not be permitted by "fundamental principles of the United States relating to the protection of human rights and fundamental freedoms." The other three defenses may be supported by a preponderance of the evidence: (1) that the petition for return was not filed within one year of the removal and the child is now well-settled in another country; (2) that the petitioner was not actually exercising his custodial rights at the time of the removal or had consented to or acquiesced in the removal; and (3) the child objects to being returned and has attained an age and degree of maturity at which it is appropriate to take account of his or her views. These defenses, or exceptions, are to be narrowly construed so that their application does not undermine the purposes of the Convention. Even if a respondent meets the burden of proving one of the defenses, the court retains the discretion to order the return of the child if it would further the aim of the Convention which is to provide for the return of a wrongfully removed child.

Federal Child Abduction Remedies Act

Congress implemented the Hague Convention with the International Child Abduction Remedies Act, 42 U.S.C. § 11601 et seq. Selected sections of the Act follow.

§ 11601. Findings and declarations.

(a) Findings

The Congress makes the following findings:

(1) The international abduction or wrongful retention of children is harmful to their well-being.

(2) Persons should not be permitted to obtain custody of children by virtue of their wrongful removal or retention.

(3) International abductions and retentions of children are increasing, and only concerted cooperation pursuant to an international agree can effectively combat this problem.

(4) ... Children who are wrongfully removed or retained within the meaning of the Convention are to be promptly returned unless one of the narrow exceptions set forth in the Convention applies. ...

(b) Declarations

The Congress makes the following declarations:

(1) It is the purpose of this chapter to establish procedures for the implementation of the Convention in the United States.

(2) The provisions of this chapter are in addition to and not in lieu of the provisions of the Convention.

(3) In enacting this chapter the Congress recognizes –

(A) the international character of the Convention; and

(B) the need for uniform international interpretation of the Convention.

(4) The Convention and this chapter empower courts in the United States to determine only rights under the Convention and not the merits of any underlying child custody claims.

§ 11602. Definitions.

For the purpose of this chapter -

(1) the term "applicant" means any person who, pursuant to the Convention, files an application with the United States Central Authority or a Central Authority of any other party to the convention for the return of a child alleged to have been wrongfully removed or retained or for arrangements for organizing or securing the effective exercise of rights of access pursuant to the Convention;

(2) the term "Convention" means the Convention on the civil Aspects of International Child Abduction, done at The Hague on October 25, 1980;

(3) the term "Parent Locator Service" means the service established by the Secretary of Health and Human Services under section 653 of this title;

(4) the term "petitioner" means any person who, in accordance with this chapter, files a petition in court seeking relief under the Convention;

(5) the term "person" includes any individual, institution, or other legal entity or body;

(6) the term "respondent" means any person against whose interests a petition is filed in court, in accordance with this chapter, which seeks relief under the Convention;

(7) the term "rights of access" means visitation rights;

(8) the term "State" means any of the several States, the District of Columbia, and any commonwealth, territory, or possession of the United States; and

(9) the term "united States Central Authority" means the agency of the Federal Government designated by the President under section 11606(a) of this title.

§ 11603. Judicial remedies.

(a) Jurisdiction of courts

The courts of the States and the United States district courts shall have concurrent original jurisdiction of actions arising under the Convention.

(b) Petitions

Any person seeking to initiate judicial proceedings under the Convention for the return of a child or for arrangements for organizing or securing the effective exercise of rights of access to a child may do so by commencing a civil action by filing a petition for the relief sought in any court which has jurisdiction of such action and which is authorized to exercise its jurisdiction in the place where the child is located at the time the petition is filed.

(c) Notice

Notice of an action brought under subsection (b) of this section shall be given in accordance with the applicable law governing notice in interstate child custody proceedings.

(d) Determination of case

The court in which an action is brought under subsection (b) of this section shall decide the case in accordance with the Convention.

(e) Burdens of proof

(1) A petitioner in an action brought under subsection (b) of this section shall establish by a preponderance of the evidence –

(A) in the case of an action for the return of a child, that the child has been wrongfully removed or retained within the meaning of the Convention; and

(B) in the case of an action for arrangements for organizing or securing the effective exercise of rights of access, that the petitioner has such rights.

(2) In the case of an action for the return of a child, a respondent who opposes the return of the child has the burden of establishing –

    (A) by clear and convincing evidence that one of the exceptions set forth in article 13(b) or 20 of the Convention applies; and

    (B) by a preponderance of the evidence that any other exception set forth in article 12 or 13 of the Convention applies.

(f) Application of Convention

For purposes of any action brought under this chapter –

(1) the term "authorities", as used in article 15 of the Convention to refer to the authorities of the state of the habitual residence of a child, includes courts and appropriate government agencies;

(2) the terms "wrongful removal or retention" and "wrongfully removed or retained", as used in the Convention, include a removal or retention of a child before the entry of a custody order regarding that child; and

(3) the term "commencement of proceedings", as used in article 12 of the Convention, means, with respect to the return of a child located in the United States, the filing of a petition in accordance with subsection (b) of this section.

(g) Full faith and credit

Full faith and credit shall be accorded by the courts of the States and the courts of the United States to the judgment of any other such court ordering or denying the return of a child, pursuant to the Convention, in an action brought under this chapter.

(h) Remedies under Convention not exclusive

The remedies established by the Convention and this chapter shall be in addition to remedies available under other laws or international agreements.

§ 11604. Provisional remedies.

(a) Authority of courts

In furtherance of the objectives of article 7(b) and other provisions of the Convention, and subject to the provisions of subsection (b) of this section, any court exercising jurisdiction of an action brought under section 11603(b) of this title may take or cause to be taken measures under Federal or State law, as appropriate, to protect the well-being of the child involved or to prevent the child's further removal or concealment before the final disposition of the petition.

(b) Limitation on authority

No court exercising jurisdiction of an action brought under section 11603(b) of this title may, under subsection (a) of this section, order a child removed from a person having physical control of the child unless the applicable requirements of State law are satisfied.

§ 11605. Admissibility of documents

With respect to any application to the United States Central Authority, or any petition to a court under section 11603 of this title, which seeks relief under the Convention, or any other documents or information included with such application or petition or provided after such submission which relates to the application or petition, as the case may be, no authentication of such application, petition, document, or information shall be required in order for the application, petition, document, or information to be admissible in court.

§ 11606. United States Central Authority.

(a) Designation

The President shall designate a Federal agency to serve as the Central Authority for the United States under the Convention.

(b) Functions

The functions of the United States Central Authority are those ascribed to the Central Authority by the Convention and this chapter. . . .

§ 11607. Costs and fees.

(b) Costs incurred in civil actions

(1) Petitioners may be required to bear the costs of legal counsel or advisors, court costs incurred in connection with their petitions, and travel costs for the return of the child involved and any accompanying persons, except as provided in paragraphs (2) and (3).

(2) Subject to paragraph (3), legal fees or court costs incurred in connection with an action brought under section 11603 of this title shall be borne by the petitioner unless they are covered by payments from Federal, State, or local legal assistance or other programs.

(3) Any court ordering the return of a child pursuant to an action brought under section 11603 of this title shall order the respondent to pay necessary expenses incurred by or on behalf of the petitioner, including court

costs, legal fees, foster home or other care during the course of proceedings in the action, and transportation costs related to the return of the child, unless the respondent establishes that such order would be clearly inappropriate.

There is no better place to begin your study of the Hague Convention than the Ninth Circuit's decision in *Cuellar v. Joyce*.

Cuellar v. Joyce

United States Court of Appeals
596 F.3d 505 (9th Cir. 2010)

Kozinski, Chief Judge:

[Leyda Cuellar] seeks the return of her daughter to Panama under the Hague Convention on the Civil Aspects of International Child Abduction. The father [Richard Joyce], opposes return; he claims that the mother is neglectful and very poor, that the child has grown used to living in America and that the child's medical needs cannot be addressed in Panama.

Richard Joyce built a sailboat and sailed it to Panama, where he met Leyda Cuellar. He's a college professor; she was an exotic dancer. They married in Panama, where she eventually gave birth to a baby girl whom we call K.C. Leyda lives in Neuva Livia, a neighborhood that Richard describes as "slum-like," "beyond the end of the road" and "very dangerous," although Leyda points out that Richard never complained when they were dating.

When K.C. was nineteen months old, Richard arranged for Leyda and K.C. to meet him in Australia. At the Sydney airport, Richard separated himself and K.C. from Leyda and flew to the United States, leaving Leyda behind without her passport. Leyda tracked Richard down in Montana, where he currently lives with K.C., and petitioned the district court there for K.C.'s return. The district court denied relief and Leyda appeals.

The Hague Convention seeks to deter parents from abducting their children across national borders by limiting the main incentive for international abduction—the forum shopping of custody disputes. A court that receives a petition under the Hague Convention may not resolve the question of who, as between the parents, is best suited to have custody of the child. With a few narrow exceptions, the court must return the abducted child to its country of habitual residence so that the courts of *that* country can determine custody.

This policy of deterrence gives way to concern for the welfare of the child only in extreme cases. Article 13(b) of the treaty provides that return need not be ordered where "there is a grave risk that ... return would expose the child to physical or psychological harm or otherwise place the child in an intolerable situation." So as not to impair the Convention's general policy, this exception is narrowly drawn, and all facts supporting the exception must be established by clear and convincing evidence. 42 U.S.C. § 11603(e)(2)(A). The exception is not license for a court in the abducted-to country to speculate on where the child would be happiest.

The district court found that "K.C. was a habitual resident of Panama and the removal or retention of K.C. did breach the rights of custody attributed to Leyda. Additionally, Leyda was exercising her custody rights at the time of the removal or retention." The district court also assumed (but did not find) that Leyda did not consent to removal. It nevertheless withheld relief under this grave risk exception. The court cited Leyda's living conditions in Panama, K.C.'s medical needs and K.C.'s psychological attachment to the United States and her father. We review the district court's factual findings for clear error, but determine de novo whether those facts establish a grave risk of harm.

The district court credited Richard's testimony about the home where Leyda lived with K.C.: that the home "has no indoor running water"; that "residents in this area use a nearby creek and outhouse for waste disposal"; and that the home "has no climate control, no refrigeration, and very little furniture." Accepting all this as true, as the district court seems to have, it comes nowhere close to establishing a grave risk of harm if K.C. were returned to Panama to live with her mother. Billions of people live in circumstances similar to those described by Richard. If that amounted to a grave risk of harm, parents in more developed countries would have unchecked power to abduct children from countries with a lower standard of living. At the time the Convention was adopted, the State Department took care to emphasize that grave risk doesn't "encompass a home where money is in short supply, or where educational or other opportunities are more limited." 51 Fed.Reg. 10494, 10510 (1986).

The district court acknowledged that poverty is not a reason to deny relief. However, it expressed additional "concerns about whether K.C. was properly nourished during the time she lived in Panama." The district court made no finding that K.C. was malnourished or that her diet in Panama had imperiled her health. Nor was there evidence that could have supported such a finding. Richard testified that K.C.'s "diet was poor, so she was kind of small and thin," and the district court noted that a professor of early childhood education called by Richard "did express concern that *perhaps* K.C. was malnourished."

This plainly does not amount to clear and convincing evidence of a grave risk of harm, and the district court erred by denying relief on that basis.

The district court also denied relief based on its conclusion that "K.C. suffered a serious head injury that was easily preventable" while in her mother's care. The district court appears to have credited Richard's testimony on this matter, which it recounted as follows: "K.C. was playing in a wheeled walker on a concrete construction platform which had no guardrails and she fell seven feet off the ground to a concrete platform, landing on her head. K.C. was unconscious from the fall and was taken to a health care facility where an x-ray was taken." The district court also relied on Richard's testimony that K.C. was sometimes cared for by a sick relative, had frequent ear infections and had unexplained burns behind her earlobes. Based on this testimony, the district court concluded that Leyda was so neglectful that to return K.C. to her custody would be "unsafe."

By drawing this conclusion about Leyda's fitness as a parent, the district court overstepped its mandate and impermissibly addressed the ultimate question of custody. Well-cared-for children do occasionally have accidents, and leaving a child with a sick relative may or may not be neglectful, depending on the circumstances. Richard's feeble showing—even if believed verbatim, as the district court seems to have done—falls far short of clear and convincing evidence of serious abuse that is a great deal more than minimal. Indeed, troubling as K.C.'s fall may be, she was subsequently given medical treatment, including an x-ray. It was not the district court's prerogative to determine whether Richard or Leyda was the better parent.

Richard tries to fashion an exception to this rule where the abducting parent believes the legal system in the country of habitual residence is too corrupt to fairly decide the issue of custody. Richard testified: "I believe that if [K.C.] goes back to Panama, she'll be lost the moment she gets off the plane. Neuva Livia is outside the bounds of what we consider a civilization, and that will just be it. I can't show up down there in some local court in Neuva Livia as the gringo and argue anything. I don't believe I'll ever see her again." It's unsurprising that Richard thinks he'll get a better shake in the courts of his home country; parents who abduct their children across international boundaries are generally driven by the same hope. But the animating idea behind the Hague Convention is to eliminate any tactical advantages gained by absconding with a child. The time to take such considerations into account is before undertaking the volitional acts that lead to conception. Once the child is born, the remote parent must accept the country where the child is habitually resident and its legal system as given. Absent a showing of grave risk, or that one of the Convention's other narrowly-drawn exceptions applies, whatever case the remote parent may have for custody must be made there. . . .

The district court also denied relief based on K.C.'s attachment to the United States and her father, and the psychological harm that would result if she were to return to Panama. This was a very serious error. The fact that a child has grown accustomed to her new home is never a valid concern under the grave risk exception, as it is the *abduction* that causes the pangs of subsequent return. Rather than allowing an abducting parent to profit from the psychological dislocation that he has caused, the Convention attempts to avoid the harm by deterring parents from abducting their children in the first place.

There's nothing special about this case; it falls squarely within the heartland of the Hague Convention. Richard has provided absolutely no evidence that should have delayed K.C.'s return to her habitual residence in Panama. Indeed, the delay in this case can only have exacerbated the harm caused by K.C.'s abduction. The Hague Convention does not allow abducting parents to resort to courts in their home country in order to thwart return of the child to its habitual residence. District courts considering Hague Convention cases are cautioned not to allow abducting parents to manipulate judicial process for purpose of delay, as Richard obviously has here.

We reverse the district court's determination that K.C. would suffer a grave risk of harm if returned to Panama.

We order Richard to transfer custody of K.C. to Leyda by 1:00 p.m. MST on the third business day following the issuance of this opinion. Within 10 days of receiving custody, Leyda shall return to Panama with K.C.; Leyda may request a limited extension upon a convincing showing of good cause. The district court shall provide Leyda with all of K.C.'s travel documents and take all steps necessary to ensure that Richard complies with this order, including, if necessary, ordering intervention of the United States Marshals Service.

Questions based on *Cuellar v. Joyce*

1. The Ninth Circuit turned a blind eye to father's argument that returning the child to Panama would cause the child psychological trauma. The court placed the blame for any trauma at father's feet. If he hadn't abducted the child in the first place, it would not be necessary for a court to order her return. But isn't that a bit harsh? It may be true that father's abduction caused the situation, but is it right to hurt the child to punish the parent?

2. The court was unsympathetic to father's argument that mother lived in poverty in Panama. How bad would conditions have to be for a court to decline to return a child? Suppose the place of return was in the throes of "war" between rival drug lords, and had the highest murder rate in the world? Would that be enough to deny return?

———————

Article 3 of the Hague Convention defines a child's removal as "wrongful" when the removal is in breach of custody rights attributed to a parent under the law of the state where the child was habitually resident immediately before the removal, and when the parent was actually exercising those custodial rights. The case of *Bader v. Kramer* provides insight into the meaning of habitual residence and the exercise of custody rights.

Bader v. Kramer

United States Court of Appeals
484 F.3d 666 (4th Cir. 2007)

Shedd, Circuit Judge.

Ulrich Bader filed this petition under the International Child Abduction Remedies Act ("ICARA"), 42 U.S.C. §§ 11601 *et seq.*, seeking the return of his daughter ("C.J.B.") to Germany. Bader alleged that his ex-wife, Sonja Kramer, violated the Hague Convention on Civil Aspects of International Child Abduction ("Hague Convention"), by taking C.J.B. to live in the United States. The district court ruled in Bader's favor and ordered C.J.B. returned to Germany. For the reasons that follow, we affirm the judgment of the district court.

Under the Hague Convention, to secure the return of an abducted child, a petitioner must prove by a preponderance of the evidence that "the child has been wrongfully removed" within the meaning of the Convention. 42 U.S.C. § 11603(e)(1). A petitioner can establish that the removal of a child is "wrongful" where: (1) the child was "habitually resident" in the petitioner's country of residence at the time of removal, (2) the removal was in breach of the petitioner's custody rights under the law of his home state, and (3) the petitioner had been exercising those rights at the time of removal.

Upon a showing of wrongful removal, return of the child is required unless the respondent establishes one of four defenses. Two of the defenses must be supported by clear and convincing evidence: (1) that return would expose the child to a "grave risk" of "physical or psychological harm or otherwise place the child in an intolerable situation" and (2) that return of the child would not be permitted by "fundamental principles of the United States relating to the protection of human rights and fundamental freedoms." The other two defenses may be supported by a preponderance of the evidence: (1) that the petition for return was not filed within one year of the removal and the child is now well-settled in another country, and (2) that the petitioner was not actually exercising his custodial rights at the time of the removal or had consented to or acquiesced in the removal. . . .

Bader is a citizen of Germany, and Kramer is a dual citizen of Germany and the United States. Bader and Kramer were married in Germany in 1998. Their only child, C.J.B., was born in 1999 in Germany. From the date of C.J.B.'s birth until Kramer left Germany on April 4, 2003, Bader, Kramer, and C.J.B. all resided continuously in Germany.

In August 2000, Bader and Kramer separated. At all times after the separation, C.J.B. resided with Kramer. Kramer was the sole source of financial support for C.J.B.

In November 2000, while employed as a foreman at a United States Army Munitions Depot, Bader was arrested for violations of the War Weapons Control Act and the Explosives Act. Bader was ultimately convicted of unauthorized transfer of the actual control of war weapons, unauthorized transportation of war weapons, and unauthorized handling of explosive substances. A German court sentenced him to a term of 42 months of incarceration and suspended his driving privileges.

During Bader's incarceration, C.J.B. continued to reside with Kramer and was supported by her. Bader received visits from C.J.B. accompanied by Kramer during the first six months of his incarceration.

Bader and Kramer were legally divorced in June 2002. C.J.B. continued to reside with Kramer and was supported financially by her subsequent to the divorce.

Bader was released from prison on December 17, 2002, and was placed on probation for a period of three years. That same day, Kramer and C.J.B. traveled to the United States with Bader's consent. They returned to Germany on January 3, 2003.

On January 9, 2003, Bader picked up C.J.B. from her school for an eight-day family ski vacation. On January 16, 2003, Kramer filed a petition in a German court seeking sole custody, and on February 6, 2003, Bader filed a petition seeking sole custody. On March 20, 2003, the German court ruled on the petitions, setting forth a visitation schedule for Bader and granting Kramer an award of child support in the amount of 177 euros per month.

On April 4, 2003, Kramer picked up C.J.B. from Bader's home and traveled with her to the United States. Kramer did not inform Bader of her intent to do so, and she did not have his consent. Kramer and C.J.B. have remained in the United States since that date.

In Germany, Bader filed a petition for sole custody in June 2003. In October 2003, Bader filed a Request for Return of Child under the Hague Convention with the Central Authority of Germany. The German Central Authority sent a letter to the American Central Authority in November 2003 stating that when Bader and Kramer "were divorced, no decision about the rights of custody was issued. So both still have parental responsibility for the child pursuant to Section 1626 of the German Civil Code (BGB)." A German court granted Bader sole custody in an order dated December 4, 2003.

Bader then filed this petition in the district court under the Hague Convention. Initially, the district court denied Bader any relief on his petition after finding that he did not have cognizable rights of custody under the Hague Convention. Bader appealed, and we reversed, holding that, under German law, Bader possessed joint custody rights to C.J.B. *Bader v. Kramer*, 445 F.3d 346, 351 (4th Cir.2006) ("*Bader I*"). This was so because German law vests both parents with joint custody of a child until a competent court enters a contrary order. We then remanded the case to the district court for a determination as to whether Bader was exercising his custody rights at the time of C.J.B.'s removal and whether any defenses apply under the Hague Convention. On remand, the district court found that Bader was actually exercising his custody rights and that no defenses precluded C.J.B.'s return to Germany. Consequently, the district court ordered C.J.B. returned to Germany. Kramer now appeals.

Bader I established that C.J.B.'s removal from Germany was in breach of Bader's custody rights under German law. Therefore, on remand, the only questions before the district court were whether Bader was actually exercising his custody rights at the time of C.J.B.'s removal and whether Kramer has established any defense precluding C.J.B.'s return to Germany. Kramer's appeal now brings these issues before us.

We first consider whether Bader was actually exercising his custody rights to C.J.B. at the time of her removal from Germany. As we noted earlier, a showing of actual exercise is a necessary element of a claim of wrongful removal under the Hague Convention. Despite this requirement, the Hague Convention does not define *exercise*. Therefore, an initial issue we face is what *exercise* means in the context of the Hague Convention. In other words, we must decide what conduct by a parent possessing custody rights is sufficient to show that he actually exercised those rights.

As other circuits have noted, this inquiry raises several serious concerns. First, it requires us either to adopt a definition of *exercise* which is drawn from that term's plain and ordinary meaning or to delve into the domestic law of the country of habitual residence in search of a meaning. Each approach is problematic. The former would require us to adopt some sort of "common law definition" of *exercise*, a definition potentially divorced from that term's meaning in the law of the country of habitual residence; and the latter is an undertaking for which we are particularly ill-suited, it requiring a determination of policy-oriented decisions concerning the application of another country's domestic law. Second, an inquiry into the exercise of custody rights pushes us toward a consideration of whether a parent's custody rights should be ignored because he or she was not acting sufficiently like a custodial parent. This would move us perilously close to a determination on the merits of the parent's underlying custody claim—a determination which is reserved for the courts of the country of habitual residence. Third, the confusing dynamics of quarrels and informal separations make it difficult to assess adequately the acts and motivations of a parent. An occasional visit may be all that is available to someone left, by the vagaries of marital discord, temporarily without the child. Often the child may be avoided, not out of a desire to relinquish the custody, but out of anger, pride, embarrassment, or fear, vis-a-vis the other parent. Reading too much into a parent's behavior during these difficult times could be inaccurate and unfair.

In light of these concerns, we find persuasive the nearly-universal approach taken by courts faced with the question of the exercise of custody rights, and we adopt it here. Accordingly, we will liberally find "exercise" whenever a parent with *de jure* custody rights keeps, or seeks to keep, any sort of regular contact with his or her child. This avoids the need to distinguish between *de jure* custody and *de facto* custody, thus obviating the concerns outlined above. Under this approach, a person who has valid custody rights to a child under the law of the country of the child's habitual residence cannot fail to "exercise" those custody rights under the Hague Convention short of acts that constitute clear and unequivocal abandonment of the child. Further, once it determines the parent exercised custody rights in any manner, the court should stop—completely avoiding the question whether the parent exercised the custody rights well or badly.

With these principles in mind, we have no difficulty affirming the district court's finding that Bader exercised his right to joint custody here. During the three months between his release from prison and C.J.B.'s removal, Bader had actual physical custody of C.J.B. on at least three occasions: a December 14-16 visit, a January ski vacation, and an April overnight stay. In fact, C.J.B. had spent the night with Bader and was at his residence when Kramer picked her up just prior to taking her to the United States. In addition, Bader paid child support to Kramer when ordered to do so and financially supported C.J.B. during the times when she was in his custody. While any one of these facts might suffice to establish that Bader did not clearly and unequivocally abandon C.J.B., their aggregation certainly does so, leading to the conclusion that Bader actually exercised his custody rights under the Hague Convention.

Notwithstanding this, Kramer maintains that, in order to establish that he was exercising his rights of custody, Bader had to "place the child in a city, suburb, or countryside; in a particular dwelling unit at some address" or provide primary care for the child. Thus, while recognizing that Bader retained the legal right to custody of C.J.B., Kramer argues that he actually exercised merely a right of access or visitation. This argument, however, requires us to engage in the exact analysis which the unequivocal abandonment standard forbids: a determination of whether Bader acted sufficiently like a custodial parent under German law. Of course, this analysis would, in turn, raise all the concerns which we earlier noted and which the unequivocal abandonment standard avoids. Having rejected this approach earlier in this opinion, we cannot accept Kramer's argument now. Because Bader did not unequivocally abandon C.J.B., he necessarily exercised his joint custody rights regardless of whether he determined C.J.B.'s place of residence or provided primary care.

We next consider whether Kramer has established any defense under the Hague Convention which precludes the return of C.J.B. to Germany. On appeal, Kramer's sole assertion in this regard is that the district court erred in failing to consider her defense under Article 13(a) of the Hague Convention. Article 13(a) provides that a child may not be returned if the removing parent proves, by a preponderance of the evidence, that the petitioner was not actually exercising his custodial rights at the time of the removal or had consented to or acquiesced in the removal. This defense, though, merely represents the converse of what Bader was required to prove to succeed on his claim that the child should be returned. Because the district court found that Bader sufficiently exercised his custody right over C.J.B. to satisfy the third prong of the Convention, it necessarily rejected Kramer's Article 13(a) defense even if it did not expressly do so. Therefore, we find no merit to Kramer's contention that the case should be remanded for a consideration of this defense.

In sum, as Bader has established, pursuant to the Hague Convention and ICARA, that C.J.B. was wrongfully removed from Germany and as no defense precludes her return, C.J.B. must be promptly returned to Germany. Accordingly, the judgment of the district court is

Affirmed.

———————

Most case law interpreting the Hague Convention is from federal courts. However, the International Child Abduction Remedies Act provides that federal *and* state courts have concurrent jurisdiction under the Convention. The following case, *Marriage of Witherspoon*, is a state court decision interpreting the Convention.

Marriage of Witherspoon

California Court of Appeal
155 Cal. App. 4th 963, 66 Cal. Rptr. 3d 586 (2007)

Aronson, J.

Danny Witherspoon challenges the trial court's order (a) requiring the return to Germany of his two children from his marriage with Julie Witherspoon under the Hague Convention on the Civil Aspects of International Child Abduction, (b) declaring California an inconvenient forum for adjudicating their custody dispute, and (c) awarding Julie temporary custody of the children pending their return to Germany. We conclude the trial court erred in failing to make factual findings regarding certain enumerated exceptions to the children's return under the Convention, and in awarding temporary custody of the children to Julie without considering whether doing so would pose a substantial risk of harm to them. We therefore reverse the order and remand for further proceedings.

Danny was a high school band teacher in California when he began a sexual relationship with 16-year-old Julie, one of his students. When rumors regarding Danny's sexual involvement with students surfaced, Julie, who was still 16 years old, moved with Danny to Florida where they lived together. In February 1994, the pair traveled to Las Vegas where Julie, then 17, married Danny, at the time 52 years old. The couple's daughter was born in September 1994, and a son was born in June 1996.

In 1995, the couple moved to Garden Grove, California, where Danny again worked as a band teacher. In 1997, Julie joined the Army reserves and later requested and received active duty orders. In August 1998, Julie left Danny and moved to Fort Hood, Texas, with her children. In December 2002, Julie was deployed to Germany, and her children followed one month later. The children attended school in Germany from January 2003 until the end of July 2006. In June 2003, Julie was transferred to Iraq, and returned to Germany in August 2004. During her Iraq deployment, Julie left the children in the care of a child care provider, assertedly because Danny refused to take them.

In July 2006, the children were hospitalized due to gastric problems. When Julie arrived to take the children home, the attending physician refused to release them because Julie was extremely intoxicated, hostile, and behaving in a bizarre fashion. According to social workers investigating the matter in Germany, Julie threatened to harm both the children and herself. As a result, the Army Community Services Offices and the Jugendamt (Youth Welfare Office) took custody of the children, and Julie was involuntarily committed to a mental institution for a brief period.

Julie's commanding officer then contacted Danny and informed him the children had been placed in a foster home because the Jugendamt would not release them to Julie. The officer informed Danny the Jugendamt would release the children to him if he went to Germany. According to Danny, Julie also called him and told him to come to Germany to pick up the children because they were in foster care and she was restricted to barracks. Danny traveled to Germany and, after speaking with those involved, returned to the United States. The children were sent to Danny shortly thereafter and, commencing in early August 2006, resided with him in Orange County.

On August 8, 2006, Danny filed for divorce in Orange County Superior Court, seeking sole legal and physical custody of the children, and requested an order denying Julie visitation absent treatment for alleged alcoholism and mental health problems. Danny included with his petition documents he received from the Army's Social Work Services Department and the Jugendamt detailing both the present and past abuse and neglect allegations relating to the children. . . .

On October 20, 2006, Julie filed an order to show cause (OSC) seeking under the Convention the return of her children to Germany, and requesting the court place the children in protective custody pending the hearing on the OSC. In her accompanying declaration, Julie accused Danny of violence toward the children and repeatedly beating her. She also accused Danny of having sex with other underage high school students, and sexually abusing a daughter from a previous marriage. Julie declared that Danny had met his three previous wives while they were his high school students. Julie also alleged that she had spoken with Beth, Danny's daughter from a previous marriage, who claimed Danny had molested her and beaten her mother, Diane, and that she witnessed Danny having sex with high school students.

Danny filed a responsive declaration denying his previous wives were ever his students, that he ever beat any of his wives, including Julie, or that he was a sexual predator. Danny filed supporting declarations from Beth, who denied ever speaking with Julie or being sexually molested, and Diane, who denied she had been Danny's student or that she had been beaten by him.

At the OSC hearing, the trial court granted Julie's Convention petition and ordered the children returned to Germany. The court also ruled that under the Uniform Child Custody Jurisdiction and Enforcement Act, California was an inconvenient forum for adjudicating child custody. The court also assumed temporary emergency jurisdiction, and removed the children from Danny's custody. The court determined the children were threatened with mistreatment or abuse in Danny's care due to the parents' extreme difference in age. . . .

The trial court based its order in part on the Convention, as implemented by the International Child Abduction Remedies Act (ICARA), 42 United States Code, sections 11601-11610. . . .

The Convention and ICARA seek to protect children internationally from the harmful effects of their wrongful removal or retention and to establish procedures to ensure their prompt return to the State of their habitual residence, as well as to secure protection for rights of access. Under Article 3 of the Convention, the removal or retention of a child is wrongful if: (a) it is in breach of rights of custody attributed to a person . . . under the law of the State in which the child was habitually resident immediately before the removal or retention; and (b) at the time of removal or retention those rights were actually exercised, . . . or would have been so exercised but for the removal or retention. The parent filing a Convention petition bears the burden of proving wrongful removal by a preponderance of the evidence. If the petitioner demonstrates that the child was wrongfully removed, the court must order the child's return to the country of habitual residence unless the respondent demonstrates that one of four narrow exceptions applies.

The parties do not dispute the children's habitual residence is Germany, where they had lived continuously for over three and one-half years. Danny, however, contends his removal or retention of the children did not breach Julie's custodial rights under German law. In support, Danny notes that German law gives both parents equal de jure custody over a child. Danny reasons that because he had equal custodial rights under German law, including the right to determine the children's residence, his removal or retention could not have been wrongful. Although Danny correctly cites German law, he misconstrues its effect under the Convention.

Under the Convention, one parent's removal or retention of a child may breach the second parent's custodial rights under the law of the children's habitual residence, even if such acts do not breach the law itself. As the Explanatory Report to the Convention instructs: "From the Convention's standpoint, the removal of a child by one of the joint holders without the consent of the other, is wrongful, and this wrongfulness derives in this particular case, not from some action in breach of a particular law, but from the fact that such action has disregarded the rights of the other parent which are also protected by law, and has interfered with their normal exercise. The Convention's true nature is revealed most clearly in these situations: it is not concerned with establishing the person to whom custody of the child will belong at some point in the future, nor with the situations in which it may prove necessary to modify a decision awarding joint custody on the basis of facts which have subsequently changed. It seeks, more simply, to prevent a later decision on the matter being influenced by a change of circumstances brought about through unilateral action by one of the parties." Thus, Danny's removal or retention of the children is considered wrongful under the Convention even if Danny's actions did not violate German law.

Danny contends that Julie was not actually exercising her rights of custody at the time of removal or retention because the Jugendamt had intervened to take physical custody of the children. Article 5a of the Convention states that the term "rights of custody," "shall include rights relating to the care of the person of the child and, in particular, the right to determine the child's place of residence." The Explanatory Report notes that in determining whether a parent exercises rights of custody, "the law of the child's habitual residence is invoked in the widest possible sense, and the sources from which custody rights derive are all those upon which a claim can be based within the context of the legal system concerned. The report also states that the Convention favors "a flexible interpretation of the terms used, which allows the greatest possible number of cases to be brought into consideration."

To determine whether Julie was exercising her rights of custody despite the Jugendamt's intervention, we consider the effect of that agency's actions upon Julie's rights under German law. . . . [U]nder German law Julie retained substantial custodial rights after the Jugendamt's emergency seizure of her children, including the right to demand their immediate return and, if the children are not returned, to require the Jugendamt to obtain a court order. We conclude Julie continued to exercise "rights of custody" under the required "flexible interpretation" of that term. Julie has thus established a prima facie case for return under the Convention. . . .

Once a petitioner under the Convention has demonstrated by a preponderance of the evidence that removal of a child was wrongful (see 42 U.S.C. § 11603(e)(1)), the other parent may assert exceptions that, if proven, will prevent the return of the child. One exception to return exists when "there is a grave risk that his or her return would expose the child to physical or psychological harm or otherwise place the child in an intolerable situation." (Convention, art. 13b) This exception must be proved by clear and convincing evidence. (42 U.S.C. § 11603(e)(2)(B).)

Courts have construed the Convention's article 13b exception as "narrowly drawn." Were a court to give an overly broad construction to its authority to grant exceptions under the Convention, it would frustrate a paramount purpose of that international agreement—namely, to preserve the status quo and to deter parents from crossing international boundaries in search of a more sympathetic court. As the U.S. State Department has explained, an "intolerable situation" was not intended to encompass return to a home where money is in short supply, or where educational or other opportunities are more limited than in the requested State. An example of an "intolerable situation" is one in which a custodial parent sexually abuses the child. If the other parent removes or retains the child to safeguard it against further victimization, and the abusive parent then petitions for the child's return under the Convention, the court may deny the petition. Such action would protect the child from being returned to an 'intolerable situation' and subjected to a grave risk of psychological harm.

Here, Danny contends Julie will place the children in an "intolerable situation" if she takes them back to Germany because the Jugendamt again will place the children in protective custody. Whether this would create an intolerable situation, however, is only part of the equation. Danny also provided evidence from Army and Jugendamt social workers detailing Julie's drunken, hostile, and suicidal acts shortly before and after Julie's children were taken from her, resulting in her involuntary commitment to a mental institution. This evidence, if accepted, would suffice to demonstrate a risk of harm to the children by clear and convincing evidence, even construing the exception narrowly. The trial court's order, however, sidestepped the issue: "There were allegations of Mother's misconduct raised in Germany. True or not true, this court has no jurisdiction to ascertain the reliability of those allegations."

Ironically, the trial court exercised emergency jurisdiction to remove the children from Danny, but refused to make any findings on the evidence demonstrating Julie posed a risk of potential harm to the children before awarding her custody. Contrary to its order, the trial court had jurisdiction to determine all of the issues raised by Julie's petition under the Convention, and erred by failing to fully consider the exceptions to return asserted by Danny and supported by the evidence.

We recognize courts should expeditiously determine Convention petitions. As one court explained: There is no requirement under the Hague Convention or under the ICARA that discovery be allowed or that an evidentiary hearing be conducted. Thus, under the guidance of the Convention and the statutory scheme, the court is given the authority to resolve these cases without resorting to a full trial on the merits or a plenary evidentiary hearing. But this case does not present the typical Convention situation. Danny did not simply abduct the children, but took them at the request of the Jugendamt, who removed them from Julie out of concern for their safety. We therefore reverse the trial court's grant of Julie's Convention petition and remand for further findings to consider whether the children may suffer harm or be exposed to an intolerable situation if returned to Germany with their mother.

Another exception to return arises where "the person, institution or other body having the care of the person of the child was not actually exercising the custody rights at the time of removal or retention, or had consented to or subsequently acquiesced in the removal or retention." (Convention, art. 13a.) This exception must be proved by a preponderance of the evidence. (42 U.S.C. § 11603(e)(2)(B).)

Danny submitted evidence that Julie agreed to have Danny take the children back to California. Specifically, Danny declared that Julie called Danny and told him he "needed to come over and get the children as they would not give them back to her and as she was restricted to barracks." In her petition, however, Julie stated that Danny took the children without her knowledge. Moreover, Julie conceded she had signed papers which apparently authorized removal of her children, but asserted she did so only under duress. On this latter issue, the trial court noted: "There were allegations of duress leading to Mother's agreement to place the children with their father. True or not true, all evidence to prove or disprove those assertions exits in the state of Germany." On remand, the trial court must determine whether Julie consented to the children's return.

The Convention also provides one additional exception to return: "The judicial or administrative authority may also refuse to order the return of the child if it finds that the child objects to being returned and has attained an age and degree of maturity at which it is appropriate to take account of its views." (Convention, art. 13.) The importance of this exception is explained in the Perez-Vera Report on the Convention: "The Convention also provides that *the child's views concerning the essential question of its return or retention may be conclu-*

sive, provided it has, according to the competent authorities, attained an age and degree of maturity sufficient for its views to be taken into account. In this way, the Convention gives children the possibility of interpreting their own interests." In applying the age and maturity exception, a court must not focus solely on the general goal of the Convention—to protect children from the harmful effects of wrongful removal—but must also carefully determine that the particular child has obtained an age and degree of maturity at which it is appropriate to take account of its views.

The couple's oldest child is 13 years old, and the youngest is now 11. Absent evidence to the contrary, the children's ages suggest they have the maturity to express their preferences. . . .

The order is reversed, and the cause remanded for further proceedings in accordance with this opinion. In the interests of justice, each party shall bear his or her own costs on this appeal.

Question based on *Marriage of Witherspoon*

Danny was a 50-year-old high school music teacher when he started a sexual relationship with his 16-year-old student, Julie. That's statutory rape! Not to mention a violation of professional ethics. Danny and Julie left California, perhaps to avoid Danny's arrest. Yet, before long, the couple returned to California and Danny got another job teaching music. Do you wonder how he managed to get another job as a music teacher?!

The concept of a child's place of "habitual residence" is central to the Hague Convention. The Seventh Circuit's decision in *Norinder v. Fuentes* offers good instruction on the meaning of habitual residence.

Norinder v. Fuentes

United States Court of Appeals
657 F.3d 526 (7th Cir. 2011)

Wood, Circuit Judge.

Although the federal courts normally have nothing to do with child custody issues, there is an exception for cases that arise under the International Child Abduction Remedies Act (the Act), 42 U.S.C. § 11601 et seq., which implements the Hague Convention on the Civil Aspects of International Child Abduction (the Convention). This is one of those cases. Petitioner, Magnus Norinder, filed this suit against his wife, Sharon Fuentes, seeking the return of their son, JRN, to Sweden. Norinder is from Sweden and Fuentes is from the United States; both countries are parties to the Convention. The Act entitles a person whose child has wrongfully been removed to the United States in violation of the Convention to petition for return of the child to the child's country of "habitual residence," unless certain exceptions apply.

The battle here is over which country—Sweden or the United States—is JRN's habitual residence. Norinder asserts that Sweden is, and that Fuentes abducted JRN to the United States in violation of the Convention. The district court agreed and ordered JRN returned to Sweden, where Norinder is living and where Fuentes and JRN lived until recently. In this appeal, Fuentes challenges the district court's conclusion and asserts that the court should have chosen the United States instead. Both for that reason, and because she charges that there is a grave risk that JRN's return to Sweden will expose him to physical or psychological harm (a defense under the Convention that the abductor may invoke to block return of a child), she argues that the district court's order should be reversed. . . .

Norinder and Fuentes, who are both physicians, met on the Internet in 2006. Norinder, a citizen of Sweden, lived in Bors, Sweden at the time; and Fuentes, who is a citizen of the United States, lived in Texas. The relationship progressed quickly: in February 2007, Fuentes visited Sweden and the couple got engaged; in April, she returned and they conceived a child; in August they were married in Sweden. After the wedding, Fuentes returned to Houston, Texas, to complete a fellowship in pathology. Norinder was chief physician of a hospital in Bors at the time. He took paternity leave in January 2008 to join Fuentes in Houston. JRN was born there the next month. In July, the whole family moved to Sweden.

It was not long before the relationship became rocky. Fuentes and Norinder had many fights, some of which escalated into physical confrontations. There are charges that JRN was harmed in the midst of these fights. On a number of occasions, Fuentes moved out of the family's house in Sweden—once to an apartment she apparently had rented in secret. Professional difficulties compounded the personal strife. Fuentes did not keep the job that Norinder secured for her at his hospital in Bors, and Norinder was suspended from work while the hospital investigated charges instigated by Fuentes that Norinder had substance abuse problems. Fuentes accused Norinder of drinking too much and abusing prescription drugs, and there is some evidence that he has had difficulty with drugs and alcohol in the past. While the two were in Sweden, divorce proceedings were initiated and then abandoned on a number of occasions. None of this, however, is directly relevant to the resolution of this case. Our authority over Norinder's petition extends only to the question whether JRN was abducted and should be returned to Sweden; we do not sit to resolve a messy domestic conflict.

The event that gave rise to this proceeding occurred after two years of the unhappiness we have just recounted. On March 17, 2010, under the guise of a two-week vacation to Texas, Fuentes traveled to the United States with JRN in tow. On April 7, 2010—the day she was scheduled to return to Sweden—Fuentes sent Norinder a text message saying that she was keeping their son and planned to remain in the United States. Norinder hired a lawyer and for about a month searched for Fuentes and JRN. They were not in Texas or any other place that he might have expected. Eventually, he found them in southern Illinois, and on May 26, 2010, his lawyer there filed the petition for return of the child that is now before us.

[Court proceedings under the Hague Convention have docket priority, and proceed quickly. It is common to go to trial within a few months of filing a petition. This speed is remarkable given the crowded docket in most courts. In the instant case, the petition was filed in late May, 2010, and the case was tried in June, 2010!] On June 30, the district court determined that JRN's habitual residence was Sweden and that Norinder had demonstrated that his rights of custody under Swedish law had been violated when Fuentes abducted JRN to the United States. The court limited the remaining proceedings, which were to take place at the end of July, to the question whether JRN would be exposed to a grave risk of harm if he was returned.

. . . On July 22, the district court held the final day of hearings to consider whether Norinder posed a threat to JRN. The court concluded that he did not, and on July 23, it issued an order requiring the return of JRN to Sweden. . . .

Fuentes presents two arguments on the merits of the district court's decision; first that it erred by finding that Sweden was JRN's habitual place of residence, and second, that it erred by finding that she failed to show by clear and convincing evidence that sending JRN back to his father will expose the child to grave harm, excusing the obligation to return him that would otherwise exist under the Act and the Convention. We address these in turn. . . .

The Act provides for the return of a child wrongfully removed to the United States in violation of the Convention. 42 U.S.C. § 11603(b). Wrongful removal is defined as removal in breach of rights of custody vested in the party who complains of the removal; to prevent forum shopping, rights of custody are defined according to the law of the country that is the child's habitual residence. The first step for a court considering a petition is to determine the child's habitual residence. The forum-shopping concern means that habitual residence must be based on the everyday meaning of these words rather than on the legal meaning that a particular jurisdiction attaches to them; for example, habitual residence is not necessarily the same as a jurisdiction's conception of "domicile." . . . The question is whether a prior place of residence (in this case, the United States) was effectively abandoned and a new residence established (here, Sweden) by the shared actions and intent of the parents coupled with the passage of time. Often parents will not agree about what their shared intentions were once litigation is underway, and so we must take account of the parents' actions as well as what they say.

This case is not a close one. Although JRN was born in Houston, Texas, the family moved to Sweden five months after the child's birth and lived there until the trip Fuentes took that triggered this lawsuit. Fuentes says that the 2008 move to Sweden was supposed to be a temporary relocation and that she never would have gone if she thought it was a permanent move. As a result, she continues, she never shared the intent to abandon the United States as her and JRN's habitual residence. The district court was unconvinced:

> The uncontroverted evidence is that Fuentes had at least 80% of her personal items shipped to Sweden in July 2008, including two automobiles. She applied for and received permanent residency status in Sweden as of the end of 2009. She was engaged in negotiations for a position at a hospital in another city in Sweden and she and Norinder had looked for homes in that city. She took Swedish lessons right up to the time she left for the United States. Notably, she did not retain a residence in the United States. She did not have a house, nor was there any evidence introduced of a driver's license, or taxes paid in the United States.

This was enough to convince the district court that Fuentes shared the intent to reside in Sweden with Norinder and JRN. It is enough to convince us as well. That Fuentes or Norinder thought that they might one day return to the United States does not mean that the United States remained the child's habitual residence. . . . An intention or hope to return does not prevent a new residence from being established. When the child moves to a new country accompanied by both parents, who take steps to set up a regular household together, the period of time the child has been in the country need not be long. The district court's determination that JRN's habitual place of residence is Sweden was not clearly erroneous.

Article 13(b) of the Convention and 42 U.S.C. § 11603(e)(2)(A) provide that when a respondent demonstrates by clear and convincing evidence that there is a grave risk that the child's return would expose the child to physical or psychological harm or otherwise place the child in an intolerable situation, the automatic return required by the Convention should not go forward. Fuentes argues that she has met this burden. She bases her assertion that Norinder poses a serious risk of harm to JRN on a handful of serious fights the couple had; an incident in which Fuentes contends that Norinder threw JRN on the ground during an argument; allegations that Norinder is addicted to prescription drugs and that he abuses alcohol; and the testimony of two psychiatrists, Drs. Roth and Woodham, who appeared on Fuentes's behalf at trial. Norinder responds that he is a fit and loving parent; he disputes that he ever threw JRN or harmed the child in any way—in fact he accuses Fuentes of dropping JRN. Norinder presented testimony from his long-time psychiatrist, Dr. Vikander, about his history of drug and alcohol abuse. He asserts that Fuentes fell far short of showing the requisite grave risk of harm required by the Convention.

The district court agreed with Norinder on every point. It found that Fuentes's testimony about Norinder's past behavior was not credible, and it expressly found Norinder's story about who dropped JRN more plausible. The court also thought that Norinder's distant history of drug and alcohol abuse did not suggest that he would harm JRN. It was not persuaded by the testimony of Fuentes's expert witnesses. While they both testified generally about the effect of substance abuse on children, neither had evaluated Norinder in any meaningful way—Dr. Woodham had seen Norinder on three occasions in 2008, and Dr. Roth had never interacted with him at all. The past fights, the court said, were best viewed as "minor domestic squabbles" rather than anything detrimental to JRN. The district court concluded, "There is no credible evidence that this return of the child to the custody of the Petitioner will, in any manner, present a grave risk of harm."

We find no fault in the lower court's factual findings. Concern with comity among nations argues for a narrow interpretation of the grave risk of harm defense; but the safety of children is paramount. Because the court in this sort of case is responsible for determining which country's courts should adjudicate the domestic dispute and not resolving the dispute itself, we have stressed that the risk of harm must truly be grave. The respondent must present clear and convincing evidence of this grave harm because any more lenient standard would create a situation where the exception would swallow the rule.

Fuentes has not met this demanding standard. She has given us no reason to doubt the district court's credibility findings, including its decision to credit Norinder's testimony over her own and its view that Norinder's long-term psychiatrist provided more accurate information than doctors who had not treated him before. As Fuentes says in her brief, "Even the most objective observer would fairly describe the trial proceedings as a swearing match between Norinder and [Fuentes]." Without some compelling evidence otherwise, we must agree with the district court's conclusion that Norinder never threw JRN on the ground, and that whatever drinking and drug problems have existed do not affect the outcome here. Based on the facts it found, the district court's decision to order JRN returned to Sweden was correct. . . .

Affirmed.

In *Norinder v. Fuentes*, the Seventh Circuit Court of Appeals grappled with whether returning a child to Sweden would expose the child to a grave risk of harm. The Seventh Circuit revisits the "grave risk" issue in *Kahn v. Fatima*. Judge Hamilton's dissenting opinion is particularly useful.

Kahn v. Fatima

United States Court of Appeals,
Seventh Circuit
680 F.3d 781 (2012)

Posner, Circuit Judge.

The International Child Abduction Remedies Act, 42 U.S.C. §§ 11601 et seq., which implements the Hague Convention on the Civil Aspects of International Child Abduction, entitles a person whose child has been removed from his custody (sole or joint) to the United States (usually by the other parent) to petition in federal or state court for the return of the child. The petitioner in this case is the father, and the respondent, his wife, is the mother. She removed the child from their joint custody and is thus the "abductor." The child is a girl not yet 4 years old, who in consideration of her privacy is referred to in the briefs and record only as ZFK.

The father, an optometrist in Edmonton, Alberta (Canada), wants to take the child back to Edmonton. He has filed for divorce in Canada on the ground of the mother's "physical or mental cruelty" to him, and seeks sole custody of the children. The mother, a U.S. citizen living in Illinois, wants to keep the children with her in the United States. The district court ordered ZFK returned to Canada with her father, and the mother appeals. The child was taken from her mother on March 9 of this year by U.S. Marshals, pursuant to an ex parte order by the district judge upon the claim of the father's lawyer that the wife is a flight risk because India, which the family was visiting when the mother flew to the United States with ZFK, is not a signatory of the Hague Convention, and so she might decide to fly back to India, taking the child with her. (Both parties are of Indian ethnicity.) Until our order of May 1, discussed below, was executed, the child was living with her father in a hotel in Chicago. The order (which was carried out on May 3) directed that she be returned to her mother's custody pending the final disposition of the appeal.

"The Hague Convention was created to discourage abductions by parents who either lost, or would lose, a custody contest.... The Convention drafters adopted a 'remedy of return'... to discourage abductions, reconnect children with their primary caretakers, and locate each custody contest in the forum where most of the relevant evidence existed. [But] while the remedy of return works well if the abductor is a noncustodial parent, it is inappropriate when the abductor is a primary caretaker who is seeking to protect herself and the children from the other parent's violence." Merle H. Weiner, "Navigating the Road Between Uniformity and Progress: The Need for Purposive Analysis of the Hague Convention on the

Civil Aspects of International Child Abduction," 33 Colum. Human Rts. L.Rev. 275, 278–79 (2002) . . . [D]omestic violence is a common inciter to "abduction"— the abused spouse flees and takes her children with her. Accusations of domestic violence figure in the present case, as we are about to see.

Article 13(b) of the Convention provides a defense to the return of the "abducted" child if "there is a grave risk that [the child's] return would expose the child to physical or psychological harm or otherwise place the child in an intolerable situation." The respondent (the abductor) must prove this defense by clear and convincing evidence, 42 U.S.C. § 11603(e)(2)(A), and Hague Convention proceedings must be conducted with dispatch. Art. 11. . . The dispatch in this case may have been excessive—the procedural adequacy of the proceedings in the district court is the principal issue presented by this appeal. The only other issue is whether the father abandoned his custodial rights during the family's trip to India; we think it clear he did not.

The parties became husband and wife in an arranged marriage two years before the birth of ZFK, their first child. During the family's visit to India that we mentioned the wife complained to the Indian police of domestic abuse. The police investigated, charged the husband, and took away his passport; and it was in April of last year, while he was thus marooned in India that the wife (pregnant at the time with a second child), flew to the United States with ZFK. Eventually the husband's passport was returned and he flew back to Canada and some months later, in February of this year, filed the petition for the return of the child. That child was born in the United States after the mother had brought ZFK here and is therefore a U.S. citizen. The father does not argue that the mother abducted that child, who continues to live with her mother.

On March 7 the father obtained an ex parte order from the district court requiring the mother to yield custody of ZFK to him pending resolution of his petition, and on the thirteenth the judge scheduled an evidentiary hearing for March 22. It was held that day, with the judge as trier of fact since it was an equitable proceeding. He issued a final order of return the next day and also ordered the wife to hand over ZFK's passport to her husband so that he could take the child back to Canada. But the judge conditioned the orders on the husband's agreeing to pay a retainer (though not necessarily any additional fees) for an attorney who would be hired by the wife to handle the divorce and custody proceeding that her husband has begun in Canada.

On the wife's motion we stayed both the order of return, and the order that she turn over the child's passport to her husband, pending the decision of her appeal. And on May 1, after hearing oral argument in the appeal the day before, we ordered the child returned to the mother pending our decision, but that both the mother's passport and the child's passport be held by the U.S. Marshals Service until further notice.

The wife's testimony, if believed, reveals that her husband has a violent, ungovernable temper, had physically abused her on many occasions, some in the presence of ZFK (and in front of the child he had told his wife he would take out her eyeballs—though the child, not quite 3 years old at the time, may not have known what "eyeballs" are), had been rough on occasion with the child—indeed terrified the child—and that the child's mood had brightened greatly when she was living apart from her father. But if the husband's testimony is believed, he was, if not a model husband, not an abuser of his wife or the child. His lawyer conducted a vigorous cross-examination of the wife, based in part on discrepancies between her testimony at the evidentiary hearing and a deposition she had given a few days earlier. She stood her ground, making few concessions to the cross examining attorney.

Rule 52(a)(1) of the civil rules requires the judge to "find the facts specially and state [his] conclusions of law separately" when he is the trier of fact. He is not excused from this duty in a proceeding under the Hague Convention. And the duty is not waived—indeed it is at its most exacting—when as in this case plaintiff and defendant testify inconsistently and it is impossible to demonstrate by objective evidence which one is telling the truth, or more of the truth. The trier of fact must decide whom to believe (and how much to believe) on the basis of the coherence and plausibility of the contestants' testimony, corroboration or contradiction by other witnesses, and other clues to falsity and veracity.

The process of fact finding in such a situation is inexact and the findings that result are doubtless often mistaken. But the judge can't just throw up his hands, as happened in this case, because he can't figure out what is true and what is false in the testimony. There is no uncertainty exception to the duty imposed by Rule 52. . . .

And if there were such an exception, it would not be available when the evidentiary hearing had lasted only a day, as in this case. The judge could have adjourned the hearing for a few days to enable additional evidence to be obtained and presented; in particular he could have had ZFK examined by a child psychologist. The wife's lawyer—his initial proposal of an expert witness having been turned down because the witness hadn't had time to examine the child (remember that the hearing was held only two weeks after the respondent learned about the suit)—offered to submit an evaluation based on an examination of the child by the end of the week. The judge refused. His final order, issued as we said the day after the hearing, is two pages long and contains no findings of fact relating to the Article 13(b) defense—just a conclusion that the wife had failed to meet her burden of proof. That was not a finding of fact, but a conclusion of law. Rule 52(a)(1) requires both: that the facts be found "specially" and the conclusions of law stated separately. It is needless to add that there is no rule exempting the judge from the duty of finding the facts in cases in which the plaintiff has a higher burden of proof than the usual civil burden of the preponderance of the evidence.

But at the end of the evidentiary hearing the judge had had a discussion with the lawyers, and from that we can piece together his thinking and extract a single, solitary fact finding.

The judge began by saying, directly after the parties' witnesses had testified (there were no closing arguments), that "neither—none of the parties to the suit are residents of Illinois." Not true; the wife is currently a resident of Illinois. The judge said that "if I send the issue of custody of the child back to Canada, the Canadian courts presumably will look and take evidence and so forth and hear essentially the same evidence, I guess, I'm hearing today and make a decision to award custody to the mother or to the father.... Under the Hague Convention the child is to be returned except where there's grave risk of harm to the child. And, now, there's—presumably, there's always some risk. All I know is what I heard here today. And I'm—there's been a he said/she said hearing today. And it's very difficult for me to say categorically one side is telling the truth and one side is not telling the truth." The judge mentioned a bruise that the mother had received on her arm in India and that had been photographed at the police station and was a basis for her complaint to the police. The judge said that if the father had inflicted the bruise—which he declined to decide one way or the other—that was a bad thing to have done but it hadn't created a "grave risk," a key term in Article 13(b). But the issue was not creating a grave risk to the mother, but a grave risk (of psychological harm) to the child. If the mother's testimony about the father's ungovernable temper and brutal treatment of her was believed, it would support an inference of a grave risk of psychological harm to the child if she continued living with him.

Very little of the wife's testimony was so much as mentioned by the judge, even though the wife had testified that she'd been beaten with a pillow (which may sound like a pillow fight, but it was a sofa pillow that he beat her with in no friendly fashion and she testified that it hurt), knocked down by him in front of ZFK, hit in the chest by a heavy wallet that he had hurled at her, choked by him twice (and she said she thought she would die) when she was pregnant with her second child, threatened as we said with having her eyeballs yanked out, and dragged bodily from the backyard into a room in the house.

Supervised Visitation Services of Chicago, funded by the City, supervises visits by noncustodial parents to their children. It supervised ZFK's visits to her mother after the marshals had transferred the child to the father's custody on March 9. One of the supervisors testified that when the visit was over and she (the supervisor) told the child that she was taking her back to her father, the child became hysterical. The supervisor testified that the child had seemed "in major distress"—"bigger than" (normal) "separation anxiety." In cross-examination she said "I do feel it wasn't just a matter of her being upset about leaving her mother. There was definitely a factor there of not wanting to go back to her dad." She was also worried by the child's having said without apparent reason when returned to her father "I am a bad girl."

Another supervisor testified that during another supervised visit the child "said 'hurt'.... She pointed to her arm, and then said something about Dad.... She said: 'I'm scared.' And I asked her to clarify who she was scared of, and she said 'Dad.' Or 'Daddy.' Something like that.... It was not very clear to me what exactly she was trying to say and what exactly was going on." About this witness the judge said "she was very, very ... was certainly very, very speculative as to—and couldn't say specifically whether anything particular happened."

The mother's testimony was corroborated by her sister and her sister's husband. The judge did not mention the testimony of those witnesses, the testimony of the supervisor from Supervised Visitation Services (the one who testified about the child's having said she "hurt"), or any testimony of the mother except about the bruise on her arm and he made no finding about whether the father had inflicted it, instead as we noted dismissing it as not evidence of a "grave risk"—to the mother. His focus on the bruise to the exclusion of any mention of the mother's testimony that her husband had choked her hard enough to make her afraid she would die, or indeed of any of her other testimony, is perplexing.

It is possible that the judge ignored the mother's testimony because so much of it was about physical and psychological abuse of her by her husband (and her husband's parents, who lived with them), rather than of the child. But much of that abuse occurred in the child's presence; and repeated physical and psychological abuse of a child's mother by the child's father, in the presence of the child (especially a very young child, as in this case), is likely to create a risk of psychological harm to the child. Whether it is a grave risk, and thus triggers the Article 13(b) defense, is a separate question, but one that cannot be addressed, let alone answered, without recognizing the potential for such a risk in the father's behavior toward the mother in the child's presence. All this the judge ignored.

Throwing up his hands at what he may have thought an incomprehensible quarrel between foreigners, the judge remarked that even if the child wouldn't be safe living with her father, "Why can't Canada any more than Illinois protect—offer her protection?" The mother's lawyer pointed out that other witnesses besides the mother had testified and that there was testimony of "multiple instances" of abuse, to which the judge replied: "Then she ultimately should prevail.... Canada should make the decision on who gets custody of the child because the child is a Canadian citizen and domiciled in Canada." The lawyer as we said asked for a few days to obtain a psychologist's evaluation of the child and the judge refused.

It seems that the judge, building on his mistaken belief that none of the parties was an Illinois resident, overlooked our warning . . . not to treat the Hague Convention as a venue statute designed to deter parents from engaging in international forum shopping in custody cases. The Convention says nothing about the adequacy of the laws of the country to which the return of the child is sought—and for good reason, for even perfectly adequate laws do not ensure a child's safety. Because of the privacy of the family and parental control of children, most abuse of children by a parent goes undetected. ZFK is not yet 4. She is hardly in a position to complain to the Mounties about her father.

If the judge's order is affirmed, the child's mother, who appears not to be employed or to have any significant financial resources, will have to hunt up a Canadian lawyer and convince the lawyer to represent her without any assurance of being fully compensated. If able to hire a lawyer she may be able to obtain interim custody of the child from a Canadian court, along with a support order, but what will she do until she obtains that relief? Move back in with the father? Let the child live with him while she returns to the United States while the custody proceeding unfolds? Suppose she eventually wins custody of the child, as is not unlikely since no one accuses her of having abused the child or being an unfit mother. Then ZFK who (until our order of May 1 was executed) had been separated from her mother only since March might not be reunited with her for an indefinite period. Unless a trier of fact determines that the mother is a thorough liar, we are concerned that continuing the child in her father's custody may inflict psychological harm on her.

But that is an aside. We are not the fact finders. The essential point is that the evidentiary hearing was inadequate. Rule 52(a) was violated; there were no findings of fact on the key issues. Decisions are frequently reversed for such omissions. The failure to allow psychological evidence was another error.

The errors were not harmless. The district court's order is therefore vacated and the case remanded for a proper hearing. Circuit Rule 36 shall apply on remand. We urge that the proceedings on remand be conducted expeditiously and we suggest that the judge to whom the case is assigned appoint a child psychologist to interview ZFK. Our May 1 order shall remain in effect until further notice.

The rulings in this opinion are procedural. We do not prejudge the merits of the Article 13(b) defense. And we remind that the burden of proving the defense is stiff. But whether the burden has been carried cannot be determined in the absence of Rule 52 fact findings.

Hamilton, Circuit Judge, dissenting:

I respectfully dissent from the decision to reverse and remand this case to the district court. My colleagues and I agree that the child's country of habitual residence is Canada and that the mother's removal of the child from India to the United States violated the father's rights as a parent. The disputed issue is the mother's "grave risk" defense to what is otherwise a rock-solid Hague Convention case for return of the child to Canada. I would affirm the district court's finding that the mother did not prove the "grave risk" defense by clear and convincing evidence and would affirm the order returning the child to Canada. I would allow that nation's courts to address this child's best interest and to decide on custody, support, visitation, and all related matters without further delay.

As I explain in detail below, the temptation we face with this case is one that was anticipated by the diplomats and family law experts who drafted the Hague Convention and by the United States Congress that enacted the implementing legislation. The temptation is to decide the merits of the underlying custody dispute, and to do so based on the best interest of the child. That sounds at first like a humane and sensible way to decide the case. But for cases involving abductions, the Convention and the legislation were drafted as tightly as possible to discourage courts from deciding the best interest of the child. The Convention and the legislation are designed to decide venue, and to decide it quickly, to deter forum shopping in custody disputes by way of international child abductions. The right venue is ordinarily the country of the child's habitual residence. Although there is an important exception where a return to that country would pose a "grave risk" to the child, that exception was drafted carefully to keep it narrow, precisely so as to prevent courts deciding Hague Convention petitions from reaching too far into the merits of the custody question.

My colleagues' decision to reverse is based on the noblest of motives, to protect a vulnerable child from a potential threat and to try to act in her best interest. Despite my colleagues' disclaimers that the reversal is only a procedural decision, though, the reversal does what Hague Convention courts are not supposed to do. The reversal is also clearly based on the view that the district judge who saw and heard the witnesses was simply wrong in his evaluation of the parties' credibility—an evaluation we can make only by reading and re-reading transcripts.

I do not know whether the district judge was right or wrong in his factual evaluation of credibility. I will cheerfully concede that, based on all we know about this troubled family, a family court judge (whether in Canada or the United States) who considers the best interest of the child is likely to award custody to her mother, at least on an interim basis while the divorce goes forward. The law could not be any clearer, however, that that is not the question for the district court or for us to decide. Our job and the district court's job is to decide only the narrow questions presented by the Hague Convention petition.

For the district court, this was a difficult case. Based on the district court's findings, our job on appeal in this case should be much easier. We should respect the district court's findings and allow the family courts in the Canadian province of Alberta to do their job, which is the more difficult one of deciding all the issues of child custody, support, and visitation in the divorce case. By instead broadening the issues in this case, as the majority does, we tend to undermine a critical provision of the Hague Convention and invite other parents who have abducted their children to do the same in future cases. To explain my reasons in more detail, I address first the "grave risk" exception as it evolved in the Hague Convention, whose proceedings show that our obligation under international law is to resist the lure of deciding custody based on a broad inquiry into the best interest of the child. I turn then to the majority's specific criticisms of the district court's handling of this case.

A close look at the proceedings that led to the Hague Convention shows that its framers and ratifiers foresaw the path my colleagues take in this case, warned against it, and drafted language as clearly as they could to prevent courts from broadening a Hague Convention case into a complete and prolonged custody battle.

The basic premise of the Hague Convention is to protect the best interests of all children by removing the incentive to abduct children involved in custody disputes and to return an abducted child to her country of habitual residence, promptly, and without attempting to determine merits of the underlying custody dispute. 42 U.S.C. § 11601(a)(4). The central provision of the Convention, Article 12, provides what is known as the return remedy: "Where a child has been wrongfully removed or retained in terms of Article 3 . . . the authority concerned shall order the return of the child forthwith." See *Abbott v. Abbott*, 130 S.Ct. 1983, 1989, (2010).

In drafting the Convention, it was recognized, of course, that there could be exceptional circumstances in which the return remedy should be denied, including cases where return would endanger the child. The drafters considered a number of different formulations for this exception. Their debates show that they recognized that if the exception were too broad, or were interpreted too broadly, it could effectively undermine the entire Convention.

The drafters first considered "substantial risk" and other, even less demanding formulations in the English texts of the proposals, such as exceptions for the best interests of the child or for the forum nation's public policy. Those less demanding standards were all rejected in favor of the "grave risk" language in Article 13(b). They were rejected precisely because they would create too great a risk that the courts would delve into the merits of the ultimate custody determination. . . .

Turning from the Hague Convention itself to its implementation by the United States, the Congress emphasized these same points, recognizing the temptation to turn Hague Convention proceedings into full-blown custody fights. Congress found that children who have been wrongfully removed or retained "are to be promptly returned unless one of the narrow exceptions set forth in the Convention applies." 42 U.S.C. § 11601(a)(4). . . .

Reasonable people may debate whether the "grave risk" standard is sufficiently sensitive to legitimate claims of abuse, without being over-sensitive to false or exaggerated claims. Some of the advocates' and scholars' law journal articles cited by the majority argue that the "grave risk" standard is too difficult for victims of domestic violence to satisfy. As the majority points out, the proportion of international child abduction cases where the abductor is herself fleeing a violent or psychologically abusive situation has grown much higher than was anticipated by the Convention or by Congress. The demanding "grave risk" standard, requiring proof by clear and convincing evidence, creates the possibility that an abusive parent could use the Convention, which was enacted to protect children, to have courts order those children back into harm's way. . . .

The district court faced the following situation. The father easily proved his prima facie case of entitlement to the return remedy. The child's habitual residence has been Canada, and the mother removed the child from the father's custody in violation of his rights as a father (under Canadian law) when she took the child during the family trip to India and flew to her parents' home in the United States. The hearing transcript shows that the judge knew he was supposed to act quickly and that his job was most emphatically not to decide the merits of the underlying custody dispute between the parents. The only serious issue was whether the mother proved by clear and convincing evidence that returning the child to her father in Canada would pose a grave risk to her physically or psychologically. On that issue, the district judge heard testimony for a day. At the end of the hearing, he stated his oral finding that the mother had not proved her defense by clear and convincing evidence. The next day he issued a short written order repeating that finding.

The majority identifies three distinct errors by the district court: (a) failing to make sufficiently specific findings; (b) overlooking a warning in one of our cases not to rely on police and laws of the country of habitual residence to protect a child; and (c) refusing to delay a ruling to give the mother's expert time to conduct a psychological evaluation of the child. As I read this record, the district judge did not commit such reversible errors.

The majority's strongest argument is that the findings were not specific enough and that the judge should have explained in more detail his view of the facts and the testimony of the witnesses. If all we had were the two-page written order, I would agree that more was needed. But we also have more detailed oral explanations that emerged at the end of the hearing as the judge announced his decision, the mother's lawyer argued that the decision was mistaken, and the judge explained his reasoning further. In my view, the transcript is sufficient to understand the judge's thinking. It shows that the judge understood the evidence, understood the law, and did not clearly err by finding that the mother had not proved by clear and convincing evidence that return would pose a grave risk to the child. . .

Did the judge say enough about the only neutral witnesses, the two visitation supervisors? The mother sought to show with their testimony that the child had been traumatized by her father's behavior and that she had spontaneously cried out that he had hurt her. The supervisors' testimony shows that the child is now much more comfortable with her mother than with her father. That is not necessarily surprising after the child's long absence from the father after the abduction and the sudden change of custody ordered by the district court, as at least one supervisor, Ms. Soto, recognized. The judge reasonably described Ms. Kelly's testimony about possible physical abuse as speculative, and he noted further: "But there's been no evidence whatsoever that anything physically was ever done to this child, possibly except squeezing an arm, and that was disputed. But even assuming that there was squeezing of an arm, that's far short of what I would consider establishing grave risk of harm." That is a reasonable view of the evidence, which was not nearly as clear or strong as the mother argues, and it is a reasonable application of the legal standard to that evidence. The judge did not specifically address the testimony of Ms. Soto, who supervised a visit two days before the hearing. Ms. Soto testified that the child was very happy to see her mother, did not want to go home with her father, and became hysterical when told it was time to meet her father. Ms. Soto testified that the child's behavior went beyond separation anxiety and she seemed traumatized. On cross-examination, however, she acknowledged that she would not expect smooth transitions from one parent to another with a young child who has been separated from one parent for 11 months, and when given the opportunity, she did not assert that she thought the child had been abused by her father. Ms. Soto's testimony was so inconclusive that I see no error in failing to address it specifically. . . .

At least for purposes of argument, . . . I will accept the majority's . . . point about possible psychological harm to the child from short-term custody with the father pending a decision by a Canadian court on interim custody. The problem is that the majority's criticism loses sight of the critical point here: the burden to prove "grave risk" to the child by clear and convincing evidence. 42 U.S.C. § 11603(e)(2)(A). With that standard of proof, the judge simply was not required to find that the mother's testimony was either true or false, accurate or mistaken. Faced with conflicting evidence from both the mother and the father, each of whose testimony was weakened by inconsistencies and the conflicting testimony of the other, it's hard to argue with the finding that the mother's evidence was not "clear and convincing." We might wish that the judge had made a crisp call of ball or strike, true or false, but that is not a realistic view of the applicable standard as applied to this conflicting evidence. The district judge was not creating a new "uncertainty exception" to Rule 52(a), as the majority suggests. He was simply applying the clear and convincing burden of proof to evidence that he found neither clear nor convincing.

By imposing the requirement of clear and convincing evidence, Congress was creating a logical space for exactly this sort of finding: the mother might be telling the truth, or so a judge might find by a preponderance of the evidence, but her evidence is still not so persuasive as to be clear and convincing. We might not like that result. . . . We might think that the Convention and the Congress should have made it easier to prove the defense. But under the controlling burden of proof, the defense to the return remedy was not proven. The district judge clearly understood the burden of proof and applied it to reject the defense. I do not see a reversible error there. A more detailed oral or written review of the conflicts in the evidence explaining in more detail why the mother's evidence was not clear and convincing would not have helped the district judge or us.

The majority next suggests that the district judge may have made a legal error, that he may have "overlooked our warning in *Van De Sande v. Van De Sande, supra*, 431 F.3d at 570–71, not to treat the Hague Convention as a venue statute designed 'to deter parents from engaging in international forum shopping in custody cases." The Hague Convention is indeed a venue statute. It is designed to deter exactly such forum-shopping and to prevent litigation of custody in the country chosen by the abducting parent. . . .

The majority suggests the judge made [a] mistake when he asked: "Why can't Canada any more than Illinois protect—offer her protection?" In context, it is clear that the judge was referring to the mother, not to the child. The question was raised as part of the judge's proper effort to satisfy himself that a Canadian family court could quickly take steps to deal with interim questions such as custody, support, including paying needed legal fees. There is no doubt that the mother here would face substantial obstacles litigating in the country of habitual residence, away from her parents. She would need to find a place to live and a lawyer, and she probably would need an award of interim support. But those obstacles are surmountable and in any event are not legitimate grounds for denying the Hague Convention's return remedy.

At the beginning of the hearing, the judge granted the father's motion to exclude testimony from the mother's psychological expert, Dr. Hatcher. Because Dr. Hatcher had not interviewed the mother or the child or anyone else involved in the case, the district court found that the proffered expert opinions would not be helpful. Near the end of the hearing, after the judge had said that grave risk had not been shown, the mother's lawyer asked for another week for Dr. Hatcher to conduct a psychological evaluation of the child and submit a report to the court. The majority finds that the district judge erred by not allowing such a delay. The judge provided a sound reason for not doing so. After discussion back and forth, the court explained: "Based upon what I know of experts, then they come up with an expert, and then you're right back where we started from. One will say that there is, and the other will say there isn't." The judge was clearly indicating that waiting for such an evaluation would lead, at a minimum, to several more weeks of delay to allow for the mother to arrange for that evaluation, for the father to arrange for a similar evaluation, for exchanges of expert reports, and for another evidentiary hearing before the district court. In other words, the judge recognized, he would be hearing a full-blown custody fight, which simply was not his job under the Hague Convention. He was correct, and he certainly did not abuse his discretion.

The finding of error on this point is the most troubling aspect of the majority's decision, in terms of the overall effectiveness of the Hague Convention. The Convention is undermined by expanding the "grave risk" exception into a thorough inquiry into the merits of the custody issue. By finding that the refusal to delay the decision for such additional expert testimony was an abuse of discretion (though the majority does not use that phrase), the expansion of virtually any "grave risk" defense into a full-blown custody hearing becomes nearly inevitable. . . .

I do not mean to exaggerate predictions of doom here. Perhaps the majority's reasoning on this point can be confined to the combination of the allegations, corroborating evidence, procedures, and findings in this case. The majority does not suggest that the refusal of more time for psychological evaluation was alone a sufficient basis to reverse. Yet the risk to the Convention and to the other children and parents it is supposed to protect is nonetheless serious. For these reasons, I would affirm the judgment of the district court and allow the Canadian courts to do their difficult job in dealing with this child and her family.

Note and Question Based on *Kahn v. Fatima*

1. Federal and state courts are congested with heavy caseloads. In some courts it takes months or years to get a case to trial. Not so with Hague Convention cases. Judges take seriously their responsibility to act promptly on Hague Convention matters.[124] Article 1 of the Convention emphasizes the importance of "prompt return of children wrongfully removed." Article 11 requires courts to "act expeditiously in proceedings for the return of children." The decision in *Kahn v. Fatima* is a good illustration of the speed at which Convention cases often fly through the judicial system. The case began in Federal District Court in March 2012. The trial judge held a trial on March 22, and made a ruling the next day. The appeal was argued on May 1, and the Court of Appeal issued its ruling on May 4, 2012. That, ladies and gentlemen, is lightning speed!

2. Which judge has the better of the argument? Judge Posner or Judge Hamilton?

Hague Convention Problems

1. Mom and dad live in France. Mom is a professor of psychology. Dad is a pediatrician. They have two kids, ages 3 and 5. Mom receives an offer to be visiting a professor at the University of California, Berkeley for a year. After mom has been in Berkeley for a semester, the kids arrive for a two week visit. Mom receives an offer of permanent employment on the Berkeley faculty. She accepts. She informs dad she is going to keep the children in the United States. Dad says no, and he files a

---

124 I represented a client with a Hague Convention matter in Federal Court in the Eastern District of California. I was extremely impressed with the efficiency and speed with which the District Court Judge, the Honorable Garland E. Burrell, Jr., handled the matter. The judge made space on his trial calendar, tried the case, and issued a final ruling very quickly.

petition under the Hague Convention for return of the children to France. What ruling should the judge make?

2. Change the facts. When mom came to Berkeley in August, mom and dad agreed the kids would live with mom for the year she was in America. In May, mom gets the offer to stay at Berkeley. Mom informs dad the kids won't be coming home. Dad files under the Convention. Different result?

C

EXPERIENTIAL ASSIGNMENT

Practice Exercise: *Problem Under the Hague Convention on the Civil Aspects of International Child Abduction*

Ellen and Joseph married January 28, 2004 at Pepper Lake City, Utep. Their child, Mary, was born May 23, 2004, in Pepper Lake City. The family lived in Pepper Lake until 2006, when they moved to Salem, Yourstate. Father's extended family, including his parents, has always lived in Salem. In January, 2007, Ellen and Mary moved to Denvil, Coloraska. Joe did not move to Denvil. Ellen and Joe separated when Ellen moved to Denvil in 2007. Ellen has always been Mary's primary custodian. Following the separation in 2007, it was Ellen and Joe's practice for the child to spend part of every summer in Salem with Joe and his parents.

While living in Denvil, Ellen commenced a proceeding for divorce. A Decree of Dissolution of Marriage was entered January 27, 2009 by the District Court in Denvil. The Decree of Dissolution awarded full custody of Mary to Ellen, with visitation to Joe. The Decree states in relevant part, "That the care, custody, and control of the minor child of the parties shall be awarded to Petitioner [Ellen], with reasonable visitation reserved in the Respondent [Joe.]" The Coloraska custody Decree has not been modified. Ellen is the sole legal custodian of Mary.

In 2012, Ellen and Mary moved to Seatol, Washissippi so Ellen could attend the University of Washissippi. While at University, Ellen worked and earned credits toward an undergraduate degree.

In 2014, Ellen received a scholarship to attend the University of Iceland. Ellen has family in Iceland, including her grandmother, four brothers, and numerous aunts, uncles, and cousins. As a child, Ellen resided briefly in Iceland with her mother. In July, 2014, Ellen moved to Iceland to attend the University. At the time of the move, Ellen abandoned Washissippi as her home. Ellen had no intent to return to Washissippi, Coloraska, Utep, or Yourstate. Ellen's primary purpose in moving to Iceland was to complete her university training in order to improve her situation for herself and Mary. When Ellen moved to Iceland, she had not made a final decision to remain in Iceland after completing college. However, the possibility of remaining in Iceland permanently was an option from the beginning. The decision to remain in Iceland with her child was formed as Ellen settled into her new home.

When Ellen moved to Iceland in July, 2014, Mary was on summer vacation with Joe in Yourstate. Mary flew home to Ellen in Iceland in the second week of August, 2014. Mary resided continuously with Ellen in Iceland from the middle of August, 2014 until July 2, 2015. While living in Iceland, Mary attended school, made friends, socialized with her extended family, and acclimated to her new home. Ellen and Mary are dual citizens of the U.S. and Iceland.

Ellen and Joe agreed that Mary would spend the 2015 summer school vacation in Salem, Yourstate. By agreement, Mary was to fly to the United States on July 2, 2015, and return to Iceland on August 15, 2015. Pursuant to the agreement, on July 2, 2015, Ellen put Mary on a plane to travel the United States for summer visitation with Joe.

Joe did not return Mary to Ellen on August 15, 2015, pursuant to the agreement. At no time did Ellen consent to Mary's presence in Salem beyond August 15, 2015.

On August 9, 2015, Joe, through counsel, filed an ex parte Petition for Custody and Protective Order in the Family Court in Salem, Yourstate. On that day, a judge of the family court awarded temporary sole custody to Joe. The judge signed an order that Ellen not remove Mary from Yourstate. Joe's petition and the temporary orders are attached.

Ellen was unaware of the ex parte proceedings in Yourstate. She received in the mail a copy of the petition and orders two weeks after the orders were signed by the judge. On August 12, 2015—unaware of what had happened—Ellen called Joe to finalize plans for Mary's return to Ellen on August 15. Mary answered the phone, and while Ellen was talking to Mary, an e-mail arrived from Joe stating, "Hi—I'll cut to the chase: Mary has made it clear, quite on her own, that she doesn't want to return to Iceland. She is adamant. For this, and for my own reasons, I have had the matter examined. At this time, the state of Yourstate has decided that no one is permitted to remove her from the state. Further information can be obtained from, and all questions regarding this can be directed to my attorney."

Upon learning that Joe would not return Mary, Ellen immediately contacted the Iceland Ministry of Justice and Human Rights. On August 20, 2015, Ellen filed with the Ministry a Request for Return of Child Under the 1980 Hague Convention on the Civil Aspects of International Child Abduction. The Ministry in Iceland contacted the U.S. Department of State, which is the Central Authority in the United States for purposes of the Convention.

You are on a State Department list of attorneys who are willing to take Hague Convention cases. The State Department gave your name to Ellen. On October 14, 2015, Ellen contacted you to determine if you would represent her in the State Court custody proceeding. You agreed to represent Ellen.

In the divorce, Joe was ordered to pay child support. Joe has not paid support, and is currently $60,000 in arrears. Child support enforcements authorities pulled Joe's passport, making it impossible for him to travel.

Assignment: In your representation of Ellen, address the following matters:

1. What, if anything, can you do about the state court orders giving Joe temporary custody and ordering Ellen not to remove Mary from Salem? Are the orders valid? Can you have the orders dismissed or vacated?

When you read the portion of Joe's Petition (see below) regarding where Mary has lived in previous years—information that is required by the UCCJEA—you note that Joe says (under oath) that Mary "resided" with Joe in Yourstate from October 2009 to the present. You believe this statement is false. You believe the statement was included in the affidavit in order to convince the family court judge that Mary has been in Yourstate more than six months. If the judge realized Mary was in Yourstate only for a summer visit with Joe, the judge probably would not have signed the orders for temporary custody and non-removal. You don't know whether Joe made an innocent mistake when he said Mary "resided" in Yourstate since 2009, or whether he deliberately lied to get an advantage in court. If it was an innocent mistake, you don't know whether the mistake was made by Joe or his attorney. If it was a deliberate lie, you don't know whether the lie was made by Joe or his attorney. It is possible that Joe, a lay person, might not understand the legal significance of "resided." But would a lawyer who is familiar with the requirements of the UCCJEA lack such understanding? Of course, it was the lawyer, not Joe, who drafted the Petition containing Joe's inaccurate statement. Or perhaps a paralegal drafted the Petition, and the attorney didn't see the mistake. What do you think you should do about this? Obviously, if the attorney intentionally misstated a critically important fact—Mary resided in Yoursate—in order to mislead the judge, this is a very serious ethical violation. Moreover, it is a violation that hurt your client. What should you do?

2. Can Ellen's rights to custody be protected under the UCCJEA alone? Do you need to invoke the Hague Convention on the Civil Aspects of International Child Abduction? Should you proceed under the UCCJEA *and* the Hague Convention?

John Jeffers
State Bar Number 98765
3100 32nd Ave.
Salem, Yourstate 96017
Telephone: 961-375-7176
Attorney for Petitioner

SUPERIOR COURT OF YOURSTATE
COUNTY OF COLUSA
SITTING AS A FAMILY COURT

Joseph Mays,	FL 3575
Petitioner,	
vs.	Ex Parte Petition for Custody and Support of Minor Children
Ellen Mays,	
Respondent.	

Petitioner, Joseph Mays, is the father of Mary Mays, born 5/23/2004. Respondent is the child's mother.

I request the following orders: Legal and physical custody of the child.

I further request that a child abduction prevention order be granted restraining Respondent, Ellen Mays, from removing the child from Yourstate.

I declare that the following facts are true and correct for purposes of child custody jurisdiction under the UCCJEA.

The child, Mary Mays, has lived at the following addresses:

October 2009 to the present, the child has resided with me at my home, 1113 Carob Ct., Salem, Yoursate.

August 2014 to July 2, 2015, the child was with Respondent in Iceland.

2012 to August 2014, the child was with Respondent in Seatol, Washissippi.

2007 to 2012, the child resided with Respondent in Devil, Coloraska.

May 23, 2004 to November 2006, the child resided with Respondent and me in Pepper Lake City, Utep.

In 2009, I was divorced from Respondent by the court in Denvil, Coloraska.

I declare under penalty of perjury under the laws of the State of Yourstate that the foregoing is true and correct.

Date: August 9, 2015.   <u>Joseph Mays</u>

SUPERIOR COURT OF YOURSTATE
COUNTY OF COLUSA
SITTING AS A FAMILY COURT

Joseph Mays,	FL 3575
Petitioner,	
vs.	Order for Temporary Custody;
	Child Abduction Prevention Order
Ellen Mays,	
Respondent.	

The Court, being fully advised, the following orders are made:

1. Temporary legal and physical custody of the minor child, Mary Mays, DOB 5/23/2004, is hereby awarded to Joseph Mays until further order of this Court.

2. Respondent, Ellen Mays, must not remove the minor child from the State of Yourstate without further order of this Court.

IT IS SO ORDERED.

Dated: August 9, 2015.   Mary Molinari, Judge

                                        Judge of the Superior Court

Visitation (Parenting Time)

A parent who is not awarded custody receives "visitation," also called "parenting time." Reasonable visitation is automatic unless the non-custodial parent forfeited the right through misconduct. Visitation is subject to modification on a showing of substantial changed circumstances. In *Collier v. Harris*,[125] the Alaska Supreme Court wrote, "We have said that a lesser showing is required for a 'change in circumstances' determination when a parent seeks to modify visitation rather than custody."

Problems on Modification of Visitation

1. Michelle and Vernon were married a short time. They separated before the birth of their daughter. In their divorce, Michelle and Vernon agreed that Michelle would have custody. Michelle intended to breast feed the baby. Michelle was unable to use a breast pump. The parties agreed that to accommodate breast feeding, until the child was 18 months old, Vernon would have visitation from 4:00 p.m. until 8:00 p.m. every Tuesday and Thursday, as well as on every other Friday, Saturday, and Sunday from 4:00 to 8:00 p.m. The agreement provided that when the child turned 18 months, Vernon would have five weeks of uninterrupted visitation each summer as well as alternating weekends and holidays. At the time of divorce, the expectation of the parties was that the child would be weaned by 18 months. As it turned out, the child was not weaned at 18 months, and Michelle continues breast feeding. Michelle desires to breast feed until the child turns two, and Michelle asked Vernon to adhere to their original 4:00 p.m. to 8:00 p.m. schedule until the child's second birthday. Vernon would not agree. Vernon insists he has a right under the original agreement to five weeks of visitation in the summer, which is fast approaching. Because Vernon will not agree to depart from the original schedule, Michelle returned to family court with a motion to modify visitation. Michelle argues she should be permitted to breast feed until the child turns two, and that the court should order adherence to the original 4:00 p.m. to 8:00 p.m. visitation schedule. How should the judge rule? *Brown v. Brown*, 2012 WL 663161 (Ark. 2012).

2. Vickie and Gordon have three daughters, ages 8, 10, and 13. Vickie and Gordon divorced three years ago. The divorce decree awarded custody to Vickie

125 261 P.3d 397 (Alaska 2011).

and visitation for Gordon. Specifically, the decree provides that the girls spend two months every summer with Gordon. During summer, when the kids are with Gordon, Vickie can take the girls to her home for a day every other week. Vickie and Gordon live about 50 miles apart. During the majority of the year, while the children live with Vickie, Gordon is entitled to visitation with them at his home every other weekend. The visitation arrangement worked well for two summers. As the third summer approached, two of the girls told Vickie they didn't want to spend the entire summer with Gordon. The 8-year-old said, "I miss you, mommy, when I'm at daddy's house. I want to stay here this summer and visit daddy on the weekends." Vickie decided it is not in the children's best interest to spend so long away from home in a city 50 miles away, removed from their friends and local activities. When Gordon would not agree to modify his summer visitation, Vickie went to court asking the judge to modify visitation. Vickie asks that during summers, the children take short visits of three or four days with Gordon. As the moving party, Vickie has the burden to prove substantial changed circumstances. On these facts, are the circumstances changed substantially? *Stellpflug v. Stellpflug,* 70 Ark. App. 88, 14 S.W.3d 536 (2000).

Visitation with Non-Parents

Do non-parents have a right to visit children with whom they have a significant relationship? Most of the law on this issue concerns grandparents. The issue of grandparent visitation reached the U.S. Supreme Court in *Troxel v. Granville.*[126] The Court affirmed the right of parents to make decisions regarding their children, including decisions about whether other persons, including grandparents, should visit the children. The Court ruled that the decision whether to allow grandparents to visit "is for the parent in the first instance. And, if a fit parent's decision of the kind at issue here becomes subject to judicial review, the court must accord at least some special weight to the parent's own determination." In *Marriage of Deuel,*[127] the California Court of Appeal discussed *Troxel v. Granville*:

> The due process clause protects the fundamental right of custodial parents to make decisions concerning the care, custody, and control of their children. A presumption exists that fit parents act in the best interests of their children. *Troxel* held that a Washington statute, under which grandparents were given visitation over the parent's

---

126　530 U.S. 57 (2000).

127　2007 WL 2318744 (Cal. Ct. App. 2007)(not reported).

objection, was unconstitutional as applied, since the trial court gave no special weight to the parent's determination of her daughters' best interest and thus violated the parent's fundamental constitutional right to make decisions for her children. *Troxel* essentially affirmed the cardinal rule, as stated by the Supreme Court, that "the custody, care and nurture of the child reside first in the parents, whose primary function and freedom include preparation for obligations the state can neither supply nor hinder." Encompassed within this well-established fundamental right of parents to raise their children is the right to determine with whom their children should associate.

Thus, a court may not disregard and overturn the decisions of fit custodial parents whenever a third party affected by the decision files a visitation petition. As to grandparents, however, a court is not precluded from granting visitation over the objection of a "fit" parent. The decision of fit parents regarding grandparent visitation is entitled to special weight, but not necessarily immunity from judicial review.

A court does not have any inherent jurisdiction or equitable power to entertain a nonparent's visitation request. Instead, grandparents' rights to court-ordered visitation with their grandchildren are purely statutory.

The Minnesota Supreme Court's decision in *Rohmiller v. Hart* provides useful analysis of non-parent visitation.

Rohmiller v. Hart

Supreme Court of Minnesota
811 N.W.2d 585 (2012)

Gildea, Chief Justice.

This case concerns Kelli Rohmiller's petition for visitation with her niece, B.H. The district court awarded Rohmiller visitation with B.H. under Minn. Stat. § 257C.08 (2010) on terms to which B.H.'s father, Andrew Hart, objects. The court of appeals reversed. Because we conclude that Rohmiller is not entitled to visitation under either Minn.Stat. § 257C.08 or the common law, we affirm.

Rohmiller is the identical twin sister of B.H.'s mother, who is now deceased. Hart and B.H.'s mother had resided together for approximately the first year of

B.H.'s life. Around B.H.'s first birthday, however, Hart injured B.H. in an incident that resulted in Hart pleading guilty to malicious punishment of a child. After this incident, Hart and the mother separated and B.H. and her mother moved to Iowa. For the next year, B.H. and her mother lived with various members of the mother's family, including Rohmiller. During that year, Rohmiller resided with B.H. for approximately 5 weeks, and otherwise saw B.H. approximately 8 hours per month. After B.H.'s mother died, a different family member (who is not a party to this case) petitioned for custody of B.H. in an out-of-state proceeding. Hart was awarded custody of B.H. in that proceeding. Hart then moved with B.H. to Minnesota. After Hart moved to Minnesota, he did not allow the Rohmiller family to visit B.H.

Rohmiller and her father, Clayton Rohmiller, petitioned the district court for visitation with B.H. "pursuant to Minn.Stat. § 257C.08, and all the laws and equities of the State of Minnesota." The district court appointed a Guardian ad Litem for B.H. and both Hart and Rohmiller were evaluated by a forensic psychologist. Although the guardian found that there was animosity between the parties, the guardian's report indicated that both Hart and Rohmiller are positive forces in B.H.'s life. The report stated that B.H. was "flourishing" under Hart's care and that B.H. and Rohmiller had a good relationship. The psychologist concluded that Hart was a "dedicated child-centered parent" and that Rohmiller also had a child-centered approach to parenting but that "it would be important if Rohmiller had visitation with B.H. that there would be clear communication and understanding of Hart's parenting goals and parental expectations." The guardian's report concluded that it would be in B.H.'s best interest for both Rohmiller and Clayton to be awarded visitation.

By the time of the evidentiary hearing on Rohmiller and Clayton's petition, Hart no longer objected to visitation between B.H. and Clayton, provided that such visitation occurred in Minnesota and subject to other conditions. Nor did Hart object to Rohmiller seeing B.H. during visits between B.H. and Clayton. But Hart argued that Rohmiller had no right to visitation with B.H. independent of Clayton.

After an evidentiary hearing, the district court "jointly granted" Rohmiller and Clayton unsupervised visitation with B.H. The court provided that the Rohmillers "do not have to both be present during visitation" and that Rohmiller could "exercise visitation without the presence of" Clayton. The court noted that Minn.Stat. § 257C.08 does not specifically grant visitation rights to aunts or uncles, but concluded that "the statute does not preclude or prohibit visitation" with classes of people outside of the statute. Turning to case law, the court cited *State ex rel. Burris v. Hiller*, 258 Minn. 491, 501,

104 N.W.2d 851, 858 (1960), for the proposition that Minnesota courts have "previously determined that aunts and uncles have certain rights with respect to visiting their nieces and nephews." Finally, the court concluded that courts sit as parens patriae in matters regarding children, and that courts have broad equitable powers in such matters. Based on these conclusions, the court decided that Minn.Stat. § 257C.08, interpreted broadly, did not preclude granting visitation to Rohmiller.

Hart appealed to the court of appeals, challenging the amount of visitation awarded to Clayton and the grant of any visitation to Rohmiller "independent of that exercised by Clayton." The court of appeals affirmed the district court's grant of visitation to Clayton. But the court of appeals reversed the award of visitation to Rohmiller, holding that Minn.Stat. § 257C.08 does not extend visitation rights to aunts generally and that she had no right to visitation under Minnesota law apart from the statute.

We granted Rohmiller's petition for review. Rohmiller urges us to reverse the court of appeals, contending that the district court properly awarded her third-party visitation under Minn.Stat. § 257C.08. Alternatively, Rohmiller argues that the district court properly awarded her visitation under the common law or the court's equitable powers.

We turn first to Rohmiller's argument that she has a right to visitation with B.H. under Minn.Stat. § 257C.08.

The statute at issue, Minn.Stat. § 257C.08, allows a court to award visitation rights to petitioners who meet specific criteria. Subdivision 1 provides for visitation by a child's grandparents and great-grandparents:

> If a parent of an unmarried minor child is deceased, the parents and grandparents of the deceased parent may be granted reasonable visitation rights to the unmarried minor child during minority by the district court upon finding that visitation rights would be in the best interests of the child and would not interfere with the parent child relationship. The court shall consider the amount of personal contact between the parents or grandparents of the deceased parent and the child prior to the application.

Minn.Stat. § 257C.08, subd. 1. Subdivision 4 provides for visitation by other persons with whom the child has resided for 2 or more years:

> If an unmarried minor has resided in a household with a person, other than a foster parent, for two years or more and no longer

resides with the person, the person may petition the district court for an order granting the person reasonable visitation rights to the child during the child's minority. The court shall grant the petition if it finds that:

> (1) visitation rights would be in the best interests of the child;
>
> (2) the petitioner and child had established emotional ties creating a parent and child relationship; and
>
> (3) visitation rights would not interfere with the relationship between the custodial parent and the child.

The court shall consider the reasonable preference of the child, if the court considers the child to be of sufficient age to express a preference.

Neither of these provisions, by their plain language, allows a court to award visitation to Rohmiller over the objections of Hart. She is neither a parent nor grandparent of B.H.'s mother and therefore does not satisfy subdivision 1. And subdivision 4 is not satisfied because Rohmiller did not show that she had established emotional ties creating a parent-child relationship with B.H. and B.H. did not reside with Rohmiller for two years.

Rohmiller urges us to look past the clear and unambiguous plain language of Minn.Stat. § 257C.08 in order to avoid an absurd result. Rohmiller contends that it would be absurd for the legislature to exclude step-parents, step-grand-parents, step-siblings, cousins, significant others, and others who had not maintained a parent-child relationship with a child for at least 2 years from gaining visitation to that child because there "is no magic relationship that is formed" after 2 years.

We are very reluctant to look past the plain language of an unambiguous statute. We will do so only when the plain meaning of a statute utterly confounds a clear legislative purpose.

In essence, Rohmiller argues that because the legislature extended visitation rights to grandparents in Minn.Stat. § 257C.08, it would be an absurd result not to extend visitation rights to other family members even though these family members do not satisfy the plain language of the statute. We disagree. Rohmiller concedes that she is not now, and never has been, in loco parentis with B.H. To the extent the legislative purpose in enacting Minn.Stat. § 257C.08 was to provide visitation rights for family members other than grandparents, the legislature specifically codified the requirement that those persons be in loco parentis with the child. Applying the plain language of the statute not to provide for a right to visitation to an aunt who does not stand in loco parentis with the child therefore does not confound the legislative purpose in enacting Minn.Stat. § 257C.08 or otherwise lead to an absurd result.

In sum, we hold that Rohmiller is not entitled to visitation with B.H. under the plain language of the statute.

We turn next to Rohmiller's argument that the district court had authority to award her visitation outside the confines of Minn.Stat. § 257C.08. Rohmiller argues, in essence, that the court had authority to grant visitation based on the equitable powers of the court. We disagree.

We turn to Rohmiller's argument that the district court, sitting as a court of equity, properly exercised its role as parens patriae in matters concerning children to grant her visitation with B.H. over the objections of B.H.'s father. Rohmiller first notes that the district court supported its determination that Rohmiller and Clayton be awarded visitation rights with B.H. with numerous detailed findings of fact. We do not disagree with Rohmiller that the court's conclusion that it would be in B.H.'s best interest for B.H. to maintain contact with her mother's family through visitation with Clayton finds support in the record. That is not the question presented for our review. Rather, the question is whether the court had authority to order visitation with Rohmiller independent of B.H.'s visitation with Clayton and over the objection of B.H.'s father. Based on our review of the record, we conclude that the court lacked this authority.

There is no question in this case that Hart has been determined to be a fit parent and that he objects to Rohmiller's visitation with B.H. independent of visitation by Clayton. Rohmiller acknowledges that a fit parent's right to make decisions concerning the care, custody, and control of his or her children is a fundamental right protected by the federal and Minnesota constitutions. *See Troxel v. Granville*, 530 U.S. 57, 65–66, 120 S.Ct. 2054 (2000). We need not decide in this case whether the district court has the equitable authority to award visitation to a petitioner who has never stood in loco parentis with the child over the objection of a fit parent because Rohmiller concedes that any such order would be subject to the United States Supreme Court's analysis in *Troxel*, and as set forth below, the district court's order providing Rohmiller with visitation independent of Clayton's visitation cannot be sustained under that analysis.

In *Troxel*, the Supreme Court discussed the relationship between a parent's fundamental right to raise his or her children and third-party visitation statutes. The Court held unconstitutional a Washington statute granting "any person" standing to petition for visitation at "any time" so long as visitation was in the best interests of the child. The Court based its decision on the "sweeping breadth" of the Washington statute but specifically declined to consider whether any non-parent visitation statute could be constitutional or to define the precise standards that would allow a visitation statute to pass constitutional muster.

In *SooHoo* [*v. Johnson*, 731 N.W.2d 815 (Minn. 2007)], we read *Troxel* to require that a third-party visitation statute adhere to three guiding principles in order to be constitutional. First, the statute must give some special weight to the fit custodial parent's decision regarding visitation. Second, there can be no presumption in favor of awarding visitation. Third, the court must assert more than a mere best-interest analysis in support of its decision to override the fit parent's wishes.

Rohmiller acknowledges that the principles from *Troxel* that we applied in *SooHoo* to Minn.Stat. § 257C.08 govern the district court's decision to grant her petition for visitation. Based on Rohmiller's concession, we assume, but do not decide, that the analysis we applied in *SooHoo* to the statute also governs the district court's decision to grant extra-statutory visitation to a petitioner such as Rohmiller, who has never stood in loco parentis with the child but seeks visitation over the objection of a fit parent. We conclude Rohmiller is not entitled to visitation under that standard.

We need look no further than the third principle. Under the third principle from *Troxel* and *SooHoo*, the district court was required to apply more than a mere "best interests" analysis to overcome Hart's visitation determination. The district court found that visitation with Rohmiller and Clayton was in B.H.'s best interests because B.H. would likely suffer emotional harm if ties to the maternal family were severed. Therefore, it appears that the court used more than a "best interests" analysis to decide that visitation with the maternal family was warranted.

But Hart is not contesting visitation with the maternal family; he is contesting only visitation between B.H. and Rohmiller independent of visitation with Clayton. The district court made no findings that B.H. would suffer emotional damage if she was not allowed to visit with Rohmiller, or any other member of the Rohmiller family, independent of visitation with Clayton. Nor do the court's findings indicate that it applied anything more than a mere "best interests" analysis in determining that Rohmiller was entitled to visitation independent of Clayton's visitation. The court's conclusion with respect to Rohmiller's visitation was simply that "visitation between Kelli Rohmiller and the child is in the child's best interest and will not interfere with the parent-child relationship of Hart and the child." In order to overcome the wishes of a fit parent, however, *SooHoo* requires more than a best interests analysis.

Because the district court made no findings to suggest that it used more than a mere "best interests" analysis in deciding to allow Rohmiller to exercise visitation independent from Clayton, we hold that the court erred. This opinion should not be read, however, to prevent Rohmiller from seeing B.H. while B.H. is visiting Clayton.

Affirmed.

——————————

In *Bowen v. Bowen*, the Arkansas Court of Appeals grapples with grandparent visitation.

Bowen v. Bowen

Court of Appeals of Arkansas
2012 WL 2406030 (2012)

Larry D. Vaught, Chief Judge.

Appellant Nicholas Bowen (Nick) argues on appeal that the circuit court erred in granting his parents, appellees Letizia and David Bowen, visitation with their grandchildren (Alex, age twelve and Kate, age ten) under Arkansas's grandparent-visitation statute. Specifically, he claims that there was insufficient evidence to support the trial court's conclusion that the court-ordered grandparent visitation was in his children's best interest. We agree and reverse.

Nick Bowen and Helene Wade divorced in 2005, and they were awarded joint custody of their two minor children—with Nick having custody in the summer and Helene having custody during the school year. The following year, the parties entered into an agreement in which they alternated care of the children on a weekly basis. In 2010, Nick and Helene agreed to homeschool their children in Nick's home. Nick's current wife, Amy Bowen, homeschooled the kids with the assistance of their mother, Helene.

In September 2010, Nick petitioned for ex parte drug testing and immediate custody of the children based on Helene's drug use. After Helene tested positive for illegal substances, the court awarded Nick sole custody of the minor children and visitation to Helene. The trial court also allowed Nick's parents, Letizia and David, to intervene and seek grandparent visitation in the underlying domestic-relations case between Nick and Helene.

The trial court set the hearing on grandparent visitation for April 2011 and ultimately ordered that Letizia and David receive visitation with their grandchildren, one weekend per month with extended time during the summer and holidays. The court further ordered that this time be taken from Nick's time with his children. It is from this order that Nick appeals. . . .

Grandparent visitation is governed by Arkansas Code Annotated section 9–13–103. Grandparent visitation is a statutorily created right and in derogation of common law; therefore, we must strictly construe the statute. Specifically, our statute states, in pertinent part:

> (b) A grandparent or great-grandparent may petition a circuit court of this state for reasonable visitation rights with respect to his or her grandchild or grandchildren or great-grandchild or great-grandchildren under this section if:
>
> > (1) The marital relationship between the parents of the child has been severed by death, divorce, or legal separation;
> >
> > ...
>
> (c) (1) There is a rebuttable presumption that a custodian's decision denying or limiting visitation to the petitioner is in the best interest of the child.
>
> > (2) To rebut the presumption, the petitioner must prove by a preponderance of the evidence the following:
> >
> > > (A) The petitioner has established a significant and viable relationship with the child for whom he or she is requesting visitation; and
> > >
> > > (B) Visitation with the petitioner is in the best interest of the child.
>
> (d) To establish a significant and viable relationship with the child, the petitioner must prove by a preponderance of the evidence the following:
>
> > (1) (A) The child resided with the petitioner for at least six (6) consecutive months with or without the current custodian present;
> >
> > > (B) The petitioner was the caregiver to the child on a regular basis for at least six (6) consecutive months; or
> > >
> > > (C) The petitioner had frequent or regular contact with the child for at least twelve (12) consecutive months; or
> >
> > (2) Any other facts that establish that the loss of the relationship between the petitioner and the child is likely to harm the child.
>
> (e) To establish that visitation with the petitioner is in the best interest of

the child, the petitioner must prove by a preponderance of the evidence the following:

(1) The petitioner has the capacity to give the child love, affection, and guidance;

(2) The loss of the relationship between the petitioner and the child is likely to harm the child; and

(3) The petitioner is willing to cooperate with the custodian if visitation with the child is allowed.

Here, Letizia and David have standing to petition for visitation because the marriage of the grandchildren's parents ended by divorce in 2005. We note that the rationale behind Arkansas's requirement that the marriage be severed before giving grandparents standing to seek visitation must (at least in great part) be in response to a concern that the custodial parent's judgment may contain animosity toward the noncustodial parent and/or the grandparents as a result of the divorce. And, with an intact marriage, the grandparents have a greater "voice" in this situation because their own child is a player in the parenting paradigm. Uniquely, we note that in this case the increased amount of visitation that Letizia and David sought (and were denied) was exclusively at their own son's discretion.

Under the statute, there is a rebuttable presumption that Nick's decision to limit the time his children spent with his parents was in his children's best interest. To rebut this presumption, Letizia and David were first required to prove by a preponderance of the evidence that they had established a significant and viable relationship with the children. The parties agreed that, prior to the divorce, in the early years of the children's lives, they were with Nick's parents a great deal. Letizia and David took the children on trips, babysat them, and assisted in transporting them to various activities and events. And, as the trial court found, after the parties' relationship became strained, the grandparents went "beyond the call of duty" to see the children at school. In fact, there is no question that the evidence supports a conclusion that Letizia and David had a significant and viable relationship with the children. Therefore, the primary issue we are concerned with on appeal is whether visitation with Letizia and David was in the children's best interest.

To prove that visitation with Letizia and David was in Alex's and Kate's best interests, the grandparents had to show (1) that they have the capacity to give the children love, affection, and guidance, (2) that the loss of the relationship between them and their grandchildren would likely cause harm to the grandchildren, and (3) that they are willing to cooperate with their son if visitation is allowed. Two of these elements are beyond question. There is no dispute that Letizia and David are capable of providing love, affection, and guidance toward Alex and Kate. There is clearly animosity between the grandparents and their son, but there is nothing in the record to show that this took away from their ability to provide love, affection, and guidance to the grandchildren. The record also unquestionably supports the finding that Letizia and David are willing to cooperate with Nick if visitation is allowed. Throughout their testimony, the grandparents stated that they would comply with any instruction given to them by the circuit court. Therefore, the question before us now is very narrowly set out. We must consider whether Letizia and David adequately carried their burden of showing that the relationship between them and their grandchildren had been lost and that the loss of the relationship would likely cause harm to Alex and Kate. . . .

The evidence showed that, after the divorce, Nick's relationship with his father deteriorated. The record establishes that Nick was fired by his father's plumbing company; Nick later married Amy; he distanced himself from his parents; and he and his parents only had contact while attending family events or the children's activities. However, the evidence also shows that at no time during the strained relationship were Nick's parents completely denied contact with the children. According to the evidence introduced at trial, the grandparents eventually settled into a weekly visit with the children during the children's school lunch hour. This continued for a five-year period, with the grandparents neither asking for nor receiving additional visitation. However, in 2010, when the decision was made to begin homeschooling the children, the grandparents were no longer able to see the children at school during lunch. In response, Letizia and David petitioned the court for grandparent visitation.

According to the record, although the grandparents were receiving visitation at the time they filed their petition (and more so after the filing), it was extremely limited. There was also testimony that Nick intended to phase his parents out of the children's lives. Nick testified that he limited his parents' relationship with his children because he had a strained relationship with his parents; he felt that his parents often interfered with his parenting decisions; and his mother was in the habit of planning and programming the children's time every weekend that his children were in his care.

As Letizia and David note in their brief, Nick said that he wants his children to have a relationship with their grandparents, "but will only do so under his terms." Based on the record before us, we are satisfied that there is sufficient evidence to support the trial court's conclusion that Nick "effectively" denied his parents visitation, which—absent a showing that the denial would harm the children—he was well within his rights as the children's sole custodial parent to do.

The trial court found that "by virtue of denying the children contact with their paternal grandparents, terrible harm is occurring to these children." In support of this conclusion, the trial court noted that the children benefited from visits with their grandparents and that they were provided "an opportunity to travel" and "gain advice from respected family members." The trial court also found that the children will be smarter and enriched if they engaged in travel during their lives. However, there was no evidence showing that the inverse will occur if the children did not frequently visit their grandparents. The record is completely void of any proof showing the children had been, or likely would be, harmed without court-mandated visitation with their grandparents.

Our statute not only has a presumption in the favor of the custodial parent—giving the parent's decision presumptive or special weight in deciding whether grandparent visitation is in the best interest of the child—the statute also requires the existence of a substantial relationship between grandchild and grandparent before the grandparent has standing to petition the court for visitation. Requiring a "substantial relationship" implies that grandparent visitation is not accepted as being beneficial, per se. And, more important, a substantial relationship does not necessarily mean the child is harmed if visitation is denied. In fact, in order to overcome the presumption that a fit parent is necessarily acting in his children's best interest, our statute requires both a showing of a substantial grandparent-grandchild relationship, and a showing that a denial of that relationship "is likely to harm the child."

In this case, the reality remains that for the five years immediately preceding Letizia and David's filing of their grandparent-visitation petition the children had only seen their grandparents on a limited basis—once a week, at lunch, during the school year. While there is no doubt that these short visits were enjoyable and perhaps even beneficial to the children, there is a substantial difference between the existence of a relationship benefiting a child and the denial of that relationship harming a child.

In formulating the threshold of proof required to show harm under Arkansas's grandparent-visitation statute, we look to other jurisdictions with similar statutory requirements. In *Moriarty v. Bradt*, the Supreme Court of New Jersey examined a visitation dispute under the harm standard. 827 A.2d 203 (N.J. 2003) (requiring a showing of harm to the child before the court will consider awarding visitation rights). In *Moriarty*, the parents divorced and remarried other people, but the children continued to spend a lot of time with the maternal grandparents. The children's mother later died of a drug overdose, and the father greatly limited visitation with the maternal grandparents because he blamed them for his ex-wife's drug addiction. The court explained that the grandparents must demonstrate harm to the children absent visitation with them, at which point the court would then consider what was in the children's best interests.

The New Jersey court found that denying the grandparents visitation rights would harm the children because the children previously had a very close relationship with the grandparents, and they had no other way to stay connected to the memory of their mother. The grandparents presented expert testimony that the children were devastated by the death of their mother and that abruptly ending visitation with the grandparents would cause severe psychological damage to the children. The grandparents further argued that, in their absence, the father might disparage the mother to the children, and therefore the children's only source of information about their mother would portray her as "evil." The court upheld the visitation order, but in doing so, set a very high bar of what constitutes "harm" to the child—the lack of connection with a deceased parent and the consequent risk that the children will suffer psychologically.

Likewise, in *Luke v. Luke*, 634 S.E.2d 439 (Ga. Ct. App. 2006), the court considered what showing of harm is required to support an award of grandparent visitation. In Luke, the children's mother and father divorced, but continued to allow visitation with all grandparents. The children spent every other weekend with their paternal grandparents, developing a very close bond. When the children's father went overseas on military duty, the mother sought to limit the paternal grandparents' visitation. The mother believed that the grandparents "shuffled" the children around too much, that the children returned from visits emotionally distressed, and that the grandmother may have slapped one of the children.

The Georgia court found that the denial of visitation would cause harm to the children and awarded visitation rights to the paternal grandparents. The grandparents explained that "with the children's father now serving with the U.S. Army, the children's ties with their paternal family would be virtually destroyed without such visitation." Further, the grandparents had developed such an intense bond with the grandchildren that cutting off visitation with the grandparents would cause the children "actual emotional harm." The harm in this case was the sudden termination of a strong, personal relationship and the threat of the children losing their memory of a parent.

Like New Jersey and Georgia—by requiring a grandparent to show that the child is likely to suffer actual harm if the requested visitation is denied—Arkansas recognizes in its grandparent-visitation statute recognizes that the right to care for and raise one's own child is a fundamental liberty interest that is protected by the Due Process Clause of the Fourteenth Amendment. . . .

In this case, the trial court substituted a benefit analysis for our required statutory presumption in favor of the parent's decision. In so doing, the trial court basically required Nick to prove that visitation would be harmful, losing sight of the fact that it is the parent who has a right to uninterrupted custody. Instead, the court should have required that Letizia and David show (1) that Nick's requiring the visitation to be "on his terms" or be effectively denied would likely harm the grandchildren and (2) that granting visitation was necessary to remedy this harm. Because these burdens were neither required by the trial court nor met by the petitioners in this case, we reverse the decision of the trial court.

Reversed.

Brown J., dissenting.

I must respectfully dissent from the majority holding in this case. . . .

As the majority acknowledges, there is no dispute that the only issue before us is whether appellees met the statutory requirement to show that the loss of the relationship between them and their grandchildren was likely to harm the children; the statute does not require a showing of actual harm. It is undisputed, either in the record below or by this court on appeal, that appellees had a significant and viable relationship with their grandchildren, that the relationship was beneficial to the children and in their best interest, and that the relationship had been effectively denied by appellant. However, the majority asserts, "There is a substantial difference between a relationship benefiting a child and the denial of that relationship harming a child."

The reasoning behind identifying such a "substantial difference" is anything but clear. How can one rationally say that the loss of a beneficial, loving, and significant relationship with a grandparent is not harmful, or at least evidence of likely harm? To say otherwise is contrary to all logic and reason, not to mention human experience and common sense. The harm is that the Bowen children have been denied a benefit they once enjoyed. At the very least, the denial of such a benefit constitutes evidence of likely harm—which is all the statute expressly requires—and provides a basis for the circuit court's ruling. If, as the majority contends, the legislature intended to set a higher burden of proof on the element of likely harm, that intent was expressed nowhere in the statute. . . .

The circuit court in this case, after evaluating the witnesses and their testimony, found that it was in the best interest of the Bowen children to order visitation with their grandparents, so that the children could once again enjoy the benefits of that relationship. Based on the evidence presented and the deference with which we are required to treat the circuit court's findings of fact and credibility, I cannot see how the court's grant of visitation can be deemed an abuse of discretion.

Question based on *Bowen v. Bowen*

Where do you come down? Majority or dissent?

Problems on Non-Parent Visitation

1. Mother and father met in San Diego when mother was a helicopter pilot for the Navy. They began living together two weeks after they met, later moving to a boat in the Chula Vista marina. They married three months after they met. They separated four years later, 10 days before the birth of their daughter, Emily. Mother filed for dissolution of marriage three months later. Mother claimed that during the marriage, father was psychologically and physically abusive to her. He hit her and called her names. On one occasion, he pushed her overboard and tried to run her over with their dinghy as she swam to shore. During an altercation when she was six months pregnant, he kicked her in the stomach. Father denied these accusations, but admitted using and selling marijuana and, on one occasion, using methamphetamine. Father also admitted striking and biting mother on several occasions that he described as mutually combative.

After Emily was born, mother stayed with a friend. She regularly took Emily to visit father. The California family court entered judgment dissolving the marriage and granting mother sole legal and physical custody of Emily. The judgment also provided that mother could move to Maryland with Emily. Father was granted supervised visitation contingent on his undergoing psychotherapy, drug testing, and attending Narcotics Anonymous meetings. A schedule was established for visitation pending mother's move to Maryland, which permitted the paternal grandparents to be present. By stipulation, the paternal grandparents were joined as parties to the action. They agreed not to interfere with the mother's scheduled move to Maryland.

After several months, the paternal grandparents filed a motion in California seeking visitation. The grandparents alleged that mother would not permit visitation absent a court order. The grandparents asked that Emily spend 10 days at their home every other month. Mother's response noted that Emily was 11 months old and was still nursing. Mother asked that all visitation take place in Maryland where she was living with her parents. A counselor conducted a mediation session in which mother participated by telephone and the parties agreed that the grandparents would visit Emily in Maryland for approximately 10 days, six times a year, with no overnight visits. Following a hearing, the court granted the grandparents visitation with Emily in Maryland with no overnight visits and without the father being present, four visits per year for up to seven days each. Six months later, mother filed a motion to terminate the grandparents' visitation rights, alleging that during a visit, the grandparents "were extremely hostile and filled with conflict" and that the visit had been detrimental to Emily. Mother declared that Emily had nightmares after the grandparents' visit, cried during her nap times, and clung to the mother "for days after the visit," all of which behavior was unusual for her. The grandparents filed a responsive declaration in which they agreed that the visits had been hostile, but placed the blame on mother.

Following a hearing, the court denied mother's motion to terminate the grandparents' visitation rights. Following this, the grandparents provided mother with 30 days' notice of their intention to visit Emily, but received no response. They traveled to the mother's residence in Maryland and discovered that mother and Emily had moved. The grandparents hired several private investigators who, many months later, located mother and the maternal grandparents in Utah. Mother had married Mark Butler, who had six children. The paternal grandparents contacted mother and she agreed to visitation, which took place soon thereafter. Later, the California court found mother in contempt for failing to comply with the court's orders that she keep the paternal grandparents informed of her current address and permit the scheduled visitation. The paternal grandparents had three, week-long visits with Emily in Utah. The paternal grandparents asked mother if they could bring Emily, then 4 years old, to California on their next visit, but mother declined, saying she was "not comfortable sending Emily to California." The paternal grandparents filed a motion to modify the visitation order to permit them to bring Emily to California for visitation and to permit overnight visits in Utah. Father joined the paternal grandparents' request for visitation in California so that father could visit Emily while she was in the care of his parents. Pursuant to court order, mother, father, and the paternal grandparents met with a counselor. Father requested unsupervised visits with Emily or, at least, visits at his parents' home. Father became so agitated and hostile during the conference that the counselor asked him to leave. The counselor recommended that father be permitted visitation only in the presence of a trained supervisor and that Emily not have contact with her father while in the care of her paternal grandparents. The counselor recommended that the paternal grandparents continue to have week-long visits with Emily four times per year until she started school. The counselor recommended that half the visits occur in California. Mother filed a declaration objecting to the recommendation that Emily visit the paternal grandparents in California on the ground that the grandparents would not be able to protect Emily from her father, who was violent, had abused mother, and had threatened to take Emily. What ruling should the court make? *Marriage of Harris,* 34 Cal. 4th 210, 96 P.3d 141, 17 Cal. Rptr. 3d 842 (2004).

2. Seven-year-old Chad is the son of Dan and May, who never married. Shortly after Chad's birth, Dan sought and received judicial recognition that he is Chad's father. Dan has visited Chad regularly throughout Chad's life. Three years ago, May married Steve. A year ago, Steve and May divorced. In the divorce, Steve and May agreed that Steve and Chad had a very strong bond. They agreed to weekly visitation between Chad and Steve. A few months ago, Steve and May had a falling out, and May filed a motion to terminate Steve's visitation with Chad. Dan joined May's request to terminate Steve's visitation. Dan and May concede that Chad refers to both Steve and Dan as "Dad." Steve testifies that he has a quasi-parental relationship with Chad and that continued contact would be beneficial to Chad. The trial court admitted a psychologist's report in which the psychologist stated that Chad desired ongoing visits with Steve and that Steve was a father figure to Chad who enhanced Chad's life. Although the psychologist concluded that conflict among the adults and some disruptive behavior by Steve made more extensive visitation inappropriate, the psychologist recommended one weekend visit between Steve and Chad every other month and one seven-day visit during the summer. How should the court rule? *Marriage of James and Claudine W.,* 114 Cal. App. 4th 68, 7 Cal. Rptr. 3d 461 (2003).

3. Beth and Jane were partners for eight years. They purchased a home together and put title in both their names. They decided they wanted a child. A friend of Jane agreed to donate sperm. Beth agreed to carry the child. Through artificial insemination, Beth became pregnant and gave birth to Carole. The baby was given Beth's last name. Jane's last name became the baby's middle name. Beth and Jane co-parented Carole. Jane remained at home while Beth returned to work full time. Carole called Jane "mama" and Beth "mommy." Carole formed close relationships with Beth and Jane's parents. Recently, Beth and Jane ended their relationship. Beth moved out and took Carole with her. Beth refuses to allow Jane to visit the child. Jane files an action in family court seeking joint custody of Carole. Jane's parents join in the action seeking third-party visitation. *Bethany v. Jones,* 378 S.W. 3d 731 (Ark. 2011).

4. Mom and dad married and lived in Rapid City, South Dakota. Mom's parents, Ellen and Keith, live on a ranch in Montana. Mom gave birth to twins. The twins were born prematurely, and Ellen and Keith helped mom and dad care for the twins during their infancy. Ellen and Keith continued to have substantial contact with the twins over the next few years. When the twins were three, mom died. After mom's death, dad arranged for the twins' continued contact with Ellen and Keith, including visitation at Ellen and Keith's ranch. After these visits, dad began to feel that Ellen and Keith had insufficient concern for the twins' exposure to heavy equipment and recreational vehicles at the ranch. Dad was also concerned about the twins' supervision when they were alone with Ellen and Keith. Dad allowed the children to travel to Montana with Ellen for a three-day visit. Ellen and Keith kept the children an extra ten days without dad's approval. Following this incident, dad advised Ellen and Keith that the children would not be allowed to return to Montana. Instead, he encouraged Ellen and Keith to visit the twins in South Dakota. Ellen and Keith visited the twins once in Rapid City, but they wanted to be able to visit with the children at their Montana ranch. Ellen and Keith filed a petition for visitation. Ellen and Keith requested, among other things, to have the children in Montana one weekend per month during the children's school year, one week during Christmas break, and four consecutive weeks during the summer. Dad did not accept Ellen and Keith's requested visitation plan. However, dad did allow visitation in Rapid City throughout the court proceedings. How should the court rule? *Beach v. Coisman,* 814 N.W.2d 135 (S.D. 2012).

CHAPTER 7

Child Support

COUNTLESS PARENTS SAY THEIR CHILDREN provide the greatest joy of their life. At the same time, kids are expensive—very expensive. Why, some kids even go to law school, and we know how expensive *that* is!

In two parent families, the family pays for diapers, then school supplies, then prom dresses or tuxedos, then, hopefully, college, and maybe, someday, a wedding. It is worth every penny, of course, but gee is it expensive. For most families there is never as much money as we'd like, but we muddle through. Single parents have it tougher. To their credit, most single moms and dads make ends meet and raise happy children.

When a marriage or domestic partnership breaks apart, the money that was barely enough to support one household must now support two—two apartment rents or mortgages, two electric bills, two water bills, two credit card balances, two of so many things that once were one. A family court judge of long experience once mused on the economic consequences of divorce, "One blanket can keep a family warm. But when the family divides in two, the blanket is not big enough for everyone. Yet, there is no money for a second blanket."

Parents have a moral and legal responsibility to support their children.[1] Arizona law, for example, provides, "Every person has the duty to provide all reasonable support for that persons' natural and adopted minor, unemancipated children . . . ."[2] California law states, "A parent's first and principle obligation is to support his or her minor children according to the parent's circumstances and

---

1   For discussion of the history of child support, *see* Michael J. Higdon, Fatherhood by Conscription: Nonconsensual Insemination and the Duty of Child Support, 46 *Georgia Law Review* 407 (2012).

2   Ariz. Rev. Stat. § 25-501.A.

station in life."[3] In Pennsylvania, "A parent has an absolute duty to support one's children . . . ."[4] The duty of child support applies whether or not parents marry.

A parent can bring an action for child support in the appropriate court, and failure to pay court-ordered support is punishable by sanctions and contempt. Chronic failure to support one's children is a crime.[5]

How Much Child Support?

In the first half of the twentieth century, the amount of child support was left to the discretion of the judge. The judge considered the number and ages of the children, which parent had custody, and the income and wealth of the parents. The judge selected a child support amount that was fair under the circumstances. We may assume this system worked reasonably well in the run of cases. Yet, because there were few standards to guide decisionmaking, and because no two judges are exactly alike, it was difficult to predict what judges would do. Given the same set of facts, one judge might set support at $100 per week, while the judge in the next courtroom might double that amount. A consensus emerged that child support decisions should be more objective and predictable. Today, states use formulas or guidelines to set child support.

Although child support formulas/guidelines differ from state to state, similarities outnumber differences. The formula/guideline considers parental income, which is defined broadly. The Florida statute, for example, defines income to include: salary or wages, bonuses, commissions, overtime, tips, all types of business income, disability benefits, worker's compensation, unemployment compensation, pensions, annuity payments, social security benefits, spousal support from a previous marriage, interest, dividends, rental income, income from royalties, trusts, or estates, reimbursements of any kind, reduced living expenses (*e.g.*, free rent), and any gains from property.[6] Can you to think of a source of money that is *not* captured by the Florida statute?

Suppose Dale owes child support. Dale's mom dies and Dale is the beneficiary of his mom's life insurance? Dale receives $300,000 in life insurance proceeds. Is the insurance money income for child support purposes? *See Marriage of Scheppers*, 86 Cal. App. 4th 646, 103 Cal. Rptr. 2d 529 (2001).

---

3   California Family Code § 4053(a).

4   In re Ciotti, 448 B.R. 694, 703 n.7 (W.D. Pa. 2011).

5   *See, e.g.*, Commonwealth v. Marshall, 345 S.W.3d 822 (Ky. 2011).

6   Fla. Stat. Ann. § 61.30(2).

Paul owes child support. Paul is hurt in a car accident and receives $100,000 in personal injury damages. Is the $100,000 income?

Mary owes child support. Mary inherits $5 million from her parents. Are the millions income? *See County of Kern v. Castle*, 75 Cal. App. 4th 1442, 89 Cal. Rptr. 2d 874 (1999).

Tom owes child support. Tom wins the lottery and is now a millionaire? Are the lottery winnings income?

Once income is established, limited deductions are allowed. In Florida, allowable deductions include: income tax deductions, self-employment tax, mandatory union dues, mandatory retirement payments, health insurance payments, court-ordered support for other children (that is actually paid) and spousal support paid to a previous spouse.[7]

In some circumstances, judges impute income to a parent that the parent doesn't actually have. The Florida statute is typical: "Monthly income shall be imputed to an unemployed or underemployed parent if such employment or underemployment is found by the court to be voluntary on that parent's part . . . . In the event of such voluntary unemployment or underemployment, the employment potential and probable earnings level of the parent shall be determined based upon his or her recent work history, occupational qualifications, and prevailing earnings level in the community if such information is available."[8] The Texas Supreme Court wrote, "A parent who is qualified to obtain gainful employment cannot evade his or her child support obligation by voluntarily remaining unemployed or underemployed."[9] The Appellate Division of the New York Supreme Court wrote, "In determining a child support obligation, a court need not rely on a party's own account of his or her finances, but may, in the exercise of its considerable discretion, impute income to a party based upon his or her employment history, future earning capacity, and educational background, and what he or she is capable of earning, based upon prevailing market conditions and prevailing salaries to individuals with the party's credentials in his or her chosen field. Further, imputation of income may be based upon the testimony of an expert regarding a party's ability to earn an income."[10]

---

7   Fla. Stat. Ann. § 61.30(2)(c).

8   Fla. Stat. Ann. § 61.30(2)(b).

9   Iliff v. Iliff, 339 S.W.3d 74 (Tex. 2011).

10   Lago v. Adrion, 93 A.D.3d 697, 940 N.Y.S. 287 (2012).

Modification of Child Support

Child support can be modified on a showing of substantial changed circumstances.[11] The parent seeking modification files a motion describing changed circumstances and asking for modification. The moving party has the burden of persuasion.[12] If the moving party carries the burden, the judge looks at support anew. As the North Carolina Court of Appeal put it in *Meehan v. Meehan*,[13] "Modification of a child support order involves a two-step process. The court must first determine a substantial change of circumstances has taken place; only then does it proceed to . . . calculate the applicable amount of support."

Often, a parent seeking lower child support has lost a job. Loss of employment can constitute substantial changed circumstances. In *Cheney v. Cheney*,[14] the Appellate Division of the New York Supreme Court wrote, "A substantial change in circumstances may be shown when, despite diligent efforts, a party fails to find new employment after a job loss."[15]

The California Court of Appeal decision in *Marriage of Cheriton* addresses child support.

Marriage of Cheriton

California Court of Appeal
92 Cal. App. 4th 269, 111 Cal. Rptr. 2d 755 (2001)

Wunderlich, J.

Appellant Iris M. Fraser (Iris) and respondent David R. Cheriton (David) were married in February 1980. They have four children, all born between 1980 and 1988.

Iris performs and teaches music. David is a professor of computer science at Stanford University. David is also a researcher and an inventor. In addition, he works as a consultant to Cisco Systems, Inc. David's business relationship with Cisco began when he and a partner sold Cisco their business, Granite Systems, Inc.

---

11 The facts that underlie the original support order are res judicata, and cannot be re-litigated. The party seeking modification must prove new facts—changed circumstances.

12 *See* Cheney v. Cheney, 86 A.D.3d 833, 927 N.Y.S.2d 696, 699 (2011)("As the party seeking modification of the existing support order, defendant bore the burden of establishing a substantial change in circumstances . . . .").

13 166 N.C. App. 369, 602 S.E.2d 21, 28 (2004).

14 86 A.D.3d 833, 927 N.Y.S.2d 696 (2011).

15 927 N.Y.S.2d at 699-700.

As a result of his work with Cisco, David received a substantial number of vested Cisco stock options, valued at more than $45 million as of the time of trial. . . .

Iris and David separated . . . in 1994. David petitioned for dissolution of the marriage. The parties stipulated that David would pay temporary child support of $2,171 per month and temporary spousal support of $689 per month. Iris and the four children moved from the family residence into a small rented house. The children shared the bedrooms, while Iris slept in the living room on a sofa bed. David remained in the family home.

Eventually, the parties stipulated to a dissolution judgment, which was filed by the court in December 1997. The judgment resolved many issues in the parties' dissolution action, including the division of property. The judgment also required David to create a trust for the children, funded by Cisco stock, to provide for specified educational and housing needs. Child support and spousal support issues were bifurcated for later trial . . . .

[Following a trial], the court . . . ordered David to pay child support of $2,292 per month for the four children; [and] set spousal support for Iris at $2,000 per month . . . .

California has a strong public policy in favor of adequate child support. That policy is expressed in statutes embodying the statewide uniform child support guideline. The guideline seeks to place the interests of children as the state's top priority. In setting guideline support, the courts are required to adhere to certain principles, including these: A parent's first and principal obligation is to support his or her minor children according to the parent's circumstances and station in life. Each parent should pay for the support of the children according to his or her ability. Children should share in the standard of living of both parents. Child support may therefore appropriately improve the standard of living of the custodial household to improve the lives of the children.

To implement these policies, courts are required to calculate child support in accordance with the mathematical formula set forth in the statute. . . . Adherence to the guidelines is mandatory, and the trial court may not depart from them except in the special circumstances enumerated in the statutes. Those special circumstances include a parent's extraordinarily high income. . . .

Iris argues generally that the trial court abused its discretion to the extent its order precluded the children from sharing in David's wealth. . . . Building on her general argument, Iris challenges the child support order on several particular grounds. She first takes issue with the trial court's decision to exclude the proceeds from David's 1997 sale of Cisco stock from the child support calculation.

In her attack on the trial court's treatment of David's 1997 stock sale proceeds, Iris first asserts that the entire net proceeds from the sale constitute income to David for purposes of child support. In considering this issue, we begin by observing that income is broadly defined for purposes of child support. Subject to certain statutory exceptions, which do not apply here, gross income means income from whatever source derived. Although it specifically lists more than a dozen possible income sources, by the statute's express terms, that list is not exhaustive. Rather, the codified income items are *by way of illustration* only. Income from other sources should properly be factored into the annual gross income computation.

The judicially recognized sources of income cover a wide gamut. (Predictable overtime and bonuses must be included in prospective income; future bonuses are properly considered income; reasonable value of rent-free housing is income; car and parent-employers' rent subsidy constitute income; . . . lottery winnings are considered income; trial court may treat inheritance as income in its discretion; gifts are not income; student loan is not income because it must be repaid.)

As pertinent here, income includes stock options granted as part of a parent's compensation. Thus, where a parent enjoys substantial income in addition to his salary and bonuses in the form of stock options, this additional income is part of his overall employment compensation and must be used to calculate child support.

Iris argues that the trial court ignored the money David received from his 1997 sale of Cisco stock in making its child support order. David disputes that contention. . . . While the trial judge was quite obviously aware that David had netted millions of dollars from the sale of a portion of his stocks in 1997, she did not factor those funds into the child support formula. . . .

David also maintains that he is not receiving incentive stock options as part of his ongoing compensation. Therefore, he argues, "even if an employee's receipt of stock options might be deemed income for the purposes of support in some other factual setting, this consideration is not pertinent in the instant matter." We disagree. First, David's attorney conceded at trial that he received the options "as compensation for work." Additionally, there is no evidence in the record to support David's factual assertion that stock options are not part of his current compensation package. Finally, even assuming David is no longer receiving stock options from Cisco, those he already owns may be subject to his child support obligation, as we discuss below.

We recognize that certain difficulties inhere in calculating support based on income from stock options. For one thing, such income may be sporadic. That impediment does not justify excluding such income from the calculation, however. The court cannot deduct predictable overtime and bonuses in determining father's prospective earnings merely because they occur sporadically. Furthermore, the Legislature specifically provided the means for overcoming that particular obstacle. Trial courts are permitted to adjust the award where the guideline monthly net disposable income figure does not accurately reflect the actual or prospective earnings of the parties. In addition, trial courts have discretion to adjust the child support order as appropriate to accommodate seasonal or fluctuating income.

There is a second, perhaps thornier obstacle that trial courts face in incorporating stock option income into the child support calculation. That difficulty lies in determining *when* stock options become income for purposes of child support. To some extent, that determination may turn on the nature of the options themselves. Federal income tax law may also affect the determination. Under California's child support statutes, as under federal tax law, the employee-parent may realize income at the time an option is exercised. At the very latest, though, income is realized when the underlying stock is sold for a gain.

In this case, the trial judge concluded that the stock options "certainly can become income upon exercise and again upon sale, but until that occurs, they are not income available for support." We agree with the court's conclusion that any proceeds from the sale of stock constitute "income available for support," after accounting for allowable deductions. Unfortunately, the court did not apply that conclusion to David's 1997 exercise of options and sale of stock, from which he grossed some $9.75 million. Instead, the trial court expressly excluded those proceeds from the child support formula . . . . [The trial court's decision was error], particularly in light of California's well-established policies requiring parents to support their children according to their ability.

Given the broad statutory definition of income, we conclude that the entire amount David received from the 1997 sale of his Cisco stock, subject to permissible deductions, constitutes gross income . . . .

Iris's next attack on the order is based on the trial court's refusal to consider David's assets in determining child support. As noted above, as of the time of trial, David's assets included stock and options worth tens of millions of dollars, principally from Cisco. The court concluded that those assets "are not income as defined in the code sections that relate to child support." Iris assigns that conclusion as error. Not surprisingly, David disagrees. He argues that the "child support guidelines are based exclusively on income, not assets."

As a general proposition, we agree that the key financial factor in the guideline formula is net disposable income. Nevertheless, relevant authority at least suggests that wealth is an appropriate consideration in setting child support. By statute, parents are required to provide child support according to their "ability," their "circumstances and station in life," and their "standard of living." It is fair to assume that in most cases assets contribute to the ability to provide support. . . .

Like its statutes, California's case law inferentially supports the consideration of assets in setting child support. For example, several cases cite a parent's "wealth" or "net worth" in connection with child support awards. Still other decisions, in discussing lifestyle, mention the parent's "financial resources" available for child support. In one case, the reviewing court found an abuse of discretion where the trial court failed to take into account husband's conceded wealth.

. . . The trial court's refusal to consider David's substantial wealth in setting child support effectively permits him to avoid his obligation to support his children according to his "ability," his "circumstances and station in life," and his "standard of living." Thus, under the current support order, the children will not benefit from the substantial assets their father received. There is no basis for concluding this was somehow in their best interests. The challenged child support order thus offends the statutory policies of this state.

We are mindful that trial courts are invested with substantial discretion in this area, and that no California authority expressly mandates the consideration of a parent's assets in awarding child support. Nevertheless, under the circumstances present here, we conclude that the trial court's refusal to consider David's substantial wealth in setting child support may have resulted in an order that is too low to be in the best interests of his children, based on an assessment of their reasonable needs. At the very least, the trial court should consider imputing reasonable income on David's assets . . . , to the extent necessary to meet the children's reasonable needs.

In this case, the court explained its assessment of the children's needs as follows: "After carefully reviewing the series of Income and Expense Declarations filed by Iris, the Court estimates the expenses of the children, as apart from Iris's expenses, and excluding those items which will be paid from the trust, to be between $3,000 and $5,000."

First, the court's analysis assumes that the children's historic expenses define their needs. But that assumption is erroneous in the case of wealthy parents, because it ignores the well-established principle that the child's need is measured by the parents' current station in life. Clearly where the child has a wealthy parent, that child is entitled to, and therefore needs something more than the bare necessities of life.

Moreover, it appears that the court calculated the children's needs by determining the household's overall expenses, then deducting expenditures attributable to Iris. That method is improper. It is error to calculate the child's needs by attributing specified monthly expenses to the custodial parent and subtracting that sum from the custodial household's total monthly expenses.

In addition, the court determined the children's needs by "excluding those items which will be paid from the trust." The court's reliance on the trust was error. In this case, it was particularly inappropriate to consider any benefit from the trust, since the trust was still inchoate at the time of the order and thus was not paying any of the children's housing or other costs.

Finally, the court was mistaken when it concluded that it was bound by the parties' stipulated judgment, which ostensibly capped the custodial household's housing costs at $3,000 per month. . . . . Parents do not have the power to agree between themselves to abridge their child's right to support. That is because the law puts the child's interests before the contractual expectations of the parents. Courts will not respect agreements that have the effect of contracting away the child's right to support.

Given the flaws in the trial court's determination of the children's needs, we conclude that remand is necessary on this issue. On remand, the trial court must properly determine the children's needs, with due regard to both parents' income and wealth.

Note and Questions based on *Marriage of Cheriton*

1. The child support obligor in *Cheriton* was wealthy, and could afford to pay enough support to maintain his kids at the standard of living they enjoyed before their parents' divorce. Most people don't have that kind of money. Indeed, after some divorces there is less money than before the divorce because what money there is has to support two households. Should an obligor spouse be required to get a second job in order to increase available income so the children can maintain the standard of living they enjoyed prior to divorce?

2. There is a difference between income and assets. Generally, child support is based on income. The *Cheriton* court ruled that it is proper, at least for some wealthy parents, to factor assets into the obligor's ability to pay child support. The California Supreme Court wrote in *Mejia v. Reed*, 31 Cal. 4th 657, 74 P.3d 166 (2003): "Assets at the time of dissolution play little part in the computation of

child support. They may enter indirectly into the calculation in two ways: (1) in assessing earning capacity, a trial court may take into account the earnings from invested assets, and (2) a court may deem assets a 'special circumstance' that may justify a departure from the guideline figure for support payments. But these are exceptional situations; the child support obligation is based primarily on actual earnings and earning capacity."

Should an obligor—wealthy or not—be required to sell assets to generate money for child support? If the obligor refuses to sell, could/should the judge impute income to the obligor that would have been realized through sale of the asset?

Does Child Support Include Paying for Private School or College?

Divorcing couples often agree to pay for a child's private school. The agreement is typically incorporated into the divorce decree, and courts enforce such agreements.[16]

It is one thing for a court to enforce a voluntary agreement between divorcing parents to pay for private school through high school. It is another to order a divorcing parent who has made no such agreement to shoulder the expense. In the case of married parents, the state cannot order them to pay for private school. Should the rule be different for divorced parents? In divorce cases, should judges have authority to order unwilling parents to pay for private school?

Some states authorize judges to order divorced parents to pay for private school.[17] The Appellate Division of the New York Supreme Court wrote in *Maybaum v. Maybaum*,[18] "The court may direct a parent to contribute to a child's education, even in the absence of special circumstances or a voluntary agreement of the parties." The South Carolina Supreme Court, wrote in *Burch v. Burch*[19] that child support "may include contributing to private school expenses where appropriate." Relevant factors include: (1) Is it in a child's best interest to attend private school? (2) Can the obligor afford the tuition? (3) Was the child

---

16 *See* Arnold v. Arnold, 177 P.3d 89 (Utah Ct. App. 2008).

17 *See, e.g.*, Short v. Short, 77 So.3d 405 (La. Ct. App. 2011)("A trial court may award child support for expenses of tuition, registration, books, and supply fees required for attending a special or private elementary or secondary school to meet the needs of the child. La. R.S. 9:315.6(1).").

18 89 A.D.3d 692, 933 N.Y.S.2d 43 (2011).

19 395 S.C. 318, 717 S.E.2d 757 (2011).

attending private school before the divorce? (4) Would private schooling have continued in the absence of divorce?

Turning from elementary and secondary education to college, may a court order divorcing parents to pay for college? Normally, the duty of support ends when children reach age 18, die, marry, or enter the military.[20] States vary on whether parents can be ordered to pay for college.[21] Madeline Marzano-Lesnevich and Scott Lattera write:

> A disparity exists among the states regarding whether a court may . . . require parents of divorce to contribute to their children's college costs, or to contribute to their children's support after high school. Moreover, even among those states that have determined that a contribution to college costs and child support for the child in college is permissible and appropriate, there still exists a significant divergence in the mechanism for defining what expenses are included in the costs of college and in determining the appropriate level of child support. . . .
>
> The majority of states contain no provision requiring parents to contribute toward their children's college costs. . . .
>
> While many states do not authorize a court to award contribution to college, the majority of those states will allow parties to voluntarily contract between themselves to create enforceable obligations to contribute to college expenses.[22]

In *McLeod v. Starnes*,[23] the South Carolina Supreme Court ruled divorced parents can be ordered to pay college expenses. The court wrote, "Requiring a parent to pay, as an incident of child support, for post-secondary education . . . is rationally related to the State's interest. While it is certainly true that not all married couples send their children to college, that does not detract from the State's interest in having college-educated citizens and attempting to alleviate the potential disadvantages placed upon children of divorced parents. Although the decision to send a child to college may be a personal one, it is not one we wish to foreclose to a child simply because his parents are divorced."

---

20 *See, e.g.,* Missouri Stat. Ann. § 452.340(3).

21 *See, e.g.,* Missouri Stat. Ann. § 452.340(5) (support can continue for child enrolled in college and getting passing grades).

22 Madeline Marzano-Lesnevich & Scott Adam Laterra, Child Support and College: What Is the Correct Result?, 22 *Journal of the American Academy of Matrimonial Lawyers* 335 (2009).

23 396 S.C. 647, 723 S.E.2d 198 (2012).

In states where child support can include payment for college, what expenses are included? Tuition, books, room, and board, clearly. What about a monthly living allowance? How about the cost of a sorority or fraternity?[24] A semester abroad? In *Marriage of Goodman*,[25] the Iowa Supreme Court wrote:

> We have recently interpreted [Iowa law] as not limiting college expenses to only tuition, room, and books. We recognized the reasonable and necessary costs of attending college surpass the costs of tuition, books, room, board, and supplies. A college education is not limited to what is learned in the classroom; it includes social, cultural, and educational experiences outside the classroom. The experiences outside the classroom impose additional expenses on the student.

> A cash allowance is necessary for a college student to participate in the social, cultural, and educational experiences outside the classroom.

Iowa has the following statute on payment for college.

1. Order of subsidy. The court may order a postsecondary education subsidy if good cause is shown.

2. Criteria for good cause. In determining whether good cause exists for ordering a postsecondary education subsidy, the court shall consider the age of the child, the ability of the child relative to post-secondary education, the child's financial resources, whether the child is self-sustaining, and the financial condition of each parent. If the court determines that good cause is shown for ordering a postsecondary education subsidy, the court shall determine the amount of subsidy as follows:

> a. The court shall determine the cost of postsecondary education based upon the cost of attending an in-state public institution for a course of instruction leading to an undergraduate degree and shall include the reasonable costs for only necessary post-secondary education expenses.

---

24 *See* Marriage of Goodman, 690 N.W.2d 279 (Iowa 2004).

25 690 N.W.2d 279 (Iowa 2004).

b. The court shall then determine the amount, if any, which the child may reasonably be expected to contribute, considering the child's financial resources, including but not limited to the availability of financial aid whether in the form of scholarships, grants, or student loans, and the ability of the child to earn income while attending school.

c. The child's expected contribution shall be deducted from the cost of postsecondary education and the court shall apportion responsibility for the remaining cost of postsecondary education to each parent. The amount paid by each parent shall not exceed thirty-three and one-third percent of the total cost of postsecondary education.

3. Subsidy payable. A postsecondary education subsidy shall be payable to the child, to the educational institution, or to both, but shall not be payable to the custodial parent.

4. Repudiation by child. A postsecondary education subsidy shall not be awarded if the child has repudiated the parent by publicly disowning the parent, refusing to acknowledge the parent, or by acting in a similar manner.

5. Obligations of child. The child shall forward, to each parent, reports of grades awarded at the completion of each academic session within ten days of receipt of the reports. Unless otherwise specified by the parties, a postsecondary education subsidy awarded by the court shall be terminated upon the child's completion of the first calendar year of course instruction if the child fails to maintain a cumulative grade point average in the median range or above during that first calendar year. Iowa Code Ann. § 598.21F.

In *Nelson v. Robinson*, the Alabama Court of Civil Appeals grapples with paying for college.

Nelson v. Robinson

Court of Civil Appeals of Alabama
74 So. 3d 979 (2011)

Thompson, Presiding Judge.

Michael Nelson ("the father") appeals from a judgment ordering him to pay half of the parties' child's postminority educational expenses. Bobbie Robinson ("the mother") was ordered to pay the other half of the child's postminority educational expenses.

The record indicates the following. On May 6, 2010, the mother filed a petition for modification of the father's child-support obligation, seeking postminority educational support on behalf of the parties' child, who graduated from high school that spring. The child reached the age of majority on June 2, 2010. On June 23, 2010, a hearing was held on the petition. At the outset of the hearing, the trial court asked the parties whether they believed the child had the ability and desire to go to college, and both parties agreed the child possessed the requisite ability and desire. The trial court also asked the father whether, if the parties had remained married, they would have "supported [the child] or helped her with college expenses?" The father said he would have assisted with those expenses. The trial court found that the mother had met the burden . . . to allow the child to receive postminority educational support.

At that point, the father's attorney noted that the father had not yet presented any evidence. The father testified that he is a construction worker and that his gross monthly income is $3,841.76. He said that he has monthly expenses of $3,858.70, including the payment on his mobile home and its furnishings, which he valued at $70,000. Including the mobile home, two older model vehicles, and his retirement account, the father estimated the total amount of his assets at $95,500. However, the father also presented evidence indicating that he owed $62,000 on the mobile home and $6,000 on one of the vehicles. He also owed $4,600 in credit-card debt, $3,600 in medical bills, and $2,000 to his retirement account. The father presented evidence of total debt of $78,200.

The father said that he could not afford to pay for the child's college education but that he was willing to continue to provide health-insurance coverage for her. He also said that he was willing to do what he could to assist the child with other expenses.

The mother, who appeared pro se at trial, is a school-bus driver. She said that the child planned to live at home and attend Alabama Southern Community College ("ASCC") in Monroeville. . . . [T]he parties stipulated that the child had been accepted at ASCC. A letter from ASCC was submitted into evidence indicating that the child's estimated tuition and fees for the fall term were $1,308. The letter also stated that the child had been awarded a Pell Grant of $2,775 for the term. The mother testified that the child's books had cost $517 for the term.

The mother testified that her gross monthly income is $1,448. She said that she had been a school-bus driver for 11 or 12 years and that she had no other job. However, she said, she had a certified-nursing-assistant license and a commercial driver's license ("CDL") that would allow her to drive "18–wheeler" trucks, but, she said, she had not made use of the CDL because when she earned the CDL, the child was small.

. . . [T]he trial court entered a judgment . . . ordering the mother and the father to each be responsible for half of the child's actual college expenses after scholarships and grants. The judgment stated that actual expenses included expenses for room, board, tuition, fees, and books. Because the child was going to continue to live at home with the mother, the trial court ordered the father to pay the mother half "of the average room and board costs listed on the web-sites of the University of Alabama and Auburn University." The father timely appealed.

The father contends that the evidence did not support the trial court's award of postminority educational support for the child. Specifically, the father argues that the trial court erred in basing the costs of room and board on the cost incurred for a student attending Auburn University ("Auburn") or the University of Alabama ("Alabama") and not on what the child's actual expenses for room and board will be. He also asserts that the mother failed to present evidence as to what those actual costs will be for the child while she is attending ASCC. In addition, the father asserts that the award subjects him to undue hardship.

. . . In an award of postminority educational support for a child of divorced parents, the trial court shall consider all relevant factors that shall appear reasonable and necessary, including primarily the financial resources of the parents and the child and the child's commitment to, and aptitude for, the requested education. . . . [T]rial courts also should consider the standard of living that the child would have enjoyed if the marriage had not been dissolved and the family unit had been preserved and the child's relationship with his parents and responsiveness to parental advice and guidance. The trial court must also determine if the noncustodial parent has sufficient estate, earning capacity, or income to provide financial assistance without undue hardship. Undue hardship does not imply the absence of personal sacrifice, because many parents sacrifice to send their children to college.

In child support cases the trial court is bound by the legal evidence or lack of it, and it may not speculate on the ability of the parties to pay nor on the needs of the children.

In this case, the undisputed evidence indicated that the child intended to live with the mother while she attended ASCC. There was no evidence presented as to what the child's living expenses might be. Nevertheless, the trial court ordered the father to pay the mother half of the room-and-board costs of a student attending Auburn or Alabama, as those costs are listed on each university's respective Web site. There is absolutely no evidence in the record to support a finding that the child's expenses while living at the mother's home will equal the cost of room and board as stated on those Web sites. Therefore, that portion of the trial court's judgment ordering the father to pay the mother half of the cost of the room-and-board expenses of a student attending Auburn or Alabama is plainly and palpably wrong and is due to be reversed.

The father also contends that the judgment ordering him to pay half of the child's college expenses subjects him to undue hardship. The trial court's judgment specifies that the mother and the father are each to be responsible for half of the child's actual expenses "after scholarships and grants." The evidence submitted at the August 11, 2010, hearing indicates that the child's tuition and books for the fall term totaled $1,825. The evidence also indicates that the child had received a Pell Grant of $2,775 for the term. Therefore, after tuition and books were paid for, the child had a surplus of $950 for the term. As discussed, the record does not include evidence of any other actual expenses the child will incur. Because no other postminority educational expenses were proven at trial, there are no other expenses for which the father could possibly be made responsible. Accordingly, after the provision ordering the father to pay to the mother an amount for room and board equivalent to half of the cost of room and board at Auburn or Alabama is removed from the judgment, as previously discussed, we conclude that, based on the record before us, the father will not suffer undue hardship under the remaining provisions of the judgment. Because of this holding, we pretermit discussion of the father's argument that the record includes insufficient evidence of the mother's financial resources.

For the reasons set forth above, we reverse that portion of the judgment ordering the father to pay an amount for room and board equivalent to half of the cost of room and board at Auburn or Alabama. The remainder of the judgment is affirmed. This cause is remanded for the trial court to enter a judgment consistent with this opinion.

Questions and Problem

1. Suppose the college freshman in *Nelson v. Robinson* was admitted to Auburn University as well as the local community college. Not to take anything away from community college, but Auburn is a fine four year university. Not surprisingly, the student chooses Auburn. Problem is, Auburn is expensive. On July 11, 2012, the Auburn website listed in-state tuition as $9,446. Room and board, $10,606. Books and supplies, add $1,100. Mom drives a school bus, dad works construction. Are the parents obligated to send their daughter to Auburn over the more affordable community college? Can/should a family court judge order either or both parents to pony up the cost of an Auburn education?

2. Following college, can divorced parents be ordered to pay for law school, medical school, or another graduate program?

3. Mom and dad divorce, and mom is awarded custody of the two kids, Brittany and Nathan. Dad is ordered to pay child support. Mom asks the court to restore her maiden name. A year later, Nathan petitions the court, asking the court to change his name to his mom's restored name. The judge cautions Nathan that under Indiana law, asking to change his name might constitute a repudiation of his relationship with his father. Nathan asks for the change. Nathan has almost no relationship with his dad. When Nathan is accepted to university, mom files a petition requesting a judge to order dad to help pay Nathan's college expenses. Should dad be ordered to help pay for Nathan's college education? Nathan wanted nothing to do with his father. *Lechien v. Wren,* 950 N.E.2d 838 (Ind. Ct. App. 2011).

Duty to Support Disabled Adult Child

Many states require parents to support adult children who are disabled.[26] In *Guardianship of MAS*, the Montana Supreme Court analyzed this duty.

Guardianship of M.A.S.

Supreme Court of Montana
363 Mont. 96, 266 P.3d 1267 (2011)

Justice Beth Baker delivered the Opinion of the Court.

M.S. (Father) appeals the First Judicial District Court's order requiring him to provide support for his disabled adult twin sons. We consider on appeal whether § 40–6–214, MCA, grants authority for the District Court's ruling.

M.A.S. and C.M.S. are the twin children of Father and V.L–S. (Mother), who divorced when the twins were eight years old. Now twenty-two years old, the twins were born with significant physical and mental disabilities and require full-time care and supervision. C.M.S. is legally blind, does not speak, cannot walk independently, and cannot take any food by mouth but instead receives a liquid diet through his abdomen. M.A.S. is autistic, has significant cognitive delays, and cannot be left alone for any length of time. Both twins live with Mother, who has modified her home to accommodate their unique needs.

Upon dissolution of his marriage to Mother, Father was ordered to pay child support. The twins graduated from high school on June 6, 2009, and turned nineteen years old approximately two months later. Pursuant to § 40–4–208(5), MCA, and in the absence of a written agreement to continue providing support beyond the age of majority, Father's obligation to provide for the twins under the child support order ceased upon their graduation from high school.

After the twins turned eighteen, Mother petitioned the court for appointment as each boy's conservator and guardian. The District Court granted Mother's petitions on March 24, 2009. The court found the twins were "incapacitated persons" in need of protection and granted Mother all powers and duties of a guardian of an incapacitated person . . . .

---

26 *See, e.g.,* Missouri Stat. Ann. § 452.340.

On June 4, 2009, Mother filed a petition in the conservatorship actions, requesting continued child support from Father once the twins turned nineteen. . . .

. . . The District Court found it had the authority to order Father to support the twins based on information he was not providing for them to the extent of his ability. The court ordered the parties to submit financial affidavits. Father appealed, contending the court lacked the statutory authority to order support. . . .

The District Court relied on § 40–6–214, MCA, codified among statutes governing the Obligations of Parents, which states, "it is the duty of the father, the mother, and the children of any poor person who is unable to provide self-maintenance by work to maintain that person to the extent of their ability." . . . Father argues his legal obligation to provide child support terminated when the twins graduated from high school or, at the latest, on their nineteenth birthday. Father cites previous rulings of this Court for the proposition that pursuant to a marital dissolution decree, a parent's obligation to provide child support terminates when the child becomes an adult.

Mother's petition, however, [was] not filed in the parents' marital dissolution proceeding but under the statutes governing a conservator and guardian. The District Court declared the twins "incapacitated persons," meaning each suffers from "physical illness or disability ... to the extent [he] lacks sufficient understanding or capacity to make or communicate responsible decisions." Mother was appointed, and continues to be, the guardian and conservator of both twins. Her rights and duties in this position are outlined in the guardianship and conservatorship statutes, which include the right to "institute proceedings to compel any person under a duty to support the ward or to pay sums for the welfare of the ward to perform that person's duty." Section 72–5–321(2)(d)(i), MCA.

Under Montana law, the relationship between parent and child extends equally to every child and to every parent, regardless of the marital status of the parents. Irrespective of the parents' prior marriage and its subsequent dissolution, the instant petitions are filed directly on behalf of Father's two adult children, not on behalf of their mother. Since the laws governing guardians and conservators grant express authority for the guardian to bring an action for support, the operative question is whether there is a duty to support the twins that may be enforced against Father in the conservatorship proceedings.

Mother claims Father's duty to provide support for the twins arises under § 40–6–214, MCA. The statute was enacted in 1895 as part of the Civil Code of Montana, but never has been applied by this Court to circumstances similar to those presented here. We find instructive the rulings of other jurisdictions that have held similar statutes impose a duty to support one's disabled adult child independent of a child support order awarded in a marital dissolution action. Courts in both Oregon and California have analyzed in detail the origins of statutes creating a parental duty of support and their applicability to an adult disabled child. *In re Haxton*, 299 Or. 616, 705 P.2d 721, 730–31 (1985)(citing cases recognizing the duty to support a disabled adult child and permitting enforcement of that duty through a direct action by the child); *Chun v. Chun*, 190 Cal. App.3d 589, 596, 235 Cal.Rptr. 553 (1987)(father owed duty of support to disabled adult child who was a "person in need who is unable to maintain herself by work" within the meaning of the statute). . . .

Other courts have articulated alternative mechanisms by which maintenance for an adult disabled child can be enforced outside the purview of a child support order granted during marital dissolution. *See, e.g., Parrish v. Parrish*, 138 Mich.App. 546, 361 N.W.2d 366, 372 (1984)(support needed for adult disabled child properly considered by trial court in fashioning alimony award notwithstanding statute precluding an award of support for adult child); *Feinberg v. Diamant*, 378 Mass. 131, 389 N.E.2d 998, 1000–02 (1979)(noting the common law rule there is no obligation on the part of parents to support adult children, but recognizing a parent may be required to support an adult disabled child not through the divorce statutes but under the court's general equity powers in guardianship proceedings); *Prosser v. Prosser*, 159 Kan. 651, 157 P.2d 544, 545–46 (1945)(upholding action to enforce common law duty of support "where a child on becoming of age is in such a feeble and dependent condition physically or mentally as to be unable to support himself").

Based on the plain language of § 40–6–214, MCA, and the construction given similar statutes, we conclude the statute has clear application to the facts of this case. No party disputes the twins are completely dependent on others and have insufficient income to be self-maintaining, aside from what benefits they may receive from government agencies and their parents. The District Court's determination of the twins' incapacity for purposes of the guardianship statutes satisfies the statute's predicate that they be unable to provide self-maintenance by work. . . . We hold the statute imposes a duty on Father to support the twins to the extent of his ability. Father's duty runs directly to the twins and is enforceable under the guardianship statutes.

Questions based on *Guardianship of M.A.S.*:

1. The Montana Supreme Court ruled father had to support his physically disabled adult children. Suppose there is one adult child. The child is not physically disabled. Rather, the child is addicted to cocaine. Should the "child's" parents be required to support the drug addicted child who can't or won't work due to addiction? Should the parents be liable for drug treatment for the child? What if the child is court-ordered into drug treatment? Should the parents be financially responsible for court-ordered drug treatment for their adult child?

2. Countless parents of severely disabled children devote themselves to their children. These parents often care for their disabled children well into adulthood. One of the greatest fears these parents have is, "What will happen to my child when I am too old to take care of her? What will happen when I die? Who will take care of her?" Ask yourself, "What role could I, an attorney, play in helping parents of disabled children plan for the future?"

Child Support Enforcement

Federal, state, and tribal governments cooperate to facilitate child support enforcement. At the federal level, Title IV-D of the Social Security Act authorizes the Child Support Enforcement Program (CSEP). The federal government provides technical assistance and money to support state and local child support enforcement. The federal government operates the Federal Parent Locator Service that tracks down obligor parents, their bank accounts, and other assets.

At the state level, states have child support enforcement offices in counties and parishes. Every state has laws to establish paternity, and a judgment of paternity brings a duty of support.

Parents receiving Temporary Assistance for Needy Families (TANF) automatically qualify for assistance from support enforcement. Parents not on TANF may request assistance from the local child support enforcement office.

Parents who owe support can have the support withheld from their wages. Federal and state income tax refunds are intercepted to pay overdue support. Child support officials place liens on obligors' property and sell obligors' property to collect support. The obligor can lose their driver's license, professional license, and passport. In *Oklahoma Bar Association v. Crane*,[27] an attorney resigned from the bar rather than face discipline for failing to pay child support.

A parent who is able to pay child support but who chronically fails to pay can be held in civil contempt. In *Turner v. Rogers*,[28] the U.S. Supreme Court discussed civil contempt intended to enforce child support:

> Civil contempt proceedings in child support cases constitute one part of a highly complex system designed to assure a noncustodial parent's regular payment of funds typically necessary for the support of his children. Often the family receives welfare support from a state-administered federal program, and the State then seeks reimbursement from the noncustodial parent. Other times the custodial parent . . . does not receive government benefits and is entitled to receive support payments herself.
>
> The Federal Government has created an elaborate procedural mechanism designed to help both the government and custodial parents to secure the payments to which they are entitled. These systems often rely upon wage withholding, expedited procedures for modifying and enforcing child support orders, and automated data processing. But sometimes States will use contempt orders to ensure that the custodial parent receives support payments or the government receives reimbursement. Although some experts have criticized this last-mentioned procedure, and the Federal Government believes that the routine use of contempt for non-payment of child support is likely to be an ineffective strategy, the Government also tells us that coercive enforcement remedies, such as contempt, have a role to play. . . .
>
> [T]he Due Process Clause does not *automatically* require the provision of counsel at civil contempt proceedings to an indigent individual who is subject to a child support order, even if that individual faces incarceration (for up to a year). In particular, that Clause does not require the provision of counsel where the opposing parent or other custodian (to whom support funds are owed) is not represented by counsel and the State provides procedural safeguards . . . .

---

27 9 P.3d 682 (Okla. 2000).

28 131 S.Ct. 2507 (2011).

Willful refusal to pay child support is a state crime. As well, it is a federal offense willfully to fail to pay support for a child in another state, or to cross state lines to avoid paying support.[29]

Under federal bankruptcy law, support obligations are not dischargeable in bankruptcy.

Uniform Interstate Family Support Act

To facilitate interstate enforcement child support, Congress mandates that all states adopt the Uniform Interstate Family Support Act (UIFSA). A goal of UIFSA is to prevent parents from moving across state lines to gain an advantage in child support litigation. Except in specified circumstances, a state that issues a child support order retains continuing, exclusive jurisdiction over child support. UISFA has parallels to the Uniform Child Custody Jurisdiction and Enforcement Act analyzed in Chapter 6. The 2008 version of UIFSA is produced below.

WARNING: The following statute may be the dullest thing you have ever read, ever! UIFSA is long and detailed. In the version provided below, quite a few sections are deleted. Even so, it will put you to sleep, guaranteed.

Article 1
General Provisions

§ 101.   Short Title.

This act may be cited as the Uniform Interstate Family Support Act.

§ 102. Definitions.

In this act:

(1) "Child" means an individual, whether over or under the age of majority, who is or is alleged to be owed a duty of support by the individual's parent or who is or is alleged to be the beneficiary of a support order directed to the parent.

(2) "Child-support order" means a support order for a child, including a child who has attained the age of majority under the law of the issuing state or foreign country.

---

29 18 U.S.C. § 228.

(3) "Convention" means the Convention on the International Recovery of Child Support and Other Forms of Family Maintenance, concluded at The Hague on November 23, 2007.

(4) "Duty of support" means an obligation imposed or imposable by law to provide support for a child, spouse, or former spouse, including an unsatisfied obligation to provide support. . . .

(8) "Home state" means the state or foreign country in which a child lived with a parent or a person acting as parent for at least six consecutive months immediately preceding the time of filing of a [petition] or comparable pleading for support and, if a child is less than six months old, the state or foreign country in which the child lived from birth with any of them. A period of temporary absence of any of them is counted as part of the six-month or other period.

(9) "Income" includes earnings or other periodic entitlements to money from any source and any other property subject to withholding for support under the law of this state.

(10) "Income-withholding order" means an order or other legal process directed to an obligor's employer or other debtor, as defined by the income-withholding law of this state, to withhold support from the income of the obligor.

(11) "Initiating tribunal" means the tribunal of a state or foreign country from which a petition or comparable pleading is forwarded or in which a petition or comparable pleading is filed for forwarding to another state or foreign country. . . .

(23) "Responding state" means a state in which a petition or comparable pleading for support or to determine parentage of a child is filed or to which a petition or comparable pleading is forwarded for filing from another state or a foreign country.

(24) "Responding tribunal" means the authorized tribunal in a responding state or foreign country. . . .

(28) "Support order" means a judgment, decree, order, decision, or directive, whether temporary, final, or subject to modification, issued a state or foreign country for the benefit of a child, a spouse, or a former spouse, which provides for monetary support, health care, arrearages, retroactive support, or reimbursement for financial assistance provided to an individual obligee

in place of child support. The term may include related costs and fees, interest, income withholding, automatic adjustment, reasonable attorney's fees, and other relief.

(29) "Tribunal" means a court, administrative agency, or quasi-judicial entity authorized to establish, enforce, or modify support orders or to determine parentage of a child.

Article 2
Jurisdiction

§ 201. Bases for Jurisdiction Over Nonresident.

(a) In a proceeding to establish or enforce a support order or to determine parentage of a child, a tribunal of this state may exercise personal jurisdiction over a nonresident individual or the individual's guardian or conservator if:

(1) the individual is personally served with citation, summons, notice within this state;

(2) the individual submits to the jurisdiction of this state by consent in a record, by entering a general appearance, or by filing a responsive document having the effect of waiving any contest to personal jurisdiction;

(3) the individual resided with the child in this state;

(4) the individual resided in this state and provided prenatal expenses or support for the child;

(5) the child resides in this state as a result of the acts or directives of the individual;

(6) the individual engaged in sexual intercourse in this state and the child may have been conceived by that act of intercourse;

(7) the individual asserted parentage of a child in the putative father registry maintained in this state by the appropriate agency; or

(8) there is any other basis consistent with the constitutions of this state and the United States for the exercise of personal jurisdiction.

(b) The bases of personal jurisdiction set forth in subsection (a) or in any other law of this state may not be used to acquire personal jurisdiction for a tribunal of this state to modify a child-support order of another state unless the requirements of Section 611 are met, or, in the case of a foreign support order, unless the requirements of Section 615 are met.

§ 203. Initiating and Responding Tribunal of State.

Under this act, a tribunal of this state may serve as an initiating tribunal to forward proceedings to a tribunal of another state, and as a responding tribunal for proceedings initiated in another state or a foreign country.

§ 205. Continuing, Exclusive Jurisdiction to Modify Child-Support Order.

(a) A tribunal of this state that has issued a child-support order consistent with the law of this state has and shall exercise continuing, exclusive jurisdiction to modify its child-support order if the order is the controlling order and:

(1) at the time of the filing of a request for modification this state is the residence of the obligor, the individual obligee, or the child for whose benefit the support order is issued; or

(2) even if this state is not the residence of the obligor, the individual obligee, or the child for whose benefit the support order is issued, the parties consent in a record or in open court that the tribunal of this state may continue to exercise jurisdiction to modify its order.

(b) A tribunal of this state that has issued a child-support order consistent with the law of this state may not exercise continuing, exclusive jurisdiction to modify the order if:

(1) all of the parties who are individuals file consent in a record with the tribunal of this state that a tribunal of another state that has jurisdiction over at least one of the parties who is an individual or that is located in the state of residence of the child may modify the order and assume continuing, exclusive jurisdiction; or

(2) its order is not the controlling order.

(c) If a tribunal of another state has issued a child-support order pursuant to the Uniform Interstate Family Support Act or a law substantially similar to that Act which modifies a child-support order of a tribunal of this state, tribunals of this state shall recognize the continuing, exclusive jurisdiction of the tribunal of the other state.

(d) A tribunal of this state that lacks continuing, exclusive jurisdiction to modify a child-support order may serve as an initiating tribunal to request a tribunal of another state to modify a support order issued in that state.

(e) A temporary support order issued ex parte or pending resolution of a jurisdictional conflict does not create continuing, exclusive jurisdiction in the issuing tribunal.

§ 206. Continuing Jurisdiction to Enforce Child-Support Order.

(a) A tribunal of this state that has issued a child-support order consistent with the law of this state may serve as an initiating tribunal to request a tribunal of another state to enforce:

(1) the order if the order is the controlling order and has not been modified by a tribunal of another state that assumed jurisdiction pursuant to the Uniform Interstate Family Support Act; or

(2) a money judgment for arrears of support and interest on the order accrued before a determination that an order of a tribunal of another state is the controlling order.

(b) A tribunal of this state having continuing jurisdiction over a support order may act as a responding tribunal to enforce the order.

§ 207. Determination of Controlling Child-Support Order.

(a) If a proceeding is brought under this act and only one tribunal has issued a child-support order, the order of that tribunal controls and must be recognized.

(b) If a proceeding is brought under this act, and two or more child-support orders have been issued by tribunals of this state, another state, or a foreign country with regard to the same obligor and same child, a tribunal of this state having personal jurisdiction over both the obligor and individual obligee shall apply the following rules and by order shall determine which order controls and must be recognized:

(1) If only one of the tribunals would have continuing, exclusive jurisdiction under this act, the order of that tribunal controls.

(2) If more than one of the tribunals would have continuing, exclusive jurisdiction under this act:

(A) an order issued by a tribunal in the current home state of the child controls; or

(B) if an order has not been issued in the current home state of the child, the order most recently issued controls.

(3) If none of the tribunals would have continuing, exclusive jurisdiction under this act, the tribunal of this state shall issue a child-support order, which controls.

(c) If two or more child-support orders have been issued for the same obligor and same child, upon request of a party who is an individual or that is a support enforcement agency, a tribunal of this state having personal jurisdiction over both the obligor and the obligee who is an individual shall determine which order controls under subsection (b). The request may be filed with a registration for enforcement or registration for modification pursuant to [Article] 6, or may be filed as a separate proceeding.

(d) A request to determine which is the controlling order must be accompanied by a copy of every child-support order in effect and the applicable record of payments. The requesting party shall give notice of the request to each party whose rights may be affected by the determination.

(e) The tribunal that issued the controlling order under subsection (a), (b), or (c) has continuing jurisdiction to the extent provided in Section 205 or 206. . . .

(h) An order that has been determined to be the controlling order, or a judgment for consolidated arrears of support and interest, if any, made pursuant to this section must be recognized in proceedings under this act.

§ 211. Continuing, Exclusive Jurisdiction to Modify Spousal-Support Order.

(a) A tribunal of this state issuing a spousal-support order consistent with the law of this state has continuing, exclusive jurisdiction to modify the spousal-support order throughout the existence of the support obligation.

(b) A tribunal of this state may not modify a spousal-support order issued by a tribunal of another state or a foreign country having continuing, exclusive jurisdiction over that order under the law of that state or foreign country.

(c) A tribunal of this state that has continuing, exclusive jurisdiction over a spousal-support order may serve as:

(1) an initiating tribunal to request a tribunal of another state to enforce the spousal-support order issued in this state; or

(2) a responding tribunal to enforce or modify its own spousal-support order.

Article 3
Civil provisions of general application

§ 301. Proceedings Under Act.

(a) Except as otherwise provided in this act, this article applies to all proceedings under this act.

(b) An individual petitioner or a support enforcement agency may initiate a proceeding authorized under this act by filing a petition in an initiating tribunal for forwarding to a responding tribunal or by filing a petition or a comparable pleading directly in a tribunal of another state or a foreign country which has or can obtain personal jurisdiction over the respondent.

§ 303. Application of Law of State.

Except as otherwise provided in this act, a responding tribunal of this state shall:

(1) apply the procedural and substantive law generally applicable to similar proceedings originating in this state and may exercise all powers and provide all remedies available in those proceedings; and

(2) determine the duty of support and the amount payable in accordance with the law and support guidelines of this state.

§ 304. Duties of Initiating Tribunal.

(a) Upon the filing of a petition authorized by this act, an initiating tribunal of this state shall forward the petition and its accompanying documents:

(1) to the responding tribunal or appropriate support enforcement agency in the responding state; or

(2) if the identity of the responding tribunal is unknown, to the state information agency of the responding state with a request that they be forwarded to the appropriate tribunal and that receipt be acknowledged.

§ 305. Duties and Powers of Responding Tribunal.

(a) When a responding tribunal of this state receives a petition or comparable pleading from an initiating tribunal or directly pursuant to Section 301(b), it shall cause the petition or pleading to be filed and notify the petitioner where and when it was filed.

(b) A responding tribunal of this state, to the extent not prohibited by other law, may do one or more of the following:

(1) establish or enforce a support order, modify a child-support order, determine the controlling child-support order, or determine parentage of a child;

(2) order an obligor to comply with a support order, specifying the amount and the manner of compliance;

(3) order income withholding;

(4) determine the amount of any arrearages, and specify a method of payment;

(5) enforce orders by civil or criminal contempt, or both;

(6) set aside property for satisfaction of the support order;

(7) place liens and order execution on the obligor's property;

(8) order an obligor to keep the tribunal informed of the obligor's current residential address, electronic-mail address, telephone number, employer, address of employment, and telephone number at the place of employment;

(9) issue a bench warrant; capias for an obligor who has failed after proper notice to appear at a hearing ordered by the tribunal and enter the bench warrant; capias in any local and state computer systems for criminal warrants;

(10) order the obligor to seek appropriate employment by specified methods;

(11) award reasonable attorney's fees and other fees and costs; and

(12) grant any other available remedy.

(c) A responding tribunal of this state shall include in a support order issued under this act, or in the documents accompanying the order, the calculations on which the support order is based.

(d) A responding tribunal of this state may not condition the payment of a support order issued under this act upon compliance by a party with provisions for visitation.

(e) If a responding tribunal of this state issues an order under this act, the tribunal shall send a copy of the order to the petitioner and the respondent and to the initiating tribunal, if any.

§ 307. Duties of Support Enforcement Agency.

(a) A support enforcement agency of this state, upon request, shall provide services to a petitioner in a proceeding under this act.

(b) A support enforcement agency of this state that is providing services to the petitioner shall:

(1) take all steps necessary to enable an appropriate tribunal of this state, another state, or a foreign country to obtain jurisdiction over the respondent;

(2) request an appropriate tribunal to set a date, time, and place for a hearing;

(3) make a reasonable effort to obtain all relevant information, including information as to income and property of the parties;

[Numerous specific tasks assigned to the Support Enforcement Agency are deleted.]

§ 311. Pleading and Accompanying Documents.

(a) In a proceeding under this act, a petitioner seeking to establish a support order, to determine parentage of a child, or to register and modify a support order of a tribunal of another state or a foreign country must file a petition. . . .

(b) The petition must specify the relief sought. The petition and accompanying documents must conform substantially with the requirements imposed by the forms mandated by federal law for use in cases filed by a support enforcement agency.

§ 315. Nonparentage as Defense.

A party whose parentage of a child has been previously determined by or pursuant to law may not plead nonparentage as a defense to a proceeding under this act.

§ 316. Special Rules of Evidence and Procedure.

(a) The physical presence of a nonresident party who is an individual in a tribunal of this state is not required for the establishment, enforcement, or modification of a support order or the rendition of a judgment determining parentage of a child.

(b) An affidavit, a document substantially complying with federally mandated forms, or a document incorporated by reference in any of them, which would not be excluded under the hearsay rule if given in person, is admissible in evidence if given under penalty of perjury by a party or witness residing outside this state.

(c) A copy of the record of child-support payments certified as a true copy of the original by the custodian of the record may be forwarded to a responding tribunal. The copy is evidence of facts asserted in it, and is admissible to show whether payments were made.

(d) Copies of bills for testing for parentage of a child, and for prenatal and postnatal health care of the mother and child, furnished to the adverse party at least 10 days before trial, are admissible in evidence to prove the amount of the charges billed and that the charges were reasonable, necessary, and customary.

(e) Documentary evidence transmitted from outside this state to a tribunal of this state by telephone, telecopier, or other electronic means that do not provide an original record may not be excluded from evidence on an objection based on the means of transmission.

(f) In a proceeding under this act, a tribunal of this state shall permit a party or witness residing outside this state to be deposed or to testify under penalty of perjury by telephone, audiovisual means, or other electronic means at a designated tribunal or other location. A tribunal of this state shall cooperate with other tribunals in designating an appropriate location for the deposition or testimony.

(g) If a party called to testify at a civil hearing refuses to answer on the ground that the testimony may be self-incriminating, the trier of fact may draw an adverse inference from the refusal.

(h) A privilege against disclosure of communications between spouses does not apply in a proceeding under this act.

(i) The defense of immunity based on the relationship of husband and wife or parent and child does not apply in a proceeding under this act.

(j) A voluntary acknowledgment of paternity, certified as a true copy, is admissible to establish parentage of the child.

§ 317. Communications Between Tribunals.

A tribunal of this state may communicate with a tribunal outside this state in a record or by telephone, electronic mail, or other means, to obtain information concerning the laws, the legal effect of a judgment, decree, or order of that tribunal, and the status of a proceeding. A tribunal of this state may furnish similar information by similar means to a tribunal outside this state.

Article 4
Establishment of support order or determination of parentage

§ 401. Establishment of Support Order.

(a) If a support order entitled to recognition under this act has not been issued, a responding tribunal of this state with personal jurisdiction over the parties may issue a support order if:

(1) the individual seeking the order resides outside this state; or

(2) the support enforcement agency seeking the order is located outside this state.

(b) The tribunal may issue a temporary child-support order if the tribunal determines that such an order is appropriate and the individual ordered to pay is:

(1) a presumed father of the child;

(2) petitioning to have his paternity adjudicated;

(3) identified as the father of the child through genetic testing;

(4) an alleged father who has declined to submit to genetic testing;

(5) shown by clear and convincing evidence to be the father of the child;

(6) an acknowledged father as provided by applicable state law;

(7) the mother of the child; or

(8) an individual who has been ordered to pay child support in a previous proceeding and the order has not been reversed or vacated.

(c) Upon finding, after notice and opportunity to be heard, that an obligor owes a duty of support, the tribunal shall issue a support order directed to the obligor and may issue other orders pursuant to Section 305.

§ 402. Proceeding to Determine Parentage.

A tribunal of this state authorized to determine parentage of a child may serve as a responding tribunal in a proceeding to determine parentage of a child brought under this act or a law or procedure substantially similar to this act.

Article 5
Enforcement of support order without registration

§ 501. Employer's Receipt of Income-Withholding Order of Another State.

An income-withholding order issued in another state may be sent by or on behalf of the obligee, or by the support enforcement agency, to the person defined as the obligor's employer under the income-withholding law of this state without first filing a petition or comparable pleading or registering the order with a tribunal of this state.

§ 503. Employer's Compliance With Two or More Income-Withholding Orders.

If an obligor's employer receives two or more income-withholding orders with respect to the earnings of the same obligor, the employer satisfies the terms of the orders if the employer complies with the law of the state of the obligor's principal place of employment to establish the priorities for withholding and allocating income withheld for two or more child-support obligees.

§ 504. Immunity from Civil Liability.

An employer that complies with an income-withholding order issued in another state in accordance with this article is not subject to civil liability to an individual or agency with regard to the employer's withholding of child support from the obligor's income.

§ 505. Penalties for Noncompliance.

An employer that willfully fails to comply with an income-withholding order issued in another state and received for enforcement is subject to the same penalties that may be imposed for noncompliance with an order issued by a tribunal of this state.

§ 506. Contest by Obligor.

(a) An obligor may contest the validity or enforcement of an income-withholding order issued in another state and received directly by an employer in this state by registering the order in a tribunal of this state and filing a contest to that order as provided in Article 6, or otherwise contesting the order in the same manner as if the order had been issued by a tribunal of this state.

(b) The obligor shall give notice of the contest to:

(1) a support enforcement agency providing services to the obligee;

(2) each employer that has directly received an income-withholding order relating to the obligor; and

(3) the person designated to receive payments in the income-withholding order or, if no person is designated, to the obligee.

§ 507. Administrative Enforcement of Orders.

(a) A party or support enforcement agency seeking to enforce a support order or an income-withholding order, or both, issued in another state or a foreign support order may send the documents required for registering the order to a support enforcement agency of this state.

(b) Upon receipt of the documents, the support enforcement agency, without initially seeking to register the order, shall consider and, if appropriate, use any administrative procedure authorized by the law of this state to enforce a support order or an income-withholding order, or both. If the obligor does not contest administrative enforcement, the order need not be registered. If the obligor contests the validity or administrative enforcement of the order, the support enforcement agency shall register the order pursuant to this act.

Article 6
Registration, enforcement, and modification of support order

§ 601. Registration of Order for Enforcement.

A support order or income-withholding order issued in another state or a foreign support order may be registered in this state for enforcement.

§ 603. Effect of Registration for Enforcement.

(a) A support order or income-withholding order issued in another state or a foreign support order is registered when the order is filed in the registering tribunal of this state.

(b) A registered support order issued in another state or a foreign country is enforceable in the same manner and is subject to the same procedures as an order issued by a tribunal of this state.

(c) Except as otherwise provided in this act, a tribunal of this state shall recognize and enforce, but may not modify, a registered support order if the issuing tribunal had jurisdiction.

§ 604. Choice of Law.

(a) Except as otherwise provided in subsection (d), the law of the issuing state or foreign country governs:

(1) the nature, extent, amount, and duration of current payments under a registered support order;

(2) the computation and payment of arrearages and accrual of interest on the arrearages under the support order; and

(3) the existence and satisfaction of other obligations under the support order.

(b) In a proceeding for arrears under a registered support order, the statute of limitation of this state, or of the issuing state or foreign country, whichever is longer, applies.

(c) A responding tribunal of this state shall apply the procedures and remedies of this state to enforce current support and collect arrears and interest due on a support order of another state or a foreign country registered in this state.

(d) After a tribunal of this state or another state determines which is the controlling order and issues an order consolidating arrears, if any, a tribunal of this state shall prospectively apply the law of the state or foreign country issuing the controlling order, including its law on interest on arrears, on current and future support, and on consolidated arrears.

§ 610. Effect of Registration for Modification.

A tribunal of this state may enforce a child-support order of another state registered for purposes of modification, in the same manner as if the order had been issued by a tribunal of this state, but the registered support order may be modified only if the requirements of Section 611 or 613 have been met.

§ 611. Modification of Child-Support Order of Another State.

(a) If Section 613 does not apply, upon petition a tribunal of this state may modify a child-support order issued in another state which is registered in this state if, after notice and hearing, the tribunal finds that:

    (1) the following requirements are met:

        (A) neither the child, nor the obligee who is an individual, nor the obligor resides in the issuing state;

        (B) a petitioner who is a nonresident of this state seeks modification; and

        (C) the respondent is subject to the personal jurisdiction of the tribunal of this state; or

    (2) this state is the residence of the child, or a party who is an individual is subject to the personal jurisdiction of the tribunal of this state, and all of the parties who are individuals have filed consents in a record in the issuing tribunal for a tribunal of this state to modify the support order and assume continuing, exclusive jurisdiction.

(b) Modification of a registered child-support order is subject to the same requirements, procedures, and defenses that apply to the modification of an order issued by a tribunal of this state and the order may be enforced and satisfied in the same manner.

(c) A tribunal of this state may not modify any aspect of a child-support order that may not be modified under the law of the issuing state, including the duration of the obligation of support. If two or more tribunals have issued child-support orders for the same obligor and same child, the order that controls and must be so recognized under Section 207 establishes the aspects of the support order which are nonmodifiable.

(d) In a proceeding to modify a child-support order, the law of the state that is determined to have issued the initial controlling order governs the duration of the obligation of support. The obligor's fulfillment of the duty of support established by that order precludes imposition of a further obligation of support by a tribunal of this state.

(e) On the issuance of an order by a tribunal of this state modifying a child-support order issued in another state, the tribunal of this state becomes the tribunal having continuing, exclusive jurisdiction.

(f) Notwithstanding subsections (a) through (e) and Section 201(b), a tribunal of this state retains jurisdiction to modify an order issued by a tribunal of this state if:

(1) one party resides in another state; and

(2) the other party resides outside the United States.

§ 612. Recognition of Order Modified in Another State.

If a child-support order issued by a tribunal of this state is modified by a tribunal of another state which assumed jurisdiction pursuant to the Uniform Interstate Family Support Act, a tribunal of this state:

(1) may enforce its order that was modified only as to arrears and interest accruing before the modification;

(2) may provide appropriate relief for violations of its order which occurred before the effective date of the modification; and

(3) shall recognize the modifying order of the other state, upon registration, for the purpose of enforcement.

§ 613. Jurisdiction to Modify Child-Support Order of Another State When Individual Parties Reside in this State.

(a) If all of the parties who are individuals reside in this state and the child does not reside in the issuing state, a tribunal of this state has jurisdiction to enforce and to modify the issuing state's child-support order in a proceeding to register that order.

(b) A tribunal of this state exercising jurisdiction under this section shall apply the provisions of Articles 1 and 2, this article, and the procedural and substantive law of this state to the proceeding for enforcement or modification. Articles 3, 4, 5, 7, and 8 do not apply.

§ 615. Jurisdiction to Modify Child-Support Order of Foreign Country

(a) Except as otherwise provided in Section 711, if a foreign country lacks or refuses to exercise jurisdiction to modify its child-support order pursuant to its laws, a tribunal of this state may assume jurisdiction to modify the child-support order and bind all individuals subject to the personal jurisdiction of the tribunal whether the consent to modification of a child-support order otherwise required of the individual pursuant to Section 611 has been given or whether the individual seeking modification is a resident of this state or of the foreign country.

(b) An order issued by a tribunal of this state modifying a foreign child-support order pursuant to this section is the controlling order.

§ 616. Procedure to Register Child-Support Order of Foreign Country for Modification.

A party or support enforcement agency seeking to modify, or to modify and enforce, a foreign child-support order not under the Convention may register that order in this state under Sections 601 through 608 if the order has not been registered. A petition for modification may be filed at the same time as a request for registration, or at another time. The petition must specify the grounds for modification.

The Washington Supreme Court's decision in *In re Schneider* demonstrates UISFA in action.

In re Schneider

Supreme Court of Washington
173 Wash. 2d 353, 268 P.3d 215 (2011)

Wiggins, J.

The Uniform Interstate Family Support Act (UIFSA) governs modification of child support obligations in Washington when the initial child support order was entered in a different state but one of the parties lives in Washington. The UIFSA provides that the duration of child support is governed by the laws of the original forum state. Jeffrey Almgren and Carol Schneider divorced in Nebraska and Schneider moved to Washington with the couple's two children. We hold that the superior court erred by extending the father's child support obligation past the age of majority by granting postsecondary support for the daughter to attend college. Nebraska law would not have allowed postsecondary support in this case, and the UIFSA provides that the law of the original forum state governs the duration of child support. We reverse the Court of Appeals, which affirmed the trial court, and remand for further proceedings consistent with this opinion.

Carol Schneider (the mother) and Jeffrey Almgren (the father) were divorced in Nebraska in 1997. The couple had two children, Amanda born December 24, 1990 and D.J.A. born October 31, 1993. The decree of dissolution set child support to continue during each child's minority. In Nebraska, the age of majority is 19 years.

The mother moved with the children to Washington, and the father moved to Minnesota. . . .

In January 2009, the mother petitioned [in Washington] for postsecondary educational support for Amanda, who was still 18 and in high school and had been accepted for admission to Eastern Washington University. The father filed a cross-motion to modify child support for the younger child downward due to the father's recent loss of his job. The trial court granted the mother's motion for postsecondary educational support for Amanda and denied the father's motion for a downward modification.

The father moved for reconsideration, raising for the first time the issue of the trial court's authority under the UIFSA to enter orders extending child support for Amanda beyond the age of majority in Nebraska. After hearing argument, the trial court denied reconsideration. . . . The Court of Appeals affirmed in an unpublished opinion.

To understand the issues presented by this case, it is helpful to understand the origin of the UIFSA. The UIFSA was developed in response to federal legislation impacting state child support enforcement laws. Prior to the development of the UIFSA, when parties in a child support action lived in different states, each state could issue its own child support orders. This potential for competing child support orders, with varying terms and duration depending on the issuing jurisdiction, resulted in a proliferation of litigation. The UIFSA addressed this "chaos" by establishing a "one-order" system for child support orders by providing that one state would have continuing exclusive jurisdiction over the order. The UIFSA enforces the one-order system in a variety of ways, including registration of out-of-state child support orders for either enforcement, modification, or both. The modification provisions of the UIFSA are mirrored in the Full Faith and Credit for Child Support Orders Act. 28 U.S.C. § 1738B.

. . . Congress required all states to adopt the UIFSA in order to remain eligible to receive federal funding for child support enforcement. All 50 states have done so. . . .

RCW 26.21A.550 defines two situations in which a Washington court may modify another state's child support order:

(1) Upon petition a tribunal of this state may modify a child support order issued in another state which is registered in this state if, after notice and hearing the tribunal finds that:

a. The following requirements are met:

(i) The child, the obligee who is an individual, and the obligor do not reside in the issuing state;

(ii) A petitioner who is a nonresident of this state seeks modification; and

(iii) The respondent is subject to the personal jurisdiction of the tribunal of this state; or

b. This state is either the state of residence of the child or of a party who is an individual subject to the personal jurisdiction of the tribunal of this state, and all of the parties who are individuals have filed consents in a record in the issuing tribunal for a tribunal of this state to modify the support order and assume continuing, exclusive jurisdiction.

[Regarding mother,] the conditions of subsection (1)(a)(ii) are not met because the mother as the petitioner is not a "nonresident of this state." Nor is subsection (1)(b) satisfied because the record does not contain the mother's or the father's consents filed in the Nebraska tribunal that issued the original child support order. Therefore, neither of the conditions that would have allowed the trial court to modify the Nebraska child support order appears to have been met. . . .

[Father] sought affirmative relief by moving to reduce support for the younger child. By making this motion, the father submitted to the personal jurisdiction of the Washington trial court. Thus, with the father as the moving party, the conditions allowing the trial court to modify the Nebraska child support order were met: (1) neither of the parties nor the child reside in Nebraska, (2) the moving party (father) does not reside in Washington, and (3) Washington has personal jurisdiction over the mother as a resident.

Once the conditions allowing a Washington Court to modify another state's child support order have been met, the UIFSA imposes restrictions on which elements may be modified:

(3) Except as otherwise provided in RCW 26.21A.570, a tribunal of this state may not modify any aspect of a child support order that may not be modified under the law of the issuing state . . . .

(4) In a proceeding to modify a child support order, the law of the state that is determined to have issued the initial controlling order governs the duration of the obligation of support. The obligor's fulfillment of the duty of support established by that order precludes imposition of a further obligation of support by a tribunal of this state. RCW 26.21A.550.

Here, the statute plainly says that (1) if an aspect of a child support order may not be modified under the law of the issuing state, a Washington court may not modify that aspect of the order and (2) when modifying the duration of an out-of-state child support order, the court must apply the law of the state that issued the initial controlling order. The initial controlling order in this case was the Nebraska child support order . . . .

[The] Washington order awarded Amanda postsecondary educational support that would continue until she reached 23 years of age, the upper limit of postsecondary educational support in Washington. . . . The original Nebraska child support order did not call for child support beyond the age of 19. . . .

. . . Nebraska law . . . provides that the obligation for child support in Nebraska continues only until the age of majority unless the dissolution decree contains a different provision or the parties reached a property settlement agreement incorporated into the decree.

In short, the duration of child support is not modifiable under Nebraska law because support extends only to age 19 absent circumstances not present here, unless the parties have agreed to postmajority support in a settlement agreement that is incorporated into the dissolution decree. The mother and the father did not enter into such a settlement agreement. Accordingly, if granting postsecondary support was a change in the duration of child support, the . . . order was erroneous under the UIFSA and RCW 26.21A .550. . . .

The New Hampshire Supreme Court has recently addressed a case similar to the case at bar. *In re Scott*, 160 N.H. 354, 999 A.2d 229 (2010). In *Scott*, the parties had been divorced in Massachusetts, after which the mother moved with the children to California and the father moved to New Hampshire. The Massachusetts child support order provided for postsecondary support under a Massachusetts law. The New Hampshire Supreme Court rejected the father's argument that he was not liable for postsecondary support under New Hampshire law, holding that "Massachusetts law governed the duration of child support because, under UIFSA, duration is a non-modifiable aspect of an issuing state's original child support order."

It may seem anomalous to deny postsecondary educational support for Amanda, who has lived in Washington for several years and attends a Washington state university. But there are two sides to this result. A child who is initially allowed the potential of postsecondary educational support in Washington will be able to receive that support even after moving to another state. Every state has adopted the UIFSA in some form and the UIFSA provides that the originating state's law applies to the duration of child support. Because the issue is durational, Washington law will apply to Washington child support orders that provide for postsecondary educational support. If the issue were not durational, other states would be free to reject the provisions for postsecondary support under Washington law.

In any event, the legislature has resolved this policy choice by adopting the UIFSA. Our responsibility under the Washington Constitution is to interpret and apply the decision of the legislature. Accordingly, we hold that postsecondary educational support is a durational aspect of child support under the UIFSA. . . .

The trial court exceeded its authority when it ordered postsecondary educational support for Amanda, and the Court of Appeals erred in affirming the trial court's order. We reverse and remand for further proceedings consistent with this opinion.

Problems on Child Support

1. Debbie and Jim were married and had two kids. They divorced after 6 years of marriage. Debbie was awarded primary physical custody of the children, and Jim was ordered to pay child support. A few years after the divorce, Jim remarried and had two kids with his second wife. For five years, Jim worked at various relatively low paying jobs—often working two jobs—to support his family and pay child support. When Jim was laid off from his most recent construction job, he decided to go to college full time to finish a degree he'd started years earlier. Jim's wife worked outside the home, and she increased her work hours to support the family. Jim went to class, studied, and took care of the kids. Because he had been laid off and had returned to school, Jim had no income. Jim petitions the family court to reduce his child support obligation to Debbie and the children of his first marriage until he finishes his degree, which will take three years. For her part, Debbie opposes Jim's petition, arguing he can work and go to school part time. Should the judge modify child support? *J.M. v. D.A., 935 N.E.2d 1235 (Ind. Ct. App. 2010). See also Little v. Little,* 193 Ariz. 518, 975 P.2d 108 (1999)(Air Force officer resigned his commission and entered law school; he sought reduction of child support amount because he was a full time law student; Supreme Court ruled against him).

2. David was an attorney. When his girlfriend Rachael became pregnant, David tried to hire a "hit man" to kill Rachael and the unborn child. The hit man turned out to be a police officer. David was convicted of two counts of solicitation of murder and sentenced to a long prison term. (He was disbarred, of course.) The baby was born and Rachel seeks an award of child support from the now-imprisoned David. David responds that he has no income in prison and no way to earn any. Should the judge enter an order for child support against David? *Mascola v. Lusskin,* 727 So. 2d 328 (Fla. Ct. App. 1999). *See also* McCall v. Martin, 34 So. 3d 121 (Fla. Ct. App. 2010).

3. Sue and Dave divorced five years ago, when their kids were 6 and 8. At the time of the divorce, Sue was a partner in a law firm and made a handsome six figure income. Dave was a high school teacher and earned roughly 25% of Sue's income. In the divorce, Sue and Dave agreed that Dave would have primary physical custody of the children, and Sue would have the children most weekends. The parties agreed that Sue would pay Dave $7,000 per month in child support, and that there would be no spousal support. In the five years since the divorce, Sue never missed a child support payment. Recently, the President of the United States appointed Sue to the federal district court bench. Sue is waiting for the Senate to confirm her appointment. There is no opposition to her nomination, and she will be confirmed. By becoming a federal judge, Sue will take a 50% pay cut. Sue asks Dave if he will agree to lower the monthly child support from $7,000 to $3,000 due to Sue's lower income, but Dave declines, telling Sue, "I know you would love to be a judge, but the needs of the children haven't changed. You could stay at the law firm and continue earning plenty of money to help support them. Even if you go on the bench, you will still be making a lot more than me. I'm sorry, but I have to have the money to pay the bills." Should Sue be able to go to family court and lower her child support obligation?

4. Change the facts in Sue and Dave's case, above. At the time of their divorce, Sue is a highly successful plastic surgeon making over $ 1 million a year. Sue decides to leave her practice for three years to work in a clinic in a war-torn country in Africa, where she will perform reconstructive surgery for children and adults wounded in war. Sue will not be paid for her work in Africa. Can Sue lower her child support payments while she is donating her time?

5. John was an electrical engineer earning $200,000 a year. John was divorced from Becky. The divorce decree obligated John to pay $2,000 per month child support. One day, John walked into work and quit, saying that he was following Jesus Christ, and that he intended to start a church. When John quit, he did not have a position as a pastor. After several months, John started his own church. It took about a year to get the church off the ground. John is the pastor and is paid $50,000 a year. John recently filed a motion in family court to reduce his child support. John argues his circumstances have changed substantially, warranting a reduction. *Andrews v. Andrews,* 719 S.E.2d 128 (N.C. Ct. App. 2011).

6. Bill has six kids from three different marriages. Despite working full time, Bill has never supported any of his children. Note a dime. After years of failing to support his children, Bill was convicted of criminal nonsupport and sent to prison for 3 years. While in prison, Bill filed a petition to lower his support obligations because he was

in prison and thus had no income with which to pay support. Should Bill's petition be granted? *Douglas v. State,* 954 N.E.2d 1090 (Ind. Ct. App. 2011).

7. When Suzanne and Michael divorced, their marriage settlement agreement (MSA) provided that Suzanne would have primary physical custody of their two kids. The MSA provided that Michael would pay monthly child support of $1,200. The MSA provided that the child support "shall be the minimum amount due for a period of no less than 33 months from the date the divorce is final, and that Michael may not file for a reduction in that amount for the full 33 months." Within a year of the divorce, Michael was laid off from his job as an engineer for the state. Michael returned to court with a motion to reduce child support. Suzanne opposes the motion, arguing the court should enforce the MSA regarding nonmodifiable child support. Michael responds that it would be against public policy to enforce the MSA. What should the judge do? *May v. May,* 339 Wis. 2d 626, 813 N.W.2d 179 (2012).

8. Referring to Suzanne and Michael from problem 7, suppose their MSA was different. Rather than set an unmodifiable floor for child support, the MSA set an unmodifiable ceiling. The MSA provided: "Michael shall pay monthly child support in the amount of $1,200 each month. This amount may not be increased for a period of at least 33 months." A year after the divorce, Suzanne files a motion to increase child support because Michael has a new, higher paying job. Michael argues the MSA should be enforced as written. What should the judge do?

9. Karla and Bill dated and had a sexual relationship. A month after they broke up, Karla discovered she was pregnant. Karla informed Bill of the pregnancy, and told him he was the father. Bill began sending Karla $2,000 a month for child support. From the outset, Karla suspected Bill was not the father. While dating Bill, Karla also dated Tom, and Karla believed Tom was the father. Bill did not know about Tom. After paying child support for two years, Bill learned for the first time he might not be the father. Genetic testing confirmed Bill's suspicion, and Bill stopped paying support. As well, Bill sued Karla for fraud, seeking reimbursement of the two years of child support. Should Bill be allowed to recover from Karla? Should it make a difference if Karla can't afford to repay the $48,000, and paying anything would undermine her ability to provide for the child? What if Karla didn't deliberately lie to Bill. Rather, from the outset, Karla believed Bill was the father, and only learned Tom was the father when the genetic testing was performed. Should this alter the outcome of Bill's lawsuit? In the first scenario, Karla lied. In the second scenario, she told the truth but she was wrong. *Dier v. Peters,* 815 N.W.2d 1 (Iowa 2012).

Emancipation

Teenagers yearn for independence from their parents. Yet, until teens turn eighteen, mom and dad normally call the shots. Below eighteen, joining the military or getting married automatically emancipates a minor from parental control. In addition to automatic emancipation, states allow minors to petition a court for a judicial determination of emancipation. California emancipation law, for example, allows minors who are at least fourteen to petition the Superior Court. The minor must establish that she does not live with her parents and that she is managing her own financial affairs. Unless the judge concludes emancipation would be contrary to the minor's best interest, the judge issues a declaration of emancipation.[30]

The New Mexico Supreme Court's decision in *Diamond v. Diamond* is a good overview of emancipation, and raises interesting questions.

Diamond v. Diamond

Supreme Court of New Mexico
283 P.3d 260 (2012)

Serna, Justice.

This appeal presents this Court with a matter of first impression: does the New Mexico Emancipation of Minors Act, NMSA 1978, §§ 32A–21–1 to –7 (1995) (the Act), which provides that a minor may be emancipated for "one or more purposes" set forth in the Act authorize a district court to declare a minor emancipated for some rather than all of those enumerated purposes? . . .

Petitioner Jhette Diamond (Daughter), then sixteen years old, petitioned the district court in January 2007 for a declaration of emancipation pursuant to the Act. Daughter left the home of her mother Adrienne Diamond (Mother) at age thirteen and had been living with several different households since that time.

The district court held a hearing on Daughter's petition in February 2007. Mother did not appear at the hearing or otherwise oppose the petition. Daughter, represented by counsel, told the district court that she had moved out of Mother's home due to domestic violence and substance abuse issues. Daughter had been working since the age of eleven, including for the past several years as a restaurant server and busser, while maintaining a high grade-point average as a sophomore

---

30 Cal. Family Code§ 7000 et seq.

at Española Valley High School. Counsel described Daughter as "focused on her future," and thriving with the support of the couple with whom she was living. Daughter had no intention of returning to live with Mother, who maintained a relationship with the man whose violent behavior and substance abuse had contributed to Daughter's decision to leave Mother's home in the first place.

The district court concluded that by all accounts Daughter was capable of making appropriate choices for herself and covering her own expenses, describing Daughter's situation as "a classic case" for emancipation. Because Mother had not provided any financial support to Daughter before or after Daughter began living apart from Mother, Daughter asked if the emancipation order could be styled to reserve her right to pursue financial support from Mother. The court agreed . . . .

The district court issued a "Declaration of Emancipation of Minor" in March 2007, finding that Daughter had been living independently and managing her own financial affairs without support from Mother, determining that emancipation would be in Daughter's best interest, and declaring Daughter "an emancipated minor in all respects, except that she shall retain the right to support from Mother" pursuant to Section 32A–21–5(D) of the Act. Mother filed a pro se motion to set aside the declaration because she had not received adequate notice of the original emancipation hearing. Mother additionally argued that she had supported Daughter even after Daughter moved out by paying for Daughter's traffic tickets, medical and dental care, and school clothes, and "was always giving Daughter spending money." Mother also disputed that Daughter was managing her own financial affairs.

The district court held a hearing on Mother's pro se motion in April 2007. Mother repeated her objections to Daughter's emancipation because, in her view, Daughter was not mature enough to act in her own best interest. The district court asked Mother for evidence or examples of Daughter's lack of maturity, and Mother could not think of any. . . .

Disputing Mother's assertions about having covered certain expenses, Daughter testified that it was actually a concerned teacher who paid for her traffic ticket, that Daughter herself paid for dental care, and that Medicaid covered the cost of medical care when Daughter broke her arm at school. Daughter acknowledged that on a single occasion Mother had purchased several items of clothing for her, but that she could not recall Mother ever providing her with spending money, contrary to Mother's claim that she "always" did so. . . .

Daughter also explained why she was seeking emancipation. Although at that point in time she had already been living apart from her Mother for two to three years, paying her own expenses, attending school, and working, Daughter testified that she had difficulty obtaining medical insurance, accessing her school report cards, or applying for a driver's permit, all of which required parental consent. Emancipated status also would allow Daughter to open a bank account. Daughter stated that she would be uncomfortable if she were required to resume living with Mother, especially because Mother's abusive boyfriend remained a presence in Mother's home, and because she was doing well on her own.

After hearing testimony from Mother and Daughter, the district court ruled from the bench that even assuming that all of Mother's contentions were true, emancipation remained in Daughter's best interest. . . .

Daughter filed a petition asking the district court to order Mother to pay retroactive and prospective child support to Daughter. . . . Mother argued that "New Mexico law does not allow child support for an emancipated minor." . . . Daughter . . . testified that since petitioning for emancipation she had graduated from high school and was now a student at New Mexico State University. . . .

A hearing officer determined that Mother had not provided a home or financial support for Daughter since Daughter's emancipation. The hearing officer recommended that Mother be ordered to make support payments to Daughter in the amount of $390.00 per month from March 1, 2008 until Daughter reached the age of eighteen or graduated from high school, whichever event occurred later. The hearing officer reserved for later determination the issue of any child support obligation predating March 1, 2008 . . . The district court affirmed the hearing officer's report over Mother's written objections, and in January 2009 directed that a portion of Mother's retirement benefit, her sole source of income, be garnished and paid to Daughter. . . .

Mother appealed the judgment entered against her in the support proceeding and a related order from the original emancipation proceeding. . . . Agreeing with Mother, the Court of Appeals held that "New Mexico law does not permit a minor emancipated pursuant to the Act to collect child support payments." . . .

The Act defines an emancipated minor as any person sixteen years of age or older who "has entered into a valid marriage, whether or not the marriage was terminated by dissolution," who "is on active duty with any of the armed forces of the United States of America," or who has received a declaration of emancipation" pursuant to the Act. The Act sets forth three prerequisites to emancipation by judicial declaration. "Any person sixteen years of age or older may be declared an emancipated minor for one or more purposes enumerated in the Act if he is [1] willingly living separate and apart from his parents, guardian or custodian, [2] is managing his financial affairs and [3] the court finds it in the minor's best interest."

. . . A minor seeking to be emancipated must file a verified petition with the children's court that "sets forth with specificity the facts" in support of such relief, and the court shall provide notice of the petition to the minor's parent, guardian or custodian. If the court determines the minor to be sixteen years of age or older and to fulfill the preconditions for emancipation, "the court may grant the petition unless, after having considered all of the evidence introduced at the hearing, it finds that granting the petition would be contrary to the best interests of the minor." . . .

As for the legal effect of emancipation, under the Act, "An emancipated minor shall be considered as being over the age of majority for one or more of the following purposes: (a) consenting to medical, dental or psychiatric care without parental consent, knowledge or liability; (b) his capacity to enter into a binding contract; (c) his capacity to sue and be sued in his own name; (d) his right to support by his parents; (e) the rights of his parents to his earnings and to control him; (f) establishing his own residence; (g) buying or selling real property; (h) ending vicarious liability of the minor's parents or; (i) enrolling in any school or college." Section 32A–21–5. . . .

In interpreting a statute, the Court's primary goal is to ascertain and give effect to the intent of the legislature. In assessing intent, we look first to the plain language of the statute, giving the words their ordinary meaning, unless the Legislature indicates a different one was intended. When interpreting a statute, all sections of the statute must be read together so that all parts are given effect. Where the language of a statute is clear and unambiguous, we must give effect to that language and refrain from further statutory interpretation.

. . . In setting forth the nine possible legal effects of emancipation, the Act refers to "one or more of the [enumerated] purposes." Daughter interprets the Act to authorize a district court to craft an order of emancipation to address only those purposes which meet the best interests of the child seeking emancipation, and asserts that there is nothing absurd about granting a minor many of the legal privileges of adulthood while in appropriate circumstances allowing that minor to pursue parental support. Mother in turn argues that where the Act refers to one or more purposes of emancipation, the phrase should be interpreted to mean all the purposes. . . .

The plain meaning of the phrase "one or more purposes" is that a minor may be declared to be emancipated under the Act for a single enumerated purpose, for all nine enumerated purposes, or for any intermediate number of enumerated purposes. . . .

We must assume the legislature chose its words advisedly to express its meaning unless the contrary intent clearly appears. Not only does the Act fail to evidence any legislative intent contrary to the plain meaning of "one or more purposes," the history of its enactment provides persuasive indications of the Legislature's intent that district courts should tailor emancipation orders to the best interests of the minor in each particular case. . . .

The Act requires that a minor must be living independently and "managing his own financial affairs" in order to be emancipated. Mother argues that in the context of the Act, "managing his financial affairs is synonymous with being financially independent, self-supporting, self-sufficient, it is axiomatic that to be emancipated you must be self-supporting and if you are self-supporting you are not in need of or entitled to support." Daughter responds that managing one's financial affairs is not the equivalent of total financial self-sufficiency. We agree with Daughter. . . .

The Court of Appeals agreed with Mother and found the district court's interpretation of the Act "paradoxical," explaining that "a minor cannot be "managing his own financial affairs" if he is receiving financial and other support from his parents." We do not see management of one's financial affairs and entitlement to support as inherently contradictory. Certainly, in other proceedings courts routinely award support without any finding or implication that the recipient is incapable of managing his or her affairs. . . .

Although we find ample support for our interpretation of the Act in its plain language and legislative intent, a brief review of several other states' emancipation statutes, illustrative rather than exhaustive, indicates a diversity in approach to defining the legal effects of emancipation. Some states have determined that emancipation should always entail a fixed rather than a flexible set of legal consequences. For example, in contrast to the Act's provision that emancipation may be ordered for "one or more purposes," California's emancipation statute directs that an emancipated minor "shall be considered as being an adult for the following purposes," Cal. Fam.Code Ann. § 7050, that is, for all of the seventeen purposes enumerated by the California statute . . . .

Consistent with California's approach and in contrast to ours, Vermont law provides that an emancipation order "shall recognize the minor as an adult for all purposes that result from reaching the age of majority, including terminating parental support and control of the minor and parental rights to the minor's income." Vt. Stat. Ann. tit. 12, § 7156(a). Pennsylvania state law does not set forth a specific statutory mechanism for a minor to obtain a declaration of emancipation, but nonetheless expressly provides that "a court shall not order either or both parents to pay for the support of a child if the child is emancipated." 23 Pa. Cons.Stat. Ann. § 4323(a).

Other states, while perhaps not favoring parental support for emancipated minors, do not foreclose it either. Under Nevada law, for example, an emancipation decree confers the right of majority for six enumerated purposes, including entering into contracts or incurring debts, Nev.Rev.Stat. § 129.130(3)(a), obtaining medical care without parental consent, and establishing the minor's own residence, but not elimination of support from a parent. Whether to award support, however, is left to the discretion of the court considering the emancipation petition, with the default under the statute for support to cease upon emancipation: "Unless otherwise provided by the emancipation decree, the obligation of support otherwise owed a minor by his or her parent or guardian is terminated by the entry of the decree."

On the other hand, New Mexico is far from the only state where a minor's emancipation does not presumptively extinguish a parent's support obligation. Montana's emancipation statute probably resembles New Mexico's most closely. If a Montana court grants a petition for emancipation, it must issue an order that "specifically sets forth the rights and responsibilities that are being conferred upon the youth, which may include but are not limited to one or more" of a list of six purposes. Mont.Code Ann. § 41–1–503(2) (2009). Those purposes include the right to live in housing of the minor's choice, the right to enter into contracts and incur debts, the right to consent to medical care, and the right to "directly receive and expend money to which the youth is entitled and to conduct the youth's own financial affairs." The Montana statute, like ours, does not define emancipation to automatically end a parent's support obligation.

At least one state goes further than New Mexico by not merely permitting but mandating parental support for emancipated minors. Under Michigan's emancipation statute, a court may declare a minor emancipated "for the purposes of, but not limited to, all of the following fourteen purposes," Mich. Comp. Laws Ann. § 722.4e(1), a list that does not include child support. Instead, Michigan law explicitly provides that "the parents of a minor emancipated by court order are jointly and severally obligated to support the minor," except that the parents are not liable for debt incurred by the minor during the period of emancipation.

The point of the foregoing review is to illustrate the wide variety of approaches states employ to determine what legal consequences emancipation should have, particularly with respect to the provision of child support. Our

Legislature . . . chose to confer authority on the district courts to determine in each particular case whether an emancipated minor is entitled to support. . . .

The Legislature's decision to allow district courts to determine the extent of an emancipated minor's rights and responsibilities also comports with our state's public policy. In New Mexico, there is a strong tradition of protecting a child's best interests in a variety of circumstances. Furthermore, it is well-settled law that when a case involves children, the trial court has broad authority to fashion its rulings in the best interests of the children. . . . More specifically, the district courts are properly invested with broad discretion and flexibility in determining an award of child support. Giving effect to the plain meaning of the Act is consistent with our state's public policy favoring judicial determination of the best interests of the minor. A district court could, for example, where appropriate declare a minor emancipated for a single purpose, such as consenting to medical, dental or psychiatric care without parental consent, knowledge or liability, or attending college. Similarly, a district court has the discretion to declare a minor emancipated for a greater number of purposes, or all of the purposes, set forth in the Act. The critical inquiry remains the best interests of the minor . . . .

The district court based its decision to order post-emancipation support on a great deal of evidence regarding Daughter's and Mother's relationship, life choices, and financial circumstances. In rendering its judgment, the district court faithfully followed the procedural requirements of the Act and reached a result consistent with the Act's plain language. Because the Court of Appeals failed to give effect to that language, we reverse.

Question based on *Diamond v. Diamond*

Does it seem fair to you that a parent who has no control over her emancipated child's life should nevertheless be on the hook to support the child? Is it right for a child to have her cake and eat it too?

CHAPTER 8

Spousal Support

THIS CHAPTER ADDRESSES SPOUSAL SUPPORT or, as it is called in some states, maintenance or alimony.[1] In *Dickert v. Dickert*,[2] the South Carolina Supreme Court described the purpose of spousal support as "a substitute for the support that is normally incidental to the marital relationship. Generally, alimony should place the supported spouse, as nearly as is practical, in the same position he or she enjoyed during the marriage." In a similar vein, the Wisconsin Supreme Court wrote in *McReath v. McReath*,[3] "There are two objectives that an award of maintenance seeks to meet. The first objective is support of the payee spouse. This objective may not be met by merely maintaining the payee spouse at a subsistence level. Rather, maintenance should support the payee spouse at the pre-divorce standard. This standard should be measured by the lifestyle that the parties enjoyed in the years immediately before the divorce and could anticipate enjoying if they were to stay married. The second objective is fairness, which aims to compensate the recipient spouse for contributions made to the marriage, give effect to the parties' financial arrangements, or prevent unjust enrichment of either party."

Historically, spousal support arose from the fact that the husband controlled all property, including wife's property. Elizabeth Warbasse observes, "The average wife, with her property under her husband's control, was completely dependent upon him for support."[4] A *quid pro quo* for male control of property was that a husband was obliged to support his wife during marriage and afterward if the marriage ended in divorce.[5] Originally, only husbands could be

---

1 Louisiana uses the term "final periodic support." Massachusetts uses "general term alimony."

2 387 S.C. 1, 691 S.E.2d 448 (2010).

3 800 N.W.2d 399, 412 (Wis. 2011).

4 Elizabeth Bowles Warbasse, *The Changing Legal Rights of Married Women: 1800-1861*, p. 21 (1987).

5 *See* Joel P. Bishop, *New Commentaries on Marriage, Divorce, and Separation* vol. 2, § 829, pp. 336-337 (1891)

ordered to pay spousal support. In *Orr v. Orr*,[6] the U.S. Supreme Court ruled this gender-based approach unconstitutional.

During the era of fault-based divorce prior to the 1970s, spousal support was generally not available to a spouse whose fault caused the breakup of a marriage. Today, there is less emphasis on fault. Yet, in many states, fault remains a factor in determining spousal support.[7] A South Carolina statute provides, "In making an award of alimony . . . , the court must consider and give weight in such proportion as it finds appropriate [to] marital misconduct or fault of either or both parties . . . ."[8] California law provides that domestic violence can be a factor influencing an award of support.

Historically, alimony was permanent, that is, for life.[9] Today, if divorcing spouses are young and able to work, the judge may award no spousal support. If support is awarded, it may be limited to a number of years, with the idea that

---

("By the unwritten law, marriage invests the husband with all the wife's available means of support, with ownership of her future earnings, and with the right to appropriate to himself her acquisitions. In return for which, it casts on him the duty, not in any considerable degree taken away by the modern statutes, suitability to maintain her, according to his ability and condition in life.").

6   440 U.S. 268 (1979).

7   *See* Diggs v. Diggs, 6 So.3d 1030 (La. Ct. App. 2009)("A spouse seeking final periodic support must 'affirmatively prove' she is free from causing the failure of the marriage. To meet this burden, she must prove she did not commit misconduct that is an independent, contributory or proximate cause of the failure of the marriage. Habitual intemperance or excesses and cruel treatment or outrages are examples of fault that can defeat a claim for final periodic support.").

8   S.C. Code Ann. § 20-3-130(C)(10).

9   *See* O'Brien v. O'Brien, 66 N.Y.2d 576, 489 N.E.2d 712, 716, 498 N.Y.S.2d 743 (1985)("Thus, the concept of alimony, which often served as a means of lifetime support and dependence for one spouse upon the other long after the marriage was over, was replaced with the concept of maintenance which seeks to allow the recipient spouse an opportunity to achieve [economic] independence.").

See also Mary Kay Kisthardtal, Re-Thinking Alimony: The AAML's Considerations for Calculating Alimony, Spousal Support or Maintenance, 21 *American Academy of Matrimonial Lawyers* 61-85 (2008). Professor Kisthardt writes:

> The initial rationale for alimony or support had its origins in the English common law system. Historically there were two remedies from the bonds of marriage. Although an absolute divorce was theoretically possible, it required an act of Parliament and was therefore hardly ever used. More commonly a plea was made for a separation from bed and board (mensa et thoro). This action, available from the ecclesiastical courts, constituted a legal separation . . . . A husband who secured such a divorce retained the right to control his wife's property and the corresponding duty to support his wife. Even after Parliament authorized the courts to grant absolute divorces, the concept of alimony remained. The initial rationale appeared to be premised on the fact that women gave up their property rights at marriage and after the marriage ended they were without the means to support themselves. The original award of alimony was similar to the wife's claim of dower, and courts used the traditional one-third of the property standard . . . . The concept of alimony came across the Atlantic with the founding of the colonies but seemingly without a corresponding rationale.

the supported spouse should endeavor to become financially self-sufficient.[10] As the Appellate Division of the New York Supreme Court explained in *Wheeler v. Wheeler*,[11] "It is settled that the purpose of maintenance is to provide temporary support while the recipient develops the skills and experience necessary to become self-sufficient." The Florida Court of Appeal wrote, "Even if a spouse is employable, an alimony award effectively rehabilitating the spouse in making the transition from married life to single status can be justified as a 'bridge-the-gap measure.'"[12] The North Dakota Supreme Court wrote in *Nuveen v. Nuveen*,[13] "A district court may award a spouse either rehabilitative or permanent spousal support. Rehabilitative spousal support is awarded to equalize the burdens of divorce or to restore an economically disadvantaged spouse to independent status by providing a disadvantaged spouse with an opportunity to acquire an education, training, work skills, or experience to become self-supporting. Rehabilitative support is appropriate when one spouse has bypassed opportunities or lost advantages as a consequence of the marriage or when one spouse has contributed during the marriage to the other's increased earning capacity or moved to further the other's career."

The introduction of the Married Women's Property Acts changed the ability of women to retain property, but alimony remained. It appears that at least one rationale was based on contract theories because, for many courts, the role of fault played a significant role. Alimony then became damages for breach of the marital contract reflected in the fact that in most states it was only available to the innocent and injured spouse. The measure of damages often approximated the standard of living the wife would have enjoyed but for her husband's breach. Alternatively it represented compensatory damages for tortious conduct.

In the 1970s the economic picture of spouses at divorce began to change. Many states adopted principles of equitable distribution allowing for property acquired during the marriage to be divided between the spouses regardless of how it was titled. This allowed economically dependent spouses to retain assets that were previously unavailable to them. Property division was used to address the inequities. These statutes resulted in decreasing spousal support awards.

In addition, women, who were historically the economically dependent spouses, joined the workforce in increasing numbers. The previous assumption that women would be unable to support themselves through employment gave way to the idea that dependence could no longer be used as a rationale for alimony. However, the practical reality of women's financial dependency remained in many marriages.

10 *See* McReath v. McReath, 800 N.W.2d 399, 413 (Wis. 2011)("The payment of maintenance is not to be viewed as a permanent annuity. Rather, maintenance is designed to maintain a party at an appropriate standard of living, under the facts and circumstances of the individual case, until the party exercising reasonable diligence has reached a level of income where maintenance is not long necessary.").

11 12 A.D.3d 982, 983, 785 N.Y.S.2d 170 (2004).

12 Demont v. Demont, 67 So. 3d 1096 (Fla. Ct. App. 2011).

13 795 N.W.2d 308, 316 (N.D. 2011).

Massachusetts ties length of alimony to length of marriage. The Massachusetts statute provides:

> (b) Except upon a written finding by the court that deviation beyond the time limits of this section are required in the interests of justice, if the length of the marriage is 20 years or less, general term alimony shall terminate no later than a date certain under the following durational limits:
>
>> (1) If the length of the marriage is 5 years or less, general term alimony shall continue for not longer than one-half the number of months of the marriage.
>>
>> (2) If the length of the marriage is 10 years or less, but more than 5 years, general term alimony shall continue for not longer than 60 per cent of the number of months of the marriage.
>>
>> (3) If the length of the marriage is 15 years or less, but more than 10 years, general term alimony shall continue for not longer than 70 per cent of the number of months of the marriage.
>>
>> (4) If the length of the marriage is 20 years or less, but more than 15 years, general term alimony shall continue for not longer than 80 per cent of the number of months of the marriage.
>
> (c) The court may order alimony for an indefinite length of time for marriages for which the length of the marriage was longer than 20 years.[14]

Permanent spousal support usually is reserved for long marriages, especially marriages in which the supported spouse has not worked in decades or at all. The North Dakota Supreme Court explained in *Nuveen v. Nuveen*,[15] "Permanent spousal support is appropriate when the economically disadvantaged spouse cannot be equitably rehabilitated to make up for the opportunities and development she lost during the course of the marriage. Permanent spousal support is awarded to provide traditional maintenance for a spouse incapable of adequate rehabilitation or self-support. Permanent spousal support may be appropriate if there is a substantial disparity in earning capacity and a substantial income disparity that cannot be adjusted through property division or rehabilitative support."[16]

---

14 Mass. Gen. Laws Ann. Ch. 208, § 49.

15 795 N.W.2d at 308 (N.D. 2011).

16 795 N.W.2d at 316.

When spousal support is requested, statutes list factors to consider. The California statute is typical:

> In ordering spousal support . . . , the court shall consider all of the following circumstances:
>
> (a) The extent to which the earning capacity of each party is sufficient to maintain the standard of living established during the marriage, taking into account all of the following:
>
>> (1) The marketable skills of the supported party; the job market for those skills; and the time and expenses required for the supported party to acquire the appropriate education or training to develop those skills; and the possible need for retraining or education to acquire other, more marketable skills or employment.
>>
>> (2) The extent to which the supported party's present or future earning capacity is impaired by periods of unemployment that were incurred during the marriage to permit the supported spouse to devote time to domestic duties.
>
> (b) The extent to which the supported party contributed to the attainment of an education, training, a career position, or a license by the supporting party.
>
> (c) The ability of the supporting party to pay spousal support, taking into account the supporting party's earning capacity, earned and unearned income, assets, and standard of living.
>
> (d) The needs of each party based on the standard of living established during the marriage.
>
> (e) The obligations and assets, including the separate property, of each party.
>
> (f) The duration of the marriage.
>
> (g) The ability of the supported party to engage in gainful employment without unduly interfering with the interests of dependent children in the custody of the party.
>
> (h) The age and health of the parties.
>
> (i) Documented evidence of any history of domestic violence . . . between the parties, including, but not limited to, consideration of

emotional distress resulting from domestic violence perpetrated against the supported party by the supporting party, and consideration of any history of violence against the supporting party by the supported party.

(j) The immediate and specific tax consequences to each party.

(k) The balance of hardships to each party.

(l) The goal that the supported party shall be self-supporting within a reasonable period of time. Except in the case of a marriage of long duration [10 years], a "reasonable period of time" for purposes of this section shall be one-half the length of the marriage. However, nothing in this section is intended to limit the court's discretion to order support for a greater or lesser length of time, based on any of the other factors listed in this section . . . and the circumstances of the parties.

(m) The criminal conviction of an abusive spouse shall be considered in making a reduction or elimination of a spousal support award [to an abusive spouse].

(n) Any other factors the court determines are just and equitable.

The trial judge has broad discretion to award appropriate spousal support.[17] As the Wisconsin Supreme Court put it in *McReath v. McReath*,[18] "It is within the circuit court's discretion to determine the amount and duration of maintenance."

An award of spousal support depends on need and ability to pay.[19] In appropriate circumstances, a judge can "impute" income to a supporting or supported spouse.[20] Thus, when a supported spouse is able to work but chooses to remain unemployed or underemployed, the judge may impute income to the supported spouse, and decrease support accordingly. The same is true for a supporting

---

17 *See* Demont v. Demont, 67 So. 3d 1096 (Fla. Ct. App. 2011)(trial court has broad discretion to determine property spousal support); Matter of Henry, 163 N.H. 175, 37 A.3d 320 (2012)("Trial courts have broad discretion in awarding alimony.").

18 800 N.W.2d 399, 412-413 (Wis. 2011).

19 A person's ability to pay spousal support is tied to the person's income and assets. Income is defined broadly. *See, e.g.,* Zickefoose v. Zickefoose, 228 W. Va. 708, 724 S.E.2d 312 (2012)(disability benefits from the Department of Veterans Affairs can be considered in determining the amount of support to be paid).

20 *See* Carr-Harris v. Carr-Harris, 98 A.D.3d 548, 949 N.Y.S.2d 707 (2012)("A court need not rely on a party's own account of his or her finances. Rather, the court may impute income to a party based on the party's past income or demonstrated earning potential. A court may based its determination on the income a parent is capable of learning by honest efforts, given his or her education and opportunities.").

spouse—the judge may impute income that would be available for support if the supporting spouse applied her or himself.

Spousal support generally ends if a supported spouse remarries or cohabits with an intimate partner.[21] In *Matter of Raybeck*, the New Hampshire Supreme Court grapples with the meaning of cohabitation.

Matter of Raybeck

Supreme Court of New Hampshire
163 N.H. 570, 44 A.3d 551 (2012)

Lynn, J.

The respondent, Bruce Raybeck, appeals an order of the Laconia Family Division, ruling that the respondent was required to continue paying alimony to the petitioner, Judith Raybeck. We vacate and remand.

The relevant facts are as follows. The parties were divorced in Texas in August 2005 after a forty-two-year marriage. The respondent was awarded property in North Carolina and Texas, and the petitioner was awarded property in Laconia, New Hampshire. The divorce decree, based upon the parties' agreement, obligated the respondent to pay the petitioner alimony of $25,000 per year for ten years, in yearly installments. That obligation would cease, however, if the petitioner "cohabitates with an unrelated adult male."

---

21 *See* Mass. General Laws Ann. Ch. 208 § 49, which provides:

(d) General term alimony shall be suspended, reduced or terminated upon the cohabitation of the recipient spouse when the payor shows that the recipient spouse has maintained a common household, as defined in this subsection, with another person for a continuous period of at least 3 months.

(1) Persons are deemed to maintain a common household when they share a primary residence together with or without others. In determining whether the recipient is maintaining a common household, the court may consider any of the following factors:

(i) oral or written statements or representations made to third parties regarding the relationship of the persons;

(ii) the economic interdependence of the couple or economic dependence of 1 person on the other;

(iii) the persons engaging in conduct and collaborative roles in furtherance of their life together;

(iv) the benefit in the life of either or both of the persons from their relationship;

(v) the community reputation of the persons as a couple; or

(vi) other relevant and material factors.

(2) An alimony obligation suspended, reduced or terminated under this subsection may be reinstated upon termination of the recipient's common household relationship; but, if reinstated, it shall not extend beyond the termination date of the original order.

Approximately three months before the January 2010 alimony payment was due, the petitioner moved out of her Laconia house and rented it to reduce her expenses. She moved into the upper level of a single family home in Plymouth owned by Paul Sansoucie, a man she had met through an online dating service. Sansoucie lived on the lower level and did not charge the petitioner for rent. She did, however, pay about $300 per month for food and often cooked for him. They also shared living space on the middle level of the house. When the respondent learned that the petitioner lived with another man, he stopped paying alimony. In response, the petitioner asked the family division to enforce the alimony agreement and require the respondent to resume his support payments.

After a hearing, the marital master recommended a finding that the petitioner was not cohabiting with Sansoucie under the terms of the divorce decree, and the family division approved the recommendation ordering the respondent to continue his alimony payments. This appeal followed.

. . . The respondent argues . . . that "the trial court below was not able to establish a workable definition of what constitutes cohabitation." [Respondent asks] this court to adopt a standard of cohabitation enacted recently by legislative initiative in Massachusetts. [The Massachusetts statute provides]:

(d) General term alimony shall be suspended, reduced or terminated upon the cohabitation of the recipient spouse when the payor shows that the recipient has maintained a common household, as defined below, with another person for a continuous period of at least 3 months.

(1) Persons are deemed to maintain a common household when they share a primary residence together with or without others. In determining whether the recipient is maintaining a common household, the court may consider any of the following factors:

(i) oral or written statements or representations made to third parties regarding the relationship of the cohabitants;

(ii) the economic interdependence of the couple or economic dependence of 1 party on the other;

(iii) the common household couple engaging in conduct and collaborative roles in furtherance of their life together;

(iv) the benefit in the life of either or both of the common household parties from their relationship;

(v) the community reputation of the parties as a couple; or

(vi) other relevant and material factors.

The petitioner argues that the trial court acted within its discretion in concluding that she was not cohabiting with another man as that term was intended in the divorce decree. . . .

Neither the legislature nor this court has had occasion to define "cohabitation" as that term is often used in a divorce decree. Because the divorce decree here reflects the parties' agreement, we will interpret the cohabitation clause according to its common meaning. The trial court applied the following standard:

> Evidence of a sexual relationship is admissible, but not necessarily required, for a finding of cohabitation. There must be more to the relationship than just occupying the same living area or sharing some or all of the expenses incurred by both parties. The evidence should reflect a common and mutual purpose to manage expenses and make decisions together about common and personal goals, and a common purpose to make mutual financial and personal progress toward those goals.

Applying this definition, the court concluded that the petitioner and Sansoucie did not cohabit. In support of that decision, the court found, among other facts, that the petitioner was forced to relocate when the respondent first announced that he would discontinue the alimony payments; that she and Sansoucie sleep on different floors of the house although they do share a common living area; that she does not pay rent but pays for food; and that their financial relationship is limited to her paying for food in exchange for shelter. The court also found, however, evidence indicating that there was a personal component to their relationship. They had, for example, shared rooms during their travels together. In a letter to her children, the petitioner stated that she and Sansoucie had discussed marriage but did not marry for "personal and financial reasons." Specifically, the petitioner wrote that "neither of us is sure if we want to remarry. Financial matters become so complicated at our age." The record also reflected that the petitioner's son-in-law referred to Sansoucie as the petitioner's boyfriend in a Christmas letter. Notwithstanding the evidence of a personal connection, the trial court ruled that the petitioner and Sansoucie did not cohabit in light of their financial situation.

Our common law lacks a definition of cohabitation as that term is used in divorce decrees and separation agreements. Dictionary definitions confirm the trial court's conclusion that to qualify a living arrangement as one of cohabitation there must be a personal connection beyond that of roommates or casual bedfellows. *Black's Law Dictionary*, for example, defines cohabitation as "the fact or state of living together, especially as partners in life, usually with the suggestion of sexual relations." *The Oxford English Dictionary* defines it as "living together as husband and wife, especially without legal marriage." *Ballentine's Law Dictionary* defines it as "a dwelling together of a man and a woman in the same place in the manner of husband and wife."

Common law standards from other jurisdictions contain similar articulations. *See, e.g., State v. Arroyo*, 181 Conn. 426, 435 A.2d 967, 970 (1980) ("Cohabitation is the mutual assumption of those marital rights, duties and obligations which are usually manifested by married people, including but not necessarily dependent on sexual relations."); *Cook v. Cook*, 798 S.W.2d 955, 957 (Ky.1990)(cohabitation is "mutually assuming the duties and obligations normally assumed by married persons"); *Fisher v. Fisher*, 75 Md.App. 193, 540 A.2d 1165, 1169 (1988)(cohabitation "envisions at least the normally accepted attributes of a marriage"); *Frey v. Frey*, 14 Va.App. 270, 416 S.E.2d 40, 43 (1992) (cohabitation "has been consistently interpreted by courts as encompassing both a permanency or continuity element and an assumption of marital duties"). . . .

After carefully reviewing these authorities, we follow them in defining cohabitation as a relationship between persons resembling that of a marriage. As such, cohabitation encompasses both an element of continuity or permanency as well as an assumption of marital obligations. As the trial court recognized, whether two people are cohabiting will depend on the facts and circumstances of each particular case. Beyond living together on a continual basis, many factors are relevant to the inquiry. Primary among them are the financial arrangements between the two people, such as shared expenses, whether and to what extent one person is supporting the other, the existence and use of joint bank accounts or shared investment or retirement plans, a life insurance policy carried by one or both parties benefiting the other, and similar financial entanglements.

We observe, however, that, in considering the financial arrangements, the age of the putative couple may be an important consideration. Where, as here, the individuals are senior citizens, support of one by the other may have less significance than with younger people not only because older individuals may be more financially secure than their younger counterparts, but also because older individuals may have estate plans in place to benefit children of prior relationships.

Also important is the extent of the personal relationship, including evidence of an intimate connection, how the people hold themselves out to others, the presence of common friends or acquaintances, vacations spent together, and similar signs of an ongoing personal commitment. Evidence of a sexual relationship should also be considered, but is not dispositive. Here too, the age of the couple may be relevant in weighing this factor; for older people, a sexual component to intimacy may not be as significant as it would be for younger couples.

In addition, the shared use and enjoyment of personal property is an indication of cohabitation, such as common use of household rooms, appliances, furniture, vehicles, and whether one person maintains personal items, such as toiletries or clothing, at the residence of the other. So, too, are indications that family members and friends view the relationship as one involving an intimate personal commitment. Taken together, these factors will support a finding of cohabitation if they indicate that two people are so closely involved that their relationship resembles that of marriage.

Because the trial court did not have the benefit of the standard we articulate here for determining whether the relationship between the petitioner and Sansoucie amounted to cohabitation, we vacate and remand the case for the master to reconsider the matter in light of the standard we have established.

Vacated and remanded.

———————————

Spousal support ends if the supported or supporting spouse dies. Massachusetts law states, "General term alimony shall terminate upon the remarriage of the recipient or the death of either spouse."[22] Of course, the parties are free in their divorce to agree otherwise. For example, the parties could agree that support will continue following the death of the supporting spouse.

Is Spousal Support Justifiable Today?

Why should spousal support *ever* be awarded? Why should one former spouse be required to support the other former spouse? The marriage is over. The parties have gone their separate ways. Shouldn't each former spouse provide for her or himself? After all, if you live with someone in a non-marital romantic relationship and the relationship ends, you don't have a legal duty to support your former lover. Why should it be different with marriage?

Scholars have explored the justifications for spousal support. An article by Mary Kay Kisthardt provides a good starting place.

———————————

22 Mass. Gen. Laws Ann. Ch. 208, § 49(a).

Re-Thinking Alimony
Mary Kay Kisthardt

21 *Journal of the American Academy of Matrimonial Lawyers* 61 (2008)

The initial rationale for alimony or support had its origins in the English common law system. Historically there were two remedies from the bonds of marriage. Although an absolute divorce was theoretically possible, it required an act of Parliament and was therefore hardly ever used. More commonly a plea was made for a separation from bed and board (mensa et thoro). This action available from the ecclesiastical courts constituted a legal separation as absolute divorce was prohibited under canon law. A husband who secured such a divorce retained the right to control his wife's property and the corresponding duty to support his wife. Even after Parliament authorized the courts to grant absolute divorces, the concept of alimony remained. The initial rationale appeared be premised on the fact that women gave up their property rights at marriage and after the marriage ended they were without the means to support themselves. The original award of alimony was similar to the wife's claim of dower, and courts used the traditional one-third of the property standard so instead of one-third of the estate at the husband's death she would receive one-third of the income of her husband at the time of the divorce. The concept of alimony came across the Atlantic with the founding of the colonies but seemingly without a corresponding rationale.

The introduction of the Married Women's Property Acts changed the ability of women to retain property, but alimony remained. It appears that at least one rationale was based on contract theories because, for many courts, the role of fault played a significant role. Alimony then became damages for breach of the marital contract reflected in the fact that in most states it was only available to the innocent and injured spouse. The measure of damages often approximated the standard of living the wife would have enjoyed but for her husband's breach. Alternatively it represented compensatory damages for tortious conduct.

In the 1970's the economic picture of spouses at divorce began to change. Many states adopted principles of equitable distribution allowing for property acquired during the marriage to be divided between the spouses regardless of how it was titled. This allowed economically dependent spouses to retain assets that were previously unavailable to them. Property division was used to address the inequities. These statutes resulted in decreasing spousal support awards.

In addition, women, who were historically the economically dependent spouses, joined the workforce in increasing numbers. The previous assumption that women would be unable to support themselves through employment gave way to the idea that dependence could no longer be used as a rationale for alimony. However, the practical reality of women's financial dependency remained in many marriages.

With the advent of no-fault divorce, alimony also lost its punitive rationale. The Uniform Marriage and Divorce Act (UMDA) changed the character of these awards to one that was almost exclusively needs based and at the same time gave spousal support a new name: maintenance. Maintenance was only available to the spouse who had an inability to meet his or her reasonable needs through appropriate employment. The marital standard of living was only one of six factors relied upon in making awards under the UMDA, where the focus was now on "self-support" even if it was at a substantially lower level than existed during the marriage. In addition, when awards were made they were generally only for a short term, sufficient to allow the dependent spouse to become "self-supporting." This spousal support reform often left wives, who were frequently the financially dependent spouses in long term marriages, without permanent support.

Maintenance was sometimes awarded for "rehabilitative" purposes such as providing income for the time it takes the recipient to acquire skills or education necessary to become self-supporting. Short term transitional awards were used to make a spouse economically self-sufficient as soon as possible.

In response to the denial of long term awards for those most in need of them, the "second wave" of reform took place in the 1990's and expanded the factors justifying an award beyond "need." This new legislation encouraged courts to base awards more on the unique facts of a case and less on broad assumptions about need and the obligation to become self-supporting in spite of the loss of earning capacity that often occurs in long term marriages. The use of vocational experts to measure earning capacity became more widespread and there were attempts to quantify the value of various aspects of homemaker services as part of a support award.

––––––––––

Cynthia Lee Starnes summarizes the various theoretical justifications for spousal support in an article in the *Family Law Quarterly*.

Alimony Theory
Cynthia Lee Starnes

45 *Family Law Quarterly* 271 (2011)

Why should anyone be forced to share income with a former spouse? If divorce severs the tie between spouses, if each spouse is entitled to a clean break and a fresh start as no-fault laws teach, what is the rationale for alimony? Surprisingly, family law offers no answers to these questions. For over thirty years, commentators have struggled to explain why alimony has survived the demise of coverture and the advent of no-fault divorce, but there is still no consensus on a contemporary rationale for alimony.

In extreme cases, the pragmatic justification for alimony is easy enough: alimony protects the state from the job of supporting a divorced spouse who, without alimony, would be thrust into poverty. Indeed, state statutes typically identify a claimant's "need" as an alimony trigger. But trial courts are given broad discretion to define "need" and state-interest does not explain cases in which alimony is awarded to a divorcing spouse who faces a decline in standard of living short of poverty. Nor does pragmatism answer the many questions to which alimony demands answers: How much? How long? To what end? On what grounds—modification or termination?

The broad discretion vested in judges to determine alimony eligibility and quantification, together with the absence of a theory to guide decisionmaking, has produced an alimony regime that is marked by unpredictability, uncertainty, and confusion. The only thing that is predictable about alimony is that it is unlikely to be awarded, a fact that is not surprising in a culture that tends to applaud self-reliance and disdain dependency. Some legal actors have responded to the dysfunction of current alimony law by endorsing alimony guidelines. While guidelines can increase predictability, the absence of an underlying theory of alimony confounds efforts to identify a mathematical formula for generating the numbers that populate these guidelines. If guideline numbers are predictable, they are not necessarily equitable or consistent among jurisdictions.

If alimony has no conceptual basis in contemporary visions of marriage, if the law of alimony is dysfunctional, just get rid of alimony or, at least, limit it to claimants near poverty. The problem with this solution is that often alimony is the only available tool for addressing cases in which marital roles have left divorcing spouses with disparate earning capacity at divorce.

Alimony theorists are remarkably consistent in their description of the problem alimony aims to address. Would-be reformers generally make two related points: (1) Disparate marital roles often produce disparate economic positioning at divorce; and (2) Inequity may result if divorce law does not address this disparity.

In 1978, Elisabeth Landes observed that wives' prioritization of household production (family labor) generates costs in the form of forgone earnings and "loss of market earning power through depreciation of market skills previously acquired, and forgone opportunities to invest in market skills."[23] In 1982, human capital theorists Elizabeth S. Beninger and Jeanne Wielage Smith stated what a number of contemporary courts were recognizing: "a wife forgoes the opportunity to develop her own career when a *couple makes the community decision* to allocate her time to housework and child care, and ... this decision limits her earning potential."[24] As Beninger and Smith reasoned, "In an intact marriage ... the wife is willing to forgo investment in her own career because she anticipates sharing her husband's future increased earnings." If the parties divorce, however, "the husband obtains the full benefit of his increased earning power and the wife sustains the full burden of the opportunity cost of her years spent in nonmarket labor."

Seven years later, Margaret Brinig and June Carbone expanded these descriptions of the problem to include primary caretakers who also work outside their homes.[25] Such a caretaker, who is typically female, may forgo her own career opportunities to further her spouse's opportunities or to rear children, but at divorce "the benefiting spouse retains the advantages of an enhanced career or properly raised children, while the contributing spouse suffers a unilateral loss."

As Jana Singer observed, there are "strong economic incentives for couples to continue to make such gendered marital investments" given the wage gap between men and women.[26] Because divorce courts "generally do not recognize career assets as marital property ... the husband, is permitted to keep most of the assets accumulated during marriage, while the wife, who has invested in her family and her husband's career, is deprived of a return on her marital investment."

In his 1989 article, *The Theory of Alimony*, Ira Mark Ellman recognized that "divorce typically burdens the wife more than her husband for two reasons: She has more difficulty finding a new spouse, and she suffers disproportionate finan-

---

23 Elisabeth M. Landes, Economics of Alimony, 7 *Journal of Legal Studies* 35, 41 (1978).

24 Elizabeth S. Beninger & Jeanne Wielage Smith, Career Opportunity Cost: A Factor in Spousal Support Determination, 16 *Family Law Quarterly*. 201, 210 (1982).

25 Margaret F. Brinig & June Carbone, The Reliance Interest in Marriage and Divorce, 62 *Tulane Law Review* 855, 869 (1988).

26 Jana Singer, Divorce Reform and Gender Justice, 67 *North Carolina Law Review* 1103, 1115 (1989).

cial loss because of her domestic role."[27] Like Singer, Ellman saw this marital division of labor as rational. Such "'specialization' makes sense," Ellman wrote, since "[i]f the spouses view their marriage as a sharing enterprise, they will usually conclude that they are both better off if the lower earning spouse spends more on their joint domestic needs, and allows the higher earning spouse to maximize his or her income." If the parties divorce, however, "the spouse who has specialized in domestic aspects of the marriage—who has invested in the marriage rather than the market—suffers a disproportionate loss."

In 1993, Joan Williams offered a powerful vision of the "dominant family ecology" that contributes to the perilous position of primary caretakers.[28] As Williams explained, this ecology consists of "an ideal-worker husband" supported by a flow of domestic services from his "marginalized-caregiver" wife, whose services support his performance as an ideal worker and simultaneously marginalize her market participation. "The ideal-worker's salary," Williams concluded, "therefore reflects the work of two adults: the ideal-worker's market labor and the marginalized-caregiver's unpaid labor." Also in 1993, I described what may be the worst-case scenario: a long-term displaced homemaker who after contributing to her family and marginalizing her own career prospects is judged by a divorce court "determined to implement the fashionable rhetoric that men and women are equal" and so sets her free to begin a new life with minimal property and little or no alimony.[29]

The problem these and other commentators described did not end with the turn of the century. Indeed, in 2002, the American Law Institute (ALI) described the problem in terms reminiscent of those used by Beninger and Smith twenty years earlier. In its *Principles of the Law of Family Dissolution* (*Principles*), the ALI noted that "wives continue in the great majority of cases to care for their children, in reliance upon continued market labor by their husbands,"[30] and that these caretaking responsibilities "typically result ... in a residual loss in earning capacity that continues after the children no longer require close parental supervision."

---

27 Ira Mark Ellman, The Theory of Alimony, 77 *California Law Review* 1, 49 (1989).

28 Joan Williams, Is Coverture Dead? Beyond a New Theory of Alimony, 82 *Georgia Law Journal* 2227, 2229 (1994).

29 Cynthia Starnes, *Divorce and the Displaced Homemaker: A Discourse on Playing with Dolls, Partnership Buyouts and Dissociation under No-fault, 60 University of Chicago Law Review* 67, 70 (1993). See also Cynthia Lee Starnes, *Victims, Breeders, Joy, and Math: First Thoughts on Compensatory Spousal Payments Under the Principles, 8 Duke Journal of Gender, Law, and Policy* 137, 138 (2001).

30 American Law Institute, *Principles of the Law of Family Dissolution: Analysis and Recommendations* § 5.05 reporter's notes cmt. c. (2002).

The ALI reasoned that in such cases the caretaker has fulfilled the couple's "joint responsibility for their children's care," allowing the other parent "to have a family while also developing his or her earning capacity." In the absence of any remedy, at divorce "the primary wage earner retains both that earning capacity and the parental status, while in the absence of any remedy the primary caretaker loses any claim upon the other spouse's earnings."

Two years later, in 2004, Carolyn Frantz and Hanoch Dagan warned that excluding earning capacity from the marital estate "exploits the spouse whose acceptance of burdens on behalf of the communal endeavor is transformed by the law into self-sacrifice."[31] The next year, I added that "[i]n a worst-case scenario, divorce exposes the undignified reality that a primary caretaker is "'just a man away from poverty.'"[32]

There is thus much common ground in the problem reformers identify. Of course, self-identified reformers may be more inclined than other observers to view the circumstances they describe as unacceptable. Nonetheless, it is difficult to dispute the point, or perhaps the intuition, that if marital roles diminish a primary caretaker's earning capacity, divorce law should not allow her husband to shed her at will, setting her "free" to alone bear the costs of family labor. As a California court observed long ago: "A woman is not a breeding cow to be nurtured during her years of fecundity, then conveniently and economically converted to cheap steaks when past her prime .... This has nothing to do with feminism, sexism, male chauvinism, or any other trendy social ideology. It is ordinary common sense, basic decency and simple justice."[33]

The next challenge is to identify a vision of contemporary marriage that provides a basis for postdivorce income sharing.

The Theories

Most reform theorists focus primarily on one of three interests: a claimant's expected gain, a claimant's loss, or a claimant's contributions to the other spouse. These foci are familiar to any student of contracts, for they suggest the three classic contract interests of expectation, reliance, and restitution. This section thus groups reform theory into three categories:

---

31 Carolyn J. Frantz & Hanoch Dagan, *Properties of Marriage*, 104 *Columbia Law Review* 75, 108 (2004)

32 Cynthia Lee Starnes, *Mothers as Suckers: Pity, Partnership, and Divorce Discourse*, 90 *Iowa Law Review* 1513, 1516 (2005). *See also* Pamela Laufer-Ukeles, *Selective Recognition of Gender Difference in the Law: Revaluing the Caretaker Role*, 31 *Harvard Journal of Law and Gender* 1, 5 (2008) (warning that divorce law leaves caretakers in distress by failing to adequately address their reduced earning capacity).

33 In re Marriage of Brantner, 136 Cal. Rptr. 635, 637 (Ct. App. 1977).

(1) Gain Theory (emphasizes expected returns on marital investments)

(2) Loss Theory (emphasizes compensation for loss experienced at divorce)

(3) Contribution Theory (emphasizes reimbursement for marital contributions)

A. Gain Theory

If gain theory is to offer a satisfactory rationale for alimony, it must also address more ordinary cases of primary caretakers. In 1978, Elisabeth Landes laid the groundwork for a more expansive view of marital investment. Landes reasoned that, "[b]y spending more time in household production, a wife directly frees some of her husband's time to the market, increasing both his current market earnings and his incentive to invest in earnings-augmenting skills." As Landes saw things, "one of the returns from the wife's investments in household production ... is the augmentation of the husband's earning capacity. The marriage contract transforms a purely general investment, the productivity of which is independent of the marital state, into marriage-specific capital."

Some gain theorists have offered rationales based on analogies to partnership. Jana Singer provides a good example. Although her income sharing proposal is not grounded in alimony, her investment partnership model is pure gain theory. Singer has reasoned that each spouse makes "an equal (although not necessarily identical) investment in a marriage." At divorce, each spouse is thus entitled to "an equal share of the fruits of the marriage." Singer stresses that "the emphasis of such an investment partnership model is not on formal equal treatment of the spouses at the time of divorce, but on each spouse receiving equal benefits from the marriage."

I have proposed a gain-based rationale for alimony built on a loose analogy to partnership buyouts:

> Like commercial partners, spouses commonly pool their labor, time, and talent to meet responsibilities and to generate income that they expect to share .... Often, the spouses' combined efforts generate enhanced human capital primarily for the husband who has invested more extensively in paid employment than his primary caretaker spouse. In such a case, it is the marital partnership, rather than the husband alone, that has produced the husband's enhanced human capital. Although divorce terminates the parties' relationship, it usually does not terminate the husband's income stream, which continues to reflect the enhanced value produced through joint marital

effort. Such a husband should therefore buy out the interest of his wife at divorce.

In an innovative proposal drawing on the law of secured transactions, Martha Ertman has analogized a primary homemaker to a creditor who extends value in the form of domestic services to the primary wage earner, who becomes her debtor.[34] Ertman's reasoning is classic gain theory: "A homemaker gives value by performing domestic services that ... benefit the marriage and family, and the primary homemaker expects that her efforts and sacrifice will be part of a lifetime joint endeavor." During marriage, "the primary homemaker/creditor gets a return on her loan by sharing in the primary wage earner's earnings ... [but] if the marriage ends, the wage earner's debt goes unpaid, and the homemaker/creditor should be able to collect on the loan just as any other creditor can collect an unpaid debt."

Another version of gain theory comes from Stephen Sugarman, who has suggested a merger of spouses' human capital over time. Sugarman reasons that the longer parties are married, "the more their human capital should be seen as intertwined rather than affixed to the individual spouse in whose body it resides."[35] Under this reasoning, each spouse's interest in the other's human capital entitles each to a share of any enhanced earning capacity fostered by the marital division of labor.

Robert Kirkman Collins's theory of "marital residuals" also evidences gain theory. Collins has called for "an equitable sharing of the residual economic benefits from work done during the marriage."[36] By way of example, he offers the vision of a couple pedaling a tandem bicycle:

> [The bicycle] will not come to a screeching halt the moment that one or both riders stops pedaling; while current efforts may cease, the momentum from their prior work continues to carry the pair forward at a gradually decreasing pace until the effects of friction (of the sort known to physicists, as opposed to that found in disintegrating marriages) eventually cause the bicycle to stop. How long the two riders will continue to coast forward will be a direct function of how fast

---

34 Martha Ertman, Commercializing Marriage: A Proposal for Valuing Women's Work Through Premarital Security Agreements, 77 *Texas Law Review* 17, 41 (1998).

35 Stephen D. Sugarman, *Dividing Financial Interests on Divorce, in* Divorce Reform at the Crossroads 130, 159-60 (1990).

36 Robert Kirkman Collins, The Theory of Marital Residuals: Applying an Income Adjustment Calculus to the Enigma of Alimony, 24 *Harvard Women's Law Journal* 23 (2001).

they were going—that is, how great their momentum had been when the joint efforts stopped.

Collins thus characterizes alimony as "a decreasing share of marital residuals."

Some gain theorists offer rationales for postdivorce income sharing but shun the label "alimony." Frantz and Dagan, for example, have argued that "[t]he joint creation of careers is often one of the most important projects of marriage ... [and that] excluding earning capacity from the marital estate ... exploits the spouse whose acceptance of burdens on behalf of the communal endeavor is transformed by the law into self-sacrifice." Joan Williams' powerful vision of the "dominant family ecology"—an ideal worker and a marginalized caretaker working together to support a family with children and together generating a family wage to which each is entitled—suggests the focus on teamwork and entitlement to returns on joint labor that signals gain theory, although she too shuns the notion of "alimony."

There is much common ground among gain theorists. Most obvious is their focus on collaboration, teamwork, and partnerships between spouses who join together to produce mutual benefits which they expect to share—income and a home with children. If their marriage ends, divorce law must impose an exit price on the spouse who takes the larger share of marital returns with him. This price will usually take the form of income sharing, and is gain theorists' rationale for alimony.

A key feature of gain theory is its general disinterest in relative spousal contributions. Gain theorists tend to assume, sometimes as a default rule drawn from visions of contemporary marriage, that spouses are equals. Equality is an assigned status that does not depend on the type or size of each spouse's contribution. As equals, spouses are entitled to equal returns on communal, joint investments—no matter who brought home the bigger paycheck and no matter who was the better cook.

Another important point about gain theory is that it does not necessarily depend on an expectation that marriage will last forever. No marriage lasts forever: all marriages end in either death or divorce. The expectation at issue is rather the expectation that each spouse will realize a return on marital investment before the marriage ends. As Lloyd Cohen so vividly described, marital gains are often not symmetrical for spouses; wage earners tend to obtain gains early on in the marriage, while homemakers tend to reap gains later in the relationship.[37] If the timing of divorce leaves spouses asymmetrically positioned, the marriage ends prematurely from the perspective of the spouse who has not yet realized expected gain. The disparately impacted spouse, often the primary caretaker, is thus entitled to compensation.

B. Loss Theory

Loss theorists focus on the reliance costs of participating in a "failed" marriage. Their aim is to put the injured spouse "in as good a position as he would have been in had the contract not been made."[38] Brinig and Carbone have described two types of reliance: (1) "a lost opportunity to marry someone else," and (2) "sacrifices in career development." They conclude that in contemporary marriage, the focus on a lost opportunity to marry someone else "is giving way to the interest in lost career opportunities."

In his 1989 article, *The Theory of Alimony*, Ira Mark Ellman argues that "[t]he main residual financial consequence of a failed marriage is a reduction in one spouse's earning capacity (usually the wife's) compared to the earning capacity she would have had if she had not married." Ellman reasons that alimony should compensate a spouse for the "residual" loss in earning capacity arising from "economically rational marital sharing behavior," since without such protection, a "rational spouse will pause before making a marital investment." The purpose of alimony, Ellman concludes, is thus "to reallocate the postdivorce financial consequences of marriage in order to prevent distorting incentives."

The ALI has offered a similar view, conceptualizing alimony as "compensation for loss" and recognizing two primary types of loss that are compensable: (1) loss of the marital standard of living in a marriage of "sufficient duration" and (2) a residual loss in earning capacity that results from primary caretaking. While the ALI goes to some trouble to identify the parameters of compensable loss, it has been criticized for its failure to explain convincingly why these losses are compensable.

Other loss theorists include Twila Perry, who has analogized alimony to strict liability in tort law, arguing that it should compensate a spouse for disproportionate economic loss caused by the "accident" of divorce,[39] and Katharine Baker, who has reasoned that in marriages with "a disproportion-

---

37 Lloyd Cohen, Marriage, Divorce, and Quasi Rents; Or, "I Gave Him the Best Years of My Life, 16 *Journal of Legal Studies* (1987).

38 Restatement (Second) of Contracts § 344(b) (1979).

39 Twila L. Perry, No-Fault Divorce and Liability Without Fault: Can Family Law Learn from Torts?, 52 *Ohio State Law Journal* 55 (1991).

ate division of household labor ... a woman relies on the security her husband can provide."[40]

Loss theory and gain theory sometimes recognize flip sides of the same coin as, for example, when a primary homemaker loses career opportunities, leaving her with a smaller share of returns on marital investments, i.e., lower earning capacity than her spouse. Loss theory and gain theory differ significantly, however, in the roles they assign alimony claimants. If the need-based approach of current alimony law casts alimony claimants as beggars, a loss-based model casts them as victims. Gain theory, by contrast, casts a claimant as an equal stakeholder in marriage. Moreover, loss theory poses difficult quantification problems that often lead loss theorists to resort to the more straightforward measurement models of gain theory. Thus, one might reasonably question whether loss theory offers any advantages over gain theory.

C. Contribution Theory

Contribution theory protects a promisee's "interest in having restored to him any benefit that he has conferred on the other party."[41] This theory is based on restitution, helpfully described by Joan Krauskopf: "The basic requirements are that one person has received a benefit at the expense of another, and that as between them it would be unjust for the recipient to retain the benefit without compensation to the other person."[42] If benefits are conferred gratuitously, there is no unjust enrichment and hence no compensation due. By way of analogy, an alimony theory based on restitution must measure the contributions a claimant made to her spouse and then ask whether that sum must be reimbursed in order to prevent unjust enrichment. Measuring contribution thus plays a key role in contribution theory.

In its narrowest form, contribution theory provides a rationale for requiring a student spouse to reimburse his/her mate for sums contributed to the student's education or training--sums that would include tuition, books, lab fees, and perhaps living expenses. Contribution theory, however, supports only a limited recovery (reimbursement) that may grossly undercompensate a supporting spouse who expects to share the return on the parties' joint marital investment, i.e., the student's enhanced earnings.

---

40   Katharine K. Baker, Contracting for Security: Paying Married Women What They've Earned, 55 *University of Chicago Law Review* 1193 (1988).

41   Restatement (Second) of Contracts § 344(c) (1979).

42   Joan M. Krauskopf, Recompense for Financing Spouse's Education: Legal Protection for the Marital Investor in Human Capital, 28 *University of Kansas Law Review* 379 (1980).

Moreover, contribution theory limits alimony to extraordinary cases. For example, the ALI Principles recognize a restitution-based rationale for alimony, which applies only to cases of short marriages in which one spouse supported the other's education or training, the education/training was completed within a limited number of years before divorce, and the education/training "substantially enhanced" the student's earning capacity. This section of the ALI Principles, and contribution theory itself, will provide a rationale for alimony only in a small number of cases.

Contribution theory might broaden its reach by expanding the concept of contribution to include family labor. Even this approach, however, will not make contribution theory an attractive option for several reasons. First, as Ellman observes, "ordinary" marital benefits are not properly recoverable under a restitution model since they are usually conferred with donative intent and thus do not unjustly enrich the other spouse. Only extraordinary benefits that suggest nondonative intent are reimbursable. Determining whether a spouse's contributions were ordinary or extraordinary invites value judgments that depend on the judge's personal view of marital roles. Additionally, as June Carbone observes, restitution is appropriate "only if the courts are willing to abandon the presumption that both spouses contribute equally to an ongoing marriage and, instead, total up and compare their individual contributions."[43]

Assessing the relative merits of various alimony theories requires inquiry into both the theory's ability to explain alimony and also its ability to identify a quantification model that will add consistency and predictability to alimony decision-making.

Conclusion

Family law has operated for too long without a satisfactory and consistent theory of alimony. Over the last thirty years, numerous commentators have offered rationales for alimony, but none has won the day. The current law of alimony remains dysfunctional.

---

43   June Carbone, Economics, Feminism, and the Reinvention of Alimony: A Reply to Ira Ellman, 43 *Vanderbilt Law Review* 1463 (1990).

Questions About Spousal Support

What is your answer to Cynthia Starnes' question, "Why should anyone be forced to share income with a former spouse?" Should spousal support be abolished as an anachronism? If not abolished, should spousal support law be changed? If so, what changes should be made?

Modification of Spousal Support

Spousal support can be modified on a showing of substantial changed circumstances. Perhaps the supporting spouse is laid off. Perhaps the supported spouse wins the lottery. The party seeking modification files a motion for modification. The moving party has the burden of proving substantial changed circumstances warranting a fresh look at support.

Planning for Retirement at Time of Divorce

Couples divorcing in their twenties or thirties probably think little about retirement decades in the future. For these couples, by the time retirement rolls around, the kids will be grown, and child support will be a faded memory. Property is divided at the time of divorce. It is true that pension issues can re-surface at retirement, but pensions, like other property, are largely settled at divorce. In many short marriages, there is no spousal support order. Even if spousal support is ordered, the typical order is not for lifetime support. It is not surprising that many young divorcing couples do not plan specifically for retirement. Beyond taking care of pensions, retirement planning is often unnecessary when young couples divorce.

But what about couples divorcing after a long marriage? The couple may be in their fifties or sixties. When older couples divorce, planning for retirement, incapacity, and death are essential. Consider spousal support. With long marriages, permanent or indeterminate spousal support is common. What happens when the supporting spouse retires and experiences decreased income? May the supporting spouse return to court and seek to lower spousal support? Suppose it is the supported spouse who retires? May the supported spouse return to court and seek increased spousal support?[44] These and other "issues of aging" should be addressed in the divorce.

Courts generally hold that retirement at normal retirement age can constitute a change of circumstances justifying reassessment of spousal support. The Colorado Court of Appeals observed in *Marriage of Swing*,[45] "The majority rule appears to be that reduced income due to a spouse's objectively reasonable decision to retire, made in good faith and not with the intention of depriving the other spouse of support, should be recognized as a basis for modifying maintenance."

In 2011, the Massachusetts Legislature passed a law dealing directly with retirement and spousal support. Massachusetts provides that an "alimony order shall terminate upon the payor attaining the full retirement age. The payor's ability to work beyond the full retirement age shall not be a reason to extend alimony . . . ."[46] Despite the law, a divorcing Massachusetts couple may agree to alimony beyond retirement. As well, the Massachusetts statute allows a judge to extend support in limited circumstances.

The Oregon Court of Appeals' decision in *Marriage of Reaves* grapples with the competing equities when a former spouse who is paying support decides to retire.

Marriage of Reaves

Court of Appeals of Oregon
236 Or. App. 313, 236 P.3d 803 (2010)

Landau, P.J.

In this domestic relations case, wife appeals a supplemental judgment terminating husband's spousal support obligation following his retirement. She

---

44 *See* Kosobud v. Kosobud, 817 N.W.2d 384 (N.D. 2012)("A spousal support obligor's nearing the age of retirement does not immunize the obligor from paying spousal support. Where, as here, the exact dates of retirement and the resulting income reductions following retirement are unknown, a court may order permanent spousal support despite the obligor's approaching retirement. The obligor's proper course of action upon voluntary retirement is to move for modification of the support obligation based on a significant change of circumstances caused by the retirement.").

45 194 P.3d 498, 501 (Colo. Ct. App. 2008)("we conclude that a Colorado court may consider an obligor spouse's reduced income as a result of early retirement, and that if the court finds (1) the obligor's decision was made in good faith, meaning not primarily motivated by a desire to decrease or eliminate maintenance, and (2) the decision was objectively reasonable based on factors such as the obligor's age, the obligor's health, and the practice of the industry in which the obligor was employed, the court should not find the obligor to be voluntarily underemployed." p. 501).

46 Mass. Gen. Laws Ann. Ch. 208, § 49(f).

argues that, although husband's retirement may warrant a reduction in support, it does not warrant termination of support entirely. Husband contends that termination of his support obligation is appropriate given that his retirement has reduced his ability to pay support. We agree with wife that the trial court erred in terminating spousal support and modify the judgment accordingly.

The parties were married for 30 years. They divorced in 1999. At the time of the dissolution, husband, then 52, worked as a psychiatrist for Lane County, earning $9,162 per month. Wife, then 53, was not employed outside the home. There are no children of the marriage.

The parties entered into a marital settlement agreement (MSA) under which husband agreed to pay monthly spousal support of $3,500 for two years, and then $3,200 indefinitely. The MSA stated that the spousal support award was "a contribution toward the support of [wife]," but did not otherwise recite a purpose for the award. Although wife was then unemployed, it was anticipated that she could earn $2,000 per month within two years. The agreement required husband to maintain $500,000 in life insurance naming wife as the beneficiary for as long as he had an obligation to pay spousal support.

In the years following the dissolution, husband continued to work for Lane County, although, in 2007, he worked 80 percent of full time. He earned approximately $13,800 per month in 2006 and $12,205 per month in 2007. Husband remarried. His current wife works as a licensed clinical social worker and psychotherapist, and earned about $3,650 per month in 2007.

Wife, meanwhile, began work teaching art half time at the University of Oregon. In 2006, she earned wages of $26,834, or $2,236 per month. Her work is contractual on an annual basis. Wife testified that she would work full time if offered the opportunity, but that opportunity has not arisen. Wife is also an artist. She does not earn any income from that work; however, maintaining a studio and showing her work are important adjuncts to her teaching.

In 2007, husband decided to retire, effective in June 2008. In light of that planned retirement, he moved to modify the dissolution judgment to terminate his spousal support obligation.

At trial, the evidence showed that husband's full PERS [Public Employee Retirement System] benefit is $2,751.96 per month, but that he has elected a survivorship benefit for his current wife, which reduces his monthly benefit to $2,234. Husband also receives $330 as an alternate payee on wife's PERS account. Husband's full federal civil service retirement benefit is $683 per month, but once again he opted for the survivorship benefit for his current wife, and so his monthly benefit was $540. Husband receives Social Security of

$1,447 per month. Husband has additional retirement investments of $350,607, from which his financial adviser estimates that he could derive monthly income of about $1,169. Considering all of these resources, husband estimates that his post-retirement income will be $5,719 per month, representing a significant reduction of his income.

Husband's uniform support affidavit shows expenses of $3,161 per month, not including spousal support, but including household expenses for his current wife. Husband notes that, upon his retirement, his monthly expenses will increase by $971 for health insurance, for a total in monthly household expenses of approximately $4,100. Thus, husband concluded, in light of those monthly expenses, his post-retirement income of $5,719 will no longer be adequate to sustain the spousal support obligation.

Wife opposed husband's motion to modify. In wife's view, husband underestimated his own post-retirement income and failed to take into account her continuing need for spousal support.

Concerning husband's post-retirement income, wife contended that, for purposes of determining husband's ability to pay spousal support, his income should include the *total* benefit available from his federal and PERS retirement accounts, rather than as reduced by the survivor benefit election. When those adjustments are applied, wife asserted, husband's monthly income is $6,380.

As for wife's own needs, the evidence at trial showed that, upon husband's retirement, she will receive benefits of $683 from husband's federal civil service retirement plan. She is also an alternate payee on husband's State of Oregon PERS retirement plan and could begin receiving $647 per month from that account, if she so elected. Wife also has her own PERS account, from which she could begin drawing $452 per month, as long as she continues to work no more than half time. Wife is also eligible to begin receiving Social Security. If she were to continue to work half time, she could draw benefits of $240 per month; if she were to retire completely, her monthly benefit would be $722. If, as wife would like, she is able to wait until her full retirement age of 66 to begin drawing Social Security benefits, her monthly benefit amount will be $909.

Wife's uniform support affidavit lists monthly expenses of $4,614. She testified that a complete termination of spousal support would be difficult for her, but she agreed that spousal support should be reduced by the $683 that she will receive from husband's federal civil service retirement account.

Husband argued that wife underestimated her own resources. In particular, he asserted that wife could increase her income by retiring now, as opposed to waiting until she is 66. Husband offered the testimony of Pope, a financial adviser, who opined that, in light of wife's limited cash flow, he would advise her to begin drawing on her PERS and Social Security benefits immediately, and perhaps put her Social Security payments in a savings account in case of an emergency. In his view, the fact that wife's monthly payments from those accounts will be smaller if she begins drawing on them now, rather than waiting until age 66, will be offset by the longer duration of payments over the course of wife's lifetime. Wife also has an IRA, from which Pope believes wife could comfortably begin withdrawing $400 per month for the rest of her life. In addition, wife owns a home and 26 acres. Pope testified that if wife were to sell the property and downsize to a smaller residence, she could invest the remaining proceeds, from which she could draw a net monthly income of $600. With that additional amount, wife's monthly income would be $5,305.

Wife responded that, when she retires, she will be entirely dependent on retirement income and spousal support. To maximize her monthly retirement benefits, she contended, it would be best to wait as long as possible to begin collecting them and not draw on her benefits until she retires at age 66. In support, wife offered the testimony of her own expert witness, Bonebrake, who recommended that wife wait until age 66 to begin drawing on her benefits. According to Bonebrake, "it's particularly important for women to maybe wait longer because women live longer than men to the tune of about eight years typically." Bonebrake explained that the "break-even point" for Social Security benefit calculation purposes is around 84 years of age, and wife's life expectancy—based on her age of 62 at the time of trial—is 91 years of age. Additionally, wife does not want to sell her property, which includes her studio. She notes that the property, which has a market value of $500,000, is encumbered by a debt of $200,000, and she is skeptical that the property would sell for its current market value.

The trial court found that there had been a substantial and unanticipated change in circumstances since the dissolution and that it was just and equitable to terminate husband's obligations to provide spousal support, life insurance, and disability insurance. In reaching that conclusion, the trial court apparently did not take into account husband's current wife's income as a resource available to him. The court also apparently did not include as part of husband's income the voluntary contributions that he makes to secure survivor benefits for his current wife. . . .

ORS 107.135 authorizes a court to modify an award of spousal support if the economic circumstances of a party have substantially changed. In this case, the trial court found such a change in the parties' economic circumstances, and wife does not challenge that finding.

If a substantial change in economic circumstances has occurred, the question becomes whether the particular modification that is sought is appropriate. Husband, as the party seeking the modification, has the burden to show that a modification of the support required by the MSA is warranted.

In this case, husband seeks termination of support. A termination of spousal support is proper when the purpose of the initial award has been met. When the award does not provide any guidance as to its purpose, the court's task is to maintain the relative positions of the parties as established in the initial decree. The ultimate inquiry, however, is whether a modification of support is "just and equitable" under the totality of the circumstances.

Determining whether the termination of support is consistent with maintaining the relative positions of the parties in the MSA necessarily depends on a determination of what those relative positions are; in other words, we must determine the nature and amount of the resources that are now available to each of the parties. That, in fact, is the focus of the parties' contentions on appeal.

We begin with husband's resources. As we have noted, husband contends that he has available to him a total of $5,719 per month in retirement and other income. Wife contends that the amount is too low, given that it fails to take into account husband's current wife's income.

. . . Where a spouse has remarried and has combined expenses and assets with a new spouse, it is appropriate to consider the additional income from the new spouse in determining an appropriate spousal support amount. . . . With his current spouse's monthly income of approximately $3,650, husband's available monthly income is approximately $9,369.

Wife also argues that it is appropriate to include the full retirement benefits that husband receives, not reduced by approximately $650 in voluntary contributions for the purchase of a survivor benefit for his current wife. Husband argues that "there is no legal or equitable basis for [wife] to argue that husband should be restricted as to what elections he chooses to make" with respect to income that is produced from his share of his retirement.

. . . Husband's retirement income is available to him to spend as he wishes. The fact that he chooses to spend part of it to secure a benefit for his current wife does not make it any less a resource that is available to him and, as a result, it may properly be considered as part of his income for support purposes. Taking those voluntary contributions into account produces a total of approximately $10,000 in monthly income.

Husband contends that, in any event, any comparison of the parties' incomes must take into account the number of people in the household. That means, he contends, that we should divide his $10,000 in monthly income by the number of people currently in his household—that is, two—producing a total income of $5,000 per month for support purposes.

We find no support in the relevant statutes or the case law for husband's proposal. Of course, it is appropriate to take into account, among other relevant considerations, the number of members of a household and the expenses that they incur. It is another thing entirely to suggest that a spouse's income, for support purposes, is simply divided by the number of household members.

Husband also argues that wife has underestimated her own resources. Specifically, husband contends that wife's income should include PERS and Social Security retirement benefits that she could elect to receive now, as well as income that could be produced by selling the real estate—her current residence and timber property—that she now owns.

We begin with husband's contention that we should attribute to wife income that she could obtain now, were she to elect to collect retirement benefits earlier than she otherwise would choose. According to husband, wife should be required to include those benefits unless she can show that she would be economically prejudiced by failing to wait to draw those benefits. In husband's view, his expert's opinion on that question established that she would be "better off" collecting the benefits now. . . .

The proper treatment of retirement benefits is set out in ORS 107.135(4)(a)(B), which provides that, in reconsidering spousal support, we are required to "consider income opportunities and benefits of the respective parties from all sources, including but not limited to retirement benefits available to the obligor and to the obligee." The statute is broad and inclusive in setting out what must be "considered" in evaluating spousal support. . . . Courts are required to take into account income opportunities, including retirement benefits, that are available from property awarded in the dissolution judgment. . . . It does not require the court to treat the availability of retirement benefits as current income. The overriding consideration in determining the appropriate amount of spousal support is what is just and equitable under the totality of the circumstances. . . .

In this case, ORS 107.135(4)(a)(B) requires that we at least consider the availability of potential retirement benefits from wife's PERS account. But we find that it would not be just and equitable to treat those potential benefits as current income to wife, in effect, requiring her to take early retirement and suffer a reduction in benefits from the amount that would be available to her were she able to retire later, as she currently plans to do. Husband's contention that, as an actuarial matter, wife would actually be better off taking the smaller amount of benefits now, as opposed to a larger amount of benefits later, is not persuasive. Among other things, wife's expert explained, it is generally better for women to wait to take retirement benefits because they have a relatively longer life expectancy.

That leaves husband's argument that, in any event, we should attribute to wife income that she could earn by the sale of her residence and timber property. In our view, however, husband's assumption that wife's property could be sold as a source of income is too speculative. Husband offered the testimony of Pope, a financial advisor, who believed that wife should sell her property and reinvest the surplus, but he did not present evidence that the property, if sold, would actually yield proceeds sufficient to allow wife to have funds to invest after purchasing a new residence.

To summarize, then, husband's current monthly income is approximately $10,000. Wife's, without spousal support, is approximately $3,300 per month. Both in absolute and in relative terms, wife's income is significantly less than what was contemplated by the original MSA.

As we noted earlier, we are not unmindful that, although husband's income now is approximately $10,000, he also has additional expenses associated with a household of two persons. But, as we also have noted earlier, husband reports that his and his current wife's combined expenses total $4,100, leaving a net of almost $6,000. Wife, on the other hand, reports expenses of $4,614, the reasonableness of which husband does not challenge. Clearly, without spousal support, she cannot continue to make ends meet, while husband enjoys ample income to continue to contribute to wife's needs.

Considering all of the circumstances of the parties, we conclude that it is just and equitable for husband to continue to pay support at the reduced amount of $1,400 per month. That amount is affordable for husband and will allow wife to meet her expenses while preserving savings that she will need when she is no longer working.

Questions based on *Marriage of Reaves*

1. At the time of the divorce, husband was 52. In the marriage settlement agreement (MSA), husband agreed to pay spousal support indefinitely. I wonder if husband and his attorney discussed the impact of retirement on husband's ability to support his soon-to-be ex-wife? Should husband have tried to negotiate a clause in the MSA that support would diminish or end at his retirement?

2. The Court of Appeals held that it was proper to consider the income of husband's second wife to calculate husband's income available to support his ex-wife. States take a variety of positions on whether a second spouse's income should factor into spousal support. California Family Code § 4323(b) provides: "The income of a supporting spouse's subsequent spouse or nonmarital partner shall not be considered when determining or modifying support." In *Moore v. Moore,* 763 N.W.2d 536, 547-548 (S.D. 2009), the South Dakota Supreme Court wrote, "While a new spouse's income might be considered to offset an obligor spouse's living expenses, thus freeing more of his or her income for alimony payments, we can find no authority in any jurisdiction in which the new spouse's income is used to supplement the obligor's *income* for alimony modification purposes. We conclude that an alimony obligor's subsequent-spouse's income may not be included as part of the obligor spouse's income." The Vermont Supreme Court wrote in *Mayville v. Mayville,* 189 Vt. 1, 12 A.3d 500, 507 (2010), "When a maintenance obligor remarries, a court may not impute income of the new spouse to the obligor for the purposes of calculating the amount of the obligor's income that is available to pay maintenance. We have previously held, however, that a trial court may properly consider the earnings of a new spouse to determine the ability of the spouse from whom maintenance is sought to meet his or her reasonable needs while meeting those of the spouse seeking maintenance." In *Marriage of Bowles,* 916 P.2d 615, 618 (Colo. Ct. App. 1995), the court wrote, "We conclude that, with the possible exception of legally required financial contributions, it is impermissible to include the financial resources of a third party in the calculation of the income of the payor spouse when determining an award of maintenance. We further conclude, however, that a limited consideration of a third party's resources is not absolutely prohibited if, as here, the existence or use of such assets is directly relevant to an allegation by the payor spouse of a substantial and continuing change of circumstances in his ability to meet his reasonable needs while meeting the needs of his former spouse."

3. Nine years after the divorce, husband is paying his ex-wife support, with no end in sight. Returning to the law review articles earlier in this chapter, does it strike you as fair that a person should have to support a former spouse forever?

Practice Note: The foregoing material highlights some of the issues that arise when a lawyer represents a divorcing client over age 50. Retirement can impact the ability to pay spousal support. Another retirement-related issue concerns the value of pre-tax retirement funds like 401(k) plans. When funds are withdrawn from such accounts, taxes must be paid, making the real value of the plan less than the face value. The true value may be in the neighborhood of 65% of the face value.

With increasing age, the possibility goes up that the supporting spouse will die. The supported spouse may think it wise to purchase a life insurance policy on the supporting spouse.

Many older divorcing clients have estate planning questions. You will need to decide whether you want to handle estate planning questions or refer the client to a specialist.

Problems on Spousal Support

1. Sue and Harry were married ten years when they divorced. In the divorce, Harry was ordered to pay Sue $4,000 per month spousal support for ten years. Two years following the divorce, Harry stopped paying spousal support because, as he said, "I'm not paying that woman another cent. She can get a job." Sue's attorney returned to court seeking to enforce Harry's support obligation. Enraged, Harry tried unsuccessfully to kill Sue *and* her attorney. Harry was convicted of two counts of attempted murder and sent to prison for 25 years to life. In prison, Harry filed a motion in family court to terminate his spousal support obligation because he no longer had a source of income. Harry stated that he had used all his savings to pay his criminal defense attorney. Should the family court judge reduce or eliminate Harry's spousal support obligation? For cases discussing the impact of incarceration on the duty to pay child support, *see Lambert v. Lambert,* 861 N.E.2d 1176 (Ind. 2007); *In re Paternity of E.C.,* 896 N.E.2d 923 (Ind. Ct. App. 2008); *Kuron v. Hamilton,* 331 N.J. Super. 561, 752 A.2d 752 (App. Div. 2000); *Herring v. Herring,* 24 A.3d 574 (Vt. 2011).

2. State law provides that the family law court must consider the earning capacity of each party in ordering spousal support. The decision whether to base a support order on a party's earning capacity rather than actual earnings is committed to the judge's discretion. At the time of her divorce from Tom, Wendy had worked as a librarian for 40 years at State University, and had risen to the position of Director of Libraries for the university. Wendy is 70 years old, but loves her job and plans to continue full time work another 5 years. Wendy's state pension is mature, and Wendy could retire any time and receive full pension benefits. Wendy has been married 41 years, and her pension is entirely marital/community property. Tom is retired and has a small pension and Social Security, the combination of which is not enough to live on comfortably. Tom seeks spousal support from Wendy. There is a dispute over Wendy's income. Wendy could increase her monthly income by retiring, taking her pension, and returning to work half time. Taking this option would increase Wendy's monthly income by $500. But retiring would require Wendy to step down from her position as Director of Libraries. She would have to return to work as a regular librarian. Because she loves the challenge of her leadership position, she does not want to retire. Tom argues that in setting spousal support, the family court judge should consider Wendy's capacity to earn an extra $500 per month. Wendy argues the judge should use her actual income. Should the judge impute an extra $500 a month to Wendy? *Marriage of Kochan,* 193 Cal. App. 4th 420, 122 Cal. Rptr. 3d 61 (2011).

3. Elizabeth has been a judge on the family court bench for 15 years, and is widely regarded as a superb judge. Elizabeth's salary as a judge is $170,000 per year. Elizabeth and her husband Dan are divorcing. Dan is a teacher, with an annual salary of $40,000. In the divorce, Dan seeks spousal support, joint custody of their fifteen-year-old daughter, and child support. Dan argues that Elizabeth could double her income by resigning from the bench and becoming a "private judge." People hire "private judges" to help resolve disputes without formal litigation. Assume Dan is right, Elizabeth could double her income by becoming a private judge. Elizabeth, however, has no interest in resigning, and plans to remain on the bench until retirement, which is at least five years in the future. In the divorce case, Dan argues that in setting spousal and child support, the judge should use what Elizabeth could earn as a private judge, not what she actually earns as a sitting judge. What should the judge do? *Marriage of Kochan,* 193 Cal. App. 4th 420, 122 Cal. Rptr. 3d 61 (2011).

4. Helen and Abe began dating when Helen was fourteen years old, and Abe was sixteen. Helen skipped her senior year of high school to join Abe at college. Upon Abe's graduation from college, the couple moved to another city so Abe could attend dental school. Helen got a college degree and starting working as a teach-

er. When their first child was born, Helen stopped working and became a stay-at-home mom. They have four children, the youngest of whom is now 18. Soon after Abe graduated from dental school, Helen and Abe bought a modest home, and in this home they raised their kids. Abe's dental practice did well, and two years ago, Helen and Abe decided to build their dream home. They invested over $1 million dollars in the home. Within months of moving into their new home, Abe started an affair with Sandy, whom he met playing golf. Abe told Helen he was in love with Sandy, and wanted a divorce. At the time of the divorce, Helen is 45 and Abe is 47. Helen has not worked in over twenty years. Abe's income from the dental practice averages in excess of $500,000 a year. Should Abe be ordered to pay spousal support to Helen? If so, how much and for how long? *Dickert v. Dickert,* 691 S.E.2d 448 (S.C. 2010).

5. Sally and Harry were married 21 years. The kids are grown. At the time of the couple's divorce three years ago, Sally had worked for the state for ten years. Harry is a carpenter. Unfortunately, Harry has a back injury that keeps him from working full time. He works "When my back will let me." In the divorce, Sally was ordered to pay Harry $300 per month spousal support. Sally has never missed a spousal support payment. Recently, to make extra money, Sally took a second job working at a Target store on weekends. When Harry found out Sally was making extra income, he returned to family court seeking an increase in spousal support. Should the judge increase spousal support?

6. Revisit Sally and Harry from problem 5. While Sally was working her part time at Target, she assisted customer Richie Rich. It was love at first sight, and within six months, Richie asked Sally to marry him. Richie Rich is indeed very rich. Once married to Richie, Sally quit her Target job, although she continues working full time for the state. When Harry learned Sally married a billionaire, Harry filed a motion in family court seeking increased spousal support. Harry argues that Sally is now wealthy and able to pay increased spousal support. Should Richie Rich's riches be considered in determining spousal support? *See* the authorities collected at Note 2, page 522.

7. Following a bitter and protracted divorce, Tim was ordered to pay Wanda $4,000 per month spousal support for ten years. Four years after the divorce, Wanda hired a "hit man" to kill Tim. Unbeknownst to Wanda, the supposed "hit man" was an undercover police officer, and Tim's life was never in danger. When Tim learned of the plot on his life, he stopped paying spousal support. Wanda was convicted of solicitation to commit murder. From her prison cell, Wanda filed a motion to enforce Tim's spousal support obligation. Wanda also seeks to collect arrears for the support Tim did not pay after he stopped paying. What result?

8. Trace and Becky divorced, and Trace was ordered to pay spousal support. After the divorce, Becky moved in with her parents. Also living in the parents' home was a teenage foster child. Trace sought to end his spousal support duty when he found out that Becky had a brief sexual relationship with the foster child. A statute provides that spousal support terminates "upon establishment by the party paying spousal support that the former spouse is cohabiting with another person." Should Trace's support obligation end? *Myers v. Myers,* 266 P.3d 806 (Utah 2011).

9. Nancy and John were married 18 years. At the time of their divorce, Nancy is 53. John is 56. Nancy has a high school diploma. John has a college degree. During the marriage, Nancy did not work outside the home. She cared for the couple's two children, Tim age 18 and Sue age 16. John is a news correspondent for a major TV network, and earns over a million dollars a year. In the divorce, the trial judge orders permanent spousal support for Nancy in the amount of $14,000 per month. John's net monthly income is $58,000. The spousal support order leaves John with $44,000 per month. Thus, Nancy has $14,000 per month and John has $44,000 per month. Nancy argues the spousal support order is too low, and will not allow her to maintain the standard of living enjoyed during the lengthy marriage. John argues the support order is correct. John points out that he is voluntarily paying for Tim's college education at a private university. Annual tuition is $52,000, plus room and board. This expense will continue for four years. John has also agreed to pay Sue's college expenses when she graduates from high school in two years. John argues that the college expenses considerably reduce his net income, making the spousal support award fair. Nancy argues that while it is praiseworthy for John to volunteer to pay the kids' college expenses, the law does not require him to do so. Nancy argues it is not fair to allow John to reduce his spousal support obligation by deducting college expenses from his income when he has no legal duty to pay for college. Spousal support should be based on John's full monthly income; not what is left over after he subtracts an expense he has no legal obligation to pay. Should John be permitted to deduct the college expenses from his income available to pay spousal support? *Quinones v. Quinones,* 84 So.3d 1101 (Fla. Ct. App. 2012).

10. Shirley and Robert were married nine years. At the time of divorce, Shirley is 62; Robert is 76. Both are in poor health. Neither works. Robert retired from the Air Force 38 years ago. After retiring from the Air Force, Robert worked 20 years for the state. Robert retired from the state before meeting Shirley. Robert's monthly income is $4,500, consisting of his Air Force and state pensions, plus Social Security retirement. In the divorce, Shirley seeks spousal support of $2,000 per month. Sally could begin receiving Social Security retirement now, but she has not applied for

Social Security. She prefers to wait to receive Social Security until she is 66. By waiting until she is 66, her monthly Social Security checks will be higher. Robert argues that in determining spousal support, the judge should consider the amount of Social Security Shirley *could* receive now, if she applied. What should the judge do? *Crossland v. Crossland,* 397 S.C. 406, 725 S.E.2d 509 (Ct. App. 2012).

Trust Income and Support Obligations

A trust is a three way fiduciary relationship in which one person holds legal title to property for the benefit of another. The person who creates and funds a trust is the settlor. The person or entity holding legal title is the trustee. The beneficiary is the person(s) for whose benefit the trust is established.

Divorcing couples sometimes agree that the spouse with support duties will establish a trust to ensure payment of spousal or child support. In most states, the judge has authority to order such a trust.[47]

A spendthrift is someone who is financially irresponsible. A spendthrift trust is established (often by the spendthrift's parents) to protect the spendthrift from her or himself. With a spendthrift trust, the beneficiary—the spendthrift—cannot sell or give away trust property.[48] Nor can the spendthrift's creditors attach the trust property to satisfy the spendthrift's debts. Of course, by no means are all beneficiaries of spendthrift trusts financially irresponsible—most are not. Nevertheless, spendthrift clauses are a common tool to protect trust assets from creditors.

When a former spouse who has child or spousal support obligations is the beneficiary of a spendthrift trust, and the beneficiary fails to make support payments, the supported spouse is a creditor. Normally, creditors cannot invade a spendthrift trust to secure payment. A supported former spouse, however, is not a "normal" creditor.[49] Most states place limits on the extent to which spendthrift trusts can defeat child or spousal support claims.[50] Thus, in some states a sup-

---

47 *See* Spicer v. Spicer, 168 N.C. App. 283, 607 S.E.2d 678 (2005)(trial court ordered dad to create a child support trust).

48 Of course, once the trustee disburses money to the beneficiary, the beneficiary is free to squander it!

49 *See* Ventura County Department of Child Support Services v. Brown, 117 Cal. App. 4th 144, 151, 11 Cal. Rptr. 3d 489, 494 (2004)(in reforming California law, "Child support creditors were elevated to the status of 'preferred creditors' and permitted to reach a beneficiary's interest in the trust, despite the existence of a spendthrift clause.").

50 *See* California Probate Code § 15305; Wis. Stat. Ann. § 701.06(4).

ported spouse can satisfy support obligations from a spendthrift trust so long as non-trust assets are first exhausted.[51] In California, the Court of Appeal in *Ventura County Department of Child Support Services v. Brown*,[52] considered the "deadbeat dad" of six children by three women. Dad didn't support any of his kids. Dad's mother established a spendthrift trust for her son. The trustee refused to disburse trust income to pay dad's child support obligations. The Court of Appeal disapproved, writing, "Even if the trust instrument contains a spendthrift clause applicable to claims for child support, it is against public policy to give effect to the provision. As a general rule, the beneficiary should not be permitted to have the enjoyment of the interest under the trust while neglecting his or her dependents."[53] In a similar vein, the Michigan Court of Appeals held in *Hurley v. Hurley*[54] that the public policy requiring parents to support their children "outweighs the public policy that an owner of property, such as the settlor of a trust, may dispose of it as he pleases and may impose spendthrift restraints on the disposition of income."[55]

A discretionary support trust is a trust set up to support/benefit a beneficiary.[56] For example, grandparents might create discretionary support trusts for their grandkids, naming themselves—grandpa and grandma—trustees. As described by the Iowa Supreme Court in *Emmet County Board of Supervisors v. Ridout*,[57] "A settlor creates a discretionary support trust when the purpose of the trust is to furnish the beneficiary with support, and the trustee has the discretion to pay the income or principal to the beneficiary, as the trustee deems necessary for the support of the beneficiary."[58]

Discretionary support trusts nearly always contain a spendthrift clause. Guided by the terms of the trust, the trustee has broad discretion to make pay-

---

51   *See* Mason v. Mason, 798 So.2d 895 (Fla. Ct. App. 2001); M.L. Cross, Trust Income or Assets as Subject to Claim Against Beneficiary for Alimony, Maintenance, or Child Support, 91 A.L.R.2d 292 (1963).

52   117 Cal. App. 4th 144, 11 Cal. Rptr. 3d 489 (2004).

53   Ventura County Department of Child Support Services v. Brown, 117 Cal. App. 4th 144, 154-155, 11 Cal. Rptr. 3d 489, 497 (2004).

54   107 Mich. App. 249, 309 N.W.2d 225 (1981).

55 107 Mich. App. at 254.

56   *See Restatement (Third) of Trusts* § 50: "(1) A discretionary power conferred upon the trustee to determine the benefits of a trust beneficiary is subject to judicial control only to prevent misinterpretation or abuse of the discretion by the trustee. (2) The benefits to which a beneficiary of a discretionary interest is entitled, and what may constitute an abuse of discretion by the trustee, depend on the terms of the discretion, including the proper construction of any accompanying standards, and on the settlor's purposes in granting the discretionary power and in creating the trust."

57   692 N.W.2d 821 (Iowa 2005).

58   *Id.* at 826.

ments from the trust for the benefit of the beneficiary. Generally, the beneficiary cannot insist on payment from the trust. It is up to the trustee to decide when, why, and how much to pay.

Suppose Hank is divorcing Sally. Some years back, Hank's parents created a discretionary support trust for Hank, containing a spendthrift provision. Hank's parents are the trustees. At the time of the divorce, Hank is not receiving any money from the trust. In the divorce, Sally seeks spousal support. Sally asks the family court judge to include in Hank' income the amount Hank *could* receive from the trust *if* the trustees decided to pay. Hank responds, "I'm not getting *any* money from the trust. I have no income from the trust, and I can't force the trustees to give me any. My income for spousal support purposes does not

include money I don't have and can't get." Sally asks the judge to impute income from the trust to Hank. What should the judge do?

Most cases dealing with trusts and duties of support involve a trust beneficiary with a duty of support.[59] But what if the trust beneficiary is the party *seeking* support? Should income from a trust be considered in calculating the need for spousal or child support? If a trustee actually distributes income to a beneficiary, the money is income. But what if the trustee of a discretionary support trust with a spendthrift provision is not distributing available income to a beneficiary? The money is sitting in the trust and *could* be distributed, but the trustee decides not to let go of the money. So long as the trustee is carrying out the terms of the trust, the beneficiary can't compel the trustee to distribute money. For spousal and child support purposes, is money that a trustee *could but doesn't* disburse income?[60] The Connecticut Appellate Court grappled with this issue in *Taylor v. Taylor.*[61] Marvin and Elinor Taylor divorced after forty years of marriage. Marvin was ordered to pay Elinor $5,000 per month alimony. Five years later, Marvin filed a motion in family court to reduce alimony because Elinor had become a beneficiary of a discretionary support trust with a spendthrift provision. The trial judge found that the trust earned more than enough income to support Elinor, and reduced alimony from $5,000 per month to $1 per year. Elinor appealed. The trustees were not actually paying trust income to Elinor— she didn't need it because she was getting alimony. In virtually eliminating

---

59 *See, e.g.,* In re Goodlander and Tamposi, 161 N.H. 490, 20 A.3d 199 (2011).

60 *See* Marriage of Rhinehart, 704 N.W.2d 677, 681 (Iowa 2005)(the supported spouse, Deborah, was the beneficiary of a trust; "Deborah has no right to the allocated, but undistributed, income from the trust. Consequently, it would not be appropriate to treat the *undistributed* income from the trust as a current source of financial support that would alleviate Deborah's need for alimony.").

61 117 Conn. App. 229, 978 A.2d 538 (2009).

Marvin's alimony obligation, the trial court considered income the trustees *could* give to Elinor *if* they decided to pay her. In essence, the trial court imputed trust income to Elinor. The Appellate Court reversed, ruling that the trial court had no authority to enter an order that basically compelled the trustees to make distributions to Elinor. The Appellate Court wrote, "The well-settled rule in this state is that the exercise of discretion by the trustee of a spendthrift trust is subject to the court's control only to the extent that an abuse has occurred. There has been no claim raised that the trustees have abused their discretion in not making any distributions to [Elinor]. The court improperly interpreted the provisions of the trust agreement when, in effect, it assumed that the trustees were obligated to distribute the income to [Elinor] . . . . Until [Elinor] receives a distribution from the supplemental spendthrift trust, the undistributed income from the trust itself cannot be considered as income to [Elinor]. . . . We conclude, therefore, that it was an abuse of discretion for the court to consider the undistributed trust assets as income to [Elinor] when the court . . . reduced [Marvin's] alimony obligation to [Elinor] to $1 per year."[62]

Do you approve the result in *Taylor*? Suppose Marvin had barely enough money to pay the $5,000 per month alimony. Suppose the trustees were sitting on millions of dollars in interest they could parcel out to Elinor without invading the trust principal or otherwise harming the trust. The trustees decide against distributing anything to Elinor *precisely because* Marvin is on the hook for $5,000 per month alimony. Fair?

---

62 978 A.2d at 543-544.

CHAPTER 9

Division of Property on Divorce

OVER THE COURSE OF A MARRIAGE or domestic partnership, property issues arise at three times. First, during intact relationships. Second, when death ends a relationship. Third, and the focus of this chapter, property issues arise when a relationship ends in divorce, legal separation, annulment, or the termination of a domestic partnership.

During intact relationships, the parties owe each other duties of honesty and fair dealing (See Chapter 1). Married couples and domestic partners can agree with each other regarding their property (See Chapter 1).

When death ends a relationship, distribution of property is governed by the law of wills, trusts, intestate succession, probate, and related topics. Property issues at death are covered in the course on wills and trusts, and are beyond the scope of this book.

Systems of Marital Property in the United States

American states employ one of two systems of marital property: equitable distribution or community property. In equitable distribution states, "marital property" is divided equitably.[1] In community property states, "community property" is divided equally or equitably, depending on the state. The two systems of marital property are increasingly similar. At this writing, 2013, the nine community property states are Arizona, California, Idaho, Louisiana, Nevada, New Mexico, Texas, Washington, and Wisconsin.

---

1 *See* Price v. Price, 69 N.Y.2d 8, 503 N.E.2d 684 (1986).

Origins of Equitable Distribution and Community Property

To understand today's equitable distribution system of marital property, it is useful to examine the law at the nation's birth. After the Revolutionary War, the original states continued their adherence to much of the English law of domestic relations. In particular, states perpetuated English law relegating married women to an inferior status vis à vie husbands. Describing the English subordination of married women, William Blackstone (1723-1780) wrote in his *Commentaries on the Laws of England*:

> By marriage, the husband and wife are one person in law: that is, the very being or legal existence of the woman is suspended during the marriage, or at least is incorporated and consolidated into that of the husband: under whose wing, protection, and cover, she performs everything; and is therefore called in our law-french a feme-covert; is said to be covert-baron, or under the protection and influence of her husband, her baron, or lord; and her condition during marriage is called her coverture . . . . Upon this principle, of an union of person in husband and wife, depend almost of the legal rights, duties, and disabilities, that either of them acquire by the marriage.

When a woman married, ownership of her personal property passed to her husband. The husband could sell the property, and his creditors could reach *her* property to satisfy *his* debts. A married woman's real property fell under her husband's control as well, although he could not sell her real property without her consent. In many states, a married woman could not enter into binding contracts. A married woman could not make a will. For many legal purposes, women were placed in the same category as children and "idiots."

Over the years, mechanisms emerged to ameliorate somewhat the wife's subordinate position regarding property. Thus, some states allowed a married couple to agree that the wife would retain control of her property. Sometimes, a woman's parents created a trust for their daughter, placing property in trust in order to remove the property from the control of the daughter's husband.[2] In some states, married women who wished to go into business were authorized to transact business and enter contacts.

---

2 *See* Homer H. Clark, Jr., *The Law of Domestic Relations in the United States*, vol. 1, § 8.1, p. 501 (2d ed. 1987) (discussing the married woman's separate estate in equity).

From early days, reformers agitated against inequitable treatment of married women.[3] Calls for reform gathered steam and reached a crescendo in 1839, when Mississippi passed the first married women's property act.[4] The act provided: "That any married woman may become seized or possessed of any property, real or personal, by direct bequest, demise, gift, purchase, or distribution, in her own name, and as of her own property . . . ."[5] Although the Mississippi law was a step forward, it by no means bestowed equality on women. Amanda Sims writes, "The 1839 [married women's property act] did nothing more than legally pass title to property to a married woman, while reserving all the privileges of ownership to her husband and providing her some recourse in retaining her separate property from his creditors, but she benefited only in the continued possession of the property, not necessarily in the enjoyment of the usual benefits of property ownership."[6] Following Mississippi's lead, other states adopted married women's property acts.[7]

Divorce was uncommon during the nineteenth century. When a divorce action was commenced, legal rules derived from England (only partially alleviated by married women's property acts) combined with then-common forms of property ownership to form a double disadvantage for women. Recall that by the old law, a married woman's property was controlled by her husband.[8] Thus, a

---

3   *See* Elizabeth Bowles Warbasse, *The Changing Legal Rights of Married Women: 1800-1861*, p. 21 (1987).

4   Intending no disrespect for Mississippi, one wonders, why did this reform for women emerge from a state in the traditionally conservative south? The answer remains a mystery. In her book *The Changing Legal Rights of Married Women 1800-1861*(1987), Elizabeth Warbasse wrote: "Colonel T.B.J. Hadley, a thirty-six-year-old planter from Hinds County, introduced this bill into the state Senate. According to tradition this senator was about to marry a wealthy widow; but, being deeply in debt did not want to involve her in his own financial ruin." The full story of the Colonel's motivation will probably never be uncovered.

5   Laws of Mississippi, Chapter 46, § 1, Feb. 15, 1839. The 1839 Mississippi act dealt in detail with ownership of slaves. The Mississippi married woman's property act was amended in 1846, 1857, and 1880. The 1880 law abolished gender-based restrictions on ownership of property.

6   Amanda Sims, *Patriarchy and Property: The Nineteenth-Century Mississippi Married Women's Property Acts.* Thesis submitted to the faculty of Brigham Young University, Department of History, August, 2007, p. 8.

7   *See* Stall v. Fulton, 30 N.J.L. 430 (N.J. 1863)(the court quotes the married women's property act of 1852: "that it shall be lawful for any married female to receive, by gift, grant, devise, or bequest, and hold to her sole and separate use, as if she were a single female, real and personal property, and the rents, issues, and profits thereof; and the same shall not be subject to the disposal of her husband, nor be liable for his debts."); Ellen Dannin, Marriage and Law Reform: Lessons from the Nineteenth-Century Michigan Married Women's Property Acts, 20 *Texas Journal of Women and the Law* 1 (2010).

8   A number of states had rules that on divorce, property that passed from wife to husband should be restored to the wife. In the 1854 divorce of Wilmore v. Wilmore, 15 B. Mon. 49, 54 Ky. 49 (1854), the Kentucky Court of Appeals noted that property still in the possession of the husband should normally be returned to the wife. In an 1855 divorce, Sharp v. Sharp, 2 Sneed 496, 34 Tenn. 496 (1855), the Tennessee Supreme Court granted wife a divorce based on cruelty, and ordered her husband to return her property. Of course, if the husband had disposed of the wife's property before the divorce—which he had the right to do—there was nothing to restore.

wife's property rested in the hands of the man she was divorcing. Add that it was common for title to property to be in the husband's name alone. Thus, the family home or farm typically stood in the husband's name. As well, some courts held that the husband was presumed to be the owner of all personal property.

Throughout the nineteenth century and into the twentieth, divorce courts in non-community property states typically assigned property based on title or ownership.[9] The American Law Institute's *Principles of the Law of Family Dissolution* observe, "Under the traditional common-law system there was no concept of marital property. Even after a long marriage the divorce court had no general authority to allocate to one spouse property whose title was held by the other spouse or which was acquired with the other spouse's earnings."[10] Under the "title theory" of marital property, the judge's job was simple: determine who held title or ownership and assign property accordingly.[11]

Consider the hypothetical couple Willodene and Henry, who married in 1920. Henry worked full time. Willodene stayed home and raised the children. They purchased a home and put title in Henry's name. All mortgage payments were from Henry's income from work. In 1930, Henry purchased a farm, putting title in his name. Mortgage payments on the farm were from Henry's earnings at work. They bought a car, a truck, and a tractor, putting title in Henry's name. Their bank account was in Henry's name. Under the title theory of marital property, when Willodene and Henry divorce, Henry owns everything! If Willodene wanted an interest in titled property, she should have taken concurrent title with

---

9 *See* Brett R. Turner, *Equitable Distribution of Property*, § 1:3, p. 6 (3d ed. 2005)("The prevailing law by the early twentieth century was thus the title theory: married women could legally own property, but upon divorce, the wife received only assets to which she owned legal title.").

10 American Law Institute, *Principles of the Law of Family Dissolution: Analysis and Recommendations*, p. 648 (2000)("Equitable doctrines such as constructive trust were occasionally employed to justify departure from these legal rules, but in many common-law states their use was closely constrained. The traditional homemaker thus could leave a 40-year marriage with essentially no property, even though her husband had created a valuable business during the marriage, relying in part on her assistance." Id.).

11 *See* Brett R. Turner, *Equitable Distribution of Property*, § 1:3, p. 5 (3d ed. 2005)("The merger of identities under early American law prevented the development of any law of property division upon divorce. Since married women had not distinct legal identity, the law viewed all property of the marriage as solely the property of the husband. From this position, it was not a great step to assume that the property rights of all women were limited, and that women had no entitlement to a property award upon divorce."); Coltea v. Coltea, 856 So.2d 1047, 1050 (Fla. Ct. App. 2003)("Fifty years ago in a divorce, property rights were usually decided solely on who held title."); Lopez v. Lopez, 206 Md. 509, 112 A.2d 466, 470 (1955)(a 1947 statute "goes no further than to empower a court of equity, in decreeing a divorce, to determine the ownership of the personal property of the parties and to apportion the property accordingly.").

See Brett R. Turner, *Equitable Distribution of Property*, § 1:3, p. 6 (3d ed. 2005)("The prevailing law by the early twentieth century was thus the title theory: married women could legally own property, but upon divorce, the wife received only assets to which she owned legal title.").

Henry.[12] Deprived of any interest in "Henry's property," Willodene's only remedy was alimony.

The divorce of Jane and Edward Wirth in 1971 is a good example of the title theory of marital property.[13] Jane and Edward lived in New York and were married 22 years. Both worked outside the home. Fifteen years before they divorced, Edward started a "crash savings program" with his paycheck, telling Jane he was saving "for the two of us for our latter days." From then on, family expenses were paid mostly with Jane's income, while Edward invested his paycheck in his own name. That is, Jane used her paycheck to support the family, while Edward saved his paycheck. On divorce, Jane argued that some of Edward's investments should be awarded to her. Under the title theory then in force in New York, however, Edward was the "owner" of his investments, and Jane was out of luck.

Chinks in the title system developed in the first half of the twentieth century.[14] Brett Turner writes, "Legislatures began passing statutes permitting the court to award the wife a share of the property to which she had directly contributed. These statutes were passed not all at once, but rather gradually over a period of years. . . . None of these enactments were equitable distribution statutes in the modern sense."[15] Turner continues, "By the mid-1960s, the American law of divorce in general was well out of line with popular notions of sex roles and marriage."[16]

In 1970, the National Conference of Commissioners on Uniform State Laws took a major step forward with promulgation of the *Uniform Marriage and Divorce Act* (UMDA). Although the UMDA is most famous for introducing no-fault divorce, UMDA also recommended abandonment of the title theory of property and adoption of equitable distribution. Turner writes, "The property division of the UMDA can fairly be called the first equitable distribution statute."[17] By the 1980s, all non-community property states had adopted some form of equitable distribution.[18]

---

12 *See* Brett R. Turner, *Equitable Distribution of Property*, § 1:3, p. 6 (3d ed. 2005)("The prevailing law by the early twentieth century was thus the title theory: married women could legally own property, but upon divorce, the wife received only assets to which she owned legal title.").

13 Wirth v. Wirth, 38 A.D.2d 611, 326 N.Y.S.2d 308 (1971).

14 *See, e.g.*, Robinson v. Robinson, 275 Mich. 420, 266 N.W. 403, 403 (1936)("There is no rigid rule of division of property in divorce proceedings, but the division must be equitable.").

15 Brett R. Turner, *Equitable Distribution of Property*, § 1:3, pp. 8-9 (3d ed. 2005).

16 *Id.* at 12.

17 *Id.* at 16.

18 American Law Institute, *Principles of the Law of Family Dissolution: Analysis and Recommendations*, p. 649

UMDA recommended a dual classification system in which property is either marital or separate. Marital property is property acquired during marriage through the effort of either spouse. Separate property is property acquired before marriage, and property acquired during marriage by bequest, devise, or gift. Upon divorce, separate property belongs to the owner, while marital property is divided equitably. Today, equitable distribution states recognize the distinction between separate and marital property. Most equitable distribution states begin with a presumption that marital property should be divided equally.[19] As the Alaska Supreme Court put it in *Jones v. Jones*,[20] "It is presumed that an equal division is equitable."

Switching from equitable distribution to community property, the history is easier to tell. Today's community property system derives not from England, where husband and wife were one, and husband was "the one," but from continental Europe. Louisiana's community property system devolved from France. Other community property states inherited their systems from Spain. France and Spain found inspiration in early German and Roman law.[21]

The hallmark of the community property system is that marriage is a partnership, and that property acquired through the effort or skill of either "partner" belongs to the community. Property that is not community is separate. Like the definition of separate property in equitable distribution states, community property jurisdictions define separate property as property acquired before marriage and acquisitions during marriage by gift, descent, or devise.

(2000)("By the mid-1980s, however, all common-law states had moved to some form of 'equitable distribution,' under which the divorce court could allocate property on a basis other than title or the source of earnings used to acquire it."); Brett R. Turner, *Equitable Distribution of Property*, § 1:3, p. 22 (3d ed. 2005)("Looking back in hindsight . . . , the size and speed of the equitable distribution revolution are almost astounding. In 1970, no American common-law state had a fair and sex-neutral property division system. Many states even had no property division system at all. By 1983, every common-law property state in the country had adopted a workable property division system.").

19 *See, e.g.*, Matter of Dube, 163 N.H. 575, 44 A.3d 556 (2012)(RSA 458:16-a, II (2004) creates a presumption that equal distribution of marital property is equitable."); McReath v. McReath, 800 N.W.2d 399, 407 (Wis. 2011) ("When engaged in dividing the marital estate, a circuit court is to proceed under the presumption of equal division. Wis. Stat. § 767.61(3).").

Equal division is the starting place in a divorce in England. *See* Radmacher v. Granatino, 2010 U.K. Supreme Court 42.

20 942 P.2d 1133 (Alaska 1997).

21 *See* George McKay, *A Commentary on the Law of Community Property* § ii, p. 36 (1910)("The strong probabilities are that the central idea of the system—a division between the spouses of the matrimonial gains—was imported into Spain from the North of Europe.").

Characterization and Division of Property

Community property states divide property into separate property and community property. Equitable distribution states divide property into separate property and marital property.[22] The details of marital/community property law vary from state to state.[23] Yet, similarities outnumber differences.

Marital/Community Property

Marital/community property is generally any property, real or personal, acquired during marriage through the time, effort, energy, or skill of a married person.[24] As defined by the New York Court of Appeals, "Marital property is broadly defined as all property acquired by either or both spouses during the marriage."[25] The Texas Court of Appeal wrote, "Under Texas law, property possessed by either spouse during or on dissolution of the marriage is presumed to be community . . . ."[26] Marriage is an economic partnership, and property gener-

---

22 *See, e.g.*, Glenn v. Glenn, 345 S.W.3d 320 (Mo. Ct. App. 2011).

The American Law Institute's *Principles of the Law of Family Dissolution* note, "Most American states distinguish at dissolution between each spouse's 'separate' property, on one hand, and their 'marital' or 'community' property, on the other." American Law Institute, *Principles of the Law of Family Dissolution: Analysis and Recommendations*, p. 646 (2000).

23 American Law Institute, *Principles of the Law of Family Dissolution: Analysis and Recommendations*, p. 646 (200 0)("Ownership rights in property acquired during marriage may vary dramatically with state law.").

24 The American Law Institute's *Principles of the Law of Family Dissolution*, § 4.03, offers the following definitions: "(1) Property acquired during marriage is marital property, except as otherwise expressly provided in this Chapter. (2) Inheritances, including bequests and devises, and gifts from third parties, are the separate property of the acquiring spouse even if acquired during marriage."

See California Family Code § 760 ("Except as otherwise provided by statute, all property, real or personal, wherever situated, acquired by a married person during the marriage while domiciled in this state is community property."); Ohio Rev. Code tit. 31, § 3105.171(A)(3)(a) ("'Marital property' means . . . all of the following: (i) All real and personal property that currently is owned by either or both of the spouses, including, but not limited to, the retirement benefits of the spouses, and that was acquired by either or both of the spouses during the marriage; (ii) All interest that either or both of the spouses has in any real or personal property, including, but not limited to, the retirement benefits of the spouses, and that was acquired by either or both of the spouses during the marriage; (iii) Except as otherwise provided in this section, all income and appreciation on separate property, due to the labor, monetary, or in-kind contribution of either or both of the spouses that occurred during the marriage . . . ."); Schmitz v. Schmitz, 88 P.3d 1116, 1124 (Alaska 2004)("Assets acquired during marriage as compensation for marital services—most commonly salaries earned by either spouse during marriage—are considered marital asserts."); Brathwaite v. Brathwaite, 58 So.3d 398, 400 (Fla. Ct. App. 2011)("An asset is marital if it is 'acquired during the marriage, created or produced by the work efforts, services, or earnings of one or both spouses.'"); In Matter of Chamberlin, 155 N.H. 13, 918 A.2d 1 (2007)(marital property is "all tangible and intangible property and assets, real or personal, belonging to either or both parties, whether title to the property is held in the name of either or both parties."); Marriage of Skarda, 345 S.W.3d 665 671 (Tex. Ct. App. 2011)("It is presumed that property possessed by spouses on the dissolution of marriage is community property.").

25 Price v. Price, 69 N.Y.2d 8, 12, 503 N.E.2d 684 (1986).

26 Sink v. Sink, 364 S.W.3d 340, 344 (Tex. Ct. App. 2012). The court went on to say, "[A] party who seeks to

ated by either partner belongs to both. Thus, a spouse's paycheck is marital/community property. As well, pension benefits that are derived from employment are marital/community property to the extent acquired during marriage.[27]

Alaska has an interesting rule regarding marital property. In *McLaren v. McLaren*,[28] the Alaska Supreme Court stated, "Property acquired by a couple prior to marriage may be considered marital if the property was acquired during premarital cohabitation. The general rule is that courts divide property acquired only during marriage. But so long as the parties do marry, the trial court is free to consider the parties' entire relationship, including any period(s) of premarital cohabitation . . . ."

Separate Property

Separate property is property acquired before marriage begins or after marriage ends, as well as property acquired during marriage by gift, bequest, devise, or descent.[29] On divorce, separate property in most states belongs to the owner.[30]

---

assert the separate character of property must prove that character by clear and convincing evidence."

27 *See* Florida Statutes § 61.076(1) ("All vested and nonvested benefits, rights, and funds accrued during the marriage in retirement, pension, profit-sharing, annuity, deferred compensation, and insurance plans and programs are marital assets subject to equitable distribution."); Parker v. Parker, 980 So.2d 323, 327 (Miss. Ct. App. 2008)("'Marital' property is any and all property acquired or accumulated during the marriage."); N.H. Res. Stat. Ann. § 458:16-a (marital "property shall include all tangible and intangible property and assets, real or personal, belonging to either or both parties, whether title to the property is held in the name of either or both parties.").

28 268 P.3d 323 (Alaska 2012).

29 California Family Code § 770(a) ("Separate property of a married person includes all of the following: (1) All property owned by that person before marriage. (2) All property acquired by the person after marriage by gift, bequest, devise, or descent. (3) The rents, issues, and profits of the property described in this section."); Fla. Stat. Ann. § 61.075(b) ("Nonmarital assets and liabilities include: 1. Assets acquired and liabilities incurred by either party prior to the marriage . . . . 2. Assets acquired separately by either party by noninterperspousal gift, bequest, devise, or descent . . . ."); Schmitz v. Schmitz, 88 P.3d 1116, 1124 (Alaska 2004)("The three primary examples of separate property are property acquired by one spouse before marriage, property acquired by gift, and inherited property."); Price v. Price, 69 N.Y.2d 8, 503 N.E.2d 684 (1986); Ohio Rev. Code tit. 31, § 3105.171(A)(6) (a) ("'Separate property' means all real and personal property and any interest in real or personal property that is found by the court to be any of the following: (i) An inheritance by one spouse by bequest, devise, or descent during the course of the marriage; (ii) Any real or personal property or interest in real or personal property that was acquired by one spouse prior to the date of the marriage; (iii) Passive income and appreciation acquired from separate property by one spouse during the marriage . . . ."); Tex. Fam. Code § 3.001.

See Glenn v. Glenn, 345 S.W.3d 320 (Mo. Ct. App. 2011); Marriage of Skarda, 345 S.W.3d 665, 671 (Tex. Ct. App. 2011)("Property a spouse owns before marriage or acquires during marriage by gift is separate property.").

30 *See* Stonehocker v. Stonehocker, 176 P.3d 476 (Utah Ct. App. 2008); American Law Institute, *Principles of the Law of Family Dissolution: Analysis and Recommendations*, p. 656 (2000) ("In the traditional community-property system, the distinction between community and separate property is critical because the divorce court has no authority to distribute one spouse's separate property to the other spouse. Most common-law states now take a similar position, particularly as to property acquired by gift or inheritance."); Pearson v. Fillingim, 332

"All Property" States

In approximately 15 states, judges have authority to divide all property, including separate property.[31] In Massachusetts, for example, "the court may assign to either husband or wife all or any part of the estate of the other . . . ."[32] Connecticut is an "all-property" state.[33] A Connecticut family court "may assign to either the husband or wife all or any part of the estate of the other."[34] Indiana law states, "In an action for dissolution of marriage, the court shall divide the property of the parties, whether: (1) owned by either spouse before marriage; (2) acquired by either spouse in his or her own right: (A) after the marriage; and (B) before final separation of the parties; or (3) acquired by their joint efforts."[35] In his book *Equitable Distribution of Property*, Brett Turner writes:

> The all-property system reaches fairer results in practice than might at first suspect. Because the court can divide any asset owned by either party, it is possible in theory that the court might divide assets which have no connection with the marital partnership. In practice, however, this is rarely done. Every all-property system includes contributions to acquisition as an equitable distribution factor, and under this factor property acquired from a nonmarital source is frequently divided unequally. When a substantial award of such property is made, the award is frequently justified by such valid equitable reasons as financial need. As a whole, therefore, decisions under the all-property system are generally consistent with the marital partnership theory and modern notions of fair division.
>
> The major weaknesses of the all-property system are predictability and consistency.[36]

S.W.3d 361 (Tex. 2011)("The Family Code provides that gifts to a spouse during marriage are that spouse's separate property.").

31   *See* Brett R. Turner, *Equitable Distribution of Property*. Vol. 1, § 2:8 (3d ed. 2005).

32   Mass. Gen. Laws. Ann. Ch. 208, § 34. *See* Williams v. Massa, 431 Mass. 619, 728 N.E.2d 932 (2000).

33   Krafick v. Krafick, 234 Conn. 783, 663 A.2d 365, 370 (1995).

34   Conn. Gen. Stat. Ann. § 46b-81(a).

35   Indiana Code Ann. § 31-15-7-4(a).

36   Brett R. Turner, *Equitable Distributin of Property*. Vol. 1, § 2:8 (3d ed. 2005).

Beginning and End of the Marital Partnership

For marital/community property purposes, a marriage begins the moment the official presiding at the wedding says, "I now pronounce you married." Thus, the marital/community property system comes into operation automatically— by operation of law—when you say, "I do." Couples who do not want the marital/ community property system to apply to them can opt out of the system with a premarital agreement (*See* Chapter 2).

The beginning date for acquisition of marital/community property is clear. But when does acquisition of marital/community property end?[37] The end date is critical because property acquired after that date is separate property.[38] States differ on the end date.[39] In California, the community ends when a couple separates and at least one of them believes the relationship is over. In Mississippi, "for purposes of classifying marital property, the marriage runs from the date of marriage until the final judgment of divorce,"[40] or until the parties obtain an order for separate maintenance or an order for temporary support. In Indiana, "the marital pot closes on the day the petition for dissolution is filed."[41]

Property Division

On divorce, a couple can divide their marital/community property however they like. They can divide it equally or unequally. Its up to them. When a divorcing couple cannot agree, and litigation is required, the court divides the marital/community property equally or equitably, depending on the jurisdiction.[42] In California, for example, the court must divide community property equally, and there are very few exceptions to equal division.[43] Wisconsin has a presumption

---

37 *See* Glenn v. Glenn, 345 S.W.3d 320 (Mo. Ct. App. 2011)(property acquired after marriage and prior to legal separation or dissolution is presumed marital property).

38 *See* American Law Institute, *Principles of the Law of Family Dissolution: Analysis and Recommendations*, § 4.03(5) (2000) ("For the purpose of this section, 'during marriage' means after the commencement of marriage and before the filing and service of a petition for dissolution" unless another date is needed to avoid injustice.").

39 *See* Fla. Stat. Ann. § 61.075(7).

40 Wheat v. Wheat, 37 So.3d 632, 637 (Miss. 2010).

41 Granzow v. Granzow, 855 N.E.2d 680, 683 (Ind. Ct. App. 2006).

42 *See* Stonehocker v. Stonehocker, 176 P.3d 476 (Utah Ct. App. 2008)(marital property is ordinarily divided equally).

43 Cal. Family Code §2550.

of equal division, but the judge may depart from equality to achieve fairness.[44] In Missouri, division of marital property need not be equal, but must be equitable.[45]

As stated earlier, most equitable distribution and community property states start with the assumption that marital/community property should be divided equally.[46] New Hampshire law, for example, states, "When a dissolution of a marriage is decreed, the court may order an equitable division of property between the parties. The court shall presume that an equal division is an equitable distribution of the property . . . ."[47] The New Hampshire statute provides that the judge may make an *un*equal division after considering the following factors:

> (a) The duration of the marriage. (b) The age, health, social or economic status, occupation, vocational skills, employability, separate property, amount and sources of income, needs and liabilities of each party. (c) The opportunity of each party for future acquisition of capital assets and income. (d) The ability of the custodial parent, if any, to engage in gainful employment without substantially interfering with the interests of any minor children in the custody of said party. (e) The need of the custodial parent, if any, to occupy or own the marital residence and to use or own its household effects. (f) The actions of either party during the marriage which contributed to the growth or diminution in value of property owned by either or both of the parties. (g) Significant disparity between the parties in relation to contributions to the marriage, including contributions to the care and education of the children and the care and management of the home. (h) Any direct or indirect contribution made by one party to help educate or develop the career or employability of the other party and any interruption of either party's educational or personal career opportunities for the benefit of the other's career or for the benefit of the parties marriage or children (i) The expectation of pension or retirement rights acquired prior to or during the marriage. (j) The tax consequences for each party. (k) The value of property that is allocated by a valid prenuptial contract made in good faith by the parties. (l) The fault of either party

---

44 *See* McReath v. McReath, 800 N.W.2d 399 (Wis. 2011).

45 Glenn v. Glenn, 345 S.W.3d 320, 326 (Mo. Ct. App. 2011).

46 *See* Fla. Stat. Ann. § 61.075(1) ("the court must begin with the premise that the distribution should be equal, unless there is justification for an unequal distribution based on all relevant factors . . . ."); Marriage of McGrath, 948 N.E.2d 1185, 1187 (Ind. Ct. App. 2011)("Pursuant to Ind. Code § 31-15-7-5, the trial court is required to divide the marital estate in a just and reasonable manner, with an equal division being presumed just and reasonable."); Matter of Henry, 163 N.H. 175, 37 A.3d 320 (2012)(presumption of equal division).

47 N.H. Rev. Stat. § 458:16-a(II).

. . . if said fault caused the breakdown of the marriage and: (1) Caused substantial physical or mental pain and suffering; or (2) Resulted in substantial economic loss to the marital estate or the injured party. (m) The value of any property acquired prior to the marriage and property acquired in exchange for property acquired prior to the marriage. (n) The value of any property acquired by gift, devise, or descent. (o) Any other factor that the court deems relevant.[48]

New Hampshire's list of factors is similar to factors considered in other states.

Role of Family Law Attorney in Property Issues

Much of the work of the family law attorney involves helping clients differentiate separate from marital/community property so they can work toward division of property *without* litigation.[49] In most cases, divorcing couples reach agreement and attorneys draft a stipulation that encapsulates the parties' property settlement, often called a marriage settlement agreement (MSA) or property settlement agreement (PSA).

Only when parties cannot agree is it necessary to litigate issues of property.[50] When litigation is necessary, the Mississippi Supreme Court described the judge's role: "The guidelines that chancellors must employ in equitable distribution are as follows: (1) classify the parties' assets as marital or separate, (2) value those assets, and (3) divide the marital assets equitably."[51]

Valuing assets can be as simple as looking up the Kelley Blue Book value of a car and as complex as valuing an international business, a professional practice, stock options, the value of investment real estate, or a Picasso. If there is a market for property, value is generally market value.[52] Family law attorneys employ accountants and appraisers to help value property.

---

48 N.H. Rev. Stat. § 458:16-a(II).

49 *See Wheat v. Wheat,* 37 So.3d 632, 637 (Miss. 2010).

50 *See Schmitz v. Schmitz,* 88 P.3d 1116, 1122 (Alaska 2004)("Equitable division of marital property involves three steps: determining what property is available for distribution, valuing the property, and allocating the property equitably.").

51 *Wheat v. Wheat,* 37 So.3d 632, 637 (Miss. 2010). *Accord see* Stonehocker v. Stonehocker, 176 P.3d 476 (Utah Ct. App. 2008).

52 *See McReath v. McReath,* 800 N.W.2d 399, 408 (Wis. 2011)("Property valued for the purpose of dividing the marital estate should be valued at its fair market value. Fair market value is the price that property will bring when offered for sale by one who desires but is not obligated to sell and bought by one who is willing but not obligated to buy.").

Debts

Married couples acquire debts as well as assets. Indeed, in some relationships there is more debt than assets. States generally characterize debts as community/marital debts or separate debts.[53] Rules for division of debts on divorce vary from state to state.

Property Division is *Res Judicata*

Once a divorce is final, some aspects of the divorce are subject to modification on a showing of substantial changed circumstances. Thus, child custody, child support, and spousal support can be modified when post-divorce circumstances change. By contrast, property division is *res judicata*.[54] As the California Court of Appeal put it in *Marriage of Thorne and Raccina*:[55]

> Generally, once a marital dissolution judgment has become final, the court loses jurisdiction to modify it later. Under the doctrine of *res judicata*, if a property settlement is incorporated in the divorce decree, the settlement is merged with the decree and becomes the final judicial determination of the property rights of the parties. In short, marital property rights and obligations adjudicated by a final judgment cannot be upset by subsequent efforts to modify the judgment. . . .

> There are three exceptions to the general rule. First, a judgment may contain an express reservation of jurisdiction authorizing the court to subsequently modify it. . . . Second, the court may divide a community property asset not mentioned in the judgment. . . . And third, the trial court may give equitable relief from an otherwise valid judgment for extrinsic fraud or mistake.

---

53 *See* American Law Institute, *Principles of the Law of Family Dissolution: Analysis and Recommendations* 652 (2000)("Debts are for the most part characterized as marital or separate by the same principles that govern assets . . . .").

54 *See* Marriage of Morris, 810 N.W.2d 880 (Iowa 2012)("We agree that a property division generally is not modifiable. Nevertheless, the district court retains authority to interpret and enforce its prior decree."); Copas v. Copas, 359 S.W.3d 471 (Ky. App. 2012).

55 203 Cal. App. 4th 492, 136 Cal. Rptr. 3d 887 (2012).

Problems on Property

1. Elizabeth and William were married eighteen years when they divorced. During marriage, Elizabeth and William established "The Elizabeth and William Chamberlin Irrevocable Charitable Trust." They created the trust to gain tax benefits and generate income for donations to charity. All monies transferred to the trust during marriage were from Elizabeth and William's income from employment. At the time of divorce, the trust contains $1 million. In the divorce, William argues that the corpus of the trust is marital property and should be awarded to Elizabeth, with other marital property of equal value awarded to him. Elizabeth argues that because the trust is irrevocable, the money in the trust does not belong to either of them, and is not marital property. Who is correct? *In Matter of Chamberlin,* 155 N.H. 13, 918 A.2d 1 (2007).

2. Rita and Dan divorced many years ago. During the marriage, Dan's parents conveyed to Dan four deeds for mineral rights. The mineral rights produce substantial dividends every year. More than 20 years ago, Rita commenced a divorce action against Dan. Dan was properly served in the divorce action, but he did not appear or participate in the divorce. The court divided the mineral rights 50-50, giving half to Dan and half to Rita. Dan did not appeal. Nor did he take any action regarding division of the mineral rights until recently, when he filed an action in court seeking a declaration that the mineral rights are his separate property because the rights were a gift to him from his parents. Dan seeks a ruling that the trial court erred 20 years ago in dividing the mineral rights 50-50. How should the judge rule on Dan's claim that the divorce court erred so long ago? *Pearson v. Fillingim,* 332 S.W.3d 361 (Tex. 2011).

3. Marian and Johnie divorced after a thirty year marriage. Johnie enjoys gambling, and in the two years prior to divorce, Johnie lost $8,000 of marital property gambling on college sports. Marian and Johnie live in an equitable distribution state where the presumption is that equal division of marital property is equitable. In the divorce, Marian argues that she should receive more than 50% of the marital property because Johnie's gambling losses amount to a waste of marital property. How should the judge rule? Should the judge depart from the presumption of equal division of marital property? *Jones v. Jones,* 942 P.2d 1133 (Alaska 1997).

4. Theresa and Aftab have been married twenty years. They have six children, four of whom are minors. Theresa and Aftab hold masters degrees. Both worked in banking. Aftab was laid off five years ago, and has not sought work since then, preferring to be a stay-at-home parent. During the marriage, Theresa started her own

finance company, specializing in the management of fixed income assets. At the time of divorce, her company has approximately $250 million of assets under management, and Theresa's net yearly income is $1 million.

The couple owns valuable real and personal property, including the family home worth more than $3 million, and two vacation homes.

Throughout the marriage, Aftab was verbally and physically abusive to Theresa and the children. Two months ago, Theresa informed Aftab that she planning to seek a divorce. Several days later, at 4:00 a.m., Aftab broke the lock on the door to Theresa's bedroom, where she slept separately from him. Aftab entered Theresa's bedroom wearing rubber gloves and carrying a metal barbell. Aftab pinned Theresa to the bed with his knee and began beating her viciously on the head, face, neck and hands with the barbell. Theresa observed her blood, teeth and bone spattering everywhere. Her screams brought their three daughters, aged 15, 12 and 10, into the room. Aftab told the girls that he had killed her mother. As one of the children called 911, Aftab attempted to renew his attack on Theresa with a long piece of pipe. The daughters held him off her until the police arrived and arrested him.

Theresa's injuries were severe. She suffered multiple contusions, a broken nose and jaw, broken teeth, multiple lacerations, and neurological damage. Her medical treatment included the surgical installation of a titanium plate over her eye, over 20 hours of painful dental procedures, and many other oral and facial surgical procedures over the next several months. Afterwards, she suffered pain, dizziness, headaches, nightmares, sleeplessness and post-traumatic stress syndrome.

Despite these problems, plus horrible bruising and scarring, Theresa was back at work on a part-time basis three weeks after the attack.

Aftab was indicted for attempted murder, pleaded guilty to assault in the first degree, and was sentenced to 8 ¼ years in prison.

Theresa commenced divorce proceedings. The value of the marital property is $13 million, including real property, cash and securities, pension and retirement benefits, jewelry, and automobiles.

The rule in this state is that marital property should be divided equally, and that fault should not be considered in determining equitable distribution. Given the extreme facts of this case, should the judge depart from the equal division rule? *Havell v. Islam,* 301 A.D.2d 339, 751 N.Y.S.2d 449 (2002).

5. Carole and George were married nearly twenty years. Carole is an attorney practicing personal injury law. At the time the couple divorced, Carole was handling five personal injury cases on a contingent fee basis. Carole had devoted hundreds

of hours to the cases (*e.g.,* depositions, motions, trial preparation), but none of the cases had settled or gone to trial when it was time to divide Carole and George's marital property. George argues that any contingent fee Carole earns from the cases is marital property because she worked on the cases during the marriage. Carole argues that any fee she earns will be received after the divorce is final, and is hers alone. Who is right? *Marriage of Kilbourne*, 232 Cal. App. 3d 1518, 284 Cal. Rptr. 201 (1991).

6. Sue and Sam met during their first year of law school. They got married during the summer before their third year. During fall semester of her senior year, Sue registered for a class on complex civil litigation. Unfortunately, the subject matter was dull and the professor was duller. One day, while daydreaming in class, Sue came up with the idea for a novel about an attorney engaged in complex civil litigation. The nature of the attorney's work involved her in romance, adventure, drama, international intrigue, car chases, five star hotels, and enormous wealth. Over the course of the semester, Sue used class time to write an outline for the novel. During spring semester, Sue wrote the first half of the novel. Unfortunately, Sue and Sam separated shortly following graduation, and Sue filed for divorce. After studying for the July bar examination, Sue devoted herself to the novel. The divorce was granted in September. The divorce decree did not mention the novel. Sue finished the novel in December. To Sue's delight, the novel was published by a major publisher and within weeks sat atop the New York Times best seller list. Large royalty checks started flowing to Sue. When Sam learned of the novel's success, he consulted an attorney to see whether he has a right to a portion of the royalties. Does he? *Marriage of Worth,* 195 Cal. App. 3d 768, 241 Cal. Rptr. 135 (1987).

The remainder of this Chapter provides analysis of specific property issues that arise in divorce.

Inception of Title vs. Source of Funds

It is common for married couples and domestic partners to acquire real or personal property partly with separate property and partly with marital/community property. If the relationship ends, how should the property be characterized? States follow either the inception of title theory or the source of funds theory. The Maryland Court of Appeals' decision in *Harper v. Harper* provides useful discussion of the two theories.

Harper v. Harper

Court of Appeals of Maryland
294 Md. 54, 448 A.2d 916 (1982)

Davidson, Judge.

This case presents two questions concerning the characterization and equitable distribution of certain property as marital property under Maryland Code § 3-6A-01(e) of the Courts and Judicial Proceedings Article. [The relevant statute is now Md. Family Law § 8-201(e)(1)]. More particularly, it initially presents the question whether real property, purchased under an installment contract and paid for in part before marriage and in part during marriage, is marital property. Additionally, it presents the question whether a marital residence constructed on that real property during marriage is marital property.

The relevant statutory provision . . . [provides]: "'Marital property' is all property, however titled, acquired by either or both spouses during their marriage." . . .

In 1950 the petitioner, Sylvester E. Harper (husband), then unmarried, purchased an unimproved parcel of real property for a purchase price of approximately $355.00. The purchase was made under a land installment contract requiring a monthly payment of approximately $6.90. Before his marriage, the husband made all of the payments that came due.

On 3 November 1951, the husband married the respondent, Amaryllis M. Harper (wife). During the marriage, the husband continued to make all of the payments that came due until all of the requisite payments had been made.

In 1967 the husband personally built a house, costing approximately $21,600.00, upon the real property. That house was used by the parties as their marital residence. Although the wife's name appeared on the mortgage and she was legally obligated under it, the husband made all of the mortgage payments that came due on the marital residence. Additionally, the husband paid for all of the expenses associated with the upkeep and repair of the marital residence. . . .

On 14 March 1980, in the Circuit Court for Anne Arundel County, the wife filed a bill of complaint for an absolute divorce. She requested, among other things, "that the Court determine the ownership of all the real property regardless of how titled, and order the sale of said real property, and divide the proceeds equitably."

At trial, there was evidence to show that there was an outstanding mortgage indebtedness of approximately $8,300.00 on the marital residence which was then appraised at a fair market value of approximately $65,500.00. There was no evidence to show the precise source and extent of the funds utilized during the marriage for payments for the land, construction of the marital residence, and its upkeep.

On 10 November 1980, a decree was entered granting the wife, among other things, an absolute divorce and a division of real property. More particularly, the trial court declared that the real property consisting of the lot with the marital residence upon it was marital property and ordered a sale in lieu of partition with each party receiving one-half of the proceeds of the sale. . . .

Courts in the majority of community property states in which the question has been considered have held that real property paid for in part before marriage and in part during marriage remains the separate property of the spouse who made the payments before marriage. The rationale underlying this rule is the inception of title theory.

A classic statement of the inception of title theory, as it applies to real property, appears in *Fisher v. Fisher*, 86 Idaho 131, 383 P.2d 840 (1963). There a husband contracted to purchase real property before marriage. While he made some payments before marriage, the remaining payments were made during marriage from community funds. The Supreme Court of Idaho stated:

> The status of property as separate or community property is fixed as of the time when it is acquired. The word "acquired" contemplates the inception of title, and as a general rule the character of the title depends upon the existence or nonexistence of the marriage at the time of the incipiency of the right by virtue of which the title is finally extended and perfected; the title when so extended and perfected relates back to that time. Stated in another way, the status of title, as belonging to one estate or the other, is determined by the status of the original right, subsequently matured into full title. Under this rule, property to which one spouse has acquired an equitable right before marriage is separate property, though such right is not perfected until after marriage.

That Court held that the real property was the separate property of the husband.

Although courts employing the inception of title theory characterize property paid for partly before marriage as separate property, they nonetheless hold that the community is entitled to some degree of compensation for community funds contributed to the separate property in the form of mortgage payments. Some of these courts have held that the community has an equitable lien for the amount of any mortgage payments made from community funds. Others have held that the community has a right to reimbursement for the amount of any mortgage payments made from community funds. Courts in such jurisdictions have held that increases in the value of a spouse's separate property, attributable solely to the normal appreciation of such property, remain a part of the separate property and require no reimbursement to the community. . . .

In *Cain v. Cain*, 536 S.W.2d 866 (Mo.App.1976), a husband purchased a farm paid for in part before marriage and in part during marriage from marital funds. The farm increased in value during the marriage. The Missouri Court of Appeals, employing the inception of title theory held that the farm and its increase in value were the husband's separate property and, therefore, nonmarital. The Court did not impose a lien or charge on the property in favor of the wife. . . . .

Courts in at least one community property state, California, have rejected the inception of title theory. In California, when real property is paid for in part before marriage from a spouse's separate funds and in part during marriage from community funds . . . , such property . . . [is] characterized as part separate and part community. Under the California rule, the spouse contributing separate funds is entitled to a pro tanto community property interest in such property . . . in the ratio of the separate investment to the total separate and community investment in the property. Similarly, the community is entitled to a "pro tanto community property" interest in such property . . . in the ratio of the community investment to the total separate and community investment in the property.

As a result of the application of the California rule, both the spouse who contributed separate funds and the community that contributed community funds each receive a proportionate and fair return on their investment. . . . .

The rationale underlying California's "pro tanto community property interest" rule is the source of funds theory. That theory is premised on the concept that it is unfair to permit a spouse who has contributed separate funds to the purchase . . . of property to enjoy all of the benefits of sole ownership of the property without regard to the fact that it had been purchased . . . in part with community funds. . . .

In at least one equitable distribution state, Maine, a court has rejected the inception of title theory and has employed the source of funds theory. In *Tibbetts v. Tibbetts*, 406 A.2d 70 (Me.1979), a case involving facts somewhat different from those here, a husband and wife purchased real property as joint tenants during the marriage. The property was paid for by an admixture of community funds and separate funds that the wife had acquired before marriage. The Supreme Judicial Court of Maine, in considering whether the property was marital or nonmarital, said:

> Such property is non-marital to the extent that it was acquired in exchange for property acquired prior to marriage. Thus a single item of property may be to some extent non-marital and the remainder marital. . . .

> The divorce court must, therefore, separate marital and nonmarital property by tracing from the evidence adduced the contributions each may have made to the acquisition of a particular item.

. . . We reject the inception of title theory . . . . Accordingly, under § 3-6A-01(e), property is not necessarily "acquired" on the date that a legal obligation to purchase is created. . . . We conclude that under the Maryland Act the appropriate analysis to be applied is the source of funds theory. Under that theory, when property is acquired by an expenditure of both nonmarital and marital property, the property is characterized as part nonmarital and part marital. Thus, a spouse contributing nonmarital property is entitled to an interest in the property in the ratio of the nonmarital investment to the total nonmarital and marital investment in the property. The remaining property is characterized as marital property and its value is subject to equitable distribution. Thus, the spouse who contributed nonmarital funds, and the marital unit that contributed marital funds each receive a proportionate and fair return on their investment. . . .

Applying these principles to the instant case produces the following result. Ordinarily, under the three-step process provided by the Maryland Act, when real property is purchased and paid for in part before marriage and in part during marriage with nonmarital and marital funds, the property is nonmarital in part and marital in part. Additionally, ordinarily, when a marital residence is constructed upon that real property during marriage by the expenditure of nonmarital and marital property, the marital residence is nonmarital in part and marital in part. The property and the marital residence are nonmarital in the ratio that the nonmarital investment in the property and the residence bears to the total nonmarital and marital investment in the property and the residence. To the extent that the property and the residence are nonmarital, their value is not subject to equitable distribution. Similarly, the property and the marital residence are marital in the ratio that the marital investment in the property and the residence bears to the total nonmarital and marital investment in the property. To the extent that the property and the residence are marital, their value is subject to equitable distribution. When making an equitable distribution of the value of the marital property, the contributions, monetary and nonmonetary of each spouse, the value of the property interests of each spouse, and the effort expended by each spouse in accumulating the marital property, among other things, shall be considered.

Of Surfboards and Million Dollar Views

All real property and some personal property (car, boat, airplane, stock), has a title document, and the way title is held can influence characterization. Many types of personal property have no title. Consider, for example, Hillary and Bill, who are married and who live in Carmel-by-the-Sea, California, just south of Monterey. Both are avid surfers. Hillary buys a surfboard for $1,000, paying $500 community property and $500 of her separate property. If Hillary and Bill divorce and can't agree about the surfboard, how will it be characterized? A surfboard has no title. As mentioned in *Harper v. Harper*, California uses the source of funds theory, and the surfboard is half separate and half community. Characterization is tied to the relative contributions of separate and marital/community property to the purchase.

The surfboard is easy: half and half. But what about the following? Before Hillary married Bill five years ago, Hillary purchased a home on Scenic Road in Carmel-by-the-Sea. Scenic Road is one of America's most exclusive and expensive addresses.[56] The home is 100 feet from the Pacific Ocean with an unobstructed and panoramic view of the beach and the water—a view worth its weight in gold. Hillary purchased the small, forty-year-old house for $7 million. She put $500,000 down and financed the balance with a loan from the bank secured by a mortgage. Before marriage, monthly mortgage payments were obviously made with separate property. When Hillary and Bill married, mortgage payments were made with earnings from Hillary's employment—community property. If Hillary and Bill divorce, how should the Scenic Road home be characterized? Title is in Hillary's name alone since she was single when she acquired the property. (If, during marriage, Hillary changed title to concurrent ownership with herself and Bill as owners, the outcome might be different). At the time of divorce, the home is worth $10 million. Should the home be treated like the surfboard?—pro rata apportionment based on the relative contributions of community and separate property? The answer in California is yes. Under the source of funds theory, California courts use a complicated formula to determine the

---

56   When I Googled Carmel-by-the-Sea, the city's website featured a photo of the ocean taken from Scenic Road, exactly the view from Hillary's home!

separate and community shares. Other states using the source of funds theory reach similar results.[57] In a state that uses the inception of title theory, the result would be different. Texas is an inception of title state,[58] and in *Miller v. Evans*,[59] the Texas Supreme Court wrote, "Property acquired during marriage acquires its status of separate or community at the time of its acquisition."

Pension Benefits

The law of pensions is complicated—*really complicated*! Miles Mason quips, "The entire process of dealing with pensions is a bugbear."[60] The California Supreme Court's decision in *Marriage of Brown* is a good starting place.

Marriage of Brown

Supreme Court of California
15 Cal. 3d 838, 544 P.2d 561 (1976)

Tobriner, J.

Since *French v. French* (1941) 17 Cal.2d 775, 112 P.2d 235, California courts have held that nonvested pension rights are not property, but a mere expectancy, and thus not a community asset subject to division upon dissolution of a marriage. . . . Upon reconsideration of this issue, we have concluded that *French v. French* should be overruled . . . . The *French* rule cannot stand because nonvested pension rights are not an expectancy but a contingent interest in property . . . . Pension rights, whether or not vested, represent a property interest; to the extent that such rights derive from employment during coverture, they comprise a community asset subject to division in a dissolution proceeding.

Before we turn to the facts of this appeal we must devote a few words to terminology. . . . The term "vested" [defines] a pension right which survives the discharge or voluntary termination of the employee. As so defined, a vested pension

---

57 *See* Hoffmann v. Hoffmann, 676 S.W.2d 817, 824 (Mo. 1984); Glenn v. Glenn, 345 S.W.3d 320 (Mo. Ct. App. 2011).

58 *See* Marriage of Skarda, 345 S.W.3d 665, 671 (Tex. Ct. App. 2011)("The separate or community character of property is determined by the inception of title to the property.").

59 452 S.W.2d 426 (Tex. 1970).

60 Miles Mason, Sr., *Accounting Deskbook: A Practical Guide to Financial Investigation and Analysis for Family Lawyers*, p. 145 (2011).

right must be distinguished from a "matured" or unconditional right to immediate payment. Depending upon the provisions of the retirement program, an employee's right may vest after a term of service even though it does not mature until he reaches retirement age and elects to retire. Such vested but immature rights are frequently subject to the condition, among others, that the employee survive until retirement.

The issue in the present case concerns the nonvested pension rights of respondent Robert Brown. General Telephone Company, Robert's employer, maintains a noncontributory pension plan in which the rights of the employees depend upon their accumulation of "points," based upon a combination of the years of service and the age of the employee. Under this plan, an employee who is discharged before he accumulates 78 points forfeits his rights; an employee with 78 points can opt for early retirement at a lower pension, or continue to work until age 63 and retire at an increased pension.

Gloria and Robert Brown married on July 29, 1950. When they separated in November of 1973, Robert had accumulated 72 points under the pension plan, a substantial portion of which is attributable to his work during the period when the parties were married and living together. If he continues to work for General Telephone, Robert will accumulate 78 points on November 30, 1976. If he retires then, he will receive a monthly pension of $310.94; if he continues his employment until normal retirement age his pension will be $485 a month.

Relying on the *French* rule, the trial court held that since Robert had not yet acquired a "vested" right to the retirement pension, the value of his pension rights did not become community property subject to division by the court. . . .

Throughout our decisions we have always recognized that the community owns all pension rights attributable to employment during the marriage. The *French* rule, however, rests on the theory that nonvested pension rights may be community, but that they are not property; classified as mere expectancies, such rights are not assets subject to division on dissolution of the marriage.

We have concluded, however, that the *French* court's characterization of nonvested pension rights as expectancies errs. The term expectancy describes the interest of a person who merely foresees that he might receive a future beneficence, such as the interest of an heir apparent, or of a beneficiary designated by a living insured who has a right to change the beneficiary. As these examples demonstrate, the defining characteristic of an expectancy is that its holder has no enforceable right to his beneficence.

. . . Since pension benefits represent a form of deferred compensation for services rendered, the employee's right to such benefits is a contractual right, derived from the terms of the employment contract. Since a contractual right is not an expectancy but a chose in action, a form of property . . . , an employee acquires a property right to pension benefits when he enters upon the performance of employment contract.

. . . In other situations when community funds or effort are expended to acquire a conditional right to future income, the courts do not hesitate to treat that right as a community asset. For example, in *Waters v. Waters* (1946) 75 Cal. App.2d 265, 170 P.2d 494, the attorney husband had a contingent interest in a suit pending on appeal at the time of the divorce; the court held that his fee, when and if collected, would be a community asset. . . .

In dividing nonvested pension rights as community property the court must take account of the possibility that death or termination of employment may destroy those rights before they mature. In some cases the trial court may be able to evaluate this risk in determining the present value of those rights. But if the court concludes that because of uncertainties affecting the vesting or maturation of the pension that it should not attempt to divide the present value of pension rights, it can instead award each spouse an appropriate portion of each pension payment as it is paid. This method of dividing the community interest in the pension renders it unnecessary for the court to compute the present value of the pension rights, and divides equally the risk that the pension will fail to vest. . . .

The judgment of the superior court is reversed and the cause remanded for further proceedings consistent with the views expressed herein.

Government Retirements Systems

For government employees at federal, state, and local levels, employers have pension plans. Go online and search a variant of "public employee retirement system." Your state's retirement system for government workers will pop up. You can then spend hours, if you are so inclined, delving into the details of your state retirement system. Civilian employees of the federal government have a retirement system, the Federal Employees Retirement System (FERS). Members of the military have a retirement system.

Private Sector Retirement Systems

Workers in the private sector may or may not have a pension at work. For those without a work-related pension, pension-like savings plans are available.

Most private sector pensions are covered by the federal Employee Retirement Income Security Act of 1974 (ERISA).[61]

Defined Benefit and Defined Contribution Plans

Traditional pensions are divided into defined benefit plans and defined contribution plans.[62] Each has many permutations. With a defined benefit plan, an employer agrees to provide pension benefits upon retirement. The pension amount for each employee is tied to a formula that typically includes length of service to the employer and the employee's salary during the final years of employment.

With many defined benefit plans, the employee contributes a portion of her or his salary each pay period to an account. The ultimate pension is determined by the formula, but the employee's contributions form part of the pension.

During the early years of employment, a defined benefit pension is typically unvested. If an employee leaves the job before a defined benefit pension vests, the employee may have no pension rights. After a number years with an employer, the pension vests, which means the employee has rights even if the employee leaves or is fired or laid off before normal retirement age. When an employee is eligible to retire, the pension is mature. If the employee retires, the pension is

---

61   David Clayton Carrad, *The Complete QDRO Handbook*, p. 1 (3d ed. 2009)("Before 1974, private pension plans were not regulated by the federal government and were only sporadically regulated by the states.").

62   *See* Lee v. Lee, 775 N.W.2d 631 (Minn. 2009). In a concurring opinion, Justice Dietzen wrote:

Retirement plans may be divided into two general categories: defined contribution and defined benefit. On the one hand, a defined contribution plan provides an individual account for each employee partici-pant, with retirement benefits based on the amount contributed to the account and any income, expenses, gains, or losses to the account. A 401k retirement plan is an example of a defined contribution plan in which employer and employee have the opportunity to contribute amounts into an individual account for the benefit of the employee. The amounts contributed to the account are invested by the plan and the balance of the account, consisting of contributions and income earned on those contributions, is available to the employee upon retirement.

On the other hand, a defined benefit plan provides qualified employees with monthly retirement benefits, the amount of which is calculated according to the plan and which are paid from plan assets as a whole. Although employees may contribute to the fund, the employer or other plan sponsor agrees to contribute as much as is required to generate the promised benefit. Thus, a defined benefit plan does not accumulate a principal amount for the employee, but rather "guarantees" a periodic payment to the employee upon retirement.

The division of the marital portion of a defined contribution plan does not—indeed, cannot—involve the division of future payments from the plan. Because future payments from a defined contribution plan depend on future contributions and future returns on those contributions—amounts that are not known at the time of the judgment and decree—the division of the marital portion of a defined contribution plan requires the division of the plan balance itself, not the division of future payments from the plan.

in "pay status." Many older workers keep working after their pension matures, postponing receipt of the pension.

With a defined contribution plan, each employee has a retirement account. Typically, the employee and the employer make regular contributions—*e.g.*, every payday—to the employee's account. At retirement, the employee's pension depends on the amount in the account. Typically, during the employee's working years, the money is invested according to the wishes of the employee.[63]

With a defined contribution plan, it is easy at any given time to tell how much money is in an employee's retirement account.[64] The plan administrator can tell at a glance the balance of the account. With a typical defined benefit plan, by contrast, the employee does not have an individual retirement account containing a set amount of money.[65] Instead, the employee has a contractual promise that at retirement age, the retirement plan will apply the applicable formula and determine, *at that time*, the amount of the pension. With defined benefit plans, it is generally not possible to tell precisely the value of a pension until the employee reaches retirement age.

If a divorcing spouse has a defined contribution pension that is partly or wholly marital/community property, it is simple to value the asset. The plan administrator can determine the value of the pension on the appropriate date. But how does one put a value on a defined benefit plan in a divorce *today*, when the employee spouse will not retire for years? Recall that with defined benefit plans there typically is no individual account with a running balance. Rather, there is a promise of benefits in the future—benefits that are tied to variables that are impossible to predict with certainty years before retirement. Determining the value *today* ("present value") of a defined benefit pension that is years from maturity requires an expert, often an accountant or an actuary. The expert makes assumptions about when the employee will retire and what the employee's pension amount will likely be at retirement (this depends, of course, on the formula used by the retirement plan and assumptions about the employee's future salary, etc.). The likely pension amount is discounted to present value. The expert factors in the possibility the employee will die—the mortality discount. Needless to say, determining present value of a defined benefit pension that will not materialize for years—if it ever materializes—is not an exact science.

---

63 The following are defined contribution retirement tools: 401(k) plans, 403(b) tax sheltered annuity plans, employee stock bonus plans, employee stock ownership plans (ESOPs), and profit sharing plans.

64 One should not get the impression there is actually money sitting in an employee's account. The pension plan invests the money it receives. Thus, the employee's money is "working" for the employee and the other employee members of the plan.

65 Some defined benefit plans do have an account for each employee.

Determining the Marital/Community
Property Share of a Pension

A pension is marital/community property to the extent it was acquired during marriage or domestic partnership.[66] Consider, for example, Mary, who enlisted in the Navy at age 18, right after high school. Mary served twenty years and retired at 38, at the rate of chief petty officer. At 39, Mary married Mike. Five years later they divorce. Mary's Navy pension is entirely her separate property because it was acquired prior to marriage. The fact that Mary receives pension checks during marriage does not change the fact that the pension was acquired before marriage. Now consider Sue and Tom, who fell in love and married in college. Following graduation, Sue entered the Navy at age 22 as an officer. After thirty years of service, Sue retired at 54, at the rank of vice admiral. Two years after retirement, Sue and Tom divorce. Sue's entire pension is marital/community because it was acquired entirely during marriage. Finally, consider John and Kim. Upon graduation from law school at age 26, Kim was commissioned as an officer in the Army Judge Advocate General's corps—an Army lawyer. Five years into her Army career, Kim married John, an Army officer. After twenty years' service, Kim retired from the Army at age 46, at the rank of colonel. A few years following retirement, Kim and John divorce. Kim's pension is part her separate property and part marital/community property because part of the pension was acquired prior to marriage and part during marriage. To be precise, 75% of the pension is marital/community, and 25% is Kim's separate property. In the divorce, Kim is entitled to the 25% that is separate, plus half the marital/community portion of the pension. In the end, Kim will have 62.5% of the pension and John will have 37.5%.

When a defined contribution plan is part separate and part marital/community, the proportions are calculated on divorce by characterizing the funds that contributed to acquiring the retirement account. Brett Turner writes, "The marital interest includes contributions from marital funds and contributions made by the employer as compensation for marital efforts, plus passive investment return. The separate interest includes contributions from separate funds, as well as contributions made by the employer as consideration for premarital or postdivorce efforts, plus passive investment return."[67] The divorce decree may provide that the administrator of the pension is to divide the pension by creating

---

66 *See* Ohio Rev. Code tit. 31, § 3105.171(A)(3)(a) ("'Marital property' means . . . all of the following: (i) All real and personal property that currently is owned by either or both of the spouses, including, but not limited to, the retirement benefits of the spouses, and that was acquired by either or both of the spouses during the marriage . . . ."); Livingston v. Livingston, 633 So.2d 1162, 1164 (Fla. Ct. App. 1994)("Premarital contributions to retirement pensions should be excluded when distributing marital assets.").

67 Brett R. Turner, *Equitable Distribution of Property*, § 6:24, pp. 143-144 (3d ed. 2005).

separate accounts for the employee and the non-employee. Each spouse obtains the benefit of appreciation on their respective account.

With defined benefit plans, division into separate and marital/community components is typically accomplished with the so-called "time rule" or the "coverture fraction."[68] The numerator of the fraction is years of service during marriage.[69] The denominator is total years during which the pension was earned. For example, Sue retired after twenty years with the highway patrol. During ten of those years, Sue was married to Paul. The numerator of the fraction is 10; the denominator is 20. Half of Sue's pension is her separate property. Half is marital/community. Sue owns half of the marital/community portion. In the end, Sue is entitled to 75% of the pension and Paul 25%.

In Sue's case, she was already retired at the time of the divorce. Thus, the denominator of the fraction—20—was established. In many divorces, however, the employee spouse is years from retirement. The employee may retire after 20 years of service, or may continue working. The denominator of the fraction cannot be determined until the employee retires. In this scenario, the divorce decree may contain the coverture fraction, with the proviso that the denominator will be filled in when the employee retires.

An important part of a lawyer's job in divorce is learning about all pension benefits of both parties. The lawyer determines whether pension benefits are separate or marital/community. The lawyer educates the client about the impact of family law on pensions. In some cases, the law's impact comes as an unpleasant surprise to the client. Consider Joe, who has worked nineteen years at a job he hates, and who can't wait to retire. Joe's divorce attorney tells Joe that nearly half his monthly pension will belong to his soon-to-be-ex-wife. In an angry voice, Joe says, "You mean to tell me I got to give half my pension to that woman?! I been going to that rotten job nearly twenty years while she stayed home with the kids having a great old time and not working at all. Now you're telling me half my pension belongs to her? I'm the one who earned that pension. Not her!" Sorry Joe, you acquired most of the pension during marriage, and that makes the pension marital/community property. Offer Joe a cup of coffee and time to calm down.

---

68 *See* Brett Turner, who writes that the time rule should not be used to characterize defined contribution pensions. He writes, "It is generally error to classify a defined contribution retirement plan using the time-based coverture fraction used to classify defined benefit plans. The time-based coverture fraction assumes that equal contributions were made to the plan in each of the employee's [years of] service. . . . Classification of defined contribution plans requires proration of funds, not proration of time." Brett R. Turner, *Equitable Distribution of Property*, § 6:24, pp. 146-147 (3d ed. 2005).

69 It is not required that the court use years. When appropriate, the court may use months or days for the numerator and denominator.

Methods of Dividing Pensions

In addition to learning about a couple's pensions, and calculating marital/community shares, attorneys help clients decide how to divide marital/community pension interests. There are several ways divorcing couples can handle pensions.[70]

Dividing a Defined Contribution Pension

Dividing a defined contribution pension is typically pretty straight forward. As explained above, the value of a defined contribution pension is usually simple to determine. If the employee is retired, periodic pension payments are divided according to the percentage of the pension that is marital/community property. If the employee spouse is still working, the administrator of the pension plan informs the parties of the balance in the employee spouse's retirement account on a specific date. The divorce decree divides the account in two—one account for each.

Dividing a Defined Benefit Pension: Cash Out or Wait and See

When a defined benefit plan is in pay status—that is, the employee spouse is retired and drawing the pension—the pension can be dividing using the time rule. When the employee spouse is yet to retire, two methods are used to divide the pension: The cash out method and the wait and see method.

With cash out, the employee spouse keeps the entire pension and the non-employee spouse receives other property equal in value to the foregone pension—the non-employee is cashed out. Consider, Rita and Juan, who married while in college. Upon graduation, Rita became a police officer, Juan became a teacher. Both have defined benefit pensions. After five years of marriage, Rita and Juan divorce. They are many years from retirement. For this couple, the best solution may be for each to keep their entire pension. If there is a difference in present value between the pensions, the spouse with the less valuable pension can receive other marital/community property to make up the difference. It is important to understand that the law does not insist that Rita and Juan leave the marriage with the same value in pension benefits. Divorcing couples are free

---

70 *See* Krafick v. Krafick, 234 Conn. 783, 663 A.2d 365, 373-374 (1995)(the Supreme Court describes in useful detail the methods of dividing pension benefits); Faber v. Herman, 731 N.W.2d 1, 7-8 (Iowa 2007)("pensions can be divided in one of two basic ways. Parties can agree the non-member will receive a share based on the present worth of the pension, or receive a share of the pension benefits at some point in the future when they become payable to the pensioner. Thus, the difference between the two methods involves the payment of an immediate amount or the payment of an amount in the future . . . . The division of a defined-benefit pension plan, such as IPERS, under the present value method requires the use of actuarial science.").

to divide their property as *they* see fit. If Rita's public safety pension is worth more than Juan's teaching pension, Juan is a free to say, "Rita, you keep your pension. I'll keep mine. I don't care if yours is worth more than mine." Although many people getting a divorce are angry, hurt, and depressed, many—hopefully, most—still care about their partner, and want what is best for them. If Juan wants to give up his portion of Rita's more valuable pension, he is free to do so, so long as his decision is voluntary and informed. It is the responsibility of Juan's attorney to explain the rights Juan has and what he is giving up. In the final analysis, the law allows divorcing couples to arrange their property according to their own lights.

When a couple decides on the cash out method, it is necessary to determine the value of the pension at the time of divorce—present value. Present value must be determined in order to figure out how much money the employee spouse must give the non-employee spouse in order to cash out the non-employee spouse. As mentioned earlier, determining the value today—present value—of a defined benefit pension that will not mature for years is not an exact science. Miles Mason writes, "The calculation of value is never 'accurate.' It is an estimate for at least two important reasons. First, no one knows exactly when the participant will die. Second, judgment is always involved when determining a discount rate. . . . There are two basic methods of estimating value. The mortality method takes into consideration probabilities of death, and is almost always handled by actuaries. The more common life expectancy method, also called the discounted to present value method, is the method must more commonly used by forensic accountants."[71]

One advantage of the employee spouse keeping her or his entire pension, and the non-employee spouse taking other property, is that the parties can make a clean break from each other. With this approach, all pension rights are disposed of at divorce. As we will see momentarily, the other method of dealing with pensions has the potential to keep divorced spouses entangled for years. A second advantage of the employee spouse retaining the entire pension is that when retirement rolls around, the employee has more money. Of course, this benefit for the employee ex-spouse may disadvantage the non-employee ex-spouse.

The second method for dealing with a martial/community interest in a defined benefit pension is to determine the interests in the pension at the time of divorce (the time rule), and wait until the employee spouse actually retires

---

71   Miles Mason, Sr., *Accounting Deskbook: A Practical Guide to Financial Investigation and Analysis for Family Lawyers*, pp. 147, 151 (2011). Mason continues: "To calculate present value, a discount rate must be chosen. Discount rates (and interest rates, for that matter) reflect an assessment of risk. . . . The greater the discount rate, the less the estimated net present value of expected benefits." p. 153.

before the non-employee spouse starts receiving their share of the pension.[72] The principle advantage of the wait and see method is that the non-employee spouse will have an income stream at a time in life when they need it—at or near their own retirement. There are disadvantages too. What if the employee spouse dies before retiring? There will be *no* pension! Or, suppose the employee retires, the non-employee starts getting checks, and the employee drops dead a few months later. The pension stops!

There are remedies for the possibility that the employee spouse dies prematurely. First, pension plans have survivor benefits, and the parties' property settlement agreement (PSA) can specify that the non-employee spouse is entitled to such benefits.[73] Sometimes, attorneys fail to state in the PSA that the non-employee spouse is entitled to survivor benefits. In *Marriage of Morris*,[74] counsel failed to specify in the PSA that wife was entitled to survivor benefits under husband's Marine Corps pension. The Iowa Supreme Court warned, "This case should serve as a vivid reminder to attorneys practicing matrimonial law to specifically address survivor rights when dividing retirement benefits."[75]

The second remedy in case the employee spouse dies is to incorporate into the PSA a requirement that the employee spouse buy life insurance with the non-employee spouse as beneficiary.

With the wait and see method, the nonemployee spouse postpones receipt of her or his share until the employee spouse retires. With this approach, it is usually unnecessary to determine the present value of the pension. The marital/community percentage of the pension is determined at the time of divorce using the time rule, and the former spouses wait until retirement to split whatever the final pension amount turns out to be.

---

72 This approach is used with defined benefit plans.

73 *See, e.g.*, Craig v. Craig, 59 Va. App. 527, 721 S.E.2d 24 (2012).

74 810 N.W.2d 880 (Iowa). *Compare* Marriage of Morris, 810 N.W.2d 880 (Iowa 2012)(attorneys failed to mention survivor benefits in property settlement agreement (PSA)), *with* Craig v. Craig, 59 Va. App. 527, 721 S.E.2d 24 (2012)(attorney specifically mentioned survivor benefits in PSA).

75 The Iowa Supreme Court wrote in *Marriage of Morris*: "Other courts in this situation [the decree does not specify whether the non-employee spouse gets survivor benefits] have adopted a default rule by holding that a decree dividing retirement benefits includes survivorship benefits. Several of these courts have allowed postdissolution orders compelling the retiree to designate his former spouse as the survivor to effectuate the division of retirement benefits in the original degree. Other courts, however, have refused to allow postdissolution orders awarding a former souse survivorship rights when the decree does not expressly contemplate the survivorship benefit."

Qualified Domestic Relations Order (QDRO)

When a divorcing couple divides the marital/community interest in a pension, an important drafting responsibility falls to the attorneys, typically the attorney for the non-employee spouse. The attorney drafts a "domestic relations order" (DRO) that becomes part of the divorce decree.[76] A DRO specifies the spouses' interests in the pension and describes how the interests are to be divided. The DRO is submitted to the pension plan, which—if everything is in order—approves the DRO, transforming it into a Qualified Domestic Relations Order or QDRO.

ERISA provides that pension benefits of employees (participants) cannot be alienated by participants.[77] Absent an exception to ERISA's anti-alienation provision, a participant's retirement benefit cannot be awarded (alienated) in a divorce to a non-employee spouse.[78] In *Ablamis v. Rober*,[79] the U.S. Court of Appeals for the Ninth Circuit explains the anti-alienation provision of ERISA:

> To secure the financial well-being of employees and their dependents, ERISA contains a spendthrift provision. That provision states that the "benefits provided under the retirement plan may not be assigned or alienated." . . . ERISA's prohibition on the assignment or alienation of pension benefits "reflects a considered congressional policy choice, a decision to safeguard a stream of income for pensioners (and their dependents), even if that decision prevents others from securing relief for the wrongs done them. If exceptions to this policy are to be made, it is for Congress to undertake that task. . . . Congress did make one important exception, however. Congress was . . . concerned with the inequities that might be suffered by women who are the economic victims of divorce or separation. To protect their interests, the [Retirement Equity Act] REA creates an express statutory

---

76   ERISA and the Internal Revenue Code define "domestic relations order" as follows: "The term 'domestic relations order' means any judgment, decree, or order (including approval of a property settlement agreement) which—(i) relates to the provision of child support, alimony payments, or marital property rights to a spouse, former spouse, child, or other dependent of a participant, and (ii) is made pursuant to a State domestic relations law (including a community property law)." 26 U.S.C. § 414(p)(1)(B); 29 U.S.C. § 1056(d)(3)(B)(ii).

Many retirement plans will examine draft DROs to see if they are acceptable.

77   29 U.S.C. § 1056(d)(1) ("Each pension plan shall provide that benefits provided under the plan may not be assigned or alienated."). There are some exceptions to ERISA's anti-alienation provision. *See* 29 U.S.C § 1056(d)(2).

See David Clayton Carrad, *The Complete QDRO Handbook*, p. 2 (3d ed. 2009)("From its enactment in 1974, ERISA has required that each pension plan ensure that the benefits it provides are not 'assigned or alienated.'").

78   ERISA is federal law, and federal law trumps state law.

79   937 F.2d 1450 (9th Cir. 1991).

exception to the prohibition on assignment and alienation in the case of distributions made pursuant to certain state court orders: ERISA's spendthrift provisions are not applicable to a "qualified domestic relations order" (QDRO). A court may divide spousal rights in pension benefits through the mechanism of a QDRO and award the non-employee spouse her appropriate share of those benefits—but only if the domestic relations order is a "qualified" one as defined in the REA.

Under REA, a QDRO is any judgment, decree, or order made pursuant to a state domestic relations law (including community property law) which (1) "creates or recognizes the existence of an alternate payee's right to, or assigns to an alternate payee the right to, receive all or a portion of the benefits payable with respect to a participant under a plan," and (2) "relates to the provision of child support, alimony payments, or marital property rights to a spouse, former spouse, child, or other dependent of a participant." Only "qualified" domestic relations orders are exempt from ERISA's spendthrift provisions; other domestic relations orders are expressly made subject to the anti-assignment provision and are, as a result, preempted. Thus, in the case of QDROs the REA provides a "limited exception" to the anti-assignment provision for certain specified types of domestic relations property allocations.

In ERISA parlance, the non-employee spouse is an alternative payee. As mentioned above, ERISA contains an exception to anti-alienation. An alternative payee *can* receive a share of a participant's retirement pursuant to a QDRO.[80] Thus, it is critical that the provisions of the divorce decree fulfill ERISA's requirements for a QDRO. Only QDROs escape ERISA's anti-alienation provision.[81]

What are the requirements for the all-important QDRO? A QDRO is a DRO that satisfies the following requirements of federal law:

(C) A domestic relations order meets the requirements of this subparagraph only if such order clearly specifies—

---

80 *See* Quijano v. Quijano, 347 S.W.3d 345, 353-354 (Tex. Ct. App. 2011)("The purpose of a QDRO is to create or recognize an alternate payee's right, or to assign an alternate payee the right, to receive all or a portion of the benefits payable to a participant under a retirement plan.").

81 29 U.S.C.§ 1056(d)(3)(A) provides: "Paragraph (1) [the anti-alienation provision] shall apply to the creation, assignment, or recognition of a right to any benefit payable with respect to a participant pursuant to a domestic relations order, except that [the anti-alienation provision] shall not apply if the order is determined to be a qualified domestic relations order. Each pension plan shall provide for the payment of benefits in accordance with the applicable requirement of any qualified domestic relations order."

(i) the name and last known mailing address (if any) of the participant and the name and mailing address of each alternative payee covered by the order.

(ii) the amount or percentage of the participant's benefits to be paid by the plan to each such alternative payee, or the manner in which such amount or percentage is to be determined,

(iii) the number of payments or period to which such order applies, and

(iv) each plan to which such order applies.

(D) A domestic relations order meets the requirements of this subparagraph only if such order—

(i) does not require a plan to provide any type or form of benefit, or any option, not otherwise provided under the plan,

(ii) does not require the plan to provide increased benefits (determined on the basis of actuarial value), and

(iii) does not require payment of benefits to an alternate payee which are required to be paid to another alternative payee under another order previously determined to be a qualified domestic relations order.[82]

It is not difficult for a lawyer drafting a DRO to obtain names and mailing addresses. Nor is it particularly challenging to specify "the amount or percentage of the participant's benefits to be paid by the plan to" the alternative payee. The tricky bit is ensuring that the DRO does not require the plan to pay any type of benefit that is not required by the plan. The Indiana Court of Appeals explained in *Evans v. Evans*,[83] "A QDRO must comply with ERISA. . . . A QDRO cannot require the plan administrator to provide any type or form of benefit, or any option, not otherwise provided under the plan." The only way to be completely sure this requirement for a valid QDRO is satisfied is obtain the actual pension plan—perhaps hundreds of pages long—and to read and understand precisely what the plan does and does not provide. The difficulty with this requirement—studying the entire plan—is the reason many family law attorneys do not draft their own QDROs, referring the task to QDRO/ERISA specialists.

David Carrad has a book on QDROs titled *The Complete QDRO Handbook*.[84] Carrad lists his "top ten QDRO mistakes":

---

82 29 U.S.C. § 1056(d).

83 946 N.E.2d 1200, 1206 (Ind. Ct. App. 2011).

84 David Clayton Carrad, *The Complete QDRO Handbook* (3d ed. 2009).

■ **Mistake # 10:** Failure to discover and divide all employee benefit plans (including nonqualified plans and benefits from prior or part-time employment). . . .

■ **Mistake # 9:** Failure to provide for cost-of-living adjustment (COLA) increases to be shared between the Participant and the Alternative Payee. . . .

■ **Mistake # 8:** Blindly following the plan's model QDRO and just "filling in the blanks" (particularly when you represent the Alternative Payee.) . . .

■ **Mistake # 7:** Failing to pro-rate contributions to Defined Contribution Plans that are made at the end of the contribution year that spans the date of separation or divorce. . . .

■ **Mistake # 6:** Limiting the division of benefits to vested benefits only, rather than to accrued benefits.

■ **Mistake # 5:** Failing to specify, when dividing a Defined Contribution Plan, whether the Alternative Payee will receive interest, dividends, gains, and losses on her share between the date of valuation and the date a separate account is established for the Alternative Payee. . . .

■ **Mistake # 4:** Not having the plan review and approve your QDRO in advance so you can bring it to court with you (with amounts or percentages left blank if necessary) or attach it as an exhibit to the separation agreement. . . .

■ **Mistake # 3:** Automatically following the Shared Interest Approach in every case. . . . Most Alternative Payees prefer the Separate Interest Approach because it gives them control over when payments from a Defined Benefit Plan begin and ensures that payments will continue for the Alternative Payee's lifetime. In contrast, the Shared Interest Approach means the Alternative Payee receives no payments at all until the Participant chooses to retire, and payments to the Alternative Payee may cease on the Participant's death.

■ **Mistake # 2:** Failing to provide a qualified preretirement survivor annuity (QPSA) benefit for ERISA plans, survivor benefit plans (SBP) for military retired pay divisions or a Former Spouse Survivor Annuity (FSSA) for federal civil service divisions for your Alternate Payee clients. . . . This is an extraordinarily common omission.

Failure to expressly provide for survivor benefits for your Alternative Payee clients at trial or in a stipulation or separation agreement can be fatal to your ability to include them in a subsequent QDRO if the Participant or his lawyer objects. Failure to include survivor benefits in the QDRO itself is always fatal. . . .[85]

■ **Mistake # 1:** Failure to follow through until your order has been accepted as a QDRO by the plan. . . . The most common form of malpractice in the QDRO area is the failure of counsel for the Alternative Payee to persevere and make sure that a QDRO is entered by the state divorce court as well as sent to and finally accepted by the plan. In my experience in plan administration, about 15-20 percent of the time when an initial QDRO application is rejected by the plan, the application is simply abandoned. The plan never hears back from the Alternative Payee's lawyers, and the Alternative Payee's rights are irrevocably lost.[86]

The Iowa Supreme Court's decision in *Marriage of Sullins* applies the pension principles discussed above. Before you read *Sullins*, it is useful to know a little about Iowa's system of equitable distribution. In *Marriage of Schriner*,[87] The Supreme Court wrote:

> Like most other states, Iowa is known as an equitable distribution jurisdiction for purposes of dividing property in a dissolution of marriage. Equitable distribution essentially means that courts divide the property of the parties at the time of divorce, except any property excluded from the divisible estate as separate property, in an equitable manner in light of the particular circumstances of the parties.
>
> In Iowa, two types of property, inherited property and gifts received by one party, are specifically excluded by statute from the divisible estate. This property is normally awarded to the individual spouse who owns the property, independent from the equitable distribution process. Yet, this exclusion is not absolute. Iowa has a unique hybrid system that permits the court to divide inherited and

---

85   *Compare* Marriage of Morris, 810 N.W.2d 880 (Iowa 2012)(attorneys failed to mention survivor benefits in property settlement agreement (PSA), *with* Craig v. Craig, 59 Va. App. 527, 721 S.E.2d 24 (2012)(attorneys specifically dealt with survivor benefits in PSA).

86   David Clayton Carrad, *The Complete QDRO Handbook* pp. 7-9 (3d ed. 2009)(for each mistake, Carrad has solutions).

87   695 N.W.2d 493 (Iowa 2005).

gifted property if equity demands in light of the circumstances of a spouse or the children. Property not excluded is included in the divisible estate. . . .

Out statute is written to define divisible property as all property of the parties, other than the two classes of excluded property. . . . .

The property included in the divisible estate includes not only property acquired during the marriage by one or both of the parties, but property owned prior to the marriage by a party. Property brought into the marriage is merely a factor to consider by the court, together with all other factors, in exercising its role as an architect of an equitable distribution of property at the end of the marriage. More importantly, the statute makes no effort to include or exclude property from the divisible estate by such factors as the nature of the property of the parties, the method of acquisition, or the owner. All property, except inherited or gifted property, is included, and the circumstances and underlying nature of the included property are generally considered factors that impact [equitable division].

Marriage of Sullins

Supreme Court of Iowa
715 N.W.2d 242 (2006)

Cady, Justice.

Ray and Donna Sullins were married on November 25, 1978. Donna was a teacher in the West Des Moines school district at the time, and Ray worked as a lawyer in the office of the Iowa Attorney General. Donna had a bachelor's degree in music education. Ray owned a house, which he contributed to the marriage. Donna contributed a car and various household items to the marriage. She had also participated in the Iowa Public Employees Retirement System (IPERS) for eight years prior to the marriage, and had acquired a tax-sheltered annuity (TSA). Ray had a variety of personal property as well as an IPERS account from his employment with the attorney general. A year into the marriage, Ray withdrew his IPERS funds and used them as a down payment on a new home. Around the same time, Ray left the attorney general's office and began to work as a lobbyist.

Donna and Ray had three children: Deborah, Stephen, and Matthew. Deborah was born in 1981, Stephen was born in 1984, and Matthew was born in 1986. Donna continued to work during this time on a part-time basis, and later returned as a fulltime teacher. Ray transitioned from lobbying into the private practice of law. Donna also took night and weekend classes, which enabled her to obtain her masters degree in 2000.

After that time, the marriage began to deteriorate. Sadly, Donna and Ray were confronted with more than their fair share of agony. Ray had a series of problems in his professional career that culminated in the revocation of his license to practice law in Iowa in 2002. That same year, Donna and Ray faced a parent's worst nightmare when Stephen, their oldest son, tragically died. They also did not escape financial difficulties. Their home was put up for tax sale on two occasions.

Donna filed for divorce in February 2003. At the time of the trial in January 2004, Donna was fifty-six, and Ray was fifty-eight. Their daughter, Deborah, was twenty-two and was a fulltime student at Northwestern College in St. Paul, Minnesota. She was in her final year of school. Matthew was eighteen and was a senior at Waukee High School. Donna was teaching fulltime, making approximately $54,000 per year. Ray was working in sales, making approximately $81,000 per year.

The district court entered its decree in April 2004. The court found Donna's annuity, which she funded entirely before the marriage, and her eight years of premarital IPERS contributions were not "part of the marital assets" and awarded both to her. The annuity was valued at $4872. The court valued the IPERS account at $57,081.47. The court awarded $35,247.81 of it to Donna, and $21,833.66 of it to Ray.[88] Including the premarital retirement savings, which the court treated as Donna's separate property, the court awarded Donna a total of $275,198.31 in assets (consisting mainly of the house and retirement accounts) and awarded Ray $57,236.16 in assets. The court ordered Donna to be responsible for $87,777.50 of the marital debt, and Ray to be responsible for $17,454.50 of the debt (in addition to a $750,000 malpractice judgment against him). To equalize the disparate equity awarded to Donna, the court ordered her to pay Ray $61,676.53. The court also ordered Ray to pay $7500 of Donna's attorney fees.

---

88 The court set aside eight thirty-fourths (23.5%) of the IPERS account ($13,414.14) for Donna as premarital property. Eight was the number of Donna's premarital contribution years, and thirty-four was the number of years she had contributed up to the divorce. The court then divided the remainder of the IPERS account ($43,667.33) equally between Donna and Ray, awarding each $21,833.67.

Iowa is an equitable distribution state. This means that courts divide the property of the parties at the time of divorce, except any property excluded from the divisible estate as separate property, in an equitable manner in light of the particular circumstances of the parties. All property of the marriage that exists at the time of the divorce, other than gifts and inheritances to one spouse, is divisible property. Importantly, the property included in the divisible estate includes not only property acquired during the marriage by one or both of the parties, but property owned prior to the marriage by a party. Property brought into the marriage by a party is merely a factor to consider by the court, together with all other factors, in exercising its role as an architect of an equitable distribution of property at the end of the marriage.

In this case, the district court set aside Donna's annuity as a premarital asset and found that it should not be considered part of the marital assets. This finding was contrary to our distribution scheme in Iowa. The property is part of the divisible estate, just as is property acquired during the marriage. The trial court may place different degrees of weight on the premarital status of property, but it may not separate the asset from the divisible estate and automatically award it to the spouse that owned the property prior to the marriage.

For the same reason, we reject Ray's argument that he should be entitled to a "credit" for the property and retirement savings he owned before the marriage and integrated into the marital coffers. While this is a factor to consider in achieving an overall equitable distribution it is one factor among many. It does not automatically require Donna's share of the property to be reduced as a reimbursement for Ray's premarital contributions. We turn now to specifically consider the district court's treatment of Donna's IPERS pension.

Pensions are divisible marital property. There are two accepted methods of dividing pension benefits: the present-value [cash out] method and the percentage [wait and see] method. Additionally, there are two main types of pension plans: defined-benefit plans and defined-contribution plans.

Although both methods of dividing pension benefits can be used with both types of pension plans, it is normally desirable to divide a defined-benefit plan by using the percentage method. The present-value method requires the present value of the benefits to be determined before allocating a portion of the benefits to the pensioner's spouse. Present value derived under this method represents the restatement in current dollars of a payment or series of payments to a current lump sum equivalent. Yet, the determination of present value of a defined-benefit plan is a complicated process that requires the use of actuarial science. . . .

. . . The value of the marital interest in defined contribution plans is the amount of contributions made during the marriage plus accumulated interest on these contributions.

The complicated nature of determining the present value of a defined-benefit plan and dividing the benefits, as well as the economic difficulty for a pensioner to pay a lump-sum amount representing the present value of a defined-benefit plan, normally makes the second method of division and distribution of pensions much more attractive for defined-benefit plans. Under the second method to divide and distribute a pension plan, the percentage method, the court awards a spouse a percentage of the pension payable in the future at the time the benefits mature.

IPERS is, of course, a defined-benefit plan. The plan uses a percentage of earnings per year of service formula, which provides a benefit that is related to the employee's earnings and length of service.

In this case, the district court divided the IPERS pension based on the current value of Donna's personal contributions to the plan over the years of the marriage at the time of the divorce. This value was not based on actuarial evidence. Instead, this value was obtained from information made available to Donna showing the amount of her personal contributions over the years and the interest earned on her personal contributions. However, the present value of her IPERS plan is more than the present value of her contributions. In fact, the amount of Donna's IPERS contributions has no relation to the present value of her future benefits because the contributions are not used to calculate benefits. Instead, the benefits are ultimately tied to a percentage of the employee's average wages. Thus, the district court's valuation and distribution of Donna's IPERS plan fell far short of our accepted methods and was inequitable. Without actuarial evidence, the district court could not have divided the retirement plan based on the present value of Donna's future benefits. On our de novo review, we conclude that the better way to divide and distribute the IPERS account is to use the percentage method normally applicable to cases involving IPERS.

Under the percentage method, the non-pensioner spouse is awarded a percentage (frequently fifty percent) of a fraction of the pensioner's benefits (based on the duration of the marriage), by a qualified domestic relations order (QDRO), which is paid if and when the benefits mature. The fraction represents the portion of the pension attributable to the parties' joint marital efforts. The numerator in the fraction is the number of years the pensioner accrued benefits under the plan during the marriage, and the denominator is the total number of years of benefit accrual.

Applying this method, we modify the decree to provide for a QDRO to divide Donna's monthly IPERS benefits when received under the following formula:

$$\text{Ray's share} = 50\% \text{ multiplied by} \quad \frac{\text{Number of quarters Donna contributed to IPERS while married}}{\text{Number of quarters Donna contributed to IPERS before retirement}} \quad \text{Multiplied by monthly benefit}$$

IPERS shall use the number of quarters in each year covered during the marriage period of November 25, 1978 through April 30, 2004.

Military Retirement

Members of the active duty military have a defined benefit retirement plan. Members of the reserve and National Guard also have a retirement system.

In 1981, in *McCarty v. McCarty*,[89] the U.S. Supreme Court ruled that state family courts could not divide military pensions. Congress abrogated *McCarty* with passage of Uniformed Services Former Spouses' Protection Act (USFSPA).[90] USFSPA allows family courts to divide military pensions on divorce. Mark Sullivan writes, "State courts can order the direct pay of pension division awards through Defense Finance and Accounting Service (DFAS) when there is ten years' overlap between the marriage and creditable military service."[91] The details of military pension law are many, and Colonel Sullivan's book is an excellent guide.

---

89   453 U.S. 210, 101 S.Ct. 2728 (1981).

90   10 U.S.C. § 1408.

91   Mark E. Sullivan, *The Military Divorce Handbook: A Practical Guide to Representing Military Personnel and Their Families* 484 (2d ed. 2011).

Social Security Retirement

Social Security retirement is available to workers who reach a pre-set age, and who have paid the required amount of payroll taxes under the Federal Income Contributions Act (FICA). Federal Social Security retirement benefits are not subject to division on divorce. The Michigan Court of Appeals explains in *Biondo v. Biondo*:

Biondo v. Biondo

Michigan Court of Appeals
291 Mich. App. 720, 809 N.W.2d 397 (2011)

Gleicher, J.

James Franklin Biondo and Mary Lynne Biondo were married for more than 40 years. Their consent judgment of divorce equally divided the marital estate and required them to "equalize their social security benefits." When Mary Biondo sought a court order compelling performance of the judgment's social security term, James Biondo asserted that federal law preempted its enforcement. The circuit court ruled that "a deal is a deal," and declined to strike the social security term from the divorce judgment. We granted leave to consider whether federal law preempts the consent judgment's social security formula. We hold that it does, reverse the circuit court ruling to the contrary, and remand for further proceedings.

The parties married in 1964, and in July 2007 consented to the entry of a divorce judgment. During the marriage, James Biondo worked for Ford Motor Company, while Mary Biondo cared for the parties' two children, now adults. The marital property included a home in Birmingham, two vehicles, and several bank accounts. A specific provision of the consent judgment, entitled "Social Security Benefits," obligated the parties to "equalize their social security benefits." After entry of the divorce judgment, the parties stipulated to the entry of a qualified domestic relations order (QDRO), which allocated to Mary Biondo 50% of James Biondo's accrued retirement benefits as of the date of the divorce. The parties agree that they intended the consent judgment's property division to equally divide the marital estate.

In July 2009, Mary Biondo filed in the circuit court a motion seeking "compliance" with the judgment's "Social Security Benefit provision." Mary Biondo averred that James Biondo had failed to make timely and full social security equalization payments. James Biondo responded that the judgment's social security formula violated federal law, and that any order enforcing the social security benefit term would be invalid. After a motion hearing, the circuit court entered an order announcing in relevant part that "the Court will enforce the property settlement provision regarding Social Security Benefits contained in the July 10, 2007 consent judgment of divorce."

James Biondo contends that the circuit court lacked subject matter jurisdiction to enforce the social security property provision of the parties' judgment of divorce. According to James Biondo, 42 USC 407 preempts state courts from transferring any of an individual's social security benefits by "any legal process to any person other than that person whom the Federal Government intended to be the recipient of those benefits."

Under the Supremacy Clause of the United States Constitution, U.S. Const, art VI, cl 2, federal law preempts state law where Congress so intends. Generally, federal law does not preempt laws governing divorce or domestic relations, a legal arena belonging to the states rather than the United States. Thus, state family and family-property law must do major damage to clear and substantial federal interests before the Supremacy Clause will demand that state law be overridden. Here, we consider whether the federal interest in social security benefits preempts enforcement of the parties' agreement to equalize their social security benefits.

We begin our analysis by consulting the specific federal statute at issue, § 407(a) of the Social Security Act: "The right of any person to any future payment under this subchapter shall not be transferable or assignable, at law or in equity, and none of the moneys paid or payable or rights existing under this subchapter shall be subject to execution, levy, attachment, garnishment, or other legal process, or to the operation of any bankruptcy or insolvency law." . . .

.[This language compels us to hold] that § 407(a) preempts the social security equalization provision in the Biondos' consent judgment . . . .

A number of state courts have addressed the extent to which a divorce court may consider social security benefits when formulating an equitable division of property. The Iowa Supreme Court has held that social security benefits may generally inform a property division:

We see a crucial distinction between: (1) adjusting property division so as to indirectly allow invasion of benefits; and (2) making a general adjustment in dividing marital property on the basis that one party, far more than the other, can reasonably expect to enjoy a secure retirement. It should not invalidate a property division if a disproportionate expectation regarding social security benefits is acknowledged in the court's assessment of the equities. *In re Marriage of Boyer*, 538 NW2d 293, 296 (Iowa, 1995).

In *Boyer*, the Iowa Supreme Court rejected the notion that "the federal pre-emption legislation requires state courts under these circumstances to purge so obvious an economic reality" as disproportionate anticipated social security benefits. Similarly, the Maine Supreme Court has reasoned:

> The court's role in property division is to accomplish a just division that takes into account all relevant factors. Just as few married couples engaged in a serious assessment of their retirement resources would ignore the availability of Social Security benefits, courts should not be required to ignore reality and fashion a distributive award of the parties' retirement and other marital assets divorced from the actual economic circumstances of each spouse at the time the division of property is to become effective. Failing to consider Social Security benefit payments a spouse can reasonably be expected to receive in the near future may result in a distorted picture of that spouse's financial needs, and, in turn, an inequitable division of the marital property. *Depot v. Depot*, 893 A.2d 995, 1002 (Me, 2006).

And the Colorado Court of Appeals has expressed, "While a trial court may not distribute marital property to offset the computed value of Social Security benefits, it may premise an unequal distribution of property—using, for example, a 60–40 formula instead of 50–50—on the fact that one party is more likely to enjoy a secure retirement." *In re Marriage of Morehouse*, 121 P3d 264, 267 (Colo App, 2005).

We join the majority of state courts that have considered this question, and hold that the circuit court may consider the parties' anticipated social security benefits as one factor, among others, to be considered when devising an equitable distribution of marital property. We caution that in endeavoring to divide the marital estate, the court may not treat social security benefits as tantamount to a marital asset. Instead, the circuit court may take into account, in a general sense, the extent to which social security benefits received by the parties affect [equitable distribution].

Reversed and remanded for further proceedings consistent with this opinion. We do not retain jurisdiction.

Question based on *Biondo v. Biondo*

If Social Security retirement cannot be divided by a state family court, but the court adjusts the division of property to account for the Social Security retirement, isn't the court doing an end run around federal law and ignoring Congress's intent?

Railroad Retirement

In *Hisquierdo v. Hisquierdo*, 439 U.S. 572, 99 S.Ct. 802 (1979), the U.S. Supreme Court ruled that state courts could not divide pensions under the Railroad Retirement Act (RRA). Congress amended the RRA to allow state divorce courts to divide certain components of RRA pensions.

Conclusion Regarding Pensions

If the preceding was complex, rest assured we barely scratched the surface. Law and practice regarding pensions and pension-like benefits—including QDROs—is extremely complicated. Overlooking a client's pension rights, and/or getting those rights wrong, is a fertile ground for legal malpractice.[92]

Use of a QDRO to Collect Child or Spousal Support

QDROs divide pensions. Additionally, a QRDO can be used to collect child or spousal support. The Virginia Court of Appeals decision in *Nkopchieu v. Minlend* is instructive.

Nkopchieu v. Minlend

Virginia Court of Appeals
59 Va. App. 299, 718 S.E.2d 470 (2011)

Beales, Judge.

In this domestic relations proceeding, the circuit court in its final order of divorce denied a motion by Cheyep Nkopchieu (mother) to enter a qualified domestic relations order (QDRO) permitting her to attach a retirement account belonging to Raymond Bernard Minlend (father) for the sole purpose of paying father's very considerable child support arrearage of over $28,000. On appeal, we hold that the circuit court committed reversible error when it found that it was constrained by this Court's decision in *Hoy v. Hoy*, 29 Va.App. 115, 510 S.E.2d 253 (1999).

The record on appeal establishes that father has completely ignored and frustrated the trial court's child support orders—and that mother's only means of obtaining the necessary child support for the parties' two children is through

---

92 *See* Faber v. Herman, 731 N.W.2d 1 (Iowa 2007)(malpractice claim related to pension); McCoy v. Feinman, 99 N.Y.2d 295, 785 N.E.2d 714, 755 N.Y.S.2d 693 (2002)(malpractice claim related to pension).

attaching father's retirement account. We find that neither *Hoy* nor any other provision of Virginia domestic relations law deprived the circuit court of authority to enter a QDRO pursuant to the procedures of the federal Employee Retirement Income Security Act (ERISA). Therefore, we reverse the portion of the circuit court's final order of divorce denying mother's motion for entry of a QDRO and remand the matter to the circuit court for further proceedings consistent with this opinion.

Mother and father were married in Virginia on February 23, 2009, approximately eleven months after the birth of their first child. They separated on or about December 15, 2009, while mother was pregnant with their second child, who was born on April 13, 2010.

Father filed a complaint for a divorce on February 25, 2010, and mother filed a cross-complaint for a divorce seeking *pendente lite* child support. In its April 16, 2010 *pendente lite* order, the trial court ordered father to make monthly child support payments in the amount of $2,000. Because the trial court determined that there was already a child support arrearage of $9,000, it ordered father to pay an additional $500 per month to begin satisfying this child support arrearage.

Father never made any of these child support payments ordered by the trial court. In fact, at some point in the divorce proceedings, father actually left the United States—and there is no indication from the record on appeal that he has ever returned to this country. Therefore, during the pendency of the divorce proceedings, the arrearage created by father's failure to make any child support payments continued to grow considerably.

Mother filed a written motion for the entry of a QDRO on January 13, 2011, when father's child support arrearage had grown to almost $28,000. Mother asserted: (a) that father had not appeared at any of the hearings in the trial court; (b) that father had left the country and was "not likely to return"; (c) that mother had not had any contact with father either "directly or through counsel"; (d) that father "was the sole income earner for the family prior to and during the marriage," leaving mother with essentially no assets; (e) that mother and the parties' two children had been forced to rely on charity and public assistance; and (f) that father's retirement account with his Virginia employer was "the only asset" of father's that mother knew of that could be used to pay the father's unpaid child support obligation. Mother contended that ERISA gives "state courts the authority to enter QDROs assigning retirement benefits to an alternate payee for the purpose of garnishing a retirement account to enforce payment" of a child support arrearage. . . .

During the divorce trial on January 21, 2011, father's counsel argued that the trial court lacked authority to enter the QDRO that mother sought. Father's counsel relied on *Hoy*, 29 Va.App. at 119, 510 S.E.2d at 255, where this Court held that a litigant's claim as a judgment creditor against her former spouse for unpaid spousal support could not be "recast" into an appropriate circumstance for entering a QDRO. In response, mother's counsel noted that *Hoy* involved an attempt to re-open a divorce case that already had been final for over two decades—in order to enter a QDRO attaching a retirement account that did not even exist at the time of the Hoys' divorce. Thus, mother's counsel argued that this Court's decision in *Hoy* did not affect the trial court's authority in this case "to assign a portion of the income" from father's retirement account "to an alternate payee" for the payment of unpaid child support.

Father's counsel also argued at the hearing in the trial court that a QDRO could not be entered because mother had expressly disavowed any property interest in husband's retirement account assets in the parties' premarital agreement. In response, mother's counsel argued:

> What we are asking the Court to do is to enter a qualified domestic relations order pursuant to ERISA to allow Ms. Nkopchieu to essentially garnish Mr. Minlend's retirement account, which is an asset, for the purpose of paying unpaid support. The Court's authority to do this stems specifically from the federal law in ERISA, which allows for the Court to enter a QDRO for two separate purposes.

> The Court is permitted to enter the QDRO as it relates to property division, which is what we would be doing in equitable distribution, which we are not in dispute that that is not before the Court today. *We are not saying she has a property interest in his retirement account, as it relates to a property division.* What we are saying is the other purpose of the QDRO, as it relates to ERISA in saying that the Court may enter a QDRO for the purpose of enforcing its child support or spousal support orders.

Mother's counsel then reiterated that mother was not seeking to create a personal "right or an interest" in father's retirement account.

In its final order of divorce, the trial court awarded mother sole legal and physical custody over the two children and increased father's monthly child support obligation to $2,035. The trial court found that father's child support arrearage had grown to $28,106.66 and ordered father "to pay this amount in full immediately." However, the trial court denied mother's motion for the entry of a

QDRO to satisfy the child support arrearage—finding that it was "bound by the Court of Appeals' decision" in *Hoy*.

On appeal, mother emphasizes (as she emphasized in the trial court) that she does not seek any *personal* interest in father's retirement assets—and that the parties' premarital agreement bars any such a claim. However, the premarital agreement also states, "Nothing in this agreement shall be construed as limiting the right of either party to make claims for child support." Mother contends that she is actually pursuing a claim of unpaid child support for her infant children. Mother asserts that she seeks a QDRO *only* in her capacity as the parent with sole legal and physical custody of the parties' children, and, therefore, as the children's guardian.

Given mother's position here, the fact that the parties were married (and are now divorced) is simply irrelevant. Mother could have made precisely the same request for the entry of a QDRO *even if the parties had never married*. This is because mother seeks to vindicate *the children's rights* to child support—not any property rights mother herself might have that resulted from the marriage with father.

In *Commonwealth ex rel. Gray v. Johnson*, 7 Va.App. 614, 622, 376 S.E.2d 787, 791 (1989), this Court noted, "An actual distinction rests in the right to child support." This Court explained:

> The duty of support of all children is owed to the child, not the mother. The amount of the support is based primarily on the needs of the child and the ability of the father to provide, not the needs of the mother. Thus, the mother does not have the same legal right of the child in seeking child support; rather, the right is solely that of the child. The mother simply has the right to act as a conduit for the payments of support to the child.

Acting solely "as a conduit for the payments of support" to the parties' children, mother seeks the entry of a QDRO in this case. She argues that ERISA and Virginia's laws pertaining to domestic relations would permit the entry of a QDRO under the specific circumstances of this case.

Under ERISA, the funds of an employee benefit plan (such as father's retirement account with his Virginia employer) generally "may not be assigned or alienated." 29 U.S.C. § 1056(d)(1). However, this general prohibition against the assignment or alienation of employee retirement benefits does not apply when a state domestic relations order "is determined to be a qualified domestic relations order." 29 U.S.C. § 1056(d)(3). ERISA states that "each pension plan shall provide for the payment of benefits in accordance with the applicable requirements of any qualified domestic relations order." 29 U.S.C. § 1056(d)(3).

According to 29 U.S.C. § 1056(d)(3)(B)(i), a "qualified domestic relations order" is a domestic relations order (I) "which creates or recognizes the existence of an alternate payee's right to, *or assigns to an alternate payee the right to*, receive all or a portion of the benefits payable with respect to a participant under a plan," and (II) which meets all of the technical requirements of "subparagraphs (C) and (D)" of 29 U.S.C. § 1056(d)(3). ERISA further defines the term "domestic relations order" as "any judgment, decree, or order" that: "(I) *relates to the provision of child support*, alimony payments, or marital property rights to a spouse, former spouse, child, or other dependent of a participant, and (II) *is made pursuant to a State domestic relations law* (including a community property law)." 29 U.S.C. § 1056(d)(3)(B)(ii) (emphasis added).

Under ERISA, the children of retirement plan participants can become plan beneficiaries and alternate payees of the plan through the entry of a QDRO. *See Boggs v. Boggs*, 520 U.S. 833, 847, 117 S.Ct. 1754 (1997). The United States Supreme Court explained in *Boggs* that one of the "central purposes" of the 1984 amendments to ERISA that created the "QDRO mechanism" was to "give enhanced protection" to plan beneficiaries such as "dependent children in the event of divorce or separation. . . ."

Therefore, under ERISA and the United States Supreme Court's explanation of that Act's purpose, the minor children of the parties in this case certainly can be listed as beneficiaries and alternate payees of the retirement account (through mother, as their guardian) in a QDRO. Furthermore, mother's request for a QDRO "relates to the provision of child support," and, therefore, satisfies another of ERISA's conditions for the entry of a QDRO.

However, the trial court never considered whether mother's draft QDRO satisfied ERISA's technical requirements for the entry of a QDRO. The trial court found that it was constrained by this Court's decision in *Hoy*—and, therefore, that it could not enter a QDRO pursuant to Virginia's domestic relations law. We disagree with the reasoning and conclusion of the trial court. . . .

Father's counsel argued in the trial court that the entry of a QDRO would be inappropriate here because "Congress has an interest in protecting these sort of retirement accounts" in order "to allow some form of support or income to folks once they retire, so the state is not burdened with that." Although it is perhaps true that the ERISA statutory scheme is designed for the protection of retirement income, this argument presents a very incomplete picture of the law.

ERISA specifically permits the parties' minor children to qualify as beneficiaries and alternate payees of father's retirement plan. . . .

Simply put, to use ERISA's *general* rule against assigning or alienating retirement assets as a way to permit father to continue to avoid his duty to pay child support would completely thwart Virginia's established principles of domestic relations law, especially the law dealing with child support. . . .

The record here establishes that a QDRO attaching father's retirement account represents *the only* actual method of enforcing the trial court's child support orders, which father has completely ignored and frustrated to the severe detriment of his own children. ERISA *and* Virginia's law on domestic relations authorized the circuit court to enter a QDRO under the specific circumstances of this case. Therefore, we reverse the circuit court's finding that it lacked authority to enter a QDRO. . . .

Reversed and remanded.

Disability Benefits

Pension benefits, to the extent acquired during marriage, are marital/community property. Disability benefits, by contrast, are generally separate property, even though acquired during marriage.[93]

In *Topolski v. Topolski*,[94] the Wisconsin Supreme Court described the difference between pension and disability benefits:

> The value of a spouse's interest in a retirement, pension, or deferred benefit account, although presenting valuation challenges, is generally classified as a divisible asset at divorce. Therefore, these assets generally must be considered in the circuit court's division of property at divorce.

> In contrast, a disability benefit is ordinarily viewed as distinct from a retirement, pension, or deferred benefit account. "Disability benefit" or "disability income," in ordinary parlance, commonly refers to a payment received when a person is unable to work, either in a chosen profession or totally, due to a physical or mental condition. Disability benefits are not ordinarily referred to as deferred compensation. Disability benefits are generally considered wage replacement,

---

93 In New Hampshire, however, disability benefits are marital property. *See* In re Sukerman, 159 N.H. 565, 986 A.2d 467, 469 (2009).

94 335 Wis. 2d 327, 802 N.W.2d 482 (2011).

that is, compensation for lost future wages because a physical or mental condition prevents the person from being gainfully employed.

Disability payments, such as Social Security disability payments or veteran's disability payments, replace the wages lost by the individual due to the disability and are generally classified as income at divorce. As such, these payments are not assets divisible at dissolution of the marriage. . . .

A disabled spouse's disability benefit may in effect be an amalgam: a portion may be a replacement for lost wages and a portion may be a replacement for deferred compensation (that is, retirement or pension benefits).

Depending on the terms of a plan, a disability benefit may encompass both a wage replacement component and a deferred compensation replacement component. In other words, under a plan, a disability benefit may in substance be both a replacement for lost future wages and a replacement for deferred compensation. The disability benefit should be viewed in light of the totality of the circumstances to determine whether all or any part of the disability benefit received by the disabled spouse replaces post-divorce lost wages or replaces deferred compensation.

When and to the extent that a disability benefit replaces the disabled spouse's post-divorce wages, the benefit should be characterized as income and will be individual property not subject to property division at divorce.

Alternatively, when and to the extent that the disability benefit replaces deferred compensation, the disability benefit should be characterized as deferred compensation and will be subject to property division at divorce.

This approach enables courts to differentiate among a multitude of disability benefits under a multitude of different circumstances that a court may encounter.

In sum, pension benefits earned during marriage are marital/community property, whereas disability benefits, even if acquired during marriage, are generally separate property. The decision of the Appellate Division of the New York Supreme Court in *Howe v. Howe* sheds light on pension versus disability benefits. The decision also discusses characterization of tort recoveries for pain and suffering and lost income.

Howe v. Howe

New York Supreme Court, Appellate Division
68 A.D.3d 38, 886 N.Y.S.2d 722 (2009)

Spolzino, J.P.

On this appeal and cross appeal, the parties raise, principally, two significant issues related to the equitable distribution of the marital estate. The plaintiff asks us to determine that a portion of his New York City Fire Department disability pension is his separate property, despite the lack of evidence in the record by which the disability and nondisability portions of the pension can be distinguished. On the cross appeal, the defendant asks us to hold that the portion of the plaintiff's September 11th Victim Compensation Fund award that is designated as compensation for economic loss does not constitute "compensation for personal injuries" within the meaning of Domestic Relations Law § 236 (B) (1) (d) (2) and is, therefore, marital property.

We conclude that, in the circumstances presented here, the disability portion of the plaintiff's pension and, consequently, his separate property interest in that pension, can be determined by the appropriate pension administrator pursuant to a properly drawn order. Therefore, we modify the judgment accordingly. As to the cross appeal, the legislative history of the Equitable Distribution Law compels the conclusion that even so much of the plaintiff's September 11th Victim Compensation Fund award as is designated as compensation for economic loss is "compensation for personal injuries" within the meaning of Domestic Relations Law § 236(B)(1)(d)(2), and therefore the separate property of the plaintiff.

The plaintiff became a New York City firefighter soon after the parties were married, and remained in that employment until approximately 16 months prior to the commencement of this action. He was disabled as a result of his service during the period immediately following September 11, 2001, and retired with a disability pension. The Supreme Court, reasoning that the plaintiff had failed to satisfy his burden of establishing the separate nature of the pension, found the entire pension to be a part of the marital estate and awarded the defendant her share. The plaintiff argues that the lack of expert testimony or evidence in the record by which the nondisability portion of the pension can be distinguished from the disability portion is not fatal to his separate property claim, since that distinction can be made by the pension administrator in the same manner as it makes the familiar calculation of the marital pension share . . . .

The manner in which disability pensions are treated for equitable distribution purposes is well established. Pension benefits or vested rights to those benefits, except to the extent that they are earned or acquired before marriage or after the commencement of a matrimonial action, constitute marital property. Thus, to the extent that the disability pension represents deferred compensation, it is subject to equitable distribution. However, to the extent that a disability pension constitutes compensation for personal injuries, that compensation is separate property which is not subject to equitable distribution. The burden of distinguishing the marital property portion of a disability pension from the separate property portion has been placed on the recipient of the pension who is resisting equitable distribution. In other words, until the contrary is demonstrated, the presumption is that the entire disability pension is marital property.

Here, the record was insufficient for the court to make this calculation. The only evidence in the record as to the nature of the plaintiff's pension was his testimony that he receives approximately $5,000 per month from a disability pension. There was no evidence of the terms of the pension plan pursuant to which the plaintiff retired and there is no statement from the plan administrator as to how the pension amount was calculated. There is nothing in the record about the plaintiff's earnings, such that a hypothetical final average salary could be determined, and there is nothing that establishes the percentage of final average salary to which the plaintiff is entitled as his pension. Thus, as the Supreme Court found, there is no record upon which it could determine the nondisability value of the plaintiff's pension.

In addition to his disability pension, the plaintiff received an award from the September 11th Victim Compensation Fund as a result of injuries he suffered in the aftermath of that tragedy. The administrator of that fund specifically designated a portion of that award, in the amount of $127,571, as compensation for economic loss. The Supreme Court held that the economic component of the award constitutes compensation for personal injuries within the meaning of Domestic Relations Law § 236 (B)(1)(d)(2) and, on that basis, treated the award as the separate property of the plaintiff. We agree with that determination, because the legislative history of the Equitable Distribution Law compels it.

It is a basic principle of the Equitable Distribution Law that marital property consists of "all property acquired by either or both spouses during the marriage and before the execution of a separation agreement or the commencement of a matrimonial action, regardless of the form in which title is held," other than property that is defined as separate. One category of property that is defined as separate is "compensation for personal injuries" (Domestic Relations Law § 236 [B][1][d][2]). For equitable distribution purposes, an award pursuant to the September 11th Victim Compensation Fund is the equivalent of a recovery in a personal injury action, the noneconomic portion of which clearly falls within this category of separate property. The only issue is whether the economic component of the award does so as well.

The purpose of the Equitable Distribution Law was to treat marriage in one respect as an economic partnership. The economic portion of a personal injury award is compensation for a loss, presumably lost earnings, that is suffered by both spouses, since the earnings that were lost during the marriage would have been marital property. Since the loss is suffered by both spouses, the compensation for that loss should be shared by both as well.

Other assets that represent compensation for the loss of marital earnings are treated in precisely this manner. There is no dispute, for example, that severance pay or a bonus earned during the marriage but paid after commencement would be treated as marital property. Similarly, in addressing the distribution of a disability pension, we distinguish between the portion of the pension that constitutes compensation for the disability and the portion that merely constitutes deferred compensation, treating the former as separate and the latter as marital.

Thus, the logic of the Equitable Distribution Law is that pain and suffering is personal and, therefore, the compensation for it is separate, but earnings are marital and, therefore, the compensation for lost earnings during the marriage should be marital as well.

While the logic of the Equitable Distribution Law thus suggests the conclusion that the economic portion of a personal injury award should be marital property, however, the legislative history compels the contrary result.

Since the legislative intent must control, the inescapable conclusion is that the Supreme Court was correct in determining that the portion of the Victim Compensation Fund award received by the plaintiff that constitutes compensation for economic loss during the marriage is the plaintiff's separate property.

Military Disability

The United States military has three disability programs: (1) Veterans Administration (VA) disability; (2) Military disability retired pay; and (3) Combat-Related Special Compensation.[95]

When a service member is sufficiently disabled such that she or he can no longer perform assigned duties, the service member may receive disability retired pay. No portion of a former service member's retirement "that is equal to

---

95 *See* Mark E. Sullivan, *The Military Divorce Handbook: A Practical Guide to Representing Military Personnel and Their Families*, p. 509 (2d ed. 2011).

the retiree's disability percentage rating at the time of retirement" can be divided in a divorce.[96]

Service members who are not sufficiently disabled to quality for military disability pay, or whose disability is detected after retirement, may qualify for VA disability benefits. The service member gives up a portion of regular retirement benefits to obtain VA disability benefits. A state court cannot divide the retired pay that a service member gives up to receive VA disability.[97]

Combat-related Special Compensation (CRSC) is available to service members who are least 10% disabled, and whose disability is related to the award of a Purple Heart or to combat. CRSC is not divisible on divorce.

The following case grapples with the disposition of military retirement and disability benefits. The court's detailed analysis introduces you to the complexity of military disability law.

Megee v. Carmine

Michigan Court of Appeal
290 Mich. App. 551, 802 N.W.2d 669 (2010)

Murphy, C.J.

Plaintiff appeals by leave granted the trial court's order that directed him to act as trustee for the benefit of defendant with respect to half of plaintiff's monthly combat-related special compensation (CRSC), 10 USC 1413a, which funds were then to be delivered to defendant. We reverse and remand.

Pursuant to a divorce judgment entered in September 1989, defendant was awarded 50 percent of plaintiff's Navy disposable retirement pay as part of the property division, and the judgment incorporated a qualified domestic relations order (QDRO) to enforce that provision. The QDRO acknowledged the 50 percent division of plaintiff's disposable retirement pay, also referred to therein as his pension, and it prevented plaintiff from making another benefit election "that would otherwise reduce the monthly pension allotment without the written consent of [defendant]." According to defendant, she began receiving her share of plaintiff's retirement pay in January 2008, although plaintiff claims

---

96 Mark E. Sullivan, *The Military Divorce Handbook: A Practical Guide to Representing Military Personnel and Their Families*, p. 509 (2d ed. 2011).

97 Mark E. Sullivan, *The Military Divorce Handbook: A Practical Guide to Representing Military Personnel and Their Families*, p. 513 (2d ed. 2011).

that defendant had been receiving her share of his retirement pay since 1994. In 2008, plaintiff was officially diagnosed, for purposes of entitlement to disability benefits, as being disabled as a result of combat-related activities and exposure to Agent Orange in Vietnam. He was declared eligible to elect CRSC, but that election would require plaintiff to waive further receipt of his retirement pay. Plaintiff elected to receive CRSC, resulting in termination of his retirement pay and thus the cessation of funds flowing to defendant under the QDRO. Defendant moved to enforce the divorce judgment and the QDRO, and the trial court entered the challenged order that effectively forces plaintiff to pay defendant half of his CRSC.

We hold that following a divorce, a military spouse remains financially responsible to compensate his or her former spouse in an amount equal to the share of retirement pay ordered to be distributed to the former spouse as part of the divorce judgment's property division when the military spouse makes a unilateral and voluntary postjudgment election to waive the retirement pay in favor of disability benefits contrary to the terms of the divorce judgment. Conceptually, and consistently with extensive case law from other jurisdictions, we are dividing waived retirement pay in order to honor the terms and intent of the divorce judgment. Importantly, we are not ruling that a state court has the authority to divide a military spouse's CRSC, nor that the military spouse can be ordered by a court to pay the former spouse using CRSC funds. Rather, the compensation to be paid the former spouse as his or her share of the property division in lieu of the waived retirement pay can come from any source the military spouse chooses, but it must be paid to avoid contempt of court. To be clear, nothing in this opinion should be construed as precluding a military spouse from using CRSC funds to satisfy the spouse's obligation if desired. In these situations, because the ordered replacement compensation must relate to the military spouse's retirement-pay obligation and not the disability pay now being received, and because the military spouse, having made the election, will no longer actually be receiving the retirement pay, it may be necessary on occasion to review and determine whether any adjustments to the retirement pay would have been made had the military spouse continued receiving the retirement pay.

Accordingly, although we agree with the trial court that plaintiff must compensate defendant, we reverse the trial court's ruling because its order required plaintiff to pay defendant from CRSC funds and required plaintiff to pay an amount equal to half of his CRSC and not half of his envisioned retirement pay. We remand for entry of an order requiring plaintiff to compensate defendant with monthly payments, from any source or combination of sources chosen, in an amount equal to 50 percent of the retirement pay that he would be receiving but for his election to waive the retirement pay in favor of disability benefits. . . .

Members of the Navy who serve for a specified period, generally at least 20 years, are entitled to retire and to receive retirement pay. 10 USC 6321 *et seq.* Military veterans in general are entitled to compensation for service-connected disabilities under 38 USC 1101 et seq., which we have referred to in this opinion as "VA disability benefits." Further, CRSC is available to an "eligible combat-related disabled uniformed services retiree who elects [such] benefits...." 10 USC 1413a(a). CRSC is "not retired pay." 10 USC 1413a(g). To be eligible for CRSC, a person must be a member of the uniformed services who is entitled to retired pay and who has a combat-related disability. 10 USC 1413a(c). . . .

Plaintiff qualified for the three different forms of benefits already discussed—disposable retirement pay, VA disability benefits, and CRSC.

Pursuant to 10 USC 1414(a)(1), "a member or former member of the uniformed services who is entitled for any month to retired pay and who is also entitled for that month to veterans' disability compensation for a qualifying service-connected disability ... is entitled to be paid both for that month." This concurrent receipt of military retirement pay and VA disability benefits is commonly referred to as CRDP, which stands for "concurrent retirement and disability pay." Because plaintiff was eligible for retirement pay and VA disability benefits, CRDP was an available option for plaintiff. A person who is qualified for CRDP and who is also qualified for CRSC, such as plaintiff, may elect to receive CRDP or CRSC, but not both. During an annual open-enrollment period, a person has the right to make an election to change from CRDP to CRSC or the reverse, as the case may be. Plaintiff elected CRSC, which effectively discontinued his retirement pay that had been subject to the QDRO, halting payments to defendant.

The Uniformed Services Former Spouses' Protection Act (USFSPA), 10 USC 1408, generally governs the distribution of a spouse's military retirement pay to a former spouse pursuant to a court order, including state court final decrees of divorce issued in accordance with the state's laws and providing for the division of property expressed as a percentage of disposable retirement pay. Section 1408(c)(1) provides, in pertinent part:

> Subject to the limitations of this section, a court may treat disposable retired pay payable to a member for pay periods beginning after June 25, 1981, either as property solely of the member or as property of the member and his spouse in accordance with the law of the jurisdiction of such court. [10 USC 1408(c)(1).]

Accordingly, disposable retired or retirement pay can be treated by a court as joint property and thus subject to division in a state court divorce decree. As used in the USFSPA, the term "disposable retired pay" is defined, in relevant part, as "the total monthly retired pay to which a member is entitled less amounts which ... are deducted from the retired pay of such member ... as a result of a waiver of retired pay required by law in order to receive compensation under title 5 or title 38." 10 USC 1408(a)(4)(B). We note that, while VA disability benefits are provided for in title 38, the right to CRSC is found in title 10, not title 5 or title 38. As we will explain in our analysis of *Mansell v. Mansell*, 490 U.S. 581, 109 S.Ct. 2023 (1989)], which involved a waiver of retirement pay in favor of title 38 VA disability benefits, the fact that CRSC is a title 10 benefit is of some significance. Finally, the total amount of the disposable retirement pay of a military spouse that a court orders payable to the other spouse "may not exceed 50 percent of such disposable retirement pay." 10 USC 1408(e)(1).

With these provisions in mind, we now proceed to our discussion of the issues presented on appeal.

We begin by first holding that, contrary to plaintiff's contention, his unilateral decision to elect CRSC was contrary to the terms and intent of the QDRO and therefore the divorce judgment, given that the judgment incorporated by reference the QDRO. The clear language in the judgment and the QDRO required a 50 percent division of plaintiff's disposable retirement pay, and plaintiff was barred from making any "other benefit election ... that would otherwise reduce the monthly pension allotment without the written consent of [defendant]." Plaintiff elected a benefit other than retirement pay when he elected CRSC to the exclusion of retirement pay, the election reduced and indeed eliminated defendant's monthly share of plaintiff's retirement pay, and there is no claim that defendant gave consent of any kind for plaintiff to make the CRSC election. The parties had also agreed that their mutual intent was to provide defendant with 50 percent of plaintiff's retirement pay. The decision to elect CRSC and to waive in its entirety the retirement pay was inconsistent with the declared mutual intent. The question now becomes one of remedy.

We find that the issue properly framed is whether a military spouse remains financially responsible to compensate his or her former spouse in an amount equal to the share of retirement pay ordered to be distributed to the former spouse as part of a divorce judgment's property division when the military spouse makes a unilateral and voluntary postjudgment election to waive the retirement pay in favor of disability benefits contrary to the terms of the divorce judgment.

In *Mansell*, a United States Supreme Court case, the husband, who had been in the military, was receiving retirement pay along with, pursuant to a waiver of a portion of the retirement pay, VA disability benefits. He was receiving both benefits at the time of the divorce. Pursuant to a property settlement that was incorporated into the divorce decree, the husband agreed to pay the wife 50 percent of his total military retirement pay, including *that portion of retirement pay that he had waived in order to receive disability benefits*. The husband then requested the trial court to modify the divorce decree by removing the provision requiring him to share his total retirement pay with his wife; he did not want to pay her a sum equal to half of the waived retirement pay. The trial court denied the request. The case made its way through the California appellate courts, with the husband arguing that the USFSPA and the statute protecting his disability benefits precluded the trial court from treating as community property that portion of his retirement pay that had been waived in favor of disability benefits.

The *Mansell* Court stated that it was being called upon to decide whether state courts, consistently with the USFSPA, "may treat as property divisible upon divorce military retirement pay waived by the retiree in order to receive veterans' disability benefits." The Court held that state courts lacked the authority to make such a division, thereby ruling in favor of the husband. The Court concluded that Congress had specifically enacted the USFSPA to change preexisting federal law that had completely preempted the application of state law to military retirement pay. The *Mansell* Court noted that the USFSPA granted state courts the authority to divide military retirement pay as property, but the section of the USFSPA defining the term "disposable retired pay" specifically and clearly excluded military retirement pay that had been waived in order to receive VA disability payments, which is a benefit found in title 38. The USFSPA's definitional section relied on and quoted by the Court was 10 USC 1408(a)(4) (B), which . . . excludes from consideration as disposable retired pay amounts waived pursuant to law "in order to receive compensation under title 5 or title 38." Once again, CRSC is compensation received under title 10, and plaintiff here did not waive his right to retirement pay in order to receive compensation under title 5 or title 38, but to receive title 10 compensation.

The *Mansell* Court ruled that, although the USFSPA now granted authority to state courts to divide as property a military spouse's disposable retirement pay in general, states continued to be federally preempted from dividing as property disposable retirement pay that had been waived in order to receive VA disability benefits. The Court ultimately held:

> . . . We realize that reading the statute literally may inflict economic harm on many former spouses. But we decline to misread the statute in order to reach a sympathetic result when such a reading requires us to do violence to the plain language of the statute and to

ignore much of the legislative history. Congress chose the language that requires us to decide as we do, and Congress is free to change it.

For the reasons stated above, we hold that the Former Spouses' Protection Act does not grant state courts the power to treat as property divisible upon divorce military retirement pay that has been waived to receive veterans' disability benefits.

We glean from *Mansell* some important, but subtle, points. First, *Mansell* did not entail an attempted division or distribution of the husband's VA disability benefits; rather, it concerned payments to the wife in an amount equal to half of the husband's total retirement pay, even though a portion of that pay was no longer being received by the husband, considering that he had waived receipt of that portion in favor of VA disability benefits. The trial court here effectively divided plaintiff's CRSC and, although *Mansell* did not directly address division of disability pay, the USFSPA clearly does not allow such a division. Subsection (c)(1) of the USFSPA, 10 USC 1408(c)(1), permits a court to treat only "disposable retired pay" as "property of the member and his spouse," and CRSC is "not retired pay," 10 USC 1413a(g). Accordingly, the trial court erred by dividing plaintiff's CRSC and forcing plaintiff to pay a portion of his CRSC to defendant. However, on the subject addressed in *Mansell*, i.e., dividing waived retirement pay, the *Mansell* decision actually supports making plaintiff in the case at bar pay defendant half of the retirement pay that he would be receiving but for his election to take CRSC. The *Mansell* Court concluded that waived retirement pay could not be divided as property in circumstances in which the pay had been waived in favor of title 38 VA disability benefits, given that the definition of "disposable retired pay" in 10 USC 1408(a)(4)(B) excludes consideration of amounts waived in order to receive title 5 or title 38 compensation. Under the reasoning and rationale of *Mansell*, there would be no prohibition here against considering for division waived retirement pay under the USFSPA because we are addressing a waiver of title 10 CRSC not mentioned in 10 USC 1408(a)(4)(B). Thus, all of plaintiff's envisioned yet waived military-retirement pay can be divided without offending the USFSPA or *Mansell*. Accordingly, there is no bar to ordering plaintiff to compensate defendant in an amount equal to 50 percent of plaintiff's envisioned retirement pay as intended under the terms of the divorce judgment after plaintiff made a unilateral and voluntary postjudgment election to waive his retirement pay in favor of disability benefits contrary to the terms of the judgment. . . .

We agree with the following sentiments expressed by the New Jersey Superior Court, Appellate Division, in *Whitfield v. Whitfield*, 373 N.J.Super. 573, 582–583, 862 A.2d 1187 (2004):

It is important to emphasize the procedural posture of this case. The issue is one of enforcement of a prior equitable distribution award, not a present division of assets. Wife does not seek to divide her former husband's disability benefits in violation of *Mansell*. Nor does she seek a greater percentage of her husband's military pension than she originally received at the time of his retirement pursuant to court order. Moreover, wife does not seek to alter the terms of her veteran-spouse's retirement plan or to compel the Department of Defense to make direct payments to her in excess of those permitted by federal law. The remedy she seeks, and that to which she is entitled, is an enforcement of the original order which was in effect before her former husband retired and unilaterally elected the waiver. The trial court appropriately accomplished that result by requiring husband to make up the shortfall in his former wife's equitable distribution award occasioned by his actions.

The trial court's determination does not hinder husband's receipt of veterans' disability benefits. Nor does it impinge upon federal statutory rights husband has under the USFSPA or violate the doctrine of pre-emption. Rather, the determination is whether under our state law the trial court has the authority to interpret and enforce a judicial decree entered prior to the retiree's unilateral election of a method of payment that has tax advantages to him and adverse consequences to his former wife. We conclude that our court does have that authority. This was an appropriate remedy to avoid the inequities that would be imposed on a spouse who had no control over, but suffered the consequences of, the other's unilateral election to switch retirement benefits to tax-free disability benefits.

. . . We hold that a military spouse remains financially responsible to compensate his or her former spouse in an amount equal to the share of retirement pay ordered to be distributed to the former spouse as part of a divorce judgment's property division when the military spouse makes a unilateral and voluntary postjudgment election to waive the retirement pay in favor of disability benefits contrary to the terms of the divorce judgment. Conceptually, and consistently with extensive case law from other jurisdictions, we are dividing waived retirement pay in order to honor the terms and intent of the divorce judgment. . . .

Accordingly, although we agree with the trial court that plaintiff must compensate defendant, we reverse the trial court's ruling because its order required plaintiff to pay defendant from CRSC funds and required plaintiff to pay an amount equal to half of his CRSC and not half of his envisioned retirement pay. . . .

Reversed and remanded for proceedings consistent with this opinion. We do not retain jurisdiction.

Question based on *Megee v. Carmine*

If you represent the spouse of a servicemember, how will you draft a marriage settlement agreement to protect your client from the servicemember's decision to waive retirement pay in favor of CRSC?

Damage Awards for Personal Injuries Suffered by a Married Person

Sue and John are married. While driving to work one morning, Sue is broadsided by a negligent driver. Sue is injured. Fortunately, Sue recovers from her injuries and returns to work. A year later, Sue settles a personal injury claim against the negligent driver and receives a check for $1 million. With the million dollars in the bank, Sue and John divorce. How should the million be characterized and divided on divorce?

States have different approaches to personal injury recoveries.[98] In California, if the cause of action arose during marriage and prior to separation, damages are community property.[99] On the other hand, if the cause of action arose before marriage or after the couple separated, damages are the separate property of the injured spouse. In Louisiana, damages due to personal injury suffered during marriage are separate property of the injured spouse, although "the portion of the damages attributable to expenses incurred by the community as a result of the injury, or in compensation of the loss of community earnings, is community property."[100] Alaska divides personal injury damages between separate and marital property.[101]

---

98 *See* Dale Joseph Gilsinger, Spouse's Cause of Action for Negligent Personal Injury, or Proceeds Therefrom, as Separate or Community Property, 80 ALR5th 533.

99 Cal. Family Code §§ 780-781.

100 La. Civ. Code Art. 2344.

101 Grace v. Peterson, 269 P.3d 663 (Alaska 2012).

Is Employment-Related Health Insurance Marital/Community Property?

One of the most valuable benefits of employment is health insurance for employees and dependents. Is employment-related health insurance property subject to valuation and division on divorce? In *Burts v. Burts*,[102] the Alaska Supreme Court wrote, "We have repeatedly recognized that health insurance benefits earned during the marriage are a marital asset of the insured spouse . . . ." In *Burts*, husband retired after 20 years in the military. Husband was eligible for TRICARE—health insurance for the rest of his life. The Alaska court ruled husband's TRICARE health insurance was marital property.

The California Court of Appeal concluded in *Marriage of Elli*[103] that husband's postretirement participation in his employer's health care plan was not property subject to division on divorce.

Severance Pay

When some employees resign or are laid off, the employee receives a "severance package." In divorce, is severance money marital/community or separate? What purpose did the severance serve? If the severance was a reward for past service to the employer, and the employee was married during the period of service, then the severance is marital/community property. On the other hand, if the severance was intended to replace lost future income after the couple separated or divorced, the severance is the separate property of the employee.

In *Wheat v. Wheat*,[104] wife resigned from her employer of more than thirty years. The employer offered wife a severance of $395,000. Not long after wife resigned, she and husband commenced divorce proceedings. The Mississippi Supreme Court ruled the severance was marital property.

Accrued Vacation Days and Sick Days

In some jobs, employees can accrue unused vacation and sick days. In some states, these days can be "cashed in" at retirement or when the employee leaves employment. In other states, accrued vacation/sick days can be added to a pension.

---

102   266 P.3d 337 (Alaska 2011).

103   101 Cal. App. 4th 400, 124 Cal. Rptr. 2d 719 (2002).

104   37 So.3d 632 (Miss. 2010).

In *Marriage of Abrell*,[105] the Illinois Supreme Court grappled with the issue of whether unused vacation or sick days should be considered marital property. The court described the diversity of opinion on the issue: "Jurisdictions are split on the issue of whether vacation and sick days are marital property. Courts have held that: (1) accrued vacation and sick days are marital property subject to division at the time of dissolution; (2) accrued vacation and sick days are marital property but are subject to distribution when received, not at the time of dissolution; and (3) accrued vacation and sick days are not marital property." For Illinois, the Supreme Court ruled that accrued vacation and sick days are not marital property. The court wrote, "The value of accrued vacation and sick days is speculative and uncertain until a party actually collects compensation for those days at retirement or termination of his employment. A party cannot receive cash for those days prior to retirement or termination. In fact, it is possible that in some cases, an employer might change its policy concerning the right to receive compensation for accrued sick days, limiting or eliminating that right entirely. Similarly, in cases where provided for in a collective-bargaining agreement, an employer might change its policy concerning the right to receive compensation for accrued vacation days. Accordingly, we find that accrued vacation and sick days are not marital property subject to distribution in a dissolution of marriage action."[106] The court noted, however, "that when a party has actually received payment for vacation and/or sick days accrued during marriage prior to a judgment for dissolution, the payment for those days is marital property subject to distribution in the marital estate."[107]

Suppose you are an Illinois family law attorney. Sue consults you about her desire for a divorce. Sue has been married twenty years, and during the entire marriage Sue worked for the same company. Sue never missed a day's work due to sickness. Nor did she take any vacation. Fortunately for Sue, her employer allows employees to accrue unused sick and vacation days. The company does not have a "use it or lose it" policy for these benefits. Sue has accumulated nearly $100,000 in accrued sick/vacation days. In addition to thinking about divorce, Sue is thinking about retirement. Should Sue postpone retirement until after the divorce is complete?

---

105   236 Ill.2d 249, 923 N.E.2d 791 (2010).

106   923 N.E.2d at 801.

107   923 N.E.2d at 801.

C

Practice Assignment: Her Honor Has a Question

You are a third year law student. You are serving an internship at the local family court, doing research for three judges. One of your judges, the Honorable Lucy Lamb, calls you to her chambers and asks you to research the following question: The judge has a divorce case before her in which the wife is claiming an interest in vacation days her husband has accumulated at his state job. According to the wife, husband has 157 days of accumulated vacation. When husband retires in five years, he can cash in the vacation days. All of the accumulated days were earned during marriage. Husband does not deny he has the 157 days. Husband argues the vacation days should not be considered property subject to division on divorce.

Assignment: Research the judge's question under the law of your state. Prepare a short memo for the judge answering her question. If your law school is in Illinois, the Illinois Supreme Court's decision quoted above provides the answer. Thus, all Illinois law students can skip this assignment and proceed to the nearest coffee shop for a well deserved break.

Pull Out Your Credit Card

Does anyone pay cash for a car, home, college education, or other "big ticket" item? For expensive purchases, most Americans rely on credit or a loan from a bank or credit union. The general rule is that property acquired during marriage on credit is presumed to be community/marital property.[108]

Businesses as Marital/Community or Separate Property

Ann and Alex marry while earning M.B.A. degrees. Upon graduation, they start a business: A & A Electron Systems (AAES). Together they invent a new method of communication—the next Facebook. Within ten years, the business is worth millions. Their marriage, however, is on the rocks. In their divorce,

---

108 *See* American Law Institute, *Principles of the Law of Family Dissolution: Analysis and Recommendations*, § 4.06(2), p. 684 (2000)("Property acquired on credit during marriage is presumed to be marital property.").

AAES is marital/community property—property acquired during marriage. The business will be valued according to the fair market value.[109]

Suppose Ann started Allied Electron Systems (AES) before she met Alex. Ann met and married Alex five years *after* AES had become a profitable business. Because AES was owned by Ann prior to marriage, it is her separate property. During their ten year marriage, Ann devoted countless hours to AES, serving as its chief executive officer. Over the course of the marriage, AES tripled in value. When the parties divorce, how should AES be characterized? Does AES remain entirely Ann's separate property? Is it part separate and part marital/community? If AES is Ann's separate property, what about the increased value during marriage? Does the increased value belong in whole or part to the marital/community estate?

Consider Bill and Tamara. When they married 10 year ago, Bill already owned a large and valuable stock portfolio that he inherited from his parents. The portfolio is separate property. During marriage, Bill did little to manage the portfolio. Bill entrusted the portfolio to a stock broker. Periodically, Bill met briefly with the stock broker, but apart from these meetings, Bill ignored the portfolio and simply enjoyed the checks sent to him by the stock broker. Between the marriage and the divorce, the portfolio doubled in value. Who owns the portfolio? What about the increased value during marriage? Change the facts. Bill managed the stock portfolio himself, devoting many hours a week to research and trading stocks. Who owns the portfolio? The increased value?

When a spouse owns a separate property business or asset that increases in value during marriage due in whole or in part to the efforts of the owner spouse, many states provide that the increased value is marital/community property to be divided on divorce.[110] The business itself remains separate property. It is the increased value attributable to efforts of the owner spouse that is marital/community property. The American Law Institute, *Principles of the Law of Family Dissolution* state: "(1) A portion of any increase in the value of separate property

---

109 *See* Nuveen v. Nuveen, 795 N.W.2d 308, 313 (N.D. 2011)("The fair market value of a business is ordinarily the property method for valuing property in a divorce. Fair market value is the price a buyer is willing to pay and the seller is willing to accept under circumstances that do not amount to coercion.").

110 *See* Schmitz v. Schmitz, 88 P.3d 1116, 1125 (Alaska 2004)("We have recognized that a spouse's premarital separate property can become marital through transmutation or active appreciation. Transmutation occurs when a married couple demonstrates an intent, by virtue of their words and actions during marriage, to treat one spouse's separate property as marital property. Active appreciation occurs when marital funds or marital efforts cause a spouse's separate property to increase in value during the marriage. . . . To find active appreciation in separate property, the court must make three subsidiary findings: First, it must find that the separate property in question appreciated during the marriage. Second, it must find that the parties made marital contributions to the property. Finally, the court must find a causal connection between the marital contributions and at least part of the appreciation.").

is marital property whenever either spouse has devoted substantial time during marriage to the property's management or preservation. (2) The increase in value of separate property over the course of the marriage is measured by the difference between the market value of the property when acquired, or at the beginning of the marriage, if later, and the market value of the property when sold, or at the end of the marriage, if sooner. (3) The portion of the increase in value that is marital property under Paragraph (1) is the difference between the actual amount by which the property has increased in value, and the amount by which capital of the same value would have increased over the same time period if invested in assets of relative safety requiring little management."[111]

Florida law provides that "marital assets" include, "The enhancement in value and appreciation of nonmarital assets resulting either from the efforts of either party during the marriage or from the contribution to or expenditure thereon of marital funds or other forms of marital assets, or both."

California courts divide increased value of separate property businesses.[112] If the increased value is due entirely to natural growth, then the entire increase is the separate property of the owner spouse. However, if the owner spouse expended more than *de minimus* effort on the business, and if at least part of the increased value is attributable to the owner spouse's efforts, then the increased value is divided between community property and separate property.[113] When the increased value is due primarily to the efforts of the owner spouse, the lion's share of the increase is community property. On the other hand, if the owner's efforts account for only a small portion of the increase—market forces account for most of the increase—most of the increase is separate property.

Two California cases guide decisionmaking in this area: *Van Camp v. Van Camp*,[114] and *Pereira v. Pereira*.[115] If the trial judge concludes the increase in value is due primarily to the efforts of the owner spouse, the judge uses *Pereira*. The judge allocates a fair return on the owner spouse's business (typically the legal interest rate) and allocates the rest of the increased value as community property arising from the owner's efforts. On the other hand, if most of the increase

---

111   American Law Institute, *Principles of the Law of Family Dissolution: Analysis and Recommendations,* § 4.05, p. 663 (2000).

112   Under the California approach, the business itself remains entirely separate property. At divorce, the focus is on the increased value of the business.

113   In most cases, it is the owner of the business who devotes time and effort to the business. In some cases, however, the non-owner spouse devotes effort to the business. In still other cases, both spouses are involved in the business. Courts apportion increased value in all these scenarios.

114   53 Cal. App. 17, 199 P. 885 (1921).

115   156 Cal. 1, 103 P. 488 (1909).

in value is due to market forces, the judge uses *Van Camp*. With *Van Camp*, the judge determines the reasonable value of the owner spouses services to the business and allocates that amount as community property. The remainder of the increase in separate property.

Problem on Increased Value of Separate Property Business

Two weeks prior to marrying Wife, Husband registered a domain name in his name to develop a website. During marriage, Husband worked many hours on the web-based business, which prospered. Most income to support the family came from the website business. After a five year marriage, Wife and Husband are divorcing. The domain name and website dramatically increased in value during marriage. Who owns the domain name and website? Can/should the increased value of the domain name and website be considered marital/community property? If so, how should value be calculated and divided? *Robertson v. Robertson*, 78 So. 3d 76 (Fla. Ct. App.2012).

Goodwill

You graduate from law school, pass the bar, and enter practice. After a few years in the legal trenches you realize your true passion is not the courtroom but the kitchen. You hang up your shingle, donate your fancy suits to charity, and move to Paris. You get a little apartment on the Left Bank with a view of the Eifel Tower, wile away the hours sipping coffee at quaint sidewalk cafes, mingle with artists, and enroll in the famous Le Cordon Bleu school of French cooking. (Hmm, sounds pretty good, doesn't it?) Upon graduation from Le Cordon Bleu, you return home to start your career as a chef. Most novices go to work at a restaurant, but not you! You decide buy a popular French restaurant. What will you pay? If the current owner owns the building, you will pay for that. Obviously, you will pay for the furniture and fittings of the restaurant— stoves, pots and pans, etc. But that's not all. A substantial portion of the purchase price will be "goodwill."

In *McReath v. McReath*,[116] the Wisconsin Supreme Court offered several definitions of goodwill:

---

116 800 N.W.2d 399 (Wis. 2011).

In its broadest sense the intangible asset called good will may be said to be reputation; however, a better description would probably be that element of value which inheres in the fixed and favorable consideration of customers arising from an established and well-conducted business.

The advantage or benefit which is acquired by an establishment beyond the mere value of the capital stock, funds, or property employed therein, in consequence of the general public patronage and encouragement which it receives from constant or habitual customers on account of its local position, or common celebrity, or reputation for skill or affluence, or punctuality, or from other accidental circumstances or necessities, or even from ancient partiality or prejudices.

Goodwill is a business's reputation, patronage, and other intangible assets that are considered when appraising the business, especially for purchase; the ability to earn income in excess of the income that would be expected from the business viewed as a mere collections of assets.

Simply stated, goodwill is an asset of recognized value beyond the tangible assets of a business.[117]

The goodwill of a traditional commercial business (*e.g.*, a laundry) is sometimes relatively simple to value: What would a willing buyer pay for the business, including goodwill?[118] Commercial goodwill is often called enterprise goodwill. Courtney Beebe writes, "Enterprise goodwill attaches to a business entity and is associated separately from the reputation of the owners. Product names, business locations, and skilled labor forces are common examples of enterprise goodwill. The asset has a determinable value because the enterprise goodwill of an ongoing business will transfer upon sale of the business to a willing buyer."[119] To the extent acquired during marriage, enterprise goodwill is marital/community property.

---

117 800 N.W.2d at 408.

118 *See* American Law Institute, *Principles of the Law of Family Dissolution: Analysis and Recommendations,* § 4.07, p. 699 (2000)("Accounting conventions usually ascribe goodwill to a business only when it is sold, at which time it is defined as the difference, if there is any, between the sale price of the business and the value of the business's tangible assets. Standard accounting practice thus gives goodwill a purely operational definition: it is no more (or less) than the amount by which the market value of a going concern exceeds the total value of its tangible assets ('asset value'). If the market value does not exceed the asset value, the business has no goodwill; if it does, it has goodwill in an amount precisely equal to that excess.").

119 Courtney E. Beebe, The Object of My Appraisal: Idaho's Approach to Valuing Goodwill as Community Property in *Chandler v. Chandler,* 39 *Idaho Law Review* 77, 83-84 (2002).

Professionals, including attorneys, accountants, physicians, dentists, engineers, and architects, can acquire goodwill. Is professional goodwill marital/community property? This is a more challenging question than enterprise goodwill. Professional goodwill is tied to an individual. You hire an architect to build your dream home based on the architect's reputation, not simply because the person has a license to practice architecture. It is the style and taste of the individual you want, not just the person's ability to put a roof over your head. Because professional goodwill is so closely linked to a particular professional, what is it worth? For example, if someone is interested in purchasing the architect's business when the architect retires, what is the value of the business's goodwill? The difficulty is that the value of the goodwill is tied to the personal attributes of the architect, and the architect is retiring!

Despite the challenge of valuing professional goodwill, most courts agree professional goodwill can be marital/community property.[120] In *McReath v. McReath*,[121] the Wisconsin Supreme Court wrote, "Originally, it was posited that goodwill did not inhere in professional businesses because professional businesses depend on the skill and reputation of the professional. However, courts and scholars now recognize goodwill in professional businesses."[122]

Some courts divide professional goodwill into two components: personal goodwill and enterprise goodwill.[123] Enterprise goodwill is the goodwill of the professional practice itself. Personal goodwill is unique to the individual.[124] In *May v. May*,[125] the West Virginia Supreme Court wrote: "There is a split of authority on whether enterprise goodwill and/or personal goodwill in a professional practice may be characterized as marital property and thus equitably dis-

---

120   *But see* Von Hohn v. Von Hohn, 260 S.W.3d 631, 638 (Tex. Ct. App. 2008)("Professional goodwill attaches to the person of the professional man or woman as a result of confidence in his or her skill and ability, and would be extinguished in the event of the professional's death, retirement, or disablement. Such professional goodwill is not property in the estate of the parties and, therefore, not divisible upon divorce. To the extent that goodwill exists in the professional practice separate and apart from the professional's personal ability and reputation, that goodwill has a commercial value and is community property subject to division upon divorce.").

121   800 N.W.2d 399 (Wis. 2011).

122   McReath v. McReath, 800 N.W.2d 399, 410 (Wis. 2011).

123   *See* Ahern v. Ahern, 938 A.2d 35, 38 (Me. 2008)("Most jurisdictions embrace a framework that distinguishes between 'enterprise' goodwill and 'personal' goodwill.").

124   *See* Von Hohn v. Von Hohn, 260 S.W.3d 631, 638 (Tex. Ct. App. 2008)("Professional goodwill attaches to the person of the professional man or woman as a result of confidence in his or her skill and ability, and would be extinguished in the event of the professional's death, retirement, or disablement. Such professional goodwill is not property in the estate of the parties and, therefore, not divisible upon to divorce. To the extent that goodwill exists in the professional practice separate and apart from the professional's personal ability and reputation, that goodwill has a commercial value and is community property subject to division upon divorce.").

125   214 W. Va. 394, 589 S.E.2d 536, 545-546 (2003).

tributed. Three different approaches have developed. A large number of courts make no distinction between personal and enterprise goodwill. These jurisdictions have taken the position that both personal and enterprise goodwill in a professional practice constitute marital property. . . . On the other hand, a minority of courts have taken the position that neither personal nor enterprise goodwill in a professional practice constitutes marital property. . . . The majority of states differentiate between enterprise goodwill and personal goodwill. Courts in these states take the position that personal goodwill is not marital property, but that enterprise goodwill is marital property."

The American Law Institute's *Principles of the Law of Family Dissolution* have this to say: "Professional goodwill earned during marriage is marital property to the extent [it has] value apart from the value of spousal earning capacity, spousal skills, or post-dissolution spousal labor."[126]

Do movie stars and professional athletes have goodwill?—celebrity goodwill? What is the value of a name like Serena or Venus Williams, David Beckham, LeBron James, Tiger Woods, Jennifer Lopez, or Michael Schumacher? Many millions to these star entertainers and athletes. But does a celebrity have goodwill that can be valued and divided on divorce? California is home to Hollywood. Given the divorce rate among actors, it is a surprise to learn that the issue of celebrity goodwill did not reach a California appellate court until 2006. In *Marriage of McTiernan and Dubrow*,[127] the California Court of Appeal ruled celebrity goodwill is not property for purposes of divorce. Courts in New Jersey and New York rule celebrity goodwill can be property subject to equitable distribution.[128]

Relationship Between Spousal Support and Property Division: The Problem of Double Dipping

Property division and spousal support serve different yet related purposes.[129] An issue at the intersection of property and support is whether income from property awarded to one spouse on divorce should be considered income for pur-

---

126   American Law Institute, *Principles of the Law of Family Dissolution: Analysis and Recommendations* § 4.07(3), p. 694 (2000).

127   133 Cal. App. 4th 1090, 35 Cal. Rptr. 3d 287 (2005).

128   *See* Piscopo v. Piscopo, 232 N.J. Super. 559, 557 A.2d 1040 (1989); Elkus v. Elkus, 169 A.D.2d 134, 572 N.Y.S.2d 901 (1991).

129   *See* McCaskill v. McCaskill, 2012 WL 1650509 (Ala. Ct. Civil App. 2012)("The issues concerning alimony and the division of property are interrelated . . . ."); Sampson v. Sampson, 62 Mass. App. 366, 816 N.E.2d 999, 1002-1003 (2004).

poses of support.[130] In *Sampson v. Sampson*,[131] the Massachusetts Appeals Court wrote, "Commentators use the phrase 'double dipping' to describe the seeming injustice that occurs when property is awarded to one spouse in an equitable distribution of marital assets and is then also considered as a source of income for purposes of imposing support obligations. Courts and commentators have often disagreed, as to what constitutes double-dipping, whether double-dipping ought to be prohibited as a matter of law, and if not so prohibited, whether it is inequitable in the circumstances of the particular divorce settlement."

Consider Sue and Tom, who were married 20 years. They divorced five years ago. During the marriage, Sue worked for the Acme Company for 15 years, and had a defined benefit pension through Acme. On divorce, the pension, which was marital/community property, was valued at $100,000, and was awarded to Sue. Tom received $50,000 in other marital/community property to equalize the property division. In the divorce, Sue was ordered to pay spousal support to Tom in the amount of $500 per month. Sue recently retired from Acme after twenty years' service and started drawing per pension. Because Sue retired, her income decreased, and Sue filed a motion in family court seeking to eliminate her $500 per month spousal support obligation. In reply, Tom argues that Sue's pension is income, and when her pension income is combined with other income, Sue has enough income to continue paying $500 a month spousal support. Sue argues it would be wrong to count her pension as income because she was awarded the pension in the division of property five years earlier. To count her pension as income now would count the pension twice, once at divorce and again at retirement.

Wisconsin courts have grappled with double counting pension awards.[132] The approach in Wisconsin is to allow the retired spouse to receive the value of the pension assigned to the spouse in the divorce—in Sue's case, $100,000— before the pension is considered income to determine support.[133]

California courts reject the double dipping argument in most scenarios. In *Marriage of White*,[134] for example, husband received his entire pension in the

---

130 *See* Grunfeld v. Grunfeld, 94 N.Y.2d 696, 731 N.E.2d 142, 709 N.Y.S.2d 486 (2000)("The primary issue on appeal in this divorce action is whether the Appellate Division erroneously based both its equitable distribution award of one half the value of defendant's law license and his obligation to pay maintenance on the same projected professional earnings. McSparron v. McSparron, 87 N.Y.2d 275, 286, 639 N.Y.S.2d 265, 662 N.E.2d 745, prescribed a rule against such double counting of income.").

131 62 Mass. App. 366, 816 N.E.2d 999, 1006 (2004).

132 *See* McReath v. McReath, 800 N.W.2d 399 (Wis. 2011).

133 *See* Olski v. Olski, 197 Wis.2d 237, 540 N.W.2d 412 (1995).

134 192 Cal. App. 3d 1022, 237 Cal. Rptr. 764 (1987).

divorce, while wife got the family home. The Court of Appeal ruled it was proper to consider husband's retirement income for purposes of determining spousal support. The court wrote, "'Double counting' of a pension occurs only on those occasions when jurisdiction is reserved over the pension, and it is divided 'in kind' as payments fall due. Then each spouse is, properly speaking, an owner of a portion of those benefits and it would be incorrect to attribute the whole to either spouse for alimony determination purposes. When, however, all marital property division is effected at divorce and one spouse is awarded the entire pension, it is not in any way improper to consider the pension benefits as entirely [the supporting spouse's] income for purposes of alimony determination.'"[135]

The Vermont Supreme Court provides a useful analysis of "double dipping" *Mayville v. Mayville*.

Mayville v. Mayville

Supreme Court of Vermont
189 Vt. 1, 12 A.3d 500 (2010)

Dooley, J.

Husband, William Mayville, who was recently laid off from his job, seeks to terminate the spousal maintenance payable to his ex-wife, Judy Mayville, pursuant to a 2003 court order. After husband filed a motion to terminate spousal maintenance, the Chittenden Family Court issued an order requiring him to pay $3000 per month—the same amount set forth in the 2003 order—until he stopped receiving unemployment compensation benefits and $1500 per month thereafter. Husband appeals from this order, alleging numerous errors. We affirm.

Husband and wife divorced in 2003, after twenty-seven years of marriage. At the time of the divorce, husband earned more than $100,000 per year working as an information technology manager for IBM. Wife is disabled and has never worked. Pursuant to an agreement made between the parties at the time of their divorce and incorporated into a court order, husband was to pay wife $3000 per month in spousal maintenance until he turned sixty-five years old. The 2003 court order granted wife fifty percent of husband's pension, among other assets, with husband retaining the other fifty percent.

Six years later, in April 2009, husband lost his job with IBM through no fault of his own. He was fifty-nine years old on the date he was laid off and had been

---

135   192 Cal. App. 3d at 1027 (quoting Grace Blumberg, Intangible Assets: Recognition and Valuation. In J. McCahey (Ed.), *Valuation and Distribution of Marital Property* 1984.).

with the company since age nineteen—for approximately forty years—working his way into a senior management position despite having only a high school education. He earned $110,000 in 2007 and $126,000 in 2008, including bonuses. Upon being laid off, husband received a severance package that included six months salary—$52,000—plus health benefits. His income for 2009, including his salary, pension, and unemployment compensation benefits, totaled $135,000; in other words, his income actually increased for 2009, the year in which he was laid off.

Husband currently lives with his new wife, who earns approximately $50,000 annually, and his major assets include a home with $136,000 equity in it and a 401(k) account valued at $150,000. Husband has made little effort to seek new employment since being laid off. He plans to retire from work and live off of his $3715 monthly pension and his unemployment compensation benefits until they expire. This plan is possible, in part, because his household expenses are reduced as a result of his new wife's contribution to them.

Wife presently lives off of her spousal maintenance and $1405 a month in Social Security benefits. She has never worked, due to her disabilities, and she incurs significant medical expenses. She was sixty-five years old at the time of the modification hearing.

On April 17, 2009, ten days before his position at IBM ended, husband filed a motion to terminate spousal maintenance with the Chittenden Family Court. . . . The court concluded that there had been no substantial change of circumstances for 2009 in that husband's annual income for that year was actually higher than the income for previous years. The court accordingly ordered husband to pay $3000 in spousal maintenance for November and December 2009. The court further concluded there would be no substantial change of circumstances during the period for which he received unemployment benefits either, as adding up his monthly pension, unemployment payments, imputed income at a minimum wage, full-time job and his wife's contribution to the household income, leaves him close to what he had been earning at the time of the final order. The court did, however, conclude that a substantial change of circumstances would occur once husband's unemployment compensation benefits ended. At that point, the court ordered that husband's maintenance obligation be reduced to $1500 per month, until he reached age sixty-five, when it would terminate completely pursuant to the 2003 court order and agreement between the parties.

Husband argues on appeal that the family court erred in concluding that the loss of his job would not result in a "real, substantial, and unanticipated change of circumstances" until his unemployment compensation benefits ran out. In particular, husband argues that the court erred by . . . considering his pension as a source of income . . . .

Husband . . . argues that the family court improperly considered his pension as a source of income. As a general matter, although pensions may be viewed as marital assets, they may also be considered as a source of income upon which an award of spousal maintenance may be based. Husband maintains, however, that pensions must be considered as either a source of income or a marital asset, but not both. Because the family court divided husband's pension between the two parties at the time of divorce, husband argues that the court erred in taking into account his income from the pension in determining whether to terminate maintenance. In his view, after the termination of unemployment compensation benefits, he must be treated as if he has no income available to pay maintenance.

We note at the outset that we can find no support for husband's theory in the statutes governing maintenance awards or in our general treatment of income-producing assets. The statutes governing maintenance authorize the court to award such amount "as the court deems just" considering "all relevant factors," including the "property apportioned to the obligee," and "the ability of the obligor to meet his or her reasonable needs while meeting those of the spouse seeking maintenance." 15 V.S.A. § 752(b). Nothing in the language suggests income from marital assets cannot be considered in determining ability of the obligor spouse to pay maintenance and the amount of such maintenance. Consistent with the statutory language, we have routinely held that in determining the amount of maintenance, the family court can consider the income available to the obligor from assets distributed as part of the property award. Under our precedents, the issue is simply whether one party has a need for maintenance and whether the other party has the ability to pay maintenance.

We see no obvious rationale for distinguishing pension income from this general rule. A pension is just another type of income-producing asset. Pension income is therefore always an important factor in determining whether alimony should be paid and how much either spouse should receive. Any source of income is material to such a determination. It was proper, then, for the family court to consider husband's portion of his pension as a source of income, for that is his money, and it is therefore a resource that he has from which to pay maintenance.

In reaching this conclusion, we recognize that a majority of courts, but not all, have reached a similar conclusion on this issue. Husband's argument is based on a "double-dipping" theory that has been widely used by litigants and adopted by a small minority of courts. The basic premise of this theory is that it would be inequitable for a party to be able to include the other party's pension income twice for his or her benefit, first for a share of equitable distribution, and second, for inclusion in the other party's cash flow for determination of an alimony base.

We note, however, that some of the courts in the minority hold so because of an explicit controlling statute.

We find nothing inequitable about taking into account the income that husband presently receives from his pension in determining whether to modify the maintenance payable to wife. We agree with the American Law Institute's *Principles of the Law of Family Dissolution*, which concludes that "under prevailing law in which maintenance is largely need-based, the double-dipping concern is unfounded." § 5.04, reporter's notes. Consideration of husband's pension would be improper only to the extent that any portion of the pension assigned to the nonemployee spouse was counted in determining the employee spouse's resources for purposes of maintenance. Such a practice would plainly be inequitable, as it would allocate, for the purposes of determining the obligor's maintenance base, assets that did not in fact belong to the obligor. That is not the situation we have here. Here, the family court considered only the portion of husband's pension that he received after the property division in determining whether he could afford to pay maintenance; the court did not allocate to husband's maintenance base the portion of the pension awarded to wife.

In conclusion, we adhere to the majority rule that in considering the amount of maintenance to award, or whether to modify a maintenance order, the family court may include as income to the obligor any income derived from assets, including a pension, awarded to the obligor in the property distribution. The family court properly applied that rule here.

Affirmed.

Is Your Law Degree Property?

The countless hours and sleepless nights you pour into your legal education will someday translate into a diploma! When you pass the bar, you will get your "ticket," your license. Hooray! If you are married, is your diploma or your license marital/community property? The majority position in the United States is that a degree or license is not property subject to division on divorce.[136] The contrary position was pioneered by the New York Court of Appeals in *O'Brien v. O'Brien*.

---

136 *See* American Law Institute, *Principles of the Law of Family Dissolution: Analysis and Recommendations*, § 4.07(2), p. 694 (2000)("Occupational licenses and educational degrees are not marital property."); Gaskill v. Robbins, 282 S.W.3d 306, 312-313 (Ky. 2009)("This Court has held that an advanced professional degree is not to be treated as marital property because it is personal to the holder and cannot be transferred to another.").

O'Brien v. O'Brien

Court of Appeals of New York
66 N.Y.2d 576, 489 N.E.2d 712, 489 N.Y.S.2d 743 (1985)

Simons, Judge.

In this divorce action, the parties' only asset of any consequence is the husband's newly acquired license to practice medicine. The principal issue presented is whether that license, acquired during their marriage, is marital property subject to equitable distribution . . . . We . . . hold that plaintiff's medical license constitutes "marital property" . . . and that it is therefore subject to equitable distribution pursuant to subdivision . . . .

Plaintiff and defendant married on April 3, 1971. At the time both were employed as teachers at the same private school. Defendant had a bachelor's degree and a temporary teaching certificate but required 18 months of postgraduate classes at an approximate cost of $3,000, excluding living expenses, to obtain permanent certification in New York. She claimed, and the trial court found, that she had relinquished the opportunity to obtain permanent certification while plaintiff pursued his education. At the time of the marriage, plaintiff had completed only three and one-half years of college but shortly afterward he returned to school at night to earn his bachelor's degree and to complete sufficient premedical courses to enter medical school. In September 1973 the parties moved to Guadalajara, Mexico, where plaintiff became a full-time medical student. While he pursued his studies defendant held several teaching and tutorial positions and contributed her earnings to their joint expenses. The parties returned to New York in December 1976 so that plaintiff could complete the last two semesters of medical school and internship training here. After they returned, defendant resumed her former teaching position and she remained in it at the time this action was commenced. Plaintiff was licensed to practice medicine in October 1980. He commenced this action for divorce two months later. At the time of trial, he was a resident in general surgery.

During the marriage both parties contributed to paying the living and educational expenses and they received additional help from both of their families. They disagreed on the amounts of their respective contributions but it is undisputed that in addition to performing household work and managing the family finances defendant was gainfully employed throughout the marriage, that she contributed all of her earnings to their living and educational expenses and that her financial contributions exceeded those of plaintiff. The trial court found that she had contributed 76% of the parties' income exclusive of a $10,000 student loan obtained by defendant. . . .

Defendant presented expert testimony that the present value of plaintiff's medical license was $472,000. Her expert testified that he arrived at this figure by comparing the average income of a college graduate and that of a general surgeon between 1985, when plaintiff's residency would end, and 2012, when he would reach age 65. After considering Federal income taxes, an inflation rate of 10% and a real interest rate of 3% he capitalized the difference in average earnings and reduced the amount to present value. He also gave his opinion that the present value of defendant's contribution to plaintiff's medical education was $103,390. Plaintiff offered no expert testimony on the subject.

The court, after considering the life-style that plaintiff would enjoy from the enhanced earning potential his medical license would bring and defendant's contributions and efforts toward attainment of it, made a distributive award to her of $188,800, representing 40% of the value of the license, and ordered it paid in 11 annual installments of various amounts beginning November 1, 1982 and ending November 1, 1992. The court also directed plaintiff to maintain a life insurance policy on his life for defendant's benefit for the unpaid balance of the award . . . . It did not award defendant maintenance.

A divided Appellate Division concluded that a professional license acquired during marriage is not marital property subject to distribution. . . .

The Equitable Distribution Law contemplates only two classes of property: marital property and separate property. The former, which is subject to equitable distribution, is defined broadly as "all property acquired by either or both spouses during the marriage and before the execution of a separation agreement or the commencement of a matrimonial action, *regardless of the form in which title is held.*" Plaintiff does not contend that his license is excluded from distribution because it is separate property; rather, he claims that it is not property at all but represents a personal attainment in acquiring knowledge. He rests his argument on decisions in similar cases from other jurisdictions and on his view that a license does not satisfy common-law concepts of property. Neither contention is controlling because decisions in other States rely principally on their own statutes, and the legislative history underlying them, and because the New York Legislature deliberately went beyond traditional property concepts when it formulated the Equitable Distribution Law. Instead, our statute recognizes that spouses have an equitable claim to things of value arising out of the marital relationship and classifies them as subject to distribution by focusing on the marital status of the parties at the time of acquisition. Those things acquired during marriage and subject to distribution have been classified as "marital property" although, as one commentator has observed, they hardly fall within the traditional property concepts because there is no common-law property interest remotely resembling marital property. . . .

Marital property encompasses a license to practice medicine to the extent that the license is acquired during marriage. . . . An interest in a profession or professional career potential is marital property which may be represented by direct or indirect contributions of the non-title-holding spouse, including financial contributions and nonfinancial contributions made by caring for the home and family. . . .

The determination that a professional license is marital property is also consistent with the conceptual base upon which the statute rests. As this case demonstrates, few undertakings during a marriage better qualify as the type of joint effort that the statute's economic partnership theory is intended to address than contributions toward one spouse's acquisition of a professional license. Working spouses are often required to contribute substantial income as wage earners, sacrifice their own educational or career goals and opportunities for child rearing, perform the bulk of household duties and responsibilities and forego the acquisition of marital assets that could have been accumulated if the professional spouse had been employed rather than occupied with the study and training necessary to acquire a professional license. In this case, nearly all of the parties' nine-year marriage was devoted to the acquisition of plaintiff's medical license and defendant played a major role in that project. She worked continuously during the marriage and contributed all of her earnings to their joint effort, she sacrificed her own educational and career opportunities, and she traveled with plaintiff to Mexico for three and one-half years while he attended medical school there. The Legislature has decided, by its explicit reference in the statute to the contributions of one spouse to the other's profession or career, that these contributions represent investments in the economic partnership of the marriage and that the product of the parties' joint efforts, the professional license, should be considered marital property. . . .

Plaintiff's principal argument . . . is that a professional license is not marital property because it does not fit within the traditional view of property as something which has an exchange value on the open market and is capable of sale, assignment or transfer. The position does not withstand analysis for at least two reasons. First, as we have observed, it ignores the fact that whether a professional license constitutes marital property is to be judged by the language of the statute which created this new species of property previously unknown at common law or under prior statutes. Thus, whether the license fits within traditional property concepts is of no consequence. Second, it is an overstatement to assert that a professional license could not be considered property even outside the context of section 236(B). A professional license is a valuable property right, reflected in the money, effort and lost opportunity for employment expended in its acquisition, and also in the enhanced earning capacity it affords its holder . . . . That a professional license has no market value is irrelevant. Obviously, a license may not be alienated as may other property and for that reason the working spouse's interest in it is limited. The Legislature has recognized that limitation, however, and has provided for an award in lieu of its actual distribution . . . .

Plaintiff also contends that alternative remedies should be employed, such as an award of rehabilitative maintenance or reimbursement for direct financial contributions. The statute does not expressly authorize retrospective maintenance or rehabilitative awards and we have no occasion to decide in this case whether the authority to do so may ever be implied from its provisions. It is sufficient to observe that normally a working spouse should not be restricted to that relief because to do so frustrates the purposes underlying the Equitable Distribution Law. Limiting a working spouse to a maintenance award, either general or rehabilitative, not only is contrary to the economic partnership concept underlying the statute but also retains the uncertain and inequitable economic ties of dependence that the Legislature sought to extinguish by equitable distribution. Maintenance is subject to termination upon the recipient's remarriage and a working spouse may never receive adequate consideration for his or her contribution and may even be penalized for the decision to remarry if that is the only method of compensating the contribution. . . .

Turning to the question of valuation, it has been suggested that even if a professional license is considered marital property, the working spouse is entitled only to reimbursement of his or her direct financial contributions. . . . If the license is marital property, then the working spouse is entitled to an equitable portion of it, not a return of funds advanced. Its value is the enhanced earning capacity it affords the holder and although fixing the present value of that enhanced earning capacity may present problems, the problems are not insurmountable. Certainly they are no more difficult than computing tort damages for wrongful death or diminished earning capacity resulting from injury and they differ only in degree from the problems presented when valuing a professional practice for purposes of a distributive award, something the courts have not hesitated to do. The trial court retains the flexibility and discretion to structure the distributive award equitably, taking into consideration factors such as the working spouse's need for immediate payment, the licensed spouse's current ability to pay and the income tax consequences of prolonging the period of payment.

If a license is property, what is it worth? In *McSparron v. McSparron*,[137] the New York Court of Appeals wrote, "The value of a newly earned license may be measured by simply comparing the average lifetime income of a college graduate and the average lifetime earnings of a person holding such a license and reducing the difference to its present value. In contrast, where the licensee has already embarked on his or her career and has acquired a history of actual earnings, the foregoing theoretical method must be discarded in favor of a more pragmatic and individualized analysis based on the particular licensee's remaining professional earning potential."

As mentioned earlier, most courts hold a degree/license is not property subject to division on divorce. This is not to say the law makes no provision for a non-licensed spouse who contributed to the degree or license by working and putting the degree holder through school. Several states provide that the court may award rehabilitative or reimbursement alimony. The California Legislature opted for a remedy that allows a non-degree holding spouse to receive reimbursement of expenses incurred to obtain the degree.[138]

Collectibles

People collect just about anything you can imagine: cars, china, baseball cards, stamps, dolls, art, jewelry, jukeboxes, clocks, beer cans, barbed wire (yes, barbed wire; check out *Barbed Wire Collector Magazine*). You name it; people collect it. Some collections are worth millions (consider late-night talk show host Jay Leno's car collection), while others are only of sentimental value. To the extent acquired during marriage, collections are marital/community property. Valuing a collection may require an expert.

Wedding Gifts

On your wedding day, you are not (hopefully) thinking about divorce. The guests arrive bearing gifts—ten pancake makers, five toasters, six waffle irons, etc. Hopefully, some guests give you cash. Suppose the marriage doesn't last.

---

137   87 N.Y.2d 275, 662 N.E.2d 745, 751, 639 N.Y.S.2d 265 (1995).

138   Cal. Family Code § 2641 provides in part: "(b) Upon dissolution of marriage or legal separation of the parties: (1) The community shall be reimbursed for community contributions to education or training of a party that substantially enhances the earning capacity of the party. The amount reimbursed shall be with interest at the legal rate, accruing from the end of the calendar year in which the contributions were made." The judge may adjust the award to achieve fairness. If the degree was earned more than ten years before the divorce, there is a presumption that the community has benefited adequately from the degree. Finally, the law defines "community contributions to education or training" as "payments made with community or quasi-community property for education or training or for the repayment of a loan incurred for education or training . . . ."

Are wedding gifts marital/community property? It depends on the intent of the donor. If Aunt Minnie intended the toaster to belong to you and you alone, it is your separate property. Most of the time, however, there is no clear evidence of donative intent.[139] In *Coppola v. Farina*,[140] the Connecticut Superior Court wrote: "Treatises have stated that if the donor's intent is not clear, there are two basic approaches for classifying wedding gifts. Those two approaches are referred to as the New York rule and the English rule. The New York rule presumes that a wedding gift is intended as a joint gift unless the gift is appropriate for the use of only one spouse or is peculiarly earmarked for one particular spouse. . . . Under the English rule, the donor is presumed to have given the gift to the party to whom he is more closely related."

Engagement Ring

Two people are in love, and one asks, "Will you marry me?" The answer is "yes." They are engaged! A small box emerges from a pocket and is opened to reveal a diamond engagement ring. Unfortunately, the engagement is broken off and the couple does not marry. Does the one who gave the engagement ring have a right to its return, or is the "gift" final? A few states have statutes on point. Courts take differing positions.[141] Many decisions hold that an engagement ring is a "gift in contemplation of marriage."[142] If the marriage does not occur, the gift must be returned. A number of decisions focus on who caused the break up. If the donor was responsible, the donee does not have to return the ring. On the other hand, if the donee was responsible, the gift is revoked. In *Campbell v. Robinson*,[143] the South Carolina Court of Appeals wrote:

> An engagement ring by its very nature is a symbol of the donor's continuing devotion to the donee. Once an engagement is cancelled,

---

139 *See* American Law Institute, *Principles of the Law of Family Dissolution: Analysis and Recommendations* 658 (2000)("Wedding gifts are sometimes said to present a special problem because they are typically received before the marriage. The usual rule classified gifts and premarital acquisitions as separate property, yet one normally assumes that wedding gifts are intended for the couple jointly. The question is whether and under what circumstances this assumption should govern. One line of cases follows an approach, sometimes called the New York rule, that treats wedding gifts as marital unless they are earmarked by the donor for one spouse alone, or consist of an item appropriate for only husband or wife. The competing approach, sometimes called the English rule, treats the source of the gift as dispositive where the donor's intent is ambiguous or uncertain, allocating it to the spouse whose relative or friend provided it.").

140 50 Conn. Supp. 11, 910 A.2d 1011, 1016-1018 (Superior Court 2006).

141 *See* Elaine Marie Tomko, Rights in Respect of Engagement and Courtship Presents When Marriage Does Not Ensue, 44 A.L.R. 5th 1 (1996).

142 *See, e.g.*, Heiman v. Parrish, 262 Kan. 926, 942 P.2d 631 (1997).

143 398 S.C. 12, 726 S.E.2d 221 (Ct. App. 2012).

the ring no longer holds that significance. Thus, if a party presents evidence a ring was given in contemplation of marriage, the ring is an engagement ring. As an engagement ring, the gift is impliedly conditioned upon the marriage taking place. Until the condition underlying the gift is fulfilled, the attempted gift is unenforceable and must be returned to the donor upon the donor's request.

The person challenging the assertions that the ring is an engagement ring and therefore impliedly conditioned upon marriage has the burden of presenting evidence to overcome those assertions. This burden may be satisfied by presenting evidence showing that the ring was not given in contemplation of marriage—it was not an engagement ring—or was not conditioned upon the marriage. If the parties do not dispute that the ring was originally an engagement ring conditioned upon the marriage, the burden may also be satisfied by presenting evidence establishing the ring subsequently became the challenger's property.

Jurisdictions differ on whether ownership of an engagement ring may be based upon fault in the breakup. Courts that do consider fault generally reason that it is unfair for a person to retain the fruit of a broken promise. In contrast, courts with a "no-fault" approach often base their decision upon the abolishment of heart balm actions, adoption of no-fault divorce, desire to limit courtroom dramatics,

and reduction of the difficulty in determining the issue of what constitutes fault in the decline of a relationship.

We hold that the consideration of fault has no place in determining ownership of an engagement ring. Generally, gift law will dictate who has the legal right to the ring.

If a couple marries and later divorces, an engagement ring is generally considered a gift to the donee.[144]

---

144 *See* Randall v. Randall, 56 So.3d 817 (Fla. Ct. App. 2011)

Tax Consequences of Divorce

Family law attorneys consider the tax consequences of divorce. If an attorney is not an expert on tax matters, referral to an accountant or tax attorney may be necessary. The following subsections briefly discuss tax consequences of divorce.

At this writing—2013—domestic partners are not "spouses" or "married persons" under federal tax law. Many state tax codes treat domestic partners and married couples the same.

Property Division

When spouses in an intact marriage transfer property to each other, no gain or loss is recognized for tax purposes (Internal Revenue Code (IRC) § 1041). The transfer is treated as a gift. The spouse receiving the property takes the transferor's basis.

The "no gain or loss" principle extends to divorcing couples. Thus, property transfers between divorcing spouses to accomplish division of property are not taxable events. This is not to say there are no tax consequences of such transfers. The transferee, after all, acquires the property with the transferor's basis, and this can have tax consequences down the line. In his book *The Forensic Accounting Deskbook: A Practical Guide to Financial Investigation and Analysis for Family Lawyers,*[145] Miles Mason writes:

> Never forget about an asset's tax basis. Tax basis is not simple and can be easily overlooked. A capital gain is the difference between the sales price (realization) less its tax basis. For some assets, rules for determining tax basis can be very, very complex. Stock and mutual fund basis calculation is fairly simple—their cost. In the divorce context, consequences can be disastrous if a party ignores built-in capital gains. For example, if one party receives a stock account worth $100,000 in exchange for another asset also worth $100,000, the spouse who ignores tax basis can be at a serious disadvantage. If the tax basis is materially different and the asset received must be sold shortly after the divorce to pay for college or debt caused by the divorce itself, the $100,000 is no longer $100,000 and may be worth significantly less.

---

145   Miles Mason, Sr., *Accounting Deskbook: A Practical Guide to Financial Investigation and Analysis for Family Lawyers*, p. 10 (2011).

Spousal Support

Spousal support (alimony) is deductible by the payor and included in the income of the payee. Two sections of the IRC govern—Sections 71 and 215.

§ 71. Alimony and separate maintenance payments.

(a) General rule. Gross income includes amounts received as alimony or separate maintenance payments.

(b) Alimony or separate maintenance payments defined. For purposes of this section—

  (1) In general. The term "alimony or separate maintenance payment" means any payment in cash if—

    (A) such payment is received by (or on behalf of) a spouse under a divorce or separation instrument,

    (B) the divorce or separation instrument does not designate such payment as a payment which is not includible in gross income under this section and not allowable as a deduction under section 215.

    (C) in the case of an individual legally separated from his spouse under a decree of divorce or of separate maintenance, the payee spouse and the payor spouse are not members of the same household at the time such payment is made, and

    (D) there is no liability to make any such payment for any period after the death of the payee spouse and there is no liability to make any payment (in cash or property) as a substitute for such payments after the death of the payee spouse.

§ 215. Alimony, etc., payments.

(a) General rule. In the case of an individual, there shall be allowed as a deduction an amount equal to the alimony or separate maintenance payments paid during such individual's taxable year.

To qualify for deductibility, alimony payments must be in cash. Payments of property or services do not qualify. Typically, the cash payment goes directly to the payee. Section 71 provides, however, that payments "on behalf of" a payee can qualify. Thus, the payor could make the monthly mortgage payment "on behalf of" the former spouse, and the payment could qualify. When spouses have separated but are not divorced or legally separated, support payments pursuant to a written agreement or court order for support can qualify.

Excess Front Loading of Alimony—Property Division Disguised as Alimony

Wife and Husband are getting divorced. Wife is a high earner. Husband has a lower paying job. Wife agrees to pay Husband $2,000 alimony per month for five years. To achieve an equal division of marital/community/property, Wife must transfer $100,000 to Husband. Property transfers between spouses on divorce are not taxable events. Thus, the $100,000 transfer to Husband is not taxable. At the same time, Wife cannot deduct the transfer. In order to give Wife a tax deduction for the $100,000 property division, the couple agree to characterize the $100,000 as additional alimony so Wife can deduct it. During the first two years of alimony, an extra $4,166 per month is added to the regular alimony payment of $2,000, and Wife deducts the entire $6,166. When the property division is accomplished, alimony drops to the regular amount of $2,000. The IRC has a formula to recapture property divisions masquerading as alimony (§ 71(f)).

Child Support

IRC § 71(c) provides that child support is neither deductible by the payor nor taxable to the payee.

§ 71(c) Payments to support children.

(1) In general. Subsection (a) shall not apply to that part of any payment which the terms of the divorce or separation instrument fix (in terms of an amount of money or a part of the payment) as a sum which is payable for the support of children of the payor spouse.

(2) Treatment of certain reductions related to contingencies involving child. For purposes of paragraph (1), if any amount specified in the instrument will be reduced—

(A) on the happening of a contingency specified in the instrument related to a child (such as a specified age, marrying, dying, leaving school, or a similar contingency), or

(B) at a time which can clearly be associated with a contingency of a kind specified in subparagraph (A), an amount equal to the amount of such reduction will be treated as an amount fixed as payable for the support of children of the payor spouse.

Dependency Exemption

Kids are expensive—very expensive! Fortunately, Uncle Sam gives parents a tax break, a tax exemption for dependent children. (IRC §§ 151(a); 152). The definition of "qualifying child" is complicated. Basically, if you want to claim Junior as a tax exemption, Junior has to live with you more than half time, you have to provide more than half of Junior's support, and Junior has to be under age 19 or a student under age 24.

When parents are divorced, if one parent has primary custody of the children, then the custodial parent is entitled to the dependency exemption. If parents share custody, the parent who has custody more than 50% of the year is entitled to the exemption. The custodial parent can "sign over" the exemption to the other parent in writing.

Filing Status—Head of Household

Taxes for single persons are generally higher than for persons entitled to file as "head of household." A divorced parent who has custody of kids more than half the year may be able to file as head of household.

Bankruptcy and Division of Property

Filing a petition for bankruptcy in U.S. Bankruptcy Court brings with it an automatic stay of other legal proceedings.[146] The automatic stay applies to the property aspects of divorce.[147] The stay does not apply to the divorce itself, actions to establish paternity, child custody or visitation proceedings, proceedings regarding domestic violence, and proceedings to establish or modify "domestic support obligations."[148] The bankruptcy code defines a domestic support obligation as a debt owed to a spouse, former spouse, or child for alimony, maintenance or support.[149] The bankruptcy judge may lift the stay on application of one or both spouses, and, with the stay lifted, the family court can proceed with property issues.

---

146 11 U.S.C. § 362(a).

147 *See* Dudley v. Dudley, 85 So.3d 1043 (Ala. Civ. App. 2011)(violations of the automatic stay are void. A bankruptcy court has authority to lift the automatic stay retroactively, validating actions that would otherwise violate the stay and be void. "When a nonbankruptcy court, however, issues an order in violation of the stay, that order is invalid, absent the bankruptcy court's retroactive approval of the order. A state court's action in a divorce proceeding taken in violation of the stay can be annulled and retroactively cured only by the bankruptcy court.").

148 11 U.S.C. § 362(b).

149 11 U.S.C. § 101(14A).

Awards of spousal and child support—domestic support obligations—are not dischargeable in bankruptcy. To qualify as a domestic support obligation, an obligation must be "in the nature of alimony, maintenance, or support . . . of [a] spouse, former spouse, or child of the debtor . . . ."[150] The bankruptcy court in *In re Swartz*[151] wrote, "In determining whether a debt is in the nature of alimony, maintenance, or child support, the crucial issue is the function the award was intended to serve." In *In re Nolan*,[152] the court explained, "Factors evaluated by courts in discerning an award's intended function include: whether the dissolution decree contains a separate provision for child or spousal support; whether the obligation is owned in a lump sum or in periodic payments; whether the obligation is conditional; the parties' relative financial conditions and employment histories; and whether a former spouse and children would have difficulty subsisting without the payments."

Debts created as part of a property division are generally not dischargeable in Chapter 7 proceedings. Such debts may be dischargeable in Chapter 13 proceedings.

The following case from the Texas Court of Appeals illustrates how bankruptcy proceedings interact with divorce litigation. The case also presents a useful review of some basic principles of marital property law.

Dickinson v. Dickinson

Court of Appeals of Texas
324 S.W.3d 653 (2010)

Livingston, Chief Justice.

Appellant Larry Dickinson appeals from the property division in a final divorce decree. . . . Appellant contends that the trial court erred by (1) divesting him of his separate property remainder interest in California real property, and (2) issuing a final decree that goes beyond the trial court's limited authority, granted by the United States Bankruptcy Court, to make a property division during the pendency of appellant's Chapter 13 bankruptcy. We affirm in part and reverse and remand in part.

---

150 11 U.S.C. § 101(14A)(B).

151 339 B.R. 497 (W.D. Mo. 2006).

152 2010 WL 3926870 (Bankruptcy D. Minn. 2010).

After filing for divorce, appellant filed a chapter 13 bankruptcy petition in the United States Bankruptcy Court for the Eastern District of Texas. The Bankruptcy Court ordered that the automatic stay be modified to allow the divorce to be finalized with respect to matters concerning "child support, custody, visitation and use of property." The order further directed the trial court "to make recommendations to the Bankruptcy Court regarding child support and the division of community property."

On August 20, 2004, a final hearing was held before the Honorable David Cleveland . . . . The parties had only personal property to divide, with the exception of appellant, who is a co-beneficiary of a trust set up by his father before his death (the Trust). The evidence at trial showed that the corpus of the Trust consists of real property located in California. Dorothy M. Cawley has a life estate in this real property; upon her death or voluntary vacancy of the property, the trustee of the Trust must distribute the property in equal fifty percent shares to appellant and his sister. If appellant dies before Cawley's life estate terminates, his share must be distributed to his sister or her issue as defined in the Trust.

On November 10, 2004, the trial court signed a decree granting the divorce and finding appellant at fault in the dissolution of the marriage. The trial court awarded appellee $500 per month in spousal support for twenty-four months, sixty percent of appellants future military pension benefits, and half of his military pension benefits that had been paid in the eighteen months before the decree was signed. The trial court recommended to the Bankruptcy Court that the parties community property be divided as follows: (1) each party would receive the personal property, bank accounts, and automobiles in his or her possession with the exception of the firearms, which were to be delivered to appellant, and the coin collection and dishes, which were to be delivered to appellee; (2) appellee would receive half of the value of the Harley Davidson motorcycle; (3) appellee would receive half of appellant's remainder interest in the real property in California; and (4) appellee would receive attorneys fees of $5,000 from appellant.

. . . Appellant filed a timely notice of appeal, but in an order dated December 6, 2005, we suspended the appeal because the bankruptcy was still pending and the Bankruptcy Court had not lifted the automatic stay for appeal. We reinstated this appeal on February 26, 2010 on appellant's motion to reinstate, which indicated that the bankruptcy has been discharged.

We first address [whether] the trial court did not have jurisdiction to effect a property division because the Bankruptcy Court's order lifting the stay allowed the trial court only to make recommendations to the Bankruptcy Court . . . .

The filing of a bankruptcy petition triggers the automatic stay under the bankruptcy code. 11 U.S.C.A. § 362(a)(1). The automatic stay deprives state courts of jurisdiction over proceedings against the debtor, and any action taken against the debtor while the stay is in place is void and without legal effect. This is true regardless of whether a party or the state court learns of the stay before taking action against the debtor. We strictly construe an order modifying the automatic stay.

Here, the Bankruptcy Court lifted the stay so that the trial court could finalize matters regarding the "use of property" but also so that it could make "recommendations" regarding the property division. The trial court stated at the end of the prove-up that the "property division is a recommendation" to the Bankruptcy Court, and the decree states, immediately before listing the property to be divided, that "the Court therefore makes the following recommendation to the Bankruptcy Court regarding the division of the property of the parties." Thus, the trial court made clear that its property division was a recommendation to the Bankruptcy Court in accordance with that court's order. Because the order lifting the stay specifically stated that the trial court was to make recommendations regarding the property division, the trial court's property division in the decree did not violate the stay; therefore, it is not void.

Appellant contends that the trial court erred by divesting him of his separate property remainder interest in the real property in California.

The trial court must divide the parties estate in a just and right manner, having due regard for each party's rights. Tex. Fam.Code Ann. § 7.001. . . . Only community property may be divided, however; a court may not divest a party of his or her separate property.

Property possessed by either spouse during or on the dissolution of the marriage is presumed to be community property. Whether property is community or separate is determined by the facts that give the property its character, and the party who asserts that property is his or her separate property must prove its separate character with clear and convincing evidence.

To overcome the presumption of community property, the burden is on the spouse claiming certain property as separate to trace and clearly identify the claimed separate property. Tracing involves using evidence showing the time and means by which the spouse originally obtained possession of the property to establish the separate origin of the property and how the spouse claimed the asset. The characterization of property is determined by the inception of title to the property. Inception of title occurs when a party first has a right of claim to the property by virtue of which title is finally vested.

The Texas constitution provides that property a spouse acquires after marriage by gift or devise is that spouse's separate property.

The evidence at trial showed that appellant's father was the settlor, trustee, and initial beneficiary of the Trust, which was fully revocable before his death. But when appellant's father died, Cawley's life estate vested, as did appellant's and his sister's remainder interests. Thus, appellant's remainder interest in the real property Trust corpus was obtained by devise.

Appellee contends that the economic interest in the increase in value of the Trust corpus constitutes community property. Generally, when separate property produces income that is acquired by a spouse, the income is community property. However, an increase in value of an item of separate property is an inherent part of the item, which cannot be separated from it. There was no evidence that appellant was entitled to receive, or that he did receive, any income from the Trust during the marriage; his only interest is the remainder interest in the real property, which he was not entitled to until his father's death and which was subject to Cawley's life estate. Rather, appellant's interest in the real property is separate property obtained by devise; thus, the property's increase in value cannot be separated from the property itself for purposes of dividing the marital estate.

Accordingly, appellant showed by clear and convincing evidence that his remainder interest in the Trust corpus was obtained by devise and is, thus, separate property that the trial court was not entitled to award to appellee. The trial court abused its discretion by mischaracterizing appellant's remainder interest as community property and awarding an interest in part of the real property to appellee.

We affirm the part of the trial court's judgment granting the divorce.

Are Pets Property?

Sue and Sam are divorcing. For the three years prior to divorce, Sue and Sam enjoyed the companionship of their two miniature dachshunds, Bindy and Chibby. Sue and Sam dearly love Bindy and Chibby, and the dogs are very attached to their owners and each other. In the divorce, Sue and Sam cannot agree on who should get the dogs. In a divorce case, are family pets property subject to division under principles of marital property law? Or are pets akin to children, which means the judge should apply a "best interests of the dog" test?

Courts traditionally have treated pets as property.[153] Three articles on pets and divorce are excerpted below.

Puppy Love: Providing for the Legal Protection of Animals When Their Owners Get Divorced

Heidi Stroh
2 *Journal of Animal Law and Ethics* 231 (2007)

Each year, at least one of every two marriages in the United States will end in divorce. Of those couples who get divorced, 39% own at least one dog and 34% have at least one cat, the most common domestic animal. Whether acting out of spite or because of their deep attachment to their beloved pets, divorcing couples often become involved in bitter disputes when deciding who will take the animals after the separation.

Recognizing that pets require protection beyond that extended by property law, Congress and the states have enacted anti-cruelty laws to ensure that animals kept as pets are treated humanely. Nevertheless, many courts across the nation base their decisions in custody disputes over animals in divorce proceedings on the principles of property law, while others consider the best interests of the pet when making such determinations. . . .

When judges must decide which spouse should retain custody of the couple's domestic animals during the divorce proceedings, they most commonly look to existing property law to guide their decision.

Typically, the utilization of property law as a framework for resolving these kinds of disputes arises from the pet's lack of human characteristics and is reinforced by the impracticability of overseeing and enforcing pet custody arrangements that the application of the "best interest of the pet" standard would entail. . . .

As many courts have acknowledged, the unfortunate side-effect of treating pets like property may be that the court's decision is not in the best interests of the pet. . . .

According to animal behaviorists, considering the psychological effect that ownership decisions will have on domestic animals is consistent with established

---

153   *See* Eric Kotloff (Note), All Dogs Go To Heaven . . . Or Divorce Court: New Jersey Un"Leashes" a Subjective Value Consideration to Resolve Pet Custody Litigation in Houseman v. Dare, 55 *Villanova Law Review* 447 (2010).

scientific principles. These experts have long known that dissension between owners can be very distressing to their pets. . . .

In addition, unlike inanimate property, pets are capable of possessing such admirable characteristics as fidelity, bravery, trust, love, and playfulness. . . .

In light of the capacity of animals to perceive, respond to, and return love and affection, courts have long recognized the tragedy inherent in awarding ownership of a pet to a party other than the one with whom the pet has formed a loving relationship. Consequently, some courts have taken a strong stance against basing pet ownership decisions on property law principles, preferring a more humane approach, which would take into account the effect of their decision on the mental and emotional health of the pet. . . .

When the welfare of the pet, including its psychological needs is not considered, the subsequent heartbreak felt by pets and owners alike is neither negligible nor harmless. Nevertheless, despite their expressions of remorse, many courts have claimed to be bound by property law principles in order to award pet ownership strictly on the basis of legal title, remaining indifferent to the negative impact their decisions might have on the psychological well-being of the animal at the heart of the dispute. . . .

Like many children, pets often have complex needs that they are unable to express. Unlike a favorite chair or pair of shoes, animals possess intelligence and sensitivity, and they are capable of enjoying and returning their owners' love. Conversely, when such love is absent or their needs are otherwise not being met, domestic animals may suffer tremendously. Obviously, the law does not consider children to be personal property; instead, it seeks to protect and shelter them in divorce actions that involve custody disputes. . . . Pets, on the other hand, often receive no such consideration when married couples seek divorce. They are frequently treated as if they are nothing more than property and therefore, by implication, no more than objects, devoid of interests that should be protected. Unfortunately, the reality is that, much like children, animals do have needs to consider, though they lack the voice to express them. . . .

Like children, the raising and maintenance of domestic animals implicates issues of care, protection, training, and personal, mutual relationships. No inanimate object or non-animal living organism can lay claim to all of these concerns. Thus, animals kept as pets are far more similar in needs to human children than they are to items of personal property, though they can be appropriately classified as neither. For this reason, new legislation must be drafted that recognizes the unique place of animals in relation to their owners.

Under a new "Uniform Domestic Animal Jurisdiction Act," courts would be empowered to hear cases relating to the custody, visitation, and support of pets. Because such proceedings would be commenced in their own right, apart from divorce actions, courts would be relieved from applying indifferent and morally questionable property law principles to pets. . . . While enacting such legislation would expand the jurisdiction of courts that are already overwhelmed, this statute would arguably contribute to the more efficient resolution of divorce proceedings by empowering courts to consider pet custody in isolation. . . .

Pursuant to the provisions of a new "Uniform Domestic Animal Custody Act," courts presiding over animal custody proceedings should consider any factor relevant to making a determination, including: (1) the wishes of the animal's owner or owners as to its custody; (2) any documented preference exhibited by the animal; (3) the interaction and interrelationship of the animal with the owners or any other person or animal who may significantly affect its best interest; (4) the prior and anticipated physical care and treatment of the animal, including the suitability of the prospective home environment in light of the animal's specific characteristics; (5) the prior and future training or use of the animal; (6) the geographic proximity of the individuals involved; (7) and the prior mental and physical health of the animal (including a consideration of the age and anticipated life span of the animal) and all other individuals involved.

In considering what is in the best interest of domestic animals and their owners, courts should, at a minimum, construe the above factors liberally. Where factors such as the prior or prospective medical or psychological condition of the animal are unclear, courts should look to professionals in animal behavior, care, and treatment for guidance. In addition, to ensure that pet custody awards receive due consideration, courts should not hesitate to expand these factors in response to the specific case before them.

An Animal is Not an iPod

Diane Sullivan and Holly Vietzke
6 Journal of Animal Law 41 (2008)

Those of us who teach animal law know one pervasive theme that resonates throughout our courses: American society's classification of animals as property, worth nothing more than a piece of merchandise—and a low-priced one at that. That treatment inevitably leads to the most basic question of how a society as great as ours can equate life—any life, much less man's best friend—with a piece of furniture or even the latest iPod. Our animal law textbooks are replete with decision after decision that makes all too clear that the law does nothing to genuinely protect animals, nor does it recognize their true value and special place in our homes and within our families. Our legal system just does not recognize the bond between people and their companion animals . . . .

Because animals are property, often divorce courts are left in the difficult position of who gets custody to be resolved typically on the basis of 'title to the property' as opposed to the best interest of the pet. Accordingly, courts generally lack the authority to grant visitation to property. In *Bennett v. Bennett*, [655 So.2d 109, 110-111 (Fla. Ct. App. 1995)] the court said, "Our courts are overwhelmed with the supervision of custody, visitation, and support matters related to the protection of our children. We cannot undertake the same responsibility for animals." This holding was despite the fact that the court also noted that many consider a dog to be a member of the family. In Maryland, however, one circuit court did uphold and enforce a divorce settlement agreement that granted one spouse visitation of the couple's dog for one month each summer. Two other courts even considered the pet's best interest. In *Raymond v. Lachman*, [695 N.Y.S.2d 308, 309 (App. Div. 1999)], the New York appeals court explained, "We think it best for all concerned that, given his limited life expectancy, Lovey, who is now almost ten years old, remain where he has lived, prospered, loved and been loved for the past four years." *Zovko v. Gregory*, [trial court decision], a Virginia case, involved roommates who shared the costs and responsibility of a cat. When the roommates parted ways, one of them took the cat, and the other charged him with theft. After a trial to determine who was the better caretaker, the court decided the cat "would be better off with Mr. Zovko."

The issues of custody and visitation are arising more and more frequently these days, and if the law begins to recognize animals as more than personal property, the "best interest" standard may eventually become the rule.

Pet Custody: Distorting Language and the Law

John DeWitt Gregory
44 *Family Law Quarterly* 35 (2010)

Pets or companion animals are the property of those who own them. In this article, I shall show that pets that are the subject of disputes between divorcing spouses or separating unmarried couples should continue to be characterized as property under a rational legal system. Proposals in the law review literature and halting, early attempts by some courts to place pets in some category other than property, which flirted with a standard derived from the prevailing best-interest-of-the-child doctrine in conventional child custody and visitation cases, are, at best, vanity. . . .

Matrimonial and family lawyers and, certainly, divorce courts should eschew the language and doctrines of child custody and visitation when addressing the treatment of companion animals. Rather, judges and lawyers should recognize and deal directly with the relevant issue and the legal task at hand in so-called "pet custody" litigation, namely, reaching a fair decision in cases that involve the equitable distribution of property at divorce. . . .

While published judicial decisions in pet custody cases are far from legion, when judges have exercised discretion in disputes over pets between unmarried persons or applied controlling equitable distribution principles in divorce proceedings where these animals are a subject of contention, the outcomes appear to be fair and the reasoning persuasive. To put it another way, there is nothing in the published decisions to suggest that the animals in issue would be better off if the law permitted courts to reject established property law principles and to adopt some doctrine of "best interest of the dog." . . .

Legal academic commentators, purporting to advocate for the interests and welfare of animals, typically argue that in divorce and separation cases in which each of the parties seeks to keep or maintain some contact with a pet that a couple shared during their relationship, courts should base their decisions on the best interest of the animal. This standard is, as the commentators acknowledge, taken directly from the long-standing family law doctrine of best interest of the child, which generally is the prevailing standard in contested cases involving child custody and visitation. . . .

It is not clear why a legal regime that emphasizes the so-called best interest of pets is even desirable . . . . The best interests approach for animals has not enjoyed significant approval or frequent application from courts. Accordingly, I believe that this failure of judges to accept the idea that best interest of the pet should be the prevailing standard in divorce cases involving pets is not regrettable in the least. . . .

The most up-to-date scientific research relating to the behavioral development of companion animals, for the most part dogs, does not appear to provide support for current academic challenges to their characterization as property in divorce proceedings and separations, or to the related quest for a "best interest of the dog" standard in these cases. . . .

As common as human declarations of love for companion animals me be, scientific behavioral research, if it addresses the issue at all, does not engender any confidence in the claim that these animals provide love in return. . . .

Courts are well equipped to make fair decisions under current law, and decisions to date suggest that they have done so.

Consider the position taken by the Florida Court of Appeal in *Bennett v. Bennett.* Do you concur?

Bennett v. Bennett

Court of Appeal of Florida
655 So.2d 109 (1995)

Wolf, Judge.

Husband, Ronald Greg Bennett, appeals from a final judgment of dissolution of marriage which, among other things, awarded custody of the parties' dog, "Roddy." The husband asserts that (1) the trial court erred in awarding the former wife visitation with the parties' dog, and (2) the trial court erred in modifying the final judgment to increase the former wife's visitation rights with the dog. We find that the trial court lacked authority to order visitation with personal property; the dog would properly be dealt with through the equitable distribution process.

A brief recitation of the procedural history will demonstrate the morass a trial court may find itself in by extending the right of visitation to personal property. The parties stipulated to all issues in the final judgment of dissolution of marriage except which party would receive possession of the parties' dog, "Roddy." After a hearing, the trial court found that the husband should have possession of the dog and that the wife should be able to take the dog for visitation every other weekend and every other Christmas.

The former husband contested this decision and filed a motion for rehearing alleging that the dog was a premarital asset. He also filed a motion for relief from final judgment and an amended motion for rehearing. The wife replied and filed a motion to strike former husband's amended motion for rehearing and a motion for contempt. The former wife requested that the trial court transfer custody of the dog because the former husband was refusing to comply with the trial court's order concerning visitation with the dog.

A hearing on these motions was held on September 27, 1993. The wife's counsel filed an ore tenus motion requesting the trial court to change custody, or in the alternative, change visitation. The trial court denied the former husband's motion for rehearing and granted the former wife's ore tenus motion to change visitation. Thus, the trial court's ruling on visitation now reads:

Dog, Roddy: The former Husband, RONALD GREGORY BENNETT, shall have custody of the parties' dog "Roddy" and the former Wife, KATHRYN R. BENNETT n/k/a KATHRYN R. ROGERS shall have visitation every other month beginning October 1, 1993. The visitation shall begin on the first day of the month and end on the last day of the month.

Based on the history of this case, there is every reason to believe that there will be continued squabbling between the parties concerning the dog.

While a dog may be considered by many to be a member of the family, under Florida law, animals are considered to be personal property. There is no authority which provides for a trial court to grant custody or visitation pertaining to personal property.

While several states have given family pets special status within dissolution proceedings, we think such a course is unwise. Determinations as to custody and visitation lead to continuing enforcement and supervision problems (as evidenced by the proceedings in the instant case). Our courts are overwhelmed with the supervision of custody, visitation, and support matters related to the protection of our children. We cannot undertake the same responsibility as to animals.

While the trial judge was endeavoring to reach a fair solution under difficult circumstances, we must reverse the order relating to the custody of "Roddy," and remand for the trial court to award the animal pursuant to the dictates of the equitable distribution statute.

A Problem

Farah and Irfan are citizens of Pakistan. They married in Pakistan pursuant to an arrangement between their families. On their wedding day, Farah was 18 and Irfan was 29. In accordance with Pakistani custom, on their wedding day, they signed a written marriage contract. The contract provided a dower of 51,00 rupees, payment of which was deferred. The contract did not contain any provisions regarding marital property. Under Pakistan law, unless a contract provides otherwise, upon divorce, all property owned by the husband on the date of the divorce remains his property, and all property owned by the wife remains hers. Shortly following marriage, the couple moved to England, where Irfan completed his Ph.D. at Oxford. They then moved to the United States, where Irfan began work at the World Bank. The couple lived nearly 20 years in the United States on diplomatic visas. Recently, Farah filed for divorce. While the divorce was pending, Irfan went to the Pakistan embassy and performed talaq (divorce under Islamic religious law and Pakistan secular law). At the embassy, Irfan executed a talaq that stated: "Now this deed witnesses that I, the said Irfan, do hereby divorce, Farah, daughter of Mahmood, by pronouncing upon her Divorce/Talaq three times irrevocably and severing all connections of husband and wife with her forever and for good. (1) I Divorce thee Farah, (2) I Divorce thee Farah, (3) I Divorce thee Farah." In the state court divorce action, Irfan argues that the talaq means he is divorced under the law of Pakistan, and that Pakistani law must be applied. Irfan emphasizes that nothing in the marriage contract alters Pakistani law. At the time of the divorce, Irfan's pension at the World Bank is valued at one million dollars. The couple owns a home valued at $850,000, title to which is in Irfan's name. Irfan argues that the state court is bound by Pakistan law, and lacks jurisdiction to characterize or divide the pension or the home. Does the state court have authority to characterize and divide the pension and the marital home? Or must the state recognize and enforce the talaq? *Aleem v. Aleem,* 404 Md. 404, 947 A.2d 489 (2008).

C

Practice Exercise: Who Gets the Goat?

Afiya and Bello met while both were Ph.D. students in archeology working on a dig in the Middle East. They married 15 years ago. After completing their doctorates, both became professors of archiology at a prestigious American university. Ten years ago, Bello purchased a small gold goat. The goat is approximately 2,000 years old and was excavated from a site in Syria. It is worth $10,000. The goat is in a glass case in Afiya and Bello's home. Both are very fond of it. It is their most prized possession. Afiya and Bello own their home. They paid the last mortgage payment last year. The home is worth $450,000. Their home is close to the university, so they don't need or own cars. They ride bikes to work. They are often abroad months at a time on archeological digs. Both have defined benefit pensions with the university. Their pensions are of equal value. In addition to the golden goat, they own other historical artefacts with a total value of $50,000. Unfortunately, Afiya and Bello are divorcing. They cannot agree on the goat. Both want it, and neither seems willing to budge. The goat is the only thing holding up the divorce. They agree to sell the home and divide the profit. They also agree on how to divide the historical artefacts. They agree they each will keep their own pension.

Assignment: Break into groups of four. One of you is Afiya's attorney. The other represents Bello. If you are not an attorney, pretend to be Afiya or Bello. You are a famous professor of archiology! Be Indiana Jones, if you like. A meeting is planned at which the lawyers will try to help the parties come to an agreement about the goat. Before the meeting, meet privately with your client and discuss their wishes about how to divide the property, including the goat. Then have the meeting to resolve the goat issue.

CHAPTER 10

Annulment

ANNULMENT ENDS MARRIAGE, and is an alternative to divorce. Why do some people prefer annulment to divorce? Historically, complete divorce (*a vinculo matrimoni*) was unavailable and annulment was the only way to terminate an unhappy marriage. Today, no-fault divorce is available. Yet, some people still prefer annulment because they can say with a straight face that in the eyes of the law they were never married, and, thus, never divorced. (*See* "relation-back" doctrine, *infra*). Some people have religious reasons to prefer annulment. In the relatively recent past, divorce was socially stigmatizing. Eyebrows rose when a woman was a "divorcee." Today, divorce is practically normative in the United States, and the stigma is disappearing.

In the twenty-first century, most unhappy couples divorce. If you practice family law, clients will ask about annulment, but few will pursue it.

Annulment is available only if grounds for annulment existed *on the day* a couple married. That is, from the very outset, there was a defect in the marriage that rendered it subject to annulment. The person seeking annulment must prove that the defect existed at the time of the marriage. Defects arising *after* a couple marries are not grounds for annulment, although they may be grounds for divorce. Unlike annulment, grounds for which exist on the wedding day, grounds for divorce arise *later*, often years later.

Marriages subject to annulment are void or voidable. Incestuous and bigamous marriages are void. A void marriage is void from the beginning—void *ab initio*. Joel Bishop, the nineteenth century authority on family law, put it this way: "A marriage is termed void when it is good for no legal purpose, and its invalidity may be maintained in any proceedings, in any court, between any parties, whether in the lifetime or after the death of the supposed husband and wife, and whether the question arises directly or collaterally."[1] As Bishop mentioned, void marriages can be annulled during the lifetimes of the couple, and can be challenged after one or both spouses has died.

Because a void marriage was never really a marriage, it is technically not necessary to bring an annulment action—there is nothing to annul; it was void *ab initio*.[2] Yet, void marriages may last years, and it is useful to bring a nullity proceeding (or a divorce) so the court can clarify the parties' marital status and adjudicate issues pertaining to children and property.

A voidable marriage is a valid marriage unless it is annulled.[3] Leaning again on Bishop: "A marriage is voidable when in its constitution there is an imperfection which can be inquired into only during the lives of both of the parties, in a proceeding to obtain a sentence declaring it null. Until set aside, it is practically valid . . . ."[4] Thus, a voidable marriage can only be annulled during the lifetime of the parties.[5] Once one spouse dies, the voidable marriage is immune from attack.

Grounds for Annulment

What are grounds for annulment?[6] As stated above, incestuous and bigamous marriages are void.[7] Incestuous marriage is marriage between parents and

---

1   Joel P. Bishop, *New Commentaries on Marriage, Divorce, and Separation*, vol. 1, § 258, p. 107 (1891).

2   *See* Marriage of Seaton, 200 Cal. App. 4th 800, 133 Cal. Rptr. 3d 50 (2011)("In California, a void marriage is invalid for all purposes from the moment of its inception, whether or not it has been so declared in a court of law, and its invalidity may be shown collaterally in any proceeding in which the fact of marriage may be material. . . . There is a fundamental difference between a judgment of dissolution and a judgment of nullity. While a judgment of dissolution terminates a valid marriage, a judgment of nullity declares that the marriage was void from its inception.").

See also Nev. Rev. Stat. § 125-290 (a marriage is "void without any decree of divorce or annulment or other legal proceedings" when either spouse has a "former husband or wife then living.").

3   *See* Marriage of Seaton, 200 Cal. App. 4th 800, 133 Cal. Rptr. 3d 50 (2011)("a voidable marriage is valid for all purposes until it is judicially declared a nullity, and may only be challenged by a party entitled by statute to assert its voidability.").

4   Joel P. Bishop, *New Commentaries on Marriage, Divorce, and Separation*, vol. 1, § 259, p. 107-108 (1891).

5   *See* Ponder v. Graham, 4 Fla. 23 (1851).

6   *See, e.g.*, Rev. Code. Wash. Ann. § 26.04.130 (on voidable marriages: "When either party to a marriage shall be incapable of consenting thereto, for want of legal age or a sufficient understanding, or when the consent of either party shall be obtained by force or fraud, such marriage is voidable, but only at the suit of the party laboring under the disability, or upon whom the force or fraud is imposed.").

7   *See* Marriage of Seaton, 200 Cal. App. 4th 800, 133 Cal. Rptr. 3d 50 (2011)("A bigamous marriage is void from the beginning.").

children, ancestors and descendants, brothers and sisters, and aunts and nephews and uncles and nieces.[8]

Bigamous marriage occurs when a married person marries a second time while the first marriage continues.[9] As stated by the Texas Court of Appeals, "A marriage is void if it is entered into when either party to the marriage has an existing marriage to another person that has not been dissolved by legal action or terminated by the death of the other spouse."[10]

When a person has been married more than once, the law presumes the most recent marriage is valid.[11] The Texas Court of Appeal discusses this presumption in *Nguyen v. Nguyen*:[12]

> When two or more marriages of a person to different spouses are alleged, we presume that the most recent marriage is valid against each marriage that precedes it, until one who asserts the validity of a previous marriage proves its validity. This presumption is one of the strongest known to law; it is, in itself, evidence; and it may even outweigh positive evidence to the contrary. The presumption's strength increases with the lapse of time, acknowledgments by the parties to the marriage, and the birth of children. . . .
>
> The party attacking the validity of the subsequent marriage must also introduce sufficient evidence, standing alone, to negate the dissolution of the previous marriage. To rebut the presumption, the proponent of the earlier marriage must prove that (1) the first spouse was alive at the time the husband married the second wife; (2) the husband never secured a divorce or annulment from the first wife; and (3) the first wife never secured a divorce or annulment from the husband.

---

8   *See* Cal. Family Code § 2200.

9   *See* Cal. Family Code § 2201; Tex. Family Code § 6.202(a); Rev. Code. Wash. Ann. § 26.04.020(1)(a).

See also Marriage of Seaton, 200 Cal. App. 4th 800, 133 Cal. Rptr. 3d 50 (2011)("Generally, a bigamous marriage is illegal and void from the beginning where the form marriage has not be dissolved or adjudged a nullity before the date of the subsequent marriage.").

10   Nguyen v. Nguyen, 355 S.W.3d 82 (Tex. Ct. App. 2011).

11   *See* Mack v. Brown, 82 A.D.3d 133, 141, 919 N.Y.S.2d 166 (2011)("Where, as here, two competing putative spouses come forward with proof of their respective marriages, there is a presumption that the second marriage is valid and that the prior marriage was dissolved by death, divorce, or annulment."); Nguyen v. Nguyen, 355 S.W.3d 82 (Tex. Ct. App. 2011).

12   355 S.W.3d 82 (Tex. Ct. App. 2011).

The following "defects" render marriage voidable: (1) The party seeking annulment was too young to consent to marriage.[13] (2) Either spouse was of unsound mind on the wedding day, thus lacking capacity to enter the marriage contract. (3) Consent to marry was obtained by fraud. Not just any old fraud will do. The fraud that suffices for annulment is discussed in *Marriage of Ramirez*, below. (4) Consent was obtained by force (so-called "shotgun wedding"). (5) Either party was, at the time of the marriage, physically incapable of entering into the marriage state.

Today, in the era of no-fault divorce, there are no viable defenses to divorce. If one spouse wants a divorce, the other spouse can't stop it. The divorce-seeker alleges irreconcilable differences or a similar ground for no-fault divorce, and the judge will not second guess the grounds. Not so with annulment. To obtain annulment, the moving party must plead and prove that a specific ground for annulment existed on the wedding day.[14] Failure to carry the burden of proof means the judge denies annulment. The party can get a divorce, but not an annulment.

In *Marriage of Ramirez*, the California Court of Appeal analyzes the type of fraud that justifies annulling a marriage.

Marriage of Ramirez

California Court of Appeal
165 Cal. App. 4th 751, 81 Cal. Rptr. 3d 180 (2008)

Ramirez, P.J.

Jorge L. Ramirez (Jorge) appeals from a judgment annulling his second marriage to Lilia Llamas (Lilia), following a bifurcated trial in which the court found the marriage void due to fraud. The trial court found the first marriage between Jorge and Lilia was a void attempt at a Mexican marriage performed in California. It found the second marriage void because of fraud, relating to the fact Jorge married Lilia even though he had begun a love affair with Lilia's sister prior to the second marriage, that he intended to continue even after the remarriage to Lilia. Jorge appeals the judgment of nullity, and the finding that Lilia was a putative spouse. We affirm.

---

13 Washington State law provides, "Every marriage entered into in which either the husband or the wife has not attained the age of seventeen years is void except where this section has been waived by a superior court judge of the county in which one of the parties resides on a showing of necessity."). Rev. Code. Wash. Ann. § 26.04.010(2).

14 *See* Stuhr v. Oliver, 363 S.W.3d 316 (Ark. 2010)(marriage "may be annulled only for causes set forth by statute.").

Jorge, an immigrant from the State of Michoacán, Mexico, lived in the United States and sought legal residence here. . . .

In 1999, Jorge and Lilia were married in a religious ceremony in Moreno Valley, California. The ceremony was performed by a priest or other official from the State of Jalisco, Mexico, and an "Acta de Matrimonia" was issued. No marriage license was issued by the State of California. In 2001, Jorge and Lilia became aware that the 1999 marriage was invalid because Lilia's prior divorce had not been final for 300 days prior to the marriage. Additionally, because it was made to look as though the parties were married in Mexico, the Mexican marriage certificate would prevent Jorge from getting his green card because it would make it appear that he had not been in continuous residence in the United States.

The parties were remarried in 2001 . . . . After the death of Jorge's mother, Lilia assumed the position as Jorge's sponsor to pursue his application for permanent residence and citizenship. In 2004, after she signed a document related to his immigration status, Jorge informed Lilia that it would be the last one. Two weeks later, in May, 2004, he took Lilia out to dinner and asked for a divorce because he was in love with someone else and always had been. In June 2004, Jorge moved out.

That same month, Lilia found out who the other woman was when she overheard a conversation between Jorge and Lilia's sister Blanca. Jorge had begun an affair with Blanca prior to the 2001 marriage, and it lasted until 2005. The intercepted conversation occurred in 2005. Lilia asked her teenaged son Victor to call Blanca, who babysat for Jorge and Lilia's daughter, on her cell phone to inquire if she would be joining them for lunch with the child. Blanca, at a restaurant with Jorge, had the cell phone in her purse. Instead of pressing the stop key, she pressed the button to answer the call, so the conversation she was having with Jorge was overheard on Victor's cell phone, which Lilia and Victor listened to by activating the loudspeaker. In this conversation, Jorge professed his love for Blanca, assured her that they would be together once he got his share of money and property from Lilia, and told her that he had only married Lilia to gain permanent residence status. This conversation occurred after Jorge had moved out.

Shortly after the parties separated, an attempt was made to reach an agreement with Jorge as to the disposition of assets. Lilia has a real estate broker's license and she and Jorge had worked together in the realty business during their marriage. Lilia's attorney prepared a proposed settlement agreement listing five parcels of real property as community property, and three as Lilia's separate property. Lilia offered Jorge one of the properties, but he declined. He then filed a petition for dissolution of the marriage on April 21, 2005.

On June 22, 2005, Lilia filed a response to the petition and a request for a judgment of nullity of marriage. At the court trial on the bifurcated trial relating to the status of the marriage, Jorge demonstrated he had obtained his permanent resident status in 2002. He denied having a relationship with Blanca, although several telephone messages left on Blanca's cell phone and retrieved by a close family friend of Blanca and Lilia—in addition to the conversation overheard by Lilia—belied his protestations.

The trial court concluded the 1999 marriage was void under the laws of Mexico and neither spouse was a putative spouse since neither acted in good faith. Although Lilia denied it, the court found she was likely the party who made the wedding arrangements since her family is from Jalisco, the ceremony was performed by an official from Jalisco, and the marriage certificate was issued by the State of Jalisco.

The court also found the second marriage was void because Jorge perpetrated a fraud on Lilia by carrying on an extramarital affair with Blanca. The court found that Jorge did not marry Lilia because he was worried about his immigration or work status; instead, the court found Jorge made false statements to Blanca about his reasons for marrying Lilia, including a need for a green card to string her along and to delay having to make a commitment to her. Thus, the fraud related to Jorge's marrying Lilia while carrying on a sexual relationship with Blanca which he intended to maintain. The court concluded Jorge wanted to "have his cake and eat it too" by carrying on sexual relationships with both women at the same time.

The trial court held that this kind of fraud goes to the heart of the marital relationship and declared the 2001 marriage void on the ground of fraud. The court also found Lilia was a putative spouse, for purposes of making a division of property at a subsequent proceeding. Jorge appeals.

Jorge contends (1) that he held a good faith belief in the validity of the 1999 marriage and should have been deemed a putative spouse of that marriage, and (2) his extramarital affair did not constitute fraud such as would render the 2001 marriage void. . . .

The 1999 Marriage

First we address Jorge's contention that he should have been deemed a putative spouse of the 1999 marriage. An innocent party to an invalid marriage may obtain relief as a putative spouse if the party believed in good faith that the marriage was valid. A putative spouse is entitled to the division of property acquired during the union as community property or quasi-community property. The determination of the party's good faith is tested by an objective standard. A subjective good faith belief alone, even by a party that is found credible and sympathetic, is insufficient. Instead, under an objective standard, a claim of putative spouse status must be based on facts that would cause a reasonable person to believe in good faith that he or she was married and that the marriage was valid under California law.

Here, regardless of whether Jorge subjectively believed the 1999 marriage was valid, a reasonable person would not have. The marriage was performed in Moreno Valley, California, by a priest or other official from the State of Jalisco, Mexico. The official issued an "Acta de Matrimonio," a marriage license, stating that the wedding was performed in Jalisco. This in itself is enough to put a reasonable person on notice that the marriage license, and hence the marriage itself, was not valid. Thus, we hold that Jorge was not a putative spouse as to the 1999 marriage.

The 2001 Marriage

A marriage is voidable and may be adjudged a nullity if the consent of either party was obtained by fraud. A marriage may be annulled for fraud only in an extreme case where the particular fraud goes to the very essence of the marriage relation. The fact represented or suppressed to induce consent to marriage will be deemed material if it relates to a matter of substance and directly affects the purpose of the party deceived in entering the marital contract. In other words, the fraud relied upon must be such as directly defeats the marriage relationship and not merely such fraud as would be sufficient to rescind an ordinary civil contract. Fraudulent intent not to perform a duty vital to the marriage state must exist in the offending spouse's mind at the moment the marriage contract is made.

A promise to be a kind, dutiful and affectionate spouse cannot be made the basis of an annulment. Instead, the particular fraudulent intention must relate to the sexual or procreative aspects of marriage. In the absence of this type of fraud, the longstanding rule is that neither party may question the validity of the marriage upon the ground of express or implied representations of the other with respect to such matters as character, habits, chastity, business or social standing, financial worth or prospects, or matters of a similar nature. Concealment of incontinence, temper, idleness, extravagance, coldness or lack of represented fortune will not justify an annulment.

Other decisions demonstrate that to void a marriage, the fraud alleged must show an intention not to perform a duty vital to the marriage, which exists in the mind of the offending spouse at the time of marriage. (*Millar v. Millar* (1917) 175 Cal. 797 [wife concealed from husband at time of marriage that she did not intend to have sexual relations with him]; *Hardesty v. Hardesty* (1924) 193 Cal. 330 [wife concealed from husband at time of marriage that she was pregnant by another man]; *Vileta v. Vileta* (1942) 53 Cal.App.2d 794 [spouse concealed known fact of sterility at time of marriage]; *In re Marriage of Liu* (1987) 197 Cal.App.3d 143 [wife married husband in Taiwan to acquire a green card, and never consummated the marriage].) Thus, historically, annulments based on fraud have only been granted in cases where the fraud relates in some way to the sexual, procreative or child-rearing aspects of marriage.

Here, the trial court specifically found that the fraud was unrelated to the husband's efforts to obtain permanent legal status. Instead, it found the fraud was based on Jorge's intent to continue the ongoing simultaneous sexual relationships with Lilia and Blanca at the time that he and Lilia entered into the 2001 marriage.

In rendering its judgment of nullity, the trial court relied on the decision in *Security-First Nat. Bank of Los Angeles v. Schaub* (1945) 71 Cal.App.2d 467 (*Schaub*). In that case, a younger woman married an older man to obtain his real property. She had been involved in an intimate relationship with another man for many years, and conspired with her lover to marry the husband, with no intention of fulfilling the obligation of marriage to consummate the marriage. This she did, while continuing her sexual relationship with her lover. The fraud was discovered when an investigator, hired by the husband, found the wife in bed with her lover, both naked.

We read *Schaub* as not standing solely on the intent not to consummate. *Schaub* does not at any point suggest that the intent not to consummate is *the* indicator of fraud. Neither does *Schaub* anywhere indicate that the intent to continue an existing relationship with a third party is enough for a finding of fraud only when accompanied by the intent not to consummate.

Further, the court in *Schaub* points out that "The marriage in itself was a contract under which each of the parties undertook the obligations of mutual respect, *fidelity* and support. The *Schaub* court then concludes that the fraud consisted of the wife's intention not to perform her marriage obligations, including the obligation of fidelity, and the concealment of that from the innocent spouse. That is just what happened here. At the time he entered into the 2001 marriage, Jorge manifestly intended not to perform his marriage obligation of fidelity. That is fraud . . . .

Finally, as stated above, historically, annulments based on fraud have only been granted in cases where the fraud relates in some way to the sexual, procreative or child-rearing aspects of marriage. Jorge's actions here, in marrying Lilia while continuing to carry on a sexual relationship with her sister Blanca, directly relates to a sexual aspect of marriage—sexual fidelity. For emphasis, we again quote from Family Code section 720, entitled "Mutual Obligations": "Husband and wife contract toward each other obligations of mutual respect, fidelity, and support." At the time of the 2001 marriage, Jorge purposely deceived Lilia into thinking that he would perform one of the central obligations of the marriage contract—the obligation of fidelity. . . . Jorge committed fraud and Lilia is entitled to a judgment of annulment.

The judgment is affirmed. Jorge is directed to pay costs on appeal.

Comment on *Marriage of Ramirez*

Under California annulment law, a putative spouse is entitled to a share of property accumulated during the annulled "marriage." Because Jorge was not a putative spouse, he may not be entitled to any of the property accumulated during the "marriage." I don't feel sorry for old Jorge. Do you?

Relation-Back Doctrine in Annulment

The relation-back doctrine is a legal fiction under which a decree of annulment is said to relate back to the date of marriage and erase the marriage. As the California Court of Appeal put it in *Marriage of Seaton*,[15] "A judgment of nullity has been said to relate back and erase the marriage and all its implications from the outset. At the same time, this legal fiction was fashioned by the courts to do substantial justice between the parties to a void or voidable marriage, and is desirable only when used as a device for achieving that purpose. In cases involving the rights of third parties, courts have been especially wary lest the logical appeal of the fiction should obscure fundamental problems and lead to unjust or ill-advised results respecting a third party's rights."

---

15 200 Cal. App. 4th 800, 133, Cal. Rptr. 3d 50 (2011).

Questions: Should Relation Back Apply?

1. Sue and Bill were married fifteen years. They divorced three years ago. In the divorce, Sue was ordered to pay Bill spousal support of $4,000 per month. The divorce decree provided that spousal support would end on Bill's death or remarriage. A year ago, Bill married Beth. Upon Bill's marriage to Beth, Sue stopped paying spousal support. Recently, Bill obtained an annulment of his marriage to Beth. As soon as the annulment was final, Bill returned to family court and filed a motion requesting the judge to order Sue to resume spousal support. Bill relies on the relation-back theory. According to Bill, the annulment relates back and wipes out the marriage to Beth. In other words, Bill did not remarry, and Sue owes him support. Should Sue be ordered to resume paying support to Bill?

2. Following a 20 year marriage, Pat and Jeff divorced. Jeff was ordered to pay Pat monthly spousal support of $3,000 for 10 years or until Pat died or remarried. Two years after the divorce, Pat was in Las Vegas on vacation. While playing a slot machine, Pat met Tom. Pat and Tom "partied" the night away, Las Vegas style. At 3:00 a.m., and while highly intoxicated, Pat and Tom decided to get married. They went to a local wedding chapel and tied the knot. By dawn, they were newlyweds! When Pat sobered up, she realized what a huge mistake she had made. She Facebooked her best friend and asked, "Can I undue this horrible mistake? I was so drunk, I didn't know what I was doing!" Jeff found out about the wedding because, despite the fact that advertisements on TV say, "What Happens in Las Vegas Stays in Las Vegas," It ain't necessarily so. Because Pat had remarried, Jeff stopped paying spousal support. Pat promptly annulled her marriage to Tom. Once annulled, Pat went to court to reinstate Jeff's support obligation. Should Jeff be ordered to resume paying support to Pat? Is this case different from number 1?

3. In *Mack v. Brown,* 82 A.D.3d 133, 919 N.Y.S.2d 166 (2011), the Appellate Division of the New York Supreme Court grappled with an unusual civil action alleging violation of the "right of sepulcher." The court wrote, "The common-law right of sepulcher gives the next of kin the absolute right to the immediate possession of a decedent's body for preservation and burial or other disposition of the remains, and damages may be awarded against any person who unlawfully interferes with that right or improperly deals with the decedent's body." Joseph Mack died in a Brooklyn hospital. The death certificate identified Regina Brown as Joseph's surviving spouse. Regina signed an authorization for cremation. On the authorization form, Regina listed herself as the surviving spouse and executor of Joseph's estate. Joseph's remains were released to a funeral home and cremated. A few months later, Shirley Mack commenced a civil action against the

funeral home (and other defendants), alleging that she, and not Regina, was the surviving spouse. Shirley argued that she had the right of sepulcher, and that she wanted Joseph buried, not cremated. Shirley sought recovery of damages for emotional distress. Shirley argued that the marriage between Joseph and Regina was bigamous and void *ab initio*. Because the marriage was void, Regina was not a surviving spouse and had no right to authorize cremation of Joseph's remains. With Regina's supposed marriage out of the way, Shirley was the surviving spouse, and Shirley did not authorize cremation. Should Shirley prevail in her suit against the funeral home?

Division of Property in Annulment

In divorce, courts divide marital/community property. What happens in annulment? How does a court divide property when a marriage is void or voidable? Should a court granting an annulment treat property the same as it would in a divorce? How can a couple have marital/community property when the marriage is void or voidable? In *Liming v. Liming*,[16] the Ohio Court of Appeals wrote, "Most courts have held that the property rights of litigants in an annulment proceeding are only those that attach to persons in an individual capacity and are not the same rights usually affiliated with a husband and wife in a divorce proceeding. A property division in annulment is not based on a legal status such as marriage but is more of an adjustment of property interests between parties similar to a dissolution of a business partnership. The judgment annulling a marriage should place the parties in the same position that they would have been in had the annulled marriage not taken place."

In some states (*e.g.*, California), the court granting annulment has authority to divide property in a manner similar to division of property on divorce.

---

16   117 Ohio App. 3d 617, 691 N.E.2d 299 (1996).

Problems on Annulment

1. Harold is in prison serving a sentence of life without the possibility of parole. Janet is a social worker for the state. Harold and Janet met and married inside the prison. The marriage was never consummated. Prior to marriage, Harold told Janet that he had applied for clemency from the governor and expected to be released from prison in a year or two. According to Janet, Harold lied about applying for clemency. After a year of marriage, Janet commenced an action to annul the marriage based on fraud. Janet argues that she married Harold based on his false statements about applying for clemency. *Meadows v. Meadows,* 330 S.W.3d 798 (Mo. Ct. App. 2011).

2. Janet and Steve were married 33 years when Janet filed for divorce. The divorce was finalized, and Steve was ordered to pay spousal support. A year after the divorce was entered, Steve filed a motion to vacate the divorce decree. Steve had obtained an annulment from a Roman Catholic tribunal. The religious tribunal ruled that the marriage was based on fraud perpetrated by Janet. In state court, Steve argues that the judge should vacate the divorce based on the religious tribunal's annulment of the marriage. With the marriage annulled, Steve argues his duty to pay spousal support should terminate. Should a ruling by a religious tribunal be controlling in state court? *Age v. Age,* 340 S.W.3d 88 (Ky. Ct. App. 2011).

3. Howard, age 72, had terminal cancer and severe dementia caused by Alzheimer's disease. Howard had several adult children. Howard lived at home. His daughter Nancy was his primary caretaker. Nancy went on a one-week vacation, and left Howard in the care of Nidia, age 58. During the one-week vacation, Nidia married Howard and transferred all his assets into her name. Howard died a few months later from cancer. Following Howard's death, Nancy brought an action seeking to have the marriage annulled because Howard was mentally incompetent to consent to marriage. Nancy's suit sought to nullify the transfers of property from Howard to Nidia. Howard's will was admitted to probate. The will left his property to his children. In the probate court, Nidia filed a right of election as a surviving spouse seeking a portion of Howard's estate. Howard's children and his doctors provided evidence that at the time of the wedding, Howard had advanced Alzheimer's and was incompetent.

Nidia provided evidence that she had known Howard 25 years, and that he had proposed marriage several times. Nidia accepted the last proposal, which just happened to occur while Nancy was on vacation. The pastor who performed the marriage stated that if he had known about Howard's medical condition he would not have performed the marriage. Can the marriage be annulled? Should the transfers of property be set aside? Is Nidia entitled to an elective share of Howard's property as a surviving spouse? *Campbell v. Thomas,* 73 A.D.3d 103, 897 N.Y.S.2d 460 (2010).

---

4. Festus is a resident of the United States, originally from Ethiopia. Betelehem is Ethiopian. Betelehem and Festus met through an internet dating site. After some months of internet communication, Betelehem told Festus she loved him wanted a marital relationship with children. The two were married after Betelehem arrived in the United States. A year after the wedding, and two days after receiving her "green card," Betelehem left Festus, claiming he abused her. Betelehem filed for divorce. Festus filed for annulment based on fraud. A cousin of Betelehem will testify that Betelehem told her, "I only married him to come to the United States." A friend of Festus will testify that Betelehem told him, "Before I came to American, I took a birth control injection because I did not want to have his baby." Is Festus entitled to an annulment? *Desta v. Anyaoha,* 371 S.W.3d 596 (Tex. Ct. App. 2012).

CHAPTER 11

Intimate Partner Violence

INTIMATE PARTNER VIOLENCE (IPV) is common in the United States and around the world. This chapter discusses legal and psychological aspects of IPV.

Brief History of Intimate Partner Violence and Law

Intimate partner violence is any use of physical force in an intimate relationship. IPV is as old as humanity.[1] During much of Western history, society not only turned a blind eye toward most IPV, the law actually approved moderate physical chastisement of a woman by her husband. In early Roman law "the husband had the power to chastise, sell or even kill the wife, having the same authority over her as over his child."[2] In England, a husband had authority to employ "moderate" physical chastisement of his wife. In 1765, William Blackstone wrote in his *Commentaries on the Laws of England* that a "husband also (by the old law) might give his wife moderate correction." Yet, Blackstone noted that as early as the reign of Charles II (1660-1685), "this power of correction began to be doubted: and a wife may now have security of the peace against her husband...."

In America, a husband's right of chastisement took shallow root, and soon withered on the vine.[3] In 1824, the Mississippi Supreme Court acknowledged the utility of chastisement, but ruled that a husband could be prosecuted for excessive force.[4] Although the Mississippi court stated that prosecution was possible, the court felt domestic squabbles should generally not be litigated in public. The court

---

1 *See* Thomas L. Hafemeister, If All You Have Is a Hammer: Society's Ineffective Response to Intimate Partner Violence, 60 *Catholic University Law Review* 919 (2011).

2 William L. Burdick, *The Principles of Roman Law and Their Relation to Modern Law*, p. 225 (1938).

3 *See* Jeannie Suk, Criminal Law Comes Home, 116 *Yale Law Journal* 2 (2006).

4 Bradley v. State, 1 Miss. 73 (1824).

wrote, "Family broils and dissentions cannot be investigated before the tribunals of the country, without casting a shade over the character of those who are unfortunately engaged in the controversy. To screen from public reproach those who may be thus unhappily situated, let the husband be permitted to exercise the right of moderate chastisement, in cases of great emergency, and use salutary restraints in every case of misbehavior, without being subjected to vexatious prosecutions, resulting in the mutual discredit and shame of all parties concerned."

In 1873, the North Carolina Supreme Court ruled that a husband had no right of physical chastisement.[5] The Court wrote, "We may assume that the old doctrine, that a husband had a right to whip his wife, provided he used a switch no larger than his thumb, is not the law in North Carolina. Indeed, the Courts have advanced from that barbarism until they have reached the position, that the husband has no right to chastise his wife, under any circumstances." Cases of serious spousal abuse were prosecuted in North Carolina. Like their colleagues on the bench in Mississippi, however, the justices of the North Carolina Supreme Court felt it was unseemly for family matters to be aired in public prosecutions. In 1868, the North Carolina court wrote, "The courts have been loath to take cognizance of trivial complaints arising out of the domestic relations — such as master and apprentice, teacher and pupil, parent and child, husband and wife. Not because those relations are not subject to the law, but because the evil of publicity would be greater than the evil involved in the trifles complained of; and because they ought to be left to family government."[6]

By 1890, the North Carolina court had changed its mind about the propriety of litigating domestic assaults in public. In *State v. Dowell*,[7] the Court wrote, "It was at one time held in our state that the relation of husband and wife gave the former immunity to the extent that the court would not go behind the domestic curtain, and scrutinize too nicely every family disturbance, even though amounting to an assault . . . But since *State v. Oliver* [1873] . . . , we have refused 'the blanket of the dark' to these outrages on female weakness and defenselessness. So it is now settled that, technically, a husband cannot commit even a slight assault upon his wife, and that her person is as sacred from his violence as from that of any other person."

---

5   State v. Oliver, 70 N.C. 60 (1873).

6   State v. Rhodes, 61 N.C. 453, 454 (1868).

7   11 S.E. 525 (N.C. 1890).

Joel Bishop, one of the nineteenth century's leading commentators on the law of domestic relations and the law of crimes, wrote in 1877, "The right of chastisement does not pertain to [husbands] in this country. . . . Therefore, [a husband] may be indicted for assault and battery committed on [his wife]."[8] The Connecticut Supreme Court wrote to similar effect in 1914, "It is now as unlawful for him to beat or falsely imprison his wife as for another to do so, and he is amenable to the criminal law for such an offense."[9]

Today, there are wide-ranging laws and social policies on IPV. These laws and policies find their roots in the 1960s and 1970s.[10] The women's movement focused national attention on violence against women.[11] Shelters for battered women sprang up around the country.[12] Deborah DeBare writes, "The first official battered woman's shelter in the modern period opened in England, the Chiswick Women's Aid in 1971. Very shortly thereafter, battered women's shelters started to develop throughout the United States. Woman House in St. Paul Minnesota, opened in 1974 . . . ."[13] Legislatures passed laws authorizing civil protection orders for battered women. Police departments rethought their approach to IPV. Prosecutors took IPV cases more seriously.

Prevalence of IPV

IPV is common.[14] The U.S. Justice Department estimated that during 2001, "There were 691,710 nonfatal violent victimizations committed by current or for-

---

8   Joel P. Bishop, *Commentaries on the Criminal Law*, pp. 497-498 (6th ed. 1877).

9   Brown v. Brown, 89 A. 880 (Conn. 1914).

10   *See* Evan Stark & Eve S. Buzawa, *Violence Against Women*, in four volumes (2009).

11   Deborah DeBare observes "Between its founding in 1939 and 1969, the leading scholarly journal in the family sciences, the *Journal of Marriage and Family*, made no reference to 'domestic violence' . . . . Thus, the 'first wave' of a public response to domestic violence came during the rebirth of the women's liberation movement of the 1960s and involved significant efforts to 'name the problem.'"). Deborah DeBare, The Evolution of the Shelter Movement. In Evan Stark & Eve S. Buzawa, *Violence Against Women*, vol. 1, pp.15-32, at 16-17 (2009).

12   *See* Sharon Rice Vaughan, The Story of the Shelter, "Women's Advocates." In Evan Stark & Eve S. Buzawa, *Violence Against Women*, vol. 1, pp.1-14 (2009)(describing the founding of a pioneering women's shelter from the perspective of a woman who was there at the time); Deborah DeBare, The Evolution of the Shelter Movement. In Evan Stark & Eve S. Buzawa, *Violence Against Women* vol. 1, pp.15-32, at 17 (2009).

13   Deborah DeBare, The Evolution of the Shelter Movement. In Evan Stark & Eve S. Buzawa, *Violence Against Women*, vol. 1, pp.15-32, at 17 (2009).

14   *See* Frank D. Fincham & Steven R. H. Beach, Marriage in the New Millennium: A Decade in Review, 72 *Journal of Marriage and Family* 630-649, at 632 (2010)("Marital conflict is a common precursor to intimate partner violence, a phenomenon that is estimated to result in nearly 2.0 million injuries and 1,300 deaths annually in the United States. A World Health Organization study across 10 countries also showed that 15% - 71% of ever-partnered women had experienced physical or sexual violence, or both, at some point in their lives by a current of former partner and that such experience was associated with increased reports of poor physical and mental health.").

mer spouses, boyfriends, or girlfriends of the victims. . . ." In 2001, intimate partner violence constituted twenty percent of violent crime against women. Between
four and thirty percent of women admitted to hospital emergency rooms are
there because of IPV. Sandra Graham-Bermann and her colleagues report, "The
annual rate of intimate partner violence in America is conservatively estimated at
between 17% and 28% of all married or cohabiting couples."[15] On a positive note,
the Department of Justice reported, "The rate of intimate violence against females
declined significantly between 1993 and 2001, dropping by nearly half." The
downward trend continues. Yet, IPV remains common and is underreported.[16]

Regarding fatal IPV, the U.S. Department of Justice reported that approximately 33% of female homicide victims are murdered by a spouse or boyfriend.
The homicide rate for males by an intimate is roughly 4%. Hilary Abrahams
observes, "Homicide statistics in both the United States and the United Kingdom
show that most women are killed by partners or ex-partners and that the danger
is greatest at the point of leaving, as he tries to stop her, or just afterward, as he
tries to find and punish her for doing so."[17]

Children Exposed to IPV

Slightly more than half of women victimized by IPV live in households with
children under age twelve. Sandra Graham-Bermann writes, "Estimates are that
11%-16% of children will be exposed to intimate partner violence each year."[18] It
is likely that more than three million children are exposed to IPV every year in
the United States. Many parents in violent relationships believe their children
are unaware of the violence, but this is usually wishful thinking.

A man who beats his wife is apt to beat his child. Studies of the co-
occurrence of IPV and child abuse indicate a co-occurrence rate of 30 percent
to 60 percent. Children are sometimes injured when they try to protect their
mother. Even when they do not intervene, children are injured accidentally during episodes of IPV.

---

15 Sandra A. Graham-Bermann, et al., Community-Based Intervention for Children Exposed to Intimate
Partner Violence: An Efficacy Trial, 75 *Journal of Consulting and Clinical Psychology* 199-209, at 199 (2007).

16 *See* Thomas L. Hafemeister, If All You Have Is a Hammer: Society's Ineffective Response to Intimate Partner
Violence, 60 *Catholic University Law Review* 919, 922 (2011)("IPV often goes unreported. One study found that
between 1994 and 2005, only fifty-eight percent of female and about fifty-two percent of male IPV victims reported their attacks to the police, and some studies indicate that rates of non-reporting may be even higher.").

17 Hilary Abrahams, Changing from Victim to Survivor. In Evan Stark & Eve S. Buzawa, *Violence Against
Women*, vol. 1, pp.33-54, at 40 (2009).

18 Sandra A. Graham-Bermann, et al., Community-Based Intervention for Children Exposed to Intimate
Partner Violence: An Efficacy Trial, 75 *Journal of Consulting and Clinical Psychology* 199-209, at 199 (2007).

Witnessing IPV isn't good for anyone. Sandra Graham-Bermann writes, "Children can be traumatized by overhearing beatings as well as by viewing them."[19] Exposure during childhood to IPV is a risk factor in adults for depression, low self-esteem, and other trauma-related symptoms.

Witnessing repeated violent attacks on one's mother, or between one's parents, is intrinsically damaging. Children exposed to such violence fear for their mother and for themselves. Living in constant apprehension of the next outburst of violence takes a toll. Abusive men often isolate their wife or girlfriend, and the isolation imposed on the woman is visited on the children, cutting off young children from sources of positive feedback and constructive adult role models. Children who grow up in violent, socially isolated homes may come to view violence as normal. Some abusive men heap psychological abuse on their children, undermining the children's sense of self-worth. Finally, some chronically abused mothers are so emotionally exhausted and depressed that they do not provide adequate parenting.

Children of all ages can be harmed by IPV. Babies can suffer neglect because their battered mother is depressed and preoccupied with violence. Babies exposed to IPV may experience attachment difficulties.

Preschoolers are aware of violence between their parents. The stress, fear, and worry they experience manifests itself in problems sleeping, nightmares, eating difficulties, acting out, withdrawal, and somatic complaints including headaches and stomachaches.

School-age children suffer the harmful effects observed in preschoolers. As well, school age children from violent homes are at risk of scholastic and behavioral problems. During the elementary school years, some children exposed to IPV develop aggressive and antisocial tendencies (externalizing behaviors), while others pull into a shell of fearfulness and inhibition (internalizing behaviors). Some children exhibit symptoms of Posttraumatic Stress Disorder.

Adolescence has rough patches. The teen years can be difficult even with supportive, loving parents who help the young person navigate the shoals separating childhood from young adulthood. The passage is more perilous for teens growing up in violent homes. Witnessing IPV during childhood is associated with increased violence by adolescents.

Fortunately some children survive horrible childhoods —including severe

---

19   Sandra A. Graham-Bermann, Child Abuse in the Context of Domestic Violence. In John E.B. Myers et al. (Eds.), *The APSAC Handbook on Child Maltreatment*, pp. 119-129, 124 (2002).

IPV and psychological abuse—apparently unscathed. How do they do it? Research on so-called resilient children reveals that many of them have some adult in their life (a grandparent, a teacher, a non-abusive parent) who provides a steady source of emotional nourishment, support, and love. This person is the child's anchor.

Exposing children to IPV can constitute neglect. In *D.W.G. v. Department of Children and Families*,[20] a father appealed a juvenile court order that his two sons were neglected. Father sexually abused one boy, and exposed both children to IPV against their mother. On appeal, father argued that the evidence did not prove the children knew of the violence, and that children must actually observe violence to be neglected. The Florida Court of Appeals disagreed, writing, "Children may be affected by domestic violence and may be aware of the violence, even if they do not see it occur with their own eyes. There was ample evidence in this case that the children were in the house when the father was abusing the mother. The mother testified that she heard the children crying when the father took her in the bathroom to abuse her. There also was evidence that the older son walked into the bathroom when the father was sexually abusing the mother. Moreover, the mother fled the home on more than one occasion with the children due to the domestic violence incidents. This evidence supports a finding that the incidents of domestic violence constituted abuse sufficient to support an adjudication of dependency."

A man who beats a woman in the presence of her children may be prosecuted for endangering the welfare of the children. The New York Court of Appeals addressed this issue in *People v. Johnson*.[21] Vanessa Parker obtained a civil order of protection against Theodore Johnson. In violation of the order, Johnson approached Parker as she walked down the street with her three daughters, aged twelve, seven, and an infant. Johnson struck Parker in the back of the head, knocking her against a fence and tipping over the baby carriage. The children started crying. Johnson yelled at Parker for having him arrested, grabbed her by the back of the neck, and dragged her to her apartment, where he knocked her head against the door. Once inside, the children escaped to their room and closed the door. Over a period of ten hours, Johnson beat Parker with his hands, his feet, and with a metal pipe. He cursed her and threatened to kill her. Johnson threw plates and glassware against walls. The children heard all this, including their mother's screams, from their room. Finally, Parker managed to call the police, and Johnson was arrested.

20　833 So.2d 238 (Fla. Ct. App. 2002).

21　95 N.Y.2d 368, 740 N.E.2d 1075 (2000).

Johnson was convicted of endangering the welfare of a child under a statute stating that a person endangers a child when "he knowingly acts in a manner likely to be injurious to the physical, mental or moral welfare of a child less than seventeen years old." On appeal, the Court of Appeals was "asked to determine whether the evidence was legally sufficient to support defendant's conviction for endangering the welfare of a child when his actions were not specifically directed at the children." Answering in the affirmative, the court stated that exposure to IPV harms children. The court noted, "Nothing in the statute restricts its application solely to harmful conduct directed at children. The statute is broadly written and imposes a criminal sanction for the mere 'likelihood' of harm. Moreover, the language provides that defendant 'knowingly' act in such a manner, further suggesting that the statute does not require that the conduct be specifically directed at a child; rather, a defendant must simply be *aware* that the conduct may likely result in harm to a child, whether directed at the child or not." The evidence was more than sufficient to prove "that defendant's assaultive conduct in this case created a likelihood of harm to the children of which he was aware."

The Batterer as Parent

Are men who beat their wives competent parents? Obviously, there is no simple answer to this question. Some complete scoundrels are doting daddies. Yet, the personal characteristics of many batterers bode ill for good parenting. In their book *The Batterer as Parent*, Lundy Bancroft and Jay Silverman report that batterers are skilled at hiding their attitudes and behavior from the outside world. "The great majority of batterers project a public image that is in sharp contrast to the private reality of their behavior and attitudes. They may impress others as friendly, calm, and reasonable people, often with a capacity to be funny and entertaining. The public reputation that a batterer can build may cause people to be reluctant to believe allegations of his battering, thus making it more difficult for his partner and children to obtain emotional support or assistance."

The predominant behavior of batterers is control, and batterers are not apt to apologize for their controlling behavior. Indeed, batterers feel it is their right to control *their* partner and *their* children. The fact that batterers feel justified makes it difficult to change their attitudes. Bancroft and Silverman write, "The woman's efforts to resist these forms of control generally meet with an escalation by the abuser, and thus the pattern of control becomes increasingly coercive over time. A batterer usually perceives his controlling behavior as justified and therefore sees his partner's reluctance to be controlled as evidence of her mental instability, volatility, or desire to control him."

Closely intertwined with control is the batterer's sense of entitlement. Bancroft and Silverman write, "Entitlement is the belief that one has special rights and privileges without accompanying reciprocal responsibilities. Batterers tend to have this orientation in specific relationship to their partners and children and do not necessarily carry it over into other contexts. . . . A primary manifestation of entitlement is that batterers expect family life to center on the meeting of their needs, often to the point of treating their partners like servants." Batterers tend to view themselves as superior, and to be selfish, self-centered, manipulative, and possessive.

Some batterers are so self-absorbed that they have little interest in their children. When they are involved with their children, batterers tend to be authoritarian and rigid. Excessive corporal punishment is common. Physical and psychological abuse are not uncommon. Bancroft and Silverman write, "The risk of physical abuse of children by a batterer rises with the severity and the frequency of his violence toward his partner. Some batterers use the threat of custody litigation to exert control over their partner. Others go to family court to intimidate or hurt the mother. Batterers express great concern about their children when they are embroiled in custody litigation. Bancroft and Lundy warn mental health professionals who conduct custody evaluations to be on guard. "A batterer's level of commitment to his children cannot be assessed on the basis of his statements or his expressions of emotion, such as the shedding of tears while talking about them or the proud showing of photographs. Such displays can be products of manipulativeness or of self-centeredness rather than of genuine connection to the child, and we have observed that our clients make recurring promises to become more consistently involved with their children, promises that they typically fail to fulfill (except during a period of custody litigation). Assessment of a batterer's potential as a parent therefore needs to rely largely on what his actual past performance has been, which varies considerably from batterer to batterer."

Psychological tests cannot determine whether someone is a batterer. Nor can tests determine the adequacy of a batterer's parenting.

When batterers discuss family problems with their children, they often blame the mother. Batterers "are commonly able to create confusion in children regarding the nature of the abuse in the home, which family members are responsible for it (leading children to blame their mothers or themselves), and who is the kinder or more concerned parent." Some children accept their father's explanation and turn against their mother. The child, especially boys, may begin treating the mother as the batterer treats her. Batterers systematically undermine the mother's parenting. Bancroft and Silverman write, "Battering leaves many emotional and physical scars on a mother, any of which can make it harder for her to care for her children."

Batterers who are motivated to change their behavior can, and for these men, treatment is effective. Many batterers, however, do not see themselves as having a problem. Lacking insight into their responsibility for violence, and short on motivation to change, few of these batterers benefit from treatment. Thousands of men are court-ordered into batterer treatment as an alternative to incarceration. For many of these men, the threat of jail keeps them in therapy. Bancroft and Silverman write, "Batterers do not continue to participate in batterer intervention or to make other serious efforts to change in the absence of outside pressure."

There is little empirical research on the effectiveness of batterer treatment, and much of what exists is discouraging. In 2003, the U.S. Department of Justice issued reports describing the results of psychoeducational batterer programs in Florida and New York.[22] The Department stated:

> For more than a decade, courts have been sending convicted batterers to intervention programs rather than to prison. But do these programs work? Two studies in Florida and New York tested the most common type of batterer intervention. Their findings raise serious questions about the effectiveness of these programs. However, problems conducting the research raise questions about the studies' findings.

> Batterer intervention programs do not change batterers' attitudes and may have only minor effects on behavior, according to these studies. The Florida study found no significant differences between those who had treatment and those who did not as to whether they battered again or their attitudes toward domestic violence. The study did find an apparent relationship between whether an offender was employed or owned a house and whether he re-offended: Those with the most to lose were the least likely to re-offend. In New York, batterers in a 26-week program were less likely to re-offend than those in an 8-week program, but neither group showed any change in attitudes toward women or domestic violence.

> Batterer intervention programs may be effective only in the context of a broader criminal justice and community response to domestic violence that includes arrest, restraining orders, intensive

22 John Ashcroft, Deborah J. Daniels & Sarah V. Hart, Do Batterer Intervention Programs Work? Two Studies. (2003). U.S. Department of Justice, Office of Justice Programs.

monitoring of batterers, and changes to social norms that inadvertently tolerate partner violence.

Bancroft and Silverman add, "Professionals need to assess carefully whether or not a batterer has made meaningful progress. Change cannot be correctly judged to have taken place just because of a recent period without physical violence. . . . In our experience, the preponderance of batterers who claim to have changed return to battering. . . . Superficially positive statements such as 'I know I'm responsible for my own actions' or 'I have done some things I'm not proud of' reveal little in themselves about the depth of a man's progress."

Parenting by Battered Women

Most victims of IPV provide competent parenting. Yet, battering takes a psychological and physical toll that can interfere with the ability to nurture children. Lucy Salcido Carter and her colleagues write, "Battered mothers may be less emotionally available to their children because they are preoccupied with the violence and trying to stay safe, and/or because they are experiencing depression."[23] John Fantuzzo and Wanda Mohr add that battered parents "may be numbed, frightened, and depressed, unable to deal with their own trauma and/or grief, and emotionally unavailable for their children."[24]

State Laws on IPV

Every state has an array of laws to respond to IPV. Thus, victims of IPV can obtain protection orders restraining IPV. In child custody litigation, a parent with a history of IPV has an uphill battle to convince a judge it is in a child's best interest to be placed with the batterer. IPV is a crime. A batterer can be prosecuted for traditional crimes such as battery, mayhem, and murder. As well, many states have specialized IPV crimes.

IPV Protective Orders

Statutory law on protective orders varies from state to state. The law of Washington State is representative. Washington defines "domestic violence" as "(a) physical harm, bodily injury, assault, or the infliction or fear of imminent physical harm, bodily injury or assault, between family or household members; (b) sexual assault of one family or household member by another; or (c) stalk-

---

23 Lucy Salcido Carter, Lois A. Weithorn & Richard E. Behrman, Domestic Violence and Children: Analysis and Recommendations, 9 *The Future of Children* 4-20, at 6 (1999).

24 John W. Fantuzzo & Wanda K. Mohr, Prevalence and Effects of Child Exposure to Domestic Violence, 9 *The Future of Children* 21-42, at 40 (1999).

ing . . . ."[25] Washington defines family or household member as present and former spouses, present and former domestic partners, persons who have a child in common, relatives, non-relatives living together, and persons in dating relationships. A "dating relationship" is "a social relationship of a romantic nature."

In Washington, a person may file a petition alleging IPV and request a protective order.[26] The petition must be accompanied by an affidavit describing the IPV. No filing fee is required, and the petitioner is not required to post a bond to obtain a protective order.

Washington judges may issue ex parte temporary orders of protection when the petition "alleges that irreparable injury could result from domestic violence if an order is not issued immediately without prior notice to the respondent."[27] An ex parte temporary order may: (1) restrain IPV; (2) restrain a person from entering the home of the petitioner or going to the petitioner's workplace or school; (3) require a person to stay a specified distance away from the petitioner; (4) restrain a person from interfering with custody of children; (5) restrain any contact with the petitioner.

An ex parte order of protection is effective for two weeks, and may be reissued. The law requires notice of the ex parte order be given promptly to the restrained person. A hearing on the petition is set for two weeks from the issuance of the temporary order.

At a hearing, a judge listens to both sides and may grant a one year restraining order. A one year order may provide the same protections as a temporary order. In addition, a one year order may require the respondent to participate in a "domestic violence perpetrator treatment program." The respondent can be ordered to pay the petitioner's costs in seeking protection, including attorneys' fees. Violation of a protective order is a crime.[28]

Protective orders are valuable, but they are not a panacea. After all, a protective order is "just a piece of paper." Some batterers are not deterred by an order, and continue harassing or battering the victim. Tragically, cases arise in

---

25 Wash. Rev. Code Ann. § 26.50.010(1).

26 Wash. Rev. Code Ann. § 26.50.020.

27 Wash. Rev. Code Ann. § 26.50.070. "The court shall hold an ex parte hearing in person or by telephone on the da y the petition is filed or on the following judicial day" § 26.50.070(3).

28 Wash. Rev. Code Ann. § 26.50.110.

See Jeannie Suk, Criminal Law Comes Home, 116 *Yale Law Journal* 2, 16 (2006)("The civil protection order, once envisioned as an alternative to criminal process, has not been subsumed by the criminalization strategy. Today, protection orders are primarily enforced through criminal misdemeanor charges. Almost every state has made the violation of a DV protection order a crime.").

which a batterer who is subject to a protective order seriously injures or kills the victim. Consider the sad case of Candy Daniels:

> [Jackie Lee Bibbs], Appellant and the victim, Candalin Daniels, also known as Candy, were paramours and had been for several years. They had a child together in 2007. However, by 2009, the relationship between the two had soured and Candy attempted to break off the relationship. Beginning in March of 2009, there were several incidents involving appellant breaking into Candy's home or being suspected of breaking into her home. Candy had reported such incidents to the Fort Worth Police Department on March 28, April 4, April 15, and May 5, 2009. Eventually, Candy sought a protective order on May 4, 2009. The ex parte protective order was signed May 5, and served on appellant that same day. The protective order provided for a hearing to be held on May 20.
>
> In addition to seeking a protective order, Candy complained about appellant's harassment and other activities to his parole officer. After discussing Candy's complaints with his supervisor, on May 5, appellant's parole officer had Candy come back to prepare a sworn statement regarding her interaction with appellant. Subsequently, on May 12, appellant's parole officer advised appellant that the terms and conditions of his parole had been amended to prohibit him from having further contact with Candy.
>
> On May 15, Candy was hosting a fish fry for family and friends at her home. Early in the evening, appellant's nephew, Andrew Bibbs, came to Candy's home and an argument ensued. Andrew was asked to leave the residence and he complied. After that, Candy's sister, Mary Ann Daniels, left the party. As Mary Ann was driving by the Sunny Food Store, which is located down the street on the corner from Candy's home, she noticed appellant's white pick-up at the store. She then called Candy to alert her.
>
> Candy decided to take her brother-in-law, Tyrone, to the store to ask appellant to quit harassing her. Eventually, a number of the guests at the party left the house and proceeded down the block toward the store. Candy and Tyrone were in front of the others by some 15 feet or so. As they were walking toward the store, appellant jumped over the fence at the corner of Candy's house with a gun in his hand. Michelle Brown and Lora Hammons both saw appellant and simultaneously yelled at Candy that appellant was coming from behind her with the

gun. Candy fled toward the store with appellant running behind her firing a gun. Candy made it to the interior of the store but could not elude appellant. Candy was shot and died from these wounds.

Candy had a protective order, but it didn't protect her. Appellant was convicted of murder and sentenced to life without parole. His conviction was affirmed.[29]

David Taylor, Maria Stoilkov and Daniel Greco discuss another concern with protective orders, particularly ex parte orders. "As the doors of the courthouse have been opened to actual victims of domestic violence, they also have inadvertently been opened to persons who are not victims of domestic violence. In fact, they have been opened to the actual abuser who seeks relief for improper motives, such as trying to gain a tactical advantage in an anticipated domestic violence proceeding or divorce action."[30]

Criminal Prosecution of IPV

Roughly half the states have laws establishing a preference for arrest when police have probable cause to believe IPV has occurred. More than half the states mandate arrest for violation of a IPV protective order. Thomas Hafemeister observes, "Mandatory-arrest laws have been extremely controversial. Supporters of mandatory-arrest laws contend that such laws force police officers to take IPV seriously and undercut the stereotypical views that otherwise downplay the gravity of IPV. . . . [C]ritics of mandatory-arrest laws say that they disempower victims of IPV by taking away their ability to decide whether the batterer should be removed or punished . . . . Critics also argue that mandatory-arrest policies harm victims in other ways. For example, they have resulted in a dramatic increase in the number of women arrested."[31]

One of the greatest impediments to prosecuting IPV is that many victims are uncooperative. Victims are initially cooperative—describing abuse to responding police officers—but later refuse to cooperate or testify. Victims change their minds for many reasons. Batterers threaten victims to change the story. Many victims love the batterer and don't want to send the batterer to jail.

---

29 Bibbs v. State, 371 S.W.3d 564 (Tex. Ct. App. 2012).

30 David H. Taylor, Maria V. Stoilkov & Daniel J. Greco, Ex Parte Domestic Violence Orders of Protection: How Easing Access to Judicial Process has Eased the Possibility for Abuse of the Process, 18 *Kansas Journal of Law and Public Policy* 83, at 85-86 (2008).

31 Thomas L. Hafemeister, If All You Have Is a Hammer: Society's Ineffective Response to Intimate Partner Violence, 60 *Catholic University Law Review* 919, at 989-990 (2011).

One way to reduce the number of uncooperative victims is to provide a robust network of social, safety, psychological, financial, and legal services for IPV victims. When victims believe the system will protect them and their children, victims are more likely to proceed with prosecution.

Many jurisdictions have so-called "no drop prosecution" policies. Prosecutors do not drop—decline to pursue—IPV cases when victims refuse to cooperate. A hard no drop policy requires prosecution whether or not the victim cooperates. If the victim won't testify voluntarily, she may be subpoenaed. Soft no drop policies afford prosecutors flexibility in deciding which cases to pursue. Critics of "no drop" prosecution, like critics of mandatory arrest, are concerned about the impact on individual victims. Linda Mills argues, "Such policies as mandatory arrest, prosecution, and reporting [of IPV], which have become standard legal fare in the fight against domestic violence and which categorically ignore the battered woman's perspective, can themselves be forms of abuse."[32]

Stalking

In *Huch v. Marrs*,[33] the Florida Court of Appeal observed, "The seriousness of stalking cannot be overstated." The U.S. Department of Justice estimated that during 2005-2006, approximately 3.4 million individuals over age 18 were stalked.[34] Most victims know their stalker. Stalking victims can obtain civil protection orders. As well, egregious stalking is a crime.

Stalking statutes prohibit a variety of acts that annoy, threaten, and frighten victims. Physical contact with the victim is not required for stalking. A threat may be made to a third person who is likely to convey the threat to the victim. Some stalkers harass the victim with phone calls, e-mails, texts, or letters.

Criminal stalking statutes generally require defendant's conduct to be intentional, purposeful, knowing, malicious, or willful. Proof of intent is usually a combination of circumstantial evidence and defendant's words and acts.

In many stalking prosecutions, defendant's conduct is so outrageous it virtually screams criminal intent. Consider *State v. Higginbotham*.[35] Defendant dated victim's daughter. While he dated the daughter, defendant lived in vic-

---

32   Linda G. Mills, Killing Her Softly: Intimate Abuse and the Violence of State Intervention, 113 *Harvard Law Review* 550 (1999).

33   858 So.2d 1202, 1204 (Fla. Ct. App. 2003).

34   Shannan Catalano, Erica Smith, Howard Snyder & Michael Rand, *Female Victims of Violence*. U.S. Department of Justice, Office of Justice Programs, Bureau of Justice Statistics (Sept. 2009).

35   790 So. 2d 648 (La. Ct. App. 2001).

tim's home. Trouble started when defendant became violent, and victim called police. After defendant moved out, he started calling victim several times a day at all hours, cursing her when she picked up the phone. During one call, defendant said, "I'm going to fuck you in the rectum 'till you die.'" In another call he threatened to kill victim. On several occasions, defendant appeared near victim's home, stared at her, shook his fist at her, and gave her "the finger." When victim obtained a restraining order, defendant said it wouldn't do any good. The *Higginbotham* court held these facts clearly demonstrated that defendant harassed the victim with intent to inflict emotional distress.

Following the victim is a common mode of stalking. The stalker may keep the victim under surveillance. In *People v. Sullivan*,[36] victim commenced divorce proceedings against her husband. When victim refused to dismiss the divorce as her husband requested, he burned her clothes in the backyard. Victim obtained a restraining order, but defendant continued contacting her. Defendant installed a global positioning device (GPS) on victim's car so he could track her. Defendant was convicted of stalking.

Stalking generally requires repeated acts. The compulsive repetition of some stalkers is frightening. Sometimes, the stalker makes no attempt to hide his identity, and it is easy to attribute repeated acts to defendant. In other cases the annoying or frightening acts are anonymous, and it is difficult to prove that defendant was responsible.

Some stalking statutes require two basic elements. First, defendant must intentionally and repeatedly follow or harass the victim. Second, defendant must make a "credible threat." Colorado's stalking statute, for example, provides, "A person commits stalking if ... the person knowingly ... makes a credible threat to another person and, in connection with the threat, repeatedly follows, approaches, contacts, or places under surveillance that person...."[37]

To constitute a "credible threat," a prosecutor does not have to prove the stalker actually intended to carry through on the threat.[38] The Alabama Court of Criminal Appeals ruled in *Hayes v. State*,[39] "The State need only show that the accused intended to cause the victim to fear for his safety or the safety of

---

36 53 P.3d 1181 (Colo. Ct. App. 2002).

37 Colorado Rev. Stat. §18-3-602.

38 *See* Hayes v. State, 717 So. 2d 30 (Ala. Crim. App. 1997); People v. Falck, 52 Cal. App. 4th 287, 60 Cal. Rptr. 2d 624 (1997); People v. Sucic, 401 Ill. App. 3d 492, 928 N.E.2d 1231 (2010).

39 717 So. 2d 30 (Ala. Crim. App. 1997).

his family." In *State v. McCauley*,[40] the Missouri Court of Appeals ruled that the Missouri stalking statute does not require proof that the defendant was actually capable of carrying out threats.

A threat does not have to be verbal. In *People v. Cross*,[41] the Colorado Court of Appeals ruled there was sufficient evidence that defendant committed a credible threat. The victim worked at a kiosk in a shopping center. For nearly two months, defendant went to the shopping center almost daily when the victim was working. He would spend several hours a day sitting on benches near victim's kiosk, staring at her. Occasionally he would circle the kiosk. Once he approached the kiosk, tapped on it, smiled at victim, and returned to the bench where he watched her for two-and-a-half hours until she got off work. One day, victim went to church only to see defendant watching her. Victim was frightened. The Court of Appeals ruled that threats do not have to be verbal to violate the stalking statute.

There are innumerable ways to threaten victims. In *Moses v. State*,[42] defendant repeatedly called his estranged wife. Eventually, victim refused to talk to him. Over the phone, defendant said, "Call me before it's too late." This threat, in conjunction with defendant's other conduct, amounted to a terroristic threat supporting a stalking conviction. In *Lowry v. State*,[43] defendant threatened to burn the victim. In *McComas v. Kirn*,[44] the Alaska Supreme Court ruled that threatening mail can constitute stalking. In *People v. Strawbridge*,[45] the Illinois Appellate Court wrote, "Any history between a defendant and a victim may be relevant to assessing whether a reasonable person in the victim's position would be in apprehension of future confinement or restraining."[46]

Some stalking statutes require proof that the victim suffered emotional distress. In *People v. Cross*, discussed above—the shopping center case—the Colorado Court of Appeals found sufficient evidence of distress. "The victim testified that defendant's behavior caused her to change her work schedule, take days off from work, and feel unsafe; she was nervous and had trouble sleeping; and she felt she was constantly being watched by defendant. The statute is clear

---

40   317 S.W.3d 132 (Mo. Ct. App. 2010).

41   114 P.3d 1 (Colo. Ct. App. 2004), rev'd on other grounds, 127 P.3d 71 (Colo. 2006).

42   72 Ark. App. 357, 39 S.W.3d 459 (2001).

43   90 Ark. App. 333, 205 S.W.3d 830 (2005).

44   105 P.3d 1130 (Alaska 2005)(former wife sought domestic violence protection order against former husband).

45   935 N.E.2d 1104 (Ill. Ct. App. 2010).

46   935 N.E.2d at 1109.

that serious emotional distress need not be such as would compel professional treatment or a breakdown."

Federal Violence Against Women Act (VAWA)

In 1994, Congress enacted the Violence Against Women Act (VAWA) to combat interstate IPV and interstate violation of IPV protection orders.[47] VAWA provides, "A person who travels in interstate or foreign commerce . . . with the intent to kill, injure, harass, or intimidate a spouse, intimate partner, or dating partner, and who, in the course of or as a result of such travel, commits or attempts to commit a crime of violence against that spouse, intimate partner, or dating partner, shall be punished . . . ."

VAWA criminalizes interstate stalking.[48] The statute provides: "Whoever travels in interstate or foreign commerce . . . with the intent to kill, injure, harass, or place under surveillance with intent to kill, injure, harass, or intimidate another person, and in the course of, or as a result of, such travel places that person in reasonable fear of death, or serious bodily injury to, or causes substantial emotional distress to that person, a member of the immediate family of that person, or the spouse or intimate partner of that person" shall be punished.

The Sixth Circuit Court of Appeals' decision in *United States v. Baggett* offers a good introduction to interstate IPV and VAWA.

United States v. Baggett

United States Court of Appeals, Sixth Circuit
251 F.3d 1087 (2001)

Cole, Circuit Judge.

Defendant, Donald Lynn Baggett, married Catherine Baggett on November 9, 1998. One week later, while riding in the car, Mrs. Baggett told her husband that she was going to leave him and that she thought their marriage had been a mistake. An altercation ensued in which Defendant told Mrs. Baggett that she was not "going anywhere," that she was his wife, and that she was not to speak to him in the way she had. The couple began to wrestle in the front seat of their car. Defendant threw Mrs. Baggett into the back seat, got into the driver's seat, and

---

47 *See* 18 U.S.C. § 2261(a).

48 18 U.S.C. § 2261A.

began driving. Mrs. Baggett jumped out of the car and tried to run away; however, Defendant caught up with her, grabbed her by the hair, and took her home, whereupon he yelled at her for approximately one hour, threw water at her, spit on her, and slapped her.

Despite this initial altercation, the couple remained together. Mrs. Baggett occasionally accompanied Defendant on his trips as a truck driver for G&H Trucking and, in May 1999, she traveled with him to California. The incident of violence at issue in this case occurred on or about May 14, 1999, during the couple's return trip to Tennessee. Mrs. Baggett testified that she overheard Defendant and another truck driver talking about a "girl in a pickup truck and her boobs," which caused Mrs. Baggett to become jealous. The couple began arguing about the girl, at which point Defendant physically attacked Mrs. Baggett. While still driving the truck, Defendant bounced Mrs. Baggett's head off the steering wheel, tore her shirt, and choked her. He then pulled into a rest area, threw her into the "sleeper" in the back of the truck cab, and continued to beat her. He slapped, punched, kicked, choked, and spat on her. He told her to stay in the sleeper and that he did not want to see or hear her. Mrs. Baggett did not feel safe or free to leave; she obeyed Defendant's instructions, and he resumed driving. Mrs. Baggett testified that this altercation occurred in Oklahoma.

Eventually, Defendant told Mrs. Baggett to return to the front of the truck. She told him that she needed to use the bathroom and he replied that he was going to pull off at an upcoming exit and that she "wasn't going any further with him." She begged him not to go on without her, because it was the middle of the night and she did not know where she was. In light of the prior altercation with her husband in November 1998, Mrs. Baggett believed that she would not be able to outrun her husband with her injuries.

After passing the exit, Defendant pulled the truck over at a rest stop and continued his physical assault. Defendant once again threw his wife into the sleeper and severely beat her, this time causing her to soil herself. Defendant then walked his wife to the restroom and permitted her to clean herself. Defendant told Mrs. Baggett to hurry and that he did not want to have to "come in there and get [her]." They then returned to the truck, and Defendant decided to take a nap. Mrs. Baggett testified that, while her husband slept, she "sat in the front seat of the truck trying to stay awake, trying to get—my ears were ringing so bad, I couldn't see right. I didn't want to lay down, I thought I had a concussion, I knew I did. I was sick, I was nauseous."

Mrs. Baggett remained in the front of the truck until sunrise. When Defendant awoke, the two talked for an hour or so. He gave her permission to lie down in the back and sleep while he drove to Memphis, their destination. He later told her that she "slept through Arkansas." When they arrived at their destination, a grocery warehouse in Memphis, he woke her up and told her to get out of the sleeper so he could go to sleep. She told him she was injured and that she needed his help, but he said he had "no sympathy" for her. She told him she needed to use a bathroom, and he told her it was in a building nearby. She went to the bathroom, felt dizzy, and vomited. Her next memory is of waking up in the hospital. According to Patricia Cantrell, the witness who found her on the floor of the bathroom, Mrs. Baggett was hysterical and bruised "from head to toe." Her nose was full of blood and she had red marks around her throat. Cantrell testified that Mrs. Baggett told her that Defendant had kept her in the truck with him for three days and that he had beaten [her] on three different occasions, once before they left to come to Memphis. And then they were in our staging area which is where the truckers park overnight and he had beaten her up there. And then when they backed into my dock door, he beat her again and that he wouldn't let her out of the truck these three days, he made her use the bathroom in a cup, he would bring her food to her."

Dr. Charles Roberson, who treated Mrs. Baggett in the emergency room of St. Francis Hospital, testified that she was frightened and in pain when he treated her, and that she had "multiple swollen areas and discolored areas about the head and face, also the neck, upper body front and back, and also the upper extremities." Medical records of Mrs. Baggett's treatment indicate that she was oriented during Dr. Roberson's examination. Mrs. Baggett told Dr. Roberson that she had been assaulted multiple times over several hours, and that the assaults had occurred in more than one place where the truck was parked. The medical records reflect that Mrs. Baggett's injuries were inflicted over a span of twenty-four hours.

James Hogan, a deputy sheriff in Shelby County, arrested Defendant after awakening him from his nap in the truck's sleeper. When Deputy Hogan told Defendant that he was arresting him for domestic assault, Defendant said, "it didn't occur there [*i.e.*, in Tennessee], it occurred in other states previous, earlier in the morning." Deputy Hogan believes that Defendant specifically mentioned Oklahoma and Arkansas.

Although Mrs. Baggett feared for her life after the May assault, she nevertheless visited Mr. Baggett and talked to him on the telephone after his arrest and prior to trial. During these telephone calls and visits, Defendant refreshed Mrs. Baggett's memory as to what transpired during their trip from California to Memphis. Specifically, Defendant told Mrs. Baggett that she slept throughout Arkansas, implying that the assault occurred only in Oklahoma.

Defendant was charged in a two-count indictment with interstate domestic violence, in violation of 18 U.S.C. § 2261(a)(2), and kidnapping, in violation of 18 U.S.C. § 1201. Defendant pleaded not guilty to both counts and the case was tried to a jury before the United States District Court for the Western District of Tennessee, at Memphis. At the close of the government's case-in-chief, defense counsel moved for a judgment of acquittal . . . . The district court reserved decision on the motion until close of all the proof, at which point Defense counsel renewed the . . . motion.

After hearing argument from counsel outside the presence of the jury, the district court decided to grant Defendant's motion for judgment of acquittal on both counts. The court stated:

As I said before it is—it is abundantly clear that—that the government has made out a case of domestic battery, domestic violence, but I don't believe that the proof has made out a case of interstate domestic violence under the federal statute which does require the forcing or causing a partner to cross state lines by force or having this conduct occur as a result of this travel. In this case the violence was really incidental to interstate travel.

The district court also found that there was insufficient proof of confinement to sustain a conviction on the kidnapping count.

The sole dispute regarding the merits of the district court's judgment of acquittal is whether the evidence was sufficient to support the jury's guilty verdict with respect to the interstate domestic violence charge.

Section 2261(a)(2) of Title 18 of the United States Code provides:

> **Causing the crossing of a State line.** A person who causes a spouse or intimate partner to cross a State line or to enter or leave Indian country by force, coercion, duress, or fraud and, in the course or as a result of that conduct, intentionally commits a crime of violence and thereby causes bodily injury to the person's spouse or intimate partner, shall be punished as provided in subsection (b).

The district court found that the government "failed to prove an essential element of the crime, to wit, that the Defendant 'by force, threats, coercion or duress caused the victim to cross state lines.'" The district court further found that the government "failed to prove that the transportation of the victim was against her will, or that she was seized, confined, etc. against her will."

We find that the district court erred in concluding that the government failed to prove that Defendant caused his wife to cross state lines by force, threats, coercion, or duress. First, Deputy Hogan testified that Defendant admitted that the assaults in question occurred in two states. This testimony contradicts one of Defendant's principal arguments on appeal, which is that he and his wife reconciled while still in Oklahoma, and thus that the interstate element of the offense could not be proved. On the basis of Deputy Hogan's testimony alone, the evidence was sufficient to permit the jury to conclude that Mrs. Baggett was forced to cross a state line. Moreover, Patricia Cantrell testified that the victim had told her that she had been beaten before arriving in Tennessee, as well as in Tennessee. Dr. Roberson's testimony further supports the jury's finding that Mrs. Baggett was beaten in more than one state, in that he reported that she was assaulted multiple times over a twenty-four-hour period, and that the assaults occurred in more than one location. Thus, the evidence was sufficient to establish the interstate element of the offense.

The evidence similarly supported a finding that Mrs. Baggett was subject to actual or threatened force of such a nature as to induce a well-founded fear of impending death or serious bodily harm from which there is no reasonable opportunity to escape. The jury was not required to conclude from the mere fact that Mrs. Baggett begged Defendant not to put her out of his truck that she did not wish to escape. To the contrary, the trial transcript indicates that Mrs. Baggett thought Defendant was "just going to sit me out of the truck but he was not going to stop." The jury could infer from that testimony that Mrs. Baggett feared Defendant was going to eject her from a moving vehicle. In any event, Mrs. Baggett also testified that she was unable to outrun Defendant at that time, given her injuries, and that she would have run away from Defendant if she had been able. This evidence demonstrates that, at the time of Defendant's assaults, Mrs. Baggett was a non-consenting participant in the interstate travel. Because a reasonable jury could have found all the elements of the offense defined in § 2261(a)(2) beyond a reasonable doubt, we conclude that the district court erred in granting Defendant's motion for judgment of acquittal.

VAWA and Cancellation of Deportation for Victims of IPV

Persons in the Unites States illegally can be removed. A married or formerly married victim of IPV who is the subject of removal proceedings may apply for cancellation of removal under VAWA. The applicant must show she or he: (1) was battered or subjected to extreme cruelty; (2) the abuser is a U.S. citizen or lawful permanent resident; (3) the victim has been continuously resident in the U.S. for at least three years; (4) good moral character; (5) the victim is not inadmissible due to criminal behavior or marriage fraud; and (6) removal of the victim would cause extreme hardship to the victim or the victim's child.[49]

The Ninth Circuit Court of Appeals' decision in *Hernandez v. Ashcroft* illustrates VAWA's impact on deportation.

Hernandez v. Ashcroft

United States Court of Appeals, Ninth Circuit
345 F.3d 824 (2003)

Paez, Circuit Judge:

While living in Mexico, Laura Luis Hernandez ("Hernandez") experienced life-threatening violence at the hands of her husband, a legal permanent resident of the United States. She fled to the United States, but her husband tracked her down, promised not to hurt her again, and begged her to return to Mexico with him. After Hernandez submitted to his demand and returned to Mexico, the physical abuse began again.

Having escaped her husband permanently, and now living without legal status in the United States, Hernandez applied for suspension of deportation under a provision of the Violence Against Women Act of 1994 ("VAWA") intended to protect immigrants who have suffered domestic violence. With the passage of VAWA, Congress provided a mechanism for women who have been battered or subjected to extreme cruelty to achieve lawful immigration status independent of an abusive spouse. However, the Board of Immigration Appeals ("BIA") affirmed the immigration judge's ("IJ's") denial of Hernandez's application because it determined that Hernandez had not "been battered or subjected to extreme cruelty *in the United States*," as the statute then required.

We interpret the phrase "extreme cruelty" as a matter of first impression. In so doing, we give deference to a regulation promulgated by the Immigration and Naturalization Service ("INS"), and conduct our inquiry in a manner mindful of Congress's intent that domestic violence be evaluated in the context of professional and clinical understandings of violence within intimate relationships. Although Hernandez was not battered in the United States, the interaction that took place in the United States presents a well-recognized stage within the cycle of violence, one which is both psychologically and practical-

---

49   *See* Immigrant Legal Resource Center, *A Guide for Immigration Advocates.* vol. 2 , pp. 11-33 to 11-41 (17th ed. 2010).

ly crucial to maintaining the batterer's control. We conclude that an abuser's behavior during the "contrite" phase of domestic violence may, and in circumstances such as those present here does, constitute "extreme cruelty." Thus, we conclude that Hernandez suffered extreme cruelty in the United States, and we determine that the BIA erred by denying her application for suspension of deportation under VAWA.

Hernandez was thirty years old when she met her future husband, Refugio Acosta Gonzalez ("Refugio"), early in 1990. Refugio frequently ate at a restaurant where Hernandez worked in Mexicali, and after a short while they began dating. Initially, the relationship seemed idyllic. Hernandez believed that Refugio "was a marvelous person, a good person .... he used to give me flowers .... everything was marvelous." After dating for a few months, the two decided to move in together. Several months later, "we were already in love and he asked me to get married." They were married in October 1990, in a small civil ceremony with a few friends present. After the wedding, they continued living in the same apartment in Mexicali.

Following the marriage, however, Refugio's behavior changed drastically. He began drinking heavily and verbally abusing Hernandez, and ultimately began physically abusing her as well. Although the verbal and physical abuse appear to have been constant throughout the marriage, Hernandez described several specific instances of particularly serious physical assault.

On the first occasion, a few months after their marriage, Refugio and Hernandez had gone to the movies. They became separated, and Hernandez was unable to find Refugio. After searching for him without success, she returned home and went to sleep. She was awakened some time later by the shattering of the bedroom window above her head. Refugio entered the darkened room through the broken window, landing on Hernandez. Seeing her, Refugio lifted her by her hair and threw her forcefully against the wall. Hernandez lay where she fell, stunned. Refugio stumbled drunkenly into the kitchen, seized a chair, and broke it across Hernandez's back. He continued hitting and kicking her while uttering insults and other verbal abuse.

Hernandez's head was wounded by the assault, and it was noted during the hearing that she still bears a visible scar from the injury. However, Refugio refused to allow her to leave the house or seek medical treatment. While testifying about this assault Hernandez became upset and began crying. She stated: "I merely cleaned my head and for two days he wouldn't let me go out. He didn't let me go to the hospital to get treatment. I was bleeding alone. He was afraid that I will denounce him to the police, that's why he wouldn't let me go out."

Following this incident Refugio became "the same man that I knew. He was very good and he will behave very well."

In December of 1992 another violent assault occurred. Intoxicated, Refugio broke through the mosquito netting of the kitchen window while Hernandez was sleeping, and again attacked her. He smashed a pedestal fan over her head, breaking it on her forehead.

Hernandez was convinced that Refugio intended to kill her. She was afraid to return to her family in Mexico, because Refugio knew where they lived, and she feared he would follow her and kill her. With the help of a neighbor, Hernandez fled to the United States, to the home of her sister who lived in Los Angeles. However, after two weeks Refugio convinced the neighbor to give him the telephone number of Hernandez's sister. Refugio began calling every day. Ultimately, Hernandez agreed to talk to him. Refugio told Hernandez that he needed her. Hernandez testified, "He was crying. He asked me forgiveness and he said that he wouldn't do it again. And he asked why I had come here.... [I responded,] if I hadn't gone, fled, he would have killed me."

Refugio came to Los Angeles. He told Hernandez that "if I would go back with him he would look for a marriage counselor so that we could save our marriage, because he didn't want to lose me and I also didn't want to leave him." Hernandez believed him, particularly because he had never previously raised the possibility of seeking professional help. Still loving him, and believing his remorse and his promises to change, she returned to Mexico with him.

Upon their return, Hernandez found a marriage counselor. However, despite his earlier promise, Refugio refused to see the counselor. After a brief period, Refugio's violence returned.

The violence culminated several months later when Refugio came home drunk one evening. He beat Hernandez savagely, broke the windows in the house, and destroyed all of the furniture. After the beating, Hernandez "stayed in the corner sitting there in the corner, because I was very hurt." The next morning, Hernandez arose and began cooking breakfast. Behaving as though nothing had occurred, Refugio got up and began helping her. Then, suddenly, Refugio lunged at her with the knife he was using to chop vegetables. Sensing the attack, Hernandez blocked the knife thrust with her arm as Refugio attempted to stab her in the back. The knife gouged Hernandez's hand, slicing through to the bone.

Despite the severity of the wound, Hernandez was unable to go to the hospital to treat the injury. Instead, Refugio kept her trapped inside the house for two days. During these two days, Refugio stayed home with her, no longer beating her. On the third day Refugio returned to work, but he placed a padlock on the front door in order to keep Hernandez locked in the house while he was gone. However, Hernandez had an extra key to the padlock, and she was able to attract the attention of a passing neighbor. She slid the key under the door, and the neighbor unlocked the padlock and released her.

Hernandez went straight to the hospital to get treatment for her hand, but the delay in treatment had resulted in permanent damage to the nerves. The hand continues to give Hernandez great pain, and her use of it is restricted. At the hearing, Hernandez showed the IJ a scar approximately an inch and a half long on her right hand between her index finger and thumb.

In fear for her life, Hernandez again fled to the United States. She did not return to her sister's house, because Refugio knew its location. She explained, "I didn't go there anymore, because he has the address of my sister. He knew where I lived and I didn't want him to—and I didn't want him to find me again. I was very afraid. In fact, I am very afraid that he will find me again and he will kill me." She stayed with a friend in the town of Huron, California, for a few months, and then moved to Salinas.

A year later, in Salinas, she met Paulino Garcia, now her domestic partner, who "has helped me economically and morally with all the problems that I have suffered from my—from the abuse of my—the constant abuse that I suffer from my husband." In 1995, she and Paulino attempted to go to Alaska to work on a fishing boat, but Hernandez was intercepted by the INS at the airport and deportation proceedings were initiated against her.

Hernandez is still married to Refugio, but she has not had any contact with him and does not want him to find her. She believes that if she were required to return to Mexico, Refugio would find her and kill her.

Hernandez was served with an Order to Show Cause on June 8, 1995. She appeared before an IJ, represented by an attorney from the Northwest Immigrant Rights Project, and conceded deportability. Her attorney informed the court that she wished to seek . . . suspension of deportation under VAWA . . . .

Following a hearing, the IJ issued a written opinion, finding Hernandez's testimony to lack credibility due to inconsistencies and the absence of corroborating testimony. The IJ denied her application for suspension of deportation because she had failed to prove she was a victim of domestic violence.

On appeal, the BIA reversed the negative credibility determination, which it determined was unfounded. Nonetheless, the BIA affirmed the IJ's denial of suspension of deportation. With regard to the application for suspension of deportation under VAWA, the BIA determined that Hernandez met the three-year continuous physical presence requirement and the good moral character requirement. However, the BIA concluded that because the acts of physical violence occurred in Mexico, Hernandez was unable to show that she was "battered or subjected to extreme cruelty in the United States," as required by the 1994 version of the statute. Due to this conclusion, the BIA did not consider whether Hernandez had demonstrated extreme hardship.

Hernandez applied for suspension of deportation under section 244(a)(3) of the Immigration and Naturalization Act (INA), 8 U.S.C. § 1254(a)(3) (1996) (now amended and recodified). The former section 244 of the INA provided a method for certain aliens to establish eligibility for a discretionary suspension of deportation and obtain a grant of lawful status. Section 244(a)(3) was added to the INA as part of the passage of the Violence Against Women Act of 1994, in order to assist certain immigrants suffering from domestic violence. This provision provided that the Attorney General had the discretion to suspend deportation proceedings against an individual who: (1) has been physically present in the United States for a continuous period of not less than 3 years immediately preceding the date of such application; (2) has been battered or subjected to extreme cruelty in the United States by a spouse or parent who is a United States citizen or lawful permanent resident; (3) proves that during all of such time in the United States the alien was and is a person of good moral character; (4) and is a person whose deportation would, in the opinion of the Attorney General, result in extreme hardship to the alien or the alien's parent or child.

Hernandez bears the burden of establishing each of these four factors in order to qualify for suspension of deportation under section 244(a)(3). The BIA concluded that Hernandez had established both continuous physical presence and good moral character, the first and third prongs. Hernandez asks us to reverse the BIA's determination that she did not "suffer extreme cruelty in the United States."

There is no dispute that the egregious abuse that Hernandez suffered in Mexico would qualify as battery or extreme cruelty. However, it is also clear that none of the acts of battery that occurred took place in the United States. Although Congress has since removed the requirement that an alien must have suffered from domestic abuse within the United States, Hernandez's case is subject to an older version of VAWA, which did include this requirement. Thus, the question presented is whether the actions taken by Refugio in seeking to convince Hernandez to leave her safe haven in the United States in which she had taken refuge can be deemed to constitute extreme cruelty.

Hernandez and amici argue that the interaction between Hernandez and Refugio in Los Angeles made up an integral stage in the cycle of domestic violence, and thus the actions taken by Refugio in order to lure Hernandez back to the violent relationship constitute extreme cruelty. Although according to common understanding, Refugio's actions might not be perceived as cruel, in enacting VAWA, Congress recognized that lay understandings of domestic violence are frequently comprised of "myths, misconceptions, and victim blaming attitudes," and that background information regarding domestic violence may be crucial in order to understand its essential characteristics and manifestations. Thus, in order to evaluate Hernandez's argument, we must first consider the nature and effects of violence in intimate relationships.

The field of domestic violence and our own case law reflect the fact that Refugio's actions represent a specific phase that commonly recurs in abusive relationships. Abuse within intimate relationships often follows a pattern known as the cycle of violence, "which consists of a tension building phase, followed by acute battering of the victim, and finally by a contrite phase where the batterer's use of promises and gifts increases the battered woman's hope that violence has occurred for the last time." Mary Ann Dutton, *Understanding Women's Responses to Domestic Violence: A Redefinition of Battered Woman Syndrome*, 21 Hofstra L. Rev. 1191, 1208 (1993); Indeed, Hernandez's relationship with Refugio reflected just such a cycle: as described in Hernandez's testimony, following each violent episode, Refugio would for a time again become the man she had loved.

The literature also emphasizes that, although a relationship may appear to be predominantly tranquil and punctuated only infrequently by episodes of violence, abusive behavior does not occur as a series of discrete events, but rather pervades the entire relationship. The effects of psychological abuse, coercive behavior, and the ensuing dynamics of power and control mean that the pattern of violence and abuse can be viewed as a single and continuing entity. Thus, the battered woman's fear, vigilance, or perception that she has few options may persist, even when the abusive partner appears to be peaceful and calm. The psychological role of kindness is also significant in understanding the impact of Refugio's actions on Hernandez, since in combination with the batterer's physical dominance, such kindness often creates an intense emotional dependence by the battered woman on the batterer. Significantly, research also shows that women are often at the highest risk of severe abuse or death when they attempt to leave their abusers.

Understood in light of the familiar dynamics of violent relationships, Refugio's seemingly reasonable actions take on a sinister cast. Following Refugio's brutal and potentially deadly beating, Hernandez fled her job, home, country, and family. Hernandez believed that if she had not fled, Refugio would have killed her. Unwilling to lose control over Hernandez, Refugio stalked her, convincing the very neighbor who helped Hernandez to escape to give him her phone number and calling her sister repeatedly until Hernandez finally agreed to speak with him. Once Refugio was able to speak with Hernandez, he emanated remorse, crying and telling Hernandez that he needed her. Refugio promised not to hurt Hernandez again, and told her that if she would go back to him he would seek counseling. Wounded both emotionally and physically by someone she trusted and loved, Hernandez was vulnerable to such promises. Moreover, Hernandez was well aware of Refugio's potential for violence. Behind Refugio's show of remorse, there also existed the lurking possibility that if Hernandez adamantly refused, Refugio might resort to the extreme violence or murder that commonly results when a woman attempts to flee her batterer. Refugio successfully manipulated Hernandez into leaving the safety that she had found and returning to a deadly relationship in which her physical and mental well-being were in danger. . . .

[T]here is no question that the relationship between Hernandez and Refugio was a violent one. Hernandez's interaction with Refugio in the United States clearly occurred within this context, an observation reaffirmed by the fact that domestic violence is not a phenomenon that appears only at brief isolated times, but instead pervades an entire relationship. Refugio's success in this "contrite" or "hearts and flowers" phase occurred because of Hernandez's emotional vulnerability, the strong emotional bond to Refugio necessitated by his violence, and the underlying threat that the failure to accede to his demands would bring renewed violence. Against this violent backdrop, Refugio's actions in tracking Hernandez down and luring her from the safety of the United States through false promises and short-lived contrition are precisely the type of acts of extreme cruelty that "may not initially appear violent but that are part of an overall pattern of violence." 8 C.F.R. § 204.2(c)(1)(vi). As a result, we hold that Hernandez has established that she was subjected to extreme cruelty in the United States.

C

Practice Exercise: Intimate Partner Violence

Sally and Harry met at a party. Both were twenty. They were immediately attracted to one another, and started dating. For the first six months, everything was roses, and Sally invited Harry to move into her apartment. After they were together a year, Sally and Harry got married while on a short vacation to Las Vegas. It is now five years later, and Sally is sitting in your office. Sally tells you the following:

Not long after we got married, Harry lost his job, and started drinking more. He stayed out late at night with his buddies, and came home drunk too many times for me to count. He started yelling at me and blaming me for his problems. I figured he was depressed for being laid off, and that when he got another job, everything would be ok. But months went by, and he didn't even bother to look for work. He just lived off me. I was waitressing, so we didn't have a lot of money. When I got paid, he took money to party with his friends. A year after we married, I got pregnant. Harry wasn't happy about it. He said, "We can't afford a baby. I don't want a kid." That's when he started getting violent. At first, he'd throw things in our apartment, always when he was drunk. Then he started hitting me. He'd pull my hair and accuse me of getting pregnant by my old boyfriend. I hadn't even seen my old boyfriend in ages. The first time he hurt me was while I was pregnant. He came home drunk and started yelling at me. He called me "bitch" and "fucking whore." Sorry, for the bad language, but he was always calling me bitch and whore, and accusing me of being with other guys. He hit me in the nose with his fist and broke my nose. I called the cops, and they arrested Harry at his parents' house. He went to jail for a few days. God was he mad at me for calling the cops. He called me and left a message on my answering machine. He said, "I'm gonna cut your fucking throat you fucking bitch. You and your fucking baby are gonna die. You deserve to die, you fucking whore." I still have the tape from the answering machine. He moved out. When the baby was born, Harry was working again, and he seemed better. He begged me to take him back. He said, "I'm sorry for what I did before. It was the alcohol. It made me crazy. I love you and I want to be a good dad." I let him move back in, and everything was ok for a while. But then he got into a fight with his boss. He attacked his boss and hurt him pretty bad. Obviously, he was fired. He was sent to jail for six months for assaulting his boss. And his boss got a restraining order against him. When he got out of jail, he came home, but he started drinking again, and he blamed me for his problems. He would hit me on the back of the head with his open hand and say, "It don't leave bruises." He'd yell at me in front of the baby, and make the baby cry. He wouldn't let me go anywhere; even to the grocery store. He'd drive me to work and then he'd pick me when I got off and drive me home. My mom and dad invited us to go camping with them, but he wouldn't let me go. He hates my folks. This went on and on. I can't count the number of times he's hit me and threatened to kill me. I just didn't know what to do. Well, a week ago, he came home drunk again. He started breaking stuff in the apartment. My daughter was there, and I put her in her room and closed the door to keep her safe. I picked up my cell phone to call for help, and he said, "Oh no you don't, bitch. Give me that fucking phone." He grabbed the phone out of my hand and broke it with his foot. He slapped me and knocked me down. He got on top of me and started choking me. I thought I was going to die. I guess a neighbor must have heard the yelling cause the police came in and pulled him off me. They took him to jail, but he bailed out the next day. I'm afraid he'll kill me. Can you help me?

Assignment: You decide to help Sally.

1. Research the law in your state regarding intimate partner violence restraining orders. If your state or county/parish has forms that victims use to obtain a restraining order, get the forms and complete them for Sally. If forms are not available, draft the necessary documents. Apply for an ex parte temporary restraining order by turning in forms in class. What is the procedure to obtain the ex parte order? Assuming an ex parte order is granted, how will the order be served on Harry?

2. You can assume Harry will deny any violence in the relationship, and will insist on a trial regarding a permanent restraining order. Think through how you will prepare for trial. What evidence—witnesses, documents—can you muster to prove the intimate partner violence? Will your evidence be admissible under the rules of evidence?

3. Harry is out of jail. Is Sally safe? A restraining order is a powerful tool, but it is just a piece of paper. Sally and her child need a safety plan. What resources exist in your community to help victims of intimate partner violence? Should Sally consult these services? Would it help Sally or the child to have therapy? (By the way, as Sally's attorney, are *you* safe?)

4. Sally wants a divorce, and she does not want Harry to have custody or visitation with the child, at least until he gets help for his violence and alcohol abuse. Draft documents to initiate a divorce and seek temporary custody for Sally, with no visitation for Harry.

Litigation Against Police for Failure to Enforce IPV Protective Order

Suppose a woman obtains an IPV protection order. The order is given to local police. Unfortunately, the police fail to protect the woman by enforcing the order. Can the woman sue the police for failing to enforce the order? In *Town of Castle Rock v. Gonzales*, the United States Supreme Court grappled with whether victims of IPV can sue police for failing to enforce protective orders.

Town of Castle Rock, Colorado v. Gonzales

United States Supreme Court
545 U.S. 748, 125 S.Ct. 2796 (2005)

Justice Scalia delivered the opinion of the Court.

We decide in this case whether an individual who has obtained a state-law restraining order has a constitutionally protected property interest in having the police enforce the restraining order when they have probable cause to believe it has been violated.

The horrible facts of this case are contained in the complaint that respondent Jessica Gonzales filed in Federal District Court. . . . Respondent alleges that petitioner, the town of Castle Rock, Colorado, violated the Due Process Clause of the Fourteenth Amendment to the United States Constitution when its police officers, acting pursuant to official policy or custom, failed to respond properly to her repeated reports that her estranged husband was violating the terms of a restraining order.

The restraining order had been issued by a state trial court several weeks earlier in conjunction with respondent's divorce proceedings. The original form order, issued on May 21, 1999, and served on respondent's husband on June 4, 1999, commanded him not to "molest or disturb the peace of [respondent] or of any child," and to remain at least 100 yards from the family home at all times. The bottom of the preprinted form noted that the reverse side contained "IMPORTANT NOTICES FOR RESTRAINED PARTIES AND LAW ENFORCEMENT OFFICIALS." The preprinted text on the back of the form included the following "WARNING":

A KNOWING VIOLATION OF A RESTRAINING ORDER IS A CRIME .... A VIOLATION WILL ALSO CONSTITUTE CONTEMPT OF COURT. YOU MAY BE ARRESTED WITHOUT NOTICE IF A LAW ENFORCEMENT OFFICER HAS PROBABLE CAUSE TO BELIEVE THAT YOU HAVE KNOWINGLY VIOLATED THIS ORDER.

The preprinted text on the back of the form also included a "NOTICE TO LAW ENFORCEMENT OFFICIALS," which read in part:

YOU SHALL USE EVERY REASONABLE MEANS TO ENFORCE THIS RESTRAINING ORDER. YOU SHALL ARREST, OR, IF AN ARREST WOULD BE IMPRACTICAL UNDER THE CIRCUMSTANCES, SEEK A WARRANT FOR THE ARREST OF THE RESTRAINED PERSON WHEN YOU HAVE INFORMATION AMOUNTING TO PROBABLE CAUSE THAT THE RESTRAINED PERSON HAS VIOLATED OR ATTEMPTED TO VIOLATE ANY PROVISION OF THIS ORDER AND THE RESTRAINED PERSON HAS BEEN PROPERLY SERVED WITH A COPY OF THIS ORDER OR HAS RECEIVED ACTUAL NOTICE OF THE EXISTENCE OF THIS ORDER.

On June 4, 1999, the state trial court modified the terms of the restraining order and made it permanent. The modified order gave respondent's husband the right to spend time with his three daughters (ages 10, 9, and 7) on alternate weekends, for two weeks during the summer, and, upon reasonable notice, for a midweek dinner visit arranged by the parties; the modified order also allowed him to visit the home to collect the children for such "parenting time."

According to the complaint, at about 5 or 5:30 p.m. on Tuesday, June 22, 1999, respondent's husband took the three daughters while they were playing outside the family home. No advance arrangements had been made for him to see the daughters that evening. When respondent noticed the children were missing, she suspected her husband had taken them. At about 7:30 p.m., she called the Castle Rock Police Department, which dispatched two officers. The complaint continues: "When the officers arrived, she showed them a copy of the TRO and requested that it be enforced and the three children be returned to her immediately. The officers stated that there was nothing they could do about the TRO and suggested that [respondent] call the Police Department again if the three children did not return home by 10:00 p.m."

At approximately 8:30 p.m., respondent talked to her husband on his cellular telephone. He told her "he had the three children at an amusement park in Denver." She called the police again and asked them to "have someone check for" her husband or his vehicle at the amusement park and "put out an all-points bulletin" for her husband, but the officer with whom she spoke "refused to do so," again telling her to "wait until 10:00 p.m. and see if" her husband returned the girls.

At approximately 10:10 p.m., respondent called the police and said her children were still missing, but she was now told to wait until midnight. She called at midnight and told the dispatcher her children were still missing. She went to her husband's apartment and, finding nobody there, called the police at 12:10 a.m.; she was told to wait for an officer to arrive. When none came, she went to the police station at 12:50 a.m. and submitted an incident report. The officer who took the report "made no reasonable effort to enforce the TRO or locate the three children. Instead, he went to dinner."

At approximately 3:20 a.m., respondent's husband arrived at the police station and opened fire with a semiautomatic handgun he had purchased earlier that evening. Police shot back, killing him. Inside the cab of his pickup truck, they found the bodies of all three daughters, whom he had already murdered.

On the basis of the foregoing factual allegations, respondent brought an action under 42 U.S.C. § 1983, claiming that the town violated the Due Process Clause because its police department had "an official policy or custom of failing to respond properly to complaints of restraining order violations" and "tolerated the non-enforcement of restraining orders by its police officers." The complaint also alleged that the town's actions "were taken either willfully, recklessly or with such gross negligence as to indicate wanton disregard and deliberate indifference to" respondent's civil rights.

Before answering the complaint, the defendants filed a motion to dismiss under Federal Rule of Civil Procedure 12(b)(6). The District Court granted the motion, concluding that, whether construed as making a substantive due process or procedural due process claim, respondent's complaint failed to state a claim upon which relief could be granted.

A panel of the Court of Appeals affirmed the rejection of a substantive due process claim, but found that respondent had alleged a cognizable procedural due process claim. On rehearing en banc, a divided court reached the same disposition, concluding that respondent had a "protected property interest in the enforcement of the terms of her restraining order" and that the town had deprived her of due process because "the police never 'heard' nor seriously entertained her request to enforce and protect her interests in the restraining order."

The Fourteenth Amendment to the United States Constitution provides that a State shall not "deprive any person of life, liberty, or property, without due process of law." Amdt. 14, § 1. In 42 U.S.C. § 1983, Congress has created a federal cause of action for "the deprivation of any rights, privileges, or immunities secured by the Constitution and laws." Respondent claims the benefit of this provision on the ground that she had a property interest in police enforcement of the restraining order against her husband; and that the town deprived her of this property without due process by having a policy that tolerated nonenforcement of restraining orders.

As the Court of Appeals recognized, we left a similar question unanswered in *DeShaney v. Winnebago County Dept. of Social Servs.*, 489 U.S. 189, 109 S.Ct. 998, (1989), another case with "undeniably tragic" facts: Local child protection officials had failed to protect a young boy from beatings by his father that left him severely brain damaged. We held that the so-called "substantive" component of the Due Process Clause does not require the State to protect the life, liberty, and property of its citizens against invasion by private actors. We noted, however, that the petitioner had not properly preserved the argument that—and we thus declined to consider whether—state child protection statutes gave him an entitlement to receive protective services in accordance with the terms of the statute, an entitlement which would enjoy due process protection."

The procedural component of the Due Process Clause does not protect everything that might be described as a "benefit": To have a property interest in a benefit, a person clearly must have more than an abstract need or desire and more than a unilateral expectation of it. He must, instead, have a legitimate claim of entitlement to it. Such entitlements are, of course, not created by the Constitution. Rather, they are created and their dimensions are defined by existing rules or understandings that stem from an independent source such as state law.

Our cases recognize that a benefit is not a protected entitlement if government officials may grant or deny it in their discretion. The Court of Appeals in this case determined that Colorado law created an entitlement to enforcement of the restraining order because the "court-issued restraining order specifically dictated that its terms must be enforced" and a "state statute commanded" enforcement of the order when certain objective conditions were met (probable cause to believe that the order had been violated and that the object of the order had received notice of its existence).

The critical language in the restraining order came not from any part of the order itself (which was signed by the state-court trial judge and directed to the restrained party, respondent's husband), but from the preprinted notice to law-enforcement personnel that appeared on the back of the order. That notice effectively restated the statutory provision describing "peace officers' duties" related to the crime of violation of a restraining order. At the time of the conduct at issue in this case, that provision read as follows:

> (a) Whenever a restraining order is issued, the protected person shall be provided with a copy of such order. *A peace officer shall use every reasonable means to enforce a restraining order.*
>
> (b) *A peace officer shall arrest, or, if an arrest would be impractical under the circumstances, seek a warrant for the arrest of a restrained person* when the peace officer has information amounting to probable cause that:
>
> > (I) The restrained person has violated or attempted to violate any provision of a restraining order; and
> >
> > (II) The restrained person has been properly served with a copy of the restraining order or the restrained person has received actual notice of the existence and substance of such order.
>
> (c) In making the probable cause determination described in paragraph (b) of this subsection (3), a peace officer shall assume that the information received from the registry is accurate. *A peace officer shall enforce a valid restraining order whether or not there is a record of the restraining order in the registry.* Colo.Rev.Stat. § 18-6-803.5(3) (emphasis added).

The Court of Appeals concluded that this statutory provision established the Colorado Legislature's clear intent "to alter the fact that the police were not enforcing domestic abuse restraining orders," and thus its intent "that the recipient of a domestic abuse restraining order have an entitlement to its enforcement." Any other result, it said, "would render domestic abuse restraining orders utterly valueless."

This last statement is sheer hyperbole. Whether or not respondent had a right to enforce the restraining order, it rendered certain otherwise lawful conduct by her husband both criminal and in contempt of court. The creation of grounds on which he could be arrested, criminally prosecuted, and held in contempt was hardly "valueless" even if the prospect of those sanctions ultimately failed to prevent him from committing three murders and a suicide.

We do not believe that these provisions of Colorado law truly made enforcement of restraining orders *mandatory*. A well-established tradition of police discretion has long coexisted with apparently mandatory arrest statutes.

Against that backdrop, a true mandate of police action would require some stronger indication from the Colorado Legislature than "shall use every reasonable means to enforce a restraining order" (or even "shall arrest ... or ... seek a warrant"), §§ 18-6-803.5(3)(a), (b). . . .

Respondent does not specify the precise means of enforcement that the Colorado restraining-order statute assertedly mandated whether her interest lay in having police arrest her husband, having them seek a warrant for his arrest, or having them "use every reasonable means, up to and including arrest, to enforce the order's terms." Such indeterminacy is not the hallmark of a duty that is mandatory. Nor can someone be safely deemed "entitled" to something when the identity of the alleged entitlement is vague. . . .

The creation of a personal entitlement to something as vague and novel as enforcement of restraining orders cannot simply go without saying. We conclude that Colorado has not created such an entitlement. . . .

We conclude . . . that respondent did not, for purposes of the Due Process Clause, have a property interest in police enforcement of the restraining order against her husband.

In light of today's decision and that in *DeShaney*, the benefit that a third party may receive from having someone else arrested for a crime generally does not trigger protections under the Due Process Clause, neither in its procedural nor in its "substantive" manifestations. This result reflects our continuing reluctance to treat the Fourteenth Amendment as a font of tort law.

The judgment of the Court of Appeals is Reversed.

Justice Stevens, with whom Justice Ginsburg joins, dissenting.

The issue presented to us is much narrower than is suggested by the far-ranging arguments of the parties and their amici. Neither the tragic facts of the case, nor the importance of according proper deference to law enforcement professionals, should divert our attention from that issue. That issue is whether the restraining order entered by the Colorado trial court on June 4, 1999, created a "property" interest that is protected from arbitrary deprivation by the Due Process Clause of the Fourteenth Amendment.

It is perfectly clear, on the one hand, that neither the Federal Constitution itself, nor any federal statute, granted respondent or her children any individual entitlement to police protection. Nor, I assume, does any Colorado statute create any such entitlement for the ordinary citizen. On the other hand, it is equally clear that federal law imposes no impediment to the creation of such an entitlement by Colorado law. Respondent certainly could have entered into a contract with a private security firm, obligating the firm to provide protection to respondent's family; respondent's interest in such a contract would unquestionably constitute "property" within the meaning of the Due Process Clause. If a Colorado statute enacted for her benefit, or a valid order entered by a Colorado judge, created the functional equivalent of such a private contract by granting respondent an entitlement to mandatory individual protection by the local police force, that state-created right would also qualify as "property" entitled to constitutional protection.

I do not understand the majority to rule out the foregoing propositions, although it does express doubts. Moreover, the majority does not contest that if respondent did have a cognizable property interest in this case, the deprivation of that interest violated due process. As the Court notes, respondent has alleged that she presented the police with a copy of the restraining order issued by the Colorado court and requested that it be enforced. In response, she contends, the officers effectively ignored her. If these allegations are true, a federal statute, 42 U.S.C. § 1983, provides her with a remedy against the petitioner, even if Colorado law does not.

The central question in this case is therefore whether, as a matter of Colorado law, respondent had a right to police assistance comparable to the right she would have possessed to any other service the government or a private firm might have undertaken to provide.

Given that Colorado law has quite clearly eliminated the police's discretion to deny enforcement, respondent is correct that she had much more than a unilateral expectation that the restraining order would be enforced; rather, she had a legitimate claim of entitlement to enforcement. Recognizing respondent's property interest in the enforcement of her restraining order is fully consistent with our precedent. This Court has made clear that the property interests protected by procedural due process extend well beyond actual ownership of real estate, chattels, or money. The types of interests protected as property are varied and, as often as not, intangible, relating to the whole domain of social and economic fact. Thus, our cases have found "property" interests in a number of state-conferred benefits and services, including welfare benefits, disability benefits, public education, utility services, government employment, as well as in other entitlements that defy easy categorization.

Police enforcement of a restraining order is a government service that is no less concrete and no less valuable than other government services, such as education. The relative novelty of recognizing this type of property interest is explained by the relative novelty of the domestic violence statutes creating a mandatory arrest duty; before this innovation, the unfettered discretion that characterized police enforcement defeated any citizen's legitimate claim of entitlement to this service. Novel or not, respondent's claim finds strong support in the principles that underlie our due process jurisprudence. In this case, Colorado law guaranteed the provision of a certain service, in certain defined circumstances, to a certain class of beneficiaries, and respondent reasonably relied on that guarantee. Surely, if respondent had contracted with a private security firm to provide her and her daughters with protection from her husband, it would be apparent that she possessed a property interest in such a contract. Here, Colorado undertook a comparable obligation, and respondent—with restraining order in hand—justifiably relied on that undertaking. Respondent's claim of entitlement to this promised service is no less legitimate than the other claims our cases have upheld, and no less concrete than a hypothetical agreement with a private firm. The fact that it is based on a statutory enactment and a judicial order entered for her special protection, rather than on a formal contract, does not provide a principled basis for refusing to consider it "property" worthy of constitutional protection.

Because respondent had a property interest in the enforcement of the restraining order, state officials could not deprive her of that interest without observing fair procedures. Her description of the police behavior in this case and the department's callous policy of failing to respond properly to reports of restraining order violations clearly alleges a due process violation.

Accordingly, I respectfully dissent.

Inter-American Commission on Human Rights

Disappointed with the U.S. Supreme Court's decision in her case, Jessica Gonzales (Lenahan) filed a petition with the Inter-American Commission on Human Rights, claiming that the failure of the Castle Rock Police Department to enforce the protective order violated her rights under the American Declaration of the Rights and Duties of Man.[50] The Commission agreed, issuing an opinion that failure to enforce the protective order constituted discrimination by the United States. An excerpt from the Commission's opinion follows:

---

50   The Inter-American Commission on Human Rights is an autonomous organ of the Organization of American States.

The Commission concludes that even though the State recognized the necessity to protect Jessica Lenahan and Leslie, Katheryn and Rebecca Gonzales from domestic violence, it failed to meet this duty with due diligence. The state apparatus was not duly organized, coordinated, and ready to protect these victims from domestic violence by adequately and effectively implementing the restraining order at issue; failures to protect which constituted a form of discrimination in violation of Article II of the American Declaration.[51]

These systemic failures are particularly serious since they took place in a context where there has been a historical problem with the enforcement of protection orders; a problem that has disproportionately affected women – especially those pertaining to ethnic and racial minorities and to low income groups – since they constitute the majority of the restraining order holders. Within this context, there is also a high correlation between the problem of wife battering and child abuse, exacerbated when the parties in a marriage separate. Even though the Commission recognizes the legislation and programmatic efforts of the United States to address the problem of domestic violence, these measures had not been sufficiently put into practice in the present case.

The Commission underscores that all States have a legal obligation to protect women from domestic violence: a problem widely recognized by the international community as a serious human rights violation and an extreme form of discrimination. This is part of their legal obligation to respect and ensure the right not to discriminate and to equal protection of the law. This due diligence obligation in principle applies to all OAS Member States.

In the case of Leslie, Katheryn and Rebecca Gonzales, the Commission also establishes that the failure of the United States to adequately organize its state structure to protect them from domestic violence not only was discriminatory, but also constituted a violation of their right to life under Article I and their right to special protection as girl-children under Article VII of the American Declaration.

The State's duty to apply due diligence to act expeditiously to protect girl-children from right to life violations requires that the

---

51 Article II provides "All persons are equal before the law and have the rights and duties established in this Declaration, without distinction as to race, sex, language, creed or any other factor."

authorities in charge of receiving reports of missing persons have the capacity to understand the seriousness of the phenomenon of violence perpetrated against them, and to act immediately. In this case, the police appear to have assumed that Jessica Lenahan's daughters and their friend would be safe with Simon Gonzales because he was Leslie, Katheryn and Rebecca's father. There is broad international recognition of the connection between domestic violence and fatal violence against children perpetrated by parents, and the [Castle Rock Police Department] CRPD officers should have been trained regarding this link. The police officers should also have been aware that the children were at an increased risk of violence due to the separation of their parents, Simon Gonzales' efforts to maintain contact with Jessica Lenahan, and his criminal background. Moreover, the Commission knows of no protocols and/or directives that were in place to guide the police officers at hand on how to respond to reports of missing children in the context of domestic violence and protection orders. The police officers' response throughout the evening was uncoordinated, and not conductive to ascertaining whether the terms of the order had been violated by Simon Gonzales.

As part of its conclusions, the Commission notes that when a State issues a protection order, this has safety implications for the women who requested the protection order, her children and her family members. Restraining orders may aggravate the problem of separation violence, resulting in reprisals from the aggressor directed towards the woman and her children, a problem which increases the need of victims to receive legal protection from the State after an order of this kind has been issued. Jessica Lenahan has declared before the Commission how she desisted from taking more actions to find her daughters that evening thinking that the State would do more to protect them, since she held a restraining order.

The Commission reiterates that State inaction towards cases of violence against women fosters an environment of impunity and promotes the repetition of violence since society sees no evidence of willingness by the State, as the representative of the society, to take effective action to sanction such acts.

Based on these considerations, the Commission holds that the systemic failure of the United States to offer a coordinated effective response to protect Jessica Lenahan and her daughters from domestic violence, constituted an act of discrimination, a breach of their obligation not to discriminate, and a violation of their right to equality before the law under Article II of the American Declaration. The Commission also finds that the State failure to undertake reasonable measures to protect the life of Leslie, Katheryn and Rebecca Gonzales, and that this failure constituted a violation of their right to life established in Article I of the American Declaration, in relation to their right to special protection contained in Article VII of the American Declaration.

CHAPTER 12

Assisted Reproduction

THOUSANDS OF PEOPLE WHO WOULD love to have a baby are unable because of infertility or another medical condition. Some people who are biologically capable of "normal" reproduction eschew traditional reproduction to avoid passing to their offspring an inheritable disease. To have the family they want, some lesbian and gay individuals pursue reproductive alternatives.

Virginia's statute on "assisted conception" provides insight into this complicated and evolving area. Virginia defines assisted conception as "a pregnancy resulting from any intervening medical technology, whether in vivo or in vitro, which completely or partially replaces sexual intercourse as the means of conception. Such intervening medical technology includes, but is not limited to, conventional medical and surgical treatment as well as noncoital reproductive technology such as artificial insemination by donor, cryopreservation of gametes and embryos, in vitro fertilization, uterine embryo lavage, embryo transfer, gamete intrafallopian tube transfer, and low tubal ovum transfer."[1]

Few states have comprehensive statutes on alternative means of reproduction, and many aspects of the subject are left to the courts. Judges are not thrilled that the issue tossed in their laps. Judges generally believe the legislature should tackle the issue. In *Marriage of Buzzanca*,[2] the California Court of Appeal implored the legislature "to sort out the parental rights and responsibilities of those involved in artificial reproduction." The Connecticut Supreme Court observed in *Raftopol v. Ramey*,[3] "The broad public policy issues raised by

---

1 Va. Code Ann. § 20-156.

2 61 Cal. App. 4th 1410, 1428 (1998).

3 299 Conn. 681, 12 A.3d 783 (2011).

modern reproductive technology . . . . more appropriately would be addressed by the legislature."

Intrauterine Insemination

Intrauterine insemination, commonly called artificial insemination, is a relatively simple process by which sperm is placed in a woman's reproductive tract to induce pregnancy.[4] The sperm donor may be the woman's partner or a donor. A non-partner sperm donor may be used if the partner is sterile or has a low sperm count. A non-partner sperm donor may be used so the partner does not pass a genetic condition to the baby. In *People v. Sorensen*,[5] the California Supreme Court ruled that when an infertile husband consents to the artificial insemination of his wife, the husband is the "lawful father" of the resulting baby because he consents to creation of the child. Similarly, Arkansas law provides, "Any child born to a married woman by means of artificial insemination shall be deemed the legitimate natural child of the woman and the woman's husband if the husband consents in writing to the artificial insemination."[6]

In Vitro Fertilization

In vitro fertilization (IVF) is a medical "procedure in which an ovum is surgically removed from a genetic mother's ovary and fertilized with the sperm of the genetic father in a laboratory procedure, with the resulting embryo implanted in the uterus of a birth mother."[7] Charles Kindregan and Maureen

---

4 *See* William M. Lopez (Note) Artificial Insemination and the Presumption of Parenthood: Traditional Foundations and Modern Applications for Lesbian Mothers, 86 *Chicago-Kent Law Review* 897 (2011)("While most people think that artificial insemination is a relatively new procedure, the process of artificial insemination can actually be traced back to 220 A.D., with the first reported human case occurring in England in 1770. In the United States, the first reported artificial insemination procedure occurred in 1866, but it was met with public outrage, and the procedure was effectively discontinued for some time. The first known case of [artificial insemination by anonymous donor] in the United States was performed in 1884. Today, artificial insemination is a popular and publicly accepted manner of producing children when a woman's partner cannot provide viable sperm, or when the mother decides to have her child without a partner."

5 68 Cal.2d 280 (1968).

6 Ark. Code Ann. § 9-10-201(a).

7 D.C. Stat. § 16-401(3).

See J.B. v. M.B., 170 N.J. 9, 783 A.2d 707, 709 (2001)("The in vitro fertilization procedure requires a woman to undergo a series of hormonal injections to stimulate the production of mature oocytes (egg cells or ova). The medication causes the ovaries to release multiple egg cells during a menstrual cycle rather than the single egg normally produced. The eggs are retrieved from the woman's body and examined by a physician who evaluates their quality for fertilization. Egg cells ready for insemination are then combined with the sperm sample and allowed to incubate for approximately twelve to eighteen hours. Successful fertilization results in a zygote that develops into a four- to eight-cell pre-embryo. At that stage, the pre-embryos are either returned to the woman's uterus for

McBrien write, "For the most part, there is no state statutory regulation of in vitro fertilization that restricts or controls choices made by medical personnel, patients, or donors."[8]

Typically with IVF, more than one egg is removed and fertilized. The "extra" embryos—sometimes called pre-embryos—are frozen for later use in case the initial effort at pregnancy fails.[9]

What should be done with unused embryos if a couple decides not to have children, divorces, separates, or dies? One of the first court decisions grappling with this question was *Davis v. Davis*,[10] handed down in 1992 by the Tennessee Supreme Court. Wife and husband divorced and agreed on everything except who was to have "custody" of seven frozen embryos. When the couple enrolled in IVF, they did not sign a document providing for disposition of unused embryos. The trial judge concluded the embryos were human beings and awarded custody to wife so she could "bring these children to term through implantation" if she so desired. The intermediate court of appeal reversed, concluding that husband had a constitutional right *not* to have children. As the case was pending before the Tennessee Supreme Court, wife changed her position and sought to donate the embryos to a couple desiring a child. Husband sought destruction of the embryos.

One issue confronting the Tennessee Supreme Court was whether the embryos were "persons" or "property." The court observed: "Three major ethical positions have been articulated in the debate over pre-embryo status. At one extreme is the view of the pre-embryo as a human subject after fertilization, which requires that it be accorded the rights of a person. . . . At the opposite extreme is the view that the pre-embryo has a status no different from any other human tissue. . . . A third view—one that is most widely held—takes an intermediate position between the other two. It holds that the pre-embryo deserves respect greater than accorded to human tissue but not the respect accorded to actual persons." The Tennessee court concluded, "Pre-embryos are not, strictly speaking, either 'persons' or 'property,' but occupy an interim category that entitled them to special respect because of their potential for human life."

---

implantation or cryopreserved at a temperature of -196 C and stored for possible future use.").

8   Charles P. Kindregan, Jr. & Maureen McBrien, *Assisted Reproductive Technology*, p. 96 (2011).

9   *See* J.B. v. M.B., 170 N.J. 9, 783 A.2d 707, 708 n.1 (2001)("A pre-embryo is a fertilized ovum (egg cell) up to approximately fourteen days old (the point when it implants in the uterus). . . . [W]e use the term 'pre-embryo' rather than 'embryo,' because pre-embryo is technically descriptive of the cells' stage of development when they are cryopreserved (frozen).").

10   842 S.W.2d 588 (Tenn. 1992).

The court concluded that disputes regarding the disposition of unused frozen embryos should be governed by the preference of the parties. If the parties disagree, a prior agreement concerning disposition should be enforced.[11] If no agreement exists, the trial judge balances the interests of the parties in using and not using the embryos. Typically, the wishes of the party who does not want a child should control, provided the other party has some other reasonable means of becoming a parent. If no other means exists, then the court considers the argument in favor of using the embryos to achieve pregnancy. However, if the party seeking to preserve the embryos intends to donate them to someone else, the wishes of the other party should prevail.

Since the wife in *Davis v. Davis* intended to donate the embryos, the husband's wish to have the embryos destroyed should control. The court concluded that the fertility clinic was free to follows its normal procedure for dealing with unused embryos.

The Louisiana Legislature tackled the question, "Is a fertilized ovum a person?" Louisiana law states, "An in vitro fertilized ovum is a juridical person which cannot be owned by the in vitro fertilization parents who owe it a high duty of care and prudent administration. If the in vitro parents renounce, by notarial act, their parental rights for in utero implantation, then the in vitro fertilized human ovum shall be available for adoptive implantation in accordance with written procedures of the facility where it is housed or stored."[12]

In 1998, in *Kass v. Kass*, the New York Court of Appeal decided whether to enforce a contract regarding disposition of frozen embryos.

Kass v. Kass

Court of Appeals of New York
91 N.Y.2d 554, 696 N.E.2d 174 (1998)

Kaye, Chief Judge.

Although in vitro fertilization (IVF) procedures are now more than two decades old and in wide use, this is the first such dispute to reach our Court. Specifically in issue is the disposition of five frozen, stored pre-embryos, or

---

11 *See* Marriage of Angle, 222 Or. App. 572, 194 P.3d 834 (2008)(husband appealed divorce judgment that ordered destruction of 6 frozen embryos; held, affirmed); Roman v. Roman, 193 S.W.3d 40 (Tex. Ct. App. 2006) (agreement providing that frozen embryos were to be discarded in event of divorce was enforceable).

12 La. Stat. Ann. tit. 9, § 130.

"pre-zygotes,"[13] created five years ago, during the parties' marriage, to assist them in having a child. Now divorced, appellant (Maureen Kass) wants the pre-zygotes implanted, claiming this is her only chance for genetic motherhood; respondent (Steven Kass) objects to the burdens of unwanted fatherhood, claiming that the parties agreed at the time they embarked on the effort that in the present circumstances the pre-zygotes would be donated to the IVF program for approved research purposes. Like the two-Justice plurality at the Appellate Division, we conclude that the parties' agreement providing for donation to the IVF program controls. The Appellate Division order should therefore be affirmed.

Appellant and respondent were married on July 4, 1988, and almost immediately began trying to conceive a child. While appellant believed that, owing to prenatal exposure to diethylstilbestrol (DES) she might have difficulty carrying a pregnancy to term, her condition in fact was more serious—she failed to become pregnant. In August 1989, the couple turned to John T. Mather Memorial Hospital in Port Jefferson, Long Island and, after unsuccessful efforts to conceive through artificial insemination, enrolled in the hospital's IVF program.

Typically, the IVF procedure begins with hormonal stimulation of a woman's ovaries to produce multiple eggs. The eggs are then removed by laparoscopy or ultrasound-directed needle aspiration and placed in a glass dish, where sperm are introduced. Once a sperm cell fertilizes the egg, this fusion—or pre-zygote—divides until it reaches the four- to eight-cell stage, after which several pre-zygotes are transferred to the woman's uterus by a cervical catheter. If the procedure succeeds, an embryo will attach itself to the uterine wall, differentiate and develop into a fetus. As an alternative to immediate implantation, pre-zygotes may be cryopreserved indefinitely in liquid nitrogen for later use. Cryopreservation serves to reduce both medical and physical costs because eggs do not have to be retrieved with each attempted implantation, and delay may actually improve the chances of pregnancy. At the same time, the preservation of "extra" pre-zygotes—those not immediately implanted—allows for later disagreements, as occurred here.

Beginning in March 1990, appellant underwent the egg retrieval process five times and fertilized eggs were transferred to her nine times. She became pregnant twice—once in October 1991, ending in a miscarriage and again a few months later, when an ectopic pregnancy had to be surgically terminated.

---

13 We use the parties' term "pre-zygotes," which are defined in the record as "eggs which have been penetrated by sperm but have not yet joined genetic material."

Before the final procedure, for the first time involving cryopreservation, the couple on May 12, 1993 signed four consent forms provided by the hospital. Each form begins on a new page, with its own caption and "Patient Name." The first two forms, "GENERAL INFORMED CONSENT FORM NO. 1: IN VITRO FERTILIZATION AND EMBRYO TRANSFER" and "ADDENDUM NO. 1–1," consist of 12 single-spaced typewritten pages explaining the procedure, its risks and benefits, at several points indicating that, before egg retrieval could begin, it was necessary for the parties to make informed decisions regarding disposition of the fertilized eggs. ADDENDUM NO. 1–1 concludes as follows:

> We understand that it is general IVF Program Policy, as medically determined by our IVF physician, to retrieve as many eggs as possible and to inseminate and transfer 4 of those mature eggs in this IVF cycle, unless our IVF physician determines otherwise. It is necessary that we decide * * * [now] how excess eggs are to be handled by the IVF Program and how many embryos to transfer. *We are to indicate our choices by signing our initials where noted below.*
>
> 1. We consent to the retrieval of as many eggs as medically determined by our IVF physician. If more eggs are retrieved than can be transferred during this IVF cycle, we direct the IVF Program to take the following action (choose one):
>
> a. The excess eggs are to be inseminated and cryopreserved for possible use by us during a later IVF cycle. We understand that our choice of this option requires us to complete an additional Consent Form for Cryopreservation.

The "Additional Consent Form for Cryopreservation," a seven-page, single-spaced typewritten document, is also in two parts. The first, "INFORMED CONSENT FORM NO. 2: CRYOPRESERVATION OF HUMAN PRE–ZYGOTES," provides:

> III. Disposition of Pre–Zygotes.
>
> We understand that our frozen pre-zygotes will be stored for a maximum of 5 years. We have the principal responsibility to decide the disposition of our frozen pre-zygotes. Our frozen pre-zygotes will not be released from storage for any purpose without the written consent of *both* of us, consistent with the policies of the IVF Program and applicable law. In the event of divorce, we understand that legal ownership of any stored pre-zygotes must be determined in a property settle-

ment and will be released as directed by order of a court of competent jurisdiction. Should we for any reason no longer wish to attempt to initiate a pregnancy, we understand that we may determine the | disposition of our frozen pre-zygotes remaining in storage.* * *

The possibility of our death or any other unforeseen circumstances that may result in neither of us being able to determine the disposition of any stored frozen pre-zygotes requires that we now indicate our wishes. THESE IMPORTANT DECISIONS MUST BE DISCUSSED WITH OUR IVF PHYSICIAN AND OUR WISHES MUST BE STATED (BEFORE EGG RETRIEVAL) ON THE ATTACHED ADDENDUM NO. 2–1, STATEMENT OF DISPOSITION. THIS STATEMENT OF DISPOSITION MAY BE CHANGED ONLY BY OUR SIGNING ANOTHER STATEMENT OF DISPOSITION WHICH IS FILED WITH THE IVF PROGRAM."

The second part, titled "INFORMED CONSENT FORM NO. 2—ADDENDUM NO. 2–1: CRYOPRESERVATION—STATEMENT OF DISPOSITION," states:

We understand that it is IVF Program Policy to obtain our informed consent to the number of pre-zygotes which are to be cryopreserved and to the disposition of excess cryopreserved pre-zygotes. *We are to indicate our choices by signing our initials where noted below.*

1. We consent to cryopreservation of all pre-zygotes which are not transferred during this IVF cycle for possible use * * * by us in a future IVF cycle. * * *

2. In the event that we no longer wish to initiate a pregnancy or are unable to make a decision regarding the disposition of our stored, frozen pre-zygotes, we now indicate our desire for the disposition of our pre-zygotes and direct the IVF program to (choose one): * * *

a. Our frozen pre-zygotes may be examined by the IVF Program for biological studies and be disposed of by the IVF Program for approved research investigation as determined by the IVF Program."

On May 20, 1993, doctors retrieved 16 eggs from appellant, resulting in nine pre-zygotes. Two days later, four were transferred to appellant's sister, who had volunteered to be a surrogate mother, and the remaining five were cryopreserved. The couple learned shortly thereafter that the results were negative and that appellant's sister was no longer willing to participate in the program. They then decided to dissolve their marriage. The total cost of their IVF efforts exceeded $75,000.

With divorce imminent, the parties themselves on June 7, 1993—barely three weeks after signing the consents—drew up and signed an "uncontested divorce" agreement, typed by appellant, including the following:

> The disposition of the frozen 5 pre-zygotes at Mather Hospital is that they should be disposed of in the manner outlined in our consent form and that neither Maureen Kass, Steve Kass or anyone else will lay claim to custody of these pre-zygotes.

On June 28, 1993, appellant by letter informed the hospital and her IVF physician of her marital problems and expressed her opposition to destruction or release of the pre-zygotes.

One month later, appellant commenced the present matrimonial action, requesting sole custody of the pre-zygotes so that she could undergo another implantation procedure. Respondent opposed removal of the pre-zygotes and any further attempts by appellant to achieve pregnancy, and counterclaimed for specific performance of the parties' agreement to permit the IVF program to retain the pre-zygotes for research, as specified in ADDENDUM NO. 2-1. By stipulation dated December 17, 1993, the couple settled all issues in the matrimonial action except each party's claim with respect to the pre-zygotes, which was submitted to the court for determination. While this aspect of the case remained open, a divorce judgment was entered on May 16, 1994. . . .

Supreme Court granted appellant custody of the pre-zygotes and directed her to exercise her right to implant them within a medically reasonable time. The court reasoned that a female participant in the IVF procedure has exclusive decisional authority over the fertilized eggs created through that process, just as a pregnant woman has exclusive decisional authority over a nonviable fetus, and that appellant had not waived her right either in the May 12, 1993 consents or in the June 7, 1993 "uncontested divorce" agreement.

While a divided Appellate Division reversed that decision, all five Justices unanimously agreed on two fundamental propositions. First, they concluded that a woman's right to privacy and bodily integrity are not implicated before implantation occurs. Second, the court unanimously recognized that when parties to an IVF procedure have themselves determined the disposition of any unused fertilized eggs, their agreement should control.

The panel split, however, on the question whether the agreement at issue was sufficiently clear to control disposition of the pre-zygotes. According to the two-Justice plurality, the agreement unambiguously indicated the parties' desire to donate the pre-zygotes for research purposes if the couple could not reach a joint decision regarding disposition. The concurring Justice agreed to reverse but found the consent fatally ambiguous. In his view, but for the most exceptional circumstances, the objecting party should have a veto over a former spouse's proposed implantation, owing to the emotional and financial burdens of compelled parenthood. A fact-finding hearing would be authorized only when the party desiring parenthood could make a threshold showing of no other means of achieving genetic or adoptive parenthood, which was not shown on this stipulated record.

While agreeing with the concurrence that the informed consent document was ambiguous, the two-Justice dissent rejected a presumption in favor of either party and instead concluded that the fate of the pre-zygotes required a balancing of the parties' respective interests and burdens, as well as their personal backgrounds, psychological make-ups, financial and physical circumstances. Factors would include appellant's independent ability to support the child and the sincerity of her emotional investment in this particular reproductive opportunity, as well as the burdens attendant upon a respondent's unwanted fatherhood and his motivations for objecting to parenthood. Finding that the record was insufficient to permit a fair balancing, and that the parties' January 9, 1995 stipulation that there would be no further submissions violated public policy because it precluded full review, the dissent would remit the case to the trial court for a full hearing.

We now affirm, agreeing with the plurality that the parties clearly expressed their intent that in the circumstances presented the pre-zygotes would be donated to the IVF program for research purposes.

We begin analysis with a brief description of the broader legal context of this dispute. In the past two decades, thousands of children have been born through IVF, the best known of several methods of assisted reproduction. Additionally, tens of thousands of frozen embryos annually are routinely stored in liquid nitrogen canisters, some having been in that state for more than 10 years with no instructions for their use or disposal . . . . As science races ahead, it leaves in its trail mind-numbing ethical and legal questions . . . .

The law, whether statutory or decisional, has been evolving more slowly and cautiously. A handful of States—New York not among them—have adopted statutes touching on the disposition of stored embryos (*see, e.g.,* Fla. Stat. Annot § 742.17 [couples must execute written agreement providing for disposition in event of death, divorce or other unforeseen circumstances]; N.H. Rev. Stat. Annot. §§ 168–B:13 – 168–B:15, 168–B:18 [couples must undergo medical exams and counseling; 14–day limit for maintenance of *ex utero* pre-zygotes]; La.Rev. Stat.Annot. §§ 9:121 – 9:133 [pre-zygote considered "juridical person" that must be implanted]).

In the case law, only *Davis v. Davis*, 842 S.W.2d 588, 604 [Tenn. 1992] attempts to lay out an analytical framework for disputes between a divorcing couple regarding the disposition of frozen embryos. . . . Having declared that embryos are entitled to "special respect because of their potential for human life" *Davis* recognized the procreative autonomy of both gamete providers, which includes an interest in avoiding genetic parenthood as well as an interest in becoming a genetic parent. In the absence of any prior written agreement between the parties—which should be presumed valid, and implemented—according to *Davis*, courts must in every case balance these competing interests, each deserving of judicial respect. In *Davis* itself, that balance weighed in favor of the husband's interest in avoiding genetic parenthood, which was deemed more significant than the wife's desire to donate the embryos to a childless couple.

Although statutory and decisional law are sparse, abundant commentary offers a window on the issues ahead, particularly suggesting various approaches to the issue of disposition of pre-zygotes. Some commentators would vest control in one of the two gamete providers (*see, e.g.,* Poole, *Allocation of Decision-Making Rights to Frozen Embryos*, 4 Am J. Fam. L. 67 [1990] [pre-zygotes to party wishing to avoid procreation]; Andrews, *The Legal Status of the Embryo*, 32 Loy. L. Rev. 357 [1986] [woman retains authority when she desires to implant]). Others would imply a contract to procreate from participation in an IVF program (*see, e.g.,* Note, *Davis v. Davis: What About Future Disputes?*, 26 Conn. L. Rev. 305 [1993]; Comment, *Frozen Embryos: Towards An Equitable Solution*, 46 U. Miami L. Rev. 803 [1992]).

Yet a third approach is to regard the progenitors as holding a "bundle of rights" in relation to the pre-zygote that can be exercised through joint disposition agreements (*see,* Robertson, *Prior Agreements for Disposition of Frozen Embryos*, 51 Ohio St. L.J. 407 [1990] ["Prior Agreements "]; Robertson, *In the Beginning: The Legal Status of Early Embryos*, 76 Va. L. Rev. 437 [1990] ["Early Embryos "]). The most recent view—a "default rule"—articulated in the report of the New York State Task Force on Life and the Law, is that, while gamete bank regulations should require specific instructions regarding disposition, no embryo should be implanted, destroyed or used in research over the objection of an individual with decision-making authority. . . .

Like the Appellate Division, we conclude that disposition of these pre-zygotes does not implicate a woman's right of privacy or bodily integrity in the area of reproductive choice; nor are the pre-zygotes recognized as "persons" for constitutional purposes . . . . The relevant inquiry thus becomes who has dispositional authority over them. Because that question is answered in this case by the parties' agreement, for purposes of resolving the present appeal we have no cause to decide whether the pre-zygotes are entitled to "special respect." . . .

Agreements between progenitors, or gamete donors, regarding disposition of their pre-zygotes should generally be presumed valid and binding, and enforced in any dispute between them. Indeed, parties should be encouraged in advance, before embarking on IVF and cryopreservation, to think through possible contingencies and carefully specify their wishes in writing. Explicit agreements avoid costly litigation in business transactions. They are all the more necessary and desirable in personal matters of reproductive choice, where the intangible costs of any litigation are simply incalculable. Advance directives, subject to mutual change of mind that must be jointly expressed, both minimize misunderstandings and maximize procreative liberty by reserving to the progenitors the authority to make what is in the first instance a quintessentially personal, private decision. Written agreements also provide the certainty needed for effective operation of IVF programs.

While the value of arriving at explicit agreements is apparent, we also recognize the extraordinary difficulty such an exercise presents. All agreements looking to the future to some extent deal with the unknown. Here, however, the uncertainties inherent in the IVF process itself are vastly complicated by cryopreservation, which extends the viability of pre-zygotes indefinitely and allows time for minds, and circumstances, to change. Divorce; death, disappearance or incapacity of one or both partners; aging; the birth of other children are but a sampling of obvious changes in individual circumstances that might take place over time.

These factors make it particularly important that courts seek to honor the parties' expressions of choice, made before disputes erupt, with the parties' overall direction always uppermost in the analysis. Knowing that advance agreements will be enforced underscores the seriousness and integrity of the consent process. Advance agreements as to disposition would have little purpose if they were enforceable only in the event the parties continued to agree. To the extent possible, it should be the progenitors—not the State and not the courts—who by their prior directive make this deeply personal life choice.

Here, the parties prior to cryopreservation of the pre-zygotes signed consents indicating their dispositional intent. While these documents were technically provided by the IVF program, neither party disputes that they are an expression of their own intent regarding disposition of their pre-zygotes. Nor do the parties contest the legality of those agreements, or that they were freely and knowingly made. The central issue is whether the consents clearly express the parties' intent regarding disposition of the pre-zygotes in the present circumstances. Appellant claims the consents are fraught with ambiguity in this respect; respondent urges they plainly mandate transfer to the IVF program.

The subject of this dispute may be novel but the common-law principles governing contract interpretation are not. Whether an agreement is ambiguous is a question of law for the courts. Ambiguity is determined by looking within the four corners of the document, not to outside sources. . . .

Applying those principles, we agree that the informed consents signed by the parties unequivocally manifest their mutual intention that in the present circumstances the pre-zygotes be donated for research to the IVF program. . . .

As they embarked on the IVF program, appellant and respondent— "husband" and "wife," signing as such—clearly contemplated the fulfillment of a life dream of having a child during their marriage. The consents they signed provided for other contingencies, most especially that in the present circumstances the pre-zygotes would be donated to the IVF program for approved research purposes. These parties having clearly manifested their intention, the law will honor it.

Accordingly, the order of the Appellate Division should be affirmed, with costs.

In *Kass v. Kass*, the parties signed an unambiguous agreement regarding disposition of their pre-embryos. By contrast, in *J.B. v. M.B.*[14] the parties' agreement was not dispositive regarding disposition, and the matter was left to the courts. The New Jersey Supreme Court wrote:

> In this area, however, there are few guideposts for decision-making. Advances in medical technology have far outstripped the development of legal principles to resolve the inevitable disputes arising out of the new reproductive opportunities now available. For infertile couples, those opportunities may present the only way to

---

14   170 N.J. 9, 783 A.2d 707 (2001).

have a biological family. Yet, at the point when a husband and wife decide to begin the in vitro fertilization process, they are unlikely to anticipate divorce or to be concerned about the disposition of pre-embryos on divorce. As they are both contributors of the genetic material comprising the pre-embryos, the decision should be theirs to make. . . .

We agree with the Tennessee Supreme Court [in *Davis v. Davis*, 842 S.W.2d 588 (Tenn. 1992)] that ordinarily, the party wishing to avoid procreation should prevail. . . . In the present case, the wife's right not to become a parent seemingly conflicts with the husband's right to procreate. The conflict, however, is more apparent than real. Recognition and enforcement of the wife's right would not seriously impair the husband's right to procreate. Though his right to procreate using the wife's eggs would be terminated, he retains the capacity to father children.

In other words, [father's] right to procreate is not lost if he is denied an opportunity to use or donate the pre-embryos. [Father] is already a father and is able to become a father to additional children, whether through natural procreation or further in vitro fertilization. In contrast, [mother's] right not to procreate may be lost through attempted use or through donation of the pre-embryos. Implantation, if successful, would result in the birth of her biological child and could have life-long emotional and psychological repercussions. Her fundamental right not to procreate is irrevocably extinguished if a surrogate mother bears J.B.'s child. We will not force [mother] to become a parent against her will. . . .

We believe that the better rule, and the one we adopt, is to enforce agreements entered into at the time in vitro fertilization is begun, subject to the right of either party to change his or her mind about disposition up to the point of use or destruction of any stored pre-embryos. . . . Only when a party notifies a clinic in writing of a change in intention should the disposition issue be reopened. . . .

Finally, if there is disagreement as to disposition because one party has reconsidered his or her earlier decision, the interests of both parties must be evaluated. Because ordinarily the party choosing not to become a biological parent will prevail, we do not anticipate increased litigation as a result of our decision.

Question on IVF

Wendy and Hank were married five years when Wendy, at age 36, was diagnosed with breast cancer. Wendy's doctor informed her that the cancer treatment might make it impossible for Wendy to become pregnant. Wendy and Hank decided to undergo in vitro fertilization (IVF) to preserve Wendy's ability to conceive a child. Wendy deferred cancer treatment several months to undergo IVF. The IVF process resulted in 13 pre-embryos using Wendy's eggs and Hank's sperm. The pre-embryos were cryopreserved and remain frozen. Wendy and Hank did not sign an agreement regarding disposition of the pre-embryos. After IVF, Wendy underwent extensive cancer treatment, including surgery, chemotherapy, and radiation. After the cancer treatment was completed successfully, Wendy was told she probably could not have children. Not long after the cancer treatment, Hank filed for divorce. Hank had become involved with Sue, and Hank and Sue's child was born before Wendy and Hank were divorced. After Wendy and Hank divorced, Hank married Sue and had a second child with Sue. Hank and Sue intend to have four children. Two years after Wendy and Hank divorced, Wendy seeks to become pregnant with a cryopreserved pre-embryo. Hank objects because he does not want to be a father with Wendy. Should Wendy be permitted to use one or more of the pre-embryos to have a baby? *Reber v. Reiss*, 42 A.3d 1131 (Pa. Super. 2012).

When Donation of Unused Embryos is Intended to Support Family-Building, Should Adoption Law Apply?

When an individual or couple decides to donate unused frozen embryos to others who desire a child, who is the parent of a resulting baby? Ohio law provides, "A woman who gives birth to a child as a result of embryo donation shall be treated in law and regarded as the natural mother of the child."[15]

Should embryo donation be treated as an adoption governed by adoption law? If an embryo is a "person," adoption law applies. Nightlight Christian Adoptions pioneered "embryo adoption" with its Snowflakes Frozen Embryo Adoption Program. Several other adoption agencies offer embryo adoption services. (*See* embryoadoption.org).

The American Society for Reproductive Medicine takes the position that

---

15 Ohio Rev. Code tit. 31, § 3111.97(A).

embryo donation should not be considered adoption.[16] The Society's Ethics Committee wrote:

> Donation of embryos to support the family-building efforts of others is an important option for patients considering the disposition of cryopreserved embryos in excess of those needed to meet the patients' own fertility goals. . . .
>
> Application of the term 'adoption' to embryos is inaccurate, misleading, and could place burdens that are not appropriate for embryos that have been donated upon infertile recipients. . . .
>
> In previous reports, this Committee has made clear its view that embryos should be accorded an elevated moral status compared with other human tissues, but that they should not be viewed as persons. . . .
>
> The use of donated embryos for family building is an established successful option for the infertile. Like gamete donation, it has resulted in the birth of many children in the more than 25 years the procedure has been in use. . . .
>
> Requiring infertile patients who need donor gametes or patients who need donor embryos to suffer the imposition of unnecessary administrative and legal trappings of adoption and the costs that accompany them is not ethically justifiable. . . . The donation of embryos for reproductive purposes is fundamentally a medical procedure intended to result in pregnancy and should be treated as such.

In a 2011 article in the *International Journal of Law, Policy and the Family* Eric Blyth and colleagues wrote:

> [The American Society for Reproductive Medicine's] endorsement of a 'one-size fits all' model of embryo relinquishment that equates it with (its own version of) gamete donation appears to us an oversimplification of what is conceptually complex, perpetuating a profession-dominated service ethic that pays scant regard to patient-centered care. . . .

---

16   American Society for Reproductive Medicine, Ethics Committee, American Society for Reproductive Medicine: Defining Embryo Donation, 92 *Fertility and Sterility* 1818 (2009).

The reality is that both embryo donation and embryo adoption are likely to continue to operate as alternative systems to facilitate the relinquishment of unused embryos for family building. . . .

In our view, there is no compelling case to justify the pre-eminence of a single model for embryo relinquishment. A dual or even multi-model system is preferable that takes into account the diversity of contemporary societies, maximizing choice for both those with unused embryos and potential recipients—which a single model would invariably restrict. The views of individuals with unused embryos indicate that it is possible to conceive of unused embryos as "unborn children" and as "unborn siblings" of existing children and yet permit their destruction or endorse a woman's right to terminate her pregnancy, thus avoiding adversely impacting women's right to choose and embroilment in abortion politics. The research evidence base suggests that for the majority of couples in the sample populations, the key to disposition decisionmaking is their kinship relationship with the embryo, rather than ideological or religious perceptions of the status of the embryo per se. And while we have no wish to minimize acknowledgement that such a choice is a *hard* choice, it is, nevertheless, not an *impossible* choice. Thus, a "right-to-choose" approach—the right of relinquishing couples to dispose of unused embryos as they see fit and the right of recipients to receive relinquished embryos for family building that does not impact on others' right to choose—seems to us the most appropriate way forward in principle for maximizing acceptable disposition options for otherwise unused embryos.[17]

If the biological "parents"—the progenitors—of a frozen embryo decide they don't want it, and prefer to help someone else have a baby, wouldn't it be good public policy to treat the embryo as a child and give the "child" the protections afforded by adoption law? The protections include home visits to ensure the adopting couple is competent to adopt. With adoption, a judge must approve the adoption, adding further protection for the child. Keeping embryo donation outside the framework of adoption means there is no supervision by the state to ensure the "child" goes to a good home. What do you think?

---

17 Eric Blyth, Lucy Frith, Marilyn S. Paul & Roni Berger, Embryo Relinquishment for Family Building: How Should It Be Conceptualized?, 25 *International Journal of Law, Policy and the Family* 260 (2011).

Surrogacy

A couple desiring a baby may consider a surrogacy contract with a woman who is willing to carry the baby to term and relinquish the infant to the couple.[18] The District of Columbia defines "surrogate parenting contract" as "any agreement, oral or written, in which: (A) a woman agrees either to be artificially

---

18   *See* Erin Y. Hisano (Comment) Gestational Surrogacy Maternity Disputes: Refocusing on the Child, 15 *Lewis and Clark Law Review* 517 (2011). The author writes:

In general, surrogacy is the practice of a third-party woman carrying a child for a couple and has been used by infertile couples as a method to conceive a child.

A. Traditional Surrogacy

Traditional surrogacy arrangements use artificial insemination (AI) to impregnate the surrogate mother's egg with the sperm of a man who is not her husband or partner. The sperm that is used is usually the intended father's sperm. AI is probably the least complicated of the assisted reproductive therapies and refers to the process of introducing sperm into the female reproductive organs by means other than sexual intercourse.

In the traditional surrogacy realm, there are two women with potential maternal rights. The traditional surrogate mother is both the genetic and gestational contributor and is legally presumed to have maternal rights. On the other hand, the wife or female companion in the arranging party is known as the "intended mother" but has no biological connection to the child. Since the intended mother does not have a genetic link to the child, she only has potential maternal rights that are guaranteed with the adoption of the child. It is common practice for the surrogate mother to relinquish her maternal rights so the intended mother can adopt the child. Without legal adoption, the intended mother has no recognized maternal rights.

B. Gestational Surrogacy

Instead of utilizing AI, gestational surrogacy uses the more complicated procedure known as in vitro fertilization. IVF refers to the process by which a doctor stimulates a woman's ovaries, removes several eggs, and fertilizes the eggs outside her body. The fertilized egg is then implanted in the gestational surrogate's uterus. Like traditional surrogates, gestational surrogates carry the child to term; however, the gestational surrogate mother never has a genetic connection to the baby.

Generally, there are three different arrangements that can arise out of a gestational surrogacy arrangement. The first—and most common—arrangement involves retrieving the egg of the commissioning female and fertilizing it with the sperm of her husband or partner. The resulting embryo is then transferred to the uterus of the gestational surrogate mother. This form of gestational surrogacy is usually used when a woman has viable eggs but cannot carry a child to term. The resulting arrangement allows both parties in the arranging couple to have a genetic link to the child. This ability to preserve a genetic link is one of the main reasons gestational surrogacy is often preferred over traditional surrogacy.

The next two variations, known as donor surrogacy arrangements, can result in the commissioning female not having any genetic links to the baby. One possible variation uses an egg donor when the intended mother is unable to produce viable eggs and is unable to carry a baby to term. The woman's husband or partner then fertilizes the egg so that at least one member of the arranging couple is genetically related to the child. This arrangement is less common than the first arrangement. The other variation of donor surrogacy arrangements creates an embryo entirely from a donor egg and sperm, resulting in neither the woman nor the man from the arranging party having a genetic link to the baby. This arrangement is the least common arrangement and is used in the unusual instance when both members of the arranging couple are unable to produce reproductive material.

See also Austin Caster (Note) Don't Split the Baby: How the U.S. Could Avoid Uncertainty and Unnecessary Litigation and Promote Equality by Emulating the British Surrogacy Law Regime, 10 *Connecticut Public Interest Law Journal* 477 (2011).

inseminated with the sperm of a man who is not her husband, or to be impregnated with an embryo that is the product of an ovum fertilized with the sperm of a man who is not her husband; and (B) A woman agrees to, or intends to, relinquish all parental rights and responsibilities and to consent to the adoption of [the] child . . . ."[19]

There are several kinds of surrogacy. With gestational surrogacy, an egg is removed from the woman who intends to be the mother. The egg is fertilized in a laboratory with sperm from the father. The fertilized egg is implanted in a surrogate. In this case, the surrogate contributes no genetic material to the baby.[20] All the baby's genetic material comes from the couple intending to be parents.

In a second type of surrogacy—traditional surrogacy—the surrogate provides the egg, and the surrogate is artificially inseminated with sperm from the intended father. The difference between the first and second forms of surrogacy, of course, is that in the second form the surrogate provides half the baby's genetic material, and is the child's biological as well as birth mother.

In a third form of surrogacy—genetic stranger surrogacy—the intended parents *as well as* the surrogate have no genetic relationship to the baby. An embryo that is genetically unrelated to the surrogate and to the intended parents is implanted in the surrogate. In *Marriage of Buzzanca*,[21] the California Court of Appeal ruled that in such a case the wife and husband are the "lawful parents" of the baby because their consent to the process brought the child into existence.

Most states lack statutes addressing surrogacy.[22] Charles Kindregan and Maureen McBrien remark, "The majority of states have no controlling decisional law, and only some states regulate surrogacy by statute."[23] A number of states forbid some or all surrogacy contracts.[24] Arizona law, for example, states,

---

19 D.C. Stat. § 16-401(4).

20 *See* Raftopol v. Ramey, 299 Conn. 681, 12 A.3d 783 (2011)(surrogate mother who had no biological relationship to child had no parental rights).

21 61 Cal. App. 4th 1410, 72 Cal. Rptr. 2d 280 (1998).

22 *See* Anne R. Dana (Note), The State of Surrogacy Laws: Determining Legal Parentage for Gay Fathers, 18 *Duke Journal of Gender Law and Policy* 353 (2011)("only a handful of states actually passed laws regarding parentage in the case of surrogacy arrangements, and today many states continue to rely on judicial determinations.").

23 Charles P. Kindregan, Jr. & Maureen McBrien, *Assisted Reproductive Technology*, p. 157 (2011).

24 *See* D.C. Stat. § 16-402 ("Surrogate parenting contracts are prohibited and rendered unenforceable in the District."); Ind. Code § 31-20-1-2 (A surrogate agreement . . . that is formed after March 14, 1988, is void."); Ky. Rev. Stat. § 199.590(4) ("A person, agency, institution, or intermediary shall not be a party to a contract or agreement which would compensate a woman for her artificial insemination and subsequent termination of parental rights to a child born as a result of that artificial insemination. A person, agency, institution, or intermediary shall not receive compensation for the facilitation of contracts or agreements as proscribed by this subsection.

"No person may enter into, induce, arrange, procure or otherwise assist in the formation of a surrogate parentage contract."[25] In Arizona, a surrogate "is the legal mother . . . and is entitled to custody . . . ."[26] New York law provides, "Surrogate parenting contracts are hereby declared contrary to the public policy of this state, and are void and unenforceable."[27] Michigan law states, "A surrogate parentage contract is void and unenforceable as contrary to public policy."[28]

Several states approve surrogacy contracts.[29] Nevada and Washington allow surrogacy so long as the surrogate is not paid anything in addition to medical expenses.[30] Illinois, Nevada, and Utah authorize gestational surrogacy.[31]

Utah allows the gestational mother and intended parents to file a petition in court to validate a gestational agreement.[32] A gestational agreement that is not

---

Contracts for agreements entered into in violation of this subsection shall be void."); La. Rev. Stat. § 2713 ("A contract for surrogate motherhood as defined herein shall be absolutely null and shall be void and unenforceable as contrary to public policy."); Neb. Stat. § 25-21,200(1) ("A surrogate parenthood contract entered into shall be void and unenforceable.").

25   Ariz. Stat. Ann. § 25-218(A).

26   Ariz. Stat. Ann. § 25-218(B).

27   McKinney's Dom Rel. N.Y. Laws Ann. § 122. The practice commentary by Alan Scheikman states, "After years of debate and study, the Legislature has declared that surrogate parenting contracts are contrary to policy, void, and unenforceable."

28   Mich. Laws Ann. § 722.855(5).

29   *See* Wash. Code Ann. § 26.26.210

30   Nev. Rev. Stat. § 126.045(3); Wash. Code Ann. § 26.26.210.

31   Ill. Stat. 750, 45/5; Nev. Rev. Stat. § 126.045(4)(a); Utah Code Ann. § 78B-15-801.

32   Utah Code Ann. § 78B-15-802. Utah law states:

(1) If the requirements of Subsection (2) are satisfied, a tribunal may issue an order validating the gestational agreement and declaring that the intended parents will be the parents of a child born during the term of the agreement.

(2) The tribunal may issue an order under Subsection (1) only on finding that:

    (a) the residence requirements of Section 78B-15-802 have been satisfied and the parties have submitted to jurisdiction of the tribunal under the jurisdictional standards of this part;

    (b) medical evidence shows that the intended mother is unable to bear a child or is unable to do so without unreasonable risk to her physical or mental health or to the unborn child;

    (c) unless waived by the tribunal, a home study of the intended parents has been conducted . . . , and the intended parents meet the standards of fitness applicable to adoptive parents;

    (d) all parties have participated in counseling with a licensed mental health professional as evidenced by a certificate signed by the licensed mental health professional which affirms that all parties have discussed options and consequences of the agreement and presented to the tribunal;

    (e) all parties have voluntarily entered into the agreement and understand its terms;

    (f) the prospective gestational mother has had at least one pregnancy and delivery and her bearing another child will not pose an unreasonable health risk to the unborn child or to the physical or men-

court approved is not enforceable.[33] When the baby is born, the intended parents notify the court and the court makes an order confirming the intended parents as the legal parents.[34] The gestational mother in Utah may receive reasonable compensation.[35] The intended parents must be married.[36]

New Hampshire allows gestational and traditional surrogacy agreements that are judicially approved.[37] New Hampshire requires the parties to a surrogacy agreement to be evaluated by a mental health professional to ensure "the ability and disposition of the person being evaluated to give a child love, affection and guidance," and to "adjust to and assume the inherent risks of the contract."[38]

In 1988, the National Conference of Commissioners on Uniform States Law promulgated the "Uniform Status of Children of Assisted Conception Act."[39] Only two states have adopted the Act, North Dakota and Virginia. Virginia's statute is the perhaps most thorough in the nation, and is reproduced below.

Virginia Statute on Surrogacy

§ 20-156. Definitions

As used in this chapter unless the context requires a different meaning:

"Assisted conception" means a pregnancy resulting from any intervening medical technology, whether in vivo or in vitro, which completely or partially replaces sexual intercourse as the means of conception. Such inter-

---

tal health of the prospective gestational mother;

(g) adequate provision has been made for all reasonable health-care expense associated with the gestational agreement until the birth of the child, including responsibility for those expenses if the agreement is terminated;

(h) the consideration, if any, paid to the prospective gestational mother is reasonable;

(i) all the parties to the agreement are 21 years of age or older;

(j) the gestational mother's eggs are not being used in the assisted reproductive procedure; and

(k) if the gestational mother is married, her husband's sperm is not being used in the assisted reproductive procedure.

33 Utah Code Ann. § 78B-15-809(1).

34 Utah Code Ann. § 78B-15-807.

35 Utah Code Ann. § 78B-15-803(h); 78B-15-808.

36 Utah Code Ann. § 78B-15-801(3). *Accord* Nev. Rev. Stat. § 126.045.

37 N.H. Rev. Stat. § 168-B:16(I)(b).

38 N.H. Rev. Stat. § 168-B:18.

39 9C *Uniform Laws Annotated* 363 (2001).

vening medical technology includes, but is not limited to, conventional medical and surgical treatment as well as noncoital reproductive technology such as artificial insemination by donor, cryopreservation of gametes and embryos, in vitro fertilization, uterine embryo lavage, embryo transfer, gamete intrafallopian tube transfer, and low tubal ovum transfer.

"Compensation" means payment of any valuable consideration for services in excess of reasonable medical and ancillary costs.

"Cryopreservation" means freezing and storing of gametes and embryos for possible future use in assisted conception.

"Donor" means an individual, other than a surrogate, who contributes the sperm or egg used in assisted conception.

"Gamete" means either a sperm or an ovum.

"Genetic parent" means an individual who contributes a gamete resulting in a conception.

"Gestational mother" means the woman who gives birth to a child, regardless of her genetic relationship to the child.

"Embryo" means the organism resulting from the union of a sperm and an ovum from first cell division until approximately the end of the second month of gestation.

"Embryo transfer" means the placing of a viable embryo into the uterus of a gestational mother.

"Infertile" means the inability to conceive after one year of unprotected sexual intercourse.

"Intended parents" means a man and a woman, married to each other, who enter into an agreement with a surrogate under the terms of which they will be the parents of any child born to the surrogate through assisted conception regardless of the genetic relationships between the intended parents, the surrogate, and the child.

"In vitro" means any process that can be observed in an artificial environment such as a test tube or tissue culture plate.

"In vitro fertilization" means the fertilization of ova by sperm in an artificial environment.

"In vivo" means any process occurring within the living body.

"Ovum" means the female gamete or reproductive cell prior to fertilization.

"Reasonable medical and ancillary costs" means the costs of the performance of assisted conception, the costs of prenatal maternal health care, the costs of maternal and child health care for a reasonable postpartum period, the reasonable costs for medications and maternity clothes, and any additional and reasonable costs for housing and other living expenses attributable to the pregnancy.

"Sperm" means the male gametes or reproductive cells which impregnate the ova.

"Surrogacy contract" means an agreement between intended parents, a surrogate, and her husband, if any, in which the surrogate agrees to be impregnated through the use of assisted conception, to carry any resulting fetus, and to relinquish to the intended parents the custody of and parental rights to any resulting child.

"Surrogate" means any adult woman who agrees to bear a child carried for intended parents.

§ 20-157. Virginia law to control

The provisions of this chapter shall control, without exception, in any action brought in the courts of this Commonwealth to enforce or adjudicate any rights or responsibilities arising under this chapter.

§ 20-158. Parentage of child resulting from assisted conception

A. Determination of parentage, generally.--Except as provided in subsections B, C, D, and E of this section, the parentage of any child resulting from the performance of assisted conception shall be determined as follows:

1. The gestational mother of a child is the child's mother.

   2. The husband of the gestational mother of a child is the child's father, notwithstanding any declaration of invalidity or annulment of the marriage obtained after the performance of assisted conception, unless he commences an action in which the mother and child are parties within two years after he discovers or, in the exercise of due diligence, reasonably should have discovered the child's birth and in which it is determined that he did not consent to the performance of assisted conception.

   3. A donor is not the parent of a child conceived through assisted conception, unless the donor is the husband of the gestational mother.

(B) Death of spouse.--Any child resulting from the insemination of a wife's ovum using her husband's sperm, with his consent, is the child of the husband and wife notwithstanding that, during the ten-month period immediately preceding the birth, either party died.

However, any person who dies before in utero implantation of an embryo resulting from the union of his sperm or her ovum with another gamete, whether or not the other gamete is that of the person's spouse, is not the parent of any resulting child unless (i) implantation occurs before notice of the death can reasonably be communicated to the physician performing the procedure or (ii) the person consents to be a parent in writing executed before the implantation.

(C) Divorce.--Any child resulting from insemination of a wife's ovum using her husband's sperm, with his consent, is the child of the husband and wife notwithstanding that either party filed for a divorce or annulment during the ten-month period immediately preceding the birth. Any person who is a party to an action for divorce or annulment commenced by filing before in utero implantation of an embryo resulting from the union of his sperm or her ovum with another gamete, whether or not the other gamete is that of the person's spouse, is not the parent of any resulting child unless (i) implantation occurs before notice of the filing can reasonably be communicated to the physician performing the procedure or (ii) the person consents in writing to be a parent, whether the writing was executed before or after the implantation.

(D) Birth pursuant to court approved surrogacy contract.--After approval of a surrogacy contract by the court and entry of an order as provided in subsection D of § 20-160, the intended parents are the parents of any resulting child. However, if the court vacates the order approving the agreement pursuant to subsection B of § 20-161, the surrogate is the mother of the resulting child and her husband is the father. The intended parents may only obtain parental rights through adoption as provided in Chapter 12 (§ 63.2-1200 et seq.) of Title 63.2.

(E) Birth pursuant to surrogacy contract not approved by court.--In the case of a surrogacy contract that has not been approved by a court as provided in § 20-160, the parentage of any resulting child shall be determined as follows:

1. The gestational mother is the child's mother unless the intended mother is a genetic parent, in which case the intended mother is the mother.

2. If either of the intended parents is a genetic parent of the resulting child, the intended father is the child's father. However, if (i) the surrogate is married, (ii) her husband is a party to the surrogacy contract, and (iii) the surrogate exercises her right to retain custody and parental rights to the resulting child pursuant to § 20-162, then the surrogate and her husband are the parents.

3. If neither of the intended parents is a genetic parent of the resulting child, the surrogate is the mother and her husband is the child's father if he is a party to the contract. The intended parents may only obtain parental rights through adoption as provided in Chapter 12 (§ 63.2-1200 et seq.) of Title 63.2.

4. After the signing and filing of the surrogate consent and report form in conformance with the requirements of subsection A of § 20-162, the intended parents are the parents of the child and the surrogate and her husband, if any, shall not be the parents of the child.

§ 20-159. Surrogacy contracts permissible

(A) A surrogate, her husband, if any, and prospective intended parents may enter into a written agreement whereby the surrogate may relinquish all her rights and duties as parent of a child conceived through assisted conception, and the intended parents may become the parents of the child as provided in subsection D or E of § 20-158.

(B) Surrogacy contracts shall be approved by the court as provided in § 20-160. However, any surrogacy contract that has not been approved by the court shall be governed by the provisions of §§ 20-156 through 20-159 and §§ 20-162 through 20-165 including the provisions for reformation in conformance with this chapter as provided in § 20-162.

§ 20-160. Petition and hearing for court approval of surrogacy contract; requirements; orders

(A) Prior to the performance of assisted conception, the intended parents, the surrogate, and her husband shall join in a petition to the circuit court of the county or city in which at least one of the parties resides. The surrogacy contract shall be signed by all the parties and acknowledged before an officer or other person authorized by law to take acknowledgments.

A copy of the contract shall be attached to the petition. The court shall appoint a guardian ad litem to represent the interests of any resulting child and shall appoint counsel to represent the surrogate. The court shall order a home study by a local department of social services or welfare or a licensed child-placing agency, to be completed prior to the hearing on the petition.

All hearings and proceedings conducted under this section shall be held in camera, and all court records shall be confidential and subject to inspection only under the standards applicable to adoptions as provided in § 63.2-1245. The court conducting the proceedings shall have exclusive and continuing jurisdiction of all matters arising under the surrogacy contract until all provisions of the contract are fulfilled.

(B) The court shall hold a hearing on the petition. The court shall enter an order approving the surrogacy contract and authorizing the performance of assisted conception for a period of twelve months after the date of the order, and may discharge the guardian ad litem and attorney for the surrogate upon finding that:

1   The court has jurisdiction in accordance with § 20-157;

2   A local department of social services or welfare or a licensed child-placing agency has conducted a home study of the intended parents, the surrogate, and her husband, if any, and has filed a report of this home study with the court;

3   The intended parents, the surrogate, and her husband, if any, meet the standards of fitness applicable to adoptive parents;

4   All the parties have voluntarily entered into the surrogacy contract and understand its terms and the nature, meaning, and effect of the proceeding and understand that any agreement between them for payment of compensation is void and unenforceable;

5   The agreement contains adequate provisions to guarantee the payment of reasonable medical and ancillary costs

either in the form of insurance, cash, escrow, bonds, or other arrangements satisfactory to the parties, including allocation of responsibility for such costs in the event of termination of the pregnancy, termination of the contract pursuant to § 20-161, or breach of the contract by any party;

6   The surrogate has had at least one pregnancy, and has experienced at least one live birth, and bearing another child does not pose an unreasonable risk to her physical or mental health or to that of any resulting child. This finding shall be supported by medical evidence;

7   Prior to signing the surrogacy contract, the intended parents, the surrogate, and her husband, if any, have submitted to physical examinations and psychological evaluations by practitioners licensed to perform such services pursuant to Title 54.1, and the court and all parties have been given access to the records of the physical examinations and psychological evaluations;

8   The intended mother is infertile, is unable to bear a child, or is unable to do so without unreasonable risk to the unborn child or to the physical or mental health of the intended mother or the child. This finding shall be supported by medical evidence;

9   At least one of the intended parents is expected to be the genetic parent of any child resulting from the agreement;

10   The husband of the surrogate, if any, is a party to the surrogacy agreement;

11   All parties have received counseling concerning the effects of the surrogacy by a qualified health care professional or social worker, and a report containing conclusions about the capacity of the parties to enter into and fulfill the agreement has been filed with the court; and

12   The agreement would not be substantially detrimental to the interests of any of the affected persons.

(A) Unless otherwise provided in the surrogacy contract, all court costs, counsel fees, and other costs and expenses associated with the hearing, including the costs of the home study, shall be assessed against the intended parents.

(B) Within seven days of the birth of any resulting child, the intended parents shall file a written notice with the court that the child was born to the surrogate within 300 days after the last performance of assisted conception. Upon the filing of this notice and a finding that at least one of the intended parents is the genetic parent of the resulting child as substantiated by medical evidence, the court shall enter an order directing the State Registrar of Vital Records to issue a new birth certificate naming the intended parents as the parents of the child pursuant to § 32.1-261.

If evidence cannot be produced that at least one of the intended parents is the genetic parent of the resulting child, the court shall not enter an order directing the issuance of a new birth certificate naming the intended parents as the parents of the child, and the surrogate and her husband, if any, shall be the parents of the child. The intended parents may obtain parental rights only through adoption as provided in Chapter 12 (§ 63.2-1200 et seq.) of Title 63.2.

§ 20-161. Termination of court-approved surrogacy contract

A. Subsequent to an order entered pursuant to subsection B of § 20-160, but before the surrogate becomes pregnant through the use of assisted conception, the court for cause, or the surrogate, her husband, if any, or the intended parents may terminate the agreement by giving written notice of termination to all other parties and by filing notice of the termination with the court. Upon receipt of the notice, the court shall vacate the order entered under subsection B of § 20-160.

B. Within 180 days after the last performance of any assisted conception, a surrogate who is also a genetic parent may terminate the agreement by filing written notice with the court. The court shall vacate the order entered pursuant to subsection B of § 20-160 upon finding, after notice to the parties to the agreement and a hearing, that the surrogate has voluntarily terminated the agreement and that she understands the effects of the termination.

Unless otherwise provided in the contract as approved, the surrogate shall incur no liability to the intended parents for exercising her rights of termination pursuant to this section.

§ 20-162. Contracts not approved by the court; requirements

(A) In the case of any surrogacy agreement for which prior court approval has not been obtained pursuant to § 20-160, the provisions of this section and §§ 20-156 through 20-159 and §§ 20-163 through 20-165 shall apply. Any provision in a surrogacy contract that attempts to reduce the rights or responsibilities of the intended parents, surrogate, or her husband, if any, or the rights of any resulting child shall be reformed to include the requirements set forth in this chapter. A provision in the contract providing for compensation to be paid to the surrogate is void and unenforceable. Such surrogacy contracts shall be enforceable and shall be construed only as follows:

1. The surrogate, her husband, if any, and the intended parents shall be parties to any such surrogacy contract.

2. The contract shall be in writing, signed by all the parties, and acknowledged before an officer or other person authorized by law to take acknowledgments.

3. Upon expiration of three days following birth of any resulting child, the surrogate may relinquish her parental rights to the intended parents, if at least one of the intended parents is the genetic parent of the child, by signing a surrogate consent and report form naming the intended parents as the parents of the child. The surrogate consent and report form shall be developed, furnished and distributed by the State Registrar of Vital Records. The surrogate consent and report form shall be signed and acknowledged before an officer or other person authorized by law to take acknowledgments. The surrogate consent and report form, a copy of the contract, and a statement from the physician who performed the assisted conception stating the genetic relationships between the child, the surrogate, and the intended parents, at least one of whom shall be the genetic parent of the child, shall be filed with the State Registrar within 180 days after the birth. The statement from the physician shall be signed and acknowledged before an officer or other person authorized by law to take acknowledgments. There shall be a rebuttable presumption that the statement from the physician accurately states the genetic relationships among the child, the surrogate and the intended parents. Where a phy-

sician's statement is not available, DNA testing establishing the genetic relationships between the child, the surrogate, and the intended parents may be substituted for the physician's statement.

4   Upon the filing of the surrogate consent and report form and the required attachments, including the physician's statement, within 180 days of the birth, a new birth certificate shall be established by the State Registrar for the child naming the intended parents as the parents of the child as provided in § 32.1-261.

(B) Any contract governed by the provisions of this section shall include or, in the event such provisions are not explicitly covered in the contract or are included but are inconsistent with this section, shall be deemed to include the following provisions:

1 The intended parents shall be the parents of any resulting child only when the surrogate relinquishes her parental rights as provided in subdivision A 3 of this section and a new birth certificate is established as provided in subdivision A 4 of this section and § 32.1-261;

2 Incorporation of this chapter and a statement by each of the parties that they have read and understood the contract, they know and understand their rights and responsibilities under Virginia law, and the contract was entered into knowingly and voluntarily; and

3 A guarantee by the intended parents for payment of reasonable medical and ancillary costs either in the form of insurance, cash, escrow, bonds, or other arrangements satisfactory to the parties, including allocation of responsibility for such costs in the event of termination of the pregnancy, termination of the contract, or breach of the contract by any party.

(C) Under any contract that does not include an allocation of responsibility for reasonable medical and ancillary costs in the event of termination of the pregnancy, termination of the contract, or breach of the contract by any party, the following provisions shall control:

1   If the intended parents and the surrogate and her husband, if any, and if he is a party to the contract, consent in writing to termination of the contract, the intended parents are

responsible for all reasonable medical and ancillary costs for a period of six weeks following the termination.

2   If the surrogate voluntarily terminates the contract during the pregnancy, without consent of the intended parents, the intended parents shall be responsible for one-half of the reasonable medical and ancillary costs incurred prior to the termination.

3   If, after the birth of any resulting child, the surrogate fails to relinquish parental rights to the intended parents pursuant to the contract, the intended parents shall be responsible for one-half of the reasonable medical and ancillary costs incurred prior to the birth.

§ 20- Miscellaneous provisions related to all surrogacy contracts

A. The surrogate shall be solely responsible for the clinical management of the pregnancy.

B. After the entry of an order under subsection B of § 20-160 or upon the execution of a contract pursuant to § 20-162, the marriage of the surrogate shall not affect the validity of the order or contract, and her husband shall not be deemed a party to the contract in the absence of his explicit written consent.

C. Following the entry of an order pursuant to subsection D of § 20-160 or upon the relinquishing of the custody of and parental rights to any resulting child and the filing of the surrogate consent and report form as provided in § 20-162, the intended parents shall have the custody of, parental rights to, and full responsibilities for any child resulting from the performance of assisted conception from a surrogacy agreement regardless of the child's health, physical appearance, any mental or physical handicap, and regardless of whether the child is born alive.

D. A child born to a surrogate within 300 days after assisted conception pursuant to an order under subsection B of § 20-160 or a contract under § 20-162 is presumed to result from the assisted conception. This presumption is conclusive as to all persons who fail to file an action to test its validity within two years after the birth of the child. The child and the parties to the contract shall be named as parties in any such action. The action shall be filed in the court that issued or could have issued an order under § 20-160.

E. Health care providers shall not be liable for recognizing the surrogate as the mother of the resulting child before receipt of a copy of an order entered under § 20-160 or a copy of the contract, or for recognizing the intended parents as the parents of the resulting child after receipt of such order or copy of the contract.

§ 20-164. Relation of parent and child

A child whose status as a child is declared or negated by this chapter is the child only of his parent or parents as determined under this chapter, Title 64.1, and, when applicable, Chapter 3.1 (§ 20-49.1 et seq.) of this title for all purposes including, but not limited to, (i) intestate succession; (ii) probate law exemptions, allowances, or other protections for children in a parent's estate; and (iii) determining eligibility of the child or its descendants to share in a donative transfer from any person as an individual or as a member of a class determined by reference to the relationship. However, a child born more than ten months after the death of a parent shall not be recognized as such parent's child for the purposes of subdivisions (i), (ii) and (iii) of this section.

Given the lack in most states of statutory guidance on surrogacy, courts have charted the territory. In 1988, the New Jersey Supreme Court handed down *Matter of Baby M.*, a surrogacy case that captured national attention and that remains a leading authority.

August 21, at Bergen County Courthouse in Hackensack, New Jersey. Mary Beth Whitehead, the surrogate mother, cries after losing custody of the infant known as "Baby M". © Bettmann/CORBIS

Matter of Baby M.

Supreme Court of New Jersey
109 N.J. 396, 537 A.2d 1227 (1988)

Wilentz, C.J.

In this matter the Court is asked to determine the validity of a contract that purports to provide a new way of bringing children into a family. For a fee of $10,000, a woman agrees to be artificially inseminated with the semen of another woman's husband; she is to conceive a child, carry it to term, and after its birth surrender it to the natural father and his wife. The intent of the contract is that the child's natural mother will thereafter be forever separated from her child. The wife is to adopt the child, and she and the natural father are to be regarded as its parents for all purposes. The contract providing for this is called a "surrogacy contract," the natural mother inappropriately called the "surrogate mother."

We invalidate the surrogacy contract because it conflicts with the law and public policy of this State. While we recognize the depth of the yearning of infertile couples to have their own children, we find the payment of money to a "surrogate" mother illegal, perhaps criminal, and potentially degrading to women. Although in this case we grant custody to the natural father, the evidence having clearly proved such custody to be in the best interests of the infant, we void both the termination of the surrogate mother's parental rights and the adoption of the child by the wife/stepparent. We thus restore the "surrogate" as the mother of the child. We remand the issue of the natural mother's visitation rights to the trial court, since that issue was not reached below and the record before us is not sufficient to permit us to decide it *de novo*.

We find no offense to our present laws where a woman voluntarily and without payment agrees to act as a "surrogate" mother, provided that she is not subject to a binding agreement to surrender her child. Moreover, our holding today does not preclude the Legislature from altering the current statutory scheme, within constitutional limits, so as to permit surrogacy contracts. Under current law, however, the surrogacy agreement before us is illegal and invalid.

In February 1985, William Stern and Mary Beth Whitehead entered into a surrogacy contract. It recited that Stern's wife, Elizabeth, was infertile, that they wanted a child, and that Mrs. Whitehead was willing to provide that child as the mother with Mr. Stern as the father.

The contract provided that through artificial insemination using Mr. Stern's sperm, Mrs. Whitehead would become pregnant, carry the child to term, bear it, deliver it to the Sterns, and thereafter do whatever was necessary to terminate her maternal rights so that Mrs. Stern could thereafter adopt the child. Mrs. Whitehead's husband, Richard, was also a party to the contract; Mrs. Stern was not. Mr. Whitehead promised to do all acts necessary to rebut the presumption of paternity under the Parentage Act. Although Mrs. Stern was not a party to the surrogacy agreement, the contract gave her sole custody of the child in the event of Mr. Stern's death. Mrs. Stern's status as a nonparty to the surrogate parenting agreement presumably was to avoid the application of the baby-selling statute to this arrangement.

Mr. Stern, on his part, agreed to attempt the artificial insemination and to pay Mrs. Whitehead $10,000 after the child's birth, on its delivery to him. In a separate contract, Mr. Stern agreed to pay $7,500 to the Infertility Center of New York ("ICNY"). The Center's advertising campaigns solicit surrogate mothers and encourage infertile couples to consider surrogacy. ICNY arranged for the surrogacy contract by bringing the parties together, explaining the process to them, furnishing the contractual form, and providing legal counsel.

The history of the parties' involvement in this arrangement suggests their good faith. William and Elizabeth Stern were married in July 1974, having met at the University of Michigan, where both were Ph.D. candidates. Due to financial considerations and Mrs. Stern's pursuit of a medical degree and residency, they decided to defer starting a family until 1981. Before then, however, Mrs. Stern learned that she might have multiple sclerosis and that the disease in some cases renders pregnancy a serious health risk. Her anxiety appears to have exceeded the actual risk, which current medical authorities assess as minimal. Nonetheless that anxiety was evidently quite real, Mrs. Stern fearing that pregnancy might precipitate blindness, paraplegia, or other forms of debilitation. Based on the perceived risk, the Sterns decided to forego having their own children. The decision had special significance for Mr. Stern. Most of his family had been destroyed in the Holocaust. As the family's only survivor, he very much wanted to continue his bloodline.

Initially the Sterns considered adoption, but were discouraged by the substantial delay apparently involved and by the potential problem they saw arising from their age and their differing religious backgrounds. They were most eager for some other means to start a family.

The paths of Mrs. Whitehead and the Sterns to surrogacy were similar. Both responded to advertising by ICNY. The Sterns' response, following their inquiries into adoption, was the result of their long-standing decision to have a child. Mrs. Whitehead's response apparently resulted from her sympathy with family members and others who could have no children (she stated that she wanted to give another couple the "gift of life"); she also wanted the $10,000 to help her family.

Both parties, undoubtedly because of their own self-interest, were less sensitive to the implications of the transaction than they might otherwise have been. Mrs. Whitehead, for instance, appears not to have been concerned about whether the Sterns would make good parents for her child; the Sterns, on their part, while conscious of the obvious possibility that surrendering the child might cause grief to Mrs. Whitehead, overcame their qualms because of their desire for a child. At any rate, both the Sterns and Mrs. Whitehead were committed to the arrangement; both thought it right and constructive.

Mrs. Whitehead had reached her decision concerning surrogacy before the Sterns, and had actually been involved as a potential surrogate mother with another couple. After numerous unsuccessful artificial inseminations, that effort was abandoned. Thereafter, the Sterns learned of the Infertility Center, the possibilities of surrogacy, and of Mary Beth Whitehead. The two couples met to discuss the surrogacy arrangement and decided to go forward. On February 6, 1985, Mr. Stern and Mr. and Mrs. Whitehead executed the surrogate parenting agreement. After several artificial inseminations over a period of months, Mrs. Whitehead became pregnant. The pregnancy was uneventful and on March 27, 1986, Baby M was born.

Not wishing anyone at the hospital to be aware of the surrogacy arrangement, Mr. and Mrs. Whitehead appeared to all as the proud parents of a healthy female child. Her birth certificate indicated her name to be Sara Elizabeth Whitehead and her father to be Richard Whitehead. In accordance with Mrs. Whitehead's request, the Sterns visited the hospital unobtrusively to see the newborn child.

Mrs. Whitehead realized, almost from the moment of birth, that she could not part with this child. She had felt a bond with it even during pregnancy. Some indication of the attachment was conveyed to the Sterns at the hospital when they told Mrs. Whitehead what they were going to name the baby. She apparently broke into tears and indicated that she did not know if she could give up the child. She talked about how the baby looked like her other daughter, and made it clear that she was experiencing great difficulty with the decision.

Nonetheless, Mrs. Whitehead was, for the moment, true to her word. Despite powerful inclinations to the contrary, she turned her child over to the Sterns on March 30 at the Whiteheads' home.

The Sterns were thrilled with their new child. They had planned extensively for its arrival, far beyond the practical furnishing of a room for her. It was a time of joyful celebration—not just for them but for their friends as well. The Sterns looked forward to raising their daughter, whom they named Melissa. While aware by then that Mrs. Whitehead was undergoing an emotional crisis, they were as yet not cognizant of the depth of that crisis and its implications for their newly-enlarged family.

Later in the evening of March 30, Mrs. Whitehead became deeply disturbed, disconsolate, stricken with unbearable sadness. She had to have her child. She could not eat, sleep, or concentrate on anything other than her need for her baby. The next day she went to the Sterns' home and told them how much she was suffering.

The depth of Mrs. Whitehead's despair surprised and frightened the Sterns. She told them that she could not live without her baby, that she must have her, even if only for one week, that thereafter she would surrender her child. The Sterns, concerned that Mrs. Whitehead might indeed commit suicide, not wanting under any circumstances to risk that, and in any event believing that Mrs. Whitehead would keep her word, turned the child over to her. . . .

The struggle over Baby M began when it became apparent that Mrs. Whitehead could not return the child to Mr. Stern. Due to Mrs. Whitehead's refusal to relinquish the baby, Mr. Stern filed a complaint seeking enforcement of the surrogacy contract. He alleged, accurately, that Mrs. Whitehead had not only refused to comply with the surrogacy contract but had threatened to flee from New Jersey with the child in order to avoid even the possibility of his obtaining custody. The court papers asserted that if Mrs. Whitehead were to be given notice of the application for an order requiring her to relinquish custody, she would, prior to the hearing, leave the state with the baby. And that is precisely what she did. After the order was entered, *ex parte*, the process server, aided by the police, in the presence of the Sterns, entered Mrs. Whitehead's home to execute the order. Mr. Whitehead fled with the child, who had been handed to him through a window while those who came to enforce the order were thrown off balance by a dispute over the child's current name.

The Whiteheads immediately fled to Florida with Baby M. They stayed initially with Mrs. Whitehead's parents, where one of Mrs. Whitehead's children had been living. For the next three months, the Whiteheads and Melissa lived at roughly twenty different hotels, motels, and homes in order to avoid apprehension. From time to time Mrs. Whitehead would call Mr. Stern to discuss the matter; the conversations, recorded by Mr. Stern on advice of counsel, show an escalating dispute about rights, morality, and power, accompanied by threats of Mrs. Whitehead to kill herself, to kill the child, and falsely to accuse Mr. Stern of sexually molesting Mrs. Whitehead's other daughter.

Eventually the Sterns discovered where the Whiteheads were staying, commenced supplementary proceedings in Florida, and obtained an order requiring the Whiteheads to turn over the child. Police in Florida enforced the order, forcibly removing the child from her grandparents' home. She was soon thereafter brought to New Jersey and turned over to the Sterns. The prior order of the court, issued *ex parte*, awarding custody of the child to the Sterns *pendente lite*, was reaffirmed by the trial court after consideration of the certified representations of the parties (both represented by counsel) concerning the unusual sequence of events that had unfolded. Pending final judgment, Mrs. Whitehead was awarded limited visitation with Baby M.

The Sterns' complaint, in addition to seeking possession and ultimately custody of the child, sought enforcement of the surrogacy contract. Pursuant to the contract, it asked that the child be permanently placed in their custody, that Mrs. Whitehead's parental rights be terminated, and that Mrs. Stern be allowed to adopt the child, *i.e.*, that, for all purposes, Melissa become the Sterns' child.

The trial took thirty-two days over a period of more than two months. It included numerous interlocutory appeals and attempted interlocutory appeals. There were twenty-three witnesses to the facts recited above and fifteen expert witnesses, eleven testifying on the issue of custody and four on the subject of Mrs. Stern's multiple sclerosis; the bulk of the testimony was devoted to determining the parenting arrangement most compatible with the child's best interests. Soon after the conclusion of the trial, the trial court announced its opinion from the bench. It held that the surrogacy contract was valid; ordered that Mrs. Whitehead's parental rights be terminated and that sole custody of the child be granted to Mr. Stern; and, after hearing brief testimony from Mrs. Stern, immediately entered an order allowing the adoption of Melissa by Mrs. Stern, all in accordance with the surrogacy contract. Pending the outcome of the appeal, we granted a continuation of visitation to Mrs. Whitehead, although slightly more limited than the visitation allowed during the trial.

Although clearly expressing its view that the surrogacy contract was valid, the trial court devoted the major portion of its opinion to the question of the baby's best interests. The inconsistency is apparent. The surrogacy contract calls for the surrender of the child to the Sterns, permanent and sole custody in the Sterns, and termination of Mrs. Whitehead's parental rights, all without qualification, all regardless of any evaluation of the best interests of the child. As a matter of fact the contract recites (even before the child was conceived) that it is in the best interests of the child to be placed with Mr. Stern. In effect, the trial court awarded custody to Mr. Stern, the natural father, based on the same kind of evidence and analysis as might be expected had no surrogacy contract existed.

Its rationalization, however, was that while the surrogacy contract was valid, specific performance would not be granted unless that remedy was in the best interests of the child. The factual issues confronted and decided by the trial court were the same as if Mr. Stern and Mrs. Whitehead had had the child out of wedlock, intended or unintended, and then disagreed about custody. . . .

On the question of best interests—and we agree, but for different reasons, that custody was the critical issue—the court's analysis of the testimony was perceptive, demonstrating both its understanding of the case and its considerable experience in these matters. We agree substantially with both its analysis and conclusions on the matter of custody.

The court's review and analysis of the surrogacy contract, however, is not at all in accord with ours. The trial court concluded that the various statutes governing this matter, including those concerning adoption, termination of parental rights, and payment of money in connection with adoptions, do not apply to surrogacy contracts. It reasoned that because the Legislature did not have surrogacy contracts in mind when it passed those laws, those laws were therefore irrelevant. Thus, assuming it was writing on a clean slate, the trial court analyzed the interests involved and the power of the court to accommodate them. It then held that surrogacy contracts are valid and should be enforced, and furthermore that Mr. Stern's rights under the surrogacy contract were constitutionally protected.

Mrs. Whitehead appealed. This Court granted direct certification. . . .

Mrs. Whitehead contends that the surrogacy contract, for a variety of reasons, is invalid. She contends that it conflicts with public policy since it guarantees that the child will not have the nurturing of both natural parents—presumably New Jersey's goal for families. She further argues that it deprives the mother of her constitutional right to the companionship of her child, and that it conflicts with statutes concerning termination of parental rights and adoption. With the contract thus void, Mrs. Whitehead claims primary custody (with visitation rights in Mr. Stern) both on a best interests basis (stressing the "tender years" doctrine) as well as on the policy basis of discouraging surrogacy contracts. She maintains that even if custody would ordinarily go to Mr. Stern, here it should be awarded to Mrs. Whitehead to deter future surrogacy arrangements.

In a brief filed after oral argument, counsel for Mrs. Whitehead suggests that the standard for determining best interests where the infant resulted from a surrogacy contract is that the child should be placed with the mother absent a showing of unfitness. All parties agree that no expert testified that Mary Beth Whitehead was unfit as a mother; the trial court expressly found that she was not "unfit," that, on the contrary, "she is a good mother for and to her older children," and no one now claims anything to the contrary.

One of the repeated themes put forth by Mrs. Whitehead is that the court's initial *ex parte* order granting custody to the Sterns during the trial was a substantial factor in the ultimate "best interests" determination. That initial order, claimed to be erroneous by Mrs. Whitehead, not only established Melissa as part of the Stern family, but brought enormous pressure on Mrs. Whitehead. The order brought the weight of the state behind the Sterns' attempt, ultimately successful, to gain possession of the child. The resulting pressure, Mrs. Whitehead contends, caused her to act in ways that were atypical of her ordinary behavior when not under stress, and to act in ways that were thought to be inimical to the child's best interests in that they demonstrated a failure of character, maturity, and consistency. She claims that any mother who truly loved her child might so respond and that it is doubly unfair to judge her on the basis of her reaction to an extreme situation rarely faced by any mother, where that situation was itself caused by an erroneous order of the court. Therefore, according to Mrs. Whitehead, the erroneous *ex parte* order precipitated a series of events that proved instrumental in the final result.

The Sterns claim that the surrogacy contract is valid and should be enforced, largely for the reasons given by the trial court. They claim a constitutional right of privacy, which includes the right of procreation, and the right of consenting adults to deal with matters of reproduction as they see fit. As for the child's best interests, their position is factual: given all of the circumstances, the child is better off in their custody with no residual parental rights reserved for Mrs. Whitehead.

Of considerable interest in this clash of views is the position of the child's guardian *ad litem*, wisely appointed by the court at the outset of the litigation. As the child's representative, her role in the litigation, as she viewed it, was solely to protect the child's best interests. She therefore took no position on the validity of the surrogacy contract, and instead devoted her energies to obtaining expert testimony uninfluenced by any interest other than the child's. We agree with the guardian's perception of her role in this litigation. She appropriately refrained from taking any position that might have appeared to compromise her role as the child's advocate. She first took the position, based on her experts' testimony, that the Sterns should have primary custody, and that while Mrs. Whitehead's parental rights should not be terminated, no visitation should be allowed for five years. As a result of subsequent developments, mentioned *infra*, her view has changed. She now recommends that no visitation be allowed at least until Baby M reaches maturity.

Although some of the experts' opinions touched on visitation, the major issue they addressed was whether custody should be reposed in the Sterns or in the Whiteheads. The trial court, consistent in this respect with its view that the surrogacy contract was valid, did not deal at all with the question of visitation. Having concluded that the best interests of the child called for custody in the Sterns, the trial court enforced the operative provisions of the surrogacy contract, terminated Mrs. Whitehead's parental rights, and granted an adoption to Mrs. Stern. Explicit in the ruling was the conclusion that the best interests determination removed whatever impediment might have existed in enforcing the surrogacy contract. This Court, therefore, is without guidance from the trial court on the visitation issue, an issue of considerable importance in any event, and especially important in view of our determination that the surrogacy contract is invalid.

We have concluded that this surrogacy contract is invalid. Our conclusion has two bases: direct conflict with existing statutes and conflict with the public policies of this State, as expressed in its statutory and decisional law.

One of the surrogacy contract's basic purposes, to achieve the adoption of a child through private placement, though permitted in New Jersey is very much disfavored. Its use of money for this purpose—and we have no doubt whatsoever that the money is being paid to obtain an adoption and not, as the Sterns argue, for the personal services of Mary Beth Whitehead—is illegal and perhaps criminal. In addition to the inducement of money, there is the coercion of contract: the natural mother's irrevocable agreement, prior to birth, even prior to conception, to surrender the child to the adoptive couple. Such an agreement is totally unenforceable in private placement adoption. Even where the adoption is through an approved agency, the formal agreement to surrender occurs only *after* birth . . ., and then, by regulation, only after the birth mother has been offered counseling. Integral to these invalid provisions of the surrogacy contract is the related agreement, equally invalid, on the part of the natural mother to cooperate with, and not to contest, proceedings to terminate her parental rights, as well as her contractual concession, in aid of the adoption, that the child's best interests would be served by awarding custody to the natural father and his wife—all of this before she has even conceived, and, in some cases, before she has the slightest idea of what the natural father and adoptive mother are like.

The foregoing provisions not only directly conflict with New Jersey statutes, but also offend long-established State policies. These critical terms, which are at the heart of the contract, are invalid and unenforceable; the conclusion therefore follows, without more, that the entire contract is unenforceable.

The surrogacy contract conflicts with: (1) laws prohibiting the use of money in connection with adoptions; (2) laws requiring proof of parental unfitness or abandonment before termination of parental rights is ordered or an adoption is granted; and (3) laws that make surrender of custody and consent to adoption revocable in private placement adoptions.

Our law prohibits paying or accepting money in connection with any placement of a child for adoption. Violation is a high misdemeanor. Excepted are fees of an approved agency (which must be a non-profit entity) and certain expenses in connection with childbirth.

Considerable care was taken in this case to structure the surrogacy arrangement so as not to violate this prohibition. The arrangement was structured as follows: the adopting parent, Mrs. Stern, was not a party to the surrogacy contract; the money paid to Mrs. Whitehead was stated to be for her services—not for the adoption; the sole purpose of the contract was stated as being that "of giving a child to William Stern, its natural and biological father"; the money was purported to be "compensation for services and expenses and in no way ... a fee for termination of parental rights or a payment in exchange for consent to surrender a child for adoption"; the fee to the Infertility Center ($7,500) was stated to be for legal representation, advice, administrative work, and other "services." Nevertheless, it seems clear that the money was paid and accepted in connection with an adoption.

The Infertility Center's major role was first as a "finder" of the surrogate mother whose child was to be adopted, and second as the arranger of all proceedings that led to the adoption. Its role as adoption finder is demonstrated by the provision requiring Mr. Stern to pay another $7,500 if he uses Mary Beth Whitehead again as a surrogate, and by ICNY's agreement to "coordinate arrangements for the adoption of the child by the wife." The surrogacy agreement requires Mrs. Whitehead to surrender Baby M for the purposes of adoption. The agreement notes that Mr. *and Mrs.* Stern wanted to have a child, and provides that the child be "placed" with Mrs. Stern in the event Mr. Stern dies before the child is born. The payment of the $10,000 occurs only on surrender of custody of the child and "completion of the duties and obligations" of Mrs. Whitehead, including termination of her parental rights to facilitate adoption by Mrs. Stern. As for the contention that the Sterns are paying only for services and not for an adoption, we need note only that they would pay nothing in the event the child died before the fourth month of pregnancy, and only $1,000 if the child were stillborn, even though the "services" had been fully rendered. Additionally, one of Mrs. Whitehead's estimated costs, to be assumed by Mr. Stern, was an

"Adoption Fee," presumably for Mrs. Whitehead's incidental costs in connection with the adoption.

Mr. Stern knew he was paying for the adoption of a child; Mrs. Whitehead knew she was accepting money so that a child might be adopted; the Infertility Center knew that it was being paid for assisting in the adoption of a child. The actions of all three worked to frustrate the goals of the statute. It strains credulity to claim that these arrangements, touted by those in the surrogacy business as an attractive alternative to the usual route leading to an adoption, really amount to something other than a private placement adoption for money.

The prohibition of our statute is strong. . . . The evils inherent in baby-bartering are loathsome for a myriad of reasons. The child is sold without regard for whether the purchasers will be suitable parents. The natural mother does not receive the benefit of counseling and guidance to assist her in making a decision that may affect her for a lifetime. In fact, the monetary incentive to sell her child may, depending on her financial circumstances, make her decision less voluntary. Furthermore, the adoptive parents may not be fully informed of the natural parents' medical history.

Baby-selling potentially results in the exploitation of all parties involved. Conversely, adoption statutes seek to further humanitarian goals, foremost among them the best interests of the child. The negative consequences of baby-buying are potentially present in the surrogacy context, especially the potential for placing and adopting a child without regard to the interest of the child or the natural mother.

The termination of Mrs. Whitehead's parental rights, called for by the surrogacy contract and actually ordered by the court, fails to comply with the stringent requirements of New Jersey law. Our law, recognizing the finality of any termination of parental rights, provides for such termination only where there has been a voluntary surrender of a child to an approved agency or to the Division of Youth and Family Services ("DYFS"), accompanied by a formal document acknowledging termination of parental rights, or where there has been a showing of parental abandonment or unfitness. . . .

In this case a termination of parental rights was obtained not by proving the statutory prerequisites but by claiming the benefit of contractual provisions . . . . It is clear that a contractual agreement to abandon one's parental rights, or not to contest a termination action, will not be enforced in our courts. . . .

Since the termination was invalid, it follows, as noted above, that adoption of Melissa by Mrs. Stern could not properly be granted.

The provision in the surrogacy contract stating that Mary Beth Whitehead agrees to "surrender custody ... and terminate all parental rights" contains no clause giving her a right to rescind. It is intended to be an irrevocable consent to surrender the child for adoption—in other words, an irrevocable commitment by Mrs. Whitehead to turn Baby M over to the Sterns and thereafter to allow termination of her parental rights. The trial court required a "best interests" showing as a condition to granting specific performance of the surrogacy contract. Having decided the "best interests" issue in favor of the Sterns, that court's order included, among other things, specific performance of this agreement to surrender custody and terminate all parental rights.

Mrs. Whitehead, shortly after the child's birth, had attempted to revoke her consent and surrender by refusing, after the Sterns had allowed her to have the child "just for one week," to return Baby M to them. The trial court's award of specific performance therefore reflects its view that the consent to surrender the child was irrevocable. We accept the trial court's construction of the contract; indeed it appears quite clear that this was the parties' intent. Such a provision, however, making irrevocable the natural mother's consent to surrender custody of her child in a private placement adoption, clearly conflicts with New Jersey law. . . .

Contractual surrender of parental rights is not provided for in our statutes as now written. . . . There is no doubt that a contractual provision purporting to constitute an irrevocable agreement to surrender custody of a child for adoption is invalid. . . .

The surrogacy contract's invalidity, resulting from its direct conflict with the above statutory provisions, is further underlined when its goals and means are measured against New Jersey's public policy. The contract's basic premise, that the natural parents can decide in advance of birth which one is to have custody of the child, bears no relationship to the settled law that the child's best interests shall determine custody. The fact that the trial court remedied that aspect of the contract through the "best interests" phase does not make the contractual provision any less offensive to the public policy of this State.

The surrogacy contract guarantees permanent separation of the child from one of its natural parents. Our policy, however, has long been that to the extent possible, children should remain with and be brought up by both of their natural parents. . . . This is not simply some theoretical ideal that in practice has no meaning. The impact of failure to follow that policy is nowhere better shown than in the results of this surrogacy contract. A child, instead of starting off its life with as much peace and security as possible, finds itself immediately in a tug-of-war between contending mother and father.

The surrogacy contract violates the policy of this State that the rights of natural parents are equal concerning their child, the father's right no greater than the mother's. . . . The whole purpose and effect of the surrogacy contract was to give the father the exclusive right to the child by destroying the rights of the mother. . . .

Under the contract, the natural mother is irrevocably committed before she knows the strength of her bond with her child. She never makes a totally voluntary, informed decision, for quite clearly any decision prior to the baby's birth is, in the most important sense, uninformed, and any decision after that, compelled by a pre-existing contractual commitment, the threat of a lawsuit, and the inducement of a $10,000 payment, is less than totally voluntary. Her interests are of little concern to those who controlled this transaction.

Although the interest of the natural father and adoptive mother is certainly the predominant interest, realistically the *only* interest served, even they are left with less than what public policy requires. They know little about the natural mother, her genetic makeup, and her psychological and medical history. Moreover, not even a superficial attempt is made to determine their awareness of their responsibilities as parents.

Worst of all, however, is the contract's total disregard of the best interests of the child. There is not the slightest suggestion that any inquiry will be made at any time to determine the fitness of the Sterns as custodial parents, of Mrs. Stern as an adoptive parent, their superiority to Mrs. Whitehead, or the effect on the child of not living with her natural mother.

This is the sale of a child, or, at the very least, the sale of a mother's right to her child, the only mitigating factor being that one of the purchasers is the father. Almost every evil that prompted the prohibition on the payment of money in connection with adoptions exists here.

In the scheme contemplated by the surrogacy contract in this case, a middle man, propelled by profit, promotes the sale. Whatever idealism may have motivated any of the participants, the profit motive predominates, permeates, and ultimately governs the transaction. . . .

Intimated, but disputed, is the assertion that surrogacy will be used for the benefit of the rich at the expense of the poor. In response it is noted that the Sterns are not rich and the Whiteheads not poor. Nevertheless, it is clear to us that it is unlikely that surrogate mothers will be as proportionately numerous among those women in the top twenty percent income bracket as among those in the bottom twenty percent. Put differently, we doubt that infertile couples in the low-income bracket will find upper income surrogates.

In any event, even in this case one should not pretend that disparate wealth does not play a part simply because the contrast is not the dramatic "rich versus poor." ...

The point is made that Mrs. Whitehead *agreed* to the surrogacy arrangement, supposedly fully understanding the consequences. Putting aside the issue of how compelling her need for money may have been, and how significant her understanding of the consequences, we suggest that her consent is irrelevant. There are, in a civilized society, some things that money cannot buy. . . . There are values that society deems more important than granting to wealth whatever it can buy, be it labor, love, or life. Whether this principle recommends prohibition of surrogacy, which presumably sometimes results in great satisfaction to all of the parties, is not for us to say. We note here only that, under existing law, the fact that Mrs. Whitehead "agreed" to the arrangement is not dispositive.

The long-term effects of surrogacy contracts are not known, but feared—the impact on the child who learns her life was bought, that she is the offspring of someone who gave birth to her only to obtain money; the impact on the natural mother as the full weight of her isolation is felt along with the full reality of the sale of her body and her child; the impact on the natural father and adoptive mother once they realize the consequences of their conduct. . . .

The surrogacy contract is based on principles that are directly contrary to the objectives of our laws. It guarantees the separation of a child from its mother; it looks to adoption regardless of suitability; it totally ignores the child; it takes the child from the mother regardless of her wishes and her maternal fitness; and it does all of this, it accomplishes all of its goals, through the use of money.

Beyond that is the potential degradation of some women that may result from this arrangement. In many cases, of course, surrogacy may bring satisfaction, not only to the infertile couple, but to the surrogate mother herself. The fact, however, that many women may not perceive surrogacy negatively but rather see it as an opportunity does not diminish its potential for devastation to other women.

In sum, the harmful consequences of this surrogacy arrangement appear to us all too palpable. In New Jersey the surrogate mother's agreement to sell her child is void. Its irrevocability infects the entire contract, as does the money that purports to buy it. . . .

Having decided that the surrogacy contract is illegal and unenforceable, we now must decide the custody question without regard to the provisions of the surrogacy contract that would give Mr. Stern sole and permanent custody. (That does not mean that the existence of the contract and the circumstances under which it was entered may not be considered to the extent deemed relevant to the child's best interests.) With the surrogacy contract disposed of, the legal framework becomes a dispute between two couples over the custody of a child produced by the artificial insemination of one couple's wife by the other's husband. Under the Parentage Act the claims of the natural father and the natural mother are entitled to equal weight, *i.e.*, one is not preferred over the other solely because he or she is the father or the mother. The applicable rule given these circumstances is clear: the child's best interests determine custody. . . .

There were eleven experts who testified concerning the child's best interests, either directly or in connection with matters related to that issue. Our reading of the record persuades us that the trial court's decision awarding custody to the Sterns (technically to Mr. Stern) should be affirmed since its findings could reasonably have been reached on sufficient credible evidence present in the record. More than that, on this record we find little room for any different conclusion. The trial court's treatment of this issue is both comprehensive and, in most respects, perceptive. We agree substantially with its analysis with but few exceptions that, although important, do not change our ultimate views.

Our custody conclusion is based on strongly persuasive testimony contrasting both the family life of the Whiteheads and the Sterns and the personalities and characters of the individuals. The stability of the Whitehead family life was doubtful at the time of trial. Their finances were in serious trouble (foreclosure by Mrs. Whitehead's sister on a second mortgage was in process). Mr. Whitehead's employment, though relatively steady, was always at risk because of his alcoholism, a condition that he seems not to have been able to confront effectively. Mrs. Whitehead had not worked for quite some time, her last two employments having been part-time. One of the Whiteheads' positive attributes was their ability to bring up two children, and apparently well, even in so vulnerable a household. Yet substantial question was raised even about that aspect of their home life. The expert testimony contained criticism of Mrs. Whitehead's handling of her son's educational difficulties. Certain of the experts noted that Mrs. Whitehead perceived herself as omnipotent and omniscient concerning her children. She knew what they were thinking, what they wanted, and she spoke for them. As to Melissa, Mrs. Whitehead expressed the view that she alone knew what that child's cries and sounds meant. Her inconsistent stories about various things engendered grave doubts about her ability to explain honestly and sensitively to Baby M—and at the right time—the nature of her origin. Although faith in professional counseling is not a *sine qua non* of parenting, several experts believed that Mrs. Whitehead's contempt for professional help, especially professional psychological help, coincided with her feelings of omnipotence in a way that could be devastating to a child who most likely will need such help. In short, while love and affection there would be, Baby M's life with the Whiteheads promised to be too closely controlled by Mrs. Whitehead. The prospects for wholesome, independent psychological growth and development would be at serious risk.

The Sterns have no other children, but all indications are that their household and their personalities promise a much more likely foundation for Melissa to grow and thrive. There is a track record of sorts—during the one-and-a-half years of custody Baby M has done very well, and the relationship between both Mr. and Mrs. Stern and the baby has become very strong. The household is stable, and likely to remain so. Their finances are more than adequate, their circle of friends supportive, and their marriage happy. Most important, they are loving, giving, nurturing, and open-minded people. They have demonstrated the wish and ability to nurture and protect Melissa, yet at the same time to encourage her independence. Their lack of experience is more than made up for by a willingness to learn and to listen, a willingness that is enhanced by their professional training, especially Mrs. Stern's experience as a pediatrician. They are honest; they can recognize error, deal with it, and learn from it. They will try to determine rationally the best way to cope with problems in their relationship with Melissa. When the time comes to tell her about her origins, they will probably have found a means of doing so that accords with the best interests of Baby M. All in all, Melissa's future appears solid, happy, and promising with them.

Based on all of this we have concluded, independent of the trial court's identical conclusion, that Melissa's best interests call for custody in the Sterns. . . .

This case affords some insight into a new reproductive arrangement: the artificial insemination of a surrogate mother. The unfortunate events that have unfolded illustrate that its unregulated use can bring suffering to all involved. Potential victims include the surrogate mother and her family, the natural father and his wife, and most importantly, the child. Although surrogacy has apparently provided positive results for some infertile couples, it can also, as this case demonstrates, cause suffering to participants, here essentially innocent and well-intended.

We have found that our present laws do not permit the surrogacy contract used in this case. Nowhere, however, do we find any legal prohibition against surrogacy when the surrogate mother volunteers, without any payment, to act as a surrogate and is given the right to change her mind and to assert her parental rights. Moreover, the Legislature remains free to deal with this most sensitive issue as it sees fit, subject only to constitutional constraints.

If the Legislature decides to address surrogacy, consideration of this case will highlight many of its potential harms. We do not underestimate the difficulties of legislating on this subject. In addition to the inevitable confrontation with the ethical and moral issues involved, there is the question of the wisdom and effectiveness of regulating a matter so private, yet of such public interest. Legislative consideration of surrogacy may also provide the opportunity to begin to focus on the overall implications of the new reproductive biotechnology-*in vitro* fertilization, preservation of sperm and eggs, embryo implantation and the like. The problem is how to enjoy the benefits of the technology—especially for infertile couples—while minimizing the risk of abuse. The problem can be addressed only when society decides what its values and objectives are in this troubling, yet promising, area.

The judgment is affirmed in part, reversed in part, and remanded for further proceedings consistent with this opinion. [The Supreme Court remanded the case to the trial court to consider visitation.]

What Happened to Baby M?

The case was remanded to the trial court, which ruled that the biological mother, Mary Beth Whitehead, would have unsupervised visitation with the child. Visitation continued until Melissa became an adult, at which time Melissa discontinued contact with Ms. Whitehead. Melissa went on to college and graduate school.

Matter of Baby M. focused on traditional surrogacy in which the surrogate provides the egg and is the child's biological and birth mother. In *Johnson v. Calvert*, the California Supreme Court dealt with gestational surrogacy, in which the surrogate is not the genetic mother. In *Johnson v. Calvert*, the surrogate mother argued that the surrogacy contract she signed violated public policy as well as her constitutional rights of privacy and procreative freedom. The version of *Johnson* printed below retains the court's analysis of the public policy argument, but deletes the constitutional analysis. In brief, on the constitutional plane, the Supreme Court ruled that the surrogate was not the baby's mother, and for that reason did not enjoy the constitutional rights of a parent.

Johnson v. Calvert

California Supreme Court
5 Cal. 4th 84, 851 P.2d 776 (1993)

Panelli, J.

In this case we address several of the legal questions raised by recent advances in reproductive technology. When, pursuant to a surrogacy agreement, a zygote[FN1] formed of the gametes[FN2] of a husband and wife is implanted in the uterus of another woman, who carries the resulting fetus to term and gives birth to a child not genetically related to her, who is the child's "natural mother" under California law? . . . [I]s such an agreement barred by any public policy of this state?

FN1 An organism produced by the union of two gametes.

FN2 A cell that participates in fertilization and development of a new organism, also known as a germ cell or sex cell.

We conclude that the husband and wife are the child's natural parents, and that this result does not offend . . . public policy.

Mark and Crispina Calvert are a married couple who desired to have a child. Crispina was forced to undergo a hysterectomy in 1984. Her ovaries remained capable of producing eggs, however, and the couple eventually considered surrogacy. In 1989 Anna Johnson heard about Crispina's plight from a coworker and offered to serve as a surrogate for the Calverts.

On January 15, 1990, Mark, Crispina, and Anna signed a contract providing that an embryo created by the sperm of Mark and the egg of Crispina would be implanted in Anna and the child born would be taken into Mark and Crispina's home "as their child." Anna agreed she would relinquish "all parental rights" to the child in favor of Mark and Crispina. In return, Mark and Crispina would pay Anna $10,000 in a series of installments, the last to be paid six weeks after the child's birth. Mark and Crispina were also to pay for a $200,000 life insurance policy on Anna's life.[FN4]

> FN4 At the time of the agreement, Anna already had a daughter, Erica, born in 1987.

The zygote was implanted on January 19, 1990. Less than a month later, an ultrasound test confirmed Anna was pregnant.

Unfortunately, relations deteriorated between the two sides. Mark learned that Anna had not disclosed she had suffered several stillbirths and miscarriages. Anna felt Mark and Crispina did not do enough to obtain the required insurance policy. She also felt abandoned during an onset of premature labor in June.

In July 1990, Anna sent Mark and Crispina a letter demanding the balance of the payments due her or else she would refuse to give up the child. The following month, Mark and Crispina responded with a lawsuit, seeking a declaration they were the legal parents of the unborn child. Anna filed her own action to be declared the mother of the child, and the two cases were eventually consolidated. The parties agreed to an independent guardian ad litem for the purposes of the suit.

The child was born on September 19, 1990, and blood samples were obtained from both Anna and the child for analysis. The blood test results excluded Anna as the genetic mother. The parties agreed to a court order providing that the child would remain with Mark and Crispina on a temporary basis with visits by Anna.

At trial in October 1990, the parties stipulated that Mark and Crispina were the child's genetic parents. After hearing evidence and arguments, the trial court ruled that Mark and Crispina were the child's genetic, biological and natural father and mother, that Anna had no parental rights to the child, and that the surrogacy contract was legal and enforceable against Anna's claims. The court also terminated the order allowing visitation. Anna appealed from the trial court's judgment. The Court of Appeal for the Fourth District, Division Three, affirmed. We granted review. . . .

Because two women each have presented acceptable proof of maternity, we do not believe this case can be decided without enquiring into the parties' intentions as manifested in the surrogacy agreement. Mark and Crispina are a couple who desired to have a child of their own genes but are physically unable to do so without the help of reproductive technology. They affirmatively intended the birth of the child, and took the steps necessary to effect in vitro fertilization. But for their acted-on intention, the child would not exist. Anna agreed to facilitate the procreation of Mark's and Crispina's child. The parties' aim was to bring Mark's and Crispina's child into the world, not for Mark and Crispina to donate a zygote to Anna. Crispina from the outset intended to be the child's mother. Although the gestative function Anna performed was necessary to bring about the child's birth, it is safe to say that Anna would not have been given the opportunity to gestate or deliver the child had she, prior to implantation of the zygote, manifested her own intent to be the child's mother. No reason appears why Anna's later change of heart should vitiate the determination that Crispina is the child's natural mother.

. . . In deciding the issue of maternity . . . , we have felt free to take into account the parties' intentions, as expressed in the surrogacy contract, because in our view the agreement is not, on its face, inconsistent with public policy.

Anna urges that surrogacy contracts violate several social policies. Relying on her contention that she is the child's legal, natural mother, she cites the public policy embodied in Penal Code section 273, prohibiting the payment for consent to adoption of a child. She argues further that the policies underlying the adoption laws of this state are violated by the surrogacy contract because it in effect constitutes a prebirth waiver of her parental rights.

We disagree. Gestational surrogacy differs in crucial respects from adoption and so is not subject to the adoption statutes. The parties voluntarily agreed to participate in in vitro fertilization and related medical procedures before the child was conceived; at the time when Anna entered into the contract, therefore, she was not vulnerable to financial inducements to part with her own expected offspring. As discussed above, Anna was not the genetic mother of the child. The payments to Anna under the contract were meant to compensate her for her services in gestating the fetus and undergoing labor, rather than for giving up "parental" rights to the child. Payments were due both during the pregnancy and after the child's birth. We are, accordingly, unpersuaded that the contract used in this case violates the public policies embodied in Penal Code section 273 and the adoption statutes. . . .

It has been suggested that gestational surrogacy may run afoul of prohibitions on involuntary servitude. Involuntary servitude has been recognized in cases of criminal punishment for refusal to work. We see no potential for that evil in the contract at issue here, and extrinsic evidence of coercion or duress is utterly lacking. We note that although at one point the contract purports to give Mark and Crispina the sole right to determine whether to abort the pregnancy, at another point it acknowledges: "All parties understand that a pregnant woman has the absolute right to abort or not abort any fetus she is carrying. Any promise to the contrary is unenforceable." We therefore need not determine the validity of a surrogacy contract purporting to deprive the gestator of her freedom to terminate the pregnancy.

Finally, Anna and some commentators have expressed concern that surrogacy contracts tend to exploit or dehumanize women, especially women of lower economic status. Anna's objections center around the psychological harm she asserts may result from the gestator's relinquishing the child to whom she has given birth. Some have also cautioned that the practice of surrogacy may encourage society to view children as commodities, subject to trade at their parents' will.

We are all too aware that the proper forum for resolution of this issue is the Legislature, where empirical data, largely lacking from this record, can be studied and rules of general applicability developed. However, in light of our responsibility to decide this case, we have considered as best we can its possible consequences.

We are unpersuaded that gestational surrogacy arrangements are so likely to cause the untoward results Anna cites as to demand their invalidation on public policy grounds. Although common sense suggests that women of lesser means serve as surrogate mothers more often than do wealthy women, there has been no proof that surrogacy contracts exploit poor women to any greater degree than economic necessity in general exploits them by inducing them to accept lower-paid or otherwise undesirable employment. We are likewise unpersuaded by the claim that surrogacy will foster the attitude that children are mere commodities; no evidence is offered to support it.

The argument that a woman cannot knowingly and intelligently agree to gestate and deliver a baby for intending parents carries overtones of the reasoning that for centuries prevented women from attaining equal economic rights and professional status under the law. To resurrect this view is both to foreclose a personal and economic choice on the part of the surrogate mother, and to deny intending parents what may be their only means of procreating a child of their own genes. Certainly in the present case it cannot seriously be argued that Anna, a licensed vocational nurse who had done well in school and who had previously borne a child, lacked the intellectual wherewithal or life experience necessary to make an informed decision to enter into the surrogacy contract. ...

The judgment of the Court of Appeal is affirmed.

Question based on *Baby M.* and *Johnson v. Calvert*

In *Baby M,* the New Jersey Supreme Court spoke with disdain about the payment of $10,000 to the surrogate, equating the payment with illegal baby selling. In *Johnson v. Calvert,* by contrast, the California Supreme Court was unperturbed by payment of the same amount to the surrogate. Who is right, the New Jersey Supreme Court or the California Supreme Court?

Assisted Reproduction for Lesbian, Gay, Bisexual and Unmarried Persons

Lesbian, gay, and bisexual individuals and couples (married, unmarried, and domestic partners) desire children. The Ethics Committee of the American Society for Reproductive Medicine wrote in 2009:

> Fertility programs often receive requests for treatment from single persons, unmarried heterosexual couples, and lesbian and gay couples, but programs vary in their willingness to accept such patients. For some programs, it is never acceptable to treat unmarried persons, whether heterosexual or gay or lesbian. Other programs that do treat single women and lesbian couples, however, make it a policy not to treat single men or gay male couples seeking to have children.

> Single individuals, unmarried heterosexual couples, and gay and lesbian couples have interests in having and rearing children. There is no persuasive evidence that children are harmed or disadvantaged solely by being raised by single parents, unmarried parents, or gay and lesbian parents. Data do not support restricting access to assisted reproductive technologies on the basis of a prospective parents' marital status or sexual orientation.[40]

Interesting issues arise when unmarried couples, including lesbian, gay, and bisexual couples, utilize assisted reproduction to have a child. Consider the California Supreme Court's decision in *K.M. v. E.G.*

K. M. v. E. G.

Supreme Court of California
37 Cal. 4th 130, 117 P.3d 673 (2005)

Moreno, J.

We granted review in this case . . . to consider the parental rights and obligations, if any, of a woman with regard to a child born to her partner in a lesbian relationship.

---

40 American Society for Reproductive Medicine, Ethics Committee, Access to Fertility Treatment By Gays, Lesbians, and Unmarried Persons, 92 *Fertility and Sterility* 1190 (2009).

In the present case, we must decide whether a woman who provided ova to her lesbian partner so that the partner could bear children by means of in vitro fertilization is a parent of those children. For the reasons that follow, we conclude that Family Code section 7613, subdivision (b), which provides that a man is not a father if he provides semen to a physician to inseminate a woman who is not his wife, does not apply when a woman provides her ova to impregnate her partner in a lesbian relationship in order to produce children who will be raised in their joint home. Accordingly, when partners in a lesbian relationship decide to produce children in this manner, both the woman who provides her ova and her partner who bears the children are the children's parents.

On March 6, 2001, petitioner K.M. filed a petition to establish a parental relationship with twin five-year-old girls born to respondent E.G., her former lesbian partner. K.M. alleged that she "is the biological parent of the minor children" because "she donated her egg to respondent, the gestational mother of the children." E.G. moved to dismiss the petition on the grounds that, although K.M. and E.G. "were lesbian partners who lived together until this action was filed," K.M. "explicitly donated her ovum under a clear written agreement by which she relinquished any claim to offspring born of her donation."

On April 18, 2001, K.M. filed a motion for custody of and visitation with the twins.

A hearing was held at which E.G. testified that she first considered raising a child before she met K.M., at a time when she did not have a partner. She met K.M. in October, 1992 and they became romantically involved in June 1993. E.G. told K.M. that she planned to adopt a baby as a single mother. E.G. applied for adoption in November, 1993. K.M. and E.G. began living together in March, 1994 and registered as domestic partners in San Francisco.

E.G. visited several fertility clinics in March, 1993 to inquire about artificial insemination and she attempted artificial insemination, without success, on 13 occasions from July, 1993 through November, 1994. K.M. accompanied her to most of these appointments. K.M. testified that she and E.G. planned to raise the child together, while E.G. insisted that, although K.M. was very supportive, E.G. made it clear that her intention was to become "a single parent."

In December, 1994, E.G. consulted with Dr. Mary Martin at the fertility practice of the University of California at San Francisco Medical Center (UCSF). E.G.'s first attempts at in vitro fertilization failed because she was unable to produce sufficient ova. In January, 1995, Dr. Martin suggested using K.M.'s ova. E.G. then asked K.M. to donate her ova, explaining that she would accept the ova only if K.M. "would really be a donor" and E.G. would "be the mother of any child," adding that she would not even consider permitting K.M. to adopt the child "for at least five years until she felt the relationship was stable and would endure." E.G. told K.M. that she "had seen too many lesbian relationships end quickly, and she did not want to be in a custody battle." E.G. and K.M. agreed they would not tell anyone that K.M. was the ova donor.

K.M. acknowledged that she agreed not to disclose to anyone that she was the ova donor, but insisted that she only agreed to provide her ova because she and E.G. had agreed to raise the child together. K.M. and E.G. selected the sperm donor together. K.M. denied that E.G. had said she wanted to be a single parent and insisted that she would not have donated her ova had she known E.G. intended to be the sole parent.

On March 8, 1995, K.M. signed a four-page form on UCSF letterhead entitled "Consent Form for Ovum Donor (Known)." The form states that K.M. agrees "to have eggs taken from my ovaries, in order that they may be donated to another woman." After explaining the medical procedures involved, the form states on the third page: "It is understood that I waive any right and relinquish any claim to the donated eggs or any pregnancy or offspring that might result from them. I agree that the recipient may regard the donated eggs and any offspring resulting therefrom as her own children." The following appears on page 4 of the form, above K.M.'s signature and the signature of a witness: "I specifically disclaim and waive any right in or any child that may be conceived as a result of the use of any ovum or egg of mine, and I agree not to attempt to discover the identity of the recipient thereof." E.G. signed a form entitled "Consent Form for Ovum Recipient" that stated, in part: "I acknowledge that the child or children produced by the IVF procedure is and shall be my own legitimate child or children and the heir or heirs of my body with all rights and privileges accompanying such status."

E.G. testified she received these two forms in a letter from UCSF dated February 2, 1995, and discussed the consent forms with K.M. during February and March. E.G. stated she would not have accepted K.M.'s ova if K.M. had not signed the consent form, because E.G. wanted to have a child on her own and believed the consent form "protected" her in this regard.

K.M. testified to the contrary that she first saw the ovum donation consent form 10 minutes before she signed it on March 8, 1995. K.M. admitted reading the form, but thought parts of the form were "odd" and did not pertain to her, such as the part stating that the donor promised not to discover the identity of the recipient. She did not intend to relinquish her rights and only signed the form so that "we could have children." Despite having signed the form, K.M. "thought she was going to be a parent."

Ova were withdrawn from K.M. on April 11, 1995, and embryos were implanted in E.G. on April 13, 1995. K.M. and E.G. told K.M.'s father about the resulting pregnancy by announcing that he was going to be a grandfather. The twins were born on December 7, 1995. The twins' birth certificates listed E.G. as their mother and did not reflect a father's name. As they had agreed, neither E.G. nor K.M. told anyone K.M. had donated the ova, including their friends, family and the twins' pediatrician. Soon after the twins were born, E.G. asked K.M. to marry her, and on Christmas Day, the couple exchanged rings.

Within a month of their birth, E.G. added the twins to her health insurance policy, named them as her beneficiary for all employment benefits, and increased her life insurance with the twins as the beneficiary. K.M. did not do the same.

E.G. referred to her mother, as well as K.M.'s parents, as the twins' grandparents and referred to K.M.'s sister and brother as the twins' aunt and uncle, and K.M.'s nieces as their cousins. Two school forms listed both K.M. and respondent as the twins' parents. The children's nanny testified that both K.M. and E.G. "were the babies' mother."

The relationship between K.M. and E.G. ended in March, 2001 and K.M. filed the present action. In September, 2001, E.G. and the twins moved to Massachusetts to live with E.G.'s mother.

The superior court granted E.G.'s motion to dismiss finding, in a statement of decision, "that K.M. knowingly, voluntarily and intelligently executed the ovum donor form, thereby acknowledging her understanding that, by the donation of her ova, she was relinquishing and waiving all rights to claim legal parentage of any children who might result from the in vitro fertilization and implantation of her ova in a recipient (in this case, a known recipient, her domestic partner E.G.). K.M.'s testimony on the subject of her execution of the ovum donor form was contradictory and not always credible."

"K.M. and E.G. agreed prior to the conception of the children that E.G. would be the sole parent unless the children were later adopted, and E.G. told K.M. prior to her ovum donation that she (E.G.) would not consider an adoption by K.M. until some years later. E.G. and K.M. agreed in advance of the ovum donation that they would not tell others of K.M.'s genetic connection to the children (they also agreed that if and when it became appropriate they would consider how to inform the children); and they abided by this agreement until late 1999."

"By voluntarily signing the ovum donation form, K.M. was donating genetic material. Her position was analogous to that of a sperm donor, who is treated as a legal stranger to a child if he donates sperm through a licensed physician and surgeon under Family Code section 7613(b). The Court finds no reason to treat ovum donors as having greater claims to parentage than sperm donors."

"The Court accepts the proposition that a child may have two legal mothers and assumed it to be the law in its analysis of the evidence herein."

"K.M.'s claim to 'presumed' parenthood rests upon her contention that she has met the criteria of Family Code section 7611(d). [Section 7611(d) provides that a person is a presumed parent when the person takes a child into her or his home and holds the child out as her or his own child]. K.M. has failed to establish either that she received the twins into her home or that she held them out as her natural children. Although K.M. treated the twins in all regards as though they were her own (and there can be no question but that they are fully bonded to her as such), the children were received into the parties' home as E.G.'s children and, up until late 1999, both parties scrupulously held confidential petitioner's natural, *i.e.*, in this case, her genetic relationship to the children."

"E.G. is not estopped by her conduct. The Court finds that petitioner was not misled by any such conduct; that she knew that respondent did not intend thereby to confer parental rights upon her."

The Court of Appeal affirmed the judgment, ruling that K.M. did not qualify as a parent "because substantial evidence supports the trial courts factual finding that only E.G. intended to bring about the birth of a child whom she intended to raise as her own." The court observed that "the status of K.M. is consistent with the status of a sperm donor under the Uniform Parentage Act, *i.e.*, treated in law as if he were not the natural father of a child thereby conceived." Having concluded that the parties intended at the time of conception that only E.G. would be the child's mother, the court concluded that the parties' actions following the birth did not alter this agreement. The Court of Appeal concluded that if the parties had changed their intentions and wanted K.M. to be a parent, their only option was adoption.

We granted review.

K.M. asserts that she is a parent of the twins because she supplied the ova that were fertilized in vitro and implanted in her lesbian partner, resulting in the birth of the twins. As we will explain, we agree that K.M. is a parent of the twins because she supplied the ova that produced the children, and Family Code section 7613(b), which provides that a man is not a father if he provides semen to a physician to inseminate a woman who is not his wife, does not apply because K.M. supplied her ova to impregnate her lesbian partner in order to produce children who would be raised in their joint home.

The determination of parentage is governed by the Uniform Parentage Act (UPA). (§ 7600 et seq.). The UPA defines the parent and child relationship, which extends equally to every child and to every parent, regardless of the marital status of the parents.

In *Johnson v. Calvert* (1993) 5 Cal.4th 84, 87, 851 P.2d 776, we determined that a wife whose ovum was fertilized in vitro by her husband's sperm and implanted in a surrogate mother was the "natural mother" of the child thus produced. We noted that the UPA states that provisions applicable to determining a father and child relationship shall be used to determine a mother and child relationship "insofar as practicable." We relied, therefore, on the provisions in the UPA regarding presumptions of paternity and concluded that "genetic consanguinity" could be the basis for a finding of maternity just as it is for paternity. Under this authority, K.M.'s genetic relationship to the children in the present case constitutes evidence of a mother and child relationship as contemplated by the Act.

The Court of Appeal in the present case concluded, however, that K.M. was not a parent of the twins, despite her genetic relationship to them, because she had the same status as a sperm donor. Section 7613(b) states: "The donor of semen provided to a licensed physician and surgeon for use in artificial insemination of a woman other than the donor's wife is treated in law as if he were not the natural father of a child thereby conceived." In *Johnson*, . . . we did not discuss whether this statute applied to a woman who provides ova used to impregnate another woman, but we observed that in a true egg donation situation, where a woman gestates and gives birth to a child formed from the egg of another woman with the intent to raise the child as her own, the birth mother is the natural mother under California law. We held that the statute did not apply under the circumstances in *Johnson*, because the husband and wife in *Johnson* did not intend to donate their sperm and ova to the surrogate mother, but rather intended to procreate a child genetically related to them by the only available means.

The circumstances of the present case are not identical to those in *Johnson*, but they are similar in a crucial respect; both the couple in *Johnson* and the couple in the present case intended to produce a child that would be raised in their own home. In *Johnson*, it was clear that the married couple did not intend to donate their semen and ova to the surrogate mother, but rather permitted their semen and ova to be used to impregnate the surrogate mother in order to produce a child to be raised by them. In the present case, K.M. contends that she did not intend to donate her ova, but rather provided her ova so that E.G. could give birth to a child to be raised jointly by K.M. and E.G. E.G. hotly contests this, asserting that K.M. donated her ova to E.G., agreeing that E.G. would be the sole parent. It is undisputed, however, that the couple lived together and that they both intended to bring the child into their joint home. Thus, even accepting as true E.G.'s version of the facts (which the superior court did), the present case, like *Johnson*, does not present a true egg donation situation. K.M. did not intend to simply donate her ova to E.G., but rather provided her ova to her lesbian partner with whom she was living so that E.G. could give birth to a child that would be raised in their joint home. Even if we assume that the provisions of section 7613(b) apply to women who donate ova, the statute does not apply under the circumstances of the present case. . . .

K.M.'s genetic relationship with the twins constitutes evidence of a mother and child relationship under the UPA and, as explained above, section 7613(b) does not apply to exclude K.M. as a parent of the twins. The circumstance that E.G. gave birth to the twins also constitutes evidence of a mother and child relationship. Thus, both K.M. and E.G. are mothers of the twins under the UPA.

It is true we said in *Johnson* that "for any child California law recognizes only one natural mother." But . . . this statement in *Johnson* must be understood in light of the issue presented in that case; "our decision in *Johnson* does not preclude a child from having two parents both of whom are women." . . .

K.M. acknowledges that E.G. is the twins' mother. K.M. does not claim to be the twins' mother *instead of* E.G., but *in addition* to E.G. . . . The parentage of the twins is determined by application of the UPA. E.G. is the twins' mother because she gave birth to them and K.M. also is the twins' mother because she provided the ova from which they were produced. . . .

The superior court in the present case found that K.M. signed a waiver form, thereby "relinquishing and waiving all rights to claim legal parentage of any children who might result." But such a waiver does not affect our determination of parentage. Section 7632 provides: "Regardless of its terms, an agreement between an alleged or presumed father and the mother or child does not bar an action under this chapter." A woman who supplies ova to be used to impregnate her lesbian partner, with the understanding that the resulting child will be raised in their joint home, cannot waive her responsibility to support that child. Nor can such a purported waiver effectively cause that woman to relinquish her parental rights.

In light of our conclusion that section 7613(b) does not apply and that K.M. is the twins' parent (together with E.G.), based upon K.M.'s genetic relationship to the twins, we need not, and do not, consider whether K.M. is presumed to be a parent of the twins under section 7611(d), which provides that a man is presumed to be a child's father if "he receives the child into his home and openly holds out the child as his natural child."

The judgment of the Court of Appeal is reversed.

Dissenting Opinion by Kennard, J.

Unlike the majority, I would apply the controlling statutes as written. The statutory scheme for determining parentage contains two provisions that resolve K.M.'s claim to be a parent of the twins born to E.G. Under one provision, a man who donates sperm for physician-assisted artificial insemination of a woman to whom he is not married is not the father of the resulting child. (Fam.Code, § 7613(b).) Under the other provision, rules for determining fatherhood are to be used for determining motherhood "insofar as practical." (§ 7650.) Because K.M. donated her ova for physician-assisted artificial insemination and implantation in another woman, and knowingly and voluntarily signed a document declaring her intention not to become a parent of any resulting children, she is not a parent of the twins. . . .

Dissenting Opinion by Werdegar, J.

The majority determines that the twins who developed from the ova K.M. donated to E.G. have two mothers rather than one. While I disagree, as I shall explain, with that ultimate conclusion, I agree with the majority's premise that a child can have two mothers. Our previous holding that "for any child California law recognizes only one natural mother" (*Johnson v. Calvert* (1993) 5 Cal.4th 84, 92, 851 P.2d 776) must be understood in the context in which it arose—a married couple who intended to become parents and provided their fertilized ova to a gestational surrogate who did not intend to become a parent—and, thus understood, may properly be limited to cases in which to recognize a second mother would inject an unwanted third parent into an existing family. When, in contrast to *Johnson*, no natural or adoptive father exists, two women who intend to become mothers of the same child may do so either through adoption or because both qualify as natural mothers under the Uniform Parentage Act, one having donated the ovum and the other having given birth. . . .

I cannot agree with the majority that the children in this case do in fact have two mothers. Until today, when one woman has provided the ova and another has given birth, the established rule for determining disputed claims to motherhood was clear: we looked to the intent of the parties. In a true egg donation situation, where a woman gestates and gives birth to a child formed from the egg of another woman with the intent to raise the child as her own, the birth mother is the natural mother under California law. Contrary to the majority's apparent assumption, to limit *Johnson's* holding that a child can have only one mother to cases involving existing two-parent families does not require us to abandon *Johnson's* intent test as the method for determining disputed claims of motherhood arising from the use of reproductive technology. Indeed, we have no other test sufficient to the task.

Furthermore, to apply *Johnson's* intent test to the facts of this case necessarily leads to the conclusion that E.G. is a mother and K.M. is not. That E.G. intended to become the mother—and the only mother—of the children to whom she gave birth is unquestioned. Whether K.M. for her part also intended to become the children's mother was disputed, but the trial court found on the basis of conflicting evidence that she did not. We must defer to the trial court's findings on this point because substantial evidence supports them. K.M. represented in connection with the ovum donation process, both orally and in writing, that she did not intend to become the children's mother, and consistently with those representations subsequently held the children out to the world as E.G.'s but not her own. Thus constrained by the facts, the majority can justify its conclusion that K.M. is also the children's mother only by changing the law. This the majority does by displacing *Johnson's* intent test—at least for the purposes of this case—with the following new rule: a woman who has supplied her ova to impregnate her lesbian partner in order to produce children who would be raised in their joint home is a mother of the resulting children regardless of any preconception manifestations of intent to the contrary.

I find the majority's reasons for not applying the *Johnson* intent test unpersuasive. The majority criticizes the test as basing the determination of parentage upon a later judicial determination of intent made years after the birth of the child. But the task of determining the intent of persons who have undertaken assisted reproduction is not fundamentally different than the task of determining intent in the context of disputes involving contract, tort or criminal law, something courts have done satisfactorily for centuries. The expectation that courts will, in most cases accurately decide factual issues such as intent, is one of the fundamental premises of our judicial system. Indeed, the majority itself expresses willingness to continue applying the *Johnson* intent test to determine whether gestational surrogacy agreements are enforceable. This position leaves no plausible basis for refusing to apply the same test to determine whether ovum donation agreements are enforceable. Ovum donation and gestational surrogacy agreements are two sides of the same coin; each involves an ovum provider, a gestator, and an agreement about who will become the parent or parents of any resulting offspring. Indeed, when two women divide in this way the genetic and gestational components of motherhood, only an examination of their intent permits us to determine whether we are dealing with an ovum donation agreement, a gestational surrogacy agreement, or neither. If courts can perform one of these tasks acceptably, they can also perform the other.

No more persuasive is the majority's suggestion that to respect the formally expressed intent of the parties to an ovum donation agreement is prohibited by the rule that parental obligations may not be waived by contract. . . . Certainly parental obligations may not be waived by contract. But *Johnson's* intent test does not enforce ovum donation and gestational surrogacy agreements; it merely directs courts to consider such documents, along with all other relevant evidence, in determining preconception intent. . . .

Question based on *K.M. v. E.G.*

Who has the better argument, the majority or the dissents?

Problems Regarding Assisted Reproduction

1. Marge underwent a hysterectomy. Marge's ovaries were left intact. Marge married John, and they decided to have a baby. Sue, a close friend of Marge and John, volunteered to be a gestational surrogate. A number of Marge's eggs were removed and fertilized with John's sperm through in vitro fertilization. One of the fertilized eggs was transferred into Sue's uterus, and she gave birth to a healthy baby. Prior to the birth, Marge, John, Sue, and Sue's husband filed a declaratory judgment action seeking a declaration that Marge and John are the parents of the child. Following birth, Sue and her husband signed documents relinquishing any parental rights to the child. A state statute provides that surrogacy contracts are unenforceable. Who are the baby's parents? How should the judge rule? *T.V. v. New York State Department of Health,* 88 A.D.3d 290, 929 N.Y.S.2d 139 (2011).

2. Sue is a single woman without a partner. Sue wishes to have a child. To save money, Sue decides against purchasing sperm from a sperm bank or using a physician to inseminate her. Sue's friend Frank donates sperm, and Sue uses a turkey baster to insert the sperm into her body. It works! Sue becomes pregnant. A few days later, Sue and Frank both sign the following "agreement": "This is a voluntary relinquishment by Frank Smith of any and all parental rights and obligations such as child support, visitation, and custody in relationship to the donation of sperm from Frank Smith to Sue Jones. Sue shall be the sole parent and provider for the child and Sue relinquishes any rights to seek financial or emotional support from Frank at any

time." When the child was born, no father was listed on the birth certificate. Will/ should a court enforce Frank's voluntary relinquishment of parental rights? Suppose Sue finds it necessary to go on public assistance for herself and the child. Are state child enforcement authorities bound by Sue and Frank's agreement, or can Frank be forced to support the child? *E.E. v. O.M.G.R.*, 420 N.J. Super. 283, 20 A.3d 1171 (Chancery 2011).

3. Guadalupe and Joanne are in a committed same-sex relationship. Same sex-marriage is not legal in their state. They decide to have a baby. Guadalupe will become pregnant through assisted reproduction. Guadalupe meets with Dr. Miles, a physician at Women's Care Medical Group. Guadalupe informs the doctor she is in a same-sex relationship with Joanne and that they intend to co-parent the child. Dr. Miles explains that it might be useful to try intrauterine insemination, in which a doctor threads a catheter through the patient's cervix and inserts semen through the catheter into the uterus. Dr. Miles says that if this procedure is used, her religious beliefs will preclude her from performing the procedure on a single woman. Dr. Miles reassures Guadalupe that other physicians in the medical practice will do the procedure. Guadalupe tries intrauterine insemination performed by another doctor, but does not become pregnant. Eventually, the other doctor employs in vitro fertilization, Guadalupe becomes pregnant, and gives birth to a healthy baby. The civil rights law of the state provides: "All persons within the jurisdiction of this state are free and equal, and no matter what their sex, race, color, religion, ancestry, national origin, disability, medical condition, or sexual orientation are entitled to the full and equal accommodations, advantages, facilities, privileges, or services in all business establishments of every kind whatsoever." Can Guadalupe and Joanne sue the medical clinic and Dr. Miles under this statute because the doctor declined on religious grounds to personally perform the intrauterine insemination? *North Coast Women's Care Medical Group. Inc. v. San Diego County Superior Court,* 44 Cal. 4th 1145, 189 P.3d 959 (2008).

CHAPTER 13

Adoption

IT IS COMMON TO SEE tears in court, but seldom tears of joy. When adoptions are finalized in court, however, tears of happiness flow. Adoptions are among the few occasions when everyone in court is smiling.

Adoption creates a new parent-child relationship. Adopting parents have all the rights and responsibilities of biological parents. An adopted child inherits from the adopting parents, and is "issue" for purposes of inheritance. Minnesota law is typical, providing: "Upon adoption, the adopted person shall become the legal child of the adopting persons and they shall become the legal parents of the child with all the rights and duties between them of birth parents and legitimate children."[1]

Not everything about adoption breeds smiles. After all, before an adoption is celebrated in court, the parent-child relationship with one or both biological parents must end. In the case of step-parent adoption, only one biological parent's rights are terminated.

The law recognizes six types of adoption: (1) Independent adoption, in which the child is placed in an adoptive home by the child's natural parent or parents; (2) Agency adoption, in which the child is relinquished to an adoption agency. The agency selects adoptive parents and places the child with the parents; (3) Stepparent adoption, in which the spouse of a child's biological parent adopts the child; (4) International adoption; (5) Adoption of adults for purposes of inheritance; (6) A small number of states have tribal customary adoption for Native American children.

---

1 Minn. Stat. Ann. § 259.59(1).

Many states provide that children of a certain age (*e.g.*, 12) must consent to adoption. Massachusetts is typical: "A decree of adoption shall not be made, except as provided in this chapter, without the written consent of the child to be adopted, if above the age of twelve."[2]

It is a crime to pay for a child to be adopted or, to put it bluntly, buy a baby.[3] It is equally a crime to sell a baby. The Oklahoma Supreme Court emphasized the policy against baby buying in *Adoption of Baby Boy*,[4] where the court wrote, "Oklahoma has a strong public policy against buying or selling children for adoption. The anti-trafficking in children statutes . . . make it a crime to accept, solicit, offer, pay, or transfer anything of value in connection with an adoption except as allowed" by statute. The law is similar in other states.

The prohibition against buying and selling children does not outlaw payment of fees to an adoption agency or an attorney providing adoption-related services. In most states, in independent adoptions, adoptive parents may pay the birth mother's living expenses while she is pregnant, as well as maternity-related medical expenses, provided such payments are not contingent on placement of the child for adoption. When payment of expenses is allowed, adopting parents must keep detailed records of adoption-related expenses, and submit the expenses to the court for approval.[5] In California, it is a misdemeanor for a mother to accept payment if she secretly plans not to go through with adoption.[6]

Is it really wrong to buy a baby for adoption? In a famous article, Elisabeth Landers and Richard Posner pondered the question. Their article is excerpted below.

---

2 Mass. Gen. Laws. Ann. Ch. 210, § 2.

3 *See* Fla. Stat. Ann. § 63.212 (1)(c) ("It is unlawful for any person to sell or surrender, or to arrange for the sale or surrender of, a minor to another person for money or anything of value or to receive such minor child for such payment or thing of value."); Ky. Rev. Stat. § 199.590(2).

4 236 P.3d 116 (Okla. 2010).

5 *See* Adoption of Baby Boy, 236 P.3d 116 (Okla. 2010)(describing Oklahoma law. In this case, the biological father fought the adoption of his baby. The adopting parents racked up nearly $150,000 in fees in their effort to adopt the baby).

6 Cal. Penal Code § 273.

The Economics of the Baby Shortage

Elisabeth M. Landers & Richard A. Posner
7 The Journal of Legal Studies 323 (1978)

Ordinarily, potential gains from trade are realized by a process of voluntary transacting – by a sale, in other words. Adoptions could in principle be handled through the market and in practice, as we shall see, there is a considerable amount of baby selling. But because public policy is opposed to the sale of babies, such sales as do occur constitute a "black market." . . .

Students of adoption agree on two things. The first is that there is a shortage of white babies for adoption; the second is that there is a glut of black babies, and of children who are no longer babies (particularly if they are physically or mentally handicapped), for adoption. . . .

Students of adoption cite factors such as the declining proportion of illegitimate children being put up for adoption as the "causes" of the baby shortage. But such factors do not create a shortage, any more than the scarcity of truffles creates a shortage; they merely affect the number of children available for adoption at any price. At a higher price for babies, the incidence of abortion, the reluctance to part with an illegitimate child, and even the incentive to use contraceptives would diminish because the costs of unwanted pregnancy would be lower while the (opportunity) costs to the natural mother of retaining her illegitimate child would rise.

The principal suppliers of babies for adoption are adoption agencies. . . . Prospective adoptive parents applying to an agency face waiting periods of three to seven years. And the (visible) queue understates the shortage, since by tightening their criteria of eligibility to adopt a child the agencies can shorten the apparent queue without increasing the supply of babies. Thus some demanders in this market must wait for years to obtain a baby, others never obtain one, and still others are discouraged by knowledge of the queue from even trying. . . .

The picture is complicated, however, by the availability of independent adoptions. An independent adoption is one that does not go through an agency. Most independent adoptions are by a relative, for example a step-father, but some involve placement with strangers and here, it would seem, is an opportunity for a true baby market to develop. However, the operation of this market is severely curtailed by a network of restrictions, varying from state to state (a few states forbid independent adoption by a nonrelative) but never so loose as to permit outright sale of a baby for adoption.

Just as a buyer's queue is a symptom of a shortage, a seller's queue is a symptom of a glut. The thousands of children in foster care are comparable to an unsold inventory stored in a warehouse. . . . We believe that the large number of children in foster care is, in part, a manifestation of a regulatory pattern that combines restrictions on the sale of babies with the effective monopolization of the adoption market by adoptive agencies . . . .

In these circumstances, the economist expects a black market to emerge. Some fraction – we do not know what – of the 17, 000 independent adoptions are indeed black-market adoptions in the sense that the compensation paid either the natural parents or the middlemen, or both, exceeds the lawful limits. However, the potential criminal and professional sanctions for the individuals involved in baby selling not only drive up the costs and hence the price of babies (and so reduce demand) but necessarily imply a clandestine mode of operation. . . .

A further consideration is that there will be more fraud in a black market for babies than in a lawful market . . . . In lawful markets the incidence of fraud is limited not only by the existence of legal remedies against the seller but also by his desire to build a reputation for fair dealing. . . .

The foregoing analysis suggests that the baby shortage and black market are the result of legal restrictions that prevent the market from operating freely in the sale of babies as of other goods. This suggests as a possible reform simply eliminating these restrictions. However, many people believe that a free market in babies would be undesirable. . . .

We begin with a set of criticisms that in reality are applicable not to the market as such, but only, we believe, to the *black* market. The first such criticism is of the high price of babies and the bad effects that are alleged to flow from a high price, such as favoring the wealthy. This criticism of the use of the price system is based on the current prices in the black market. There is no reason to believe that prices would be so high were the sale of babies legalized. On the contrary, prices for children of *equivalent quality* would be much lower.

The current black-market price is swollen by expected punishment costs which would not be a feature of a legalized baby market. In a legal and competitive baby market, price would be equated to the marginal costs of producing and selling for adoption babies of a given quality. These marginal costs include certain well-known items, such as the natural mother's medical expenses and maintenance during pregnancy and the attorney's fee for handling the legal details of the adoption proceedings. The question marks are the additional fees that would be necessary (1) to compensate a woman either for becoming pregnant or, if she was pregnant already, for inducing her to put the baby up for adoption rather than abort or retain it, and (2) to cover the search costs necessary to match baby and adoptive parents. . . .

Because the adoption agencies give substantial emphasis to the employment and financial situation of adoptive parents, a baby market might actually provide more opportunities for the poor to adopt than non-price rationing does. If we are correct that the (acquisition) costs of babies in a lawful and competitive market would often be small, perhaps no more than the cost of an automobile, low-income families who would normally be considered financially ineligible by adoption agencies would be able in a free market to obtain a child.

Another prevalent criticism of the market, and again one that pertains primarily to the operations of the black market, is that fraud and related forms of dishonesty and overreaching pervade the market method of providing children for adoption. It is contended, for example, that the health of the child or of the child's mother is regularly misrepresented and that frequently after the sale is completed the seller will attempt to blackmail the adoptive parents. Such abuses are probably largely the result of the fact that the market is an illegal one. . . .

To be sure, there are probably inherent limitations on the use of legal remedies to protect purchasers even in a legal baby market. For example, consideration of the welfare of the child might lead courts to refuse to grant rescission to a buyer as a remedy for breach of warranty (*i.e.*, allow him to return the child). And courts might be reluctant to order specific performance of a contract to put up a child for adoption. . . .

We now consider criticisms of baby selling that are applicable to a legal market rather than just to the present illegal market. The first is that the rationing of the supply of babies to would-be adoptive parents by price is not calculated to promote the best interests of the children, the objective of the adoption process. This criticism cannot be dismissed as foolish. . . .

Very simply, the question is whether the price system would do as good a job as, or a better job than, adoption agencies in finding homes for children that would maximize their satisfactions in life. . . .

One valuable function agencies may perform is screening out people whose interest in having children is improper in an uncontroversial sense—people who wish to have children in order to abuse or make slaves of them. The criminal statutes punishing child abuse and neglect would remain applicable to babies adopted in a free market, but the extreme difficulty of detecting such crimes makes it unlikely, at least given current levels of punishment, that the criminal statutes alone are adequate. This may make some prescreening a more effective method of prevention than after-the-fact punishment. But the logical approach, then, is to require every prospective baby buyer to undergo some minimal background investigation. This approach would be analogous to licensing automobile drivers and seems as superior to the agency monopoly as licensing is to allocating automobiles on a non-price basis.

Moreover, concern with child abuse should not be allowed to obscure the fact that abuse is not the normal motive for adopting a child. And once we put abuse aside, willingness to pay money for a baby would seem on the whole a reassuring factor from the standpoint of child welfare. Few people buy a car or a television set in order to smash it. In general, the more costly a purchase, the more care the purchase will lavish on it. . . .

A further point is that today some fetuses are probably aborted because the cost to the mother of carrying them to term and placing them for adoption exceeds the permissible return. In a free adoption market, some of the 900,000 fetuses aborted in 1974 would have been born and placed for adoption. If the welfare of these (potential) children is included in the calculation of the welfare of adopted children, both actual and potential, the heavy costs imposed on the market by adoption regulation may actually decrease child welfare. . . .

Other objections to legalizing the market in babies are more symbolic than pragmatic. For example, to accord a property right in the newborn child to the natural parents seems to some observers to smack of slavery. But allowing a market in adoptions does not entail giving property rights to natural parents for all purposes. Laws forbidding child abuse and neglect would continue to be fully applicable to adoptive parents even if baby sales were permitted. Further, we are speaking only of sales of newborn infants, and do not suggest that parents should have a right to sell older children. . . .

The antipathy to an explicit market in babies may be part of a broader wish to disguise facts that might be acutely uncomfortable if widely known. Were baby prices quoted as prices of soybean futures are quoted, a racial ranking of these prices would be evident, with white baby prices higher than nonwhite baby prices. . . .

Some people are also upset by the implications for the eugenic alteration of the human race that are presented by baby selling. Baby selling may seem logically and inevitably to lead to baby breeding, for any market will generate incentives to improve the product as well as to optimize the price and quantity of the current quality level of the product. . . .

The emphasis placed by critics on the social costs of a free market in babies blurs what would probably be the greatest long-run effect of legalizing the baby market: including women who have unintentionally become pregnant to put up the child for adoption rather than raise it themselves or have an abortion. . . .

The symbolic objections to baby sale must also be compared with the substantial costs that the present system imposes on childless couples, aborted fetuses (if they can be said to incur costs), and children who end up in foster care. In particular, many childless couples undergo extensive, costly, and often futile methods of fertility treatment in order to increase their chances of bearing a child. Some people produce unhealthy offspring (due to various genetic disorders) because of their strong desire to have children. And no doubt many people settle for childlessness because of the difficulties of obtaining an adopted child. . . .

The most vocal and organized opponents of the baby market are the adoption agencies. . . . Assuming that agencies would have no cost or efficiency advantage over private firms in an unregulated market, they would be reduced to operating at the competitive margin if such a market were permitted. They might even be competed out of the market. . . .

Potentially allied to the agencies and the social welfare professionals who staff them in opposition to baby selling are those prospective adoptive parents who by virtue of their contacts and general sophistication are able to jump to the head of the queue or procure a baby easily in the (lawful) independent market, either way paying less than they would have to pay in the free market. . . .

The potential supporters of baby selling are difficult to organize in an effective political coalition. They consist of unborn babies, children in foster care, taxpayers (each only trivially burdened by the costs of foster care), and people who have only a low probability of ever wanting to adopt a baby, as well as couples currently wanting to adopt one.

———————————

Nearly a decade after the "baby selling" article, Judge Posner returned to the subject, in part to respond to critics.

The Regulation of the Market in Adoptions

Richard A. Posner
67 Boston University Law Review 59 (1987)

Whenever critics of the law-and-economics movement want an example of its excesses they point to what is popularly known as the "baby selling article," which Dr. Elisabeth Landes and I wrote almost a decade ago. The article is usually, although incorrectly, described as advocating a free market in babies....

Another profound misconception about the article is that in discussing the pros and cons of using the market to equilibrate the demand for and supply of babies for adoption, Dr. Landes and I were proposing a radical break with existing ethical norms. Actually, wholly apart from the black market in babies for adoption, the market is used, though in a stunted form, to allocate babies for adoption. Adoption agencies charge fees, often stiff ones, to adoptive parents, and part of the agencies' fee income goes to pay the medical expenses and other maintenance expenses of the natural mother; thus the adoptive parents pay the natural mother, albeit indirectly and at a regulated price, to give up her child. In "independent" adoptions, which are arranged through a lawyer or obstetrician, the element of sale is even more transparent, and indeed the system of independent adoption is often referred to as the "gray market." Dr. Landes and I were simply trying to consider how changes in the law might make the existing market in babies for adoption operate more efficiently—and more equitably....

The purpose of our article was not to make an extrapolation at once mechanical and unsound from the market in goods to the market in babies but to use the analytical tools of economics to explore a pressing social problem—the imbalance between the demand for and supply of babies for adoption....

Both adoption through an agency and independent adoption favor the wealthy and well connected....

The difficulty of satisfying the potential demand for babies for adoption would be easier to accept if the supply of babies were inherently quite limited in relation to the demand, as it would be if premarital sex were rare—for the usual source of babies for adoption is illegitimate births. But sex outside marriage is rampant in our society....

For heuristic purposes (only!) it is useful to analogize the sale of babies to the sale of an ordinary good, such as an automobile or a television set. We observe, for example, that although the supply of automobiles and of television sets is rationed by price, not all the automobiles and television sets are owned by wealthy people. On the contrary, the free market in these goods has lowered prices, through competition and innovation, to the point where the goods are available to a lot of people. There is even less reason for thinking that if babies could be sold to adoptive parents the wealthy would come to monopolize babies. Wealthy people (other than those few who owe their wealth to savings or inheritance rather than to a high income) have high costs of time. It therefore costs them more to raise a child—child rearing still being a time-intensive activity—than it costs the nonwealthy. As a result, wealthy couples tend to have few rather than many children. This pattern would not change if babies could be bought. . . .

Thus far I have implicitly been speaking only of the market for healthy white infants. There is no shortage of nonwhite and of handicapped infants, and of any children who are no longer infants, available for adoption. Such children are substitutes for healthy white infants, and the higher the price of the latter, the greater will be the demand for the former. The network of regulations that has driven up the full price (including such nonmonetary components of price as delay) of adopting a healthy, white infant may have increased the willingness of childless couples to consider adopting a child of a type not in short supply, though how much (if at all) no one knows. . . .

As soon as one mentions quality, people's hackles rise and they remind you that one is talking about a traffic in human beings, not in inanimate objects. The observation is pertinent, and at least five limitations might have to be placed on the operation of the market in babies for adoption. The first, already mentioned and already in place, is that the buyers can have no right to abuse the thing bought, as they would if the thing were a piece of steel or electronics. This really should go without saying. . . .

[A]ll adoptive parents are, in theory anyway, screened for fitness. Adoption agencies are charged with this responsibility, and if we moved toward a freer market in babies the agencies could be given the additional function of investigating and certifying prospective purchasers, who would pay the price of the service.

But let us not make too much of screening. The idea that a significant number of people are lurking about who if given the chance would buy babies for criminal purposes is a bogeyman. . . .

[S]ince we do not screen natural parents, and any proposal to do so would be met with justifiable protests against governmental intrusion into private matters, the case for screening adoptive parents can hardly be considered self-evident. . . .

The third limitation on a baby market concerns remedies for breach of contract. In an ordinary market a buyer can both reject defective goods and, if the seller refuses to deliver and damages would be an inadequate remedy for the refusal, get specific performance of the contract. Natural parents are not permitted to reject their baby, either when it is born or afterward, because it turns out to be handicapped or otherwise not in conformity with their expectations; no more should adoptive parents who buy their babies. Nor should the adoptive parents be able to force the natural mother to surrender the baby to them if she changes her mind, unless some competent authority determines that the baby would be better off adopted. The child is an interested third party whose welfare would be disserved by a mechanical application of the remedies available to buyers in the market for inanimate goods.

For the same reason (the child's welfare) neither natural nor adopting parents should be allowed to sell their children after infancy, that is, after the child has established a bond with its parents. Nor should the natural mother be allowed to take back the baby after adoption, any more than a seller of a conventional good or service can (except in extraordinary circumstances) rescind the sale after delivery and payment in accordance with his contract with the buyer, unless, once again, a competent authority decides that the baby's welfare would be increased.

The last limitation on the baby market that I shall discuss relates to eugenic breeding. Although prospects still seem remote, one can imagine an entrepreneur in the baby market trying to breed a race of Übermenschen who would command premium prices. The external effects of such an endeavor could be very harmful, and would provide an appropriate basis for governmental regulation.

I am not so sanguine about the operation of a baby market, even with the limitations I have discussed, that I am prepared to advocate the complete and immediate repeal of the laws forbidding the sale of babies for adoption. That such a market might give somewhat greater scope for child abusers and might encourage weird and potentially quite harmful experiments in eugenic breeding should be enough to give anyone pause. But to concentrate entirely on the downside would be a mistake. One million abortions a year is a serious social problem regardless of where one stands on the underlying ethical issues; so is a flourishing black market in babies combined with a severe shortage in the lawful market. . . .

Even if partial deregulation of the baby market might make practical utilitarian sense along the lines just suggested, some will resist on symbolic grounds. If we acknowledge that babies can be sold, the argument goes, we open the door to all sorts of monstrous institutions—including slavery. We regularly resist this type of argument in analogous contexts, and I have difficulty understanding why it stubbornly persists in this one. . . .

One should always be suspicious of arguments against the market when they are made by people who have no desire to participate in it themselves, people who want to restrict the availability of goods to other people. . . .

The opponents of "baby selling" are unwilling to acknowledge that what we have today, even apart from the black market, is closer to a free market in babies than a free market in babies would be to slavery or torture. As I said at the outset, adoption agencies do lawfully "sell" babies, and many charge thousands of dollars. Moreover, in independent adoptions, the mother herself may "sell" her baby, for it is not considered unlawful to use a part of the fee paid by the adoptive parents to defray the medical and other maintenance costs of the mother during pregnancy. . . .

So we have legal baby selling today; the question of public policy is not whether baby selling should be forbidden or allowed but how extensively it should be regulated. I simply think it should be regulated less stringently than is done today.

Question based on Landers and Posner

What are your thoughts? Do you agree with Judge Posner and Dr. Landers?

Independent Adoption

Independent adoption is also called private adoption or direct placement.[7] Most states allow independent adoption. Delaware and Massachusetts do not.[8] The primary distinction between agency adoption and independent adoption is

---

7 *See* Mich. Comp. Laws Ann. § 710.22(o) ("'Direct placement' means a placement in which a parent or guardian selects an adoptive parent for a child, other than a stepparent or an individual related to the child within the fifth degree of marriage, blood, or adoption, and transfers physical custody of the child to the prospective adoptive parent.").

8 Del. Code Ann. tit. 13 § 904; Mass. Gen. Laws ch. 210 § 2A.

that with independent adoption, placement of the child in the adoptive home is made by the parents—usually the birth mother—rather than an adoption agency. The birth mother personally selects the adoptive parents.[9] Michigan law is typical, providing: "A parent or guardian shall personally select a prospective adoptive parent in a direct placement. The selection shall not be delegated."[10] A direct connection exists between the birth mother and the adopting parents. The adopting parents often attend the birth and take custody of the baby at the hospital. A petition for adoption is filed following birth.

An adoption agency plays a role in independent adoption. In many states, a social worker from an adoption agency counsels the birth parent about giving up the child for adoption. An agency investigates the adoptive parents and files a report with the court.

As mentioned, in independent adoption, the mother personally places the baby with the adoptive parents. But how does a young pregnant woman find a couple to adopt her baby? Craigslist? eBay? Facebook? In some cases, the child is placed with members of the mother's family. In other cases, a professional assists the mother locate adoptive parents. Professionals who specialize in independent adoptions—often attorneys—maintain files of prospective adoptive parents, and provide names and background information to birth parents considering adoption. In some states, limited advertising is allowed.

Can an attorney ethically represent both the birth parent and the adoptive parents in an independent adoption? Experienced adoption attorneys say no.[11] In California the answer is yes, but subject to limitation. California law provides: "The Legislature declares that in an independent adoption proceeding, whether or not written consent is obtained, multiple representation by an attorney should be avoided whenever a birth parent displays the slightest reason for the attorney to believe any controversy might arise."[12]

When birth parents and adoptive parents live in different states, the laws of both jurisdictions must be satisfied. As well, compliance with the Interstate Compact on the Placement of Children (ICPC) is required. The ICPC is discussed in Chapter 14.

---

9 Michigan law requires that the mother be provided information about the adoptive parents. Mich. Comp. Laws Ann. § 710.23a(3).

10 Mich. Comp. Laws Ann. § 710.23a(2).

11 *See* Jennifer Fairfax, *The Adoption Law Handbook*, pp. 93-94 (2011).

12 Cal. Fam. Code § 8800(c).

Every year, thousands of women—typically young, unmarried women—make the agonizing decision to give up their baby for adoption. One of these cases turned into a cause celebre, capturing the nation's attention. The case involved a protracted battle over a little girl named Jessica. The protagonists were the child's biological parents, living in Iowa, and the married couple who hoped to adopt Jessica, living in Michigan. The battle over "Baby Jessica" wound up in the supreme court of both states. An excerpt from the Michigan Supreme Court's decision follows.

Baby Girl Clausen

Supreme Court of Michigan
442 Mich. 648, 502 N.W.2d 649 (1993)

Per Curiam.

[This case arises] out of a child custody dispute involving the competing claims of the child's natural parents (Cara and Daniel Schmidt) and the third-party custodians with whom the child now lives (Roberta and Jan DeBoer).

. . . We sum up our analysis of the competing arguments by reference to the words of the United States Supreme Court: "No one would seriously dispute that a deeply loving and interdependent relationship with an adult and a child in his or her care may exist even in the absence of blood relationship." *Smith v. Organization of Foster Families*, 431 U.S. 816, 843-844, 97 S.Ct. 2094, 2109-2110 (1977). But there are limits to such claims. In the context of foster care, the Court has said:

There are also important distinctions between the foster family and the natural family. First, unlike the earlier cases recognizing a right to family privacy, the State here seeks to interfere, not with a relationship having its origins entirely apart from the power of the State, but rather with a foster family which has its source in state law and contractual arrangements. The liberty interest in family privacy has its source, and its contours are ordinarily to be sought, not in state law, but in intrinsic human rights, as they have been understood in this Nation's history and tradition. Here, however, whatever emotional ties may develop between foster parent and foster child have their origins in an arrangement in which the State has been a partner from the outset. . . .

Likewise, the DeBoers acquired temporary custody of this child, with whom they had no prior relationship, through the power of the state and must be taken to have known that their right to continue custody was contingent on the completion of the Iowa adoption. Within nine days of assuming physical custody and less than one month after the child's birth, the DeBoers learned of Cara Schmidt's claim that the waiver of rights procured by the attorney acting on behalf of the DeBoers was unlawful because she had not been afforded the seventy-two hour waiting period required by Iowa law. Within two months of the child's birth, the DeBoers learned of Daniel Schmidt's claim of paternity when on March 27, 1991, he filed a petition to intervene in the DeBoers' adoption proceeding. . . .

On February 8, 1991, Cara Clausen gave birth to a baby girl in Iowa. Proceedings in Iowa have established that defendant Daniel Schmidt is the child's father. On February 10, 1991, Clausen signed a release of custody form, relinquishing her parental rights to the child. Clausen, who was unmarried at the time of the birth, had named Scott Seefeldt as the father. On February 14, 1991, he executed a release of custody form.

On February 25, 1991, petitioners Roberta and Jan DeBoer, who are Michigan residents, filed a petition for adoption of the child in juvenile court in Iowa. A hearing was held the same day, at which the parental rights of Cara Clausen and Seefeldt were terminated, and petitioners were granted custody of the child during the pendency of the proceeding. The DeBoers returned to Michigan with the child, and she has lived with them in Michigan continuously since then.

However, the prospective adoption never took place. On March 6, 1991, nine days after the filing of the adoption petition, Cara Clausen filed a motion in the Iowa Juvenile Court to revoke her release of custody. In an affidavit accompanying the request, Clausen stated that she had lied when she named Seefeldt as the father of the child, and that the child's father actually was Daniel Schmidt. Schmidt filed an affidavit of paternity on March 12, 1991, and on March 27, 1991, he filed a petition in the Iowa district court, seeking to intervene in the adoption proceeding initiated by the DeBoers.

On November 4, 1991, the district court in Iowa conducted a bench trial on the issues of paternity, termination of parental rights, and adoption. On December 27, 1991, the district court found that Schmidt established by a preponderance of the evidence that he was the biological father of the child; that the DeBoers failed to establish by clear and convincing evidence that Schmidt had abandoned the child or that his parental rights should be terminated; and that a best interests of the child analysis did not become appropriate unless abandonment was established. On the basis of these findings, the court concluded that the termination proceeding was void with respect to Schmidt, and that the DeBoers' petition to adopt the child must be denied. Those decisions have been affirmed by the Iowa appellate courts.

On remand from the Iowa Supreme Court, the district court ordered the DeBoers to appear on December 3, 1992, with the child. The DeBoers did not appear at the hearing; instead, their Iowa attorney informed the court that the DeBoers had received actual notice of the hearing but had decided not to appear. In an order entered on December 3, 1992, the district court terminated the DeBoers' rights as temporary guardians and custodians of the child. The court found that, "Mr. and Mrs. DeBoer have no legal right or claim to the physical custody of this child. They are acting outside any legal claim to physical control and possession of this child."

On the same day their rights were terminated in Iowa, the DeBoers filed a petition in Washtenaw Circuit Court [in Michigan], asking the court to assume jurisdiction under the [Uniform Child Custody Jurisdiction Act] UCCJA. The petition requested that the court enjoin enforcement of the Iowa custody order and find that it was not enforceable, or, in the alternative, to modify it to give custody to the DeBoers. On December 3, 1992, the Washtenaw Circuit Court entered an ex parte temporary restraining order, which directed that the child remain in the custody of the DeBoers, and ordered Schmidt not to remove the child from Washtenaw County.

On December 11, 1992, Schmidt filed a motion for summary judgment to dissolve the preliminary injunction and to recognize and enforce the Iowa judgment. The Washtenaw Circuit Court held a hearing on Schmidt's motion on January 5, 1993. It found that it had jurisdiction to determine the best interests of the child. It denied Schmidt's motion for summary judgment, and directed that the child remain with the DeBoers until further order of the court.

On March 29, 1993, the Court of Appeals reversed the Washtenaw Circuit Court's denial of Schmidt's motion for summary judgment, concluding that that court lacked jurisdiction under the UCCJA, and that . . . the DeBoers lacked standing to bring the action. . . .

[The Michigan Supreme Court ruled that under the UCCJA, Michigan courts had no jurisdiction to award custody to the DeBoers. The court concluded that Michigan was required to enforce the Iowa custody order giving custody to the biological parents.].

We direct the Washtenaw Circuit Court to enter an order enforcing the custody orders entered by the Iowa courts. In consultation with counsel for the Schmidts and the DeBoers, the circuit court shall promptly establish a plan for the transfer of custody, with the parties directed to cooperate in the transfer with the goal of easing the child's transition into the Schmidt home. The circuit court shall monitor and enforce the transfer process, employing all necessary resources of the court, and shall notify the clerk of this Court 21 days following the release of this opinion of the arrangements for transfer of custody. The actual transfer shall take place within 10 days thereafter.

To a perhaps unprecedented degree among the matters that reach this Court, these cases have been litigated through fervent emotional appeals, with counsel and the adult parties pleading that their only interests are to do what is best for the child, who is herself blameless for this protracted litigation and the grief that it has caused. However, the clearly applicable legal principles require that the Iowa judgment be enforced and that the child be placed in the custody of her natural parents. It is now time for the adults to move beyond saying that their only concern is the welfare of the child and to put those words into action by assuring that the transfer of custody is accomplished promptly with minimum disruption of the life of the child.

Levin, Justice (dissenting).

I would agree with the majority's analysis if the DeBoers had gone to Iowa, purchased a carload of hay from Cara Clausen, and then found themselves in litigation in Iowa with Daniel Schmidt, who also claimed an interest in the hay. It could then properly be said that the DeBoers "must be taken to have known" that, rightly or wrongly, the Iowa courts might rule against them, and they should, as gracefully as possible, accept an adverse decision of the Iowa courts. Michigan would then have had no interest in the outcome, and would routinely enforce a decree of the Iowa courts against the DeBoers.

But this is not a lawsuit concerning the ownership, the legal title, to a bale of hay. This is not the usual *A v B* lawsuit; *Schmidts v. DeBoers*, or, if you prefer, *DeBoers v. Schmidts*.

There is a *C*, the child, "a feeling, vulnerable, and about to be sorely put upon little human being": Baby Girl Clausen, also known as Jessica DeBoer, who will now be told, "employing all necessary resources of the Washtenaw Circuit Court," that she is not Jessie, that the DeBoers are not Mommy and Daddy, that her name is Anna Lee Schmidt, and that the Schmidts, whom she has never met, are Mommy and Daddy. This child might, indeed, as the circuit judge essentially concluded, have difficulty trying that on for size at two and one-half years, she might, indeed, suffer an identity crisis. The judge said: "We had different degrees of testimony from the experts. All the way from permanent, serious damage, she would never recover from, down to the child would recover in time. But every expert testified that there would be *serious traumatic injury to the child at this time.*"

The majority's analysis, that the DeBoers should have known when they filed their petition for adoption in Iowa that they might lose, overlooks that the child did not choose to litigate in Iowa, over four hundred miles from her only home, the legal and factual issues that would decide whether her world would be destroyed, and know that she might lose. . . .

The majority's analysis focusing on the contest between the Schmidts and the DeBoers for possession of the child misfocuses on whether biological parents or persons acting as parents have the better "legal right," better "legal title," not to a carload of hay, but to a child. . . .

The superior claim of the child to be heard in this case is grounded not just in law, but in basic human morality. Adults like the Schmidts and the DeBoers make choices in their lives, and society holds them responsible for their choices. When adults are forced to bear the consequences of their choices, however disastrous, at least their character and personality have been fully formed, and that character can provide the foundation for recovery, the will to go on.

The character and personality of a child two and one-half years old is just beginning to take shape. To visit the consequences of adult choices upon the child during the formative years of her life, and to force her to sort out the competing emotional needs of the Schmidts and DeBoers, is unnecessarily harsh and without legal justification.

Jessica appeared on the cover of *Time* magazine, nestled in the arms of her adoptive mother—the woman who raised her, and who, when the picture was taken, was about to lose her. For *Time*, reporter Nancy Gibbs wrote:

Mother and Father can take down the pictures and store the rocking horse in the attic, pluck the magnetic alphabet off the refrigerator door. Maybe they can find some other use for the room with the yellow wallpaper. Or they could close it up and seal it like a tomb so they can go about their grieving for the merry little girl they love and are about to lose.

Time & Life Pictures/Getty Images

In the tidy backyard of the Cape Cod-style house with the cranberry shutters, Jessica DeBoer is having a picnic with her dog Miles. Her mother watches her through the blinds on the kitchen window. Everything feels so very normal. But the clock ticks loudly and the blinds all stay down and an answering machine screens the phone calls. Reporters keep calling—and sad friends, and adoption experts—and strangers who feel sorry for them.

When the Michigan Supreme Court ruled that Jan and Roberta DeBoer, a printer and a homemaker, had no right to keep the baby they have tried to adopt for more than two years, it lit a long, scorching fuse on a time bomb. The DeBoers were given a month to turn her over to her biological parents in Iowa, Dan and Cara Schmidt. This afternoon they have 26 days left.

"I sit here and count the stupid hours and the days and mark them off a dumb calendar as to my last moment, my last hour, my last kiss." Roberta sits in the forest-green dining room, sipping herbal tea out of a mug decorated with little footprints, hearts and the words IT'S A GIRL. How is she holding herself together? "'People can't understand,'" she says. "'They think I'm falling to pieces nonstop in front of Jessie. But I would never do that.'" And then Robby DeBoer breaks down, heaving and weeping. The cries are not plaintive, not whimpers, but sobs that send her body shaking and her voice coming from deep inside her. And she is angry.

"We let our government make irrational decisions for children to suffer and be condemned." She wants to take the case to the U.S. Supreme Court. "'They're going to walk away just like Michigan did and say, 'Wish we could have done something but there's nothing to do because our laws dictate otherwise.' I wonder if they could take their little two-year-old kids and walk into a black forest and just leave the child and walk away . . . And not feel the pain . . . How not to feel the pain . . .?"

In this case, everyone feels the pain. Here are Jessica's two sets of parents, those who conceived her and those who have raised her, fighting a passionate battle over who gets to keep her. Then there are all the other adoptive parents in the U.S., many of whom have been watching this ghastly spectacle unravel in the courts and go to sleep wondering whether their precious child will stay their child. And finally, of course, there is Jessica, the one party to the case who has most at stake and the smallest voice and is at the mercy of judges whose rulings at times have seemed little better than suggesting that she be sawed in half.

Writing for *People* magazine, Bill Hewitt wrote on May 31, 1993:

A Toddler's Future Hangs in the Balance
Amid a Bitter Struggle Over Her Adoption

As best she can, Roberta Deboer, 35, tries to maintain a semblance of normality around her home in Ann Arbor, Mich. Each weekday, after her husband, Jan, 40, sets out for work as a printer, she plays with Jessica, the 28-month-old girl she hopes to adopt. Other times the toddler loves frolicking with the family's golden retriever, Miles. In the afternoons, Robby, as she is known, usually puts Jessica down for a nap. But while the little girl sleeps, it is Robby who tries to ward off a nightmare—poring over legal documents in a desperate attempt to prevent authorities from taking away the baby she calls her own. "She is my child," Robby has said. "I did not birth her, but in every respect she is my child. When she cries, I am there. When she is happy, I'm a part of that happiness."

The way things look now, however, there may be precious little happiness ahead for the DeBoers. After more than two years of legal wrangling, one of the most closely watched—and agonizing—adoption cases ever seems to be moving to a climax. Last March an appeals court in Michigan ruled that the DeBoers must return Jessica, whom they have raised since she was a week old, to the girl's biological mother and father, Cara Schmidt, 30, and her husband, Dan, 41, of Blairstown, Iowa. The Schmidts have waged a fierce campaign to win back the daughter they call Anna, who they contend was unfairly taken from them. "This is like a death," said Robby at the time of the decision. The Schmidts, who are expecting another child in June, pronounced themselves "overjoyed."

Yet for both sides in this painful dispute, the misery goes back a long way. In January 1991, after years of looking for a baby to adopt because she was unable to have children herself, Robby got a call from a friend who worked as an attorney in Iowa, telling her about a single woman named Cara Clausen, then 28, who lived in the tiny farming community of Blairstown, near Cedar Rapids, and worked at a nearby trucking company. Cara was pregnant and wanted to put her child up for adoption because she didn't feel equipped to care for it on her own. The DeBoers hired a local lawyer, John Monroe, who made contact with Cara and worked out the necessary details to have the baby handed over at birth. Six days after the child was born, on Feb. 14, Robby and her mother drove through a heavy snowstorm to Cedar Rapids to pick up her new daughter.

Holding the little girl—whom she had decided to name Jessica—for the first time, Robby felt blessed. "I just fell made in love with her immediately," she said in an interview. "She was gorgeous." At a court hearing on Feb. 25, attorney

Monroe presented a judge with Cara's signed release of custody. Monroe also handed over a signed release from Scott Seefeldt, whom Cara had identified as the baby's father. The judge officially terminated Clausen and Seefeldt's parental rights, and within five days the elated DeBoers had become the legal guardians of Jessica and returned to Ann Arbor.

Their bliss lasted exactly one week. On March 8 a lawyer called to tell them that Cara had changed her mind and wanted her baby back. As Cara later explained, the whole pregnancy had been enormously stressful for her. Fearful that her parents, who also live in Blairstown, would disapprove, she had not even told them she was expecting a child until three days before the birth. "I was in denial," she recently told the Ann Arbor Observer. "I guess I felt ashamed." It turned out that her parents were strongly supportive and wanted her to keep the baby. More to the point, in court papers filed to win back her child, Cara also claimed that she had thought that Monroe had been working for her, not for the DeBoers, and that when he brought her papers to sign hours after the birth she was still in a daze.

But the real bombshell came a few days later when Dan Schmidt, a local truck driver and former boyfriend of Cara's, came forward, declared that he was Jessica's biological father and sued to establish his parental rights. (Tests have confirmed Schmidt's paternity.) Since then Schmidt and Clausen have married. Why Cara had originally named Seefeldt as the father is unclear. Whatever the reason, though, the net effect was plain enough: The paternal rights of the biological father had not been signed away after all. Thus the DeBoers were presented with the terrible dilemma of whether or not to hand back the child they had obtained in good faith.

Quickly they decided to fight. And so began the bitter custody battle that has seesawed back and forth—while Jessica has grown more aware of her world and more vulnerable to the trauma of dislocation. After a raft of appeals and rulings in both Michigan and Iowa, the DeBoers won what appeared to be a crucial victory last February when Michigan Judge William Ager Jr., stressing the best interests of the child over the traditional rights of biological parents, decreed that they should get custody of Jessica. Handing down his decision, he implored the Schmidts to abandon any further appeals, in order to spare Jessica. "Think of the possibility of saying, 'Enough!'" he urged.

Certainly both couples have taken their share of emotional hits as embarrassing and occasionally troubling details surfaced about them. It emerged, for instance, that in his youth, Jan, who was born in the Netherlands, had been in several scrapes with the law, including a conviction for illegal entry. Meanwhile some people in Blairstown looked askance at Cara and Dan's newly minted family values. "[She was] a woman who did her own thing, who lived her whole life just like she wanted," local resident Nancy Stults told a reporter from Ann Arbor. As for Dan, a former girlfriend, Barbara Schlicht, finds it strange that he should suddenly express such paternal concern for Jessica when he has all but ignored Amanda, the 13-year-old daughter they had together out of wedlock. "He says he wanted visitation with Jessica, when Mandy was only 25 miles from him her whole life," says Schlicht. As a measure of opinion in Iowa, a recent poll by a Cedar Rapids television station showed those surveyed favoring the DeBoers by a 2-to-1 margin over the Schmidts.

Supporters of the DeBoers believe that Cara and Dan are being manipulated in their quest to get Jessica back. Some believe the Schmidts have fallen under the spell of a group called Concerned United Birthparents, which crusades for the rights of biological parents. Although several CUB members have befriended the couple, Cara and Dan staunchly deny that they are puppets of the organization and in any case, in late March the Michigan Court of Appeals overturned Judge Ager's ruling and ordered the DeBoers to return Jessica to the Schmidts on the grounds that Iowa courts which have generally supported the Schmidts had jurisdiction in the case.

Although the DeBoers will have a chance to argue their case before the Michigan Supreme court on June 3, even their lawyer acknowledges that their prospects for victory appear rather dim. Though the DeBoers indicated that they would return Jessica to the Schmidts if they lose, they now seem determined to take the case to the U.S. Supreme Court if necessary. In addition to the emotional toll, each of the couples has run up legal bills approaching $100,000. And as always, the real victim in the case is the child. "We've got to bury the hatchet," said Jan recently. "We've got to bury the animosity between the two parties. Because in Jessie's eyes, she's got to see us as friendly couples."

Questions based on *Baby Girl Clausen*

1. Should Jessica have been allowed to remain with the DeBoers?

2. Was it selfish or praiseworthy for the birth parents to fight for Jessica when they knew she was happy, loved, and in a good home?

The Alabama Court of Civil Appeals decision in *A.E.C v. J.R.M., Jr., and J.A.M.* provides insight into the emotional and legal issues that can arise in independent adoptions.

A.E.C. v. J.R.M., Jr., and J.A.M.

Court of Civil Appeals of Alabama
46 So. 3d 481 (2009)

Bryan, Judge.

This is an adoption case in which A.E.C. ("the birth mother") appeals the Jefferson Probate Court's denial of the contest she filed challenging the adoption of A.J.M. ("the child") by J.R.M., Jr., and J.A.M. ("the adoptive parents"). The birth mother's contest and appeal are based, in large part, on her assertion that the prebirth-consent form used for the adoption is invalid.

On September 7, 2006, Jefferson County Probate Judge Mark Gaines signed an order confirming the prebirth consent for adoption signed by the birth mother.[13] The order states, in part, that

The Court having explained the legal effects of the execution of the consent/relinquishment herein, and of the time limits and procedures for withdrawal of the said consent/relinquishment and the Court having provided the aforesaid expectant mother with a form for withdrawing the consent/relinquishment, . . . and the Court being satisfied that the aforesaid expectant parent fully understands the consent/relinquishment herein, and has executed it voluntarily and unequivocally.

The birth mother signed the consent form, which stated in part:

2. I am executing this document voluntarily and unequivocally thereby consenting to the adoption of said minor;

3. I understand that by signing this document and the subsequent court order to ratify the consent, I will forfeit all rights and obligations to said minor unless said petitioner is my spouse; and that I understand the consent to adoption and execute it freely and voluntarily;

4. I understand that the consent to adoption may be irrevocable, and

---

13 The biological father of the child also signed a consent-for-adoption form, which was identical to the form the birth mother signed. The biological father did not withdraw his consent for adoption, and he is not a party to this action.

I should not execute it if I need or desire psychological or legal advice, guidance or counseling;

* * *

8. I understand that notice of withdrawal of consent must be mailed to the Probate Court of Jefferson County and that such withdrawal must be mailed within five days after birth of said minor or the execution of this document, whichever comes last.

The birth mother signed an affidavit on September 7, 2006, stating that she had "received no money or other things of value or been paid for giving the said minor up for adoption." Likewise, the adoptive parents signed an affidavit stating that they had "paid no money or other things of value to any party in connection with this adoption proceeding except that which has been approved by the Court."[14]

The child was born on December 20, 2006. On December 22, 2006, the adoptive parents took custody of the child at the hospital where the birth mother had delivered the child. The adoptive parents filed a petition for adoption on January 2, 2007. Also on January 2, 2007, 13 days after the child was born, the birth mother filed a petition to withdraw her consent for adoption. . . .

In the adoption-contest petition, the birth mother alleged that the adoptive parents had obtained her consent for the adoption by fraud, duress, mistake, or undue influence, and that, therefore, her consent is invalid . . . . The birth mother further alleged that R.S., a family friend of the birth mother's, was the agent of the adoptive parents and was also a perpetrator of the alleged fraud, duress, mistake, or undue influence. . . .

The probate court conducted an ore tenus hearing on the birth mother's withdrawal of consent and adoption contest over seven days during April and June 2008. On October 13, 2008, the probate court held that adoption of the child by the adoptive parents was in the best interest of the child [and] that "undue influence was not manifested by [R.S.] or any other person." Thus, the probate court denied the adoption contest filed by the birth mother. . . . She filed her notice of appeal to this court on October 16, 2008. . . .

The probate court gave a detailed summary of its specific findings of fact in its final order as follows:

---

14 On July 21, 2006, the probate court approved the adoptive parents' request to provide support to the birth mother in the amount of $798 a month; this amount was to cover the birth mother's living expenses, such as transportation, utilities, food, and clothing.

The sworn testimony from the birth mother is that she began using illegal drugs when she was 16 years of age. She used marijuana, cocaine, prescription pills (Xanax), LSD and ecstasy. By the time she became pregnant, she testified that she had been sexually active with ten men. The birth mother attempted suicide twice, in March and April, 2003, and cut herself with scissors when she was 16. As a teenager she told her parents that she was hearing voices, but now says that was not true. She testified that she was reaching out for attention. Upon learning that she was pregnant in May, 2006, her testimony was that she immediately stopped using all illegal substances. This appears to be undisputed.

Her parents were having marital problems when the birth-mother learned she was pregnant. Two days after finding out she was pregnant the birth mother moved back in with her parents; however, two days later her mother and younger sister moved out. The birth mother testified that her parents told her she needed to give up her baby for adoption. She also testified that her mother and father informed her that "it would be better if she found somewhere to live."

On or about May 30, 2006, the birth mother had a meeting with R.S., who was a longtime friend of the birth mother's parents. The birth mother has known R.S. since she was in the second grade. R.S. testified that he has known the birth mother's father for 42 years. Through the years the two families went on vacations to the beach and to Disney World together. She recalls that R.S. informed her that he knew a wonderful couple who were looking to adopt a child.

The birth mother's father lost his job at some point in time and on or about June 16, 2006, he was admitted to a Birmingham hospital. Upon being released from the hospital after one week, her dad took her to Lifeline Village, a home for unwed mothers in St. Clair County, but she did not wish to stay there.

At this point, the birth mother's mom and younger sister were living in an apartment together, and her dad was still not doing well. R.S. attempted to arrange living arrangements for the birth mother with a couple and their daughter but that fell through. Finally, in early July, 2006, the birth mother moved in with R.S. and his wife and their daughter.

The birth mother contends that R.S. exerted undue influence over her. Shortly after moving in with R.S. and his wife and their daughter, the birth mother went to Gulf Shores with them. R.S. and his wife paid for everything. The daughter and the son of R.S. and his wife and the son's girlfriend were also at the beach with them. The birth mother also contends that R.S. was an agent of either the adoptive parents, the birth mother's family or some group of people who were in favor of the adoption.

A petition for pre-approval of fees was filed and the Court approved the payment in the amount of $798.00 for the adoptive parents to remit each month. The birth mother testified that the monthly payment was made to R.S., and he used the funds to pay her automobile note, cell phone and other bills. The birth mother was given the remainder as an allowance. The birth mother testified that she felt "controlled" by R.S. during the months she lived with his family from July, 2006 through November 29, 2006. Beginning in August or September, the birth mother began spending weekends with her mother. Later, on or about November 29, 2006, she left R.S.'s home and moved in with her mother with whom she now has a good relationship.

The birth mother and R.S. both testified that he solicited some contributions from men at his church, in November, 2006, to assist the birth mother's dad financially. R.S. also paid the tuition for the birth mother's sister to continue attending school when she was a senior (which was in 2006 while the birth mother was residing with R.S. and his family). The tuition paid by R.S. was in the range of $6,000.00.

R.S. has been active in his church for many years. He has known the birth mother and her dad and mom and sister for years. The birth mother grew up referring to R.S. as "Mr. B.". R.S. has a long history of church and prison fellowship work. He testified that he made charitable contributions of $50,000.00-$60,000.00 in 2007.

R.S. testified that he never encouraged the birth mother to proceed with the adoption. He saw the birth mother after the delivery, and did not see any signs that she was having second thoughts. R.S. had supper with the birth mother on December 29, 2006, and he doesn't remember her saying anything about changing her mind.

The birth mother testified that R.S. and her dad were with her in the courtroom at the Pre-Birth Consent hearing before Probate Judge Mark Gaines. The birth mother testified that she began crying during the hearing. After a short break, she testified that Judge Gaines told her how proud he was of her, and that the baby would be taken care of. . . .

The birth mother is now attending a Community College and she lives with her mother and her sister. She testified that she is making good grades, and has taken parenting classes.

The background on the adoptive parents, J.A.M. and J.R.M., Jr., is as follows: J.A.M., the adoptive mother, completed her education in 2000, in the field of occupational therapy. At the present time she does not work outside the home. J.A.M. was diagnosed with rheumatoid arthritis in 1997, which is controlled by medication. J.A.M. and J.R.M., Jr. were married in 2001. Her mom and dad reside in Virginia.

J.R.M. Jr., the adoptive father, graduated from university, was honorably discharged as a Naval Officer, earned a graduate degree, and works in Birmingham where he was raised. The adoptive parents testified that neither has been arrested, received psychiatric treatment, or used illegal drugs. The parents of the adoptive father reside in Birmingham, and the parents of the adoptive mother visit from Virginia whenever possible.

The birth mother's OB-GYN, Dr. Ceciha Stradtman, testified during the hearing. Dr. Stradtman met with the birth mother on June 19, 2006, and said that the birth mother planned to give her child up for adoption from the beginning. Dr. Stradtman testified that the adoptive mother was a patient of hers in the past, and the birth mother's mother is a patient of hers and a friend. Dr. Stradtman said that the birth mother was emotional throughout the pregnancy but "did quite well." The birth mother was not under the influence of illegal drugs, and she was mentally competent during the pregnancy. Dr. Stradtman testified that during the pregnancy the birth mother did not mention any reservations about giving up the baby. She felt like the birth mother was making the decision with a clear mind and, while pregnant, wanted to do everything right for her baby. The birth mother never voiced any doubts to her, pre-birth, about the adoption. Dr. Stradtman delivered the baby on December 20, 2006. The doctor said that the birth mother was very emotional, post-birth.

A child psychologist, Dr. Karen Turnbow, also testified at the hearing. Dr. Turnbow testified that "attachment develops most strongly over an extended period of time." She said that attachment refers to a child's feelings toward parents. In positive attachment there is an impact throughout life. The majority of development occurs during the first year of life. The quality of care is the determining factor in a child's first year, not whether the caregiver is the birth mother or adoptive mother and father. An infant relates by smell, touch, sound, and a broad spectrum of factors. Dr. Turnbow said that stability needs to be preserved for an infant. She stated that if an infant has positively attached to the caregivers, then, in that event, an infant would grieve and have a painful emotional response for the rest of its life were it removed from the caregivers.

The attorney for the birth mother brought up the fact that the adoptive parents gave gifts to the birth mother during the pregnancy. The testimony and evidence were that the adoptive mother first met the birth mother in the hospital, post-birth, on December 22, 2006; however, a gift bag with candy, snacks, and school supplies was delivered to her in August, 2006, a pumpkin container with candy and snacks was delivered to her in October, 2006, a birthday card with Bath & Bodyworks lotion was delivered in November, 2006, a candle was delivered in December, 2006, and flowers were delivered, post-birth, to the birth mother in the hospital. The total cost of the items was slightly less than $112.00, with the flowers being the most expensive at a cost of $43.60.

The birth mother is a young woman who made some poor lifestyle choices prior to becoming pregnant. Afterwards, during the most crucial time in her life, her parents' marital discord reached a crescendo. Her mother and sister moved out and her father, having experienced job related and marital problems, was hospitalized. There was no safety net for the birth mother. The closest substitute was R.S..

The birth mother has, it appears, matured and her life is more stable than it was in 2006.

The adoptive parents are a little older than the birth mother, and they have maintained responsible, stable lives both prior to and since their marriage in 2001. . . .

The Court considers the candy and snacks to be a non-issue. The adoptive mother was merely attempting to be kind and supportive during the pregnancy, nothing more.

The birth mother contends that R.S. exerted undue influence over her. Yet, the birth mother, who was an adult, began spending weekends with her mother in August/September, and moved out of the S. residence on or about November 29, 2006, to live full time with her mother. The birth mother was not around R.S. for three weeks immediately prior to the birth. R.S. visited the birth mother in the hospital on the day of delivery, December 20, 2006, but he was not present on December 22, 2006, which was the day of the hand-off of the baby at the hospital from the birth mother to the adoptive parents. Regarding the agency contention, the court finds that R.S. was not working on behalf of anybody. At the time of the pregnancy, R.S. had known the birth mother for over a decade, and was a longtime friend of her dad and mom. R.S. was only trying to be helpful in the face of less than the best of circumstances. The Court finds that no other person or groups of persons were involved in any agency relationship in any way.

Section 26-10A-14, Ala.Code 1975, sets forth the time limitations for withdrawing a signed consent-for-adoption form, as follows: "(a) The consent or relinquishment, once signed or confirmed, may not be withdrawn except: (1) As provided in Section 26-10A-13; or (2) At any time until the final decree upon a showing that the consent or relinquishment was obtained by fraud, duress, mistake, or undue influence on the part of a petitioner or his agent or the agency to whom or for whose benefit it was given."

In her adoption-contest petition, the birth mother alleged that the adoptive parents personally, or through their agent, R.S., committed acts of fraud, duress, mistake, or undue influence in order to obtain her consent for adoption. On appeal, the birth mother alleges 15 specific examples of fraud, duress, or undue influence committed by the adoptive parents or R.S. However, since we are affirming the probate court's finding that R.S. was not the agent of the adoptive parents, we review only the claims of fraud, duress, and undue influence alleged by the birth mother on the part of the adoptive parents. In doing so, we keep the attendant presumption that, because the evidence was heard ore tenus, the probate court's findings are presumed correct.

First, the birth mother alleges that the adoptive father agreed to pay for the birth mother's college education if she went through with the adoption. Although the birth mother stated that R.S. told her that the adoptive father would probably pay for her education if she went through with the adoption, the adoptive father testified that he did not recall agreeing to pay for the birth mother's education and did not recall discussing the matter with R.S.. R.S. also denied that the adoptive parents had ever said that they would pay for the birth mother's education after the adoption went through.

Next, the birth mother argues that she felt "controlled" by the fact that the adoptive parents mailed the court-approved support payment to R.S., who then paid the birth mother's expenses and gave the remaining amount to the birth mother as an allowance. R.S. testified that the birth mother's mother put together a "starter kit" for him that contained all the birth mother's bills that could be paid for by the court-approved support from the adoptive parents; some of the bills were already overdue, including the bill for the birth mother's cellular telephone, which had been turned off. R.S. also testified that the payments from the adoptive parents on behalf of the birth mother were sent to him, at his private post office box, to protect the identity of the adoptive parents. R.S. gave the birth mother's counsel a spreadsheet that accounted for "every penny" of the money sent to R.S. by the adoptive parents on behalf of the birth mother, to the satisfaction of the birth mother's counsel.

The birth mother further argues that she suffered "pressures" at the hospital from the adoptive parents when she delivered the child. The birth mother insisted on handing the child directly to the adoptive parents at the hospital, despite their desire for confidentiality. Two days after the birth of the child the adoptive parents came to the hospital to take custody of the child; the birth mother testified that she was very emotional during this encounter. The birth mother further testified that she and the adoptive mother decided what outfit the child would wear and that anything said between the parties was very brief. The adoptive mother testified that when she and the adoptive father arrived at the birth mother's hospital room, everyone was very emotional. She stated that she and her husband left the room for a short period so that the birth mother "could have a little bit more time with her mom." The adoptive parents returned to the birth mother's room after a nurse called them in; the birth mother handed the child to the adoptive mother, and, as they were leaving, the adoptive mother recalled the birth mother saying "thank you." This event took place after the birth mother had signed the consent-for-adoption form, and it is unclear how it affected her decision to sign the prebirth-consent form three months earlier.

The birth mother also states that the number of telephone communications between R.S. and the adoptive parents, including a time of prayer together, is evidence of fraud, duress, or undue influence. The amount of communication between the adoptive parents and R.S. throughout the pregnancy in and of itself is not an example of fraud, duress, or undue influence. The testimony cited by the birth mother is of R.S. and the adoptive parents failing to recollect the specifics of their conversations; these are not examples of fraud, duress, or undue influence. The birth mother also points out that the adoptive parents provided lunch for R.S. and had a time of prayer with R.S. at some point during her pregnancy, but she fails to show how these circumstances amounted to fraud, duress, or undue influence on her.

Finally, the birth mother argues that the adoptive parents' delay in taking the child to their home was "in recognition of [the birth mother's] tentativeness." The testimony of both of the adoptive parents was that they left the child with the adoptive father's parents for several days after they took custody of the child because they knew that the birth mother had the absolute right to withdraw her consent to the adoption at any time during the five days following the birth of the child. They testified that it was to "protect their heart," not because they knew that the birth mother was feeling tentative about going through with the adoption. Regardless, it is unclear how this act of the adoptive parents, which occurred after the birth mother had given her consent to the adoption some three months earlier, is an example of fraud, duress, or undue influence on the birth mother. . . .

We conclude that the record supports the dismissal of the birth mother's adoption contest and the finding of the probate court "that undue influence was not manifested by R.S. or by any other person."

In her adoption contest, the birth mother alleged that R.S. and his family "provided for me, shelter and sustenance during my pregnancy in exchange for placing my child for adoption" with the adoptive parents. She further stated that R.S. and his family "acted at all times on behalf of the prospective adoptive parents and acted to influence the birth mother's action in favor of adoption." She also stated in her petition that she "was at a loss of what to do, and I was made to feel that I had no other option but to place my child for adoption, or I would incur the ill will and disfavor of R.S. and his family and the adoptive couple and all their friends." . . .

The evidence presented in the record supports the probate court's finding that R.S. was not the agent of the adoptive parents. The record reveals that the adoptive parents saw R.S. as a representative of the birth mother and her family. The probate court specifically found that R.S. and his family were long-time friends of the birth mother and her family. The birth mother's father and R.S. were "best friends," and their families had been on vacations together to the beach and to Disney World.

The record indicates that R.S. first attempted to arrange for the birth mother to live with other friends but that, when that fell through, he offered his own home to the birth mother. We further note that the adoptive parents did not know R.S. before he contacted the adoptive father's mother about the possible adoption.

The adoptive parents argue that "there is no citation to authority which would establish that any of the actions or inactions of R.S. and the adoptive parents indicate an agency relationship under Alabama law ...." We agree; the record supports the trial court's finding that R.S. was not the agent of the adoptive parents and that he "was only trying to be helpful in the face of less than the best of circumstances."

Affirmed.

Questions based on *A.E.C. and J.R.M., Jr. v. J.A.M.*

1. The biological mother's recollection of what happened differed markedly from that of the adoptive parents and other witnesses. Do you think someone was deliberately lying—committing perjury? If not, how do you account for such dramatically different perspectives on the truth?

2. Could the attorney who supervised the biological mother's "consent" have taken any additional steps to ensure that the mother understood what she was doing? Could the attorney have taken additional steps to document the "signing ceremony" in order to make it clear that the mother understood what she was doing?

Agency Adoption

With agency adoption, a biological parent who is thinking about "giving up" her child for adoption is counseled by an employee of an adoption agency. If the parent decides adoption is the way to go, she gives custody to the agency and signs a relinquishment form. The agency then locates prospective adoptive parents and places the child in their home.[15] Adoption agencies are either government or private.

---

15 *See* Mich. Comp. Laws Ann. § 710.22(d) (" 'Agency placement' means a placement in which a child placing agency, the department, or a court selects the adoptive parents for the child and transfers physical custody of the child to the prospective adoptive parent.").

The primary difference between agency adoption and independent adoption is that in independent adoption the birth mother herself places the child with the adoptive parents. In an agency adoption, the birth parent relinquishes the child to an adoption agency. The agency places the child in the adoptive home. In the typical agency adoption, the birth parent has no idea who the adoptive parents are.

Interracial Adoption

Before the civil rights movement of the 1960s, interracial adoption was uncommon. Several states, for example, Louisiana and Texas, had outright bans on interracial adoption. Most social workers believed it was important to place children with adoptive parents of the same ethnic background. During the 1960s, courts struck down laws against interracial adoption, and increasing numbers of white parents adopted children of color.

During the 1970s, critics of interracial adoption campaigned against the practice, led by the National Association of Black Social Workers. In 1972, the Association issued a position paper based on the premise that America is racist. The paper stated in part: "Black children should be placed only with Black families in foster care of for adoption. Black children belong, physically, psychologically and culturally in Black families in order that they receive the total sense of themselves and develop a sound projection of their future. Human beings are products of their environment and develop their sense of values, attitudes and self-concept within their family structures. Black children in white homes are cut off from the healthy development of themselves as Black people."

Opposition to interracial adoption was effective. Unfortunately, children of color, particularly African American children, are overrepresented in foster care, and African American foster children tend to wait longer for adoption than white children. During the 1980s and 1990s, pressure mounted to lower racial barriers to adoption, and in 1994, Congress passed the Multiethnic Placement Act or MEPA. Congress replaced MEPA with the Removal of Barriers to Interethnic Adoption Act, which mandates that agencies that are involved in foster care or adoption, and that receive federal funds, are prohibited from denying to any person the opportunity to become an adoptive or a foster parent on the basis of the race, color, or national origin of the person or the child.

Stepparent Adoption

Stepparent adoption typically arises when mom and dad divorce, mom gets custody, mom remarries, stepdad forms a great relationship with his step kids, bio dad is not close to the kids, and mom and stepdad decide stepdad will adopt the kids. The primary issue in such cases is whether the biological father will consent to the adoption. If he will—and consenting ends his child support obligation—no problem. If he refuses consent, stepparent adoption can go forward only if the biological father's parental rights are terminated against his will.

The following case illustrates how stepparent adoption plays out when a biological father refuses consent to adoption.

Adoption of Allison C.

California Court of Appeal
164 Cal. App. 4th 1004, 79 Cal. Rptr. 3d 743 (2008)

Ikola, J.

John C. (father) appeals from a judgment terminating his parental rights and freeing his daughter, Allison C. (now seven years old) from his custody and control due to abandonment. Dario A. (stepfather) filed the petition as a precursor to adopting Allison without father's consent. Father contends (1) insufficient evidence supports the court's finding he abandoned Allison, and (2) the court misapplied the law in reaching this determination. We disagree and affirm the judgment.

When Allison was conceived, her mother (mother) was dating father while married to his brother. After Allison's birth in March 2001, mother and Allison lived with father on and off for about 110 days during the child's first six months of life. But in the summer of 2001, father struck mother as she held Allison, causing mother to move to a relative's home with the child and to stop all contact with father. From October 2001 through February 2003, father was incarcerated for domestic violence. After father's release from prison in February 2003, he visited Allison (without mother's knowledge) at his brother's house every weekend through September 2003. Mother, upon learning of these visits, informed father's brother that he (father's brother) could see Allison only with mother present. Starting in September 2003, father was incarcerated for second degree burglary. He testified that while incarcerated, he sent Allison cards until "notified by the prison" at some unspecified time that stepfather or mother had advised the prison father was not allowed to contact the child.

Meanwhile, stepfather had been involved in Allison's life since early 2003; in February 2005, he married mother. In April 2005, stepfather filed with the court a request to adopt Allison, then four years old.

A July 2005 DNA test showed father was Allison's biological father. Also that month, father was released from prison.

Orange County Probate Court Services (PCS), in its August 2005 adoption report, concluded stepfather had been a "stable and suitable parent for" Allison and was a "fit and proper person to adopt" her. Stepfather had no criminal record and no substance abuse or domestic violence concerns, was in good health, made a good income, provided Allison with "suitable living accommodations," and had "been involved with all aspects of Allison's parenting" since 2003. PCS concluded "stepparent adoption appeared to be in Allison's best interests." But PCS reported father had informed the agency that "at no time would he ever consent to the adoption."

Also in August 2005, the court issued a restraining order against father to protect both mother and Allison. The order allowed father "to have supervised visitation with Allison" for two hours every Saturday commencing in September 2005. Mother then asked father's parole officer to have father "drug tested at least a couple of times a week," for Allison's safety if father visited the child. Father's parole officer responded by prohibiting father from seeing Allison, but the special parole condition allowed father to contact the child by telephone or mail with a "supervising parole agent's prior approval." Father never tried to obtain such approval, but did file an inmate parolee appeal and a citizen's complaint contesting the parole officer's action.

In September 2005, stepfather and mother petitioned . . . for a determination of father's parental rights over Allison, asking whether father's consent was necessary for stepfather's adoption of the child. The court found father to be Allison's presumed father under [the Uniform Parentage Act] section 7611(d) (receives child into home and holds child out as natural child), because father had custody of the child for 110 days during her first eight months of life.

From May to September of 2006, father was incarcerated for violating parole.

In October 2006, stepfather petitioned the court to declare Allison free from father's parental custody and control under section 7822 (parental abandonment) or section 7825 (parent convicted of felony). Specifically, stepfather and mother sought to have father's parental rights terminated under section 7822, alleging father had left Allison in mother's custody for at least four years, had "*never* paid or offered to pay child support since Allison's birth," and had "not had any' contact with Allison for a period exceeding one year." Alternatively, stepfather and mother sought to have father's parental rights terminated under section 7825(a), alleging father was a "habitual criminal" who had been convicted of and sentenced to prison for at least one felony. Stepfather alleged Allison lived "in a loving and nurturing home" with stepfather and mother, and it was in her best interest to be declared free from father's parental custody and control so she could be adopted by stepfather. . . .

From October 2006 to April 2007, father was incarcerated for driving under the influence of alcohol. . . .

The court granted stepfather's petition after finding by clear and convincing evidence that father had left Allison with mother for over a year without communication or support and with the intention to abandon the child, and that Allison's best interest required father's parental rights to be terminated.

Father contends insufficient evidence supports the court's findings (1) he left Allison in mother's care and custody, (2) he did not support or communicate with her, and (3) he intended to abandon Allison.

Under section 7822, a court may declare a child free from a parent's custody and control if the parent has abandoned the child. Abandonment occurs when a parent has left the child in the care and custody of the other parent for a period of one year without any provision for the child's support, *or* without communication from the parent, with the intent on the part of the parent to abandon the child. Thus, a section 7822 proceeding is appropriate where three main elements are met: (1) the child must have been left with another; (2) without provision for support or without communication from his parent for a period of one year; and (3) all of such acts are subject to the qualification that they must have been done with the intent on the part of such parent to abandon the child. The failure to provide support, or failure to communicate is presumptive evidence of the intent to abandon. If the parent has made only token efforts to support or communicate with the child, the court may declare the child abandoned by the parent.

On appeal father contests the court's findings on all three elements of the section 7822 determination of abandonment. He first contends insufficient evidence supports the court's finding he left Allison in another's care and custody for at least one year. He argues the term "left" connotes voluntary action and therefore abandonment does not occur when the child is taken from parental custody against the parent's wishes. While acknowledging he was incarcerated at different time periods from 2001 through 2007, father argues his incarceration was involuntary. He further asserts mother left father and tried "at every turn to cut off any contact between Father and his daughter," including by discontinuing Allison's visits to father's brother's house, obtaining a restraining order against father, and persuading father's parole officer to disallow visitation. He concludes petitioners failed to prove at trial that Father voluntarily allowed Mother to assume custody.

. . . We conclude substantial evidence supports the court's finding he did just that. In the summer of 2001 father, by his voluntary act of domestic violence, left Allison in mother's care and custody. Thereafter, he never sought to take parental responsibility for Allison's care, and instead chose to let the child stay with mother. In other words, he was content to leave to mother all real parental responsibility for Allison. His actions underlying his incarcerations for domestic violence, burglary, and driving under the influence were voluntary, and in any case, being incarcerated does not, in and of itself, provide a legal defense to abandonment of children. Even when father was out of prison in 2003 and routinely visited Allison at his brother's house, he did so secretly, rather than seeking custody or visitation rights. Mother's efforts to curtail father's communication with Allison, while relevant to an assessment of whether father *intended* to abandon the child by noncommunication, do not negate the reality he never sought to take custody or care of the child after mid-2001. In sum, he voluntarily abdicated the parental role. Thus, the court did not err by finding father left Allison in mother's care and custody from 2003 to October 2006.

We next examine whether substantial evidence supports the court's finding father failed to support Allison from September 2003 to December 2006. Father testified he never paid "any child support for Allison," but gave his brother "close to $800" in 2003 because they "had her on the weekends," and brought the child toys, food and clothes when visiting her during that year. He also testified that, at the time of the section 7822 hearing, he had saved "about $300" for Allison.

The court found that, even giving father credit for $1,100 in monetary support, this amount was "de minimis," insufficient, and "token" for the period from March 2003 through October 2006 (the date of stepfather's section 7822 petition), in light of the cost of "medical care, food, clothing and shelter" for a child in Orange County. The court recognized father's ability to provide support was limited due to his incarceration but noted that if incarceration were an acceptable excuse for nonsupport, "a child could conceivably never be adopted." The court further noted a parent's incarceration results from his or her own actions.

Substantial evidence supports the court's finding father failed to support Allison from September 2003 through December 2006. Other than the $300 father claimed to have saved for Allison, father provided her with no support after September 2003, *i.e.* a period of over three years; the statute requires only a one-year period of nonsupport.

Finally, father contests the court's finding he intended to abandon Allison. He first argues his nonsupport of Allison cannot serve as presumptive evidence he intended to abandon the child because mother "apparently" never obtained a support order and never asked him for "money or supplies" for Allison. He argues "failure to contribute support in the absence of demand does not prove an intent to abandon," and "evidence of a parent's inability to pay support rebuts presumption of abandonment." In response, stepfather argues: Although a parent's failure to contribute to his child's support absent demand does not necessarily show abandonment, such failure coupled with failure to communicate, may do so.

Here, the court found father failed to communicate with Allison from September 2003 to December 2006. The court explained that after 2003 father had no direct contact with Allison, failed to make adequate efforts to communicate by letters, and therefore had not bonded with her. The court noted father's incarceration had removed him from contact with the child. As to father's testimony he tried to send Allison cards and letters "all through her life," the court was entitled to disbelieve or discount that testimony (and apparently did so, since it expressly found father made inadequate efforts to communicate by letters). Finally, father failed to seek permission to contact Allison by telephone or mail in late 2005, despite the special parole condition entitling him to do so.

The court's finding father failed to communicate with Allison from September 2003 to December 2006, coupled with its finding of nonsupport for the same period, are sufficient to show father intended to abandon her for that period. . . .

We are more than satisfied the court correctly applied the law. . . . The court did not err in finding father abandoned Allison for at least one year under section 7822.

The judgment is affirmed.

Note on the Incarcerated Parent

Parental rights cannot be terminated simply because a parent is incarcerated. The flip side is that incarceration is not an excuse to stop communication with a child. The Appellate Division of the New York Supreme Court observed, "Incarceration does not absolve him of his responsibility for supporting the child or for maintaining regular contact."[16] To avoid a finding of abandonment, a parent who is incarcerated for a substantial period must take reasonable steps to maintain a relationship with the child.

$$\mathcal{C}$$

EXPERIENTIAL ASSIGNMENT

Practice Exercise: Stepparent Adoption

You have been retained by Laura Martinez to help her adopt her two stepchildren, Stephen, who is 8, and Juanita, who is 6. Laura and Carlos have been married ten years. They have a new baby of their own. Laura has raised Stephen and Juanita since they were 3 and 1. Laura treats Stephen and Juanita as her own children, and they think of her as their mom.

Laura and Carlos live in a small town in an area of the state that is heavily agricultural. Laura is a stay at home mom, and appears to be a great parent to the three kids. During harvest season, Carlos drives a large truck for farmers, taking crops— rice and tomatoes—to processing plants. When the truck driving job is not available, Carlos works construction. Laura and Carlos live in a small rental house owned by Laura's dad. They attend church, are active in the kids' school, and support the children in Future Farmers of America (FAA) and sports.

Stephen and Juanita's biological mother is Stephanie. Carlos and Stephanie never married, but they lived together during the time Stephen and Junanita were born. Stephanie lives in different small town, ten miles away from Carlos and Laura. Stephanie has a long history of drug abuse, including marijuana, cocaine, methamphetamine, and prescription drugs. Since she was a teenager, she's liked to "party." She has been convicted three times of misdemeanor possession of illegal drugs and twice for driving under the influence. Stephanie has tried drug treatment quite a few times, but drops out of treatment when she starts hanging around her friends who are into drugs and partying. Stephanie has a spotty employment record.

Stephanie has never provided financial support for Stephen and Juanita. For the past year and a half, Stephanie has had almost no contact with the kids. Six months ago she saw them briefly at the county fair.

---

16   In re Harold Ali D.-E., 94 A.D.3d 449, 942 N.Y.S.2d 50 (2012).

Three months ago Stephanie had a baby. The baby's father is not in the picture. With the birth of her new child, Stephanie is trying to straighten out her life. Stephanie is in drug treatment and is staying sober. She is supporting herself with welfare, food stamps, and Medicaid. She has a part time job at the local community college and is doing well. She wants to get her high school equivalency and then enroll in college classes at the community college.

A month ago, Stephanie called told Carlos and told him she was getting her act together and wants to get back in her kids' lives. Stephanie asks for regular visitation. It was Stephanie's request for visitation that prompted Laura and Carlos to contact you about the possibility of stepparent adoption. Laura and Carlos believe it will be traumatic for the children to have regular contact with Stephanie. Laura says, "I'm the only mom they have known since they were babies. I want to adopt them so they are legally our children. I'm their mom, not just a baby sitter until Stephanie decides to suddenly reappear out of nowhere."

Assignment: Research the law in your state on stepparent adoption. Assume Stephanie will not consent to adoption, and you will have to bring an action to terminate her parental rights. What pleading do you file to commence termination proceedings? What will you have to prove? Prepare the following:

1. Draft the pleading necessary to commence the termination proceeding.

2. Draft the summons required to inform Stephanie of the proceeding.

3. Draft the portion of a Memorandum of Points and Authorities that describes for the court the governing law.

International (Intercountry) Adoption

Intercountry adoption is complicated and expensive for adoptive parents, who must comply with four sets of laws: (1) Law of the country of the child's birth; (2) Law of the U.S. state where the adoptive parents live; (3) U.S. immigration law; and (4) In many cases, international law including the Hague Convention on Intercountry Adoption. More than 75 countries have joined the Hague Convention.

Before an American may bring an adopted child home from abroad, U.S. Citizenship and Immigration Services—the immigration service—must determine that the adopting adult is capable of providing a loving home for the child.

Some nations require adopting parents to formally adopt the child in the child's birth country. Once the child is brought to America, experts recommend re-adopting the child in this country. In her book *The Adoption Law Handbook*, Jennifer Fairfax writes:

> In a re-adoption, the adoptive parents are already the legally recognized parents based on the final decree of adoption from the foreign country. . . .

> The re-adoption process has routinely been recommended in these cases for the following reasons: the adoptive parents' home state does not recognize a foreign adoption decree, the adoptive parents wish to change the child's name, to obtain a state-issued birth certificate in order to avoid using the only birth certificate they have from the child's birth country, or to obtain a state-issued adoption decree so they do not have to use the only one issued by the child's birth state.

> However, for the children adopt[ed] from a Hague Country and arriv[ing] on a IH-3 Visa, they may opt to obtain a Hague Adoption Certificate issued by the U.S. Department of State in its role of U.S. Central Authority for the Convention. Hague Adoption Certificates certify that a U.S. adoption has been completed in accordance with the Convention and the Intercountry Adoption Act (IAA). The *Hague Adoption Certificate* entitles the adoption to recognition in the United States and other Convention countries. Thus, a child who has a Hague Adoption Certificate should have his or her adoption recognized in every state in the United States, is a U.S. citizen for all purposes, and should not have to be re-adopted. However, many families still go through the re-adoption process for the reasons previously stated.

> Thus, re-adoption remains the standard recommendation to obtain a U.S.–issued birth certificate and adoption decree and to change the child's name if desired.[17]

Open Adoption

Open adoption allows a biological parent to continue a relationship with a child *after* the child is adopted. In her book on adoption law, Jennifer Fairfax describes open adoption.

---

17 Jennifer Fairfax, *The Adoption Law Handbook* pp. 96-98 (2011).

The Adoption Law Handbook
Jennifer Fairfax

It has become increasingly common for birth parents and adoptive parents to have some form of contact after the adoptive placement has been made and the adoption finalized. This practice is called "open adoption," but the degree of openness and enforceability of agreements to have contact can vary significantly. This is a change from the historical "closed adoption," where there was no post-adoption contact and often no contact prior to the adoption. Now, birth and adoptive parents often meet before the baby is born or at the time of placement. They either have no further contact, or the families maintain some level of ongoing contact throughout the child's life, such as exchanging photos or letters or having face-to-face meetings, which exemplifies the extremes of an open adoption. Negotiating a post-adoption contact agreement has become a "must know" for adoption attorneys in almost every state, regardless of their enforceability. Knowing the laws regarding enforceability is important in protecting a clients rights and explaining whether the parties are legally bound or morally bound. Clients, however, should never enter into a post-adoption contact agreement they do not intend to honor regardless of enforceability.

Post-adoption contact agreements (PACAs) are arrangements that allow for some kind of contact between a child's adoptive family and members of the child's birth family or other persons with whom the child has an established relationship, such as a foster parent, after the child's adoption has been finalized. These arrangements, sometimes referred to as cooperative adoption, continual contact agreements, or open adoption agreements, can range from informal, mutual understandings between the birth and adoptive families to written, formal contracts.

Typical agreements include precise descriptions of the number and type of contacts per year. Some people choose to write letters through a third party or an attorney, and some agreements contain promises to update contact information as necessary. Often, the parties stipulate that until the child is 18 years old, all communication from the birth mother will be through the adoptive parents and not directly to the child, and that when the child turns 18, he or she will determine the nature of future contact. Some agreements allow phone, written, or in-person contact and visits throughout the child's life. No particular terms are required. Rather, the contents of the agreement simply reflect the mutual wishes of the birth mother and the adoptive family. If the parties agree that other biological relatives can visit the child or receive updates, the contract should provide for that as well as setting parameters.

Every post-adoption contact agreement, whether legally enforce-able or not, makes clear that failing to comply with its terms does not provide a basis for invalidating the adoption. Although they are enforceable in court, such agreements are not designed to set the stage for legal proceedings. Rather, such agreements ensure that the birth family and adoptive family have the same understanding about what is going to happen in the future. Therefore, as an attorney advocating for the birth parents or adoptive parents, the attorney must ensure that the clients understand the level of contact they are agreeing to and that they should adhere to the contract terms. Advocating for a client to put the post-adoption plan in writing establishes clear and reliable expectations and can eliminate awkward requests or hard feelings and protect the child—even if the agreement is not enforceable. As with any contact agreement, the attorney must pay close attention to the choice of law issues. If the attorney represents a birth mother in New Hampshire but the adoptive parents reside in Tennessee, and one state allows for a PACA but the other state does not, this becomes a negotiation regarding the law that will apply to the adoption and also a question of whether the parties will or can agree to a contract enforceable in one state even though the adoption might be finalized in another state.

The increasing use of social media to make and maintain contact with friends provides another avenue for lawyers to think about when drafting post-adoption contact agreements, as well as placement agreements. Many years ago, adoptive parents worried that a birth parent might find out where they lived and show up on their doorstep. Then, as open adoption started to evolve, adoptive parents and birth parents would agree on the level of contact, and the adoptive parents would be able to monitor the contact because it generally was by telephone, letters by mail, or even prescheduled in person meetings. Recently, with the development of not only social media, but online services to assist biological relatives to locate each other, it is becoming more difficult to ensure contact is not being made between adoptive children and biological relatives through the Internet without the adoptive parents' approval. Discussing social media and even drafting clauses in post-adoption contact agreements addressing Internet or other avenues of social media or digital contact becomes a necessary part of an attorney's repertoire of clauses. Attorneys for adoptive or birth parents must think beyond the norms of current issues and anticipate the future, although it is not very likely that a birth parent would make unwanted or unmonitored contact with a very young child. It is increasingly more likely that as children grow up and have increasing access to the Internet, accidental or even intentional contact by a birth parent will be made. Recent contracts regarding social media have included clauses such as:

So long as the child is under the age of 18 and has access to a computer, phone, PDA, or other electronic or digital device allowing Internet or social media access the birth parent(s) agree that they shall NOT initiate any contact with child through any social media, Internet, or digital avenue and should the child initiate contact with the birth parent(s), they shall not respond to the child and shall immediately notify the adoptive parents that the child has attempted to contact them.

In general, state laws do not prohibit post-adoption contact or communication; however, they may not enforce the contract should there be no laws allowing for them. Because adoptive parents have the right to decide who may have contact with their adopted child, they can allow any amount of contact with birth family members, and such contacts often are arranged by mutual understanding without any formal agreement. A written contractual agreement between the parties to an adoption can clarify the type and frequency of the contact, set parameters regarding the contact or communication and can provide a way for the agreement to be legally enforced. Approximately 24 states currently have statutes that allow written and enforceable contact agreements. The written agreements are signed by the parties to an adoption prior to finalization and often made part of the final decree.

Disputes over compliance and requests for modification of the terms that the parties cannot resolve must be brought before the court in states that enforce the contracts. Any party to the agreement may petition the court to modify, order compliance with, or void the agreement. In states where the contract is not enforceable, there are no options to force compliance. The court may do so if the parties agree or circumstances have changed, and the action is determined to be in the best interests of the child. A sample clause to use regarding court modifications to contracts is:

> In the event that a Court of competent jurisdiction takes any action regarding this agreement, it is the express intent of the parties that any such modification shall not affect the adoption. Any breach, modification or invalidation of any part of this agreement shall not affect the validity of the adoption. A court-imposed modification of a previously approved Agreement may limit, restrict, condition or decrease contact between the birth mother and the child, but in no event shall a court-imposed modification serve to expand, enlarge or increase the amount of contact between the birth mother and the child or place new obligations on the adoptive parents.

The modes of contact can range from an exchange of information about the child between adoptive and birth parents, to the exchange of cards, letters, and photos, phone calls, texts, to personal visits with the child by birth family members. Many adoption professionals require that updates are at least one page long containing relevant, current information about the child's developmental progress and social development and that there be a minimum number of photos so that the contact is meaningful to and respectful of the birth parents.

In most states that permit enforceable post-adoption contact agreements, contact is permitted for any adoptive child as long as the nature and frequency of contact is deemed by the court to be in the "child's best interest" and designed to protect the safety of the child and the rights of all the parties to the agreement. Some states limit the enforceability of such agreements based on such factors as the type of adoption, the age of the adoptive child, or the nature of the contact. For example, Connecticut and Nebraska limit agreements to children who have been adopted from foster care. Indiana limits enforceable contact agreements to children ages 2 and older. For children in Indiana under age 2, nonenforceable agreements are permitted as long as the type of contact does not include visitation. Some states also allow other birth relatives who have significant emotional ties to the child to be included in the agreement, including grandparents, aunts, uncles, or siblings. For example, Minnesota permits former foster parents to petition for contact privileges. In a few states, when the case involves an Indian child, members of the child's tribe are included among the eligible birth relatives. Thus, it is important to research the potential parties to a contract when a PACA is considered. Other states have provisions for sibling participation in an agreement. The most important aspect is that the contact be in the child's best interest. PACA laws are one of the most recent types of laws being implemented and therefore confirming the current status of the law in a particular state should be done at the beginning of any adoption case. It is possible that an adoption plan is put into place where there are no post-adoption contact laws but during the plan period, the law goes into effect. In this case, the clients should be advised of the change in the law so that they can carefully consider the terms to which they are agreeing to be legally bound.

Many states have statutes authorizing open adoption.[18] The Minnesota statute provides:

---

[18] *See, e.g.*, Nev. Rev. Stat. Ann. § 127.187 et seq.

Adoptive parents and a birth relative or foster parents may enter an agreement regarding communication with or contact between an adopted minor, adoptive parents, and a birth relative or foster parents under this section. An agreement may be entered between:

(1) adoptive parents and a birth parent;

(2) adoptive parents and any other birth relative or foster parent with whom the child resided before being adopted; or

(3) adoptive parents and any other birth relative if the child is adopted by a birth relative upon the death of both birth parents.

For purposes of this section, "birth relative" means a parent, stepparent, brother, sister, uncle, or aunt of a minor adoptee. This relationship may be by blood, adoption, or marriage. For an Indian child, birth relative includes members of the extended family as defined by the law or custom of the Indian child's tribe . . . .

a. An agreement regarding communication with or contact between minor adoptees, adoptive parents, and a birth relative is not legally enforceable unless the terms of the agreement are contained in a written court order entered in accordance with this section. . . . The court shall not enter a proposed order unless the court finds that the communication or contact between the minor adoptee, the adoptive parents, and a birth relative as agreed upon and contained in the proposed order would be in the minor adoptee's best interests. . . .

b. Failure to comply with the terms of an agreed order regarding communication or contact that has been entered by the court under this section is not grounds for:

(1) setting aside an adoption decree; or

(2) revocation of a written consent to an adoption after that consent has become irrevocable.

c. An agreed order entered under this section may be enforced by filing a petition or motion with the family court that includes a certified copy of the order granting the communication, contact, or visitation, but only if the petition is accompanied by an affidavit that the parties have mediated or attempted to mediate any dispute under the agreement or that the parties agree to a proposed modification. The prevailing party may be awarded reasonable attorney's fees and costs. The court shall not modify an agreed order under this section unless it finds that the modification is necessary to serve the best interests of the minor adoptee, and:

(1) the modification is agreed to by the parties to the agreement; or

(2) exceptional circumstances have arisen since the agreed order   was entered that justify modification of the order.[19]

The Alaska Supreme Court's decision in *Adoption of S.K.L.H.* discusses open adoption. The decision provides insight into the deep emotions surrounding adoption.

Adoption of S.K.L.H.

Supreme Court of Alaska
204 P.3d 320 (2009)

Winfree, Justice.

Biological parents consented to their baby's adoption and the superior court entered a final adoption decree. Six months later the biological mother petitioned to set aside the adoption decree, alleging that her consent was invalid. The superior court granted her petition, finding first that there had not been a "meeting of the minds" (which the court on reconsideration later characterized as "mistake") about the biological mother's relationship with the child after the adoption decree, and second that it was in the child's best interests to be with her biological mother.

Because we do not recognize mere mistake about post-adoption visitation as a ground to invalidate adoption consent or an adoption decree, we reverse the superior court's decision and reinstate the adoption decree. But because: (1) the adoption consent form prepared by the attorney for the adoptive parents and signed by the biological mother provided that the biological mother understood she would have the right to visitation with the child after the adoption; (2) the findings of fact and conclusions of law prepared by the attorney for the adoptive parents and entered by the court with the adoption decree confirmed the parties' contemplated visitation rights for the biological mother following the adoption; and (3) the superior court has the authority to enforce a visitation framework in the best interests of the child, we remand with direction to consider appropriate visitation for the biological mother in this open adoption.

---

19 Minn. Stat. Ann. § 258.58.

Donna was barely eighteen years old when she gave birth to a baby girl in October 2006. The child's biological father was seventeen years old and resided in Iowa with no intent to move to Alaska. He is not a party to this litigation.

During her pregnancy Donna expressed an intent to give up her child for adoption. About one week before giving birth, she approached her father and stepmother (the Smiths) about adopting the child. Donna changed her mind about adoption after the child was born, and she and the child moved in with Donna's stepsister. About three weeks later Donna changed her mind again. Donna asked her stepsister and her stepsister's boyfriend to adopt the child, but they declined. Donna again approached the Smiths about adopting the child. The Smiths agreed.

The child was placed in the Smiths' care and custody on November 9, 2006. Both Donna and the biological father were required to give consent before the adoption could be completed, and on November 13 Donna and the Smiths met with the Smiths' attorney for Donna to review and sign her consent form. Donna was not represented by an attorney at this meeting, but before she signed her consent form the Smiths' attorney read and discussed each paragraph of the document with her.

Paragraph six of Donna's consent form provided: "I understand that, by signing this consent, I am giving up all of my rights to the care, custody and control of the minor child, and that I am giving up these rights permanently. I will also be permanently relieved of all responsibility for the child. I will have legal relationships to the child including for purposes of inheritance; and I will have full right to visitation with the child after the adoption."

Donna's consent form also provided that her consent could be withdrawn up to ten days after signing the consent form, but thereafter could be withdrawn "only upon a finding by the Court, after a hearing, that withdrawal of the consent is in the child's best interests." It also provided that once the adoption decree was entered, consent no longer could be withdrawn "at all." Donna signed the consent form that day, and it was filed with the court. Donna later contacted the child's biological father to solicit his consent to the adoption; his written consent, which was not conditioned upon maintenance of any legal relationships or visitation rights, was also filed with the court.

The Smiths' attorney lodged proposed findings of fact and conclusions of law and a proposed decree. Relevant findings and conclusions were that: (1) Mr. Smith (Donna's father) was forty-nine years old and Mrs. Smith (Donna's stepmother) was nearly forty years old; (2) the Smiths had seven children other than Donna; (3) Donna voluntarily consented to the Smiths' adoption of her child; (4)

Donna "shall retain visitation rights with the minor child following the adoption"; (5) all required consents had been filed or excused and all appropriate notices had been given; and (6) the adoption was in the best interests of the child. The findings and conclusions and the adoption decree were entered as presented after a brief hearing on December 18, 2006.

Donna visited the child freely in the weeks following the adoption, but the Smiths then began imposing restrictions and limitations that Donna characterizes as preventing "meaningful contact" with the child. In late June 2007 Donna filed a verified petition to set aside the adoption, alleging that: (1) her consent had been "obtained by misrepresentation and/or undue influence," specifically that the Smiths "falsely stated that [Donna] could have her child back when she was ready"; (2) the Smiths had "failed to obtain [Donna's] proper consent" and "failed to give required notice of the adoption petition"; (3) she had not signed the consent "voluntarily, knowingly or intelligently" and had not received a copy of it as required by statute; and (4) it was "in the best interests and welfare of the minor child to have the parental relationship with [Donna] restored."

An evidentiary hearing was held on December 5 and 6, 2007. The superior court orally entered its decision to set aside the adoption on December 6. The court first noted that it had jurisdiction because the petition was filed within one year of the decree. The court found that Donna's consent had not been obtained by fraud or misrepresentation because "there was no question" that the Smiths' attorney "did his job" making sure that Donna understood what was going on and that "he did it well." The court made no specific note or findings either of "duress" or "undue influence" affecting Donna's consent, or of any procedural infirmities during the adoption process. While not finding that Donna lacked capacity when she signed the consent, the court stated that "considering her age, immaturity, lack of education, and mental situation that she found herself in" Donna "was not in a state of mind to be buying a car, and certainly not signing consents" for adoption of her child. The court concluded that even if Donna's assumptions about the adoption were "unreasonable" and "foolish," these factors fatally undermined the "strength" of Donna's consent.

The superior court stated that "the legislature is a little coy, and so is the supreme court in telling me exactly what sort of grounds I could rely upon to invalidate a consent," but that "it generally seems to be done in the same fashion as an analysis of a contract because we've talked about misrepresentations, and fraud and duress, and I guess a mistake." The court then applied a contract analysis and found that there had not been a "meeting of the minds" with respect to the post-decree relationship among the Smiths, Donna, and the child: "[Donna] and her parents were on different tracks entirely. They really intended to become this child's parents and I really think that [Donna had] some vague concept whereby they were going to be the grandparents who raised her kid for a while at least, and maybe for the full 18 years."

The superior court stated that it needed to "reopen this and have a look and see what was in the best interest of this child." The court applied the best interests analysis . . . generally applicable in divorce-like proceedings, to determine whether Donna or the Smiths should raise the child. In Donna's favor, the court found that: (1) there was a natural bond between Donna and her child; Donna had matured in the year since giving up the child for adoption; Donna was the one more willing to allow the other to play a role in the child's life; and Donna was the more age-appropriate parent. In the Smiths' favor, the court found that because the couple had custody of the child for more than a year, they had bonded with her and she with them, and that they clearly were more experienced as parents. The court ultimately concluded that it was in the child's best interests to be raised by Donna.

The Smiths appealed. Pending resolution of the appeal we ordered that in lieu of a stay of the superior court's order, the superior court establish a visitation schedule for the Smiths and the child. . . .

The superior court may set aside an adoption decree if it is challenged within the first year. But there is a presumption favoring the validity and regularity of an adoption decree, and the burden is on the challenging party to show by a preponderance of the evidence that the decree is invalid. Ambiguities in an adoption decree are to be construed in favor of validity of the decree. In this case the validity of the adoption decree turns on the validity of Donna's consent, because withdrawal of her consent was prohibited once the decree was entered.

We first note that an adoption decree should not be set aside lightly. The clear policy of the adoption statutes is to hold a biological parent to the terms of a signed consent and to the adoption decree, except under limited circumstances. This is evidenced by the fact that after a year has elapsed from the entry of a decree, it cannot be challenged for any reason, even one as egregious as fraud or misrepresentation . . . .

In response to Donna's collateral attack on the adoption decree in this case, the superior court found "mistake" in the adoption process, specifically the lack of a "meeting of the minds" about the post-decree relationship among Donna, the Smiths, and the child. The court thought Donna "maybe foolishly misunderstood what was happening," and "she may have unreasonably assumed that she would come and go as mom, with grandparents raising the children"; while the Smiths felt the need to "maintain the fiction" that "they're the parents and [Donna's] not the parent anymore." After implying that this "mistake" invalidated Donna's consent, the court went on to apply a best interests analysis to determine whether the adoption decree should be set aside. The court concluded that "the best interest of the child would be served by returning [her to Donna]."

The Smiths argue that invalidation of an adoption decree is limited to the grounds mentioned in AS 25.23.140(b), namely fraud, misrepresentation, failure to give required notice, and lack of jurisdiction. None of these grounds was found by the superior court. But that provision states only that "upon the expiration of one year after an adoption decree is issued, the decree may not be questioned in any manner upon any ground, including fraud, misrepresentation, failure to give any required notice, or lack of personal or subject matter jurisdiction." This does not necessarily preclude other grounds for a challenge brought before the one-year period expires. That interpretation would be inconsistent with our view that adoption consent provisions should be construed to protect the rights of biological parents.

But we note that confusion, mistake about the finality of the agreement, and a "change of heart" are generally insufficient grounds to invalidate consent to an adoption. We also note that the most recent version of the Uniform Adoption Act provides that the validity of an adoption decree may not be challenged for failure to comply with an open adoption agreement.

The legislature took specific action to allow open adoptions in Alaska by enacting AS 25.23.130(c) after a decision by this court that Alaska's adoption statutes did not allow open adoption agreements. That provision states that nothing in the adoption statutes "prohibits an adoption that allows visitation between the adopted person and that person's natural parents or other relatives." We subsequently noted that although this statute does not give biological parents an inherent right to post-adoption visitation, it does authorize courts to fashion open adoption decrees securing visitation rights to a biological parent if it is in the child's best interests to do so, *with or without* an agreement between the biological and adopting parents.

The superior court found that there was not much "strength" in Donna's consent because of her lack of maturity and that her "foolish" misunderstanding about her post-adoption relationship with the child was a "mistake." But even if Donna was laboring under a "mistake" (and not simply having a "change of heart"), this mistake is insufficient to invalidate Donna's consent.

First, if the adoption decree's underlying conclusion that Donna "shall retain visitation rights" is ambiguous because of a lack of detail, ambiguities are construed in favor of validity of the adoption decree. Second, the contours of an open adoption are subject to the best interests of the child, regardless of the detail and content of an agreement by the parties. We therefore agree with the current Uniform Adoption Act that post-decree disputes about details of an open adoption cannot be grounds to set aside an adoption decree. If the parties cannot resolve post-decree disputes about the boundaries of a biological parent's relationship with an adopted child, these boundaries can be determined by the court.

The Smiths also argue that it was error to apply a best interests analysis to set aside the adoption decree. We agree. . . .

Donna testified that she went with the Smiths to their attorney's office to sign some papers on November 13 but did not know what she was signing—she "thought it was help so they could take the child to the doctor and if something happened ... make sure she was okay." She testified that her "mental state really wasn't there, I mean, I was restless, I was very upset." She testified that she had no recollection of anything the attorney told her. Donna testified that she thought that if she did not go with the Smiths to the attorney's office they would not help her, although she had no idea what would have happened if she had not signed the paperwork.

According to the Smiths' attorney: (1) he read and discussed the consent form with Donna; (2) he believed Donna understood the terms of the adoption and of the consent, as did the Smiths; (3) he gave Donna the chance to reflect on her consent before she signed it. Mrs. Smith and the attorney testified that Donna was not restless and upset, but rather was normal, pleasant, and even eager and happy to sign the consent. Donna admitted she was not forced to sign anything. . . .

Donna's claims of duress and undue influence also must fail on this record. A fair reading of the superior court's oral decision reflects that the court implicitly found no duress or undue influence by the Smiths, and these findings are supported by substantial evidence and are not clearly erroneous. There is no evidence in the record to suggest that the Smiths somehow threatened and aroused such fear in Donna that she could no longer exercise her free will to refuse her consent to the adoption. Similarly there is no evidence in the record to suggest that the Smiths assumed control of Donna's free will, precluded Donna from exercising her own free and deliberate judgment about her options and about consenting to the Smiths' adoption of the child, or coerced her into an adoption to which she otherwise would have not have agreed. Even if the superior court did not implicitly address undue influence or duress, as a matter of law this record cannot support such claims. . . .

We accept Donna's arguments that: (1) she was in a difficult situation; (2) she was young, inexperienced, and immature; (3) she was "stressed-out" trying to be a mother to her child; and (4) she needed help. We also accept Donna's argument that the Smiths were in a position to influence Donna's decisions. But these arguments overlook a critical component for Donna's claims of duress and undue influence—Donna must show that the Smiths did something wrongful. The Smiths certainly did nothing to put Donna in her difficult situation; the evidence actually reflects that the Smiths tried as best they could to help her in her time of need. Donna did not present any evidence that the Smiths threatened her or tried to force her to give up her child for adoption. Nor has Donna suggested a motive for the Smiths to do anything wrongful—the only evidence in the record about motive is Mr. Smith's testimony that the Smiths agreed to adopt the child because it was what Donna wanted, because it would avoid Donna and the family losing the child completely, and because it was "what families do for family."

We therefore reject Donna's argument that the superior court's decision can be affirmed on alternative grounds of actual or constructive fraud or misrepresentation, duress, or undue influence.

The decision to invalidate the adoption decree cannot be sustained. The adoption decree must be reinstated, and the child must be returned to the Smiths. If Donna and the Smiths cannot agree on post-adoption visitation, the superior court must consider an appropriate visitation framework for Donna.

We note that the child's living situation will tend to foster the kind of open adoption that must have been contemplated: (1) the parties live in a small community; (2) the child will be raised by her biological grandparents; (3) Donna has seven siblings who will be the child's biological aunts and uncles as well as adoptive brothers and sisters; and (4) Donna will be the child's adoptive sister as well as biological mother. Under these circumstances it is very likely the child will become aware of her natural place in her extended family at an early age. The Smiths expected this and were planning for it by keeping two baby books, one reflecting the child's biological parents and their families. If the parties leave it to the court to fashion a visitation framework, these circumstances will no doubt play a significant role in its determination.

We also note that in fashioning a visitation framework the superior court must be mindful of addressing three potentially competing interests: (1) Donna is entitled to reasonable visitation with the child; (2) the Smiths are the child's legal parents and Donna's visitation may not unreasonably interfere with the Smiths' parental rights; and (3) the visitation framework must reasonably reflect the best interests of the child in light of the adoption and all other relevant family circumstances. Because the superior court did not attempt to fashion a visitation framework and the parties therefore have not discussed visitation in their briefing to us, we do not address legal issues that may be implicated in recognizing and accommodating these interests. If the superior court must fashion a visitation framework over the objection of an interested party, the court's decision should be supported by appropriate findings of fact and conclusions of law to allow appellate review.

We reverse the court's order setting aside the adoption decree and remand with directions to return the child to the Smiths' custody and to consider a visitation framework for Donna that takes into account the Smiths' parental rights, Donna's right to visitation, and the best interests of the child.

Note on Open Adoption

Is an open adoption agreement enforceable? Jennifer Fairfax addressed this subject in *The Adoption Law Handbook, supra.* Courts have reached varying conclusions on the enforceability of open adoption contracts. *See, e.g., Birth Mother v. Adoptive Parents*, 118 Nev. 972, 59 P.3d 1233 (2002)(post-adoption contact agreement not enforceable because not incorporated into adoption decree); *Quets v. Needham*, 198 N.C. App. 241, 682 S.E.2d 214 (2009)(open adoption agreement not enforceable); *Fast v. Moore*, 205 Or. App. 630, 135 P.3d 387 (2006) (post adoption contact agreement not enforceable because it was not approved by the adoption court); Danny R. Veilleux, Postadoption Visitation by Natural Parents, 78 A.L.R. 4th 218 (1990).

Equitable and Virtual Adoption

Courts in some states employ "equitable adoption" to avoid injustice to a child who everyone thought was adopted. Consider the following case: Harry and Mary marry. They have two children. Their baby nephew is orphaned when his parents are killed in a car crash. Harry and Mary take the nephew into their home, and treat him as one of their children. Harry and Mary decide to formally adopt the nephew.

Unfortunately, unbeknownst to Harry and Mary, there is a defect in the adoption, so the adoption is not legal. Harry and Mary treat the nephew as a member of the family. Mary dies. A few years later, Harry dies intestate, leaving a large estate. Harry and Mary's two biological children learn of the defect in the adoption and seek to exclude the nephew from inheriting.

Equitable adoption allows a person like nephew, who was treated as an adopted child, to share in inherited property from the person's "equitable" parent. There must be evidence of: (1) An agreement to adopt; (2) Evidence the decedent intended to adopt (*e.g.*, an invalid attempt to adopt); and (3) Conduct by the parties indicating their recognition of a parent-child relationship.

Georgia recognizes "virtual adoption," described by the Supreme Court "an equitable remedy utilized when the conduct of the parties creates an implied adoption without a court order."[20]

Adoption of Adults

One adult may adopt another, usually for purposes of inheritance.

Tribal Customary Adoption

In the typical adoption, a court terminates the parental rights of the biological parents.[21] Native American children can be adopted this way, so long as the Indian Child Welfare Act (ICWA) is satisfied. IWCA is discussed in Chapter 14.

A few states have a special form of adoption for Native American children. This special adoption allows a child to be adopted by Native American adoptive parents *without* terminating the parental rights of the biological parents. In California, this form of adoption is called "tribal customary adoption." The California statute provides: "Tribal customary adoption means adoption by and through the tribal custom, traditions, or law of an Indian child's tribe. Termination of parental rights is not required to effect the tribal customary adoption."[22]

Adoption Failure

Despite the best efforts of social workers to ensure a good "fit" between a child and adoptive parents, some adoptions don't work. Perhaps the child and the adoptive parents do not bond. Tragically, some abused and neglected children are so damaged that adoptive parents simply cannot nurture and control the child.

If an agency adoption "fails" before it is legally finalized, the child can be returned to the agency in what is sometimes called "disrupted adoption." The national rate of disruption is 10 to 20%.

---

20 Morgan v. Howard, 285 Ga. 512, 678 S.E.2d 882, 883 (2009).

21 Of course, this is not the case with step-parent adoption. In step-parent adoption, only parental rights of one parent are terminated.

22 Cal. Welfare & Institutions Code § 366.24(a).

When an agency adoption breaks down after the adoption is legally finalized, the law in most states allows the adoption to be dissolved by a judge, and here too the child is returned to the agency. Nationally, 1 to 10% of final adoptions dissolve.

The following case involved an effort by adoptive parents to set aside an intercountry adoption.

Adoption of M.S.

California Court of Appeal
181 Cal. App. 4th 50, 103 Cal. Rptr. 3d 715 (2010)

Sims, J.

This is a tragic case in which there can be no good ending for anyone.

Appellants Eleanor P. and Martin S. appeal from an order denying their petition to set aside their Ukrainian adoption of a Ukrainian girl, M.S. The petition was opposed by the California Department of Social Services (the Department or DSS). Appellants contend the trial court erred in construing Family Code section 9100, which authorizes the court to vacate adoptions, as inapplicable to an "intercountry adoption" completed in Ukraine.

Section 9100 provides:

(a) If a child adopted pursuant to the law of this state shows evidence of a developmental disability or mental illness as a result of conditions existing before the adoption to an extent that the child cannot be relinquished to an adoption agency on the grounds that the child is considered unadoptable, and of which conditions the adoptive parent or parents had no knowledge or notice before the entry of the order of adoption, a petition setting forth those facts may be filed by the adoptive parents or parent with the court that granted the adoption petition. If these facts are proved to the satisfaction of the court, it may make an order setting aside the order of adoption.

(b) The petition shall be filed within five years after the entry of the order of adoption.

(c) The court clerk shall immediately notify the department at Sacramento of the petition. Within 60 days after the notice, the department shall file a full report with the court and shall appear before the court for the purpose of representing the adopted child.

This is a case with equities on both sides. However, when we apply the governing statutes enacted by the Legislature, we conclude the trial court was correct. We shall affirm the judgment.

In early 2003, appellants began the process to adopt a foreign-born child. Appellants engaged a California lawyer and a private California adoption agency, Heartsent Adoptions, Inc. (Heartsent), which was licensed by the Department to provide noncustodial intercountry adoption services.

In late 2003, appellants spent several weeks in Ukraine for the adoption. On December 15, 2003, by decree of a Ukrainian court, appellants adopted M.S., a three-year-old Ukrainian girl. The Ukrainian court decree stated in part: "It was found out from the case documents that the child's biological mother is mentally sick. She left the child at the hospital and never visited her. The place of father's residence was not identified. Since February 2002 the child has been made the ward of the government. The medical history of the girl says that she is almost healthy though psychologically delayed." A hospital record says the mother has epilepsy.

Appellants' declarations assert they believed M.S. was healthy, were not aware of this medical background information until after the adoption was finalized, and the documents were not translated for them until after the adoption was completed.

Appellants brought M.S. to live in their Davis home. They did not "readopt" M.S. in California.

In California, various evaluations were performed due to M.S.'s low level of functioning. Healthcare professionals diagnosed her with spastic cerebral palsy, reactive attachment disorder, oppositional defiance disorder, moderate mental retardation, global development delay, ataxia, fetal alcohol syndrome or effect, microcephaly, and post-traumatic stress disorder. Appellants assert M.S. cannot live in a normal home environment, is unadoptable, and has been living in intensive foster care placement in Arizona since 2005.

On May 20, 2008, appellants filed in Yolo County Superior Court a "MOTION TO SET ASIDE ORDER OF ADOPTION UNDER FAMILY CODE SECTION 9100" (the petition). This petition was served on the Department, which filed an opposition. The opposition argued section 9100 is inapplicable to intercountry adoptions; the statutory remedy is not appropriate because the child could not be returned to Ukraine; the records gave notice of potential problems; and the Department did not have access to underlying investigative reports or documentation it would need to fulfill its obligation to make a full report to the court.

On October 31, 2008, after hearing oral argument, the superior court issued an "ORDER DENYING PETITION TO SET ASIDE INTERCOUNTRY ADOPTION PURSUANT TO FAMILY CODE SECTION 9100." The order denied the petition on the ground the court lacked jurisdiction to make a ruling on the matter.

Appellants cite no legal authority for un-doing the Ukraine adoption except section 9100. Section 9100 authorizes the superior court to vacate an adoption of a child "adopted pursuant to the law of this state."

Appellants contend the superior court erred in construing section 9100's language "pursuant to the law of this state" to mean that an adoption must have occurred within California's borders in order to be afforded section 9100 relief to vacate the adoption.

However, the language of section 9100 . . . clearly shows that section 9100 is limited to un-doing adoptions that were granted by California state courts.

We conclude that section 9100 applies only to adoptions granted by a California state court. This is the law that must be applied in this difficult case. The trial court correctly found that section 9100 could not be used to undo the Ukrainian adoption.

The judgment (order) is affirmed.

Wrongful Adoption

In a small number of cases, adoptive parents sue adoption agencies claiming that social workers did not inform them of their child's medical or psychiatric history. The adoptive parents seek monetary damages against the agency to help pay the child's medical or psychiatric bills. In so-called "wrongful adoption" cases, the adoptive parents do not seek to end the adoption. Rather, they claim that the agency deliberately or carelessly withheld vital information.

The first wrongful adoption case, *Burr v. Board of County Commissioners*,[23] was decided in 1986 by the Ohio Supreme Court. Russell and Betty Burr contacted the county adoption agency in 1964, expressing their desire to adopt. A few days later, an adoption worker phoned the Burrs and told them a seventeen-month-old boy was available for adoption. The caseworker told the Burrs the child was born to an eighteen-year-old single mother who relinquished the child

---

23 491 N.E.2d 1102 (Ohio 1986).

to the agency. The caseworker told the Burrs the child was "a nice big, healthy, baby boy." The Burrs adopted the child. As the years passed, the child developed numerous medical and psychiatric problems, including twitching, a speech impediment, and learning problems. In high school, the child developed hallucinations. Eventually, the child was diagnosed with Huntington's Disease, a genetically inherited disease that damages the nervous system.

In 1982, the Burrs got a court order opening the sealed records of their son's medical history prior to adoption. For the first time, they learned that the things the adoption worker told them were false. The records disclosed that the child's mother was not a healthy eighteen-year-old but a thirty-one-year-old mental patient at a state psychiatric hospital. The identity of the biological father was unknown, but he was presumed to be a mental patient. The mother was psychotic and mildly mentally retarded. The adoption agency knew this but did not tell the Burrs. As well, the agency knew the child had a fever at birth and was developing slowly. This information too was withheld from the Burrs. Apparently, the adoption worker fabricated the story of the birth mother.

To recoup the more than $80,000 they had spent on their son's medical care, the Burrs sued the county, the adoption agency, and the caseworker. The jury concluded the adoption agency committed fraud against the Burrs and awarded them $125,000. On appeal, the Ohio Supreme Court approved the jury's decision.

Burr established that an adoption agency cannot *deliberately lie* about a child's history. But what of a scenario in which an adoption agency does *not* intentionally lie, but rather mistakenly fails to tell adoptive parents some detail of a child's medical history? Judges have difficulty deciding whether adoptive parents should be able to sue adoption agencies that try to act responsibly, but that make mistakes or act negligently.

Adoption by Lesbian, Gay, and Bisexual Individuals

In the past, adopting parents were heterosexual married couples. Lesbian, gay, and bisexual individuals were not allowed to adopt. In 1995, the New York Court of Appeals grappled with adoption by gay and straight unmarried couples.

Matter of Jacob

Court of Appeals of New York
86 N.Y.2d 651, 660 N.E.2d 397 (1995)

Kaye, Chief Judge.

Under the New York adoption statute, a single person can adopt a child. Equally clear is the right of a single homosexual to adopt. These appeals call upon us to decide if the unmarried partner of a child's biological mother, whether heterosexual or homosexual, who is raising the child together with the biological parent, can become the child's second parent by means of adoption.

Because the two adoptions sought—one by an unmarried heterosexual couple, the other by the lesbian partner of the child's mother—are fully consistent with the adoption statute, we answer this question in the affirmative. To rule otherwise would mean that the thousands of New York children actually being raised in homes headed by two unmarried persons could have only one legal parent, not the two who want them.

In *Matter of Jacob*, Roseanne M.A. and Jacob's biological father (from whom she is divorced) separated prior to the child's birth and Roseanne M.A. was awarded sole custody. Jacob was a year old when Stephen T.K. began living with him and his mother in early 1991. At the time of filing the joint petition for adoption three years later, Stephen T.K. was employed as a programmer/analyst with an annual income of $50,000, while Roseanne M.A. was a student at SUNY Health Center. Jacob's biological father consented to the adoption.

Though acknowledging that "the granting of an adoption in this matter may be beneficial to Jacob," Family Court dismissed the petition for lack of standing on the ground that Domestic Relations Law § 110 does not authorize adoptions by an unmarried couple. The Appellate Division affirmed . . . .

In *Matter of Dana,* appellants are G.M. and her lesbian partner, P.I., who have lived together in what is described as a long and close relationship for the past 19 years. G.M. works as a special education teacher in the public schools earning $38,000 annually and P.I., employed at an athletic club, has an annual income of $48,000. In 1989, the two women decided that P.I. would have a child they would raise together. P.I. was artificially inseminated by an anonymous donor, and on June 6, 1990, she gave birth to Dana. G.M. and P.I. have shared parenting responsibilities since Dana's birth and have arranged their separate work schedules around her needs. With P.I.'s consent, G.M. filed a petition to adopt Dana in April 1993.

In the court-ordered report recommending that G.M. be permitted to adopt, the disinterested investigator described Dana as an attractive, sturdy and articulate little girl with a "rich family life," which includes frequent visits with G.M.'s three grown children from a previous marriage "who all love Dana and accept her as their baby sister." Noting that G.M. "only has the best interest of Dana in mind," the report concluded that she "provides her with a family structure in which to grow and flourish."

As in *Matter of Jacob*, Family Court, while conceding the favorable results of the home study and "in no way disparaging the ability of [G.M.] to be a good, nurturing and loving parent," denied the petition for lack of standing. In addition, the court held that the adoption was further prohibited by Domestic Relations Law § 117 which it interpreted to require the automatic termination of P.I.'s relationship with Dana upon an adoption by G.M. Despite its conclusion that G.M. had standing to adopt, the Appellate Division nevertheless affirmed on the ground that Domestic Relations Law § 117 prohibits the adoption. We granted leave to appeal.

. . . [W]e conclude that appellants have standing to adopt under Domestic Relations Law § 110 and are not foreclosed from doing so by Domestic Relations Law § 117. There being no statutory preclusion, we now reverse the order of the Appellate Division in each case and remit the matter to Family Court for a factual evaluation and determination as to whether these adoptions would be in the best interest of the children. . . .

[S]ince adoption in this State is solely the creature of statute, the adoption statute must be strictly construed. What is to be construed strictly and applied rigorously in this sensitive area of the law, however, is legislative purpose as well as legislative language. Thus, the adoption statute must be applied in harmony with the humanitarian principle that adoption is a means of securing the best possible home for a child. . . . In strictly construing the adoption statute, our primary loyalty must be to the statute's legislative purpose—the child's best interest. . . .

This policy would certainly be advanced in situations like those presented here by allowing the two adults who actually function as a child's parents to become the child's legal parents. The advantages which would result from such an adoption include Social Security and life insurance benefits in the event of a parent's death or disability, the right to sue for the wrongful death of a parent, the right to inherit under rules of intestacy, and eligibility for coverage under both parents' health insurance policies. In addition, granting a second parent adoption further ensures that two adults are legally entitled to make medical decisions for the child in case of emergency and are under a legal obligation for the child's economic support.

Even more important, however, is the emotional security of knowing that in the event of the biological parent's death or disability, the other parent will have presumptive custody, and the children's relationship with their parents, siblings and other relatives will continue should the coparents separate. . . .

———————

The New York court's 1995 decision in *Matter of Jacob* helped change the rule that unmarried couples—gay and straight—could not adopt. Courtney Joslin and Shannon Minter report, "As of January 2011, no state bars all lesbian and gay individuals from adopting children. There are, however, a small number of states that limit the ability of lesbian and gay people to adopt or become foster parents. Most commonly these states prohibit people living in nonmarital relationships from adopting and/or serving as foster parents."[24]

In 2008, voters in Arkansas approved a ballot initiative entitled "An Act Providing That an Individual Who is Cohabiting Outside of a Valid Marriage May Not Adopt or Be a Foster Parent of a Child Less Than Eighteen Years Old." The initiative provided in part:

BE IT ENACTED BY THE PEOPLE OF THE STATE OF ARKANSAS:

Section 1: Adoption and foster care of minors. (a) A minor may not be adopted or placed in a foster home if the individual seeking to adopt or serve as a foster parent is cohabiting with a sexual partner outside of a marriage which is valid under the constitution and laws of this state. (b) The prohibition of this section applies equally to cohabiting opposite-sex and same-sex individuals.

Section 4: Public policy. The public policy of the state is to favor marriage, as defined by the constitution and laws of this state, over unmarried cohabitation with regard to adoption and foster care.

Section 5: Finding and declaration. The people of Arkansas find and declare that it is in the best interest of children in need of adoption or foster care to be reared in homes in which adoptive or foster parents are not cohabiting outside marriage.

———————

24 Courtney G. Joslin & Shannon P. Minter, *Lesbian, Gay, Bisexual and Transgender Family Law*, § 2:10, p. 97 (2011)(West).

Questions based on *Matter of Jacob*

Do you believe the Arkansas initiative is good policy? Do you think the initiative is constitutional? The Arkansas Supreme Court didn't. In *Arkansas Department of Human Services v. Cole*,[25] the Supreme Court ruled the law unconstitutional.

In *Adoption of X.X.G. and N.R.G.*,[26] the Florida Court of Appeal struck down as unconstitutional a Florida statute banning adoption by homosexuals.

---

25 380 S.W.3d 429 (Ark. 2011).

26 45 So. 3d 79 (Fla. Ct. App. 2010).

CHAPTER 14

Juvenile Court

Child Abuse, Neglect, and Juvenile Delinquency

AMERICA'S JUVENILE COURTS play a central role in protecting children from maltreatment, and providing guidance and reform for children who break the law. This chapter discusses the day-to-day work of juvenile court, or, as it is called in some states, family court. Before describing juvenile court, the chapter offers a brief history of America's child welfare system.

Child Protection from the Colonial Period to 1875

As early as 1642, Massachusetts had a law authorizing magistrates to remove children from parents who did not "train up" their children properly. In 1655, a tradesman from Plymouth was convicted for causing the death of his young servant. In 1735, an orphan girl in Georgia was sexually abused in several homes until she was finally rescued and "placed with a reliable woman." In 1809, a New York City shopkeeper was prosecuted for brutality against a slave and her three-year-old daughter. Homer Folks wrote, "From about 1825 there came a more and more general recognition and practical application of the principle that it is the right and duty of the public authorities to intervene in cases of parental cruelty, or gross neglect seriously endangering the health, morals, or elementary education of children, and to remove the children by force if necessary, and place them under surroundings more favorable for their development."[1]

---

1   Homer Folks, *The Care of Destitute, Neglected, and Delinquent Children.* pp. 168-169. 1902. New York: MacMillan Co.

Almshouses

America's first institution to provide for large numbers of dependent children was the almshouse.[2] At first, the almshouse was considered an advance. Some residents could work or learn a trade. Others would be cared for by staff and by each other. Any notion that the almshouse was a suitable place for children faded quickly. In 1856, a New York Senate committee reported that almshouses were "the most disgraceful memorials of public charity. . . . Filth, nakedness, licentiousness, general bad morals . . . gross neglect of the most ordinary comforts and decencies of life" were rampant. The committee concluded that for children, almshouses were "the worst possible nurseries."[3] By the middle of the 1800s, an increasing drumbeat of criticism called for removal of children from almshouses.

Orphanages

For children who could not remain at home, or who had no home, the orphanage was a significant improvement over the almshouse. America's first orphanage was established in New Orleans in 1728 by Ursuline nuns. The first public orphanage opened in Charleston, South Carolina in 1790. By 1800, there were five orphanages. The number of orphanages grew steadily during the first half of the nineteenth century, fueled by increasing immigration, economic downturns, disease, and growing urban poverty. In 1822, the Society of Friends opened the first orphanage for African American children. By 1850, there were more than seventy orphan asylums. The Civil War created thousands of orphans and half-orphans (a child with one living parent). By 1880, some six hundred orphanages dotted the national map. By 1900, 100,000 children lived in orphanages.

---

2 By 1700, the colonial population reached 250,000, and as the population expanded, so did the number of people unable to fend for themselves, including dependent children, the infirm elderly, the mentally ill, the retarded, the chronically poor, and the seriously or terminally ill. Traditional methods of providing for the poor (outdoor relief, apprenticeship) proved inadequate. Turning to England for solutions, colonists began erecting almshouses, also called the poor house, the workhouse, or the county farm. Care in an almshouse was called "indoor relief." One of the first American almshouses was erected in New York State in 1653. Most almshouses were built after 1700, and the pace of construction was brisk during the nineteenth century. By 1823, one New York City almshouse was "home" to more than five hundred children.

3 *See* Sophonisba P. Breckinridge, *Public Welfare Administration in the United States: Selected Documents.* pp. 146, 169. 1927. Chicago, IL: University of Chicago Press.

Charles Loring Brace
and the New York Children's Aid Society

Charles Loring Brace is a towering figure in American child welfare. He was born 1826 in Connecticut. At sixteen, Brace entered Yale, where he studied religion and moral philosophy. He decided on the ministry, and upon graduation from Yale, he attended Union Theological Seminary during 1848 and 1849.

College and seminary behind him, Brace had to make a choice between the comfortable life of a preacher or the arduous existence of a missionary to the poor. He settled on the latter, joining a long tradition of religiously inspired assistance to New York City's poor. Brace took up his duties in the notorious slum known as Five Points.

Brace soon realized that to make a difference he must work with children. Many adults of Five Points and similar haunts were beyond redemption. Thousands of Yew York City children lived in rundown, unsanitary, crowded, airless, rat-infested, tenements. Brace wrote, "The influence of overcrowding has been incredibly debasing. When we find half a dozen families—as we frequently do—occupying one room, the old and young, men and women, boys and girls of all ages sleeping near each other, the result is inevitable. The older persons commit unnatural crimes; the younger grow up with hardly a sense of personal integrity or purity; the girls are corrupted even in childhood; and the boys become naturally thieves, vagrants, and vicious characters." Brace's allusion to sexual abuse is repeated elsewhere in his writing. He wrote, "Of the young girls in the city, driven to dishonest means of living, it is most sad to speak. Privation, crime, and old debasement in the pure and sunny years of childhood." Like others of his time, Brace was well aware of child sexual abuse, but felt constrained to hint at it rather than describe it forthrightly. Brace was equally aware of physical abuse, and he understood the relationship between poverty and maltreatment. Brace knew that substandard parenting can be passed from parent to child in what scholars today call intergenerational transmission.

While thousands of children lived in tenements, thousands more had no home at all. In 1852, more than 3,000 New York City children were homeless. Some street children were orphans. Others had one or both parents living, but preferred the streets to conditions at home.

Brace and a group of older colleagues discussed creation of a "general organization" for poor children. Following a planning meeting, Brace received a letter inviting him to lead the new "mission to the children." Accepting what he thought would be a one year commitment, Brace embarked on the work of a lifetime. In February, 1853, Brace took the reins of the newly created New York

Children's Aid Society (CAS). The Society was not a child protection agency. Its mission was broader—to help poor children. Although the CAS did not focus on maltreatment, it saved thousands of children from neglect and cruelty.

Brace created "industrial schools" where poor children were taught useful occupations. By 1890, the CAS operated twenty-two industrial schools, instructing nearly 10,000 children. In addition to industrial schools, Brace founded night schools in poor neighborhoods so children who worked all day could obtain an education. Brace wrote, "Young girls and lads, who have been working from seven o'clock till six, have been known to go without their supper in order not to miss the evening lessons. The stormiest weather and the worst walking do not keep them from these schools. In various night schools of the Children's Aid Society will be found hundreds of little ones from six to thirteen who have been working very hard the whole day, and who are now just as eager to learn their little lessons."

In 1854, Brace started the Newsboys' Lodging-House, which provided lodging, food, a bath, night-school, and guidance for homeless lads, many of whom hawked newspapers to eke out a living. By 1890, the CAS operated five lodging-houses for homeless boys and one for girls. In addition to lodging-houses, night schools, and industrial schools, Brace's Society operated kindergartens, free reading rooms, Sunday schools, baths, gymnasiums, and homes for sick children. To give city kids a breath of fresh air, Brace created seaside homes where groups of poor children enjoyed week-long romps.

Although Brace and the Children's Aid Society accomplished many things in New York City, Brace is best remembered for the so-called orphan trains that relocated ("placed out") nearly 100,000 children in new homes in the Midwest between 1854 and 1929.[4] Brace believed that for many poor, abandoned, and neglected children, the only hope lay in a fresh start in the wholesome environs of Midwestern farms and small towns. Brace believed in a clean break from the degrading influences of the City. He was also motivated by his opposition to institutional care for children. Brace was one of the nineteenth century's most forceful critics of institutional care for dependent children.

Some of the "orphan trains" riders were indeed orphans. Other children had one or both parents living. These children could not be placed without parental consent, and employees of the Society visited parents to obtain the necessary permission. Some parents agreed, hoping to improve their child's prospects. Others withheld consent.

---

4   Brace did not invent placing out. Colonial officials used the technique. Brace, however, put placing out on a grand scale.

Small groups of children were gathered, fed, bathed—some for the first time, many for the first time in months—given decent clothes to replace their rags, and sent to the train station with an agent of the Society. The agent accompanied the children on the journey to one or more preselected destinations, where local citizens' committees, which were established in advance for the purpose, were ready to receive them. Several weeks prior to the children's arrival, circulars were distributed informing farmers and townsfolk of the date and time of the train's arrival. A crowd welcomed the train, and everyone walked to the town hall or other meeting place for the big event. The children were introduced one by one, and adults were allowed to select a child of their liking. If the committee approved, the child went home with his or her new "foster parents."

If this procedure seems highly informal, remember these were small communities where people knew their neighbors. The local committee responsible for placing children was usually made up of the minister and perhaps a judge, lawyer, doctor, or leading merchant. These individuals, with input from other residents, were in a good position to block most inappropriate placements. Ill-considered placements occurred, of course, and some orphan train children were abused. In the main, however, placements worked well.[5]

Although many applauded the orphan trains, Brace had no shortage of critics. The most cogent criticism of the orphan trains was that the Children's Aid Society did not adequately monitor its far-flung charges to ensure proper care. Brace acknowledged the weakness, and took steps to increase supervision.

Charles Loring Brace was a remarkable individual, and deserves to be remembered as one of childhood's great friends and protectors. His tireless efforts to save children, his antipathy toward institutional care, and his pioneering efforts to place unfortunate children in good homes, helped shape the child welfare system of the twentieth century.

---

5 The parents of many orphan train children were Catholic, and Brace was accused of converting Catholic children by sending them to Protestant homes. Brace was also attacked by those who believed in the superiority of orphanage care. Some criticized the informality of Brace's placement procedures, and the lack of follow-up to make sure children were well cared for. Finally, some accused Brace of ridding the City of "bad seeds," who grew up to populate Midwestern prisons.

Between 1884 and 1985, four independent investigations confirmed that most of the children fared well. If you should be interested in the details of these studies, *see* my book *A History of Child Protection in American* (2004).

Birth of Organized Child Protection—1875

Organized child protection began in 1875. In that year, the New York Society for the Prevention of Cruelty to Children (NYSPCC) was incorporated. From 1875 through the early decades of the twentieth century—more than half a century—privately funded child protection societies pulled the laboring oar in child protection. It was not until the second half of the twentieth century that government agencies assumed the leadership of child protection.

Rescue of Mary Ellen Wilson

The New York Society for the Prevention of Cruelty to Children resulted from the rescue of a little girl named Mary Ellen Wilson, and no telling of American child protection is complete without this dramatic case. Mary Ellen's mother, Francis Conner, arrived in New York City from London in 1858. Francis married Thomas Wilson, who died fighting in the Civil War. Now a poor pregnant widow, Francis struggled to survive. After Mary Ellen's birth in 1863, Francis found work as a hotel maid. She boarded Mary Ellen with a woman named Score, paying Score eight dollars a month for Mary Ellen's care.

In 1864, Mary Ellen's mother disappeared, and the money for the baby's care dried up. Score took Mary Ellen to the Department of Charities, where the child lived until 1866 when she was indentured to Thomas McCormack and his wife Mary. Soon thereafter, Mr. McCormack died, and Mary took a new husband, Francis Connolly.

Mary Ellen spent eight long years with Mary and Francis Connolly, years filled with neglect and cruelty. Mary Ellen was not permitted to play with other children. Nor was she allowed outside, except occasionally at night. She was beaten routinely. When the Connolly's went out, Mary Ellen was locked in. She had only one item of clothing, a threadbare dress over an undergarment. She slept on a piece of carpet on the floor.

In late 1873, a religious missionary to the poor named Etta Angell Wheeler was visiting a women in the tenements of Hell's Kitchen, one of New York's worst slums. The woman told Wheeler that a little girl who used to live nearby "was often cruelly whipped and very frequently left alone the entire day with the windows darkened."[6] The girl's family had recently moved a few blocks away. Wheeler investigated, but when she knocked at the door, no one answered. She inquired next door, where she encountered a young women recently arrived

---

6 Etta Angell Wheeler, *The Story of Mary Ellen: Which Started the Child Saving Crusade Throughout the World.* p. 1. No date. Denver, CO: American Humane Association.

from Germany, and very ill. The young women told Wheeler she often heard a child being beaten and crying, "Oh, Mamma! Mamma!" Wheeler returned to the apartment and knocked again. This time the door opened slightly and a woman's voice asked, "What do you want?" Wheeler cajoled her way into the apartment, where, in Wheeler's own words, she "saw a pale, thin child, bare-footed, in a thin, scanty dress, so tattered that I could see she wore but one garment besides. It was December and the weather was bitterly cold. She was a tiny mite, the size of five years, though as afterward appeared, she was then nine. Across the table lay a brutal whip of twisted leather strands and the child's meager arms and legs bore many marks of its use. But the saddest part of her story was written on her face, in its look of suppression and misery, the face of a child unloved, of a child that had seen only the fearsome side of life."[7]

Etta Wheeler was determined to rescue Mary Ellen. She went to the police, but they said there was nothing they could do without more evidence of assault. Wheeler visited several child-helping charities, but they declined because they lacked authority to intervene in the family. In April, 1874, after four months of futile efforts, Wheeler was running out of ideas. She had thought several times of asking help from Henry Bergh, the influential founder of the American Society for the Prevention of Cruelty to Animals, "but had lacked courage to do what seemed absurd." Wheeler's niece encouraged her to contact Bergh, saying, You are so troubled over that abused child, why not go to Mr. Bergh? She is a little animal, surely." Wheeler plucked up the courage and went to Bergh's office, where he listened courteously. The next day, Wheeler visited the sick woman living next door to Mary Ellen, where she encountered an investigator sent by Henry Bergh.

Bergh contacted the lawyer for the animal protection society, Elbridge Gerry, and asked Gerry to find a legal means to rescue Mary Ellen from the Connollys. Gerry drew up the necessary papers and asked Judge Abraham Lawrence to issue a warrant authorizing the police to take Mary Ellen into custody. The judge obliged, and on Thursday, April 9, 1874, New York City police officer Christian McDougal, assisted by Alanzo Evans from the animal protection society, went to the Connolly's apartment and whisked Mary Ellen to safety. Outside it was chilly, and they wrapped the child in a carriage blanket to keep her warm. Mary Ellen was taken to police headquarters where the matron took a

---

7   Etta Wheeler, Report to the 37th Annual Meeting of the American Humane Association, October 13-16, 1913. Rochester, N.Y. Reprinted under the title Child Protection Begins, *The National Humane Review*, 50, 16-17. January-February, 1962. Ms. Wheeler provided another version of the case, different in a few details, in a publication titled "The Story of Mary Ellen: Which Started the Child Saving Crusade Throughout the World," available from the American Humane Association in Denver, Colorado.

scrub brush to her. The child was filthy; her hair matted and filled with vermin. It took several tubs of hot water to remove the dirt caked on Mary Ellen's body.

Later that morning, Officer McDougal carried Mary Ellen into Judge Lawrence's courtroom bundled in the carriage blanket. When the blanket was removed, the judge was shocked at the sight of the little girl, clad in her tattered dress and covered with cuts and bruises, including a fresh gash on her face where Mrs. Connolly cut her with scissors.

Elbridge Gerry informed the judge of the case while Henry Berg and Etta Wheeler listened. In the judge's chambers, Mary Ellen told the judge her sad story. She said she could not remember ever "having been kissed by any one— have never been kissed by mamma. I do not want to go back to live with mamma, because she beats me so."

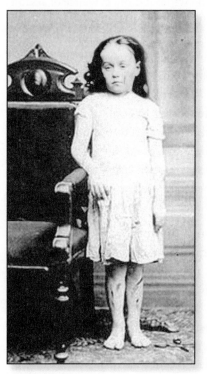

Mary Ellen, shortly following rescue.
Note her injuries.

The next day, everyone was back in court, and by this time Mary Ellen's story was front-page news. Reporters and curious onlookers filled the courtroom and crowded the hallway. Mrs. Connolly was present, and was questioned by Gerry. After several days of testimony from various witnesses, Judge Lawrence removed Mary Ellen from the Connolly's custody.

Later in 1874, Mrs. Connolly was prosecuted before a different judge for assaulting Mary Ellen with scissors. Etta Wheeler testified, as did Mary Ellen. Although it was very difficult for Mary Ellen to speak in the courtroom, she managed to describe how Mrs. Connolly cut her face with scissors while they worked on a quilt. Mrs. Connolly was convicted and sent to prison for a year.

A legend grew up around the rescue of Mary Ellen. According to legend, when Etta Wheeler informed Henry Bergh of the animal protection society of Mary Ellen's plight, Bergh said, "The child is an animal. If there is no justice for it as a human being, it shall at least have the right of the cur lost in the street. It shall not be abused."[8] Thus was born the idea that Mary Ellen was rescued under animal protection laws. What a powerful irony! A society existed to protect animals, but not children. It is a good story, but it is not what happened. Henry Bergh did indeed facilitate the rescue of Mary Ellen, but not under animal protection laws or the auspices of the Society for the Prevention of Cruelty to Animals.[9] Bergh acted as a concerned private citizen.

What became of Mary Ellen? No relatives could be found, so Judge Lawrence placed her in the Sheltering Arms, an institution for homeless children. Etta Wheeler did not believe an institution was the place for Mary Ellen, so Wheeler asked the judge if Mary Ellen could live with Wheeler's own mother on a farm near Rochester, New York. Judge Lawrence approved, and in June, 1875, Mary Ellen was trundled off to the farm. Etta Wheeler's mother died shortly thereafter, but one of Etta's sisters stepped in and raised Mary Ellen as a daughter.

Following her rescue, Mary Ellen enjoyed a happy childhood. At twenty-four, she married Lewis Schutt, who worked for the railroad. In 1897, Mary Ellen gave birth to her first child, Etta—named, of course, for Mary Ellen's guardian angel, Etta Angell Wheeler. A second child, Florence, was born four years later. Both of Mary Ellen's daughters attended college and became teachers. Mary Ellen died October 30, 1956, at ninety-two.

Creation of the New York Society for the Prevention of Cruelty to Children

With Mary Ellen safe, Elbridge Gerry and Henry Bergh discussed the need for an organization to protect children. Laws were on the books to begin the work, but no government agency or private organization had specific responsibility for child protection. The Children's Aid Society and other charities helped many abused and neglected children, but they did not view themselves as child protection agencies. The police often stepped in, but child protection was not the focus of police work. Special courts for children lay twenty-five years in the future.

As Gerry and Bergh discussed the problem, they drew on their experience protecting animals. Bergh had founded the American Society for the Prevention of Cruelty to Animals (ASPCA) in 1866, and Gerry was the Society's lawyer. Both men believed animal protection was best accomplished through private

---

8 *See* Sidney H. Coleman, *Humane Society Leaders in America.* p. 74. 1924. Albany, N.Y.: American Humane Association.

9 *See* Lela B. Costin, Unraveling the Mary Ellen Legend: Origins of the "Cruelty" Movement, Social Service Review 65(2), 203-223. June 1991.

organizations rather than government agencies. Bergh and Gerry took a law enforcement approach to animal protection. Although ASPCA agents were not police officers, they had limited police power delegated by the City. ASPCA agents received reports of animal cruelty, conducted investigations, wore badges, made arrests, and prosecuted animal abusers in criminal court. Gerry and Bergh transported the law enforcement/prosecution model into child protection.

Gerry took the lead in planning a child protection society, and the New York Society for the Prevention of Cruelty to Children (NYSPCC) opened for business in 1875. Gerry assumed the presidency, and served in that capacity until 1901.

Spread of Nongovernmental Child Protection Societies

News of the New York SPCC spread rapidly, and reformers in other cities created nongovernmental child protection societies. In many communities, child protection was accomplished by expanding the role of existing animal protection societies. Other cities established societies devoted exclusively to child protection. By 1880, there were thirty-seven child protection societies in the United States. In 1902, the number was 161, and by 1910 some 250 nongovernmental societies were protecting children or children and animals. At the high water mark,1922, the number exceeded 300. Although 300 is impressive, many cities and nearly all rural areas had little or no access to an SPCC.

SPCCs were nongovernmental charities, and depended for survival on contributions. Although many SPCCs received government subsidies, SPCC administrators and boards of directors were constantly raising funds. To tug the heartstrings of the public, and to open pocketbooks, SPCCs publicized the plight of abused and neglected children. Their most potent fund raising tool was the "before and after" photograph of an abused child. The "before" photo shows a sad-faced, dirty, battered urchin immediately following rescue, while the "after" photo depicts the smiling, plump, well-dressed result of intervention. The most famous "before and after" photos are of Mary Ellen herself.

What Was the Role of the Government During this Period?

Early child protection societies were nongovernmental. Why did child protection fall to private organizations rather than public officials as it does today? There are several explanations. Apart from their traditional responsibility for poor relief, cities and counties in the nineteenth century played a limited role in social welfare. State governments were even less involved. It was not until the late nineteenth and early twentieth centuries that most states created state-level departments of social services. In the nineteenth century, social work as a profession did not exist. What we think of today as social work was carried out primarily by private citizens like Charles Loring Brace, Etta Wheeler, and Elbridge Gerry. Most nineteenth century child protection workers believed private organizations could do a better job of child protection than government, a view shared by most politicians.

Child Protection from 1900 to 1962

Late nineteenth and early twentieth century child protection occurred during the Progressive Era, a period of agitation on numerous social fronts, including efforts to help children, women, and poor and working class people.

Emergence of Social Work, Psychology, Psychiatry, and Pediatrics

Today, child protection is the domain of social work, with supporting roles for law enforcement, mental health, medicine, nursing, law, and education. When organized child protection began in 1875, however, social work had not emerged as a profession. This is not to say that social work was not practiced. The nineteenth century saw a proliferation of private charitable organizations such as the New York Children's Aid Society and associations to improve the condition of the poor. Employees and volunteers of these societies were not called social workers, although many of them did wonderful social work.

In 1877, the first Charity Organization Society (COS) was established at Buffalo, New York. Eventually, more than one hundred COSs were scattered across the country. The COSs improved the administration of poor relief by coordinating voluntary and public efforts. Gradually, COSs hired full time workers to replace middle class volunteers. Of course, full time workers need training. Early training was informal and on-the-job. Eventually, however, more formal training was needed. Nathan Cohen wrote that in 1898, the "New York Charity Organization Society expanded its in-service training program into a more organized effort and established the first school for training social workers. It was called the New York School for Philanthropy."[10] Today, the school is the influential School of Social Work at Columbia University. With increasingly full time, trained staffs, COSs contributed to the professionalization of social work.

---

10 *See* Nathan E. Cohen, *Social Work in the American Tradition*. pp. 68-69. 1958. New York: Dryden Press. Cohen wrote, "By the end of the century the charity organization societies began to employ paid workers, to engage in social reform, and to recognize the need for trained staff. Many of these societies established training courses for their workers." (pp. 68-69).

Another contributor to the professionalization of social work was the settlement movement, described below. Like their colleagues in COSs, settlement workers needed training. Ralph and Muriel Pumphrey wrote, "The COS and the settlement movements were the primary places where an interest in method and education moved workers and the emerging field of social work toward professionalization. . . . In the forty years between the [economic] panic of the [1890s] and the depression of the [1930s], social work became a recognized profession."[11] In 1919, there were seventeen social work schools; by 1930 the number exceeded thirty.

Pediatrics emerged as a specialty in the second half of the nineteenth century. One of the fathers of pediatrics was Abraham Jacobi. In 1860, Jacobi established a clinic for children at the New York Medical College, where he was professor of infantile pathology and therapeutics. Along with other doctors, Jacobi founded the pediatric section of the American Medical Association (AMA). In 1930, the American Academy of Pediatrics was formed by pediatricians who were upset with the AMA's opposition to the federal Sheppard-Towner Act, a law that provided money to assist in the promotion of maternal and infant health.

Psychology developed during the last quarter of the nineteenth century, with clinical psychology emerging during the early twentieth century. Psychiatry came to the fore in the first decades of the twentieth century. With the professions of social work, pediatrics, clinical psychology, and psychiatry in place, the cast of characters was in place for the emergence of child protection as we know it today.

Settlement Movement

The first settlement house was established in 1885 in London's East End slums. This experiment in assisting the poor was created by Oxford and Cambridge students working under the guidance of Samuel Barnett, a young clergyman of the Church of England. The first settlement was christened Toynbee Hall to honor historian Arnold Toynbee, an advocate for the poor who chose to live in humble surroundings.

Stanton Coit of New York City visited Toynbee Hall and came home inspired to create a settlement. Along with Charles Stover, Coit established the Neighborhood Guild of New York City in 1886, America's first settlement. America's most famous settlement, Hull House in Chicago, was started in 1889

---

11 Ralph E. Pumphrey & Muriel W. Pumphrey, *The Heritage of American Social Work*. pp. 202, 255. 1961. New York: Columbia University Press.

by Ellen Starr and Jane Addams following Addams' visit to Toynbee Hall. By 1920, more than four hundred settlements operated in the United States.

Jane Addams was an extraordinary leader. In 1931, she was awarded the Nobel Peace Prize for her efforts to avert World War I. During the early twentieth century, Addams had an enormous impact on social policy in general and child welfare in particular. Addams' Hull House was home to many leading social workers, and Addams was their inspiration and mentor. Thus, Julia Lathrop of Hull House was the first director of the U.S. Children's Bureau, and the first woman to lead a federal agency. Grace Abbott succeeded Lathrop at the Children's Bureau. Edith Abbott, Grace's sister, was one of social work's most brilliant intellectuals and researchers. Sophonisba Breckinridge (Nisba to her friends) was involved in a host of social issues. Edith Abbott and Sophonisba Breckinridge played key roles in creating the University of Chicago's School of Social Service Administration. Florence Kelley was at the forefront of the child labor movement. These remarkable individuals were deeply involved in women's suffrage, child labor, working conditions in industry, public health and sanitation, and other issues.

Settlements created "kindergartens, child-welfare clinics, homemaking programs, handicrafts, play groups, and the involvement of workers in preschool education, juvenile courts, and child and labor legislation. . . . American settlers were at the forefront of the demands for labor legislation, especially for women and children, and they were as much responsible for its passage as any group in the Progressive Period."[12]

Orphanage Care vs. Foster Family Care

During the second half of the nineteenth and the first half of the twentieth centuries, there was debate over the relative merits of institutional care versus foster family care for dependent children. In the nineteenth century, two types of foster family care predominated: free homes and board homes. In free homes, foster parents were not compensated; thus, home was "free." In most free homes, children worked, popularizing this arrangement in farming communities. In 1920, Lawrence Royster wrote, "The choice of a home is of vast importance. Too many children have been taken out of institutions and given apparently good homes, only to become servants. Not that such children should be reared in indolence, but they should be given education, religious training and recreation,

---

12   Robert C. Reinders, Toynbee Hall and the American Settlement Movement. *Social Service Review*, 56, 39-54, at pp. 45-46 and 49. March, 1982.

and their activities not limited to drudgery. To accomplish this best, a trained observer should investigate every home."[13]

In board homes, foster parents were compensated. Children too young to work were more easily placed in board homes, as were troubled or disabled youngsters. As child labor diminished in the twentieth century, free homes where children worked decreased. By the middle of the twentieth century, some 300,000 children were in foster care, most of it compensated, and by the end of the twentieth century, compensation was the norm.

During the nineteenth century, orphanages grew rapidly. In 1825, New York State had two orphanages; by 1866, it had sixty. By 1904, there were more than 1,000 orphanages and children's homes in the United States.

The quality of care in orphanages varied. In 1910, Hastings Hart observed:

There still survive orphan asylums where children are kept in uniform, with shaved heads; where they do not have individual clothing, but have clothing distributed to them promiscuously from week to week; where lice and bedbugs prevail; where food is meager and of inferior quality; where good and willing girls are kept scrubbing floors month after month because they do not complain; where sleeping rooms are insanitary; where thin straw beds let the tender bodies down upon hard wooden slats; where cuffs and abuse are more freely distributed than kind words.

But on the other hand there are children's homes and orphan asylums where tenderness and love prevail; where mirth and jollity are contagious; where weary heads find a pillow on gentle bosoms; where generous diet is prescribed by medical advice and served with liberal hands; where foster homes are constantly sought as a better haven than even the good and homelike shelter of such an institution.[14]

Supporters of orphanage care highlighted the order, cleanliness, and discipline of the institution. Children were educated, fed, clothed, and instructed in morality and piety. As the nineteenth century wore on, however, criticism of orphanage care grew. Opponents argued that the most humble home was better than the finest institution. Institutional life deprived children of love and lessons only families provide. Charles Birtwell of the Boston Children's Aid Society put it this way, "I know what I should want for my little boy if my wife and I were

---

13 Lawrence T. Royster, The Care of the Dependent Child, *National Humane Review*, 8, p. 113, June, 1920. Royster was President of the Norfolk Society for the Prevention of Cruelty to Children in Norfolk, Virginia.

14 Hastings H. Hart, *Preventive Treatment of Neglected Children*. pp. 67-68. 1910. New York: Charities Publication Committee. Reprinted in 1971 as part of David J. Rothman (Advisory Ed.), *Poverty, U.S.A.: The Historical Record*. New York: Arno Press and the New York Times.

blotted from his life. If he should fall into the hands of charity I should pray God to guide him to an agency that would open for him at once the door to family life."[15] Charles Loring Brace of the New York Children's Aid Society was a relentless critic of institutional care for children. With Brace leading the way, momentum gathered to place dependent children in foster homes rather than orphanages.

Supporters and opponents of orphanage care agreed on one thing, children should be removed from almshouses. In 1873, Michigan passed the first law against children in almshouses. In 1875, New York passed similar legislation, as did Massachusetts in 1879. Other states followed.

Increasing Role of Government in Social Services

The role of government in social services in general, and child welfare in particular, changed substantially over time. From colonial times until the Civil War, care of dependent children was the responsibility of local officials, assisted by the increasing number of private charitable organizations like the New York Children's Aid Society. By the twentieth century, the number of nongovernmental child helping organizations reached the point that Lillian Wald quipped, "The air is murky with many organizations."[16] Although state legislatures had long appropriated funds to support private charities and the efforts of local officials, it was not until the 1860s that state governments began assuming leadership roles.

Massachusetts created the first State Board of Charities in 1863 to coordinate the work of various charities. Other states followed suit, creating state-level departments with oversight of public and private charities receiving state funds. In 1869, Massachusetts created the first state department of health. State-level oversight of social services, child welfare, and health took years to develop, and was not complete until the middle of the twentieth century.

Social Security Act of 1935

Prior to 1935, the federal government played an insignificant role in child welfare policy and funding. It was the Great Depression of the 1930s that stimulated the sea change in the federal government's role in social programs. With

---

15   Address of Charles W. Birtwell at the 1909 White House Conference on the Care of Dependent Children. *Proceedings of the Conference on the Care of Dependent Children: Held at Washington, D.C. January 25, 26, 1909.* pp. 133-134, at p. 134. Senate Documents, 60th Congress, 2nd Session. Volume 13.

16   Address of Lillian D. Wald at the 1909 White House Conference on the Care of Dependent Children. *Proceedings of the Conference on the Care of Dependent Children: Held at Washington, D.C., January 25, 26, 1909.* p. 171. Senate Documents, 60th Congress, 2nd Session. Volume 13. 1909.

the economy in shambles, bold action was required. Franklin Delano Roosevelt brought the necessary leadership to the White House when he took office on March 4, 1933. Roosevelt assembled a cadre of advisors to formulate rescue plans for the nation. Calling his vision for economic recovery the "New Deal," Roosevelt asked and received Congress's help. Meeting in special session from March 9, 1933 to June 16, 1933—the so-called Hundred Days—Congress passed a broad array of economic laws to cope with the depression.

Building on the first wave of reform, in June, 1934, President Roosevelt created the Committee on Economic Security to "study problems relating to the economic security of individuals."[17] Edwin Witte was appointed executive director of the Committee.[18] Witte worked with hundreds of individuals to draft the Social Security Act. The Act became law in 1935.

The Social Security Act "marked the beginning of the federal government's participation in a broad range of social-insurance and public-welfare programs. This act has had implications for almost every American family and for many of our social institutions."[19] In addition to old-age pensions, unemployment insurance, and vocational and rehabilitation services, the Social Security Act created the Aid to Dependent Children program (ADC).

To be eligible for federal ADC funds, states had to abide by conditions set forth in the Social Security Act. In other words, Congress attached "strings" to ADC funds. Each state desiring ADC funds was required to submit a plan to the federal government describing its ADC program and promising to comply with the strings attached to the money. The technique of attaching strings to federal money gives Congress tremendous leverage to shape public policy in the states. Congress passes laws making billions of federal dollars available to states that are willing to abide by the strings attached to the money. Since few states can afford to forego federal largess, Congress exerts wide ranging influence over state policy and practice.

The Social Security Act authorized the Children's Bureau "to cooperate with State public-welfare agencies in establishing, extending, and strengthening, especially in predominantly rural areas, [child welfare services] for the protection and care of homeless, dependent, and neglected children, and children in

---

17 President Franklin D. Roosevelt, Executive Order Number 6757. June 29, 1934.

18 *See* Edwin E. Witte, *The Development of the Social Security Act*. 1962. Madison, WI: University of Wisconsin Press. Mr. Witte prepared the manuscript of his book as he worked on the Social Security Act. The book is a fascinating first-hand account of the making of the Social Security Act.

19 Wilbur J. Cohen & Robert J. Lampman, Introduction. In Edwin E. Witte, *The Development of the Social Security Act*. pp. xi-xvi, at xii.1962. Madison, WI: University of Wisconsin Press.

danger of becoming delinquent."[20] This provision of the Social Security Act was an important shot in the arm for the nascent field of child welfare, and a modest step toward what, in the 1970s, became a central role for the federal government in child protection policy and funding. By 1939, every state had a child welfare plan approved by the Children's Bureau. The preference for rural areas dropped away in 1958.

Summary of Progressive Era Reforms

Progressive Era reforms had a direct impact on children. The emergence of the helping professions created the work force needed to advance the fields of child welfare and children's mental and physical health. The effort to limit child labor dovetailed with the spread of compulsory public education. Children put down factory tools and picked up school books. The debate over orphanage versus foster care tipped in favor of the latter. State governments slowly assumed leadership in the provision of social services. Finally, the Progressive Era saw an end to the long-held tradition that the federal government had no role to play in social issues.

Transition from Nongovernmental SPCCs to Government Child Protection

During the early twentieth century, calls arose to shift child protection from nongovernmental SPCCs to government agencies. Writing in 1929, Ray Hubbard stated, "Leaders in the field of child protection now generally agree that such work should become a public function and be made a part of a state-wide program with county units under state supervision or control."[21] In 1935, Douglas Falconer wrote, "For many years responsibility for child protection was left almost entirely to private agencies . . . . They were generally independent, autonomous, local units, only loosely gathered into national federations, if indeed they had any such national relationship. Great sections of child population were untouched by them and in many other places the service rendered was perfunctory and of poor standard."[22]

The call for government child protection coincided with the increasing role

---

20 *See* the Social Security Act, U.S. Statutes at Large, Volume 49, Part 1, Title V, Part 3, Section 521, 74th Congress, First Session, Chapter 531, August 14, 1935.

21 Ray S. Hubbard, Child Protection. In Fred S. Hall (Ed.), *Social Work Yearbook*, vol. 1, pp. 65-67, at 67. 1929. New York: Russell Sage Foundation.

22 Douglas P. Falconer, Child and Youth Protection. In Fred S. Hall (Ed.), *Social Work Yearbook*, vol. 3, pp. 63-66, at 65. 1935. New York: Russell Sage Foundation.

of state governments in social services. As discussed earlier, prior to the twentieth century, there were relatively few state-level departments of social services. What government services there were, primarily outdoor relief (welfare), were the province of local government, i.e., towns, cities, and counties. During the first half of the twentieth century, states created or strengthened state departments of welfare, social services, health, and labor.

By 1935, half the states had child welfare divisions within the state department of welfare or social services. At the county level, counties developed welfare departments and slowly added child welfare workers. In 1959, half the counties in the United States had no social workers providing full-time child welfare services.

The Great Depression, which began with the Stock Market crash of 1929, and persisted through the 1930s, hastened the demise of nongovernmental SPCCs. The charitable contributions that were the lifeblood of SPCCs dried up with the economy, and only the heartiest SPCCs weathered the economic drought. In the 1930s and 1940s, many SPCCs merged with children's aid societies or family social work agencies, or went out of business altogether. In some communities, child protection was assumed by the juvenile court or the police department, while in other communities organized protective work ceased.

World War II, from 1941 to 1945, caused major dislocations in American life, as thousands of fathers went off to war, and thousands of mothers entered the labor force. Neglect and delinquency increased, but the number of foster homes remained stagnant or, in some places, declined. In some communities, war increased pressure to merge social agencies. Child welfare services, including child protection, were stretched thin.

In 1954, Vincent De Francis, director of the Children's Division of the American Humane Association, conducted a national inventory of child protective services.[23] De Francis wrote letters to child welfare professionals throughout the United States, asking them to describe child protection in their state,

---

23 Vincent De Francis was one of the twentieth century's foremost authorities on child protection. De Francis was born in New York City on Christmas Eve, 1907. He graduated from City College of New York in 1929, and studied law at Fordham, graduating in 1932. De Francis practiced law in New York until 1941, when he accepted a position with the Brooklyn Society for the Prevention of Cruelty to Children doing casework with families and prosecuting abuse cases in court. The Brooklyn SPCC had long favored the social work approach to child protection, and this tradition rubbed off on the young lawyer. De Francis realized his legal training and experience did not adequately equip him to help children and families, so he took social work classes at the New York School of Social Work. In 1946, De Francis became Executive Director of the Queensboro Society for the Prevention of Cruelty to Children, a position he held until 1954, when he was appointed director of the Children's Division of the American Humane Association in Denver, Colorado. De Francis remained at American Humane from 1954 until his retirement in 1977. Under De Francis, AHA's Children's Division became one of America's most influential organizations addressing child protection.

county, city, or town. The responses to De Francis' letter provide valuable insight into child protection midway through the twentieth century. De Francis found eighty-four nongovernmental SPCCs, down from the high of three hundred early in the century. Thirty-two states had no SPCC. In these states, and in states with only partial SPCC coverage, government agencies were gradually assuming responsibility for child protection.

De Francis found fifteen states where the law did not clearly impose responsibility for child protection on a state agency. Lack of a specific state law did not mean, of course, that children were unprotected. De Francis' finding, however, provides insight into the unfinished business of government child protective services midway through the twentieth century.

When government assumed responsibility for child protection, the usual practice was to assign the task to the county department of welfare or social services. Until the 1960s and 1970s, many departments lacked social workers trained in child welfare, let alone specialized units focused on child protection. Protective work was typically part of an undifferentiated social work caseload. In the 1950s, a number of large cities and a smattering of smaller communities established separate child protection units. At mid-century, many communities had no agency clearly in charge of child protection.

A decade after his 1956 research, De Francis again took the pulse of American child protection.[24] By 1967, the number of states with SPCCs was down to ten. De Francis wrote, "Responsibility for provision of Child Protective Services under voluntary agency auspices, like the old soldier it is, is slowly fading away."

As of 1967, "protective Services under public welfare auspices [were] reported to exist in 47 states." Yet, De Francis complained, "No state and no community has developed a Child Protective Service program adequate in size to meet the service needs of all reported cases of child neglect, abuse and exploitation."

Thus, for the first six decades of the twentieth century, protective services in most communities were inadequate and, in some places, nonexistent. Yet, despite tremendous obstacles, professionals protected children. In 1958, Claire Hancock described the dedication common among child protection workers then and now. "Day after day, the staff, under great pressure, were faced with staggering problems. They were attempting to make suitable plans for children whose lives were all tangled up, whose needs were desperate, often

---

24 Vincent De Francis, *Child Protective Services: A National* Survey. 1967. Denver, CO: American Humane Association.

beyond the resources available to meet them. Their endurance, their consistent effort to do the very best they could under the circumstances, commands one's admiration as well as sympathy for the strain and discouragement that was common experience."[25]

Race in American Child Welfare

Prior to the 1960s, children of color were often treated insensitively or excluded altogether from the child welfare system. It did not dawn on many nineteenth and early twentieth century professionals that it was wrong to treat children of color differently.[26] Yet, throughout our history, enlightened professionals cared for children across color lines.[27] Charles Loring Brace's New York Children's Aid

---

25 Claire R. Hancock, *A Study of Protective Services and the Problem of Neglect of Children in New Jersey.* p. 36. 1958. State of New Jersey, Department of Institutions and Agencies, State Board of Child Welfare.

26 Examples of racial insensitivity abound. In the Child Welfare League of America *Bulletin* for June 15, 1928, there is a story of the funding of Ellis College, a private "institution for white, fatherless girls under the age of thirteen . . . ." Vol. 7(6), p. 1.

In 1934, Carol Hayes, the principal of a "school for Negroes" in Birmingham, Alabama gave a moving speech at the Southern Regional Conference of the Child Welfare League of America. Carol Hayes, The Negro Child in Our Social Pattern, Child Welfare League of America, *Bulletin*, 8(9), 1, 4-6. November, 1934. The *Bulletin* published excerpts of Hayes' speech. The *Bulletin* editor introduced the speech with the following: "Speech, in part, made at Southern Regional Conference of the Child Welfare League of America, Birmingham, Alabama, October 13. The speaker, himself a Negro, is principal of one of the public schools for Negroes in Birmingham. The Conference was held in a leading hotel, the Tutwiler, which permitted attendance of Negroes."

The system of boarding schools for Native American children, originally designed to undermine Native American culture, had a long history. *See* Margaret Connell Szasz, Federal Boarding Schools and the Indian Child: 1920-60. In N. Ray Hiner & Joseph M. Hawes, *Growing Up in America: Children in Historical Perspective.* pp. 210-218. 1985. Chicago: University of Illinois Press. Szasz wrote that Congress funded the first off-reservation schools in 1882. Szasz observed that by 1928, "There were seventy-seven boarding schools with an enrollment of 21,000. By 1941 only forty-nine boarding schools remained with an enrollment of 14,000." (p. 213).

27 *See* California Society for the Prevention of Cruelty to Children, *Twenty-Seventh Annual Report.* 1902. In the Director's Address to the members of the Society, he reported on the founding of a "Colored Children's home."

See also Carol Hayes, The Negro Child in Our Social Pattern, Child Welfare League of America, *Bulletin*, 8(9), 1, 4-6. November, 1934. Hayes was the principal of a school "for Negroes in Birmingham." In an eloquent speech that was careful not to offend the largely white audience, but which powerfully described the racial injustice of the South, Hayes praised the Birmingham Children's Aid Society for helping African American as well as white children.

See also Priscilla Ferguson Clement, Families and Foster Care: Philadelphia in the Late Nineteenth Century. In N. Ray Hiner & Joseph M. Hawes, *Growing Up in America: Children in Historical Perspective.* pp. 135-146.1985. Chicago: University of Illinois Press. Clement described the practices of the Philadelphia Children's Aid Society and the Home Missionary Society of Philadelphia, both of which placed children in foster homes. Clement wrote:

The majority of children in the care of both agencies were native-born Protestants, and, in addition, about 90 percent were Caucasian. Still, there is no evidence that either society deliberately discriminated against non-whites. Actually the opposite may have been true since both agencies cared for a higher percentage of blacks than their proportion of the city's population would warrant. Between 1870 and 1890 the number of blacks in Philadelphia hovered at just under 4 percent of the total population, while 10 percent of the boys and girls assisted

Society helped children of all races. The 1930 White House Conference on Child Health and Protection devoted considerable attention to inequities tied to race.[28] Ira Reid, on behalf of the White House Subcommittee on the Negro in the United States, wrote, "Though constituting but 10 per cent of the total population of the United States, the Negro forms a much larger percentage of the dependent population. The problems of such a situation are both created and augmented by the prevailing racial situation in which the Negro suffers grave economic and social injustices. In many communities efforts are made to ameliorate these conditions,

---

by the Children's Aid and Home Missionary societies were black. The extreme poverty of the city's nonwhite population in the late nineteenth century, which has been well documented elsewhere, may in part account for the relatively significant minority of black youths in the care of the two agencies. (pp. 140-141).

See also Crystal M. Potter, The Institutional Care of Negro Children in New York City, Child Welfare League of America, Bulletin, 25(6), 1-5. June, 1946. Potter was Second Deputy Commissioner in the New York City Department of Welfare. Her article described how institutions in New York City worked to comply with a 1942 rule called the Race Discrimination Amendment which prohibited distribution of government funds to institutions that discriminated on the basis of color. Speaking in general terms about racial prejudice, Potter wrote:

We have accepted the basic principles that the problems with which human beings struggle are universal; that those of a particular group are not unique; and that a Negro child is not fundamentally different from any other child except insofar as he may be more deprived. Our dilemma as child welfare workers arises when we try to insure the welfare of an individual Negro child living in a community in which these principles are accepted in theory only, or not accepted at all. Our services to the individual Negro child are obstructed by the fact that the Negro people as a group are disadvantaged as to their housing, their living standards, their educational and employment opportunities, their rights and privileges as Americans! Their children by and large cannot feel part of the community; their sense of belonging is warped and undeveloped. The homeless Negro children in general are not given the same care, treatment, and opportunity as other children under similar circumstances. As child welfare workers, we find ourselves entangled in this mesh of unfairness, discrimination, and segregation. Every day, we see at firsthand what is happening to individual children and what deprivation does to them. This deprivation will continue not only for the Negro child but for the majority of our children as long as there is the cultural lag between our knowledge of what is necessary for the well-being of children and what is actually provided for them. A child's fundamental needs and rights should not be compromised, but this is our national practice. (p. 1).

See also Richard Paul, Negro Children at the Leake and Watts School, Child Welfare League of America, *Bulletin*, 25(6), 5-7, 12. June, 1946.

See also Patricia M. Collmeyer, From "Operation Brown Baby" To "Opportunity": The Placement of Children of Color at the Boys and Girls Aid Society of Oregon, *Child Welfare*, 74, 242-263. January-February, 1995.

See also Paul H. Stuart, The Kinsley House Extension Program: Racial Segregation in the 1940s Settlement Program. *Social Service Review*, 66(1), 112-120. March, 1992. The Abstract reads, "In this article, I review the experience of a settlement house that conducted a biracial recreation program in a southern city from 1945 to 1949. The Kingsley House Extension Program, while innovative, was controversial and was, ultimately, abandoned. The program's fate was a harbinger of events to come in the South during the height of the civil rights movement in the 1950s and early 1960s."

28 *See* Ira DeA. Reid, Child Dependency as Affected by Race, Nationality, and Mass Migration. In *White House Conference on Child Health and Protection*. Section IV—The Handicapped: Prevention, Maintenance, Protection. Carl C. Carstens, Chair. Committee on Socially Handicapped—Dependency and Neglect. Homer Folks, Chair. J. Prentice Murphy, Vice-Chair. pp. 279-350. 1933. New York: Appleton-Century.

In addition to discussing problems affecting African American children, Reid discussed "The Mexican in California," writing, "Among a majority of Americans racial prejudices exist against the Mexican which manifests itself in the common classification of the Mexican as *not white*, and the Mexican, sensitive to this social ostracism, does not force himself where he feels the pressure against him." (p. 312. Emphasis in original).

but such efforts are often based upon racial distinction which tends to perpetu-ate rather than to eliminate the problems of dependency."[29] The Subcommittee asserted, "It is the responsibility of every community to see that full resources for care be available for Negro children as well as for white children. . . . Lower standards of care for Negro children than those available for white children in the same community can in no way be condoned."

Decline of the Orphanage

The number of children in orphanages peaked during the Great Depression at roughly 144,000. Following World War II, orphanages declined, and by 1980, Americans viewed the orphanage as a relic of the past.

As orphanages slowly disappeared, foster care grew. In 1933, forty-seven percent of children who could not live at home were in foster homes, while fifty-three percent lived in institutions. By 1972, eighty percent of children needing out-of-home care lived in foster homes or group homes, and twenty percent lived in institutions.

Relative Obscurity of Child Protection from 1929 to 1962

From Mary Ellen's rescue in 1874 until the Great Depression of the 1930s, impressive achievements occurred in child protection. Although most Americans knew little about societies to prevent cruelty to children, profession-als were well aware of child abuse and neglect. SPCCs made no secret of their work, publicizing heartrending cases in the press and in fund raising appeals. Thus, child protection was out in the open for all to see. Then came the stock market crash of 1929 and the Great Depression. SPCCs declined. Attention shift-ed from the reforms of the Progressive Era to economic survival of the Nation. Overseas, a plethora of issues, dominated by the rise of fascism, preoccupied government and public alike. America, it seemed, was headed again for war, less than twenty years after World War I, "the war to end all wars." In this climate, child protection did not cease, but it retreated into relative obscurity.

The end of Progressive reforms, the Great Depression, World War II, Korea, and the Cold War, with its omnipresent threat of nuclear annihilation, were not the only reasons for the relative obscurity of child protection from

---

29   Ira DeA. Reid, Child Dependency as Affected by Race, Nationality, and Mass Migration. In *White House Conference on Child Health and Protection*. Section IV—The Handicapped: Prevention, Maintenance, Protection. Carl C. Carstens, Chair. Committee on Socially Handicapped—Dependency and Neglect. Homer Folks, Chair. J. Prentice Murphy, Vice-Chair. p. 279. 1933. New York: Appleton-Century.

the 1930s to the 1960s. As child protection shifted to government agencies, the highly specialized and visible SPCCs disappeared. Child protection became simply one of the many functions of government social workers. Few communities had special units responding to child maltreatment, and child abuse disappeared into an undifferentiated child welfare caseload. Moreover, many social workers disliked abuse and neglect cases, involving, as they often do, confrontation and courts.

Loss of a specialized identity was not the only byproduct of the transformation from private SPCCs to government child protection. Unlike SPCCs, which *sought* public attention to raise money, government agencies such as departments of social services and juvenile courts eschew public attention and are shrouded in confidentiality. Under government auspices, child protection "officially" disappeared from public view.

Additional factors contributed to the relative obscurity of child protection from the 1930s to the 1960s. Except in cases of obvious brutality, physicians and nurses were not particularly adept at differentiating accidental from nonaccidental injuries, particularly in young children and babies. Medical professionals were apt to accept a parent's explanation for a child's injuries. Regarding sexual abuse, professionals were aware of the problem. Yet, it was not until the late 1970s that America opened it eyes to the reality of child sexual abuse.

Child Protection from 1962 to the Present

From 1900 through the 1960s, child protection was an incomplete patchwork of nongovernmental societies to prevent cruelty to children (SPCCs) and government agencies. Many communities lacked organized child protection. Apart from occasional headlines recounting horrendous abuse, the public was blissfully ignorant. The 1960s and 1970s, however, witnessed an explosion of interest in child abuse. This explosion was triggered by physicians who alerted the medical profession to physical abuse of young children. Discoveries by doctors attracted the media. Increased media and professional interest spurred passage of laws requiring professionals to report abuse to authorities. The first reporting laws appeared in 1963 and quickly spread across the country. In 1974, Congress assumed a leadership role with passage of the Child Abuse Prevention and Treatment Act (CAPTA). Through CAPTA and other laws, Washington financed and shaped child protection policy from the 1970s to the twenty-first century. In the 1960s and 1970s, attention focused primarily on physical abuse and neglect. During the 1980s, sexual abuse came to the fore. Because child sexual abuse raises unique issues, it is discussed in a separate chapter.

Medical Profession "Discovers" Child Physical Abuse

The medical profession played a key role in kindling interest in child physical abuse. Of course, physicians have always known of child abuse.[30] Prior to the 1960s, however, medical schools provided little or no training on the topic. There was a dearth of medical literature on physical abuse.

In 1946, pediatrician and radiologist John Caffey published a groundbreaking article titled, "Multiple Fractures in the Long Bones of Infants Suffering from Chronic Subdural Hematoma."[31] Caffey's article created a spark that smoldered for sixteen years, gradually building heat until it ignited in 1962. In his article, Caffey described six young children with subdural hematoma (bleeding inside the skull) and twenty-three fractures of the legs or arms. Although Caffey did not expressly state that any of the children were abused, he hinted at it. He commented, "In not a single case was there a history of injury to which the skeletal lesions could reasonably be attributed." Caffey wrote that for two of the children, "fresh fractures appeared shortly after the patient had arrived home after discharge from the hospital. In one of these cases the infant was clearly unwanted by both parents and this raised the question of intentional ill-treatment of the infant; the evidence was inadequate to prove or disprove this point." Following his 1946 article, Caffey often called attention to the traumatic origin of fractures and subdural hematoma in infants.[32]

Following Caffey's paper, a series of articles in the medical literature pointed with increasing confidence to child abuse as an explanation for certain injuries in young children. Finally, sixteen years after Caffey's groundbreaking paper, in 1962, Drs. Henry Kempe, Frederic Silverman, Brandt Steele, William Droegemueller, and Henry Silver advanced the journey with their article, "The Battered-Child Syndrome."[33] Kempe and his colleagues reported the results of a year-long survey of hospitals and prosecuting attorneys. The hospitals reported 302 cases of physical abuse of young children. Thirty-three of the children died, and eighty-five suffered permanent damage. Prosecutors reported 447 cases.

---

30 In 1860, French physician Ambroise Tardieu, professor of legal medicine at the University of Paris, described a condition remarkably similar to battered child syndrome. *See* Frederic N. Silverman, Rigler Lecture: Unrecognized Trauma in Infants, the Battered Child Syndrome, and the Syndrome of Ambroise Tardieu. *Radiology*, 104, 337-353. 1972.

31 John Caffey, Multiple Fractures in the Long Bones of Infants Suffering from Chronic Subdural Hematoma. *American Journal of Roentgenology*, 56, 163-173. August, 1946.

32 *See* John Caffey, Some Traumatic Lesions in Growing Bones Other Than Fractures and Dislocations: Clinical and Radiological Features. *The British Journal of Radiology*, 33(353), 225-238. May, 1957.

33 C. Henry Kempe, Frederic N. Silverman, Brandt F. Steele, William Droegemueller, & Henry K. Silver, The Battered-Child Syndrome. *Journal of the American Medical Association*, 181(1), 17-24. July 7, 1962.

Forty-five children died of their abuse, and twenty-nine suffered brain damage. Kempe and his colleagues described Battered Child Syndrome:

> The battered-child syndrome may occur at any age, but, in general, the affected children are younger than 3 years. In some instances the clinical manifestations are limited to those resulting from a single episode of trauma, but more often the child's general health is below par, and he shows evidence of neglect including poor skin hygiene, multiple soft tissue injuries, and malnutrition. One often obtains a history of previous episodes suggestive of parental neglect or trauma. A marked discrepancy between clinical findings and historical data as supplied by the parents is a major diagnostic feature of the battered-child syndrome. . . . Subdural hematoma, with or without fracture of the skull, is, in our experience, an extremely frequent finding even in the absence of fractures of the long bones. . . . The characteristic distribution of these multiple fractures and the observation that the lesions are in different stages of healing are of additional value in making the diagnosis.

The first author of the Battered Child Syndrome, Henry Kempe, played a leading role in bringing child abuse to national attention during the 1960s and 1970s. Kempe was the head of the Department of Pediatrics at the University of Colorado School of Medicine in Denver. As head of pediatrics, Kempe was responsible for pediatric services at four Denver hospitals. He grew increasingly disturbed at the number of children with unexplained injuries. Kempe lost patience with the false excuses offered to explain fractures, bruises, burns, head trauma, and other injuries. Thus, it was in Denver that Henry Kempe focused on child abuse.

John Caffey, Henry Kempe, and other physicians alerted the medical profession to physical abuse of young children. The growing medical literature—particularly the Battered Child Syndrome—joined forces with the factors described below to stir national interest in child abuse and neglect.

1962 Amendments to the Child Welfare Provisions of the Social Security Act

The 1935 Social Security Act provided limited funds for child welfare services, which the Act defined as services "for the protection and care of homeless, dependent, and neglected children, and children in danger of becoming delinquent." In 1959, an Advisory Council on Child Welfare Services recommended expanding the definition, and in 1962, Congress obliged, redefining child welfare services under the Social Security Act as "public social services which supplement, or substitute for, parental care and supervision for the purpose of

(1) preventing or remedying, or assisting in the solution of problems which may result in, the neglect, abuse, exploitation, or delinquency of children, (2) protecting and caring for homeless, dependent, or neglected children, (3) protecting and promoting the welfare of children of working mothers, and (4) otherwise protecting and promoting the welfare of children, including the strengthening of their own homes where possible or, where needed, the provision of adequate care of children away from their homes in foster family homes or day-care or other child-care facilities."[34] The 1962 definition focused squarely on abuse and neglect. Vincent De Francis remarked that the 1962 amendments "for the first time, identified Child Protective Services as part of all public child welfare."[35]

In addition to clarifying the definition of child welfare services, the 1962 amendments required states seeking child welfare funds under the Social Security Act to pledge that by 1975, they would make child welfare services available state wide. This requirement fueled the expansion of child welfare services, including protective services.

Growing Public Awareness of Abuse

The 1960s witnessed increased media attention on child abuse and neglect. Although local media had always covered noteworthy cases, as when a child died or was horribly mistreated, coverage of physical abuse and neglect in national media outlets was uncommon prior to the 1960s. During the 1960s, however, national media coverage grew. In August, 1960, for example, *Newsweek* described three Canadian children who "spent eleven years in prison—at home," confined for the most part to a single room.[36] In April, 1962, *Newsweek* published an article titled, "When They're Angry . . ."[37] Quoting Katherine Oettinger, chief of the Children's Bureau, the article stated, "'Since 1959, [the Bureau has] been receiving an increasing number of reports from pediatricians and hospitals about physical abuse of children by their parents. We're now giving the problem of the battered child top priority.'" The article described Battered Child Syndrome and quoted Dr. Kempe saying, "'One day last November, we had four battered children in our pediatrics ward. Two died in the hospital and one died at home four weeks later. For every child who enters the hospital this badly beaten, there must

---

34 Public Welfare Amendments of 1962, Public Law 87-543, Section 528. Statutes at Large, vol. 76, p 172.

35 Vincent De Francis, *Child Protective Services: A National Survey.* p. 4. 1967. Denver, CO: American Humane Association.

36 Their 'Prison' Was Home. *Newsweek*, p. 43. August 8, 1960. *Life* described the same three children in its August 29, 1960 issue, vol. 49, pp. 29-30.

37 'When They're Angry . . .' *Newsweek*, p. 74. April 16, 1962.

be hundreds treated by unsuspecting doctors. The battered child syndrome isn't a reportable disease, but it damn well ought to be.'"

In July, 1962, *Time* magazine reported, "To many doctors, the incident is becoming distressingly familiar. A child, usually under three, is brought to the office with multiple fractures—often including a fractured skull. The parents express appropriate concern, report that the baby fell out of bed, or tumbled down the stairs, or was injured by a playmate. But X rays and experience lead the doctor to a different conclusion: the child has been beaten by his parents."[38]

In June, 1963, *Life* published a story titled, "Cry Rises from Beaten Babies."[39] The article contained disturbing photographs. The text stated, "The atrociously battered little boy at left bears wounds inflicted by his own father. Suddenly, across the U.S. . . . there is an upsurge in discoveries of brutal cases of child beating. Beyond doubt many cases never come to the attention of doctors. Of those that do, the cause of injury is often written off as accidental. Even if the truth is suspected, it may be ignored because the doctors are unwilling either to believe the evidence or to get involved in legal complications."

In March, 1964, *Good Housekeeping* published a powerful description of abuse.[40] Four-year-old Christopher was playing outside in his new sandbox. He carried a pail of sand into the house and accidentally spilled it on his mother's freshly-waxed floor. "Chris' body suddenly became rigid as he stared at the disaster before him. Suddenly a heavy blow caught him across the upper part of his back and knocked him ten feet across the kitchen floor. The boy looked up to see his mother advancing upon him with the handle of the dust mop. He stiffened his body as more blows were rained upon his arms, legs and back. Not once did he utter a sound, although his mother screamed all the time she was hitting him that he was a 'horrible child' and 'bad clear through.' Minutes later, her arms exhausted, Kate stopped the beating and stormed from the kitchen. Chris lay on the floor, his body quivering, his large eyes staring."[41]

Thus, a steady stream of news stories on child abuse—usually mentioning Battered Child Syndrome and Dr. Kempe—brought the issue to the fore in American society.[42] Child abuse was a hot topic.

---

38 Battered-Child Syndrome. *Time*, p. 60. July 20, 1962.

39 Cry Rises from Beaten Babies. *Life*, pp. 38-39. June 14, 1963.

40 *Good Housekeeping*, pp. 87-89, 195. March, 1964. This article was impressive for its thoroughness and objectivity.

41 *Good Housekeeping*, pp. 87-88. Chris' mother got psychiatric help for her anger.

42 *See* Charles Flato, Parents Who Beat Children. *Saturday Evening Post*, 235, 30-35. October 6, 1962. This was

Growth in Professional Literature

Prior to 1962, there was little professional research and writing on physical abuse. In 1963, Elizabeth Elmer wrote, "The amount of systematic research on the problem of child abuse and neglect is conspicuously scant."[43] Following publication of the Battered Child Syndrome in 1962, however, a trickle of writing became a torrent. In 1964, pediatrician Vincent Fontana published the first American medical text on abuse, *The Maltreated Child*.[44] Fontana wrote, "In discussing this problem with other physicians, it became apparent that a blind spot existed concerning the importance or frequency of [child abuse]. . . . The maltreatment of children has not been considered important enough to be included in the curricula of medical schools; it has not been given notice in any of the major pediatric textbooks, and it has been ignored by both society and physicians for many years."

Child Abuse Reporting Laws

In 1959, Henry Kempe stated, "The battered child syndrome isn't a reportable disease, but it damn well ought to be." Kempe was about to get his wish. In January, 1962, the Children's Bureau sponsored a small meeting of child abuse experts. Kempe was there, as was Vincent De Francis of American Humane. According to De Francis, the purpose of the meeting was "to look into the medical aspects of the abuse of children."[45] The experts discussed the complexity of diagnosing physical abuse, and steps the Children's Bureau could take to better inform professionals. At a follow-up meeting in May, 1962, experts discussed the need for laws encouraging doctors to report physical abuse to child protection or police agencies.

Out of the Children's Bureau meetings and similar gatherings, pressure mounted for laws requiring physicians to report suspected abuse. In 1963, ten states passed reporting laws, and by 1967 every state had reporting legislation on the books.

---

an in-depth article that included compelling photographs of abused children.

43 Elizabeth Elmer, Identification of Abused Children. *Children*, 10(5), 180-184. September-October, 1963.

44 Vincent J. Fontana, *The Maltreated Child: The Maltreatment Syndrome in Children*. 2nd ed., 2nd printing. 1972. Springfield, IL: Charles C. Thomas.

45 Vincent De Francis, Who Said There's No More Cruelty to Children? *The National Humane Review*, 50, 18-19. March-April, 1962.

Federal Leadership in Child Protection

Prior to the 1970s, the federal government played a useful but minor role in child protection. The Children's Bureau was created in 1912, although the Bureau devoted little attention to maltreatment until the 1960s. The Social Security Act of 1935 created Aid to Dependent Children and authorized the Children's Bureau "to cooperate with State public-welfare agencies in establishing, extending, and strengthening, especially in predominantly rural areas, [child welfare services] for the protection and care of homeless, dependent, and neglected children, and children in danger of becoming delinquent."[46] Yet, as late as 1973, Senator Walter Mondale wrote, "Nowhere in the Federal Government could we find one official assigned full time to the prevention, identification and treatment of child abuse and neglect."[47] It was not until 1974 that the federal government assumed a leadership role in responding to child abuse and neglect.

1974—Child Abuse Prevention and Treatment Act

In 1973, hearings were conducted in the U.S. Senate and House of Representatives on bills to create the Child Abuse Prevention and Treatment Act (CAPTA). In January, 1974, President Nixon signed CAPTA into law. CAPTA authorized federal funds to improve the response to physical abuse, neglect, and sexual abuse. CAPTA provided funds to train professionals, funds for multidisciplinary centers on child abuse and neglect, and money for demonstration projects.

1980—Adoption Assistance and Child Welfare Act

The child abuse reporting laws and enhanced awareness of abuse produced an increase in intervention. By the mid-1970s, a rising number of children in foster care set off alarm bells in Congress, resulting in the Adoption Assistance and Child Welfare Act of 1980. The Act required states seeking federal foster care funds—all states—to make "reasonable efforts" to avoid removing children from maltreating parents. When removal was necessary, reasonable efforts were required to reunite families. Every child in foster care had to have a "permanency plan" to return the child home or move toward termination of parental rights.

---

46 *See* the Social Security Act, U.S. Statutes at Large, Volume 49, Part 1, Title V, Part 3, Section 521, 74th Congress, 1st Session, Chapter 531, August 14, 1935.

47 Letter of Transmittal from Walter F. Mondale to Harrison A. Williams dated March 15, 1974. Located at Child Abuse Prevention and Treatment Act, 1974. Public Law 93-247 (S. 1191). Questions and Answers, Analysis, and Text of the Act. Prepared for the Subcommittee on Children and Youth of the Committee on Labor and Public Welfare, United States Senate. 93rd Congress, 2nd Session. Page VII. April, 1974.

For children who could not go home, Congress provided financial incentives for adoption. Finally, the Act provided financial support for adoptive parents who adopted children with special needs.

The effort to preserve families was a key component of the Adoption Assistance and Child Welfare Act, and "family preservation" was the dominant paradigm of child welfare in the 1980s.

Family preservation programs worked well for many families. In the 1990s, however, critics argued that over-reliance on family preservation sometimes led to tragedy. One forceful critic of family preservation was Richard Gelles, who challenged the effectiveness of family preservation in his 1996 book, *The Book of David: How Preserving Families Can Cost Children's Lives.*[48] Gelles criticized the research supporting programs like Homebuilders. Gelles argued for a shift in policy toward what he called "A New Child-Centered Policy." Gelles wrote, "The essential first step in creating a safe world for children is to abandon the fantasy that child welfare agencies can balance the goals of protecting children and preserving families, adopting instead a child-centered policy of family services. This is not a new policy, but rather a return to the policy of the early 1960s that established child safety as the overriding goal of the child welfare system. It is time to abandon the myth that 'the best foster family is not as good as a marginal biological family.' The ability to make a baby does not ensure that a couple have, or ever will have, the ability to be adequate parents. The policy of family reunification and family preservation fails because it assumes that *all* biological parents can become fit and acceptable parents if only appropriate and sufficient support is provided."

1997—Adoption and Safe Families Act

The 1980 Adoption Assistance and Child Welfare Act helped many children and parents. Yet, the number of children in foster care did not decline. Too many children languished in out-of-home care. Moreover, Richard Gelles and others charged that the reasonable efforts and family preservation requirements caused social workers to leave children in dangerous homes. Congress responded with the Adoption and Safe Families Act of 1997 (ASFA). Although ASFA did not abandon family preservation, it made child safety the top priority. When children were placed in foster care, ASFA established strict time lines to return them to their parents or terminate parental rights so children could be adopted. In cases of sexual abuse and chronic physical abuse, ASFA authorized states to

---

48   Richard J. Gelles, The Book of David: How Preserving Families Can Cost Children's Lives. 1996. New York: Basic Books.

dispense with efforts to reunify the family, and to move directly to termination of parental rights.

Across the history of child protection, we see pendulum swings in the debate over family privacy versus intervention. These swings are reflected in the federal legislation described above. The Child Abuse Prevention and Treatment Act of 1974 contained fairly broad definitions of maltreatment, encouraging greater intervention. By contrast, the Adoption Assistance and Child Welfare Act of 1980, with its emphasis on family preservation, pushed the pendulum away from intervention. Finally, the Adoption and Safe Families Act of 1997 placed top priority on child safety, once again shifting the emphasis toward intervention. The intervention pendulum swings back and forth, never reaching the extremes, and never standing still.

Conclusion

The period from 1962 to 2000 witnessed remarkable progress. For the first time, child protective services were available across America—in small towns, farm country, reservations, and cities. The late twentieth century system was not perfect. Far from it. Yet, despite flaws and overwhelming caseloads, professionals kept their heads above water, and swam in the same direction.

Juvenile Court

Today, every state has a juvenile court with authority over three groups of children: abused and neglected children, juvenile delinquents, and status offenders. A status offense is misbehavior that is not delinquency, but that nevertheless brings a child under the authority of the juvenile court. The traditional status offenses are truancy, smoking and drinking under age, running away, curfew violations, and so-called ungovernable behavior.

America's first juvenile court was established in 1899. The Progressive Era reformers who created the juvenile court were concerned primarily with the criminal justice system's harsh treatment of delinquent children. Prior to the juvenile court, children who broke the law were arrested, jailed, brought to trial, and punished similarly to adults. Children as young as six languished in jail with adult criminals.

What stood the Chicago juvenile court apart from earlier reforms was that it removed youthful offenders *altogether* from the criminal justice system. Rather than subject children to trial, conviction, and punishment as criminals, proceedings in juvenile court were civil. The juvenile court adjudicated the youngster a delinquent rather than a criminal, and provided individualized treatment rather than punishment. The goal in juvenile court was to save the child from a downward spiral leading to a life of crime. The reformers who created the juvenile court believed rehabilitation was superior to the retribution meted out by criminal law. Julian Mack, an early judge of the Chicago juvenile court put it this way in 1909, "Why is it not just and proper to treat these juvenile offenders . . . as a wise and merciful father handles his own child whose errors are not discovered by the authorities? Why is it not the duty of the state, instead of asking merely whether a boy or girl has committed a specific offense, to find out what he is, physically, mentally, morally, and then if it learns that he is treading the path that leads to criminality, to take him in charge, not so much to punish as to reform, not to degrade but to uplift, not to crush but to develop, not to make him a criminal but a worthy citizen."[49]

In addition to delinquency, the Chicago juvenile court had authority over neglected and dependent children, which the 1899 law defined as any child under sixteen "who for any reason is destitute or homeless or abandoned; or dependent upon the public for support; or has no proper parental care or guardianship; or who habitually begs or receives alms; or who is found living in any house of ill fame or with any vicious or disreputable person; or whose home, by reason of neglect, cruelty or depravity on the part of its parents, guardian or other person in whose care it may be, is an unfit place for such child."[50] This definition became the model for juvenile court laws across the United States.

Juvenile courts spread quickly across the United States. By 1919, all states but three had juvenile court laws, and eventually every state fell in line. The early juvenile court was as much social agency as law court. For that reason, the formal procedures of the courtroom were relaxed in favor of informality. In many juvenile courts, the judge sat at a desk rather than on an elevated bench. The child and interested adults sat at the desk with the judge. Usually, the child had no attorney. Everyone provided input, and the judge decided what was needed to turn the young offender away from crime. Most delinquents were placed on probation. Some were sent to reform schools or other institutions. In cases of abuse or neglect, the judge could remove children from home or leave them at home under the supervision of the court's probation officers.

In the 1960s, the U.S. Supreme Court decided two cases dealing with the juvenile court—*Kent v. United States* and *In re Gault*. The decisions discuss the

---

49 Julian W. Mack, The Juvenile Court. *Harvard Law Review*, 23, 104-122, at 107. 1909. Judge Mack became a federal judge on the United States Court of Appeals for the Seventh Circuit.

50 Illinois Juvenile Court Law, Section 1.

strengths and weaknesses of the juvenile court. Both decisions shaped America's juvenile courts for the twentieth century and the twenty-first.

Kent v. United States

United States Supreme Court
383 U.S. 541, 86 S. Ct. 1045 (1966)

Mr. Justice Fortas delivered the opinion of the Court.

This case is here on certiorari to the United States Court of Appeals for the District of Columbia Circuit. The facts and the contentions of counsel raise a number of disturbing questions concerning the administration by the police and the Juvenile Court authorities of the District of Columbia laws relating to juveniles.

Because we conclude that the Juvenile Court's order waiving jurisdiction of petitioner was entered without compliance with required procedures, we remand the case to the trial court.

Morris A. Kent, Jr., first came under the authority of the Juvenile Court of the District of Columbia in 1959. He was then aged 14. He was apprehended as a result of several housebreakings and an attempted purse snatching. He was placed on probation, in the custody of his mother who had been separated from her husband since Kent was two years old. Juvenile Court officials interviewed Kent from time to time during the probation period and accumulated a "Social Service" file.

On September 2, 1961, an intruder entered the apartment of a woman in the District of Columbia. He took her wallet. He raped her. The police found in the apartment latent fingerprints. They were developed and processed. They matched the fingerprints of Morris Kent, taken when he was 14 years old and under the jurisdiction of the Juvenile Court. At about 3 p. m. on September 5, 1961, Kent was taken into custody by the police. Kent was then 16 and therefore subject to the "exclusive jurisdiction" of the Juvenile Court. He was still on probation to that court as a result of the 1959 proceedings.

Upon being apprehended, Kent was taken to police headquarters where he was interrogated by police officers. It appears that he admitted his involvement in the offense which led to his apprehension and volunteered information as to similar offenses involving housebreaking, robbery, and rape. His interrogation proceeded from about 3 p. m. to 10 p. m. the same evening.

Sometime after 10 p. m. petitioner was taken to the Receiving Home for Children. The next morning he was released to the police for further interrogation at police headquarters, which lasted until 5 p. m.

The record does not show when his mother became aware that the boy was in custody, but shortly after 2 p. m. on September 6, 1961, the day following petitioner's apprehension, she retained counsel.

Counsel, together with petitioner's mother, promptly conferred with the Social Service Director of the Juvenile Court. In a brief interview, they discussed the possibility that the Juvenile Court might waive jurisdiction and remit Kent to trial by the District Court. Counsel made known his intention to oppose waiver.

Petitioner was detained at the Receiving Home for almost a week. There was no arraignment during this time, no determination by a judicial officer of probable cause for petitioner's apprehension.

During this period of detention and interrogation, petitioner's counsel arranged for examination of petitioner by two psychiatrists and a psychologist. He thereafter filed with the Juvenile Court a motion for a hearing on the question of waiver of Juvenile Court jurisdiction, together with an affidavit of a psychiatrist certifying that petitioner "is a victim of severe psychopathology" and recommending hospitalization for psychiatric observation. Petitioner's counsel, in support of his motion to the effect that the Juvenile Court should retain jurisdiction of petitioner, offered to prove that if petitioner were given adequate treatment in a hospital under the aegis of the Juvenile Court, he would be a suitable subject for rehabilitation.

At the same time, petitioner's counsel moved that the Juvenile Court should give him access to the Social Service file relating to petitioner which had been accumulated by the staff of the Juvenile Court during petitioner's probation period, and which would be available to the Juvenile Court Judge in considering the question whether it should retain or waive jurisdiction. Petitioner's counsel represented that access to this file was essential to his providing petitioner with effective assistance of counsel.

The Juvenile Court judge did not rule on these motions. He held no hearing. He did not confer with petitioner or petitioner's parents or petitioner's counsel. He entered an order reciting that after "full investigation, I do hereby waive" jurisdiction of petitioner and directing that he be "held for trial for the alleged offenses under the regular procedure of the U. S. District Court for the District of Columbia." He made no findings. He did not recite any reason for the waiver. He made no reference to the motions filed by petitioner's counsel. We must assume that he denied *sub silentio*, the motions for a hearing, the recommendation for hospitalization for psychiatric observation, the request for access to the Social Service file, and the offer to prove that petitioner was a fit subject for rehabilitation under the Juvenile Court's jurisdiction.

Presumably, prior to entry of his order, the Juvenile Court judge received and considered recommendations of the Juvenile Court staff, the Social Service file relating to petitioner, and a report dated September 8, 1961 (three days following petitioner's apprehension), submitted to him by the Juvenile Probation Section. The Social Service file and the September 8 report were later sent to the District Court and it appears that both of them referred to petitioner's mental condition. The September 8 report spoke of "a rapid deterioration of petitioner's personality structure and the possibility of mental illness." As stated, neither this report nor the Social Service file was made available to petitioner's counsel.

The provision of the Juvenile Court Act governing waiver expressly provides only for "full investigation." It states the circumstances in which jurisdiction may be waived and the child held for trial under adult procedures, but it does not state standards to govern the Juvenile Court's decision as to waiver. The provision reads as follows:

> If a child sixteen years of age or older is charged with an offense which would amount to a felony in the case of an adult, or any child charged with an offense which if committed by an adult is punishable by death or life imprisonment, the judge may, after full investigation, waive jurisdiction and order such child held for trial under the regular procedure of the court which would have jurisdiction of such offense if committed by an adult; or such other court may exercise the powers conferred upon the juvenile court in this subchapter in conducting and disposing of such cases.

Petitioner appealed from the Juvenile Court's waiver order to the Municipal Court of Appeals, which affirmed, and also applied to the United States District Court for a writ of habeas corpus, which was denied.

At trial, petitioner's defense was wholly directed toward proving that he was not criminally responsible because "his unlawful act was the product of mental disease or mental defect." Durham v. United States, 214 F. 2d 862, 875 (D.C. 1954). Extensive evidence, including expert testimony, was presented to support this defense. The jury found as to the counts alleging rape that petitioner was "not guilty by reason of insanity." Under District of Columbia law, this made it mandatory that petitioner be transferred to St. Elizabeth's Hospital, a mental institution, until his sanity is restored. On the six counts of housebreaking and robbery, the jury found that petitioner was guilty.

Kent was sentenced to serve five to 15 years on each count as to which he was found guilty, or a total of 30 to 90 years in prison. The District Court ordered that the time to be spent at St. Elizabeths on the mandatory commitment after the insanity acquittal be counted as part of the 30- to 90- year sentence. Petitioner appealed to the United States Court of Appeals for the District of Columbia Circuit. That court affirmed.

It is to petitioner's arguments as to the infirmity of the proceedings by which the Juvenile Court waived its otherwise exclusive jurisdiction that we address our attention. Petitioner attacks the waiver of jurisdiction on a number of statutory and constitutional grounds. He contends that the waiver is defective because no hearing was held; because no findings were made by the Juvenile Court; because the Juvenile Court stated no reasons for waiver; and because counsel was denied access to the Social Service file which presumably was considered by the Juvenile Court in determining to waive jurisdiction.

We agree that the order of the Juvenile Court waiving its jurisdiction and transferring petitioner for trial in the United States District Court for the District of Columbia was invalid. . . . The issue is the standards to be applied upon such review.

We agree with the Court of Appeals that the statute contemplates that the Juvenile Court should have considerable latitude within which to determine whether it should retain jurisdiction over a child or—subject to the statutory delimitation—should waive jurisdiction. But this latitude is not complete. At the outset, it assumes procedural regularity sufficient in the particular circumstances to satisfy the basic requirements of due process and fairness, as well as compliance with the statutory requirement of a full investigation. The statute gives the Juvenile Court a substantial degree of discretion as to the factual considerations to be evaluated, the weight to be given them and the conclusion to be reached. It does not confer upon the Juvenile Court a license for arbitrary procedure. The statute does not permit the Juvenile Court to determine in isolation and without the participation or any representation of the child the critically important question whether a child will be deprived of the special protections and provisions of the Juvenile Court Act. It does not authorize the Juvenile Court, in total disregard of a motion for hearing filed by counsel, and without any hearing or statement or reasons, to decide—as in this case—that the child will be taken from the Receiving Home for Children and transferred to jail along with adults, and that he will be exposed to the possibility of a death sentence instead of treatment for a maximum, in Kent's case of five years, until he is 21.

We do not consider whether, on the merits, Kent should have been transferred; but there is no place in our system of law for reaching a result of such tremendous consequences without ceremony—without hearing, without effective assistance of counsel, without a statement of reasons. It is inconceivable that a court of justice dealing with adults, with respect to a similar issue would proceed in this manner. It would be extraordinary if society's special concern for children, as reflected in the District of Columbia's Juvenile Court Act, permitted this procedure. We hold that it does not.

The theory of the District's Juvenile Court Act, like that of other jurisdictions, is rooted in social welfare philosophy rather than in the *corpus juris*. Its proceedings are designated as civil rather than criminal. The Juvenile Court is theoretically engaged in determining the needs of the child and of society rather than adjudicating criminal conduct. The objectives are to provide measures of guidance and rehabilitation for the child and protection for society, not to fix criminal responsibility, guilt and punishment. The State is *parens patriae* rather than prosecuting attorney and judge. But the admonition to function in a "parental" relationship is not an invitation to procedural arbitrariness.

Because the State is supposed to proceed in respect of the child as *parens patriae* and not as adversary, courts have relied on the premise that the proceedings are "civil" in nature and not criminal, and have asserted that the child cannot complain of the deprivation of important rights available in criminal cases. It has been asserted that he can claim only the fundamental due process right to fair treatment. For example, it has been held that he is not entitled to bail; to indictment by grand jury; to a speedy and public trial; to trial by jury; to immunity against self-incrimination; to confrontation of his accusers; and in some jurisdictions that he is not entitled to counsel.

While there can be no doubt of the original laudable purpose of juvenile courts, studies and critiques in recent years raise serious questions as to whether actual performance measures well enough against theoretical purpose to make tolerable the immunity of the process from the reach of constitutional guaranties applicable to adults. There is much evidence that some juvenile courts, including that of the District of Columbia, lack the personnel, facilities and techniques to perform adequately as representatives of the State in a *parens patriae* capacity, at least with respect to children charged with law violation. There is evidence, in fact, that there may be grounds for concern that the child receives the worst of both worlds: that he gets neither the protections accorded to adults nor the solicitous care and regenerative treatment postulated for children.

This concern, however, does not induce us in this case to accept the invitation to rule that constitutional guaranties which would be applicable to adults charged with the serious offenses for which Kent was tried must be applied in juvenile court proceedings concerned with allegations of law violation. The Juvenile Court Act and the decisions of the United States Court of Appeals for the District of Columbia Circuit provide an adequate basis for decision of this case, and we go no further.

It is clear beyond dispute that the waiver of jurisdiction is a critically important action determining vitally important statutory rights of the juvenile. The statutory scheme makes this plain. The Juvenile Court is vested with "original and exclusive jurisdiction" of the child. This jurisdiction confers special rights and immunities. He is, as specified by the statute, shielded from publicity. He may be confined, but with rare exceptions he may not be jailed along with adults. He may be detained, but only until he is 21 years of age. The court is admonished by the statute to give preference to retaining the child in the custody of his parents "unless his welfare and the safety and protection of the public cannot be adequately safeguarded without removal." The child is protected against consequences of adult conviction such as the loss of civil rights, the use of adjudication against him in subsequent proceedings, and disqualification for public employment.

The net, therefore, is that petitioner—then a boy of 16—was by statute entitled to certain procedures and benefits as a consequence of his statutory right to the "exclusive" jurisdiction of the Juvenile Court. In these circumstances, considering particularly that decision as to waiver of jurisdiction and transfer of the matter to the District Court was potentially as important to petitioner as the difference between five years' confinement and a death sentence, we conclude that, as a condition to a valid waiver order, petitioner was entitled to a hearing, including access by his counsel to the social records and probation or similar reports which presumably are considered by the court, and to a statement of reasons for the Juvenile Court's decision. We believe that this result is required by the statute read in the context of constitutional principles relating to due process and the assistance of counsel.

Accordingly, we hold that it is incumbent upon the Juvenile Court to accompany its waiver order with a statement of the reasons or considerations therefore. We do not read the statute as requiring that this statement must be formal or that it should necessarily include conventional findings of fact. But the statement should be sufficient to demonstrate that the statutory requirement of "full investigation" has been met; and that the question has received the careful consideration of the Juvenile Court; and it must set forth the basis for the order with sufficient specificity to permit meaningful review.

Correspondingly, we conclude that an opportunity for a hearing, which may be informal, must be given the child prior to entry of a waiver order. The child is entitled to counsel in connection with a waiver proceeding, and counsel is entitled to see the child's social records. These rights are meaningless—an illusion, a mockery—unless counsel is given an opportunity to function.

The right to representation by counsel is not, a formality. It is not a grudging gesture to a ritualistic requirement. It is of the essence of justice. Appointment of counsel without affording an opportunity for hearing on a "critically important" decision is tantamount to denial of counsel. There is no justification for the failure of the Juvenile Court to rule on the motion for hearing filed by petitioner's counsel, and it was error to fail to grant a hearing.

We do not mean by this to indicate that the hearing to be held must conform with all of the requirements of a criminal trial or even of the usual administrative hearing; but we do hold that the hearing must measure up to the essentials of due process and fair treatment.

With respect to access by the child's counsel to the social records of the child, we deem it obvious that since these are to be considered by the Juvenile Court in making its decision to waive, they must be made available to the child's counsel.

We do not agree with the Court of Appeals' statement, attempting to justify denial of access to these records, that counsel's role is limited to presenting "to the court anything on behalf of the child which might help the court in arriving at a decision; it is not to denigrate the staff's submissions and recommendations." On the contrary, if the staff's submissions include materials which are susceptible to challenge or impeachment, it is precisely the role of counsel to "denigrate" such matter. There is no irrebuttable presumption of accuracy attached to staff reports. If a decision on waiver is "critically important" it is equally of "critical importance" that the material submitted to the judge—which is protected by the statute only against "indiscriminate" inspection—be subjected, within reasonable limits having regard to the theory of the Juvenile Court Act, to examination, criticism and refutation. While the Juvenile Court judge may, of course, receive *ex parte* analyses and recommendations from his staff, he may not, for purposes of a decision on waiver, receive and rely upon secret information, whether emanating from his staff or otherwise. The Juvenile Court is governed in this respect by the established principles which control courts and quasi-judicial agencies of the Government.

For the reasons stated, we conclude that the Court of Appeals and the District Court erred in sustaining the validity of the waiver by the Juvenile Court.

Appendix to Opinion of the Court

[The Supreme Court attached the following Appendix, which was a document prepared by the presiding judge of the D.C. District Court]

The authority of the Judge of the Juvenile Court of the District of Columbia to waive or transfer jurisdiction to the U. S. District Court for the District of Columbia is contained in the Juvenile Court Act (§ 11-914 D. C. Code, 1951 Ed.). This section permits the Judge to waive jurisdiction "after full investigation" in the case of any child "sixteen years of age or older who is charged with an offense which would amount to a felony in the case of an adult, or any child charged with an offense which if committed by an adult is punishable by death or life imprisonment."

The statute sets forth no specific standards for the exercise of this important discretionary act, but leaves the formulation of such criteria to the Judge. A knowledge of the Judge's criteria is important to the child, his parents, his attorney, to the judges of the U. S. District Court for the District of Columbia, to the United States Attorney and his assistants, and to the Metropolitan Police Department, as well as to the staff of this court, especially the Juvenile Intake Section.

An offense falling within the statutory limitations will be waived if it has prosecutive merit and if it is heinous or of an aggravated character, or—even though less serious—if it represents a pattern of repeated offenses which indicate that the juvenile may be beyond rehabilitation under Juvenile Court procedures, or if the public needs the protection afforded by such action.

The determinative factors which will be considered by the Judge in deciding whether the Juvenile Court's jurisdiction over such offenses will be waived are the following:

> The seriousness of the alleged offense to the community and whether the protection of the community requires waiver.

> Whether the alleged offense was committed in an aggressive, violent, premeditated or willful manner.

> Whether the alleged offense was against persons or against property, greater weight being given to offenses against persons especially if personal injury resulted.

> The prosecutive merit of the complaint, i. e., whether there is evidence upon which a Grand Jury may be expected to return an indictment (to be determined by consultation with the United States Attorney).

The desirability of trial and disposition of the entire offense in one court when the juvenile's associates in the alleged offense are adults who will be charged with a crime in the U. S. District Court for the District of Columbia.

The sophistication and maturity of the juvenile as determined by consideration of his home, environmental situation, emotional attitude and pattern of living.

The record and previous history of the juvenile, including previous contacts with the Youth Aid Division, other law enforcement agencies, juvenile courts and other jurisdictions, prior periods of probation to this Court, or prior commitments to juvenile institutions.

The prospects for adequate protection of the public and the likelihood of reasonable rehabilitation of the juvenile (if he is found to have committed the alleged offense) by the use of procedures, services and facilities currently available to the Juvenile Court.

It will be the responsibility of any officer of the Court's staff assigned to make the investigation of any complaint in which waiver of jurisdiction is being considered to develop fully all available information which may bear upon the criteria and factors set forth above. Although not all such factors will be involved in an individual case, the Judge will consider the relevant factors in a specific case before reaching a conclusion to waive juvenile jurisdiction and transfer the case to the U. S. District Court for the District of Columbia for trial under the adult procedures of that Court.

Transfer to Adult Court

Some teenagers commit serious, calculated, callous crimes. Some of these teens deserve to be punished like adult criminals. Moreover, some teens are already committed to a life of crime and are unlikely to benefit from the therapeutic approach of the juvenile court. The law allows such "hardened" youth to be transferred from juvenile court to criminal court where they are prosecuted as adults. In making the transfer decision, the juvenile court judge considers the minor's age and IQ, the nature and seriousness of the crime, whether the youth is naive or sophisticated in the ways of crime, whether the minor has been in trouble before, and the likelihood the minor can be rehabilitated in juvenile court.

In re Gault

United States Supreme Court
387 U.S. 1, 87 S. Ct. 1428 (1967)

Mr. Justice Fortas delivered the opinion of the Court.

This is an appeal affirming the dismissal of a petition for a writ of habeas corpus. The petition sought the release of Gerald Francis Gault, appellants' 15-year-old son, who had been committed as a juvenile delinquent to the State Industrial School by the Juvenile Court of Gila County, Arizona.

On Monday, June 8, 1964, at about 10 a.m., Gerald Francis Gault and a friend, Ronald Lewis, were taken into custody by the Sheriff of Gila County. Gerald was then still subject to a six months' probation order which had been entered on February 25, 1964, as a result of his having been in the company of another boy who had stolen a wallet from a lady's purse. The police action on June 8 was taken as the result of a verbal complaint by a neighbor of the boys, Mrs. Cook, about a telephone call made to her in which the caller or callers made lewd or indecent remarks. It will suffice for purposes of this opinion to say that the remarks or questions put to her were of the irritatingly offensive, adolescent, sex variety.

At the time Gerald was picked up, his mother and father were both at work. No notice that Gerald was being taken into custody was left at the home. No other steps were taken to advise them that their son had, in effect, been arrested. Gerald was taken to the Children's Detention Home. When his mother arrived home at about 6 o'clock, Gerald was not there. Gerald's older brother was sent to look for him at the trailer home of the Lewis family. He apparently learned then that Gerald was in custody. He so informed his mother. The two of them went to the Detention Home. The deputy probation officer, Flagg, who was also superintendent of the Detention Home, told Mrs. Gault "why Jerry was there" and said that a hearing would be held in Juvenile Court at 3 o'clock the following day, June 9.

Officer Flagg filed a petition with the court on the hearing day, June 9, 1964. It was not served on the Gaults. Indeed, none of them saw this petition until the habeas corpus hearing on August 17, 1964. The petition was entirely formal. It made no reference to any factual basis for the judicial action which it initiated. It recited only that "said minor is under the age of eighteen years, and is in need of the protection of this Honorable Court"; (and that) said minor is a "delinquent minor." It prayed for a hearing and an order regarding "the care and custody of said minor." Officer Flagg executed a formal affidavit in support of the petition.

On June 9, Gerald, his mother, his older brother, and Probation Officers Flagg and Henderson appeared before the Juvenile Judge in chambers. Gerald's father was not there. He was at work out of the city. Mrs. Cook, the complainant, was not there. No one was sworn at this hearing. No transcript or recording was made. No memorandum or record of the substance of the proceedings was prepared. Our information about the proceedings and the subsequent hearing on June 15, derives entirely from the testimony of the Juvenile Court Judge, Mr. and Mrs. Gault and Officer Flagg at the habeas corpus proceeding conducted two months later. From this, it appears that at the June 9 hearing Gerald was questioned by the judge about the telephone call. There was conflict as to what he said. His mother recalled that Gerald said he only dialed Mrs. Cook's number and handed the telephone to his friend, Ronald. Officer Flagg recalled that Gerald had admitted making the lewd remarks. Judge McGhee testified that Gerald "admitted making one of these (lewd) statements." At the conclusion of the hearing, the judge said he would "think about it." Gerald was taken back to the Detention Home. He was not sent to his own home with his parents. On June 11 or 12, after having been detained since June 8, Gerald was released and driven home. There is no explanation in the record as to why he was kept in the Detention Home or why he was released. At 5 p.m. on the day of Gerald's release, Mrs. Gault received a note signed by Officer Flagg. It was on plain paper, not letterhead. Its entire text was as follows: "Mrs. Gault: Judge McGHEE has set Monday June 15, 1964 at 11:00 a.m. as the date and time for further Hearings on Gerald's delinquency."

At the appointed time on Monday, June 15, Gerald, his father and mother, Ronald Lewis and his father, and Officers Flagg and Henderson were present before Judge McGhee. Witnesses at the habeas corpus proceeding differed in their recollections of Gerald's testimony at the June 15 hearing. Mr. and Mrs. Gault recalled that Gerald again testified that he had only dialed the number and that the other boy had made the remarks. Officer Flagg agreed that at this hearing Gerald did not admit making the lewd remarks. But Judge McGhee recalled that "there was some admission again of some of the lewd statements. He—he didn't admit any of the more serious lewd statements." Again, the complainant, Mrs. Cook, was not present. Mrs. Gault asked that Mrs. Cook be present "so she could see which boy that done the talking, the dirty talking over the phone." The Juvenile Judge said "she didn't have to be present at that hearing." The judge did not speak to Mrs. Cook or communicate with her at any time. Probation Officer Flagg had talked to her once—over the telephone on June 9.

At this June 15 hearing a "referral report" made by the probation officer was filed with the court, although not disclosed to Gerald or his parents. This listed the charge as "Lewd Phone Calls." At the conclusion of the hearing, the judge committed Gerald as a juvenile delinquent to the State Industrial School "for the period of his minority (that is, until 21), unless sooner discharged by due process of law." An order to that effect was entered. It recites that "after a full hearing and due deliberation the Court finds that said minor is a delinquent child, and that said minor is of the age of 15 years."

No appeal is permitted by Arizona law in juvenile cases. On August 3, 1964, a petition for a writ of habeas corpus was filed with the Supreme Court of Arizona and referred by it to the Superior Court for hearing.

At the habeas corpus hearing on August 17, Judge McGhee was vigorously cross-examined as to the basis for his actions. He testified that he had taken into account the fact that Gerald was on probation. He was asked "under what section of the code you found the boy delinquent?" In substance, he concluded that Gerald came within ARS § 8—201, which specifies that a "delinquent child" includes one "who has violated a law of the state or an ordinance or regulation of a political subdivision thereof." The law which Gerald was found to have violated is ARS § 13--377. This section of the Arizona Criminal Code provides that a person who "in the presence or hearing of any woman or child uses vulgar, abusive or obscene language, is guilty of a misdemeanor." The penalty specified in the Criminal Code, which would apply to an adult, is $5 to $50, or imprisonment for not more than two months. The judge also testified that he acted under ARS § 8--201, which includes in the definition of a "delinquent child" one who, as the judge phrased it, is "habitually involved in immoral matters."

Asked about the basis for his conclusion that Gerald was "habitually involved in immoral matters," the judge testified, somewhat vaguely, that two years earlier, on July 2, 1962, a "referral" was made concerning Gerald, "where the boy had stolen a baseball glove from another boy and lied to the Police Department about it." The judge said there was "no hearing," and "no accusation" relating to this incident, "because of lack of material foundation." But it seems to have remained in his mind as a relevant factor. The judge also testified that Gerald had admitted making other nuisance phone calls in the past which, as the judge recalled the boy's testimony, were "silly calls, or funny calls, or something like that."

We do not in this opinion consider the . . . totality of the relationship of the juvenile and the state. We do not even consider the entire process relating to juvenile "delinquents." For example, we are not here concerned with the procedures or constitutional rights applicable to the pre-judicial stages of the juvenile process, nor do we direct our attention to the post-adjudicative or dispositional process. We consider only the problems presented to us by this case. These relate to the proceedings by which a determination is made as to whether a juvenile is a "delinquent" as a result of alleged misconduct on his part, with the consequence that he may be committed to a state institution. As to these proceedings, there appears to be little current dissent from the proposition that the Due Process Clause has a role to play. The problem is to ascertain the precise impact of the due process requirement upon such proceedings.

From the inception of the juvenile court system, wide differences have been tolerated—indeed insisted upon—between the procedural rights accorded to adults and those of juveniles. In practically all jurisdictions, there are rights granted to adults which are withheld from juveniles. In addition to the specific problems involved in the present case, for example, it has been held that the juvenile is not entitled to bail, to indictment by grand jury, to a public trial or to trial by jury. It is frequent practice that rules governing the arrest and interrogation of adults by the police are not observed in the case of juveniles.

The history and theory underlying this development are well-known, but a recapitulation is necessary for purposes of this opinion. The Juvenile Court movement began in this country at the end of the last century. From the juvenile court statute adopted in Illinois in 1899, the system has spread to every State in the Union. . . .

The early reformers were appalled by adult procedures and penalties, and by the fact that children could be given long prison sentences and mixed in jails with hardened criminals. They were profoundly convinced that society's duty to the child could not be confined by the concept of justice alone. They believed that society's role was not to ascertain whether the child was "guilty" or "innocent," but "What is he, how has he become what he is, and what had best be done in his interest and in the interest of the state to save him from a downward career." The child—essentially good, as they saw it—was to be made "to feel that he is the object of (the state's) care and solicitude," not that he was under arrest or on trial. The rules of criminal procedure were therefore altogether inapplicable. The apparent rigidities, technicalities, and harshness which they observed in both substantive and procedural criminal law were therefore to be discarded. The idea of crime and punishment was to be abandoned. The child was to be "treated" and "rehabilitated" and the procedures, from apprehension through institutionalization, were to be "clinical" rather than punitive.

These results were to be achieved, without coming to conceptual and constitutional grief, by insisting that the proceedings were not adversary, but that the state was proceeding as *parens patriae*. The Latin phrase proved to be a great help to those who sought to rationalize the exclusion of juveniles from the constitutional scheme; but its meaning is murky and its historic credentials are of dubious relevance. The phrase was taken from chancery practice, where, however, it was used to describe the power of the state to act in *loco parentis* for the purpose of protecting the property interests and the person of the child. But there is no trace of the doctrine in the history of criminal jurisprudence. At common law, children under seven were considered incapable of possessing criminal intent. Beyond that age, they were subjected to arrest, trial, and in theory to punishment like adult offenders. In these old days, the state was not deemed to have authority to accord them fewer procedural rights than adults.

The right of the state, as *parens patriae*, to deny to the child procedural rights available to his elders was elaborated by the assertion that a child, unlike an adult, has a right "not to liberty but to custody." He can be made to attorn to his parents, to go to school, etc. If his parents default in effectively performing their custodial functions—that is, if the child is "delinquent"—the state may intervene. In doing so, it does not deprive the child of any rights, because he has none. It merely provides the "custody" to which the child is entitled. On this basis, proceedings involving juveniles were described as "civil" not "criminal" and therefore not subject to the requirements which restrict the state when it seeks to deprive a person of his liberty.

Accordingly, the highest motives and most enlightened impulses led to a peculiar system for juveniles, unknown to our law in any comparable context. The constitutional and theoretical basis for this peculiar system is—to say the least—debatable. And in practice, the results have not been entirely satisfactory. Juvenile Court history has again demonstrated that unbridled discretion, however benevolently motivated, is frequently a poor substitute for principle and procedure. . . . The absence of substantive standards has not necessarily meant that children receive careful, compassionate, individualized treatment. The absence of procedural rules based upon constitutional principle has not always produced fair, efficient, and effective procedures. Departures from established principles of due process have frequently resulted not in enlightened procedure, but in arbitrariness.

Failure to observe the fundamental requirements of due process has resulted in instances, which might have been avoided, of unfairness to individuals and inadequate or inaccurate findings of fact and unfortunate prescriptions of remedy. Due process of law is the primary and indispensable foundation of individual freedom. It is the basic and essential term in the social compact which defines the rights of the individual and delimits the powers which the state may exercise. As Mr. Justice Frankfurter has said: "The history of American freedom is, in no small measure, the history of procedure." But, in addition, the procedural rules which have been fashioned from the generality of due process are our best instruments for the distillation and evaluation of essential facts from the conflicting welter of data that life and our adversary methods present. It is these instruments of due process which enhance the possibility that truth will emerge from the confrontation of opposing versions and conflicting data. "Procedure is to law what 'scientific method' is to science."

It is claimed that juveniles obtain benefits from the special procedures applicable to them which more than offset the disadvantages of denial of the substance of normal due process. As we shall discuss, the observance of due process standards, intelligently and not ruthlessly administered, will not compel the States to abandon or displace any of the substantive benefits of the juvenile process. But it is important, we think, that the claimed benefits of the juvenile process should be candidly appraised. Neither sentiment nor folklore should cause us to shut our eyes, for example, to such startling findings as that reported in an exceptionally reliable study of repeaters or recidivism conducted by the Stanford Research Institute for the President's Commission on Crime in the District of Columbia. This Commission's Report states:

In fiscal 1966, approximately 66 percent of the 16- and 17-year-old juveniles referred to the court by the Youth Aid Division had been before the court previously. In 1965, 56 percent of those in the Receiving Home were repeaters. The SRI study revealed that 61 percent of the sample Juvenile Court referrals in 1965 had been previously referred at least once, and that 42 percent had been referred at least twice before.

Certainly, these figures and the high crime rates among juveniles could not lead us to conclude that the absence of constitutional protections reduces crime, or that the juvenile system, functioning free of constitutional inhibitions as it has largely done, is effective to reduce crime or rehabilitate offenders. We do not mean by this to denigrate the juvenile court process or to suggest that there are not aspects of the juvenile system relating to offenders which are valuable. But the features of the juvenile system which its proponents have asserted are of unique benefit will not be impaired by constitutional domestication. For example, the commendable principles relating to the processing and treatment of juveniles separately from adults are in no way involved or affected by the procedural issues under discussion. Further, we are told that one of the important benefits of the special juvenile court procedures is that they avoid classifying the juvenile as a "criminal." The juvenile offender is now classed as a "delinquent." There is, of course, no reason why this should not continue. It is disconcerting, however, that this term has come to involve only slightly less stigma than the term "criminal" applied to adults. It is also emphasized that in practically all jurisdictions, statutes provide that an adjudication of the child as a delinquent shall not operate as a civil disability or disqualify him for civil service appointment. There is no reason why the application of due process requirements should interfere with such provisions.

Beyond this, it is frequently said that juveniles are protected by the process from disclosure of their deviational behavior. As the Supreme Court of Arizona phrased it in the present case, the summary procedures of Juvenile Courts are sometimes defended by a statement that it is the law's policy "to hide youthful errors from the full gaze of the public and bury them in the graveyard of the forgotten past." This claim of secrecy, however, is more rhetoric than reality. Disclosure of court records is discretionary with the judge in most jurisdictions. Statutory restrictions almost invariably apply only to the court records, and even as to those the evidence is that many courts routinely furnish information to the FBI and the military, and on request to government agencies and even to private employers. Of more importance are police records. In most States the police keep a complete file of juvenile "police contacts" and have complete discretion as to disclosure of juvenile records. Police departments receive requests for information from the FBI and other law-enforcement agencies, the Armed Forces, and social service agencies, and most of them generally comply. Private employers word their application forms to produce information concerning juvenile arrests and court proceedings, and in some jurisdictions information concerning juvenile police contacts is furnished to private employers as well as government agencies.

In any event, there is no reason why, consistently with due process, a State cannot continue if it deems it appropriate, to provide and to improve provision for the confidentiality of records of police contacts and court action relating to juveniles. It is interesting to note, however, that the Arizona Supreme Court used the confidentiality argument as a justification for the type of notice which is here attacked as inadequate for due process purposes. The parents were given merely general notice that their child was charged with "delinquency." No facts were specified. The Arizona court held, however, as we shall discuss, that in addition to this general "notice," the child and his parents must be advised "of the facts involved in the case" no later than the initial hearing by the judge. Obviously, this does not "bury" the word about the child's transgressions. It merely defers the time of disclosure to a point when it is of limited use to the child or his parents in preparing his defense or explanation.

Further, it is urged that the juvenile benefits from informal proceedings in the court. The early conception of the Juvenile Court proceeding was one in which a fatherly judge touched the heart and conscience of the erring youth by talking over his problems, by paternal advice and admonition, and in which, in extreme situations, benevolent and wise institutions of the State provided guidance and help "to save him from downward career." Then, as now, goodwill and compassion were admirably prevalent. But recent studies have, with surprising unanimity, entered sharp dissent as to the validity of this gentle conception. They suggest that the appearance as well as the actuality of fairness, impartiality and orderliness—in short, the essentials of due process—may be a more impressive and more therapeutic attitude so far as the juvenile is concerned. . . . While due process requirements will, in some instances, introduce a degree of order and regularity to Juvenile Court proceedings to determine delinquency, and in contested cases will introduce some elements of the adversary system, nothing will require that the conception of the kindly juvenile judge be replaced by its opposite, nor do we here rule upon the question whether ordinary due process requirements must be observed with respect to hearings to determine the disposition of the delinquent child.

Ultimately, however, we confront the reality of that portion of the Juvenile Court process with which we deal in this case. A boy is charged with misconduct. The boy is committed to an institution where he may be restrained of liberty for years. It is of no constitutional consequence—and of limited practical meaning—that the institution to which he is committed is called an Industrial School. The fact of the matter is that, however euphemistic the title, a "receiving home" or an "industrial school" for juveniles is an institution of confinement in which the child is incarcerated for a greater or lesser time. His world becomes "a building with whitewashed walls, regimented routine and institutional hours." Instead of mother and father and sisters and brothers and friends and classmates, his world is peopled by guards, custodians, state employees, and "delinquents" confined with him for anything from waywardness to rape and homicide.

In view of this, it would be extraordinary if our Constitution did not require the procedural regularity and the exercise of care implied in the phrase "due process." Under our Constitution, the condition of being a boy does not justify a kangaroo court. The traditional ideas of Juvenile Court procedure, indeed, contemplated that time would be available and care would be used to establish precisely what the juvenile did and why he did it—was it a prank of adolescence or a brutal act threatening serious consequences to himself or society unless corrected? Under traditional notions, one would assume that in a case like that of Gerald Gault, where the juvenile appears to have a home, a working mother and father, and an older brother, the Juvenile Judge would have made a careful inquiry and judgment as to the possibility that the boy could be disciplined and dealt with at home, despite his previous transgressions. Indeed, so far as appears in the record before us, except for some conversation with Gerald about his school work and his "wanting to go to Grand Canyon with his father," the points to which the judge directed his attention were little different from those that would be involved in determining any charge of violation of a penal statute. The essential difference between Gerald's case and a normal criminal case is that safeguards available to adults were discarded in Gerald's case. The summary procedure as well as the long commitment was possible because Gerald was 15 years of age instead of over 18.

If Gerald had been over 18, he would not have been subject to Juvenile Court proceedings. For the particular offense immediately involved, the maximum punishment would have been a fine of $5 to $50, or imprisonment in jail for not more than two months. Instead, he was committed to custody for a maximum of six years. If he had been over 18 and had committed an offense to which such a sentence might apply, he would have been entitled to substantial rights under the Constitution of the United States as well as under Arizona's laws and constitution. The United States Constitution would guarantee him rights and protections with respect to arrest, search, and seizure, and pretrial interrogation. It would assure him of specific notice of the charges and adequate time to decide his course of action and to prepare his defense. He would be entitled to clear advice that he could be represented by counsel, and, at least if a felony were involved, the State would be required to provide counsel if his parents were unable to afford it. If the court acted on the basis of his confession, careful procedures would be required to assure its voluntariness. If the case went to trial, confrontation and opportunity for cross-examination would be guaranteed. So wide a gulf between the State's treatment of the adult and of the child requires a bridge sturdier than mere verbiage, and reasons more persuasive than cliché can provide. The rhetoric of the juvenile court movement has developed without any necessarily close correspondence to the realities of court and institutional routines.

We now turn to the specific issues which are presented to us in the present case.

Notice of Charges

. . . We cannot agree that adequate notice was given in this case. Notice, to comply with due process requirements, must be given sufficiently in advance of scheduled court proceedings so that reasonable opportunity to prepare will be afforded, and it must set forth the alleged misconduct with particularity.

Right to Counsel

Appellants charge that the Juvenile Court proceedings were fatally defective because the court did not advise Gerald or his parents of their right to counsel, and proceeded with the hearing, the adjudication of delinquency and the order of commitment in the absence of counsel for the child and his parents or an express waiver of the right thereto. The Supreme Court of Arizona pointed out that "there is disagreement (among the various jurisdictions) as to whether the court must advise the infant that he has a right to counsel." The court argued that "the parent and the probation officer may be relied upon to protect the infant's interests." Accordingly it rejected the proposition that "due process requires that an infant have a right to counsel." It said that juvenile courts have the discretion, but not the duty, to allow such representation; it referred specifically to the situation in which the Juvenile Court discerns conflict between the child and his parents as an instance in which this discretion might be exercised. We do not agree. Probation officers, in the Arizona scheme, are also arresting officers. They initiate proceedings and file petitions which they verify, as here, alleging the delinquency of the child; and they testify, as here, against the child. And here the probation officer was also superintendent of the Detention Home. The probation officer cannot act as counsel for the child. His role in the adjudicatory hearing, by statute and in fact, is as arresting officer and witness against the child. Nor can the judge represent the child. There is no material difference in this respect between adult and juvenile proceedings of the sort here involved. . . . A proceeding where the issue is whether the child will be found to be "delinquent" and subjected to the loss of his liberty for years is comparable in seriousness to a felony prosecution. The juvenile needs the assistance of counsel to cope with problems of law, to make skilled inquiry into the facts, to insist upon regularity of the proceedings, and to ascertain whether he has a defense and to prepare and submit it. The child "requires the guiding hand of counsel at every step in the proceedings against him."

We conclude that the Due Process Clause of the Fourteenth Amendment requires that in respect of proceedings to determine delinquency which may result in commitment to an institution in which the juvenile's freedom is curtailed, the child and his parents must be notified of the child's right to be represented by counsel retained by them, or if they are unable to afford counsel, that counsel will be appointed to represent the child.

Confrontation, Self-Incrimination, Cross-Examination

. . . It would indeed be surprising if the privilege against self-incrimination were available to hardened criminals but not to children. The language of the Fifth Amendment, applicable to the States by operation of the Fourteenth Amendment, is unequivocal and without exception. And the scope of the privilege is comprehensive.

. . . Against the application to juveniles of the right to silence, it is argued that juvenile proceedings are "civil" and not "criminal," and therefore the privilege should not apply. . . .

It would be entirely unrealistic to carve out of the Fifth Amendment all statements by juveniles on the ground that these cannot lead to "criminal" involvement. In the first place, juvenile proceedings to determine "delinquency," which may lead to commitment to a state institution, must be regarded as "criminal" for purposes of the privilege against self-incrimination. To hold otherwise would be to disregard substance because of the feeble enticement of the "civil" label-of-convenience which has been attached to juvenile proceedings. . . .

It is also urged, as the Supreme Court of Arizona here asserted, that the juvenile and presumably his parents should not be advised of the juvenile's right to silence because confession is good for the child as the commencement of the assumed therapy of the juvenile court process, and he should be encouraged to assume an attitude of trust and confidence toward the officials of the juvenile process. This proposition has been subjected to widespread challenge on the basis of current reappraisals of the rhetoric and realities of the handling of juvenile offenders.

In fact, evidence is accumulating that confessions by juveniles do not aid in "individualized treatment," as the court below put it, and that compelling the child to answer questions, without warning or advice as to his right to remain silent, does not serve this or any other good purpose. . . . It seems probable that where children are induced to confess by "paternal" urgings on the part of officials and the confession is then followed by disciplinary action, the child's reaction is likely to be hostile and adverse—the child may well feel that he has been led or tricked into confession and that despite his confession, he is being punished.

We conclude that the constitutional privilege against self-incrimination is applicable in the case of juveniles as it is with respect to adults. We appreciate that special problems may arise with respect to waiver of the privilege by or on behalf of children, and that there may well be some differences in technique—but not in principle—depending upon the age of the child and the presence and competence of parents. The participation of counsel will, of course, assist the police, Juvenile Courts and appellate tribunals in administering the privilege. If counsel was not present for some permissible reason when an admission was obtained, the greatest care must be taken to assure that the admission was voluntary, in the sense not only that it was not coerced or suggested, but also that it was not the product of ignorance of rights or of adolescent fantasy, fright or despair.

The "confession" of Gerald Gault was first obtained by Officer Flagg, out of the presence of Gerald's parents, without counsel and without advising him of his right to silence, as far as appears. The judgment of the Juvenile Court was stated by the judge to be based on Gerald's admissions in court. Neither "admission" was reduced to writing, and, to say the least, the process by which the "admissions," were obtained and received must be characterized as lacking the certainty and order which are required of proceedings of such formidable consequences. Apart from the "admission," there was nothing upon which a judgment or finding might be based. There was no sworn testimony. Mrs. Cook, the complainant, was not present. The Arizona Supreme Court held that "sworn testimony must be required of all witnesses including police officers, probation officers and others who are part of or officially related to the juvenile court structure." We hold that this is not enough. No reason is suggested or appears for a different rule in respect of sworn, testimony in juvenile courts than in adult tribunals. Absent a valid confession adequate to support the determination of the Juvenile Court, confrontation and sworn testimony by witnesses available for cross-examination were essential for a finding of "delinquency" and an order committing Gerald to a state institution for a maximum of six years.

. . . We now hold that, absent a valid confession, a determination of delinquency and an order of commitment to a state institution cannot be sustained in the absence of sworn testimony subjected to the opportunity for cross-examination in accordance with our law and constitutional requirements.

Judgment reversed and cause remanded with directions.

Day-to-Day Practice with Delinquency Cases

Juvenile delinquency is illegal conduct by a minor that would be a crime if committed by an adult. When a minor is suspected of delinquency, police investigate. The minor may be questioned and searched. If the investigation points to the minor, an arrest may follow. Once arrested on a serious matter, the minor is typically taken to the county juvenile detention center. At the detention center, an intake worker—often a probation officer—interviews the minor, considers the police report, and decides whether the minor should be released or detained. Simultaneously, the intake worker and/or a prosecutor decides whether to file formal delinquency charges against the minor. If charges are filed and the minor is detained, the minor must be taken before a juvenile court judge as soon as possible so the judge can rule on the legality of the detention.

Once a minor is charged with delinquency, the minor has the right to an attorney. Because most minors (and their parents) cannot afford to hire private defense attorneys, the judge assigns the public defender's office to represent the minor. The public defender meets with the minor, explains the charges, listens to the minor's side of the story, and helps the minor decide whether to admit or deny guilt. The state is represented by a prosecutor.

Plea bargaining occurs in juvenile court delinquency proceedings, and most minors plead guilty. Only a small percentage of minors deny guilt and insist on a trial, or, as it is called in many states, an adjudicatory hearing. A juvenile court adjudicatory hearing regarding delinquency looks much like the trial of an adult. The minor is represented by counsel. A prosecutor represents the government. Formal rules of evidence and procedure apply. Witnesses are called and cross-examined. The minor has the right to testify but cannot be compelled to do so.

Adults charged with serious crimes have a right under the U.S. Constitution to trial by jury. In juvenile court, however, the U.S. Supreme Court ruled in *McKeiver v. Pennsylvania*[51] that minors accused of delinquency do not have a constitutional right to jury trial. The Supreme Court reasoned that the constitutional right to a jury trial in criminal cases does not apply in juvenile court because delinquency proceedings are civil not criminal.

Since the Supreme Court's 1971 decision in *McKeiver* that the Constitution does not require juries in delinquency cases, there has been a movement across the country to "get tough" on juvenile delinquents. As a result, defense attorneys have renewed the argument that minors accused of delinquency should have the right to trial by jury in juvenile court. In 2008, the Kansas Supreme Court agreed, ruling in *In re L.M.*[52] that Kansas minors accused of delinquency have a constitutional right to a jury. In 2009 the Louisiana Supreme Court rejected the argument that minors accused of delinquency have a constitutional right to a jury trial in juvenile court.[53]

If a minor pleads guilty or is found guilty following an adjudicatory hearing, the judge decides the appropriate disposition. Unlike criminal prosecutions against adults, where the sentencing judge imposes punishment in the

---

51 403 U.S. 528 (1971).

52 186 P.3d 164 (Kan. 2008).

53 In re A.J., 27 So.3d 247 (La. 2009).

form of incarceration, a fine, or, if the defendant is deserving, probation, the juvenile court judge is concerned more about rehabilitation than punishment. The judge, aided by a report from the juvenile probation officer, and input from counsel, fashions a disposition that is intended to turn the young offender away from crime. Most youth are placed on probation and may be ordered to go to school, obey their parents, perform community service, and stay away from bad influences. If the youth has mental health or substance abuse issues, the disposition may include therapy. To the extent it will teach a lesson, punishment is part of disposition in juvenile court. The goal of disposition is individualized intervention to turn the youth away from the negative influences pulling in the direction of crime.

The overarching theory of juvenile court is that youth are malleable. With the right package of individualized services, most youth can be saved from the downward spiral that leads to crime as a career. Sadly, there are times when the theory of the juvenile court gets lost in crowded court dockets, overworked professionals, and underfunded programs. Today's juvenile court is stretched to the breaking point. Yet, few argue that the juvenile court should be abandoned as a failure. Every day, dedicated judges, probation officers, social workers, and attorneys pour their energies into turning kids away from crime. Failure is depressingly common, but success stories abound. Thousands of minors benefit from interaction with the juvenile court.

Status Offenses

As conceived at the beginning of the 20th century, the juvenile court was intended as a refuge for a broad range of children in difficulty. Thus, the court had jurisdiction over delinquent children, abused and neglected children, and children who were simply poor. In addition, the juvenile court had jurisdiction over so-called status offenders. A status offense is conduct by a minor that is not a crime but that nevertheless justifies intervention by the juvenile court. The traditional status offenses include running away from home, truancy, and smoking and drinking under age. In addition, the juvenile court had authority over so-called "ungovernable children"—that is, older children who refused to obey the "reasonable" demands of their parents. A parent at wits' end with their teenager's disobedience could ask a juvenile court judge to assume control of the child and order the child to behave or face the possibility of commitment to a reform school or some other institution.

The extent to which juvenile courts dealt with status offenses varied from place to place. In the closing decades of the 20th century, expert commissions recommended narrowing or eliminating juvenile court authority over status offenses. In particular, experts called for an end to the practice of placing status offenders in the same institutions with delinquents. Congress responded to the experts in 1974 with passage of the Juvenile Justice and Delinquency Prevention Act. This law required states receiving federal funds to stop institutionalizing status offenders in facilities for juvenile delinquents.

Today, juvenile courts in many states retain authority over status offenses. As before, however, the degree of juvenile court involvement with these children varies. In many communities, juvenile courts are so overwhelmed with delinquency and maltreatment cases that little time and few resources are available to help status-offending youth.

Protecting Children from Abuse and Neglect: Dependency Proceedings in Juvenile Court

The juvenile court has authority to intervene in the family to protect children from abuse and neglect. Definitions of abuse and neglect vary slightly from state to state. The following definitions are typical:

Physical abuse is nonaccidental physical injury inflicted on a child by an adult. Physical abuse takes many forms: hitting with hands, fists, or weapons; kicking; burning; poisoning; twisting arms or legs; squeezing; drowning; stabbing; and strangling. Devastating and often fatal brain injuries are inflicted when babies are shaken by frustrated caretakers, resulting in Shaken Baby Syndrome. Much physical abuse results from "corporal punishment" that goes too far.

Sexual abuse is sexual activity between a child and an adult. Sexual abuse also includes sexual activity between a child and an adolescent. Sexual activity includes inappropriate sexual touching, penetration, and use of children in pornography.

Psychological abuse is a pattern of adult behavior that conveys to a child the idea that the child is worthless, unloved, unwanted, or all three. Sexual abuse is essentially psychological abuse. Many physically abused or neglected children are also psychologically abused. Every year, millions of children witness domestic violence. Witnessing domestic violence is a form of neglect.

Neglect occurs when a caretaker deliberately or inadvertently fails to provide a child with essential food, clothing, shelter, medical care, or love. At its core, neglect occurs when the "care" is missing from "caretaker."

Decision to Involve the Juvenile Court

Cases of possible child abuse and neglect come to official attention when reports of suspected maltreatment are received by CPS. Approximately one third of initial reports are screened out because they do not involve maltreatment. For cases that are screened in, CPS workers conduct an investigation. If no maltreatment is detected, the case is closed. On the other hand, if abuse or neglect is substantiated, CPS workers make a series of decisions. How serious is the maltreatment? What is the risk the child will be hurt again? Is it safe to leave the child at home, or must the child be removed and placed with relatives or in a foster home? Can the case be handled safely and effectively without involving juvenile court? In quite a few cases—particularly neglect cases—CPS workers decide juvenile court is not needed, and CPS offers services to alleviate neglect.

The juvenile court is invoked when maltreatment is serious, when the abused or neglected child is at risk, when it is unsafe to leave the child at home, or when maltreating parents increase the risk to the child by refusing to cooperate.

Formal proceedings in juvenile court are commenced by filing a petition. The petition contains a brief description of the facts of the case and an allegation that the child is abused or neglected and in need of the court's protection. A copy of the petition is given to the parents.

Emergency Removal of the Child From Home

One difficult decision CPS workers make is whether to remove a child on an emergency basis from an unsafe home. Often this decision is made in the middle of the night, in chaotic circumstances, and with less than complete information.

CPS agencies have procedures for assessing risk and determining when a child needs to be removed on an emergency basis. In addition to mastering the principles and practice of risk assessment, safety evaluation, and casework, CPS workers need to understand that the Constitution places limits on emergency removal. The Fourteenth Amendment to the Constitution guarantees all citizens due process of law, and the U.S. Supreme Court has interpreted the Fourteenth Amendment to protect parental rights. As The Federal Court of Appeals for the Ninth Circuit put it in *Wallis v. Spencer*,[54] "Parents and children have a well-established constitutional right to live together without governmental interference."

In addition to the Fourteenth Amendment, the Fourth Amendment protects citizens from unreasonable searches and seizures by police and government social workers. Removing a child from parents is a "seizure" for Fourth Amendment purposes. Under the Constitution, CPS may not remove a child from parents unless (1) parents consent to removal or (2) before removal CPS obtains a court order or warrant authorizing removal or (3) absent a court

---

54   202 F.3d 1126, 1136 (9th Cir. 2000).

order or warrant, a genuine emergency exists that necessitates immediate removal to protect the child from serious harm or death. The emergency exception to the requirement of a preremoval warrant is known as the exigent circumstances exception.

When it comes to emergency removal, CPS workers balance the need for child protection against the right of parents to custody of their children free from unwarranted government intrusion. The federal Court of Appeals for the Fifth Circuit discussed the delicate balancing of interests in *Gates v. Texas Department of Protective and Regulatory Services*[55]:

> There is no doubt that child abuse is a heinous crime, and the government's interest in stopping abuse and removing children from abusive situations is paramount. . . . Deciding what is reasonable under the Fourth Amendment will require an assessment of the fact that the courts are dealing with a child who likely resides in the same house, and is under the control of, the alleged abuser. The analysis cannot be divorced from that fact, but that fact does not override all other Fourth Amendment considerations.

> Therefore, we hold that the government may not seize a child from his or her parents absent a court order, parental consent, or exigent circumstances. Exigent circumstances in this context means that, based on the totality of the circumstances, there is reasonable cause to believe that the child is in imminent danger of physical or sexual abuse if he remains in his home. This is a flexible inquiry that considers all of the facts and circumstances with no one factor being dispositive. . . . Whether there was time to obtain a court order is . . . . one factor that informs the reasonableness analysis. . . . Other non-exclusive factors . . . are the nature of the abuse (its severity, duration, and frequency), the strength of the evidence supporting the allegations of abuse, the risk that the parent will flee with the child, the possibility of less extreme solutions to the problem, and any harm to the child that might result from the removal. (p. 429)

On rare occasions, parents whose child was removed sue the removing CPS worker.[56] In such lawsuits, parents claim that removal violated their constitutional rights under the Fourteenth and Fourth Amendments.

---

55 537 F3d 404 (5th Cir. 2008).

56 *See e.g.*, Gates v. Texas Department of Protective and Regulatory Services, 537 F.3d 404 (5th Cir. 2008); Rogers v. County of San Joaquin, 487 F.3d 1288 (9th Cir. 2007); Doe v. Kearney, 329 F3d 1286 (11th Cir. 2003); Tenenbaum v. Williams, 193 F3d 581 (2d Cir. 1999).

When a child is removed in an emergency, the law requires CPS to immediately file a petition in juvenile court. Within a short time—often the next day—a hearing is held before a juvenile court judge (or referee or commissioner). The purpose of the hearing is to determine whether the child should remain in out-of-home care or be returned to the parents. At the hearing—which goes by various names, including detention hearing and initial hearing—the judge informs the parents of the nature of the proceedings, including the specific allegations in the petition.

At the detention hearing, CPS is represented by a government attorney. The judge assigns attorneys for the parents and, in many states, for the child. After listening to the attorneys, the CPS worker, and the parents, the judge decides whether CPS made a reasonable effort to avoid removing the child from the home. Assuming reasonable efforts were made, the judge decides whether to "detain" the child in out-of-home care or return the child to the parents. The detention hearing is often quick—on the order of a few minutes to an hour.

With the detention hearing out of the way, the attorneys get down to the task of resolving the case or preparing for trial, often called an adjudicatory hearing. As is true with all types of litigation, few juvenile court cases go all the way to a contested adjudicatory hearing. Most cases settle. The attorney for CPS negotiates with the attorneys for the parents and the child in the effort to reach a solution that is acceptable to all parties. In cases that settle, the parents acknowledge they need help. The parents, CPS, and the child's attorney agree that the child meets one or more of the definitions of maltreatment. The agreement is presented to the judge, who typically approves the agreement and makes a ruling that the child is subject to the juvenile court's authority. The child is then called a "dependent of the court" or a "child in need of protection."

Once the judge rules that a child is a dependent of the court, the next step is disposition—what is the goal for this child and family? CPS typically prepares a report for the judge outlining the agencies' goals for the family and the services that will be provided to help the parents achieve the goals. In most cases, the goal is reunification of the family.

Adjudication

Cases that do not settle go to contested adjudicatory hearing before a juvenile court judge, referee, or commissioner. In most states, there is no jury in juvenile court. At the adjudicatory hearing, CPS is represented by its attorney. The parents have the right to hire an attorney of their choosing. Most parents, however, cannot afford to hire an attorney, and the judge appoints an attorney to represent the parents.

Does the child need an attorney? The practice in many states until recently was not to appoint attorneys for children in juvenile court dependency proceedings. Rather, the judge appointed a guardian ad litem to look after the child's interests. A guardian ad litem is an individual—not necessarily an attorney—assigned to safeguard a child's interests in litigation. Today the trend is to appoint an attorney for the child. Although there is some disagreement about the proper role for a child's attorney, in most states the attorney conducts an investigation, communicates with the child, and advocates in court for the position the attorney believes is best for the child.

In addition to an attorney for the child, juvenile courts in many states appoint a court-appointed special advocate (CASA) for children in dependency proceedings. CASAs are nonattorney volunteers—college students, retirees, parents, etc.—who are interested in helping abused and neglected children. CASAs receive training about child maltreatment, the child protection system, and juvenile court. Typically, each CASA volunteer is assigned only one or two children. The CASA gets to know the child, and, in most communities, the CASA goes to court when their child's case comes up. Juvenile court judges often place great stock in the opinions of CASA volunteers because it is common for the CASA to know the child better than any of the professionals assigned to the case.

Disposition

If the judge sustains the petition and rules the child was maltreated, the next step is disposition. The judge receives recommendations from CPS, considers the parents' wishes, consults the child if the child is old enough to have a useful opinion, and listens to the attorneys.

If the child can live safely at home, then home placement is the preferred disposition. The judge's dispositional order outlines the services the parents will receive to keep the child safe and reduce the likelihood of further maltreatment. The order may provide that the child receive therapy or other intervention.

If the child cannot live safely at home, the dispositional order provides for the child's placement and approves a plan to work toward family reunification. In some cases of severe maltreatment, there is no realistic hope of reunification, and the disposition is to move expeditiously toward termination of parental rights.

Post-Adjudication Placement and Review

Every year, some half a million children enter America's foster care system. A rural county may have a dozen children in out-of-home care, while a large urban county has thousands. Keeping track of these children and providing services to the children and their families is one of the greatest challenges facing child welfare.

CPS workers have myriad rules and regulations to keep kids from falling through cracks in the foster care system. In tandem with efforts by CPS workers, the juvenile court retains authority over the children it adjudicates and the court holds periodic post-adjudication hearings to review progress. The timing of review hearings varies from state to state, but a common approach is to review progress every 6 months.

To prevent children from languishing in out-of-home care, the federal Adoption and Safe Families Act (ASFA) requires states to consider termination of parental rights for children who have been in foster care 15 of the previous 22 months. ASFA's push toward termination is not required for children in the care of relatives and in cases where termination is not in a child's best interest. ASFA's time limits keep pressure on CPS workers and judges to reunite families or move toward adoption.

Termination of Parental Rights

The law of every state has detailed provisions governing termination of parental rights. The party seeking termination—CPS in juvenile court—has the burden of proof and must establish grounds for termination by clear and convincing evidence. To terminate the parent–child relationship, CPS must establish serious parental fault such as abandonment of the child, mental illness or intellectual disability that is incompatible with minimally adequate parenting, or serious maltreatment that is likely to persist. If fault is established, the judge determines whether termination of parental rights is in the child's best interest.

A judgment terminating parental rights permanently severs the legal parent–child relationship. The "parent" no longer has rights to custody, visitation, or even contact with the child. Severance of the parent–child relationship frees the child for adoption.

The Massachusetts Supreme Judicial Court's decision in *Adoption of Ilona* addresses termination of parental rights.

Adoption of Ilona

Supreme Judicial Court of Massachusetts
944 N.E.2d 115, 459 Mass. 53 (2011)

Gants, J.

The Department of Children and Families (department) filed a petition alleging that Ilona was a child in need of care and protection. After five days of trial, a judge in the Juvenile Court found that Ilona's mother and father were "currently unfit, unable and unavailable to further the welfare and best interest of Ilona" and that their unfitness was "likely to continue into the indefinite future to a near certitude." The judge concluded that Ilona was a child in need of care and protection, and dispensed with the need for her parents' consent to adoption, guardianship, custody, or other disposition of the child pursuant to G.L. c. 119, § 26. The judge ordered that Ilona be committed to the custody of the department, and found that Ilona's best interest would be served by the department's plan of adoption, which proposed that Ilona be adopted by her current foster parents. The judge also found that a significant attachment existed between Ilona and her mother and that continued contact between them was in Ilona's best interest, but declined to enter an order as to the frequency or extent of contact between them, concluding that these decisions were "best left to the informed decisionmaking" of Ilona's preadoptive parents.

The mother makes two arguments on appeal. First, while she does not dispute that she is currently unfit as a parent, she claims that there is a reasonable likelihood her unfitness would be temporary if the department provided her with adequate support services, and that the decision to terminate her parental rights before such services were provided was improper. Second, she claims that the judge abused his discretion in declining to order visitation with Ilona after finding that continued contact between them was in Ilona's best interest.

The Appeals Court concluded that the judge did not err in terminating the mother's parental rights but that he abused his discretion in not ordering visitation with the mother. We granted the applications for further appellate review filed by Ilona and the mother. We agree with the Appeals Court that the judge did not err in terminating the mother's parental rights, but do not agree that, in the circumstances of this case, he abused his discretion in declining to order visitation with the mother and leaving decisions about visitation to the sound judgment of the preadoptive parents.

Ilona was born in 1997 and is the mother's only child; Ilona's father left the mother after she became pregnant and has had no contact with the mother or child. Ilona first came to the department's attention in March and October, 2001, when two reports that the mother had physically abused Ilona were filed, and were found to be supported after investigation. The mother participated in a parenting class in 2000 and 2001, but her physical abuse of Ilona continued.

A third report was filed on December 27, 2006, after the police responded to a 911 telephone call from a neighbor who reported hearing screams and banging on the walls coming from the mother's apartment. When the police arrived, they found nine year old Ilona in shock, with redness and bruising on her face, hips, and arms. Ilona told the police that her mother had hit her with a belt because she did not eat her dinner, and disclosed a history of regular physical abuse by the mother. The mother initially denied physically abusing Ilona, but later admitted she hit her because Ilona had refused to eat her food. As a result of this incident, the mother was charged with assault and battery by means of a dangerous weapon, and assault and battery on a child resulting in injury. After admitting sufficient facts for a finding of guilt as to both charges, the mother was given a continuance without a finding and placed on probation for eighteen months.

The department removed Ilona from her mother's home on the day of the incident, and on December 28, 2006, filed the instant care and protection petition in the Suffolk County Division of the Juvenile Court Department. The department was granted temporary custody of Ilona and placed her that same day in the home of the foster parents who now wish to adopt her and in whose home she continues to reside.

Before the December 27, 2006, incident, the mother had been attending weekly individual sessions with a therapist, which began in November, 2005, and monthly individual sessions with a psychiatrist, which began in May, 2006. She was diagnosed with major depression and a learning disorder, not otherwise specified. Apart from a six-month break in her therapy sessions, these weekly and monthly sessions continued after the incident and through the time of trial.

After the incident, in January, 2007, the department began providing the mother with services intended to improve her parenting skills and teach her alternative forms of discipline. In the first half of 2007, the mother completed a sixteen-week nurturing class that taught parenting skills and techniques, and a twelve-week one-on-one anger management counseling program. Although both programs were conducted in Spanish, representatives of the programs reported that the mother had difficulty understanding the concepts that were taught. The mother did not demonstrate any of the skills or concepts taught in the nurturing class or make any significant change to her parenting as a result of the class. The department also recommended that the mother participate in a

Department of Mental Health day program, which was designed to help with job training and job placement, but the mother declined.

Throughout its temporary custody of Ilona, the department arranged biweekly visits between Ilona and her mother, supervised by a department social worker. The social worker observed that, during most of the visits at the mother's apartment in early 2007, the mother did not initiate any conversation or express any interest in Ilona's life, but instead watched television, cooked, or cleaned. Ilona asked her mother's permission for everything she did during a visit, including using the bathroom and getting food. When the mother prepared food for her, Ilona would eat what she was given but never ask for more, even when she was hungry, because she feared her mother's reaction. The social worker worked with the mother in order to increase her interaction with Ilona and improve her responsiveness to the child during these visits.

By August 14, 2007, the department had changed its goal for Ilona from reunification to adoption. At a permanency hearing held on November 29, 2007, a judge (who was not the trial judge) determined that the department's "efforts to place the child in a timely manner in accordance with the permanency plan for the child, other than reunification, were reasonable."

Two Juvenile Court clinicians issued reports that were considered by the trial judge. In a report dated June 20, 2007, a clinician who had twice interviewed the mother concluded that she had a cognitive impairment, with over-all intellectual ability in the low range. While he did not make a parenting evaluation, he noted that parents with her cognitive limitations "often experience significant difficulty in adequately caring for a child, especially as the child becomes older and the developing needs of the child become more complex."

A second Juvenile Court clinician conducted a parenting evaluation after interviewing the mother twice and observing two visits between the mother and Ilona. In her April 30, 2008, report, she noted that the mother blamed Ilona for disclosing the abuse to the authorities, and had limited insight into her parenting problems and her relationship with Ilona. The clinician noted that, during the visits, there was little conversation between the mother and Ilona, and it appeared they had nothing to talk about. The clinician wrote, "It appears that in addition to being physically abusive, the mother was not able to meet her daughter's emotional needs and nurture her."

When Ilona first arrived at her foster home, she could not read or write, was failing all subjects in school, and displayed significant behavioral problems. The foster mother received services and learned behavioral modification techniques to use with Ilona, and Ilona participated in family therapy with her foster mother. By the time of trial, Ilona's performance in school had vastly improved and she was a "different girl"—polite, affectionate, and happy.

Ilona told social workers that she wanted to be adopted by her foster family, but that she still loves her mother and wants to continue seeing her. Her foster mother, who is "very warm and nurturing," supports continued contact between Ilona and her mother, and would continue to allow such contact as long as it did not hurt Ilona.

In deciding whether to terminate a parent's rights, a judge must determine whether there is clear and convincing evidence that the parent is unfit and, if the parent is unfit, whether the child's best interests will be served by terminating the legal relation between parent and child. Here, the mother does not contest the judge's finding that she is currently unfit, but argues that there is a reasonable likelihood that her unfitness would be temporary if the department fulfilled its obligation to make reasonable efforts to provide her with the necessary services.

Because termination of a parent's rights is an extreme step, a judge must decide both whether the parent is currently unfit and whether, on the basis of credible evidence, there is a reasonable likelihood that the parent's unfitness at the time of trial may be only temporary. A judge may consider evidence that provides a reason to believe that a parent will correct a condition or weakness that currently disables the parent from serving his or her child's best interests. Because childhood is fleeting, a parent's unfitness is not temporary if it is reasonably likely to continue for a prolonged or indeterminate period.

Before seeking to terminate parental rights, the department must make reasonable efforts aimed at restoring the child to the care of the natural parents.

Where a parent, as here, has cognitive or other limitations that affect the receipt of services, the department's duty to make reasonable efforts to preserve the natural family includes a requirement that the department provide services that accommodate the special needs of a parent.

The judge determined that the department's efforts to make it possible for Ilona to return safely to her parent were reasonable, and that the mother's unfitness was likely to continue into the indefinite future to a near certitude.

Nor did the judge clearly err in finding no reasonable likelihood that the mother's unfitness would be temporary, or abuse his discretion in concluding that termination of the mother's parental rights was in Ilona's best interest.

The judge found that a significant attachment existed between Ilona and her mother, and that continued contact is currently in Ilona's best interest. The judge noted the preadoptive mother's willingness to allow visitation between

Ilona and her biological mother, but he did not enter an order requiring visitation, leaving the extent and frequency of contact between them to the "informed decisionmaking" of the preadoptive parents. The Appeals Court concluded that the judge abused his discretion in not ordering visitation after he found that continued contact between Ilona and her mother was in Ilona's best interest.

We have repeatedly recognized the equitable authority of a judge to order visitation between a child and a parent whose parental rights have been terminated, where such visitation is in the child's best interest. A judge may order visitation in the child's best interest in cases where the biological parents' rights are terminated but there is no family waiting to adopt the child, and in appropriate cases where a family is ready to adopt the child on termination of the rights of the biological parents.

In determining whether to exercise the authority to order visitation, a judge must ask two questions: First, is visitation in the child's best interest? Second, in cases where a family is ready to adopt the child, is an order of visitation necessary to protect the child's best interest, or may decisions regarding visitation be left to the judgment of the adoptive family?

As to the first question, a judge should consider, among other factors, whether there is a significant, existing bond with the biological parent whose rights have been terminated. A judge may also take into account whether a preadoptive family has been identified and, if so, whether the child "has formed strong, nurturing bonds" with that family.

Where visitation is in the best interest of the child, a judge must then decide whether an order of visitation is warranted. We have recognized that even where the child's custodian is supportive of visitation with the terminated parent, an order of visitation provides clarity and security to a child who may be worried about the loss of a relationship with the biological parent. However, we have also recognized that, while a judge cannot order visitation unless it is in the child's best interest, the best interest of the child does not by itself answer the question whether an order of visitation should enter.

Adoptive parents have the same protected interest in their relationship with the adoptive child as biological parents, and are entitled to the same presumption they will act in the best interest of the child in making decisions regarding the child, including decisions about visitation. Therefore, once a preadoptive family has been identified, a judge must balance the benefit to the child of an order of visitation that will provide assurance that the child will be able to maintain contact with a biological parent, with the intrusion that an order imposes on the rights of the adoptive parents, who are entitled to the presumption that they will act in their child's best interest. A judge should issue an order of visitation only if such an order, on balance, is necessary to protect the child's best interest.

Here, the judge concluded that there was a significant bond between the child and biological parent and that continued contact between them was in the child's best interests. However, in this case, the judge also found that Ilona had a very warm and nurturing preadoptive mother, and that Ilona was thriving under her care. In addition, the judge found that the preadoptive mother was supportive of continued contact between Ilona and her mother, and would continue to allow such contact unless it began to harm Ilona. There is no reason to question the presumption that Ilona's preadoptive parents will act in her best interest in evaluating—now and in the future—whether continued contact with her mother is in Ilona's best interest; nor is there any compelling reason requiring that a visitation order be entered in order to protect the best interests of the child. The judge therefore did not abuse his discretion in leaving the issue of visitation to the sound judgment of loving adoptive parents who will be in the best position to gauge whether such visits continue to serve Ilona's best interest, rather than issuing a specific visitation order setting forth the frequency and extent of such visits.

Decree affirmed.

Impact of Incarceration on Termination of Parental Rights

The fact that a parent is incarcerated is not sufficient reason to terminate parental rights.[57] That said, lengthy incarceration can be the deciding factor in termination. The Pennsylvania Supreme Court wrote in *Adoption of S.P.*,[58] "We now definitively hold that incarceration, while not a litmus test for termination, can be determinative of the question of whether a parent is incapable of providing essential parental care, comfort or subsistence and the length of the remaining confinement can be considered as highly relevant to whether the conditions and causes of the incapacity, abuse, neglect or refusal cannot or will not be remedied by the parent."

----

57 *See* In re Audrey S., 182 S.W.3d 838, 866 (Tenn. Ct. App. 2005)(parental incarceration is merely a "triggering mechanism that allows the court to take a closer look at the child's situation to determine whether the parental conduct that resulted in incarceration is part of a broader pattern of conduct that renders the parents unfit or poses a risk of substantial harm to the child.").

58 47 A.3d 817 (Pa. 2012).

Foster Care

Foster care is intended to be an interim stop, a short layover on the journey to permanence for children removed from home. Most foster children eventually are reunified with their parents. When reunification is impossible, the journey takes a different turn, often in the direction of adoption—the creation of a new family.

Children who cannot remain safely at home are placed in out-of-home care. The federal government defines foster care broadly to include "24-hour substitute care for children outside their own homes."[59] Under the federal definition, foster care includes children living with relatives, nonrelative foster family homes, group homes, institutions, and preadoptive homes. State definitions of foster care vary.

The number of children in foster care fluctuates over time. Until recently there were few national statistics on foster care, making it difficult to tell how many children were in care at any given point in time. Across the 20th century, approximately 1% of American children were in foster care at any given time. The percentage of poor children in foster care always exceeded 1%.

Today, the foster care population hovers around 500,000. Although a half million children is unacceptably high, it is well to remember that foster children make up a tiny fraction of the total child population. Most children are not abused or neglected, and most who are not in foster care.

African American children are overrepresented in the child welfare system. African Americans make up 15% of the U.S. population but 32% of the foster care population. American Indian and Alaskan Natives represent 1% of the U.S. population but 2% of children in foster care. Whites are 60% of the population but 40% of the foster care population.

In 2006, approximately 289,000 children left foster care. How long did they stay in out-of-home care? Fifteen percent of the children were away from the home less than a month. Thirty-four percent were in care up to 1 year. Nearly a quarter lived in foster care from 1 to 2 years. Twenty-eight percent were in care more than 2 years.

Every year, approximately 20,000 foster children reach age 18, and "age out" of the child welfare system Unfortunately, many of these young people do not

---

59   45 C.F.R. § 57.

fare well. Children who age out of foster care have increased rates of homelessness, incarceration, and mental illness. Some sell drugs to earn money. Others sell their body. In 2005, Courtney and his colleagues described a longitudinal study of former foster youth in Illinois, Iowa, and Wisconsin:

> In summary, youth making the transition from foster care are faring worse than their same-age peers, in many cases much worse, across a number of domains of functioning. They approach the age of majority with significant educational deficits and relatively few of them appear to be on a path that will provide them with the skills necessary to thrive in today's economy. They are less likely to be employed than their peers, and earnings from employment provide few of them with the means to make ends meet. This is reflected in the economic hardships many of them face and the need that many of them have for government assistance. A large number continue to struggle with health and mental health problems. Too many of them have children for whom they cannot provide a home. They are much more likely than their peers to find themselves involved with the criminal justice system.[60]

To help foster youth prepare for adulthood, Congress in 1986 created the Independent Living Program. The program provides federal funds to states to help foster youth achieve independence. In 1999, Congress strengthened the program with the Foster Care Independence Act, including the John H. Chafee Foster Care Independence Program. Under the Chafee program, federal funds allow states to pay educational expenses for foster youth aging out. Additional funds are available to extend Medicaid eligibility to age 21. Money is available to assist former foster youth with housing.

It is important to keep in mind that foster care itself is not responsible for all the difficulties children experience. Berzin compared outcomes for foster youth and similarly situated youth who were not in care. Berzin's findings, "suggest that youth with foster care experience and matched youth do not differ to a statistically significant degree on any of the outcomes measured. This finding differs from the results of previous research, which suggests that many educational and employment outcomes are worse for youth with foster care experience than for other youth. This study does not find such differences. . . . The results challenge the notion that foster care placement is uniquely responsible for nega-

---

60   M.E. Courtney, A. Dworsky, G. Ruth, T. Keller, J. Havicek, & N. Bost, Midwest Evaluation of the Adult Functioning of Former Foster Youth: Outcomes at Age 19. *Chapin Hall Working Paper*, University of Chicago. p. 71 (2005).

tive outcomes. . . . [V]ulnerabilities for foster youth seem to stem from characteristics that existed well before youth's placement in care."[61]

The earliest in-depth research on foster care was Henry Maas and Richard Engler's 1959 classic *Children in Need of Parents*.[62] Maas and Engler studied hundreds of foster children in nine urban and rural communities. Mass and Engler documented that many children live for years in foster care. They wrote:

> Of all the children we studied, better than half of them gave promise of living a major part of their childhood years in foster families- and institutions. Among them were children likely to leave care only when they came of age, often after having had many homes—and none of their own—for ten or so years. Children who move through a series of families or are reared without close and continuing ties to a responsible adult have more than the usual problems in discovering who they are. They are the children who learn to develop shallow roots in relationships with others, who try to please but cannot trust, or who strike out before they can be let down.

Maas and Engler found low rates of adoption from foster care. When adoption did occur, the child was usually a baby. Older children, children with mental or physical handicaps, and children of color were seldom adopted.

Why did so many children languish so long in foster care? Maas and Engler attributed foster care drift to several factors. First, in the 1950s, the law made it difficult to terminate parental rights so children could be freed for adoption. Second, child welfare agencies did not push adoption. Third, agencies received money for children in out-of-home care, creating incentives to keep children in care. Fourth, in many communities, little effort was made to reunify children with parents. Fifth, many agencies didn't know how many children were in care. Sixth, for children of color, discrimination was a roadblock to adoption.

The second classic study of foster care was David Fanshel and Eugene Shinn's 1978 *Children in Foster Care: A Longitudinal Investigation*.[63] In Fanshel and Shinn's study of 624 foster children, 36% were in care more than 5 years. Of children in long-term care, more than half were not visited by their parents.

---

61 S.C. Berzin, Difficulties in the Transition to Adulthood: Using Propensity Scoring to Understand What Makes Foster Youth Vulnerable, 82 *Social Service Review* 171-196, 19-191 (2008).

62 Henry S. Mass & Richard E. Engler, Jr., *Children in Need of Parents* p. 356 (1959).

63 David Fanshel & Eugene B. Shinn, Children in Foster Care: A Longitudinal Investigation (1978).

How did the children in long-term care fare? Contrary to expectations, Fanshel and Shinn did not find that long-term foster care was inevitably harmful. Indeed, when Fanshel and Shinn compared outcomes for children who remained in foster care with outcomes for children who returned to parents, they found

> Continued tenure in foster care is not demonstrably deleterious with respect to IQ change, school performance, or the measures of emotional adjustment we employed. We do not say that the children are in a condition that is always reassuring—but staying in care as opposed to returning home does not seem to compound the difficulties of the children. (p. 491)

Fanshel and Shinn certainly did not advocate long-term foster care for children. Between 25% and 33% of Fanshel and Shinn's foster children showed signs of emotional impairment. Along with other child welfare experts, Fanshel and Shinn urged greater resources to prevent the problems that lead to out-of-home care. Yet, Fanshel and Shinn remind us that for many abused and neglected children, a good foster home is better than a dysfunctional, drug infested, and abusive biological family.

Unfortunately, many children in long-term foster care are moved from home to home. It is hardly surprising that moving children from one home to another can be detrimental. In 2009, Fernandez wrote:

> Research into the relationship between placement disruption and children's psychosocial problems notes that children who experience multiple moves tend to develop elevated emotional and behavioral problems which in turn trigger placement breakdown. Children's vulnerability to the loss of significant attachments is also documented. Repeated moves exacerbate the sense of loss they have experienced through separation from birth parents threatening their evolving sense of security and belonging.[64]

Finding permanent homes for children in foster care means working toward reuniting children with parents or—when reunification is unwise—moving toward adoption, guardianship, or long-term foster care. For most abused or neglected children in out-of-home care, the plan is to work toward reunifying the family. Services are offered to help parents overcome the problems that led to

---

64 E. Fernandez, Children's Wellbeing in Care: Evidence from a Longitudinal Study of Outcomes, 31 Children and Youth Service Review 1092-1100, 1092 (2009).

removal. Unfortunately, following reunification, some children are abused again and returned to foster care.

When efforts to reunify a family fail, social workers seek another stable arrangement for the child, with formal adoption the ideal for many children. The federal Adoption Assistance and Child Welfare Act of 1980 established the goal of reducing the time it takes to move foster children to adoption. In 1997, the federal Adoption and Safe Families Act (ASFA) reinforced this goal. ASFA requires states to seek termination of parental rights for foster children who have been abandoned and for children in foster care for 15 of the most recent 22 months.

Since passage of ASFA in 1997, states have worked to speed adoption. In 2003, Cornelia Ashby wrote, "The annual number of adoptions have increased by 57 percent from the time ASFA was enacted through fiscal year 2000."[65] The Pew Charitable Trusts reported in 2003, "From 1998 to 2002, states placed over 230,000 children in adoptive homes. More children were adopted during this five-year period than the previous 10 years combined."[66]

Guardianship is an increasingly popular option for foster children who cannot return to parents and for whom adoption is unlikely. Often, the guardian is a member of the child's extended family such as a grandparent, aunt, or uncle. Guardianship is a legal relationship established by a judge. A child's guardian receives legal custody of the child, including the decision-making authority normally exercised by parents. Once formal guardianship is established, the child leaves the child welfare system. Guardianship lasts until the child turns 18. The principal advantage of guardianship is that the child has a permanent family. An additional advantage in many cases is that the biological parents can remain part of the child's life because guardianship does not terminate parental rights.

Many family members who are willing to become guardians cannot afford the expense of raising a child. Subsidized guardianship provides an answer. Massachusetts established the first subsidized guardianship program in 1983, and today many states have subsidized guardianship programs.

In the literature on foster care, we seldom hear from children themselves. An early exception was the 1885 Annual Report of the Massachusetts Society for

---

65 Cornelia M. Ashby, Foster Care: States Focusing on Finding Permanent Homes for Children, But Long-Standing Barriers Remain. Testimony before the Subcommittee on Human Resources, Committee on Ways and Means, U.S. House of Representatives (2003).

66 Pew Charitable Trusts, Fostering Results: Nation Doubles Adoptions from Foster Care (2003).

the Prevention of Cruelty to Children. A motherless girl was rescued by the society from a brutal and drunken father. Following her placement in a rural foster home, she wrote the society:

> I had a lovely time last winter, sliding down hill. I went to private school last winter. I have been may-flowering and got some lovely ones. I sent you a box of them, which I hope you received all right. I think I am a happy girl, and would not exchange for anything of my own accord.

Another little girl was removed from an "intemperate mother," who forced the child to sing in saloons. From her foster home in the country, the child wrote:

> I like my place very much. I love Mr. and Mrs. C. and call them papa and mamma. I have been going to school. The teacher is Miss C. and she is very nice. We spelt for headmarks and I got the second prize. I can play "Sweet By and By" and "Yankee Doodle" on the organ, and mamma is learning me the notes. I had a splendid Christmas and New Years. I have four pets; two pigs, a chicken and a calf.

We would hardly expect the Massachusetts Society to publish children's letters longing for parents or complaining about foster care. Some children weren't happy, and unfortunate placements occurred. Child welfare isn't perfect. Yet, these touching letters attest success.

What do today's foster children say about their circumstances? A report on California's foster care system compiled in 2000 provides insights.[67] Foster children were asked a series of questions, including "In what ways has your social worker been helpful to you?" Among children's answers we find a 12-year-old saying, "Every Monday she takes me to the library, she takes me shopping, and she came to my graduation." A 7-year-old said, "She helped me because she came to my school and talked to my teacher." A 10-year-old remarked, "She takes me places. She makes sure I get to see my mom, I have what I need, that I'm happy." An 8-year-old stated, "She helps my mommy learn to take care of us better." A 10-year-old said, "She takes care of things when I have a problem. She plays with me and always answers my questions."

Obviously being away from parents is difficult for children. Foster youth were asked, "Is there anything else that you think I should know about what it's like for children who live separate from their birth mother?" An 11-year old

---

67 A. Fox, K. Frasch & J.D. Berrick, *Listening to Children in Foster Care* (2000).

spoke for many when she said, "It's sad. It's not fun. You cry sometimes. You miss them a lot. You want to be with them every day." A 10-year-old remarked, "It's scary, and you don't know what's gonna happen." One child said simply, "I miss my mom."

When asked what they liked about foster care, a 12-year-old said, "They are taking care of me. They treat us right. They do not beat us." An 8-year old replied, "I have friends. I love my sisters." A 9-year-old's answer was "It has lots of toys and food, and my mom cooks good too." A 13-year-old said, "I like it good. We eat chicken every day. Good house. Clothes on my back." An 8-year-old stated, "My foster mom is the best. She treats me well. When she puts me in the corner I know why. And I like it here a lot." A 13-year-old said, "I feel how it is to have a family that loves you."

Every foster child has a story. Some are happy, some sad. Research tells us that for many foster children the passage into adulthood is stormy. Yet, as we read the quotes from these and other foster children, we see young people who are better off in foster homes than their own homes. We see children who are cared for and in many cases loved by substitute moms and dads. We see children with a future thanks to foster care.

It is sad that some children cannot live safely with their parents. Earlier in our history, such children were indentured or apprenticed. Thousands were consigned to almshouses and orphanages, and thousands lived on the street. Gradually, reformers won the argument that such children deserve something better; they deserve a substitute family, a foster family. The foster care system has faults: Too many children are in care too long, and too many children are shifted from home to home. Despite the problems, we are fortunate that hundreds of thousands of adults open their homes and hearts to abused and neglected children. The great majority of foster parents provide competent, stable homes. Caring for children who have been through so much is stressful, yet foster parents persist and give children the tremendous gift of a "normal" home where a kid can be a kid. Although researchers, policymakers, and legislators must continue efforts to improve foster care, they should devote just as much effort to supporting the existing system. The foster parents, foster children, and professionals in the child welfare system deserve praise and support.

Foster care is not ideal for children. No one doubts that children are better off with loving biological parents than with substitute caretakers. Yet, there are biological parents who parent in name only: parents who are so incompetent, stoned, drunk, perverted, mentally ill, or violent that they cannot or will not provide what children need. Children in such "families" are better off in foster care.

Some people view foster care as a problem rather than a solution. They lament that a half million children live in foster care. This is a legitimate concern, yet we should not lose sight of the fact that for many abused and neglected children, foster care is better than whence they came. Joseph Reid observed long ago: "For thousands of children foster care is preferable to their being in their own homes, for there simply is no own home and no possibility for one. . . . The need for foster care programs cannot be eliminated and communities should not blame themselves for this necessity."[68]

Foster care works well for thousands of children. The goal is not elimination of foster care but reducing the number of children who need such care.

Indian Child Welfare Act (ICWA)

Prior to 1978, as many as 25% to 35% of Native American children were removed from their parents for alleged abuse or neglect. The majority of these children were placed in non-Indian foster homes, adoptive homes, and institutions. In 1974, Congress held hearings on the issue. Calvin Isaac, Chief of the Mississippi Band of Choctaw Indians, testified before Congress:

> One of the most serious failings of the present system is that Indian children are removed from the custody of their natural parents by non-tribal government authorities who have no basis for intelligently evaluating the cultural and social premises underlying Indian home life and childrearing. Many of the individuals who decide the fate of our children are at best ignorant of our cultural values, and at worst contemptuous of the Indian way and convinced that removal usually to a non-Indian household or institution; can only benefit an Indian child.

Congress enacted ICWA in 1978. The law is intended to reduce the number of Native American children inappropriately removed from their homes. Congress reported, "The wholesale separation of Indian children from their families is perhaps the most tragic and destructive aspect of Indian life today." ICWA provides:

§ 1901. Congressional findings

Recognizing the special relationship between the United States and the

---

68 Joseph H. Reid, Next Steps: Action Called For—Recommendations. In H.S. Mass & R.E. Engler, Jr. Children in Need of Parents pp. 378-397, at 388-389 (1959).

Indian tribes and their members and the Federal responsibility to Indian people, the Congress finds—

(1) that clause 3, section 8 article I of the United States Constitution provides that "The Congress shall have Power . . . To regulate Commerce . . . with Indian tribes" and, through this and other constitutional authority, Congress has plenary power over Indian affairs:

(2) that Congress, through statutes, treaties, and the general course of dealing with Indian tribes, has assumed the responsibility for the protection and preservation of Indian tribes and their resources;

(3) that there is no resource that is more vital to the continued existence and integrity of Indian tribes than their children and that the United States has a direct interest, as trustee, in protecting Indian children who are members of or are eligible for membership in an Indian tribe;

(4) that an alarmingly high percentage of Indian families are broken up by the removal, often unwarranted, of their children from them by non-tribal public and private agencies and that an alarmingly high percentage of such children are placed in non-Indian foster and adoptive homes and institutions; and

(5) that the States, exercising their recognized jurisdiction over Indian child custody proceedings through administrative and judicial bodies, have often failed to recognize the essential tribal relations of Indian people and the cultural and social standards prevailing in Indian communities and families.

§ 1902. Congressional declaration of policy

The Congress hereby declares that it is the policy of this Nation to protect the best interests of Indian children and to promote the stability and security of Indian tribes and families by the establishment of minimum Federal standards for the removal of Indian children from their families and the placement of such children in foster or adoptive homes which will reflect the unique values of Indian culture, and by providing for assistance to Indian tribes in the operation of child and family service programs.

§ 1903. Definitions

For the purposes of this chapter, except as may be specifically provided otherwise, the term—

(1) "child custody proceeding" shall mean and include-

> "foster care placement" which shall mean any action removing an Indian child from its parent or Indian custodian for temporary placement in a foster home or institution or the home of a guardian or conservator where the parent or Indian custodian cannot have the child returned upon demand, but where parental rights have not been terminated;

> "termination of parental rights" which shall mean any action resulting in the termination of the parent-child relationship;

> "preadoptive placement" which shall mean the temporary placement of an Indian child in a foster home or institution after the termination of parental rights, but prior to or in lieu of adoptive placement; and

> "adoptive placement" which shall mean the permanent placement of an Indian child for adoption, including any action resulting in a final decree of adoption.

Such term or terms shall not include a placement based upon an act which, if committed by an adult, would be deemed a crime or upon an award, in a divorce proceeding, of custody to one of the parents.

(1) "extended family member" shall be as defined by the law or custom of the Indian child's tribe or, in the absence of such law or custom, shall be a person who has reached the age of eighteen and who is the Indian child's grandparent, aunt or uncle, brother or sister, brother-in-law or sister-in-law, niece or nephew, first or second cousin, or stepparent;

(2) "Indian" means any person who is a member of an Indian tribe, or who is an Alaska Native and a member of a Regional Corporation as defined in section 1606 of Title 43;

(3) "Indian child" means any unmarried person who is under age eighteen and is either (a) a member of an Indian tribe or (b) is eligible for membership in an Indian tribe and is the biological child of a member of an Indian tribe;

(4) "Indian child's tribe" means (a) the Indian tribe in which an Indian child is a member or eligible for membership or (b), in the case of an Indian child who is a member of or eligible for membership in more than one tribe, the Indian tribe with which the Indian child has the more significant contacts;

(5) "Indian custodian" means any Indian person who has legal custody of an Indian child under tribal law or custom or under State law or to whom temporary physical care, custody, and control has been transferred by the parent of such child;

(6) "Indian organization" means any group, association, partnership, corporation, or other legal entity owned or controlled by Indians, or a majority of whose members are Indians;

(7) "Indian tribe" means any Indian tribe, band, nation, or other organized group or community of Indians recognized as eligible for the services provided to Indians by the Secretary because of their status as Indians, including any Alaska Native village as defined in section 1602(c) of Title 43;

(8) "parent" means any biological parent or parents of an Indian child or any Indian person who has lawfully adopted an Indian child, including adoptions under tribal law or custom. It does not include the unwed father where paternity has not been acknowledged or established;

(9) "reservation" means Indian country as defined in section 1151 of Title 18 and any lands, not covered under such section, title to which is either held by the. United States in trust for the benefit of any Indian tribe or individual or held by any Indian tribe or individual subject to a restriction by the United States against alienation;

(10) "Secretary" means the Secretary of the Interior; and

(11) "tribal court" means a court with jurisdiction over child custody proceedings and which is either a Court of Indian Offenses, a court established and operated under the code or custom of an Indian tribe, or any other administrative body of a tribe which is vested with authority over child custody proceedings.

§ 1911. Indian tribe jurisdiction over Indian child custody proceedings

(a) Exclusive jurisdiction

An Indian tribe shall have jurisdiction exclusive as to any State over any child custody proceeding involving an Indian child who resides or is domiciled within the reservation of such tribe, except where such jurisdiction is otherwise vested in the State by existing Federal law. Where an Indian child is a ward of a tribal court, the Indian tribe shall retain exclusive jurisdiction, notwithstanding the residence or domicile of the child.

(b) Transfer of proceedings; declination by tribal court

In any State court proceeding for the foster care placement of, or termination of parental rights to, an Indian child not domiciled or residing within the reservation of the Indian child's tribe, the court, in the absence of good cause to the contrary, shall transfer such proceeding to the jurisdiction of the tribe, absent objection by either parent, upon the petition of either parent or the Indian custodian or the Indian child's tribe: Provided, that such transfer shall be subject to declination by the tribal court of such tribe.

(c) State court proceedings; intervention

In any State court proceeding for the foster care placement of, or termination of parental rights to, an Indian child, the Indian custodian of the child and the Indian child's tribe shall have a right to intervene at any point in the proceeding.

(d) Full faith and credit to public acts, records, and judicial proceedings of Indian tribes

The United States, every State, every territory or possession of the United States, and every Indian tribe shall give full faith and credit to the public acts, records, and judicial proceedings of any Indian tribe applicable to Indian child custody proceedings to the same extent that such entities give full faith and credit to the public acts, records, and judicial proceedings of any other entity.

§ 1912. Pending court proceedings

(a) Notice; time for commencement of proceedings; additional time for preparation

In any involuntary proceeding in a State court, where the court knows or has reason to know that an Indian child is involved, the party seeking the foster care placement of, or termination of parental rights to, an Indian child shall notify the parent or Indian custodian and the Indian child's tribe, by registered mail with return receipt requested, of the pending proceedings and of their right of intervention. If the identity or location of the parent or Indian custodian and the tribe cannot be determined, such notice shall be given to the Secretary in like manner, who shall have fifteen days after receipt to provide the requisite notice to the parent or Indian custodian and the tribe. No foster care placement or termination of parental rights proceeding shall be held until at least ten days after receipt of notice by the parent or Indian custodian and the tribe or the Secretary: Provided, that the parent or Indian custodian or the tribe shall, upon request, be granted up to twenty additional days to prepare for such proceeding.

(b) Appointment of counsel

In any case in which the court determines indigency, the parent or Indian custodian shall have the right to court-appointed counsel in any removal, placement, or termination proceeding. The court may, in its discretion, appoint counsel for the child upon a finding that such appointment is in the best interest of the child. Where State law makes no provision for appointment of counsel in such proceedings, the court shall promptly notify the Secretary upon appointment of counsel, and the Secretary, upon certification of the presiding judge, shall pay reasonable fees and expenses out of funds which may be appropriated pursuant to section 13 of this title.

(c) Examination of reports or other documents

Each party to a foster care placement or termination of parental rights proceeding under State law involving an Indian child shall have the right to examine all reports or other documents filed with the court upon which any decision with respect to such action may be based.

(d) Remedial services and rehabilitative programs; preventive measures

Any party seeking to effect a foster care placement of, or termination of parental rights to, an Indian child under State law shall satisfy the court that active efforts have been made to provide remedial services and rehabilitative programs designed to prevent the breakup of the Indian family and that these efforts have proved unsuccessful.

(e) Foster care placement orders; evidence; determination of damage to child

No foster care placement may be ordered in such proceeding in the absence of a determination, supported by clear and convincing evidence, including testimony of qualified expert witnesses, that the continued custody of the child by the parent or Indian custodian is likely to result in serious emotional or physical damage to the child.

(f) Parental rights termination orders; evidence; determination of damage to child

No termination of parental rights may be ordered in such proceeding in the absence of a determination, supported by evidence beyond a reasonable doubt, including testimony of qualified expert witnesses; that the continued custody of the child by the parent or Indian custodian is likely to result in serious emotional or physical damage to the child.

§ 1913. Parental rights; voluntary termination

(a) Consent; record; certification matters; invalid consents

Where any parent or Indian custodian voluntarily consents to a foster care placement or to termination of parental rights, such consent shall not be valid unless executed in writing and recorded before a judge of a court of competent jurisdiction and accompanied by the presiding judge's certificate that the terms and consequences of the consent were fully explained in detail and were fully understood by the parent or Indian custodian. The court shall also certify that either the parent or Indian custodian fully understood the explanation in English or that it was interpreted into a language that the parent or Indian custodian understood. Any consent given prior to, or within ten days after, birth of the Indian child shall not be valid.

(b) Foster care placement; withdrawal of consent

Any parent or Indian custodian may withdraw consent to a foster care placement under State law at any time and, upon such withdrawal, the child shall be returned to the parent or Indian custodian.

(c) Voluntary termination of parental rights or adoptive placement; withdrawal of Consent; return of custody

In any voluntary proceeding for termination of parental rights to, or adoptive placement of, an Indian child, the consent of the parent may be withdrawn for any reason at any time prior to the entry of a final decree of termination or adoption, as the case may be, and the child shall be returned to the parent.

(d) Collateral attack; vacation of decree and return of custody; limitations

After the entry of a final decree of adoption of an Indian child in any State court, the parent may withdraw consent thereto upon the grounds that consent was obtained through fraud or duress and may petition the court to vacate such decree. Upon a finding that such Consent was obtained through fraud or duress, the court shall vacate such decree and return the child to the parent. No adoption which has been effective for at least two years may be invalidated under the provisions of this subsection unless otherwise permitted under State law.

§ 1914. Petition to court of competent jurisdiction to invalidate action upon showing of certain violations

Any Indian child who is the subject of any action for foster care placement or termination of parental rights under State law, any parent or Indian custodian from whose custody such child was removed, and the Indian child's tribe may petition any court of competent jurisdiction to invalidate such action upon a showing that such action violated any provision of sections 1911, 1912, and 1913 of this title.

§ 1915. Placement of Indian children

(a) Adoptive placements; preferences

In any adoptive placement of an Indian child under State law, a preference shall be given, in the absence of good cause to the contrary, to a placement with (1) a member of the child's extended family; (2) other members of the Indian child's tribe; or (3) other Indian families.

(b) Foster care or preadoptive placements; criteria; preferences

Any child accepted for foster care or preadoptive placement shall be placed in the least restrictive setting which most approximates a family and in which his special needs, if any, may be met. The child shall also be placed within reasonable proximity to his or her home, taking into account any special needs of the child. In any foster care or preadoptive placement, a preference shall be given, in the absence of good cause to the contrary, to a placement with-

(i) a member of the Indian child's extended family;

(ii) a foster home licensed, approved, or specified by the Indian child's tribe;

(iii) an Indian foster home licensed or approved by an authorized non-Indian licensing authority; or

(iv) an institution for children approved by an Indian tribe or operated by an Indian organization which has a program suitable to meet the Indian child's needs.

(c) Tribal resolution for different order of preference; personal preference considered; anonymity in application of preferences

In the case of a placement under subsection (a) or (b) of this section, if the Indian child's tribe shall establish a different order of preference by resolution, the agency or court effecting the placement shall follow such order so long as the placement is the least restrictive setting appropriate to the particular needs of the child, as provided in subsection (b) of this section. Where appropriate, the preference of the Indian child or parent shall be considered: Provided, that where a consenting-parent evidences a desire for anonymity, the court or agency shall give weight to such desire in applying the preferences.

(d) Social and cultural standards applicable

The standards to be applied in meeting the preference requirements of this section shall be the prevailing social and cultural standards of the Indian community in which the parent or extended family resides or with which the parent or extended family members maintain social and cultural ties.

(e) Record of placement; availability

A record of each such placement, under State law, of an Indian child shall be maintained by the State in which the placement was made, evidencing the efforts to comply with the order of preference specified in this section. Such record shall be made available at any time upon the request of the Secretary or the Indian child's tribe.

§ 1916. Return of custody

(a) Petition; best interests of child

Notwithstanding State law to the contrary, whenever a final decree of adoption of an Indian child has been vacated or set aside or the adoptive parents voluntarily consent to the termination of their parental rights to the child, a biological parent or prior Indian custodian may petition for return of custody and the court shall grant such petition unless there is a showing, in a proceeding subject to the provisions of section 1912 of this title, that such return of custody is not in the best interests of the child.

(b) Removal from foster care home; placement procedure

Whenever an Indian child is removed from a foster care home or institution for the purpose of further foster care, preadoptive, or adoptive placement, such placement shall be in accordance with the provisions of this chapter, except in the case where an Indian child is being returned to the parent or Indian custodian from whose custody the child was originally removed.

§ 1917. Tribal affiliation information and other information for protection of rights from tribal relationship; application of subject of adoptive placement; disclosure by court

Upon application by an Indian individual who has reached the age of eighteen and who was the subject of an adoptive placement, the court which entered the final decree shall inform such individual of the tribal affiliation, if any, of the individual's biological parents and provide such other information as may be necessary to protect any rights flowing from the individual's tribal relationship.

§ 1918. Reassumption of jurisdiction over child custody proceedings

(a) Petition; suitable plan; approval by Secretary

Any Indian tribe which became subject to State jurisdiction pursuant to the provisions of the Act of August 15, 1953 (67 Stat. 588), as amended by Title IV of the Act of April 11, 1968 (82 Stat. 73, 78), or pursuant to any other Federal law, may reassume jurisdiction over child custody proceedings. Before any Indian tribe may reassume jurisdiction over Indian child custody proceedings, such tribe shall present to the Secretary for approval a petition to reassume such jurisdiction which includes a suitable plan to exercise such jurisdiction.

(b) Criteria applicable to consideration by Secretary; partial retrocession

(1) In considering the petition and feasibility of the plan of a tribe under subsection (a) of this section, the Secretary may consider, among other things:

(i) whether or not the tribe maintains a membership roll or alternative provision for clearly identifying the persons who will be affected by the reassumption of jurisdiction by the tribe;

(ii) the size of the reservation or former reservation area which will be affected by retrocession and reassumption of jurisdiction by the tribe;

(iii) the population base of the tribe, or distribution of the population in homogeneous communities or geographic areas; and

(iv) the feasibility of the plan in cases of multitribal occupation of a single reservation or geographic area.

(2) In those cases where the Secretary determines that the jurisdictional provisions of section 1911(a) of this title are not feasible, he is authorized to accept partial retrocession which will enable tribes to exercise referral jurisdiction as provided in section 1911(b) of this title, or, where appropriate, will allow them to exercise exclusive jurisdiction as provided in section 1911(a) of this title over limited community or geographic areas without regard for the reservation status of the area affected.

(c) Approval of petition; publication in Federal Register; notice; reassumption period; correction of causes for disapproval

If the Secretary approves any petition under subsection (a) of this section, the Secretary shall publish notice of such approval in the Federal Register and shall notify the affected State or States of such approval. The Indian tribe concerned shall reassume jurisdiction sixty days after publication in the Federal Register of notice of approval. If the Secretary disapproves any petition under subsection (a) of this section, the Secretary shall provide such technical assistance as may be necessary to enable the tribe to correct any deficiency which the Secretary identified as a cause for disapproval.

(e) Pending actions or proceedings unaffected

Assumption of jurisdiction under this section shall not affect any action or proceeding over which a court has already assumed jurisdiction, except as may be provided pursuant to any agreement under section 1919 of this title.

§ 1919. Agreements between States and Indian tribes

(a) Subject coverage

States and Indian tribes are authorized to enter into agreements with each other respecting care and custody of Indian children and jurisdiction over child custody proceedings, including agreements which may provide for orderly transfer of jurisdiction on a case-by-case basis and agreements which provide for concurrent jurisdiction between States and Indian tribes.

(b) Revocation; notice; actions or proceedings unaffected

Such agreements may be revoked by either party upon one hundred and eighty days' written notice to the other party. Such revocation shall not affect any action or proceeding over which a court has already assumed jurisdiction, unless the agreement provides otherwise.

§ 1920. Improper removal of child from custody; declination of jurisdiction; forthwith return of child: danger exception

Where any petitioner in an Indian child custody proceeding before a State court has improperly removed the child from custody of the parent or Indian custodian or has improperly retained custody after a visit or other temporary relinquishment of custody, the court shall decline jurisdiction over such petition and shall forthwith return the child to his parent or Indian custodian unless returning the child to his parent or custodian would subject the child to a substantial and immediate danger or threat of such danger.

§ 1921. Higher State or Federal standard applicable to protect rights of parent or Indian custodian of Indian child

In any case where State or Federal law applicable to a child custody proceeding under State or Federal law provides a higher standard of protection to the rights of the parent or Indian custodian of an Indian child than the rights provided under this subchapter, the State or Federal court shall apply the State or Federal standard.

§ 1922. Emergency removal or placement of child; termination appropriate action

Nothing in this subchapter shall be construed to prevent the emergency removal of an Indian child who is a resident of or is domiciled on a reservation, but temporarily located off the reservation, from his parent or Indian custodian or the emergency placement of such child in a foster home or institution, under applicable State law, in order to prevent imminent physical damage or harm to the child. The State authority, official, or agency involved shall insure that the emergency removal or placement terminates immediately when such removal or placement is no longer necessary to prevent imminent physical damage or harm to the child and shall expeditiously initiate a child custody proceeding subject to the provisions of this subchapter, transfer the child to the jurisdiction of the appropriate Indian tribe, or restore the child to the parent or Indian custodian, as may be appropriate.

ICWA provides that only tribal courts can decide abuse and neglect cases involving Native American children whose permanent home is a reservation, although state juvenile courts can make emergency orders to protect Indian children found off the reservation. For children who do not live on a reservation, state juvenile courts can make decisions about removal from parents, but the child's tribe must be notified, and the tribe has the right to join in the juvenile court proceedings.

A state court judge cannot place a Native American child in foster care unless the need for out-of-home care is established by clear and convincing evidence and is supported by expert testimony.

When a Native American child is removed from parental custody, ICWA requires efforts to place the child with the child's extended family or with foster or adoptive parents approved by the child's tribe. Active efforts must be "made to provide remedial services and rehabilitative programs designed to prevent the breakup of the Indian family."[69]

The Montana Supreme Court's decision in *Matter of J.W.C.* illustrates ICWA at work.

Matter of J.W.C.

Supreme Court of Montana
363 Mont. 85, 265 P.3d 1265 (2011)

Cotter, J.

The mother of four Indian children appeals from the order of the Thirteenth Judicial District Court, Yellowstone County, Montana, terminating her parental rights to J.W.C., L.W.C., K.W.C., and C.W.C. (children). S.W.C. (Mother) had moved to transfer the case to the Fort Peck Tribal Court, as allowed under the Indian Child Welfare Act (ICWA). 25 U.S.C. § 1911(b). However, the case was never transferred. The District Court maintained jurisdiction, terminated Mother's and C.W.C.'s (Father) parental rights, and denied Mother's request to continue the termination hearing and appoint counsel for the children.

Mother appeals. She argues that the District Court failed to comply with the jurisdictional ICWA transfer requirements because the Tribal Court should have had jurisdiction over the proceedings upon her petition to transfer jurisdiction....

Mother, Father, and their four children are members of the Fort Peck Assiniboine and Sioux Tribes (Tribes). In August 2009, the four children were between the ages of one and nine years old. Father was incarcerated and Mother could not provide food or shelter for the children. Mother voluntarily placed the children in foster care on August 26, 2009, and they were all returned to Mother's care by August 31, 2009, when she was able to secure temporary housing for herself and the children at the Gateway House in Billings. They resided there until September 3, 2009, when Mother was taken to an emergency room for reportedly taking pills and making suicidal threats. Mother was then arrested on an existing warrant and banned from returning to the Gateway House for six to twelve months due to drug paraphernalia found in her room. The children were returned to foster care.

Later that month, the Department's Child and Family Services Division

---

69 25 U.S.C. § 1912.

filed a petition in the Thirteenth Judicial District Court for emergency protective services, adjudication as youths in need of care (YINC), and temporary legal custody for the four children. As required by ICWA, notice of the involuntary child custody proceedings was sent to the Tribes. 25 U.S.C. § 1912(a). On September 9, 2009, the District Court appointed one attorney to be both the guardian ad litem (GAL) and legal counsel for the children, and ordered the assignment of counsel to Mother and Father. The District Court granted emergency protective services for the children and set a show cause hearing. In March 2010, the Tribes filed a Notice of Appearance and Intervention to assist the court in its deliberations and reserve its right to move for a transfer of jurisdiction if necessary. The court granted the Tribes' motion to appear at the hearings telephonically.

On May 6, 2010, Mother moved to transfer the cases to the Fort Peck Assiniboine and Sioux Tribal Court, as allowed under 25 U.S.C. § 1911(b), and neither Father nor the GAL objected. The Tribes advised the District Court that they were seriously considering a transfer of jurisdiction, but they needed more time to make an informed decision. The GAL argued that a delay was not in the best interests of the children, and the District Court, while recognizing this, allowed the Tribes an additional six weeks to file the motion. The Tribes did not file documents for a jurisdictional transfer within the six weeks, so the District Court granted the Department's request to vacate further consideration of the transfer. The District Court acknowledged that the Tribes could still file a motion with the District Court for transfer but noted the Tribes did not seem interested in taking jurisdiction at that point.

At a hearing on June 17, 2010, all parties except Mother stipulated that the alleged facts were sufficient for the District Court to find that the children had been abused, neglected, or abandoned, that the children were YINC, and that the Department should be given temporary legal custody of the children. Mother was not present at the hearing. Mother had disappeared after being released from custody on other charges, and she failed to maintain contact with anyone. Mother's counsel was present and did not object to the stipulation.

The following month, the District Court found that the children had been exposed to physical neglect, and consequently adjudicated them as YINC, granted the Department temporary legal custody, and ordered a treatment plan for Mother. Again, Mother's attorney did not object. Mother was assigned new counsel in August 2010 but her counsel was unable to contact her. Though the Department attempted to work with Mother and Father towards reunification, the lack of contact with Mother and her absence from hearings, her lack of visitation with the children, and her inability to finish the treatment plan led the Department to work toward termination of parental rights. Moreover, neither

Mother nor Father appeared for the subsequent permanency hearing in October.

At the termination hearing on February 24, 2011, the GAL recommended terminating Mother's and Father's parental rights. Counsel for Mother requested a continuance of the hearing so counsel could be appointed for the children, and the District Court denied the motion, reasoning that Mother had numerous previous opportunities to request counsel for the children, and she had not done so. Additionally, in order to expedite the process for the sake of the children, the court stated it would assume the children wished to be returned to their parents, as the GAL reported that the three older children had expressed that preference and the youngest one was too young to express a preference. The ICWA director for the Tribes testified that the current foster care placements of the children complied with ICWA. She further testified that though the Tribes had made an affirmative decision about transferring the case to tribal jurisdiction, the necessary paperwork had not been done. Again, neither Mother nor Father was present for the hearing.

The District Court concluded that the children had been adjudicated as YINC, the treatment plan for Mother was appropriate, Mother failed to complete the required treatment plan, and Mother's unfitness was unlikely to change within a reasonable time. The court awarded the Department permanent legal custody after determining that termination was in the best interests of the children.

Mother appealed. The cases of the four children were consolidated, and this Court appointed independent appellate counsel for the children.

On appeal, Mother argues that the District Court should have transferred the case to the Tribal Court upon her motion, and it committed jurisdictional error when it did not do so. The State argues that the Tribes were on actual notice of all the state court proceedings, as required by ICWA's notice provisions, and declined the jurisdictional transfer by failing to request a transfer. Further, the State asserts that Mother "anticipated that a tribal court order accepting jurisdiction would be a prerequisite for the transfer of jurisdiction to the Tribes." While ICWA provides for concurrent jurisdiction between state and tribal courts, we conclude that the District Court should have transferred jurisdiction to the Tribal Court, or determined after a hearing that there was good cause not to do so.

The policy of ICWA is "to protect the best interests of Indian children and to promote the stability and security of Indian tribes and families by the establishment of minimum Federal standards for the removal of Indian children from their families and the placement of such children in foster or adoptive homes which will reflect the unique values of Indian culture." 25 U.S.C. § 1902.

An "Indian child," as defined by 25 U.S.C. § 1903(4), is "any unmarried person who is under age eighteen and is either (a) a member of an Indian tribe or (b) is eligible for membership in an Indian tribe and is the biological child of a member of an Indian tribe." It is undisputed that the children are Indian children under this definition.

Jurisdiction over Indian child custody proceedings is at the heart of ICWA. *Miss. Band of Choctaw Indians v. Holyfield*, 490 U.S. 30, 36, 109 S.Ct. 1597, 1601 (1989). Specifically, ICWA provides:

(a) Exclusive jurisdiction. An Indian tribe shall have jurisdiction exclusive as to any State over any child custody proceeding involving an Indian child who resides or is domiciled within the reservation of such tribe, except where such jurisdiction is otherwise vested in the State by existing Federal law. Where an Indian child is a ward of a tribal court, the Indian tribe shall retain exclusive jurisdiction, notwithstanding the residence or domicile of the child.

(b) Transfer of proceedings; declination by tribal court. In any State court proceeding for the foster care placement of, or termination of parental rights to, an Indian child not domiciled or residing within the reservation of the Indian child's tribe, the court, in the absence of good cause to the contrary, shall transfer such proceeding to the jurisdiction of the tribe, absent objection by either parent, upon the petition of either parent or the Indian custodian or the Indian child's tribe: Provided, that such transfer shall be subject to declination by the tribal court of such tribe.

(c) State court proceedings; intervention. In any State court proceeding for the foster care placement of, or termination of parental rights to, an Indian child, the Indian custodian of the child and the Indian child's tribe shall have a right to intervene at any point in the proceeding. 25 U.S.C. § 1911(a)-(c).

Since the case at hand involves Indian children apparently residing in Billings, not on the Tribes' reservation, we apply 25 U.S.C. § 1911(b) to these proceedings. Therefore, upon petition of a parent, the custodian, or the tribe, and unless good cause to the contrary is shown, a parent objects, or the tribal court declines the transfer, the proceedings must be transferred to the jurisdiction of the tribe. 25 U.S.C. § 1911(b). This section creates concurrent but presumptively tribal jurisdiction in the case of children not domiciled on the reservation. Consequently, the extraterritorial jurisdiction of the tribe created by ICWA must first be adjudicated in a transfer hearing before a request for the transfer of jurisdiction can be granted or denied.

We look to the guidelines promulgated by the Bureau of Indian Affairs in 1979 to help state courts interpret and apply ICWA. [hereinafter Guidelines]. This Court has previously determined that these Guidelines are persuasive and that we will apply them when interpreting ICWA.

The Guidelines' commentary regarding petitions for jurisdictional transfers to tribal court states: "Although ICWA does not explicitly require transfer petitions to be timely, it does authorize the court to refuse to transfer a case for good cause. When a party who could have petitioned earlier waits until the case is almost complete to ask that it be transferred to another court and retried, good cause exists to deny the request." Guidelines, C.1. Commentary, 44 Fed. Reg. at 67590.

The Guidelines for ruling on 25 U.S.C. § 1911(b) transfer petitions state:

(a) Upon receipt of a petition to transfer by a parent, Indian custodian or the Indian child's tribe, the court *must* transfer unless either parent objects to such transfer, the tribal court declines jurisdiction, or the court determines that good cause to the contrary exists for denying the transfer.

(b) If the court believes or any party asserts that good cause to the contrary exists, the reasons for such belief or assertion shall be stated in writing and made available to the parties who are petitioning for transfer. The petitioners shall have the opportunity to provide the court with their views on whether or not good cause to deny transfer exists. Guidelines, C.2. Criteria and Procedures for Ruling on 25 U.S.C. § 1911(b) Transfer Petitions, 44 Fed.Reg. at 67590–91 (emphasis added).

Regarding a tribal court's declination of transfer, the Guidelines state:

(a) A tribal court to which transfer is requested may decline to accept such transfer.

(b) Upon receipt of a transfer petition the state court shall notify the tribal court in writing of the proposed transfer. The notice shall state how long the tribal court has to make its decision. The tribal court shall have at least twenty days from the receipt of notice of a proposed transfer to decide whether to decline the transfer. The tribal court may inform the state court of its decision to decline either orally or in writing. Guidelines, C.4. Tribal Court Declination of Transfer, subsections (a)-(c), 44 Fed.Reg. at 67592 (emphasis added).

. . . An important distinction we recognize is the difference between "Indian tribe" and "tribal court." They are separate entities, and are separately defined by ICWA. 25 U.S.C. § 1903(8), (12). "'Indian tribe' means any Indian tribe, band, nation, or other organized group or community of Indians recognized as eligible for the services provided to Indians by the Secretary because of their status as Indians." 25 U.S.C. § 1903(8). "'Tribal court' means a court with jurisdiction over child custody proceedings and which is either a Court of Indian Offenses, a court established and operated under the code or custom of an Indian tribe, or any other administrative body of a tribe which is vested with authority over child custody proceedings." 25 U.S.C. § 1903(12). . . . It is the *tribe* which has the right to intervene under 25 U.S.C. § 1911(c), and it is the tribal *court* which must decline to exercise jurisdiction over a case transferred to it under § 1911(b). Under the clear language of § 1911(b) and as explained in the Guidelines, the district court, upon petition of either parent, *shall* transfer the proceeding to the jurisdiction of the tribe, absent circumstances not present here. If the tribal court decides not to accept jurisdiction, it is incumbent on the tribal court to affirmatively decline the transfer. It is the tribal court, and not the Tribes, which must decline the transfer of jurisdiction in order for the state court to thereafter proceed. Because the Tribal Court did not affirmatively decline to receive this case, it remains ripe for transfer from the District Court to the Tribal Court.

The guidelines indicate that once a state court is asked to transfer jurisdiction, the court has an obligation to ascertain whether the tribal court is declining jurisdiction. The circuit court must first ascertain whether the tribal court will accept jurisdiction. If the tribal court indicates that it will accept jurisdiction, then the circuit court must transfer jurisdiction unless it determines that good cause exists for denying the transfer. The trial court therefore must transfer the case to tribal court unless it either obtains a declination of jurisdiction from the tribal court or makes a finding that good cause exists not to transfer the case to the tribal court.

For a jurisdictional transfer to be precluded for good cause, the State must provide clear and convincing evidence that the best interests of the child would be injured by such a transfer. In the case at hand, the issue of good cause was never reached, so we need not further address this exception.

We conclude that the District Court misinterpreted the ICWA requirement to require an affirmative acceptance of the transfer by the Tribes. Instead, an affirmative declination of the transfer by the *Tribal Court* was required, and this did not occur. Mother petitioned for a transfer early in the proceedings, no one objected to Mother's petition, and the State did not argue good cause existed so as to preclude the transfer to the Tribal Court. The Guidelines provide that "upon receipt of a transfer petition the state court shall notify the tribal court in writing of the proposed transfer" and the tribal court then has at least twenty days to decide whether to accept or decline the transfer. Guidelines, C.4. Tribal

Court Declination of Transfer, subsection (b), 44 Fed.Reg. at 67592. However, the state court notified the Tribes, not the Tribal Court, and as we have already stated, these are separate entities. We therefore conclude that under the clear language of 25 U.S.C. § 1911 and the Guidelines, the District Court was obligated to obtain a declination of jurisdiction from the Tribal Court, or make a finding that good cause existed not to transfer the case to the Tribal Court. Because neither course of action was taken, we must reverse and remand in order that the requisites of ICWA may be met.

Finally, the District Court must hold a jurisdictional transfer hearing before it can grant or deny a request for a jurisdictional transfer of Indian children to tribal custody. Mother filed her motion to transfer jurisdiction to the Tribal Court on May 6, 2010, and all parties were willing to transfer the case at that time. However, the State changed its position by the June 17 hearing and sought to vacate the transfer of jurisdiction hearing portion of the case. While Mother argues that these two hearings were sufficient to satisfy the procedural requirement of holding a transfer hearing and that a new transfer hearing is unnecessary, we decline to make that determination.

We therefore reverse the District Court's conclusion as to the jurisdictional ICWA transfer requirements and remand so that jurisdiction may properly be determined according to our findings and a transfer hearing may be held. . . .

For the foregoing reasons, we reverse and remand for further proceedings consistent with this Opinion.

———————

The impact of ICWA on adoption is addressed in the Kansas Supreme Court's decision in *Matter of T.S.W.*

Matter of T. S. W.

Supreme Court of Kansas
276 P.3d 133 (2012)

The opinion of the court was delivered by Moritz, J.:

Cherokee Nation, Intervenor, challenges the district court's decision under the Indian Child Welfare Act (ICWA), 25 U.S.C. § 1901 et seq., to deviate from ICWA's placement preferences, *see* 25 U.S.C. § 1915(a), based upon the biological non-Indian mother's preference that her child be placed with a non-Indian family. Because we conclude that absent a request for anonymity by a biological parent, a parent's placement preference cannot override ICWA's placement factors, we reverse the district court's determination.

D.R.W. (Mother) gave birth to T.S.W. on September 14, 2009. Approximately 2 months before T.S.W.'s birth, Mother decided to place her child for adoption. She contacted Adoption Centre of Kansas, Inc. (the Agency) to assist her in that process, and she identified two possible fathers of her child, one of whom was J.A.L.

In early August 2009, J.A.L.'s mother notified the Agency that J.A.L. was a member of Cherokee Nation (the Tribe). Because of the child's potential eligibility for membership in the Tribe, the Agency requested that the Tribe provide profiles of potential adoptive families.

In early September, employees of the Agency exchanged several e-mails with employees of the Tribe. In these e-mails, the Agency advised that because the Tribe had no families that could pay the Agency's $27,500 flat fee, the Agency wished to place Mother's child with one of its own families. However, the Agency expressed concern that the Tribe might seek to remove the child at a later time. The Agency also pointed out that Mother had her own criteria for any adoptive family, including that the couple be Caucasian, childless, financially secure, and open to postadoption visitation.

The Tribe responded that it had identified several certified families that could meet Mother's adoption criteria but that it had no families capable of paying the Agency's $27,500 fee. The Tribe also pointed out that "agency fees are not a reason to deviate from federal law."

Eventually, on September 9, 2009, the Agency's counsel, through an e-mail sent by an Agency employee, advised the Tribe that Mother would consider family profiles that met Mother's "criteria" and the Agency would "base fees and cost on an appropriate sliding scale." However, the Agency's counsel noted that the Agency's fees and costs could not be calculated absent information as to the prospective adoptive family's overall financial condition. The following day, September 10, 2009, the Tribe sent profiles of two potential adoptive families to the Agency.

Mother gave birth to T.S.W. on September 14, 2009. On September 15, 2009, the Agency filed a petition in district court seeking to terminate the parental rights of the two potential biological fathers. The petition specifically noted: "Subsequent to this petition for termination of parental rights, a petition for the adoption of the subject minor child will be filed."

After court-ordered paternity testing conclusively determined that J.A.L. (Father) was T.S.W.'s biological father, the Agency filed an amended petition on October 1, 2009, seeking termination of Father's parental rights. Also on October 1, 2009, the court granted temporary custody of T.S.W. to the Agency.

Father filed a handwritten objection to the petition, noting that although he was in jail, his mother was willing to raise T.S.W. However, the Agency did not contact any of Father's family members regarding T.S.W.'s placement because Mother did not want T.S.W. to be placed with Father's family.

Meanwhile, the Agency had not communicated with the Tribe regarding the Indian family profiles provided by the Tribe. Consequently, on September 28, 2009, the Tribe requested an update from the Agency on T.S.W.'s placement. On September 30, 2009, the Agency responded that T.S.W. had been born on September 14, 2009; that paternity testing had confirmed that J.A.L. was T.S.W.'s biological father; that J.A.L. planned to contest the adoption; and that Mother had selected one of the two families provided by the Tribe as a possible adoptive family for T.S.W.

Based on T.S.W.'s status as an Indian child, on October 21, 2009, the Tribe moved to intervene in the action to terminate Father's parental rights. The record on appeal contains no ruling on this motion. Nevertheless, on November 5, 2009, the Tribe filed both an answer to the Agency's amended petition to terminate parental rights and a counter-petition requesting application of ICWA to the proceedings.

By November 2, 2009, both of the families proposed by the Tribe had withdrawn from consideration as potential adoptive families for T.S.W. . . . .

In any event, upon learning of the unavailability of these families, the Agency requested that the Tribe provide profiles of other available adoptive families. But before the Tribe could do so, the Agency reviewed with Mother the profiles of several of its own families. From these profiles, Mother chose a non-Indian family to adopt T.S.W.

Apparently unaware that Mother had selected a non-Indian family, on November 9, 2009, the Tribe provided the Agency with an additional 17 to 20 Indian family profiles. Mother reviewed those profiles, but according to an Agency employee, Mother did not prefer any of the Indian families over the non-Indian family she had already selected. Mother later testified that had she not been permitted to place T.S.W. with the family of her choice, she would have withdrawn her consent to T.S.W.'s adoption.

Meanwhile, on November 18, 2009, the Agency filed a pleading entitled "Petition" seeking to deviate from ICWA's placement preferences in the pending action to terminate Father's parental rights. Although to this point no adoption proceeding had been filed, the Agency recited that it sought to deviate from ICWA's placement preferences. The pleading did not indicate whether the Agency sought to deviate from ICWA's temporary or adoptive placement preferences, nor did it indicate whether an adoption petition had been filed or was forthcoming. Further, although the "petition" mentioned ICWA, it contained no statutory reference to the Act, nor did it identify or discuss ICWA's placement preferences.

The docket sheet indicates the district court conducted a temporary placement hearing on December 4, 2009, although the transcript of the hearing is not included in the record on appeal. The hearing apparently resulted in T.S.W.'s prospective adoptive placement with the non-Indian family selected by Mother. It is unclear from the record whether the district court considered if good cause existed to deviate from ICWA's foster care and preadoptive placement preferences under 25 U.S.C. § 1915(b) before issuing a temporary placement order.

The record on appeal contains a pretrial order filed on January 12, 2010, reflecting a pretrial conference held on December 29, 2009. The pretrial order identifies the "Nature of hearing" as a "Termination of Parental Rights."

Also on January 12, 2010, the district court conducted a hearing on the Agency's petition to terminate Father's parental rights. Again, although the record on appeal contains no transcript of the hearing, it appears that at the conclusion of the hearing, the district court ruled from the bench, terminating Father's parental rights. However, the district court did not issue a written order terminating Father's parental rights until March 11, 2010.

On January 26 and 27, 2010, the district court conducted a hearing on the Agency's petition to deviate from ICWA's placement preferences. At the close of the hearing, the district court orally ruled from the bench, deviating from ICWA's placement preferences based primarily upon Mother's desire that the child be placed with the adoptive couple she had chosen and Mother's threat to withdraw her consent to the adoption if her choice was not approved.

At the close of the hearing, the district court asked the Agency's counsel to draft and circulate a journal entry memorializing the court's finding within 10 days and indicated that if the parties did not sign the journal entry within 4 days after circulation, the court would sign the journal entry without signatures. The court stated: "I wanna make sure that this case keeps moving and it's not sitting around for a couple of months waiting for the journal entry."

However, the journal entry formalizing the district court's decision was not filed until more than 2 months later, on April 15, 2010. In the meantime, as discussed below, counsel for the Agency in this case apparently filed a separate adoption proceeding in district court. In that separate proceeding, counsel represented the adoptive parents chosen by Mother and, without notice to the Tribe, obtained a final decree of adoption of T.S.W.

In its April 15, 2010, journal entry, the district court found good cause existed to deviate from ICWA. Like the "petition" for deviation filed by the Agency, the journal entry contains neither a statutory reference to ICWA nor a description of ICWA's placement preferences. Further, the journal entry does not specify whether the deviation is for temporary or adoptive placement. Nevertheless, in the journal entry the district court held: "Birth parents can revoke their consent at any time for any reason; and the birth Mother has final say." Further, the district court conclusively stated that the "birth mother's preference is good cause under ICWA to deviate from the prescribed placement preferences."

The Tribe appealed the district court's April 15, 2010, order granting a deviation from ICWA's placement preferences. The appeal was transferred from the Court of Appeals to this court . . . .

Prior to oral argument, this court issued a show cause order advising the parties that the record contained insufficient information for the court to verify its jurisdiction to hear the appeal. Specifically, the court noted the record contained no petition for adoption or final adoption decree, and the court directed the parties to address the finality of the order appealed from under K.S.A. 2011 Supp. 59–2401a(a)(1).

In response to the show cause order, the Tribe pointed out that the district court's journal entry finding good cause to deviate from ICWA's placement preferences was the final docket entry in the district court, other than appeal-related filings. The Tribe also noted that while the Agency had advised the Tribe that T.S.W. was adopted "a long time ago," the Tribe received no notice of the adoption and assumed it occurred "under a different case number." Finally, the Tribe advised that it had requested that the Agency provide confirmation of T.S.W.'s final adoption, but the Agency had not responded to its request.

In its "Response to Show Cause Order and Motion to Dismiss Appeal," the Agency argued this appeal should be dismissed for lack of jurisdiction because the Tribe did not appeal the termination of Father's parental rights and because the court's decision regarding placement deviation was not an appealable order under K.S.A. 59–2401 or K.S.A. 60–2102. However, the Agency's response did not address whether a separate adoption proceeding had been filed or a final adoption decree issued.

Nevertheless, during oral argument in this appeal, counsel for the Agency conceded that prior to the expiration of the appeal time in this action, he filed a petition to adopt T.S.W. in a separate proceeding and in that proceeding, he represented the adoptive parents chosen by Mother. Counsel represented at argument that the same judge that granted the deviation from ICWA in this case also entered a final adoption decree in the adoption proceeding. Finally, the Agency's counsel conceded he did not notify or communicate with the Tribe about T.S.W.'s adoption until after this court entered its show cause order, when he advised the Tribe's counsel that the adoption "happened a long time ago."

On appeal, the Tribe argues the district court erred in finding good cause to deviate from ICWA's placement preferences as set forth in 25 U.S.C. § 1915. But before considering this issue, we must determine whether we have jurisdiction to hear this appeal in light of the unique procedural posture presented by this case. [The court's lengthy discussion of jurisdiction is omitted. The court concluded it had jurisdiction to hear the appeal.]

On appeal, the Tribe argues the district court abused its discretion in finding good cause to deviate from ICWA's placement preferences because the Agency: (1) failed to make reasonable efforts to seek placement within ICWA's placement preferences beyond requesting the Tribe provide families that complied with the preferences and could meet the Agency's fees of $27,500; (2) failed to impartially consider T.S.W.'s relatives for placement; and (3) offered non-ICWA placement options to Mother prior to offering the remaining ICWA-compliant families offered by the Tribe.

Further, the Tribe contends the district court erred in basing its good cause finding on Mother's promise to withdraw her consent to the adoption if she was not allowed to choose the adoptive family. The Tribe contends Mother's threat to withdraw her consent and/or her choice of adoptive parents cannot override ICWA's mandatory placement preferences. Instead, the Tribe reasons that Mother's preferences are relevant only in limited circumstances not present here.

The Agency does not argue that it complied with ICWA's placement preferences. Rather, the Agency essentially contends that while it attempted to comply with the second placement preference, Mother's preference to place her child with non-Indian parents ultimately provided good cause to deviate from ICWA's preferences. Alternatively, the Agency argues ICWA does not apply to a non-Indian biological parent's voluntary placement of their child with a non-Indian adoptive family. . . .

Before considering whether the district court correctly applied ICWA's placement preferences here, we first briefly consider what appears to be an alternative argument by the Agency. Although not precisely formulated, the Agency contends ICWA's placement preferences should not be applied to the situation presently before us, *i.e.*, where a non-Indian biological parent has voluntarily consented to the placement of her Indian child with a non-Indian family. Without benefit of authority, the Agency reasons:

> The most troubling aspect to the Cherokee Nation's position is the attempt to use the Act to usurp the prenatal rights of a fit non-Indian mother to determine the best interest of her child. The Act was designed to prevent the unfair forcible removal of Indian children from their own homes and place them with non-Indian adoptive parents. Here, the Cherokee Nation attempts to use the placement preferences in an involuntary removal to overrule the placement desires of the fit non-Indian mother in a voluntary placement.

But the Agency's argument is contrary to the explicit language of 25 U.S.C. § 1915(a), which makes ICWA's placement preferences applicable to "any adoptive placement of an Indian child." Moreover, this issue was resolved, albeit in a different context, by the United States Supreme Court in *Mississippi Choctaw Indian Band v. Holyfield*, 490 U.S. 30, 109 S.Ct. 1597 (1989). There, the Mississippi Band of Choctaw Indians argued ICWA's jurisdictional provisions applied to an attempt by the biological Indian parents of twins to consent to their adoption by a non-Indian family. The tribe argued that the twins, like their parents, were "domiciled" on the reservation and the tribe had exclusive jurisdiction over their placement.

In *Holyfield*, the Supreme Court found that at the time of their birth, the twins were domiciled—like their parents—on the reservation. In so holding, the Court noted that tribal jurisdiction under ICWA "was not meant to be defeated by the actions of individual members of the tribe, for Congress was concerned not solely about the interests of Indian children and families, but also about the impact on the tribes themselves of the large numbers of Indian children adopted by non-Indians." The Court reasoned:

> It is clear that Congress' concern over the placement of Indian children in non-Indian homes was based in part on evidence of the detrimental impact on the children themselves of such placements outside their culture. Congress determined to subject such placements to the ICWA's jurisdictional and other provisions, even in cases where the parents consented to an adoption, because of concerns going beyond the wishes of individual parents.

Thus, the Supreme Court in *Holyfield* held ICWA's jurisdictional provisions apply even when both biological parents voluntarily attempt to place their Indian child with a non-Indian family. Further, the Court expressly extended its jurisdictional holding to ICWA's "other provisions," which include the placement provision at issue here, 25 U.S.C. § 1915(a).

We also reject the Agency's implied suggestion that ICWA's placement preferences apply only when the parental rights of Indian parents are at issue. Simply stated, this argument is inconsistent with our recent holding in *In re A.J.S.* There, we abandoned the existing Indian family doctrine and held ICWA's placement preferences applied to the placement of A.J.S., who had both Indian and non-Indian heritage.

Although the district court's order deviating from ICWA's placement preferences did not identify or discuss the preferences, the language of the statute at issue, 25 U.S.C. § 1915(a), is a good place to start with our analysis. That statute provides:

> In any adoptive placement of an Indian child under State law, a preference shall be given, in the absence of good cause to the contrary, to a placement with (1) a member of the child's extended family; (2) other members of the Indian child's tribe; or (3) other Indian families.

It is undisputed that T.S.W. is an Indian child as defined in ICWA. See 25 U.S.C. § 1903(4)(an "Indian child" is an unmarried person under the age of 18 who is eligible for membership in an Indian tribe and is the biological child of a member of an Indian tribe). Thus, in any adoptive placement involving T.S.W., ICWA required the court to consider the three placement preferences specified in § 1915(a) in the order specified in the statute absent good cause to the contrary. Further, the burden was on the Agency, as the party urging deviation from the preferences, to establish good cause to do so.

In this case, we need not extensively consider whether the Agency followed the placement preferences before seeking a deviation from those preferences. It did not. While the Agency made some effort to satisfy the second placement preference when it requested the Tribe provide available adoptive family profiles, the Agency impermissibly qualified its request in at least two ways. First, the Agency provided the Tribe with Mother's extensive "criteria" for any prospective adoptive family. Second, the Agency specified that prospective adoptive families be able to pay the Agency's $27,500 fee requirement. And while the Agency eventually indicated a willingness to modify its fee based on an unspecified sliding scale, the parties never agreed as to the parameters of that scale because Mother chose a non-Indian family based on profiles presented to her from the Agency.

Essentially, the Agency grafted its substantial fee requirement as well as Mother's placement criteria (which ironically specified that the adoptive parents be Caucasian) onto ICWA's placement preferences. Common sense dictates that ICWA's placement preferences cannot be undermined in this manner. In fact, the Agency's actions appear to fly in the face of Congress' intent in enacting ICWA. *See Holyfield*, 490 U.S. at 37, 109 S.Ct. 1597 (ICWA "seeks to protect the rights of the Indian child as an Indian and the rights of the Indian community and tribe in retaining its children in its society by establishing a Federal policy that, where possible, an Indian child should remain in the Indian community" and ensuring that Indian child welfare determinations are not based on a white, middle-class standard that often forecloses placement with an Indian family).

Moreover, even if we could conclude that the Agency appropriately and thoroughly attempted to comply with ICWA's second placement preference, it is undisputed that it made no effort to comply with ICWA's first and third preferences. Regarding the first preference—placement with the child's extended family—an Agency employee testified that because Mother did not want T.S.W. to be placed with Father's extended family, the Agency did not ascertain whether such placement was possible. Further, it is undisputed that the Agency made no effort to ascertain the availability of placement with other Indian families—the third placement preference.

Instead, the district court found "good cause" under this statute to deviate from the placement preferences, permitting T.S.W.'s placement with a non-ICWA compliant family. Therefore, we are asked to decide whether a biological parent's preference for placement of an Indian child can provide good cause to override ICWA's placement preferences.

This is not an issue of first impression for this court. In *B.G.J.*, we considered whether the district court abused its discretion in finding good cause to deviate from ICWA's adoptive placement preferences in granting a non-Indian family's petition to adopt an Indian child. Both parties here rely on *B.G.J.* to support their opposing positions regarding whether the district court properly found good cause to deviate from ICWA's placement preferences in this case. For reasons discussed below, we conclude *B.G.J.* does not support the district court's deviation from ICWA here.

In *B.G.J.*, the tribe offered placement of the Indian child, B.G.J., with four of her biological mother's relatives. But the mother, who was one-half Indian, selected a non-Indian family profile from an adoption agency because she "did not want a member of the Tribe to raise B.G.J." 281 Kan. at 555, 133 P.3d 1. After the prospective adoptive couple petitioned to adopt B.G.J., the district court found good cause to deviate from ICWA's placement preferences.

On review, this court held the district court did not abuse its discretion in finding good cause to deviate from ICWA's placement preferences. The court first noted that 25 U.S.C. § 1915(c) provides that where appropriate, the preference of the Indian child or parent shall be considered and that the tribe contended that appropriateness must be assessed in light of the congressional intent to protect the best interest of Indian children and promote the stability of Indian tribes and families. .

But the *B.G.J.* court pointed out that while placing Indian children with Indian families is a priority under ICWA, the legislation also provides that for good cause, courts may deviate from the placement preferences, allowing the state courts flexibility in the placement of Indian children. The court then noted that the BIA Guidelines, specifically BIA Guideline F.3., permit a court to rely on "parental preference" in deviating from ICWA's placement preferences. The *B.G.J.* court noted:

> It [BIA Guideline F.3] states that the good cause determination "shall be based on one or more of the considerations." It does not limit the consideration which may be given to the mother's preference. Here, the mother knowingly and with full knowledge of the ICWA preferences executed her relinquishment. She was adamant that her child be placed with the adoptive parents, and not with her extended family or the Tribe.

Relying upon this language in this case, the Agency contends *B.G.J.* supports the district court's decision to deviate from ICWA based upon Mother's "strong desire to place with the adoptive couple of her choosing." However, we do not read *B.G.J.* so narrowly.

While *B.G.J.* emphasized the mother's preference, it also specifically noted that the district court based its determination on two of the three factors suggested by BIA Guideline F.3. as a basis for deviation from the guidelines. The court concluded:

> B.G.J. had no extraordinary physical or emotional needs. Hence, the trial court based its determination on the other two factors. Giving as much if not more weight to the unavailability of suitable families offered by the Tribe for placement as to the birth mother's request, the trial court determined that good cause existed to deviate from the statutory preferences. The trial court's analysis is in accord with the federal statutes and guidelines. We hold the district court did not abuse its discretion in finding that good cause existed to deviate from ICWA's placement preferences.

Thus, this court in *B.G.J.* did not base its decision to deviate from ICWA's placement preferences solely, or even mostly, on the mother's placement preference. But to the extent our opinion in *B.G.J.* can be read to suggest that a parent's preference can solely override ICWA's placement preferences, we disapprove that language as dicta. . . .

In this case the district court made no . . . findings regarding the availability of placement with either natural parent's extended family or the availability of Tribe families. Instead, the court expressly noted that "neither of the birth mother's or birth father's families were considered as the birth mother did not want placement with them." And regarding the Cherokee Nation families offered by the Tribe, the court held: "An additional seventeen (17) to twenty (20) families were presented which the birth mother did not like and rejected." Significantly, the court further commented that "there is no evidence to show that any of these families were disqualified for any legal or practical reason."

Thus, the district court in this case did not rely upon the unavailability of either T.S.W.'s extended family or the families offered by the Tribe. Instead, the court permitted Mother's desire not to place T.S.W. with extended family or any of the potential adoptive Tribe families to override these preferences. . . .

The Agency points out that the district court in this case also referenced "the best interest of the child" in deviating from the placement factors. However, . . . the district court's reference to the best interest of the child in this case was not made in the context of an adoption proceeding, since no such proceeding had been filed. In fact, the court's order makes no reference whatsoever to T.S.W.'s temporary placement or to the potential adoptive parents other than to indicate that the "subject minor child has been with the prospective adoptive couple since December 2009." Thus, the court's reference to the "best interest of the child" is confusing at best and appears to be based, like the court's other conclusions, on Mother's placement preference.

. . . We conclude *B.G.J.* does not support the district court's decision in this case to deviate from ICWA based solely on Mother's preference to place T.S.W. with a non-Indian family of her choice. Therefore, we next consider whether the district court's holding can stand under the factual circumstances of this case.

The Tribe contends the parental preference referred to in 25 U.S.C. § 1915(c) has only limited application and is not meant to entirely override the placement preferences of § 1915(a). Specifically, the Tribe argues that parental preference can support a finding of good cause to deviate from the order of consideration of ICWA's placement preferences only in the limited situation in which the consenting parent desires anonymity. In support, the Tribe points to the complete text of 25 U.S.C. § 1915(c), BIA Guidelines F.1. and F.3., and the commentary to those guidelines.

Notably, the Agency entirely fails to respond to this argument and instead relies simply on this court's decision in *B.G.J.* as support for its contention that 25 U.S.C. § 1915(c) permits a parent's preference to override the placement preferences of 25 U.S.C. § 1915(a). But we were not presented in *B.G.J.* with the argument that the parental preference provision of 25 U.S.C. § 1915(c) is limited to situations in which a consenting parent requests anonymity with respect to the placement of the child. Nor are we precluded from considering that issue now.

Significantly, in *B.G.J.* we recognized that 25 U.S.C. § 1915(c) provides in part that where appropriate, in considering the placement preferences of 25 U.S.C. § 1915(a), the preference of the Indian child or parent shall be considered. But we did not consider the entire text of subsection (c). Instead, we omitted the proviso to that subsection which lends context and meaning to the scope of the parental preference language. Specifically, § 1915(c) states in full:

> In the case of a placement under subsection (a) or (b) of this section, if the Indian child's tribe shall establish a different order of preference by resolution, the agency or court effecting the placement shall follow such order so long as the placement is the least restrictive setting appropriate to the particular needs of the child, as provided in subsection (b) of this section. Where appropriate, the preference of the Indian child or parent shall be considered: Provided, that where a consenting parent evidences a desire for anonymity, the court or agency shall give weight to such desire in applying the preferences.

Thus, the entire text of 25 U.S.C. § 1915(c) indicates that a district court should modify the order of preferences in 25 U.S.C. § 1915(a) when (1) the tribe establishes a different order under certain circumstances or (2) a consenting parent seeks anonymity with respect to the placement of the child.

This interpretation is bolstered by BIA Guideline F.1. That guideline, which also was not discussed in *B.G.J.*, closely tracks 25 U.S.C. § 1915(a) and (c). BIA Guideline F.1.(c) provides: "Unless a consenting parent evidences a desire for anonymity, the court or agency shall notify the child's extended family and the Indian child's tribe that their members will be given preference in the adoption decision."

... In light of the text of 25 U.S.C. § 1915(c), BIA Guidelines F.1. and F.3., and the commentary to both of those guidelines, we are persuaded that the "parental preference" referred to in § 1915(c) was not intended to permit a biological parent's preference for placement of a child with a non-Indian family to automatically provide "good cause" to override the adoptive placement preferences of 25 U.S.C. § 1915(a). Instead, a parent's request for anonymity with respect to placement of the child must be considered along with other relevant factors, including the best interest of the child, in deciding whether to modify the order of consideration of ICWA's placement references.

Returning to the facts of this case, we note that the record contains no indication that Mother requested confidentiality with respect to T.S.W.'s placement. Rather, Mother simply did not want T.S.W. placed with Father's extended family members or members of the Tribe. Applying the above analysis, we conclude the district court erred in permitting Mother's preference to override ICWA's placement factors absent some request for confidentiality. Accordingly, we reverse the district court's decision deviating from ICWA's placement preferences in this case.

Questions Based on *Matter of T.S.W.*

1. The Supreme Court was not impressed with the state of the record in the trial court. This case illustrates the importance of making sure the trial court record contains all necessary information about proceedings, orders, findings, etc.

2. Reading between the lines, do you get the impression the adoption agency was trying to stall the Tribe? I get that impression, but maybe I'm misreading the opinion.

Interstate Compact on the Placement of Children (ICPC)

Juvenile courts sometimes place children across state lines. When they do, it is necessary to comply with the Interstate Compact on the Placement of Children (ICPC), which is in force in all states. The purpose of the ICPC is to enhance cooperation between states to the end that children are placed in appropriate foster homes, institutions, or adoptive homes. Social workers seeking to place a child in another state send a detailed form to social workers in the receiving state. The placement does not occur until social workers in the receiving state notify social workers in the sending state "that the proposed placement does not appear to be contrary to the interests of the child."[70] Once a child is placed across state lines, the sending state retains authority over the child as well as financial responsibility for the child.

The ICPC does not apply to cross-border placements with parents and other close relatives.[71] As the California Court of Appeal put it in *In re Z.K.*,[72] "The ICPC governs conditions for out-of-state placement in foster care or as a preliminary to a possible adoption. . . . The ICPC is applicable only to foster care and possible adoption—neither of which would involve natural parents. Accordingly, compliance with the ICPC is not required for placement with an out-of state parent." The ICPC does not play a role in child custody litigation in family court.

Conclusion

Do you think you might want to practice in juvenile court? You can do enormous good for children and families. The work is difficult but satisfying. I practice in juvenile court, representing abused and neglected children. I've been an attorney and law professor 36 years. Nothing in my professional life has been more rewarding than serving as counsel for abused and neglected children. Give it a try. I think you'll like it. I know the kids you represent will benefit from your energy, your intellect, and your commitment to justice and to them.

---

70 ICPC Article III(d).

71 ICPC Article VIII(a).

72 201 Cal. App. 4th 51, 133 Cal. Rptr. 3d 597, 611 (2011).

CHAPTER 15

Ethical and Business Issues in Family Law

ETHICAL ISSUES PERVADE LAW PRACTICE. You will plumb the depths of legal ethics in your Professional Responsibility course. This chapter touches on ethical issues of special relevance to family law. The chapter also examines legal malpractice in family law. Finally, the chapter touches on the business side of practicing law.

Dual Representation

Married couples getting divorced may ask a lawyer to represent both of them. The couple typically says, "Our divorce is amicable, and we can't afford two lawyers. Will you represent both of us?" Dual representation is a bad idea, even in uncontested cases. The potential for conflict of interest is too high. According to Michael Frazee, in Massachusetts "attorneys are prohibited from representing both members of a divorcing couple."[1] The better practice is to represent one spouse. Encourage the other spouse to get their own lawyer.

In *Marriage of Newton*,[2] husband had an initial consultation with attorney Gund about the possibility of divorcing wife. During the consultation, husband discussed divorce-related matters with Mr. Gund. Later, Gund signed a retainer to represent wife. Husband filed a motion to disqualify Mr. Gund and his law firm based on a conflict of interest. The motion to disqualify was appealed.

---

1 Michael A. Frazee, Ethical Issues for Divorce and Family Lawyers, Massachusetts Continuing Legal Education (2012).

2 353 Ill. Dec. 105, 955 N.E.2d 572 (2011).

Eventually, wife sought some $250,000 in attorneys fees from husband, including fees for appellate work. The Illinois Court of Appeal ruled that Mr. Gund was disqualified from representing wife, and that the retainer agreement was invalid. Because the agreement was invalid, Mr. Gund was not entitled to any attorneys fees from husband. The Court of Appeal noted that an attorney-client relationship can be established in an initial consultation between a prospective client and an attorney.

Diligence and Communication

Clients are deeply personally concerned about their case. It is vital to keep clients informed of all developments. Regular communication—even when nothing new is happening—is respectful to the client and helps the client understand you are not ignoring them. When clients contact the office, make sure you or someone on your staff gets back to the client promptly.

You Don't Have to be a Pit Bull to be a Good Advocate

The adversary system of justice is, well, adversarial. Yet, even in contested cases, attorneys are expected to act professionally toward witnesses, the judge, and each other. The California Court of Appeal, in *Marriage of Davenport*,[3] offers good advice: "Zealous advocacy does not equate with 'attack dog' or 'scorched earth'; nor does it mean lack of civility. Zeal and vigor in the representation of clients are commendable. So are civility, courtesy, and cooperation. They are not mutually exclusive."

The State Bar of California promulgated *Attorney Guidelines of Civility and Professionalism*, which state, "As officers of the court with responsibilities to the administration of justice, attorneys have an obligation to be professional with clients, other parties and counsel, the courts and the public. This obligation includes civility, professional integrity, personal dignity, candor, diligence, respect, courtesy, and cooperation, all of which are essential to the fair administration of justice and conflict resolution. . . . In family law proceedings an attorney should seek to reduce emotional tension and trauma and encourage the parties and attorneys to interact in a cooperative atmosphere, and keep the best interest of the children in mind." The Massachusetts Bar Association issued *Civility Guidelines for Family Law Attorneys*. The Massachusetts guidelines remind us, "Civility and professionalism are hallmarks of a learned profession. Uncivil, abrasive, abusive, hostile and obstructive conduct impedes our

---

3 194 Cal. App. 4th 1507, 125, Cal. Rptr. 3d 292 (2011).

ability as domestic relations attorneys to resolve disputes rationally, peacefully and efficiently."

Zealous advocacy and civility are not mutually exclusive. Indeed, as you gain experience, you will find that the most competent and respected members of the profession are often the most courteous and professional.

"I'm Beginning to Understand the Law, But I Have No Idea How to Run a Business"

The vast majority of law students have no experience running a business. Yet, most family law attorneys are sole practitioners or members of small firms. Not only do you have to mold yourself into a good lawyer, you have to mold yourself into a competent business person. Like the owners of the local flower shop, dentist office, and gas station, you will be running a business. For some young lawyers the idea of running their own business—being your own boss—is exciting, liberating. For others, its a very scary proposition.

How do you start your own practice? There are countless things to think about. Fortunately, many state bar associations offer help. The State Bar of California, for example, has an excellent book titled *The California Guide to Opening and Managing a Law Office*. To give you an idea of the issues awaiting you, consider the Table of Contents from the California book:

Chapter 1 – The Big Decision to Open Your Law Office
- Personal considerations in going solo—Is it for you?
- Basic financial considerations—Can you afford this?
- Choosing your practice area—
    Market and practice area considerations

Chapter 2 – Creating a Business Plan
- Creating a business plan

Chapter 3 – Finding Office Space and Location
- Leasing and subleasing
- Office sharing and executive suites
- Office design, layout, and furnishings
- Home offices, and virtual offices

Chapter 4 – Law Office Systems and Procedures
- Law office systems and procedures
- Sample written fee agreement forms

Chapter 5 – Finance and Cash Management
- Initial funding for your solo practice
- Cash flow
- Managing overhead
- Becoming your own risk manager
- Fees and billing/collecting fees
- Mandatory fee arbitration
- Client trust accounting
- Tax issues related to the solo practitioner

Chapter 6 –Technology
- Assessing technology needs and return on investment
- Computers and peripherals
- Legal software
- E-mail
- Computer security, privacy, and ethics concerns
- eFiling
- Data backup and management
- Tech support
- A paperless office
- Records retention and destruction

Chapter 7 – Solo Practice Management
- Basic management principles and procedures
- How to make requests, delegate work,
  and give productive feedback
- Finding, recruiting, and hiring staff, clerks, and attorneys
- Retaining, motivating, and managing staff, clerks, and attorneys
- Using temps and contract attorneys; outsourcing work
- Training staff, clerks, and attorneys
- Sharing staff

- HR consultants

- Lawyers as employers—The tax and legal basics

- Solo practice management: Human resources director

Chapter 8 – Business Development
- Business development: Chief marketing officer

- Ethical considerations in the business development context

- Website development, internet marketing, blogs, and other electronic media

Chapter 9 – Professional Development
- Overcoming the fear of networking

- Becoming involved with your local bar association

- Join a section/write articles/speak at CLE events

- Join boards/community activities

- Legal specializations

Chapter 10 – Customer Service
- Customer service

Chapter 11 – Quality of Life
- The myth of the "solo practitioner"—
  Creating your very own support system

- Personal health

- Maintaining personal relationships

- Work-life balance

- How to take vacations and breaks

- What to do (ahead of time) when health problems arise

- Learning to say NO and to set boundaries and expectations

- Dealing with stress, anxiety, depression, and addictive behavior

- Lawyer assistance programs and other available help

If you are not at least a little bit frightened by the Table of Contents and the thought of hanging out your shingle, you are not paying attention! It is huge challenge figuring out how to be a lawyer—a million things to learn that you didn't learn in law school. And if becoming a competent attorney isn't enough, you also have to learn to manage a business.

Add to the burdens of becoming a competent lawyer and business owner the enormous professional responsibility you are about to assume. Your clients entrust you with their families, their fortunes, and their futures. They put their lives in your hands. It is a tremendous privilege to be entrusted with such responsibilities, but the weight can be crushing. In my own practice (I'm a full time professor and a part time practitioner), when I'm preparing for court on a contested family law matter, I don't sleep well. At two in the morning, I awake with the details of the case rushing through my mind. There are few things more satisfying than helping a client achieve the result she deserves, but it is not easy—never easy. It isn't simple, but it *is* worth it.

Communication with Opposing Spouse Who is Not Represented by an Attorney

An attorney representing one spouse must be careful when communicating with the opposing spouse who is not represented by counsel. First, encourage the opposing spouse to get a lawyer. Second, emphasize that you are not neutral, and that you represent only your client. Third, make sure the opposing spouse understands you cannot offer legal advice.

Communication with Opposing Spouse Who is Represented by an Attorney

An attorney may not communicate with a person whom the attorney knows is represented by counsel unless the opposing attorney permits communication. Consider the Wyoming Supreme Court's decision in *Wyoming State Bar v. Melchior.*

Wyoming State Bar v. Melchior

Supreme Court of Wyoming
269 P.3d 1088 (Wyo. 2012)

Kite, M., Chief Justice.

This matter came before the Court upon a "Report and Recommendation," filed herein December 22, 2011 by the Board of Professional Responsibility for the Wyoming State Bar. The Court, after a careful review of the Board of Professional Responsibility's Report and Recommendation and the file, finds that the Report and Recommendation should be approved, confirmed and adopted by the Court, and that Respondent D. Stephen Melchior should be publicly censured for his conduct, which is described in the attached Report and Recommendation. It is, therefore,

ADJUDGED AND ORDERED that the Board of Professional Responsibility's Report and Recommendation, which is attached hereto and incorporated herein, shall be, and the same hereby is, approved, confirmed, and adopted by this Court; and it is further

ADJUDGED AND ORDERED that D. Stephen Melchior shall receive a public censure for his conduct, and he shall be publicly censured in a manner consistent with the recommended censure contained in the Report and Recommendation . . . .

Respondent is an attorney licensed to practice law in Wyoming since 1991.

In July of 2010, after Respondent's client represented to Respondent that she and her husband had reached an agreement regarding all matters relative to their divorce, Respondent filed a divorce complaint on behalf of his client against her husband, with the expectation that Respondent would subsequently be filing a signed copy of a Property Settlement Agreement that Respondent had prepared and understood reflected the agreement of the parties relative to all issues pertaining to the parties' divorce. After Respondent filed such divorce complaint on behalf of his client, the husband hired Cheyenne attorney Deborah Ford Mincer to represent him in the divorce. Ms. Mincer thereafter filed an answer and counterclaim on behalf of the husband, a copy of which was served upon Respondent.

In the course of the divorce case, Respondent made revisions to said settlement documents at his client's request, including to the property settlement agreement and a confidential financial affidavit in the husband's name. Respondent did not initially inform Ms. Mincer of these facts, nor did he initially provide Ms. Mincer with copies of the documents.

On or about February 7, 2011, the husband signed a stipulated property settlement, child custody and child support agreement (both redacted and unredacted versions), and a confidential financial affidavit, all of which were prepared by Respondent. The husband's lawyer, Deborah Ford Mincer, was not informed by Respondent that he had been making revisions to the parties' said settlement documents at his client's direction or that Respondent knew, based upon his client's representations to him, that the parties were meeting together on their own for the purpose of trying to reach agreement relative to the terms of their divorce.

After the husband signed the documents, he called his lawyer, Deborah Ford Mincer, and told her he had signed some sort of agreement. Ms. Ford Mincer immediately advised Respondent not to file the agreement and requested a copy of it.

On February 8, 2011, Respondent wrote to Ms. Ford Mincer and told her that her client had signed the stipulated divorce settlement, and that her client had also signed a financial affidavit. In Respondent's letter, he told Ms. Ford Mincer:

My client has come to me several times in the last couple of weeks with edits to a proposed PSA [property settlement agreement] that it is my understanding the parties have been working off of. I made final edits to the PSA yesterday after my client came into my office and told me that [the husband] had just a few more changes before he would sign. Shortly after I presented a final edited version of such PSA to my client, she returned to my office with the PSAs (unredacted and redacted versions) bearing [the husband's] signatures. I also received a signed copy of [the husband's] Confidential Financial Affidavit. Rest assured that I would not have and will not file with the Court any of the documents that [the husband] has signed without first obtaining your approval or unless I receive an Order from the Court announcing that you no longer serve as [the husband's] attorney. This I have been clearly explaining to my client for the last several weeks.

In response to Respondent's February 8, 2011 letter, Ms. Ford Mincer instructed Respondent to have no communications with her client, not to obtain any additional documents from her client, and to file nothing that concerns her client. Respondent replied in an E-mail dated February 9, 2011, in which he stated as follows:

[I] told my client that I could not file any signed PSA or documents bearing [the husband's] signature without first providing you with a copy of the same for review and not until you gave me the green light to do so; and my client told me that she communicated the same to [the husband] several times. That is how I operate. That is how I have always operated. That is how I will continue to operate.

Ten days later, on February 19, 2011, Respondent wrote to Ms. Ford Mincer:

After giving the matter much thought, I am of the opinion that the documents our clients negotiated between themselves and which our clients signed ... constitute a valid and enforceable contract between the parties. I was not involved in the parties' settlement negotiations. My client provided to me fully executed documents. I had no communications with your client whatsoever about any aspect of the parties' divorce or their agreement, and never "negotiated" anything with your client.

On February 22, 2011, Respondent filed, on behalf of his client, a motion for order acknowledging as valid and enforceable the parties' settlement agreement.

On February 25, 2011, Ms. Ford Mincer submitted a complaint to Bar Counsel in which she alleged that Respondent had violated Rules 4.2 and 8.4 of the Wyoming Rules of Professional Conduct.

Respondent has acknowledged that his conduct violated Rule 4.2 of the Rules of Professional Conduct for Attorneys at Law, which provides, "In representing a client, a lawyer shall not communicate [either directly or indirectly] about the subject of the representation with a person or entity the lawyer knows to be represented by another lawyer in the matter, unless the lawyer has the consent of the other lawyer or is authorized to do so by law or a court order." Comment 3 to the Rule states, "The Rule applies even though the represented person initiates or consents to the communication. Regardless of who commences the communication, a lawyer must immediately terminate communication with a person if the lawyer learns that the person is one with whom communication is not permitted by this Rule." Comment 4 to the Rule states, "A lawyer may not make a communication prohibited by this Rule through the acts of another."

Respondent has acknowledged that he violated this Rule when he created and gave to his client a divorce settlement agreement and a confidential financial statement at a time when Respondent knew or reasonably should have known that there was a substantial risk that she would deliver them to the husband, whom Respondent knew was being represented by counsel.

Respondent has acknowledged that his conduct also violated Rule 8.4(d), which provides, "It is professional misconduct for a lawyer to ... engage in conduct that is prejudicial to the administration of justice." Respondent violated this Rule when he presented the divorce settlement agreement to the Court for enforcement after assuring Ms. Ford Mincer that he would not file the agreement without her approval, despite his client directing Respondent to do so.

Respondent has expressed remorse for the poor judgment he exhibited in violating the Rules of Professional Conduct as set forth herein, and has vowed not make similar mistakes in the future. . . .

Melchior stipulated to the public censure and agreed to pay an administrative fee and certain costs of the disciplinary action to the Wyoming, State Bar.

Legal Malpractice

Lawyers practicing family law can be sued for malpractice. Obviously, the lawyer's client can sue. Some malpractice claims are brought by non-clients, including children and the former spouse of the client. The Idaho Supreme Court's decision in *Stephen v. Sallaz & Gatewood* is a good introduction to legal malpractice in family law.

Stephen v. Sallaz & Gatewood

Supreme Court of Idaho
150 Idaho 521, 248 P.3d 1256 (2011)

J. Jones, Justice.

This is an appeal from a legal malpractice judgment entered against attorney Scott Gatewood and the law firm of Sallaz & Gatewood, Chtd. Appellants argue the district court erred in finding that professional malpractice had occurred. We affirm.

This case arises from a malpractice action brought by Pamela Joerger Stephen ("Pamela") against the law firm of Sallaz & Gatewood, Chtd., Scott Gatewood ("Gatewood") and Dennis Sallaz ("Sallaz") (all three of the defendants are herein collectively referred to as "Appellants"). Pamela's ex-husband, Gary Stephen ("Stephen"), filed for divorce in May of 2003. During the divorce proceedings, Stephen retained attorney Ann Shepard to represent him, and Pamela retained Sallaz & Gatewood, Chtd. Pamela claims the Appellants committed malpractice by failing to make inquiries into her mental status during the divorce proceedings and by failing to properly investigate, inform, and advise her regarding the fair market value of real property that was part of the settlement agreement, which resulted in her receiving less than her equitable share of the community property.

The district court found that Gatewood was liable for malpractice in his representation of Pamela for (1) failing to inquire into Pamela's mental status prior to trial or for failing to seek a continuance, and (2) failing to investigate, inform, and advise her with respect to the value of the couple's Crescent Rim property. The court determined that Sallaz & Gatewood, Chtd., was also liable for the malpractice judgment.

With regard to the first finding, the district court noted that Gatewood had many indications of Pamela's alleged mental incapacity. Specifically, Pamela disclosed to Gatewood during a June 2003 meeting that she suffered from bi-polar disorder, that she had attempted suicide on two separate occasions, and that she was taking medications for her condition. The court also noted that Pamela was living in an unstable environment at the time of the divorce proceedings because she was residing in the couple's Crescent Rim property with another man while Stephen made payments on the property. Pamela was also receiving income from the couple's rental property at the time, but failed to make mortgage payments or pay other expenses on the rental property. Gatewood was also aware that Pamela had been involuntarily hospitalized approximately one week before the trial was scheduled to begin but "did not inquire of [Pamela] where she had been hospitalized, for what reason or by what doctor." Stephen's attorney also advised Gatewood that Pamela was using methamphetamine. Finally, the court noted that Gatewood had to personally visit Pamela's residence on several occasions in an effort to speak to her. Gatewood even filed a motion to withdraw as Pamela's attorney in July of 2004, identifying a "total communication breakdown" as the basis for the motion. Although the motion was ultimately withdrawn, Pamela testified that she received very little correspondence, court pleadings or discovery information from Gatewood during the divorce proceedings.

On the second issue, the district court found that because Pamela was never informed of Stephen's valuation of the couple's Crescent Rim property, she undervalued the property for purposes of settlement. The parties exchanged discovery requests in September of 2003, including interrogatories seeking, among other things, the other's valuation of the Crescent Rim property. Stephen was the first to respond, and he disclosed the property value to be $500,000. Pamela testified that Gatewood never informed her of this valuation and Gatewood testified he could not recall if he had. Pamela subsequently valued the property at only $385,500. This final valuation was used in the couple's final settlement agreement. There was also evidence that a judgment lien against the Crescent Rim property had been paid prior to trial, but the amount of the lien was nonetheless credited to Stephen in the settlement.

On the first day of the divorce trial, the parties informed the district court that they had reached a proposed settlement agreement. When the court asked Pamela if she understood the agreement, Pamela responded that she was in agreement "as far as I know." However, Gatewood testified that Pamela was "clear in her thoughts and understanding" at the time of the proceedings and that he "did not believe that she was impaired as a result of methamphetamine use and/or mental health issues."

In the subsequent malpractice action against Appellants, the court found that Gatewood breached duties owed to Pamela and imposed liability in the amount of $27,435.00 against Gatewood, personally, as well as against Sallaz & Gatewood, Chtd. However, the district court declined to assess any personal liability against Sallaz because the court found that he had never provided any legal services to Pamela, nor had he acted in a supervisory capacity over Gatewood. The court made this finding despite Sallaz being named as an attorney in documents filed with the court during the divorce proceedings and despite Sallaz's affiliation with Sallaz & Gatewood, Chtd. . . .

On appeal, Appellants argue that the district court erred in its determination of the duties owed to Pamela, and contend that there was no evidence establishing a breach of any duties. They also argue that Pamela's malpractice claim is barred by judicial estoppel and judgmental immunity, and that liability cannot be imposed upon a law firm. Pamela argues that the final damage award is in error, and that Sallaz should be personally liable for the malpractice judgment. . . .

Appellants contend the district court erred in finding that Gatewood committed legal malpractice in his representation of Pamela. Specifically, they argue that the district court misapprehended the duty owed to Pamela as a client with a diminished capacity, and that there was no evidence to support the finding of breach in that regard. Additionally, they argue that Gatewood had no duty to investigate the value of the Crescent Rim property because there was not a significant difference in the values provided by the parties, and because attorneys are permitted to rely on the valuations provided by their clients.

Pamela argues that Gatewood breached the duties he owed to her by failing to properly investigate, inform, and advise her as to the value of the Crescent Rim property, separate and apart from his breach for failing to investigate her diminished capacity. She argues that Gatewood never told her about the $500,000 valuation made by Stephen and that no competent attorney would have knowingly advised a client to provide a substantially lower valuation. Pamela also argues there was sufficient evidence to support the malpractice finding regarding her diminished capacity.

The district court found that Gatewood breached duties he owed to Pamela by failing to investigate, inform, and advise her regarding the value of the Crescent Rim property when such a disparity existed between the valuations provided by the parties. The court found that Gatewood's failure to inquire into Pamela's mental state and to take appropriate protective measures also breached the duties he owed her.

We affirm the district court's finding that Gatewood committed legal malpractice by failing to investigate, inform, and advise Pamela regarding the value of the Crescent Rim property. Therefore, it is unnecessary to address the district court's finding that Gatewood committed malpractice by failing to adequately inquire into Pamela's alleged diminished capacity. For this reason, we also decline to address Appellants' judicial estoppel and judgmental immunity arguments.

A legal malpractice action is based on a combination of tort and contract theories. The attorney-client relationship is generally based on contract principles, while the negligence standard is based on tort principles.

The elements of a legal malpractice action are: (a) the existence of an attorney-client relationship; (b) the existence of a duty on the part of the lawyer; (c) failure to perform the duty; and (d) the negligence of the lawyer must have been a proximate cause of the damage to the client. . . .

The existence of a duty of care is a question of law over which this Court exercises free review. An attorney's duty arises out of the contract between the attorney and his or her client. In this case, Pamela retained Gatewood's firm "to represent [her] interests in connection with a divorce and related matters." A requisite component of a divorce action is the valuation of property making up the community estate. Therefore, because Pamela retained the firm for assistance with her divorce proceedings, this representation implicitly included assistance with the valuation of the Crescent Rim home.

In providing such assistance, Gatewood owed Pamela the duties of competent and diligent representation, as well as adequate communication. In order to provide competent representation, an attorney must use the legal knowledge, skill, *thoroughness*, and preparation reasonably necessary for the representation. To be adequately prepared and thorough, the attorney must make "inquiry into and analysis of the factual and legal elements of the problem. Additionally, an attorney must be diligent in providing representation, and zealously pursue the client's objectives as defined by the scope of the representation. Finally, in terms of communication, an attorney must keep the client informed about the matter for which the attorney was retained, and must also explain the matter to the client so that the client can make informed decisions.

There is substantial evidence in the record that Gatewood violated these duties in regard to the Crescent Rim property. Pamela testified, and Gatewood was unable to rebut, that she was never informed of Stephen's initial $500,000 valuation of the property. Without this information, Pamela relied on an "old appraisal" to make her estimation of the property's value, and ultimately provided a value that was over one-hundred-thousand dollars less than Stephen's valuation. This does not appear to be an informed decision on Pamela's behalf, as there is no rational explanation for allowing Pamela to undercut the value of the couple's most valuable real property community asset, when Stephen had previously provided a higher valuation. Indeed, the discovery response containing the $500,000 valuation was submitted upon Stephen's oath, making it difficult for him to later assert a lesser value. While it is ordinarily true that an attorney can accept the client's valuation of property without performing an independent investigation thereof, an attorney in a divorce proceeding must also pursue the most equitable division of community assets for his or her client. Accepting Stephen's proposed value, or making a minimal investigation into the value of the Crescent Rim property because Pamela provided him a substantially lower value, would have demonstrated the diligence and competence that is expected of an attorney in Gatewood's position. At the very least, Gatewood was obligated to advise Pamela of Stephen's higher valuation and discuss the legal implications of her proposing a lesser value. Instead, Gatewood failed to provide Pamela with information that was critical for her to make an informed decision.

There is also evidence that Stephen was credited for a $28,000 judgment lien against the Crescent Rim property, when it had been paid off nearly two months before the settlement. Gatewood testified that he had no knowledge that the debt had been paid prior to settlement and further testified that, even if he had known, it would not have changed the settlement agreement because he believed Pamela was receiving adequate temporary maintenance. This justification does not embody the type of zealous representation that is expected of an attorney in reaching the most equitable property distribution in a divorce case, nor does it embody the type of thoroughness and investigation that would be expected of a competent attorney in Gatewood's position.

Because the district court's finding that Gatewood breached his duties to Pamela by failing to investigate, inform, and advise her regarding the value of the Crescent Rim property is supported by substantial, albeit conflicting, evidence, we affirm the district court's holding that Gatewood committed legal malpractice in his representation of Pamela.

The most common malpractice claim against family law attorneys relates to property division.[4] The Iowa Supreme Court's decision in *Faber v. Herman* illustrates the issue.

---

4 *See* Ronald E. Mallen & Jeffrey M. Smith, *Legal Malpractice* § 28:8, p. 1277 (2011)("The most commonly alleged error against a family lawyer concerns the property settlement agreement or how the marital property is divided in the divorce proceedings.").

Faber v. Herman

Iowa Supreme Court
731 N.W.2d 1 (Iowa 2007)

Cady, Justice.

In this appeal from a judgment against a lawyer in a legal malpractice action based on claims of negligence while representing a former client in a dissolution proceeding, we conclude the claims of malpractice did not cause the damages sought as a matter of law. We vacate the decision of the court of appeals and reverse the judgment of the district court.

Douglas Herman is an Iowa lawyer. He represented Steven Faber in an action to dissolve his marriage to Karen Faber. Karen was represented by attorney Karl Moorman.

The Fabers were married for nineteen years at the time the dissolution action was commenced. The divorce presented many challenging issues, not the least of which was the equitable division of their marital property. The parties and their attorneys worked to resolve these issues, which ultimately resulted in a stipulated decree for dissolution of marriage.

One item of property divided under the stipulation and decree was Steven's retirement account with the Iowa Public Employer's Retirement System (IPERS). Steven began working for the State of Iowa two years after the marriage. He worked at the Anamosa state penitentiary as a corrections officer, and continued to be employed in that capacity until after the divorce.

Based on information provided by IPERS during the pendency of the divorce, Steven learned the "investment value" of his retirement account was $38,179.38, and the "death benefit" was $63,785.94. The "death benefit" represented the amount to be distributed to Karen, as the designated beneficiary, in the event of Steven's death. The "investment value" represented the amount Steven would receive in a lump sum payment if he retired from his employment with the State of Iowa on the day the value was determined. Steven was vested in the pension plan, and therefore the "investment value" represented all of his personal contributions during the course of his employment plus a portion from his employer.

Steven and Karen agreed to divide the IPERS account equally. To accomplish this division, they considered the "investment value" to be the value of the account, and they sought to divide the account by means of a qualified domestic relations order (QDRO) that required IPERS to immediately pay Karen one-half of the investment value, or $19,100. Specifically, the stipulation required Steven to "immediately pay $19,100.00 to Karen from his I.P.E.R.S. retirement account pursuant to a separate Qualified Domestic Relations Order issued by the Court."

Steven and Karen also prepared an itemization of the division of all their property by listing each item of property received by each party in separate columns, with a corresponding value assigned to each item. This itemization was attached to the written stipulation signed by the parties. Steven's column included "IPERS (one-half)" with a value of "$19,100." Likewise, Karen's column included "IPERS (one-half)" with a value of "$19,100." The stipulation was signed by Steven and Karen in May 1999, and the decree was entered by the court.

Moorman then drafted a proposed QDRO to divide the IPERS account pursuant to the stipulation. This proposed order essentially directed IPERS to create a separate interest for Karen in the amount of $19,100, payable to her as a participant under the plan. Moorman then sent the order to the administrator of IPERS for approval. IPERS rejected the proposed QDRO because it allowed Karen to acquire independent rights in the account. IPERS informed Moorman that Karen could not receive any benefits until Steven began to receive benefits or died. IPERS also informed Moorman that Karen had no right to independently select a distribution option and begin receiving benefits, or to have a separate account set aside in her name.

Moorman then drafted a new QDRO that abandoned the lump-sum division approach agreed to by the parties under their stipulation. The new QDRO provided for the benefits to be distributed to Steven and Karen upon Steven's retirement under a formula based on the length of the marriage and the length of employment. The QDRO provided:

IPERS is directed to pay benefits to [Karen] as a marital property settlement under the following formula: Fifty percent (50%) of the gross monthly or lump sum benefit payable at the date of distribution to [Steven] multiplied by the "service factor." The numerator of the service factor is 70 and the denominator is [Steven's] total quarters of service covered by IPERS.

Under the QDRO the benefits were to inure to Karen as an alternate payee for Steven's life, and were not to begin until "[Steven] begins to receive benefits from IPERS or when the death benefits become payable, whichever occurs first." IPERS approved this QDRO, and it was signed by Herman, Moorman, and the court in July of 1999.

Herman did not directly participate in drafting the QDRO, but he did approve it. Herman acknowledged his approval in a letter to Steven in September of 1999. The letter informed Steven the QDRO had been finalized, and it divided his IPERS account "consistent with the stipulation." Herman did not tell Steven that IPERS rejected the lump-sum payment approach agreed to under the stipulation, and he did not explain the percentage method of distribution ultimately used to divide the pension. Consequently, Steven understood at the conclusion of his divorce that his IPERS account had been divided pursuant to the stipulation.

In 2000, the Iowa legislature amended the law governing IPERS to permit in-service disability benefits. Steven subsequently applied to IPERS for disability retirement as a result of exposure to mace and second-hand smoke while working at the prison. IPERS approved his application in January 2001, and eventually informed him that due to the QDRO on file he would receive monthly benefits of $1,209.77, and Karen, as the alternate payee, would receive $962.31 each month.

Steven was surprised to learn Karen would receive a portion of the monthly benefits, and he wrote a letter to Herman expressing his displeasure with the distributions from IPERS. As a result, Herman tried several times to modify the QDRO to provide Steven with a more favorable result. Ultimately, Herman's efforts were unsuccessful and the distributions under the QDRO remained the same.

Steven then brought a legal malpractice action against Herman. He claimed Herman was negligent in preparing and drafting the stipulation and QDRO, and in advising him in the division of the pension. He sought damages based on the amount of benefits Karen would receive in excess of the amount she was entitled to recover under the stipulation.

The case proceeded to trial. The jury found Herman seventy percent negligent and Faber thirty percent negligent. It also found past damages of $20,984.47, and future damages of $88,349.93.

Herman argues the grounds of negligence alleged by Steven could not have caused the damages sought because Steven and Karen intended to divide the pension equally at the time of the divorce, which is exactly what the parties ultimately received. Thus, Herman claims any claim of negligence supported by the evidence was not a cause of the damages sought by Steven.

Causation is an essential element in a cause of action based on negligence.

Causation in a negligence action must be analyzed in the context of the relationship between those theories of negligence supported by the evidence and the theory of damages sought by the plaintiff. Actual causation, as well as legal causation, must exist between the breach of the duty of care and the damages sought. The theory of damages alleged by Steven was based on the amount of benefits Karen would ultimately receive under the QDRO in excess of the $19,100

Karen was to receive under the stipulation. Steven claims this amount represents his compensatory damages because the excess benefits received by Karen should have been received by him.

The jury was instructed on four claims of negligence. They included: (1) Drafting a stipulation (to provide for an immediate payment to Karen of $19,100) contrary to the terms of the IPERS plan. (2) Failing to prepare a QDRO to provide Karen with a specific dollar amount.(3) Failing to advise Steven that he could have divided the pension with non-pension assets worth $19,100. (4) Failing to advise Steven that the QDRO approved by IPERS and entered by the court divided the pension by a different method than agreed under the stipulation.

In analyzing each claim of negligence, we begin with the fundamental principle that pensions can be divided in one of two basic ways. Parties can agree the non-member will receive a share based on the present worth of the pension, or receive a share of the pension benefits at some point in the future when they become payable to the pensioner. Thus, the difference between the two methods involves the payment of an immediate amount or the payment of an amount in the future. We have previously identified this difference by using the terms "present value method" and "percentage method."

The division of a defined-benefit pension plan, such as IPERS, under the present value method requires the use of actuarial science. For this reason, it is normally desirable to divide a defined-benefit plan by using the percentage method. Additionally, it is usually too difficult for a pensioner to pay a lump sum amount representing the present value of a defined pension plan. It is difficult because the lump sum amount is normally paid through an award of non-pension benefits. In this case, Steven's IPERS account was ultimately divided using the normally desirable percentage method.

The future division of IPERS benefits does not usually require actuarial science, but it does require a QDRO. A QDRO is necessary because a future division divides the member's benefits. Without a QDRO, the member's benefits would be distributed to the member according to the terms of the pension plan. The QDRO directs the distribution of future benefits to the former spouse as an alternate payee.

Generally, a QDRO can divide an IPERS account between a member and a nonmember spouse in a divorce in three basic ways: A straight percentage method, a service factor percentage method, and a dollar amount method. A straight percentage method divides the member's lump sum or gross monthly benefit according to a percentage determined by the parties. A service factor percentage method divides the pension according to a percentage multiplied by a factor based on the member's service during the marriage and the member's total service. Finally, a dollar amount method divides the member's lump sum or gross monthly benefits based on a specific dollar amount awarded to the alternate payee. Thus, an IPERS account can be divided in a divorce by one of these three basic methods, or by means of non-pension assets based on the present value of the pension at the time of the divorce.

Our analysis in this case turns on the realization that a one-half division under each method of division produces the same basic result. In other words, if the parties agree to divide a pension equally, an equal division will occur regardless of the method of division selected so long as the methods are properly applied. Of course, an equal division under some of the methods would involve an extremely complex analysis and would be difficult to achieve. This difficulty underscores our previous observation that the service factor percentage approach is the preferred method, even though no method of division can be precise in carrying out the parties' agreement. It is in this light that we consider whether the claims of negligence caused the damages Steven alleges.

The first claim of negligence is that Herman drafted a stipulation (providing for an immediate payment of $19,100 from the IPERS account by means of a QDRO) that could not be carried out pursuant to a QDRO because it was contrary to the IPERS regulations. While Herman was clearly negligent in drafting a stipulation to provide for a division of the pension by a means not permitted by law, it is equally clear that this negligence was not a factual cause of the damages claimed by Steven. The damages claimed by Steven are based on the amount of payments Karen has received and will continue to receive under the service factor percentage method of division in excess of $19,100. Yet, Steven would have suffered this same damage if Herman had drafted a stipulation based on an approved method of division.

The important point is the stipulation clearly expressed the intention of the parties to divide the pension equally. A defined-benefit pension plan such as IPERS can only be divided in one of several methods. If the parties agree to split the pension equally, any method of division will produce the same basic result if properly done. Importantly, there is no claim of negligence raised by Steven that the method ultimately used in this case was misapplied. Thus, the damages claimed by Steven would have occurred in any "one-half" division under our approved methods of division. Steven would have suffered the same harm he now claims if Herman had drafted the stipulation to equally divide the pension under any approved method of division. The causation element was not satisfied as a matter of law.

The next ground of negligence concerns Herman's failure to draft a QDRO that would limit Karen's share to a specific dollar amount. More specifically, Steven claims Herman could have drafted a QDRO to limit the amount of future benefits available to Karen under the IPERS plan. Yet, Steven would again suffer the same damage he now claims (the amount of benefits Karen has received and will receive in excess of $19,100) if Herman had drafted a QDRO with a specific dollar limitation. While a QDRO can limit the benefits to an alternate payee, any limitation on the future benefits available to Karen in this case would need to represent one-half of the value of the pension. This amount would be the practical equivalent of the amount Karen is receiving now. Steven overlooks that the pension was to be split in "one-half" shares, and that under any allowable method of division, "one-half" would equal more than the $19,100 he claims. Although the parties believed the value of the pension was $38,200, that figure only represented the value of the pension as a liquid asset. The pension could only be divided into equal shares of $19,100 as a liquid asset. However, as a benefit payable in the future, its present value was not equivalent to its investment value. Thus, if Herman had properly prepared a QDRO to cap Karen's future benefits as Steven claimed he should have done, then Herman would have been required to determine a cap based upon an equal division of the pension as a future benefit. Such a limitation would far exceed $19,100. Consequently, this claim of negligence does not satisfy the causation element because Steven would have suffered the same harm he now claims if Herman had drafted a QDRO to limit Karen's future distribution. Such a method of division would have achieved a "one-half" division amounting to more than $19,100, and which would be, for all intents and purposes, the same as the division the parties have received.

The next ground of negligence concerns the claim that Herman failed to tell Steven that he could have divided the pension with non-pension benefits instead of dividing the pension under a QDRO. Armed with this advice, Steven claims he could have preserved the pension for himself by giving Karen $19,100 in non-pension assets.

This ground of negligence also fails to support causation because Steven would have suffered the same harm he now claims if the pension had been divided using non-pension assets. Steven's claim of negligence overlooks that if Herman would have drafted a stipulation to divide the pension with non-pension assets, the value of the pension under this method of division would far exceed $38,200. When a pension is divided by means of non-pension assets, the non-pensioner spouse gives up a future interest in the pension and must consequently receive non-pension assets equal to the present value of that future interest.

The final ground of negligence was that Herman failed to inform Steven of the change in the method of dividing the pension from an immediate lump sum payment to the percentage method of division. As with the other grounds of negligence, however, Steven would have suffered the same harm he now claims if Herman had told him of the change in the method of division. This result occurs because any method of division ultimately used to divide a pension equally will, when properly used, achieve an equal division. Of course an equal division was the outcome sought by Steven and the outcome he ultimately obtained.

The common theme with all four claims of negligence is that the parties desired an equal division of the pension, and the only time such a result will not be achieved is when the method employed is erroneously utilized. This was not the case here. Karen received a one-half share in the normally desirable way, and Steven has essentially suffered the same harm he would have suffered had Herman not been negligent. In other words, whatever method Steven would have preferred to use to divide his IPERS pension, a one-half division under any method would have yielded the same result. While the division could have been accomplished by different methods, each with its own advantages and disadvantages, a division by one-half under any method is the practical equivalent for the purposes of determining causation under Steven's theory of compensatory damages. Thus, in the end the negligence of Herman in failing to advise Steven about the methods to equally divide a pension and to draft a stipulation and QDRO to fully protect his one-half interest was not a cause of the damage claimed because the method of division ultimately used by Herman gave Steven his equal division of the pension. This division was not what Steven expected, but his expectation or misunderstanding of the method of distribution was not a cause of the damages claimed. The negligence of Herman in failing to advise Steven of the change may have caused some damages, such as incidental and consequential damages, but not the compensatory damages (difference between the amount of benefits under the stipulation and the amount of benefits under the QDRO that was entered) sought by Steven.

The district court erred by failing to grant Herman's motion for judgment notwithstanding the verdict. As a matter of law, there was no causation between the theories of negligence alleged by Steven and his theory of damage. . . . We vacate the decision of the court of appeals and reverse the judgment entered by the district court.

Problems

1. Harry and Wendy decided to divorce. Wendy retained Attorney to represent her in the divorce. Attorney filed the necessary papers to commence the divorce. At Wendy's request, Attorney drew up a property settlement agreement (PSA) for the couple. At no time did Attorney meet with Harry or advise him about the agreement. Harry and Wendy agreed that Harry would pay half of Attorney's fee for drafting the PSA. Harry sent a check to Attorney for half of Attorney's fee. Wendy gave the agreement to Harry. Harry read and signed it and returned it to Wendy. Attorney filed the agreement with the court. A few weeks later, Harry decided he didn't like some terms of the PSA. Harry filed a motion in court to set aside the agreement. Harry also asked the judge to order Attorney to withdraw from the case because, according to Harry, Attorney had a conflict of interest because Attorney accepted payment for the PSA from Harry. Does Attorney have a conflict of interest? If you face a situation like this in a divorce case, will you accept payment from your client's spouse? *Helms v. Helms,* 317 Ark. 143, 875 S.W.2d 849 (1994).

2. Tim and Tera were married and had two kids. Tim was injured in a traffic accident. Tim and Tera retained Attorney to represent them in a personal injury suit arising out of the accident. Attorney obtained a personal injury settlement for Tim and Tera. While the settlement was pending, Tera met with Attorney. Tera asked Attorney to represent her in a divorce from Tim. Attorney filed the papers to commence a divorce. Not long thereafter, Attorney and Tera began a sexual relationship. While he was sleeping with Tera, Attorney finalized the personal injury settlement. In the divorce, Attorney drafted a marriage settlement agreement (MSA) for Tim and Tera. The MSA dealt with child custody, child support, and property division. Before the divorce was granted, Tim was arrested for various motor vehicle offenses. Attorney agreed to represent Tim on these charges. While the criminal charges were pending, the divorce was granted. The MSA was incorporated into the divorce decree. After the divorce was entered, Tim learned that Tera and Attorney were sleeping together. Tim fired Attorney as his criminal attorney. Tim threatened to kill Attorney. Can Tim return to family court and set aside the divorce decree based on Attorney's behavior with Tera? Can Tim sue Attorney? If Attorney and Tera break up, can Tera sue Attorney? Should the State Bar discipline Attorney? *Nebraska State Bar Association v. Freese,* 259 Neb. 530, 611 N.W.2d 80 (2000).

3. Here's a True/False question for you:

> It is a good idea to have sex with a client.   ___ True   ___ False

CHAPTER 16

Final Practice Exercise:

A "Simple" Divorce from Start to Finish

AS YOU WORKED YOUR WAY through this book, you learned a lot of family law. Of course, you barely scratched the surface of what you need to know. Nevertheless, you have travelled a good distance on the road toward understanding. This final chapter contains a practice problem that affords you the opportunity to apply much of what you have learned. The problem involves Ellen and Bill and gives you an opportunity to work through a "simple" divorce.

Ellen and Bill grew up in Jolly City, in the State of Misanni. They met and dated in high school. Upon graduation, Bill got an entry level job with the state highway department. Ellen started community college and worked at a coffee shop. Ten years ago, when they were twenty, they married. Today they have one child, Justin, age 6. Throughout the marriage, Bill worked full time for the state highway department. He intends to work for the department until he retires. Bill has been promoted to supervisor, and makes $65,000 a year. Bill's job requires him to travel around the state quite a bit, so he is often away from home for periods of a day or two up to several weeks. Ellen worked and went to school until Justin was born, at which point she stopped working and left school to take care of the baby. When Justin was 4, Ellen went back to work part time. She also resumed her college studies. Today, Ellen has about one year left to earn a bachelor's degree. Ellen works 20 hours a week as a receptionist at a doctor's office. She earns $12,000 a year.

Seven years ago, Ellen and Bill purchased a home for $250,000 (see deed below). They took title as joint tenants with right of survivorship. They made the down payment with $10,000 Ellen inherited from her father. There are two mortgages on the home. The first mortgage is with First Bank. Both Ellen and

Bill signed the promissory note and the first mortgage. The balance due on the first mortgage is $180,000. Two years ago, Ellen and Bill took out a $10,000 loan from the state employees credit union to pay off credit card and other debt. The credit union debt is secured by the second mortgage. They both signed the promissory note and the second mortgage for the $10,000 loan. The balance due on the second mortgage is $8,000. The monthly payment on the first mortgage is $1,000. The monthly payment on the second is $300.

Bill has a defined benefit retirement plan with the state. Bill's pension is vested. When Bill retires, his pension will be determined based on a formula that considers how long he works for the state and his average monthly salary for the last three years of employment.

Ellen does not have a retirement plan through her employment.

Bill has medical insurance through his employment. His family is covered by his medical insurance.

Ellen and Bill have a term life insurance policy on Bill's life in the amount of $300,000. Monthly premium payments on the policy are $100.

Ellen and Bill have two cars, a two-year-old Toyota Prius and a ten-year-old Toyota Corolla. The Corolla is paid off. Monthly payments on the Prius are $400.

Assignment: Ellen and Bill have decided to divorce. You represent Ellen. Your assignment is to draft (1) a petition/complaint for dissolution of marriage and accompanying summons, (2) a marriage settlement agreement (MSA), (3) a qualified domestic relations order (QDRO) to divide Bill's pension, (4) the final divorce decree/judgment, which will incorporate the MSA and the QDRO, (5) a deed transferring ownership of the family home to Ellen, and (6) a document to sever the joint tenancy so that it becomes a tenancy in common.

▪ Petition/Complaint and Summons

Many states have forms for the petition and summons in family law cases. If your state uses forms, utilize the forms. If your state does not require forms, draft a Petition in pleading form, along with a summons. Bill will file a general appearance and a response. You don't have to draft Bill's documents.

▪ The MSA

To help you draft the MSA, refer to the Client Intake Form below, filled out by Ellen before her first appointment with you. In drafting the MSA, assume the parties have agreed on the following matters.

Child custody. Ellen and Bill agree on joint legal custody of Justin, with primary physical custody to Ellen. They agree that Bill will have limited physical custody and liberal visitation. They would like to retain as much flexibility as possible regarding custody and visitation because they feel they can work cooperatively regarding parenting.

Child support. Ellen and Bill agree Bill will pay Ellen $300 per month child support.

Spousal support. Ellen and Bill agree there will be no spousal support.

Property. Ellen and Bill agree that Ellen will have sole ownership of the family home. Ellen will assume payment of both mortgages. To be able to make the mortgage payments, Ellen will quit school and find full time employment. While Ellen is working, Justin will either be in school or taken care of by his grandparents, who live nearby.

Bill is personally liable for both mortgages (he signed the promissory notes on both). Because Bill is willing to give his interest in the family home to Ellen, he would like to know if it is possible for him to be relieved of his personal liability on the two mortgage debts. That is, will the bank and the credit union agree to relieve Bill of his indebtedness? Research this issue and prepare language for the MSA.

As for Bill's pension, Ellen and Bill agree they will wait until Bill retires to receive their respective shares of the pension. Draft a Qualified Domestic Relations Order (QDRO) to submit to Bill's employer for approval. To draft the QDRO, you will need to study the materials reproduced below: (1) State Miscellaneous & Industrial Benefits: What You Need to Know About Your MisPERS Benefits the Model Order Packet, and (2) MisPERS Community Property Model Order Package Draft the QDRO.

Draft language to incorporate the QDRO into the MSA.

Medical insurance. Bill has medical insurance through his employer. Ellen and Justin are covered by the insurance while Bill and Ellen are married. Bill's state health insurance falls under the federal Consolidated Omnibus Reconciliation Act of 1985 (COBRA). Draft language for the MSA that will continue medical coverage for Ellen and Justin after the divorce.

Life insurance. Draft language that obligates Bill to maintain the life insurance policy on his life, with the child as beneficiary.

The cars. Draft language giving the Prius to Ellen and the Corolla to Bill.

The bank accounts. Draft language to split funds in bank accounts.

Debts. Draft language to divide responsibility for debts.

■ Decree/Judgment of Divorce

Draft a final decree/judgment of divorce that incorporates the MSA.

■ Deed

Draft a deed transferring the family home to Ellen.

■ Document to Sever Joint Tenancy

Ellen and Bill own their home as joint tenants with right of survivorship. If one of them dies before the divorce is final, the divorce action abates. The survivor will own the home by right of survivorship. To avoid this possibility, prepare a document that will sever the joint tenancy. You will need to find out the law and the procedure in your state governing severance of joint tenancy. The severance document will be filed with the land records in the county.

GRANT DEED

This Deed, made this 3rd day of May, [7 years ago], in consideration of the sum of One Dollar ($1.00) and other good and valuable consideration now paid, the receipt of which is acknowledged, witnesses that, Arnold R. Porter Does hereby grant, bargain, sell and convey to Ellen and Bill Peterson, wife and husband, as joint tenants with right of survivorship, the following described real property:

Parcel No. 10, as set forth on the map recorded in Book 332, Page 17, Blue Bird County, Misanni. 234 Maple St. Jolly City, Misanni.

To have and to hold in fee simple absolute, with all the reservations, remainders, tenements, hereditaments, and appurtenances thereto forever.

This Deed was executed on the date of last acknowledgment.

Arnold R. Porter, Grantor

State of Misanni
County of Blue Bird

This instrument was acknowledged before me
on 4 June, [7 years ago]

By Arnold R. Porter, Grantor   Grace Abbott

      SEAL   Notary Public

My Commission expires:

Client Intake Form[1]

Before you come to the office for your
appointment, please take whatever time you need to fill out this form.
Our office can only help you when we have complete information.
We realize it is an inconvenience for you
to fill out this lengthy form, but please understand that in the long
run, doing a thorough job on this form will save
you time and money.

1. Names and descriptions of spouses/domestic partners

Your full name: *Ellen Peterson.*

Your spouse/partner's full name: *William (Bill) Peterson*

Have you or your spouse/partner ever used any other names or aliases?
If yes, please list:
No.

Will you want to resume use of your former surname after termination of
your relationship? What is the name you wish to resume?
No, I want to keep Peterson.

Please provide the following information regarding your spouse/
partner: employer (name and address), working hours, current income from
employment:
*Bill started working for the state highway department right after high
school. He works 40 hours a week. Bill is a supervisor. His yearly gross
salary is $65,000.*

2. Residence and contact information

Your current address: *234 Maple St., Jolly City, Misanni.*

Name and relationship to you of every person living with you:
Bill, spouse. Justin Peterson, our son.

---

1 The client intake form is borrowed from *California Family Law Practice and Procedure* (2d ed. 2012)(Matthew Bender).

How long have you lived at this address?
We bought the house seven years ago.

Your previous addresses going back 5 years:
NA.

Your phone number(s), FAX, and email address:
(123) 456-7890. No FAX. Email: epeterson@sbc.net.

Your spouse/partner's current address:
*We live together, but Bill will be moving out soon to an apartment.
I don't know the address.*

Contact information for your spouse/partner:
*Bill's cell number is (234) 567-8899. His office address is: State Highway
Department, Maintenance Yard, 7483 Yale Blvd., Jolly City, Misanni.*

3. Birth information

Your date of birth:
May 23, 1980.

Your spouse/partner's date of birth:
January 5, 1980.

4. Citizenship and immigration status

Immigration status of anyone who is not a U.S. citizen. Please supply
details of permanent residency or naturalization. If not in the U.S. legally, please
inform me of this fact. Keep in mind that information you provide to me in
confidence is confidential:
We are U.S. citizens.

5. Social Security numbers

Your Social Security number:
123-45-6789.

Your spouse/partner's Social Security number:
987-65-4321.

6. Information about your marriage/domestic partnership

Date of marriage or registration as domestic partners:
We were married June 15, [10 years ago].

Place (city) where you celebrated your marriage/partnership:
Jolly City, Misanni.

County where marriage license obtained:
Blue Bird.

7. Ending your relationship

Please explain in a few words, why you are thinking of ending your marriage/partnership:

This has been coming a long time. It makes me very sad to say, but we don't love each other anymore. Bill has never been violent with me; he's just cold and distant. We've talked about it a hundred times, but it never does any good. We agree that at this point we want to go our separate ways. We are concerned about the impact of a divorce on Justin, of course. But we feel that if we can do this amicably and cooperate, then it won't be too hard on him. Bill and I want to remain active in Justin's life.

Would you like to "save" your marriage/partnership, if possible?
Please explain:

No, it is over.

What about your spouse/partner? To the best of your knowledge, does your spouse/partner want to end the relationship?

We agree it is over. We talked about this last night and agreed.

Do you think it would be a good idea to consult a marriage counselor?
Please explain:

We tried marriage counseling a couple of years ago, and it seemed to help for a little while, but not for long. No, I don't think it is worth trying again.

Are you separated from your spouse/partner? If so, please describe when you separated and the circumstances of the separation (*e.g.*, who moved out, what was said about separation, etc.):

Like I said earlier, Bill is planning to move out soon into an apartment. He signed a lease that starts one week from today.

Were there previous separations and reconciliations? Is yes, please describe and provide dates:

No, no previous separations.

8. Domestic Violence

In your marriage/partnership, has there ever been any violence between you and your spouse/partner? If yes, please describe: *No.*

9. Previous marriages/domestic partnerships

Have you been previously married or in a partnership? If yes, please describe, including relevant dates: *No.*

Has your spouse/partner been previously married or in a partnership? If yes, please describe, including relevant dates: *No.*

10. Children

Please provide the full name, age, date of birth, place of birth, gender, and Social Security number for all of your children. For each child, state: (1) Are you the child's biological parent? (2) Who is the other biological parent? (3) If you are a step-parent, please explain. (4) If you adopted any of your children, please explain.

Justin is our only child.

With whom does each child live?

He lives in our home. We plan to share custody. Because Bill has to be on the road a lot, we agree that I should have primary physical custody. Bill could have partial custody and all the visits he wants.

Please describe any special medical, dental, or mental health needs of your children: *None.*

Please list all insurance currently in place for your children:

Health insurance through Bill's work.

Have you and your spouse/partner discussed or agreed upon how you wish to handle child custody and visitation?

As I mentioned above, I'd like primary physical custody.

11. Health issues

Do you or your spouse/partner have any special health issues? Please explain:

No, both of us are in good health.

Describe any insurance that you have:

We have good medical insurance through Bill's work. What will happen to the insurance coverage for me if we get a divorce?

12. Property

Please provide a list of all interests you and your spouse/partner have in property. Property includes real estate, bank accounts, stock, retirement/pension plans, cars, life insurance. If you have deeds or other documents of title regarding property, please provide a copy.

Our family home. I have attached a copy of the deed. There are two mortgages on the house. Bill and I are both responsible for the debt on these two mortgages. The first mortgage is with First bank, and we owe $180,000. The second mortgage is with the state employees credit union, and we owe $8,000.

We have two cars. An old Toyota Corolla (Bill's car) that is paid off. The Corolla is a 2001. It has 150,000+ miles on it, but it never breaks because it is a Toyota. We have a 2011 Toyota Prius (my car). It has 20,000 miles. We owe $15,000 on the Prius, and the monthly payment is $400.

I don't have any pension.

Bill has his pension with the state.

Through the state, we have a term life insurance policy on Bill for $300,000, and we pay $100 per month for that.

We have a joint checking account at First Bank. The current balance is $1,000. We live pretty much pay check to pay check, and the balance in the account is always about $1,000. We have a savings account with First Bank, and we have saved $2,500.

13. Debts

Please list all your debts:
First mortgage: $180,000. One thousand a month.

Second mortgage: *$8,000. $300 a month.*

Utilities on the house: *$350 per month.*

Car payment each month: *$400.*

Food and clothing: *$400 month.*

Transportation:
Bill gets to use a state car and the state pays for his gas. Our Prius gets great mileage, so our monthly gas bill is only about $100.

Fortunately we paid off a large credit card bill we had. We used the loan from the credit union to pay off that debt. Now we try really hard to pay off our VISA card every month. Right now we don't have any credit card debt!

Materials Regarding Bill's State Pension

Below you will find two documents related to Bill's state pension. First, a brief description of the MisPERS pension program. Second, a document prepared by the state to help people draft QDROs regarding state pensions.

State Miscellaneous & Industrial Benefits:

What You Need to Know
About Your MisPERS Benefits

MisPERS members make a monthly retirement contribution to MisPERS that equals approximately 5-11 percent of salary, although the amount can vary for different employee bargaining units. The member also earns retirement service credit.

There are three types of retirement benefits:

- Service Retirement or "Normal" Retirement

- Disability Retirement

- Industrial Disability Retirement

Service Retirement or "Normal" Retirement

To be eligible for service retirement, you must be at least age 50 and have a minimum of five years of MisPERS-credited service.

Disability Retirement

This type of retirement applies to you if you become disabled and can no longer perform the duties of your job. Disability retirement has no minimum age requirement, and your disability does not need to be job related.

Industrial Disability Retirement

This type of retirement applies to you if you become disabled from a job-related injury or illness and can no longer perform the duties of your job. Industrial disability retirement has no minimum age or service credit requirement.

How Your Retirement is Funded

Three sources fund a defined benefit retirement plan like MisPERS. First, employees generally make contributions into the System. The percentage of your contribution is fixed by statute and varies from about 5 to about 11 percent of your earnings, depending on the plan type and whether you are covered by Social Security. The second funding source is earnings from the investment of System assets in stocks, bonds, real estate, and other investment vehicles. The amount contributed from this source fluctuates from year to year. The balance of the funding is provided by employer contributions. Employer contributions decline when investment returns rise and increase when investment returns decline.

In a defined benefit retirement plan, you will receive a lifetime benefit determined by a set formula. For State members, MisPERS uses your credited years of service, age at retirement, and highest one-year compensation or three-year compensation while employed. This contrasts with a defined contribution plan (such as a 401(k) plan), in which the benefits are determined not by a formula, but solely by the amount of contributions in an account, plus earnings.

How Your Retirement Benefit is Calculated

Now that you understand the basic building blocks of a defined benefit retirement system, it's time to learn how to calculate your retirement benefit. Three factors are multiplied together to calculate your service retirement:

- Service Credit

- Benefit Factor

- Final Compensation

Service Credit

You earn service credit for each year or partial year you work for the State.

In some cases, you may be eligible for other types of service credit that can help you maximize your retirement benefits.

Other types of service include:

- Unused sick leave at retirement

- Unused education leave at retirement

- Redeposit of contributions you previously withdrew from MisPERS

- Additional Retirement Service Credit (ARSC)

Benefit Factor

Your benefit factor is the percentage of pay to which you are entitled for each year of service. It is determined by your age at retirement and the retirement formula for your classification. This guide explains the following State miscellaneous and individual retirement formulas.

- 2% at 55

- 2% at 60

- 1¼ % at 65

Final Compensation

Final compensation is your average full-time monthly pay rate and special compensation for the last consecutive 12 or 36 months of employment.

Your Options at Retirement

At retirement, you can choose to receive the highest benefit payable, which is referred to as the Unmodified Allowance. The "Unmodified Allowance" provides a monthly benefit to you that ends upon your death.

You also have the choice of requesting a reduction in the Unmodified Allowance to provide a lump sum or monthly benefit for a beneficiary upon your death.

Option 1

This retirement option provides a lump sum payment of your remaining member contributions to your beneficiary after your death. The reduction to your monthly benefit to provide this payment is based on your life expectancy at retirement and the amount of your contributions. You can name one or more beneficiary(ies), and can name a new beneficiary at any time. If you name someone other than your spouse or registered domestic partner as your Option 1 beneficiary(ies), upon your death your spouse or domestic partner may still be entitled to a community property share of any remaining contributions.

Option 2

The same retirement allowance you receive will be paid to your beneficiary for life.

Option 3

In this option, one-half of your monthly retirement allowance will be paid to your beneficiary for life.

Option 4

Option 4 is a somewhat flexible option. There are several unique variations of Option 4, each specifically designed to mesh with various situations that might apply to you such as the ability to name more than one beneficiary.

Cost-of-Living Adjustments

Cost-of-living adjustments are provided by law and are based on the Consumer Price Index for all United States cities. Cost-of-living adjustments are paid the second calendar year of your retirement on the May 1 check and then every year thereafter.

The Standard cost-of-living adjustment is a maximum of 2 percent per year.

Member Services Division
P.O. Box 9689
Capitol City, Misanni 98765
Telecommunications Device for the Deaf - (123) 123-1234
(123) 456-7890

MISPERS COMMUNITY PROPERTY
MODEL ORDER PACKAGE

The purpose of this package is to provide you with information concerning the Misanni Public Employees' Retirement System's ("MisPERS" or "System") procedures for processing and implementing domestic relations orders that are designed to allocate and award a portion of a member's retirement benefits to a nonmember spouse. The following documents are included in this package:

MisPERS Procedures to Determine the Status of Domestic Relations Orders

MisPERS Instructions for Completion of Model Domestic Relations Order

MisPERS Model Domestic Relations Orders:

Model Order A — Separation of Account for members not retired
Model Order B — Division of Benefits for members not retired
Model Order C — Division of Benefits for retired members only

PLAN INFORMATION

The plan administered by MisPERS is a "governmental plan" as defined in section 414(d) of the Internal Revenue Code of 1986, and is not subject to the provisions of section 414(p) of the Internal Revenue Code and section 206(d) of ERISA which govern "qualified domestic relations orders." The terms of the plan are set forth in the Misanni Public Employees' Retirement Law ("PERL"), which can be found at section 258908, et seq., of the Misanni Government Code.

The administrator of the plan is the MisPERS Board of Administration. The plan is a defined benefit plan and most members contribute a percentage of their salary to the System. Member contributions are separated into individual member accounts and may be withdrawn, with any interest which has accrued, upon permanent termination of MisPERS covered employment. If the member withdraws his or her contributions, the member will not be entitled to a monthly retirement allowance. If the member does not withdraw his or her contributions, the member may, at retirement, elect to receive an unmodified monthly allowance paid for the life of the member or elect to reduce the allowance and receive one of the optional settlements. The member's contributions, if any, will fund the "annuity" portion of any monthly allowance elected.

The employer also contributes a percentage of the member's salary to the System, and may contract with MisPERS to provide other benefits as well; e.g., certain death benefits. Unlike member contributions, employer contributions are not separated into individual member accounts and are not subject to withdrawal upon termination of MisPERS covered employment.

As noted above, if the member has not previously withdrawn his or her member contributions, the member, when eligible, may elect to receive a monthly retirement allowance. The employer contributions are used to fund the "pension" portion of the member's monthly retirement allowance. On the other hand, if the member does withdraw his or her member contributions, the member will not receive a monthly retirement allowance or the benefit of any of the employer contributions which were made on the member's behalf.

The Public Employees' Retirement Law (PERL) is complex. The above description of the plan is merely intended to summarize how the plan operates. For a complete description of the plan, the parties and their respective counsel are strongly advised to review the PERL and the appropriate member booklet. The member booklet provides a summary of the various benefits available to the member. If one was not included with this package, you may request a member booklet from any MisPERS office.

MISPERS MODEL DOMESTIC RELATIONS ORDER PACKAGE

In accordance with applicable law, MisPERS has determined that it is in the best interest of the System, its members, and their spouses to provide for certain procedures designed to efficiently and effectively process and implement domestic relations orders that require the System to allocate and assign a portion of a member's benefits to his or her nonmember spouse. A domestic relations order ("order") will only be processed if such order is acceptable under the terms of the PERL and other applicable law.

The enclosed procedures are designed to inform you of the steps that MisPERS will undertake to process any order you may submit. The model domestic relations order is intended as a sample only and is provided to assist you in the preparation of an order that is acceptable to MisPERS. You may, of course, use other language; however, any order must be consistent with the terms of the PERL. In the event that MisPERS determines that an order is not consistent with the terms of the PERL, MisPERS will require that the parties modify the order in all necessary respects.

The instructions for completing the model domestic relations order provide some additional information regarding the options available for dividing the community's interest in a member's benefits.

REQUEST FOR INFORMATION / CONFIDENTIALITY

By law, the contents of a member's retirement file are confidential, except to the member or his or her authorized representative. The member's spouse and/or the attorney may obtain information, if the request includes the member's written authorization or if MisPERS has been joined as a party to the dissolution. To obtain the information, the System must receive either:

A Subpoena Duces Tecum. Upon receipt of a subpoena, the contents of a member's file will be photocopied and the requested calculations completed. Pursuant to section 1563 of the Misanni Evidence Code, the System charges $10 an hour clerical costs, plus $.10 per page copying costs. This amount represents actual costs incurred in locating and making the records available. The System will accept service of subpoena by mail, if joined. If not joined, we require personal service of the subpoena which may be personally served to our Legal Office at 400 P Street, 3rd Floor, Capitol City, Misanni. Please be sure to include a Proof of Service and Notice to Consumer; OR

A written request outlining the specific data needed. All correspondence with MisPERS must include the member's name and Social Security number. Upon receipt of a written request, MisPERS may provide the following information:

- A statement as to the member's accumulated contributions and interest for a specified period. If specific dates are not requested, a current statement will be provided. Due to agencies' reporting requirements, a current statement will reflect contributions two to four months in arrears.

- A statement as to the member's years of service credit. Again, if a specific period is not requested, a current statement will be provided.

- A statement as to the membership classification; i.e., safety or miscellaneous member, state or local member, and the applicable benefit formula.

- A statement as to retiree's option selected at retirement, the beneficiary designated, the amount of monthly allowance and any death benefit payable.

MisPERS will not provide:

- Actuarial valuations of retirement benefits. Although a private actuary may provide a valuation of the pension plan, MisPERS will not accept an order which provides for payment of benefits not authorized by the Government Code.

- Employment data, salary, payroll, and earnings or personnel records. You must contact the employer directly for this information.

HEALTH BENEFIT INFORMATION

This information applies only to members or retirees enrolled in a MisPERS-sponsored health plan under the Public Employees' Medical and Hospital Care Act (PEMHCA). The nonmember spouse loses eligibility for health benefit coverage under the member's insurance at midnight the last day of the month in which the marriage terminated. The nonmember spouse may, however, elect to continue coverage under the employer's group health plan at his or her own expense for a period of up to 36 months from the date coverage would otherwise be lost as a result of the divorce pursuant to the Consolidated Omnibus Budget Reconciliation Act of 1985, ("COBRA").

For more information regarding COBRA rights, please contact the member's Personnel Office if the member is currently employed under a PEMHCA agency. If the member is retired and has MisPERS-covered insurance, please contact:

Health Benefit Services Division
P.O. Box 942714
Capitol City, Misanni
Telephone: (123) 456-9876

The nonmember spouse may also obtain health insurance by requesting a conversion policy underwritten by the member's current health benefits plan or insurance carrier. The nonmember spouse should contact the carrier within 30 days of the termination date of group coverage for information on the coverage and cost of the policy.

It is the responsibility of the employee or retiree to report a dissolution of marriage which results in the loss of insurance coverage for the nonmember spouse to their personnel office or, if retired, to MisPERS, within 60 days of the date that the marriage was terminated. Otherwise, there is no eligibility for COBRA coverage.

The MisPERS Community Property Unit in the Member Services Division is responsible for processing domestic relations orders. If you have any questions regarding the enclosed documents or MisPERS' procedures for processing domestic relations orders, please contact:

Misanni Public Employees' Retirement System
Attn: Community Property Unit
P.O. Box 2056
Capitol City, Misanni
Telecommunication Device for the Deaf: (124) 795-4567
Telephone: (124) 877-5551

PROCEDURES FOR PROCESSING MisPERS
DOMESTIC RELATIONS ORDERS

The plan administered by the Misanni Public Employees' Retirement System ("MisPERS" or "System") is a "governmental plan" as defined in section 414(d) of the Internal Revenue Code of 1986, as amended ("Code") and section 3(32) of the Employee Retirement Income Security Act of 1974, as amended ("ERISA") and is thus not subject to the provisions of section 414(p) of the Code and section 206(d) of ERISA which govern "qualified domestic relations orders." See Code section 401(a) (final paragraph of the section); Code section 411(e)(1)(A) and ERISA section 4(b)(1). The terms of the plan are set forth in the Misanni Public Employees' Retirement Law ("PERL"), which can be found at section 258908, et seq., of the Misanni Government Code.

The administrator of the plan is the MisPERS' Board of Administration. A domestic relations order ("order") that is designed to allocate and award a portion of a member's retirement benefits to his or her nonmember spouse will only be processed if such order is acceptable under the terms of the PERL and other applicable law.

MisPERS has determined that it is in the best interests of the System, its members and their spouses to provide certain procedures designed to efficiently and effectively process such orders.

MisPERS shall review and administer all orders received with respect to benefits provided by the System. When administratively practicable, MisPERS shall act pursuant to the following procedures:

Procedures Prior to Receipt of an Order

Section 755 of the Misanni Family Code provides, among other things, a procedure whereby a person who claims an interest in a member's retirement benefits ("nonmember spouse") may seek to protect that interest by providing written notification to MisPERS of such interest.

MisPERS must be joined as a party to the applicable proceeding, in accordance with Misanni Family Code sections 2060-2074. MisPERS should not be joined if the dissolution action is filed in a state other than Misanni.

Upon receipt of notice of a claim under section 755, a properly filed summons (joinder), or a proposed (draft) court order, MisPERS shall notify both parties, or their representatives, in writing, of the receipt of such notice, joinder or order, along with a copy of these procedures and shall not permit any distributions from the affected member's benefits unless and until such time as the claim has been resolved to the satisfaction of MisPERS or MisPERS has received an acceptable filed court order.

Upon receipt of a claim, joinder, or order which proposes to divide a retired member's pension, MisPERS will continue to pay the retired member one-half of his or her retirement allowance pending receipt of a filed court order or other resolution of the community property claim. The party, who placed the claim, filed the joinder or submitted the proposed order, may notify MisPERS in writing to continue to pay the full allowance to the member. However, if full benefits continue to be paid to the member, any benefit awarded to the nonmember spouse will be paid on a prospective basis after the filed court order has been received and approved by MisPERS.

Procedures Upon Receipt of a Proposed or Draft Order

A. Upon receipt of a proposed or draft copy of an order, MisPERS shall:

If the provisions of the order are acceptable, MisPERS shall notify all persons named in the order and their attorneys ("interested parties") that a determination has been made that the order is acceptable. If an original order is submitted requiring MisPERS signature, the order will be signed by MisPERS staff and returned to the requesting party for filing with the court. Please note that although MisPERS' model order includes a signature block for the approval of the order by MisPERS staff, we will sign the order only after it has been signed by both parties.

If the order is not acceptable, MisPERS shall notify all interested parties that a determination has been made that the order is not acceptable. The notice shall state the reason the order is not acceptable to MisPERS.

PROCEDURES UPON RECEIPT OF A FILED COURT ORDER

A. Within 30 days of receipt of a filed order, MisPERS shall make a final determination as to whether or not the order is acceptable.

If the order is acceptable, MisPERS shall follow the terms of the order as soon as administratively practicable following the date MisPERS determines that the order is acceptable and shall notify all interested parties in writing that such order is acceptable.

If a final determination is made that the order, as written, is not acceptable, MisPERS shall so notify all interested parties. MisPERS shall require the parties to take any such action as is necessary to modify the order.

Supplemental Procedure

MisPERS is authorized to take whatever action it deems appropriate to arrive at a final determination as to the status of each order. In general, MisPERS shall determine whether the order, as written, can be effectively administered pursuant to the terms of the PERL. In accordance with the foregoing, all interested parties shall promptly respond to any request by MisPERS for additional information or documentation. Any failure to provide such information or documentation will delay the determination process.

The order must be acceptable to MisPERS at the time benefit distributions to either party are to commence. MisPERS shall review the order and confirm that the order is acceptable prior to the time benefit distributions are to commence. It shall be the responsibility of the parties to advise if the order has been amended subsequent to the Board's initial determination that the order was acceptable.

All written communication with the member and the nonmember spouse or other interested party shall be sent by first class mail to the addresses provided in the order or to the address maintained by MisPERS, unless MisPERS receives written notice of a change of address

INSTRUCTIONS FOR COMPLETION OF
MODEL DOMESTIC RELATIONS ORDER

Enclosed with these instructions is a model domestic relations order ("model") prepared by the Misanni Public Employees' Retirement System ("MisPERS" or "System"), which offers provisions that conform with the benefit provisions of the Public Employees' Retirement Law ("PERL"), section 258908, et seq., of the Misanni Government Code, and other applicable law.

Completion of the model will expedite the process for determining whether a domestic relations order can be administered by the System and will ensure that the provisions of such order conform with the PERL. The model order is to be used as a guide when preparing an order to divide the retirement benefits of a MisPERS member. **The model is not to be used as a fill in form. The model is only intended to provide suggested language. The parties may, of course, agree to, or a court may order, other language, provided the ultimate order is consistent with the terms of the PERL and other applicable law. The parties and their respective counsel are also advised to review the applicable provisions of the PERL and the applicable member booklet, which provide a summary description of the benefits to which a member in a particular employment category may be entitled. Some benefits described in the booklet may only apply to a given member if his or her employer has contracted with the System to provide such benefits. The parties and their counsel are responsible for determining exactly what benefits a member is entitled to and how each method available for dividing those benefits will affect those benefits. This sample order is not, nor can it be, a substitute for reviewing the terms of the PERL and the applicable member booklet. The System does not provide legal, tax or other advice regarding the division of a member's benefits.**

As you will note, the provisions of the model reflect Misanni community property law and may need to be revised to accommodate other state domestic relations laws.

As discussed in more detail below, the model contains three separate ORDERS which may be used to divide the community property interest in a MisPERS member's pension plan. These will be referred to as ORDER A, B and C. ORDER A and B apply only to members who have not yet retired. ORDER C applies to retired members ONLY. All three ORDERS are included as samples only. When the actual ORDER is filed, only one of the sample orders, EITHER A, B, OR C, should be included in the final package.

INSTRUCTIONS

The initial blanks on page one of the model must be completed as provided by the court with respect to case number, matter of the marriage, judicial district, county and date. Also note that in the first full paragraph of the model, counsel must provide the names of petitioner and respondent. Important information relative to the System is as follows:

Governing Law:	Misanni Public Employees' Retirement Law, section 258908, et seq., of the Misanni Government Code
Administrator:	Board of Administration of the Misanni Public Employees' Retirement System
Address:	Misanni Public Employees' Retirement System Member Services Division Attn: Community Property Unit P.O. Box 2056 Capitol City, Misanni
Type of Plan:	Defined Benefit Plan

The model is designed to allocate and award a nonmember spouse a portion of a member's interest in the System. The model is broken down into three sections, Recitals, Stipulation and Order. These instructions follow that format.

RECITALS

Paragraph 1: Indicate the date of marriage, the date of separation and the date the court entered a judgment of dissolution of marriage (if applicable).

Paragraph 2: States that the court has personal jurisdiction over both the Petitioner and Respondent and the subject matter of the action.

Paragraph 3: States that the System was properly joined as a party to the action pursuant to sections 2060 through 2065 of the Misanni Family Code (if applicable).

STIPULATION

A stipulation by the Respondent, the Petitioner and the System that this domestic relations order is acceptable under the terms of the PERL and can be administered by the System. For more information refer to the PERL and the applicable member booklet.

ORDER

Paragraph 4: Provides that the domestic relations order was entered pursuant to the Misanni Family Code. If this is not the appropriate cite for the order, please cite the applicable domestic relations law pursuant to which the order is to be entered.

MEMBERS WHO HAVE NOT YET RETIRED:
ORDER A OR ORDER B

There are two methods by which the community property interest of a MisPERS member who has not yet retired may be divided; both methods are provided for in the model and explained in these instructions for completing the model. However, it is the sole responsibility of the parties and their respective counsel to determine which method would be the most advantageous based upon the parties' obligations, needs, and desires.

ORDER A
DIVISION OF MEMBER'S ACCUMULATED CONTRIBUTIONS AND
SERVICE CREDIT BY SEPARATION OF ACCOUNT

The first method is an order made pursuant to sections 2667(c) of the Family Code and sections 21299 through 21310 of the Government Code which allow the community property interest in a member's pension to be divided by separating the service credit and member contributions accrued during the marriage into two separate and distinct accounts, one in the name of the member and one in the name of the nonmember spouse. **The parties and their respective counsel are advised to review sections 21299 through 21310 of the Government Code for a complete description of this method of dividing a member's account.**

If the member was vested on the date of dissolution, the nonmember would have the right to receive a monthly allowance from the nonmember account, independent of the member, when both reach the minimum retirement age. The monthly allowance payable to the nonmember spouse would be based on the service credited to the nonmember account, the nonmember's age at retirement and the salary (final compensation) earned by the member prior to the dissolution of the marriage.

In lieu of a monthly allowance, the nonmember spouse would have the right to withdraw, by direct refund or rollover, the member contributions and interest credited to the nonmember account, plus interest earned at 6% per year through date of payment. The taxable portion of the benefit would be subject to 20% federal withholding, unless it was rolled over to an IRA. If the member was not vested on the date of dissolution, the nonmember's only right would be to withdraw his or her contributions by a direct refund or rollover.

Some MisPERS members, such as State Miscellaneous Second-Tier, do not contribute to MisPERS. In that case, there would be no contributions available for the nonmember to refund. The nonmember could receive a monthly allowance, when eligible, but only if the member was vested on the date of the parties' dissolution of marriage.

If the nonmember chooses to withdraw the contributions and interest credited to the nonmember account, the member would have the right to purchase that service credit and redeposit those contributions, plus interest, in order to restore the service credit and contributions to the member account. Any such election to redeposit the contributions and service must be made prior to a member's retirement. If, however, the nonmember chooses to leave the funds on deposit or if the nonmember elects to receive a monthly allowance, the member cannot purchase the contributions and service credit transferred to the nonmember account.

After a separation of account occurs, the benefits payable to the member at retirement or payable upon the member's death prior to retirement will be based on the actual service credit and/or contributions remaining in his or her member account.

However, Government Code section 21251.15 provides for a new calculation method for any member whose account was divided in accordance with Government Code 21290 and who retires on or after January 1, 2004, if the nonmember spouse (1) qualifies to retire from the nonmember account **and** (2) has NOT received a refund prior to the member's retirement date. The new calculation provides that a member's retirement allowance shall be equal to the **difference** between (1) the allowance that would have been payable to the member had the separation of the account not occurred, and (2) the unmodified allowance payable to the nonmember spouse, less an actuarial adjustment if the nonmember spouse retires before the member. For further information, please refer to Government Code 21251.15, or contact the Community Property Unit directly.

PARAGRAPHS 5 THROUGH 10 OF ORDER A
ILLUSTRATE THIS METHOD OF DIVIDING THE COMMUNITY
PROPERTY INTEREST IN A MisPERS PENSION:

Paragraph 5: States that the parties have a community interest in the member's pension plan and defines that interest as the member's accumulated retirement contributions and service credit attributable to periods of service in the System from the parties' date of marriage up to the date of separation.

Paragraph 6: States that 50% of the member's accumulated retirement contributions and service credit is to be allocated and awarded to the nonmember spouse as his or her "System Interest." The order may specify a percentage higher or lower than 50%, provided that such percentage is acceptable to MisPERS. Paragraph 3 also provides that any contributions and service credit not awarded to the nonmember spouse shall be the sole and separate property of the member.

MisPERS WILL NOT accept an order, entered in accordance with Government Code sections 21299 through 21310, which provides for either a specific dollar amount or specific years of service credit to be used to establish the nonmember spouse's interest, or which attempts to divide only contributions without service credit.\

*IMPORTANT INFORMATION REGARDING ELECTIVE SERVICE CREDIT for Model Order A: All community property, including the issue of elective service credit, needs to be specifically addressed in the court order. Unless otherwise provided for in the order, any elective service credit and contributions, such as military service, service prior to membership, redeposit of previously refunded contributions, or additional retirement service credit will be divided according to when the service and contributions were credited and paid to the member's account. For example, if the member earned military service credit prior to his or her marriage, **but elected and paid for that service during the marriage,** MisPERS would divide the service and contributions proportionately to both the member and nonmember. If elective 'service credit is not addressed in the court order, any service purchased or redeposited after the date of marital separation, will be treated as the member's separate property.*

Paragraph 7: In accordance with section 21299 of the Government Code, paragraph 7 provides that MisPERS shall establish separate accounts for the member and the nonmember for the interests awarded to each of them pursuant to paragraph 6 of the order.

Paragraph 8: Following the date that separate accounts have been established for the member and the nonmember spouse, paragraph 8 provides that the nonmember spouse shall be entitled to all rights permitted under section 21299(c) of the Misanni Government Code, as summarized in paragraphs 8.a. through 8.e. The parties and their respective counsel are once again advised to review the provisions of the Government Code affecting the rights of the nonmember spouse with respect to his or her System Interest.

Paragraph 9: Illustrates how the parties may provide for the nonmember spouse's interest to go to a beneficiary if the nonmember spouse should die prior to receiving his or her System Interest.

Paragraph 10: Provides, in accordance with section 21299(g) of the Government Code, that the nonmember spouse will receive a refund of the nonmember spouse's accumulated contributions and any interest that has accrued to such contributions, as soon as administratively practicable, following the date an account was established for the nonmember spouse if the member did not have the necessary minimum credited service to retire as of the parties' dissolution or legal separation.

Paragraph 11: **SUPPLEMENTAL PROVISIONS**: Apply to orders A, B and C. Please refer to page 19 for instructions on paragraph 11 through 21.

----------* * * *----------

ORDER B
DIVISION OF COMMUNITY PROPERTY INTEREST
AT THE TIME BENEFITS BECOME PAYABLE TO THE MEMBER

— TIME-RULE METHOD —

The second method used to divide the community property interest in the pension plan of a MisPERS member who has not yet retired, provides for the nonmember spouse to receive his or her community property interest at the time benefits become payable to the member. Benefits become payable to a member only upon the member's retirement or termination of membership. Pursuant to sections 2610(a) and (b) of the Family Code, the court may also order the division of any benefits payable upon the death of the member and/or order the member to elect a survivor benefit annuity or other similar election for the benefit of the nonmember spouse.

Under this method of dividing community property, the nonmember spouse's "System Interest" can **only** be paid by MisPERS at the time that benefits become payable. If the nonmember spouse wishes to receive his or her community property interest from MisPERS prior to the time that benefits become payable, the parties should consider using ORDER A: DIVISION OF MEMBER'S ACCUMULATED RETIREMENT CONTRIBUTIONS AND SERVICE CREDIT BY SEPARATION OF ACCOUNT.

IMPORTANT INFORMATION REGARDING ELECTIVE SERVICE CREDIT for Model Order B: All community property, including any elective service credit, must be specifically addressed in the court order. Unless otherwise provided for in the order, any elective service credit and contributions, such as military service, service prior to membership, redeposit of previously refunded contributions or additional retirement service credit will be applied to the calculation according to when the service and contributions were credited and paid to the member's account. For example, if the member earned military service credit prior to his or her marriage, but elected and paid for that service during the marriage, MisPERS would consider this service as having been earned during the marriage, If elective service credit is not addressed in the court order, any service purchased or redeposited after the date of marital separation, will be treated as the member's separate property for purposes of calculating the nonmember spouse's "system interest." Although any additional service credit may be treated as the member's separate property, the purchase of elective service credit will usually result in an increase in the benefit upon which the nonmember's spouse's "system interest" is applied.

PARAGRAPHS 5 THROUGH 10 OF ORDER B ILLUSTRATE THIS METHOD OF DIVIDING A MEMBER'S BENEFITS:

Paragraph 5: States that the community has an interest in the member's retirement benefits and defines that interest as those retirement benefits attributable to the member's service in the System during the period from the parties' date of marriage up to the date of separation.

Paragraph 6: Illustrates how the nonmember spouse's share of the member's retirement benefits may be calculated. This is the usual, although not required, language encountered with this method for dividing a member's benefits and is commonly referred to as the "time rule." This benefit allocation formula is only an example. The parties may, of course, provide another method (or percentage) of allocating the member's retirement benefits provided the method is consistent with the terms of the PERL and other applicable law. Paragraph 6 also illustrates how the parties may provide for MisPERS to divide all benefits payable pursuant to the formula provided in this order.

Benefits, for purposes of this order, include a refund of the Member's accumulated retirement contributions, service retirement, disability retirement, industrial disability retirement, and/or any death benefits payable, as provided in paragraph 9 a. and b. of the ORDER.

Misanni case law may exempt certain disability retirement benefits from community property considerations; thus, it is the parties' responsibility to determine the appropriate division of any disability or industrial disability pension and modify this order accordingly. In this model, unless the parties modify the order to the contrary, the community property percentage will be applied to all benefits, including disability or industrial disability retirement allowances. The parties may, of course, agree to provide for the division of only certain benefits or certain types of retirement or modem this paragraph to reflect the wishes and desires of the parties or to reflect case law which may be appropriate to an individual case. MisPERS will comply with the provisions of any order to the extent provided in the Government Code. The court cannot order MisPERS to pay a benefit not provided for, or which is contrary to the PERL.

Paragraph 7: Requires the member, at retirement, to select optional settlement four (4) and name the nonmember spouse as the beneficiary **to the extent of the nonmember spouse's community property interest.** The community property interest shall be determined by MisPERS at the time the member retires using the method described in paragraph 6. This method insures that the nonmember spouse will receive a <u>lifetime</u> benefit equal to his or her community property interest.

The selection of option four will not jeopardize the member's right to name another lifetime beneficiary *for any remaining option portion*. The member can make this request at the time of retirement. <u>There are some plan limitations which may affect the amount available to **a second lifetime** beneficiary under this option.</u>

> *THE ACTUAL ELECTION OF AN OPTIONAL SETTLEMENT CAN ONLY BE MADE BY THE MEMBER AT THE TIME OF RETIREMENT AND ONLY IF BOTH PARTIES ARE LIVING. IT IS THE MEMBER'S RESPONSIBILITY TO COMPLY WITH THE TERMS OF THIS ORDER AT THE TIME OF RETIREMENT.*

The parties may, of course, agree to elect one of the other optional settlements available to the member at retirement, such as optional settlements 2, 2W, 3, or 3W. If the order specifies that the member is to select one of these options at retirement and designate the nonmember spouse, then the nonmember spouse will be the only beneficiary to receive benefits at the member's death with respect to that benefit. The amount available to the nonmember spouse under options 2, 2W, 3, and 3W will be determined based on the combined ages of the member and beneficiary, not on the amount of the nonmember spouse's System Interest. The parties should carefully consider how this may affect future choices before selecting this method to provide a lifetime benefit to the nonmember spouse.

> If the member is not required to provide the nonmember spouse with a continuing monthly allowance, paragraph 7 may be deleted. If deleted, the nonmember spouse's System Interest would be applied to the member's monthly retirement allowance, while living, and to the death benefits after retirement as provided in paragraph 9.b.

Paragraph 7 is not applicable if the member dies prior to retirement as discussed in paragraph 9. a. or if the member terminates membership and receives a refund of his or her contributions and interest. In addition, paragraph 7 is not applicable if the nonmember spouse predeceases the member prior to retirement.

Paragraph 8: Provides for the nonmember spouse to receive his or her "System Interest" directly by separate warrant at the time the member receives benefits or as soon as administratively practicable following the member's death.

Paragraph 9: Illustrates how the parties may provide for the nonmember spouse to receive a share of any benefits payable at the member's death. Paragraph 9. a. provides for the nonmember spouse to receive his or her System Interest in the event of the **member's death prior to retirement.** Paragraph 9.b. provides for the nonmember spouse to receive his or her System Interest in the event of the **member's death after retirement.**

Paragraph 9.a. Specifically provides for the nonmember spouse to receive his or her "System Interest" in any death benefit payable upon the death of a member prior to retirement. Unless the order provides otherwise, MisPERS will pay to the nonmember spouse his or her System Interest from any benefit otherwise payable at the time of the member's death. This includes any lump sum or monthly allowance which may be payable by designation or by statute. Any choice regarding the type of benefit payable (lump sum or monthly) will belong to the person (or persons) determined to be entitled to those benefits. The nonmember spouse cannot be designated as a surviving spouse and WILL NOT receive a monthly allowance based on his or her life expectancy.

The parties and their counsel may wish to review the applicable member booklet to determine which of the **pre-retirement death benefits** are applicable with respect to the member. The **pre-retirement death benefits** vary for a number of reasons, including the member's employment status, the employer's contract with MisPERS, whether the member is vested, and whether the member is legally married or has minor children at the time of death.

Paragraph 9.b: Provides for the nonmember spouse's "System Interest" in any lump sum death benefit payable upon the death of the member after retirement. Paragraph 9.b. also provides for the nonmember spouse to receive his or her "System Interest" in any monthly allowance payable after the death of the member, unless the nonmember spouse is entitled to receive a monthly benefit for his or her own life based on the member's election and designation of the nonmember spouse as a beneficiary under optional settlement 2, 2W, 3, 3W or 4.

If authorized by the court order, MisPERS will divide any benefit payable after the member's death, including any monthly allowance, but only as long as those benefits are payable. Of course, if there are no benefits payable after the member's death, there will be no benefits from which to pay the nonmember spouse's System Interest.

> **A NONMEMBER SPOUSE CANNOT BE CONSIDERED A "SURVIVING SPOUSE" FOR ANY PURPOSE UNDER THE PERL.**

The parties and their counsel may wish to review the applicable member booklet in order to determine which of the post-retirement death benefits are applicable with respect to the member. The post-retirement death benefits vary for a number of reasons, including the member's election at retirement, the employer's contract with MisPERS and whether the member has a "surviving spouse" or minor children.

Paragraph 10: Illustrates how the parties may provide for the nonmember spouse's "System Interest" to be paid to a beneficiary if the nonmember spouse should die prior to the member. Should the parties elect to make such a provision, MisPERS must be provided with the beneficiary's name, current mailing address and Social Security number. If such beneficiary predeceases the nonmember spouse, any "System Interest" shall be paid to the nonmember spouse's next of kin as provided under Government Code section 21493. If the nonmember spouse dies before the member has retired, his or her System Interest will be paid to such beneficiary, if living, from any monthly allowance payable when the member retires, from any refund of contributions payable when the member terminates membership, or from any Pre-Retirement Death Benefits if the member should die prior to retirement.

If the parties desire to have the nonmember spouse's interest revert back to the member after the nonmember spouse's death, instead of continuing to the nonmember spouse's beneficiary for the life of the member, paragraph 10 will need to be changed to provide for this provision.

Paragraph 11: **SUPPLEMENTAL PROVISIONS:** Apply to orders A, B and C. Please refer to page 19 for instructions on paragraph 11 through 21.

> *Again, if any portion of ORDER B is unacceptable to the parties, model ORDER A, separation of accounts provides the nonmember spouse with the right to retire, if the member was vested as of the date of dissolution, and receive a monthly allowance when both parties reach the minimum retirement age. The nonmember would have the right at retirement to select an optional settlement which would provide either a lump sum benefit or a monthly allowance to a beneficiary, upon the nonmember's death.*

----------* * * *----------

ORDER C
RETIRED MEMBERS ONLY

ORDER C illustrates the standard method for dividing the member's monthly retirement allowance between the member and the nonmember spouse and also addresses how any death benefits are to be divided.

It is important that the parties understand the effect that a dissolution of marriage may have on the benefits the member selected at retirement and on the death benefits which may be payable, particularly if the survivor continuance benefit is applicable. If you are unable to determine whether or not the survivor continuance benefit is applicable, this information may be obtained from MisPERS. Please see page 3, Request for Information, for instructions on how to obtain information from MisPERS.

The survivor continuance benefit provides a monthly allowance payable by statute to certain "eligible survivors." An eligible survivor, for purposes of the survivor continuance benefit, is defined under the PERL as a surviving spouse who was married to the member for a continuous period beginning at least one year (or less than one year in certain cases) prior to the member's effective retirement date and ending on the date of the member's death. If there is no surviving spouse, the benefit can be paid to the member's minor children.

> Upon dissolution of marriage, a nonmember spouse ceases to be the "surviving spouse" for purposes of the survivor continuance benefit and would no longer be eligible to receive this benefit upon the member's death. **A NONMEMBER SPOUSE CANNOT BE CONSIDERED A "SURVIVING SPOUSE" FOR ANY PURPOSE UNDER THE PERL.**

Paragraph 5: States that the community has an interest in the member's retirement benefits and defines that interest as those retirement benefits attributable to the service credit accrued by the member during the period from the parties' date of marriage up to the date of separation, or retirement, whichever is earlier. A member ceases to accrue service credit at retirement.

Paragraph 6: Provides the amount of the monthly benefit currently being paid to the member, the option selected, and the member's named beneficiary, if any. This information may be obtained from MisPERS. Please see page 3, Request for Information, for instructions on how to obtain information from MisPERS.

> *If the nonmember spouse was named as a beneficiary under optional settlement 2, 2W, 3, 3W or 4, the member cannot change his or her beneficiary or his or her option unless the entire interest in the pension plan is awarded to the member as his or her sole and separate property.*

Paragraph 7: Sets forth how the nonmember spouse's share of the member's retirement benefits are to be calculated. The benefit allocation formula described in the model is only an example. The parties may, of course, provide another method (or percentage) of allocating the member's retirement benefits among the parties provided the method is consistent with the terms of the PERL and other applicable law.

Paragraph 8: Provides that benefit payments will commence to the nonmember spouse by separate check as soon as administratively practicable following the date MisPERS determines that the order is acceptable.

Paragraph 9: The nonmember spouse's "System Interest" in the member's monthly retirement allowance will cease to be payable upon the death of the member. Paragraph 9 provides for the nonmember spouse to receive his or her "System Interest" in any lump sum death benefit payable upon the death of the member after retirement. Paragraph 9 also provides for the nonmember spouse to receive his or her "System Interest" in any monthly allowance payable after the death of the member, unless the nonmember spouse is entitled to receive a monthly benefit for his or her own life based on the member's election and designation of the nonmember spouse as a beneficiary under optional settlement 2, 2W, 3, 3W or 4.

> *MisPERS will divide any benefit payable after the member's death, including any monthly allowance, but only as long as those benefits are payable. Of course, if no benefits are payable after the member's death, there will be no benefits from which to pay the nonmember spouse's System Interest.*

The parties and their counsel may wish to review the <u>member's election and beneficiary designation, and the applicable member booklet</u> in order to determine which of the post-retirement death benefits are applicable with respect to the member or whether this paragraph is applicable.

Paragraph 10: Illustrates how the parties may provide for the nonmember spouse's System Interest to be paid to a beneficiary if the nonmember spouse should die and benefits are still payable to the member. Should the parties elect to make such a provision, MisPERS must be provided, either in the order or in a separate document, with the beneficiary's name, current mailing address and Social Security number. If the beneficiary predeceases the nonmember spouse, any "System Interest" shall be paid to the nonmember spouse's next of kin as provided under Government Code section 21493.

If the parties desire to have the nonmember spouse's interest revert back to the member after the nonmember spouse's death instead of continuing to the nonmember spouse's beneficiary for the life of the member, paragraph 10 will need to be changed to provide for this provision.

----------* * *----------

SUPPLEMENTAL PROVISIONS: ALL ORDERS

The following provisions are commonly included in orders affecting a member's benefits. The parties and their counsel should review these provisions to determine whether such provisions are consistent with the parties' objectives.

Paragraph 11: Provides that the nonmember spouse's "System Interest" in any monthly allowance will increase with any cost-of-living increase or other similar increases in accordance with the terms of the PERL.

Paragraph 12: Standard language in accordance with the terms of the Internal Revenue Code.

Paragraph 13: Indicate the member's full name, current mailing address, telephone number, Social Security number and date of birth.

Paragraph 14: Indicate the nonmember spouse's full name, current mailing address, telephone number, Social Security number and date of birth.

Paragraph 15: Sets forth information about the administration of the System and the manner in which the nonmember spouse is to communicate with the System.

Paragraph 16: Standard language in accordance with the terms of the PERL.

Paragraph 17: Provides that the System may provide the nonmember spouse and/or his or her agents and attorneys with information regarding the member's benefits until such time as the nonmember spouse has received his or her entire interest in the System.

Paragraph 18: Contains standard language in accordance with the terms of the PERL and other applicable law.

Paragraph 19: Is designed to address the situation where alternate payee or participant receive funds to which the other is entitled under the order.

Paragraph 20: Provides for amending the order in the event subsequent changes to applicable law result in the order no longer being acceptable to the System. Paragraph 20 further provides that the nonmember spouse and the member shall be responsible for any of the costs and/or expenses associated with any such amendment.

Paragraph 21: Provides for amending the court's continuing jurisdiction to modify the order in any and all necessary respects. IMPORTANT: In the event such modification proves necessary or advisable, any related fees, taxes and/or penalties will be assessed against the parties who then have an interest payable from the System.

IMPORTANT: MisPERS model order includes a signature block for the approval of the order by MisPERS staff. MisPERS will sign the order only after it has been signed by both parties. Model orders which have been modified should be sent to MisPERS in draft form with a cover letter explaining which provisions were changed.

[NAME OF COUNSEL]
[ADDRESS OF COUNSEL]
[CITY, STATE]
[PHONE NUMBER]

ATTORNEY FOR [PETITIONER/RESPONDENT]

MODEL ORDER PROVISIONS

CAUTION: THE DISPOSITION OF RETIREMENT BENEFITS IN DO-
MESTIC RELATIONS PROCEEDINGS INVOLVES COMPLEX MARITAL
RIGHTS AND TAX ISSUES. THE FOLLOWING IS A MODEL ORDER
WHICH DEMONSTRATES SEVERAL METHODS OF SPLITTING RE-
TIREMENT BENEFITS PROVIDED TO MEMBERS OF THE MISANNI
PUBLIC EMPLOYEES' RETIREMENT SYSTEM. OTHER METHODS OF
SPLITTING SUCH BENEFITS ARE AVAILABLE AND THIS MODEL OR-
DER MAY BE INAPPROPRIATE FOR YOU.

THIS SAMPLE IS PROVIDED AS A COURTESY ONLY, AS NEITHER THE
MISANNI PUBLIC EMPLOYEES' RETIREMENT SYSTEM, NOR ITS AGENTS
OR CONSULTANTS ARE AUTHORIZED TO GIVE LEGAL ADVICE AND THEY
MAKE NO REPRESENTATION AS TO ITS SUFFICIENCY UNDER APPLICABLE
FEDERAL OR STATE LAW OR AS TO ITS LEGAL CONSEQUENCES.

SUPERIOR COURT OF THE STATE OF MISANNI
COUNTY OF _____

_____	)	Case No. _____
In re the Marriage of	)	
	)	***MODEL ORDER A***
Petitioner: _____	)	STIUPLATED DOMESTIC
	)	RELATIONS ORDER RE:
and	)	DIVISION OF MISANNI
	)	PUBLIC EMPLOYEES'
Respondent: _____	)	RETIREMENT SYSTEM BENEFITS
	)	
_____	)	

Petitioner, _____, and Respondent, _____, and
the Board of Administration of the Misanni Public Employees' Retirement
System ("Administrator") as administrator of the Public Employees' Retirement
System ("MisPERS" or "System") hereby stipulate as follows:

RECITALS

Petitioner and Respondent were married to each other on _____.
They separated on _____, and this Court entered a judgment of
dissolution of marriage in the action on _____.

2. This Court has personal jurisdiction over both Petitioner and
Respondent and jurisdiction over the subject matter of this Order and the dissolution of marriage action.

3. MisPERS was properly joined as a party to the Petitioner and
Respondent's dissolution of marriage action pursuant to sections 2060 through
2065 of the Misanni Family Code.

STIPULATION

This Order is acceptable under the Public Employees' Retirement
Law ("PERL"), which is set forth at section 258908, et seq., of the Misanni
Government Code.

IT IS HEREBY ORDERED BY THE COURT THAT:

4. This Order is entered pursuant to the Misanni Family Code.

5. **[Respondent or Petitioner]** ("Member") and **[Respondent or
Petitioner]** ("Nonmember Spouse") have acquired a community interest in the
Member's accumulated retirement contributions and service credit attributable
to periods of service in the System during the period from the Date of Marriage
up to the Date of Separation.

6. Pursuant to section 21290 of the Misanni Government Code, the Court
allocates and awards to the Nonmember Spouse 50% of the accumulated retirement contributions and service credit attributable to the Member's service
in the System during the period from the Date of Marriage up to the Date of

Separation ("System Interest") as the Nonmember Spouse's sole and separate property. All accumulated retirement contributions and service credit attributable to the Member's service in the System not awarded to the Nonmember Spouse pursuant to this Order shall be the Member's sole and separate property.

7. Pursuant to section 21290(b) of the Misanni Government Code, the Administrator shall divide the Member's accumulated retirement contributions and service credit in accordance with Paragraph 6 of this Order and establish a separate and distinct account for the interest awarded to the Member and the Nonmember Spouse as soon as administratively practicable after the Administrator determines that this Order is acceptable under the PERL.

8. From and after the date that the Administrator has divided the Member's accumulated retirement contributions and service credit pursuant to Paragraph 7 of this Order, the Nonmember Spouse shall be entitled to all applicable rights permitted under section 21290(c) of the Misanni Government Code, including:

     a. The right to a service retirement allowance, including the right to elect an optional settlement and the right to name a beneficiary, provided that the Nonmember Spouse is otherwise eligible for such an allowance in accordance with section 21295 of the Misanni Government Code;

     b. The right to a refund of that portion of the Nonmember Spouse's System Interest which represents accumulated Member retirement contributions in accordance with section 21292 of the Misanni Government Code, including any interest which has accrued on such contributions through the date of payment;

     c. The right to redeposit the Nonmember's System Interest in any accumulated retirement contributions attributable to the Member's service during the period from the Date of Marriage up to the Date of Separation which would otherwise have been eligible for redeposit by the Member under sections 20750 and 20752 of the Misanni Government Code, in accordance with section 21293 of the Misanni Government Code;

     d. The right to purchase the Nonmember's System Interest in any additional service credit earned during the period from the Date of Marriage up to the Date of Separation which would otherwise have been eligible for purchase by the Member under Article 4 (commencing with section 20990 of the Misanni Government Code) and-Article 5 commencing with section 21020 of the Misanni Government Code) of Chapter 11, in accordance with section 21294 of the Misanni Government Code;

e. The right to designate a beneficiary to receive that portion of the Nonmember Spouse's System Interest which represents accumulated Member contributions and any interest on such contributions payable at death prior to the Nonmember Spouse's retirement and to receive any unpaid monthly retirement allowance payable at death after the Nonmember Spouse's retirement; and

9. If the Nonmember Spouse fails to designate a beneficiary pursuant to paragraph 8.e. of this Order or the designated beneficiary does not survive the Nonmember Spouse, any portion of the Nonmember Spouse's System Interest which is payable after his or her death shall be paid in accordance with section 21493 of the Misanni Government Code.

10. Notwithstanding any other provision of this Order, if the Member does not have the necessary minimum credited service to retire as of the date of dissolution or legal separation, the Nonmember Spouse shall receive a refund of that portion of the Nonmember Spouse's System Interest which represents accumulated, Member contributions and any interest that has accrued to such contributions as soon as administratively practicable following the date an account was established for the Nonmember Spouse pursuant to paragraph 7 of this Order in accordance with section 21292(g) of the Misanni Government Code.

11. The Nonmember Spouse's System Interest will be applied to any cost-of-living increases or other similar increases, but only to the extent permitted under the PERL.

12. The Member and the Nonmember Spouse shall be responsible for and pay any taxes due in connection with his or her receipt of distributions from the System.

13. Member's Name. For purposes of making any benefit payments provided by the terms of this Order or providing any notice required by the terms of this Order, Member's name, current mailing address, telephone number, Social Security number and date of birth are as follows:

Name:_____

Address: _____

_____

Telephone No.: (   )_____

Social Security Number: _____-_____-_____

Date of Birth: _____

14. Nonmember Spouse's Name. For purposes of making any benefit payments required by the terms of this Order or providing any notice required by the terms of this Order, the Nonmember Spouse's name, current mailing address, telephone number, Social Security number and date of birth are as follows:

Name:_____

Address: _____

_____

Telephone No.: (   )_____

Social Security Number: _____-_____-_____

Date of Birth: _____

15. Notice of change of address shall be made in writing to the System, addressed as follows, or as the Administrator may specify in a written notice to Nonmember Spouse:

Misanni Public Employees' Retirement System
Attn: Community Property Unit
P.O. Box 2056
Capitol City, Misanni

Notice of change of address or telephone number shall be made in writing to the Administrator, addressed as indicated above, or as the Administrator may specify in a written notice to the Nonmember Spouse. No notice or document shall be deemed to be given to the System unless such notice or document is sent by certified mail, return receipt requested, at the above address.

16. The Member and the Nonmember Spouse shall sign all forms, letters and other documents as required to effect the distribution(s) described herein and the intent of this Order.

17. The Nonmember Spouse, the Nonmember Spouse's agents and attorneys are authorized to receive any and all information concerning the Member's benefits until such time as the Nonmember Spouse has received the Nonmember Spouse's System Interest.

18. Notwithstanding any other provision of this Order, the Order shall not be construed as to require the System:

(a) to provide any form of benefit or any option not otherwise provided under the PERL;

(b) to provide increased benefits (as determined based on actuarial value) not available to the Member;

(c) to provide benefits to the Nonmember Spouse which are required to be paid to another nonmember spouse under another Order previously entered by a Court of competent jurisdiction and acceptable under the PERL;

(d) to provide payment to the Nonmember Spouse of benefits forfeited by the Member; or

(e) to change the benefit election of the Member once the Member has retired.

19. It is further ORDERED that the Member shall act as constructive trustee of any benefits assigned to the Nonmember Spouse under this Order which may be paid to or received by the Member. The Member, as trustee, shall promptly pay or transmit any such benefits to the Nonmember Spouse at the Nonmember Spouse's last known address. It is also ORDERED that the Nonmember Spouse shall act as constructive trustee of any benefits assigned to the Member under this Order which may be paid to or received by the Nonmember Spouse. The Nonmember Spouse, as trustee, shall promptly pay or transmit any such benefits to the Member at the Member's last known address.

20. This Order shall be administered and interpreted in conformity with the PERL and other applicable law. If the PERL is amended, then Member and the Nonmember Spouse shall immediately take the steps necessary to amend this Order to comply with any such amendments, changes and/or modifications, or, if permissible under any such change, amendment, or modification to the PERL, the Administrator may treat this Order as acceptable. The Member and the Nonmember Spouse shall be responsible for any of the costs and/or expenses associated with any such amendment.

21. The Member, the Nonmember Spouse, the Administrator, and the Court intend that this Order meets all requirements of a domestic relations order under the PERL and other laws of the State of Misanni, and the Court shall reserve jurisdiction to modify this Order for the purpose of meeting or monitoring its implementation. The Court's reservation of jurisdiction shall be liberally construed to effect the provisions of this Order and to resolve any disputes that may arise among the parties and the Administrator concerning benefit payments or any other aspect of this Order. If any portion of this Order is rendered invalid, illegal, unconstitutional or otherwise unenforceable, the Court reserves jurisdiction to make an appropriate adjustment to effectuate the intent of the parties. Any future fees, taxes, and/or penalties will be assessed against the parties who then have an interest payable from the System.

It is so Stipulated:

Dated: _____   _____
                                         [NAME]
                                         Petitioner

Dated: _____   _____
                                         [NAME]
                                         Attorney for Petitioner

Dated: _____   _____
                                         [NAME]
                                         Respondent

Dated: _____   _____
                                         [NAME]
                                         Attorney for Respondent

Dated: _____   _____
                                         Administrator of the Misanni Public Employees' Retirement System.

ORDER

The parties having stipulated thereto and good cause appearing therefore.

IT IS SO ORDERED.

Dated: _____   _____
                                         JUDGE OF THE SUPERIOR COURT

[**NAME OF COUNSEL**]
[**ADDRESS OF COUNSEL**]
[**CITY, STATE**]
[**PHONE NUMBER**]
ATTORNEY FOR [**PETITIONER/RESPONDENT**]

MODEL ORDER PROVISIONS

CAUTION: THE DISPOSITION OF RETIREMENT BENEFITS IN DOMESTIC RELATIONS PROCEEDINGS INVOLVES COMPLEX MARITAL RIGHTS AND TAX ISSUES. THE FOLLOWING IS A MODEL ORDER WHICH DEMONSTRATES SEVERAL METHODS OF SPLITTING RETIREMENT BENEFITS PROVIDED TO MEMBERS OF THE MISANNI PUBLIC EMPLOYEES' RETIREMENT SYSTEM. OTHER METHODS OF SPLITTING SUCH BENEFITS ARE AVAILABLE AND THIS MODEL ORDER MAY BE INAPPROPRIATE FOR YOU.

THIS SAMPLE IS PROVIDED AS A COURTESY ONLY, AS NEITHER THE MISANNI PUBLIC EMPLOYEES' RETIREMENT SYSTEM, NOR ITS AGENTS OR CONSULTANTS ARE AUTHORIZED TO GIVE LEGAL ADVICE AND THEY MAKE NO REPRESENTATION AS TO ITS SUFFICIENCY UNDER APPLICABLE FEDERAL OR STATE LAW OR AS TO ITS LEGAL CONSEQUENCES.

SUPERIOR COURT OF THE STATE OF MISANNI
COUNTY OF _____

_____	) Case No. _____
	)
In re the Marriage of	)
	) ***MODEL ORDER A***
Petitioner: _____	) STIUPLATED DOMESTIC
	) RELATIONS ORDER RE:
and	) DIVISION OF MISANNI
	) PUBLIC EMPLOYEES'
Respondent: _____	) RETIREMENT SYSTEM BENEFITS
	)
_____	)

Petitioner, _____, and Respondent, _____, and the Board of Administration of the Misanni Public Employees' Retirement System ("Administrator") as administrator of the Public Employees' Retirement System ("MisPERS" or "System") hereby stipulate as follows:

RECITALS

Petitioner and Respondent were married to each other on _____. They separated on _____, and this Court entered a judgment of dissolution of marriage in the action on _____.

2. This Court has personal jurisdiction over both Petitioner and Respondent and jurisdiction over the subject matter of this Order and the dissolution of marriage action.

3. MisPERS was properly joined as a party to the Petitioner and Respondent's dissolution of marriage action pursuant to sections 2060 through 2065 of the Misanni Family Code.

STIPULATION

This Order is acceptable under the Public Employees' Retirement Law ("PERL"), which is set forth at section 258908, <u>et seq.</u>, of the Misanni Government Code.

IT IS HEREBY ORDERED BY THE COURT THAT:

4. This Order is entered pursuant to the Misanni Family Code.

5. [**Respondent or Petitioner**] ("Member") and [**Respondent or Petitioner**] ("Nonmember Spouse") have acquired a community interest in the Member's accumulated retirement contributions and service credit attributable to periods of service in the System during the period from the Date of Marriage up to the Date of Separation.

6. The Member is currently receiving $ _____ [**Enter amount**] a month under option _____ [**Enter option selected at retirement**] with _____ [**Name of Beneficiary**] named as beneficiary of any benefits payable under such option at the Member's death.

7. <u>Calculation of Nonmember Spouse's Interest</u>. The Court allocates and awards to the Nonmember Spouse an interest in any and all of the Member's "retirement benefits" calculated as follows:

> Member's credited service in the
> System from Date of Nonmember Marriage
> until Date of Spouse's Retirement
> X <u>Separation</u> X 50% = System Benefits
> Member's total credited Interest service in the System

For purposes of this Order, the term "retirement benefits" shall include any refund of the Member's accumulated retirement contributions, any service retirement benefits, any disability retirement benefits, any industrial disability retirement benefits and any death benefits (as provided in paragraph 9 a. and b. of this ORDER). The portion of the Member's retirement benefits which are allocated and awarded to the Nonmember Spouse pursuant to the terms of this paragraph shall hereinafter be referred to as the Nonmember Spouse's "System Interest." All retirement benefits attributable to the Member's service in the System not awarded to the Nonmember Spouse pursuant to this Order shall be the Member's sole and separate property.

7. <u>Form of Retirement Benefit.</u> At the time the Member retires, the Member Spouse shall elect Optional Settlement method no. 4, naming the Nonmember Spouse as beneficiary to the extent of his or her community property interest. The community property interest will be determined at the Member's retirement based on the formula provided in paragraph 6.

8. <u>Commencement of Benefits to the Nonmember Spouse.</u> The Nonmember Spouse shall commence to receive the Nonmember Spouse's System Interest by separate warrant directly from the System beginning on the earlier of the date the Member commences to receive his or her retirement benefits or as soon as administratively practicable following the Member's death.

9. <u>Benefits payable at Member's Death.</u>

a. <u>Pre-retirement death benefits.</u> If the Member dies prior to retirement, the Administrator shall pay by separate warrant, directly to the Nonmember Spouse, the Nonmember Spouse's System Interest as applied to any death benefit payable as a result of the Member's death, whether lump sum or monthly.

b. <u>Post-retirement death benefits.</u> If the Member dies after retirement, and a lump sum death benefit is payable from the System, the Administrator shall pay by separate warrant, directly to the Nonmember Spouse, 'the Nonmember Spouse's System Interest as applied to such benefit. In addition to any lump sum death benefit which may be payable to the Nonmember Spouse pursuant to the preceding sentence, if the Nonmember Spouse was not designated as beneficiary under an optional settlement and thus, not entitled to a monthly allowance in his or her own right, the Administrator shall pay by separate warrant directly to the Nonmember Spouse the Nonmember Spouse's System Interest in any monthly allowance otherwise payable for as long as that benefit is payable to the Member's beneficiary or survivor.

10. <u>Benefits Payable at Nonmember Spouse's Death.</u> If the Nonmember Spouse dies prior to the time that the Nonmember Spouse has received or commences to receive the Nonmember Spouse's System Interest, and benefits are payable to the Member at any time in the future, the Administrator shall pay the Nonmember Spouse's System Interest to the beneficiary named below by separate warrant directly to such beneficiary as soon as administratively practicable after the date that benefits are payable. If the designated beneficiary is not living at the time benefits are payable, such Interest shall be paid in accordance with section 21493 of the Misanni Government Code.

Beneficiary: _____

Address: _____

_____

Social Security Number: _____-_____-_____

11. The Nonmember Spouse's System Interest will be applied to any cost-of-living increases or other similar increases, but only to the extent permitted under the PERL.

12. The Member and the Nonmember Spouse shall be responsible for and pay any taxes due in connection with his or her receipt of distributions from the System.

13. <u>Member's Name.</u> For purposes of making any benefit payments provided by the terms of this Order or providing any notice required by the terms of this Order, Member's name, current mailing address, telephone number, Social Security number and date of birth are as follows:

Name:_____

Address: _____

_____

Telephone No.: (   )_____

Social Security Number: _____-_____-_____

Date of Birth: _____

14. <u>Nonmember Spouse's Name.</u> For purposes of making any benefit payments required by the terms of this Order or providing any notice required by the terms of this Order, the Nonmember Spouse's name, current mailing address, telephone number, Social Security number and date of birth are as follows:

Name:_____

Address: _____

_____

Telephone No.: (   )_____

Social Security Number: _____-_____-_____

Date of Birth: _____

15. Notice of change of address shall be made in writing to the System, addressed as follows, or as the Administrator may specify in a written notice to Nonmember Spouse:

Misanni Public Employees' Retirement System
Attn: Community Property Unit
P.O. Box 2056
Capitol City, Misanni

Notice of change of address or telephone number shall be made in writing to the Administrator, addressed as indicated above, or as the Administrator may specify in a written notice to the Nonmember Spouse. No notice or document shall be deemed to be given to the System unless such notice or document is sent by certified mail, return receipt requested, at the above address.

16. The Member and the Nonmember Spouse shall sign all forms, letters and other documents as required to effect the distribution(s) described herein and the intent of this Order.

17. The Nonmember Spouse, the Nonmember Spouse's agents and attorneys are authorized to receive any and all information concerning the Member's benefits until such time as the Nonmember Spouse has received the Nonmember Spouse's System Interest.

18. Notwithstanding any other provision of this Order, the Order shall not be construed as to require the System:

> (a) to provide any form of benefit or any option not otherwise provided under the PERL;
>
> (b) to provide increased benefits (as determined based on actuarial value) not available to the Member;
>
> (c) to provide benefits to the Nonmember Spouse which are required to be paid to another nonmember spouse under another Order previously entered by a Court of competent jurisdiction and acceptable under the PERL;
>
> (d) to provide payment to the Nonmember Spouse of benefits forfeited by the Member; or
>
> (e) to change the benefit election of the Member once the Member has retired.

19. It is further ORDERED that the Member shall act as constructive trustee of any benefits assigned to the Nonmember Spouse under this Order which may be paid to or received by the Member. The Member, as trustee, shall promptly pay or transmit any such benefits to the Nonmember Spouse at the Nonmember Spouse's last known address. It is also ORDERED that the Nonmember Spouse shall act as constructive trustee of any benefits assigned to the Member under this Order which may be paid to or received by the Nonmember Spouse. The Nonmember Spouse, as trustee, shall promptly pay or transmit any such benefits to the Member at the Member's last known address.

20. This Order shall be administered and interpreted in conformity with the PERL and other applicable law. If the PERL is amended, then Member and the Nonmember Spouse shall immediately take the steps necessary to amend this Order to comply with any such amendments, changes and/or modifications, or, if permissible under any such change, amendment, or modification to

the PERL, the Administrator may treat this Order as acceptable. The Member and the Nonmember Spouse shall be responsible for any of the costs and/or expenses associated with any such amendment.

21. The Member, the Nonmember Spouse, the Administrator, and the Court intend that this Order meets all requirements of a domestic relations order under the PERL and other laws of the State of Misanni, and the Court shall reserve jurisdiction to modify this Order for the purpose of meeting or monitoring its implementation. The Court's reservation of jurisdiction shall be liberally construed to effect the provisions of this Order and to resolve any disputes that may arise among the parties and the Administrator concerning benefit payments or any other aspect of this Order. If any portion of this Order is rendered invalid, illegal, unconstitutional or otherwise unenforceable, the Court reserves jurisdiction to make an appropriate adjustment to effectuate the intent of the parties. Any future fees, taxes, and/or penalties will be assessed against the parties who then have an interest payable from the System.

It is so Stipulated:

Dated:_____   _____
             [NAME]
             Petitioner

Dated:_____   _____
             [NAME]
             Attorney for Petitioner

Dated:_____   _____
             [NAME]
             Respondent

Dated:_____   _____
             [NAME]
             Attorney for Respondent

Dated:_____   _____
             Administrator of the Misanni Public Employees' Retirement System.

ORDER

The parties having stipulated thereto and good cause appearing therefore.

IT IS SO ORDERED.
Dated: _____   _____
             JUDGE OF THE SUPERIOR COURT

[**NAME OF COUNSEL**]
[**ADDRESS OF COUNSEL**]
[**CITY, STATE**]
[**PHONE NUMBER**]
ATTORNEY FOR [**PETITIONER/RESPONDENT**]

MODEL ORDER PROVISIONS

<u>CAUTION</u>: THE DISPOSITION OF RETIREMENT BENEFITS IN DOMESTIC RELATIONS PROCEEDINGS INVOLVES COMPLEX MARITAL RIGHTS AND TAX ISSUES. THE FOLLOWING IS A MODEL ORDER WHICH DEMONSTRATES SEVERAL METHODS OF SPLITTING RETIREMENT BENEFITS PROVIDED TO MEMBERS OF THE MISANNI PUBLIC EMPLOYEES' RETIREMENT SYSTEM. OTHER METHODS OF SPLITTING SUCH BENEFITS ARE AVAILABLE AND THIS MODEL ORDER MAY BE INAPPROPRIATE FOR YOU.

THIS SAMPLE IS PROVIDED AS A COURTESY ONLY, AS NEITHER THE MISANNI PUBLIC EMPLOYEES' RETIREMENT SYSTEM, NOR ITS AGENTS OR CONSULTANTS ARE AUTHORIZED TO GIVE LEGAL ADVICE AND THEY MAKE NO REPRESENTATION AS TO ITS SUFFICIENCY UNDER APPLICABLE FEDERAL OR STATE LAW OR AS TO ITS LEGAL CONSEQUENCES.

SUPERIOR COURT OF THE STATE OF MISANNI
COUNTY OF _____

_____	) Case No. _____
	)
In re the Marriage of	)
	) ***MODEL ORDER A***
Petitioner: _____	) STIUPLATED DOMESTIC
	) RELATIONS ORDER RE:
and	) DIVISION OF MISANNI
	) PUBLIC EMPLOYEES'
Respondent: _____	) RETIREMENT SYSTEM BENEFITS
	)
_____	)

Petitioner, _____, and Respondent, _____,
and the Board of Administration of the Misanni Public Employees' Retirement
System ("Administrator") as administrator of the Public Employees' Retirement
System ("MisPERS" or "System") hereby stipulate as follows:

RECITALS

Petitioner and Respondent were married to each other on _____.
They separated on _____, and this Court entered a judgment of
dissolution of marriage in the action on _____.

2. This Court has personal jurisdiction over both Petitioner and
Respondent and jurisdiction over the subject matter of this Order and the
dissolution of marriage action.

3. MisPERS was properly joined as a party to the Petitioner and
Respondent's dissolution of marriage action pursuant to sections 2060 through
2065 of the Misanni Family Code.

STIPULATION

This Order is acceptable under the Public Employees' Retirement
Law ("PERL"), which is set forth at section 258908, <u>et seq.</u>, of the Misanni
Government Code.

<u>IT IS HEREBY ORDERED BY THE COURT THAT:</u>

4. This Order is entered pursuant to the Misanni Family Code.

5. [**Respondent <u>or</u> Petitioner**] ("Member") and [**Respondent <u>or</u>
Petitioner**] ("Nonmember Spouse") have acquired a community interest in the
Member's accumulated retirement contributions and service credit attributable
to periods of service in the System during the period from the Date of Marriage
up to the Date of Separation.

6. The Member is currently receiving $ _____ [**Enter amount**] a month
under option_____[**Enter option selected at retirement**] with
_____[**Name of Beneficiary**] named as beneficiary of any benefits
payable under such option at the Member's death.

Calculation of Nonmember Spouse's Interest. The Court allocates and awards to the Nonmember Spouse an interest in any and all of the Member's "retirement benefits" calculated as follows:

Member's credited service in the
System from Date of Nonmember Marriage
until Date of Spouse's Retirement

X Separation X 50% = System Benefits

Member's total credited Interest service in the System

For purposes of this Order, the term "retirement benefits" shall include any service retirement benefits, any industrial disability, retirement benefits, any disability retirement benefits and any death benefits (as provided in paragraph 9 of this Order). The portion of the Member's retirement benefits which are allocated and awarded to the Nonmember Spouse pursuant to the terms of this paragraph shall hereinafter be referred to as the Nonmember Spouse's "System Interest." All retirement benefits attributable to the Member's service in the System not awarded to the Nonmember Spouse pursuant to this Order shall be the Member's sole and separate property.

8. Commencement of Benefits to the Nonmember Spouse. The Nonmember Spouse shall commence to receive the Nonmember Spouse's System Interest by separate warrant directly from the System as soon as administratively practicable following the date the Administrator determines that this Order is acceptable under the PERL.

9. Benefits payable at Member's Death. Upon the Member's death after retirement, and if a lump sum death benefit is payable from the System, the Administrator shall pay by separate warrant, directly to the Nonmember Spouse, the Nonmember Spouse's System Interest as applied to such benefit. In addition to any lump sum death benefit which may be payable to the Nonmember Spouse pursuant to the aforementioned sentence, if the Nonmember Spouse was not designated as beneficiary under an optional settlement and thus, not entitled to a monthly allowance in his or her own right, the Administrator shall pay by separate warrant, directly to the Nonmember Spouse, the Nonmember Spouse's System Interest as applied to any monthly allowance otherwise payable for as long as the benefit is payable to the Member's beneficiary or survivor.

10. <u>Benefits Payable at Nonmember Spouse's Death.</u> If benefits are still payable to the Member at the time of the Nonmember Spouse's death, the Administrator shall continue to pay the Nonmember Spouse's System Interest by separate warrant directly to the beneficiary named below. If such beneficiary does not survive the Nonmember Spouse, such Interest shall be paid in accordance with section 21493 of the Misanni Government Code.

Beneficiary: _____

Address: _____

_____

Social Security Number: _____-_____-_____

11. The Nonmember Spouse's System Interest will be applied to any cost-of-living increases or other similar increases, but only to the extent permitted under the PERL.

12. The Member and the Nonmember Spouse shall be responsible for and pay any taxes due in connection with his or her receipt of distributions from the System.

13. Member's Name. For purposes of making any benefit payments provided by the terms of this Order or providing any notice required by the terms of this Order, Member's name, current mailing address, telephone number, Social Security number and date of birth are as follows:

Name:_____

Address: _____

_____

Telephone No.: (   )_____

Social Security Number: _____-_____-_____

Date of Birth: _____

14. <u>Nonmember Spouse's Name.</u> For purposes of making any benefit payments required by the terms of this Order or providing any notice required by the terms of this Order, the Nonmember Spouse's name, current mailing address, telephone number, Social Security number and date of birth are as follows:

Name:_____

Address: _____

_____

Telephone No.: (   )_____

Social Security Number: _____-_____-_____

Date of Birth: _____

15. Notice of change of address shall be made in writing to the System, addressed as follows, or as the Administrator may specify in a written notice to Nonmember Spouse:

Misanni Public Employees' Retirement System
Attn: Community Property Unit
P.O. Box 2056
Capitol City, Misanni

Notice of change of address or telephone number shall be made in writing to the Administrator, addressed as indicated above, or as the Administrator may specify in a written notice to the Nonmember Spouse. No notice or document shall be deemed to be given to the System unless such notice or document is sent by certified mail, return receipt requested, at the above address.

16. The Member and the Nonmember Spouse shall sign all forms, letters and other documents as required to effect the distribution(s) described herein and the intent of this Order.

17. The Nonmember Spouse, the Nonmember Spouse's agents and attorneys are authorized to receive any and all information concerning the Member's benefits until such time as the Nonmember Spouse has received the Nonmember Spouse's System Interest.

18. Notwithstanding any other provision of this Order, the Order shall not be construed as to require the System:

> (a) to provide any form of benefit or any option not otherwise provided under the PERL;

> (b) to provide increased benefits (as determined based on actuarial

value) not available to the Member;

(c) to provide benefits to the Nonmember Spouse which are required to be paid to another nonmember spouse under another Order previously entered by a Court of competent jurisdiction and acceptable under the PERL;

(d) to provide payment to the Nonmember Spouse of benefits forfeited by the Member; or

(e) to change the benefit election of the Member once the Member has retired.

19. It is further ORDERED that the Member shall act as constructive trustee of any benefits assigned to the Nonmember Spouse under this Order which may be paid to or received by the Member. The Member, as trustee, shall promptly pay or transmit any such benefits to the Nonmember Spouse at the Nonmember Spouse's last known address. It is also ORDERED that the Nonmember Spouse shall act as constructive trustee of any benefits assigned to the Member under this Order which may be paid to or received by the Nonmember Spouse. The Nonmember Spouse, as trustee, shall promptly pay or transmit any such benefits to the Member at the Member's last known address.

20. This Order shall be administered and interpreted in conformity with the PERL and other applicable law. If the PERL is amended, then Member and the Nonmember Spouse shall immediately take the steps necessary to amend this Order to comply with any such amendments, changes and/or modifications, or, if permissible under any such change, amendment, or modification to the PERL, the Administrator may treat this Order as acceptable. The Member and the Nonmember Spouse shall be responsible for any of the costs and/or expenses associated with any such amendment.

21. The Member, the Nonmember Spouse, the Administrator, and the Court intend that this Order meets all requirements of a domestic relations order under the PERL and other laws of the State of Misanni, and the Court shall reserve jurisdiction to modify this Order for the purpose of meeting or monitoring its implementation. The Court's reservation of jurisdiction shall be liberally construed to effect the provisions of this Order and to resolve any disputes that may arise among the parties and the Administrator concerning benefit payments or any other aspect of this Order. If any portion of this Order is rendered invalid, illegal, unconstitutional or otherwise unenforceable, the

Court reserves jurisdiction to make an appropriate adjustment to effectuate the intent of the parties. Any future fees, taxes, and/or penalties will be assessed against the parties who then have an interest payable from the System.

Dated:_____   _____

                                         [NAME]
                                         Petitioner

Dated:_____   _____

                                         [NAME]
                                         Attorney for Petitioner

Dated:_____   _____

                                         [NAME]
                                         Respondent

Dated:_____   _____

                                         [NAME]
                                         Attorney for Respondent

Dated:_____   _____

                                         Administrator of the Misanni Public Employees' Retirement System.

ORDER

**The parties having stipulated thereto and good cause appearing therefore.
IT IS SO ORDERED.**

Dated: _____   _____

                                         JUDGE OF THE SUPERIOR COURT

Index

References are to pages